Professional Linux Programming

Neil Matthew
Richard Stones

Christopher Browne
Brad Clements
Andrew Froggatt
David J. Goodger
Ivan Griffin
Jeff Licquia
Ronald van Loon
Harish Rawat
Udaya A. Ranawake
Marius Sundbakken
Deepak Thomas
Stephen J. Turnbull
David Woodhouse

Wrox Press Ltd.

Professional Linux Programming

wrox

Published by Wrox Press Ltd,
Arden House, 1102 Warwick Road, Acocks Green,
Birmingham, B27 6BH, UK
Printed in Canada
ISBN 1861003013

Trademark Acknowledgments

Wrox has endeavored to provide trademark information about all the companies and products mentioned in this book by the appropriate use of capitals. However, Wrox cannot guarantee the accuracy of this information.

Credits

Authors
Neil Matthew
Richard Stones

Contributing Authors
Christopher Browne
Brad Clements
Andrew Froggatt
David J. Goodger
Ivan Griffin
Jeff Licquia
Ronald van Loon
Udaya Ranawake
Harish Rawat
Marius Sundbakken
Deepak Thomas
Stephen J. Turnbull
David Woodhouse

Technical Architect
Louay Fatoohi

Technical Editors
David Mercer
Dan Squier

Technical Reviewers
Robert Applebaum
Jason Bennett
Jonathon Blank
Michael Boerner
Wankyu Choi
Brad Clements
Andrew Froggatt
Chris Harshman
Dave Hudson
Dave Jewel
Giles Lean
Marty Leisner
Bill Moss
Mike Olson
Jonathon Pinnock
Gavin Smyth
Paul Spencer

Technical Reviewers
Chris Tregenza
Ronald van Loon
Bruce Varney
Paul Warren
Mark Wilcox
Peter Wright

Category Manager
Viv Emery

Author Agent
Lynne Basset

Proof Readers
Lisa Rutter
Christopher Smith
Keith Westmoreland

Production Manager
Laurent Lafon

Project Administrator
Nicola Phillips

Production Coordinator
Tom Bartlett

Design/Layout
Tom Bartlett

Illustrations
Shabnam Hussain

Chapter Divider Artwork
Fidget

Cover
Chris Morris
Shelley Frazier

Index
Alessandro Ansa

About the Authors

Neil Matthew

Neil has been programming computers of one sort or another since 1974, but doesn't feel that old. Keen on programming languages and the ways they can be used to solve different problems he has written his fair share of emulators, interpreters, and translators, including ones for Basic, BCPL, FP (Functional Programming), Lisp, Prolog, and the 6502 microprocessor hardware at the heart of the BBC Microcomputer. He graduated from the University of Nottingham, England with a degree in Mathematics, but got stuck into computers straight away.

He has used UNIX since 1978, including most academic and commercial variants, some now long forgotten. Highlights include UNIX versions 6 and 7 on PDP 11/34 and 11/70, Xenix on PDP 11/23 and Intel 286 and 386, BSD 4.2 on DEC VAX 11/750, UNIX System V on MicroVAX and Intel 386, Sun SunOS4 on Sparc, and Solaris on Sparc and Intel. He now collects Linux distributions to run on his home network of six PCs.

Neil's first Linux was a 0.99.11 kernel based SLS system that was shipped across the Atlantic in boxes and boxes of floppy disks in August 1993. He has been using Linux ever since, both at home and at work, programming mainly in C, C++, Icon, and Tcl. He uses and recommends Linux for Internet connections, usually as a proxy caching server for Windows LANs and also as a file and print server to Windows 9x/NT using SAMBA. He's sold a number of Internet firewall systems to UK companies (including to Wrox in their early days!).

Neil says that Linux is a great development environment, as it offers all of the flexibility and power of traditional UNIX systems, but it manages to combine the strengths of just about all of the disparate UNIX variants (such as System V and BSD). Programs written for just about any UNIX will port to Linux with little or no effort. You can also "get under the hood" with Linux as the source code is freely available.

As Head of Software and Principal Engineer at Camtec Electronics in the 1980s Neil programmed in C and C++ for real-time embedded systems. Since then he's worked on software development techniques and quality assurance both as a consultant in communications software development with Scientific Generics and as a software QA specialist with GEHE UK. Linux has played an increasing role in the work that he has undertaken over the years, from file servers, through Internet gateways to forming the platform for a distributed radio communications system.

Neil is married to Christine and has two children, Alexandra and Adrian. He lives in a converted barn in Northamptonshire, England. His interests include computers, music, science fiction, chess, motor sport, and not doing it yourself.

Richard Stones

Richard started programming in the early days, when a BBC with 32k on RAM was a serious home computer. He graduated from Nottingham University, England with an Electronics degree, but decided that software was more fun.

He has worked for a variety of companies over the years, from the very small with just two dozen employees, to the American multinational EDS. Along the way he has worked on a wide variety of interesting projects. These have ranged from communications network management systems, embedded real time systems, and multi-gigabyte help desk and user management systems, through to more mundane accountancy systems. He has always done his best to get Linux running as part of his projects, and usually finds a niche for Linux somewhere. In many projects, especially those requiring embedded software, Linux has been used as the main development platform. He has also installed Linux as file and print servers and Internet gateways.

He first met UNIX style operating systems on a PDP 11/23+, after which BSD 4.2 on a VAX seemed like a big leap forward. He has used many of the various commercial UNIX offerings, and bemoans the unnecessary differences between them. He first discovered Linux when Slackware CDs of the 0.99 kernel became available, and was amazed at how much quicker it ran than the commercial versions of UNIX he had previously worked on, without compromising functionality. He hopes that Linux distributions never fragment in the way the commercial offerings did.

He programs mainly in C or Java, but has also worked in C++, SQL, PHP, Perl, various assembly languages, and some proprietary real time languages, and under duress will admit that he's quite familiar with Visual Basic, but claims he only used it because it was a lesser evil than the alternatives available at the time.

He is currently employed as a systems architect for GEHE, who are the UK's largest pharmaceutical wholesaler and retailer, as well as the largest pharmaceutical wholesaler in both France and Germany, and active in many other European countries.

Rick lives in a Leicestershire village, in England, with his wife Ann, children Jenny and Andrew, and two cats. Outside computers his passion is for classical music, especially early church music. He tries to find time to practice the piano, but it always seems to be last on the list of things to do.

Rick and Neil co-authored *Instant UNIX (Wrox Press)*, and *Beginning Linux Programming (Wrox Press)* and have contributed chapters to one or two other Wrox books. They also spoke at the first Bang!inux conference in Bangalore in February 2000.

AUTHORS' ACKNOWLEDGMENTS

We, Richard and Neil, would like to thank our families:

Neil's wife Christine for her unfailing support and understanding, and his children Alexandra and Adrian for thinking that it's cool to have a Dad who can write books.

Rick's wife Ann, and children, Jenny and Andrew, for their patience during the many evenings and weekends while the book was written. He would also like to thank them for being so understanding about the decision to do more writing.

We would also like to thank the many people who made this book possible.

Firstly the people who enjoyed *Beginning Linux Programming*, making it the success it has been, providing useful feedback and spurring us on to write a sequel. We have taken their suggestions for ways to extend and improve *BLP*, and this is the result – a book that we hope takes Linux application development to the next level. We have tried to introduce some more advanced topics and show how programs can be made robust, flexible, secure, and extensible, ready to be distributed and maintained in a professional manner.

We would like to thank the team at Wrox for their hard work on the book, especially Louay, David M, Dan S, Richard, James, Nicola, Lynne, Rob, Dan M, Andrew P, and last, but not least, John for buying the pizza, as well as the others who worked behind the scenes.

We would also like to thank the people who have contributed additional material to the book; they provided some excellent material.

Special thanks are also due to the team of reviewers who worked on our chapters. They provided comments and suggestions of the highest quality, and went to efforts above and beyond the call of duty to improve the book. Thank you very much one and all. Any errors that have slipped through are, of course, entirely our own fault.

We, Neil and Rick, would also like to thank our employers, GEHE, for their support while we were writing this book.

We would also like to pay homage to Linus for the Linux platform, RMS for the excellent set of GNU tools and the GPL, and the ever expanding throng of unsung heroes who choose to make their software freely available.

Christopher Browne

Christopher is a consultant with Sabre Inc., in the Human Resources and Payroll Systems organization supporting these systems for AMR (American Airlines). He has been involved since 1996 with conversions at AMR to use SAP R/3 for financial accounting and for HR and payroll systems. He was previously a Systems Engineer with SHL Systemhouse (now EDS) in their SAP R/3 practice. He is also the treasurer of the North Texas Linux Users Group (NTLUG).

Chris holds a Bachelor of Mathematics degree from the University of Waterloo, Joint Honors Co-op Chartered Accountancy and Computer Science, and a Master of Science degree in Systems Science from the University of Ottawa, Canada.

Brad Clements

Brad Clements is the president of MurkWorks, Inc., a software consulting company based in Potsdam, New York, USA. He has over two decades experience developing software for a wide variety of operating systems, handheld gauges, and embedded devices. A firm believer of "use the best tool for the job", he has found Python to be an elegant, powerful solution for an increasing number of projects.

While attending Clarkson University as a Physics major, he caught the entrepreneurial spirit and ran off to join a startup firm developing an airport bomb detection device. Later, he worked as a Sr. Network Engineer for five years before forming his own consulting business.

Although he spends much of his time managing the company, he still finds time to develop new software, study emerging technologies, and collaborate with other open source developers.

An avid horseman, dog lover, and pilot, he enjoys show jumping and flying. He has recently begun building his own airplane – a Sonex. Brad lives in the Adirondack mountain region of northern New York with his wife, Marsha and two lovely daughters Rachael and Rhiannon. You can reach him on the Internet at bkc+plip@MurkWorks.com

Andrew Froggatt

Andrew is a student at Cambridge University, England, reading Experimental and Theoretical physics. His first encounter with computers was with a trusty BBC Micro at the age of six, with which he first programmed with BBC BASIC (the best language ever). He also learned the important life skill of how to adjust the cassette player volume level to load games such as Elite or Stryker's Run first time.

Andrew discovered Linux around ten years later, and immediately took to it because he thought it was really cool to enter a password to use your own computer. Now he can say he's written dozens of large and small programs with C, Java, ML, Perl, and even Fortran, all on various platforms.

Having gone to Cambridge and studied a little Computer Science, he found himself one summer working for Wrox Press, and they've pestered him several times to write and technically review for them since – something that he's very happy to do. Despite all this, Andrew does not know what to do after he graduates.

David J. Goodger

David is a programmer, systems administrator, and consultant. He collects programming languages but loves Python best. He has worked in education (teaching English in Japan), government (two years as an embassy employee in Tokyo), and industry.

His hobbies include Go, puzzles, bicycling, reading (and aspiring to writing), good science fiction, and poker. He helped his wife produce two beautiful children, and they all live happily in Kitchener, Ontario, Canada. This is his first professionally published work.

Ivan Griffin

Ivan works for Parthus Technologies plc, on some really crazy bleeding edge technology. His most recent project has been embedded development on Bluetooth, the 2.4 GHz short range wireless radio system – where lower power, low MIPs and low RAM requirements are essential.

Previously, he worked on a research project for the University of Limerick, Ireland. This project involved dynamically reconfigurable telecomms systems through the use of migratable CORBA/Java agents.

Ivan has developed on many different platforms – from various flavors of UNIX to Windows to Z80 and ARM7 embedded systems. He stumbled across Linux 0.99 sometime in '92/93 as an undergraduate, and has been hooked on the environment ever since.

Aside from computers, Ivan has keen interests in swimming, skiing, and mountain-biking.

Jeff Licquia

Jeff has been working in the information industry for over 10 years in many diverse roles. He discovered Linux in its early days (before it could boot multi-user), and has professionally deployed Linux since 1993. Currently, he is the network administrator for Springfield Clinic, a health clinic in his home town of Springfield, Illinois, USA.

Outside of work, he enjoys being active in the Debian project, as well as spending time with his wife and two children.

Ronald van Loon

Ronald is currently working as an IT Architect for IBM Global Services in Amsterdam, The Netherlands. A neighbor (who had built a computer for himself) first introduced him, at the age of 12, to computers. Soon after that he owned his first computer (a Commodore 64) and started to experiment with it. He now has a Masters degree in Computer Science and has about 12 years of work experience in several fields, ranging from medical imaging to video-on-demand applications.

Ronald has broad interests with a weak spot for multimedia and route planning. He was the developer of the TMF (a Dutch commercial broadcasting channel) Cyberchoice program, a standalone interactive play-out video system that works without human intervention.

In his leisure time he sings in a choir, goes to the theatre, looks after Bas (a little teddy bear), and lives and loves together with his girlfriend Marjolijn in their combined apartments in Amersfoort. You can reach him by email: mail@rvl.nu

Udaya A. Ranawake

Udaya is a research scientist at Goddard Earth Sciences and Technology (GEST) Center at NASA GSFC, USA. He has more than ten years of experience developing software for parallel computers.

Currently, he is working on the Hive project at NASA GSFC the goal of which is to build a low cost high performance parallel computer using commodity hardware and freely available software packages.

Udaya holds a BSc degree in Electrical Engineering from University of Moratuwa, Sri Lanka, and MSc and PhD degrees in Electrical & Computer Engineering from Oregon State University, USA.

Harish Rawat

Harish is a Software Developer at the Oracle Corporation, USA. He has eight years of experience in systems programming. His technical areas of interest include XML, Java, and Network Protocols.

Marius Sundbakken

Marius received a Software Engineering degree from the college of Buskerud in Kongsberg, Norway. After a year of study at Washington State University, USA, he received a Bachelor of Computer Science degree. He plans to get his Masters in Computer Science, in the near future.

His main interest in computing is object-oriented software design, especially using Qt. C++ is his favorite language, although he uses C and Java if he has to. He bought his first computer, an Amiga, at the age of sixteen, and learned a wide variety of languages, ranging from C, AREXX, 680x0 assembly, to C++.

Marius first noticed Qt in 1996, and has been programming Linux applications using Qt in his spare time. He made QtVu, an image viewer based on Qt (www.qtvu.org), and is currently writing an email client called Mailliam (www.mailliam.org) , which is also Qt based.

Thanks to Jan Borsodi at eZ Systems for technical assistance.

Deepak Thomas

Deepak Thomas works for Oracle corporation at Redwood Shores, CA, USA. His areas of interest include PHP, Linux, and several Java related technologies. He co-authored *Professional PHP Programming* for Wrox press.

Stephen J. Turnbull

Stephen daylights as an economist. He moved to Japan in 1990, and discovered that the Japanese have four different ways to encode ASCII, let alone the multiple ways they encode the three native character sets. That left him no alternative to learning about internationalization of software in detail.

Steve was dual booting Linux and DESQview/X in the months before January 1995; he started leaving Linux running 24x7 on January 17, and for the next four days his web page was the Internet's main broadband window on the Kobe earthquake disaster.

Now he lives a quieter life, occasionally working on multilingual features of Xemacs, and advocating better internationalization for Linux.

David Woodhouse

David is a Linux kernel hacker, working for Red Hat on embedded Linux technology. He is responsible for the Memory Technology Device drivers in the Linux kernel, which handle solid state storage devices such as Flash chips. He encountered Linux while studying Computer Science at the University of Cambridge, England, and hasn't done any "real work" since then.

He is often suspected of being schizophrenic – long periods of languishing in front of a computer in the dark are punctuated with a violent desire to get outside and climb mountains.

David lives near Cambridge, which is a shame because there are no mountains there.

Online discussion at http://www.p2p.wrox.com

Table of Contents

Table of Contents

Table of Contents

Table of Contents

Table of Contents

Table of Contents

Table of Contents

Table of Contents

Table of Contents

Online discussion at http://www.p2p.wrox.com

Introduction

Welcome

Welcome to the exciting world of Linux Programming.

If you are one of the many readers of our authoritative book *Beginning Linux Programming* then be prepared for another enjoyable and informative journey into the world of Linux. If this is your first encounter with our Linux programming book series, then you'll shortly be convinced that you have got the right book.

Who is This Book for?

This book is for experienced Linux programmers and those aspiring to become developers for one of the most exciting Operating Systems around. This book covers topics that have been carefully chosen, based on the knowledge of what professional developers usually encounter during their careers. This includes practical information on libraries, techniques, tools and applications for Linux programmers.

Versatility, and breadth of choice, ensure that you are more than likely to find something that is of particular interest to you. Depth of coverage is what professional developers can expect to find when consulting this book, and we have made every effort to strike the right balance between the type of topics that we cover and the depth of our coverage.

Whether an experienced Linux programmer or on your way to be so, this book is for you.

What's Covered in This Book?

In both editions of our first Linux programming book, *Beginning Linux Programming (ISBN 1861002971)*, we covered many tools, libraries and techniques that every Linux programmer should be familiar with. In this book, we tackle new, more advanced topics that professional Linux programmers are bound to deal with. *Professional Linux Programming* is the natural sequel to *Beginning Linux Programming*.

Maintaining the style that we followed in *Beginning Linux Programming*, this book takes a practical approach. Whenever necessary, examples are called upon to support and explain theory. Again, following in the path of *Beginning Linux Programming*, this book adopts a central application example that is developed as the book progresses. To be precise, we use a DVD rental store application to introduce the various tools, libraries and techniques.

We have divided the chapters into two categories: theme chapters, which discuss topics that progress the DVD store application theme, and take-a-break chapters. The latter are standalone chapters that tackle a variety of topics of interest to professional developers. Rather than having a continuous flow of 17 theme chapters followed by 11 non-theme chapters, we have used the take-a-break chapters as "stopping stations" between the theme chapters.

The distinction between the two types of chapter does not imply that the topics covered by one group of chapters are more important. Additionally, the theme chapters differ to an extent in how much they revolve around the DVD store application theme. Both kinds of chapter are practical tutorials that use examples to put the theory into practice. So, what are those chapters about?

We start off Chapter 1 with an overview of issues involved in application design. Next, we discuss the DVD store application that is developed and used in the theme chapters. We explain how to determine and formalize the requirements of our application. The objective of the chapter is achieved when we translate those requirements into APIs.

When working with a project of any size, there is always a need to track changes to our code. While it is possible to do this manually when we work on our own and when our project is small, we certainly need a better and more efficient way of doing this when managing large projects and/or working within a team. Chapter 2 introduces us to a powerful source control system: the Concurrent Versions System (CVS). We show how to install and use CVS, and we investigate one of the most powerful advantages that CVS has over its competitors: its ability to operate across networks, including the Internet.

Having already decided to use a relational database for our DVD store, Chapter 3 takes a very brief look at mSQL, MySQL and PostgreSQL, and compares them with each other. After picking PostgreSQL, we take a look at installing and commissioning the database, as well as basic commands. We then explore data normalization in relational databases and take a peek at some data management commands.

Chapter 3 showed you how to access PostgreSQL using a command line tool called psql, and Chapter 4, teaches you how to access PostgreSQL from C code. The chapter covers both ways of doing this: using the library libpq and embedded SQL. Now, we can design the backend of the database for the DVD store.

Chapter 5 is the first of our take-a-break chapters. Although we made the decision that PostgreSQL is the database for our DVD store application, MySQL is an equally powerful database that would be ideal to use in many applications. In this chapter we learn about installing, configuring, and administering MySQL. Finally, we see how we an access MySQL from C.

When writing an application, it is inevitable that errors begin to creep into our code. Chapter 6 introduces some tools and techniques that we can use to clean our code. Efficient reporting of errors is a great help in tackling bugs. There is a discussion of the various ways to include debug statements in code followed by a section on using assertions. We then learn how to add tracing functionality to our program to follow the path that it takes. The last part of the chapter introduces the GNU debugger, GDB, showing some of its commands.

There are situations where it is more appropriate to use an LDAP directory server than a database. Our second take-a-break introduces various concepts and conventions used with LDAP servers, and then focuses on an open source LDAP directory server called OpenLDAP. We take a peek at installing, configuring and running the server, and see how data is structured inside a directory server. Then we look in detail into how to access OpenLDAP using code, including manipulating and searching data.

Chapter 8 talks us through a powerful set of GUI libraries: GTK+ and GNOME. We learn first about glib which provides the GTK+ and GNOME libraries with their underlying data management functionality. The chapter then takes us on a journey into GTK+ and GNOME showing us how to build simple as well as sophisticated GUIs using these powerful libraries. There is also a description of the GNOME source tree and session management.

The previous chapter paved the road to another theme chapter in which we build a GUI front end for our DVD store application using GTK+/GNOME. We first introduce Glade, a powerful interface builder for GTK+/GNOME, before embarking on a detailed description of a GUI that we have developed for our application using Glade.

Now it is the time for another break, this time with Flex and Bison. Flex is an open source generator of lexical analyzers or scanners. Bison is the GNU writer of parsers. In Chapter 10 we learn how to use these two utilities and see the power they offer.

Using the DVD store application, the next chapter investigates various techniques and tools that can be used for testing the applications we write. Issues covered in this chapter include memory and performance testing, and the installation and use of the mpatrol library.

In another take-a-break chapter, we investigate aspects of secure programming in Linux. We take a look at filesystem security, user authentication, Pluggable Authentication Modules (PAM), cryptography, and secure network programming. We also explore in Chapter 12 some of the security issues concerning C/C++, Perl, Python, and PHP.

GTK+ and GNOME are not the only sets of libraries that can be used for developing GUIs on Linux. The C++ based Qt and KDE are very powerful and popular GUI libraries. In Chapter 13, we learn how to install and use Qt and KDE.

Having introduced Qt/KDE in the previous chapter, we can now proceed to use these libraries to develop another GUI for the DVD store application, along the same lines as the one that we developed earlier using GTK+/GNOME.

Then we take a break with Python. Python is a popular, high-level, interpreted, object-oriented language. We show how to install Python and its various running modes. Then we take a look at the built-in data types and operators of this language and its syntax.

Chapter 16 explores one of the most popular server-side scripting languages, PHP. The chapter covers installing and configuring PHP, as well as its syntax. We then use PHP to develop an interface for our DVD store application.

The following take-a-break chapter extends the Python knowledge that we acquired from Chapter 15, showing us how to embed and extend Python with C/C++. We use the Simplified Wrapper Interface Generator (SWIG) and the Python C API to extend Python.

Chapter 18 shows us first how applications can communicate across the network through the use of sockets. It then moves to its main topic, Remote Procedures Calls (RPC). Assuming that we wanted to open another branch of our DVD store but use a single centralized database, this chapter shows us how to accomplish this using RPC.

In Chapter 19 we take another break to have a look at multi media programming in Linux. This is one area where Linux is lagging behind other OSs. The main reason for this is the lack of device drivers. We see how to handle audio devices and take a quick look at Linux support for video and animation.

While RPC is useful, CORBA is much better at constructing distributed object-based applications. Chapter 20 is an introduction to CORBA. We learn about the various component and layers of CORBA and how they interact with each other.

In the next chapter we apply our newly acquired CORBA knowledge to our DVD store application using the GNOME ORB, ORBit. The chapter also covers CORBAServices.

In Chapter 22, we put aside our DVD store application to learn about diskless systems and how to implement them using Linux.

Chapter 23 tackles one of the most exciting topics in computing today: XML. There is an introduction to the structure and syntax of XML documents using an XML catalog of our DVD store. XML is ideal for importing catalogs to our DVD database. The concept of valid XML is defined and DTD is explained. We then investigate how to parse XML documents using the Simple API for XML (SAX).

Our next break is with Beowulf clusters, where we learn about their architecture and software configuration. We then explore programming of Beowulf clusters using two popular message-passing libraries, the Message Passing Interface (MPI) and the Parallel Virtual Machine (PVM).

Documentation is an essential aspect of software development. Chapter 25 explains the types of documentation required by different users. There is coverage of a wide range of the different types and formats of documentation including manpages, HTML, XML, TeX, DocBook, Plain Old Document (POD) and PDF. The chapter also covers literary programming.

Chapter 26 talks about an important topic in kernel programming, device drivers. The chapter also explains how the Linux kernel handles PCI devices.

Preparing an application for distribution is something of interest to every developer. Chapter 27 explores the RedHat Package Manager (RPM), including installing, upgrading and uninstalling RPM packages. We also show how to build an RPM package that distributes our DVD store application. There is also coverage of the use of `configure`, `autoconf` and `automake` to create a standard source code directory ready for distribution, as well as creating patches.

A worthy topic to end our journey through the world of Linux programming is Internationalization. Chapter 28 tackles various models, techniques and issues involved in making any application portable to other languages.

What You Need to Use This Book

You need a Linux box with the set of packages that are required by the different chapters of the book. These include GTK+, GNOME, Glade, Qt, KDE, PostgreSQL, MySQL, LDAP, Flex, Bison, Python, SWIG, ORBit-Python, MPICH and many others. Although the vast majority of required packages are bundled with the common Linux distributions, where a package is not present, or you wish to install the very latest version, the relevant information for obtaining these packages and installing them is given in the appropriate places in the book.

You'll also need to have an Internet connection to download the source code for the book if you want to see the full source code behind all of the chapters, or avoid typing in the many self-contained example code examples

You are presumed to have knowledge of programming in C and Linux. If you find that you need some help in familiarizing yourself with programming in Linux, then you might find our book *Beginning Linux Programming* (*ISBN 1861002971*) very helpful. Certain chapters presume a limited knowledge of C++.

Source Code

We have tried to provide example programs and code snippets that best illustrate the concepts being discussed in the text. The complete source code from the book is available for download from:

http://www.wrox.com

It's available under the terms of the GNU Public License. We suggest you get hold of a copy to save yourself a lot of typing, although almost all the code you need is listed in the book.

Conventions

To help you get the most from the text and keep track of what's happening, we've used a number of conventions throughout the book.

> *This style is used for asides to the current discussion.*

We use several different fonts in the text of this book:

- ❏ File names, and words you might use at a command prompt, in code or type into a configuration file are shown like this: `struct pci_driver`, `main.c`, or `rpcinfo -p localhost`.

- ❏ URLs are written like this: www.gnome.org

We show commands typed at the command line like this:

```
$ gcc -I/usr/include/xml sax1.c -lxml -lz -o sax1
```

Commands which must be executed as root are shown with a # prompt like this:

```
# make install
```

And when we list the contents of files, we'll use the following convention:

```
Lines which show concepts directly related to the surrounding text are shown on a
grey background
But lines which do not introduce anything new, or which we have seen before, are
shown on a white background.
```

Online discussion at http://www.p2p.wrox.com

1

Application Design

Overview

The development of professional quality applications is best achieved through a reasonably balanced and planned approach, understanding your aims, and understanding your tools. Nobody likes getting things wrong unexpectedly and being forced to start over. Taking care with planning your application before you start coding can save a great deal of grief.

Linux is a great platform to develop applications on. It's open architecture and the availability of its source code has made writing applications for Linux truly attractive.

This book is not intended as an academic textbook on systems development. We are not going to spend time teaching project management or much time on any particular software methodology. There are many other good books that can do that. Some ideas for further reading can be found in the *Resources* section at the end of this chapter.

As software developers, the authors have come to appreciate that we can save time and effort by applying some simple techniques and tools to our work. In this chapter we will consider how to avoid some of the pitfalls that can trap the unwary when developing real applications (but are also useful for applications written just for fun). We will cover requirements capture, use cases, application architecture, and interface specification. Later in the book we will cover source code control, debugging, testing, documentation, as well as implementation topics such as databases and graphical user interfaces.

Throughout the book we will be using an application to demonstrate the tools, techniques, and libraries we will be covering. The development of a single application will provide us with a useful thread linking many of the chapters together. It will begin as a loosely defined set of requirements, progressing through a more rigorous design and ultimately blossoming into a professionally developed, robust, and potentially deployable basis for a software system.

The application we are going to develop over the course of this book is not intended to be a complete commercial product. In some ways the example is contrived, and many system designers are likely to disagree with the decisions we have made for its implementation, quite possibly with good reasons.

The application we have chosen is one for helping to manage a DVD or video rental store. We will begin in the early stages with a simple application for storing details of DVDs available to rent. We will then add functionality such as a graphical user interface with searching facilities. We will see how we might add the ability to implement business rules, for example to enable charging different rates depending on different factors (such as allowing a discount for Mondays through Thursdays). Eventually we will add a Web-based interface to allow customers to pre-book their rentals.

We will start with a couple of implementation choices already made.

We have elected to develop the application in C. Despite the advent and rise in popularity of newer and more exotic languages such as C++, Java and Perl, C remains more than capable of supporting most of the programming tasks we are likely to undertake, especially in a Linux environment. After all, C is the language of UNIX, and the Linux kernel is written in it – there are interfaces from C to just about every feature of the system. The Linux application interface is effectively designed for use in C programs. You can access databases from C and even program graphical user interfaces in C using GNOME and GTK+.

We have also taken the decision to implement the application using a full-strength database, even though the scope of the example system is not really wide enough to fully warrant it. This is a little contrived, but allows us to demonstrate database and GUI interfaces late in the book.

The detail of the application is also a compromise. When discussing its requirements and design we will skip over some issues that would need to be resolved in the real world. For example, some choices have been made to use fixed length fields where variable length might be more appropriate. Some of the detailed design is a little inflexible.

This chapter is in three parts. In the first part we talk briefly about methodologies, and how they are evolving to meet ever-changing challenges. In the next section, we describe how a real world exercise in requirements capture and analysis might proceed, showing how we would convert user requirements into more formal statements that could be used as a basis for creating a system design. Finally we will present a basic application architecture and API (Application Programming Interface) designed to meet those requirements, which will act as our theme application for this book. Later chapters will use these APIs to illustrate topics covered earlier in this chapter.

Requirements Capture

We mentioned earlier that we would start with a loosely defined set of requirements. That was not intended as a statement of intent, rather as an acceptance of the real world. For many projects the process of determining precisely what the customer wants is a fraught one and the source of many problems further down the road. There are few things worse than completing a system only to find out that some underlying assumption was incorrect. In the worst case it is possible that all the development will have been wasted, the customer won't pay, and might even sue!

If we do not take care to think about what our application has to do, we can end up with a raft of problems. These might include:

- ❏ expanding or changing requirements (feature creep)
- ❏ ambiguous requirements
- ❏ missing or assumed requirements
- ❏ incorrect requirements
- ❏ a lack of flexibility in the design and implementation

Feature creep can occur when we rush to start coding an application. We have a basic idea of what we are trying to do and press on with development. Then we discover that we need to add another feature, change that function or support another interface. If we haven't agreed with our customer precisely what we are going to do for him, he may keep on asking for more and more. We might never finish what we started! However, there are ways of coping with this situation.

Ambiguous requirements arise when we are sloppy about the terms we use, or when the same terms mean different things to different parties. There are many English words that have more than one meaning. A 'store' might refer to a sales outlet, or a storage facility. If we design a system for the wrong type of store we could be in big trouble. It is therefore important to define terms carefully and avoid industry jargon as much as possible.

Assumed requirements can be very tricky. These might cause a problem if we are working in unfamiliar territory. For example, we might not realize that book numbers (ISBN numbers) include a check digit, and design a system that did not generate them. Our customer – a book publisher – may neglect to tell us this requirement because it's well known in the industry. All publishing systems have to cope with this; it is an assumed requirement.

Other examples abound. In Australia and New Zealand all cash prices are rounded to the nearest five cents, because a five-cent piece is the smallest coin in circulation in both countries. Woe to the retail supplier who doesn't cater for this! Similarly, countries with value added taxes would expect point of sale systems to calculate them according to the local rules.

We can go a long way to mitigate the effects of these kinds of problems by taking care, recording our requirements in a formal way, and by prioritizing them so that we always know what is most important.

If we agree on the functionality of the application before we get too far into implementation we can avoid feature creep later on. Or at least, be compensated for the extra effort needed to extend the application in an agreed way. To keep control of changing requirements we can use a 'wish list' to keep track of feature creep, advising the client of the costs and implications of any changes he wants to consider.

If we make sure that we concentrate on as much detail as we can when capturing requirements, we can reduce the likelihood of being caught out by missing or assumed requirements.

We can also reduce ambiguity by establishing a common vocabulary, defining what we mean by each of the specialist terms used in the requirements. We should take care to word the requirements in short sentences, using words like 'shall' and 'must' for things that we *have* to do - the mandatory requirements - and 'should' or 'may' when describing optional features that our application might have, given sufficient time and money. All requirements should be testable, that is, it should be possible to construct a test to tell whether or not a system meets a particular requirement. For example, being 'fast' is not testable, but 'responding in under a second' is.

When developing for an end user, gaining a good understanding of the requirements can be frustrating, as we have noted earlier. It is important to remember however, that the user (or sponsor) is our customer, and has the freedom to do more or less as he or she pleases in terms of indicating what they want. A scribble on a napkin may be all that we get. As professional developers we must be able to cope with the variable nature of user requirements. However, just because our customer is not inclined to produce a well-structure statement of requirements, it's no excuse for us to be lax in this regard.

In general, requirements fall into one of several categories:

- ❏ functionality (what needs to be done)
- ❏ performance (how quickly, how many)
- ❏ usability (screen layouts, downtime needed)
- ❏ compatibility (what the system needs to interface with)
- ❏ price
- ❏ quality

Once the requirements are collected, it is essential that both parties agree on what is required – a formal requirement document signed by the client can be of great value.

Development Models

The Waterfall model

One classical approach to development is the 'waterfall' model. Each activity in the waterfall should be complete before moving on to the next. The diagram below illustrates this approach:

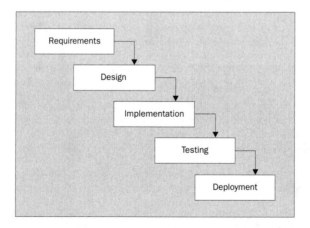

Disadvantages to the waterfall method include an inability to react to changes in requirements, except by breaking from the model. Another is the risk associated with leaving testing until near the end. If you discover that you have made a mistake in some interface or other, the consequences could be disastrous.

Some variations on the waterfall model allow re-visiting of earlier stages, swimming upstream, but these are not usually planned activities and their inclusion simply shows that the pure model does not fit well with reality.

Iterative development

Iterative development is a more modern style of software development, challenging the 'waterfall' model and its strict boundaries between stages.

Iterative development plans for a situation where the requirements change as the project proceeds. A small number of iterations are planned from the start, to allow the end product to be refined. This embodies the realization that the customers will change their minds, even if they were sure what they wanted in the first place. Flexible software, such as GUI's or sophisticated decision-making processes support, will often find themselves subject to loose requirements or feature creep. We have to find a way of countering the all too frequent cry 'I'll know what I want when I see it', or worse 'I've just thought of another use, can we make it do this?' The iterative model allows the requirements to be re-visited, provides the user with early sight of a version of the software and allows the developer to 'pipe clean' his development environment.

The general plan is to schedule the highest priority mandatory requirements into earlier iterations (release 1.0). The methodology promotes a modular construction, with shallow GUIs and replaceable data access methods.

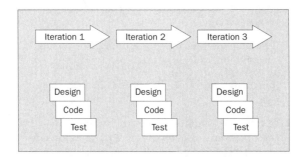

We can see from this diagram that in the iterations of our development we are performing tasks taken from all phases in the waterfall model. Typically you would plan for a small number of iterations, implementing a defined subset of requirements in each iteration. Larger projects in a changing environment may need some re-implementation, but this is always planned before the start of each iteration.

It is worth emphasizing that design (and requirements refining) is an ongoing process throughout the development process, while testing starts about a third of the way through the project and not right at the end.

'Fast Track' Development

To overcome the 'I'll know what I want when I see it' problem, it is often useful to start designing and implementing a minimal application as soon as a basic requirement set is known. This will result in a basic application that may not function terribly well – and will certainly be missing major areas of functionality – but it does provide feedback to the requirements capture effort.

Note that this is not quite the same as a disposable prototype. We are not developing a mock-up application that we will throw away (although that might happen if the requirements were way off). It is intended to be real code, but only enough to verify that we are on the right track. Our project plan will show two or three such subset implementations being refined as we go, not thrown away and re-written. An exception might be made for fake screens, laid out just to get agreement on look-and-feel.

Test Early, Test Often

Once we have an initial design we can begin our test processes. The way that we intend to handle all of the types of testing that will be necessary can usefully be documented in a written test plan. We can validate the design by performing a review of what we have against the requirements as they stand at that stage.

Furthermore, we can formulate a test strategy for the application. We can decide how we are going to test, what tools we will need, and what support in the application itself will make testing more productive.

We will need to cover testing of:

❑ Code components (**unit testing**)

❑ Interfaces between components (**integration testing**)

❑ The complete system (**system testing**)

As changes are made we will need to retest to ensure that new problems have not been introduced. This is known as **regression testing**.

Finally we will need to show the customer that the finished system does indeed meet the agreed requirements. This is **acceptance testing**.

Before we start on an initial implementation we can test our development environment, making sure our compilers and libraries are present and working correctly.

Once we have an initial implementation we can test it, making sure that our testing strategy works and that all the tools we need to test with are available and functioning properly.

Basically, the idea is to test everything, and to reduce risk by doing so as early as possible. The waterfall model can be vulnerable if all of the testing activities take place at the end. By then it's too late to decide that implementation in an exotic language was a mistake because the debugger you thought you could use doesn't work on your hardware, or the interpreter you are using cannot run fast enough to meet the performance targets!

We will have more to say about testing in Chapter 11.

The DVD Store

To provide an example system development, let's imagine a local DVD rental store, that's almost entirely paper based, and that the owner decides he wants a system to help manage his day-to-day operations. There will probably be a number of problems that he faces, and he would like them taken away.

The owner of the DVD store is not a real person. We will be putting words into his mouth; especially regarding the cost limits (which do not include our labor), and the desire to use Open Source software. We will also assume that he at least understands that 'Operating System' does not automatically mean Windows.

Given that this is a book about application development using Linux, it would be rather unfortunate if the example application ended up being closed-source, using a proprietary database on Windows NT. However, there is of course no inherent restriction when it comes to programming for Linux. You are always free to develop proprietary solutions using commercial products.

We need to ask the store manager to tell us about how the store works, so as to get a basic understanding of the problem. It will be valuable to observe the store in operation, and talk to customers too. We need a good understanding of the context in which the system will be developed – its users and its environment.

At this point in requirements capture, you will almost always discover that the user wants to tell you *how* they do things at present, not *what* they do. It's very important to try and talk about what is being done, or you will end up designing a computer system that simply computerizes the existing problems, instead of developing a computer system to solve the existing problems.

Initial Requirements

Talking to the storeowner, we can get some initial user requirements. Notice that we record each requirement with a unique reference. For user requirements we prefix a requirement number with the letters 'UR':

> **UR1** – People leave returned DVDs in my mail box first thing in the morning before the store is opened; when there are several copies of the same film out I have no idea which copy has been returned.

> **UR2** – I can't find which DVDs are out on rental without looking in the back of the shop to check, and it annoys people when they have to put the box back on the shelf because the video is out.

> **UR3** – It must be friendly.

> **UR4** – I want to keep the cash drawer I already have, because I only just purchased it.

> **UR5** – I've heard about this thing where developers let people have the code for computer systems; I want the code for any system you sell to me.

> **UR6** – I can't justify spending more than $1000, we'll do a separate deal for your labor.

Notice that the requirements are pretty vague and could be fulfilled in many different ways. The principle task in the requirements capture phase is to clarify and refine the requirements, possibly splitting complex ones into a number of simpler ones. We have also numbered the requirements to make them easier to track later on. We should not be too focused on the design of the eventual system at this stage, although we might be able to determine that some requirements will ultimately be impractical or too costly.

This is not a bad list as a starting point, but there is one obvious omission that we need to find out about: just how many DVDs and members does the store application need to support? We can get an idea from the current situation.

This gives us our seventh and eighth user requirements:

> **UR7** – I have 5000 different titles, and 7000 actual disks.

> **UR8** – I just gave out membership card 9000, though I suppose a few of those must have moved away and never got round to canceling their membership.

Analyzing the User Requirements

Now we have some user requirements as a starting point, we can leave the store owner to get on with his job, while we try and understand these requirements, and express them in a more exact way.

We will start with **UR1**, and **UR7**:

> **UR1** – People leave returned DVDs in my mail box first thing in the morning before the store is opened, and when there are several copies of the same film out I have no idea which copy has been returned.

> **UR7** – I have 5000 different titles, and 7000 actual disks.

There is a very important fact lurking in these two statements: the DVD store has multiple copies of many movies, and it's very important to be able to tell which member returned a particular disk, just knowing which title was returned is not enough. If we had missed the subtle point that a DVD title (the film "2001") needs to be handled differently to a DVD disc (copy number 3 of the film "2001") we could have been in for a lot of reworking later on.

We can state these more formally, expanding them into more succinct requirement statements, and allowing some room for growth:

> **R1: The store must support more than 5000 different titles.**
>
> **R2: The store must support more than 7000 different disks.**
>
> **R3: We need to support at least 5 different physical copies of each title.**
>
> **R4: We need to be able to tell from a returned disk which member rented it.**

Let's move on to **UR2**:

> **UR2** – I can't find which DVDs are out on rental without looking in the back of the shop to check, and it annoys people when they have to put the box back on the shelf because the DVD is out.

This is a tricky one. There are several ways this problem could be solved, not all of them involving a computer. The problem is that members are selecting a DVD case off the shelf, then getting to the counter, having to wait while the person behind the counter checks in the back of the store, then being told there are no copies available and having to put the case back. We can also deduce from the little we have seen of the existing paper based system, that it's almost impossible for the person behind the counter to know if any of the copies are due back in soon.

A solution that didn't involve the computer might be to put a tag on each case of rented DVD, saying that it was out on loan. This would certainly help, but might be rather labor intensive.

We could add a facility to our proposed computer system, to tell the user that all copies are out and perhaps when the first one is due back in. This should be pretty easy, since it's difficult to see how any sensible system would not know which disks are currently rented out. The only drawback is that people are still getting to the counter with a DVD case, only to be told it's not available. At least now the rejection of the rental is quicker, providing there is no queue at the counter. Based on personal experience we (unfortunately!) know this isn't always the case.

If we think a bit more radically, we could take this a step further. Suppose we put a customer terminal in the store, one that allows members to check for themselves if a DVD was available? This would shorten the queue at the counter, and reduce the workload and perhaps the number of staff in the store. Hey, we could take this idea a lot further – they could search for new releases or DVDs with their favorite star in? The owner might like this approach, if we can do it cheaply enough... but we need to keep an eye on the dreaded feature creep.

We will avoid going much further with this idea, we need to talk to the storeowner again and see how he reacts to this suggestion. For now we will keep the requirements open:

> **R5: There needs to be an efficient way of discovering that all copies of a title are currently unavailable, and where they are.**
>
> **R6: There should be a way of searching the database for titles available.**

We can come back to clarify (and perhaps prioritize) these requirements later.

Let's move on to **UR3**:

> **UR3** – It must be friendly.

This is not an easy one to pin down. We cannot really justify ignoring it either. Does it mean that it is intuitive to use so no training is required? Does it mean that the system takes you through the steps needed to perform different actions in an intuitive fashion? There are probably some assumptions about performance of the system lurking in this statement as well - slow systems are not friendly! Perhaps the best thing would be to consider a design using graphical user interface that makes the common functions as obvious as possible Then, when we have an initial implementation we can seek the owner's agreement that the structure of the application will satisfy the requirement.

The next requirement is **UR4**:

> **UR4** – I want to keep the cash drawer I already have, because I only just purchased it.

We need to clarify what the storeowner means, does he mean that the system needs to integrate with his existing cash drawer, or does he just mean he doesn't want us to replace it and charge him more? It is important, not only to avoid missing requirements, but also to avoid implementing non-existent requirements.

After talking to the owner we discover that what the owner means is that he expects the new rental management system to be separate from the cash drawer – all it needs to do is display on the screen the amount to be collected. This is a big win for us as it involves less work, and gives us:

> **R7: The system only needs to display the amount of money to be collected, not to interface to a cash drawer.**

Think how much work we could have done if we had assumed that this requirement meant that we needed to interface to a cash drawer in some way.

The next requirement is **UR5**:

> **UR5** – I've heard about this thing where developers let people have the code for computer systems; I want the code for any system you sell to me. That way if anything goes wrong or I need changes I can hire anyone I like to do the work.

We assume here that he is referring to some form of Open Source, though clearly that has a number of different meanings. That's not a problem for the code we were going to write, the customer can stipulate any reasonable condition, but it might pose a problem for some other parts of the system. For now we will assume that it's going to be sufficient to give him the source to all the new code we write, but other components might not have their source code available. At this stage we don't want to rule too much out, though a Linux based solution is looking interesting, as the entire system could potentially be Open Source.

> **R8: We must make the source code of the application available to the storeowner.**
>
> **R9: The source for other components should be available.**

Here we are setting a mandatory requirement **R8**, and an optional requirement **R9**. The mandatory requirements must be achieved before the storeowner will accept delivery. We would prefer the system to have the complete source code available, but can live without it if we have to. The use of the word 'must' and 'should' differentiates the requirement types.

Moving onwards to **UR6**:

> **UR6** – I can't justify spending more than $1000.

Well we didn't expect to be able to retire rich on one job did we? This is a reasonably tight budget, and is probably going to rule out many commercial packages we might have considered.

> **R10: The total cost of the system must be less than $1000 on hardware and software licenses.**

We take the next pair of user requirements, **UR7** and **UR8** together, since they are both to do with sizing:

> **UR7** – I have 5000 different titles, and 7000 actual disks.
>
> **UR8** – I just gave out membership card 9000, though I suppose a few of those must have moved away and never got round to canceling their membership.

In fact, we have already captured the first requirement in **R1**, **R2** and **R3**. We just need to add a memberships number requirement, and some growth requirement:

> **R11: The system must support at least 9000 members, be able to add further new members and delete members that move away.**
>
> **R12: The system must be capable of growing to at least twice the size of the initially installed system.**

At this point we might want to suggest some requirements of our own, things that the owner didn't mention, but that we think are important for one reason or another; perhaps adding flexibility, or making it more useful to other stores. Examples might include some non-functional requirement types such as performance (how fast must it run when the database is fully populated), and quality (it must not crash regardless of whatever keys the user presses).

Although best placed in the 'wish list' category, there are a few other potential requirements that could crop up in the future. First, Web access:

> **R13: The system must be expandable to incorporate a web interface that could be accessible from the Internet.**

Next, XML is growing rapidly as a format for many types of structured data.

> **R14: The system must be extendable to import data from XML data sources, as the DVD supplier is planning to make an XML feed available.**

The other interesting trend is LDAP. Maybe in the future there could be online directory servers with local residents' data in, or maybe up and coming DVD titles?

> **R15: The system must be extendable to access data from LDAP directory servers.**

We will see how these technologies can be integrated into our applications in Chapters 7, 16 and 23.

So far we have said almost nothing about the people that use the system, but until we have clarified **UR2**, and how **R5** and **R6** might solve it, we don't know if members should ever be allowed to interact with the system directly. Even if the user likes the idea, it will require a second computer system in the store for members to use, which is going to be difficult in the budget available.

Now we have thought about the requirements, we can go back to the store owner, and see if we can be more precise about **R5** and **R6**, check to see who will use the system, and ask about the format of the disk numbers and membership numbers. Since it seems unlikely the owner will want to re-code all their disks, and re-issue 9000 membership cards, the system had better cope with the existing numbering scheme.

We also need to see if there are any requirements we have missed that can now be uncovered, since the earlier we fully discover our requirements the better.

Back in the store, we notice that the price of film rental has been changed. It seems that disk rental is cheaper on some days of the week, and over the summer holidays, when it's quiet; the owner often does discounts for multiple rentals. Better add that as a requirement:

> **R16: The system shall be able to cope with discounts for multi-rentals, and different rental prices for different days of the week.**

After talking again to the storeowner about our understanding of the requirements, we find he was very keen on the idea of some simple user interface that people could use in the store to check if a title is available or had been reserved. This is interesting, since we had not considered the idea of reserving disks in advance. Unfortunately the owner didn't want to pay much more for a member kiosk in store. They thought it might be worth another $200 at most. That's going to be a problem. The only way we could see to build a kiosk for that sort of money would be to re-use a 'scrap' PC, perhaps a diskless one that could be booted across the network.

We also discovered that the owner did not see any particular reason to differentiate between himself using the system and staff using the system, and that any web or kiosk access would just be the same, but with fewer functions available. This makes things easier for us, it means we probably don't need to worry about security beyond any login security, and the application does not need to cater in any complex way for different types of user of the main system.

We also asked him about the possibility of adding barcode labels to the disk cases, and adding a scanner to the system to avoid typing. This idea went down well, until the price of the hardware was mentioned. We won't add barcode labels and a scanner as a requirement for now. Maybe that's a future project.

We can now re-write **R5** and **R6**, and also add **R17**, to cope with reservations:

> **R5: The system must indicate that all copies of a disk are rented out if a member tries to rent a disk that is not available.**
>
> **R6: The system should, if possible for less than $200, be capable of having a publicly available terminal added to it that could be used for searching and checking availability of titles.**
>
> **R17: The system must cater for reserving titles; each member can reserve at most one title, one week in advance. There is no charge for reservations, but the title must be collected before 4pm on the day for which it is reserved, or it becomes available again.**

The answer to the question (in relation to **R11**) about the format of disk and membership numbers was simple; disks have a 5-digit number, as does each member. We also checked what happened if a member forgot their membership card. It turns out that happens all the time, and then the staff in the shop ask them for their post code and name, and look them up. If the member's details check out they are allowed to rent a disk even without the card. That's three more requirements:

> **R18: The system must support 5 digit numeric disk numbers.**
>
> **R19: The system must support the existing 5 digit numeric membership numbers.**
>
> **R20: The system must have a way of determining a membership number from information a member would know, even if they have forgotten their membership card.**

Statement of Requirements

We think we have now teased out most requirements so let's restate them in a precise manner, being careful to use 'must' and 'shall' as appropriate. We would normally expect to incorporate these into a formal document and ask the customer to sign it:

R1: The system must support more than 5000 different titles.

R2: The system must support more than 7000 different disks.

R3: The system must support at least 5 different physical copies of each title.

R4: The system must be able to tell from a returned disk number which member rented it.

R5: The system must indicate that all copies of a disk are rented out if a member tries to rent a disk that is not available.

R6: The system shall be capable of having a publicly available terminal added to it that could be used for searching and checking availability of titles, the cost of this additional terminal must not exceed $200.

R7: The system must display the amount of money to be collected, but does not need to interface to a cash drawer.

R8: We must make the source code of the application available to the client.

R9: The source for other components shall be available.

R10: The total cost of the system must be less than $1000.

R11: The system must support more than 9000 members.

R12: The system must be capable of growing to at least twice the size of the initially installed system.

R13: The system must be expandable to incorporate a Web interface that could be accessible from the Internet.

R14: The system shall be extendable to import data from XML data sources.

R15: The system shall be extendable to access data from LDAP directory servers.

R16: The system must be able to cope with discounts for multi-rentals, and different rental prices for different days of the week.

R17: The system must cater for reserving titles; each member can reserve at most one title, one week in advance. There is no charge for reservations, but the title must be collected before 4pm on the day for which it is reserved, or it becomes available again.

R18: The system must support 5 digit numeric disk numbers.

R19: The system must support 5 digit numeric membership numbers.

R20: The system must have a way of determining a membership number from information a member can remember while in the store.

The first thing we must check is that all the original user requirements appear in our more formal list. At this point we discover a big hole – we have omitted anything about:

> **UR3** – It must be friendly.

At the very least we should add something about a graphical user interface, and performance:

> **R21: The system shall have a GUI**
>
> **R22: The system shall respond to all user actions in less than 2 seconds.**

Requirement **R21** is still too vague. In a real-world application we would probably try to make this testable in some way – perhaps by creating some storyboards, drawings that show interactions with the graphical interface. When the customer is happy with the look-and-feel and the screen layouts we can keep the drawings and check that the final system does indeed confirm to our initial ideas.

There are many other possible requirements we have omitted here to keep the application simple. Let's just say that barcode scanners, more flexible rental arrangements, wide screen variants of DVDs, and so on have been left for phase 2!

Notice that for the requirements we have made the wording more formal, and there are representatives of the different types of requirement we mentioned earlier. We have:

- ❑ functionality – it caters for reservations
- ❑ performance – responding to user action in less than 2 seconds
- ❑ usability – a GUI
- ❑ compatibility – caters for existing number formats
- ❑ price – a maximum delivered cost

Most lists of requirements that you capture will have this type of mix. If you ever generate a list of requirements that has no entry relating to one of these main categories you should be concerned that you may have missed some important aspects during your requirement capture.

At this point we need to identify the people who interact with our proposed system; either 'real' people or external interfaces.

Use Cases

In system design parlance, the people who interact with the system are called **actors**. The ways in which they interact with the system are called **Use Cases**. These were first used by Ivar Jacobson, and are now incorporated into the unified modeling language, UML.

We also need to uncover the next layer of functionality. For example, how do new titles get into the store?

Let's try for a first cut of ideas, which we can then show to the storeowner to validate our understanding. Here is an example of a Use Case diagram that can be used to communicate the basic functionality of the system.

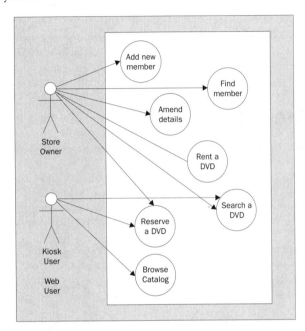

There are three actors: the Store Staff or Owner, a store customer using the Kiosk and a customer connecting via the Web. These last two are combined in the diagram as they have the same Use Cases.

The Store Owner can perform the following functions:

- ❏ add a new member, and issue a membership card

- ❏ amend member details

- ❏ lookup member by number

- ❏ lookup member by name and address

- ❏ lookup DVD title by name, disk number or title number

- ❏ record a rental

- ❏ make a reservation, recording DVD title against date and member number

The in-store Customer (using the kiosk terminal) can:

- ❏ browse DVD titles

- ❏ search by title

- ❏ search by category (Thriller, Comedy, etc)

- ❏ create an advance rental booking

The Web Customer is just the same as the in-store Customer, only accessing the system via an internet Web browser.

The functions that we have allocated to the different users are incomplete, but serve as an example. We can use Use Cases to discuss the system behavior with the customer and the end users. They are quite expressive and easy to understand. As a result we might gain a better understanding of the requirements and refine them further.

From the Use Cases we will derive a functional specification of the application, a description of all of the things the system has to do, and from that we can begin to see how we might structure the application and create its architecture.

Application Architecture

Now we have some basic requirements nailed, we can think how we might build this system.

We will use the information gleaned from the requirements capture and Use Case analysis to think about how the system might decompose into components that co-operate to perform the required functions. The architecture of the system needs to be documented so that it provides a guide for detailed design, and be of help for maintaining the system after it is delivered.

Many factors will influence the precise architecture choice. In our example there is logical division between a graphical front end and records of DVDs and members. By splitting the application we can run the two parts on separate machines to create a multi-user or web-enabled system. We also have some quite severe restraints in terms of cost.

The tight price and requirement for providing the source certainly suggest a Linux solution. Its ability to run on budget hardware will also keep costs down. Then the in-store kiosk part of the project has a very tight budget. About the only way we can think of doing this is a free web browser on some very cut down, and perhaps even second-hand, hardware. As we said earlier, a diskless workstation that boots across a network would be cheap and would also have the advantage that we could remove the floppy disk drive, which would stop members 'playing' with the kiosk.

A database of some sort will clearly be required. There are a number of choices that run on Linux, both commercial and free, ranging from flat files through simple index files to industrial strength products.

We have chosen to use PostgreSQL, since it is a fully featured SQL-capable database that just happens to be free as well. Choosing a standard like SQL leaves open the possibility of moving to another database should the need arise. Some of the factors that influence the choice of data storage mechanisms are discussed in Chapter 3.

The architecture of the application will look like this:

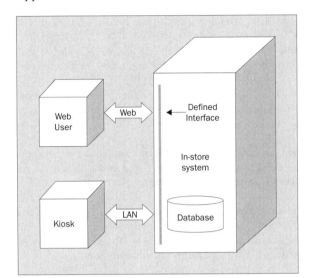

We shall need to consider data integrity issues if we have more than one user of the application at the same time. What will happen if a web user makes a reservation for a DVD at the same time as the in-store system tries to do the same? As far as we are concerned we don't mind which 'wins', perhaps as long as at the end of the day the correct number of people have rented or reserved the correct number of disks.

At this point we need to think about dividing our application up a little.

Let's imagine that several different people, who live in geographically diverse locations, will write the application. Ideally we would like to make the base functionality as separate as possible from the GUI, so that in the future other people could write totally different GUI interfaces to the same basic system if they wished to customize it in different ways. We will see how this pays off when we see multiple implementations of the GUI and database functions in later chapters. We will also see ways of dealing with many developers working on the same system when we look at a source code control system in Chapter 2.

What we need to do here is separate the programming interface needed for the GUI from the underlying business rules and database implementation. We need to define a set of APIs.

Detailed Design

We will construct our application by creating functionality that meets our requirements **R1** through **R22** by writing software that implements our Use Cases. In a complete example, we would have expanded our Use Cases further and made more detailed descriptions of the functions needed.

At this point we will leap forward slightly, and present the API that will act as an interface between the User Interface and our backend processing. It should be reasonably clear how the API, once implemented, would enable a GUI component to meet the requirements of our application. The APIs are directly related to the low-level functions that are needed by the Use Cases we developed earlier. As we have chosen to implement in C, the APIs are defined in terms of C function calls.

To keep the application manageable we have used a simplistic approach to API design, including some fixed structures. We can imagine that this API forms part of a first iteration implementation, used to check that the API set is sufficient to support all of the system's functions.

We can now proceed with the development of the database, GUI and Web interfaces independently. We will discuss the physical layout of the database into tables in Chapter 4.

These notes describe how to use the DVD database functions. All structures, constants and functions described here are made available by including the file dvd.h and linking with an implementation of the interface.

Note that we are not trying to create a library of functions for the general public with this API. Its purpose is to provide the definition of an interface that a small number of developers need to conform to in order to write the components of our application.

A reference implementation or the core API can be found in flatfile.c. It is a simplistic flat file approach that is not optimized at all. For large collections of disks and members (in the thousands) it will rapidly become very slow as it contains linear searches. However, it will allow development and testing of a GUI and a database backend to proceed independently.

The main implementation of the APIs using a real database will be covered in Chapter 4.

Unless otherwise stated, the functions return an error status and pass outputs via parameter pointers. Error status will be DVD_SUCCESS if everything is OK, or DVD_ERR_NOT_FOUND if a lookup fails, for example if a DVD disk has been retired or the relevant membership has lapsed.

Note that search functions may create an empty list of matches and still return DVD_SUCCESS.

Data Access Functions

Before calling the functions described here you must initialize the connection to the data store. This is done with a call to dvd_open_db:

```
int dvd_open_db()
```

which opens the database connection. It returns DVD_SUCCESS if everything is OK, otherwise an error code, DVD_ERR_*.

Alternatively, you can specify a user name and password if the connection to the database is to be made with a particular user identity rather than the default (namely, the user running the application). To do this, call dvd_open_db_login instead:

```
int dvd_open_db_login(const char *user, const char *password)
```

To decode an error value from a database function you can use dvd_err_text:

```
int dvd_err_text(const int error, char **message)
```

Given a DVD error number, `dvd_err_text` re-writes the given pointer to point to a static string containing a human readable error description. This returns DVD_SUCCESS.

The application must call `dvd_close_db` before it terminates, to allow the backend processing to perform any tidying up that may be required:

```
int dvd_close_db()
```

This returns DVD_SUCCESS if everything is OK.

Member Functions

The DVD store rents disks to members only. Members have a card that includes a unique membership number on it. This is allocated automatically by the system when the member record is created. The system uses an internal, integer, membership ID to access member details.

All the character arrays are NULL terminated, as this will make the application code easier to write.

The member structure, `dvd_store_member`, is:

```
typedef struct {
    int member_id;                        /* internal id [1..] */
    char member_no[MEMBER_KNOWN_ID_LEN];  /* number the member knows */
    char title[PERSON_TITLE_LEN];         /* Mr Mrs Ms Dr Sir */
    char fname[NAME_LEN];                 /* first name */
    char lname[NAME_LEN];                 /* last name */
    char house_flat_ref[NAME_LEN];        /* i.e. 5, or 'The Elms' etc. */
    char address1[ADDRESS_LEN];           /* Address line 1 */
    char address2[ADDRESS_LEN];           /* Address line 2 */
    char town[ADDRESS_LEN];               /* Town/City */
    char state[STATE_LEN];                /* needed in US only */
    char phone[PHONE_NO_LEN];             /* +44(0)123 456789 */
    char zipcode[ZIP_CODE_LEN];           /* LE1 1AA or whatever */
} dvd_store_member;
```

A new member is created with `dvd_member_create` :

```
int dvd_member_create(dvd_store_member *member, int *member_id);
```

The application must create a proto-member by assigning all fields of a `dvd_store_member` except `member_id` and `member_no`. A call to `dvd_member_create` will add the member to the database and return via the output parameter a newly allocated `member_id`. This will be used to fetch member details from the database. A new membership number will be created and added to the member details in the database. Note that the passed `dvd_store_member` structure is not updated. To retrieve the new membership number a call to `dvd_member_get` is required.

```
int dvd_member_get(const int member_id, dvd_store_member *member);
```

Updates the member structure with details of the record that matches the given member ID.

To recap, the sequence needed to add a member is:

❑   collect details into a dvd_store_member

❑   call dvd_member_create

❑   call dvd_member_get

❑   add membership number to member's card and issue it

dvd_member_get_id_from_number retrieves an internal member ID from a membership number on the member's card:

```
int dvd_member_get_id_from_number(const char *member_no, int *member_id);
```

This extracts the membership number from a character array pointed to by member_no (five characters plus a trailing NULL) and writes the corresponding member ID into the integer pointed to by member_id.

To alter an existing member's details use a call to dvd_member_set:

```
int dvd_member_set(const dvd_store_member *member);
```

This updates the database record to match **exactly** the member structure provided. To ensure that the record contains correct internal fields it must be initialized via a call to dvd_member_get.

So, to update a member's details:

❑   Read the membership number from the member's card.

❑   Call dvd_member_get_id_from_number.

❑   Call dvd_member_get.

❑   Change the relevant details.

❑   Call dvd_member_set.

To find a member's details without a membership number, use dvd_member_search:

```
int dvd_member_search(const char *name, int *ids[], int *count);
```

This function takes part of a surname, the string name, and searches for all members that have surnames (the lname field in the member structure) that contain the given string. The number of matches found (including zero) is written to the integer pointed to by count. The result, an array of member IDs, is allocated and the pointer ids re-written to point at it. The ids pointer must be passed to free to deallocate the memory it occupies.

To identify a member:

❑   Ask the member his name.

❑   Call dvd_member_search.

❑   For each result, call dvd_member_get.

❑   Verify the member's details.

A member can be deleted with a call to dvd_member_delete:

```
int dvd_member_delete(const int member_id);
```

The member ID may or may not be retired – that is, made available for reallocation (it is not in the reference implementation). However, in general, reusing IDs is not a good idea if it can be easily avoided. Old IDs can occasionally carry accidental 'baggage' such as outstanding rentals, and using a new ID each time is a simple, if rather brute force way of avoiding such problems. Phase 2 of the application might include functions to 'time out' member numbers or scan for rentals outstanding for a long time.

Title Functions

Each disk that the DVD store rents is a copy of a title. We may have several, or no copies of each title. A set of APIs allows the system to maintain a database of DVD titles, recording details of its production (director, actors, etc.) The title structure is public:

```
typedef struct {
    int title_id;                       /* internal ID [1..] */
    char title_text[DVD_TITLE_LEN];     /* 'The silence of the lambs' */
    char asin[ASIN_LEN];                /* 10 digit reference number */
    char director[NAME_LEN];            /* restricted to a single name */
    char genre[GENRE_LEN];              /* 'Horror', 'comedy', etc. */
                                        /* API for standard list later */
    char classification[CLASS_LEN];     /* API for standard list later */
    char actor1[NAME_LEN];              /* 'Jeremy Irons' */
    char actor2[NAME_LEN];              /* 'Ingmar Bergman' */
    char release_date[DAY_DATE_LEN];    /* YYYYMMDD plus the null */
    char rental_cost[COST_LEN];         /* rental cost for this title $$$.cc */
} dvd_title;
```

The title handling APIs work in exactly the same manner as the member APIs, using an internal title_id as a key.

```
int dvd_title_set(const dvd_title *title_record_to_update);
int dvd_title_get(const int title_id, dvd_title *title_record_to_complete);
int dvd_title_create(dvd_title *title_record_to_add, int *title_id);
int dvd_title_delete(const int title_id);
```

The genre and classification fields of a title must be set to one of a limited set of standard strings used for film type and rating. These can be obtained from the utility functions dvd_get_genre_list and dvd_get_classification_list:

```
int dvd_get_genre_list(char **genre_list[], int *count);
int dvd_get_classification_list(char **class_list[], int *count);
```

The search function is slightly different as it allows searching on the name of the film and people involved in it separately:

```
int dvd_title_search(const char *title, const char *name, int *result_ids[],
                                                           int *count);
```

This function returns a list of matching title IDs. The `title` string is sub-string matches against the file title. If it is `NULL` it will match no titles, if `' '` (the empty string) it will match all titles. The `name` string is substring matched against the director and actor names. If either finds any matches they are included in the results.

Disk Functions

We deal with DVD titles and physical DVD disks separately because while we rent a specific physical disk, we will only wish to reserve a DVD title for a future date – and we do not care which physical disk we are given. The system for renting disks will allocate a physical disk when we ask for a title.

Each physical DVD disk has a unique identifier. The idea is that each copy will be labeled with this number. For each physical disk the database records which DVD title it is a copy of. This must be setup by the storeowner when disks are obtained.

The disk record structure is public:

```
typedef struct {
    int disk_id;        /* internal ID [1..] (not related to title_id) */
    int title_id;       /* the title_id of which this is an instance */
} dvd_disk;
```

The disk handling APIs work in exactly the same way as those for titles. The identifier is allocated internally. The search function returns a list of disk IDs for a given title ID:

```
int dvd_disk_set(const dvd_disk *disk_record_to_update);
int dvd_disk_get(const int disk_id, dvd_disk *disk_record_to_complete);
int dvd_disk_create(dvd_disk *disk_record_to_add, int *disk_id);
int dvd_disk_delete(const int disk_id);
int dvd_disk_search(const int title_id, int *result_ids[], int *count);
```

Rental Functions

Each member is allowed to rent as many DVD disks as he desires. Each rental is recorded along with the date the rental was made. Each member may make one reservation, for one title, for a particular date.

Date format used in the system is YYYYMMDD and the current date may be obtained from the utility function `dvd_today`. This function re-writes a passed string pointer to point at a static location containing the current date in the correct form:

```
int dvd_today(char **date);
```

To check if a particular title will be available on a given date call `dvd_title_available`. The date must be in the form YYYYMMDD.

```
int dvd_title_available(const int title_id, const char *date, int *count);
```

The `count` is updated to indicate the number of copies of the DVD title expected to be available on the given date (including zero).

A DVD title can be rented, and a physical disk allocated by a call to `dvd_rent_title`.

```
int dvd_rent_title(const int member_id, const int title_id, int *disk_id);
```

A physical disk copy of the given title ID (if available) is allocated and returned in `disk_id`. A record of the rental to the member whose member ID is given is made. `DVD_ERR_NOT_FOUND` will be returned if no disks are available.

A DVD disk on loan can be queried and returned with calls to `dvd_disk_rental_info` and `dvd_disk_return`.

```
int dvd_rented_disk_info(const int disk_id, int *member_id, char *date_rented);
int dvd_disk_return(const int disk_id, int *member_id, char *date_rented);
```

Given a disk ID these functions return the member ID of the member who rented it, and the date that the rental began. In the case of `dvd_disk_return` the rental record is cleared.

A title is reserved with a call to `dvd_reserve_title` and a reservation cancelled with a call to `dvd_reserve_title_cancel`:

```
int dvd_reserve_title(
    const char *date, const int title_id, const int member_id);
int dvd_reserve_title_cancel(const int member_id);
```

Making a second reservation for any member will cancel any previous reservation for that member.

A member's last reservation request may be retrieved by a call to `dvd_reserve_title_query_by_member`:

```
int dvd_reserve_title_query_by_member(const int member_id, int *title_id);
```

Additional functions not implemented in the reference implementation and still under consideration include:

```
int dvd_reserve_title_query_by_titledate(
    const int title_id, const char *date, int *member_ids[])
```

Return a list of members who have reserved this title on this date. A `NULL` date means any date:

```
int dvd_overdue_disks(
    const char *date1, const char *date2, int *disk_ids[], int *count)
```

Scan the rental table for disks whose rented date is after `date1` and before `date2`. `NULL` dates for these mean beginning of time (actually 1st January 1970, the start of the UNIX epoch) and tomorrow respectively.

Reference Implementation

For applications that are divided into a number of co-operating components, like our DVD store, it can be extremely worthwhile producing a reference implementation for the defined interface. In this case an almost complete, if inefficient, implementation was created so that the GUI implementers could work independently of the database and create a working application that returned meaningful results for searches and so on.

For the DVD store we created an implementation of all of the APIs using simple flat files rather than a fully-fledged database. The code is very simple, the idea being to test that the APIs would be sufficient to support a full implementation. The code is similarly not optimized, and would be too slow for anything other than very small numbers of DVDs. It needed to be correct, not quick, so it was easy to follow and debug. However, it is pretty much fully functional and allowed the graphical user interface to be developed against working code while the database work was still under way. It also allowed the database implementation to be checked against a known working implementation.

A reference implementation may impose a number of restrictions such as database size. In our case in the reference implementation all searches are case sensitive, so it is recommended that the application force text input to have each word capitalized, or all upper case, and that match strings be suitably specified.

A command line test program was also developed to check out the flat file implementation. Once done, it was also used to test the database version. We will see more of the test program in Chapter 11.

Resources

Here are some suggestions for further reading on systems development and design:

Rapid Development, by Steve McConnell, Microsoft Press *(ISBN 1-55615-900-5)*

eXtreme Programming Explained, by Kent Beck, Addison Wesley *(ISBN 0-201-61641-6)*

Clouds to Code, by Jesse Liberty, Wrox Press *(ISBN 1-861000952)*

The Cathedral and The Bazaar, by Eric S. Raymond, O'Reilly & Associates (*ISBN 1-56592-724-9*)
http://www.tuxedo.org/~esr/writings/cathedral-bazaar

Instant UML, by Pierre-Alain Muller, Wrox Press *(ISBN 1-861000871)*

Object-Oriented Systems Analysis and Design, by Bennet, McRobb & Farmer, McGraw Hill *(ISBN 0-07-709497-2)*

Summary

In this chapter we have very quickly followed through the first steps in producing an application in a structured way. Using the DVD store example that we shall see a lot more of in the course of this book we have seen how to set about specifying and designing the bones of a usable system.

We have considered requirements of different types and problems associated with them. We took a quick look at how to plan an implementation in an iterative way.

We established an architecture for the system that separates the user interface from the main body of the application. Finally we defined in detail the interface that binds the two parts of the system together.

We are now just about ready to start cutting some code.

Online discussion at http://www.p2p.wrox.com

2

CVS

One of the things you should do at an early phase in your project is to set up a way of tracking changes to your project. This might just be the source code, or you might have some documents you wish to track as well. You should be tracking these items for two reasons: firstly so that you can discover what a build or document looked liked at some point in time, and secondly so that you can identify changes over time.

Of course you could just copy items to duplicated directories, with names corresponding to the date, but such a simple solution quickly becomes unmanageable where multiple developers are involved, and the timescale is longer than a few weeks.

If you are a developer working on your own, you may be tempted to think that source code control doesn't offer you much; after all, no one else is going to change the code, so you have full control. However, even the best developers make mistakes occasionally and need to go back to previous versions. Users may report a bug introduced in a minor revision, and rather than just track it down in the traditional way, it might be much more productive to have a look at how the code has changed in the affected area since the last release before the bug appeared. A source code control system can be an invaluable aid in these circumstances, allowing the tracking of exactly when, and how, code was changed.

Where there are multiple developers, the case is even stronger. Not only are there all the reasons that exist for single developers, but new and important reasons relating to peoples' ability to see who has changed what and when – it's then much easier to wind back changes in the event that another developer has 'got it wrong'. Providing people properly comment their changes, it's also possible to discover *why* they changed things, which can sometimes be very enlightening.

In short, there are *many* very good reasons to use a source code control system, and very *few* excuses for not doing so, given the choice of quality free tools available on Linux.

In this chapter we will:

❑ set up CVS

❑ explore using CVS to manage a project

❑ network CVS to enable true collaborative projects

Tools for Linux

Initially there was only one mainstream choice for source code control on Linux, which was **RCS** (the Revision Control System) from the GNU software tool set. Whilst RCS was, and still is, a very good and reliable revision control system, a lot of people (particularly on projects with several developers or with distributed development environments) have moved to use a newer tool – **CVS**, the Concurrent Versions System.

CVS originated as a number of shell scripts in 1986. Today's CVS code is mostly based on the work of Brian Berliner since 1989. There are three principal features that have allowed CVS to displace RCS as the tool of choice for managing changes to source code:

❑ Its ability to be configured easily to operate across networks, including the internet.

❑ Its ability to allow multiple developers to work on the same source file simultaneously, in many cases being able to merge changes made to a project by many different developers automatically.

❑ Its significant improvements, over RCS, in handling of collections of files.

Add to this the fact that CVS is completely free, and you have a winning tool that you should probably consider learning how to use. In the course of this chapter, we're going to have a look at:

❑ setting up and using CVS for a single user on a local machine

❑ setting up and using CVS for multiple-users across a network

❑ useful features and extensions to CVS, including network configuration and graphical clients

CVS is a rather complex system, and we will not have the space in a single chapter to cover every last detail of its use. However, we hope to show sufficient details that 95% of your needs will be met. You should then be well placed to investigate some of the more obscure features of CVS, should your needs be more exacting than those we've had space to cover.

In this chapter we will be concentrating on using CVS to manage source code. However you should remember that it's just as effective at managing changes to test data, configuration files or the utility scripts that your project is using. Indeed all aspects of your project can be stored in CVS.

CVS can also store your specifications, which are often even more valuable than the source code. However, if any of these are written in binary format, then you must tell CVS that the file is binary, and CVS will not be able to automatically report differences between versions. We will talk more about managing binary files later in the chapter.

Terminology

Before we get started, it's worth just briefly covering some CVS terminology:

- ❑ **Check Out** – to take a copy of one or more files from the master source with the intention of changing them.

- ❑ **Commit** – to integrate locally made changes to a source file into the master copy of the source.

- ❑ **Project** – a collection of files that together comprise an application.

- ❑ **Repository** – the place where CVS keeps its master copy of the source code.

- ❑ **Revision** – each change to a file is a revision. This term is often used to mean different versions of a final released executable, but in this chapter we will use it in the specific CVS meaning, of an identifiable change to a single source file.

Later on, we will need some more terms, but for now that's enough terminology to be going on with.

The Repository

CVS comes with all main Linux distributions, so in this chapter we will concentrate on configuring CVS. In the very unlikely event that your distribution is missing CVS, the Resources section at the end of the chapter lists some starting points where you can locate a downloadable copy.

The first thing you must do before you can start using CVS is to create a repository, which CVS can use both for holding its master copy of your source files, and also the internal administrative files that it needs.

Where you put the repository is largely a matter of personal choice. However, since it holds the master copy of your source code, putting it somewhere safe that will be backed up regularly would be a good idea! It's perfectly feasible to have multiple repositories on the same machine, and each repository can hold source trees for multiple projects. Each of these could have many sub-directories, so there is plenty of scope for flexibility.

In this chapter we are going to use a CVS repository in /usr/local/cvsrep. If you are hosting a large CVS project you may wish to devote a disk partition, and mount point, specifically for your CVS repository. To keep control of access to CVS, which is mostly governed by permissions to write to the CVS repository, we will create a new group especially for users of the CVS system.

To keep it memorable we will use the group cvs-user, which we have created specifically for this purpose. Any users that we wish to have access to our CVS repository must belong to the group cvs-user. Before we add users to this group, we need to set up our repository. Firstly, as root, we create the group:

```
# groupadd cvs-user
```

and then the directory:

```
# mkdir /usr/local/cvsrep
```

Now we have made a directory for CVS to use, we tell it to create the administration files that it will use in the repository. We do this as root, with the `cvs init` command:

```
# cvs -d /usr/local/cvsrep init
```

CVS will silently create a CVSROOT directory under /usr/local/cvsrep, and populate it with the various administration files it needs.

Now we change into the directory, and change the owning group to cvs-user for the CVS repository directory and all the files in it:

```
# cd /usr/local/cvsrep
# chmod g+w .
# chgrp -R cvs-user .
```

Now all users on the system who are members of the group cvs-user should be able to make full use of the repository. For those who are UNIX users of old, remember that Linux is like most modern UNIX flavors and allows users to be members of multiple groups, so having to be a member of the group cvs-user is not too restrictive.

Single User CVS projects

We will now look at working with a CVS repository as the only user of that repository. Along the way we will see how CVS manages our source code for us.

CVS Command Format

CVS is a command line tool, and that is the interface we will concentrate on in this chapter. Later in the chapter we show some of the various GUIs that have been developed that sit on top of CVS.

All CVS commands are in a standard format, which is:

```
cvs [standard options] command [command specific options] [filenames]
```

As you can see, they take an argument that specifies the actual operation required. This opens up a whole new namespace for CVS, and thus helps to keep the command names simple. The standard options are available on almost all CVS commands, and we list the principal ones here:

`-d <repository>`	Specifies the repository to use. As we will see in the next section, unless you are working with a number of repositories it's often more convenient to set an environment variable. The -d option will override the environment variable CVSROOT (explained shortly), and so provides a convenient way of accessing repositories that are infrequently used.
`-e <editor>`	Specifies an editor to use when CVS needs to prompt for input, for example for log entries.
`--help, -H`	Provide help on a specific command.

-n	No action. Lets you see what CVS would do, without actually doing it.
-q, -Q	Run quietly (-q) or very quietly (-Q). Suppresses some informative output from CVS.
-t	Trace execution.
-v, -version	Print the CVS version.
-z <level>	Used across a network, it compresses the data being transferred. A level of 1 is least compression, 9 is maximum. Generally 4 is a good compromise between CPU use and network bandwidth.

Environment Variables

Before we see CVS in action, we should take a quick look at a small number of rather useful environment variables that CVS commands recognize. (CVS actually knows a few more, but only three are generally useful.) These are:

CVSROOT	controls the repository that CVS commands should use
CVSEDITOR	sets the editor that CVS will invoke if it needs you to type in some text
CVSIGNORE	defines a list of filenames and patterns to ignore when performing CVS commands

The environment variable CVSROOT can always be overridden with -d option as we saw in the previous section. We will set these before we go any further. The following commands assume you are using a BASH-like shell; csh users need to use setenv instead.

```
$ export CVSROOT=/usr/local/cvsrep
$ export CVSEDITOR=emacs
$ export CVSIGNORE="foo bar *.class"
```

From now on, we will default to using /usr/local/cvsrep as the repository, emacs as our editor when using CVS commands, and CVS commands will always ignore files called foo, bar or ending in .class.

In practice, CVS already knows about many types of intermediate file, including those ending in .o, .a and ~, as well as files called core, and ignores them automatically.

Importing a New Project

Let's start at a very early stage in our project, when we just have three files, each of which contain SQL:

```
create_tables.sql
drop_tables.sql
insert_data.sql
```

It's not much of a project so far, but it's good to start use of CVS early in a project. The first thing we need to decide is a name for our project. CVS will use this name as a directory, so we must pick a name that is also a valid directory name. We will call our project plip-app, and since it is for Wrox, we will also classify it under a directory name wrox.

We import our rather minimal initial set of files with the cvs import command. The only option we generally need to use with this is –m, which specifies a log message; although if you don't specify a message, CVS will prompt for it anyway. People familiar with RCS often find the import –b option useful, which allows you to specify a starting number sequence.

> *For the curious reader, other less frequently used options can be found in the* man *and* info *pages for CVS, and further CVS resources which are given at the end of the chapter.*

The parameters to the import command are the name of the project, a vendor tag, and a release tag. The vendor tag is not often used; it's most common use is to specify the original source for external software. Since it is a mandatory parameter, you must always think of a tag name to use, even if you don't actually need to use it. The release tag allows us to group sets of changes together, for example where a group of files have been changed to add a feature, we could use the release tag to identify points in their history where that feature was added. It's common simply to use start as the release tag when importing a project for the first time. We will learn more about tags and how useful they can be, later on in the chapter.

To summarize, the syntax of cvs import is:

```
cvs import [options] project-name vendor-tag release-tag
```

The cvs import command looks at all the files in the current directory, and imports them one at a time. For our import we will use the –m option to specify a log message, use a vendor tag of stixen, and a release tag of start:

```
$ cvs import -m"Initial version of demonstration application for PLiP"
                                          wrox/plip-app stixen start
```

CVS responds with something like:

```
N wrox/plip-app/create_tables.sql
N wrox/plip-app/drop_tables.sql
N wrox/plip-app/insert_data.sql
I wrox/plip-app/create_tables.sql~

No conflicts created by this import
```

This command has several types of response, generally the first letter tells you the type, and this is followed by a file name. Often there is additional informative text at the end. The response types that various commands (not just import) can give you are:

C	conflict – the file already existed in the repository, but was different from the local file so needs manually merging
I	ignored – the file was ignored
L	link – the file is a symbolic link and was therefore ignored (CVS does not handle symbolic links)
M	modified – the file was modified in the repository
N	new – a new file was added to the repository
R	removed – the file was removed
U	updated – the file was updated
?	query – a file was found locally that is not in the repository, nor marked to be ignored

In our case, you can see that three new files were added to the repository, and an emacs editor backup file (create_tables.sql~) was ignored, because the pattern *~ is automatically recognized by CVS as being a pattern indicating files to ignore.

If, later on in the project we add additional files (as seems quite likely, given our starting point), then there are two ways these can be added to an existing project. If the project is checked out and being worked on, we can use the cvs add command which we will meet later. If the project is not being currently worked on, then cvs import can add additional files. Suppose when we imported our sources we immediately noticed that we had forgotten to write a README file. We can create it in the current directory and immediately add it with the cvs import command, like this:

```
$ cvs import -m"Added README" wrox/plip-app stixen start
U wrox/plip-app/create_tables.sql
U wrox/plip-app/drop_tables.sql
U wrox/plip-app/insert_data.sql
N wrox/plip-app/README
I wrox/plip-app/create_tables.sql~

No conflicts created by this import
```

CVS notices the existing files, but only adds the new README file to the repository.

Starting Work on Our Project

Now we have created our project, we should move to a clean directory, and check out a copy to work on. In theory we could now delete the directory and all the files we just imported into CVS, however the authors usually like to leave it around, usually renamed, at least till they are sure all is well in the CVS repository, and they haven't forgotten to check any files in.

In reality CVS has not lost a file for the authors yet, but we tend to err on the side of caution.

To get files back out of the repository we use the cvs checkout command. This takes several options; only the generally useful ones are shown here.

-D <date>	Check out the project as it was at a certain date. Normally the date is specified either in the ISO form "1999-09-24 16:05", which is the format we would recommend, or you can also use "24 Sep 1999 16:05" or even some special phrases, such as "yesterday" and "last Monday".
-d <dir>	Check the project out into a named directory. By default, as we said earlier, the project name is used as a directory.
-p	Write the file to standard output, rather than saving it in the directory, which is the default.
-r <tag>	Check out the project as it was when tagged with the specified tag name. We will come back to tags shortly.

In addition, you must specify the project you want checked out, and you can optionally specify one or more files to check out. By default all the files in the project are checked out.

After moving to a clean directory, we can check out our project out again, ready to start work:

```
$ cvs checkout wrox/plip-app
cvs checkout: Updating wrox/plip-app
U wrox/plip-app/README
U wrox/plip-app/create_tables.sql
U wrox/plip-app/drop_tables.sql
U wrox/plip-app/insert_data.sql
```

A directory `wrox/plip-app` is created and the most recent version of each file is created in that directory, ready for us to work on. You will notice that an extra directory, CVS (note the capitals), has also been created alongside the project files in this directory. This is CVS's own working directory; you should never need to edit files or delete files in the directory, though some documentation tells you how to take short cuts by doing so. We strongly suggest you stick to the official commands, even if it occasionally involves more typing.

Checking Our Changes Against the Repository

Once we have a checked out copy of our project, we can continue to work on it. Suppose some hours later we have been working away, and have reached another stable point, where we have completed making and testing a set of changes, and wish to save them back to the repository. Before we do this it's always a good idea to double-check what changes have been made; it's always sensible to take one last look before saving changes.

We can look at the changes we have made using the `cvs diff` command. This takes several options:

-c	Do a context `diff`, where surrounding lines are shown, making it easier to identify visually the lines that have changed.
-b	Ignore whitespace differences inside a particular line.
-B	Ignore the insertion or deletion of blank lines.

-D *<date>*	Look for differences against the version in the repository at the specified date.
-r *<tag>*	Compare against a numbered version for a particular file, or against a tag name for all the files in a project.
	You can specify two -r tag options, in which case cvs diff tells you about changes internal to the repository between two different versions, and ignores the local files.

You can also optionally provide a list of file names. If you do provide a list, cvs diff will show differences for the listed files. If you don't provide a list it will show differences between all files in the project and in the current directory.

Be aware that if you have created a new file in the directory that is not in the repository, cvs diff will ignore it, since it only checks files it knows are in the project. While this might at first appear a poor default behavior, in practice it is the right default, since it avoids cluttering the output with complaints about temporary project files that are not in the repository.

After editing two of our files, we run cvs diff and can see the changes we have made, comparing the current working copies with those in the CVS repository:

```
$ cvs diff -B
cvs diff: Diffing .
Index: create_tables.sql
===================================================================
RCS file: /usr/local/cvsrep/wrox/plip-app/create_tables.sql,v
retrieving revision 1.1.1.1
diff -B -r1.1.1.1 create_tables.sql
47a50,55
> );
>
> create table genre (
>         genre_id              INT NOT NULL,
>         genre_name            CHAR(21),
>         CONSTRAINT            genre_id_uniq UNIQUE(genre_id)
Index: drop_tables.sql
===================================================================
RCS file: /usr/local/cvsrep/wrox/plip-app/drop_tables.sql,v
retrieving revision 1.1.1.1
diff -B -r1.1.1.1 drop_tables.sql
10a11
> drop table genre;
```

As you can see, each file that has changed has been listed, along with the actual changes. You will notice there is a reference to RCS in the output. Older versions of CVS relied on RCS 'under the hood', and CVS still uses many of the same ideas and file names.

Another way of looking at the changes in the local copy is to use cvs status, which provides a list of files that have been changed. For a complete breakdown of the status, use cvs status -v, which provides more verbose output.

At this point you may decide that you are not keen on the changes you have made, and want to abandon them. The easiest way to do this is simply to delete the local copy of the file, and use the cvs update command, which we'll see more of later, to refresh the local directory with a clean copy of the file from the repository.

Updating the Repository with Our Changes

Assuming we are happy with the changes we have made, we can then put our files back in the repository. This is called committing a change, and not surprisingly there is a cvs commit command to perform the action.

The cvs commit command has only two commonly needed options:

-m <message>	Attach a message to the check in. If you don't specify a message, CVS will invoke the editor that is specified with the environment variable CVSEDITOR, or failing that, EDITOR, or a system default editor (usually vi) to prompt you for a message.
-r <rev>	Commit changes to a specific revision. This is only relevant where the project has branches, which we will come back to later in the chapter.

When you run cvs commit, it tells you what files it is changing in the repository:

```
$ cvs commit
```

At this point, since we failed to specify a log message on the command line, but set CVSEDITOR to emacs, emacs is started automatically by CVS, and is asking for a log message:

```
CVS: -----------------------------------------------------------
CVS: Enter Log.  Lines beginning with 'CVS:' are removed automatically
CVS:
CVS: Committing in .
CVS:
CVS: Modified Files:
CVS:    create_tables.sql drop_tables.sql
CVS: -----------------------------------------------------------
```

Once we provide a message and exit emacs (after saving the file of course), the cvs commit command resumes and the commit proceeds:

```
Checking in create_tables.sql;
/usr/local/cvsrep/wrox/plip-app/create_tables.sql,v  <--  create_tables.sql
new revision: 1.2; previous revision: 1.1
done
Checking in drop_tables.sql;
/usr/local/cvsrep/wrox/plip-app/drop_tables.sql,v  <--  drop_tables.sql
new revision: 1.2; previous revision: 1.1
```

As you can see, CVS can determine automatically what files need processing.

Releasing the Project

If we have stopped working on the project, we should release it so that CVS knows it is no longer being worked on. In practice this doesn't matter for single user, or simple multi-user projects, but it's a good habit to get into. We do this simply by changing up one level of directory, so we are no longer in the `plip-app` directory, and running `cvs release`. This has only one commonly used option:

-d	Delete the released directory automatically.

The `cvs release` command will warn you if you have changes in the directory that have not been put back into the repository, and allow you to abandon the release if you wish.

If you ever want to look back and list the changes in a project, you can use the `cvs history` command. This gives an overview of the project history, in perhaps not the most user-friendly form.

Here is a brief example of our project so far:

```
$ cvs history -e -a
O 04/15 17:23 +0000 rick wrox/plip-app =wrox/plip-app= ~/wrox/plip-app
M 04/15 21:15 +0000 rick 1.2 create_tables.sql wrox/plip-app == ~/wrox/plip-app
M 04/15 21:15 +0000 rick 1.2 drop_tables.sql   wrox/plip-app == ~/wrox/plip-app
F 04/15 21:20 +0000 rick                 =plip-app=       ~/wrox/*
```

As you can see, it's not difficult to guess the general history of the project from the output. The principal options to CVS history are:

-a	Show history for all users.
-D <date>	Show changes since date.
-e	Show everything (by default only checkouts are shown).
-r <rev>	Show changes since a named revision.
-u <user>	Show changes made by a particular user.

Reviewing Changes

Now we have a set of changes in the repository, we can review what was changed, using the `cvs log` command. We need to change back into the project directory first, so CVS can tell which project we are working on. The output can be rather long-winded, so we will just show a brief extract here:

```
$ cd plip-app
$ cvs log create_tables.sql
---------------------------
revision 1.2
date: 2000/04/15 21:15:08;  author: rick;  state: Exp;  lines: +8 -0

Added the genre table.
---------------------------
revision 1.1
date: 2000/04/15 15:57:22;  author: rick;  state: Exp;
branches:  1.1.1;
Initial revision
```

If you omit the filename argument, CVS log will show you the log for all files in the project. The CVS log command has a couple of useful options:

`-D <date>`	Show changes since date.
`-h`	Show only the header information for each file.

Adding and Removing Files from a Project

As a project progresses, it almost invariably acquires additional files. These need to be added to the project in the CVS repository. As you might guess, there is a `cvs add` command to do this, which takes the name of the file as a parameter. It has three useful options:

`-kb`	The file is binary.
`-ko`	Don't expand keyword strings (see below).
`-m <message>`	Add a reason *message* to the CVS log.

When you add a new file to the project, this does not immediately add the file to the repository. What it does is add the file to the list of files that need to be checked next time the `cvs commit` command is run.

In a similar fashion there is `cvs remove`. This removes a file from the project. If the file still exists in the local directory, `cvs remove` will fail unless you use the `-f` option, when `cvs remove` deletes the local copy of the file. Like `cvs add`, the repository is not actually changed until a `cvs commit` command is run.

If you delete a file, and commit the change, then decide you want the file back again, CVS has not quite deleted all traces of the file, it's remnants can still be found in the `Attic` subdirectory of the CVS repository. You will however, have to copy it to a new location and perform some edits to recreate your original file.

Keyword Substitution

One very useful feature of CVS is its ability to perform keyword substitution in a file that is being checked out. This feature was inherited from RCS, and CVS behaves in a very similar manner. The following 'magic' strings are processed when files are checked out or committed to the repository:

`$Author$`	Expand to login name.
`$Date$`	Expand to date of last commit.
`$Header$`	Expand to some standard header information.
`$Id$`	Expand to some standard header information, without pathnames.
`$Log$`	Expand to an ever increasing set of log messages.
`$Name$`	Expand to any tag name used to check out this file.
`$Revision$`	Expand to the revision number.
`$State$`	Not generally used.

The easiest way of explaining these is simply to see what happens when they are expanded:

```
$Author: rick $
$Date: 2000/04/16 17:38:08 $
$Header: /usr/local/cvsrep/wrox/plip-app/README,v 1.4 2000/04/16 17:38:08 rick Exp
$
$Id: README,v 1.4 2000/04/16 17:38:08 rick Exp $
$Log: README,v $
Revision 1.4  2000/04/16 17:38:08  rick
Added keyword strings
$Name:  $
$Revision: 1.4 $
$State: Exp $
```

CVS will automatically re-expand these strings each time the file is checked out from CVS, so you never need to modify them.

Generally it is useful to have at least one of the strings visible in the final compiled version of the application, and assigning the string to a static variable can help to ensure that the string appears in the final executable, though optimizing compilers will often try and remove it again, unless the string is actually used. The authors often find it useful to allow the string to appear when the version of a program is displayed, and usually find the Id string is the most useful to use. Even if you don't want any of the strings to appear in your final program, it's often handy to have at least some of them appearing as comments in the source files. Have a look at the man pages for the ident command (from RCS) that can search for strings of this format in executable files.

Revisions, Tags and Branches

Up until now, although we have briefly mentioned revisions and branches, and have seen that some commands can refer to a tag, we haven't specified too precisely what we mean by all this. Let's put that right now.

Revisions

Each time we commit a change to a file in CVS we create a new revision of that file. These are generally numbered 1.1, 1.2, 1.3 etc. Although it's possible to change the first number, this is in many ways a bit of a hang over from RCS, and in CVS there is generally no need. Where revision numbers would have been used in RCS, we can use a tag in CVS, a much more flexible approach, as we are about to see.

You will have noticed in the output above, that CVS sometimes refers to branch numbers, with several numbers separated by dots, and also revision numbers, which are generally just two numerals separated by a dot. This looks rather confusing, but, unless you are using branches, which we will cover shortly, you only need to take notice of the revision numbers, such as 1.1, 1.2 etc.

Tags

Normally when we release a version of a project it will consist of many files, each file at various revision levels. It is very important that we have some way not only of capturing the version of each source file that went into making a released version of the project, but also to be able to retrieve all the files at exactly the right revision. We can do this by adding a tag name to a project across the whole set of files in that project, regardless of the actual version of the file.

Suppose we wish to do a release of our plip-app project now. Admittedly it's not in much of a state yet, but we might want to release to someone our database creation SQL, so they can create their own copy to work on. Of course, since the project is far from finished, there is a risk that we will need to change our tables, so it's important we have a record of what we released to people, so we can warn them if we need to make changes.

Currently we have just 4 files, but they are not all at the same revision number. The files `create_tables.sql` and `drop_tables.sql` are at revision 1.2, while the rest are only at 1.1. Of course with only 4 files the problem is quite easy, but in a large project with dozens of files, each file potentially at a different revision, it is a real headache.

What we can do is add a tag to the project, which is effectively like a textual revision mark that sits alongside the default numeric revision number that CVS assigns automatically. We create a tag on a project with the `cvs tag` command, which has quite a few useful options.

`-b`	Create a branch. We will come back to branches in the next section.
`-c`	Check that all changes have been committed to the repository. If they haven't, the tag command will fail.
`-D <date>`	Tag revisions, providing they are no later than a given date.
`-d`	Delete a tag. Beware there is no revision history on tags, once they are deleted there is no trace of them.
`-F`	Force a rename of an existing tag if there is a clash of tag names.
`-r <rev>`	Tag by revision (which could be a tag itself, though that wouldn't seem to be very useful).

Let's tag the current state of our project, ready to provide a first rush of the schema to our customer.

```
$ cvs tag -c release-schema-to-wrox-01
cvs tag: Tagging .
T README
T create_tables.sql
T drop_tables.sql
T insert_data.sql
```

This simply adds a tag to each file in the project. Notice we used the `-c` option, to check that all changes had been committed. This is a good habit to get into.

We can see the tag by looking at part of the log history for one of the files:

```
$ cvs log -h create_tables.sql
RCS file: /usr/local/cvsrep/wrox/plip-app/create_tables.sql,v
Working file: create_tables.sql
head: 1.2
branch:
locks: strict
access list:
symbolic names:
        release-schema-to-wrox-01: 1.2
        start: 1.1.1.1
        stixen: 1.1.1
keyword substitution: kv
total revisions: 3
=============================================================
```

Now we can give a copy to our sponsors, and continue working on the files.

By way of demonstration, we change some CHAR field definitions to VARCHAR types, committing our changes to the repository. Later on, Wrox ask if there have been any updates since the version we sent them. We can get at the changes in several ways. Generally the most useful is to have a look at the output of cvs log to check the name of the tag we used, then use cvs diff to tell us the changes. Since cvs diff works across the whole project, we don't even need to specify which files we are interested in:

```
$ cvs diff -r release-schema-to-wrox-01
cvs diff: Diffing .
Index: create_tables.sql
===================================================================
RCS file: /usr/local/cvsrep/wrox/plip-app/create_tables.sql,v
retrieving revision 1.2
retrieving revision 1.3
diff -r1.2 -r1.3
8,10c8,10
<         fname              CHAR(26),
<         lname              CHAR(26) NOT NULL,
<         house_flat_ref     CHAR(26) NOT NULL,
---
>         fname              VARCHAR(26),
>         lname              VARCHAR(26) NOT NULL,
>         house_flat_ref     VARCHAR(26) NOT NULL,
60c60
<         err_text           CHAR(50)
---
>         err_text           VARCHAR(50)
```

As you can see, CVS not only identifies the file (or files) that have changed, it also shows us the changes we made, in standard diff format output.

The other thing we might want to do is to allow a different user to get a copy of the project as it was at the time a tag was created. This is very easy; as we can just use -r <tagname> with the cvs checkout command. Unfortunately CVS doesn't always seem to get file permissions quite right, and you may need to double check that the files in the CVS repository have the correct group of cvs-user.

If they do not, you may need to manually correct it, as the CVS administrator, using chgrp -R cvs-user in /usr/local/cvs-rep. You may also notice when you check files out, that permissions are sometimes not identical to those in place when a file was checked in. Hopefully these minor quirks will be fixed in later versions of CVS.

Here is a second user, neil, checking out a copy of our project, in the same state as when it was given to Wrox. Be careful to do this in an empty directory, or you may accidentally overwrite some existing files:

```
$ cvs checkout -r release-schema-to-wrox-01 wrox/plip-app
cvs checkout: Updating wrox/plip-app
U wrox/plip-app/README
U wrox/plip-app/create_tables.sql
U wrox/plip-app/drop_tables.sql
U wrox/plip-app/insert_data.sql
```

If we check the file `create_tables.sql`, we do indeed find that our later changes to VARCHAR types are not present.

> *We gave the user* `neil` *a* CVSROOT *environment variable that specified our repository. Alternatively we could have used the* `-d` *option on the CVS command line.*

That's essentially all there is to basic tags in CVS. However don't let the simplicity of tags make you think they are not important, they are a very useful way of identifying islands of stability in the lifetime of your project.

Branches

Occasionally we wish to split the development stream into two or even more versions that can be worked on independently. An example is when a release of a project is made to which bug fixes and patches must be created, without getting in the way of new feature development for the next release of the project. This allows both old and new versions of the project to be worked on independently.

This could be solved simply by having a pair of projects, one for the old release and one for the new one, except for one very important consideration – we need to be absolutely sure that bugs fixed in the old release stay fixed in the next release. This means we need to merge bug fix changes from the older release into the new release, automatically if possible. CVS can help us achieve this.

Suppose that we had found a need to change the SQL commands we have given to Wrox, independently of our mainstream changes. Rather than simply take a complete copy of the source, just in case we ever needed it, we could have planned ahead and created a branch when we did the `cvs tag` command, by adding the `-b` (branch) option to the `cvs tag` command. Then, when a user checks out a working copy based on the tag name, they are working on a branch, rather than the mainstream copy.

Consider the changes a file in our application goes through as it is being developed. If we are using CVS is probably has nice simple incremented version numbers, like this:

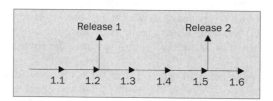

What must happen if people are to continue working on the release 1 code while others work on the code for release 2, is to have a branch, like this:

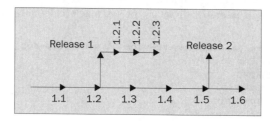

Here we have branch versions 1.2.1, 1.2.2 etc. that develop independently of our mainstream development path, which is 1.2, 1.3 etc.

However, all is not lost. We can retrospectively decide that our tag should have been a branch, and not just a simple tag. Suppose the user `neil` wants to start with a clean copy of the project, as released to Wrox. The simplest way of doing this is to use `cvs release` to discard the existing copy, and then do `cvs checkout -r release-schema-to-wrox-01 wrox/plip-app` again, to ensure we have a pristine copy of the project.

Now we can tag the version we have as branch, using the `cvs tag` command.

```
$ cvs tag -b release-schema-to-wrox-01-branch
cvs tag: Tagging .
T README
T create_tables.sql
T drop_tables.sql
T insert_data.sql
```

At this point you need to be very careful. What we've done here is mark in the repository that all files at the version we've checked out in this directory (`release-schema-to-wrox-01`) belong to a branch off the main development. We haven't actually made the current working copy a branch – this is a bit of a catch for the unwary.

So how do we update the local copy? We need to check out the current copy again, so that our local copy of the project knows it is part of the branch. First, release the existing files:

```
$ cvs release -d wrox/plip-app
```

Now we can make the local copy a copy of the branch we tagged:

```
$ cvs checkout -r release-schema-to-wrox-01-branch wrox/plip-app
cvs checkout: Updating wrox/plip-app
U wrox/plip-app/README
U wrox/plip-app/create_tables.sql
U wrox/plip-app/drop_tables.sql
U wrox/plip-app/insert_data.sql
```

At this point, instead of the usual chatty response, you might get an error message about permissions on a `val-tags` file. What may have happened is that the first user to create some tags has caused the `val-tags` file to be created in the CVS repository control file area. However if that user's main group is not `cvs-user`, it may well be that the file did not get created with sufficient permissions for other `cvs-user`'s to modify it, and we need, as CVS administrator, to apply a minor permissions update.

All that's needed is to change working directory into the CVS repository, and correct the group ownership (to `cvs-user`) and permissions on the `val-tags` file to match the others files in the CVSROOT directory.

Now we have a local copy of the project, as given to Wrox, that is a branch from the main development. You can see the branch tag by using the `cvs status` command. If we do this first as user `rick`, whom you will remember is working on the latest mainstream version. We see:

```
$ cvs status create_tables.sql
File: create_tables.sql Status: Up-to-date

    Working revision:    1.3      Sat Apr 15 22:59:50 2000
    Repository revision: 1.3      /usr/local/cvsrep/wrox/plip-
app/create_tables.sql,v
    Sticky Tag:          (none)
    Sticky Date:         (none)
    Sticky Options:      (none)
```

If we do the same command for user `neil`, working on the Wrox branch of the project, we get:

```
File: create_tables.sql Status: Up-to-date

    Working revision:    1.2      Sat Apr 15 21:15:08 2000
    Repository revision: 1.2      /usr/local/cvsrep/wrox/plip-
app/create_tables.sql,v
    Sticky Tag:          release-schema-to-wrox-01-branch (branch: 1.2.2)
    Sticky Date:         (none)
    Sticky Options:      (none)
```

As you can see, they are working on different versions of the same file. The 'Sticky Tag' line tells us that the local copy is marked as being part of a tagged release. It is 'Sticky' because subsequent CVS commands will automatically take account of this status. We can see this if we make a simple change to the file, and do a `cvs diff`:

```
$ cvs diff create_tables.sql
Index: create_tables.sql
===================================================================
RCS file: /usr/local/cvsrep/wrox/plip-app/create_tables.sql,v
retrieving revision 1.2
diff -r1.2 create_tables.sql
29a30
>         actor3          CHAR(51),
60c61
<         err_text            CHAR(50)
---
>         err_text            CHAR(75)
```

As you can see, `cvs diff` automatically took account of the fact that we are working on a branch, and compared our changes to the latest version in the repository on that branch, rather than the latest version of the main stream of development in the repository. If we manually compare the copy of the file `neil` is working on, with the copy `rick` is working on, there are actually rather more differences:

```
$ diff ~rick/wrox/plip-app/create_tables.sql create_tables.sql
```

```
8,10c8,10
<         fname           VARCHAR(26),
<         lname           VARCHAR(26) NOT NULL,
<         house_flat_ref VARCHAR(26) NOT NULL,
---
>         fname           CHAR(26),
>         lname           CHAR(26) NOT NULL,
>         house_flat_ref CHAR(26) NOT NULL,
29a30
>         actor3          CHAR(51),
60c61
<         err_text                VARCHAR(50)
---
>         err_text                CHAR(75)
```

For the purposes of illustration, `neil` also makes a change to the file `insert_data.sql`, which is not changed by `rick`. We can now commit our changes to the repository, using `cvs commit`. You will see CVS remembers (it was 'Sticky') that we are working on a branch, and does something slightly different when `neil` checks in changes to the Wrox version:

```
$ cvs commit -m"Fix minor bugs in Wrox version"
cvs commit: Examining .
Checking in create_tables.sql;
/usr/local/cvsrep/wrox/plip-app/create_tables.sql,v  <--   create_tables.sql
new revision: 1.2.2.1; previous revision: 1.2
done
Checking in insert_data.sql;
/usr/local/cvsrep/wrox/plip-app/insert_data.sql,v  <--   insert_data.sql
new revision: 1.1.1.1.2.1; previous revision: 1.1.1.1
done
```

You can see CVS created a new version with nested version numbers. At this point it's only fair to point out that CVS does not restrict you to a single branch. You can have several different branches off the mainstream and you can even have branches off branches. However, just because CVS gives you this flexibility it doesn't make it a good idea to use it. You should consider carefully before branching your code in the first place, and you should question long and hard any suggestions for having more than a single active branch in a project at any one time.

We can now give Wrox the minor changes to their version, keeping them separate from the changes we are making to our mainstream development version.

Now we are ready for the complex part of the operation, re-merging the branch with the mainstream, or 'trunk' as some people might prefer to call the mainstream development version. We need to re-merge the branch, which may well have important bug fixes we need in release 2, back into our mainstream development path.

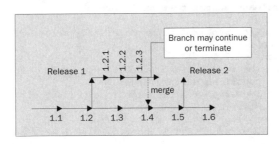

Back as user `rick`, the first thing to do is take stock of where we are with the project. Using `cvs status -v` gives a clear picture of the status of files in our project. We need the `-v` option because by default `cvs status` doesn't tell us about branches. The actual output from `cvs status` is rather long, but here is a short extract to give the general idea:

```
File: create_tables.sql Status: Up-to-date

    Working revision:      1.3       Sat Apr 15 22:59:50 2000
    Repository revision: 1.3         /usr/local/cvsrep/wrox/plip-
app/create_tables.sql,v
    Sticky Tag:            (none)
    Sticky Date:           (none)
    Sticky Options:        (none)

    Existing Tags:
        release-schema-to-wrox-01-branch         (branch: 1.2.2)
        release-schema-to-wrox-01         (revision: 1.2)
        start                             (revision: 1.1.1.1)
        stixen                            (branch: 1.1.1)
```

We know that when we try and put things back together, there is going to be a problem. We have changed `create_tables.sql` in both versions, and, worse, we know that some changes are incompatible. For example from our earlier `diff` we saw:

```
60c61
<           err_text                   VARCHAR(50)
---
>           err_text                   CHAR(75)
```

Which version is correct? There is no automatic way of sorting this out. However CVS can do a lot to sort out other changes, where they are less ambiguous. Indeed, CVS's ability to automatically merge changes is one of its great features.

We can safely allow CVS to try an automatic merge of the two development streams, because we have two safety nets. Firstly, CVS will not automatically merge changes where there is a clear conflict, and secondly, we can always review the changes against the master repository version. We do however suggest that you double check that both the mainstream and branch versions have been committed into the repository before you start merging changes.

To merge the branches we use a new CVS command, `cvs update`, which we will see more of when we talk about multi-user development shortly. What we need is to join two threads of development together, which requires the `-j` (join) flag, which takes a tag parameter to tell it which branch in the repository to merge with the current project directory.

As user `rick` (who you will remember has the latest mainstream sources checked out), we use CVS update to join the branch back to the current version:

```
$ cvs update -j release-schema-to-wrox-01-branch
cvs update: Updating .
RCS file: /usr/local/cvsrep/wrox/plip-app/create_tables.sql,v
retrieving revision 1.2
retrieving revision 1.2.2.1
Merging differences between 1.2 and 1.2.2.1 into create_tables.sql
rcsmerge: warning: conflicts during merge
RCS file: /usr/local/cvsrep/wrox/plip-app/insert_data.sql,v
retrieving revision 1.1.1.1
retrieving revision 1.1.1.1.2.1
Merging differences between 1.1.1.1 and 1.1.1.1.2.1 into insert_data.sql
```

As you can see, CVS warned us about a conflict in the create_tables.sql file. This is not unexpected, we know both parties made several changes, and at least one of the changes had a conflict between versions.

If we have a look at the result of the merging, by opening create_tables.sql in an editor, we only see one section that clearly hasn't worked:

```
create table errtext (
        err_code          INT,
<<<<<<< create_tables.sql
        err_text          VARCHAR(50)
=======
        err_text          CHAR(75)
>>>>>>> 1.2.2.1
);
```

Apart from that, CVS appears to have merged changes with an uncanny accuracy. We need to edit create_tables.sql and resolve the conflict, so the file is how we want it to appear on the mainstream. Since both versions are in the source file, clearly identified, this is very easy. As a double check that we are happy with the automatic merging, we can then run cvs diff, to check that we are indeed sure, before we finally commit the merge to the repository:

```
$ cvs commit -m"Merge changes from release-schema-to-wrox-01-branch to mainstream"
Checking in create_tables.sql;
/usr/local/cvsrep/wrox/plip-app/create_tables.sql,v  <--  create_tables.sql
new revision: 1.4; previous revision: 1.3
done
Checking in insert_data.sql;
/usr/local/cvsrep/wrox/plip-app/insert_data.sql,v  <--  insert_data.sql
new revision: 1.2; previous revision: 1.1
done
```

It's always a good idea to ensure that the merger of a branch goes into the repository as a single identifiable change. Don't ever be tempted to 'slip in' an extra change on the side. You may also find it helpful to add a tag to both the branch and the mainstream versions at this point, to allow tracing of the merge easier in the future.

Now our branch changes are re-integrated with the mainstream, and we can develop with a single set of source code files again.

Multi-user CVS

In our examination of branches we touched on the multi user aspects of CVS, but they deserve a more detailed look.

Most source code control tools assume that only one developer is working on a source file at any one time, and lock other users from changing files that are being edited, though a few are now starting to provide the option of allowing concurrent development as an alternative. CVS starts from the opposite premise – it assumes you may have multiple developers working on a project at once, and that in practice they will sometimes need to alter the same source file.

The problems with multi-user changes are a bit like those of having a branch compounded by the possibility that there are often many users, and people may want to partially merge working copies at any time.

Depending on the number of users, and the degree of communication between them, there are two ways to work in a multi-user mode with CVS. If you have a smallish number of users sharing the files, and they are all collaborating closely, then you don't need CVS to do much work for you, you can just work in a collaborative mode. If there are many developers, or they do not work in a particularly collaborative way, CVS can do more work for you, to help developers watch more closely who is changing what. There are not actually distinct CVS modes, just different ways of using CVS to achieve the same goals.

Working Collaboratively

In this way of working, users use CVS much as they would in single user mode, except they use the `cvs update` command to update their local working copies with other users' changes.

The principal options to `cvs update` are:

`-A`	Clear any sticky options, as though this was a fresh copy of the mainstream project.
`-D <date>`	Update to versions of files as far as a specified date.
`-d`	Retrieve missing directories.
`-j <rev>`	Joins two branches together.
`-p`	Write files to standard output rather than to the directory.
`-r <rev>`	Update to revisions of files up to a specified revision or tag.

Suppose our two developers, `rick` and `neil`, both check out a copy of the README file, and then both edit it. Also `rick` changes `create_tables.sql`, and `neil` changes `drop_tables.sql`.

At this point neither can see changes made by the other, because neither set of changes has been committed to the repository. Suppose user `neil` commits his changes first. His changes are stored in the repository with no problems, since it is a case of first come, first served. When `rick` is ready to put his changes in, he checks that no one has beaten him to updating his files, by running `cvs status`. What he sees is output like this:

```
File: README            Status: Needs Merge

   Working revision:    1.1.1.1 Sat Apr 15 16:13:02 2000
   Repository revision:1.2   /usr/local/cvsrep/wrox/plip-app/README,v
   Sticky Tag:          (none)
   Sticky Date:         (none)
   Sticky Options:      (none)


===================================================================
File: create_tables.sqlStatus: Locally Modified
```

```
     Working revision:    1.4    Sun Apr 16 12:21:34 2000
     Repository revision:1.4     /usr/local/cvsrep/wrox/plip-app/create_tables.sql,v
     Sticky Tag:          (none)
     Sticky Date:         (none)
     Sticky Options:      (none)


     ===================================================================
File: drop_tables.sql    Status: Needs Patch

     Working revision:    1.2    Sat Apr 15 21:15:08 2000
     Repository revision:1.3     /usr/local/cvsrep/wrox/plip-app/drop_tables.sql,v
     Sticky Tag:          (none)
     Sticky Date:         (none)
     Sticky Options:      (none)


     ===================================================================
File: insert_data.sql    Status: Up-to-date

     Working revision:    1.2    Sun Apr 16 12:21:34 2000
     Repository revision:1.2     /usr/local/cvsrep/wrox/plip-app/insert_data.sql,v
     Sticky Tag:          (none)
     Sticky Date:         (none)
     Sticky Options:      (none)
```

This tells him that:

- ❑ README has been modified both by himself and someone else

- ❑ create_tables.sql has been modified by himself, but no one else

- ❑ drop_tables.sql has been modified by someone else, but not by him

- ❑ insert_data.sql has not been locally modified nor changed in the repository.

It's all looking a bit of a mess. However, as we have already seen, CVS is good at automatically sorting out incompatible changes. The first step is to allow CVS to do a local merge of as many of the changes as it can:

```
$ cvs update
cvs update: Updating .
RCS file: /usr/local/cvsrep/wrox/plip-app/README,v
retrieving revision 1.1.1.1
retrieving revision 1.2
Merging differences between 1.1.1.1 and 1.2 into README
rcsmerge: warning: conflicts during merge
cvs update: conflicts found in README
C README
M create_tables.sql
U drop_tables.sql
```

What CVS is telling us is that README needs some hand editing to resolve a conflict, create_tables.sql was automatically merged, and the copy of drop_tables.sql was updated with the later version found in the repository.

Once we have edited by hand the README, which has incompatible changes marked (just like we saw when we merged a branch back to the mainstream), rick can then run cvs diff to check that he is happy with all the changes, and then use cvs commit to put them back in the repository. In practice some testing to ensure that the changes where truly compatible would be wise, CVS is good, but it can't understand the logic of your application code, just watch for obvious conflicting changes.

Working with Watches

There is an advanced set of CVS commands, the 'watch' commands, which allow developers to be registered to be notified (usually via email) as files in a CVS repository are edited and modified. This mode of working is very much an advanced topic that is rarely needed, and we don't have the space to cover in detail here. Consult the information sources at the end of the chapter for more information on this topic.

More Fun with CVS

There are still many CVS commands and features that we've not had a chance to look at. Here are some that we really should cover before moving on.

Binary Files

CVS is very good, but nothing is perfect, and binary files are one area where CVS is currently not as strong as it might be. CVS is quite happy to store binary files, but you are responsible for telling CVS the file is actually a binary.

There are two ways of telling CVS a file is binary. You can use -kb with the cvs add command, as we saw earlier, or you can use cvs admin -kb filename. Unfortunately this only affects files in the repository, not local copies, so it's best to start again with a clean local copy after fixing binary files problems.

Currently CVS is also unable to sensibly diff binary files.

Correcting Bad Annotations

People, being people, sometimes put the wrong, or just inappropriate, message in a log file when they make changes to the repository. This is such a common mistake that CVS has a way to correct it. To change the log message on a revision of a file you simply use:

```
$ cvs admin -mrev:"New message"
```

However this is not logged, and the old log message is gone forever, so use it with care.

Accessing CVS Across a Network

One of the most useful things about CVS is its ability to operate across a network. There are several ways of doing this, but by far the most common is pserver, which is short for password authenticating server.

The CVS service is normally run on port 2401. You can change the port number if you need to, but that's unlikely. Since starting the CVS service is not normally a major performance concern, each time a remote CVS command is issued, the inetd daemon provides the best way to run the service, and will monitor the port and start the service for you as and when required.

Firstly you need to check that the service is correctly defined, and is using the standard port. Check that your /etc/services file has an entry:

```
Cvspserver  2401/tcp
```

If it doesn't, add an entry like the one shown. You may also find an entry for UDP, but TCP is the normal method of access. If there is already a line for cvspserver on UDP, there is no need to remove it.

Next we need to update inetd's configuration file, to tell it what to do when it encounters a request on the CVS service port – start the server.

use xinetd instead

In /etc/inetd.conf add a line (it must be all on one line) like this: *see xinetd.org .*

```
cvspserver stream tcp nowait root /usr/bin/cvs cvs --allow-root=/usr/local/cvsrep
pserver
```

-f

Remember to check the path to your CVS binary, and insert the appropriate path to the repository you wish to allow access to across the network. The allow-root option tells the CVS server that remote users are allowed to access a particular repository. You can specify multiple allow-root options if you need to.

Now you need to tell inetd to re-read its configuration file.

```
# killall -HUP inetd
```
/etc/init.d/inet restart.

At this point we can check the service is running, by using telnet to connect to the port. We are not going to be able to access CVS this way, but it is an interim check that all is well.

```
$ telnet localhost 2401
```

When you press *Return* a couple of times, you should see something like:

```
Trying 127.0.0.1...
Connected to localhost.
Escape character is '^]'.

cvs [pserver aborted]: bad auth protocol start:

Connection closed by foreign host.
```

We now have the cvs pserver service accessible on port 2401.

To access a remote repository, we use a special form of the repository specifier, in the following format:

```
:pserver:username@remote-machine:path-to-repository command
```

Let's try a network login as `rick` to the machine gw1:

```
$ cvs -d :pserver:rick@gw1:/usr/local/cvsrep login

(Logging in to rick@gw1)
CVS password:

$
```

From now on, we can do CVS commands across the network accessing the remote repository. CVS has actually stored the users password away in `~/.cvspass`, so we will not need it again until we logout. Easy wasn't it? However there are a couple of drawbacks. The most obvious one is that we have significantly loosened security on our server. People are accessing our server across the network using their normal passwords, and the method `pserver` uses for transmitting passwords, although not plain text, is far from secure. We can improve security by separating CVS user names from real usernames, and also by explicitly listing users allowed to read and/or write the repository.

Suppose we want to allow user `rick` to access the repository, but using a separate username and password. What we need to do is create a file in `/usr/local/cvsrep/CVSROOT` called `passwd`.

Each entry in here gives a CVS login name, an encrypted password, and the real login ID to use. Currently there doesn't seem to be any easy way of generating encrypted passwords from the command line on Linux, so you may have to resort to changing your password temporarily to the one you want to use for CVS, then copying it from `/etc/shadow` (assuming that's where passwords live on your system) back into the `CVSROOT/passwd` file.

To create a CVS-only login for a user `rick-cvs`, the file would look something like:

`rick-cvs:HhyGFguuGuyiuhgiuGiuiuUhh:rick`

Now the user `rick` can remotely login to the CVS server using the login ID `rick-cvs`, with a different password from his normal login. If you simply want to configure alternate passwords for remote users, but leave the login name the same, simply omit the final 'real user ID' and CVS will default to using the one used to login to CVS.

This method is the same one we use to enable anonymous login to the CVS server – we create a real login ID on the system, then map the CVS login `anonymous` to this real ID in the `CVSROOT/passwd` file.

Of course, what we actually don't normally want is anonymous CVS users having write access to our repository. What we need is to specify a list of users actually allowed to read and write the repository remotely. This is very easy, we create two new files in `CVSROOT`, one called `readers` and one called `writers`. All CVS logins listed in readers only have read only access to the system, and only CVS logins listed in the `writers` file will have write access. Since the very existence of a CVS `writers` file automatically disables write access for users not listed in it, you should always create a `writers` file. Both files are a simple one CVS login per line format. So, for example, to restrict both `neil` and `anonymous` to read only access, but `rick` both read and write access, we create a `readers` file like this:

```
neil
anonymous
```

and a `writers` file like this:

```
rick
```

GUI CVS Clients

Up to now we have restricted ourselves to local and network command line clients. However several GUI clients are now becoming available. Here, for example is a Tk interface to CVS, which can be found at http://tkcvs.sourceforge.net/

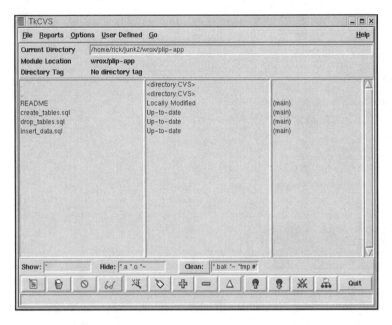

Since CVS operates across a network, you don't have to be on a UNIX, or Linux, machine to access it. Here is WinCVS from http://www.wincvs.org/

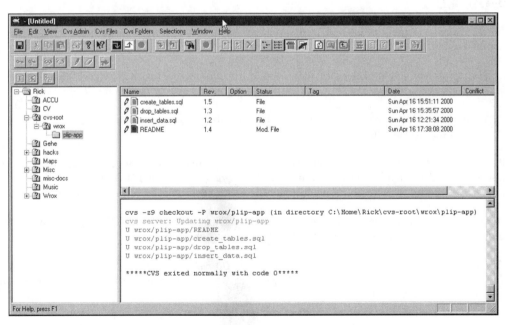

For ultimate portability, there is even a Java client, which you can find at http://www.jcvs.org/

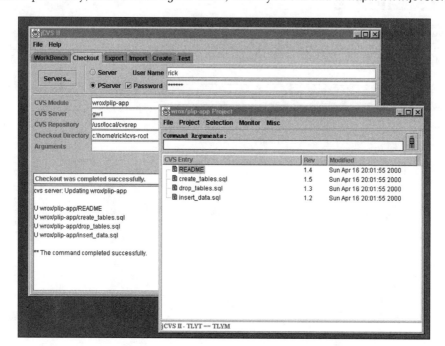

The other, rather interesting possibility, is to use a web-only client, which you can find at
http://stud.fh-heilbronn.de/~zeller/cgi/cvsweb.cgi/

Resources

There are a large number of CVS resources on the Internet, as well as a few probably already installed on your Linux machine.

For a start, try the manual pages with man cvs, or the info pages with info cvs. If that fails, have a look in /usr/doc/cvs-<version number> where you'll probably find more documents.

A good starting point on the Web can be found in the GNU project pages, at
http://www.gnu.org/software/cvs/cvs.html.

http://www.cyclic.com is another good starting point. In particular, look out for an excellent document known as the 'Cederqvist' (after it's author, Per Cederqvist). Also on the Web at
http://www.sourcegear.com/CVS/Dev/interface is a list of user interfaces you can use with CVS.

There is an interesting paper on managing third-party source code with CVS by Luke Mewburn at
http://goanna.cs.rmit.edu.au/~lukem/papers/3rdparty-and-cvs.html.

One book on CVS that's well worth looking out for is *Open Source Development with CVS* by Karl Fogel (Coriolis, *ISBN 1-57610-490-7*). Parts of this book are also available on the Web – have a look at the Coriolis web site at www.coriolis.com.

Summary

In this chapter, we've seen how to use CVS – the Concurrent Versions System – a powerful, free tool for tracking code changes during software development. Its support for multiple users and network configuration has made it the version management tool of choice for many programmers.

We've seen what's involved in setting up and using CVS with a single user on a local machine, and also with multiple users across a network.

We've also looked briefly at some of the graphical clients that are available for CVS.

Since CVS has such a large range of commands, here is a quick summary of the main ones you'll need to use:

add	add a new file/directory to the repository
admin	administration front end for rcs
checkout	check out sources for editing
commit	check files into the repository
diff	show differences between revisions
history	show repository access history
init	create a CVS repository if it doesn't exist
log	print out history information for files
release	indicate that a module is no longer in use
remove	remove an entry from the repository
status	display status information on checked out files
tag	add a symbolic tag to checked out version of files
update	bring work tree in sync with repository

You can always get more help on any of these commands with cvs -H <command>.

CVS commands are always in the format:

```
cvs general-option command command-specific-option [file names]
```

The general options, available in most CVS commands, are:

-d *<repository>*	specify the repository to use
-e *<editor>*	specify an editor to use
--help, -H	provide help on a specific command
-n	no action
-q, -Q	quiet
-t	trace execution
-v, --version	print the CVS version
-z *<level>*	compression level when used across a network

Online discussion at http://www.p2p.wrox.com

3

Databases

Almost all applications have a need to store data. This can range from quite basic requirements such as storing a small number of startup options, to huge complex databases like those needed for managing census data for an entire country. Equally importantly, the storage requirements can vary between the need to store basic fixed length text, and large binary objects.

It's important to choose an appropriate solution to your problem. There is no point in using a large complex database server to store the background image used on your Linux desktop. Equally it would not be sensible to try and store all the data needed for tracking stock in a large warehouse in a single text file.

The appropriate choice depends on both the volume and type of data. Where data contains a large amount of essentially 'single objects' (using the object word in it's general sense) to be stored, a flat file, or an indexed flat file, might be the more appropriate solution. If the data is very hierarchical, a tree type structure like that used in an LDAP server might be more appropriate(we will meet LDAP servers later on).

Where data consists of several different types of objects, related to each other by virtue of their properties, then a relational database is probably a good choice. Relational databases are very flexible, and you can store most types of data structures, including trees, in them if that is appropriate.

On Linux, we are lucky in that we have a wide range of ways to manage our data, so we can pick a solution that is appropriate to our needs. At the simplest level we can just use flat files, either using the low level APIs, or perhaps if it is a Gnome application using the gnome_config API which simplifies access. If our needs are simple, but we require rapid access to indexed data, we might consider using the ndbm routines. These allow the storage of reasonably arbitrary data, but provide retrieval via an index so we can access data very efficiently. These routines are described in *Beginning Linux Programming*, published by Wrox Press. However such solutions are not suitable for more complex needs, and we won't be considering them further.

Further up the scale we have three principal choices, mSQL, MySQL, PostgreSQL, which we will discuss further. We could also consider InterBase, which is formally a commercial product. However, at the time of writing it was available on Linux at no cost, complete with source code. If our needs are more extreme, then we might have to consider using a Linux port of one of the non-open source commercial databases, such as DB2, Sybase or Oracle. Fortunately few people have needs that are quite so demanding, and most should be more than happy with the more common open source solutions such as MySQL or PostgreSQL for their database needs.

Choosing a Database

Before we move on to more technical issues, it's worth briefly considering three most popular open source 'SQL based' solutions available on Linux, and which one would be an appropriate choice for meeting your database needs. At the time of writing, source code is available for all three of these databases, and MySQL and PostgreSQL are free of all license fees. It's possible that license restrictions may have eased, or become more restrictive, or even that some later versions of the sources are no longer available. You should check the web sites for the exact current license requirements.

mSQL

David Hughes, a PhD researcher at Bond University in Australia, was working on a network management project called Minerva, which required a database. He wanted to use the standard query language SQL, but the only 'free' database available at the time was Postgres, which used its own query language, PostQUEL. David's solution was to write an interface program that took basic SQL statements, converted them to PostQUEL, and passed them on to a Postgres server. This was called miniSQL, or mSQL. After a while it became clear that the Postgres server and the translation was more complex a solution than was actually needed, and he enhanced mSQL so that it no longer needed the Postgres backend server. This standalone mSQL is still available today, and it can be found at http://www.hughes.com.au/.

MySQL

MySQL came about in a remarkably similar way to mSQL. A company called TcX was developing web-based applications using an in-house database, and realized that an SQL based approach would be more appropriate. They decided to base their API on the mSQL one, and came up with a product called MySQL. Over time MySQL and mSQL APIs have diverged a little as MySQL has been developed, but they still have many similarities that makes moving code from mSQL to MySQL reasonably easy. MySQL can be found at http://www.MySQL.com/.

PostgreSQL

PostgreSQL has its origins in Ingres (a database originally written at the University of California at Berkeley). At the time of writing it was still available commercially from Computer Associates. Another database called Postgres was also developed at Berkeley not long after Ingres, to experiment with object relational ideas. Initially Postgres did not use SQL at all, but around 1995 Jolly Chen and Andrew Yu added SQL to Postgres, and released a new version called Posgres95.

In late 1996, development had moved out into the open source community, and the product was renamed again, this time to PostgreSQL, it continues to be actively developed. Since it has no commercial ties, PostgreSQL can be freely distributed and appears on many Linux distributions. PostgreSQL can be found at http://www.postgresql.org/.

Which is Right for Me?

Given three midrange databases, all having source code available, which one is the right choice for your project? As always – it depends! There is no single right answer. At the time of writing, the easiest choice is between mSQL and MySQL. MySQL has better support for the SQL standard, and its license is slightly more open, so it's the favorite. However by the time you read this, it's possible that mSQL will have retaken the lead, since both databases continue to be actively developed.

Choosing between MySQL (or perhaps mSQL) and PostgreSQL depends much more on your requirements. If what you need is a lightweight database with fast queries for internal or personal use, but are not too worried about transaction support (which we will explain later), or other more advanced features of SQL, then MySQL is probably your best choice. Indeed it is widely used behind many web servers where transaction support is much less of a concern than the speed of data retrieval. This is because most web servers require exclusively read only data to be passed to clients, and updates to that data need only happen rarely.

If however, you want to distribute an application with a database, and you are concerned about transaction support, then PostgreSQL is probably the one to go for. To decide between those two extremes, have a look at the web sites, and make up your own mind. All are excellent products.

PostgreSQL

For the rest of this chapter, and the next, we are going to concentrate on PostgreSQL, for four reasons:

1. It is available under a very relaxed license, and can be used without fee. Here is a brief extract of the license, which gives you the general idea:

```
Copyright (c) 1994-8 Regents of the University of California


Permission to use, copy, modify, and distribute this software and its
documentation for any purpose, without fee, and without a written agreement is
hereby granted, provided that the above copyright notice and this paragraph
and the following two paragraphs appear in all copies.
```

(The rest of the paragraphs are standard disclaimers).

2. It is already included in many Linux distributions, so chances are, if you are running Linux, you either already have PostgreSQL installed, or at least have it on a CD in an installable format.

3. It also has support for transactions, which allows you to execute several data updates, then decide if you want all or none of the updates to go ahead. For multi-user use, where data is being updated, this can be a very important consideration. Even in single user applications, the availability of transaction support can be very useful.

4. Finally, it has better support for ANSI SQL than the others, so you can explore the more complex areas of SQL with it.

Installation and Commissioning

We are not going to say much about PostgreSQL installation, because the chances are you either already have it installed, or it came with your Linux distribution. If not then a download and install from the PostgreSQL site http://www.postgresql.org may be called for. Both source and binaries are available, though we would normally recommend a binary install, since it's easier and quicker.

When PostgreSQL is initialized for the very first time, only one database exists, template1, and this is the database you must connect to. The only user permitted to access the server by default is probably the database administrator user, postgres, which will have been created when PostgreSQL was installed.

Once you have PostgreSQL installed, you need to make sure that the server process is running, and that the server database has been initialized. To initialize the database, first make sure you are the root user, then make the directory /usr/local/pgsql/data. Change the ownership of this directory to the postgres user by typing:

> # **chown postgres /usr/local/pgsql/data.**

Change to the postgres user by typing:

> # **su - postgres**

and then initialize PostgreSQL as follows:

> # **/usr/local/pgsql/bin/initdb -D /usr/local/pgsql/data**

Check that there is a **postmaster** process running (this the server process for PostgreSQL):

> # **ps axw""**

If your postmaster process is running, then depending on your setup you will get something like this:

> 474 p1 S 0:00 /usr/local/pgsql/ bin /postmaster –D/usr/local/pgsql/data

If there is no postmaster process running, then start one:

> # **usr/local/pgsql/bin/postmaster -D /usr/local/pgsql/data**

Of course, if you have already set $PATH to include /usr/local/pgsql/bin, or the equivalent, then you need not type in the path, just:

> # **postmaster –D usr/local/pgsql/data**

It is a good idea to set your $PATH variable, as it will generally save you a lot of time later on.

Normally, distributions ensure that the first time the postmaster server is started, if the PostgreSQL database has not already been initialized, then the initdb command is automatically invoked to initialize PostgreSQL for first time use. You may need to check the run level configuration of your system once you have installed PostgreSQL, to check the PostgreSQL daemon is automatically started and shutdown.

On some older distributions, notably Red Hat 6.0, the initdb *function was not automatically invoked to create an empty database for first time use, however the manual process is documented on the Red Hat web site, and in Professional Linux Deployment by Wrox.*

Once you are confident the postmaster process is running, it's time to try and connect to the server. When you connect to the server, you must connect to a database. Like many other true database servers, PostgreSQL can serve many different databases from the same server process.

PostgreSQL comes with a handy command line tool for accessing databases, **psql**, and this is tool we will use for experimenting with PostgreSQL, before we get on to access from a programming language.

To check that your server is running correctly, you must first become the database admin user. Login at root, then execute:

```
# su - postgres
```

Now you should be able to connect to the server, using the command:

```
$ psql template1
```

With a bit of luck, you should get a sequence similar to this:

```
$ psql template1
Welcome to psql, the PostgreSQL interactive terminal.

   Type:   \copyright for distribution terms
           \h for help with SQL commands
           \? for help with internal slash commands
           \g or terminate with semicolon to execute query
           \q to quit

template1=#
```

This is success! You have connected to a running PostgreSQL server. Of course by the time you read this, there have probably been upgrades to the versions, but the general idea is unlikely to change.

Creating Users

The first thing to do is quit the psql session, because normally you should not access the server as the administrative user, just like you should not use Linux as 'root' any more than you have to. To exit psql enter:

```
Template1=# \q
```

and you should return to the command prompt. We will come back to the many '\' commands shortly.

Now we know that the server is well, we need to create a user of the server. It's normally convenient to make the username match your normal login, though you don't have to do this. Creating PostgreSQL users is done with the createuser command. Initially we need to do this as the postgres user, since when the server is first initialized, this is the only user with administration privileges on the server. It is also the only user the PostgreSQL server knows about.

```
$ createuser rick
'Shall the new user be allowed to create databases? (y/n) y""
Shall the new user be allowed to create more new users? (y/n) n""
CREATE USER
$
```

If we need to delete the user again, we can do this with the `dropuser` command.

Now we should be able to login as ourselves, and run `psql template1` to connect to the server. Notice that we allowed the user we just created to create new databases. By default only the administrative user can create databases.

Creating Databases

It's normally convenient to allow users to create the databases they need. That way they become the administrator of their own databases, and don't need to bother the PostgreSQL administrator (or if it's yourself, save you swapping logins!). It also minimizes the amount of use you need to make of the `postgres` administration user account.

Now we have permissions as an ordinary Linux user, we can run **psql**, connect to the `template1` database, and create ourselves a database to use. Databases are normally created and deleted inside the **psql** command shell in the normal SQL standard way, using the following commands:

```
template1=# CREATE DATABASE <Dbname>;
template1=# DROP DATABASE <Dbname>;
```

Notice that the commands have semicolons at the end. All the SQL commands you issue to PostgreSQL are not considered complete until a ';' has been entered, just pressing return is not good enough. As an alternative you can terminate lines with '\g', but ';' is a more common SQL convention. This ability to write many lines, that are a single SQL command, is useful when you want to write longer SQL statements, such as those found when creating tables.

If you, as the PostgreSQL administrator, want to create and delete databases outside the psql shell, this can be done from the shell command line:

```
$ createdb <Dbname>
$ dropdb <Dbname>
```

In this case you will be the database administrator for any new databases you create. You may find that some older distributions of PosgreSQL start with no database, and you must run `createdb` before you can use psql to connect to the server.

If you run the `psql` command and don't specify a database, then by default psql will try and connect you to a database with the same name as your user name. As a result, it's often convenient to create a database with that name, even if you only use it for experimenting with.

Backing Up Databases

Having created databases, now is probably a sensible place to mention backing them up. The command

```
$ pg_dump [-a -d -s -t table ] database_name
```

is probably the best way to do this. The main options are:

-a	dump only data in a database, not it's structure
-d	dump data in the form of SQL commands for re-adding it later
-s	dump only the definition of the database, not it's data
-t table	dump for a named table only

The online manual that comes with PostgreSQL has full details. Remember, you put your data in a database because it was important – so it's also important to have a backup of the data!

Remote Access

Before we leave the issues of installation and commissioning of PostgreSQL, it's perhaps worthwhile making a quick mention of remote access. PostgreSQL is a 'proper' client server database, and can be accessed on other Linux machines from across a network using TCP/IP. Indeed you can access it from Microsoft Windows if you like, the source of PostgreSQL comes with a version of psql that can be built with Visual C++, and there is also a nice GUI Interactive PostgreSQL program that can be found at http://www.zeos.dn.ua, so even hardened Windows GUI people can access your server:

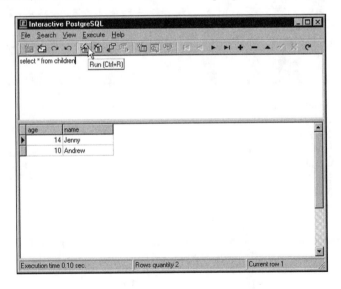

Local users who prefer a GUI are also catered for – see pgaccess, which you can find at http://www.flex.ro/pgaccess, or Mpsql, which can be found at http://www.mutinybaysoftware.com. By way of comparison to MS-Windows, here is pgaccess running on a Red Hat system:

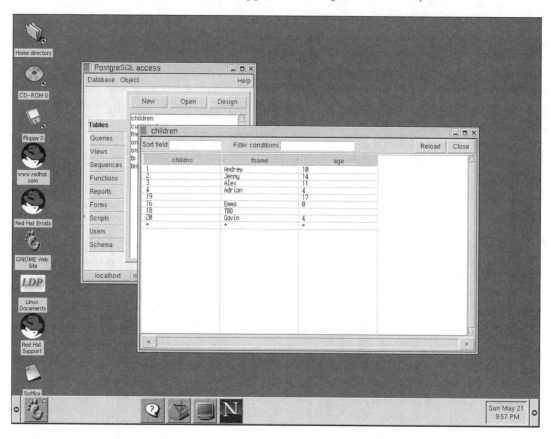

Before you access PostgreSQL across a network, there is some configuration needed. PostgreSQL, by default does not permit remote connections, a very sensible default. To enable this you must manually edit the configuration file /var/lib/pgsql/data/pg_hba.conf to permit remote access. Depending on your installation this file may sometimes be found in the /usr/local hierarchy. If it's not in any of the obvious places, the locate or find commands should help you out. The file is well commented, and it's very easy to add an additional line at the bottom, to permit remote connections. For example we added:

```
host        all        192.168.100.0   255.255.255.0    trust
```

This allows access from all machines on our local network, which is a Class C network using 192.168.100 as the network part. Normally you will not need to restart the PostgreSQL server for this change to take effect. Edits are immediately effective, unlike MySQL that normally requires a reload for configuration changes to take effect.

Database Fundamentals

At this point experienced database people might like to skip forward to the next section, *Using psql*, because we are going to have a very quick look at the fundamentals of databases.

Relational databases were born out of work Dr. E. F. Codd did in the early 1970s, when he applied set theory to the storage and retrieval of large amounts of data. Before then databases had been mostly either hierarchical or based on a network model. Although these databases worked, they were not very flexible, and the relational model was a great step forward. The new vogue, some would claim 'the way forward', are Object databases. However, currently they are not taking the world by storm, and many Object systems still use relational databases for their persistent storage needs.

In a relational database, all data is stored in tables, which are sometimes referred to as 'relations'. Tables are in many ways like the spreadsheet (which was in fact designed after the relational database), in that it is composed of records (often called rows, or sometimes tuples) and fields (a single column in a row, sometimes called an attribute). A database will normally be composed of many tables, each with many rows and columns. The real power of relational databases comes from the way the data is broken down into its smallest elements, and the manner in which data from one table can be related to data in a different table in a very flexible way.

When deciding how to break data down to store it in a database, you must work through a design process to 'normalize' your data, and design the tables, rows, and columns. There are several increasing levels, or forms of normalization, each form being more rigorous than the last. In practice only the first three forms are commonly used, and those are the only three we will look at here.

First Normal Form

This is reasonably easy to understand, and basically says that there must only be one value in each field, and that your tables must be rectangular. The reason for the first part of this is quite apparent – don't try and store a persons name in the same field as their age for example. This is pretty much common sense, since intuitively we can that see that this would be like having a 'C' structure where we didn't properly break down the data into separate members.

The second part is also reasonably easy – it stops us having repeated columns. So, if we had a table for storing book information, it tells us that we can't have some rows with one author column, and some rows with several author columns where a book had more than one author. Again this seems pretty sensible, after all, how could we ever know in advance how many authors a book could have? As we are writing this, we don't know for certain how many authors will contribute to this book, though we do have a pretty reasonable idea.

How far do you take this breakdown of data? In the course of reviewing this book one of the reviewers kindly pointed out that in Dutch a lastname can be preceded with an interjection. In the case of the author this would be "van". However this part of his name should not be used for sorting. Alphabetically he should not be found under the Vs. This means that for the Netherlands we should break the last name down into two separate components, because we might need to sort data based on only the last component of the name.

Experience suggests that breaking it down just a bit more than you believe is required is often advisable, but it's often difficult to predict in advance the optimal breakdown of data.

Second Normal Form

The second rule is that all the data in a row should depend on a primary key. This means that each row in your table should have one key piece of data (that is the information on which all the other data in the row depends); usually it is in a single column, but can occasionally be the combination of several columns. For example, you should not have a row containing information about authors where the key column was a first name, as there are bound to be several authors sharing a first name. A combination of first name and last name might do, but this is still not a great idea, because it may not be unique. Something like a passport number, however, is guaranteed to be unique, at least for citizens of the same country, and might make a good key. We say might, because how many people know their passport number from memory? Also some people don't have passports at all, so in practice even this would not be a good key to choose.

In circumstances where there is no obvious unique key, we often create a unique value for each row, which has no meaning beyond that of providing a way to refer uniquely to each row of data. We will see this in a later chapter, where we create some '_id' fields for guaranteed uniqueness.

Third Normal Form

This is the hardest one of the three to explain. It says that each column in a row must only depend on the contents of the primary unique key column or columns, not on any other column's data. Suppose we had a book table with information about books in it. We might reasonably choose to use the ISBN as a primary key since it's well known and unique, and perhaps store the book title and publisher name in the rows. Now suppose later on we want to store the web address of the publisher. It would be tempting to simply add an extra column to our book table to store this extra piece of information. The web address would depend on the primary key, since it depends on the ISBN. However, this would break third normal form since in fact the web address actually depends only on the column containing the publisher's name, which is not the primary key.

Intuitively we can see that this would not have been a great decision, since we could end up storing the web address of the same publisher many times, which would be wasteful. We should break the storage of the web address out to a new separate table. We can then 'join' the data between the two tables when we require the web address.

De-normalization

You will sometimes hear people talking about de-normalizing the database to improve its performance. You should only ever do this once you have fully normalized your data and decided that you do in fact have a performance problem. Even then, it's much more likely your performance problem is due to poor application design, not over-normalization of data. Analyze where your performance problem is, and consider very carefully if it might not stem from a higher-level design flaw, rather than the way the data is stored. Always beware of trying to 'improve' the design of data arranged in third normal form!

A Simple Database

Well, enough of theory, what does this mean in practice? Let us suppose we want to build a database for books, authors and publishers. It's been done before, but it's a nice example because it's easy to understand.

It's reasonably intuitive to see the first three tables – author, book, and publisher, so let's start by designing them. We will keep the data we need to store very basic, and just store names and book titles.

Let's start with authors. As we mentioned, names are not a good unique value to use, so we will invent a unique ID to use, which we will call `author_id`. This will be our primary key for the table. Here is our first stab at the author table:

author_id	Fname	Lname
1	Richard	Stones
2	Neil	Matthew
3	Andrew	Froggatt
4	Peter	Wainwright
5	Simon	Cozens
6	Iain	Banks

As you can see, we have separated the first and last names, in case we ever need to access them independently at some point in the future, but (sorry!) we have not catered for Dutch names specifically. We have shown the rows ordered by `author_id`, but you should remember that this is just for our convenience – the database internally is free to store them in any order it chooses. Actually some databases have a 'clustered' option, to force the storage order, but we won't consider that here. If the order of rows extracted from a table matters to you, you must specify the order you require when you retrieve the data.

The book table is also easy, since this time we know that books do have a unique reference, the ISBN:

ISBN	Title	pub_year
1874416656	Instant UNIX	1995
1861002971	Beginning Linux Programming 2e	1999
1861003021	Professional Apache	1999
0349101779	The Wasp Factory	1985

Publisher should be even easier:

publisher_name	web_address
Wrox	www.wrox.com
Addison-Wesley	www.aw.com
Abacus	

although this is a case where we might consider generating a unique _id column for publishers, to keep the length of the primary key column short, which is more efficient. Since we know there are not a huge number of publishers (at least in database terms), and to keep it simple, we decide to just use the name here.

There is one other problem. As you can see, we don't have a web address for Abacus. Now they may well have a web address, in fact they probably do, but it's not printed on the back of the book I own, so currently I don't know what it is. This means that for the web_address column of Abacus, we need to use a NULL value. This is a special database value that means 'unknown'. It doesn't mean there isn't a web address, or that the web address is an empty string, it just means it's unknown. We might also have to use NULL if we were storing data from a survey, and some people had refused to state their gender – we may use a NULL to indicate that we don't know the answer. It's very important to remember that two NULLs are not the same as each other – if we had had another publisher whose web address we didn't know, we would have set this to NULL as well. The two NULLs are different, since we could be fairly sure both publishers actually had different web addresses.

As you can see, we have three nice clean tables, each is rectangular, each has only one piece of data in each cell, and each has all the data in the row depending on a single key. We have kept the key in the first column, since this makes the tables much easier to understand. Unfortunately, this doesn't tell us all we need to know.

Suppose we want to know who the publisher was for each book. We can't tell from the current data, but this is easy to correct – we just need to add a publisher_name column to the book table so that each book has a publisher. That way if we know a publisher, we can just search the book table for all the entries having that publisher name. Alternatively if we know the book title and want a web address, we search for the book title in the book table, then use the publishers name to locate the entry in the publisher table that will contain the web address (or NULL if we are unlucky!).

The publisher_name column in the book table is called a foreign key, because it stores a value that appears in a different table as a primary key.

Since each book only ever has one publisher, what we have here is a many to one relationship between books and publishers (many books could be published by one publisher), but each book is published by exactly one publisher. OK, in practice this might not always be true, but it's sufficient for our purposes.

This structure still doesn't tell us anything about who wrote each book. Suppose we want to find the books Peter Wainwright contributed to. You might be tempted to add an extra column to the book table, to store `author_id`. We would then have a relationship between the book table and author table, like this:

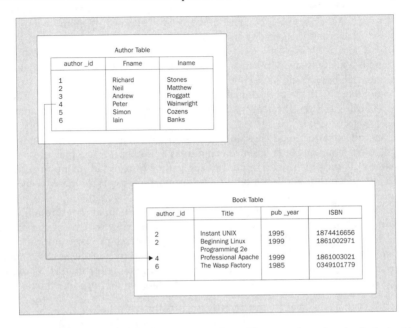

Now suppose we want to add the data for Neil Matthew. He contributed to both *Instant UNIX* and *Beginning Linux Programming*. In this case we would have two links, because the `author_id` for Neil Matthew, 2, would appear twice in the book table, once against *Instant UNIX*, and once against *Beginning Linux Programming*:

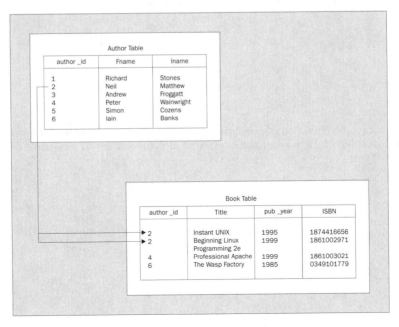

But wait a minute; you may have noticed that in the diagram before we only put one author ID per row. *Instant UNIX* had two authors, Neil Matthew and Rick Stones. How do we show they both contributed to the book? We might be tempted to add an extra column with `author_id2` to the book table, but this would be a very bad idea. *Professional Java Server Programming* lists fifteen authors – clearly adding an extra column for each author is excessive, and how would we know how many columns to add? Suppose we added fifteen and then we found a book with sixteen authors? Disaster.

What we have here is a many-to-many relationship between books and authors, each author could contribute to many books, and each book could have contributions from many authors. Unfortunately many to many relationships are not directly usable in relational databases. We solve this conundrum by adding an extra table, which we will call `author_book`, and will have just two columns, `author_id` and `Isbn`.

This adding of an additional table, to cater for many-to-many links is very common in relational database design, and the new table is often referred to as a link table. As a pair these columns are unique, since we would only ever need to put in each author-book relationship once. This new 'link' table will act to join the author and book tables, and support our many-to-many relationship.

Each row in this new table describes a single relationship between an author and a book, so there will be one entry with `author_id` 2 and isbn 1874416656, one entry with `author_id` 1 and isbn 1874416656. That way knowing the ISBN of a book we can search the table and find both `author_id`s, and hence the author names for *Instant UNIX*, and by starting with an author name, we could find their `author_id` and then search the `author_isbn` table for the ISBNs of books they had contributed to. The data in `author_book` for our sample data would look like this:

author_id	Isbn
1	1874416656
2	1874416656
1	1861002971
2	1861002971
5	1861002971
4	1861003021
6	0349101779

As you can see, each combination of columns is unique, and is called a composite key, and this joining table allows us to relate many books to one author, and many authors to one book.

Our final database structure looks like this:

Author Table				Author _book Table			Book Table			
author _id	Fname	lname		author _id	ISBN		author _id	ISBN	Title	pub _year
1	Richard	Stones		1	1874416656		2	1874416656	Instant UNIX	1995
2	Neil	Matthew		2	1874416656		2	1861002971	Beginning Linux Programming 2e	1999
3	Andrew	Froggatt		1	1861002971					
4	Peter	Wainwright		2	1861002971		4	1861003021	Professional Apache	1999
5	Simon	Cozens		5	1861002971		6	0349101779	The Wasp Factory	1985
6	Iain	Banks		4	1861003021					
				6	0349101779					

Publisher Table	
publisher _name	web _address
Wrox	www.wrox.com
Addison - Wesley	www.aw.com
Abacus	

That was, of necessity, a very brief look at database design, which is a complex subject, on which many books have been written. If you want to know more about database design, then a good starting place is *Database Design for Mere Mortals*, by Michael J. Hernandez, pub. Addison-Wesley, *ISBN 0201694719*.

Using psql

After that aside into database design, let us get back to PostgreSQL, and see what we can do with it.

We don't have the space in this chapter to teach SQL in any depth. If you want more detail about SQL, we suggest a couple of books you might like to consider, *Instant SQL*, by Joe Cleko, pub. Wrox; *The Practical SQL Handbook*, J Bowman et al., pub. Addison-Wesley; and *PostgreSQL Introduction and Concepts*, available online from the PostgreSQL web site. What we will do here is work through some of the basic SQL commands that should cover your basic needs.

There are three types of commands we can issue to psql – data definition commands, data manipulation commands, both of which affect data in the database, and '\' commands, which are commands to psql itself. We will look at these in turn.

Commands to psql

A list of these are available by typing \? at the psql command prompt. We will list them all here, for ease of reference, then will look in slightly more detail at the commands you are most likely to use.

```
\?             -- help
\a             -- toggle field-alignment (currently on)
\C [<captn>]   -- set html3 caption
\connect <dbname|-> <user> -- connect to new database
\copy table {from | to} <fname>
\d [<table>]   -- list tables and indices, columns in <table>, or * for all
\da            -- list aggregates
\dd [<object>]- list comment for table, field, type, function, or operator.
\df            -- list functions
\di            -- list only indices
\do            -- list operators
\ds            -- list only sequences
```

```
\dS            -- list system tables and indexes
\dt            -- list only tables
\dT            -- list types
\e [<fname>]   -- edit the current query buffer or <fname>
\E [<fname>]   -- edit the current query buffer or <fname>, and execute
\f [<sep>]     -- change field separator (currently '|')
\g [<fname>]   [|<cmd>] -- send query to backend [and results in <fname> or pipe]
\h [<cmd>]     -- help on syntax of sql commands, * for all commands
\H             -- toggle html3 output
\i <fname>     -- read and execute queries from filename
\l             -- list all databases
\m             -- toggle monitor-like table display
\o [<fname>]   [|<cmd>] -- send all query results to stdout, <fname>, or pipe
\p             -- print the current query buffer
\q             -- quit
\r             -- reset(clear) the query buffer
\s [<fname>]   -- print history or save it in <fname>
\t             -- toggle table headings and row count
\T [<html>]    -- set html3.0 <table ...> options
\x             -- toggle expanded output
\w <fname>     -- output current buffer to a file
\z             -- list current grant/revoke permissions
\! [<cmd>]     -- shell escape or command
```

The main ones you will need to know are:

\?	This simply lists the list above.
\c table {from | to} <fname>	Copies the data from a table to a flat file, or loads a table from a flat file. Often the copy 'in' to the database is done using SQL insert statements, but the copy command does provide a good way of backing up database data at the table level.
\d <table>	On it's own , \d lists the tables in your database. If you give it the optional table name parameter, then it lists the columns in that table.
\e	Edits the current buffer. When you type into psql, you can type in multiple lines before you execute them. This is quite handy, but annoying when you make a mistake early on, and don't discover it till later. The \e command lets you edit the buffer. You can override the default editor by exporting the environment variable EDITOR before starting psql. You can also use the up and down arrows for moving through your command history.
\h <cmd>	This lists the syntax of SQL commands. If you give it a partial command, such as create, it will even tell you the possible more specific commands you may have been interested in, such as create table, create index etc.
\i <fname>	Executes commands from a file.
\l	Lists all databases in the current server.
\q	Quits.
\r	Resets the buffer you are typing into, so you can start over quickly.

As with all of PostgreSQL, you will find more information on the web site and in the installed documentation under /usr/doc/postgresql-version.

Data Definition Commands

These are commands that define the structure of your database, rather than the data in it. The most common example is creating tables to store data in. Experienced users of SQL will find most of this section gratifyingly familiar, because PostgreSQL does follow the SQL92 standard reasonably closely (although with a few omissions, which reduce with every release). Most of the differences are down to PostgreSQL's extensions, which you don't have to use if you don't need them.

Experienced SQL users may still find just reading quickly through this section worthwhile, because there are some slight differences from what they may be used to. If you use a CASE tool, you may find that they can often generate DDL (Data Definition Language) for creating databases directly from a design in the case tool, and this can be a very efficient way of generating your database.

In this chapter, we will do all of our work with psql from the command line, typing in commands as we go. In practice, it almost always better to create some ordinary text files containing the SQL for your data manipulation, then feed them to psql like this:

```
$ psql -d databasename -f command-file.sql
```

That way, it's much easier to modify your database design. Just edit the command file, dropping the existing table (saving the data first if needed!), and then re-executing the modified command file.

Creating and Dropping Tables

First let's look at the syntax for creating a new table. The easiest way of getting a summary of the syntax is actually to ask psql, with \h CREATE TABLE, which gives us the following syntax summary:

```
Command:     CREATE TABLE_
Description: Creates a new table
Syntax:
CREATE   [TEMPORARY | TEMP] TABLE table (
column type
[NULL | NOT NULL] [UNIQUE] [DEFAULT value]
[column_constraint_clause | PRIMARY KEY } [ ... ]]
[, ... ]
[, PRIMARY KEY ( column [, ... ] ) ]
[, CHECK ( condition ) ]
[, table_constraint_clause ]
) [ INHERITS ( inherited_table [, ... ] ) ]
```

People with SQL skills will notice this is not quite standard SQL, though it is very close. In particular the 'INHERITS' keyword is not in normal SQL syntax. This is part of PostgreSQL's object relational extensions, and lets you do fascinating things, such as inherit column definitions from other tables. Sadly we don't have the space in this chapter to explore these features. The rest of the syntax is fairly standard. As an example, we will create a very simple table, to store the ages and first names of some children. All you need to do is type this in at the psql prompt:

```
Dbname=# CREATE TABLE children (
Dbname(# fname VARCHAR,
Dbname(# age INTEGER
Dbname(# );
```

being sure not to forget the trailing semi colon, and not to put a comma before the closing brace. psql responds with the word CREATE telling you the table was successfully created. We can ask psql about the table we just created by entering

```
Dbname=# \d children;
```

it responds with:

```
                      Table      "children"
+-------------------------------+-------------------+----------+
|          Attribute            |       Type        | Modifier |
+-------------------------------+-------------------+----------+
| fname                         | varchar()         |          |
| age                           | integer           |          |
+-------------------------------+-------------------+----------+
```

We can drop the table again with drop table children, which simply throws the table away. The drop table command has the following syntax:

```
DROP TABLE class_name1, ... class_nameN
```

If there was any data in the table, that gets thrown away too, so be careful!

At the moment there is nothing that constrains the data in the table, providing the types are correct. It would be perfectly reasonable as it stands to insert data about the same child twice, or many times. When working with databases, we invariably need to ensure that there is a unique way of referring to a single row in a table. Often this is done by making the value in a single column unique, though sometimes it is a combination of two or more columns that provides a unique reference or key. If we want to ensure that we only allow each child's name to appear once, then we can ask the database to enforce this rule (always a much better idea than relying on application code or worse, users!) by specifying a **constraint** that fname is a primary key.

```
Dbname=# CREATE TABLE children (
Dbname(# fname VARCHAR PRIMARY KEY,
Dbname(# age INTEGER
Dbname(# );
```

psql warns us that to implement the primary key, it has created an index. This is fine.

```
NOTICE:  CREATE TABLE/PRIMARY KEY will create implicit index 'children_pkey' for
table 'children'
Dbname=#
```

Although we have not yet got onto manipulating data in tables, we can jump ahead for a moment, and check that all is well, by trying to insert some data into our new table:

```
Dbname=# INSERT INTO children VALUES ('jenny', 14);
INSERT 20195 1
Dbname=# INSERT INTO children VALUES ('jenny', 15);
ERROR:  Cannot insert a duplicate key into a unique index
```

The numbers you see after the first insert will be different – you can ignore these for now. As you can see, PostgreSQL is enforcing the rule about uniqueness for us. Sometimes it is not a single column that needs to be unique, but a combination of two or more columns. Suppose we wanted to ensure that it was only the combination of fname and age that was unique. We do this with a similar syntax, but using the CONSTRAINT keyword at the end of the list of columns for our table, and specifying which combination of columns must be unique:

```
Dbname=# CREATE TABLE children (
Dbname(# fname VARCHAR,
Dbname(# age INTEGER,
Dbname(# CONSTRAINT fname_age PRIMARY KEY(fname, age)
Dbname(# );
```

psql responds (providing you remembered to drop any earlier versions of the table first!):

```
NOTICE:  CREATE TABLE/PRIMARY KEY will create implicit index 'fname_age' for table
'children'
CREATE
```

Now PostgreSQL will allow us two rows with the same fname, so long as the age is different:

```
Dbname=# INSERT INTO children VALUES ('jenny', 14);
INSERT 20195 1
Dbname=# INSERT INTO children VALUES ('jenny', 14);
ERROR:  Cannot insert a duplicate key into a unique index fname_age
Dbname=# INSERT INTO children VALUES ('jenny', 15);
INSERT 20228 1
```

The next important restriction we can impose on data in our tables is to prevent NULL values. This is very simple, just put 'NOT NULL' after the column type, since by default NULL values are usually allowed. Suppose we went back to our original table definition, but wanted to ensure the fname could never be NULL. The syntax we need is simply:

```
Dbname=# CREATE TABLE children (
Dbname(# fname VARCHAR NOT NULL,
Dbname(# age INTEGER
Dbname(# );
```

The last special constraint we will look at is automatically creating an incrementing value in a column. This is such a common requirement that there is a special syntax for creating columns with values that automatically get incremented when data is inserted – just like we used in our author table earlier, when we wanted an author_id that was unique. To do this we define the column type as SERIAL, like this:

```
Dbname=# CREATE TABLE children (
Dbname(# childno SERIAL,
Dbname(# fname VARCHAR,
Dbname(# age INTEGER
Dbname(# );
```

When you run this, psql warns you something special is happening:

```
NOTICE:  CREATE TABLE will create implicit sequence 'children_childno_seq' for
SERIAL column 'children.childno'
NOTICE:  CREATE TABLE/UNIQUE will create implicit index 'children_childno_key' for
table 'children'
CREATE
```

This rather strange sequence of messages is because PostgreSQL is using another lower level facility it has called **sequences**, in order to implement the SERIAL column type. In general it's not important to know about sequences, except, as we shall see in a moment, when you drop and recreate tables that use SERIAL column types.

This time when we insert data, we need to explicitly avoid adding data to the SERIAL column:

```
Dbname=# INSERT INTO children (fname, age) VALUES ('Andrew', '10');
INSERT 20327 1
Dbname=# INSERT INTO children (fname, age) VALUES ('Jenny', '14');
INSERT 20328 1
Dbname=# SELECT * FROM children;
Childno |fname  |age
--------+-------+---
      1 |Andrew | 10
      2 |Jenny  | 14
(2 rows)
```

Don't worry about the new command 'select' we will be explaining it shortly. For now all you need to know is that it retrieves data from a table for you.

As you can see, PostgreSQL automatically creates an incrementing value for us. However, there are a couple of things to be aware of. The first is if we try and drop the table children, and then recreate it exactly as before, we get a rather strange error message:

```
ERROR:  Relation 'children_childno_seq' already exists
```

This is because although we dropped the table, PostgreSQL did not drop the sequence it automatically created. We must do it ourselves before we can recreate the table:

```
Dbname=# DROP SEQUENCE children_childno_seq;
```

This is an unfortunate consequence of the way PostgreSQL currently implements SERIAL columns, and may be changed in later releases. It's only a minor annoyance, once you know what the error message means and how to correct it. If you are not sure what sequences have been left around in your database, you can list them with the psql command \ds, which will provide a list.

You should also be aware of a couple of other features of SERIAL columns. Firstly, if you try and insert a value into a SERIAL field, then providing it's a unique number, PostgreSQL will not prevent you. Secondly, if you delete all the rows from a table and then insert some new ones, the serial number will not reset and start counting from one again. This is often a good thing, because it ensures that even if you had left some other tables, which used the unique numbers in the table you just dropped, you will not add new rows that the old stale data could accidentally refer to.

There is much, much more you can do to impose rules on the data in your tables, but those are the main features that you will need to know.

PostgreSQL Data Types

The last area we need to look at when creating tables is data types. Up to now we have confined ourselves to INTEGER, which is self-explanatory, and VARCHAR, which as you probably guessed, is just a variable length character string. Since we didn't specify a maximum length PostgreSQL allows the array to grow to an internal limit.

PostgreSQL has an unusually large range of data types, and even allows you to add your own if you need additional ones. Here we will just list the main ones:

bool	Boolean. Stores true or false. On input, 'y', '1', 'yes', and 'true' are all taken to mean true; 'n', '0', 'no', and 'false' are all taken to mean false, independently of the case used.
char(N)	stores up to N characters in a fixed length field.
date	a date (without time)
float	a floating point number
integer	a signed 32-bit integer
numeric(p, d)	a number with a specified number of digits and precision
time	a time (without date)
timestamp	a combined date and time
varchar(N)	a variable length string up to N characters. Unlike char(N) unused space is not stored in the database.

There are other types, including some unusual ones such as polygons and Ethernet MAC addresses, however almost all applications can manage with the set above.

Data Manipulation Commands

We have now seen how to create tables, and had a sneak look at adding and retrieving data from tables, but now it's time to look more fully at the data storage and retrieval parts of PostgreSQL. Readers who know SQL already will be pleased to discover that PostgreSQL's support for SQL92 in this area is very good, and all the syntax we will be covering here is standard. PostgreSQL, unlike some databases, is not case sensitive to table names, nor does it matter what case is used for SQL commands. The authors of this chapter tend to type all upper case on the command line, and always use lower case for all table and column names, partly because it's quicker, and partly for consistency.

When writing SQL that is embedded in procedural code, you may find it makes the SQL easier to read if you put SQL key words in upper case, while keeping table and column names lower case. We do strongly recommend you avoid camel case (i.e. names like AuthorBooks) because it may cause you problems if you ever need to port to a database that is case sensitive, and you have not been perfectly consistent. PostgreSQL would not have noticed the inconsistency, since it takes no account of the case in the first place.

Inserting Data

The first thing we need to cover is inserting data into tables. After all, it's going to be difficult to demonstrate much to do with manipulating data until we have some.

The SQL command for adding data is very simple, it's INSERT and it only allows you to insert data into a single table with each command. PostgreSQL has a more complex version, which allows you to insert data extracted from another table, but it's not commonly used, so we omit it here.

The basic syntax is:

```
Dbname=# INSERT INTO class_name [(attr1, …attrN)] VALUES (expr1, …exprN);
```

Notice that PostgreSQL uses the word 'class_name' where 'table_name' would be more conventional. This is just how the syntax is displayed, and doesn't affect how it is used.

Notice the optional attributes; these are the names of the columns. If we simply want to insert data into all the columns in a table, we can omit the column names, and just provide values. However, we recommend that you avoid this shortened form in production code, and always explicitly name your columns. This is much safer because it will catch any mistakes you might make if you re-order columns in your table, and also allows you to avoid accidentally inserting values into SERIAL columns. If you don't specify data for a column when you insert data, then it will be given the value NULL.

The following session, using some very short names (so that a later display fits on the page better), demonstrates an insert. In real code we would, of course, use much more descriptive names.

```
Dbname=# CREATE TABLE tb (
Dbname(# b bool,
Dbname(# cn char(5),
Dbname(# d date,
Dbname(# f float,
Dbname(# i integer,
Dbname(# n numeric(5, 3),
Dbname(# t time,
Dbname(# v varchar(32),
Dbname(# v0 varchar
Dbname(# );
CREATE
Dbname=# \d tb;
```

```
                                Table = "tb"
+--------------------------------+----------------------------------+-----------+
|           Attribute            |               Type               | Modifier  |
+--------------------------------+----------------------------------+-----------+
| b                              | boolean                          |           |
| cn                             | char(5)                          |           |
| d                              | date                             |           |
| f                              | float                            |           |
| i                              | integer                          |           |
| n                              | numeric(5,3)                     |           |
| t                              | time                             |           |
| v                              | varchar(32)                      |           |
| v0                             | varchar()                        |           |
+--------------------------------+----------------------------------+-----------+
```

```
Dbname=# INSERT INTO tb (b, cn, d, f, I, n, t, v, v0) VALUES ('y', 'CH', 'June 1
2000', '12.3', '45', '3.45', '15:32', 'It\'s', 'Hello world, how are you today?');
INSERT 20412 1
Dbname=# SELECT * FROM tb;
 b|cn  |           d| f| i|  n|t       |v     |v0
-+-----+-----------+----+--+-----+--------+-----+-----------------------------
 y|CH   |2000-06-01|12.3|45|3.450|15:32:00|It's  |Hello world, how are you today?
(1 row)
```

As you can see, there is not a lot to the INSERT statement. Remember to escape single quotes with a '\', and dates are safest when they are unambiguous, because not everyone agrees which order months and days should come in! We used a month name 'June' in our INSERT statement, PostgreSQL stores and reports this as numeric month, 6.

Retrieving Data from a Single Table

Now we have some data in tables, we might reasonably want to try and get it back out again, and this is where SQL comes into it's own with the SELECT statement. For our purposes we only need to use a tiny part of the SELECT syntax, if you want to know more we suggest you take a look at one of the references.

The basic syntax for SELECT is:

```
SELECT [DISTINCT] expr1, ... ,exprN
FROM table_list
WHERE qualifier
[ORDER BY attr1 [ASC|DESC], ... ,attrN];
```

This apparently simple syntax enables you to do most of what you will need for data retrieval. The expr fields let you choose the columns you want, or * which selects all columns. The qualifier allows you to select a subset of rows, and the ORDER clause allows you to order the result. In more formal terms we could say that the expr terms allows you to project a subset of columns, and the where clause selects a subset of rows. It's a straightforward syntax, so let's look at a few examples of selecting data from a single table. First we insert some rows, so we have a table with data like this:

```
Dbname=# SELECT * FROM children;
 childno|fname  |age
--------+-------+---
      1|Andrew|  10
      2|Jenny  |  14
      3|Alex   |  11
      4|Adrian|   5
      5|Allen  |   4
(5 rows)
```

First let's select the child number and the age:

```
Dbname=# SELECT childno, age FROM children;
 childno|age
--------+---
      1|  10
      2|  14
      3|  11
      4|   5
      5|   4
(5 rows)
```

We can also impose an order:

```
Dbname=# SELECT childno, age FROM children ORDER BY age;
childno|age
-------+---
      5|  4
      4|  5
      1| 10
      3| 11
      2| 14
(5 rows)
```

Now let's have a subset, ordered by an alphanumeric field in descending order:

```
Dbname=# SELECT fname, age FROM children WHERE age <= '10' ORDER BY fname DESC;
fname |age
------+---
Andrew| 10
Allen |  4
Adrian|  5
(3 rows)
```

As you can see, simple SELECT commands are easy to work with.

There are a small number of 'special' expressions you can select, one of which is particularly useful. Quite often you will find that you need to know how many rows match a query, but don't actually need to retrieve the data. For example you might want to know how many rows there are in the children table. This is such a common need that there is a special way of retrieving just the row count, which is to use the expression COUNT(*) as the expression in your SELECT statement, like this:

```
Dbname=# SELECT COUNT(*) FROM children WHERE age < '6';
count
-----
    2
(1 row)
```

One other 'trick' that comes in handy is to name the columns in the output of the selection. You do this by simply adding 'as name' where 'name' is the name you want the column to be displayed as. You can name all or just some columns, as you wish. For example we can force the name of the column 'fname' to be displayed as 'firstname' like this:

```
Dbname=# SELECT age, fname AS firstname FROM children WHERE age < '6';
age|firstname
---+---------
  5|Adrian
  4|Allen
(2 rows)
```

Retrieving Data Combined from Several Tables

Life gets slightly more complicated when we want to combine data from more than one table.

The extension of SELECT to multiple tables is deceptively simple – you just list columns from more than one table, specify multiple tables in the FROM clause, and use a WHERE clause to specify how the columns in different tables are related.

Suppose we have two tables in a sales order application. One table called 'customer' has customer_id and customer_name columns, and a table called 'placed_order' has order_id, and customer_id. The intention is that given an order_id, you can discover the customer's name by looking up the related customer_id in the customer table. We need to know one slight extension to the syntax, which is that to specify a column from a particular table, where there are columns with the same name in more than one table, we write table_name.column_name.

If you were writing procedural code, you would write something like:

```
Fetch customer_id from placed_order where order_id = 4 into customer_id_variable
Fetch customer_name from customer where customer_id = customer_id_variable into
customer_name_variable
```

However in SQL, you should write this all as one statement, because that allows the SQL engine to process the query much more efficiently. The SQL equivalent is:

```
Dbname=# SELECT customer_name FROM customer, ORDER WHERE (placed_order.order_id =
4) AND (placed_order.customer_id = customer.customer_id);
```

Let's try this out. We start with our two tables with data like this:

```
Dbname=# SELECT * FROM placed_order;
order_id|customer_id
--------+-----------
       1|          3
       2|          1
       3|          2
       4|          1
       5|          3
(5 rows)

Dbname=# SELECT * FROM customer;
customer_id|customer_name
-----------+-------------
          1|Rick Stones
          2|Neil Matthew
          3|Simon Cozens
(3 rows)
```

Suppose we want to know the name of the customer for order number 4. We just ask:

```
Dbname=# SELECT customer_name FROM customer, placed_order WHERE
placed_order.customer_id = customer.customer_id AND placed_order.order_id = '4';
customer_name
-------------
Rick Stones
(1 row)
```

It doesn't matter which way round the statements are in the 'where' clause, the answer will still be the same. Nor does it matter which way round the tables are, we can ask the question 'What orders were placed by Rick Stones?' like this:

```
Dbname=# SELECT order_id FROM customer, placed_order WHERE
placed_order.customer_id = customer.customer_id AND customer.customer_name = 'Rick
Stones';
order_id
--------
       2
       4
(2 rows)
```

Extending this to three tables is easy. Suppose we additionally had an orderdate table that contains order IDs and dates. We could find both the order IDs and dates for Rick Stones like this:

```
Dbname=# SELECT placed_order.order_id, orderdate.order_date FROM customer,
placed_order, orderdate WHERE placed_order.customer_id = customer.customer_id AND
orderdate.order_id = placed_order.order_id AND customer.customer_name = 'Rick
Stones';
order_id|order_date
--------+----------
       2|03-07-2000
       4|05-04-2000
(2 rows)
```

Notice that we now also specify the table names we want the columns to be selected from. In this particular case it would not have mattered, since the value for order_id would have been the same in both tables, but it does serve to illustrate the point.

Updating Data in a Table

Updating data in a table is very similar to selecting it, except that we can only work on one table at a time. The basic syntax is:

```
UPDATE table_name SET attr1 = expr1, ... ,attrN = exprN [WHERE qualifier];
```

Suppose the date in our last example for order_id 2 was wrong, and we want to correct it. All we need is to update the column, specifying the rows to be updated:

```
Dbname=# UPDATE orderdate SET order_date = 'March 8 2000' WHERE order_id = '2';
```

If we don't specify a WHERE clause all rows get updated. This is rarely what is required, so be careful!

Deleting Data

Deleting data is easy, perhaps too easy.... It's just the same as an update, except all you need is a table and an optional condition to specify the rows to be deleted:

```
DELETE FROM table_name [WHERE qualifier];
```

Like the update command, delete only works on one table at a time. So to delete all records relating to Rick Stones, we would have to do it in three steps, in order:

1. DELETE the `orderdate` entries

2. DELETE the `placed_order` entries

3. DELETE the `customer` entries

At first sight it looks like a bit of a problem. Since we can only specify one table, we apparently need some procedural logic to determine which `order_ids` belong to Rick Stones first, and then delete the rows in the other tables.

Actually we can do this in SQL, it's just that we need what is called a subquery, in this case the `'where'` clause is actually a `select` statement. Sub-selects are, at the time of writing, one of the standard SQL features that PostgreSQL possesses that are missing from many of it's competitors. In general you can use a sub-select in a `where` clause in any type of SQL statement, including `select` statements, and sometimes that is the natural way of writing the query. However, it is generally in DELETE statements that they are most often needed. In pseudo code a sub-select looks like:

```
Delete from table where order_id in (select statement)
```

Notice that rather than writing `'order_id='` as we did before in the `where` clauses, we write `'order_id in'`. This is a very important distinction – it tells the database engine that the `select` statement may return more than one row, and we want to delete all the matching rows.

Let's do it for real, and tidy up Rick Stones, who has left us as a customer. Since delete can only work on one table at a time, we still need to execute three SQL statements in the correct order, but at least we don't need any procedural logic to tie them together.

First we remove the entries for order date:

```
Dbname=# DELETE FROM orderdate WHERE order_id IN (SELECT placed_order.order_id
FROM placed_order WHERE placed_order.customer_id = customer.customer_id AND
customer.customer_name = 'Rick Stones');
DELETE 2
```

Then we tidy up the `order_ids` in a similar way:

```
Dbname=# DELETE FROM placed_order WHERE order_id IN (SELECT placed_order.order_id
FROM placed_order WHERE placed_order.customer_id = customer.customer_id AND
customer.customer_name = 'Rick Stones');
DELETE 2
```

Finally a simple delete to remove the customer entry:

```
Dbname=# DELETE FROM customer WHERE customer_name = 'Rick Stones';
DELETE 1
```

Transactions

There is one short but very important topic we have barely mentioned so far, that of transaction support. PostgreSQL's support for transactions is, at the time of writing, one of the main features that other open source databases lack.

By default, when we execute data manipulation statements on PostgreSQL each statement acts on its own, and either succeeds or fails. What it never does is partially succeed, because PostgreSQL ensures that all statements either execute to successful conclusion, or do not change the data at all.

Sometimes we need this type of behavior across several different SQL statements, particularly, as is often the case, where more than one user might be using the database at any one time. Suppose in our DVD store we had a 'for sale' section, and we periodically moved old stock from the rental section to the for sale section. This would probably involve at least two SQL statements, one to remove the DVD from the rental section, and one to add it to the for sale section. If something happened to the application in the middle, the DVD could be lost, unless we made either both SQL statements succeed, or neither SQL statement succeed.

This is done with transactions, and conceptually is very simple. Before executing the first of our SQL data manipulation statements we execute the command BEGIN WORK. After the last SQL command we can either decide to allow both of them to succeed, using the COMMIT statement, or make them both fail, with the ROLLBACK command.

Underneath the hood, PostgreSQL is doing a lot of work to support this apparently simple idea, but fortunately we generally don't have to worry about it. There is, however, one thing you should be aware of – if another user looks at the database after the first SQL statement, but before the COMMIT or ROLLBACK, it may appear as though the data has been changed. If a ROLLBACK is performed the data will appear to go back to its previous value. However, PostgreSQL will not let you see 'new' data another process is inserting but which has not yet been committed.

> *Note for advanced users. PostgreSQL defaults to a transaction isolation level which allows non-repeatable reads, and phantom reads, but not dirty reads.*

Non-advanced users (i.e. most of us!) just need to be aware that occasionally in multi-user situations data can appear to change when you don't expect it to. The reason for this apparently strange behavior is to maximize performance. We don't have the space in this chapter to go into the complex subject of transaction isolation levels, and the merits and drawbacks of PostgreSQL's default behavior.

Here is a quick look at BEGIN, COMMIT and ROLLBACK in action:

```
Dbname=# BEGIN WORK;
BEGIN
Dbname=# INSERT INTO children (fname, age) VALUES ('Fred', '1');
INSERT 20479 1
Dbname=# INSERT INTO children (fname, age) VALUES ('Freda', '2');
INSERT 20480 1
Dbname=# ROLLBACK;
ROLLBACK
Dbname=# SELECT * FROM children;
childno|fname |age
-------+------+---
```

```
        1|Andrew|  10
        2|Jenny |  14
        3|Alex  |  11
        4|Adrian|   5
        5|Allen |   4
(5 rows)
```

If we wanted to save our changes, we would have done a COMMIT, like this:

```
Dbname=# BEGIN WORK;
BEGIN
Dbname=# INSERT INTO children (fname, age) VALUES ('Fred', '1');
INSERT 20481 1
Dbname=# INSERT INTO children (fname, age) VALUES ('Freda', '2');
INSERT 20482 1
Dbname=# COMMIT;
COMMIT
Dbname=# SELECT * FROM children;
childno|fname |age
-------+------+---
        1|Andrew|  10
        2|Jenny |  14
        3|Alex  |  11
        4|Adrian|   5
        5|Allen |   4
        9|Fred  |   1
       10|Freda |   2
(7 rows)
```

Notice that there are now some 'holes' in the serial field because we rolled back some inserts. This is the way PostgreSQL works, and is not a bug, you must allow for non-contiguous numbers in serial fields.

From a user perspective transactions are very important, and you should be careful to wrap your SQL in transactions if an inconsistency could arise should one of a sequence of SQL statements fail. You should be aware however, that like most commercial databases, there is no support for nested transactions – once you have used BEGIN WORK, you must either COMMIT or ROLLBACK.

And that concludes our lightning tour of SQL. There is far, far, more to SQL than we have shown here, but you should find that this limited subset of the syntax is sufficient for most of your needs.

Database Design Tips

Having learnt about the basics of databases and SQL, now would be a good time for a few basic tips about designing databases. Whole books have been written about database design, all we present here are some tips that the authors have found helpful, and hope you do too.

❏ Naming tables – Keep table names to the singular, so a table that holds product records is called 'product' not 'products'. Stick to single case table names – generally the authors prefer lowercase for table names. Avoid key words in table names, they may occasionally be allowed, but it can be confusing.

- ❑ Column order – Try and make the primary key column (or columns for composite keys) appear first in the table, it makes it much easier to look at the tables later and understand which columns are the important ones.

- ❑ Column names – If your primary key column is an 'invented' unique numeric key perhaps generated automatically by SERIAL, call it tablename_id. If the key is an external code, such as a country code, call it tablename_code.

- ❑ Foreign key names – Foreign keys (i.e. where a column in one table refers to the primary key of another table) names should use the name of the column in the primary table to which they relate, where possible.

- ❑ Normalization – Always finish your 'perfect' database design before you try and optimize performance. If you don't have to, don't optimize at all, beyond adding a few indexes to critical columns.

- ❑ NULL – Be very careful about the use of NULL. NULL means 'unknown'. It is not zero or an empty string, it is a distinct, but unknown, value.

- ❑ VARCHAR – Where character fields are short, and have a well bounded upper length, use CHAR rather than VARCHAR, since wasting a small number of characters on some rows is better than making the database always track the length of a column. Conversely, if the length varies considerably, you should use VARCHAR, rather than store many empty character spaces.

- ❑ Types – It's normally better to use the built in database types, rather than have your own personal format for storing special data types. For example if there is a database type 'date' it's usually better to use that than define your own format for dates and store them in character strings.

- ❑ Lookups – Never provide free-form input fields to the user where you could provide a lookup and force the user to pick from a known set of values. A common example is 'color'. If you allow people free reign to enter their own text, you will end up with a wide variety of weird and wonderful colors, including the inevitable typing mistakes. Much better to provide a lookup table. After all you can always add extra entries into the lookup table later if more options are needed, which is much easier than cleaning up poor quality data after hundreds of rows have been entered. Keeping the lookup in a table also means you can change the options, without having to change your application.

- ❑ Unless it's a one-off experiment, always create your tables using the Data Definition Language, rather than just typing into psql. When you want to change the structure it will be a lot easier if you have the SQL file that created the table originally.

That's far from a complete list of database DOs and DON'Ts, but hopefully will help you make some of your design decisions.

Resources

Instant Sql Programming, by Joe Celko, published by Wrox, ISBN: 1-874416-50-8

The Practical Sql Handbook : Using Structured Query Language, by Judith S. Bowman, Sandra L. Emerson, Marcy Darnovsky, published by Addison-Wesley, ISBN: 0-201447-87-8

Database Design for Mere Mortals : A Hands-On Guide to Relational Database Design by Michael J. Hernandez, published by Addison-Wesley, ISBN: 0-201694-71-9

Joe Celko's SQL for Smarties: Advanced SQL Programming by Joe Celko, published by Morgan Kaufmann Publishers, ISBN: 1-558605-76-2

The PostgreSQL documentation is available online at http://www.postgresql.org and often in /usr/doc on your Linux Installation.

Some related sites are:

> http://www.phpwizard.net/phpPgAdmin
>
> http://www.pgadmin.freeserve.co.uk/

Last, but certainly not least, the *PostgreSQL Introduction and Concepts* book, available online from the PostgreSQL web site, also due to be published by Addison-Wesley.

Summary

In this chapter we have had a very brief look at SQL and relational databases, from the specific point of view of PostgreSQL. We looked at the basics of creating users and databases, and then how to create tables in those databases. We then moved on to look at the main data types that PostgreSQL offers us, how to insert data into tables, and, more importantly, how to select it back out again. We also looked at how to select data specifying an order, and joining data between two or more tables.

Now we know how to build tables and access PostgreSQL from the command line, the next chapter takes us on to accessing PostgreSQL from C – so we can build compiled programs that access our database.

Online discussion at http://www.p2p.wrox.com

4

PostgreSQL Interfacing

Now that we know the basics of how to use SQL to interactively access PostgreSQL from the psql interpreter, we can move on to accessing a database from program code. The good news is that it is very similar, and you can put all that command line knowledge to work almost immediately.

Accessing PostgreSQL from Code

PostgreSQL is accessible from many different programming languages. We know of at least:

- ❏   C
- ❏   C++
- ❏   Java
- ❏   Perl
- ❏   Python
- ❏   PHP
- ❏   Tcl

It's probable that there are even more languages supported that we don't know about.

There is also an ODBC driver, which opens the door to access from many other systems, including clients on MS-Windows that can talk to ODBC data sources, such as Access.

Even though the main examples in this book will be coded in C, and that is the language from which we wish to access our PostgreSQL database, there are still two ways we could approach the problem of accessing PostgreSQL from our code.

❑ The first is a traditional style library, called **libpq**. To use this your code calls library functions to access the database.

❑ The second way is called embedded SQL, or **ecpg** in PostgreSQL terms, where SQL statements are embedded in the C code, and processed by a pre-processor before the resulting C code is compiled. The approach is broadly similar to the C pre-processor that handles #include and #define before the main C compiler sees the program. This will be familiar to users of some commercial products such as Oracle's PRO*C and Informix's ESQLC because all of these follow, to a greater or lesser extent, the ANSI standard for embedding SQL.

In this chapter we will see both ways in use, and you will be able to choose the method that is most appropriate for your needs, or with which you feel most comfortable.

Libpq

In general the functions in libpq fall into one of three groups:

❑ Managing connections

❑ Executing SQL statements

❑ Obtaining results from queries

We will look at each of these in turn. The libpq library has accumulated some obsolete functions over the years – these are maintained for backward compatibility. We will generally ignore these, and present only the ones that should be used in newer programs. If you do look through some older libpq code and see some unfamiliar library calls, you can always look them up in the documentation downloadable from the PostgreSQL web site, http://www.postgresql.org.

To use any of the libpq functions you must:

❑ Include the header file libpq-fe.h

❑ Add the pgsql include directory to the include path when you compile

❑ Link with the pq library

In case you are wondering, the 'fe' in libpq-fe stands for 'front end'. Therefore, to compile a file that uses libpq, you would generally use a compile command such as:

```
$ gcc -o program -I/usr/include/pgsql program.c -lpq
```

depending of course on the exact installation directories on your system. If they are in a different place you may need to alter the include directory, and specify an alternative library directory, by adding an additional option of the form -L/usr/local/pgsql/lib.

Database Connection Routines

The preferred method of connecting to a PostgreSQL database is using the `PQconnectdb` command. Incidentally, you should use the '`-i`' option when starting the postmaster so that it listens for TCP/IP sockets as well as UNIX domain sockets.

```
PGconn *PQconnectdb(const char *conninfo);
```

The `conninfo` string is a general-purpose string that can contain a sequence of parameters and values, each separated by white space. Where a value needs to contain white space itself, then it must be enclosed in single quotes. Parameters that are not set explicitly default to NULL, and the library function will generally use default values, or values defined in environmental variables instead. The parameters that may be set are:

host	the name of the host to connect to. By default this will be the local host.
port	the port number to connect on. By default this will be the standard PostgreSQL port which is 5432.
dbname	the name of the database to connect to. By default the same as the current Linux login name.
user	the user name to use. By default the same as the login name.
password	the password to use.
options	any tracing options required.
tty	the file or terminal for debug output from the backend processor.

Each parameter is followed by an equals sign, then the value to which it should be set. So to connect to a database `template1`, on a machine `gw1`, we would use a command like this:

```
conn = PQconnectdb("host=gw1 dbname=template1");
```

A NULL pointer is only returned if the library fails to allocate a connection object. Even if you get a non-NULL pointer back you must still check if the connection was successful using the `PQstatus` function.

```
ConnStatusType PQstatus(PGconn *conn);
```

This returns one of two enums, either CONNECTION_OK or CONNECTION_BAD, which have the obvious meanings. Once a good connection has been established, it will usually remain 'good', unless there are network problems, or the remote database is shut down.

If there is a problem with the connect, a meaningful error message can be retrieved with:

```
char *PQerrorMessage(PGconn *conn);
```

This returns a pointer to static space, so the text may be overwritten if you make further calls to libpq routines. When you have finished with a connection, either because your program has finished or because the connection failed, you must call:

```
void PQfinish(PGconn *conn);
```

to close the connection. You must always call this routine, even if the connection failed. This is because it not only closes open connections, but it also releases memory and other resources associated with the connection. Failing to correctly close the connection will cause your program to accidentally consume system resources.

Once the connection object has been 'finished', the connection pointer no longer points anywhere meaningful, and must not be passed as a parameter to any more routines. A good defensive coding technique would be to set the connection pointer to NULL immediately after calling PQfinish.

Now we know those few routines, we are in a position to write our first C program to connect to a PostgreSQL server. It's not very useful, all it does is test the connection, but it's a first step. Remember to change the server name and login to your own local values, and you must have created a database with the same name as your login id, which we saw how to do in the last chapter.

```
#include <stdlib.h>
#include <stdio.h>
#include <libpq-fe.h>

int main()
{

    PGconn *conn;
    const char *connection_str = "host=localhost dbname=template1";

    conn = PQconnectdb(connection_str);
    if (PQstatus(conn) == CONNECTION_BAD) {
        fprintf(stderr, "Connection to %s failed, %s", connection_str,
PQerrorMessage(conn));
    } else {
        printf("Connected OK\n");
    }
    PQfinish(conn);
    return EXIT_SUCCESS;
}
```

This should be quite easy to follow. We set up a connection string to connect to the database template1 on the server localhost, attempt a connection, print an error if it fails, then close the connection again before exiting.

Executing SQL Statements

Executing a query against the server is surprisingly simple. There is only one function to call, and three functions to check the result and access error information. To execute an SQL command you call:

```
PGresult *PQexec(PGconn *conn, const char *sql_string);
```

This routine can return a NULL pointer in exceptional circumstances, so this must be trapped – otherwise the result can be obtained by passing the result pointer to another routine:

```
ExecStatusType *PQresultStatus(PGresult *result);
```

The result is an enum of type `ExecStatusType`, with one of the following values:

PGRES_EMPTY_QUERY	Nothing was done.
PGRES_COMMAND_OK	The command completed successfully, but no data could have been returned because the command was not a SELECT command.
PGRES_TUPLES_OK	The command completed successfully, and some data may have been returned.
PGRES_COPY_OUT	A copy to an external file was in progress.
PGRES_COPY_IN	A copy from an external file was in progress.
PGRES_BAD_RESPONSE	Something unexpected happened.
PGRES_NONFATAL_ERROR	A non-fatal error occurred.
PGRES_FATAL_ERROR	A fatal error has occurred.

Notice the careful definition of PGRES_TUPLES_OK. Receiving this response means that a SELECT SQL statement executed successfully, but it doesn't mean that any data has been returned. We shall find out in the next section how to check for returned data. The COPY errors relate to the database being loaded or backed up.

If you want a textual error message, then you need:

```
const char *PQresultErrorMessage(PGresult *result);
```

Notice that this is different from error relating to connections, where we use PQerrorMessage to get a textual error message.

It's often useful to know the number of rows that have been affected by an SQL command. This is particularly true for DELETE commands, because if you execute a DELETE command that is syntactically correct, but doesn't actually delete any rows, then PostgreSQL considers the command to have executed successfully.

For INSERT, UPDATE and DELETE commands, we can find the number of rows affected with PQcmdTuples.

```
const char *PQcmdTuples(PGresult *result);
```

Notice that this returns a char *result, containing a NULL-terminated string of digits in character format, not the integer you might have expected. We will see how to obtain the number of rows returned by a SELECT statement later, since this is rather more complex.

After we have finished with a result object we need to tell the library, so that its allocated memory can be released. Just like connection objects, failure to do this will result in memory leaks in your application.

```
void PQclear(PGresult *result);
```

One other function that fits into this section that can be useful for debugging:

```
const char *PQresStatus(ExecStatusType status);
```

converts a status enum into a descriptive string.

We now know just enough to write our first C program that executes SQL. Since we don't yet know how to retrieve results from a query, we will stick to executing a DELETE. Here is our first C routine that does something useful, del1.c, which extends our original con1.c. This time we are connecting to a database rick, on a server called gw1.

Throughout this chapter we will be experimenting with a single table in our database called children, which we created in the previous chapter. If you need to re-create the table, the SQL to type into psql is:

```
CREATE TABLE children (
  childno SERIAL,
  fname VARCHAR,
  age INTEGER
);
```

The lines we changed between con1.c and del1.c are highlighted:

```
#include <stdlib.h>
#include <stdio.h>
#include <libpq-fe.h>

int main()
{

    PGconn *conn;
    PGresult *result;
    const char *connection_str = "host=gw1 dbname=rick";

    conn = PQconnectdb(connection_str);
    if (PQstatus(conn) == CONNECTION_BAD) {
        fprintf(stderr, "Connection to %s failed, %s", connection_str,
PQerrorMessage(conn));
    } else {
        printf("Connected OK\n");
    }

    result = PQexec(conn, "DELETE FROM children WHERE fname = 'freda'");

    if (!result) {
        printf("PQexec command failed, no error code\n");
    } else {
        switch (PQresultStatus(result)) {
        case PGRES_COMMAND_OK:
          printf("Command executed OK, %s rows
                affected\n",PQcmdTuples(result));
          break;
```

```
        case PGRES_TUPLES_OK:
          printf("Query may have returned data\n");
          break;
          default:
        printf("Command failed with code %s, error message %s\n",
          PQresStatus(PQresultStatus(result)),
          PQresultErrorMessage(result));
        break;
        }
    PQclear(result);
    }



    PQfinish(conn);
    return EXIT_SUCCESS;
}
```

If we ensure that there is a row in a table `children` with an fname column of `freda`, then when we compile and execute this program we see:

```
[rick@gw1 psql]$ ./del1
Connected OK
Command executed OK, 1 rows affected
```

Now there is no row to be deleted matching this criterion. If we execute the program again, it still executes successfully, but this time no rows are affected:

```
[rick@gw1 psql]$ ./del1
Connected OK
Command executed OK, 0 rows affected
```

You must be careful to distinguish between a statement that works, but affects no rows, and a statement that fails because it is syntactically incorrect.

Obtaining Results from Queries

We now come to both the most used part of **libpq**, and also the most complex – retrieving data.

When we retrieve data, we potentially have a bit of a problem. In general we will not know in advance how many rows will be retrieved. If we were to execute a SELECT statement using '*' as the column name to retrieve all columns, we may not even know how many fields or what type of data there is in the rows we are retrieving. Catering for these circumstances is what makes this part of the API more complex. Don't worry, there is no rocket science here, just a few more API calls to get to know.

Let's first convert our del1.c test program into a query that returns data, and while we are at it we will restructure it slightly, so it is easier to add new functionality after the SQL statement is executed. This new file is sel1.c:

```
#include <stdlib.h>
#include <stdio.h>
#include <libpq-fe.h>
```

```
PGconn *conn = NULL;

void tidyup_and_exit();

int main()
{
    PGresult *result;
    const char *connection_str = "host=gw1 dbname=rick";

    conn = PQconnectdb(connection_str);
    if (PQstatus(conn) == CONNECTION_BAD) {
        fprintf(stderr, "Connection to %s failed, %s", connection_str,
                PQerrorMessage(conn));
        tidyup_and_exit();
    } else {
        printf("Connected OK\n");
    }

    result = PQexec(conn, "SELECT age, fname FROM children WHERE age < '6'");

    if (!result) {
        printf("PQexec command failed, no error code\n");
        tidyup_and_exit();
    } else {
        switch (PQresultStatus(result)) {
        case PGRES_COMMAND_OK:
            printf("Command executed OK, %s rows affected\n", PQcmdTuples(result));
            break;
        case PGRES_TUPLES_OK:
            printf("Query may have returned data\n");
            break;
        default:
            printf("Command failed with code %s, error message %s\n",
                PQresStatus(PQresultStatus(result)),
                PQresultErrorMessage(result));
            PQclear(result);
            tidyup_and_exit();
            break;
        }
    }

/* New code will get added here */

    if (result) PQclear(result);
    PQfinish(conn);
    return EXIT_SUCCESS;
}


void tidyup_and_exit() {
    if (conn != NULL) PQfinish(conn);
    exit(EXIT_FAILURE);
}

}
```

What we have done is to add a new routine, `tidyup_and_exit`, which allows us to abandon our program when database actions fail. This is obviously not how we should write it for production code, since aborting an application because a single SQL statement failed is a bit drastic to say the least, but for test purposes it's easier to work with the code this way. We have also changed the DELETE to a SELECT statement that returns some data.

If we run this version of the program, we can see that our code is correctly identifying that data may have been returned:

```
[rick@gw1 psql]$ ./sel1
Connected OK
Query may have returned data
```

The first thing we can do is to find out how many rows were actually returned. We can do this with a call to PQntuples (remember PostgreSQL refers to rows as 'tuples'):

```
int PQntuples(PGresult *result);
```

Changing `sel1.c` into `sel2.c`, we just need to change one line where we check the return code from PQresultStatus:

```
case PGRES_TUPLES_OK:
    printf("Query was OK and returned %d rows\n", PQntuples(result));
    break;
```

When we run the query now, we get the result:

```
[rick@gw1 psql]$ ./sel2
Connected OK
Query was OK and returned 3 rows
```

That's all very well, but clearly what we now need to do is access the data being returned. For now we'll start with the quickest and easiest way, which is simply to use one of libpq's special functions for outputting all the data to a file stream. It has the benefit of being easy to use, and is great for debugging.

The function we need is PQprint, which looks like this:

```
void PQprint(FILE *stream, PGresult *result, PQprintOpt *options);
```

This is easy to use – we need to provide an output stream, the result pointer we got back from executing our SQL, and a pointer to an options structure.

The options structure as defined in `libpq-fe.h` looks like this:

```
typedef struct _PQprintOpt
{
    pqbool  header;         /* print output field headings and row count */
    pqbool  align;          /* fill align the fields */
    pqbool  standard;       /* old brain dead format */
    pqbool  html3;          /* output html tables */
```

```
    pqbool  expanded;        /* expand tables */
    pqbool  pager;            /* use pager for output if needed */
    char  *fieldSep;      /* field separator */
    char  *tableOpt;      /* insert to HTML <table ...> */
    char  *caption;       /* HTML <caption> */
    char  **fieldName;    /* null terminated array of replacement field names */
} PQprintOpt;
```

These options allow you some control over how the result data is output. You may notice that in the header file there are several other output functions for writing to streams – generally you should use PQprint, which has superceded some earlier methods.

Now we can adapt our program to output the data we have retrieved to an output stream. We will send the output to /dev/tty, which directs it to the controlling terminal. This file is sel3.c, but we only show the modified lines here:

At the start of main, we need two new variables:

```
    FILE *output_stream;
    PQprintOpt print_options;
```

Then once the data has been retrieved, we can print it out:

```
    output_stream = fopen("/dev/tty", "w");
    if (output_stream == NULL) {
        PQclear(result);
        tidyup_and_exit();
    }

    memset(&print_options, '\0', sizeof(print_options));
    print_options.header = 1;        /* print headers */
    print_options.align = 1;         /* align fields */
    print_options.html3 = 0;         /* output as html tables */
    print_options.fieldSep = "|";    /* field separator */
    print_options.fieldName = NULL; /* alternate field names */

    PQprint(output_stream, result, &print_options);
```

Notice that we don't need to explicitly set all the fields of the PQprintOpt structure, the memset provides a reasonable default for the values we do not need. However you should be aware that at the time of writing it is important to specify a field separator for fieldSep.

When we run this version of the program, we get:

```
[rick@gw1 psql]$ ./sel3
Connected OK
Query was OK and returned 3 rows
age|fname
---+------
    5|Adrian
    4|Allen
    1|fred
(3 rows)
```

our first bit of embedded SQL code that retrieves data.

Unfortunately, there are a couple of snags with this. Firstly, outputting the data to a file stream is great for debugging, but not so good for actually processing the data. Secondly, we are retrieving all the data in one go, which is fine for small amounts of data, but will quickly become unwieldy for larger data sets.

Cursors

Suppose our program was accessing a large database, with thousands of rows, and we executed a query that returned all those rows. Our program could suddenly need a very large amount of memory indeed, to store all those results. Since potentially this is all happening across a network as well, clearly we need a way of retrieving the data in smaller quantities, say a row at a time. There is a standard way of doing this, and it is how you would normally fetch data from an SQL database into a C program, (or indeed programs coded in many other languages). What we need is a cursor.

A cursor is a feature we have not met so far, because they are normally only applicable either when using SQL embedded in an external program, or within procedural language function stored in the database, often referred to as 'stored procedures'. Cursors are not generally used from the command line. The SQL92 standard only defines cursors for use in embedded programs, so in most database environments this is the only place you can use them, although in an extension to the SQL standard PostgreSQL does allow them from the command line as well.

A cursor is a way of scrolling through a set of results, fetching returned data in discrete blocks. To use a cursor, you declare it – with a name that has an associated SELECT statement. You then FETCH the results, usually one row at a time, though you can fetch many rows at a time.

The SQL92 standard, and many other implementations of cursors, require an additional step, an OPEN cursor command, between the DECLARE and the FETCH. The PostgreSQL libpq does not need it, the DECLARE is taken as an implicit command. When we get onto ecpg (the alternative way of embedding SQL in C code), you will see that we need to write the OPEN CURSOR command in the source code.

In pseudo code, the sequence looks something like:

```
BEGIN A TRANSACTION
DECLARE CURSOR mycursor FOR SELECT-statement
[OPEN mycursor]
DO {
      FETCH some data from mycursor
      Process the row(s) retrieved
} WHILE the FETCH command found data
CLOSE mycursor
COMMIT WORK
```

There are two new SQL commands here, DECLARE CURSOR and FETCH, both of which we need to look at before we can write some program code that fetches data using a cursor.

The syntax for declaring a cursor is very straightforward:

```
DECLARE cursor_name [BINARY] CURSOR FOR <SELECT-statement>
```

This creates, and implicitly opens in libpq, a cursor with the given name. Notice that the cursor is bound to a single SELECT statement. This cursor name is now effectively another way of referring to the SELECT statement. We only need the BINARY option when we wish to retrieve binary data stored in a column, an advanced topic that you will rarely need, so we are not considering it here. SQL92 experts will have noticed some keywords from the SQL standard are missing, notably SCROLL and FOR READ ONLY or FOR UPDATE. In PostgreSQL all cursors can scroll, so the keyword SCROLL, whilst accepted, has no effect. PostgreSQL also only supports 'read only' cursors, so we cannot use a cursor for updating the database, so the FOR clause is equally redundant, though the syntax FOR READ ONLY is accepted for compatibility with the standard.

The syntax of FETCH is very simple:

```
FETCH [FORWARD|BACKWARD] [number|ALL|NEXT] [IN cursor_name];
```

Normally FORWARD or BACKWARD is omitted, the default is FORWARD. We use a number, or ALL, to tell the FETCH that we wish to retrieve all, or just a fixed number, of rows. The keyword NEXT is the same as giving a number of 1. The SELECT statement specified when we declared the cursor determines the actual rows that can be fetched.

Now we have seen the principle, it's time to try it out in practice. This is sel4.c, which fetches data using a cursor:

```c
#include <stdlib.h>
#include <stdio.h>
#include <string.h>
#include <libpq-fe.h>

PGconn *conn = NULL;

void tidyup_and_exit();
int execute_one_statement(const char *stmt_to_exec, PGresult **result);


int main()
{
    PGresult *result;
    int stmt_ok;
    const char *connection_str = "host=gw1 dbname=rick";

    FILE *output_stream;
    PQprintOpt print_options;

    conn = PQconnectdb(connection_str);
    if (PQstatus(conn) == CONNECTION_BAD) {
        fprintf(stderr, "Connection to %s failed, %s", connection_str,
PQerrorMessage(conn));
        tidyup_and_exit();
    } else {
        printf("Connected OK\n");
    }

    stmt_ok = execute_one_statement("BEGIN WORK", &result);
    if (stmt_ok) {
```

```
        PQclear(result);
        stmt_ok = execute_one_statement("DECLARE age_fname_cursor CURSOR FOR
                                        SELECT age, fname FROM children
                                        WHERE age < '6'", &result);

        if (stmt_ok) {
          PQclear(result);
          stmt_ok = execute_one_statement("FETCH ALL IN age_fname_cursor",
                                          &result);
        if (stmt_ok) {
          PQclear(result);
          stmt_ok = execute_one_statement("COMMIT WORK", &result);
          }
        }
    }
    if (stmt_ok) PQclear(result);
    PQfinish(conn);
    return EXIT_SUCCESS;
}


int execute_one_statement(const char *stmt_to_exec, PGresult **res_ptr) {
    int retcode = 1;
    const char *str_res;

    PGresult *local_result;

    printf("About to execute %s\n", stmt_to_exec);

    local_result = PQexec(conn, stmt_to_exec);
    *res_ptr = local_result;

    if (!local_result) {
       printf("PQexec command failed, no error code\n");
       retcode = 0;
    } else {
       switch (PQresultStatus(local_result)) {
    case PGRES_COMMAND_OK:
       str_res = PQcmdTuples(local_result);
       if (strlen(str_res) > 0) {
         printf("Command executed OK, %s rows affected\n", str_res);
       } else {
         printf("Command executed OK, no rows affected\n");
       }
       break;
    case PGRES_TUPLES_OK:
       printf("Select executed OK, %d rows found\n", PQntuples(local_result));
       break;
       default:
       printf("Command failed with code %s, error message %s\n",
         PQresStatus(PQresultStatus(local_result)),
         PQresultErrorMessage(local_result));
       PQclear(local_result);
       retcode = 0;
       break;
```

```
        }
    }
    return retcode;
} /* execute_one_statement */


void tidyup_and_exit() {
    if (conn != NULL) PQfinish(conn);
exit(EXIT_FAILURE);

}
```

The main changes from the previous version are highlighted. We have removed the printing of the output, shortly we will see a more useful way of accessing the retrieved data than simply printing it out.

When we run this, we get:

```
Connected OK
About to execute BEGIN WORK
Command executed OK, no rows affected
About to execute DECLARE age_fname_cursor CURSOR FOR SELECT age, fname FROM
children WHERE age < '6'
Command executed OK, no rows affected
About to execute FETCH ALL IN age_fname_cursor
Select executed OK, 3 rows found
About to execute COMMIT WORK
Command executed OK, no rows affected
```

It is now trivial to fetch the rows one at a time, simply by changing the ALL to a 1 in the FETCH statement, and checking that rows are actually returned. A FETCH, just like a SELECT, can succeed, but return no data.

The changed lines in sel5.c, are:

```
    conn = PQconnectdb(connection_str);
    if (PQstatus(conn) == CONNECTION_BAD) {
        fprintf(stderr, "Connection to %s failed, %s", connection_str,
tidyup_and_exit();
    } else {
        printf("Connected OK\n");
    }
    stmt_ok = execute_one_statement("BEGIN WORK", &result);
    if (stmt_ok) {
        PQclear(result);
    stmt_ok = execute_one_statement("DECLARE age_fname_cursor CURSOR FOR SELECT
age, fname FROM children WHERE age < '6'", &result);
    stmt_ok = execute_one_statement("FETCH 1 IN age_fname_cursor", &result);
        while(stmt_ok && PQntuples(result) > 0) {
            PQclear(result);
            stmt_ok = execute_one_statement("FETCH NEXT IN age_fname_cursor",
                                    &result);
        }
        stmt_ok = execute_one_statement("COMMIT WORK", &result);
    }
```

```
        if (stmt_ok) PQclear(result);
        PQfinish(conn);
        return EXIT_SUCCESS;
    }
```

The output is:

```
[rick@gw1 psql]$ ./sel5
Connected OK
About to execute BEGIN WORK
Command executed OK, no rows affected
About to execute DECLARE age_fname_cursor CURSOR FOR SELECT age, fname FROM
children WHERE age < '6'
Command executed OK, no rows affected
About to execute FETCH 1 IN age_fname_cursor
Select executed OK, 1 rows found
About to execute FETCH NEXT IN age_fname_cursor
Select executed OK, 1 rows found
About to execute FETCH NEXT IN age_fname_cursor
Select executed OK, 1 rows found
About to execute FETCH NEXT IN age_fname_cursor
Select executed OK, 0 rows found
About to execute COMMIT WORK
Command executed OK, no rows affected
```

As you can see, it's actually very easy to retrieve our data one row at a time. The only drawback, which usually doesn't matter, is that we don't know until we have retrieved all the data how many rows there were. This is because PQntuples(result), not unreasonably for a FETCH of one row, has a value of one when a row is retrieved.

Now we have our data being retrieved in a more manageable format, we can progress to access individual parts of that information.

Getting column information

The first piece of information that it's useful to extract from the returned data, is the column information (both the column names and data types). This is quite easy to do with three functions, one to discover how many columns there are, one for the name of each column, and one for the data size of that column. Of course, you could specify by name each of the columns you want, but then, in theory, you know in advance the type of each column that will be returned.

In general, it is a good idea to specify by name each column you require. The reason for this is to prevent your code from being 'surprised' if the database has new columns added. If columns are to be deleted, then at least a 'grep' through the code will show that the names of the columns to be deleted are used in the code. Assuming the column type in code is less clear cut – it may be that determining the type at run time means your code can then automatically take account of any changes of column type. Conversely you are writing more code, which increases the risk of a bug and slightly decreases performance.

We find the number of columns in the returned result with PQnfields:

```
int PQnfields(PGresult *result);
```

We find the name of an individual column using `PQfname` function, and passing the `field_index`, where the first column is at index 0:

```
char *PQfname(PGresult *result, int field_index);
```

We can get an idea of the size of the data with `PQfsize`. We use the word 'idea' because it returns only the amount of space that PostgreSQL has used internally, and even then is -1 for variable length fields, such as `VARCHAR`.

```
int PQfsize(PGresult *result, int field_index);
```

The obvious omission in this set is the type of the column being returned. Unfortunately, the routine that appears to do this, `PQftype`, returns an `Oid` type (actually a `typedef` for an unsigned integer). This gives only an internal representation of the type, and is not externally documented anywhere, which makes it almost useless. For this reason we will not use it here, though hopefully in a later release PostgreSQL, or at least the libpq library, will develop a more useful routine for discovering the type being returned.

We can now use this knowledge to extend our `sel5.c` program into `sel6.c`, by retrieving the column information. It doesn't matter which row of the retrieved data we use to extract the column header information from, indeed even if the `SELECT` statement returned no rows, we could still access the column information.

The changes are very minor, so we just show the additions here, rather than repeat all the code.

First we add a prototype for our new function:

```
void show_column_info(PGresult *result);
```

Then we call it when data is retrieved. We allow it to be called each time data is returned, to show that this works, though of course we would not do this in production code.

```
if (stmt_ok) {
    PQclear(result);
    stmt_ok = execute_one_statement("FETCH 1 IN age_fname_cursor",
                                    &result);
    if (stmt_ok) show_column_info(result);
    while(stmt_ok && PQntuples(result) > 0) {
        show_column_info(result);
        PQclear(result);
        stmt_ok = execute_one_statement("FETCH NEXT IN age_fname_cursor",
                                        &result);
    }
    stmt_ok = execute_one_statement("COMMIT WORK", &result);
}
```

Finally, here is the implementation of show_column_info:

```
void show_column_info(PGresult *result) {
    int num_columns;
    int i;

    if (!result) return;

    num_columns = PQnfields(result);
    printf("%d columns in the result set\n", num_columns);
    for(i = 0; i < num_columns; i++) {
        printf("Field %d, Name %s, Internal size %d\n",
            i,
            PQfname(result, i),
            PQfsize(result, i));
    }
} /* show_column_info */
```

When we execute this, we get output like this:

```
About to execute FETCH NEXT IN age_fname_cursor
Select executed OK, 1 rows found
2 columns in the result set
Field 0, Name age, Internal size 4
Field 1, Name fname, Internal size -1
```

We have abbreviated the full output, to save space. Notice that the size of fname is reported as -1, because it is a variable size field type, a VARCHAR.

Accessing the retrieved data

Last, but certainly not least, we need to access the data we have retrieved. As we mentioned before, type information of the data being returned is not available in any sensible fashion, so you may be wondering how we are going to manage this in code. The answer is very simple – libpq always returns a string representation of the returned data, which we can convert ourselves. (Actually this isn't quite true, for BINARY cursors binary data is returned, but very few users will need such advanced PostgreSQL features.)

What we can discover is the length of the representation of the data that will be returned when we fetch the data, this is done with PQgetlength:

```
int PQgetlength(PGresult *result, int tuple_number, int field_index);
```

Notice that this has a tuple_number field, which you will recall is PostgreSQL speak for a row. This is because we might have not used a cursor (as we saw earlier) and retrieved all the data in one go, or asked for more than one row at a time, as we did in the last example. Without this parameter, retrieving several rows at once would have been pointless, since we could not have accessed the data in any but the last row retrieved.

We get the string representation of the data with PQgetvalue:

```
char *PQgetvalue(PGresult *result, int tuple_number, int field_index);
```

This returns a NULL terminated string. The actual string is inside a PGresult structure, so you must copy the data out if you want it accessible after doing anything else with the result structure. At this point the astute amongst you may have spotted a snag – how do you distinguish between an empty string being returned because the string in the database had no length, and an empty string being returned because the database column was a NULL value (which we're sure you remember means 'unknown', rather than empty). The answer is a special function, PQgetisnull, which is used to separate the two database values:

```
int PQgetisnull(PGresult *result, int tuple_number, int field_index);
```

This returns 1 if the field was NULL in the database, otherwise 0.

Now, at last, we are in a position to write our final version of our test code, which returns data from the database row by row, displaying the column information and data as it goes. Before we run this, we set one of the rows we will retrieve to have a NULL value, so we can check our code detects NULLs correctly. Depending on the data you put into the children table, you may have to use a different childno. I had a childno of 9, with an age of 1, where we set the fname field to NULL, by executing this statement in psql:

```
UPDATE children set fname = NULL where childno = 9;
```

Now here is the final version of our SELECT from C code, sel7.c. The principal changes are highlighted, and some 'debug' type lines have also been removed, in order to clean up the output a little:

```
#include <stdlib.h>
#include <stdio.h>
#include <string.h>
#include <libpq-fe.h>

PGconn *conn = NULL;

void tidyup_and_exit();
int execute_one_statement(const char *stmt_to_exec, PGresult **result);

void show_column_info(PGresult *result);
void show_one_row_data(PGresult *result);

int main()
{
    PGresult *result;
    int stmt_ok;
    char *connection_str = "host=gw1 dbname=rick";

    FILE *output_stream;
    PQprintOpt print_options;

    conn = PQconnectdb(connection_str);
    if (PQstatus(conn) == CONNECTION_BAD) {
        fprintf(stderr, "Connection to %s failed, %s", connection_str,
                PQerrorMessage(conn));
        tidyup_and_exit();
    } else {
        printf("Connected OK\n");
    }
```

```
        stmt_ok = execute_one_statement("BEGIN WORK", &result);
    if (stmt_ok) {
        PQclear(result);
        stmt_ok = execute_one_statement("DECLARE age_fname_cursor CURSOR FOR
                                    SELECT age, fname FROM children WHERE
                                    age < '6'", &result);

        if (stmt_ok) {
          PQclear(result);
          stmt_ok = execute_one_statement("FETCH 1 IN age_fname_cursor",
                                        &result);
        if (stmt_ok) show_column_info(result);
        while(stmt_ok && PQntuples(result) > 0) {
          show_one_row_data(result);
          PQclear(result);
          stmt_ok = execute_one_statement("FETCH NEXT IN age_fname_cursor",
                                        &result);
        }
        stmt_ok = execute_one_statement("COMMIT WORK", &result);
        }
    }
    if (stmt_ok) PQclear(result);
    PQfinish(conn);
    return EXIT_SUCCESS;
}


int execute_one_statement(const char *stmt_to_exec, PGresult **res_ptr) {
    int retcode = 1;
    const char *str_res;

    PGresult *local_result;

    printf("About to execute %s\n", stmt_to_exec);

    local_result = PQexec(conn, stmt_to_exec);
    *res_ptr = local_result;

    if (!local_result) {
        printf("PQexec command failed, no error code\n");
        retcode = 0;
    } else {
        switch (PQresultStatus(local_result)) {
        case PGRES_COMMAND_OK:
          str_res = PQcmdTuples(local_result);
        if (strlen(str_res) > 0) {
            printf("Command executed OK, %s rows affected\n", str_res);
        } else {
          printf("Command executed OK, no rows affected\n");
        }
        break;
    case PGRES_TUPLES_OK:
        printf("Select executed OK, %d rows found\n", PQntuples(local_result));
        break;
    default:
        printf("Command failed with code %s, error message %s\n",
          PQresStatus(PQresultStatus(local_result)),
          PQresultErrorMessage(local_result));
        PQclear(local_result);
```

```
        retcode = 0;
        break;
        }
    }
    return retcode;
} /* execute_one_statement */

void show_column_info(PGresult *result) {
    int num_columns = 0;
    int i;

    if (!result) return;

    num_columns = PQnfields(result);
    printf("%d columns in the result set\n", num_columns);

    for(i = 0; i < num_columns; i++) {
        printf("Field %d, Name %s, Internal size %d\n",
            i,
            PQfname(result, i),
            PQfsize(result, i));
    }
} /* show_column_info */
```

```
void show_one_row_data(PGresult *result) {
    int col;

    for(col = 0; col < PQnfields(result); col++) {
        printf("DATA: %s\n", PQgetisnull(result, 0, col) ? "<NULL>":
PQgetvalue(result, 0, col));
    }
} /* show_one_row_data */
```

```
void tidyup_and_exit() {
    if (conn != NULL) PQfinish(conn);
    exit(EXIT_FAILURE);

}
```

Notice we check for NULLs in all columns. When we run this, we get:

```
Connected OK
2 columns in the result set
Field 0, Name age, Internal size 4
Field 1, Name fname, Internal size -1
DATA: 4
DATA: Adrian
DATA: 4
DATA: Allen
DATA: 1
DATA: <NULL>
```

And that concludes our tour of the libpq library. We have seen how we can use the libpq library to access data in the database, retrieving it row by row using cursors. We have also seen how to extract column information, and handle NULL values in the database.

ECPG

Now it's time to look at the alternative way of combining SQL and C, by embedding SQL statements in the C code, and then pre-processing them into something the C compiler can understand, before invoking the C compiler. There is still a library to interface C calls to the database, but the details are hidden away behind a pre-processor.

PostgreSQL's ecpg follows the ANSI standard for embedding SQL in C code, and what follows will be familiar to programmers who have used systems such as Oracle's PRO*C or Informix's ESQL-C. At the time of writing some of the less used features of embedded SQL are not supported, and the standard documentation for ecpg that ships with PostgreSQL is somewhat limited.

Since we have now worked through many of the basics of SQL, this section will actually be quite short. The first problem that has to be tackled is how to delimit sections in the file that the ecpg pre-processor needs to process. This is done with the special sequence in the source that starts 'exec sql', then contains the SQL you want to execute, and ends with a ';'. Depending on the exact syntax, as we shall see in a moment, this can either be a single line that needs to be processed, or it can be used to mark a section that needs pre-processing.

If we want to write a simple C program that performs a single UPDATE statement in the middle of some C code, we need to do only one thing in the source code – embed the UPDATE SQL statement.

What could be easier? Let's write a very simple C program with some embedded SQL that updates a table. By convention these have a file extension of pgc. Here is upd1.pgc:

```
#include <stdlib.h>

exec sql include sqlca;

main() {

exec sql connect to  'rick@gw1';

exec sql BEGIN WORK;

exec sql UPDATE children SET fname = 'Gavin' WHERE childno = 9;

exec sql COMMIT WORK;

exec sql disconnect all;

return EXIT_SUCCESS;

}
```

At first sight, this hardly looks like C at all. However, if you ignore the lines that start exec sql, you can see it is just a minimal C program. To compile this program we need a two-stage process. First we must run the ecpg pre-processor, then we compile the resulting C file, linking it with the ecpg library. To compile this you may need to add a -I option to ecpg, to tell it where to look for the include file, depending on your installation. For this program, upd1.pgc, the commands are:

```
$ ecpg -t -I/usr/include/pgsql upd1.pgc
$ gcc -o upd1 -I/usr/include/pgsql upd1.c -lecpg -lpq
```

The ecpg command pre-processes the file, leaving a `.c` file, which we then compile in the normal way, linking with two PostgreSQL libraries. The `'-t'` on the command line for ecpg tells ecpg that we wish to manage our own transactions with explicit BEGIN WORK and COMMIT WORK statements in the source file. By default ecpg will automatically start a transaction when you connect to the database. There is nothing wrong with this, it's just that the authors prefer to explicitly define transaction blocks.

You will notice the connect string is `'rick@gw1'`. This requests a connection to the database `'rick'` on server `'gw1'`. No password is needed since that's a local machine, and I am already logged in as user rick. However in the general case you can specify the connection in a URL style format, in which case the format is

```
<protocol>:<service>://<machine>:<port>/<dbname> as <connection name> as <login
name> using <password for login>
```

A concrete example makes this much clearer. Suppose we want to connect using `tcp` to the `postgresql` service on the `dbs6` machine, port `5432`, connecting to the database `rick`, using the database login name `neil`, who has a password `secret`. The connect line we would put in our program would be:

```
exec sql connect to tcp:postgresql://dbs6:5432/rick as connect_2 user neil using
secret;
```

If we want to separate out the different elements, then we can use the same style of connect request, but using "host variables", which you will notice always start with a `':'`. We will see more about host variables later in the chapter; for now just imagine them as normal C variables.

```
exec sql BEGIN DECLARE SECTION;
        char connect_str[256];
        char as_str[25];
        char user_str[25];
        char using_str[25];

exec sql END DECLARE SECTION;

        strcpy(connect_str, "tcp:postgresql://localhost:5432/rick");
        strcpy(as_str, "connect_2");
        strcpy(user_str, "neil");
        strcpy(using_str, "secret");

exec sql connect to :connect_str as :as_str user :user_str using :using_str ;

        if (sqlca.sqlcode != 0) {
            pg_print_debug(__FILE__, __LINE__, sqlca, "Connect failed");
            return DVD_ERR_BAD_DATABASE;
        }
```

Now we have seen the basics, let's look in slightly more detail at what ecpg does.

The first feature that we almost always need when writing an ecpg program is to include a header file that gives us access to errors and status information from PostgreSQL. Since we need this file to be pre-processed by the ecpg processor, before the C compiler runs, a normal `include` will not do. What we need is to use the `exec sql include` command. Since there is just a single file called `sqlca`, which we almost always need to include, `pgc` files usually start with:

```
exec sql include sqlca;
```

This causes the ecpg command to include the file `sqlca.h`, which is (by default) found in the `/usr/include/pgsql` directory, though depending on your installation this may of course be different. This important include file declares an `sqlca` structure, and variable of the same name, that allows us to determine results from our SQL statements. The `sqlca` structure is a standard structure used when embedding SQL in C code, though implementations vary slightly. For our install of PostgreSQL the structure is declared to be:

```
struct sqlca
{
        char            sqlcaid[8];
        long            sqlabc;
        long            sqlcode;
        struct
        {
                int             sqlerrml;
                char            sqlerrmc[70];
        } sqlerrm;
        char            sqlerrp[8];
        long            sqlerrd[6];
        char            sqlwarn[8];
        char            sqlext[8];
};
```

Actually interpreting the contents of `sqlca` can seem a little odd. The implementation of ecpg that comes with PostgreSQL does not implement as much of the `sqlca` functionality as some commercial packages such as Oracle. This means some members of the structure are unused, however all the important functions are implemented, so it is perfectly usable.

When processing an `sqlca` structure you first need to check `sqlca.sqlcode`. If it is less than zero then something serious went wrong, if it's zero all is well, and if it's 100 then no data was found, but that was not an error.

When an INSERT, UPDATE or SELECT statement succeeds, `sqlca.sqlerrd[2]` will contain the number of rows that were affected.

If `sqlca.sqlwarn[0]` is 'W', then a minor error occurred, usually data was retrieved successfully, but was not transferred correctly into a host variable (we will meet these later in the chapter).

When an error occurs `sqlca.sqlerrm.sqlerrmc` contains a string describing the error.

Commercial packages use more fields, that can tell you a notional 'cost' and other information, but these are not currently supported in PostgreSQL. However since such information is only occasionally useful, it's omission is not generally missed.

Let's just summarize that explanation:

`sqlca.sqlcode`	Contains a negative value for serious errors, zero for success, 100 for no data found.
`sqlca.sqlerrm.sqlerrmc`	Contains a textual error message.
`sqlca.sqlerrd[2]`	Contains the number of rows affected.
`sqlca.sqlwarn[0]`	Is set to 'W' when data was retrieved, but not correctly transferred to the program.

Let's try this out, by modifying our upd1.pgc file to include sqlca, and also deliberately making it fail, by using an invalid table name:

```
#include <stdlib.h>
#include <stdio.h>

exec sql include sqlca;
main() {

exec sql connect to  'rick@gw1';

exec sql BEGIN WORK;

exec sql UPDATE XXchildren SET fname = 'Emma' WHERE age = 0;

printf("error code %d, message %s, rows %d, warning %c\n", sqlca.sqlcode,
        sqlca.sqlerrm.sqlerrmc, sqlca.sqlerrd[2], sqlca.sqlwarn[0]);

exec sql COMMIT WORK;

exec sql disconnect all;

return EXIT_SUCCESS;

}
```

This is upd2.pgc. The highlighted lines show the important changes. Compile it as before:

```
$ ecpg -t -I/usr/include/pgsql upd2.pgc
$ gcc -g -o upd2 -I /usr/include/pgsql/ upd2.c -lecpg -lpq
```

This time when we run it, an error is generated:

```
error code -400, message Postgres error: ERROR:  xxchildren: Table does not exist.
line 10., rows 0, warning
```

As you can see, it's a little basic but does the job.

Now we have seen the basics, we can get to important issue – how do we access data that SQL statements embedded in .pgc files return?

The answer is actually quite simple, and relies on variables called host variables, which are accessible to both the statements delimited by exec sql ... ; and to the ordinary C compiler.

We do this by having a declare section, usually near the start of the file, that is processed by both the ecpg processor, and the C compiler. This is achieved by declaring C variables inside a special declare section, which also tells the ecpg processor to process them. We use the delimiting statements:

```
exec sql begin declare section;
```

and

```
exec sql end declare section;
```

Suppose we wanted to declare two variables, child_name and child_age, that are intended to be accessible in both the embedded SQL and in the C code for use in the rest of the program.
What we need is:

```
exec sql begin declare section;

int child_age;
VARCHAR child_name[50];

exec sql end declare section;
```

You will notice two odd things here, firstly the 'magic number' 50 as a string length, and secondly that VARCHAR is not a normal C type. We are forced to use literal numbers here, because this section of code is being processed by ecpg before the C compiler runs, so it is not possible to use either a #define or a constant. The reason for VARCHAR is because the SQL type of the fname column in children is not a type that maps directly to a C type. We must use the PostgreSQL type in our declaration, which is then converted into a legal C structure by the ecpg pre-processor, before the C compiler sees it. The result of this line in the source file is to create a structure called child_name, with two members, a char array 'arr', and an integer len, to store the length. So what the C compiler sees from this one line is actually:

```
struct varchar_child_name {int len; char arr[50];} child_name;
```

Now we have two variables, visible both in SQL and in C. We use a slight extension of the SQL syntax, the 'into' keyword, to retrieve data from the table into named variables, which are denoted by having a ':' prepended to the name. This is so they cannot be confused with values or table names. Notice this 'into' is not the same as the extension some vendors support to allow interactive selecting of data from one table into another. The 'into' keyword has a slightly different meaning when using embedded SQL.

```
exec sql SELECT fname into :child_name FROM children WHERE age = :child_age;
```

The epgc pre-processor converts this to C, which we compile in the normal way. So our complete code is now in `selp1.pgc`, and looks like this:

```
#include <stdlib.h>
#include <stdio.h>

exec sql include sqlca;

exec sql begin declare section;

int child_age;
VARCHAR child_name[50];

exec sql end declare section;

main() {

    exec sql connect to  'rick@gw1';

   exec sql BEGIN WORK;

    child_age = 14;

    exec sql SELECT fname into :child_name FROM children WHERE age =
              :child_age;

    printf("error code %d, message %s, rows %d, warning %c\n", sqlca.sqlcode,
          sqlca.sqlerrm.sqlerrmc, sqlca.sqlerrd[2], sqlca.sqlwarn[0]);

    if (sqlca.sqlcode == 0) {
       printf("Child's name was %s\n", child_name.arr);
    }

    exec sql COMMIT WORK;

    exec sql disconnect all;

    return EXIT_SUCCESS;
}
```

The important changes are highlighted. Notice we need to use `child_name.arr` to access the returned data. However you only need to use VARCHAR declarations when you want to get data **out** of the database – when you want to store data into a VARCHAR field you should use a NULL terminated C string in the normal way.

However there is a potential problem with this program. You will see that we had to declare our `child_name` VARCHAR to be a fixed size, even though we could not know in advance how large the answer might have been. What will happen if we make `child_name` only 3 long, and the name stored in the database is longer than this? In this case ecpg will only retrieve the first 3 characters, and will set the warning flag. If we change the declaration to VARCHAR `child_name[3]` and run the program we get:

```
error code 0, message , rows 1, warning W
Child's name was Jen
```

(You may also see some corruption, we will explain why in a moment.)

As you can see, the sqlca.sqlwarn[0] warn character was set to 'W', and the returned name truncated. However since our declaration of child_name is translated into a structure containing a character array of exactly 3 characters, there is no location for the string terminator to be stored. It's lucky our printout worked at all, though we could have been decidedly cleverer with the printf format string. To be certain of getting a VARCHAR into a normal C string we should always check that sqlca.sqlwarn[0] is not set, and then copy the string away to a separate location, adding the NULL terminator explicitly. A more secure version of the program is selp3.c, which has the following changes:

```
#include <stdlib.h>
#include <stdio.h>

exec sql include sqlca;

exec sql begin declare section;

int child_age;
VARCHAR child_name[50];

exec sql end declare section;

main() {

    exec sql connect to  'rick@gw1';

    exec sql BEGIN WORK;
    child_age = 14;
    exec sql SELECT fname into :child_name FROM children WHERE age =
            :child_age;

    printf("error code %d, message %s, rows %d, warning %c\n", sqlca.sqlcode,
            sqlca.sqlerrm.sqlerrmc, sqlca.sqlerrd[2], sqlca.sqlwarn[0]);

    if (sqlca.sqlcode == 0) {
       child_name.arr[sizeof(child_name.arr) -1] = '\0';
       printf("Child's name was %s\n", child_name.arr);
    }

    exec sql COMMIT WORK;
    exec sql disconnect all;

    return EXIT_SUCCESS;
}
```

Now we can retrieve data, it's time to see how we use cursors with ecpg where we want to specify, at run time, the condition for the SELECT, and also retrieve data into C variables. Unlike the libpq example, ecpg, (at least in the version used while writing this chapter), required an explicit OPEN statement to open the cursor, before data could be fetched. This example is selp4.pgc, it's noticeably shorter than the libpq equivalent:

```c
#include <stdlib.h>
#include <stdio.h>

exec sql include sqlca;

exec sql begin declare section;

int child_age;
VARCHAR child_name[50];
int req_age;

exec sql end declare section;

main() {

    exec sql connect to  'rick@gw1';

    exec sql BEGIN WORK;

    req_age = 6;

    exec sql DECLARE mycursor CURSOR FOR SELECT age, fname FROM children
            WHERE age > :req_age;

    exec sql OPEN mycursor;

    exec sql FETCH NEXT IN mycursor into :child_age, :child_name;

    if (sqlca.sqlcode < 0)
        printf("error code %d, message %s, rows %d, warning %c\n", sqlca.sqlcode,
sqlca.sqlerrm.sqlerrmc, sqlca.sqlerrd[2], sqlca.sqlwarn[0]);

    while (sqlca.sqlcode == 0) {
        if (sqlca.sqlcode >= 0) {
            child_name.arr[sizeof(child_name.arr) -1] = '\0';
            printf("Child's name and age %s, %d\n", child_name.arr, child_age);
            }

        exec sql FETCH NEXT IN mycursor into :child_age, :child_name;

        if (sqlca.sqlcode < 0) printf("error code %d, message %s, rows %d, warning
%c\n", sqlca.sqlcode, sqlca.sqlerrm.sqlerrmc, sqlca.sqlerrd[2], sqlca.sqlwarn[0]);

    }

    exec sql CLOSE mycursor;

    exec sql COMMIT WORK;

    exec sql disconnect all;

    return EXIT_SUCCESS;
}
```

When we run this, we get the expected output:

```
Child's name and age Andrew, 10
Child's name and age Jenny, 14
Child's name and age Alex, 11
```

You may be thinking that all this messing with VARCHARS is a bit pointless, and providing your strings are known to be reasonably consistent in size, it would be much easier to use fixed length strings. Unfortunately this gives rise to a different problem – PostgreSQL does not store the \0 in CHAR columns. What it does do is fill the field to the maximum size with spaces. So if you store "Foo" in a CHAR(10), when you get the data back you actually get "Foo   ", and you have to strip the spaces yourself. It does however add a \0 when you retrieve the string, so you do get a conventional C string returned to you.

There is one last ecpg feature we need to look at, how to detect NULL values. Doing this in ecpg (and indeed the standard way for embedded SQL) is slightly more complex than in libpq, but it's not difficult. Remembering that NULL means unknown, it's clear we can't use a magic string, or special integer value to show NULL, since any of these values could actually occur in the database.

What we have to do is to declare an extra variable, often called an indicator variable, that goes alongside the variable we will use to retrieve the data. This additional indicator variable is set to indicate if the data value retrieved was actually NULL in the database. These are often named ind_nameofrealvariable, or sometimes nameofrealvariable _ind, but could have any name. They are always integers – a negative value indicating that the associated variable has a NULL value.

For example, suppose in our earlier example we needed to detect if age was NULL. What we would do is declare an extra variable in the declare section like this:

```
int ind_child_age;
```

Then when we do the FETCH from the cursor, we specify both the real variable, and the indicator variable, joined by a colon, like this:

```
exec sql FETCH NEXT IN mycursor into :child_age:ind_child_age, :child_name;
```

Then if ind_child_age is not negative, we know that child_age is correctly filled in – otherwise the data in it is not valid because the database value was a NULL. For our final example of ecpg, let's convert our example so it correctly detects NULL values.

First we update our 'children' table, so we have examples of both NULL ages and fnames. The test data we start with looks like this:

```
SELECT * from children;
childno|fname |age
-------+------+---
      1|Andrew| 10
      2|Jenny | 14
      3|Alex  | 11
      4|Adrian|  5
     19|      | 17
     16|Emma  |  0
     18|TBD   |
     20|Gavin |  4
(8 rows)
```

As you can see, we have a seventeen year old with an unknown name, and an unborn child whose name is still to be decided, and doesn't have an age yet.

This is `selp5.pgc`. By way of example, we have also used the alternate form of connection string.

```c
#include <stdlib.h>
#include <stdio.h>

exec sql include sqlca;

exec sql begin declare section;

int child_age;
int ind_child_age;
VARCHAR child_name[50];
int ind_child_name;

exec sql end declare section;

main() {

    exec sql connect to  tcp:postgresql://localhost:5432/rick as rick user rick
using secretpassword;

    exec sql BEGIN WORK;

    exec sql DECLARE mycursor CURSOR FOR SELECT age, fname FROM children;

    exec sql OPEN mycursor;

    exec sql FETCH NEXT IN mycursor into :child_age:ind_child_age,
            :child_name:ind_child_name;

    if (sqlca.sqlcode < 0)
        printf("error code %d, message %s, rows %d, warning %c\n", sqlca.sqlcode,
sqlca.sqlerrm.sqlerrmc, sqlca.sqlerrd[2], sqlca.sqlwarn[0]);

    while (sqlca.sqlcode == 0) {
    if (sqlca.sqlcode >= 0) {
        if (ind_child_name >= 0) {
          child_name.arr[sizeof(child_name.arr) -1] = '\0';

        } else {
          strcpy(child_name.arr, "Unknown");
        }
        if (ind_child_age >= 0) {
          printf("Child's name and age %s, %d\n", child_name.arr, child_age);
        } else {
          printf("Child's name %s\n", child_name.arr);
        }
     }

        exec sql FETCH NEXT IN mycursor into :child_age:ind_child_age,
              :child_name:ind_child_name;
```

```
    if (sqlca.sqlcode < 0)
        printf("error code %d, message %s, rows %d, warning %c\n", sqlca.sqlcode,
sqlca.sqlerrm.sqlerrmc, sqlca.sqlerrd[2], sqlca.sqlwarn[0]);

    } /* end of while loop */

    exec sql CLOSE mycursor;

    exec sql COMMIT WORK;

    exec sql disconnect all;

    return EXIT_SUCCESS;
}
```

The sections related to checking for NULL values are highlighted. When we run this, we get:

```
Child's name and age Andrew, 10
Child's name and age Jenny, 14
Child's name and age Alex, 11
Child's name and age Adrian, 4
Child's name and age Unknown, 17
Child's name and age Emma, 0
Child's name TBD
Child's name and age Gavin, 4
```

As you can see, we correctly detect and handle NULL values now.

And that concludes our look at the ecpg, the embedded SQL pre-processor for PostgreSQL.

Which Method to Use?

So given two methods of accessing PostgreSQL from 'C', which is the right one to use? As usual, there is no right answer; use whichever you feel fits the problem and your way of working best. However we would advise you not to mix and match inside a single project – pick a preferred way of working and stick to it.

Advantages of libpq:

❑ It uses a familiar call library function paradigm, which is familiar to many people.

❑ It's reasonably well documented.

Disadvantages:

❑ It requires a lot of code.

❑ The SQL is difficult to spot in the middle of the surrounding C code.

Advantages of ecpg:

❑ It's a standard for embedding SQL.

❑ The SQL is much easier to read when it is not embedded in library calls.

Disadvantages:

❑ Debugging can be difficult, because the file is pre-processed before the C compiler sees it. This means that errors from the C compiler can be harder to track down, and debugging with gdb can get very confusing because the line numbers can appear to be wrong. Ecpg inserts #line directives in the resulting 'C' file, which normally help, because error messages refer to the original .pgc file line numbers. However this is not always what you want, and can also confuse gdb. You can work round this, by allowing ecpg to generate a .c file, use grep -v '^#line' > _1.c, copy the _1.c back to the .c file that ecpg created, then continue compiling. This strips the line setting commands out, and so error messages from the compiler, and commands in gdb now work with line numbers from the .c file, rather than the .pgc file. This difficulty is not specific to ecpg, most other embedded SQL systems have similar quirks.

❑ To many people, it is probably not as familiar a technique as standard library usage.

❑ You must know in advance the number and types of the columns you will retrieve in SELECT statements.

If you have a progam that is mostly C code, with only a small amount of SQL, then the added difficulties of debugging pre-processed code are a distinct disadvantage.

The Application

Now we have learnt the basics of accessing the PostgreSQL database from 'C', it's time to see how we can implement the backend of our database for the DVD store.

The first, and probably most important thing we need to do, is design our database tables. Well, we need a table for storing member information, so there is our first table. We also need to think about the actual DVDs. It's important to realize that there are two different types of information to be stored – information about a film that is on DVD, for example, the film 'Death and the Maiden' starring 'Sigourney Weaver', which has a director, a release date and so on, and the actual DVD disks available in the shop. The film exists independently of an available DVD disk; there could be zero, one or many disks with that film title actually available in the shop. This tells us that we should separate the film information from the disk information using two separate tables. Clearly they are related pieces of information, but they are not the same.

The next piece of information to store is to relate member bookings to titles. We do this by adding an additional table, 'member_booking, which stores a member ID and a title ID, along with the booking date. This acts as the link between a member and the title they have booked. This also allows more than one member to have reserved the same title on the same day, a classic many-to-many relationship. (The application must check how many disks are actually available of course!)

When we come to disks actually rented, we could do a similar thing, by adding a table between the 'disk' and 'member' tables, we could link disks to members when they are rented. However we notice an obvious optimization – there can only ever be no link, or a one to one link between a particular disk the store owns, and a member renting that disk. So we could store the 'renting' related information directly in the 'disk' table, using a NULL member ID when the disk is not rented. This is called de-normalizing, and should only be done when you are sure you have properly analyzed your data structures. We do it here as much for the purposes of demonstration as any valid optimization technique, though it does slightly simplify the code.

Finally, we need three additional tables for utility information, one for error messages, one for the film genre categories, and one for film classifications. Both the genre and film classifications relate directly to a film title, and are the only values that should appear there. Here we have another set of choices to make. We could either directly store the genre and classification text in the 'title' table against a film, relying on the application to lookup the allowed text from the utility table. Alternatively we could store only an ID, with links in the database back to the actual table where the text is stored.

If the text is very short, and we are confident we can rely on the application only to use a valid text string, then it's probably better to simply store the actual text in the title table, since it makes the database design simpler, and the SQL easier to write. However, if the text is longer, and we want to be absolutely certain that no illegal values could be stored, then we should store the ID for the text, and store the text in a different table. This reduces the storage, since each unique string is only stored once. For the purposes of demonstration in this application, we store the classification directly, but keep the genre stored separately, so you can compare the two techniques.

In a real application however, we would always recommend storing only a link to the table with the real data. This is because it's much more conducive to maintaining the quality of your data, which in a database should always be your number one concern. A brilliantly designed database, that stores incorrect data, is little better than no database at all.

To make managing our table easier, we store the SQL we need to create the tables in a separate file, so we can edit the file and re-create the database easily. You can run SQL commands from a file in psql with the \i file.sql command. Here is the SQL code that creates our database:

```
create table member (
        member_id  SERIAL,
        member_no  CHAR(6) NOT NULL,
        title          CHAR(4),
        fname          CHAR(26),
        lname          CHAR(26) NOT NULL,
        house_flat_ref CHAR(26) NOT NULL,
        address1       CHAR(51) NOT NULL,
        address2       CHAR(51),
        town           CHAR(51) NOT NULL,
        state          CHAR(3),
        phone          CHAR(31),
        zipcode        CHAR(11) NOT NULL,
        CONSTRAINT     member_no_uniq UNIQUE(member_no)
);

create table title (
        title_id       SERIAL,
        title_text     CHAR(61) NOT NULL,
        asin           CHAR(11),
        director       CHAR(51),
        genre_id       INT,
        classification CHAR(11),
        actor1         CHAR(51),
        actor2         CHAR(51),
        release_date   CHAR(9),
        rental_cost    CHAR(7)
);
create table disk (
        disk_id        SERIAL,
        title_id       INT NOT NULL,
```

```
        member_id        INT,      /* set if rented out otherwise NULL */
        rented_date      CHAR(9)
);


create table member_booking (
        member_id        INT NOT NULL,
        title_id         INT NOT NULL,
        date_required    CHAR(9) NOT NULL
);

create table filmclass (
        class_name       CHAR(11)
);

create table genre (
        genre_id         INT NOT NULL,
        genre_name       CHAR(21),
        CONSTRAINT       genre_id_uniq UNIQUE(genre_id)
);

create table errtext (
        err_code         INT,
        err_text         CHAR(50)
);
```

You should notice some extra 'constraints' have been added, for example:

```
        CONSTRAINT       genre_id_uniq UNIQUE(genre_id)
```

We did not want to make the genre_id a SERIAL column, because if we ever need to reload the data it's very important that we re-create each genre_id with the same value we had before, or all the information it relates to in the title table will be wrong. On the other hand, it's very important that the value is unique. We trade off these two conflicting demands by adding a constraint that allows us to pick the value of genre_id – so long as the value we pick does not currently exist in the database.

Below is a graphical representation of the database structure:

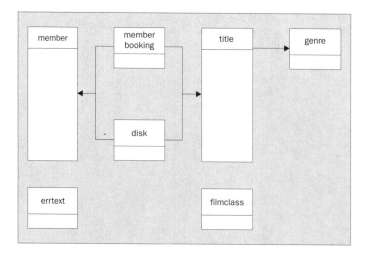

We don't have anything like the space required here to reproduce all the code, so we just show a few small snippets to give you a flavor of how the application was developed. These code pieces are the lowest level of the application, and are called after general sanity checking (such as ensuring we have a database connection, and that pointer parameters were not NULL) has been performed.

For example, here is the code that takes a structure with the title details in it, finds the appropriate genre_id, and adds the row to the title table.

```c
int pg_title_insert(dvd_title *title_ptr) {

    exec sql BEGIN WORK;

    strcpy(title_text, title_ptr->title_text);
    strcpy(asin, title_ptr->asin);
    strcpy(director, title_ptr->director);
    sprintf(genre_name, "%s%c", title_ptr->genre, '%');
    strcpy(classification, title_ptr->classification);
    strcpy(actor1, title_ptr->actor1);
    strcpy(actor2, title_ptr->actor2);
    strcpy(release_date, title_ptr->release_date);
    strcpy(rental_cost, title_ptr->rental_cost);

    /* Find the genre_id */
    exec sql SELECT genre_id INTO :genre_id:genre_id_ind FROM genre WHERE
genre_name LIKE :genre_name;
    if ((sqlca.sqlcode < 0) || (sqlca.sqlcode == 100) || (genre_id_ind == 1)) {
        pg_print_debug(__FILE__, __LINE__, sqlca, "Unknow genre\n");
        exec sql ROLLBACK WORK;
        return DVD_ERR_BAD_GENRE;
    }

    exec sql INSERT INTO title(
                        title_text, asin,
                        director, genre_id, classification,
                        actor1, actor2, release_date,
                        rental_cost)
        VALUES (
            :title_text, :asin,
            :director, :genre_id, :classification,
            :actor1, :actor2, :release_date,
            :rental_cost);

if (sqlca.sqlcode < 0) {
    pg_print_debug(__FILE__, __LINE__, sqlca, "insert into title failed\n");

    exec sql ROLLBACK WORK;

    return DVD_ERR_BAD_TITLE_TABLE;
} else {
    if (sqlca.sqlerrd[2] != 1) {
        pg_print_debug(__FILE__, __LINE__, sqlca, "insert into title
                    failed\n");

        exec sql ROLLBACK WORK;
```

```
        return DVD_ERR_BAD_TITLE_TABLE;
    }
}

exec sql SELECT MAX(title_id) INTO :title_id FROM title;
if (sqlca.sqlcode < 0) {
    pg_print_debug(__FILE__, __LINE__, sqlca, "select max title
                   failed\n");

    exec sql ROLLBACK WORK;
    return DVD_ERR_BAD_TITLE_TABLE;
}

exec sql COMMIT WORK;

/* Update the member structure with the now known fields */
title_ptr->title_id = title_id;
return DVD_SUCCESS;

} /* pg_title_insert */
```

The code that looks up the appropriate genre_id is highlighted. Notice we check that not only did the SQL statement succeed (sqlca.sqlcode was not < 0), but also that data was returned (sqlca.sqlcode was not == 100), and the genre_id we recovered was not a NULL value (genre_id_ind was not 1). It's always good to have a belt and braces approach to checking return status information. Hiding this use of the genre_id means that unless the application tries to insert an invalid string, it is not aware of how the data is actually stored; this is a valuable separation of responsibility.

Here is the code that retrieves title information. It also hides the details of the data storage, and illustrates how we join tables (select from more than one table at a time) to recover information from both the title table and genre table in a single SELECT statement:

```
int pg_title_get(int req_title_id, dvd_title *title_ptr) {

    title_id = req_title_id;

    exec sql BEGIN WORK;

    exec sql SELECT
        title_id, title_text, asin,
        director, genre_name, classification,
        actor1, actor2, release_date,
        rental_cost
    INTO
        :title_id:ind_title_id, :title_text, :asin,
        :director, :genre_name, :classification,
        :actor1, :actor2, :release_date,
        :rental_cost
    FROM title, genre WHERE title.title_id = :title_id AND title.genre_id
                                                = genre.genre_id;
```

```
        if (sqlca.sqlcode < 0) {
            pg_print_debug(__FILE__, __LINE__, sqlca, "title get failed\n");
            exec sql ROLLBACK WORK;
            return DVD_ERR_BAD_TITLE_TABLE;
        }

        if ((sqlca.sqlcode == 100) || (ind_title_id != 0)) {
            pg_print_debug(__FILE__, __LINE__, sqlca, "title get failed - no
                                                        entry\n");
            exec sql ROLLBACK WORK;
            return DVD_ERR_NOT_FOUND;
        }

        title_ptr->title_id = title_id;
        strcpy(title_ptr->title_text, title_text);
        strcpy(title_ptr->asin, asin);
        strcpy(title_ptr->director, director);
        strcpy(title_ptr->genre, genre_name);
        strcpy(title_ptr->classification, classification);
        strcpy(title_ptr->actor1, actor1);
        strcpy(title_ptr->actor2, actor2);
        strcpy(title_ptr->release_date, release_date);
        strcpy(title_ptr->rental_cost, rental_cost);

        exec sql COMMIT WORK;

        return DVD_SUCCESS;

    } /* pg_title_get */
```

One other 'interesting' section of code that deals with titles is the searching. The API allows clients to
search on a film title, and/or actors names. It might be tempting to write these as separate functions, but
in SQL it is very easy to express the selection in a single statement. Provided of course you know that '%'
is the string matching character in SQL.

```
    int pg_title_search(char *title_to_find, char *name_to_find, int *result_ids[], int
    *count) {

        int result_size = 0;
        int *results = NULL;

        if (title_to_find == NULL) strcpy(title_text, "%");
        else sprintf(title_text, "%c%s%c", '%', title_to_find, '%');
        if (name_to_find == NULL) strcpy(actor1, "%");
        else sprintf(actor1, "%c%s%c", '%', name_to_find, '%');

        exec sql BEGIN WORK;
        exec sql DECLARE mycursor CURSOR FOR SELECT title_id from title WHERE
                (title_text LIKE :title_text) AND ((actor1 LIKE :actor1) OR
                (actor2 LIKE:actor1)) ORDER by title_text, actor1,actor2;

        exec sql OPEN mycursor;
```

```
        if (sqlca.sqlcode < 0) {
           pg_print_debug(__FILE__, __LINE__, sqlca, "mycursor");
           exec sql ROLLBACK WORK;
           return DVD_ERR_BAD_TABLE;
        }

        exec sql FETCH NEXT in mycursor INTO :title_id;
        while (sqlca.sqlcode == 0) {
           result_size++;
           results = (int *)realloc(results, sizeof(int) * result_size);
           if (results == NULL) { /* Major error, we don't attempt a recovery */
             exec sql ROLLBACK WORK;
             return DVD_ERR_NO_MEMORY;
           }
           results[result_size - 1] = title_id;

           exec sql FETCH NEXT in mycursor INTO :title_id;
        } /* while */
        if (sqlca.sqlcode < 0) {
           pg_print_debug(__FILE__, __LINE__, sqlca, "mycursor");
           exec sql ROLLBACK WORK;
           return DVD_ERR_BAD_TABLE;
        }

        exec sql COMMIT WORK;

        *result_ids = results;
        *count = result_size;
        return DVD_SUCCESS;

     } /* pg_title_search */
```

We even order the output by `title` and `actor1`, the most likely items to be correct.

The rest of the application code, like most of the code snippets from this book, is available on the Wrox web site.

Summary

In this chapter we have looked at two ways of accessing a PostgreSQL database from C code. Firstly we looked at a conventional library based method, then we looked how SQL could be embedded more directly in C code. We compared these two techniques, and saw that both had advantages and disadvantages. Finally we looked at a small section of our example application, which implemented access to data stored in a PostgreSQL database for our imaginary DVD store.

MySQL

We decided earlier that MySQL was not the ideal choice of backend database for our particular application, but there are many applications where this very popular database is more than adequate. Generally, this is where query speed is very important, but you don't need transactions or other more advanced SQL support. Since that covers a significant number of applications, we're going to have a look at it anyway.

In this chapter, we will provide an overview of installing MySQL. We will then look at:

❑   basic administration commands you will need to maintain your MySQL installation

❑   major differences between the SQL support in PostgreSQL and that in MySQL

❑   writing C programs that access MySQL databases

Installation and Commissioning

Installing MySQL is very easy. If your Linux distribution did not come with a copy, then the MySQL web site (http://www.mysql.com) has both source and binary distributions (including RPM packages) for many platforms. Generally you will find a pre-built installation suitable for your needs, though source is also available if you prefer.

Pre-compiled Packages

The RPM package is currently distributed as four RPMs:

❑   The **main server package**, with a name of the form

```
MySQL-<version>.<architecture>.rpm
```

This contains the main binaries and manual pages, as well as multi-language support files. You *must* install this package.

❑   The **client package**, with a name of the form

```
MySQL-client-<version>.<architecture>.rpm
```

This contains several standard client programs, which you should generally install along with the server. It's packaged separately, so that if you have several machines which only need to act as clients, accessing a MySQL server on a different machine, you can avoid installing the server components unnecessarily.

❑   The **shared component package**, with a name of the form

```
MySQL-shared-<version>.<architecture>.rpm
```

which contains shared libraries required by some clients.

❑   The **development package**, with a name of the form

```
MySQL-devel-<version>.<architecture>.rpm
```

which contains the headers and additional library files for developing applications that communicate with a MySQL server.

If you decide to start developing programs to access a MySQL server, you will need to install all of the packages on your development system.

During installation, an initial database will have been created for you automatically by the installation scripts. You will also have an init.d script, mysql, for starting and stopping the server. Generally the easiest way to find the database files on your specific distribution is to locate this script in your init.d directory, and have a look through it. Standard paths and defines are early in the script, and it's very easy to see where files have been located. For example, on our binary installation of Red Hat RPMs, the 'shell variables' section of the mysql script contains this:

```
bindir=/usr/bin
datadir=/var/lib/mysql
pid_file=/var/lib/mysql/mysqld.pid
mysql_daemon_user=mysql  # Run mysqld as this user.
```

This is nice and easy to follow. The installation will also create the user 'mysql', which is the user name that the MySQL server daemon runs under. Depending on the version of MySQL you're using, the installation may also start the server for you. To check this, use:

```
$ ps -el | grep mysqld
```

If you see some `mysqld` processes running, the server has been started. If not, you can get it started by running the mysql script (in `init.d`) as the mysql user, with the argument `start`. Depending on your distribution the command will be similar to:

```
# su - mysql
$ /etc/rc.d/init.d/mysql start
```

Building from Source

Installing from the source is only slightly harder than using a pre-built package. Download and unpack the sources in the usual way, then run:

```
$ ./configure --help
```

to check if there are any configuration options you wish to change. Assuming the defaults are fine, the sequence to build and install the server is:

```
$ ./configure
$ make
$ su -
# make install
```

If all is well, you can now run (as root) the install script `scripts/mysql_install_db` to initialize the server for first time use:

```
# scripts/mysql_install_db
```

Depending on your version of MySQL, this script may start the server automatically. If it doesn't, you will have to start it by hand, using the script `mysql.server`, which you will find in the support-files directory. The `mysql_install_db` script creates some required base tables, and also initializes permissions. It's a straightforward shell script, so if you're interested, you can always have a look to see what is being done.

Before the script completes, you will be given a message about how to cause MySQL to automatically start when the system boots. You'll also receive a warning about setting an initial password for the 'root' MySQL user. (Confusingly MySQL has a user with the name 'root' who is, by default, the server administrator.) Don't worry if you miss these messages, you can always have a look in the script for them afterwards.

The final step in a source install is to configure the server to automatically start and stop with the system. In the support-files directory you will find a helpful script `mysql.server`, which you can copy to `init.d`, then create links for automatic start and stop to the appropriate `rc.d` script. Alternatively you can always run the script with the start or stop parameter by hand if you prefer. However, always be careful (just as with PostgreSQL) to ensure that the database server is shutdown before the system is halted.

Post-install Configuration

If all went well, you've installed the default configuration with `mysql_install_db` and have started the MySQL server demon using the script in `init.d`. It's now time to check the server is running:

```
$ mysql -u root mysql
```

You should get a 'Welcome to the MySQL monitor' message, followed by a `mysql>` prompt. The good news is that your server is running. The bad news is that *anyone* can connect to it *with administrator privileges.* You exit the mysql prompt by typing `quit`.

An alternative way to check if the server is running is to use the `mysqladmin` command, like this:

```
$ mysqladmin -u root version
```

This will not only tell you if the server is running, but also which server version is in use and how long it has been running.

If the connection failed when you used `mysql`, firstly check the server is actually running, by using `ps` and searching for `mysqld` processes. If it's not running, but you believe you started it, try the `safe_mysqld` program with the `--log` option to start the server. This will generate a log file in a file name with the same name as your hostname, with `.log` appended, in the directory where MySQL is installed, often `/var/lib/mysql`.

If the server is running, but you cannot connect, then have a look in the `mysql_install_db` script, or the `inid.d/mysql` script to see where the database is installed. The directory `/var/lib/mysql`, in a sub-directory `mysql` is a common location. There should be some file with the extensions `.frm` `.ISD` and `.ISM`.

If all else fails, try stopping the server; manually delete the database files, and run the `mysql_install_db` script manually to recreate the database. Finally restart the server. Hopefully, all will then be well. If not, you can find further debugging suggestions for the more unlikely problems in the comprehensive documentation that comes with MySQL. If you installed a binary version, you will probably find them in `/usr/doc/MySQL-<version>`. Alternatively have a look at the MySQL web pages.

A very confusing bug can be seen if the permissions on the database files do not match the `mysql` user created automatically by the installation, or the `mysqld` processes are running with the wrong user ID. If you find that `mysql` allows you to connect, but other programs (such as `mysqladmin` and `mysqlshow`) fail, double-check the ownership of the database files and the user under which the `mysqld` processes are running; it's probable that there is a mismatch. If this happens, you need to change the ownership of all the database files to be owned by the `mysql` user.

Our next task is to set up an administrator (or root) password for the database server. We do this with the `mysqladmin` command, like this:

```
$ mysqladmin -u root password newpassword
```

This will set an initial password of *newpassword*. Now try `mysql` again, and it should fail, unless you also supply a user and a password, like this:

```
$ mysql -u root -psecretpassword mysql
```

Notice the syntax is a little unusual – there must be no space between the `-p` and the actual password. The final parameter, `mysql`, is the database to select. If you don't give a password (by using just `-p`) `mysql` will prompt for one. Since putting passwords on the command line is generally a bad idea (other people can read them, using `ps` and other methods), it's normally much better to omit the actual password, and use this format:

```
$ mysql -u root -p mysql
```

Which will get `mysql` to prompt you for a password. Once you are running `mysql`, you can check that the test database is present, by typing, at the `mysql` prompt:

```
mysql> select host, db, user from db;
```

You should get a list like this:

```
+------+----------+------+
| host | db       | user |
+------+----------+------+
| %    | test     |      |
| %    | test\_%  |      |
+------+----------+------+
2 rows in set (0.00 sec)
```

You can then type `quit` to exit `mysql`.

MySQL Administration

A small number of utility programs come with MySQL that you need to know about in order to administer the system. The one you will need most often is `mysqladmin`, but for completeness, we will briefly run through the others as well, before moving on to writing MySQL client programs.

Commands

All of the commands except `mysqlshow` take three standard parameters:

❑   `-u` `username`

❑   `-p` `[password]`

❑   `-h` `host`

The `-h` parameter is for connecting to a server on a different host, and can always be omitted for local servers. If `-p` is given but the password is omitted, then the password is prompted for. If the `-p` parameter is not present, then MySQL commands assume no password is needed.

isamchk

This is a utility that checks and repairs the underlying data tables used by MySQL. To run this utility you should be the same user as the mysql pseudo-user, and then change to the subdirectory under the main mysql directory (probably /var/lib/mysql) with the name of the database you wish to check. For example, to check a database fud, then you should be in /var/lib/mysql/fud. The isamchk utility has many options, which are listed if you run it with no parameters.

In general, you run it with one or more options, followed by *.ISM to ask it to work on all the tables present. The main options are:

-a	analyze the files
-e	do extended checking
-r	recover (correct) errors found
-s	run silently unless an error is found

For more information, invoke isamchk with no parameters, and look through the extensive help message.

Hopefully you will never need this utility. However, if you do suffer an uncontrolled power down, or shutdown the machine without shutting down the mysql daemon, it's possible you will manage to corrupt the underlying database storage files. This is the tool you will need when you come to try and repair the damage.

mysql

This is the standard command line tool, and can be used for many administration and permission tasks, which we will cover later.

The mysql command takes an additional argument, which must come after the options, the database name to connect to. For example, for rick, with a password bar, to start mysql with the database foo already selected, we need:

```
$ mysql -u rick -pbar foo
```

It's generally convenient to specify the database you wish to connect to in this way. Other options can be displayed by invoking mysql with the -h option.

You can also ask mysql to process commands from a file, by simply redirecting standard input from a file, like this:

```
$ mysql -u rick -pbar foo < sqlcommands.sql
```

Once the file has been processed, mysql will exit.

mysqladmin

This is the main administration utility. Apart from the normal -u *user* and -p to ask it to prompt you for a password, there are four main commands you will need:

`create databasename`	create a new database
`drop databasename`	delete a database
`password newpassword`	change a password (as we saw earlier)
`status`	provide the status of the server
`version`	provide the version number of the server, as well as how long it has been running

If you invoke it with no parameters, it will provide a helpful list of the commands it accepts.

mysqlbug

Hopefully you will never need this utility! It gathers information about your installation and sets up a standard report to be mailed to the maintainers, once you have edited-in details of your problem.

mysqldump

This is a very handy utility that allows you to dump a database (either all tables or selected tables) to a file. It writes standard SQL commands to the file, which can be executed by making it the input to `mysql`, as we saw earlier, or using `mysqlimport`, which we will meet shortly. The parameters are a database, and optionally a list of one or more table names from the database. Apart from the standard -u and -p options, the main two options you will find useful are:

`--add-drop-table`	add SQL commands to the output file to drop (delete) any tables before the commands to create them
`-t`	dump only the data from tables
`-d`	dump only the table structure

The information is produced on the standard output, so you'll probably need to redirect it to a file.

You can use this utility to make periodic backups, or export data for migration to a different database. The output is in straight ASCII and is very easy to read; it even incorporates comments. For example, to dump the database `rick` to a file `rick.dump`, we would use the command:

```
$ mysqldump -u rick -p rick > rick.dump
```

The resulting file, which on our system has only a single table in the `rick` database, looks like this:

```
# MySQL dump 7.1
#
# Host: localhost    Database: rick
#--------------------------------------------------------
# Server version 3.22.32-log
```

143

```
#
# Table structure for table 'children'
#
CREATE TABLE children (
    childno int(11) DEFAULT '0' NOT NULL auto_increment,
    fname varchar(30),
    age int(11),
    PRIMARY KEY (childno)
);

#
# Dumping data for table 'children'
#

INSERT INTO children VALUES (1,'Jenny',14);
INSERT INTO children VALUES (2,'Andrew',10);
INSERT INTO children VALUES (3,'Gavin',4);
INSERT INTO children VALUES (4,'Duncan',2);
INSERT INTO children VALUES (5,'Emma',0);
INSERT INTO children VALUES (6,'Alex',11);
INSERT INTO children VALUES (7,'Adrian',5);
```

mysqlimport

This is, as you probably guessed, the partner to `mysqldump`, and allows database tables to be recreated from text files, normally those created by `mysqldump` (though you could always write your own by hand if you wanted to). Generally, the only parameters you need are a database name and a text file to read the commands from.

It's also possible to perform SQL commands from a text file by simply running `mysql` with input redirected from a file.

mysqlshow

This is a very handy little utility that displays useful information about a server, a database, or a table, depending on the parameters you give it:

❑   With no parameters, it lists all available databases.

❑   With a database as a parameter, it lists the tables in that database.

❑   With both a database and a table name, it lists the columns in that table.

❑   With a database, table and column, it lists the details of the specified column.

Generally there is not much point in providing a column name, since all the information about each column is shown at the table level anyway.

Creating Users, and Giving Them Permissions

The most common administration need, apart from backing up important data, is setting up user permissions. From version 3.22 of MySQL, user privileges should be managed with two SQL commands: grant and revoke. Both of these are run inside the mysql command utility.

grant

MySQL's grant command is similar to that of the SQL92 standard, but with some significant differences. The general format is:

grant privilege **on** object **to** user [user-password] [option]**;**

There are several privileges that can be granted, which are:

Alter	alter tables and indexes
Create	create databases and tables
Delete	delete data from the database
Drop	remove databases and tables
Index	manage indexes
Insert	add data to the database
Select	retrieve data
Update	modify data
All	do anything

There are also several special administration privileges, but these do not concern us here.

The object on which you grant these privileges is identified as:

databasename.tablename

and a * matches all, so rick.* matches all tables in the rick database. As a consequence of the way MySQL is implemented, you can grant privileges on a database that does not yet exist. This might seem a little odd, but in practice it gives the user the right to create that database, which can be useful.

The specified user name can either be that of an existing user or, if you want, a new one, automatically causing that user to be created. Client users of the MySQL server are always identified as username.host, even if it's the local machine, in which case you should set the host name to localhost.

The special identifier % means 'any host'. If you prefer though, you can invoke the grant command several times, once for each of the machines from which the user wishes to access the server. If you want to grant connect permissions to a group of hosts in a domain, just use % for the host, specifying the domain as something like:

```
rick@"%.docbox.co.uk"
```

Notice that we now need quotes.

Using the 'identified by' clause sets the password for the user name. Normally, if you are creating a new user, you should set a password immediately; otherwise you are leaving your database rather insecure.

with grant

The with grant option allows the user to pass on the privileges you just granted them. Normally you would not use this option, unless you are setting up an administrator account.

Enough of the theory, let's create a user rick, who can connect from any machine, set his password to bar, and allow him to create a database foo. The command inside mysql that we need is:

```
mysql> grant all on foo.* to rick@"%" identified by "bar";
```

Remember the trailing ; necessary in SQL commands.

This creates the user rick with password bar. This user can connect from any machine and can create and then manage a database foo. Once you've granted rick permission to create a database foo, he can cause it to be physically created using the normal create database SQL command.

revoke, delete

While we are looking at permissions, it's sensible to look at how we take privileges away again. Generally it is done with the revoke command, which has the syntax:

```
revoke a-privilege on an-object from a-user;
```

in a similar format to the grant command. For example:

```
revoke insert on foo.* from rick@"%";
```

There is, however, one slight oddity; even if you revoke all privileges from a user, they still have *connect* permission on your database, which probably isn't what you want. To get rid of the user completely, you must also delete them from the user table of the MySQL database, and then force mysql to reload its permission tables, like this:

```
mysql> use mysql
mysql> delete from user where User = "rick" and Host = "%";
mysql> flush privileges;
```

Passwords

If you forget to specify a password, you can always set it later on. You'll need to be logged on as `root`, and have the `mysql` database selected. If you enter:

```
mysql> select host, user, password from user;
```

you should get a list like this:

```
+-----------+----------+------------------+
| host      | user     | password         |
+-----------+----------+------------------+
| localhost | root     | 67457e226a1a15bd |
| %         | rick     | 7c9e0a41222752fa |
| .%        | foo      |                  |
+-----------+----------+------------------+
2 rows in set (0.00 sec)
```

[handwritten: this database is called user is FreeBSD S 1]

Say you want to assign the password `bar` to user `foo`; you can do so like this:

```
mysql> update user set password= password('bar') where user= 'foo';
```

Display the relevant columns in the `mysql.user` table again:

```
mysql> select host, user, password from user;
+-----------+----------+------------------+
| host      | user     | password         |
+-----------+----------+------------------+
| localhost | root     | 67457e226a1a15bd |
| %         | rick     | 7c9e0a41222752fa |
| .%        | foo      | 7c9e0a41222752fa |
+-----------+----------+------------------+
2 rows in set (0.00 sec)
mysql>
```

and sure enough, it's there; the same encrypted password as we defined earlier for user `rick`.

Creating a Database

Let's play around with a **database** called `rick`. First, as the `mysql` root user we must give ourselves permission to create the database:

```
mysql> grant all on rick.* to rick@% identified by "bar";
```

This will give user `rick` all permissions on database `rick` from all machines.

[handwritten: grant all on ViewCVS. to root;]*

We can now quit `mysql`, start it again as user `rick`, and create the database:

```
mysql> quit
Bye
$ mysql -u rick
mysql> create database rick;
```

We then switch to using the `rick` database, with the `use` command:

```
mysql> use rick
```

Now we are in a position to create any tables we require.

You may remember from the PostgreSQL chapter, we used a table 'children' for some examples. The SQL to create it was this:

```
create table children (
  childno SERIAL,
  fname VARCHAR,
  age INTEGER
);
```

If we try and create this in MySQL, we immediately run into the first minor incompatibility: MySQL doesn't support the SERIAL keyword. Fortunately, correcting this is very easy – see the *'Differences'* section later. The equivalent SQL for MySQL is:

```
create table children (
        childno INTEGER AUTO_INCREMENT NOT NULL PRIMARY KEY,
        fname VARCHAR(30),
        age INTEGER
);
```

which is an easy change. Inserting data is done in the same way as with PostgreSQL; we must specifically ignore the auto-incremented column:

```
insert into children(fname, age) values("Jenny", 14);
insert into children(fname, age) values("Andrew", 10);
```

with appropriate data for as many rows as needed.

SQL Support in PostgreSQL and MySQL

In Chapter 3 we covered the basics of SQL, mostly from the viewpoint of PostgreSQL. MySQL's support for SQL is similar to that in PostgreSQL. Although we note below the main differences that apply to the SQL commands we covered earlier, you will find that the basic SQL coverage is the same. Most mainstream SQL will work on both platforms. Remember that both servers are actively being developed, so this difference list may change significantly in the future. Of course, these aren't the only differences, but we've mentioned the main ones you are likely to encounter.

❏   MySQL does not currently support **subqueries**, though they are planned for a future release. As we saw in PostgreSQL, these can be very useful in a few special cases, but normally it's possible to re-write the SQL statement to avoid using sub-queries if you want to be able to use the same SQL or port from one database to the other.

❏   MySQL considers table names to be **case-sensitive**, unlike PostgreSQL which is not case-sensitive. MySQL relies on the Operating System file system using one file per table for table storage and considers table names with the same case-sensitivity as the underlying OS. Therefore, table names are case-sensitive under Linux. This is not generally a problem, but is unusual, so you should be careful never to make case the only distinguishing feature between two table names. In general, we suggest you confine tables names to lower case.

❏   MySQL does not currently support the SERIAL column type, though it's easy to work round. Replace the SERIAL keyword with INTEGER AUTO_INCREMENT NOT NULL PRIMARY KEY. It's a bit more typing, but is almost identical in operation to PostgreSQL's SERIAL keyword; it also has the advantage that dropping a table with such a type doesn't require any additional work to tidy up stray sequences, as you must do with PostgreSQL. Bear in mind though, that the SERIAL keyword is the more common usage in SQL.

❏   MySQL has a lock command:

```
lock tables tablename READ | WRITE [,tablename READ | WRITE ...];

unlock tables;
```

Actually PostgreSQL has a lock command as well, but in PostgreSQL it should almost never be used, since you should always use transactions to solve the problem of automically updating data. Since MySQL doesn't currently support transactions (see below), the lock command is more commonly needed.

Locking a table for read prevents any updates to the table. Locking a table for write prevents others reading *or* writing the table, but the current thread of execution can both read and write it. Lock commands do not nest; if you execute another lock command, any currently locked tables will be unlocked automatically before the new list of tables is locked.

❏   MySQL has no **transactions**. This is the main difference between the two, and is the most difficult to work around. For simple updates you can sometimes work around this in one of two ways:

Firstly, by making updates specify all column values of the row being updated. If, for example, you wanted to adjust the balance in a user's account, which has a customer first name, customer last name, a unique account number and amount, and want to update the amount from 3 to 4, then rather than writing:

```
update account set amount = 4 where accnum = 3013;
```

put: 518 929 2290

```
update account set amount = 4 where
                   accnum=3013 and customerfn = "Bilbo" and
                   customerln = "Baggins" and amount = 3;
```

That way, if any column in the row has already been updated between you discovering the value in the account was 3, and wanting to make it 4, the update will fail because a column value has been changed, and, providing you check and handle the failure, you can make an intelligent decision about what should happen next.

Secondly you can use the `lock tables` command to prevent other users accessing tables you wish to update. This is simpler, but much more difficult to get right than using transactions; also, it can badly hurt database performance where there are several users and frequent updates are being performed.

These are the main differences you are most likely to come across, given the subset of SQL we have presented in this book.

Accessing MySQL Data from C

Like PostgreSQL, MySQL can be accessed from many different languages. We know of:

- ❑   C
- ❑   C++
- ❑   Java
- ❑   Perl
- ❑   Python
- ❑   REXX
- ❑   Tcl
- ❑   PHP

There's also an ODBC driver for access on the Microsoft Windows platform, though there are also Linux ODBC drivers, so we can use that method on Linux as well.

> *At time of writing there are some potential security issues with ODBC, so it should not generally be your first choice of access method.*

In this chapter we will only look at the C interface, not because it is better than the others in any way, simply that C is the main focus of this book. The C programming interface to MySQL is very comprehensive, and similar in many ways to the `libpq` interface for PostgreSQL. However, there is no equivalent of the embedded SQL method of accessing data from C, which PostgreSQL offers with its `ecpg` command and library.

Connection Routines

There are two steps involved in connecting to a MySQL database from C:

- ❑   initializing a connection handle structure
- ❑   physically making the connection

To initialize a connection handle, we must use `mysql_init`:

```
MYSQL *mysql_init(MYSQL *);
```

Normally you pass NULL to the routine, and a pointer to a newly allocated connection handle structure is returned. If you pass an existing structure, it will be re-initialized. On error, NULL is returned.

MySQL actually provides two ways of connecting to the database, but `mysql_connect`, which you may see in older code, is deprecated, so we will not consider it here.

At this point, all we have done is allocate and initialize a structure; we have not yet provided any parameters to enable connection to a database. These parameters are set, and the actual connection made, with the `mysql_real_connect` routine:

```
MYSQL *mysql_real_connect(MYSQL *connection,
const char *server_host,
const char *sql_user_name,
const char *sql_password,
const char *db_name,
unsigned int port_number,
const char *unix_socket_name,
unsigned int flags);
```

The connection pointer must be a pointer to a structure that was earlier initialized with `mysql_init`. The `server_host` is the name, or IP address, of the server machine on which the MySQL server is running. If you want to connect to the local machine, you should use `localhost` rather than a machine name, as that allows MySQL to optimize the connection type.

`sql_user_name` and `sql_password` are login credentials to the database. If the login name is NULL then the current login ID is assumed. If the password is NULL, you will only be able to access data on the server that's accessible without a password. The password is encrypted before being sent across the network.

The port number and `unix_socket_name` should be 0 and NULL respectively, unless you have special reasons for needing non-standard values. They will default to appropriate values.

Finally, the flag parameter allows you to OR together some bit-pattern defines, allowing you to alter certain features of the protocol being used. The only two you're likely to need to use are:

❑ CLIENT_ODBC – this should be set if you know that ODBC is being used for the remote database.

❑ CLIENT_FOUND_ROWS – this is rather subtle, and to understand it we have to jump slightly ahead of ourselves.

You will remember from the chapters on PostgreSQL that you can determine the number of rows affected by INSERT, UPDATE and DELETE statements. For UPDATE statements, MySQL is subtly different to PostgreSQL (and most other mainstream databases).

When PostgreSQL returns the number of rows an UPDATE statement affected, what it actually returns is the number of rows in which the WHERE clause matched. For MySQL, the value is the number of rows changed, which might be slightly different.

Suppose we had a table with three children called Ann, one aged 3, one 4 and one 5. In PostgreSQL, a statement like:

```
UPDATE age SET age = 3 WHERE name = 'Ann'
```

would report 3 rows – the number of children with the name Ann. MySQL, on the other hand, would report 2 – the number of rows actually changed. By passing this flag to the connect routine, the default behavior is changed to be more like PostgreSQL, in that the number of rows matched is returned.

Other, less frequently used flags are documented in the manual.

If the connection fails, NULL is returned. To discover the underlying cause of the error, we can use mysql_error, which we will meet shortly.

To close the connection when you have finished with it (normally this would only be at the end of a program), you use mysql_close:

```
void mysql_close(MYSQL *connection);
```

This closes the connection down. If the connection structure was allocated by mysql_init (because you passed NULL when you called mysql_init originally), the structure is freed; the pointer is now invalid and must not be used again.

Closely associated with the connection routines (since it can only be called between mysql_init and mysql_real_connect) is mysql_options, a routine for setting options:

```
int mysql_options(MYSQL *connection, enum option_to_set,
                               const char *argument);
```

Since it can only set one option at a time, you have to call this routine as many times as you need, providing you only call it between mysql_init and mysql_real_connect. Some of the options take arguments that are not of type char; for these you will have to cast the value to const char *. There are several possible options, and we will look at the main three you may need to know. The full list is, as usual, included in the extensive online manual, the documentation that is normally installed with MySQL (in the /usr/doc directory), and the downloadable pdf format manual file.

enum option	Actual Argument Type	Meaning
MYSQL_OPT_ CONNECT_TIMEOUT	Const unsigned int *	The number of seconds to wait before timing out a connection.
MYSQL_OPT_COMPRESS	None, use NULL	Use compression on the network connection
MYSQL_INIT_COMMAND	Const char *	Command to send each time a connection is established

On success, zero is returned. Since all the routine is doing is setting flags in the connection handle structure, a failure means you used an invalid option.

To set the connection timeout to seven seconds, we would use a fragment of code such as this:

```
unsigned int timeout = 7;
...
connection = mysql_init(NULL);
ret = mysql_options(connection, MYSQL_OPT_CONNECT_TIMEOUT, (const char
*)&timeout);

if (ret) {
    /* Handle error */
    ...
}

connection = mysql_real_connect(connection …
```

Now we've seen the basics of setting up and closing a connection, let's write a short program, just to test it out.

This is connect1.c, which connects to a server on the local machine, as user `rick` with password `bar`, to the database called `rick`.

```c
#include <stdlib.h>
#include <stdio.h>

#include "mysql.h"

int main(int argc, char *argv[]) {
    MYSQL *conn_ptr;

    conn_ptr = mysql_init(NULL);
    if (!conn_ptr) {
        fprintf(stderr, "mysql_init failed\n");
        return EXIT_FAILURE;
    }

    conn_ptr = mysql_real_connect(conn_ptr, "localhost", "rick", "bar",
                                  "rick", 0, NULL, 0);

    if (conn_ptr) {
        printf("Connection success\n");
    } else {
        printf("Connection failed\n");
    }

    mysql_close(conn_ptr);

    return EXIT_SUCCESS;
}
```

Now we need to compile it. Depending on how you installed MySQL, you may need to add both the include path and a library path, as well as specifying that the file needs linking with the library module `mysqlclient`. On our install from RPMs, the required compile line is:

```
$ gcc -I/usr/include/mysql connect1.c -L/usr/lib/mysql -lmysqlclient -o connect1
```

When we run it, we simple get a message saying the connection succeeded.

```
$ ./connect1
Connection success
$
```

As you can see, getting a connection to a database is very easy.

Error Handling

Before we progress to more useful programs, we need to look at how MySQL manages errors. All errors are indicated by return codes, and the details reported via the connection handle structure. There are only two routines to know:

```
unsigned int mysql_errno(MYSQL *connection);
```

and

```
char *mysql_error(MYSQL *connection);
```

If a `mysql` function returns an integer code indicating an error – generally any non-zero value – you can retrieve the error code by calling `mysql_errno`, passing the connection structure. Zero is returned if the error code has not been set. This code is updated each time a call is made to the library. You can therefore only retrieve the error code for the last command you executed, with the exception of these two error routines, which do not cause the error code to be updated.

The return value is the error code, which you will either find defined in the `errmsg.h` include file, or in `mysqld_error.h`, both in the mysql-specific `include` directory. The former is for client type errors, such as losing a connection, and the latter for server type errors, such as passing an invalid command.

If you prefer a textual error message, then you can call `mysql_error`, which provides a meaningful text message instead. The message is in internal static space, so you need to copy it elsewhere if you want to save the error text.

If we add some basic error handling to our connection tester program, we can see how this works in practice. However, you may have noticed we are about to have a problem. If `mysql_real_connect` returns a `NULL` connection pointer when it fails, how do we get at the error code? The answer is to make the connection handle a variable; then we can still access it if `mysql_real_connect` fails.

Here is `connect2.c`, which illustrates both how we use the connection structure when it isn't dynamically allocated, and also shows how we might write some basic error handling code. The changes are highlighted:

```
#include <stdlib.h>
#include <stdio.h>

#include "mysql.h"

int main(int argc, char *argv[]) {
    MYSQL my_connection;

    mysql_init(&my_connection);
    if (mysql_real_connect(&my_connection, "localhost", "rick",
                                           "bar", "rick", 0, NULL, 0)) {
        printf("Connection success\n");
        mysql_close(&my_connection);
    } else {
        fprintf(stderr, "Connection failed\n");
        if (mysql_errno(&my_connection)) {
            fprintf(stderr, "Connection error %d: %s\n", mysql_errno(&my_connection),
mysql_error(&my_connection));
        }
    }

    return EXIT_SUCCESS;
}
```

We could in fact have solved our problem quite simply; we'd simply have to avoid overwriting our connection pointer with the return result if `mysql_real_connect` failed. Nevertheless, this serves our purposes as an illustration of the other way of using connection structures. If we force an error, perhaps by putting in an incorrect password, we will get an error code and error text, much as we would have seen from the interactive `mysql` tool.

Executing SQL Statements

Now we have a connection, and know how to handle errors, it's time to look at doing some real work with our database. The principal keyword for executing SQL statements of all types is `mysql_query`:

```
int mysql_query(MYSQL *connection, const char *query)
```

As you can see, there is very little to it. It takes a pointer to a connection structure and a text string containing the SQL to be executed; unlike the command line tool, no terminating semicolon should be used. On success, zero is returned. In the special case that you need to include binary data, you can use a related function, `mysql_real_query`. For the purposes of this chapter though, we only need to look at `mysql_query`.

SQL Statements That Return No Data

We will look first at UPDATE, DELETE and INSERT statements. Since they return no data from the database, they are easier to use.

The other important function that we will introduce here is a function to check the number of rows affected:

```
my_ulonglong mysql_affected_rows(MYSQL *connection);
```

Probably the most obvious thing about this function is the rather unusual return result. For portability reasons, this is a special unsigned type. For use in `printf`, you're recommended to cast to unsigned long, with a format specification of `%lu`. This function returns the number of rows affected by the previous UPDATE, INSERT or DELETE query executed using `mysql_query`.

Unusually for `mysql_` functions, a return code of zero indicates no rows affected; a positive number is the actual result, normally the number of affected rows.

As we mentioned earlier, there can be some 'unexpected' results when using `mysql_affected_rows`. Let's look first at the number of rows affected by INSERT statements, which do behave as expected. We add the following code to our `connect2.c` program, and call it `insert1.c`:

```
#include <stdlib.h>
#include <stdio.h>

#include "mysql.h"

int main(int argc, char *argv[]) {
    MYSQL my_connection;
    int res;

    mysql_init(&my_connection);
    if (mysql_real_connect(&my_connection, "localhost",
                           "rick", "bar", "rick", 0, NULL, 0)) {
        printf("Connection success\n");

        res = mysql_query(&my_connection, "INSERT INTO children(fname, age)
                                           VALUES('Ann', 3)");
        if (!res) {
            printf("Inserted %lu rows\n",
                        (unsigned long)mysql_affected_rows(&my_connection));
        } else {
            fprintf(stderr, "Insert error %d: %s\n", mysql_errno(&my_connection),
                                            mysql_error(&my_connection));
        }

        mysql_close(&my_connection);
    } else {
        fprintf(stderr, "Connection failed\n");
        if (mysql_errno(&my_connection)) {
        fprintf(stderr, "Connection error %d: %s\n",
                    mysql_errno(&my_connection), mysql_error(&my_connection));
        }
    }

    return EXIT_SUCCESS;
}
```

As expected, the number of rows inserted is one.

Now we change the code, so the 'insert' section is replaced with:

```
mysql_errno(&my_connection), mysql_error(&my_connection));
    }
  }

    res = mysql_query(&my_connection, "UPDATE children SET AGE = 4
                                       WHERE fname = 'Ann'");
    if (!res) {
       printf("Updated %lu rows\n",
                       (unsigned long)mysql_affected_rows(&my_connection));
    } else {
       fprintf(stderr, "Update error %d: %s\n", mysql_errno(&my_connection),
                                  mysql_error(&my_connection));
    }
```

and call it update1.c.

Now suppose our children table has data in it, like this:

```
+---------+--------+------+
| childno | fname  | age  |
+---------+--------+------+
|       1 | Jenny  |   14 |
|       2 | Andrew |   10 |
|       3 | Gavin  |    4 |
|       4 | Duncan |    2 |
|       5 | Emma   |    0 |
|       6 | Alex   |   11 |
|       7 | Adrian |    5 |
|       8 | Ann    |    3 |
|       9 | Ann    |    4 |
|      10 | Ann    |    3 |
|      11 | Ann    |    4 |
+---------+--------+------+
```

Where we execute update1, we would expect the number of rows affected to be reported as 4, but in practice the program reports 2, since it only had to change 2 rows, even though the WHERE clause identified 4 rows. If we want mysql_affected_rows to report the result as 4, which may be the result people familiar with other databases will expect, we need to remember to pass the CLIENT_FOUND_ROWS flag to mysql_real_connect, as in update2.c, like this:

```
    if (mysql_real_connect(&my_connection, "localhost",
                   "rick", "bar", "rick", 0, NULL, CLIENT_FOUND_ROWS)) {
```

If we reset the data in our database, then run the program with this modification, it reports the number of affected rows as 4.

The function mysql_affected_rows has one last oddity, which appears when we delete data from the database. If we delete data with a WHERE clause, then mysql_affected_rows returns the number of rows deleted, as we would expect. However, if there is no WHERE clause, and all rows are therefore deleted, the number of rows affected is reported as zero. This is because an optimization deletes the whole table for efficiency reasons. This behavior is not affected by the CLIENT_FOUND_ROWS option flag.

Statements That Return Data

It's now time to look at the most common use of SQL, the SELECT statement for retrieving data from a database.

> *MySQL also supports SHOW, DESCRIBE and EXPLAIN SQL statements for returning results, but we're not going to be considering these here. As usual, the manual contains explanations of these statements.*

You will remember from the PostgreSQL chapter that we could either retrieve the data from SQL SELECT statements in a PQexec, where all the data was fetched at once, or use a cursor, where we retrieved data from the database row by row, so that large data sets did not overload the network or client.

MySQL has almost exactly the same choice of retrieval methods, for exactly the same reasons, although it does not actually describe the row-by-row retrieval in terms of cursors. However what it does offer is an API with far fewer differences between the two methods, which will generally make it easier to swap between the two methods, should you ever need to.

Generally there are four stages in retrieving data from a MySQL database:

- ❑   issue the query
- ❑   retrieve the data
- ❑   process the data
- ❑   perform any tidy up required

We issue the query with mysql_query, as we did earlier. Retrieving the data is done with either mysql_store_result or mysql_use_result, depending on how we want the data retrieved, followed by a sequence of mysql_fetch_row calls to process the data. Finally we must call mysql_free_result to allow MySQL to perform any required tidying up.

Functions for all-at-once data retrieval

We can retrieve all the data from a SELECT (or other statement that returns data), in a single call, using mysql_store_result:

```
MYSQL_RES *mysql_store_result(MYSQL *connection);
```

This function must be called after a mysql_query has retrieved data, to store that data in a result set. This function retrieves all the data from the server and stores it in the client immediately. It returns a pointer to a structure that we haven't met before – a **result set structure**. A NULL is returned if the statement failed.

> **As with the PostgreSQL equivalent, be aware that returning a NULL means an error has occurred, and that this is different from no data being retrieved. Even if the returned value is not NULL, it does not mean there is data present to process.**

Providing NULL was not returned, you can then call mysql_num_rows and retrieve the number of rows actually returned, which may of course be zero.

```
my_ulonglong mysql_num_rows(MYSQL_RES *result);
```

This takes the result structure returned from mysql_store_result, and returns the number of rows in that result set, which may be zero. Providing mysql_store_result succeeded, mysql_num_rows will always succeed.

This combination of mysql_store_result and mysql_num_rows is an easy and intuitive way to retrieve data. Once mysql_store_result has returned successfully, all the query data has been stored on the client, and we know that we can retrieve it from the result structure without risk of further database or network errors occurring, since all the data is now local to our program. We also get to discover the number of rows returned immediately, which can make coding easier. As mentioned earlier, this sends all the results back to the client at once. For large result sets, this can consume enormous quantities of server, network and client resources. For these reasons, when working with larger data sets, it's often better to retrieve the data as we need it. We will see how to do this shortly, using the mysql_use_result function.

Once the data has been retrieved, we can retrieve it with mysql_fetch_row, and also jump around the result set with mysql_data_seek, mysql_row_seek, mysql_row_tell. Before we move on to retrieving the data in stages, let's have a look at these functions.

mysql_fetch_row

```
MYSQL_ROW mysql_fetch_row(MYSQL_RES *result);
```

This function takes the result structure we obtained from store result, and retrieves a single row from it, returning the data in a row structure that it allocates for you. When there is no more data, or an error occurs, NULL is returned. We will come back to processing the data in this row structure later.

mysql_data_seek

```
void mysql_data_seek(MYSQL_RES *result, my_ulonglong offset);
```

This function allows you to jump about in the result set, setting the row that will be returned by the next fetch row operation. The offset value is a row number, and must be in the range zero to one less than the number of rows in the result set. Passing zero will cause the first row to be returned on the next call to mysql_fetch_row.

mysql_row_tell, mysql_row_seek

```
MYSQL_ROW_OFFEST mysql_row_tell(MYSQL_RES *result);
```

This function returns an offset value, indicating the current position in the result set. It is not a row number, and you can't use it with mysql_data_seek. However you can use it with:

```
MYSQL_ROW_OFFSET mysql_row_seek(MYSQL_RES *result, MYSQL_ROW_OFFSET offset);
```

which moves the current position in the result set, and returns the previous position.

This pair of functions can sometimes be useful for jumping between known points in the result set. Be careful *never to mix up* the **offset value** used by row tell and row seek with the **row number** used by data_seek. These are not interchangeable, and your results will not be what you were hoping for.

mysql_free_result

There is one last function we need to know before we can use these new functions in anger, and that is mysql_free_result.

```
void mysql_free_result(MYSQL_RES *result);
```

When you've finished with a result set you **must always** call this function, to allow the MySQL library to tidy up the objects it has allocated.

Retrieving the data

We are now in a position to write our first program that retrieves data from the database. We're going to select the contents of all rows for which age is greater than 5. Unfortunately we don't know how to process this data yet, so all we can do it loop round retrieving it. This is select1.c:

```c
#include <stdlib.h>
#include <stdio.h>

#include "mysql.h"

MYSQL my_connection;
MYSQL_RES *res_ptr;
MYSQL_ROW sqlrow;

int main(int argc, char *argv[]) {
    int res;

    mysql_init(&my_connection);
    if (mysql_real_connect(&my_connection, "localhost", "rick",
                                           "bar", "rick", 0, NULL, 0)) {
    printf("Connection success\n");

    res = mysql_query(&my_connection, "SELECT childno, fname,
                                       age FROM children WHERE age > 5");

    if (res) {
        printf("SELECT error: %s\n", mysql_error(&my_connection));
    } else {
        res_ptr = mysql_store_result(&my_connection);
        if (res_ptr) {
          printf("Retrieved %lu rows\n", (unsigned long)mysql_num_rows(res_ptr));
          while ((sqlrow = mysql_fetch_row(res_ptr))) {
            printf("Fetched data...\n");
          }
          if (mysql_errno(&my_connection)) {
            fprintf(stderr, "Retrive error: %s\n", mysql_error(&my_connection));
          }
```

```
        }
        mysql_free_result(res_ptr);
    }
    mysql_close(&my_connection);

} else {
    fprintf(stderr, "Connection failed\n");
    if (mysql_errno(&my_connection)) {
        fprintf(stderr, "Connection error %d: %s\n",
                mysql_errno(&my_connection), mysql_error(&my_connection));
    }
}

return EXIT_SUCCESS;
}
```

The important section, where we retrieve a result set and loop through the retrieved data, is highlighted.

Retrieving the data one row at a time

To retrieve the data row by row, as we require it, rather than fetching it all at once and storing it in the client, we can replace the `mysql_store_result` call with `mysql_use_result`:

```
MYSQL_RES *mysql_use_result(MYSQL *connection);
```

This function also takes a connection object and returns a result set pointer, or NULL on error. Like `mysql_store_result`, this returns a pointer to a result set object; the crucial difference though, is that it hasn't actually retrieved any data into the result set when it returns, just initialized the result set ready to receive data.

> To actually retrieve the data you must call `mysql_fetch_row` repeatedly, as we did before, until all the data has been retrieved. If you fail to fetch all the data from a **use result** call, then subsequent data retrieval will be corrupted.

What if we use `mysql_use_result`? Although we have potentially a major benefit, in that we've minimized both the client and network resources being used, there's a tradeoff – we can't use functions `mysql_num_rows`, `mysql_data_seek`, `mysql_row_seek` and `mysql_row_tell` along with `mysql_use_result`. Actually that's not strictly true: `mysql_num_rows` can be called, but won't return the number of available rows until the last one has been retrieved with `mysql_fetch_result`. It's therefore not very useful.

We've also increased the latency between row requests, since each time we ask for the next row, it now has to be fetched across the network. Another problem is that we have left ourselves open to the possibility of the network connection failing before we have finished retrieving all the data; this will prevent us actually *accessing* that data, since it isn't stored locally any more.

However we still have some big benefits: we've smoothed our network traffic load, and significantly reduced a potentially very large storage overhead from the client. For larger data sets, the row-by-row fetch of `mysql_use_result` is almost always to be preferred.

Changing `select1.c` into `select2.c` (which will use the `mysql_use_result` method) is easy, so we just show the changed section here with changed lines highlighted:

```
if (res) {
    printf("SELECT error: %s\n", mysql_error(&my_connection));
} else {
    res_ptr = mysql_use_result(&my_connection);
    if (res_ptr) {
        while ((sqlrow = mysql_fetch_row(res_ptr))) {
            printf("Fetched data...\n");
        }
        if (mysql_errno(&my_connection)) {
            printf("Retrive error: %s\n", mysql_error(&my_connection));
        }
    }
    mysql_free_result(res_ptr);
}
```

Notice that we can no longer discover the number of rows retrieved immediately after obtaining a result. Furthermore, our earlier error-checking technique – using the fact that `mysql_errno(&my_connection)` would be zero unless an error occurred – made this change very easy to apply. If you write code using `mysql_store_result`, but think there's a chance that you'll need to go back and change to using `mysql_use_result`, you can make the change much easier by coding the original with this in mind, and code defensively by checking the return results from all functions.

Processing Returned Data

Retrieving the data is not of much use unless we can do something with it afterwards. Just like PostgreSQL, there are two types of data return:

❑   the actual information from the database that was retrieved

❑   data about the data, so called **metadata**

First let's see how we would recover and print the data out, before we worry about determining column names and other information about the data.

In newer versions of MySQL you can use the function `mysql_field_count`, which takes a connection object and returns the number of fields in the result set:

```
unsigned int mysql_field_count(MYSQL *connection);
```

This function can also be used in more generic processing, for example, to determine why a `mysql_store_result` call failed. If `mysql_store_result` returns NULL, but `mysql_field_count` returns a number greater than zero, you know there should have been some columns in the result set, but that there was an error retrieving them. On the other hand, if `mysql_field_count` returns zero, there were no columns to retrieve, and that will be why attempting to store the result has failed.

This is more likely to be used where the SQL statement is not known in advance, or where you wish to write a completely generic query processing module.

In code written for older versions of MySQL, you may see `mysql_num_fields` *being used. These could take either a connection structure or a result structure pointer and return the number of rows.*

In newer code you should generally use `mysql_field_count`, *unless you know that your code needs to execute on older versions of MySQL.*

If we simply want to get at the result information in an unformatted text format, then we now know enough to print out the data directly, using the MYSQL_ROW structure returned from mysql_fetch_row. We can add a very simple function, display_row, to our select2.c program, to print out the data.

Notice we have made the connection, result, and row information returned from `mysql_fetch_row` *all global, to simplify the example. In production code we would not recommend this.*

Here is our very simple routine for printing out the data:

```c
void display_row() {
    unsigned int field_count;

    field_count = 0;
    while (field_count < mysql_field_count(&my_connection)) {
        printf("%s ", sqlrow[field_count]);
        field_count++;
    }
    printf("\n");
}
```

Append it to select2.c, and add a declaration and a function call:

```c
void display_row();

int main(int argc, char *argv[]) {
    int res;

    mysql_init(&my_connection);
    if (mysql_real_connect(&my_connection, "localhost", "rick",
                                        "bar", "rick", 0, NULL, 0)) {
    printf("Connection success\n");

    res = mysql_query(&my_connection, "SELECT childno, fname,
                                    age FROM children WHERE age > 5");

    if (res) {
        printf("SELECT error: %s\n", mysql_error(&my_connection));
    } else {
        res_ptr = mysql_use_result(&my_connection);
        if (res_ptr) {
        while ((sqlrow = mysql_fetch_row(res_ptr))) {
            printf("Fetched data...\n");
            display_row();
        }
```

Now save the finished product as `select3.c`. Finally, compile and run `select3` as follows:

```
$ gcc -I/usr/include/mysql select3.c -L/usr/lib/mysql -lmysqlclient -o select3
$ ./select3
Connection success
Fetched data...
1 Jenny 14
Fetched data...
2 Andrew 10
Fetched data...
6 Alex 11
$
```

Well, that shows it's working, although the formatting is rather basic. We've also not taken account of possible NULL values in the result. If we wanted to display the output in a table, for example, we would need to obtain both the data, and information about the data, in a more structured form. So how do we do this?

Rather than use the row object (defined as a `char **`) that `mysql_fetch_row` returned directly, we can fetch the information, one field at a time, into a structure containing both data and **metadata** (data about the returned data). This is done with the `mysql_fetch_field` function:

```
MYSQL_FIELD *mysql_fetch_field(MYSQL_RES *result);
```

You need to call this repeatedly to step though the fields, one at a time. NULL is returned when there are no more fields to process. The pointer to the field structure returned can be used to access various information about the column, stored in the field structure. This is defined in `mysql.h`:

Field in **MYSQL_FIELD** structure	Meaning
`char *name;`	The name of the column, as a string.
`char *table;`	The name of the table from which the column came. This tends to be more useful where your select uses multiple tables. Beware that for calculated values, such as MAX will have an empty string for the table name.
`char *def;`	If you call the `mysql_list_fields` (which we are not covering here), then this will contain the default value of the column.
`enum enum_field_types type;`	Type of the column. See below.
`unsigned int length;`	The width of the column, as specified when the table was defined.
`unsigned int max_length;`	If you used `mysql_store_result` then this contains the longest actual column length found. It is not set if you used `mysql_use_result`.

Field in `MYSQL_FIELD` structure	Meaning
`unsigned int flags;`	Flags. These tell you about the definition of the column, not about the data actually found. The common flags have obvious meanings, and are: NOT_NULL_FLAG, PRI_KEY_FLAG, UNSIGNED_FLAG, AUTO_INCREMENT_FLAG, BINARY_FLAG. The full list can be found in the documentation.
`unsigned int decimals;`	The number of decimals, valid only numeric fields.

Column types are quite extensive. The full list can be found in `mysql_com.h`, and in the documentation. The common ones are:

❑   `FIELD_TYPE_DECIMAL`

❑   `FIELD_TYPE_LONG`

❑   `FIELD_TYPE_STRING`

❑   `FIELD_TYPE_VAR_STRING`

One particularly useful macro that is defined is `IS_NUM`, which returns true if the type of the field is numeric, like this:

```
if (IS_NUM(myslq_field_ptr->type)) printf("Numeric type field\n");
```

Before we update our program, we should mention one extra function:

```
MYSQL_FIELD_OFFSET mysql_field_seek(MYSQL_RES *result,
                                    MYSQL_FIELD_OFSET offset);
```

This allows us to override the current field number, which is internally incremented each time `mysql_fetch_field` is called, and by passing an offset of zero jump back to the first column in the result. The previous offset is returned.

We now know enough to update our select program, to show all the additional data that is available about a column. This would also enable us to produce a more stylish output, if we so desired.

This is `select4.c`; we print the whole file here, so you get a complete example to look at. Notice that it does not attempt an extensive analysis of the column types, it just demonstrates the principles required.

```
#include <stdlib.h>
#include <stdio.h>

#include "mysql.h"

MYSQL my_connection;
MYSQL_RES *res_ptr;
MYSQL_ROW sqlrow;
```

```
void display_header();
void display_row();


int main(int argc, char *argv[]) {
    int res;
    int first_row = 1;

    mysql_init(&my_connection);
    if (mysql_real_connect(&my_connection, "localhost", "rick",
                                       "bar", "rick", 0, NULL, 0)) {
        printf("Connection success\n");

        res = mysql_query(&my_connection, "SELECT childno, fname,
                                age FROM children WHERE age > 5");

        if (res) {
            fprintf(stderr, "SELECT error: %s\n", mysql_error(&my_connection));
        } else {
            res_ptr = mysql_use_result(&my_connection);
            if (res_ptr) {
                display_header();
                while ((sqlrow = mysql_fetch_row(res_ptr))) {
                    if (first_row) {
                        display_header();
                        first_row = 0;
                    }
                    display_row();
                }
                if (mysql_errno(&my_connection)) {
                 fprintf(stderr, "Retrive error: %s\n",
                                mysql_error(&my_connection));
                }
            }
            mysql_free_result(res_ptr);
        }
        mysql_close(&my_connection);
    } else {
        fprintf(stderr, "Connection failed\n");
        if (mysql_errno(&my_connection)) {
          fprintf(stderr, "Connection error %d: %s\n",
                                mysql_errno(&my_connection),
                                mysql_error(&my_connection));
        }
    }

    return EXIT_SUCCESS;
}


void display_header() {
    MYSQL_FIELD *field_ptr;

    printf("Column details:\n");
```

```
        while ((field_ptr = mysql_fetch_field(res_ptr)) != NULL) {
            printf("\t Name: %s\n", field_ptr->name);
            printf("\t Type: ");
            if (IS_NUM(field_ptr->type)) {
                printf("Numeric field\n");
            } else {
                switch(field_ptr->type) {
                    case FIELD_TYPE_VAR_STRING:
                        printf("VARCHAR\n");
                    break;
                    case FIELD_TYPE_LONG:
                        printf("LONG\n");
                    break;
                    default:
                        printf("Type is %d, check in mysql_com.h\n", field_ptr->type);
                } /* switch */
            } /* else */

            printf("\t Max width %d\n", field_ptr->length);
            if (field_ptr->flags & AUTO_INCREMENT_FLAG)
                printf("\t Auto increments\n");
            printf("\n");
        } /* while */
}


void display_row() {
    unsigned int field_count;

    field_count = 0;
    while (field_count < mysql_field_count(&my_connection)) {
        if (sqlrow[field_count]) printf("%s ", sqlrow[field_count]);
        else printf("NULL");
        field_count++;
    }
    printf("\n");
}
```

Where we compile and run this, the output we get is:

```
$ ./select4
Connection success
Column details:
        Name: childno
        Type: Numeric field
        Max width 11
        Auto increments

        Name: fname
        Type: VARCHAR
        Max width 30

        Name: age
        Type: Numeric field
        Max width 11
```

```
Column details:
1 Jenny 14
2 Andrew 10
6 Alex 11
$
```

It's not particularly stylish, but is at least informative.

There are other functions that allow you to retrieve arrays of fields, and jump between columns. Generally all you need is the routines shown here, the interested reader can find more information in the MySQL manual.

Miscellaneous Functions

There are a few API functions that do not fit into the categories we have covered so far, but are useful to know. Where possible you should do as much of your work on the database through the `mysql_query` interface. For example there is an API `mysql_create_db` for creating databases, however it's generally easier to use the `CREATE DATABASE` command in conjunction with `mysql_query`, since then you only need to know the SQL for creating a database, rather than a larger number of specialized API calls.

Additional API calls that you may find useful are:

`mysql_get_client_info`	`char *mysql_get_client_info(void);`
	Returns version information about the library that the client is using.
`mysql_get_host_info`	`char *mysql_get_host_info(MYSQL *connection);`
	Returns server connection information.
`mysql_get_server_info`	`char *mysql_get_server_info(MYSQL *connection);`
	Returns information about the server that we are currently connected to.
`mysql_info`	`char *mysql_info(MYSQL *connection);`
	Returns information about the most recently executed query, but only works for a few query types, generally `INSERT` and `UPDATE` statements. Otherwise returns `NULL`.
`mysql_select_db`	`int mysql_select_db(MYSQL *connection, const char *dbname);`
	Change the default database to the one given as a parameter, providing the user has appropriate permissions. On success zero is returned.
`mysql_shutdown`	`int mysql_shutdown(MYSQL *connection);`
	If you have appropriate permissions, shuts down the database server you are connected to. On success zero is returned.

Resources

The main resource for MySQL is quite simply the main web site at http://www.mysql.com

Books that you may wish to look at include: *MySQL*, by Paul DuBois, New Riders (*ISBN 0-7357-0921-1*) and *MySQL & mSQL*, by Randy Jay Yarger, George Reese and Tim King, O'Reilly & Associates (*ISBN 1-56592-434-7*).

Summary

In this chapter we have taken a brief look at MySQL. Although not as fully featured as PostgreSQL, it is nonetheless a very capable product, with a comprehensive C-based API.

We saw how to install and configure a basic MySQL database, some of the relevant utility commands, and then looked at the API for C, just one of the many programming languages that can access data in a MySQL database.

MySQL's main advantage over PostgreSQL is its performance. For read-only access, as is common on many web sites, MySQL is very fast indeed. Its main drawbacks are weaker support for standard SQL, and the lack of support for transactions.

Online discussion at http://www.p2p.wrox.com

6

Tackling Bugs

In this chapter we are going to take a look at some of the tools and techniques we can use to make our application robust. We will consider some of the errors that creep into our programs and what we can do to try to prevent them, find them quickly and remove them.

We will cover debug print statements, assertions, tracing functions and using a debugger.

Before we get on to the tools, such as the debuggers and special libraries, let's consider why it is that our programs don't always do what we want them to. Some of this may seem quite obvious, but one man's everyday observation is another man's blinding revelation. Hopefully you will glean some useful nuggets from the tips and techniques in this chapter.

Error Classes

Before we get started it is useful to consider classes of errors. We will keep it simple here by mentioning just two of the most common classes of error, faulty input and faulty programming.

The first class occurs when something out of the ordinary happens to our program. Perhaps the user of an image viewing application asks to view a database file and an error occurs because the file format is not as expected. The application should react gracefully to this and prompt to the user to re-select. This class of error can and should always be handled by the software.

The second class of errors occurs when the software is at fault. Perhaps, because the check for correct file format mentioned earlier is missing, the image viewer goes on to crash as a result of reading garbage data. Another example might be a financial calculator program that routinely calculates an incorrect repayment for a loan.

We shall see in the course of this chapter a number of techniques that can be used both to minimize the effect of the first class of error (user or environment error) and reduce the time it takes to track down the cause of the second (software error).

Reporting Errors

If you want to save yourself a lot of time and effort tracking down bugs in your programs there is one thing that you really ought to make a golden rule.

> **Always, always, check return results.**

It is all too easy for programmers to lapse into bad habits brought on by laziness or poor assumptions. To be fair, many books and courses skip over error handling so as not to clutter up an example program with unnecessary details. Once past the learning stage a professional programmer will want to do better. Whenever you use a function written by someone else it is up to you to make sure that you understand what that function does, what assumptions it makes about its arguments or environment and under what conditions it might fail. If you do not check that the function succeeded you will only store up trouble. Your program must be able to cope with errors that occur in functions that you call.

A simple example is found in the standard I/O library.

The fopen function opens a file for reading or writing or both. It returns a stream pointer that can be used in future read or write operations. If the file cannot be opened a NULL is returned. Just about anyone who uses fopen knows to check the return result or risk a program crash trying to read a file that does not exist.

Many programmers who use the fwrite function will be aware that the function may not write all of the data that you pass to it. When this happens it may or may not be an error. If your hard disk is full it's probably an error. If you are writing across a network or to a device driver it's possible that the write operation has succeeded in writing part of your data (perhaps just a single packet). It may be quite happy enough to accept more data at some later point in time, even immediately if it is simply writing packet by packet - you just have to call fwrite again with the remaining non-written data.

A program that is written to maximize the chance of discovering a genuine error as close as possible to the point at which it occurs will be coded in such a way that it deals with all three of the possible outcomes of calling fwrite. These are: success in writing all data, partial success in writing some of the data, or failure. It will also be in a position to handle any error in the most appropriate way.

Almost no program checks the return result from calling fclose.

Why is this?

Well, some say that fclose never returns an error in practice. Some say there is nothing you can do to retrieve the situation if there is an error closing a file. If your application depends on knowing that your data has been safely written away then you better had check that closing the file succeeded, or find some other way to determine that all is well with your data. (The functions fstat and fflush can be helpful in this case.)

It is possible that on a networked file system, or anywhere where writes are asynchronous that data buffering in the system may allow the final write to appear to succeed, the failure only being picked up when the buffers are flushed on closing the file. An example might be the case when exceeding a disk quota. An application sensitive to this may retain its data in memory and on failure try to write the data to a different location - at least giving the user a chance to rectify the situation. That must be better than failing silently, leaving corrupt information to lead to failures later, and a long, cold, trail back to the original culprit.

Many functions, especially in the standard C library, make use of the error variable, `errno`. This integer variable is set to one of a number of error codes when a function fails. The manual page is a good place to start when looking for information about return results and possible error conditions for functions you are using.

For example, the manual page for `fclose` reminds us that `fclose` may fail, and set the `errno` variable, for any of the reasons that `close` may fail. In turn, the manual page for `close` actually contains a warning that it is a serious, but common error to ignore the result of a close, especially when using the network file system NFS. We have been alerted to it only by considering return results.

Remember that just because your program today is only ever run writing to a hard disk, that's no guarantee that a user in the future won't find a new use for it running over a network.

Continuing our analysis we find that `fclose` might fail and set `errno` to values that include:

EBADF	stream pointer or underlying file descriptor is invalid
ENOSPC	no space left on device
EIO	a low-level I/O operation failed
EPIPE	the stream is connected to a pipe or socket that has closed

We can, and should, test the value of `errno` against any of these error values defined in `errno.h`. To help inform the user of the problem we have encountered we can use the library functions `strerror` to obtain a string describing the error or `perror` to print a message. `perror` writes to the standard error stream, `stderr`, text describing the last error encountered - the one that caused `errno` to be set.

Fastidiously checking return results helps keep errors from spreading – it is part of coding *defensively*. If a function you call returns an unexpected value, your function might use it and generate its own errors. This is sometimes called error propagation, or knock-on errors. If you take care to check the return result of every function you call, you can be sure that you will spot any error as soon as it occurs.

In your own functions it is a good idea to establish a method for dealing with errors and their propagation right from the start. Define a common set of error values that your functions can share. Make each function consistent in its use of the error values, and make the error values meaningful. Here is an example taken from the reference implementation of the DVD store application APIs:

```
/* Error definitions */
#define DVD_SUCCESS               0
#define DVD_ERR_NO_FILE          -1
#define DVD_ERR_BAD_TABLE        -2
#define DVD_ERR_NO_MEMBER_TABLE  -3
#define DVD_ERR_BAD_MEMBER_TABLE -4
#define DVD_ERR_BAD_TITLE_TABLE  -5
#define DVD_ERR_BAD_DISK_TABLE   -6
#define DVD_ERR_BAD_SEEK         -7
#define DVD_ERR_NULL_POINTER     -8
#define DVD_ERR_BAD_WRITE        -9
#define DVD_ERR_BAD_READ        -10
#define DVD_ERR_NOT_FOUND       -11
```

```
#define DVD_ERR_NO_MEMORY         -12
#define DVD_ERR_BAD_RENTAL_TABLE  -13
#define DVD_ERR_BAD_RESERVE_TABLE -14

static int file_set(FILE *file, long file_position, int size, void *data)
{
  if(fseek(file, file_position, SEEK_SET) != 0)
    return DVD_ERR_BAD_SEEK;

  if(fwrite(data, size, 1, file) != 1)
    return DVD_ERR_BAD_WRITE;

  return DVD_SUCCESS;
}
...
FILE *member_file;
...
int dvd_member_set(dvd_store_member *member_record_to_update)
{
  if(member_record_to_update == NULL)
    return DVD_ERR_NULL_POINTER;

  return
    file_set(member_file,
             sizeof(dvd_store_member) * (member_record_to_update -> member_id),
             sizeof(dvd_store_member),
             (void *) member_record_to_update);
}
```

All functions in the reference implementation return a status value. Any data that needs to be passed or returned is done through arguments and pointers. This is an important point. By reserving return results for success or error indications we separate the control and data flow. This is generally a good thing as we avoid 'special values', otherwise valid results that are used for special purposes. The design of some of the UNIX system is poor is this respect. Take getchar as an example. It returns the next character that can be read from the standard input. But the return result is not a char, it's an int. This is because it needs to have a special value, EOF, to indicate the end of file has been reached. EOF is defined as -1 so that it is outside the range of valid character values. So we end up with a function that confuses in its return type the data that it's returning and a status that would be used to control the flow of the program by way of a test for EOF.

In our example from the reference API implementation, the function member_set writes a structure to a flat file database. As with all other functions in this implementation it will return either DVD_SUCCESS if all is well or an error indication, in this case one of DVD_ERR_NULL_POINTER, DVD_ERR_BAD_SEEK or DVD_ERR_BAD_WRITE. It used a data structure passed to it as an argument. Notice that it is coded defensively. It checks first that the pointer it has been given is not NULL, although this is not really a strong enough test to be sure that it is valid - but that's another story. This is an example of a pre-condition test. We'll cover those in more detail shortly. If we have a NULL pointer we return with the result DVD_ERR_NULL_POINTER, otherwise we pass control to a helper function file_set.

Making a program detect and report errors in the functions it calls as soon as possible will help identify bugs. Making it robust to errors, taking appropriate action when things don't quite go to plan – like closing opened files when reads fail – will make the application a better one. Robust applications tend to live longer in the software community, and get used more widely than ever thought possible.

Detecting Software Errors

Even if we are careful to build our application correctly and meticulously record every change we make as we go along problems still occur. It is a fact of life that our applications have bugs in them. It is possible to find these bugs, errors or defects just by informally reading the source or by performing more formal code inspections. Very often they are only found when we come to use the program, either in testing before release, or when users find new ways of using the application that we didn't think of.

Sometimes these bugs can be difficult or time consuming to track down, but there are a few things that we can do before we get to the testing stage that will help squash those bugs quickly.

Most importantly we can adopt a coding style that will help with debugging. In this chapter we shall see why you should add debug support to your program and how to go about it. Adding debug messages and other functions that support debugging is much easier to do as you write the program than it is later on, usually when you are really busy trying to fix a nasty problem.

Once you have a well-structured application coded with debugging in mind, testing it and fixing it will be much easier. We will cover testing in more detail in a later chapter.

Types of Software Error

During the testing stage of application development we will discover bugs, mistakes that we have made somewhere along the line. These errors could have crept in at any stage.

The simplest error is a plain and simple coding error. Perhaps we misspelled something, used the wrong variable, or passed an incorrect parameter, or got the order of the statements in some function transposed. These coding errors are usually quite easy to fix, once you've found out where they are. If you've coded the application along the lines we mentioned earlier, that should be no problem. Some higher-level languages, especially those more strongly typed than C, can spot some of these issues at compile time.

Sometimes we make larger errors. It might turn out that we have misunderstood how some library works, or how to deal with some other system we need to communicate with. These design errors can be hard to put right. We may have to re-think how we are going to perform a certain task and we may have to re-write a portion of our application.

You can try to prevent design errors by making sure that you fully understand how your application is going to work. It is definitely worth spending some time writing down how your program is split into modules, what each module will do, and how it talks to other modules. Consider drawing some diagrams that show the relationships between modules and the data they use.

The worst kind of error is the specification error. This can happen if the purpose of the application is not understood or communicated accurately. Sometimes the customer does not make it clear what is wanted, or changes his or her mind. When this happens you can end up with a finished application that works, has been tested and debugged, but does not do what it should. In the worst case you might have to throw it away and start all over again. All this effort might have been saved if we spent longer talking to the end user, or thinking about what the application should do.

You can see that the effort that might be needed to fix each of these types of error increases sharply as development proceeds. It is estimated that you need about ten times more effort to fix a problem for each stage of development you go through before finding that you have an error.

The key to successful development is to try hard to get a good understanding of the requirements of the application, design it carefully and code in a way that helps debugging and testing. Studies show that errors will always crop up, possibly as many as 5 per 100 lines of code. If we take care we can make sure that they are mainly simple to fix.

So let's look at how to track down and avoid coding errors.

Debug Statements

To track down where a program is going wrong we need to be able to see what it is doing. Sometimes this might be very clear, if for example the bug is in some user interface screen we might see an incorrect display and immediately deduce the fault. Very often things are not so straightforward. If a spreadsheet calculates an incorrect value in the bottom right-hand corner of a complex worksheet we probably need to know more about the route the program has taken through its code, how exactly it reached the wrong result.

The simplest way of discovering where a program has been is to introduce debug statements in the code. There are a number of ways of doing this, and the best method will depend on the size and complexity of your program. For small programs a simple approach may work sufficiently well. Larger projects may need a sophisticated strategy for debugging information. Others again might fall between these two extremes. Here we will take a look at a range of options looking at the advantages and disadvantages of each.

The easiest way to introduce debug information is perhaps to use `fprintf` at key points in the code. For example:

```
fprintf(stderr, "calling important function with %d\n", arg);
result = important(arg);
fprintf(stderr, "important function returned %d\n", result);
```

This approach is clearly easy to do and may be a good choice for small programs, but it has some disadvantages. For a start we have no way of controlling it – we get it all the time.

When we run our program we get the debug messages mixed up with the normal program output, but we can redirect them independently of the normal output using a shell redirection:

```
$ ./prog 2>stderr.log   # send debug messages to the file stderr.log
```

This shell command runs the program, `prog`, redirecting any output it sends to `stderr` to the file `stderr.log`. This is not very convenient if we want to view the output as the program runs, but we can use

```
$ tail -f stderr.log
```

in another terminal session if we wish.

We can ignore the debug output if we need to by redirecting it to the 'bit bucket', /dev/null, which will just discard it.

```
$ ./prog 2>/dev/null
```

To control the debug output itself we can use conditionals. For reasons that will become apparent shortly when we look at assertions, we could reasonably choose only to produce debug information if the macro NDEBUG (for No Debug) is not set. Our debug statements would then look like this:

```
#ifndef NDEBUG
        fprintf(stderr, "calling important function\n");
#endif
```

This is perhaps rather cumbersome, and in fact has limitations. To turn debug information on and off we still need to recompile, although now we no longer have to edit the code. We just pass the flag -DNDEBUG (Define NDEBUG) to the C compiler when we compile any source file we want to disable debug information for. While this has the advantage of eliminating any overhead incurred by the additional debug statements themselves it means that the debug version and non-debug version of our program are different binaries. If our intention was to test with debug enabled and then distribute a binary package with no debug we run a risk because the tested program and the released one are different.

The NDEBUG flag is also a very coarse tool. We either get all debug information, or none at all. This might be all you need, but with a little thought we can do a little better. If we create a binary variable, say debug_level, we can use that to activate or deactivate debug information at run time.

```
        int debug_level = 0; /* Default to no debug */

...

if( arguments contain -d )
  debug_level = 1;

if(debug_level)
  fprintf(stderr, "calling important function\n");
```

Here we add code to process a debug argument to our program, -d is a good choice, and use its presence to set the debug_level variable to control the debug information. Now we can run the program normally and get no debug information and run it with a -d argument and get the debug information. One disadvantage to this approach is that we incur additional overhead in our program compared with the compile-time switched version. We have also allowed our users to turn on debugging information, which may not always be desirable.

Sometimes it is useful to create many different levels of debug information. We may decide that to begin with we need to know exactly what steps our program is taking. Later, as the program develops we might want to know less, perhaps just those occasions when something unexpected happens. Later again, when we have handled all the 'normal errors' we might want to know only about severe or fatal errors.

We can implement debug levels as an extension of our debug variable technique. We could allow the debug_level variable to be an integer variable – the higher it is set the more detail we require. We could allow the -d flag to take an argument to set the variable and then use this to decide whether or not to execute the debug statement.

```
        if(debug_level >= 3)
            fprintf(stderr, "some routine information\n");

        if(debug_level >= 1)
            fprintf(stderr,"some critical information\n");
```

It would be sensible to create some constants with meaningful names for the values of the debug_level variable to make the code more readable.

We could also consider the debug_level variable as a bit mask. For each type of debug information we want to be produced we define a bit in the debug bit mask, and each statement tests for its own bit to decide whether to execute or not. In this way, each module of a complex program can have its own, independently switched, debug information.

```
    #define DEBUG_UI      1   /* Debug information for user interface */
    #define DEBUG_DB      2   /* Debug information for the database */
    #define DEBUG_LOC     4   /* Debug information for program location */

      if(debug_level & DEBUG_DB)
          fprintf(stderr, "database opened with handle %d\n",...);

      if(debug_level & DEBUG_LOC)
          fprintf(stderr, "just entered function func\n");
```

Multiple levels of information make it very straightforward to separate any error messages your program might produce from additional statements meant solely to aid debugging, especially if your messages contain an indication of their level:

```
      if(debug_level & DEBUG_DB)
          fprintf(stderr, "DB: database open\n");
```

An alternative way of setting the debug level is to use the value of an environment variable. This is especially useful for programs that are started with no command line arguments, for example via a graphical user interface.

The C pre-processor has a number of facilities that can help with creating debug statements. A macro can be used to cut down on the repetition involved in testing debug variables:

```
    #define debug_db(x) {if(debug_level & DEBUG_DB)
                              fprintf(stderr, "DB: " ## x ## "\n");}

    ...

        debug_db("database opened");
```

The standard error will contain the line:

```
    DB: database opened
```

when this code is executed.

Note that the string concatenation operator (##) has been used to automatically prepend the correct debug level identifier to the message that is being logged. A debug statement macro can also make use of pre-processor defines that are available at compile time. These include the current file name and line number (__FILE__ and __LINE__ respectively).

```
#include <stdio.h>

#define debug_db(x)  if(debug_level & DEBUG_DB) { 
                           fprintf(stderr, "DB: " __FILE__ "(%d): ", __LINE__);
                           fprintf(stderr, x ## "\n");
                     }

#define DEBUG_DB 1

main()
{
  int debug_level = DEBUG_DB;

  debug_db("error message");
}
```

Here we use the file and line number information to add to the debug message being produced so that the standard error in this case would contain:

```
DB: debug.c(15): error message
```

If you are using the GNU C compiler, which is likely with almost all Linux distributions, you can also take advantage of a third location macro defined in the C pre-processor, __PRETTY_FUNCTION__, which expands to be the current function name. To keep things portable protect your use of this GNU-specific extension with #ifdefs.

Linux and UNIX support the idea of multiple levels of seriousness for messages with the syslog facility. This is a standard facility for adding messages to the system error log. It should be used very sparingly during development, as there is typically only one set of log files collecting log information for the entire computer system. However, it can be invaluable for recording fatal errors, like being unable to start, or abnormal termination. Check out the manual pages for syslog(3) and syslog.conf(5).

One trick that might come in handy when deciding how to handle debug information is to redirect the standard error within the program, rather than rely on a shell redirection. This can be useful if a shell script you'd rather not edit starts your program. If you execute

```
stderr = freopen("stderr.log", "w", stderr);
```

then the standard error will be redirected to the file stedrr.log from this point forward. You will need to check that the return result is not NULL in which case the freopen call failed. The log file will be created if it does not exist, and truncated to zero length if it does.

Assertions

You can extend the idea of error detection a stage further by adding statements to check pre- and post-conditions, and invariants in general. These are conditions that are assumed to be true when a function starts and when it finishes. For example, if a function you write expects a pointer that must never be NULL, add debug code to check this. The same goes for parameters that must be in a valid range. When your function is about to return a value that must be in a certain range, check that too.

The standard C library supports the concept of assertions. These are defined as conditions that are supposed to be true and describe the assumptions that have been made in the code. They are ideal for pre- and post-conditions for function parameters and return results. They are used to check for things that should never happen.

Let's take a look at a simple use of assertions.

If we were writing a square root function we might only wish to deal with positive arguments. We might document that our function must *only* be used with positive arguments. We assert that the argument *is* positive. The assert function in the C library allows us to implement this assertion in a straightforward way. Here is a program that does just that.

```c
#include <stdlib.h>
#include <assert.h>
#include <math.h>
#include <stdio.h>

double mysqrt(double x)
{
    /* Example use of an assertion */
    assert(x >= 0);
    return sqrt(x);
}

int main()
{
    double value = -1.0;
    printf("mysqrt returns %g\n", mysqrt(value));
    exit(EXIT_SUCCESS);
}
```

The function mysqrt must only be called with positive or zero arguments. The call to assert says that the expression x>=0 must always be true whenever this code is executed. If the test ever fails our program will immediately halt. The exact implementation of the assert function may vary from system to system, in the UNIX98 standard it is in fact a macro. Usually assert will print a message before ending the program with a call to abort. In our example in main we call mysqrt with a negative argument. Let's compile and run to see what happens.

```
$ gcc -o asserts asserts.c -lm
$ ./asserts

asserts: asserts.c:9: mysqrt: Assertion 'x >= 0' failed.
Aborted
```

You can see that the `assert` function has detected that our test has failed and printed a message. This is an assertion failure. The message `Aborted` has come from the shell reporting an abnormal termination of our program. If the assertion does not fail, in the case where we pass a positive value, the `assert` function does nothing (apart from evaluate the test expression).

While assertions can be useful when developing a program they are not at all user friendly after the application is released. Halting a program immediately a problem arises can cause considerable inconvenience to the user. We might leave behind a corrupt file or invalid data in a database. It is almost always better to try to allow the user to save his work before quitting. However, assertions do have their place, not least in documenting the assumptions made in the code. Assertions are disabled by defining the constant `NDEBUG` before including `assert.h`. This has the effect of redefining the assert function to do nothing. In this way we can leave assertions in the source code, enable them during development and test, and possibly disable them before release (if we have added sufficient error recovery).

Unlike most headers, `assert.h` is designed to be included multiple times, and `#define #undef` `NDEBUG` before its inclusion can turn off and on assertion checking.

A simple way to define the `NDEBUG` macro is on the compiler command line:

```
$ gcc -o asserts -DNDEBUG asserts.c -lm
$ ./asserts
mysqrt returns nan
$
```

Here we can see that the assertion had no effect, even though we know the test will have failed. The `sqrt` function is called with a negative argument and in turn returns an invalid result. In this case the special value NaN is used to mean 'Not a Number'. The `printf` function is called to display this invalid result and prints "nan".

Assertions are useful to police what might be described as a contract between a function and its caller. The function user has to promise to abide by the conditions set out in the assertions within the function. If an assertion is used on the function return result it has the effect of ensuring that the function in turn holds up its end of a bargain with respect to results.

Where Are You?

Copious amounts of debug information can be very useful, but also difficult to sift through, although adopting a consistent style of error message and a judicious application of `grep` can help.

Sometimes it is appropriate to limit the amount of information to certain key points, perhaps when an error occurs. In this case it may be helpful to know more about how it was that the error arose. We'd like to know the path the program took to reach this point. With full debug information enabled that is possible, but we can also implement a utility that will tell us where we are, without having to produce mounds of information.

The idea is a simple one. If we add some tracing functionality to our program and record it, we can print it out when we need it. Let's take a look at one possible implementation. As we write our program we are going to add a call to our trace function to each function. We will call one function when we enter and another when we leave. We will in fact use macros so that we can capture the filename and function name as before, but this time instead of printing them we will keep a record of them in a stack, removing them as our code returns. It's probably easier to see with an example. We want to write our code, like this:

```
int main()
{
   trace_in();
   function();
   trace_out();
}

void function()
{
   trace_in();
   ...
   if(error)
      trace_print();

   trace_out();
}
```

When an error occurs and we call `trace_print` we want to see output like this:

```
main.c: main in
main.c: function in
```

We can therefore see that we came to be in `function` via the call in `main`. This is effectively the same as a stack trace that we could get from a debugger if we ran the program under the debugger's control and set a break point at the place the error occurred. Here though, we do not have to use a debugger, or stop the program.

A simple implementation of the trace logging functionality might look like this:

```
#include <stdio.h>
#include <assert.h>
#include <signal.h>

void handle_signal(int sig)

{
  trace_print();
}

#define debug_db(x) if(debug & DEBUG_DB) {
                        fprintf(stderr, "DB: " __FILE__ "(%d): ", __LINE__);
                        fprintf(stderr, "in " __PRETTY_FUNCTION__ ": " ## x ##
"\n");
                    }

#define DEBUG_DB 1

int trace_idx = 0;
#define TRACE_STACK 100
char *trace_stack[TRACE_STACK];


#define stringify(x) str2(x)
```

```
#define str2(x) #x
#define trace_in()
{
  assert(trace_idx < TRACE_STACK);
  trace_stack[trace_idx++] = __FILE__ ":" stringify(__LINE__) ": "
__PRETTY_FUNCTION__ " in\n";
}

#define trace_out()
{
  trace_idx--;
}

trace_print()

{
  int idx = 0;
  while(idx < trace_idx)
    fprintf(stderr, trace_stack[idx++]);
}
```

We allow space in a stack for 100 entries, after which the program will abort with an assertion failure. This level of stack depth should be sufficient for most programs. If the stack is exceeded it will probably be an indication that the program is stuck in a recursive loop, or that there is a route out of a function that does not include a call to trace_out. In fact, to help detect the loop it might be even better to print out the stack before aborting!

An alternative implementation might choose to record the last 100 trace_in records, rather than use a simple stack. This would give a trace that listed the most recent functions entered.

Finally for this section we can consider ways of making our errant program give up its secrets without having to decide in advance what we want to know. If we arrange to catch a signal in our program we can use it to get the program to tell us where it is. This can be an extremely useful technique for debugging programs that have long computations that you suspect may be 'stuck'. You can send a signal to probe for status information, such as the trace_print that we just looked at.

A reasonable signal to choose for status information would be one of the user-defined signals, either SIGUSR1 or SIGUSR2. To do this we just add the following code to our application:

```
#include <signal.h>

void handle_signal(int sig)
{
  trace_print();
}

main()
{
  struct sigaction act;
  act.sa_handler = handle_signal;
  sigemptyset(&act.sa_mask);
  act.sa_flags = 0;
  sigaction(SIGUSR1, &act, 0);
  ...
}
```

Now if we want to find out where our program is at whilst it is busy, we can send it a signal and it'll dutifully report its whereabouts.

```
$ ./debug &
[1] 1835
$ kill -USR1 1835
debug.c: main in
debug.c: function in
```

Using signals bring it's own complications. You must make sure that you are prepared to handle the consequences of the interrupt occurring. Specifically if your program is interrupted while executing one of many system calls you will see the call fail, probably setting the error variable, errno, to the value EINTR or possibly EAGAIN. This error value is used to indicate that a system call was interrupted and that the program should reissue the call. As long as you are careful to check return results and act on them accordingly all will be well.

Generally speaking it is best to keep the amount of processing you perform using interrupt handlers to a minimum, if possible limiting them to setting a global variable that can be tested in the main program code. If you are trying to locate a hard to find bug though, this technique can be very useful.

There are many alternatives for handling debug output that we do not have space to cover here. One such is to write debug output to a socket connection that can be received by another process created for the purpose. One advantage of this approach is that you can use the fact that 'writes to sockets' will fail if there is no process listening and this might be one way to eliminate unwanted output.

Backtrace

For Linux users prepared to give up some flexibility and portability there is an alternative way to obtain information about a program's whereabouts. The GNU C library now contains a number of functions that allow a program to probe its own executable file as it is running. These functions are available in GLIBC 2.1 or later and require a Linux kernel version of 2.2 or later and best results are obtained if you are using the GNU C compiler version 2.95.1 or later. Other UNIX platforms have similar facilities, although they are often highly compiler specific and not well documented, if at all. Our trace functions developed earlier will work on a wider range of system versions, including most UNIX systems.

The functions are declared like this:

```
#include <execinfo.h>

int backtrace(void **array, int size);
char **backtrace_symbols(void **array, int count);
void backtrace_symbols_fd(void **array, int count, int fd);
```

The function backtrace stores up to count return addresses from the program stack into the given array. These addresses represent the point in the program that the last function was called, and where that function was called from and so on all the way back to main. In fact, to where main is called from the C library startup code. The backtrace function returns the number of addresses actually written into array.

To translate the raw addresses returned by backtrace into program locations we use one of the symbol functions. The function backtrace_symbols returns an array of strings describing the locations given by the addresses in the array. The count parameter must be the number of valid addresses, as returned by backtrace. The array of strings is held in memory allocated by malloc, and therefore should be deallocated by a call to free.

The function `backtrace_symbols_fd` writes the strings directly to an open file and avoids the use of `malloc` altogether. The `fd` parameter must be a file descriptor for a file open for writing.

Here is the layout of an example program using `backtrace`.

```
/* backtrace.c */

#include <stdio.h>
#include <execinfo.h>

/*
 Example program to illustrate the use of backtrace
*/

void dumptrace()
{
#define maxdepth 10
  static void *addresses[maxdepth];
  int naddresses = backtrace(addresses, maxdepth);
  char **names = backtrace_symbols(addresses, naddresses);
  int i = 0;
  for(i; i < naddresses; i++)
    fprintf(stderr, "%d: %s\n", i, names[i]);
  free(names);
}

func3()
{
  dumptrace();
}

func2()
{
  func3();
}

func1()
{
  func2();
}

int main()
{
  func1();
}
```

The program simply illustrates the use of `backtrace` called from inside a small number of nested function calls. The output reflects the stack frames at the time `backtrace` is called.

The output from this program will vary according to the versions of the kernel, compiler and libraries as mentioned earlier. At the time of writing, `backtrace` information is only provided for locations in shared objects. So, to get meaningful information we must build our application using a shared object for our code. This is quite simple – we just need an extra link step, like this:

```
$ gcc -c backtrace.c
$ ld -shared -o backtrace.so backtrace.o
$ gcc -o backtrace backtrace.so
```

Now when we run the program `backtrace` it will dynamically link to our shared object `backtrace.so` that contains all of our code. We just need to make sure that the dynamic loader can locate it. The easiest way is to set the environment variable `LD_LIBRARY_PATH` to include the current directory when we run our program.

```
$ LD_LIBRARY_PATH=. ./backtrace
0: ./backtrace.so(dumptrace+0x12) [0x40015322]
1: ./backtrace.so (func3+0x8) [0x400153a8]
2: ./backtrace.so (func2+0x8) [0x400153b8]
3: ./backtrace.so (func1+0x8) [0x400153c8]
4: ./backtrace.so (main+0x8) [0x400153d8]
5: /lib/libc.so.6(__libc_start_main+0x103) [0x4003b313]
6: [0x8048411]
```

Preparing to Debug

Debugging and testing really go hand in hand. A productive testing session will reveal that an application has problems, or defects, that have to be fixed. That's only the start.

Bugs have a nasty habit of being tricky to track down. Sometimes they appear to come and go, or only appear in odd places.

The next thing we have to do is stabilization. That is, make the bug appear every time we run a particular test. To do this we have to experiment and try to work out what operations make the bug appear. We could try different data, different order of operation, or a combination. Once we have developed a test that reliably fails, then we can track down the bug.

Determining exactly why a program is not functioning as it should requires a scientific approach to be most effective. Debugging is about collecting information, forming a theory about what is happening, and then testing the theory by making changes.

It is sensible to make sure that you have looked at all of the data you have available before reaching for a debugger program. It is best to locate your problem first, if you can. Finding out exactly where the bug is hiding is called localization. Here's where we can use our debug statements to find out what is going on and where.

A debugger program comes into its own when theories about a program are hard to form, maybe the flow of control is unknown, or the application crashes and dumps core. If you have a suspect function, you can use a debugger to go right to it. We can use a debugger program to run the application, stopping at various places to see exactly what is going on and try out fixes.

Using the Debugger

Once we are on the trail of a bug and decide to use a debugger there is one additional step we can take to make life easier.

When a compiled program is running, it is separated from its source code – it's now just a set of CPU instructions. If we want to be able to control the application and view the data it's using we need to prepare a special version.

With just about any C compiler you can compile and link your application with the –g flag. This tells the compiler to include extra information in the object files that will allow the debugger to relate processor instructions to the source code. We will be able to tell the debugger to stop the application at a particular line of code and the debugger will know the exact instruction to stop the program.

There is a lesson lurking in the paragraph above. Note that we can tell the debugger to stop a program at a particular line of code. This can be a problem. If the line of code is a very complex one we will not easily be able to execute it piece by piece in the debugger. There are ways of stepping through code right down to the machine code level, but it is easier if we keep all our code statements simple and on a line by themselves. It is then easier to step through. In the same vein the compiler does not produce line number information for pre-processor macros. If your macro contains code, even if it is split over multiple lines, at the place where it is expanded it appears as if on a single line. It is a good idea to keep macros that contain code as simple as possible, or avoid them altogether.

There are a number of good debuggers available for Linux. A personal favorite of the authors is the GNU debugger, GDB. This debugger has been available since the early days of the GNU project and can be used in a number of different ways. It is a command line program, although graphical front ends like xxgdb and DDD have been written. Here is the KDE equivalent, Kdbg:

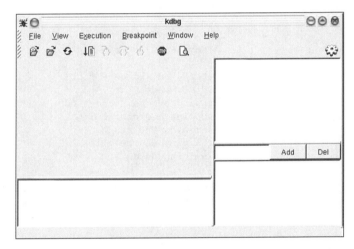

GDB can be run inside an Emacs session. Both the traditional GNU Emacs and the graphical XEmacs support a GDB mode that allow you to view your source code and a debug session at the same time. GDB can even attach itself to a program that is already running, as we shall see.

Simple GDB Commands

Using GDB is reasonably simple. You run GDB on the debug version of your application. GDB is used to start the program with the run command.

If you need to stop execution at a specific place you can set breakpoints with the break command.

When the program is stopped you can continue the program line-by-line with the step command, or function-by-function with the next command. You can examine variables with the print command.

You can let the program carry on to the next breakpoint with the cont (for Continue) command.

Other commands let you see the source code being executed (the `list` command) and how the application got to that point (the `backtrace` command).

There is a tutorial on the use of GDB in the companion volume to this book – *Beginning Linux Programming* (also from Wrox Press) or you can read the GDB manual on-line with the `info` command:

```
$ info gdb
File: gdb.info,  Node: Top,  Next: Summary,  Prev: (dir),  Up: (dir)

Debugging with GDB
******************

    This file describes GDB, the GNU symbolic debugger.

    This is the Seventh Edition, February 1999, for GDB Version 4.18.

    Copyright (C) 1988-1999 Free Software Foundation, Inc.

* Menu:

* Summary::                     Summary of GDB

* Sample Session::              A sample GDB session

* Invocation::                  Getting in and out of GDB
* Commands::                    GDB commands
* Running::                     Running programs under GDB
* Stopping::                    Stopping and continuing
* Stack::                       Examining the stack
* Source::                      Examining source files
* Data::                        Examining data
```

All we really want to cover here is the GDB trick we alluded to earlier, that of attaching to a program that is already running. Here is the full code of the debug sample tracing program we have been developing so far.

```c
#include <stdio.h>
#include <assert.h>
#include <signal.h>

void handle_signal(int sig)

{
  trace_print();
}

#define debug_db(x) if(debug & DEBUG_DB) {
                      fprintf(stderr, "DB: " __FILE__ "(%d): ", __LINE__);
                      fprintf(stderr, "in " __PRETTY_FUNCTION__ ": " ## x ##
"\n");
                    }

#define DEBUG_DB 1
```

```
int trace_idx = 0;
#define TRACE_STACK 100
char *trace_stack[TRACE_STACK];


#define stringify(x) str2(x)

#define str2(x) #x
#define trace_in()
{
  assert(trace_idx < TRACE_STACK);
  trace_stack[trace_idx++] = __FILE__ ":" stringify(__LINE__) ": "
__PRETTY_FUNCTION__ " in\n";
}

#define trace_out()
{
  trace_idx--;
}

trace_print()
{
  int idx = 0;
  while(idx < trace_idx)
    fprintf(stderr, trace_stack[idx++]);
}

main()
{
  int debug = DEBUG_DB;
  (void) signal(SIGUSR1, handle_signal);
  trace_in();
  function();
  /* stderr = freopen("stderr.log", "w", stderr); */
  /* debug_db("error message"); */
  trace_out();

}

function()
{

  int snooze = 30;

  trace_in();

  while(snooze)

    snooze = sleep(snooze);

  trace_out();
}
```

The function `function` is intended to simulate a long and complex calculation. You can see that it just in fact sleeps for 30 seconds. Notice that the call to `sleep` is in a loop. This is because `sleep` will return if it is interrupted. The return value from `sleep` is the number of seconds left to sleep. We can run this program and send it signals as before, or we can stop it in its tracks with GDB and probe its state.

Let's compile the program ready for debugging, and then start it running in the background.

```
$ gcc -o debug -g debug.c
$ ./debug &
[1] 1943
```

We will now start up GDB with the intention of finding out what is happening with our program, now running as process 1943. (If you try this you will need to use the process number reported by the shell.)

```
$ gdb
GNU gdb 4.18
Copyright 1998 Free Software Foundation, Inc.
GDB is free software, covered by the GNU General Public License, and you are
welcome to change it and/or distribute copies of it under certain conditions.
Type "show copying" to see the conditions.
There is absolutely no warranty for GDB.  Type "show warranty" for details.
This GDB was configured as "i386-suse-linux-gnu".
(gdb) file debug
Reading symbols from debug...done.
```

We start up GDB and tell it that the application we are going to debug is `debug`. We do this with the `file` command. GDB then reads the debug information from the copy of the executable that we have in the current directory. Now we can attach to the running program, which will immediately halt, just as if it had hit a breakpoint.

```
(gdb) attach 1943
Attaching to program: /home/neil/PLiP/chapter06/debug, Pid 1943
Reading symbols from /lib/libc.so.6...done.
Reading symbols from /lib/ld-linux.so.2...done.
0x400b5621 in __libc_nanosleep () from /lib/libc.so.6
(gdb) where
#0  0x400b5621 in __libc_nanosleep () from /lib/libc.so.6
#1  0x400b559d in __sleep (seconds=30) at ../sysdeps/unix/sysv/linux/sleep.c:78
#2  0x8048609 in function () at debug.c:58
#3  0x8048585 in main () at debug.c:45
```

Here we have used the `where` command in GDB to find out exactly where the program has got to. We can see from the stack trace that we are in the function `function` called from `main`. We actually interrupted the program while in a function used by `sleep` to do its work. The exact format of this stack trace beyond `function` will vary from system to system and by library version.

To allow the program to proceed we can use the usual breakpoint and continue functions in GDB if we wish. When we are done, we can allow our program to continue once more on its own by using the `detach` command. This releases the captive process that then continues as before.

```
(gdb) detach
Detaching from program: /home/neil/PLiP/chapter06/debug, Pid 1943
(gdb) quit
$
```

Other GDB Features

You can run GDB and other debuggers on a program after it has crashed, if it has dumped core. This will allow you to examine the contents of global data structures at the time the application died. To do this run GDB with the command:

```
$ gdb application core
```

Within a GDB session you can call any function contained within your application or libraries you have used. Just use the `call` command with a valid C function call as argument.

```
(gdb) call printf("hello\n")
hello
$2 = 5
(gdb) call dumptrace()
0: ./backtrace.so(dumptrace+0x12) [0x40015322]
...
```

GDB will allow you to set watchpoints, a type of breakpoint that only triggers when the value of an expression changes. This will slow down execution, but can be a lifesaver. Check out the GDB manual or on-line help for more details.

Resources

There are many other tools, tricks and tips used by experienced programmers that we don't have the space to cover in any detail here. Here are a few suggestions that we have found useful.

The `strace` utility prints all of the system calls that a program makes as it runs. It can also record the signals that the application receives. This can be especially useful tracking down problems with files, since all of the low-level open, read and write calls are shown. Other UNIX-like systems have similar tools - the BSD-based systems have `ktrace`, Solaris has `truss` and `sotruss`.

It is possible to replace a library function with one of your own devising – perhaps that logs more information about its operation. This is often done with the memory allocation routines, `malloc` and friends. There are many replacement implementations available that help to track down memory problems. Some of these are covered in Chapter 11.

On Linux you have access to the source code, so you can even build your own version of the complete C library if you wish!

If your application can run over a network, doing so with a network traffic 'sniffer' running can be useful. Programs such as `tcpdump` log the packets that are crossing the network, and can be configured to record just one particular type of exchange.

Using telnet on the appropriate port can often access applications such as web servers that listen for network connections on a TCP port. This approach may allow you to check out server functionality independently of a client application.

Performance tools like `top` and system administration tools like `lsof` can provide a viewport into what a process is up to. Don't forget `ps` too! It can show how much memory a process is using; very helpful.

If a program exists in different versions, try them out. This can often be a clue.

Running a buggy application on a different machine can help. Perhaps run on an Alpha for a 64 bit system or a SPARC or PA-RISC machine for a big-endian machine. If a libc problem is suspected try the application on a commercial UNIX system, or a BSD-based system and compare.

Finally, once a bug is found, add a test for it to the regression suite for the application, so that it doesn't come back! Do the same thing with OS bugs. Finding bugs your vendor has re-introduced (even if your vendor is Open Source) is very painful.

If a program is behaving oddly and you've no idea at all, try a different optimization level or a different compiler. Compiler bugs are rare – this is not the first thing to try – but they do happen, and your boss won't be impressed that they are rare, he or she will just ask how you are going to get back on schedule!

Summary

In this chapter we have looked at the different types of error your application has to contend with. It has to deal with problems that arise in the environment it finds itself in, and it has to help you to track down errors made in its construction.

We have looked at ways of making programs robust to run-time errors by checking return results and error values.

We saw ways of providing information to help track down bugs, including debug statements, location reporting and stack traces. We also took a quick look at some features in the C library that can help with error reporting and tracing.

We finished up by considering how to employ a debugger to home in on elusive bugs.

Online discussion at http://www.p2p.wrox.com

7

LDAP Directory Services

What is a Directory Service?

For larger organizations, there are significant benefits in having a centralized service for employee data, logon authorization, looking up phone numbers and e-mail address, determining user groups and printer rights, and many similar tasks. Organizations are starting to turn to directory servers to act as a central point of access for information in the organization, and increasingly to LDAP based servers.

In this chapter we will:

- ❑ outline the strengths and weakness of LDAP
- ❑ go through basic installation and configuration
- ❑ introduce the LDAP schema definition
- ❑ use the LDAP C API to query and manipulate data from the server

Directory services themselves are not new. Many Linux and UNIX users will be familiar with NIS (the facility originally known as 'yellow pages') that Sun invented to provide network-wide account management on UNIX flavor machines, allowing a single point of logon and administration for user accounts. Similar centralized administration facilities exist for Novell networks, and Microsoft NT domain administration. Unfortunately all of these solutions are somewhat vendor specific, and in the heterogeneous environment that is today's network, none of these can provide a simple solution across an organization of any size or complexity. What is needed is a server that can look up generally useful things; such as addresses, logins, e-mail addresses, and validate logins for many heterogeneous systems across the enterprise, from a central location, using a standardized open protocol.

At first sight, a directory server seems much like a database server. They both hold data, and they both let you ask questions which result in data being returned. You might reasonably ask why anyone would bother with a directory server, when they could simply use a database. Getting further into directory services, one thought that occurs to most database experts is that directory servers are actually less flexible than databases. Many directory servers actually use more conventional relational or other databases as part of their implementation. So a reasonable opening question for the chapter is: 'Why use a directory server in the first place?'

The answers are speed, more speed, redundancy and standardization of the protocol. Directory servers are blindingly fast at processing searches, because unlike general-purpose databases, they are heavily optimized to solve a very specific problem – fast searching over a network. Directory servers are also normally replicated, with two or more servers seamlessly providing service even in the event of a failure of any single server. One of the authors once worked with a large directory server that stored the profiles of tens of thousands of staff, their computers, departments and many other details. It was a huge amount of data, and yet the directory server could answer queries, even very complex ones, almost instantaneously.

The other benefit, standardization, is perhaps less immediately apparent, since for databases SQL is already a well-established standard. However, there is no standard way of storing data beyond the basic data types. SQL for retrieving data about people, for example, will depend on exactly how the database designer arranges the table and column names. In addition the protocol that the SQL server uses for clients to access them is not standardized, so, for example, a Sybase client cannot talk to an Oracle database. With a directory server, much of this storage dependency is hidden away, and what is presented is a standard way of asking for data, and a standard format for receiving the answer, with standard object types, such as people, having a well-defined standard set of base attributes. The protocol is also standardized, so you should be able to mix and match your servers and clients using the combination that suits you.

X.500 and LDAP

The solution to this rather confusing mix was intended to be a directory service designed by the ITU (International Telecommunications Union) called X.500. This was to be a universal solution for directory services, with multiple servers around the world collaborating to provide different branches of a universal directory tree; a very ambitious idea indeed.

Unfortunately, there were three big problems with X.500. Firstly, it was designed to use OSI protocols, which were one of those great networking ideas that never happened. This was largely because TCP/IP was already well established, supported on a wide variety of machines, and was, perhaps decisively, the protocol of the Internet. Secondly, X.500 is complicated. It is hard to implement and X.500 servers are hard to manage. At the time it was proposed, it required (for the time) serious computing resources to support an X.500 server. The final problem with OSI protocols is that it would cost people money just to *see* the specification, a very different approach from the Internet RFCs, with their very open approach to standards.

To get around the first of these problems, a protocol called LDAP (Lightweight Directory Access Protocol) was invented at the University of Michigan, which allowed X.500 servers to be accessed over TCP/IP protocols. This opened up the accessibility of X.500 servers to smaller machines on a TCP/IP network. It also hid the complexities of X.500, making implementation of the client much easier. LDAP very successfully addressed the client end of the directory service problem, and in a sense the server end too. The implementation details of the server are completely hidden by the LDAP protocol, so it doesn't actually matter if the server supports X.500 or not – all that matters is that the LDAP protocol is supported.

LDAP is specified in RFC 1777 (v.2 of the protocol) and more recently in RFC 2252 (see also the *Resources* section at the end of the chapter), which specifies v.3 of the protocol. This specification has widespread vendor support, including SUN, Microsoft, Netscape and Novell. There is no licensing cost; anyone is free to read the specifications and develop their own implementation. Perhaps just as importantly, the University of Michigan released a free reference implementation, which allowed others to see how such servers could be built.

The mantle of a free LDAP-based server has now passed to the OpenLDAP group, at http://www.openldap.org, who are now making an excellent attempt at doing for LDAP what Apache did for web servers – providing a high quality, free, open source solution for everyone.

Structure of a Directory Server

Data in an LDAP directory server is laid out in a tree structure. The root is the starting point for all data held in the tree. However, LDAP servers often support a 'referral' service, where requests that are outside the scope of the tree on the local server can be referred to another server.

Let's consider a company. It must be registered in a country, along with other companies in that country. It probably has some departmental structure, perhaps an architecture department, a development department, and almost certainly an accounts department. These departments may be sub-divided, for example development might have separate divisions for communications and applications. Suppose we have a (mythical as far as we know) company called Stixen. We can easily draw this as a tree:

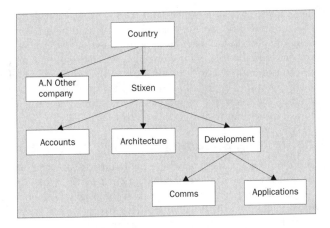

This is almost exactly how a company would be represented in an LDAP directory.

There is, however, a slight problem. The initial X.500 idea was to have the top level of each tree a country, and inside the country was a group of unique organizations. The problem with this has turned out to be ensuring absolute uniqueness of names. More recently, as the Internet expanded, an alternative scheme became popular, which used Internet domain names to designate uniqueness. After all, an Internet domain name is already guaranteed to be unique, so it's an easy starting point. To make life even more complex, there are two ways of using an Internet domain name in an LDAP directory, as we shall see in a moment.

The Naming of Parts...

The easiest way to think about the nodes of an LDAP tree is as objects. Each object in an LDAP directory has to have a unique name. In LDAP parlance, this is called a 'Distinguished Name', or dn. (Note that although an acronym, it is normally written in lowercase.) The dn of any component of an LDAP tree is made up of the unique attributes of all the objects above it in the tree, plus an additional attribute of its own. Each of these separate components is called a Relative Distinguished Name, or rdn. Consequently no two objects at the same level in the tree can have the same rdn. For our company the rdn is o=Stixen, since that is the organization name. The country is defined using a two character country code, notionally the ISO 3166 country code, though the United Kingdom, tends to be uk, rather than the ISO code gb, since that's the Internet domain it uses. In an LDAP directory the dn for the UK is shown as c=uk. The company in the country, notionally Stixen, is an organization, so is identified with o=Stixen. Putting these two together, gives not only a path to the company object, but also its dn: 'o=Stixen, c=uk'.

Don't worry about the magic strings c= and o= parts for now, we will come back to them shortly.

dn Naming

The precise method of generating dns is not currently standardized. There are three common ways which we describe below. The names are not official names for the naming schemes, but they do give us a convenient way to refer to them.

X.500 Naming Scheme

The original X.500 scheme is the easiest to understand, and is exactly as we have shown above. We simply paste together the country code and the company name, and bingo, we have a dn. Unfortunately, as we mentioned earlier, determining uniqueness of a company name is not always a trivial task in some countries, and the issue of trademarks, which are often similar, but different, to company names is also a consideration. For example, companies with very similar names, Such as 'Olympic Motorcycles' and 'Olympic Office Supplies' might want to use the same organization, o=Olympic. An added complication is that in some countries (until recently, including Australia) business names do not have to be unique across the country.

X.500 with Domains Naming Scheme

This is a slight variation on the original scheme, where the company, or organization, name, the o= part, is simply replaced with the domain name of the company. In our case this would give a dn of 'o=stixen.co.uk, c=uk'. This has the advantage over the original scheme that determining uniqueness of an Internet domain name is trivially easy. However it's a bit 'unclean' in that the country now appears to be encoded twice; we can see from the o= part that the company must be a UK company, although the trend for companies to register as a .com, even if not based in the US, confuses the issue somewhat. It also causes problems in determining which LDAP server should hold the master entry for that company; one in the country where it's based, or one in the US where its domain entry is held?

Domain Component Naming Scheme

An alternative scheme is also used, where the country code part is omitted, and the domain name broken down into components. In this scheme, the company domain, stixen.co.uk, is considered to consist of an ordered set of Domain Component (dc) parts, so the dn would be 'dc=stixen, dc=co, dc=uk'.

In this chapter we will use what we have termed the 'X.500 with domains' naming scheme, because it has the advantage of simplicity, even if it's not a pure naming scheme. For the interested, RFC2377 contains an excellent and detailed explanation of the different naming schemes.

Object Components

If all we could do with a directory server were to name the objects in it, it would not be very useful. In practice, objects in an LDAP directory have many attributes of various types. It is also possible for an object to have many attributes of the same type with different names, a sort of unordered collection.

For example, we might wish to identify someone in our organization who is a person, works in the development department, and is also a director. We would manage this by giving them several ou (organizational unit) attributes, like this:

```
dn: cn=Bill O'Neill, ou=People, o=mythical.co.uk, c=uk
cn: Bill
sn: O'Neill
givenname: Bill
uid: bon
ou: Development
ou: People
ou: Director
objectclass: top
objectclass: person
```

Don't worry too much about the details, we will be finding out more about this representation of entries (known as ldif files) very shortly. For now it's just important to realize that although the dn must be unique, it's possible for other attributes to have multiple values, as in the case of the ou attribute above. Notice that there are also two objectclass values – there is no limit on the number of attributes that can have multiple values.

The definitions of objects in an LDAP schema are quite complex, and, at first sight, unnecessarily so. However, as we mentioned earlier, one of the benefits of LDAP is the standardization – all LDAP servers should support a base set of object types and attributes in a standard form.

The OpenLDAP server, which we will be using throughout this chapter, comes with two object schema configuration files, slapd.oc.conf and slapd.at.conf.

The at file defines a set of attributes and the type each attribute has, while the oc file defines the object classes – which attributes can be contained in each object. The overall schema for LDAP is defined in RFC 2256, where you will find some very detailed specifications. One thing you will notice is that each data format has a dotted number associated with it, for example the attribute serialNumber has a number 2.5.4.5 associated with it. These numbers are Object Identifiers, or OIDs, and are guaranteed to be unique throughout the world. If you follow the links from the OpenLDAP home page you will find not only definitions of OIDs, but links where you can register your own.

When you run an LDAP server, one of the important configuration options is to decide if you wish to enforce schema checking. If this is turned on, then adding objects to the directory server will be slower, but the server will check that all your objects conform to the schema. For experimentation purposes it's easier to leave schema checking turned off, and that's what we will assume for the rest of this chapter. For production use you should turn schema checking on.

Standard Types and Attributes

Even working inside the default schema, there are a set of standard defined types and attributes that you can use, that will be sufficient for many server needs. For the rest of this chapter we will be working with the standard types and attributes. Whilst defining your own types, attributes and extending the LDAP schema is possible, it's an advanced topic, which we don't have the space to cover here. For more information see the documentation that comes with the OpenLDAP server.

Standard types

There are only a few standard types of attributes that you need to know. The common ones that you will see are:

Type	Meaning
cis	Case Ignore String
ces	Case Enforce String
bin	Binary Data
dn	Distinguished Name

In this chapter we are only concerned with strings, and distinguished names.

Standard Attributes

The list of standard attributes is extensive, but again only a small number are essential. Some common attributes are listed below.

Attribute	Meaning
C	The two letter ISO 3166 country code
Cn	Common Name. For a person this would normally be the name by which they are known. For example Norma Jean Baker is normally known as Marilyn Monroe, so that would be the common name in a directory server.
GivenName	A person's given, or non-family, name.
Member	Can appear multiple times, and contains a dn, thus allowing an object to be associated with many other objects. For example a person may be a member of the development team, and also a member of the management team.
O	The name of the organization.
ObjectClass	The type of object. This is a multi-valued attribute. Each object, although it can only appear once in the directory tree, can 'belong' to multiple types. As a minimum each object must have an entry with ObjectClass set to 'top'.

Attribute	Meaning
Organizational Unit, or ou	A type of grouping defined within an organization, for example 'Support Group'.
PostalAddress	A postal address.
PostalCode	A post, or ZIP, code for the location.
SerialNumber	A serial number.
Sn	A surname, containing the family name for a person.
TelephoneNumber	A telephone number.
UserPassword	The user's password for accessing the LDAP server.

This is only a short list to give you the general idea, the full list of standard attributes can be found in RFC2256. Local LDAP servers may also extend the scheme. A good place to look for more standard schema items is http://www.hklc.com/ldapschema/.

The actual types of the attribute are defined in the schema for the directory server you are using, as are any mandatory attributes. In general a dn is always required, as is ObjectClass. Others may be omitted, depending on the schema in use.

LDAP Directory Tree

Now we have the general idea of what an LDAP directory can contain, we can show, in a simplified way, what a very simple LDAP directory might look like.

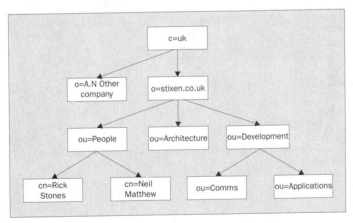

We have removed the 'Accounts' department to give us more room on the diagram, and also added an organizational unit, 'People'. Adding a special group for 'People' might seem a little odd, why did we not put people under the departments in which they work? In LDAP schemas it is common practice to separate people from the actual departments they work in, because this minimizes changes as people move departments, as they invariably do. If we had put a person under a department, and then they move, that person's complete Distinguished Name would be wrong, and we would have a major schema update to perform.

Changing an attribute is a minor operation on a directory server, changing the structure is a major undertaking. Instead we class people in a separate group, and link them to departments by giving them multiple ou attributes. That way we allow people to be members of two groups, such as Architecture and Management, and a move of that person from Architecture to Development would only entail the update of a single attribute in the person object, rather than a move of the object within the LDAP directory tree.

LDIF Files

Drawing an LDAP directory visually is very nice, and easy to understand, but not a practical way of transporting data around, or preparing data for loading into an LDAP server. A simple text representation is what is needed, and indeed there is such a format, called LDAP Data Interchange Format, or LDIF. (Don't you love these embedded acronyms?) The format is very simple. Each object starts with a dn: line. This is followed by as many lines as needed to specify the attributes of the object, one per line, after which a new dn: line marks the start of a new object.

Here is a short ldif file, that expresses the structure shown above, as well as adding more details to each object. This is available in the download bundle as plip.ldif

```
dn: o=stixen.co.uk, c=uk
o: stixen.co.uk
objectclass: top
objectclass: organization

dn: ou=People, o=stixen.co.uk, c=uk
ou: People
objectclass: top
objectclass: organizationalunit

dn: ou=Architecture, o=stixen.co.uk, c=uk
ou: Architecture
objectclass: top
objectclass: organizationalunit

dn: ou=Development, o=stixen.co.uk, c=uk
ou: Development
objectclass: top
objectclass: organizationalunit

dn: ou=Communications, ou=Development, o=stixen.co.uk, c=uk
ou: Communications
objectclass: top
objectclass: organizationalunit

dn: ou=Applications, ou=Development, o=stixen.co.uk, c=uk
ou: Comms
objectclass: top
objectclass: organizationalunit
```

```
dn: cn=Rick Stones, ou=People, o=stixen.co.uk, c=uk
cn: Rick Stones
sn: Stones
givenname: Richard
uid: stonesr
mail: Rick.Stones@mythicalcompany.co.uk
userpassword: bangalore
title: Systems Architect
objectclass: top
objectclass: person
ou: Architecture
ou: People
postalAddress:1 School Street, Newtown
postalCode:NT1 1AA
telephoneNumber:01234 987654321

dn: cn=Richard Neill, ou=People, o=stixen.co.uk, c=uk
cn: Richard Neill
sn: Neill
givenname: Richard
uid: neillr
mail: rjn@mythicalcompany.co.uk
userpassword: ulsoor
title: Specialist
objectclass: top
objectclass: person
ou: Development
ou: People
postalAddress:2 Thatched Street, Newtown
postalCode:NT1 2BB
telephoneNumber:01234 876543210

dn: cn=Neil Matthew, ou=People, o=stixen.co.uk, c=uk
cn: Neil Matthew
sn: Matthew
givenname: Neil
uid: matthewn
mail: Neil.Matthew@mythicalcompany.co.uk
userpassword: lalbagh
title: Software Specialist
objectclass: top
objectclass: person
ou: Architecture
ou: People
postalAddress:3 Barn Street, Newtown
postalCode:NT1 3CC
telephoneNumber:01234 765432109
```

An alternative is DSML, a markup language for representing directory services in XML, although at the time of writing LDIF files are much more common. See the *Resources* section for more information.

Installing and Configuring an LDAP Server

Now that we have had a very brief look at the theory behind LDAP, it's time to move onto the more practical aspects of an LDAP server. However, first we must find a server to work with, and get some base data loaded into it.

The server we use in this chapter is OpenLDAP, which is freely downloadable, and complete with source code. The source can be compiled for many platforms, including Linux, FreeBSD, AIX, Solaris, HP-UX, and others. Some of the clients in the source distribution have also been ported to Windows 9x/NT. There are also pre-compiled versions, in various formats, but if your distribution isn't supported, or you simply prefer to install from source, you can compile it yourself.

We will only cover the essential steps of installing OpenLDAP from source here, for two reasons. Firstly it's very easy indeed, and secondly there is a very informative LDAP Linux HOWTO (see the *Resources* list at the end of the chapter), which provides more details if you need them. You should be aware that you normally need an implementation of the dbm libraries installed before you start, the GNU set, gdbm, is fine, and installed by most Linux distributions. There is also a chapter in the book *Professional Linux Deployment*, also published by Wrox Press, which provides some information on installing OpenLDAP.

Steps in Installing OpenLDAP

In case you were worried that installing OpenLDAP might be complicated, worry not. It's possible that your Linux distribution came with one already, look for a startup script ldap in the standard init.d directory. Even if there isn't one, or you want to run the very latest version, installation follows the standard steps:

❑ Fetch the latest stable OpenLDAP sources from http://www.openLDAP.org.

❑ Run **tar zxvf** on the source tarball.

❑ Change to the unpacked directory and run **./configure**.

❑ Run **make depend** to setup the dependencies.

❑ Run **make** to build the components.

❑ As root, run **make install** to install the server.

❑ As root, **cd tests** then **make** to execute the tests.

Assuming all went well, you now have an installation of OpenLDAP, probably in /usr/local. Well, we did say it was easy!

Configuring OpenLDAP

Now the server is installed, you need to perform some basic configuration, before it can be used. OpenLDAP comes with some default configuration files, which are an excellent starting point, but we still need to make a few decisions and minor edits before we are up and running.

Firstly we need to decide if we wish to run the LDAP service from inetd, or as a standalone service. Unless you have some very special need, standalone is normally recommended, for several reasons. If you are in development mode, you may need to stop and restart the service several times, and with a standalone service this is slightly easier. In production a standalone service is usually recommended, because the default backend implementation of OpenLDAP is to use dbm, and allowing it to run continuously allows it to perform some caching. In addition, one of the main benefits of LDAP is its incredible response speed, and running it via inetd significantly impacts those response times.

For the rest of this chapter we assume you will be using standalone execution, and that you have installed the standalone ldap daemon (slapd) server under /usr/local. If this is not where the server has been installed, you will need to adjust the paths shown as appropriate. The main configuration file is probably in /usr/local/etc/openldap/slapd.conf, if you built from sources, or /etc/openldap /slapd.conf for most Red Hat distributions if you installed the provided distribution. Other distributions may use other locations. We suggest you make a copy of the default, before making any changes.

The default file that comes with the sources, which is nice and short, looks like this:

```
#
# See slapd.conf(5) for details on configuration options.
# This file should NOT be world readable.
#
include         /usr/local/etc/openldap/slapd.at.conf
include         /usr/local/etc/openldap/slapd.oc.conf
schemacheck     off
#referral       ldap://root.openldap.org/

pidfile         /usr/local/var/slapd.pid
argsfile        /usr/local/var/slapd.args

#####################################################################
# ldbm database definitions
#####################################################################

database        ldbm
suffix          "dc=my-domain, dc=com"
#suffix         "o=My Organization Name, c=US"
rootdn          "cn=Manager, dc=my-domain, dc=com"
#rootdn         "cn=Manager, o=My Organization Name, c=US"
rootpw          secret
# cleartext passwords, especially for the rootdn, should
# be avoided.  See slapd.conf(5) for details.
Directory       /usr/tmp
```

The version on your local machine will probably vary slightly, especially if you installed a version of LDAP that came with your Linux distribution. In particular the pid files may have alternate locations, such as /var/run, and the configuration files will probably be under /etc/openldap.

The first section is the global configuration, then there can be one or more 'database' sections, The first two lines refer to the `attribute` and `objectclass` configuration files, the configuration of which is an advanced topic, beyond the scope of a single chapter. However it is instructive to have a look at the files, as the default contents are reasonably easy to understand. The line `schemacheck off` tells the server not to check objects being added against the schema. As we said before, this is a convenient default during development, but should be changed before the system is put into production.

Next comes a commented out `referral` line, which allows you to configure your LDAP server to pass on queries it can't answer to a different server.

The next two lines tell `slapd` where to place its process identifier (`pid`) and arguments. The `pid` file is useful when shutting the `slapd` daemon down, as we will see in a moment.

The next section of the file is a database section. It's possible to have multiple back end databases for different branches of an LDAP tree, but normally only one is required.

The first line of the section specifies the database type to be used. Your choices are `ldbm`, `shell`, or `passwd`, which control the 'back end' implementation of the data retrieval. Normally you should choose `ldbm`.

The `suffix` line tells the LDAP server which part or parts of the global LDAP namespace this database will serve. At least one suffix line must be present in each database section, since otherwise there is no point in having the database at all, but you can have multiple suffix lines if required.

The `rootdn` and `rootpw` lines provide a 'bootstrap' login ID and password for the server that is always valid, and has administrator privileges on the server. Now you know why the comment at the top of the file warns against having this file world readable! The password can be in cleartext, as it is here, crypt or MD5 format. Whilst cleartext is fine while you are developing, we strongly suggest that you don't use it on a production server.

The final control line, `directory`, tells the `ldbm` database backend where to store the data and index files. You probably want to change this value to something less temporary than the default, we use `/var/local/<meaningful-name>`.

There are other options, particularly for running multiple LDAP servers and using replication to keep them in synchronization. In this case you will have producer and consumer LDAP servers, but the ones presented here are sufficient for everyday needs.

A more detailed explanation can be found in the online `slapd.conf` manual page, or in the Administrator's guide, which can be found at http://www.umich.edu/~dirsvcs/ldap/doc/guides/. Although the guide is intended for the University of Michigan LDAP server, it's still a recommended read, as much of the information is still relevant.

Once we customize the file to our local needs, it looks like this:

```
#
# See slapd.conf(5) for details on configuration options.
# This file should NOT be world readable.
#
include    /usr/local/etc/openldap/slapd.at.conf
include    /usr/local/etc/openldap/slapd.oc.conf
schemacheck off
```

```
pidfile    /usr/local/var/slapd.pid
argsfile   /usr/local/var/slapd.args

######################################################################
# ldbm database definitions
######################################################################

database    ldbm
suffix     "o=stixen.co.uk, c=uk"
rootdn     "cn=root, o=stixen.co.uk, c=uk"
rootpw     secret
directory   /var/local/stixen
#
```

Running the Server

Now that we have configured the `slapd.conf` file, and made sure that the directory specified in the file exists, it's time to fire up the server and see if we can connect to it. If your system came with `slapd` already configured in the `init.d` directory, you may find that the server is already running, or at least has a script to start it. If so look for the shutdown script in the `init.d` directory and manually stop it before restarting in a fashion appropriate to your system.

First, as root, run up the `slapd` server, passing the configuration file as a parameter:

```
# /usr/local/libexec/slapd -f /usr/local/etc/openldap/slapd.conf
```

Hopefully you will just get a prompt back, since `slapd` automatically runs in the background. If you run **ps -el** you should see some `slapd` processes running. Now we need to load some data into the server, to check it's accessible.

As an ordinary user, create a file `test.ldif` that contains:

```
dn: o=stixen.co.uk, c=uk
o: stixen.co.uk
objectclass: top
objectclass: organization
```

Now we can load this into the server. We specify the host to use with -h, the port 389 (the default LDAP port) with -p, -D is the `rootdn` we specified in the `slapd.conf` file, -w is the password we specified, and -f is the file to load:

```
$ /usr/local/bin/ldapadd -h localhost -p 389 -D "cn=root, o=stixen.co.uk, c=uk" -w
secret -f test.ldif
```

And you will hopefully get:

```
adding new entry o=stixen.co.uk, c=uk
```

Check that you can retrieve the data:

```
$ /usr/local/bin/ldapsearch -h localhost -p 389 -D "cn=root, o=stixen.co.uk, c=uk"
-w secret -b "o=stixen.co.uk, c=uk" 'objectclass=*'
```

And you should get:

```
o=stixen.co.uk, c=uk
o=stixen.co.uk
objectclass=top
objectclass=organization
```

Congratulations, you now have a running LDAP server. If you have a look in /var/local/stixen, you will see that slapd has created several files for its own use. The online manual contains more detailed specifications for these and other parameters to ldapadd and ldapsearch.

It's important that you always shutdown the LDAP server in a graceful manner. You might even want to add the shutdown into your /etc/rc.d scripts, to ensure you don't forget. Closing the server down is very simple, you just run:

```
# kill -TERM `cat /usr/local/var/slapd.pid`
```

If your LDAP server doesn't seem to be working, don't worry, it's most probably that you have a minor typing mistake somewhere in the configuration. Kill the slapd server (as shown above) and restart it in debug mode, by adding -d256 to the command line. It should stay in the foreground and print debugging information as it runs. Then run both ldapadd and ldapsearch adding the -v option to the parameters shown above, which turn on verbose output. Hopefully the cause of your problems should soon be apparent. The online OpenLDAP manual provides more detail on running slapd in debug mode, and other parameters you might wish to use.

If you want to wipe your ldap database and start again, this is very easy. First shutdown your slapd server, then remove all the files in the database directory as specified as directory entry of slapd.conf (here /var/local/stixen), and you are back to an empty directory again.

We have now learned a little about directory servers, and seen how to create a basic OpenLDAP server configuration and get the LDAP server daemon running. It's time to move on to some programming.

Accessing LDAP from C

It's taken us a few steps to get a here, but the good news is that writing code to talk to your newly installed LDAP server is quite easy. However, if you have installed an LDAP server from a distribution, it's possible that the programming includes and libraries have not been installed, even if the server was. You may need to check your distribution, and if all else fails install the OpenLDAP server from sources, which does include the programming interface files. All the examples are designed to work with plip.ldif.

There are two distinct sets of APIs, a synchronous set and an asynchronous set. The synchronous set has the same names as the asynchronous set with an s appended to the name. The advantage of the asynchronous set is that it allows you to initiate a query on the LDAP server, and then continue other processing before returning to retrieve the results. The drawback, as I'm sure you guessed, is increased complexity. Since generally the synchronous set is sufficient, that is the set we will concentrate on in this chapter.

Initialize the LDAP Library

The routines we will be using to write client programs for accessing our LDAP server come with OpenLDAP, and are in libraries ldap, lber, and the include file ldap.h. The first stage in talking to the LDAP server is to initialize the library. The function ldap_init is the preferred method, and the only one we will consider here, although in older code you may come across lpad_open which acts in a very similar way, but is now a deprecated interface. The prototype for ldap_init is:

```
#include <lber.h>
#include <ldap.h>

LDAP *ldap_init(char *host, int port);
```

The LDAP structure to which the function returns a pointer can be found in ldap.h, for those interested. If the routine fails, NULL is returned and errno set appropriately. The actual parameters to ldap_init can be specified in two ways. The most common way is to specify a host where the server lives as a simple string, such as ldap_host.stixen.co.uk, and the port to use, which would normally be the default port, 389, available as a define LDAP_PORT. However, where an LDAP server is a critical part of the infrastructure, it may be that there are two or more LDAP servers, any of which could satisfy the request, and we don't actually care which one is used. We can specify this by making the host string a list of space-separated hosts, each with an optional port number. If no port number is specified then the port given in the second parameter is used. As an example, the call:

```
ldap_init("ldap_master ldap_slave ldap_master:10389", LDAP_PORT);
```

This tells the LDAP library that we want it to first try port 389 on the host ldap_master, then try port 389 on ldap_slave, and finally port 10389 on ldap_master. The library takes care of the actual details of selecting a server for us.

Bind to the LDAP Server

Having initialized the LDAP library, the next stage is to bind to it, which is done with a call to ldap_bind_s. There are actually a whole group of closely related bind calls, but this one is the only one you will generally need. The prototype is:

```
#include <lber.h>
#include <ldap.h>

int ldap_bind_s(LDAP *ld, char *who, char *credentials, int method);
```

You may have noticed that some parameters that are probably const *are not actually specified as such. The original C API for LDAP (RFC1823) defined them in Kernigan and Ritchie style, and this is still how the prototype appears in the OpenLDAP include files.*

The ld pointer is the pointer returned from the earlier ldap_init call. The rest of the parameters depend somewhat on the authentication method being used, which is defined by the parameter passed in the method parameter. The normal method, set by passing LDAP_AUTH_SIMPLE, is the most commonly used and is the one we will consider here. The alternative is Kerberos authentication, which is also freely available for Linux.

The who parameter specifies the user who wishes to connect. You will remember we specified a rootdn user in our slapd.conf file of cn=root, o=stixen.co.uk, c=uk, and this is the user we will use here. For simple authentication the credentials parameter is just a password, in this case the rootpw from slapd.conf, but in the general case the userPassword attribute of the LDAP entry is used.

The call to ldap_bind_s will return LDAP_SUCCESS if all is well, otherwise it will return an LDAP specific error code, which we will come to shortly.

When your program has finished with the connection to an LDAP server you must call ldap_unbind_s to release the connection to the server and other resources associated with the link before your program exits. The prototype is:

```
#include <lber.h>
#include <ldap.h>

int ldap_unbind_s(LDAP *ld);
```

The ld parameter is a pointer to the structure returned from the ldap_init call. Once you have called ldap_unbind_s the connection to the LDAP server will have been closed, and the ld structure invalidated, so you must start back at the ldap_init stage if later in your program you wish to initiate another LDAP operation. The return value will be LDAP_SUCCESS unless there was a problem. We will be seeing the LDAP specific error codes next.

LDAP Error Handling

Before we go any further, we need to look at error handling. Generally the ldap_functions calls return an integer value, which is either LDAP_SUCCESS if all is well, or an error code. The LDAP structure also contains a member, ld_errno, which will, conveniently, contain the same error number. The error codes are defined in ldap.h, generally with well-chosen names that make the meaning obvious. In addition there are three useful routines, which you can use for obtaining more information. These are:

```
#include <lber.h>
#include <ldap.h>

void ldap_perror(LDAP *ld, char *message);

char *ldap_err2string(int err);

int ldap_result2error(LDAP *ld, LDAPMessage *result, int freeit);
```

The simplest of these is ldap_perror, which works in a very similar way to perror. You pass ldap_perror a pointer to an LDAP structure, and an additional text string. This routine converts the error number in the LDAP structure to a meaningful message, combines it with the additional string passed in, and prints the result on the standard error stream.

The ldap_err2string routine is similar, except it simply returns a pointer to the human readable string, giving you more control over how the error is displayed. The pointer returned points to static data and must not be modified, as it will be overwritten next time ldap_err2string is called.

The third routine, ldap_result2error, is used in a situation we have not yet met, when a search on an LDAP server needs processing to determine the error code. We mention it here since it logically fits with the other LDAP error utility functions. By passing an LDAPMessage structure (which we meet later) to the routine, the error code is extracted, returned and set in the LDAP structure. If freeit has a non-zero value then the LDAPMessage structure is automatically freed afterwards.

A First LDAP Client Program

We now know enough about the LDAP library to write our first program to access our LDAP server. It's not very useful, but ties together what we have learnt so far, by initializing a connection to an LDAP server, binding to that connection, then releasing the resources again. Here is ldap1.c:

```
#include <stdio.h>
#include <stdlib.h>
#include <unistd.h>

#include <lber.h>
#include <ldap.h>

int main() {
  LDAP *ld;
  int res;

  int  authmethod = LDAP_AUTH_SIMPLE;

  char *ldap_host = "locahost";

  char *user_dn = "cn=root, o=stixen.co.uk, c=uk";
  char *user_pw = "secret";

  if ((ld = ldap_init(ldap_host, LDAP_PORT)) == NULL ) {
    perror( "Failure of ldap_init" );
    exit( EXIT_FAILURE );
  }

  if (ldap_bind_s(ld, user_dn, user_pw, authmethod) != LDAP_SUCCESS ) {
    ldap_perror( ld, "Failure of ldap_bind" );
    exit( EXIT_FAILURE );
  }


  res = ldap_unbind_s(ld);
  if (res != 0) {
    fprintf(stderr, "ldap_unbind_s failed: %s\n", ldap_err2string(res));
    exit( EXIT_FAILURE );
  }

  return EXIT_SUCCESS;
} /* main */
```

This file is quite simple; it just exercises most of the functions we have used so far. To compile this file you may need to force the inclusion of additional include and library path directories, as well as linking with the ldap and lber libraries. The compile line for our 'installed from source' LDAP server was:

```
$ gcc -Wall -g -I/usr/local/include ldap1.c -o ldap1 -L/usr/local/lib -lldap -llber
```

Go ahead and try this, including changing some of the parameters so the initialize or bind fails, so you can see the errors that are returned. If the program runs silently, you have successfully connected to an LDAP server.

Searching

The main reason for using an LDAP server is to hold data that you need to search, but need the results quickly. There are two main ways to restrict the results from an LDAP directory search, which are usually combined.

Selecting the Scope

The first way is to determine which part of the directory you wish to search. As you will remember from earlier in the chapter, LDAP directories are best thought of as tree structures. When you execute a search on a directory, you can specify two parameters. The first is the start point, or base of the search, which might be the top of the tree, or some levels down. The second is the depth of the search, which can be one of three depths, or 'scopes' as they are termed. The base of the search is always expressed as a dn, a distinguished name, and the scope as one of three constants:

LDAP_SCOPE_BASE	this causes the search to be made only on the object specified by the base dn. This is normally used if you already know the entry you wish to retrieve, and just need to retrieve some or all of its attributes.
LDAP_SCOPE_ONELEVEL	this allows the search to work on the object pointed to by the base dn, and all the objects at one level of the tree beneath the base object.
LDAP_SCOPE_SUBTREE	this allows the search to work on the object pointed to by the base dn, and all objects underneath it in the tree.

It might seem odd that you can't specify a particular number of levels, except for one, but that's just the way it is.

Filtering the Results

The other way of restricting the results from an LDAP search is to filter the results by specifying a pattern, or patterns, that attributes of the required objects must possess. For example you might wish to find only objects of type 'person', so you would set the filter to be (objectclass=person).

The format of LDAP filters is specified formally in RFC2254, here we will present a less formal specification, but hopefully in an easier to read format.

LDAP filters are always enclosed in round parentheses, and can be either a simple filter, such as checking that a particular attribute has a given value, or are combined, to check for example that attribute1 has a particular value, and attribute2 has a particular value. We will look at simple filters first, and then see how they can be combined.

The tests that can be applied to an attribute are:

=	equals
~=	approximately equals
>=	greater than
<=	less than
=*	attribute is present in the object
= string*	attribute value starts with string
= *string	attribute value ends with string
= *string*	string occurs in the attribute's value

Notice that the operators > and < are not valid. The definition of 'approximately equals' seems to be left to the implementers of LDAP servers, so results using this may vary slightly between servers. The filter does not control the issue of case sensitivity – rather it is determined by how the attribute type was defined. You will recall from the beginning of the chapter that string attribute types could be 'Case Ignore String' or 'Case Enforce String', and this controls how matching is performed.

Here are a few examples of simple filters:

(cn=Rick Stones)	The common name is "Rick Stones".
(cn=*Stones)	The common name ends in "Stones".
(ou=Architecture)	The organizational unit is "Architecture".
(postalCode=*)	The postalCode attribute is present in the object.

Occasionally you need to search for something where one of the special characters appears in the string. You can do this by using a standard escape, which is a backslash (\) followed by the hexadecimal value of the ASCII character. The characters *, (,), \, and NULL must always be escaped. Here are some examples:

(cn=*\2a*)	The common name contains a '*' (0x2a) character.
(ou=\28Architecture\29)	The organizational unit is "(Architecture)", including the parentheses.

Simple filters are useful, but often need to be combined with Boolean operators to be truly useful. The three operators allowed are:

- ❏ & (and)
- ❏ | (or)
- ❏ ! (not)

Filters are combined in a prefix notation, where the Boolean operator precedes the two filters it combines. You can combine as many filters as you need to narrow down your criteria. For example, to search for objects that represent people who work in the organizational unit Architecture group, we need to combine the filter (objectClass=Person) with the filter (ou=Architecture), like this:

```
(&(objectClass=Person)(ou=Architecture))
```

The not operator simply negates a filter, so we search for objects which don't have the attribute title set to Systems Architect like this:

```
(!(title= Systems Architect))
```

You can combine filters, just paste together the required filters with more operators. For example, to find people with a surname of "Stones" or "Matthew", we would use:

```
(&(objectClass=Person)(|(sn=Stones)(sn=Matthew)))
```

As you can see, although the way filters are expressed may not be quite what you are used to, it is simple and unambiguous. If you want to experiment, you can always use the ldapsearch program provided as part of the OpenLDAP distribution. Do beware, however, of repeatedly performing sub-tree searches on a large production directory server that returns a large volume of results – you might well be causing an administrator somewhere to wonder what has suddenly happened to the performance of his server!

As an example of using ldapsearch, here is a query that will list all the objects in our server:

```
$ ldapsearch -D "cn=root, o=stixen.co.uk, c=uk" -w secret
             -b "o=stixen.co.uk, c=uk" 'objectclass=*'
```

The -D and -w, as you can probably guess, are our connection credentials. Notice we have to specify the base of our search, using the -b option. This is not the sort of query you want to run on a production server, but on our test server the output, abbreviated to save space, starts:

```
o=stixen.co.uk, c=uk
o=stixen.co.uk
objectclass=top
objectclass=organization

ou=People, o=stixen.co.uk, c=uk
ou=People
objectclass=top
objectclass=organizationalunit

ou=Architecture, o=stixen.co.uk, c=uk
ou=Architecture
objectclass=top
objectclass=organizationalunit

ou=Development, o=stixen.co.uk, c=uk
ou=Development
objectclass=top
objectclass=organizationalunit
```

and so on till all the objects have been shown.

A more sensible search, which lists all the attributes for people with a surname of Stones, would be:

```
$ ldapsearch -D "cn=root, o=stixen.co.uk, c=uk" -w secret -b "o=stixen.co.uk,
c=uk" '(&(sn=Stones)(objectclass=person))'
```

Searching Using the API

Now we know how to search an LDAP server, we can have a look at writing some code to execute our searches. Searching is reasonably complex, because not only do we have more details to specify, but also we must handle multiple results being returned.

The basic search API is:

```
#include <lber.h>
#include <ldap.h>

int ldap_search_s(LDAP *ld, char *base_dn, int scope, char *filter, char
*attrs_required[], int attributesonly, LDAPMessage **result);
```

This is the synchronous version, which only returns when all results are available, and is generally the most useful. However there are two closely related calls, ldap_search, which is an asynchronous search, and ldap_search_st, which is synchronous, but has a timeout to force a return after a given interval, even if no results are available. We will only consider the synchronous version of the search here; the manual pages contain more information about the other variants of the search function.

Let's look at the parameters in turn:

- ❑ The first parameter, ld, is the pointer to the structure bound to the LDAP server.

- ❑ base_dn is a pointer to the object where searching should start. This could be the top of the tree, or some lower point, for example "ou=Development, o=stixen.co.uk, c=uk", which is one level into the directory tree of the test data loaded in our test server.

- ❑ scope is one of the three defines we saw before, LDAP_SCOPE_BASE, LDAP_SCOPE_ONELEVEL or LDAP_SCOPE_SUBTREE.

- ❑ filter is a filter, such as (postalCode=NT1*).

- ❑ attrs_required is a NULL terminated array of the attributes that should be returned. For example we may only be interested in the sn and uid attributes of a person, and it would be wasteful to return all the others. If you specify NULL then all attributes will be returned.

- ❑ attributesonly, if set to 1, will cause only the attribute types to be returned. Normally it is 0 which allows both types and values to be returned.

On success LDAP_SUCCESS is returned, otherwise an LDAP-specific error code is returned.

You must free the result set afterwards, which is done with ldap_msgfree:

```
#include <lber.h>
#include <ldap.h>

int ldap_msgfree(LDAPMessage *msg);
```

Unusually, the returned value is the type of message freed, not a result code, and is not generally of interest.

Having performed a search, we need to process the results. This is done with a set of three routines:

```
#include <lber.h>
#include <ldap.h>
```

```
int ldap_count_entries(LDAP *ld, LDAPMessage *result);

LDAPMessage *ldap_first_entry(LDAP *ld, LDAPMessage *result);

LDAPMessage *ldap_next_entry(LDAP *ld, LDAPMessage *result);
```

These functions parse the result chain, and allow us to extract each result in turn. We will see shortly how to extract the actual values from the results. Once all results have been fetched the ldap_next_entry returns a NULL.

The routine ldap_count_entries is simply a convenience, to allow us to tell how many results we have obtained; you normally only need to use ldap_first_entry and ldap_next_entry to process those results. The sequence in pseudo code is:

```
Initialize an LDAP structure
Bind to an LDAP server
Execute a search
Obtain the first result message
WHILE (result message) DO
    Process the LDAP message
    Free the message structure
    Get the next result message
DONE
UNBIND from the server
```

Let's update our program (as ldap2.c) to do a search, even though we are not in a position to process the results yet. Just to show we are obtaining results, we will use one function we will meet in the next section, ldap_get_dn, which returns the distinguished name of the object found. The important changes are highlighted:

```
#include <stdio.h>
#include <stdlib.h>
#include <unistd.h>

#include <lber.h>
#include <ldap.h>

int main() {
  LDAP *ld;
  int res;
  LDAPMessage *ldap_message_set, *ldap_one_message;
```

```
char *attributes[4] = {"sn",
        "ou",
        "title",
        NULL};

int  authmethod = LDAP_AUTH_SIMPLE;

char *ldap_host = "localhost";

char *user_dn = "cn=root, o=stixen.co.uk, c=uk";
char *user_pw = "secret";

char *base_dn = "o=stixen.co.uk, c=uk";
char *filter = "(objectClass=Person)";


if ((ld = ldap_init(ldap_host, LDAP_PORT)) == NULL ) {
  perror( "Failure of ldap_init" );
  exit( EXIT_FAILURE );
}

if (ldap_bind_s(ld, user_dn, user_pw, authmethod) != LDAP_SUCCESS ) {
  ldap_perror( ld, "Failure of ldap_bind" );
  exit( EXIT_FAILURE );
}

res = ldap_search_s(ld, base_dn, LDAP_SCOPE_SUBTREE, filter,
                              attributes, 0, &ldap_message_set);
if (res != LDAP_SUCCESS) {
  ldap_perror( ld, "Failure of ldap_search_s" );
  exit( EXIT_FAILURE );
}

printf("There were %d objects found\n", ldap_count_entries(ld,
                                        ldap_message_set));

ldap_one_message = ldap_first_entry(ld, ldap_message_set);
while (ldap_one_message) {
  char *dn_str;
  dn_str = ldap_get_dn(ld, ldap_one_message);
  printf("Found DN %s\n", dn_str);
  free(dn_str);
  ldap_one_message = ldap_next_entry(ld, ldap_one_message);
}
(void)ldap_msgfree(ldap_message_set);

res = ldap_unbind_s(ld);
if (res != 0) {
  fprintf(stderr, "ldap_unbind_s failed: %s\n", ldap_err2string(res));
  exit( EXIT_FAILURE );
}

return EXIT_SUCCESS;
} /* main */
```

When we run this we see:

```
There were 3 objects found
Found DN cn=Rick Stones, ou=People, o=stixen.co.uk, c=uk
Found DN cn=Richard Neill, ou=People, o=stixen.co.uk, c=uk
Found DN cn=Neil Matthew, ou=People, o=stixen.co.uk, c=uk
```

Now we can move on, and extract the actual attributes and values. Apart from the special case of ldap_get_dn that we had a sneak preview of, there are first and next routines to step through the attributes, and a routine to access the value(s) of each attribute.

```
#include <lber.h>
#include <ldap.h>


char *ldap_first_attribute(LDAP *ld, LDAPMessage *entry,
                                       BerElement **ber_element);

char *ldap_next_attribute(LDAP *ld, LDAPMessage *entry,
                                       BerElement *ber_element);

char *ldap_get_dn(LDAP *ld, LDAPMessage *entry);

char **ldap_get_values(LDAP *ld, LDAPMessage *entry, char *attribute);

void ldap_value_free(char **value);
```

Notice the subtle difference between ldap_first_attribute and ldap_next_attribute, where there is an additional level of indirection on the ldap_first_attribute third parameter. You also need to be aware that internal to the library ldap_next_attribute arranges to free memory that ldap_first_attribute allocated once the end of the list of attributes is reached. You need to be aware that if for some reason you do not call ldap_next_attribute to retrieve all the attributes (that is, until it returns a NULL), you need to call a routine ber_free, passing the ber_element and a zero, thus ber_free(ber_element, 0). Since normally you will use ldap_next_attribute until all the attributes are exhausted, you do not need to worry about this, so we will not discuss it here.

Again, we can see, in pseudocode, the sequence required on each LDAPMessage retrieved:

```
Get first attribute
WHILE (attribute)  DO
   Get values for attribute
   Release memory used for attributes
   Get the next attribute
DONE
```

Let's modify our program for a third time, to show the code required. This is ldap3.c:

```
#include <stdio.h>
#include <stdlib.h>
#include <unistd.h>

#include <lber.h>
#include <ldap.h>
```

```
int main( int argc, char *argv[] ) {
  LDAP *ld;
  int res;
  LDAPMessage *ldap_message_set, *ldap_one_message;
  char *attributes[4] = {"sn",
          "ou",
          "title",
          NULL};

    char *attribute;
    char **values;
    BerElement *ber_element_ptr;
    int i;

    int  authmethod = LDAP_AUTH_SIMPLE;

    char *ldap_host = "gw1";

    char *user_dn = "cn=root, o=stixen.co.uk, c=uk";
    char *user_pw = "secret";

    char *base_dn = "o=stixen.co.uk, c=uk";
    char *filter = "(objectClass=Person)";


    if ((ld = ldap_init(ldap_host, LDAP_PORT)) == NULL ) {
      perror( "Failure of ldap_init" );
      exit( EXIT_FAILURE );
    }

    if (ldap_bind_s(ld, user_dn, user_pw, authmethod) != LDAP_SUCCESS ) {
      ldap_perror( ld, "Failure of ldap_bind" );
      exit( EXIT_FAILURE );
    }

    res = ldap_search_s(ld, base_dn, LDAP_SCOPE_SUBTREE, filter, attributes,
                                          0, &ldap_message_set);
    if (res != LDAP_SUCCESS) {
      ldap_perror( ld, "Failure of ldap_search_s" );
      exit( EXIT_FAILURE );
    }

    printf("There were %d objects found\n", ldap_count_entries(ld,
                                          ldap_message_set));

    ldap_one_message = ldap_first_entry(ld, ldap_message_set);
    while (ldap_one_message) {
      char *dn_str;
      dn_str = ldap_get_dn(ld, ldap_one_message);
      printf("Found DN %s\n", dn_str);
      free(dn_str);

      attribute = ldap_first_attribute(ld, ldap_one_message,
                                    &ber_element_ptr);
```

```
       while (attribute != NULL) {
         if ((values = ldap_get_values(ld, ldap_one_message,
                                              attribute))!=NULL){
          for (i=0; values[i] != NULL; i++) {
            printf("%s: %s\n", attribute, values[i]);
          }
          ldap_value_free(values);
          }
          attribute = ldap_next_attribute(ld, ldap_one_message,
                                              ber_element_ptr);
       }

    ldap_one_message = ldap_next_entry(ld, ldap_one_message);
    printf("\n");
  }
  ldap_msgfree(ldap_message_set);

  res = ldap_unbind_s(ld);
  if (res != 0) {
    fprintf(stderr, "ldap_unbind_s failed: %s\n", ldap_err2string(res));
    exit( EXIT_FAILURE );
  }

  return EXIT_SUCCESS;
} /* main */
```

The important changes have been highlighted.

When we run it on our test data, the output is:

```
There were 3 objects found
Found DN cn=Rick Stones, ou=People, o=stixen.co.uk, c=uk
sn: Stones
title: Systems Architect
ou: Architecture
ou: People

Found DN cn=Richard Neill, ou=People, o=stixen.co.uk, c=uk
sn: Neill
title: Specialist
ou: Development
ou: People

Found DN cn=Neil Matthew, ou=People, o=stixen.co.uk, c=uk
sn: Matthew
title: Software Specialist
ou: Architecture
ou: People
```

Notice that the ou attribute occurs more than once, and that only attributes we requested in our attributes array were retrieved.

Sorting Returned Objects

There is one last feature relating to searching that we should cover, and that is sorting the results, since it's a common requirement, and the LDAP library gives us an elegant way to sort entries.

The function we need is `ldap_sort_entries`, which looks like this:

```
#include <lber.h>
#include <ldap.h>

int ldap_sort_entries(LDAP *ld, LDAPMessage **msg, char *attr_to_sort_on,
                                                   int (*cmp)());
```

This takes the `LDAPMessage` chain we got back from `ldap_search_s`, and uses the `cmp` function to sort the entries. The `cmp` function uses a similar convention to `qsort`, in that it passes pointers to a pair of strings, and the function should return a negative, zero, or positive number to indicate the relative order of the strings. Often the function `strcmp` is all that is required. We can sort our returned results by including `string.h`, and immediately before we call `ldap_first_entry`, add just four lines of additional code:

```
res = ldap_sort_entries(ld, &ldap_message_set, "sn", strcmp);
if (res != LDAP_SUCCESS) {
  ldap_perror( ld, "Failure of ldap_sort_entries" );
}
```

Now our results are sorted by surname. Sorting of results doesn't come much easier than that.

Changing the Data

Just occasionally we need to change the data in the LDAP directory server. As we saw earlier, there are utility routines provided to do this, such as `ldapadd`, `ldapmodify`, and `ldapdelete`. Not surprisingly there are also library functions for performing these tasks from C. We would however suggest that the best way of adding a group of entries is to build an `ldif` file, and use the provided `ldapadd` utility, as we saw earlier.

Adding a New Entry

We will start by adding a new entry to our data. During this we will also learn of the data structures that we will need to modify operations, as the two operations are carried out in a very similar manner.

To add a new entry, we first need to construct a structure with all the attributes and values needed for that entry. Only then can we add it to our directory server. Since the data structure of an object in an LDAP directory is quite flexible (it just needs to conform to the schema, if schema checking is enabled), this leads to an array of structures, some of which themselves contain arrays.

The basic building block of an LDAP entry is an `LDAPMod` structure. This contains the building block for a single attribute within an object. The actual definition is:

```
typedef struct ldapmod {
        int mod_op;
        char *mod_type;
        union {
         char **modv_strvals;
         struct berval **modv_bvals;
        } mod_vals;
        struct ldapmod *mod_next;
} LDAPMod;
#define mod_values mod_vals.modv_strvals
#define mod_bvalues mod_vals.modv_bvals
```

Don't worry, it's easier to use than it looks. In practice we only need to set three fields, because we are only using string attributes in this chapter, so we can ignore modv_bvals, and mod_next is only for use by the library. The mod_op value is one of LDAP_MOD_ADD, LDAP_MOD_DELETE, LDAP_MOD_REPLACE.

Before we can create an LDAPMod structure, we need to set up an array of strings for the attribute values, for assignment to mod_values (or mod_vals.modv_strvals). It has to be an *array* of strings because some attributes have several values; for example objectClass and ou quite often have two or more values.

Let's start by declaring the arrays of strings we need:

```
char objectClass_vals[] = {"top", "person", NULL};
char ou_vals[] = {" Development", "People", NULL};
char cn_vals[] = {"Jenny Stones", NULL};
...
```

Now we can declare some LDAPMod structures, which use these arrays:

```
LDAPMod cn_attribute, objectclass_attribute
...
```

We can then set up each LDAPMod structure with the appropriate values:

```
cn_attribute.mod_op = LDAP_MOD_ADD;
cn_attribute.mod_type = "cn";
cn_attribute.mod_values = cn_vals;

objectclass_attribute.mod_op = LDAP_MOD_ADD;
objectclass_attribute.mod_type = "objectClass";
objectclass_attribute.mod_values = objectClass_vals;
...
```

Last in the sequence of setting up the data structure we need, we build an array of the attributes our new directory object needs:

```
LDAPMopd *mods[8];

mods[0] = &cn_attribute;
mods[1] = &objectclass_attribute;
...
mods[7] = NULL;
```

After all that setting up of data, you will be pleased to know that the actual function for adding a new entry is quite simple:

```
#include <lber.h>
#include <ldap.h>
```

```
int ldap_add_s(LDAP *ld, char *new_dn, LDAPMod *mods[]);
```

We just need to pass it the LDAP structure, which needs to have been bound to an LDAP server, the dn to create as a string, and our array of attribute structures.

In many ways, the description of how to add a new dn is harder than the actual code. So here is ldap_add_one.c, which creates a new entry in our server:

```
#include <stdio.h>
#include <stdlib.h>
#include <unistd.h>
#include <string.h>


#include <lber.h>
#include <ldap.h>

int main( int argc, char *argv[] ) {
  LDAP *ld;
  int res;

  int  authmethod = LDAP_AUTH_SIMPLE;

  char *ldap_host = "gw1";

  char *user_dn = "cn=root, o=stixen.co.uk, c=uk";
  char *user_pw = "secret";

  char *new_dn = "cn=Jenny Stones, ou=People, o=stixen.co.uk, c=uk";

  char *cn_vals[] = {"Jenny Stones", NULL};
  char *sn_vals[] = {"Stones", NULL};
  char *givenname_vals[] = {"Jenny", NULL};
  char *uid_vals[] = {"stonesj", NULL};
  char *title_vals[] = {"Programmer", NULL};
  char *objectClass_vals[] = {"top", "person", NULL};
  char *ou_vals[] = {"Development", "People", NULL};

  LDAPMod cn_attribute, sn_attribute, givenname_attribute, uid_attribute,
                   title_attribute, objectClass_attribute, ou_attribute;

  LDAPMod *mods[8];

  cn_attribute.mod_op = LDAP_MOD_ADD;
  cn_attribute.mod_type = "cn";
  cn_attribute.mod_values = cn_vals;
```

```
  sn_attribute.mod_op = LDAP_MOD_ADD;
  sn_attribute.mod_type = "sn";
  sn_attribute.mod_values = sn_vals;

  givenname_attribute.mod_op = LDAP_MOD_ADD;
  givenname_attribute.mod_type = "givenname";
  givenname_attribute.mod_values = givenname_vals;

  uid_attribute.mod_op = LDAP_MOD_ADD;
  uid_attribute.mod_type = "uid";
  uid_attribute.mod_values = uid_vals;

  title_attribute.mod_op = LDAP_MOD_ADD;
  title_attribute.mod_type = "title";
  title_attribute.mod_values = title_vals;

  objectClass_attribute.mod_op = LDAP_MOD_ADD;
  objectClass_attribute.mod_type = "objectClass";
  objectClass_attribute.mod_values = objectClass_vals;

  ou_attribute.mod_op = LDAP_MOD_ADD;
  ou_attribute.mod_type = "ou";
  ou_attribute.mod_values = ou_vals;

  mods[0] = &cn_attribute;
  mods[1] = &sn_attribute;
  mods[2] = &givenname_attribute;
  mods[3] = &uid_attribute;
  mods[4] = &title_attribute;
  mods[5] = &objectClass_attribute;
  mods[6] = &ou_attribute;
  mods[7] = NULL;

  if ((ld = ldap_init(ldap_host, LDAP_PORT)) == NULL ) {
    perror( "Failure of ldap_init" );
    exit( EXIT_FAILURE );
  }

  if (ldap_bind_s(ld, user_dn, user_pw, authmethod) != LDAP_SUCCESS ) {
    ldap_perror( ld, "Failure of ldap_bind" );
    exit( EXIT_FAILURE );
  }

  if (ldap_add_s(ld, new_dn, mods) != LDAP_SUCCESS) {
    ldap_perror( ld, "Failure of ldap_add_s" );
  }

  res = ldap_unbind_s(ld);
  if (res != 0) {
    fprintf(stderr, "ldap_unbind_s failed: %s\n", ldap_err2string(res));
    exit( EXIT_FAILURE );
  }

  return EXIT_SUCCESS;
} /* main */
```

As you can see, the support code is identical to our initial ldap1.c, and the bulk of the effort is in setting up the rather complex data structures.

Modifying an Entry

Now we have learnt how to add an entry, simply modifying an entry is easy to understand. We build an array of LDAPMods in much the same way as we did before, except we can now use LDAP_MOD_REPLACE for attributes we wish to modify, or stick to LDAP_MOD_ADD, for attributes that are new to the object. Then we just call ldap_mod_s, which is almost identical to ldap_add_s:

```
#include <lber.h>
#include <ldap.h>
```

```
int ldap_mod_s(LDAP *ld, char *new_dn, LDAPMod *mods[]);
```

Again, it's easiest to see it in action, so here is ldap_mod_one.c, which updates the person's title, and adds a telephone number. The changes are highlighted:

```
#include <stdio.h>
#include <stdlib.h>
#include <unistd.h>
#include <string.h>


#include <lber.h>
#include <ldap.h>

int main( int argc, char *argv[] ) {
  LDAP *ld;
  int res;

  int  authmethod = LDAP_AUTH_SIMPLE;

  char *ldap_host = "gw1";

  char *user_dn = "cn=root, o=stixen.co.uk, c=uk";
  char *user_pw = "secret";

  char *new_dn = "cn=Jenny Stones, ou=People, o=stixen.co.uk, c=uk";

  char *title_vals[] = {"Supervisor", NULL};
  char *phone_vals[] = {"01234 654310987", NULL};


  LDAPMod title_attribute, telephoneNumber_attribute;

  LDAPMod *mods[3];


  title_attribute.mod_op = LDAP_MOD_REPLACE;
  title_attribute.mod_type = "title";
  title_attribute.mod_values = title_vals;

  telephoneNumber_attribute.mod_op = LDAP_MOD_ADD;
  telephoneNumber_attribute.mod_type = "telephoneNumber";
  telephoneNumber_attribute.mod_values = phone_vals;
```

```
    mods[0] = &title_attribute;
    mods[1] = &telephoneNumber_attribute;
    mods[2] = NULL;


  if ((ld = ldap_init(ldap_host, LDAP_PORT)) == NULL ) {
    perror( "Failure of ldap_init" );
    exit( EXIT_FAILURE );
  }

  if (ldap_bind_s(ld, user_dn, user_pw, authmethod) != LDAP_SUCCESS ) {
    ldap_perror( ld, "Failure of ldap_bind" );
    exit( EXIT_FAILURE );
  }

  if (ldap_modify_s(ld, new_dn, mods) != LDAP_SUCCESS) {
    ldap_perror( ld, "Failure of ldap_modify_s" );
  }

  res = ldap_unbind_s(ld);
  if (res != 0) {
    fprintf(stderr, "ldap_unbind_s failed: %s\n", ldap_err2string(res));
    exit( EXIT_FAILURE );
  }

  return EXIT_SUCCESS;
} /* main */
```

We can test that all is well, using the utility `ldapsearch` function:

```
$ ldapsearch -v -h localhost -p 389 -D "cn=root, o=stixen.co.uk, c=uk" -w secret -
b "o=stixen.co.uk, c=uk" 'objectclass=person'
$
```

This returns four objects; for sake of brevity, only the last of these is shown below:

```
cn=Jenny Stones, ou=People, o=stixen.co.uk, c=uk
cn=Jenny Stones
sn=Stones
givenname=Jenny
uid=stonesj
objectclass=top
objectclass=person
ou=Development
ou=People
title=Supervisor
telephonenumber=01234 654310987
```

As you can see, we have changed the title and added a phone number.

Deleting an Entry

Last, but not least, deleting an entry is simplicity itself. We just need:

```c
#include <lber.h>
#include <ldap.h>
```

```c
int ldap_delete_s(LDAP *ld, char *dn_to_delete,);
```

Just for completeness, here is `ldap_delete_one.c`:

```c
#include <stdio.h>
#include <stdlib.h>
#include <unistd.h>
#include <string.h>


#include <lber.h>
#include <ldap.h>

int main( int argc, char *argv[] ) {
  LDAP *ld;
  int res;

  int authmethod = LDAP_AUTH_SIMPLE;

  char *ldap_host = "gw1";

  char *user_dn = "cn=root, o=stixen.co.uk, c=uk";
  char *user_pw = "secret";

  char *dn_to_delete = "cn=Jenny Stones, ou=People, o=stixen.co.uk, c=uk";

  if ((ld = ldap_init(ldap_host, LDAP_PORT)) == NULL ) {
    perror( "Failure of ldap_init" );
    exit( EXIT_FAILURE );
  }

  if (ldap_bind_s(ld, user_dn, user_pw, authmethod) != LDAP_SUCCESS ) {
    ldap_perror( ld, "Failure of ldap_bind" );
    exit( EXIT_FAILURE );
  }

  if (ldap_delete_s(ld, dn_to_delete) != LDAP_SUCCESS) {
    ldap_perror( ld, "Failure of ldap_delete_s" );
  }

  res = ldap_unbind_s(ld);
  if (res != 0) {
    fprintf(stderr, "ldap_unbind_s failed: %s\n", ldap_err2string(res));
    exit( EXIT_FAILURE );
  }

  return EXIT_SUCCESS;
} /* main */
```

Again the principal changes are highlighted, not that there is much to change!

The Application

As you can probably appreciate, using an LDAP server to fully implement our DVD store database would not be a good idea. An essential part of the functionality requires us to store details that are subject to change, such as who rented a disk, but the write performance of an LDAP server is generally pretty terrible – it's not what LDAP servers were designed to do particularly well. They also have no concept of transactions, which (as we saw in Chapter 4) can be very important when we need multi-user updates to data.

We could use an LDAP server to store items like usernames and addresses, and possibly the base details of DVDs, such as the title, actors, and directors, the details of which are fairly static and well defined. It's conceivable that in the future there may be publicly accessible LDAP servers on the Internet, possibly with basic address details for the local region, and perhaps even an online DVD catalogue with an LDAP interface. We could then remove most of the attributes from our DVD store database, rather storing a distinguished name, which we could use to retrieve additional details from LDAP servers as required.

Resources

RFCs can be found at many locations on the Internet, such as http://www.rfc.net. The primary ones of interest in the LDAP area are RFC1777 (which replaces the earlier RFC 1487), RFC2251, RFC2252, RFC2255, RFC1778, RFC1779, RFC 1823, RFC1959, RFC1960, RFC2247, RFC2377 and RFC1558.

The OpenLDAP project can be found at http://www.openldap.org and has many useful resources and links.

The LDAP Linux HOWTO can be found on the http://www.linuxdoc.org server, at http://www.linuxdoc.org/HOWTO/LDAP-HOWTO.html.

The configuration guide for the standalone LDAP server can be found at http://www.umich.edu/~dirsvcs/ldap/doc/guides/.

Some standard schema items can be found at http://www.hklc.com/ldapschema/, and information about DSML, and alternative markup scheme based on XML, can be found at http://www.dsml.org/.

If you're interested in books on the subject, we recommend the excellent *Implementing LDAP* by Mark Wilcox, *(ISBN 1-861002-21-1)*, also published by Wrox.

Summary

In this chapter we have introduced some theory and concepts about the OpenLDAP directory server. We installed and provided basic configuration for this server, and looked briefly at its schema definition. We looked at how queries, the most important feature of a directory server, are expressed.

We then moved onto programming and looked at the C API for accessing LDAP servers, using the tools that come with the OpenLDAP sources. We learned how to query and manipulate data in the server.

The open source OpenLDAP server is a very complete and competent LDAP server, which will hopefully become as ubiquitous and well respected in the directory server world as Apache is in the web server world.

The information about LDAP in this chapter is of necessity rather superficial in some areas, notably when configuring OpenLDAP. There is a substantial amount of information available on the Internet, particularly in the Linux `LDAP HOWTO`, the `LDAP FAQ` and numerous RFCs, most of which come bundled with the OpenLDAP distribution.

Online discussion at http://www.p2p.wrox.com

GUI programming with GNOME/GTK+

GNOME is the GNU Network Object Model Environment, a thriving part of the GNU free software project. The aims of the GNOME project are to build a complete, easy-to-use desktop environment for the user, and a powerful application framework for the software developer. By allowing close integration of desktop tools with a powerful and flexible development framework, the GNOME and GTK+ libraries (on which the graphical elements of GNOME are largely based) provide an increasingly attractive choice for developing professional GUI applications in Linux.

Graphical toolkits such as Tk, Qt, Motif, and so on, have long been around to hide the underlying The X Window system API from the GUI programmer, so precisely what are some of the advantages of the GNOME/GTK+ libraries?

❑ Licensed under the GPL, they are, always have been, and always will be completely free software. One major advantage that they have had over KDE for example, is that, unlike KDE, they do not make use of any proprietary, or even semi-proprietary libraries in their underlying architecture.

❑ With an emphasis on portability, they are written in C, implementing a sophisticated Object and Type system, to provide a complete object-oriented framework. This framework encourages language bindings: already you can use C, C++, Python, Guile, and Perl to program with GNOME/GTK+.

❑ A core element of the architecture in new and forthcoming releases of GNOME is *Bonobo*; this technology allows the implementation of embeddable, reusable software components similar to ActiveX and Java Beans. This will allow, for instance, the embedding of a graphical, or word processing component in a spreadsheet program.

The GNOME desktop is both user-friendly and highly customizable. Menus come preconfigured with an intuitive layout and well designed, attractive icons. GNOME is independent of the window manager, but does supply 'hints' to compliant window managers, so as to interact appropriately with GNOME features such as the panel.

Assuming basic knowledge of GNOME/GTK+ we will in the course of this chapter cover the core GNOME/GTK+ material; we'll summarize familiar topics, and take an overview of some more advanced ideas. The aim is to reach a level where we can comfortably implement a GNOME/GTK+ GUI for the DVD Store application. We'll be working exclusively in C, which as we'll see, fits surprisingly well with GTK+/GNOME's object-oriented structure.

If you're totally new to GNOME/GTK+, you may first want to check out some of the introductory resources listed at the end of the chapter.

We'll look at:

❑   the GTK+/GNOME libraries

❑   glib – the C utility library

❑   GTK+ – the underlying toolkit

❑   the basics of GNOME

❑   the GNOME source tree

❑   configuration saving

❑   command line parsing

❑   session management

❑   getting more information on GNOME/GTK+

The GTK+/GNOME libraries

In this chapter and the next, we'll be dealing almost exclusively with the following libraries:

❑   glib

❑   GTK+ (along with GDK)

❑   GNOME

glib

glib provides the backbone to much of GTK+ and GNOME. It's a multi-faceted library that provides all manner of support features for C programmers, including memory functions, data storage and sorting functions. It also contains many improved alternatives to the standard system and C library functions. We'll explore in more detail in a following section, where we'll explain what's meant by 'improved alternatives'.

GTK+

GTK+, the GIMP ToolKit, is the GUI toolkit used by GNOME to provide a layer of abstraction between the programmer and the underlying window system (be it X or Win32) to make for more pain-free GUI programming. Supporters of GTK+ point to its powerful container layout system (see the *Containers* section, later on in this chapter) for designing windows; also the straightforward system used to link user events to code.

> **In the X Window system, events are called signals; these are totally different from (and not to be confused with) low-level UNIX signals.**

GDK

GDK is the GIMP Drawing Kit, which provides a thin layer between applications and the Xlib primitive drawing routines. When you develop with GTK+ you are actually using a wrapper on top of GDK, which in turn wraps X. This means that the GDK library is an essential component in the development of a GTK+/GNOME application for Linux.

There are several more very powerful libraries associated with GNOME. While these are strictly outside the scope of this book, they are so commonly used and referred to in GNOME circles, it would be criminal not to mention them. These are:

❑   Imlib

❑   ORBit

❑   libGnorba

Imlib

Imlib is a powerful image handling library, capable of manipulating a large number of image formats, such as JPGs and PNGs. GNOME uses the GDK version of the library. In future, Imlib will be replaced by the even better `gdk_pixbuf` library.

ORBit

ORBit is a free implementation of a CORBA 2.2 ORB, designed for speed and simplicity. ORBit also supports the C language, and is therefore an appropriate choice of ORB for GNOME. You can read more about CORBA in Chapters 20 and 21.

libGnorba

libGnorba provides GNOME with links to ORBit, including mechanisms for object activation and security.

glib

glib is a general C utility library that provides robust, low level elements essential to the portability of applications between different UNIX type systems and Windows. glib brings a standard set of utility functions and data types to programmers on all platforms, reducing the need for wheel-reinvention in your code and consequently reducing both development time and memory usage. Furthermore, it can increase the stability of your code in that you don't need to learn a new set of standards for each platform you want to develop on. Even if you're just wanting to develop Linux applications, then it has the edge by being just so darn helpful.

The functionality glib provides is impressive by any standard; a complete discussion is well beyond the scope of this chapter. Fortunately, as is typical of GNU projects, glib is very well documented, both on its parent web site, www.gtk.org and in the header file glib.h. Even if you aren't the sort that loves reading header files, there's a lot of really useful information to be gleaned from them, and it's sometimes actually quicker to look it up in the header than it is to browse the help files or web pages.

GNOME and GTK+ themselves rely heavily on the types, functions and debugging macros that glib provides, so a good understanding of glib should be the cornerstone of any aspiring GNOME/GTK+ programmer's training.

The features covered in this section are:

❑ glib types

❑ macros

❑ memory routines

❑ string handling functions

❑ lists

Types

One important but easily forgotten aspect of C is that the sizes of certain primitive types are platform-dependent. For example, an int will usually occupy 32 bits of memory, but on some machines it can be more or less than this. Of course there are fairly simple coding methods you can use to ensure that this doesn't cause problems, but mistakes do happen.

Therefore, to make our lives easier, glib defines its own set of primitive types of guaranteed length, together with new boolean, string and void pointer types for complete convenience. For example gint16 is a signed integer of length 16 bits, and guint16 its unsigned partner.

glib type	Description
gint8, gint16, gint32, gint64	signed integer of guaranteed length
guint8, guint16, guint32, guint64	unsigned integer of guaranteed length
gboolean	boolean type, TRUE/FALSE also defined by glib

glib type	Description
gint	equivalent to int
gshort	equivalent to short
gchar	equivalent to char
gfloat	equivalent to float
gdouble	equivalent to double
gpointer	equivalent to void *

Note that gint64 and guint64 only exist if the platform can support them. If it can, then glib will define G_HAVE_GINT64.

gint, gshort, gchar, gfloat and gdouble are simple wrappers around the existing C types, and are included purely for consistency. Given their identical nature, you might wonder what benefits there are in using gint over int, or gchar over char. The fact is that technically there aren't any; in terms of good programming practice though, we're maintaining consistency, a habit that we should try to reinforce whenever we have the opportunity. It's particularly important to use common coding style and maintain overall consistency when writing cross-platform code, so although gint versus int won't make any difference to your compiled code, it may well help *you* in more subtle ways.

Macros

glib defines several macros to aid with general programming and debugging, most of which will be familiar to C programmers. To complement the gboolean type, there are TRUE and FALSE macros. NULL is predefined as a void pointer: (void *)0 in ANSI C.

There are also several simple macros provided to help with numerical juggling, principally there to help speed up coding and help with code legibility.

Macro	Description
FALSE	#define FALSE (0)
TRUE	#define TRUE (!FALSE)
NULL	#define NULL ((void *) 0)
ABS(x)	Returns the absolute value of x
MIN(a,b)	Returns the smaller of a and b
MAX(a,b)	Returns the larger of a and b
CLAMP(x, low, high)	Returns x if x is between low and high. Returns low if x<low or high if x>high

According to the machine's processor, the macro G_BYTE_ORDER is set to G_LITTLE_ENDIAN, G_BIG_ENDIAN or G_PDP_ENDIAN (byte orderings 4321, 1234 and 3412 respectively).

Debugging macros

glib provides us with a set of macros that can be used to test assumptions made in the code, allowing bugs to be caught early. Place these macros in code check conditions and make assertions, which upon failure, print a warning to the console. They can force an immediate return to the calling function or even force the application to quit.

These functions are divisible into two types: those which are commonly used to check that the calling function has supplied us with valid arguments, and those used to check conditions within the function itself.

Checking valid arguments is often the first thing done at the beginning of a function – so called precondition checks. The two macros g_return_val_if_fail(condition, retval) and g_return_if_fail(condition) print a warning if (condition!=TRUE) and return from the function. The former is used in void functions, while the latter returns retval, and must be used in non-void functions.

You don't have to look hard to find examples in the GNOME source – here's a snippet from the GNOME panel implementation:

```
void
panel_clean_applet(AppletInfo *info)
{
        g_return_if_fail(info != NULL);

        if(info->widget) {
            if(info->type == APPLET_STATUS) {
                status_applet_put_offscreen(info->data);
            }
            gtk_widget_destroy(info->widget);
        }
}
```

Without g_return_if_fail, panel_clean_applet would run into problems if info was passed NULL. With the assertion macro in place, g_return_if_fail returns the error:

```
** CRITICAL **: file panel.c: line 227 (panel_clean_applet):
                assertion 'info != NULL' failed.
```

which directs us straight to the problem. Checking internal consistency within functions is most often done with the assertion macro:

```
g_assert(condition)
```

If the condition fails, abort is called and a core dump is generated

```
** ERROR **: file test.c: line 9 (assert_test):
                assertion failed: (pointer != NULL)
aborting...
Aborted (core dumped)
$
```

Since g_assert ends program execution, it's preferable to use g_return_if_fail within a function in cases where failure would be non-fatal.

To denote a region of code that should never be executed, glib provides:

```
g_assert_not_reached()
```

which aborts with the error:

```
** ERROR **: file search_window.c: line 733 (update_search_clist):
                  should not be reached
aborting...
Aborted (core dumped)
$
```

if ever reached. This proves useful in conditional statements where one or more conditions should never be met. For instance, in this code fragment:

```
current_page = gtk_notebook_get_current_page (GTK_NOTEBOOK (search_notebook));

switch (current_page)
  {
  case TITLE_PAGE:
    clist = lookup_widget (GTK_WIDGET (button), "title_search_clist");
    break;
  case MEMBER_PAGE:
    clist = lookup_widget (GTK_WIDGET (button), "member_search_clist");
    break;
  case DISK_PAGE:
    clist = lookup_widget (GTK_WIDGET (button), "disk_search_clist");
    break;
  default:
    g_assert_not_reached();
  }
```

we make sure that current_page is equal to either TITLE_PAGE, MEMBER_PAGE or DISK_PAGE in the switch statement.

GNOME and GTK+ frequently use these macros in their source; this is one of the reasons they are so easy to program with, and why spotting errors is very straightforward when using them. Learn by example – using debugging macros will halve the time you spend searching for NULL pointers and other irritating bugs.

String functions

String handling in C is an awkward task, as every C programmer knows. Dealing with character arrays, pointers to characters, pointers to arrays, arrays of pointers, and so on, requires consistent, flawless programming.

Running over memory boundaries and incorrect use of pointers form the backbone of runtime errors, and it doesn't help that the standard string functions in string.h are as unforgiving as they are. glib provides cleaner, safer, portable alternatives, and includes helpful extra functions when it comes to chopping, changing, and general string manipulation.

A good example of glib's robust string library is g_snprintf. This function is equivalent to sprintf but it will copy only the first n characters of the formatting string to buf and guarantees to NULL-terminate the string. Note that the n characters include the NULL terminator.

```
gint g_snprintf(gchar *buf, gulong n, const gchar *format, ...)
```

Before using g_snprintf though, you must allocate enough space for the formatted string:

```
gchar *msg = g_malloc(50);
g_snprintf(msg, 50 , "Error %d occurred. %s", err, action);
```

In this case, a more convenient method is to use g_strdup_printf:

```
gchar * g_strdup_printf(const gchar * format, ...)
```

g_strdup_printf allocates the correct space to hold the formatted string, removing the need to guess or calculate the required length:

```
gchar *msg = g_strdup_printf("Error %d occurred. %s", err, action);
```

In both cases, the allocated buffer must still be freed with g_free after use:

```
g_free(msg);
```

We'll look at more of glib's memory management functions later.

glib makes strcasecmp and strncasecmp available on all platforms in the form of two functions:

```
gint g_strcasecmp(const gchar *s1, const gchar *s2)
gint g_strncasecmp(const gchar *s1, const gchar *s2, guint n)
```

g_strcasecmp compares two given strings, and g_strncasecmp the first n characters of two strings, returning 0 if they match, a negative value if s1 < s2, and a positive value if s1 > s2. Note that the comparison is case-insensitive.

glib also provides functions for in-situ string modification. To convert a string to upper or lower case, call strup and strdown respectively. The order of characters in a string is reversed using g_strreverse, so that g_strreverse("glib") will return a pointer to "bilg".

```
void g_strup(gchar *string)
void g_strdown(gchar *string)
gchar * g_strreverse(gchar *string)
```

g_strchug removes leading spaces in a string; similarly g_strchomp removes trailing spaces.

```
gchar * g_strchug(gchar *string)
gchar * g_strchomp(gchar *string)
```

To copy a string to a newly allocated string we have g_strdup, g_strndup and g_strdup_printf as mentioned previously. g_strdup copies the complete string, g_strndup only the first n characters:

```
gchar * g_strdup(const gchar *str)
gchar * g_strndup(const gchar * format, guint n)
```

Finally in our quick tour of the most commonly used string functions, are a couple of functions to concatenate strings:

```
gchar * g_strconcat(const gchar *s1, ...)
gchar * g_strjoin(const gchar * separator, ...)
```

g_strconcat returns a newly allocated string containing the concatenation of the arguments. g_strjoin works in a similar fashion, but places separator between elements of the concatenation.

Memory Allocation

glib irons out any potential problems with the C malloc and free memory functions by wrapping them with its own equivalents: g_malloc and g_free. The glib pair also provides useful memory profiling when used with the --enable-mem-profile compilation option. Calling g_mem_profile prints handy information on the memory use of your program to the console. Specifically, g_mem_profile outputs the frequency of allocations of different sizes, the total number of bytes that have been allocated, the total number freed, and the difference between these values; that is, the number of bytes still in use. Memory leaks become easy to spot.

g_malloc will sensibly deal with a 0 size allocation request, unlike malloc, by returning a NULL pointer. g_malloc will immediately abort the program if the allocation fails, thereby circumventing the need to check for a NULL pointer. This can be seen as a disadvantage, as there's no scope for fallback in the case of failure. g_free happily ignores NULL pointers given to it, unlike free.

As the two allocators malloc and g_malloc may use separate pools of memory, it's essential to match g_free with g_malloc, likewise free and malloc must be used in pairs.

```
gpointer g_malloc(gulong size)
void g_free(gpointer mem)
```

g_realloc is a glib mirror of the familiar realloc, to reallocate a buffer to a new size. Consistent with g_malloc, g_realloc returns a NULL pointer if passed a zero-length buffer. g_memdup copies a block of memory into a newly allocated buffer.

```
gpointer g_realloc(gpointer mem, gulong size)
gpointer g_memdup(gconstpointer mem, guint bytesize)
```

Lists

Storage of data in singly or doubly linked lists is a very common programming requirement, and glib provides excellent resources for implementing both in a clean and efficient manner.

The doubly linked list struct GList contains pointers to both the previous and next elements:

```
/* Doubly Linked List */
struct GList
{
  gpointer data;
  GList *next;
  GList *prev;
};
```

Unlike the singly linked list GSList, Glist enables the possibility of traversing the list both forwards and backwards.

```
/* Singly Linked List */
struct GSList
{
  gpointer data;
  GSList *next;
};
```

Note that the data in both lists is stored as gpointers, but you can easily store integers using the macros GINT_TO_POINTER, GPOINTER _TO_INT, GUINT_TO_POINTER and GPOINTER_TO_UINT.

To create an empty singly linked list, just initialize a NULL pointer:

```
GSList* single_list = NULL;
```

Similarly, a doubly linked list is created with:

```
GList *double_list = NULL;
```

Both use an identical API, with the exception of a leading 'S' in the case of singly linked list functions, which makes sense given that doubly linked lists are a superset of singly linked ones. For instance, g_slist_append adds an element to a singly linked list, and g_list_append adds an element to a doubly linked list. There is no singly linked equivalent of g_list_previous though.

To add items to a list, use g_slist_append, making sure to update the GSList pointer with the returned value in case the start of the list has changed.

```
GSList * g_slist_append (GSList *list, gpointer data);
```

For example, to add a string and integer as elements to the end of a list we would write:

```
GSList *single_list = NULL;
single_list = g_slist_append(single_list, "The answer is:");
single_list = g_slist_append(single_list, GINT_TO_POINTER (42));
```

noting of course that we need to be careful with the subsequent code if we have elements holding different datatypes in the same list.

To add elements to the start of the list, use g_slist_prepend:

```
single_list = g_slist_prepend(single_list, "This appears at the start");
```

And finally to free the list, call g_slist_free:

```
g_slist_free(single_list);
```

This frees up the list cells, but not the contents of the cells. You have to free the contents of a list manually if necessary, to avoid memory leaks.

To retrieve the contents of a cell, simply access the data element of the GSList struct directly:

```
gpointer data = single_list->data;
```

and to move to the next cell in the list, call g_slist_next:

```
single_list = g_slist_next(single_list);
```

Naturally, we can also move backwards in the list with doubly linked lists:

```
double_list = g_list_previous(double_list);
```

We often need to add items at a specific position in the list; likewise we may well need to grab data from a certain position in the list. For these purposes we have:

```
GSList * g_slist_insert(GSList *list, gpointer data, gint position)
gpointer g_slist_nth_data(GSList *list, guint n)
```

Also of great use is g_slist_remove, which removes the element containing data:

```
GSList * g_slist_remove(GSList *list, gpointer data)
```

Other functions to grab data from the list return the list at the element specified. The three listed below respectively allow you to specify the element by its contents, its position from the start, or simply the fact that it's the last element in the list:

```
GSList * g_slist_find(GSList *list, gpointer data)
GSList * g_slist_nth(GSList *list, guint n)
GSList *g_slist_last(GSList *list)
```

GTK+

The GIMP ToolKit, GTK+, has its roots in providing the user interface for the GNU Image Manipulation Program, known as the GIMP. GTK+ has since gone from strength to strength, and is now a well featured, easy to use, lightweight, non-desktop specific Toolkit. None of its features place any demands on the actual desktop environment; for instance, it doesn't include the ability to interact with desktop menus or save state between sessions. This is entirely by design, as it enables GTK+ to be ported between OS platforms; successful ports include those to Windows, Sloaris and BeOS.

As GNOME is based upon GTK+, a good working knowledge of GTK+ is a prerequisite for aspiring GNOME programmers. The information that appears in this section is only a small fraction of what we could conceivably present, but as you'll find, the key to understanding GNOME/GTK+ lies in an appreciation of the general concepts, rather than in the details of individual widgets.

Widgets

A **widget** is an X Windows term for any user interface element, as originally coined by the MIT Athena project; widgets can be labels, frames, entry boxes, windows, buttons, whatever else you happen to need. GTK+ is an object-oriented toolkit, and all widgets in GTK+ are derived from the GtkWidget base class (itself derived from the base object GtkObject). As mentioned earlier, GTK+ is written in C, and includes a comprehensive Object and Type System to deal with class properties, inheritance, typecasting and storage and retrieval of arbitrary object data.

A typical widget life-cycle involves five steps:

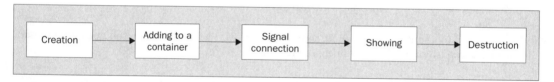

Widget Creation

A widget is typically created with a GtkWidget *gtk_widgetname_new function, which returns a pointer of type GtkWidget for convenience.

```
label = gtk_label_new("Hello World");
```

To use label in a label widget-specific function such as gtk_label_set_text we would need to use the casting macro GTK_LABEL:

```
gtk_label_set_text(GTK_LABEL(label), "Goodbye World");
```

You can find a full description of the Object and Type system, together with examples on writing your own widgets in *GTK+/GNOME Application Development*, details of which are given at the end of the chapter.

Containers

A GTK+ container is a widget that can physically contain other widgets. GtkContainer is an example of such a widget, whose purpose is to provide extra functionality to its children; that is, widgets derived from GtkContainer have the ability to 'contain' other widgets.

It's this ability that GTK+ uses to create the layout of widgets on screen. Rather than positioning widgets in a window using a fixed coordinate system, each widget is added to a parent container using the function:

```
void gtk_container_add(GtkContainer *container, GtkWidget *widget)
```

The position and size of a widget on screen is determined by the properties of the container. This approach is hugely flexible, resulting in the intelligent sizing of widgets within windows, regardless of window size.

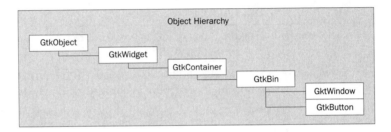

Looking at the widget hierarchy above, we see the window widget GtkWindow and button widget GtkButton are amongst those derived from GtkContainer. Therefore to make a GtkWindow contain a GtkButton, and have that GtkButton contain a GtkLabel, we can write:

```
GtkWidget *window = gtk_window_new(GTK_WINDOW_TOPLEVEL);
GtkWidget *button = gtk_button_new();
GtkWidget *label = gtk_label_new("Hello World");

gtk_container_add(GTK_CONTAINER(button), label);
gtk_container_add(GTK_CONTAINER(window), button);
```

GtkWindow and GtkButton are descendants of GtkBin, another abstract widget class that has been designed to hold a single child widget only. To create more complicated layouts, we use the direct descendants of GtkContainer, which can hold multiple widgets in any one of several formats.

Packing Boxes

GtkHBox and GtkVBox are containers that divide an occupied portion of a window into rows and columns respectively. Each of these 'packing boxes' can hold all the usual widgets, including more packing boxes. This is the key to flexible arrangement of widgets in windows; it allows you to subdivide a simple window in complex but still well-defined ways. The relative size and spacing of widgets in the box are controlled by the properties of the HBox and VBox widgets.

The relevant creation functions require two overall properties: homogeneous, dictating whether child widgets are given equal space, and spacing, the spacing in pixels between adjacent widgets.

```
GtkWidget *gtk_hbox_new(gboolean homogeneous, gint spacing)
GtkWidget *gtk_vbox_new(gboolean homogeneous, gint spacing)
```

Individual widget spacing properties are specified upon adding the child widget to the Vbox or Hbox:

```
void gtk_box_pack_start(GtkBox *box, GtkWidget *child,
                        gboolean expand, gboolean fill, gint padding)

void gtk_box_pack_end(GtkBox *box, GtkWidget *child,
                      gboolean expand, gboolean fill, gint padding)
```

gtk_box_pack_start will add a child to the top of a GtkVBox or the left of a GtkHBox. Conversely, gtk_box_pack_end adds to the bottom or right.

Quite a complicated interplay takes place between packing box and child widgets in order to determine their spacing. The three arguments passed when adding each child are easy to understand:

Argument	Type	Description
expand	gboolean	If TRUE, the child widget expands to fill the available space, otherwise it remains its default size.
fill	gboolean	If TRUE, the child widget expands to fill the allocated space, otherwise it adds more padding around the widget.
padding	gint	The space, in pixels, with which to surround the child widget.

Bear in mind that if the packing box is homogeneous, the expand parameter is irrelevant.

It's well worth experimenting with these properties, and probably easiest using Glade, a program which we'll be looking at in some depth in the next chapter.

Tables

A common layout for dialog boxes uses rows of label and entry widgets, for input from the user. One method of creating this layout would be to pack each label/entry pair into a GtkHBox, and pack rows of these into a GtkVBox. However, aligning columns of label and entry widgets proves rather tiresome unless the text for all the labels is of the same length.

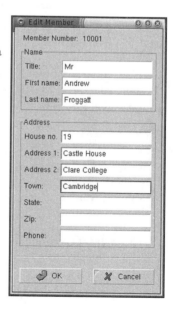

It turns out that in this case, it's easier to use a GtkTable. As its name suggests, a GtkTable consists of a layout table, with cells divided into rows *and* columns, to which widgets can be attached. Widgets can be made to span more than one row or column if necessary. GtkTable aligns rows and columns for neatness, and gives similar flexibility for individual widget placing to GtkHBoxes and GtkVBoxes.

```
GtkWidget *gtk_table_new(guint rows, guint columns, gboolean homogeneous)
```

The first two arguments to gtk_table_new specify the initial number of rows and columns of the table, although the table will automatically expand as needed, if a widget is added to the table outside its current limits. As with boxes, homogeneous specifies whether each cell will be forced to occupy the same area.

Adding a widget to the table involves a call to gtk_table_attach, to which we give the row and column bounding edges, two gtkAttachOptions, and padding to surround the widget.

```
GtkWidget * gtk_table_attach(GtkTable *table, GtkWidget *child,
                    guint left_column, guint right_column,
                    guint top_row,      guint bottom_row,
                    GtkAttachOptions xoptions,
                    GtkAttachOptions yoptions,
                    guint xpadding,     guint ypadding)
```

The position of each child widget in the table is specified in terms of the row and column lines that form the widget's bounding box. For example, in a table with 3 columns and 2 rows, there are 4 column lines (numbered 0 to 3) and 3 row lines (numbered 0 to 2).

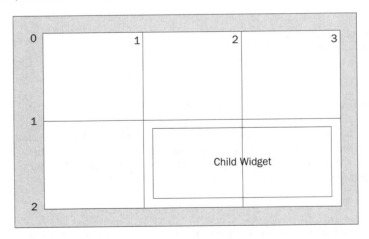

To place a child widget in the shown position, we would thus set left_column to 1, right_column to 3 respectively, and top_row and bottom_row to 1 and 2 respectively.

The GtkAttachOptions arguments take one or more of three enum values to give the table more information on how to space the widget. The values are bitmasks, so to specify two or more simultaneously, use the bitwise OR: for example, GTK_EXPAND|GTK_FILL

GtkAttachOptions	Description
GTK_EXPAND	This section of the table expands to fill the available space.
GTK_FILL	The child widget will expand to fill the space allocated when this is used with GTK_EXPAND. It has no effect unless GTK_EXPAND is also used.
GTK_SHRINK	If there is insufficient space for the child widget and GTK_SHRINK is set, the table forcibly shrinks the child. If unset, the child will be given its requested size, which may result in clipping at the boundaries.

We might write something like this:

```
table = gtk_table_new(2,1, FALSE);
label1= gtk_label_new("Label One");
label2 = gtk_label_new("Label Two");

gtk_table_attach(GTK_TABLE(table), label1,
    0, 1,
    0, 1,
    GTK_FILL,
    GTK_FILL,
    0,
    0);

gtk_table_attach(GTK_TABLE(table), label2,
    0, 1,
    1, 2,
    GTK_FILL | GTK_EXPAND | GTK_SHRINK,
    GTK_FILL | GTK_EXPAND | GTK_SHRINK,
    0,
    0);
```

We'd then have to add table itself to a container.

Manually writing layout code is undeniably rather tedious and repetitive, especially for complicated windows. Consider using a user interface builder (such as Glade) to design your interface. Not only are they WYSIWYG – What You See Is What You Get – but offer far more flexibility, such as the possibility of dynamically loading GUI designs.

Signals

Generating responses to user actions is an integral part of all GUI programming. When something interesting happens, typically a user clicking on a widget, or typing in an entry box, that widget will emit a signal. (As we mentioned before, signals in the GTK+ sense are wholly different from low level UNIX signals.) Each widget can emit signals specific to its type, and all of those specific to its parent widgets in its hierarchy.

Signals are referred to by string identifiers. For example, when a GtkButton is clicked, it emits the "clicked" signal. To take action on this signal, we connect a **callback** function, which is executed on the emission of that signal:

```
gint id = gtk_signal_connect(GTK_OBJECT(button),
                    "clicked",
                    GTK_SIGNAL_FUNC(button_clicked_callback),
                    NULL);
```

Here, gtk_signal_connect connects the function button_clicked_callback to the "clicked" signal of button. We have the option to pass arbitrary user data as the fourth parameter in the form of a gpointer; here we choose not to, and pass NULL instead. gtk_signal_connect returns a unique signal connection ID; this is rarely used, but necessary if we later want to disconnect the signal.

The prototype for a typical callback function looks like this:

```
void button_click_callback( GtkButton *button, gpointer data);
```

Certain signals require slightly different callback functions though, as we'll see for GNOME dialogs later. We are always passed a pointer to the widget emitting the signal as the first argument.

To disconnect a signal, we need to pass the GtkObject and connection ID:

```
gtk_signal_connect(GTK_OBJECT(button), id);
```

Showing, Sensitivity and Hiding

To make widgets visible on screen, we must call gtk_widget_show on each widget. More conveniently, we can call gtk_widget_show_all on the top level widget, which recursively shows all of its children:

```
void gtk_widget_show(GtkWidget *widget)
void gtk_widget_show_all(GtkWidget *widget)
```

We often want a widget to appear shaded, or grayed out; in GTK parlance, we want its **sensitivity** set to FALSE; effectively we want to deactivate the widget. We can adjust the sensitivity with a call to:

```
void gtk_widget_set_sensitive(GtkWidget *widget, gboolean setting)
```

We can also *hide* a widget temporarily, with a call to gtk_widget_hide:

```
void gtk_widget_hide(GtkWidget *widget)
```

Destruction

Destroying widgets that are no longer needed keeps memory usage to a minimum:

```
void gtk_widget_destroy(GtkWidget *widget)
```

gtk_init and gtk_main

All GTK+ programs must be initialized with a single call to `gtk_init`, which connects to the X server and parses GTK+ specific command line options. Simply pass `argc` and `argv`, and `gtk_init` removes the options it recognizes from `argv`, and decrements `argc` appropriately:

```
gtk_init(&argc, &argv);
```

Having created and laid out the primary window, a typical GTK+ application passes control to the event handling loop with a call to `gtk_main`, which takes no arguments. When `gtk_main` is called, the program interacts with the user only through the signal and event callback functions, until such time as `gtk_main_quit` is called:

Example GTK+ Application

This is a very simple application, using the principles we've seen so far in this chapter:

```c
/*
 * A hello world application using GTK+
 */

#include <gtk/gtk.h>

static void
on_button_clicked(GtkWidget *button, gpointer data)
{
  g_print("The button was clicked - Hello World!\n");
}

static gint
on_delete_event(GtkWidget *window, GdkEventAny *event, gpointer data)
{
  gtk_main_quit();
  return FALSE;
}

gint
main(gint argc, gchar *argv[])
{
  GtkWidget *window;
  GtkWidget *vbox;
  GtkWidget *label;
  GtkWidget *button;

  gtk_init(&argc, &argv);

  window = gtk_window_new(GTK_WINDOW_TOPLEVEL);
  vbox = gtk_vbox_new(TRUE, 10);
  label = gtk_label_new("This label is placed first into the VBox");
  button = gtk_button_new_with_label("Click Me!");

  gtk_box_pack_start(GTK_BOX(vbox), label, FALSE, FALSE, 0);
  gtk_box_pack_start(GTK_BOX(vbox), button, FALSE, FALSE, 0);
```

```
      gtk_container_add(GTK_CONTAINER(window), vbox);

      gtk_window_set_title(GTK_WINDOW(window), "The Title");

      gtk_signal_connect(GTK_OBJECT(window), "delete_event",
                  GTK_SIGNAL_FUNC(on_delete_event),
                  NULL);

      gtk_signal_connect(GTK_OBJECT(button), "clicked",
                  GTK_SIGNAL_FUNC(on_button_clicked),
                  NULL);

      gtk_widget_show_all(window);

      gtk_main();

      return 0;

}
```

The Makefile for `basic_gtk_app.c` looks like this:

```
CC=gcc

all: basic_gtk_app.c
    $(CC) 'gtk-config --libs --cflags' -o basic_gtk_app basic_gtk_app.c
```

GNOME Basics

In this section we're going to look at some important aspects of GNOME and GNOME programming, including:

❑   GNOME widgets

❑   building menus and toolbars with GNOME

❑   GNOME dialog boxes

As mentioned in the chapter introduction, GNOME builds on GTK+ in two ways: it adds widgets that extend the functionality of existing GTK+ widgets, for example, `gnome_entry` enhances `gtk_entry`; it also replaces the GTK+ routines used to build menus, toolbars and dialogs with a new set of functions, which are not only more powerful, but also easier to use.

All of the GNOME, GTK+, GDK, etc. header files are #included with:

```
#include <gnome.h>
```

gnome_init

This function is analogous to `gtk_init`; an application must pass a short version of its name and version number (along with the usual command line parameters) to `gnome_init` in order to initialize both GNOME and GTK+. It therefore replaces the need to call `gtk_init` in GNOME programs. It should (that is, it doesn't at present, but may do in future) return non-zero if the call fails; current versions of GNOME abort on failure instead.

```
gint gnome_init(const char *app_id, const char *app_version,
                             gint argc, char **argv)
```

gnome_init will not change argc and argv in the way that gtk_init does. Command line parsing in gnome applications is best done using gnome_init_with_popt_table.

popt is a specialized command line parsing library, about which we'll say more later.

GnomeApp

Almost all GNOME applications make use of the GnomeApp widget for their main window. GnomeApp is a subclass of GtkWindow, and provides the basis for easy menu, toolbar and status bar creation. What's great about GnomeApp is that it gives the application a large amount of extra functionality at no cost:

❑ Menu and toolbars can be detached and 'docked' in horizontal and vertical positions on the GnomeApp. GNOME automatically saves the docking configuration between sessions.

❑ Users can configure global preferences that determine the properties of menus and toolbars.

Creating a GnomeApp widget requires a call to gnome_app_new, passing the same app_id that we passed to gnome_init and a string to be placed in the window title:

```
GtkWidget *gnome_app_new(gchar *app_id, gchar *title)
```

Once a GnomeApp exists, adding a menu, toolbar and status bar is simply a matter of setting up the required menu and toolbar structs, creating a status bar, and then calling:

```
void gnome_app_set_menus(GnomeApp *app, GtkMenuBar *menubar)
void gnome_app_set_toolbar(GnomeApp *app, GtkToolbar *toolbar)
void gnome_app_set_statusbar(GnomeApp *app, GtkWidget *statusbar)
```

Menus and Toolbars

The GNOME method of creating menus and toolbars is to define each menu and toolbar item using a GnomeUIInfo struct:

```
typedef struct {
 GnomeUIInfo type;
  gchar* label;
  gchar* hint;
  gpointer moreinfo;
  gpointer user_data;
  gpointer unused_data;
  GnomeUIPixmapType pixmap_type;
  gpointer pixmap_info;
  guint accelerator_key;
  GdkModifierType ac_mods;
  GtkWidget* widget;
 } GnomeUIInfo;
```

In fact, we rarely have to fill in this struct ourselves, as GNOME has plenty of predefined `GnomeUIInfo` structs; it's useful nevertheless to have an understanding of its innards.

❏ `type` is a type marker relating to one of the `GnomeUIInfoType` enums; its value controls the interpretation of the fourth parameter, `moreinfo`, as shown below:

Type	**Moreinfo** interpreted as	Description
GNOME_APP_UI_ITEM	callback function	Standard menu/toolbar item
GNOME_APP_UI_TOGGLE_ITEM	callback function	Toggle or Check item
GNOME_APP_UI_RADIOITEMS	array of radio items in the group	Radio item group
GNOME_APP_UI_SUBTREE	GnomeUIInfo array that forms a subtree	Submenu
GNOME_APP_UI_SEPARATOR	NULL	Separator between items
GNOME_APP_UI_HELP	help node to load	Help item
GNOME_APP_UI_ENDOFINFO	NULL	GnomeUIInfo array terminator

❏ `label` contains the text of the menu or toolbar item.

❏ `hint` points to some additional descriptive text; in the case of a button this will be displayed as a tooltip, whereas for menu items it can be made to appear in the status bar. Make tooltips long if necessary, sufficient to explain the function of the item. In any case, don't just repeat `label`.

❏ `moreinfo` is dependent on `type`, as shown above; if it contains a callback function, then the next parameter...

❏ ...`user_data` is passed to the callback function.

❏ `unused_data` is reserved for future use, and should be set to `NULL`.

❏ `pixmap_type` and `pixmap_info` specify a pixmap to be used in the menu or toolbar item, one dictating the interpretation of the other as follows:

pixmap_type	**pixmap_info** interpreted as	Description
GNOME_APP_PIXMAP_STOCK	name of a stock GNOME pixmap	Use a GNOME-provided pixmap
GNOME_APP_PIXMAP_DATA	pointer to a GdkPixmap	Use an application-specific pixmap
GNOME_APP_PIXMAP_FILENAME	filename of a pixmap	Use the pixmap found at `filename`
GNOME_APP_PIXMAP_NONE	NULL	No pixmap

❑ accelerator_key and ac_mods define the keyboard shortcuts that apply to this item. The former can be a character such as 'a', or a value taken from gdk/gdkkeysms.h. The latter is a mask (like GDK_CONTROL_MASK) that controls the modifier keys (or combinations thereof) that can be used with the shortcut.

❑ widget should be left NULL; on passing GnomeUIInfo to gnome_app_create_menus, GNOME fills widget with a pointer to an actual widget of that menu or toolbar item. This pointer is used to specify the menu or toolbar item during program execution. A common use would be to gray out the item by passing widget to gtk_widget_sensitivity.

Here's an entry for an 'Undo' item, as a concrete example:

```
GnomeUIInfo undo = {GNOME_APP_UI_ITEM,
                    N_("_Undo"),
                    N_("Undo the last action"),
                    on_undo_clicked,
                    NULL,
                    GNOME_APP_PIXMAP_DATA,
                    undo_pixmap,
                    'z',
                    GDK_CONTROL_MASK};
```

The N_ macro surrounding the on-screen text strings facilitates internationalization, a topic that we'll cover in chapter 28.

Menus and toolbars are built from arrays of GnomeUIInfo structs, followed by a call to either gnome_app_create_menus and gnome_app_create_toolbar, as appropriate.

```
void gnome_app_create_menus(GnomeApp *app, GnomeUIInfo *uiinfo)
void gnome_app_create_toolbar(GnomeApp *app, GnomeUIInfo *uiinfo)
```

While GnomeUIInfo structs provide complete control over menu and toolbar definition, complete control is not always necessary, or indeed desirable. Many GUI applications follow a File, Edit, View, Help format of top level menus, and most of those that don't really ought to. Once inside the top level menus, there are more conventions as to which menu items appear where, and in what order. For example New, Open, and Exit items are conventionally placed first, second and last in the File menu.

With standardization in mind, GNOME provides a whole set of macros that define GnomeUIInfo structs for commonly used menu items; they can set out the label, tooltip, pixmap and accelerator for you. Standard menu design is therefore very quick and easy.

Each top level menu on the menubar consists of an array of GnomeUIInfo structs, and the menu definitions are combined to form the complete menu tree by including pointers to these arrays, using the GNOMEUIINFO_SUBTREE macro. You can find these definitions in libgnomeui/gnome-app-help.h

GnomeAppbar

The GnomeApp widget can optionally hold a status bar; these are the strips that often lie along a window's bottom edge, which convey information about the application's status. GnomeApps can also hold a progress bar, giving a graphical indication of progress for a time consuming operation. For instance, Netscape uses its progress bar to show the approximate percentage of a web page or email that has currently been downloaded.

On creating a GnomeAppbar, we use booleans to specify whether it consists of a status bar, progress bar, or both. There's also an interactivity term, which in future versions of GNOME may allow for further interaction with the user. Until this feature is developed though, the recommended setting is GNOME_PREFERENCES_USER.

```
GtkWidget *gnome_appbar_new(gboolean has_progress,
                            gboolean has_status,
                            GnomePreferencesType interactivity)
```

This creates the appbar; to then add it to the GnomeApp window, we require the function:

```
void gnome_app_set_statusbar(GnomeApp *app, GtkWidget *statusbar)
```

Text in the status bar is treated as a stack system. Adding text means pushing it onto the stack with:

```
void gnome_appbar_push(GnomeAppBar  appbar, const gchar *text)
```

Text pushed onto the top of the stack remains visible until either new text is pushed on top or the stack is popped with a call to gnome_appbar_pop. In the latter case, the text held one position lower in the stack is displayed.

```
void gnome_appbar_pop(GnomeAppBar *appbar, const gchar *status)
```

Should the stack become empty, the default text is displayed; this is normally an empty string. You can change this text using:

```
void gnome_appbar_set_default(GnomeAppBar *appbar, const gchar *default_text)
```

The entire stack can be cleared quickly and simply with gnome_appbar_clear_stack. Although the stack is useful for allowing different parts of your application to use the status bar simultaneously without risk of interference, you'll often just need to display temporary information without recourse to the stack. You can add **transient** text using gnome_appbar_set_status, which remains visible until either new transient text is added, or the stack is pushed, popped, cleared, or refreshed with a call to gnome_appbar_refresh.

```
void gnome_appbar_clear_stack(GnomeAppBar *appbar)
void gnome_appbar_set_status(GnomeAppBar *appbar, const gchar *status)
void gnome_appbar_refresh(GnomeAppBar *appbar)
```

As the mouse pointer highlights menu items, GNOME allows the display of menu tooltips on the status bar for the cost of one call to:

```
void gnome_app_install_menu_hints(GnomeApp *app, GnomeUIInfo *uiinfo)
```

The GnomeUIInfo struct must previously have been created with a call to one of the menu creation functions, so that its widget field is filled in.

Progress Bar

The progress bar consists of a `GtkProgress` widget, and providing the `GnomeAppBar` has been created with the optional progress bar, a pointer to the `GtkProgress` can be returned with:

```
GtkProgress *gnome_appbar_get_progress(GnomeAppBar *appbar)
```

Finally, and most importantly, you can add contents to a `GnomeApp` widget with:

```
void gnome_app_set_contents(GnomeApp *app, GtkWidget *contents)
```

This is equivalent to using `gtk_container_add` with a conventional `gtk_window`.

Dialogs

Dialogs form an essential part of any GUI application, allowing the user to select or enter data, and report to the user all manner of information such as errors, general messages and help text. In a typical application, there are many more dialog boxes than central windows, so the easy programming of dialogs is an essential requirement for any modern toolkit.

Dialog boxes have certain distinctions from normal windows:

❑ They always have one or more buttons that signal to the application to invoke or cancel the operation of the dialog.

❑ They have no minimize tab on the window decoration.

❑ They have the option of being *modal*, that is, preventing use of the rest of the application until the dialog is dismissed.

Recognizing these distinctions, GNOME implements dialogs by extending `GtkWindow` to a dialog base class, `GnomeDialog`. This forms a ready-built dialog template complete with assorted functions; making dialogs with GNOME is therefore a wholly civilized affair.

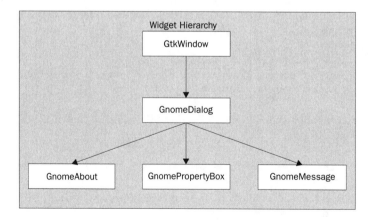

However, GnomeDialog isn't the end of the story. There are also three special dialog types:

❑   GnomeAbout

❑   GnomePropertyBox

❑   GnomeMessageBox

These make it quicker and easier to create commonly used dialog boxes for more specific purposes. What's more, they're derived from GnomeDialog, share its functionality and help maintain consistency across GNOME applications. Let's look in more detail at GnomeDialog.

Creating a *GnomeDialog*

To create a GnomeDialog widget, call gnome_dialog_new and pass the window title and a NULL-terminated list of buttons (to be placed inside the dialog box) as arguments:

```
GtkWidget *gnome_dialog_new(const gchar *title, ...)
```

The buttons list is a list of strings to be used as text for the buttons. Rather than pass simple strings, it's a much better idea to use the GNOME macros for commonly used buttons. Just like menu/toolbar macros, it provides pixmaps to standardize the interface.

The macro list is held in libgnomeui/gnome-stock.h and includes:

❑   GNOME_STOCK_BUTTON_OK

❑   GNOME_STOCK_BUTTON_CANCEL

❑   GNOME_STOCK_BUTTON_YES

❑   GNOME_STOCK_BUTTON_NO

❑   GNOME_STOCK_BUTTON_CLOSE

❑   GNOME_STOCK_BUTTON_APPLY

❑   GNOME_STOCK_BUTTON_HELP

❑   GNOME_STOCK_BUTTON_NEXT

❑   GNOME_STOCK_BUTTON_PREV

❑   GNOME_STOCK_BUTTON_UP

❑   GNOME_STOCK_BUTTON_DOWN

❑   GNOME_STOCK_BUTTON_FONT

> *These macros equate to simple strings, so be aware that if you create a button with the text of one of these strings, you'll probably end up with an icon as well as text.*

Creating a simple OK/Cancel dialog would look something like this:

```
GtkWidget *dialog = gnome_dialog_new(
                    _("A GnomeDialog with Ok and Cancel buttons"),
                    GNOME_STOCK_BUTTON_OK,
                    GNOME_STOCK_BUTTON_CANCEL,
                    NULL);
```

Buttons are filled in the dialog from left to right, and given numbers starting from 0, which represents the leftmost button.

GnomeDialogs are automatically created with a GtkVBox widget in the main part of the window, accessible as the vbox member of the dialog struct. Adding widgets to a newly created GnomeDialog is just a matter of packing widgets into that GtkVBox:

```
GtkWidget *label = gtk_label_new(_("This label is placed in the dialog"));

gtk_box_pack_start(GTK_BOX(GNOME_DIALOG(dialog)->vbox)),
                                              label, TRUE, TRUE, 0);
```

Showing a GnomeDialog

Having created and filled the dialog, we need to put it into action by showing it on the screen. The mechanisms for showing the dialog and waiting for user response are very different for modal and non-modal dialogs. You should set its modality before showing it, by calling gtk_window_set_modal. Windows and dialogs are non-modal by default.

```
gtk_window_set_modal(GtkWindow *window, gboolean modality)
```

Non-modal dialogs

Non-modal dialogs are the type that don't restrict usage of other windows. As this allows normal operation of the rest of your application, you must connect callbacks to the GnomeDialog that inform you when a button is clicked or the dialog is closed. Once a non-modal GnomeDialog has been created and filled, use gtk_widget_show as normal to make the dialog visible on screen.

```
gtk_widget_show(dialog);
```

Rather than connect handlers to individual buttons, it is best to make use of GnomeDialog's own signals. It emits two signals: "clicked" and "close" in addition to those provided by its parent classes; it is these signals that you should connect to in order to provide dialog functionality.

❑   The "clicked" signal is emitted when a dialog button is clicked. The callback function connected to "clicked" is provided with three arguments, a pointer to the dialog, the number of the button that was clicked, and user data. Be aware that the GnomeDialog "clicked" signal is different from the "clicked" signal of the buttons themselves.

❑   The "close" signal is emitted when gnome_dialog_close is called, and has a default handler provided by GNOME. This handler by default destroys the dialog by calling gtk_widget_destroy, unless gnome_dialog_close_hides is invoked passing setting as TRUE.

```
void gnome_dialog_close_hides(GnomeDialog *dialog, gboolean setting)
```

In this case, the "close" handler will hide the dialog with gtk_dialog_hide. This simply means that you won't have to recreate it should you want to show it again. This is ideal for complicated dialogs, or situations where you want to preserve the state of the widgets in the dialog between dialog operations.

You can also connect your own handler to "close"; it could put up an "Are you sure?" message, the return value of which tells GNOME whether or not to execute the default action.

It is useful to have the "close" signal emitted when a button is clicked, as this removes the need to destroy or hide the dialog yourself. To make GnomeDialog emit "close" as well as "clicked" when a button is clicked, call gnome_dialog_set_close with setting as TRUE.

```
void gnome_dialog_set_close(GnomeDialog *dialog, gboolean setting)
```

Modal Dialogs

Modal dialogs prevent the user from interacting with other windows until the dialog has been dealt with. Using modal dialogs is sometimes essential to prevent the user from changing critical settings while the dialog is in place, or to force the user into making an immediate decision. Since the rest of the application is frozen while the dialog is being shown, it's possible for your code to wait for user input without compromising the functionality of the rest of the application. In other words, we don't need to use callbacks, as we simply display the dialog and wait for something to happen.

This makes it much easier to write modal dialogs than their non-modal equivalents, a fact that makes them very popular with programmers, even in situations where a non-modal dialog would be more appropriate. To use a modal dialog, create and show the GnomeDialog as usual, and call either gnome_dialog_run or gnome_dialog_run_and_close. They both show a GnomeDialog and return the number of the button pressed (or –1 if the dialog was closed by the window manager). The run_and_close variant destroys the dialog when returning if the dialog is not destroyed by the normal means.

```
gint gnome_dialog_run(GnomeDialog *dialog)
gint gnome_dialog_run_and_close(GnomeDialog *dialog)
```

These calls automatically make the dialog modal – we don't need to use gtk_window_set_modal beforehand. Remember that the buttons are numbered starting from 0, in the order that they were given to gnome_dialog_new:

```
GtkWidget *dialog;
gint result;

    dialog = gnome_dialog_new ( _("Do you really want to quit?"),
                    GNOME_STOCK_BUTTON_YES,
                    GNOME_STOCK_BUTTON_NO,
                    NULL );

        gtk_widget_show(dialog);
result = gnome_dialog_run_and_close ( GNOME_DIALOG (dialog) );
switch  (result)
    {
        case 0: g_print("You clicked Yes\n");
    break;
    case 1: g_print("You clicked No\n");
    break;
    default: g_print("You closed the dialog\n");
    }
```

GnomeAbout

We mentioned when talking about GnomeDialog that it has three descendants, which provide further specialization. GnomeAbout is the first of these, a template for the ubiquitous 'About' dialog, which gives information about the application version, authors, copyright and other comments. For extra professionalism, we can even add a logo!

```
GtkWidget gnome_about_new(const gchar *title,
                          const gchar *version,
                          const gchar *copyright,
                          const gchar **authors,
                          const gchar *comments,
                          const gchar *logo)
```

The only mandatory field is authors, an array of strings. GnomeAbout contains an OK button which destroys the dialog when clicked.

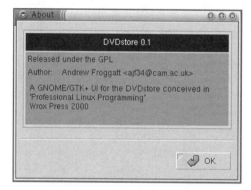

A GnomeAbout dialog should be set up to appear when the 'About' item is clicked in the Help menu.

GnomePropertyBox

GnomePropertyBox is a much greater extension of GnomeDialog than GnomeAbout. As the name suggests, this is a template for a Property or Preferences dialog box. It contains a GtkNotebook widget to enable separation of Preferences into pages, and four buttons: OK, Apply, Cancel and Help.

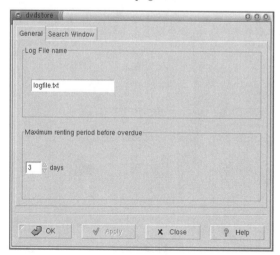

GnomePropertyBox helps you along with coding the dialog by emitting "apply" and "help" signals. It also closes the dialog automatically if the **OK** or **Cancel** buttons are clicked. Creating a GnomePropertyBox involves calling gnome_property_box_new, which takes no arguments. Like **GnomeAbout**, the dialog title is set by default to the name of the application.

```
GtkWidget * Gnome_property_box_new()
```

The **Apply** button is initially set **insensitive** – that is, it's grayed out to indicate there are no outstanding changes in the preferences. If any widget on any of the pages is modified, then it's the programmer's responsibility to make the **Apply** button sensitive. To do this, we simply call gnome_property_ box_changed in response to the "changed" signal of widgets in the GnomePropertyBox.

```
void gnome_property_box_changed(GnomePropertyBox *box)
```

Of course, first we must add pages to the dialog, using gnome_property_box_append_page, which returns the number of the page just added:

```
gint gnome_property_box_append_page(GnomePropertyBox *box,
                                    GtkWidget *page, GtkWidget *tab)
```

page is the widget to be added to a new page, and will most likely be a GtkFrame or container widget to make the page look presentable, even if it only contains one widget. tab is the widget placed in the tab of the notebook, and it lets us use pixmaps as well as text to identify each page.

GnomePropertyBox emits the "apply" signal when either the **Apply** or **OK** buttons are clicked; in response, our code should then read the state of the widgets in the pages, and apply preferences accordingly. If the button clicked was **Apply**, GnomePropertyBox sets the **Apply** button insensitive once again.

In the unlikely event that you need to set the state of this 'changes pending' flag manually, you can use gnome_properties_box_set_state where passing setting as TRUE indicates there are indeed changes pending:

```
void gnome_properties_box_set_state(GnomePropertyBox *box, gboolean setting)
```

The callback prototype for the "apply" and "help" signals should look like this:

```
void property_box_handler(GtkWidget *box, gint page_num, gpointer data);
```

For the "help" signal handler, page_num holds the number of the current open page, allowing context-sensitive help to be displayed. For the "apply" signal though, things aren't quite as straightforward. In fact, the "apply" signal is emitted once for each page, and one final time, passing page_num as −1. Your handler needn't distinguish between pages; it simply needs to wait for the −1 page number to be emitted, and then update the properties relating to all pages.

GnomeMessageBox

The final descendant of GnomeDialog is GnomeMessageBox, a simple dialog subclass that displays a short message together with an appropriate title and icon, determined by the message box type. The creation function is the only one special to GnomeMessageBox, and in calling it, you specify the text content, type, and NULL-terminated button list:

```
GtkWidget * gnome_message_box_new(const gchar *message,
                                  const gchar *messagebox_type,
                                  ...)
```

GNOME gives us macros to supply for the messagebox_type, which are self-explanatory:

❑   GNOME_MESSAGE_BOX_INFO

❑   GNOME_MESSAGE_BOX_WARNING

❑   GNOME_MESSAGE_BOX_ERROR

❑   GNOME_MESSAGE_BOX_QUESTION

❑   GNOME_MESSAGE_BOX_GENERIC

Here's an example, using the question type GnomeMessageBox:

```
GtkWidget *dialog;
gint reply;

dialog = gnome_message_box_new(_("Delete this Member?"),
                               GNOME_MESSAGE_BOX_QUESTION,
                               GNOME_STOCK_BUTTON_OK,
                               GNOME_STOCK_BUTTON_CANCEL,
                               NULL);
    gtk_widget_show(dialog);
    reply = gnome_dialog_run(GNOME_DIALOG(dialog));

    if (reply == GNOME_OK)
      {
          /* User clicked OK */
      }
```

Example GNOME Application

Before we move on any further, let's put some of what we've talked about into action, in the form of a simple GNOME application. This example creates a GnomeApp widget, populates it with several menu and toolbar items, and connects the appropriate callbacks to indicate which menu item was clicked.

```
#include <gnome.h>

const static gchar *app_id = "Gnome Example";
const static gchar *version = "0.1";
```

```
static void
on_menu_item_clicked(GtkWidget *button, gpointer data)
{
  gchar *text = (gchar*) data;
  g_print("The %s menu item was clicked\n", text);
}

/* File menu structures */
static GnomeUIInfo filemenu[] = {
    GNOMEUIINFO_MENU_NEW_ITEM ( "New", "This is the Hint", on_menu_item_clicked,
"New"),
    GNOMEUIINFO_MENU_OPEN_ITEM ( on_menu_item_clicked, "Open" ),
    GNOMEUIINFO_END
    };

static GnomeUIInfo custom_menu[] = {
    {GNOME_APP_UI_ITEM, "Item One", "Item One Hint", NULL, NULL, 0, 0},
    {GNOME_APP_UI_ITEM, "Item Two", "Item Two Hint", NULL, NULL, 0 ,0},
    GNOMEUIINFO_END
    };

static GnomeUIInfo menu[] = {
    GNOMEUIINFO_MENU_FILE_TREE (filemenu),
    GNOMEUIINFO_SUBTREE ("Custom", custom_menu),
    GNOMEUIINFO_END
    };

static gint
on_delete_event(GtkWidget *window, GdkEventAny *event, gpointer data)
{
  gtk_main_quit();
  return FALSE;
}

gint main(gint argc, gchar *argv[])
{
  GtkWidget *window;

  gnome_init(app_id,  argc, argv);

  window = gnome_app_new (app_id, "This is the window Title");
  gtk_window_set_default_size(GTK_WINDOW(window), 300, 300);

  gtk_signal_connect(GTK_OBJECT(window), "delete_event",
              GTK_SIGNAL_FUNC(on_delete_event),
              NULL);
  gnome_app_create_menus(GNOME_APP(window), menu);
  gnome_app_create_toolbar(GNOME_APP(window), custom_menu);
  gtk_widget_show(window);
  gtk_main();
  return 0;
}
```

The Makefile for this GNOME example is also very simple:

```
CC=gcc

all: basic_gnome_app.c
        $(CC) `gnome-config --libs --cflags gnomeui` -o basic_gnome_app
basic_gnome_app.c
```

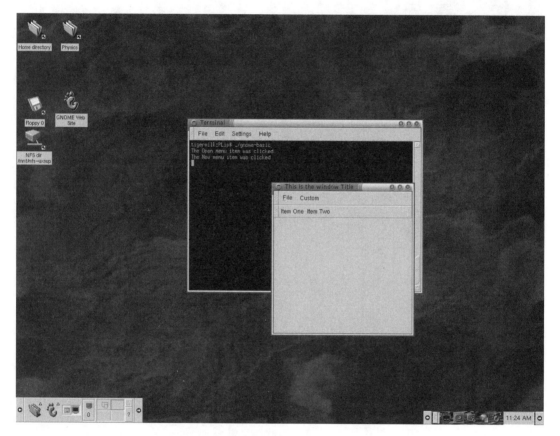

The GNOME Source Tree

Developing the source code for a GNOME application can appear to be one of the most time consuming components of the development cycle, but the most crucial component is that of ensuring that the application is well-structured in every respect. If we anticipate distributing our application, either throughout the world or just to another computer, it is essential that we build a source tree for our application; this is best done before a single line of code is written.

GNOME source trees elements follow a number of conventions that differ little from those of typical GNU software source trees. While the tree consists of many files and subdirectories, most can simply be copied from other GNOME apps without alteration. The remaining files we create ourselves using templates.

1. The first step in manually creating a GNOME source tree is to create the directory structure, consisting of a top level directory (named appropriately for the application) and subdirectories src, macros, docs and pixmaps (assuming your GNOME application will ship with pixmaps).

2. Next create the text files AUTHORS, NEWS, COPYING, README and ChangeLog. Each one should contain relevant, appropriately formatted information, consistent with other GNOME applications – go check some source files. Fill them up, and place in the top level directory.

3. Create an empty file called stamp.h.in. This is needed by configure.in for use with the AM_CONFIG_HEADER macro.

4. Write configure.in and acconfig.h files and place them in the top level directory. Write a Makefile.am file for the top level directory, listing each directory that contains source code. Then write an individual Makefile.am for each of those directories.

5. Run the gettextize executable that comes with the GNU gettext package. This will create the intl and po directories that deal with internationalization. In po/POTFILES.in, list the source files containing strings that should be scanned for translation.

6. Copy the contents of the macro directory, and copy autogen.sh from another GNOME application.

7. Finally, run autogen.sh to call automake, autoconf, autoheader, aclocal and libtoolize.

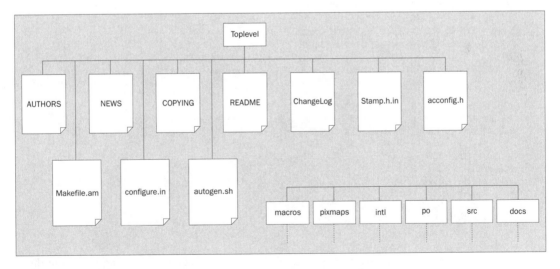

Now, for the files we need to write ourselves: configure.in and Makefile.am.

configure.in

`configure.in` is a template that `autoconf` uses to create the configure script, and consists of m4 macros that are expanded into shell scripts.

The example `configure.in` script here is the one used for our GNOME DVD Store frontend. There are only three GNOME-specific macros here: GNOME_INIT, GNOME_COMPILE_WARNINGS and GNOME_X_CHECKS, which are expanded into shell scripts from files held in the `macros` directory.

```
dnl Process this file with autoconf to produce a configure script.
AC_INIT(configure.in)
AM_INIT_AUTOMAKE(dvdstore, 0.1)
AM_CONFIG_HEADER(config.h)

dnl Pick up the Gnome macros.
AM_ACLOCAL_INCLUDE(macros)

GNOME_INIT
AC_ISC_POSIX
AC_PROG_CC
AM_PROG_CC_STDC
AC_HEADER_STDC

GNOME_COMPILE_WARNINGS
GNOME_X_CHECKS

dnl Add the languages which your application supports here.
ALL_LINGUAS=""
AM_GNU_GETTEXT

dnl Set PACKAGE_LOCALE_DIR in config.h.
if test "x${prefix}" = "xNONE"; then
  AC_DEFINE_UNQUOTED(PACKAGE_LOCALE_DIR,
"${ac_default_prefix}/${DATADIRNAME}/locale")
else
  AC_DEFINE_UNQUOTED(PACKAGE_LOCALE_DIR, "${prefix}/${DATADIRNAME}/locale")
fi

dnl Subst PACKAGE_PIXMAPS_DIR.
PACKAGE_PIXMAPS_DIR="`gnome-config --datadir`/pixmaps/${PACKAGE}"
AC_SUBST(PACKAGE_PIXMAPS_DIR)

AC_OUTPUT([
Makefile
macros/Makefile
src/Makefile
intl/Makefile
po/Makefile.in
])
```

❑ GNOME_INIT is responsible for adding GNOME-specific command line arguments to the configure script, by making extensive use of the `gnome-config` program.

❑ GNOME_COMPILE_WARNINGS turns on all appropriate compiler checking flags.

❑ GNOME_X_CHECKS carries out simple checks on the X11 server, and checks for the Xpm library.

This `configure.in` script also creates and exports the PACKAGE_PIXMAPS_DIR environment variable (using the AC_SUBST macro) for our code to locate any installed pixmaps.

Makefile.am

automake reads the Makefile.am files in the top level directory and each source-containing subdirectory, and processes them into Makefile.in. Remember that automake is called when you execute autogen.sh. The top level Makefile.am may only contain a SUBDIRS pointer to the subdirectories. In the makefile for the GNOME DVD Store frontend, shown below, there's also an entry to install a .desktop file and a couple of extra make options defined: install-data-local and dist-hook.

```
## Process this file with automake to produce Makefile.in

SUBDIRS = intl po macros src

EXTRA_DIST = \
    dvdstore.desktop

Applicationsdir = $(gnomedatadir)/gnome/apps/Applications
Applications_DATA = dvdstore.desktop

install-data-local:
    @$(NORMAL_INSTALL)
    if test -d $(srcdir)/pixmaps; then \
      $(mkinstalldirs) $(DESTDIR)@PACKAGE_PIXMAPS_DIR@; \
      for pixmap in $(srcdir)/pixmaps/*; do \
        if test -f $$pixmap; then \
          $(INSTALL_DATA) $$pixmap $(DESTDIR)@PACKAGE_PIXMAPS_DIR@; \
        fi \
      done \
    fi

dist-hook:
    if test -d pixmaps; then \
      mkdir $(distdir)/pixmaps; \
      for pixmap in pixmaps/*; do \
        if test -f $$pixmap; then \
          cp -p $$pixmap $(distdir)/pixmaps; \
        fi \
      done \
    fi
```

A .desktop file tells GNOME how and where to place an entry for the application in the GNOME menus. dvdstore.desktop looks like this:

```
[Desktop Entry]
Name=DVDStore
Comment=DVD Store GUI
Exec=dvdstore
Icon=dvdstore.png
Terminal=0
Type=Application
```

The `.desktop` file is made up of a series of key-value pairs:

- ❑ `Name` is the name of the application as it appears in the default locale.
- ❑ `Comment` appears as its tooltip.
- ❑ `Exec` specifies the command line statement used to execute the program.
- ❑ `Icon` is the icon to place alongside the entry in the GNOME menu.
- ❑ `Terminal` is a boolean; if non-zero the application will execute in a terminal window.
- ❑ `Type` should be set to `Application`.

The `Makefile.am` file in the `src` directory for `dvdstore` informs `automake` of the source files and libraries that must be compiled and linked:

```
## Process this file with automake to produce Makefile.in

INCLUDES = \
        -I$(top_srcdir)/intl \
        $(GNOME_INCLUDEDIR)

bin_PROGRAMS = dvdstore

dvdstore_SOURCES = \
        flatfile.c dvd.h \
        main.c \
        support.c support.h \
        interface.c interface.h \
        callbacks.c callbacks.h \
            dvd_gui.c dvd_gui.h

dvdstore_LDADD = $(GNOME_LIBDIR) $(GNOMEUI_LIBS) $(INTLLIBS)
```

The process of creating and compiling the source tree is represented by the following diagram:

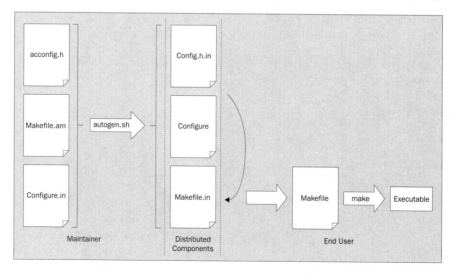

Configuration Saving

An important feature for any GUI application is the ability to save configuration and user preferences. GNOME makes it very easy to store and retrieve data in all common data types, and provides a comprehensive API under the namespace gnome_config precisely for this purpose. Configuration data is stored as key/value pairs in a plain text file, which resides by default in the root/.gnome directory.

Storing data

Saving data to a configuration file involves passing a key path, along with the data we want stored, to the appropriate gnome_config_set function. This key path is made up of three '/'-separated sections:

❑   the name of the config file, conventionally that of the application,

❑   the section, an arbitrary label describing the key category,

❑   and the key itself: ./<filename>/<section>/<key>.

Therefore, to save an integer value to the path application/General/number, simply call gnome_config_set_int, followed by gnome_config_sync to actually write the data to disk.

```
gint value = 42;
gnome_config_set_int("/application/general/number", value);
gnome_config_sync();
```

There are similar functions for other datatypes:

```
void gnome_config_set_string(const gchar *path, const gchar *value)
void gnome_config_set_float(const gchar *path, gdouble value)
void gnome_config_set_bool(const gchar *path, gboolean value)
void gnome_config_set_int(const gchar *path, gint value)
void gnome_config_set_translated_string(const gchar *path,
                                        const gchar *value)
void gnome_config_set_vector(const gchar *path, gint argc,
                             const gchar *const argv[])
```

There are an equivalent set of functions that save data under the directory ~/.gnome_private that begin with gnome_config_private_set. This directory should only be readable by the user, so gnome_config_private functions can be used to save sensitive data, such as passwords.

Reading the Stored Data

Conveniently, data is returned in the return values of the gnome_config functions:

```
gchar *gnome_config_get_string(const gchar *path)
gdouble gnome_config_get_float(const gchar *path)
gboolean gnome_config_get_bool(const gchar *path)
gint gnome_config_get_int(const gchar *path)
gchar *gnome_config_get_translated_string(const gchar *path)
void gnome_config_set_vector(const gchar *path, gin *argcp, gchar ***argvp)
```

We can therefore retrieve our previously stored int simply with:

```
g_print("The answer is %d\n",
        gnome_config_get_int("/application/general/number"));
```

giving us:

```
The answer is 42
```

If the configuration file has not been created, or the key doesn't yet exist, the gnome_config_get functions return 0, NULL or FALSE, according to the type. For convenience, you can provide a default value to be returned in case the key is not found, by appending =default to the path. This also removes the possibility of gnome_config returning a NULL pointer.

```
gchar *msg;
msg = gnome_config_get_string("/application/general/string=Default_Text");
g_print("The stored string is %s\n", msg);
g_free(msg);
```

gnome-config provides the gnome_config_push_prefix and gnome_config_pop_prefix functions, which let us avoid having to specify the complete path for every call. Also, the session manager can pass a prefix to a suitable file to save configuration data between sessions; this is described in the next section.

```
gnome_config_push_prefix("/application/general");
gnome_config_get_int("number=42");
gnome_config_pop_prefix();
```

Session Management

Session management is the process of saving the state of the desktop at the end of a session, and recreating it at the start of a new session.

Desktop state refers to current open applications, position and size of their windows, open documents etc. as well as desktop components, such as panel position.

It is your responsibility as an application writer to interact with the session manager, and when requested, save enough information about your application's state to enable us to restart (or clone it) in the same state.

The GNOME session manager gnome-session uses the X session management specification for compatibility with other desktop environments such as CDE and KDE. gnome-session communicates with GNOME applications through signals:

❑ It emits the "save-yourself" signal when an application must save its current state;

❑ "die" when an application should immediately exit.

You should note that although GNOME generates GTK signals within the application, those used by the session manager are not GTK signals.

The amount of information an application should save between sessions will depend on the application type. A word processor, for instance, might save the current open document, the cursor position, the undo/redo stack, etc., etc., whereas a small utility may save nothing at all. In some cases, saving the state might have security implications, such as in a password protected database program.

In GNOME, the user normally has to actively request that the session be saved, by checking a toggle button on the logout window.

GnomeClient

To connect to the signals from gnome-client, first grab a pointer to the **master client** object, then connect the callback functions as normal:

```
GnomeClient *client = gnome_master_client ();

gtk_signal_connect(GTK_OBJECT(client), "save_yourself",
        GTK_SIGNAL_FUNC(on_session_save), argv[0]);

gtk_signal_connect(GTK_OBJECT(client), "die",
        GTK_SIGNAL_FUNC(on_session_die), NULL);
```

In the save_yourself callback, the application must save the appropriate information for restarting in the next session. There are two usual methods of saving data:

Command Line Arguments

If there's not a lot of information, and it can easily be represented by command line arguments, then you can pass gnome-session whatever arguments are needed to start up your application in the required state.

Here's an example where two parameters, --username and --password, together with their current values, user and passwd, are passed to gnome-session in an argv array. At the start of the next session, gnome-session will restart the application, passing --username user --password passwd as arguments. Our application should then take appropriate action; in this case, it's probably to open the GUI with the application-specific username and password previously entered.

```
static gint
on_session_save(GnomeClient *client, gint phase, GnomeSaveStyle save_style,
    gint is_shutdown, GnomeInteractStyle interact_style, gint is_fast,
    gpointer client_data)
{
  gchar **argv;
  guint argc;

  if ( !(argv = malloc( sizeof(char *) * 6 )) {
    perror("malloc() failed") ;
    exit( errno );
  }
  memset( argv, 0, (sizeof(char *) * 6) ) ;
  argv[0] = client_data;
  argc = 1;
```

```
    If (connected)
        {
    argv[1] = "--username";
    argv[2] = user;
    argv[3] = "--password";
    argv[4] = passwd;
    argc = 5;
    }

    gnome_client_set_clone_command (client, argc, argv);
    gnome_client_set_restart_command (client, argc, argv);

    return TRUE;
}
```

The gnome-config API

Using command line arguments to store information between sessions is only really convenient when the amount of information is small. When there is more substantial data, an alternative method is to use the gnome-config API, asking gnome-session to provide a suitable prefix. Retrieving information on restart doesn't then require you to parse command line arguments. Let's give it a try.

Use gnome_client_get_config_prefix to grab the prefix:

```
static gint
save_yourself (GnomeClient *client, gint phase, GnomeSaveStyle save_style,
               gint is_shutdown, GnomeInteractStyle interact_style,
               gint is_fast, gpointer client_data)
{
        gchar* args[4] = { "rm", "-r", NULL, NULL };

        gnome_config_push_prefix (gnome_client_get_config_prefix (client));

        gnome_config_set_string("/username", user);
        gnome_config_set_string("/password", passwd);

        gnome_config_pop_prefix ();

        args[2] = gnome_config_get_real_path
                      (gnome_client_get_config_prefix (client));
        gnome_client_set_discard_command (client, 3, args);

        return TRUE;
}
```

By using gnome_client_set_discard_command, we delete any information saved as part of the session that was in progress when the discard command was set.

The "die" callback is much simpler; all we have to do is exit neatly:

```
static gint
on_session_die(GnomeClient *client, gpointer client_data)
{
    gtk_main_quit;
    return TRUE;
}
```

With these two signals handled correctly, GNOME applications will happily reinstate themselves automatically at the start of a new session. The definitive reference sources on gnome-session are the files session-management.txt and gnome-client.h, both found in the GNOME libraries. They include details on user interaction during session saves, and avoiding race conditions during startup with the use of priority levels.

Command Line Parsing Using popt

The sensible way to parse command line options that have been passed to your GNOME application, is to use the popt library. By default, this handles many GNOME and GTK+ options; to add custom options we use popt tables, which consist of an array of poptOption structs.

Parsing argv and argc with popt involves replacing gnome_init with gnome_init_with_popt_table:

```
gint gnome_init_with_popt_table(const char *app_id,
                                const char *app_version,
                                gint argc,
                                char **argv,
                                const struct poptOption *options,
                                gint flags,
                                poptContext *return_ctx)
```

app_id, app_version, argc and argv are identical in meaning to their gnome_init counterparts. An array of poptOptions follows, terminated by a NULL poptOption (its elements are 0 or NULL). Each element details the name and properties of a command line argument. poptOption is defined as:

```
struct poptOption {
    const char *longName;
    char shortName;
    int argInfo;
    void *arg;
    int val;
    char *descrip;
    char *argDescrip;
};
```

The first two elements are the long and short names of the option, giving the user both a shorthand and more descriptive name. arginfo indicates the type of the table entry, and can be one of seven macros:

arginfo	Description
POPT_ARG_NONE	The option is a simple switch, like -help, and takes no argument.
POPT_ARG_STRING	The option holds a string value, such as --username="Andrew".
POPT_ARG_INT	The option holds an integer value.
POPT_ARG_LONG	The option holds a long integer value.

arginfo	Description
POPT_ARG_INCLUDE_TABLE	Not an option, but a pointer to another table.
POPT_ARG_CALLBACK	Specifies that all options in the popt table are handled by a callback function. This should be placed first in the array if present.
POPT_ARG_INTL_DOMAIN	Indicates (when specified) a language to use for translation of on-screen text.

The meaning of arg is dependent on the arginfo type:

If POPT_ARG_NONE is used, then popt sets arg to point to a boolean, indicating whether or not that option was present on the command line.

If arginfo is POPT_ARG_STRING, POPT_ARG_INT, or POPT_ARG_LONG, then arg should point to a variable of that argument type. popt then fills the pointer with the argument passed on the command line.

In the case of POPT_ARG_INCLUDE_TABLE, arg is a pointer to a sub-table to include.

For POPT_ARG_CALLBACK and POPT_ARG_INTL_DOMAIN, arg should point to a callback and translation domain string respectively.

> val acts as an option identifier, which may be useful if a callback is used to parse the option; usually though, it's unused and set to 0.

descrip and argDescrip are the final members of poptOption, and contain strings used for generating help output when the --help option is invoked. (This is one of the default options provided by popt.) descrip is a short description of the option, and argDescrip acts as an argument identifier. For a username and password option, the poptOption array might read:

```
struct poptOption options[] = {
    {
        "username",
        'u',
        POPT_ARG_STRING,
        &user,
        0,
        N_("Specify a username"),
        N_("USERNAME")
    },
    {
        "password",
        'p',
        POPT_ARG_STRING,
        &passwd,
        0,
        N_("Specify a password"),
```

```
            N_("PASSWORD")
        },
        {
            NULL,
            '/0',
            0,
            NULL,
            0,
            NULL,
            NULL
        }
    };
```

The `--help` option output would then read:

```
$ dvdstore --help
Usage: dvdstore [OPTION...]

GNOME Options
  --disable-sound               Disable sound server usage
  --enable-sound                Enable sound server usage
  --espeaker=HOSTNAME:PORT      Host:port on which the sound server to use is
                                running

  --version

Help options
  -?, --help                    Show this help message
  --usage                       Display brief usage message

GTK options
  --gdk-debug=FLAGS             Gdk debugging flags to set
  --gdk-no-debug=FLAGS          Gdk debugging flags to unset
  --display=DISPLAY             X display to use
  --sync                        Make X calls synchronous
  --no-xshm                     Don't use X shared memory extension
  --name=NAME                   Program name as used by the window manager
  --class=CLASS                 Program class as used by the window manager
  --gxid_host=HOST
  --gxid_port=PORT
  --xim-preedit=STYLE
  --xim-status=STYLE
  --gtk-debug=FLAGS             Gtk+ debugging flags to set
  --gtk-no-debug=FLAGS          Gtk+ debugging flags to unset
  --g-fatal-warnings            Make all warnings fatal
  --gtk-module=MODULE           Load an additional Gtk module

GNOME GUI options
  --disable-crash-dialog

Session management options
  --sm-client-id=ID             Specify session management ID
  --sm-config-prefix=PREFIX     Specify prefix of saved configuration
  --sm-disable                  Disable connection to session manager

dvdstore options
  -u, --username=USERNAME       Specify a username
  -p, --password=PASSWORD       Specify a password
$
```

The custom `username` and `password` options appear at the bottom – most of these options are common to all GNOME applications.

We return finally to the two remaining `gnome_init_with_popt_table` parameters. However, only one of these is really of interest; `flags` can be ignored as it's not useful in GNOME applications.

`return_ctx` provides a pointer to the current context, which enables us to parse the remaining arguments of the command line – that is, the arguments not relating to any options such as filenames, libraries, etc. We just call `poptGetArgs` on the current context, to grab the `NULL`-terminated argument array. Remember to free the context with `poptFreeContext` once you're done.

```
popContext context;
gint i;
char **args;

gnome_init_with_popt_table(APP, VERSION, argc, argv, options, 0, &context);

args = poptGetArgs(context);

if (args != NULL)
    {
        while (args[i] != NULL)
        { i++;
        }
    }

poptFreeContext(context);
```

GNOME/GTK+ Resources

The growing popularity of GNOME ensures a growing wealth of high quality documentation, tutorials, FAQs and beginners' guides, both online and in printed form.

- ❑ The first stop for news and information is the GNOME project's home page at www.gnome.org. Also, check out the developers' site at developer.gnome.org. You'll find all manner of links to documentation, API references, and a GNOME/GTK+ software map with links to most popular GNOME applications.

- ❑ Don't forget that the GNOME/GTK+ header files often contain a great deal of useful information. A good rule of thumb is: "if in doubt, consult the source".

Finally, there are several books dedicated to GNOME/GTK+, although most approach it at a beginners level. Two highly recommended books are:

- ❑ *Beginning GTK+/GNOME* by Peter Wright, Wrox Press (*ISBN 1-861003-81-1*), giving a comprehensive introduction to the world of GTK+ and GNOME.

- ❑ *GTK+/GNOME Application Development* by Havoc Pennington, New Riders (*ISBN 0-7357-0078-8*); the most advanced book available on the subject, this is the final word in GNOME programming, written by a core GNOME hacker. This book is published under the GPL and you can freely download the text from www.gnome.org.

Summary

In this chapter, we've taken a look at some of the most common issues involved in GNOME/GTK+ programming. We looked first at glib; its complete set of portable variable types, macros, functions for string handling and memory allocation, and its support for list storage.

We then moved on to GTK+, introducing the idea of widgets, and describing GTK's use of containers and signals to support simple but powerful interface building, concluding with a small but functional example.

We then introduced GNOME, looking at its basic functions and widgets, and how they facilitate building menus, toolbars and dialog boxes. Finally, we looked at building a GNOME source tree, configuration saving and session management.

Online discussion at http://www.p2p.wrox.com

9

GUI Building with Glade and GTK+/GNOME

We're now going to look at **Glade**, a powerful tool designed for the rapid development of graphical user interfaces under GNOME/GTK. In the course of this chapter we shall look at various features of Glade and the different ways it can be used, and then take a step-by-step look at how we can use Glade to quickly build a GUI front end to the DVD store application. Along the way, we'll see all the features of GNOME, GTK+ and glib that were mentioned in the previous chapter, but now applied in the context of a real program.

Before we dive in though, a word of caution – getting to grips with the complexity required of a real-world GUI is one of the biggest challenges facing the inexperienced GUI builder. We'll therefore be building a relatively complex front end; it's not light on features, it *is* quite code heavy and is admittedly rather ambitious for a demonstration application.

It's our intention that you should see for yourself just how important it is to consider that most unpredictable of elements – the end user – who can (and *will*) expect the GUI to do everything predictably, consistently, and safely. Building big, we'll start to see some of the more subtle problems that dog the unwary GUI builder.

The structure of the chapter will be as follows:

- ❑   an overview of Glade
- ❑   a Glade tutorial
- ❑   `libglade`
- ❑   building the GNOME DVD Store front end

Overview of Glade

Glade is a user interface builder for Linux, which allows developers to design layouts of windows, dialogs, menus and toolbars in a point-and-click fashion, in the same vein as a paint package. In fact, the paint package analogy is quite appropriate – just as the responsibility for icons and other artwork is best put in the hands of skilled graphics designers using such tools as The GIMP, user interface builders such as Glade allow user interfaces to be created by designers without a technical background, by separating the interface design from the back end code.

Glade is the most advanced RAD tool for GNOME/GTK+ and is similar to Windows-based tools such as Power Builder and the Visual C++ Resource Editor. Once we've put together a design, Glade can generate a skeleton source tree, complete with code to create that design, packaging each window and dialog within a creation function.

As an alternative to this, we can use a library called `libglade` in our GUI application, which can load an XML-formatted Glade design at runtime. This dynamic interface loading is a very powerful feature, as it permits different interfaces to be used according to the circumstances, something we'll be looking at in detail later on.

> *This is actually a much broader concept than the familiar 'skins' functionality of programs like Winamp. Skins allow you to modify the appearance of an interface with customized graphics, rather akin to changing the theme of your X window manager, a purely aesthetic change. On the other hand,* `libglade` *allows you to adapt interfaces at a functional level as well, offering much more flexibility.*

Glade can be used as a GUI prototyping program, or as an excellent learning tool for GNOME/GTK+. With Glade, we have instant access to all the common GNOME/GTK+ widgets, along with their properties that we can adjust in real time, and hence see the effects instantaneously.

A Word on GUI Design

The success of an application lies to a great extent with the quality of its user interface – that's nothing revolutionary. If an interface appears complicated, confusing or just plain ugly to a new user, then the product will fail to impress, regardless of the quality of the rest of the product. Now quite what makes a good user interface is far from clear-cut.

Whole books exist on the subject, filled with "do's and don'ts of GUI design", but it's not uncommon to find popular applications consistently breaking several of these so-called 'rules'. Take for example buttons in toolbars, the original purpose of which was to replicate commonly used menu items for quicker access. Now along comes Internet Explorer 5; you press the *Mail* toolbar button and it gives you a submenu! Now, you may personally consider this a bad thing, or you may think that breaking rules to make a program better for the user can't be all that bad a thing to do. However you feel about a given set of 'rules', one simple fact remains – an inconsistent interface is a confusing interface. If the user expects some feature to operate in a particular way, make sure you have a very good reason before going and changing it!

> **Just as word usage, spelling and grammar evolve, so does acceptable GUI design, usually led by a few very popular packages. If a rule of thumb is possible, it's to make your design as similar as possible to other established programs while remembering the key buzzwords *intuitive, user-friendly, easy-to-use*.**

A Glade Tutorial

In this section we're going to explore Glade's features by creating a simple application, called `Example`, which lets us enter text into a `GtkEntry` widget, and displays it in a message dialog box. In the process, we will:

❏ see how to use Glade's editing features

❏ describe the skeleton source tree that Glade builds

❏ see how to link our Glade design to the code that reads the text and creates the dialog box

Glade is included as part of the packages that make up GNOME, so you'll typically find it included with your distribution. As with most GNOME/GTK+ software at this time, the current status of Glade (at the time of writing version 0.5.7) is best described as 'stable, but not yet finished'. It's therefore worth looking at the latest version (available from the Glade web site: glade.pn.org) to get the latest features and bug fixes. You can also find details of how to join the Glade mailing list, as well as up-to-date developers' guides, FAQs and links to existing Glade-built software.

Assuming we've correctly installed Glade, we can start it up from the GNOME panel menu, as Glade installs a shortcut in the *development* submenu. Alternatively type **glade** in a terminal window.

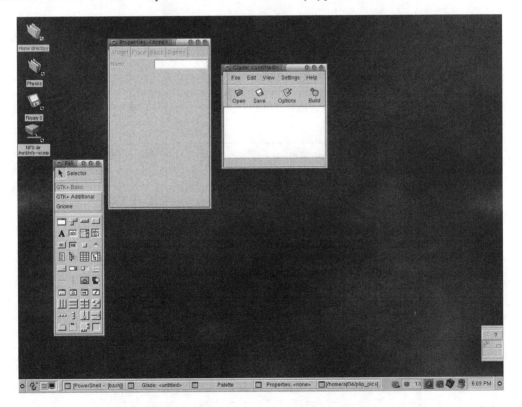

Glade starts up displaying three windows – the **main project window**, the **widget palette**, and the **properties editor**.

Main Window

The main window contains the (initially empty) list of windows, dialogs and menus associated with the currently open project. Start a new project by clicking on File | New Project and open the Project Options dialog box by clicking on the appropriate toolbar button, or File | Project Options.

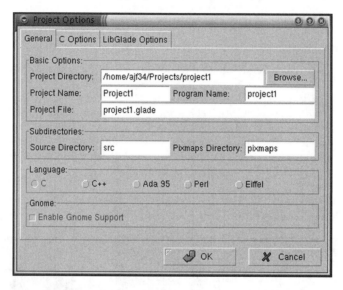

On the General tab, we can specify the project's name and directory, and the filename that Glade uses to save its XML representation of the project. A group of radio buttons lets us choose the language that Glade writes the source code in, and a toggle button to enable GNOME support, without which we are limited to using GTK+.

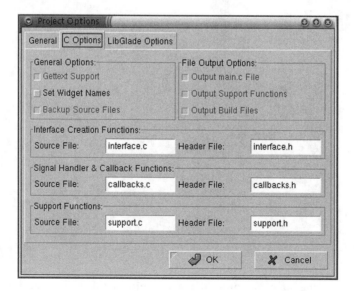

On the C Options and libglade tabs, there are options to specify further details about the Glade C source code saving and libglade options.

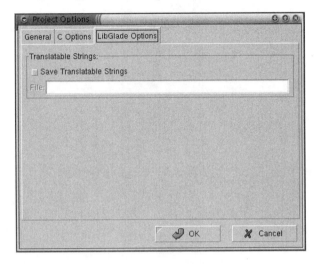

The Palette

The Palette holds the widgets we can use in our interface, and is separated into three tabs: Basic, Additional, and Gnome.

❑ GTK+ Basic contains the most commonly used basic GTK+ widgets, such as labels, entry boxes, frames, and packing widgets.

❑ **GTK+ Additional** holds the more specialized GTK+ widgets such as the scale and ruler widgets.

❑ **GNOME** holds all of the Glade-supported GNOME widgets.

There are a plethora of widgets represented in these tabs, and not all of them are easily identifiable from their icons. To avoid confusion, pop-up hints describe whichever icon the mouse is positioned over.

The action of selecting an item in the palette depends on whether you select one of the top-level widgets (GtkWindow, GnomeApp, GtkDialog and GnomeDialog) or another (such as GtkLabel or GtkButton). This is because labels and buttons can only be placed inside these top-level widgets. Selecting a window widget creates a new instance of that item, and then adds a reference to it in the list in the main window.

> *Notice the potential confusion between the terms 'window', 'dialog', 'GtkWindow',*
> *'GtkDialog' and so on, especially since a GtkDialog is a window, but is not a GtkWindow*
> *(although it is a descendant thereof).*
>
> *To makes things a little clearer, we'll refer to the GtkWindow, GnomeApp, GtkDialog and*
> *GnomeDialog widgets by the generic term **window** when the distinction between a window and a*
> *dialog is not important, but refer to them explicitly by widget name when the distinction is important.*

By double-clicking on an item in the main window, Glade displays that window so that we can begin populating it with packing boxes, and other widgets. Closing a window or dialog will only hide it from view, to re-display simply double-click its reference again. In fact the only way to permanently delete an item in the window list is to highlight it, and select Edit | Cut from the main window menu.

Let's now add a window. From the Gnome tab, select the GnomeApp icon to create a new GnomeApp widget that instantly springs to life. You'll notice how a menu, toolbar, and status bar are already present – Glade creates them automatically as part of the GnomeApp widget.

One rather nice feature of Glade is that any region that *can* hold a child widget, such as the main area of a GnomeApp widget or the cells of a GtkTable, appears as a gray cross-hatched area unless it actually *does* contain a child widget. You can place any child widget (except for windows) in such an area by selecting the widget on the palette, and then clicking in that area.

Try experimenting with all the types of widgets, and notice how the Properties window changes its available options to reflect the currently highlighted widget. Right-click over widgets to give access to the usual 'cut and paste' editing features.

The Properties Window

This is the most important window in Glade, and is where we set properties for individual widgets such as name, border width, dimensions, as well as defining accelerators and connecting signals.

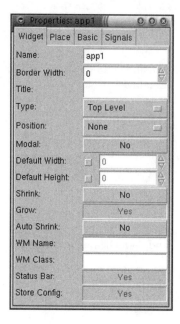

Properties fields are *context-sensitive* – in other words they adjust which options are available according to which widget is currently selected. You can learn a lot about widgets using Glade to experiment with modifying these properties.

For example, let's add a fourth button to the GnomeApp toolbar, and connect a callback function to its 'clicked' signal. Select the toolbar, and bring up the Widget tab of the property editor. The size field controls the number of widgets on the toolbar – increment this by one to add space for a fourth button.

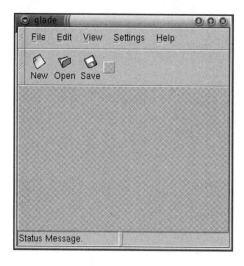

A small cross-hatched area should now appear on the toolbar. From the Basic tab on the Palette, select the button widget (identifiable from the icon with 'OK' in, or from the pop-up hints) and click onto the cross-hatched area to place on the toolbar. With the new button selected, change the name field to 'quit_button' and the label field to 'Quit' and also select the 'quit' icon from the icon combo box in the property editor. Notice how the label and icon change in response in the GnomeApp window.

Select the Place tab, and toggle the New Group option to read Yes – this adds a vertical separator to the left of the icon. Now select the Signals tab, and add a callback to the 'clicked' signal as follows:

❑ Click the ellipsis button at the right of the signal name entry box to bring up the list of signals appropriate to the GtkButton widget.

❑ Choose the 'clicked' signal and press OK.

❑ Click Add to add the handler to the signal handler list.

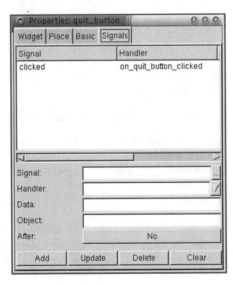

Glade automatically fills the **Handler** entry box with the name of the default callback function, which is of the format `'on_<widget name>_<signal>'`. Since our button is now called `quit_button`, Glade chose the handler name `on_quit_button_clicked`. You can see now why it's sensible to change the default widget name, since the default handler name is more recognizable than it would be otherwise.

Let's add some contents to the main area of the GnomeApp window. Add a frame widget, and then a vertical box widget (both from the **Basic** tab of the Palette) to the large crosshatched area. Glade queries the number of rows we want in our vertical packing box; select two. Into these spaces add a button and text entry widget.

Now let's fine-tune the layout. Select **View | Show Widget Tree** from the main window to bring up the widget tree.

> *This dialog box is really useful for general manipulation since you can expand the tree to display the parent-child relationships of all the widgets in your project. Selecting a widget in the Widget Tree also selects it in the open window and the Properties window; this makes for very straightforward navigation, particularly when you're dealing with many widgets, some of which may not be highly visible.*

Expand `dock1` to display the three dock items in the `GnomeApp` widget – namely the menubar, toolbar, and frame widgets we just added. Select the frame, and adjust its properties to make it look neat. For example, you might want to add a label and increase the border width.

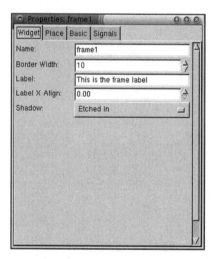

Finally, we adjust the properties for our Button and Text Entry widgets.

Select the Button, and change its name (`"click_me_button"`), label (`"Click Me"`) and padding values, adding a callback to the clicked signal as before. Finally select the Text Entry, and change its name to `"text_entry"` and add some default text: `"Enter Some Text!"` seems appropriate.

Now we've finished designing the user interface of our basic Glade application, save the project as `Example`, using the **Save** button on the main window toolbar. Before we go any further and build the code, let's discuss some of the details of a Glade-built project.

The Glade-built Source Tree

When a C-based project is built, Glade creates a complete GNOME source tree in the project directory and automatically writes C code that creates the Glade design. We can specify the pathname of the project directory, the name of the project, and the names of the various `.c` files using the Project Options dialog. Usually all we need to do is to change the project name to something appropriate, as the defaults for the remaining options are quite sensible.

Consequently, there are several things we need to know:

- ❑ the format of the generated code

- ❑ where Glade puts that code

- ❑ how we can manipulate Glade-designed widgets

- ❑ where it's safe to add our own code without the risk of Glade overwriting it should we wish to change our design and rebuild the interface

Let's build the project and figure these out. First, edit the Project Options dialog in Glade, and click Build to create our example project. Now have a look at the files Glade has created in the project directory.

You should find a `.glade` file; this is Glade's project save file, which is in XML.

We'll see more on XML in Chapter 23 which deals with handling XML in Linux (specifically `gnome-xml`, *the library that Glade uses to parse the XML structure).*

Here's the section in our example program, `example.glade`, that defines the frame and button widgets. It's easy to get an idea of how Glade represents a design in XML by looking at this file.

```
...
<class>GtkFrame</class>
        <child_name>GnomeDock:contents</child_name>
        <name>frame1</name>
        <border_width>10</border_width>
        <label>This is the frame label</label>
        <label_xalign>0</label_xalign>
        <shadow_type>GTK_SHADOW_ETCHED_IN</shadow_type>

        <widget>
        <class>GtkVBox</class>
        <name>vbox1</name>
        <homogeneous>False</homogeneous>
        <spacing>7</spacing>

        <widget>
          <class>GtkButton</class>
          <name>click_me_button</name>
          <can_focus>True</can_focus>
          <signal>
            <name>clicked</name>
            <handler>on_click_me_button_clicked</handler>
          </signal>
    ...
```

In the `src` directory are the source files for the project, which are by default:

Filename	Description	User modifiable?
src/interface.h src/interface.c	Contains functions you can call to create the windows and dialogs that were built in Glade.	NO
src/support.h src/support.c	Support functions for Glade, including `lookup_widget` which you can use to get pointers to widgets.	NO
src/main.c	Contains `main`. Initially creates and displays one of each window and dialog for demonstration. Not overwritten by Glade on subsequent builds.	YES
src/callbacks.h src/callbacks.c	Initially contains empty callback functions that were connected to signals in the Signals tab of the Properties Dialog.	YES

The interface and support files contain code built by Glade that are overwritten when rebuilding, so *never* add code to these files. That way you'll guarantee that `interface.c` can always be reconstructed from the `.glade` file. On adding further callbacks to an already built project, Glade graciously appends (rather than overwrites) the appropriate declarations and empty callback functions to `callbacks.h` and `callbacks.c` respectively, allowing concurrent code and Glade GUI design development.

If you delete a file that is normally generated by Glade, such as `callbacks.c`, then Glade will create a new copy from scratch.

In `interface.c`, creation functions exist for each window or dialog designed in Glade. In our example we have a GnomeApp widget called App1, and the function to create it, called `create_app1`, is in `interface.c`. Here's the start of it:

```
GtkWidget*
create_app1 (void)
{
  GtkWidget *app1;
  GtkWidget *dock1;
  GtkWidget *toolbar1;
  GtkWidget *tmp_toolbar_icon;
  GtkWidget *button1;
  GtkWidget *button2;
  GtkWidget *button3;
  ...
```

For each window in a design, there is a corresponding function `create_<windowname>` in `interface.c`. This function only returns a pointer to the new window, so we have to call `gtk_widget_show` to actually put the window on screen.

lookup_widget

One of the most common questions asked by newcomers to Glade is this: how do you grab pointers to widgets buried in Glade-created windows or dialogs, in order that we can manipulate those widgets? Why is this? Well, as we've just seen, `interface.c` contains creation functions for each window designed in Glade. These functions return a widget pointer to that window and there's therefore no obvious mechanism for getting pointers to widgets contained within those top-level widgets. For instance, the `GtkWidget` pointer in our example is local and private to the `create_app1`.

The solution lies in the `lookup_widget` function in `support.c`, a source file automatically written by Glade. Suppose we want a pointer to a widget named `text_entry`, contained in the dialog `message_box`. We use `lookup_widget` to get that pointer, passing it the name of the widget to which we want a pointer, as well as a pointer to `message_box`.

The prototype for `lookup_widget` looks like this:

```
GtkWidget* lookup_widget (GtkWidget *widget, const gchar *widget_name)
```

and an example might read:

```
GtkWidget *entry;
entry = lookup_widget(GTK_WIDGET(message_box), "text_entry");
```

The widget name – in this case it's `"text_entry"` – will be whatever you set it to in the Properties dialog box. `widget` doesn't have to be a pointer to this widget's parent: it can be a pointer to *any* other widget contained in the same window, or indeed a pointer to that window itself.

This is an essential feature, since we often don't have easy access to a parent widget pointer (at least not without resorting to global variables), but do have easy access to a related widget pointer. For example, in a typical callback function we're given a pointer to the widget that emitted the signal, but if we need to modify or query a second widget, we might use `lookup_widget` as a quick solution.

Let's add some code to our example Glade application and put `lookup_widget` to use.

Adding Code

The `src/main.c` file in our built example should look something like this, depending on the options set in Glade:

```
/*
 * Initial main.c file generated by Glade. Edit as required.
 * Glade will not overwrite this file.
 */

#ifdef HAVE_CONFIG_H
#  include <config.h>
#endif

#include <gnome.h>
```

```
#include "interface.h"
#include "support.h"

int
main (int argc, char *argv[])
{
  GtkWidget *app1;

  bindtextdomain (PACKAGE, PACKAGE_LOCALE_DIR);
  textdomain (PACKAGE);

  gnome_init ("example", VERSION, argc, argv);

  /*
   * The following code was added by Glade to create one of each component
   * (except popup menus), just so that you see something after building
   * the project. Delete any components that you don't want shown initially.
   */
  app1 = create_app1 ();
  gtk_widget_show (app1);

  gtk_main ();
  return 0;
}
```

Our GnomeApp window, **app1**, is created with a call to create_app1, and is then displayed with gtk_widget_show. In this simple case, the Glade-written main is just what we want, so we can leave main.c alone.

If we now open up callbacks.c, we find a dozen or so empty callback functions. Recall that the GnomeApp widget has several toolbar and menu items already present with callback functions defined, and we didn't delete any of them. Of course the other two are the callbacks we set up in Glade ourselves: on_quit_button_clicked and on_click_me_button_clicked.

Add the following code to these functions, noting that since the button name was changed to 'click_me_button', the callback function is called on_click_me_button_clicked:

```
void
on_quit_button_clicked                    (GtkButton        *button,
                                           gpointer          user_data)
{
  gtk_main_quit();
}


void
on_click_me_button_clicked                (GtkButton        *button,
                                           gpointer          user_data)
{
  GtkWidget *entry, *dialog;
  const gchar *text;

  entry = lookup_widget(GTK_WIDGET(button), "text_entry");
  text = gtk_editable_get_chars(GTK_EDITABLE(entry), 0, -1);
```

```
    dialog = gnome_ok_dialog(text);
    gtk_widget_show(dialog);

}
```

Calling `gtk_main_quit` in `on_quit_button_clicked` makes the application do as the button suggests – quit. Often we'll want to check that the user really wanted to quit using a dialog box, we'll see a good method of doing this later.

In `on_click_me_button_clicked`, we grab a pointer to the text entry widget, using `lookup_widget`, and get the contents of `text_entry` which we then pass to a `gnome_ok_dialog`. (We use `gtk_editable_get_chars` to grab the contents of `text_entry`, because the native `gtk_entry_get_text` method returns a pointer that points to internally allocated storage in the widget and must not be freed, modified or stored. `GtkEntry` is descended directly from `GtkEditable`.)

To compile the example application the first time, you need to first run the `autogen.sh` script:

```
./autogen.sh
make
./src/example
```

and you should see something like this:

Click on the button, and you'll get a message:

We've created a simple Gnome application very quickly and painlessly using Glade. In fact the steps we've covered are all that are needed to understand how our rather more complicated GNOME DVD store application is put together. Before we begin the dvdstore frontend, we'll take a brief look at libglade, an alternative method of using of Glade designs.

libglade

In the example Glade application above, we got Glade to build source code from the XML .glade representation. However, this step is theoretically redundant: the XML data *completely* describes the interface design – for a given .glade file, Glade will always output an identical interface.c. The process of building turns the neat XML statements into language-specific, library-specific code, with a corresponding loss of generality.

What if, rather than parsing of the Glade XML at build time, we want to allow GNOME applications to interpret the XML at run time – this is precisely what we can do with libglade.

Using libglade, applications can dynamically load an interface design – expressed as a Glade XML file – at runtime. This makes it possible to alter the design without recompiling, even allowing an application to choose from several different front ends according to which is the more appropriate.

Making use of libglade is quite simple. We just load the .glade file, and create each window using the libglade API when necessary. Connecting signals is also easy, since libglade is intelligent enough to locate the callback functions in your code that correspond to the callbacks defined with Glade.

To see how this works, we'll now use libglade in our Glade program to interpret our example.glade file. Since Glade is no longer creating a source tree for us, we'll have to create our own directory and makefile.

1. Create a new directory called libglade_example, and copy example.glade (or whatever you called the project), callbacks.c, and callbacks.h into it from the example project directory.

We're actually going to cheat and use the previous callback.c to save ourselves the effort of rewriting the callback functions. In fact, to show how simple a program can be using libglade, we'll rename callbacks.c as libglade_example.c, and write main in the same file.

2. Rename callbacks.h as libglade_example.h.

3. Edit callbacks.c, changing the include directives to remove interface.h, support.h and modify callbacks.h as above. Add a global GladeXML variable declaration and save this file as libglade_example.c.

```
#include <glade/glade.h>
#include <gnome.h>

#include "libglade_example.h"

GladeXML *xml;
. . .
```

The GladeXML object xml is an instance of an XML interface description. We declare xml as a global variable so we have access to it later in a callback function. We could alternatively have passed xml as the user data argument to the callback, but this method is used for simplicity, and to maintain complete compatibility between the two versions of the example.

4. Now add `main` to `libglade_example.c`:

```
gint main(gint argc, gchar *argv[])
{
  GtkWidget *app1;

  gnome_init("libglade_example", "0.1", argc, argv);
  glade_gnome_init();

  xml = glade_xml_new("example.glade", NULL);
  if (!xml)
    {
      g_warning("Could not load interface");
      return 1;
    }
  app1 = glade_xml_get_widget(xml, "app1");
  gtk_widget_show(app1);

  glade_xml_signal_autoconnect(xml);
  gtk_main();
  return 0;
}
```

The first thing new in main is `glade_gnome_init`, which initializes Glade and the widget building routines. We then ask libglade to load example.glade with a call to `glade_xml_new`, which has the prototype:

```
GladeXML*    glade_xml_new          (const char *fname, const char *root);
```

The second argument allows us to build only a section of the interface from the root widget downwards; useful if we only want to build, say, the toolbar of a window.

`glade_xml_get_widget` is the libglade equivalent of `lookup_widget`; it returns a pointer to the named widget given as its second argument. We use it to get a pointer to app1, which we then show on the screen.

We connect signals to their handlers by calling `glade_xml_signal_autoconnect`; this matches signal handler names (as given in the interface description) to the appropriate callback functions. For this to work, the callback functions must appear in the symbol table of the application, and cannot therefore be declared as static.

In our example, this connects our two button-click signals. We just need to make a small alteration to the `click_me_button` handler, so that it uses `glade_xml_get_widget` instead of `lookup_widget` to get the pointer to the `GtkEntry` widget.

Finally we need a Makefile.

5. Edit on_click_me_button_clicked in libglade_example.c to read:

```
void
on_click_me_button_clicked                    (GtkButton      *button,
                                               gpointer        user_data)
{
   GtkWidget *entry, *dialog;
   const gchar *text;

   entry = glade_xml_get_widget(xml, "text_entry");
   text = gtk_editable_get_chars(GTK_EDITABLE(entry), 0, -1);

   dialog = gnome_ok_dialog(text);
   gtk_widget_show(dialog);
}
```

6. Finally, create a Makefile that reads:

```
CC = gcc

CFLAGS = -g -Wall `gnome-config --cflags gnomeui libglade`
LDFLAGS = `gnome-config --libs gnomeui libglade`

all: libglade_example

clean:
        rm -f *.o libglade_example
```

To run our libglade example, we just type:

$ **make**
$ **./libglade_example**

This libglade example is functionally identical to the previous one; now though, we can load example.glade back into Glade, adjust the layout of the widgets, and save and re-run the example to witness the changes – all without any need to recompile.

The DVD Store GNOME GUI

This section is where we put all that we've talked about into action, and code the frontend for the DVD store, using Glade for the user interface design. We shall build the project in C (rather than using libglade) so that it's similar in form to the majority of existing GNOME applications.

As planned, our GNOME frontend will require no knowledge of the backend implementation, as this is completely hidden by the DVD API. Our program will essentially just pass data from various dialogs via the DVD API to the backend, and vice-versa. In fact, writing the GNOME frontend is totally straightforward, the only problem being as to which parts of the API we can fully support given the limitations of space inherent in the confines of a single chapter.

Several GNOME applications exist that are generic database clients designed to connect and interact directly with databases. gnome-db is one of these very powerful tools, featuring support for PostgreSQL, MySQL, ODBC, Oracle, and others, and the client program is itself written as a widget. Glade supports gnome-db from versions 0.5.9 onward. We could imagine including this widget as part of our GNOME DVD Store UI, giving us direct access to powerful database queries. This also gives us a good excuse not to try implementing some of the data-reporting API functions and concentrate on the core API functions of renting, returning, and searching for DVD titles.

The features we will include in our frontend are:

- Authentication to the database via login dialog or command line.

- A record of each transaction displayed in a log window and saved to a log file.

- Facilities for adding, editing and deleting members.

- Facilities for adding, editing and deleting titles.

- Facilities for adding disks to titles.

- Ability to search for titles and members.

- Ability to determine the rental status of a disk.

- Renting of titles to members.

- Returning of particular disks displaying whether overdue or not.

- Reserving of titles.

- Configuration saving.

- Session management.

Design

We'll refer to our GNOME DVD Store frontend as project dvdstore.

We won't spend any time going through how the Glade GUI design was put together, but you can see for yourself by downloading the Glade design and code from the Wrox web site (www.wrox.com) and seeing it in action. By loading the dvdstore.glade file into Glade, and using the Properties and Widget Tree dialogs, you can quickly unravel how each window has been designed, and see how and where different widget signals have been connected.

The menu and toolbar items have been chosen, grouped, and given icons and keyboard accelerators simply according to common sense and convenience. dvdstore isn't a typical application (with New, Open, Close items on a File menu and so on), so it's a case of having to choose the nearest equivalent items. A good rule of thumb when designing GUIs is to copy unashamedly from similar applications, checking of course that the design doesn't look odd, awkward or confusing in GNOME. For instance the size of a GNOME toolbar is set to the width and height of the largest button, so keeping the button text to a minimum will make for a more compact toolbar.

Compiling and Running dvdstore

Explaining the substantial amount of code behind dvdstore is potentially very confusing, simply because of the volume, rather than the complexity of the code. First, we'll run through how to use dvdstore, then look at the overall code structure behind the dialogs, and finally look in detail at important bits of the code.

First, download dvdstore from the Wrox web site; untar the source, compile, install and run by the usual means:

```
$ ./configure
$ make
$ su -
Password:
# make install
# dvdstore
```

The make file src/Makefile.am is configured by default for the PostgreSQL implementation. However, dvdstore will quite happily work with the flat-file implementation by alteration of src/Makefile.am.

The make install is optional, and must normally be done by a privileged user. If you decide to use it, the dvdstore.desktop file is copied into $(gnomedatadir)/gnome/apps/Applications so that a DVD Store entry will appear in the applications submenu of the GNOME panel menu.

When we run dvdstore, the application starts without a database connection, menu and toolbar items grayed out, and Not Connected displayed in the status bar.

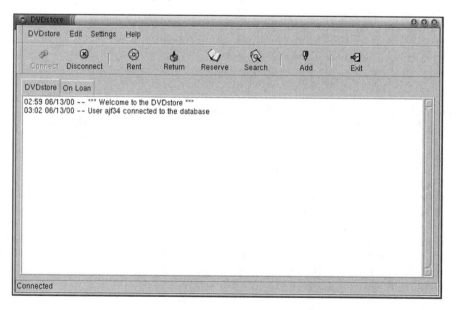

Click on Connect (or type *Ctrl-C*) to bring up the login dialog, enter the username with which you created the PostgreSQL database, and click on OK. All being well, dvdstore will connect, update the sensitivity of the menu and toolbar items, add a line to the log message window, and display Connected in the status bar.

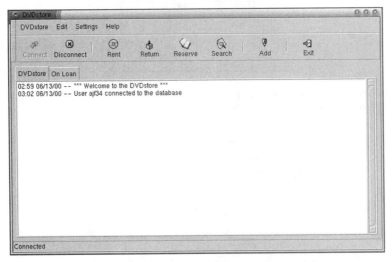

Now try adding a new title. Select DVDstore | New Title to bring up the Title dialog. Now enter the details of your favorite film and click Add. A message dialog informs us of the new title ID, and a log message is added.

Next, let's add a disk to the new title, selecting DVDstore | New Disk and entering the Title ID. Another message box pops up, informing us of the new Disk ID once we've clicked on Add.

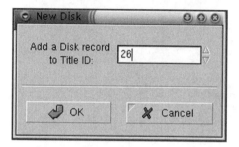

Now add a new member by bringing up the new member dialog, either using menu item DVDstore | New Member or the appropriate toolbar button.

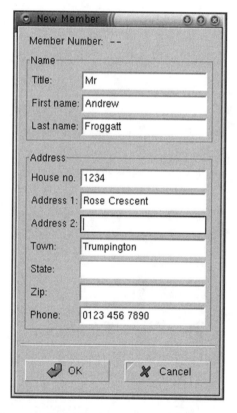

Try out the search features by using Edit | Find or the Search toolbar button to bring up the search window. There are three tabs on which we can search: Titles, Members, and Disks. Notice also the status bar, which tells us the number of items a search request succeeds in matching.

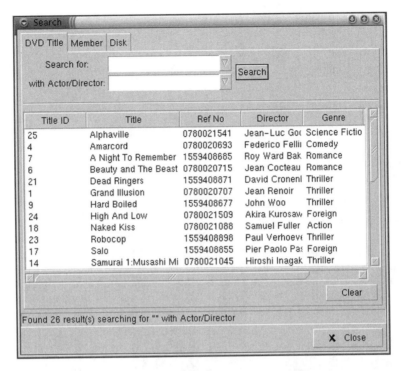

On both Title and Member search tabs, clicking with the right mouse button over an entry displays a drop down menu, which gives us the option to Rent, Reserve, Edit or Delete that item. In the case of Members, we can Rent or Reserve an item *for* the selected member.

Next, try renting out a Title. Enter a valid Member ID and a list of Title IDs into the Edit | Rent dialog appropriate to the movie you wish to rent. When you're happy with your choices, click Rent, and the rent report dialog appears with the list of Titles; each of these will have a tick and Disk ID if the rent was successful, or a cross if not.

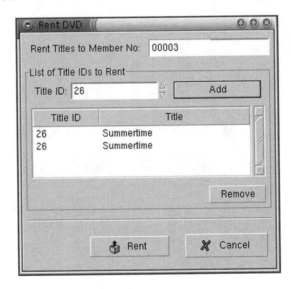

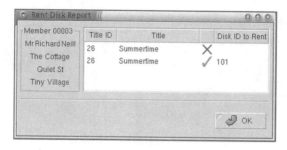

Here, we've tried to rent two copies of our new Title, but since we only created one Disk for that title, only one request has been successful.

Now try returning disks. Display the return dialog by clicking the Return button, and enter a list of disk IDs to return. Only disks that are currently on loan can be added to the list.

The status column displays whether each disk is overdue or not. How does dvdstore know whether a disk is overdue? Open up the preferences dialog (Settings | Preferences) and you'll see the Number of Days Renting before overdue field. The program adds this number of days to the date on which the disk was rented, and compares it to the current date. The disk status is labeled as OVERDUE if the current date is later this date, or as OK if the same or before this date.

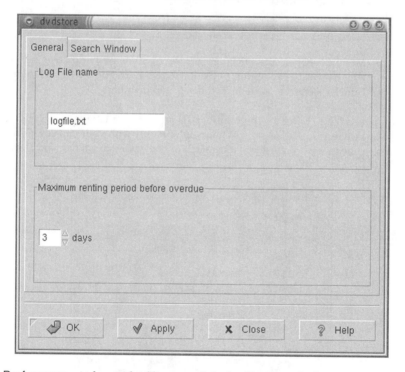

Also in the Preferences window is the filename of the logfile, into which copies of log messages are saved, and in the second tab, a series of toggle buttons controlling which of the fields Title or Member are displayed in the search window.

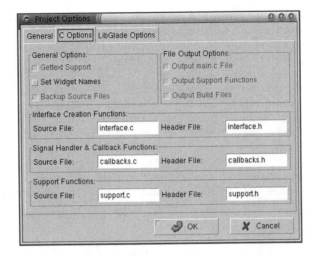

Structure

Having now used the `dvdstore` application, we can start looking behind the scenes, to see how it all works. Now is a good time to load the glade interface definition file `dvdstore.glade` into Glade and to explore. Tabulated here is a short description of each of the windows and menus designed in Glade that make up the `dvdstore` application.

Widget Name	Widget Type	Callback Code File	Description
dvdstore	GnomeApp	callbacks.c	Main window
about_dialog	GnomeAbout	--	Author About dialog
member_dialog	GnomeDialog	member_dialog.c	Member adding/editing
rent_dvd_dialog	GnomeDialog	rent_dvd_dialog.c	Rent Title dialog
return_dvd_dialog	GnomeDialog	return_dvd_dialog.c	Return Disk dialog
reserve_dialog	GnomeDialog	reserve_dialog.c	Reserve Title dialog
dvd_dialog	GnomeDialog	title_dialog.c	Title adding/editing
member_optionmenu	GtkMenu	--	Member search options
search_window	GtkWindow	search_window.c	Search window
dvd_popup_menu	GtkMenu	search_window.c	Search list popup menu
disk_dialog	GnomeDialog	disk_dialog.c	Add disk dialog
rent_report_dialog	GnomeDialog	--	Rent result dialog
preferences	GnomePropertyBox	properties.c	Preferences
login_dialog	GnomeDialog	--	Login dialog

You may be wondering what the `member_optionmenu` item is. On the **Member** tab of the search window, there's a `GtkOptionmenu` widget that allows you to choose between searching by Member ID or by Member Surname with the aid of a dropdown menu. This widget takes a `GtkMenu` as input for its options, and we've chosen to define that menu, called `member_optionmenu`, with Glade.

As we've seen, the design is centered around two windows, the main `GnomeApp` window that holds the menu, toolbar and log report window, and the search window that enables the staff member to bring up information on titles, members and disks. There are then several dialogs to handle the inputting of data from the user, and one dialog, `rent_report_dialog` that outputs data only: namely which disks, if any, to give to the customer.

Each of the dialogs has its related code contained in separate `.c` files, the names of which are tabulated above. The remaining source files contain `main`, along with miscellaneous support functions:

File	Description
`main.c`	Contains functions to deal with command line option parsing, initialization and creation of the `dvdstore` application.
`dvd_gui.h`	Contains global variables for the program.
`misc.c`	Contains functions to connect and disconnect to the database, to toggle the sensitivity of widgets, to handle exiting the application neatly, to deal with the logging facilities, to handle errors, to calculate whether a disk is overdue, and finally to display the **About** dialog box.
`session.c`	Contains functions to deal with session management.

Code

Let's begin our description of the code at the obvious place – `main.c`.

main.c

Following the necessary header files, we create the `poptOption` structure:

```
struct poptOption options[] =
{
  {
    "username", 'u', POPT_ARG_STRING, &user, 0,
    N_("Specify a user"), N_("USER")
  },
  {
    "password", 'p', POPT_ARG_STRING, &passwd, 0,
    N_("Specify a password"), N_("PASSWORD")
  },
  {
    NULL, '\0', 0, NULL, 0,
    NULL, NULL
  }
};
```

Notice the use of N_ macros to surround text that will appear on the screen. They will be very useful if we decide to internationalize the frontend, as they help us to substitute other languages in these fields.

In main, we set up the text domain for internationalization (see Chapter 28), and call gnome_init_with_popt_table, which initializes GNOME and parses the command line options:

```
int
main (int argc, char *argv[])
{
  GnomeClient *client;

 #ifdef ENABLE_NLS
  bindtextdomain (PACKAGE, PACKAGE_LOCALE_DIR);
  textdomain (PACKAGE);
 #endif
  gnome_init_with_popt_table("dvdstore", VERSION, argc, argv,
                                             options, 0, NULL);
```

Next, we set up the session management callbacks:

```
  /* Session Management */
  client = gnome_master_client();
  gtk_signal_connect (GTK_OBJECT(client),
              "save_yourself",
              GTK_SIGNAL_FUNC(save_session),
              argv[0]);
  gtk_signal_connect (GTK_OBJECT(client),
              "die",
              GTK_SIGNAL_FUNC (session_die),
              NULL);
```

Now we create the main window, connect its delete_event signal to exit_dvdstore (in misc.c), and open the log file to which we save log messages:

```
  main_window = create_dvdstore ();
  gtk_signal_connect(GTK_OBJECT(main_window),
              "delete_event",
              GTK_SIGNAL_FUNC(exit_dvdstore),
              NULL);

  open_log_file();
```

Before displaying main_window, we update its appbar to indicate current status and sensitize menu and toolbar widgets to be in the 'Not Connected' state. We then add a 'welcome' log message and, if a user has been specified on the command line, attempt to connect to the database:

```
  gnome_appbar_push(GNOME_APPBAR(lookup_widget(main_window, "appbar1")),
                                              "Not Connected");

  sensitize_widgets (main_window, FALSE);
  gtk_widget_show (main_window);
  add_log_message(_("*** Welcome to the DVDstore ***"));
  if (user)
    dvd_store_connect();
  gtk_main ();
  return 0;
}
```

callbacks.c

As we've already seen, `callbacks.c` contains the callback functions for the menu and toolbar items on the GnomeApp main window, grouped in a single file for convenience only. All of these callbacks are simply redirectors to functions contained within other source files.

For example, the callback for the **Rent Title** toolbar button calls `do_rent_dvd_dialog` in `rent_dialog.c` to display the renting dialog box:

```
void
on_rent_button_clicked              (GtkButton    *button,
                                     gpointer     user_data)
{
   do_rent_dvd_dialog(NULL, 0);
}
```

Rather than print `callbacks.c` verbatim, we've summarized the callbacks in this table:

	Callback function	Function that callback calls	Source file of function
MENU ITEMS	on_connect_activate	dvd_store_connect	misc.c
	on_disconnect_activate	dvd_store_disconnect	misc.c
	on_add_member_activate	do_member_dialog	member_dialog.c
	on_add_dvd_activate	do_dvd_dialog	title_dialog.c
	on_new_disk_activate	do_new_disk_dialog	disk_dialog.c
	on_exit_activate	exit_dvdstore	misc.c
	on_search_activate	do_search_dialog	search_window.c
	do_return_dvd_activate	do_return_dvd_dialog	return_dialog.c
	on_rent_dvd_activate	do_rent_dvd_dialog	rent_dialog.c
	on_reserve_activate	do_reserve_dialog	reserve_dialog.c
	on_preferences_activate	do_property_box	properties.c
	on_about_activate	do_about_dialog	misc.c

	Callback function	Function that callback calls	Source file of function
TOOLBAR BUTTONS	`on_connect_button_clicked`	`dvd_store_connect`	`misc.c`
	`on_disconnect_button_clicked`	`dvd_store_disconnect`	`misc.c`
	`on_rent_button_clicked`	`do_rent_dvd_dialog`	`rent_dialog.c`
	`on_return_button_clicked`	`do_return_dvd_dialog`	`return_dialog.c`
	`on_add_member_button_clicked`	`do_member_dialog`	`member_dialog.c`
	`on_search_button_clicked`	`do_search_dialog`	`search_window.c`
	`on_reserve_button_clicked`	`do_reserve_dialog`	`reserve_dialog.c`
	`on_exit_button_clicked`	`exit_dvdstore`	`misc.c`

So why do we bother having the intermediate functions? Isn't it better to connect the signals directly to the functions? Well, there's no reason why we couldn't do this, but there's a simple reason why we don't.

As we've seen, Glade appends an empty callback function for each new callback we create, together with its prototype, to `callbacks.c` and `callbacks.h` respectively. We could move these callbacks to any source file we wanted, but it's easier for a casual code browser to locate them if they're all kept together. This is especially true if they know that the application was written with Glade, and therefore know the origin and purpose of `callbacks.c`.

member_dialog.c and title_dialog.c

`member_dialog.c` and `title_dialog.c` are the source files that deal with adding and editing members and DVD titles respectively. They're very similar, so we're just going to look in detail at the first.

`member_dialog.c` contains only two functions: one creates a dialog and fills in contents as necessary; the other is a callback, which is connected to the 'clicked' signal of that dialog. One Glade dialog template is used both for creating and editing members, two different operations that require the same fields. We also use a single function, `do_member_dialog`, to handle creating and editing members.

We're going to see a lot of instances of needing to update the text in a GtkEntry widget (the widget displaying the member's name for example) with the value of the corresponding member element (in this case `member.name`), and vice-versa. We therefore define two macros that will take care of these jobs, and save us a lot of typing.

`ENTRY_SET_TEXT(field)` sets the text of the widget called `field` to the value of the element `member.field`:

```
#define ENTRY_SET_TEXT(field)
            gtk_entry_set_text(
                GTK_ENTRY(lookup_widget(member_dialog, #field)),
                member.field
            )
```

`ENTRY_GET_TEXT(field)` sets the element `member.field` to the value of the widget `field`:

```
#define ENTRY_GET_TEXT(field, field_len)
            strncpy(
                (member.field),
                gtk_entry_get_text(
                    GTK_ENTRY(lookup_widget(GTK_WIDGET(gnomedialog), #field))
                ),
                field_len
            )
```

> **These macros only work because we purposely set the names of the GtkEntry widgets in the Glade member dialog to be the same as the names of the elements of the DVD member struct.**

One additional feature of the otherwise equivalent `do_dvd_dialog` in `title_dialog.c` is the ability to set the items of the Genre and Classification combo boxes with those values retrieved using the API.

do_member_dialog

`do_member_dialog` takes a single argument, which should either be the member ID we want to edit, or zero if we want to create a new member. It then checks the validity of the ID, and if it exists, fills the dialog fields with current values for the corresponding member. To make it clear to the user that the dialog is 'editing' and not 'creating', we also change the dialog title, and fill in the otherwise blank member ID field.

```
void
do_member_dialog(gint member_id_to_edit)
{
    dvd_store_member member;
```

First, we declare a `member_dialog` pointer as `static`, thus ensuring that only one copy of the member dialog can be open at one time:

```
static GtkWidget* member_dialog = NULL;
```

`member_dialog` is set `NULL` when the window is destroyed from connection to the "destroy" signal. If it isn't `NULL`, then it must exist somewhere, maybe minimized or iconized; we can then try to raise it and bring it to the front. This is the only time at which we need to use any low-level `gdk_window` methods.

```
if (member_dialog != NULL)
  {
    /* Try to raise and de-iconify dialog
     */
    gdk_window_show(member_dialog->window);
    gdk_window_raise(member_dialog->window);
  }
else
  {
    /* Call the glade created function to create
     * the dialog and connect callbacks
     */
    member_dialog = create_member_dialog ();

    gtk_signal_connect(GTK_OBJECT(member_dialog),
                "destroy",
                GTK_SIGNAL_FUNC(gtk_widget_destroyed),
                &member_dialog);
    gnome_dialog_set_parent(GNOME_DIALOG(member_dialog),
                GTK_WINDOW(main_window));
    gnome_dialog_set_close(GNOME_DIALOG(member_dialog),
                TRUE);
```

We use `dvd_member_get` to look up the member whose ID was passed to the function, and fill all relevant fields with the appropriate values. In the case of an unsuccessful lookup (the ID is zero or otherwise hasn't been assigned), these fields are left unchanged.

```
if (dvd_member_get(member_id_to_edit, &member) == DVD_SUCCESS)
    {
      /* member number is valid - fill the fields with current values */
      gtk_label_set_text(GTK_LABEL(lookup_widget(member_dialog,
                                    "member_no")), member.member_no);
      ENTRY_SET_TEXT(title);
      ENTRY_SET_TEXT(fname);
      ENTRY_SET_TEXT(lname);
      ENTRY_SET_TEXT(house_flat_ref);
      ENTRY_SET_TEXT(address1);
      ENTRY_SET_TEXT(address2);
      ENTRY_SET_TEXT(town);
      ENTRY_SET_TEXT(state);
      ENTRY_SET_TEXT(zipcode);
      ENTRY_SET_TEXT(phone);

      gtk_window_set_title(GTK_WINDOW(member_dialog), _("Edit Member"));
    }
    gtk_widget_show (member_dialog);
  }
}
```

on_member_dialog_clicked

This is the callback function for the dialog 'clicked' signal, emitted whenever any button or window decoration is clicked on. arg1 is the undescriptive name used by Glade for the variable that holds the number of the relevant dialog button. We look to see if it was the OK button that was clicked on; if so, the member details are updated (or created) accordingly:

```
void
on_member_dialog_clicked               (GnomeDialog    *gnomedialog,
                                        gint           arg1,
                                        gpointer       user_data)
{
  GtkWidget *message_box;
  gchar *msg;
  gchar *member_no;
  gint member_id = 0;
```

We test to see if the OK button was the one that was pressed, and if so, get the contents of the dialog:

```
if (arg1 == GNOME_OK)
  {
    dvd_store_member member;

    gtk_label_get(
      GTK_LABEL(lookup_widget(GTK_WIDGET(gnomedialog), "member_no")),
      &member_no
    );

    strncpy((member.member_no), member_no, MEMBER_KNOWN_ID_LEN);

    ENTRY_GET_TEXT(title, PERSON_TITLE_LEN);
    ENTRY_GET_TEXT(fname, NAME_LEN);
    ENTRY_GET_TEXT(lname, NAME_LEN);
    ENTRY_GET_TEXT(house_flat_ref, NAME_LEN);
    ENTRY_GET_TEXT(address1, ADDRESS_LEN);
    ENTRY_GET_TEXT(address2, ADDRESS_LEN);
    ENTRY_GET_TEXT(town, ADDRESS_LEN);
    ENTRY_GET_TEXT(state, STATE_LEN);
    ENTRY_GET_TEXT(zipcode, ZIP_CODE_LEN);
    ENTRY_GET_TEXT(phone, PHONE_NO_LEN);
```

If the dialog is currently editing an existing member, then the member_no label will contains their member number. If we're successful in getting their ID from the value in this label, then we know we're editing an existing member and can pass the member struct to dvd_member_set.

```
    if (
      dvd_member_get_id_from_number(member_no, &member_id) == DVD_SUCCESS
      )
    {
      member.member_id = member_id;
      dvd_gui_show_result("member_set", dvd_member_set(&member));
    }
```

If `dvd_member_get_id_from_number` fails, we know to create the member, get the new member ID, and display the new member number in a message dialog.

```
  else
{
  dvd_gui_show_result("member_create",
                    dvd_member_create(&member, &member_id));

  dvd_gui_show_result("member_get",
                    dvd_member_get(member_id, &member));

  msg = g_strdup_printf(_("%s %s %s added as new member, no. %s"),
                    member.title, member.fname,
                    member.lname, member.member_no);

  message_box = gnome_message_box_new (msg, GNOME_MESSAGE_BOX_INFO,
                                    GNOME_STOCK_BUTTON_OK,
                                    NULL);

  gtk_widget_show(message_box);
```

`add_log_message` prints `msg` in the log window and appends it to the logfile.

```
  add_log_message(msg);
  g_free(msg);
  }
 }
}
```

rent_dialog.c and return_dialog.c

The requirements of the DVD store are such that we need to be able to rent and reserve titles and disks in sets, rather than individually, so that we can return a total price (or total fine!) for any given transaction. As we've seen, dvdstore's solution is to have a **list widget** in the dialog. This holds a list of such titles or disks, which we can add to and subtract from; useful if we make a mistake. We can then rent out (or return) the entire list in one go, by clicking either the Rent or Return button.

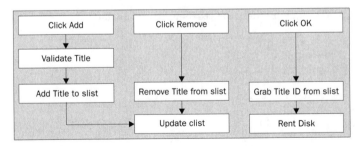

The rent and reserve dialog boxes work in very similar ways, although `rent_dialog.c` contains additional code to display the rent report dialog telling the staff which disks to give to members. Once again, due to this similarity, we'll look at the code for just one of this pair of dialogs, in this case `rent_dialog.c`.

There are several components to the rent dialog that need careful explanation. We use the GtkClist widget for the title list, as its API is more comprehensive and flexible than the simpler GtkList widget.

Where we use GtkClist, we only use it as a display element, and not a data storage device. In other words, we only write elements, and never re-read the contents of cells. Unusually for a GTK+ widget, GtkClist is, at time of writing, rather cumbersome to use, with a huge API but not nearly as much flexibility as that would suggest. A new widget is expected in GTK+ 1.4 that unifies tree and list displays into something much more powerful.

For demonstration purposes, we rely on a dedicated data list rather than a display widget for data storage. It makes sense to hold our list of items in a glib singly linked list, and update the GtkClist to reflect the linked list contents in a separate function: update_rent_dvd_disk_clist.

PIXMAP_HEIGHT defines the row height of the rent report clist, so that the tick and cross pixmaps are not clipped. LABEL_SET_TEXT is another convenient macro used to save repetition.

```
#define PIXMAP_HEIGHT 19
#define LABEL_SET_TEXT(field) \
        gtk_label_set_text( \
                GTK_LABEL(lookup_widget(rent_report_dialog, #field)), \
                g_strdup(member.field) \
        )
```

rent_disk_slist is the glib linked list that holds the list of titles to rent.

```
static GSList *rent_disk_slist;
```

do_rent_dvd_dialog

This displays the rent dialog, and takes as arguments optional member and title IDs to fill the dialog entry widgets with before display. This allows you to search for a member or title in the search window and select one of the search results in the list. By choosing the **Rent** item in the popup menu, the member or title ID of the selected item is then automatically filled in the rent dialog.

```
void
do_rent_dvd_dialog(gchar *default_member, gint default_title)
{
  GtkSpinButton *title_id;
  GtkWidget *member_no;
  static GtkWidget *rent_dialog;

  g_slist_free(rent_disk_slist);
  rent_disk_slist = NULL;
  if (rent_dialog != NULL)
    {
      /* Try to raise and de-iconify dialog
       */
      gdk_window_show(rent_dialog->window);
      gdk_window_raise(rent_dialog->window);
    }
  else
    {
      rent_dialog = create_rent_dvd_dialog();
```

We check whether the arguments contain non-NULL IDs, and if so fill the appropriate widget contents:

```
    title_id = GTK_SPIN_BUTTON(lookup_widget(rent_dialog,
                               "titleid_spinbutton"));
  member_no = lookup_widget(rent_dialog, "member_no_entry");

  if (default_title)
  gtk_spin_button_set_value(title_id, (float) default_title);

  if  (default_member != NULL)
  gtk_entry_set_text(GTK_ENTRY(member_no), default_member);

  gtk_signal_connect(GTK_OBJECT(rent_dialog),
             "destroy",
             GTK_SIGNAL_FUNC(gtk_widget_destroyed),
             &rent_dialog);
  gnome_dialog_set_parent(GNOME_DIALOG(rent_dialog),
                 GTK_WINDOW(main_window));
  gnome_dialog_set_close(GNOME_DIALOG(rent_dialog),
                 TRUE);
  gtk_widget_show(rent_dialog);
  }
}
```

on_rent_dvd_dialog_clicked

This is where all the action happens, getting called in response to *any* button click in the dialog. After having checked that **OK** was pressed, we grab the member number and exit if it's not valid.

```
void
on_rent_dvd_dialog_clicked          (GnomeDialog    *gnomedialog,
                                     gint           arg1,
                                     gpointer       user_data)
{
  GtkWidget *rent_report_dialog;
  GtkCList *rent_result_clist;
  GdkPixmap *tick;
  GdkPixmap *cross;
  GdkBitmap *tick_mask;
  GdkBitmap *cross_mask;
  dvd_title title;
  dvd_store_member member;
  gchar *msg;
  gchar *text[4];
  gchar *pathname;
  gchar *member_no;
  gint member_id, title_id, disk_id;
  gint result, count;

  if (arg1 == GNOME_OK)
    {
      member_no = gtk_entry_get_text(GTK_ENTRY(lookup_widget
                              (GTK_WIDGET(gnomedialog),
                           "member_no_entry"))));
```

Here we load the 'tick' and 'cross' XPM pixmaps into memory for use in the rent report `GtkClist`:

```
pathname = gnome_pixmap_file("yes.xpm");
tick = gdk_pixmap_colormap_create_from_xpm ( NULL,
                        gtk_widget_get_default_colormap(),
                        &tick_mask,
                        NULL,
                        pathname );
pathname = gnome_pixmap_file("no.xpm");
cross = gdk_pixmap_colormap_create_from_xpm ( NULL,
                        gtk_widget_get_default_colormap(),
                        &cross_mask,
                        NULL,
                        pathname);
g_free(pathname);
```

We check that the user entered a valid member number:

```
result = dvd_member_get_id_from_number(member_no, &member_id);
if (result != DVD_SUCCESS)
{
  dvd_gui_show_result(_("The member number is not valid"), result);
  return;
}
```

Now we create the rent report dialog, and fill in the member's details in the dialog:

```
rent_report_dialog = create_rent_report_dialog();
rent_result_clist = GTK_CLIST(lookup_widget(rent_report_dialog,
                            "rent_result_clist"));

dvd_member_get(member_id, &member);

LABEL_SET_TEXT(title);
LABEL_SET_TEXT(fname);
LABEL_SET_TEXT(lname);
LABEL_SET_TEXT(house_flat_ref);
LABEL_SET_TEXT(address1);
LABEL_SET_TEXT(address2);

gtk_frame_set_label(GTK_FRAME(lookup_widget(rent_report_dialog,
        "member_frame")), g_strdup_printf("Member %s",member_no));
```

Next, we cancel any reservations the member may have made:

```
dvd_gui_show_result("dvd_reserve_title_cancel",
                    dvd_reserve_title_cancel(member_id));
```

Now for each Title ID stored in the list, we attempt to rent it out, adding an entry for each in the rent report GtkClist:

```
count = g_slist_length(rent_disk_slist);
while (count--)
{
  title_id = GPOINTER_TO_INT(g_slist_nth_data(rent_disk_slist, count));
  dvd_title_get(title_id, &title);

  text[0] = g_strdup_printf("%d", title_id);
  text[1] = g_strdup_printf("%s", title.title_text);
  result = dvd_rent_title(member_id, titleid, &disk_id);
```

If the rent was successful, then we add to the clist the disk ID to be handed over to the customer, and print a message to the log file. If unsuccessful, we leave the disk ID cell blank.

```
if (result == DVD_SUCCESS)
  {
    text[3] = g_strdup_printf("%d", disk_id);
    msg = g_strdup_printf(_("Rented disk %d to Member: %s"), disk_id,
                                          member_no);
    add_log_message(msg);
    g_free(msg);
  }
else
  text[3] = "";
```

Next we prepend the row to the clist, and add the appropriate pixmap. Note that we must add the text of the new row (using gtk_clist_prepend) before we can add the pixmap.

```
gtk_clist_prepend(rent_result_clist, text);
if (result == DVD_SUCCESS)
  gtk_clist_set_pixmap(rent_result_clist, 0, 2, tick, tick_mask);
else
  gtk_clist_set_pixmap(rent_result_clist, 0, 2, cross, cross_mask);
}
```

Finally, we set the row height, call gnome_dialog_set_close so that the dialog is destroyed on clicking any button, and show the dialog.

```
gtk_clist_set_row_height(rent_result_clist, PIXMAP_HEIGHT);
gnome_dialog_set_close(GNOME_DIALOG(rent_report_dialog),
            TRUE);
gtk_widget_show(rent_report_dialog);
}
}
```

on_rent_dvd_dialog_add_clicked

This is a callback function connected to the 'clicked' signal of the dialog's Add button. Its job is to read the Title ID entered into the GtkSpinButton in the rent dialog, and if it's valid, add it to the list of titles to rent (rent_disk_slist) and update the GtkClist to reflect this change.

```
void
on_rent_dvd_dialog_add_clicked          (GtkButton       *button,
                                         gpointer        user_data)
{
  GtkCList *disk_clist;
  GtkWidget *titleid_spinbutton;
  gint titleid;
  dvd_title title;

  disk_clist = GTK_CLIST(lookup_widget(GTK_WIDGET(button),
                                "rent_dvd_dialog_disk_clist"));
  titleid_spinbutton =  lookup_widget(GTK_WIDGET(button),
                                "titleid_spinbutton");
  titleid = gtk_spin_button_get_value_as_int
                                (GTK_SPIN_BUTTON(titleid_spinbutton));


  if (dvd_title_get(titleid, &title) == DVD_SUCCESS)
    {
      rent_disk_slist = g_slist_append(rent_disk_slist,
                                GINT_TO_POINTER(titleid));
      update_rent_dvd_diskid_clist(disk_clist);
    }
}
```

on_rent_dvd_dialog_remove_clicked

This responds to a click on the Remove button by deleting the last entered Title ID from the list. We use g_slist_nth_data to get the zeroth item in the rent_disk_slist, which we then remove with g_slist_remove.

There's actually no need for us to convert the data from gpointer to int and back again between calls, but doing so serves to emphasize the fact that the list contains title IDs.

```
void
on_rent_dvd_dialog_remove_clicked       (GtkButton       *button,
                                         gpointer        user_data)
{
  gint titleid;

  titleid = GPOINTER_TO_INT(g_slist_nth_data(rent_disk_slist, 0));
  rent_disk_slist = g_slist_remove(rent_disk_slist, GINT_TO_POINTER(titleid));
  update_rent_dvd_diskid_clist(disk_clist);
}
```

update_rent_dvd_diskid_clist

This, the last function in rent_dialog.c, updates the GtkClist in the rent dialog:

```
void
update_rent_dvd_diskid_clist(GtkCList *disk_clist)

{
 gchar *text[2];
 dvd_title title;
 gint title_id;
 gint count;

 count = g_slist_length(rent_disk_slist);
 gtk_clist_clear(disk_clist);

 while (count--) {
   title_id = GPOINTER_TO_INT (g_slist_nth_data(rent_disk_slist, count));

   if (dvd_title_get(title_id, &title) == DVD_SUCCESS)
  {
     text[0] = g_strdup_printf("%d", title_id);
     text[1] = title.title_text;

     gtk_clist_prepend(disk_clist, text);
   }
 }
}
```

search window.c

The search window is the most complicated window in dvdstore. The window is a GtkWindow, with a GtkNotebook widget, which has three pages in which we can search for titles, members and disks. Together with a status bar, a clear button and a popup menu there's quite a lot going on.

In a continuing bid to keep the code listing compact and easy to navigate, we'll cut out a few bits that are very similar to other code we're looking at, and consequently don't explain anything new. For example, the three functions update_title_search_clist, update_member_search_clist, and update_disk_search_clist, do equivalent operations of updating a clist with search results.

First, we define two enums to aid readability: search_page allows us to refer to the GtkNotebook tabs by name rather than number; likewise member_search_type reflects the state of the GtkOptionMenu, which we use to choose between searching for a member by member number or by surname.

```
enum search_page {
   TITLE_PAGE,
   MEMBER_PAGE,
   DISK_PAGE };

enum _member_search_type {
   MEMBER_NO,
   LAST_NAME }
member_search_type;
```

selected_row holds the number of the selected GtkClist row, used by the popup menu. The title, member and disk search slists are used to hold the search results for each type; title IDs, member IDs and disk IDs as ints respectively:

```
static gint selected_row;

GSList *title_search_slist;
GSList *member_search_slist;
GSList *disk_search_slist;

void
do_search_dialog()
{
  GtkWidget *member_optionmenu;
  GtkWidget *member_menu;
```

We'd rather not lose our search results when we close the window, so we *hide* rather than *destroy* search_window when it's closed:

```
if (search_window != NULL)
  {
    gtk_widget_show(search_window);
  }
else
  {
    /* Call the glade created function to create
     * the window, setup optionmenus and connect callbacks
     */

    search_window = create_search_window ();
```

We now set up the GtkOptionmenu with the Glade-designed menu, member_optionmenu:

```
    member_optionmenu = lookup_widget(search_window, "member_optionmenu");

    member_menu = create_member_optionmenu();

    gtk_option_menu_remove_menu (GTK_OPTION_MENU(member_optionmenu));

    gtk_option_menu_set_menu(GTK_OPTION_MENU(member_optionmenu),
                             member_menu);

    gtk_signal_connect(GTK_OBJECT(search_window), "delete_event",
              GTK_SIGNAL_FUNC(gtk_widget_hide), &search_window);

    gtk_window_set_default_size(GTK_WINDOW(search_window), 500, 500);
    update_search_window_preferences();
    gtk_widget_show (search_window);
  }
}
```

update_title_search_clist

Here's the first of the three functions that refreshes the GtkClist. We set count to the length of the list, and loop round filling in rows of the clist:

```
void
update_title_search_clist()
{
  dvd_title title;
  GtkCList *clist;
  gint count;
  gint id;
  gchar *text[10];

  count = g_slist_length(title_search_slist);

  clist = GTK_CLIST(lookup_widget(search_window,
                        "title_search_clist"));
  gtk_clist_clear(clist);
  gtk_clist_freeze (clist);

  while (count--) {
    id = GPOINTER_TO_INT (g_slist_nth_data(title_search_slist, count));
    dvd_title_get(id, &title);

    text[0] = g_strdup_printf("%d", id);
    text[1] = title.title_text;
    text[2] = title.asin;
    text[3] = title.director;
    text[4] = title.genre;
    text[5] = title.classification;
    text[6] = title.actor1;
    text[7] = title.actor2;
    text[8] = title.release_date;
    text[9] = title.rental_cost;

    gtk_clist_prepend(clist, text);
  }
  gtk_clist_thaw (clist);
}
```

As noted previously, update_member_search_clist and update_disk_search_clist each take a similar form.

The function on_search_clicked is the real meat of search_window.c, getting called when the **Search** button is clicked. It must first query the GtkNotebook to see which of the three pages is open and whether we're searching for a title, member or disk:

```
void
on_search_clicked                        (GtkButton      *button,
                                          gpointer        user_data)
{
  GtkWidget *entry1, *entry2, *menu, *active_item, *member_optionmenu;
```

```
gchar *entry1_text;
gchar *entry2_text;
gchar member_no[6];
gchar *appbar_text = NULL;

gint diskid, current_page, id, count, member_search_type;
gint i = 0;
gint *ids;

current_page = gtk_notebook_get_current_page(
                    GTK_NOTEBOOK (
                        lookup_widget(GTK_WIDGET (button),
                              "search_notebook")
                        )
                    );
```

Assuming we're on the Title search page, we know we should be searching for a title. We get the contents of the two GnomeEntry widgets in the title page, and pass the values to dvd_title_search:

```
if (current_page == TITLE_PAGE)
  {
    /* Search for a DVD Title */

    entry1 = lookup_widget(GTK_WIDGET (button), "title_entry");

    entry1_text = gtk_entry_get_text(
                    GTK_ENTRY(gnome_entry_gtk_entry(GNOME_ENTRY(entry1)))
                        );

    entry2 = lookup_widget(GTK_WIDGET (button), "actor_entry");

    entry2_text = gtk_entry_get_text(
                    GTK_ENTRY(gnome_entry_gtk_entry(GNOME_ENTRY(entry2)))
                        );

    dvd_gui_show_result("dvd_title_search", dvd_title_search(entry1_text,
                                        entry2_text, &ids, &count));
```

Next we summarize the search result in the status bar of the search window:

```
appbar_text = g_strdup_printf(
                    _("Found %d result(s) searching
                        for" \"%s\" with Actor/Director %s"),
                    count, entry1_text, entry2_text
                        );

gnome_appbar_set_status(GNOME_APPBAR (
                    lookup_widget(GTK_WIDGET(button),"search_appbar")
                            ),
                    appbar_text
                        );
```

Then we clear the previous contents of the title search list and add the title IDs from the result of the new search. To display the result, we call `update_title_search_clist`:

```
        g_slist_free(title_search_slist);
        title_search_slist = NULL;

        while (count--)
        title_search_slist = g_slist_append(title_search_slist,
                                GINT_TO_POINTER(ids[i++]));
        update_title_search_clist();
        free(ids);
    }

if (current_page == MEMBER_PAGE)
    {
```

The next four lines get the currently selected item of the `GtkOptionmenu`. Unfortunately, since there's no ready-made API, we have to use this rather cumbersome method:

```
        member_optionmenu = lookup_widget(GTK_WIDGET(button),
                                    "member_optionmenu");

        menu = GTK_OPTION_MENU(member_optionmenu)->menu;

        active_item = gtk_menu_get_active(GTK_MENU(menu));

        member_search_type = g_list_index(GTK_MENU_SHELL(menu)->children,
                                        active_item);

        entry1 = lookup_widget(GTK_WIDGET (button), "member_entry");

        entry1_text = gtk_entry_get_text(GTK_ENTRY(gnome_entry_gtk_entry(
                                        GNOME_ENTRY(entry1))));
        g_slist_free(member_search_slist);
        member_search_slist = NULL;
```

If we're searching for a member's details by entering the member number, we just call `dvd_member_get_id_from_number`. If this is successful, the member's ID is added to the list. Searching by member number can only produce one successful result.

```
        if (member_search_type == MEMBER_NO)
    {
        strncpy(member_no, entry1_text, 6);
        if (dvd_member_get_id_from_number (member_no, &id) == DVD_SUCCESS)
            member_search_slist = g_slist_append(member_search_slist,
                                GINT_TO_POINTER(id));

        appbar_text = g_strdup_printf("Found 1 result searching for
                                    \"%s\"", entry1_text);

        gnome_appbar_set_status(GNOME_APPBAR (lookup_widget(
                    GTK_WIDGET (button), "search_appbar")), appbar_text);
    }
```

```
  else
{
  dvd_gui_show_result("member_search",
                    dvd_member_search(entry1_text, &ids, &count));

  appbar_text = g_strdup_printf("Found %d result(s) searching for
                                  \"%s\"", count, entry1_text);

  gnome_appbar_set_status(GNOME_APPBAR (
                    lookup_widget(GTK_WIDGET (button), "search_appbar")
                                      ), appbar_text);

  while (count--)
  member_search_slist = g_slist_append(member_search_slist,
                          GINT_TO_POINTER(ids[i++]));
}
  update_member_search_clist();
  if (member_search_type == LAST_NAME)
    free(ids);
}
```

Searching for a disk will list all disks associated with a particular title and, if rented out, display the member number of the member to whom each one is rented out:

```
if (current_page == DISK_PAGE)
  {
  entry1 = lookup_widget(GTK_WIDGET (button), "diskid_spinbutton");
  diskid = gtk_spin_button_get_value_as_int (GTK_SPIN_BUTTON (entry1));
  clist = GTK_CLIST(lookup_widget(GTK_WIDGET(button),
                                  "disk_search_clist"));

  dvd_gui_show_result("disk_search",
                    dvd_disk_search(diskid, &ids, &count));

  g_slist_free(disk_search_slist);
  disk_search_slist = NULL;

  appbar_text = g_strdup_printf("Found %d Disk(s) for Title ID %d",
                                  count, diskid );

  gnome_appbar_set_status(GNOME_APPBAR (
                    lookup_widget(GTK_WIDGET (button), "search_appbar")
                                      ), appbar_text);

  while (count--)
    disk_search_slist = g_slist_append(disk_search_slist,
                                  GINT_TO_POINTER(ids[i++]));
  update_disk_search_clist();

  }
g_free(appbar_text);
}
```

on_search_close_clicked

```
void
on_search_close_clicked                    (GtkButton      *button,
                                            gpointer        user_data)
{
  gtk_widget_hide(search_window);
}
```

on_search_clear_clicked

This function clears the contents of the clist on the currently open page:

```
void
on_search_clear_clicked                    (GtkButton      *button,
                                            gpointer        user_data)
{
  gint current_page;
  GtkWidget *search_notebook;
  GtkWidget *clist;

  search_notebook = lookup_widget (GTK_WIDGET (button), "search_notebook");

  current_page = gtk_notebook_get_current_page (
                                    GTK_NOTEBOOK(search_notebook));

  switch (current_page)
    {
    case TITLE_PAGE:
      clist = lookup_widget (GTK_WIDGET (button), "title_search_clist");
      break;
    case MEMBER_PAGE:
      clist = lookup_widget (GTK_WIDGET (button), "member_search_clist");
      break;
    case DISK_PAGE:
      clist = lookup_widget (GTK_WIDGET (button), "disk_search_clist");
      break;
    default:
      g_assert_not_reached();
    }
  gtk_clist_clear (GTK_CLIST (clist));
  gnome_appbar_set_status(GNOME_APPBAR (
                  lookup_widget(GTK_WIDGET (button), "search_appbar")
                                    ), "Cleared");
}
```

on_dvd_search_clist_button_press_event

This function displays a relevant popup menu whenever the right-hand mouse button is clicked inside the title or member clists.

```
gboolean
on_dvd_search_clist_button_press_event (GtkWidget       *widget,
                                        GdkEventButton  *event,
```

```
                                           gpointer        user_data)
{
  GtkWidget *menu;
  GtkCList *clist;
  gint row, column;

  g_return_val_if_fail(widget != NULL, FALSE);

  menu = create_dvd_popup_menu();
  if (event->type == GDK_BUTTON_PRESS)
    {
       GdkEventButton *buttonevent = (GdkEventButton *) event;

       if ( buttonevent->button == GDK_BUTTON1_MASK )
       {
         clist = GTK_CLIST(widget);
         if (gtk_clist_get_selection_info(clist,
                              buttonevent->x,
                              buttonevent->y,
                              &row,
                              &column)) {

           gtk_clist_select_row(clist, row, column);
           selected_row = row;

           gtk_menu_popup ( GTK_MENU (menu), NULL, NULL, NULL, NULL,
                                      buttonevent->button, 0 );
           return TRUE;
         }
       }
     }
  return FALSE;
}
```

The remaining functions are the callbacks for the four menu items of the popup menu, Rent, Reserve, Edit and Delete respectively.

on_search_menu_rent_activate

This determines whether the title or member page is open, and calls do_rent_dvd_dialog passing either the title or member ID of the selected row as arguments:

```
void
on_search_menu_rent_activate            (GtkMenuItem    *menuitem,
                                         gpointer        user_data)
{
  gint current_page;
  gint id;

  dvd_store_member member;

  current_page = gtk_notebook_get_current_page (GTK_NOTEBOOK
              (lookup_widget(search_window, "search_notebook")));
  if (current_page == TITLE_PAGE)
    {
```

```
        g_return_if_fail (title_search_slist != NULL);
        id = GPOINTER_TO_INT(g_slist_nth_data(title_search_slist,
                              selected_row));
        do_rent_dvd_dialog(NULL, id);
    }
  if (current_page == MEMBER_PAGE) {
    g_return_if_fail (member_search_slist != NULL);
    id = GPOINTER_TO_INT(g_slist_nth_data(member_search_slist,
                          selected_row));
    dvd_member_get(id, &member);
    do_rent_dvd_dialog(member.member_no, 0);
  }
}
```

on_search_menu_edit_activate

```
void
on_search_menu_edit_activate               (GtkMenuItem    *menuitem,
                                            gpointer        user_data)
{
 gint current_page;
 gint id;
  g_return_if_fail (search_window != NULL);

  current_page = gtk_notebook_get_current_page (GTK_NOTEBOOK
                      (lookup_widget(search_window, "search_notebook")));
  if (current_page == TITLE_PAGE)
    {
      g_return_if_fail (title_search_slist != NULL);
      id = GPOINTER_TO_INT(g_slist_nth_data(title_search_slist,
                            selected_row));
      do_dvd_dialog(id);
    }
  if (current_page == MEMBER_PAGE)
    {
       g_return_if_fail (member_search_slist != NULL);
       id = GPOINTER_TO_INT(g_slist_nth_data(member_search_slist,
                             selected_row));
       do_member_dialog(id);
    }
}
```

on_search_menu_delete_activate

The delete_activate function queries the user with a Gnome message dialog box before deleting the selected title or member:

```
void
on_search_menu_delete_activate             (GtkMenuItem    *menuitem,
                                            gpointer        user_data)
{
  GtkWidget *dialog;
  gint id;
```

```
      gint reply;
      gint current_page;

      g_return_if_fail (search_window != NULL);

      current_page = gtk_notebook_get_current_page (GTK_NOTEBOOK
(lookup_widget(search_window,
                                              "search_notebook")));
   if (current_page == TITLE_PAGE)
     {
        g_return_if_fail (title_search_slist != NULL);
        id = GPOINTER_TO_INT(g_slist_nth_data(title_search_slist,
                             selected_row));
        dialog = gnome_message_box_new(_("Delete this Title?"),
                        GNOME_MESSAGE_BOX_QUESTION,
                        GNOME_STOCK_BUTTON_YES,
                        GNOME_STOCK_BUTTON_NO,
                        NULL);
        gtk_widget_show(dialog);
        reply = gnome_dialog_run(GNOME_DIALOG(dialog));

        if (reply == GNOME_OK) {
        dvd_title_delete(id);
        title_search_slist = g_slist_remove (title_search_slist,
                             GINT_TO_POINTER(id));
        update_title_search_clist();
        }
   }
   if (current_page == MEMBER_PAGE)
     {
        g_return_if_fail (member_search_slist != NULL);
        id = GPOINTER_TO_INT(g_slist_nth_data(member_search_slist,
                             selected_row));
        dialog = gnome_message_box_new(_("Delete this Member?"),
                        GNOME_MESSAGE_BOX_QUESTION,
                        GNOME_STOCK_BUTTON_OK,
                        GNOME_STOCK_BUTTON_CANCEL,
                        NULL);
        reply = gnome_dialog_run(GNOME_DIALOG(dialog));

        if (reply == GNOME_OK)
        {
          dvd_member_delete(id);
          member_search_slist = g_slist_remove (member_search_slist,
                             GINT_TO_POINTER(id));
          update_member_search_clist();
        }
      }
   }
```

on_search_menu_reserve_activate

```
      void
      on_search_menu_reserve_activate        (GtkMenuItem    *menuitem,
                                              gpointer       user_data)
      {
```

```
    gint current_page;
    gint id;
    g_return_if_fail (search_window != NULL);

    current_page = gtk_notebook_get_current_page (GTK_NOTEBOOK
                            (lookup_widget(search_window,"search_notebook")));
    if (current_page == TITLE_PAGE)
      {
        g_return_if_fail (title_search_slist != NULL);
        id = GPOINTER_TO_INT(g_slist_nth_data(title_search_slist,
                                selected_row));
        do_reserve_dialog(0, id);
      }
    if (current_page == MEMBER_PAGE)
      {
        g_return_if_fail (member_search_slist != NULL);
        id = GPOINTER_TO_INT(g_slist_nth_data(member_search_slist,
                                selected_row));
        do_reserve_dialog(id, 0);
      }
  }
```

misc.c

The final source file we'll delve into is misc.c, containing various miscellaneous functions. Here we initialize the log file descriptor, and a gboolean indicating the state of the connection to the backend. SET_SENSITIVE is a macro that sets the widget sensitivity to the value of sensitive:

```
    static FILE *logfile;
    static gboolean connected = FALSE;

    #define SET_SENSITIVE(widget)
            gtk_widget_set_sensitive(GTK_WIDGET(
                                lookup_widget(main_window, #widget)
                                            ), sensitive)
```

dvd_store_connect

This handles authentication and logging into the backend. user is a global variable, filled in by the command line option parsing if the --username option is specified:

```
    void
    dvd_store_connect()
    {
      GtkWidget *login_dialog;
      GtkWidget *gtk_username_entry;
      gchar *msg;
      gint reply;
      gint result;
```

If --username wasn't specified, then user is NULL, and we create the login dialog to grab the user and password from the staff member:

```
    if (!user)
      {
```

```
         login_dialog = create_login_dialog();
         gnome_dialog_set_default(GNOME_DIALOG(login_dialog), GNOME_OK);
         gnome_dialog_editable_enters(GNOME_DIALOG(login_dialog),
                                      GTK_EDITABLE(lookup_widget(login_dialog,
                                                                 "password")));
         reply = gnome_dialog_run(GNOME_DIALOG(login_dialog));
         if (reply != GNOME_OK)
           {
             gtk_widget_destroy(login_dialog);
             return;
           }

         gtk_username_entry = gnome_entry_gtk_entry(GNOME_ENTRY(
                                  lookup_widget(login_dialog, "username")
                                                      ));

         user = g_strdup(gtk_entry_get_text(GTK_ENTRY(gtk_username_entry)));

         passwd = g_strdup(gtk_entry_get_text(GTK_ENTRY(
                              lookup_widget(login_dialog, "password")
                                                 )));
         gtk_widget_destroy(login_dialog);
       }
     result = dvd_open_db_login(user, passwd);
```

If successful in connecting, this toggles the sensitivity of the menu and toolbar items, changes the status bar message, and adds a log message:

```
     if (result == DVD_SUCCESS)
       {
         connected = TRUE;
         sensitize_widgets();
         gnome_appbar_push(GNOME_APPBAR(lookup_widget (main_window,"appbar1")),
                           _("Connected"));

         msg = g_strdup_printf(_("User %s connected to the database"), user);
         add_log_message(msg);
         g_free(msg);
       }
     else
       {
         dvd_gui_show_result(_("Cannot connect to the database. Check the
                               Username and\n Password are correct and that
                               the database is set up correctly"), 0);
         user = NULL;
         passwd = NULL;
       }
   }
```

dvd_store_disconnect

This deals with the somewhat simpler task of disconnection:

```
void
dvd_store_disconnect()
{
  g_return_if_fail(connected);

  dvd_close_db();
  connected = FALSE;
  user = NULL;
  passwd = NULL;
  sensitize_widgets();
  gnome_appbar_push(GNOME_APPBAR(lookup_widget (main_window,
                                "appbar1")),_("Not Connected"));
  add_log_message(_("Disconnected from the database"));
}
```

sensitize_widgets

This toggles the sensitivity of database-related menu and toolbar items, so that they are grayed out and unresponsive when not connected.

```
void
sensitize_widgets()
{
  static gboolean sensitive = FALSE;

  SET_SENSITIVE(menu_disconnect);
  SET_SENSITIVE(add_member);
  SET_SENSITIVE(new_title);
  SET_SENSITIVE(new_disk);
  SET_SENSITIVE(menu_search);
  SET_SENSITIVE(rent_dvd);
  SET_SENSITIVE(return_dvd);
  SET_SENSITIVE(reserve);
  SET_SENSITIVE(disconnect_button);
  SET_SENSITIVE(rent_button);
  SET_SENSITIVE(return_button);
  SET_SENSITIVE(add_member_button);
  SET_SENSITIVE(search_button);
  SET_SENSITIVE(reserve_button);

  gtk_widget_set_sensitive (GTK_WIDGET(lookup_widget(main_window,
                            "connect_button")), !sensitive);
  gtk_widget_set_sensitive (GTK_WIDGET(lookup_widget(main_window,
                            "menu_connect")), !sensitive);
  sensitive = !sensitive;
}
```

exit_dvdstore

This function handles quitting from the application, and is called when the delete_event signal is emitted. It checks that we're sure we want to quit, and ensures we disconnect neatly from the database if we do. Notice that the return value is somewhat counter-intuitive – we return FALSE if we want to quit.

```
gboolean
exit_dvdstore(void)

{
  GtkWidget *dialog;
  gint reply;

  dialog = gnome_message_box_new(_("Are you sure you want to quit?"),
                     GNOME_MESSAGE_BOX_QUESTION,
                     GNOME_STOCK_BUTTON_YES,
                     GNOME_STOCK_BUTTON_NO,
                     NULL);
  reply = gnome_dialog_run(GNOME_DIALOG(dialog));
  if (reply != GNOME_OK)
    return TRUE;

  if (connected)
    dvd_store_disconnect();

  gtk_main_quit ();
  return FALSE;
}
```

open_log_file

This opens up the logfile for modification, the filename of which is specified in the **Preferences** window, and is saved under the configuration name of logfile_name:

```
void
open_log_file(void)
{
  if ((logfile = fopen(gnome_config_get_string_with_default(
    "/dvdstore/general/logfile_name=logfile.txt", NULL) ,"a")) == NULL)
    {
      dvd_gui_show_result(_("Cannot open logfile"), 0);
    }
}
```

add_log_message

This adds the textual message msg to the log window, also appending it to the logfile along with the time and date:

```
void
add_log_message(gchar *msg)
{
  GtkText *textbox;
  gchar *text;
```

```
gchar time_text[50];
struct tm *time_now = NULL;
time_t the_time;

textbox = GTK_TEXT(lookup_widget(main_window, "text_box"));

the_time = time(NULL);
time_now = localtime(&the_time);
strftime(time_text, sizeof(time_text), "%R %x", time_now);

text = g_strdup_printf("%s -- %s\n", time_text, msg);
gtk_text_insert(textbox, NULL, NULL, NULL, text, -1);
if (logfile != NULL)
   fprintf(logfile, "%s -- %s\n", time_text, msg);
}
```

dvd_gui_show_result

This is our primitive error handling function. If the error number is DVD_SUCCESS, then msg is printed to the standard output; otherwise a warning dialog is shown to the user with msg and error text displayed:

```
void
dvd_gui_show_result(char *msg, int err)
{
  gchar *err_msg;
  gchar *dialog_text;
  GtkWidget *dialog;

  (void) dvd_err_text(err, &err_msg);
  if (err == DVD_SUCCESS)
  g_print("%s: %s\n", msg, err_msg);
  else
    {
      dialog_text = g_strdup_printf(_("DVDStore Error:\n %s: %s"),
                          msg, err_msg);
      dialog = gnome_message_box_new(dialog_text,
                    GNOME_MESSAGE_BOX_WARNING,
                    GNOME_STOCK_BUTTON_OK,
                    NULL);
      gtk_widget_show(dialog);
    }
}
```

date_overdue

This returns an integer value indicating whether a disk rented on date is overdue. This would be a difficult task without glib's calendar functions, as otherwise there's no easy way to add a number of days to a date and then compare to another, accounting for possible month and year boundaries and leap year considerations. Using glib, we turn each date into a GDate object (with sscanf), add the number of allowed days rent (with g_date_add_days), and then compare the dates, by using g_date_compare:

```
gint
date_overdue(gchar *date)
{
  gchar *date_today;
  gint day, month, year;
  gint overdue;
  GDate *g_rent_date;
  GDate *g_date_today;

  dvd_today(&date_today);
  sscanf(date_today, "%04d%02d%02d", &year, &month, &day);
  g_date_today = g_date_new_dmy(day, month, year);

  sscanf(date, "%04d%02d%02d", &year, &month, &day);
  g_rent_date = g_date_new_dmy(day, month, year);

  g_date_add_days(g_rent_date, gnome_config_get_int_with_default
                              ("/dvdstore/general/days_rent=3", NULL));

/* g_date_compare returns Zero for equal dates , less than zero if
 * g_rent_date is less than g_date_today and greater than zero if g_rent_date
 * is greater than g_date_today
 */
  overdue = g_date_compare(g_rent_date, g_date_today);
  g_date_free(g_rent_date);
  g_date_free(g_date_today);
  return overdue;
}
```

do_about_dialog

Finally, we have a function to display the 'about' dialog. Note that Glade-created about dialogs are modal:

```
void
do_about_dialog()
{
  GtkWidget* about_dialog = NULL;

  about_dialog = create_about_dialog ();
  gtk_widget_show (about_dialog);
}
```

We've now finished our look at the dvdstore source code.

Summary

In this chapter we've looked at Glade in detail, and walked through the development of an example application. We've demonstrated many of Glade's features, and how complicated programs can be built quickly using a skeleton framework together with the simple yet powerful GNOME/GTK+ libraries.

We looked at the `lookup_widget` method of pointer retrieval, and applied `libglade` to our example before moving on to the implementation a Graphical User Interface for the DVD Store Application in GNOME/GTK+.

10

Flex and Bison

A typical computer program does three things. It reads some input, performs some action and writes some output. Applications that we write in C can call upon many library functions to help with all three of these tasks. The standard I/O library (`stdio`) contains many functions for both input and output that will be familiar to all C programmers. These range from basic data input and output with `fread` and `fwrite` to more sophisticated routines for reading and writing slightly more complex things like numbers and strings with `printf` and `scanf`.

Very often applications have to read data that is more structured, like names and addresses, configuration files, mathematical formulae, or programming language expressions. Although the input will be made up of characters, numbers or strings that can be read individually by `stdio` functions, there is no real support for easily reading more structured data.

In this chapter we will discuss structured input and meet two tools that can be very useful to developers working with complex data. First developed in the 1970s for use in compiler construction, the programs `lex` and `yacc` became popular with programmers writing all kinds of applications in C. They are now part of the POSIX standard for UNIX utilities.

Versions of these tools – or their free equivalents `flex` and `bison` – are available for UNIX, and of course Linux. You can use the tools for applications written in other languages, and there is a version of `yacc` specifically for Perl. Almost all distributions of Linux contain them, but they are often overlooked, being seen as difficult to understand and use. A glimpse at the manual page for `yacc` doesn't generally give the impression of a utility that is going to be easy to learn; but as we shall see, appearances can be deceptive.

We don't have space in a single chapter to cover every aspect of using these two programs. Our aim here is to give a flavor of the tools, and how they can be used. As always, complete information can be found elsewhere, including some useful Internet resources (which we've listed at the end of the chapter) and, of course, the on-line documentation that's provided with your Linux distribution.

Input Structure

Before we dive into the details of using the tools, let's consider what programs need to do with their input. Take a look at this input for a program:

```
program hello(input,output);

(* A simple example program *)

const alength = 7;
      bindex = 3;

var left, right: integer;
    a : array[1..alength] of real;

begin
    if a[bindex] > 32.613 then
    begin
        writeln(left:5, a[bindex]:10:2);
        left = 6 + right*21
    end
end.
```

As experienced developers, we may well recognize this as a computer program written in the Pascal programming language. We may even be able to tell that it fully conforms to the rules of the Pascal language (although if you tried to run it, you would find that it doesn't do anything very useful).

An application that has to read this input will see it very differently indeed. At a low-level a program will see just a stream of characters, like this:

```
'p' 'r' 'o' 'g' 'r' 'a' 'm' ' ' 'h' ... 'e' 'n' 'd' '.'
```

The internal representation within a program that reads the input will bear little relation to a Pascal program as recognized by a developer. It is not significantly different from any other stream of random characters. Depending on the application, this may be sufficient. In fact, programs like text editors may very deliberately treat their input as a stream of characters, imposing no structure at all. Word processors may treat their input as lines of text, and might therefore view this same input as a sequence of strings, each ending with a newline character:

Line[1] is "program hello(input,output);"

Line[2] is ""

Line[3] is "(* A simple example program *)"

and so on.

Some editors use syntax-directed highlighting, giving special elements of the text different on-screen attributes (such as coloring keywords in red). They might wish to view the input as a sequence of keywords interspersed with other text, like this:

```
KEY(program) "hello(input,output);"
...
        KEY(if) "a[bindex] > 32.613" KEY(then)
```

A 'folding editor' takes this idea a stage further – it might want to manipulate the separate sections of the input, allowing the user to move whole blocks of code at a time. Therefore, it may wish to view the input like this:

```
    ...
    BLOCK(
      begin
          if a[bindex] > 32.613 then
          BLOCK(
            begin
                writeln(left:5, a[bindex]:10:2);
                left = 6.1 + right*21
            end
          )
      end.
    )
```

Finally, a compiler for the Pascal language will need to view the program almost as a human does: as a sequence of declarations and statements, using constants and variables to describe a sequence of actions to be taken:

```
...
ASSIGNMENT(VARIABLE("left"),EXPRESSION(ADD(NUMBER(6.1),EXPRESSION(TIMES(VARIABLE("
right"),INTEGER(21))))))
...
```

Scanners and Parsers

The tools that we will take a look at in this chapter allow a developer to write programs that handle input data with a reasonably complex structure. Even if you are not planning to write a compiler, there are many instances where structured input handling can be of great help. Examples include command recognition in a program that has to interact with a user (like a command line file transfer client), recognizing arithmetic expressions in a debugger, writing a specification for a screen layout, and checking the format of data (for example, reading HTML).

The task of recognizing different kinds of items in an input stream is called lexical analysis. A program that reads input and provides an indication of which items (also called tokens) have been encountered is called a lexical analyzer, or scanner. lex and its free equivalent, flex, are applications that write scanners for us. We give them a description of the tokens (such as keywords, numbers or tags) we wish to identify, plus some code we want to execute when those tokens are seen. They write the code to recognize the tokens and call our code.

The secondary task is that of recognizing higher-level structure in a sequence of tokens, such as program blocks, assignment statements, arithmetic expressions, or complete HTML constructs. This is called parsing, and a program that does this is called a parser (after the technique once taught in schools for breaking down an English or Latin sentence into verbs, nouns, adjectives, and so on). yacc and its GNU equivalent, bison, are applications that write parsers for us. They are called parser generators, or compiler-compilers.

The name yacc *comes from 'Yet Another Compiler Compiler' (reflecting the popularity of parser applications at the time), while* bison *gets its name from a weak pun on being another sort of Yak.*

How Generators Work

We use a parser generator by giving it a description of the structures we want to recognize (using a particular type of grammar) and code to execute whenever those structures are seen (usually to build some internal representation of the input – perhaps a tree structure representing an entire HTML page or a complex calculation). The parser generator then produces a function that creates the appropriate structure from the input that it's given.

Although parsers require a lexical analyzer to provide their input, you don't have to use lex or flex to create one. Often for simpler tasks, a hand-crafted lexical analyzer is sufficient. However, these can be difficult to write such that they handle all combinations of input correctly. Therefore flex may prove to be an easier solution in the longer term, since its code generation has already been debugged by many previous users.

The process of reading structured input can be summarized as follows. For written English we might have:

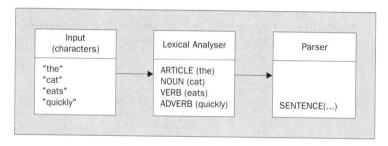

For our computer input we might have:

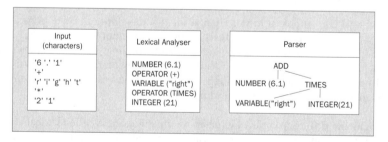

Reading from left to right, we see that the raw input is transformed into a representation of its structure. The lexical analyzer is responsible for reading the lowest form of input we have, recognizing words and their types. The parser recognizes larger structures such as sentences and statements.

We'll now move on to look at implementing scanners and parsers.

Scanners

We will not make a distinction between lex and flex, as flex can be considered a superset of lex and can be used on systems that do not have a version of lex installed. Of course, since flex is available under the BSD License, its source code is available and it can be compiled and installed on just about all UNIX-like systems, including Linux. It's usually part of the development set of packages though, so it may not be installed by default.

It is worth noting that flex also conforms much more closely to the POSIX standard for the lex command than many implementations of lex.

If you need to write specifications for scanners that will be generated by lex, you can invoke a 'lex-compatibility' mode for flex by specifying the -l option to flex when you run it.

This has the advantage that your generated scanner will be very similar to one that would have been created by lex. It has the disadvantage of turning off all of the performance advantages and extensions that flex has over lex.

On Linux systems, lex is sometimes implemented as a small shell script that invokes flex with this compatibility option.

By default, scanners created with flex simply read the standard input, executing any code fragments associated with tokens they have been programmed to recognize. Any characters read that don't form part of a token are copied to the standard output.

A Simple Scanner

Here is a complete, trivial example that corrects a common spelling error, namely the misspelt surname of one of the authors.

```
%%
Mathews       printf("Matthew");
%%
int main()
{
    yylex();
    return(0);
}
```

Save this file as matthew.l and create a scanner with the following incantation. We will look more closely at what happens when we do this shortly.

```
$ flex matthew.l
$ gcc -o matthew lex.yy.c -lfl
```

We now have a program, called matthew, which will correct that spelling error. Let's try it out.

```
$ ./matthew
Dear Mr Mathews,
Dear Mr Matthew,
How is Mrs Matthew today?
How is Mrs Matthew today?
^D
$
```

337

As you can see, wherever the string "Mathews" is encountered it is replaced in the output by the string "Matthew". The match is case sensitive and the string must match exactly. Any characters not matching are copied to the standard output unchanged, as is the case when the spelling is correct (as in the second line entered).

What the scanner does is to look for regular expressions (just like sed and grep do) in the input. For input that matches an expression, a fragment of code is executed. Any input that doesn't match is (by default) output unchanged. The stdin and stdout streams are used for default input and output.

Scanner Specifications

The general form of a scanner specification consists of three sections, separated by lines consisting of a pair of percent signs.

The first section, omitted in our initial demonstration program, is used for definitions. These are either specifications of macros for flex, or C code to be included in the scanner; typically #include directives and declarations of variables and functions with static or global scope that we want to use in the rules section code fragments.

The second section specifies the scanner rules and code to be executed when the regular expression specified in the rule is matched. In our program, this matches the misspelt name and specifies the code to be executed whenever it's found.

The third section contains user code that will be included verbatim in the generated scanner. Generally this section is used for the bulk of our code, the first being conventionally reserved for include files and declarations. In our example we've declared a simple main program. This does nothing more than to call the generated scanner function, which by default has the rather arcane name yylex.

The generated scanner file lex.yy.c automatically includes stdio.h. So in our example we didn't need to create a definitions section to contain a #include directive. We would normally have done this, since our scanner code fragments call printf.

Let's take a closer look at what happened when we generated our scanner.

First, we ran flex on our specification file matthew.l. flex read the rules and generated the code for a scanner that would perform the actions we specified. This code is written to a file called lex.yy.c by default. We then compiled this C file and linked it with the flex library (-lfl), which contains a number of functions that the generated scanner needs to do its job.

If you are using lex rather than flex, the lex library will have a different name (typically linked with -ll).

The C code in the file lex.yy.c defines the scanner function itself. This function (yylex) reads all of the input, matching the rules as it goes. Our main program will hand over control to yylex and will call our code as required. This is similar in many ways to the notion of callbacks in GUI applications programming. Since yylex essentially loops through all of the input, our main program just has to call it once and then exit. All of the code we need to execute (as the tokens are recognized) must be called from code fragments in the rules section.

Let's take a look at a more complex example. Below is a specification for a scanner to recognize numbers. It will handle three types of number:

- integers of the form 123

- decimals of the form 123.456

- real numbers in scientific notation, such as 1.23e45

Here's how we do it:

```
/* LEX specification for numbers */

%{
#include <stdlib.h>
%}

EXP        "E"|"e"
DIGIT      [0-9]
DECIMAL    "."
SIGN       "+"|"-"

%option main
%%
{DIGIT}+{DECIMAL}{DIGIT}*{EXP}{SIGN}?{DIGIT}+   {
          printf("REAL(%s -> %g)", yytext, atof(yytext));
                                      }
{DIGIT}+{DECIMAL}{DIGIT}*   {
          printf("DECIMAL(%s -> %g)", yytext, atof(yytext));
                                }
{DIGIT}+ {
           printf("INTEGER(%s -> %d)", yytext, atoi(yytext));
         }
%%
```

This is numbers.l and generates a scanner that recognizes numbers in the forms we need, including whole numbers, decimals and exponents.

Note that the specification does not accept numbers with a leading plus or minus sign. This is because in a full-blown application that handles arithmetic expressions we need to deal with the monadic operators + and - in a consistent way.

There are a few new concepts introduced here so we will go through them one by one.

We can comment lex (and flex) specification files using C-style comments, as shown in the definitions section of this example:

```
/* LEX specification for numbers */
```

In the definitions section we add some C commands to be included early in the code for the generated scanner. Any text that flex finds between decorated brackets, %{ and %}, is copied into the scanner code verbatim. In this example we have inserted code to include the standard header file stdlib.h to provide declarations of the functions atof and atoi that we use later on.

The remaining definitions give names to some regular expressions that we want to use as part of our scanner specification. The regular expression format should be familiar, particularly to anyone who has used sed or egrep. We define the expression EXP to match either a lower case or upper case letter E:

```
EXP       "E"|"e"
```

The expression DIGIT matches any decimal digit in the range zero through nine:

```
DIGIT     [0-9]
```

The expression DECIMAL matches a period used as an indicator of the decimal point in floating point numbers:

```
DECIMAL   "."
```

The expression SIGN matches either a plus or minus sign:

```
SIGN      "+"|"-"
```

We will come back to the rules for constructing regular expressions shortly.

In the rules section, we define three kinds of numbers that we're interested in recognizing. The first are those containing both a decimal point and an exponent – the regular expression we try to match is:

```
{DIGIT}+{DECIMAL}{DIGIT}*{EXP}{SIGN}?{DIGIT}+
```

This can be read as:

- ❏ "**one or more digits**, followed by
- ❏ **a decimal point**, followed by
- ❏ **zero or more further digits**, followed by
- ❏ **an exponent indicator**, followed by
- ❏ **an optional sign**, followed by
- ❏ **one or more further digits**"

The operators +, *, and ? specify that parts of the number are optional or can occur several times. We will see these again shortly. We expect that this expression will match numbers like this:

```
12.34e3
1.e-04
```

Note that we do not cater for numbers with an exponent but no decimal point in this example. Neither do we deal with explicit plus or minus signs at the start of the number.

The second form of number we want to recognize is a floating-point number without an exponent. This is just a simpler form of the first rule:

```
{DIGIT}+{DECIMAL}{DIGIT}*
```

This corresponds to the statement:

- ❏ "**one or more digits**, followed by
- ❏ **a decimal point**, followed by
- ❏ **zero or more further digits**"

We expect this rule to match numbers like this:

```
0.645
768.
```

The third form we want to capture is an integer, a simple case of "**one or more digits**", hence our third rule:

```
{DIGIT}+
```

We expect this to be triggered by input of numbers like these:

```
456
1
```

We have used a flex-specific extension to the POSIX standard in this specification, that of %option. This is used to guide flex in its generation of a scanner. The option we have used here is:

```
%option main
```

This causes flex to generate a main function for us automatically, so that we can omit it from the user code section. The generated main does exactly what our first example did, calling yylex and returning. However, if portability is a high priority, you should probably try to avoid the use of %option.

Within the rules section of a scanner specification we define a number of separate rules. Each rule has the same basic form:

```
expression    code-fragment
```

The expression is simply the regular expression that we're trying to match. It must begin in the first column of a line. The code fragment must be valid C code that begins on the same line as the expression, but may extend over multiple lines if enclosed in braces, as shown in our example.

The code fragment may be omitted, in which case an input that matches the regular expression is simply discarded. This is often used for eliminating blank lines or white space in the input. We will see an example of this later.

In the code fragments, we write the code to be executed when the expression is matched. In our case we make use of one of the variables that flex and lex provide for use within the scanner code fragments. The variable yytext is a NULL-terminated character array that contains the input that matched the regular expression. Here we use it to extract the value of the number either with atof or atoi depending on the expression matched.

It is important to realize that the yytext variable cannot be stored – it changes with each execution of a code fragment. It is typically implemented via a pointer into the middle of an input buffer, which is constantly updated as the scanning proceeds. If you need to store the input for a particular match you'll have to copy it out of yytext and store it elsewhere.

Let's compile and run the scanner:

```
$ flex numbers.l
$ cc -o numbers lex.yy.c
$ ./numbers
12.34e3
REAL(12.34e3 -> 12340)
1.e-04
REAL(1.e-04 -> 0.0001)
0.645
DECIMAL(0.645 -> 0.645)
768.
DECIMAL(768. -> 768)
456
INTEGER(456 -> 456)
1
INTEGER(1 -> 1)
ABC123DEF
ABCINTEGER(123 -> 123)DEF
^D
$
```

As before, unmatched input is copied to the standard output.

Longest Match Principle

You will probably have noticed that our specification of numbers is potentially ambiguous. If we are presented with the input "123.45E67" this could be interpreted as an integer (123) matching our third rule, followed by some more characters. How does flex know that it is a real number and match it as such?

The scanners that lex and flex produce try to match the longest possible input string. They keep on trying to match all rules until the match begins to fail. So faced with a long string of digits the scanner keeps accumulating them in yytext until all possible matches begin to fail. So given "123", we don't get a sequence of single-digit integers, but a single three-digit one. Similar rules apply for floating point numbers.

The scanner will not give up and 'settle' for a simple decimal. It will look ahead to see if an exponent is coming and try to match a floating-point number of that form. If that fails, it will return a match for decimal and carry on with the used input. For example:

```
$ ./numbers
123.45E*12
DECIMAL(123.45 -> 123.45)E*INTEGER(12 -> 12)
```

Here the scanner tries to match a floating-point number with an exponent, but the characters after the E do not fit the definition. So instead we get a match for a decimal (123.45) followed by the characters E and *, and then we get another match for an integer from the remaining digits.

It is important to understand that `flex` uses this 'longest possible match' principle to disambiguate its specification rules, as it can sometimes have unforeseen consequences, especially for command line programs. For example, if you allow the input of multiple lines and have optional trailing components of a command, then `flex` will keep reading until it knows for sure that the option has not been specified. This will not occur until it has seen the start of the *next* command. To avoid this we'd need to make sure that all commands are terminated, possibly with a newline or a period.

Although we wrote our rules in 'longest first' order – to avoid any possible problem with leading substrings of our input matching more than one rule – we need not have worried too much. The effectively generated scanner matches all rules at once, automatically using the longest match principle to determine which rule to match with. However, human readers sometimes need some help in reading scanner specifications, so it's helpful to structure your specifications with the longest match specification first. That way, the reader can interpret the specification as meaning:

- ❑ A number has digits, a decimal point and an exponent.

- ❑ Failing that, it may have just digits and a decimal point.

- ❑ Failing that it may just have digits.

In the case where two rules match the same length string in the input stream, `flex` will match the rule that occurs first in the specification.

Regular Expressions

Anyone who has used `grep`, `sed`, `awk` or `perl` will be familiar with regular expressions. If not, suffice to say that they provide a way of describing strings of characters in terms of their parts, such as three 'a's optionally followed by a 'b'. They are used by `emacs` for searching within files, and here they are used to specify how to recognize tokens in input streams. Generally, regular expressions used by `lex` and `flex` follow these character matching rules:

RegExp	Matches
a	literal character 'a' (unless one of the special characters below)
[abc]	matches any of the characters a, b, or c
[a-z]	matches any of the characters a through z
[^x]	matches any character except x, which may be a single character or a group as above
"xyz"	matches the literal sequence of characters x, y and z
\\<char>	escaped character – as in C, this matches control characters in the input. <char> may be one of a, b, f, n, r, t or v – for example, \n matches a newline, and \t matches a tab character
\0	NULL character (ASCII value zero)
\123	character with ASCII code octal 0123
\x12	character with ASCII code hexadecimal 0x12
.	any character

The character classes shown here can also be combined. For example, [^a-z] matches any characters *not* included in the range a through z, while [i-kx-zA] matches any of the characters i, j, k, x, y, z and A.

flex provides some special abbreviations for commonly used character classes, including alphanumeric characters and whitespace. These are bracketed with [: and :], and must appear within the normal character class square brackets whenever used. These classes include [:alnum:], [:alpha:] and [:xdigit:]. In general there's a class for each of the is<class> functions defined for standard C in ctype.h. The class [:alnum:] represents one of the characters for which the function isalnum returns true. The list of classes supported by flex includes:

alnum	alpha	blank	cntrl	digit	graph
lower	print	punct	space	upper	xdigit

So our rule for digits could be written:

```
DIGIT        [[:digit:]]
```

Regular Expression Combination

If re represents a regular expression, including the character matches above, then using expression operators as shown below, we can create more complex expressions:

re*	zero or more occurrences of the match defined by re
re+	one or more occurrences of re
re?	zero or one matches of re
re{N}	exactly N instances of re
re{N,}	at least N instances of re
re{N,M}	between N and M (inclusive) instances of re
{name}	matches the regular expression given the name "name" in the definition section of the scanner specification
(re)	matches an instance of re – parentheses are used to enforce precedence rules, especially when using optional expressions
re1re2	matches an instance of re1 followed by an instance of re2
re1|re2	matches either re1 or re2
re1/re2	matches an re1 only if followed by an re2 (which is itself not consumed by the match)
^re	matches an instance of re occurring at the start of a line (only)
re$	matches an instance of re occurring at the end of a line

The operators used to combine regular expressions are listed above in order of precedence. Parentheses may be used to override the normal order of evaluation, in the same way as arithmetic expressions.

> *There are a few other ways to combine regular expressions that are rarely used. Details can be found in the* flex *manual pages.*

When writing patterns for the rules, it's important that you don't leave any whitespace between parts of the expression, as `flex` will interpret this as signifying the end of the expression and the start of the action code fragment.

As an example of the expressive power of character classes and regular expressions, here are a couple of samples taken from the source code for the `xboard` application. This manages two chess playing programs and interprets the output that they give. These are:

```
[RrBbNnQqKkPp][/]?[a-h][1-8][xX:-]?[a-h][1-8](=?\(?[RrBbNnQqKk]\)?)? {
    /*
     * Fully-qualified algebraic move, possibly with promotion
     */
    ...
}
```

and:

```
(([Ww](hite)?)|([Bb](lack)?))" "(([Rr]esign)|([Ff]orfeit))(s|ed)?  {
    return (int) (ToUpper(yytext[0]) == 'W' ? BlackWins : WhiteWins);
}
```

The first expression matches moves such as N/g1-f3 and Ph7-h8=Q. The second expression matches messages at the end of the game such as 'White Resigns' or 'black forfeit'.

Actions

We've seen some simple examples of actions being taken as the result of matching expressions in the input. To help with common tasks, `flex` also defines some macros and variables that can be used in the code fragments associated with matches:

`yytext[]`	character array containing the text that matched the expression
`yyleng`	the length of the string held in `yytext`
`YYLMAX`	a `#define` that states the maximum possible length of `yytext` – it is set to a reasonable, fairly large value – as this affects the maximum size of a token it can be overridden in your scanner by including a suitable `#define` in the definitions section of your specification
`ECHO;`	copies the current content of `yytext` to the scanner's output
`REJECT;`	causes the scanner to fail in matching this rule, and proceed with the next best matching other rule – using `REJECT` has performance implications for the scanner and is best avoided
`unput(c);`	places the character c back on the input stream – it will be the next character read – this action will invalidate the current token if you are using `flex` in its default mode, so use this only after taking actions that use the contents of `yytext`
`yymore();`	causes the scanner to add to `yytext` rather than replacing it when it matches its next rule
`yyless(n);`	places the trailing part of the current token back on the input stream to be re-read – only the first n characters are consumed
`input();`	returns the next character (as an `int`) from the input stream

The macro `yymore` can be used to scan prefixes that can occur multiple times. For example:

```
%option main
%%
"grandfather"     { printf("paternal ancestor: %s", yytext); }
"great-"          { yymore(); }
%%
```

When the scanner sees "great", it continues scanning but remembers the prefix (as part of `yytext`). When "grandfather" is matched, we've therefore collected all the prefixes at once.

```
$ ./great
grandfather
paternal ancestor grandfather
great-great-great-grandfather
paternal ancestor great-great-great-grandfather
^D
$
```

Redirecting Scanner Input and Output

The scanners generated by `flex` and `lex` will automatically read from the standard input and write to the standard output. This behavior is easily overridden by assigning input and output streams to the two variables `yyin` and `yyout`:

```
FILE *yyin = stdin;
FILE *yyout = stdout;
```

Say we have a program that uses a scanner to read input from a file given on the command line. It might execute code similar to this (with added error checking of course!):

```
yyin = fopen("filename", "r");
yylex();
```

Similarly, for redirecting output, the variable `yyout` can be re-assigned to a suitable output stream pointer.

When the scanner reaches the end of the input file, it calls a function called `yywrap`. If this is not defined in the user code within the specification, a default will be provided when the program is linked with the `flex` library. This is why we had to link with `-lfl` in our examples above. The return value from `yywrap` is used to decide whether or not the scanner has finished its work. If `yywrap` returns a non-zero value the scanner terminates.

If we wish to continue scanning – perhaps using another file as input – we can provide our own `yywrap` function. One use of this would be to scan a number of files whose names are passed as arguments to our main program. `yywrap` would then be used to open the next file, assign the stream pointer to `yyin` and return zero. The scanner would then just carry on as if the input from the new file was an extension of the input just read.

The scanner can also be directed to **nest** inputs (such as would be needed for processing `#include` directives in a C compiler) using a stack of input streams to create a combined input. Details of using multiple input streams can be found in the `flex` manual page.

Furthermore, input can be taken from sources other than files by overriding the low-level input functions used by the generated scanner. Again, details may be found in the manual page.

Returning Tokens

Often in an application, we don't need the lexical analyzer to consume all the input at once, but rather just provide us with the next available token. To do this, we simply execute a `return` in the action that corresponds to the match we wish to stop at.

For example, we may wish to eliminate blank lines and other whitespace in our input, and return matching keywords to a calling program. Here is a very small example that does just this. It also returns an indication of unmatched input to the caller:

```
%{
#define TOKEN_GARBAGE   1
#define TOKEN_PROGRAM   2
#define TOKEN_BEGIN     3
/* and so on */
%}

%%
"program"   { return TOKEN_PROGRAM; }
"begin"     { return TOKEN_BEGIN; }
[ \t\n]+    /* ignore whitespace */
.           { return TOKEN_GARBAGE; }
%%
int main()
{
    int token;

    while(token = yylex())
            printf("got token #%d\n", token);
}
```

When we generate a scanner and run it, we see that the program functions as intended:

```
$ flex token.l
$ cc -o token lex.yy.c -lfl
$ ./token
  program
got token #2


begin
got token #3


    1
got token #1
^D
$
```

Every time `yylex` is called, it starts from where it left off and tries to match against the full set of rules again. We will see more of this type of use of the lexical analyzer function, in conjunction with a parser generated by `yacc` or `bison`.

Context Sensitive Scanners

Sometimes it is necessary to write a scanner that needs to have some idea of state; that is, respond to matches in different ways depending on what has been matched previously. One example would be matching a quoted string in a C program, since we treat backslashes and quotes differently when inside a string to when we encounter them outside.

Constructing a regular expression capturing the rules for 'quoting inside a string' is very difficult. However we can quite easily divide the scanner into two or more phases, one for use outside of strings and the other for use inside. We can build a state-enabled scanner by using what flex and lex refer to as **start conditions**.

Each rule in a lex specification can be prefixed with a **state** in angled brackets, indicating that the rule is only to be applied when the scanner is in that state. In fact, a rule may be prefixed with a *list* of states for which it's valid. A macro BEGIN(state); can be used within actions to switch from one state to the next.

Here is an example from the manual page, which deals with discarding C comments:

```
%x comment
%%
"/*" BEGIN(comment);

<comment>[^*\n]*        /* Eat up anything that's not a '*' */
<comment>"*"+[^*/\n]*   /* eat up '*'s not followed by a '/' */
<comment>\n             line_num++;
<comment>"*"+"/"        BEGIN(INITIAL);
```

Note that the scanner has to cope with multiple stars at the beginning and end of comments.

Options to flex

There are quite a few options to the flex program, controlling either the scanner's behavior or the method used to store the data tables that it uses for interpreting the scan rules. Some of those most likely to be used are:

-d	debug mode – generated scanner includes additional debug statements that will be output to the standard error stream as the rules are matched
-f	fast mode – generated scanner runs more quickly, but consumes more memory
-h	help – prints a brief synopsis of the available options
-i	case insensitive – generated scanner matches input regardless of case
	(contents of yytext will have the original case as it appears in the input)
-l	lex compatible mode
-t	write generated scanner to standard output rather than file lex.yy.c
-I	interactive – generated scanner suitable for interactive applications
	(for efficiency, flex will read as much input as it can to help decide which rule matches – sometimes this can have an impact on programs intended to be used interactively – this option causes the scanner to be more conservative in its read-ahead, but still sufficient to successfully scan the rules as intended)
-ofile	write generated scanner code to the named file rather than lex.yy.c

One of the most useful options when things don't go quite to plan is the debug option -d. Debug statements take the form:

```
--accepting rule at line <n> ("string")
```

indicating which portion of the input has matched which rule. The 'grandfather' example produces this output when run with a debug-enabled scanner:

```
$ ./great
--(end of buffer or a NUL)
great-great-grandfather
--accepting rule at line 4 ("great-")
--accepting rule at line 4 ("great-great-")
--accepting rule at line 3 ("great-great-grandfather")
paternal ancestor great-great-grandfather
--accepting default rule ("
")
--(end of buffer or a NUL)
^D
--EOF (start condition 0)
$
```

Parsers

It's now time to move up a level and look at parsers. A parser is a program that determines whether or not a sequence of lexical tokens conforms to a given specification. Simply put, it takes a word or group of words and tests their compliance with a set of grammatical rules.

Strictly speaking, the 'word' can be anything that we've specified as a lexical token. In that sense it's much like the lexical analyzer, which determines whether a *sequence of characters* constitutes a *token* (and if so, which one). However, the structures that a parser deals with are typically records, expressions, and commands – anything with some definable syntax.

In a sense it is true to say that any computer program that requires input (and performs actions based on that input) defines an input language that it accepts. As we have already mentioned, this may be as complex as a high-level programming language (in the case of a compiler) or as simple as a sequence of letters and digits.

Languages are specified by grammars; sets of rules stating which arrangements of words (known as sentences, strangely enough) are valid. In fact, languages are *defined* by the set of *all* of their sentences, but rules of grammar let us neatly summarize the valid sentences in a variety of languages, especially well-defined artificial ones like those we'll consider here.

We can consider rules for specifying dates in a particular way – one such rule might be:

```
<date> = <month-name> <day> ',' <year>
```

Here <date>, <month-name>, <day> and <year> represent structures of interest in the input process – we presume that they are defined elsewhere. The comma is in quotes to illustrate that we require it to appear literally in the input. With proper definitions, the input

```
July 4, 1776
```

can therefore be matched by our rule for dates.

There's often considerable leeway in deciding whether to recognize input components in a lexical analyzer or a parser. In this case, we might arrange for the lexical analyzer to return tokens of one sort representing individual month names, and another sort (with associated values) for single digits. Our subsidiary rules might then look something like this:

```
<month-name> = JANUARY | FEBRUARY | ... | DECEMBER
<day> = DIGIT | DIGIT DIGIT
<year> = DIGIT DIGIT DIGIT DIGIT
```

Alternatively, we might arrange for the lexical analyzer to return a month *number* according to which month name was recognized, along with some integers representing the day number and year.

Striking the right balance between lexical analysis and parsing can be tricky. A useful rule of thumb is to do as much as you can in the lexical analyzer, without making the regular expressions too complex. Parsers should only be used where the complexity of the structure exceeds the ability of regular expressions to readily describe them. Try to return tokens that have meaning for the grammar being used in the parser.

Generating Parsers

As we mentioned earlier, a parser generator is a program that writes a parser from a set of grammar rules – yacc and bison are two well-known examples. It is of course possible to create a parser 'by hand'. In our example it's fairly easy to construct a function that called the lexical analyzer to collect tokens and check whether the date format is valid. For more complex grammar though, handcrafted parsers can be tiresome to build and difficult to modify if the grammar changes.

In a grammar specification, each rule defines a structure known as a **non-terminal**, giving it a name, like date in our example above. Non-terminals are made up of tokens, also called **terminal symbols**, and other non-terminals. It is possible, and indeed very common, to create recursive sets of rules, where rules refer to themselves either directly or indirectly through other rules.

Here is an example of a recursive set of rules, taken from a grammar specification for the Pascal programming language:

```
<statement> = <identifier> ":=" <expression>
            | IF <expression> THEN <statement>
            | IF <expression> THEN <statement> ELSE <statement>
            | BEGIN <statements> END

<statements> = <statement>
             | <statement> ';' <statements>
```

These lines embody the rule that a Pascal statement may take several forms, some of which include other statements. With appropriate definitions of the other non-terminals, these rules for a statement could match the following fragments of Pascal programs:

```
fred := 2+bill

if fred-7 > 34
then x := x+1
else
        begin
        y := y-1;
        bill := 2-fred
    end
```

Note that the rule defining <statements> will match any group of statements separated by semi-colons. As with flex, the parsers generated by bison try to match the longest possible sequence of their input. When trying to match a <statements> structure the parser will try to match a <statement> and then rather than accept that as a <statements> structure as allowed by the rule, will carry on trying to match another <statements> structure, which will lead eventually to a group of statements being recognized. In our two examples, the parser will match the code fragments like this:

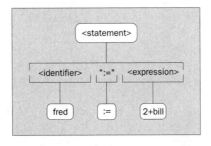

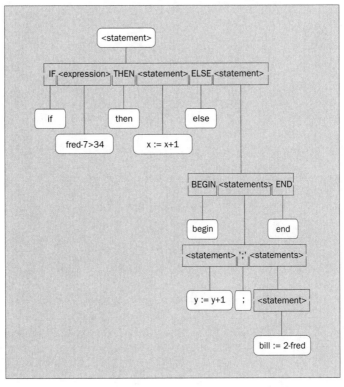

Here, we've abbreviated the second diagram a little – each of the assignments will be represented by a structure <identifier> := <expression>.

The parser reads tokens from the input and replaces them with structures as defined in the grammar rules. This technique is called **shift-reduce** parsing. The tokens (terminals) and non-terminals already matched are shifted from the input into a parse buffer. When enough of them taken together match a rule, they are **reduced** to an indication that a (non-terminal) structure has been recognized. Eventually all of the input is consumed and there is only one structure left – the start symbol, in this case a single <statement>.

When we write a specification for yacc or bison, we are able to write actions – fragments of C code – much like those we used for lex and flex. When a rule is reduced the code associated with the rule that matches is executed.

It's probably time for an example. Just below are the beginnings of a grammar specification for the subset of Pascal used in our example code fragment. It is in fact a complete, valid input for yacc or bison – let's call it pascal.y. (By convention, grammar files written to be processed with either yacc or bison are given the extension .y.)

```
%{
#include <stdio.h>
%}

%token tBEGIN
%token tEND
%token tIF
%token tTHEN
%token tELSE
%token tASSIGN
%token tIDENTIFIER
%token tNUMBER

%start statement
%left '>'
%left '+'
%left '-'

%%

statement:    tIDENTIFIER tASSIGN expression
            | tIF expression tTHEN statement
            | tIF expression tTHEN statement tELSE statement
            | tBEGIN statements tEND
    ;

statements:   statement
            | statement ';' statements
    ;

expression:   tNUMBER
            | tIDENTIFIER
            | expression '+' expression
            | expression '-' expression
            | expression '>' expression
    ;

%%
```

```
int main()
{
  yyparse();
}

int yyerror(char *s)
{
  fprintf(stderr, "%s\n", s);
  return 0;
}

int yylex()
{
  return 0;
}
```

As with `lex` specifications, the parser specification is split into three sections:

❑   definitions

❑   rules

❑   additional code

Once again, the sections are separated by lines consisting of two percent signs.

Definitions

Just as with `flex`, we use the definitions section to arrange for C declarations to be made available to code used later on:

```
%{
#include <stdio.h>
%}
```

and for definitions to guide the generation of the parser program itself:

```
%token tBEGIN
%token tEND
%token tIF
%token tTHEN
%token tELSE
%token tASSIGN
%token tIDENTIFIER
%token tNUMBER

%start statement
%left '>'
%left '+'
%left '-'
```

These are known as **directives**.

The main purpose of `yacc` and `bison` is to generate a parser function, which will be called `yyparse`. This function calls another function, `yylex`, to fetch tokens from the input stream. The tokens that `yylex` is expected to return are declared in the definition section of the grammar specification.

Lines starting `%token` declare names for tokens we're interested in, and generate constants for them that we can use in a scanner. The line starting `%start` tells the generator to make a parser that tries to match a statement. Without a `%start` directive the parser will try to match the structure defined by the first rule in the specification.

> When choosing token names, try to avoid possible clashes with defines that might be used elsewhere in the program, including the generated scanner and parser. This can be a problem, especially with keywords. You cannot have a token called **else** which is returned when a scanner sees the input "else", as that would clash with the keyword in C. Simply capitalizing is not enough either. Remember that the token names will just be **#defines** in the code, and the scanner and parser define some constants of their own, including **BEGIN**! That is why we have chosen here to make all the token names distinctive with a prefix.

We will return to the remaining directives (`%left`) when we consider the parsing of arithmetic expressions and the issues involved with them.

Rules

The rules section looks very similar to our informal specification of structures:

```
statement:    tIDENTIFIER tASSIGN expression
            | tIF expression tTHEN statement
            | tIF expression tTHEN statement tELSE statement
            | tBEGIN statements tEND
    ;

statements:   statement
            | statement ';' statements
    ;

expression:   tNUMBER
            | tIDENTIFIER
            | expression '+' expression
            | expression '-' expression
            | expression '>' expression
    ;
```

The general form of a grammar rule is:

```
thing:        components1
            | components2
            | components3
              ...
    ;
```

where components are sequences of other non-terminals, lexical tokens and literal characters. The rule is read as "a non-terminal called thing is made up of either components1 or components2 or...". There need not be any alternatives in which case the rule is essentially shorthand for a sequence of other items. One of the alternatives may be empty, indicating that it is possible for the non-terminal to match the empty string. In these cases it is conventional to indicated that the alternative is empty with a comment, like this:

```
<optional_comma>: ','
                | /* empty */
   ;
```

Additional Code

The additional code section contains C declarations and function definitions that will be copied verbatim into the parser source file:

```
int main()
{
  yyparse();
}

int yyerror(char *s)
{
  fprintf(stderr, "%s\n", s);
  return 0;
}
int yylex()
{
  return 0;
}
```

We define a main program that calls the parser function yyparse, and a lexical analyzer function called yylex that is called by yyparse. At the moment this analyzer function is a stub, returning the token zero, which indicates end of file. We will replace this with a genuine lexical analyzer shortly.

The third function we must supply is called yyerror. Its purpose is to handle any errors that occur during parsing. The parser will call yyerror if it's unable to match the input with the grammar specified. It is often enough to just print this message with the standard error, as we've done here.

It is possible to use yyerror along with other associated functions to initiate an error recovery scheme, where the parser tries to re-synchronize with the input and carry on. In a full-blown compiler for example, we would want to try to find as many errors as we can. For simpler applications it will be OK to stop parsing at the first error, as here. For details of error recovery actions see the yacc and bison manual pages, and the bison info pages.

Creating a Syntax Tester

Let's use our `pascal.y` example to create a program that will test the syntax of our code fragment; that is, parse a Pascal statement as defined in the grammar specification.

To start with, we need to create the parser itself – the function `yyparse`. This is the job of `yacc` and `bison`. The default behavior is enough to get started, so let's try it:

```
$ yacc pascal.y
yacc: 1 shift/reduce conflict.
$
```

Alternatively, if you're using `bison`, you can use the `-y` option to make `bison` behave in the same way as `yacc`:

```
$ bison -y pascal.y
conflicts: 1 shift/reduce
$
```

Both utilities report the number of potential problems that may be present in the grammar specification. We will cover grammar conflicts a little later. In this case the conflict is not a problem.

The parser function itself will have been written to a file called `y.tab.c`. Don't you just love these file names? If you take a peek inside `y.tab.c` you will see some quite complex code and some tables of integers. This is the parser itself, and the tables are used to guide the matching of tokens and structures. At any given time the parser will be in one of several defined states. Depending on the next token read, it might (or might not) move into another state.

For example, before we've seen any input we are in state zero. The next tokens valid for this state are `tIDENTIFIER` (the first token in an assignment), `tBEGIN` (the first token in a block), and so on. When a token is seen, say `tIF`, the parser moves into a state in which it expects to match an expression. Once an expression has been matched, the parser will continue by looking for a `tTHEN` token, and so on. The parser will accumulate a stack of these states, so that it can resume matching a rule after matching components within that rule.

To turn our `pascal.y` example into a program that we can run, we need to write the lexical analyzer function `yylex`. It will need to read the input and produce the tokens `tBEGIN`, `tNUMBER`, and other friends. The token names are translated into C constants by means of `#defines` within the parser file `y.tab.c`. They are normally integer values from around 256 and up. This range is chosen so that the lexical analyzer can return single character tokens as small integers in the range 1 to 255, and end of file as 0.

We can make use of these token values in a `yylex` function defined in the grammar specification, as the additional code section will form part of `y.tab.c`. To make use of the token values in a lexical analyzer defined in a separate file we can make use of a header file that contains just these defines. It is `y.tab.h`, but is not generated automatically. We have to ask for it by specifying the `-d` (for defines) option to `yacc` or `bison`:

```
$ yacc -d pascal.y
$ cat y.tab.h
#define tBEGIN 257
#define tEND 258
#define tIF 259
#define tTHEN 260
#define tELSE 261
#define tASSIGN 262
#define tIDENTIFIER 263
#define tNUMBER 264
$
```

We can now proceed and write a lexical analyzer function as we wish. Of course, this is precisely what lex and flex are for, so it seems reasonable to use them for this. Here is a specification for a suitable scanner. Let's call it pascal.l:

```
/* (f)lex specification for Pascal subset */

%{
#include "y.tab.h"
%}

ID [A-Za-z][A-Za-z0-9]*

%%

"begin"    { return tBEGIN; }
"end"      { return tEND; }
"if"       { return tIF; }
"then"     { return tTHEN; }
"else"     { return tELSE; }
":="       { return tASSIGN; }
{ID}       { return tIDENTIFIER; }
[0-9]+     { return tNUMBER; }
[ \t\n]    /* ignore whitespace */
.          { return *yytext; }

%%
```

Notice that we return any characters we do not recognize as tokens as single characters by returning the next character in the input buffer yytext as the result. This will not clash with the other token values as those are arranged to be outside the range of valid characters.

If we run flex on this specification we will generate a function yylex in the file lex.yy.c. We could compile it separately, or #include into in our grammar specification, in place of our dummy yylex. Here is the additional code section from pascal2.y, which does just that – the rest of the file is the same as pascal.y:

```
int main()
{
  yyparse();
}
```

```
int yyerror(char *s)
{
  fprintf(stderr, "%s\n", s);
  return 0;
}


#include "lex.yy.c"
```

We simply include the generated scanner code file instead of defining our own. We have two files that contain code that needs to be compiled: `lex.yy.c` containing the scanner, and `y.tab.c` which contains the parser, and also #includes the scanner code too, so it's all we have to deal with.

Now we can compile and execute our complete parser. Here are all of the steps that are needed:

```
$ yacc -d pascal2.y
$ flex pascal.l
$ gcc -o pascal y.tab.c -lfl
```

You might be wondering how useful this program can possibly be given that we have essentially written no code at all. Well, we can use it to check the syntax of Pascal statements (the subset of them that we have defined anyway), because if there are any errors `yyerror` will be called, print a message and the parse will stop. If all is well, we will not see any output at all. Try it out!

```
$ ./pascal
fred := 2
^D
$
```

The parser is happy with the simple assignment statement. Let's try something we haven't defined yet – negative numbers.

```
$ ./pascal
fred := -2
parse error
$
```

In this case the program terminates without us having to enter *Ctrl-D* for end of file. It prints the message `'parse error'` to indicate that the statement was not syntactically correct. Let's try something a little more complex:

```
$ ./pascal
    if fred-7 > 34
    then x := x+1
    else
        begin
            y := y-1;
            bill := 2-fred
        end
^D
$
```

The parser is perfectly happy that this complex statement conforms to the grammar we wrote. We could, if we wished, continue to add more grammar rules and enlarge the lexical analyzer to create a program that would recognize an entire Pascal program. We'll leave this as an exercise. What we need to do next is consider what useful actions our programs can take as a result of recognizing tokens and larger structures.

Token Types

Our examples so far have not passed any values between the scanner and the parser. Although the program checked that the grammar was correct, we couldn't have compiled or executed our Pascal code, since the parser had no knowledge of the numbers or variable names that the lexical analyzer was processing. In more realistic programs we will want to make use of token values. The prime example here is the numeric value associated with numbers that we return as token tNUMBER.

The bison generated parser defines a variable called yylval that it makes itself available to the lexical analyzer to communicate token values. It is by default an int. We could change our scanner specification to return a value associated with the token tNUMBER by changing the rule to read:

```
[0-9]+    { yylval = atoi(yytext); return tNUMBER; }
```

This is fine, as long as all token values can be safely stored in an integer variable. What about identifiers though? We might want to get scanner code to store identifiers it sees in a table, and return a pointer to that table entry. That would enable the parser to maintain information about which variables have been declared, and store values with each of them.

In general, tokens will have different types, so we need a yylval that's sufficiently general to meets our needs, A C union would be a good choice, and yacc and bison allow us to create a yylval type that is a union – we'll need to augment our grammar specification a little though. The token definitions now become:

```
%union {
    int    numval;
    char   *idval;
}
%token tBEGIN
%token tEND
%token tIF
%token tTHEN
%token tELSE
%token tASSIGN
%token <idval> tIDENTIFIER
%token <numval> tNUMBER
```

The scanner actions need to assign token values to the appropriate members of the yylval union, like this:

```
{ID}      { yylval.idval = strdup(yytext); return tIDENTIFIER; }
[0-9]+    { yylval.numval = atoi(yytext); return tNUMBER; }
```

Note that we have to extract the value we need from yytext, as its contents change as the input stream is consumed. Here, to keep this simple we're just copying the name of the identifier and returning it as the token value for tIDENTIFIER. A complete program would probably maintain a symbol table containing names and values.

Notice that we have to declare the type of each token that is going to be assigned a value. This allows yacc and bison to generate the correct code for accessing the yylval union. The type is indicated by adding the union member name in angled brackets in the %token directive as shown:

```
%token <idval> tIDENTIFIER
%token <numval> tNUMBER
```

The next step is to make use of the token values in the parser.

Actions in Rules

Each rule in a `bison` grammar specification can contain code fragments in a similar way to those in the scanner specification. These are normally placed at the end of each alternative in a rule. Let's change a few of the grammar rules to contain simple actions, just to demonstrate:

```
statement:      tIDENTIFIER tASSIGN expression { printf("assignment seen\n"); }
              | tIF expression tTHEN statement
              | tIF expression tTHEN statement tELSE statement
              | tBEGIN statements tEND
      ;

statements:     statement
              | statement ';' statements
      ;

expression:     tNUMBER { printf("number seen: %d\n", $1); }
              | tIDENTIFIER { printf("identifier seen: %s\n", $1); }
              | expression '+' expression
              | expression '-' expression
              | expression '>' expression
      ;
```

Here, we print out a message when an assignment statement is recognized. We also print out a message whenever we see an identifier or number in an expression. We can access the value of the token by using the shorthand $1, which is expanded as the correct reference to the `yylval` union. (In fact it's a reference to an element on the parser-maintained stack of values, but that's another story.) Other tokens in a rule would be referred to as $2, $3, and so on, according to their position in the rule. So, for example, in the rule fragment:

```
| expression '-' expression
```

the semantic value of the first expression is $1, the second is $3.

The non-terminals also have values associated with them, and we can define the type in a similar way to that of tokens. The directive is `%type`, and it lives in the declarations section of the grammar specification. If we were writing a calculator, we might want to calculate the value of an expression as it was recognized. We could arrange for this to happen with the following grammar fragments:

```
%type <numval> expression

statement:      tIDENTIFIER tASSIGN expression
                     { printf("assignment seen, value is %d\n", $3); }
              | tIF expression tTHEN statement
              | tIF expression tTHEN statement tELSE statement
              | tBEGIN statements tEND
      ;

expression:     tNUMBER { $$ = $1; }
              | tIDENTIFIER { $$ = 0; /* would be lookup($1); see text */; }
              | expression '+' expression { $$ = $1 + $3; }
              | expression '-' expression { $$ = $1 - $3; }
              | expression '>' expression { $$ = $1 > $3; }
      ;
```

We state that expressions have the type `numval` – that is, their value is to be stored as an integer in the `numval` member of the `yylval` union. We can then use the value of the expression in the message that we print out on identifying an assignment. That is, as long as we take care to produce one!

To do this, we must make sure that all the alternatives in the rule for this expression will return a numeric value. The actions shown here do that. We use the shorthand `$$` to refer to the value that will be returned as the value of the non-terminal – in this case the expression. Once again, we use the value of sub-expressions by referring to `$1` and `$3` where expressions are combined.

In this simple example, we simply return zero for identifiers. In a fuller application we'd look up the value of the variable in the symbol table. We could also store e value when seeing it used as the target of an assignment statement.

In some cases we might want the value of the non-terminal to be of a type not used as a type for tokens. For example, we might want to build a data structure corresponding to an input structure, and then act on that structure as a whole (rather than build a result as we go). This might be the case in a calculator application.

We can do this, but we have to add another type to the `%union` declaration, and declare our non-terminals with that type. Let's complete our example of parsing Pascal by building a syntax tree (an internal data structure) and printing it out once we've read in a complete statement.

Our structure will be a classic abstract data type, the binary tree. The structure will be made up of nodes. Each node will have a type and branches left and right representing sub-trees. Some examples should make this clearer. The expression `fred - 7 > 34` will be represented like this.

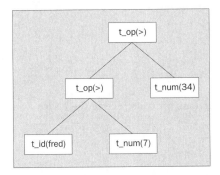

An assignment statement will consist of a node with type `t_assign`, its two branches being the identifier and expression being assigned. An `if-then-else` statement will consist of two nodes like this:

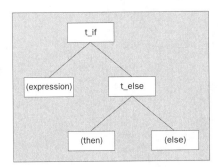

The {else} part will be NULL if there was no else present in the statement.

Here is tree.h, defining the interface to our tree building functions:

```
/* tree.h - definitions for syntax tree */

/* Tree types */
typedef enum {
            t_block,  /* For statements in a block */
            t_join,   /* For statements within a block */
            t_if,     /* For if statements */
            t_else,   /* For else parts of if statements */
            t_assign, /* For assignments */
            t_op,     /* For expressions with an operator */
            t_num,    /* For numbers */
            t_id,     /* For identifiers */
} treetype;

typedef struct t {
  treetype type;
  int op;
  union {
    int numval;
    char *idval;
  } value;
  struct t *left;
  struct t *right;
} tree;

tree *mknum(int);
tree *mkid(char *);
tree *mknode(treetype, int, tree *, tree *);
```

Here is tree.c, containing functions for constructing the nodes from other nodes and terminals (such as numbers and identifiers):

```
/* Tree function definitions */

#include <stdio.h>
#include <stdlib.h>
#include "tree.h"

tree *mkid(char *id)
{
  tree *t = mknode(t_id, 0, NULL, NULL);
  t -> value.idval = id;
  return t;
}

tree *mknum(int num)
{
  tree *t = mknode(t_num, 0, NULL, NULL);
  t -> value.numval = num;
  return t;
}
```

```
tree *mknode(treetype type, int op, tree *l, tree * r)
{
  tree *t = malloc(sizeof(tree));
  t -> type = type;
  t -> op = op;
  t -> left = l;
  t -> right = r;
  return t;
}

print_tree(tree *t)
{
    /* To be defined */
}
```

To keep this example as brief as possible, we have omitted error checking and a function to free the memory used in our node structures.

We leave definition of a tree-traversing function until a little later. First let's look at how to construct the program. Here's the scanner definition p2c.l:

```
/* lex specification for Pascal subset */

%{
#include <string.h>
%}

ID [A-Za-z][A-Za-z0-9]*

%%

"begin"   { return tBEGIN; }
"end"     { return tEND; }
"if"      { return tIF; }
"then"    { return tTHEN; }
"else"    { return tELSE; }
":="      { return tASSIGN; }
{ID}      { yylval.idval = strdup(yytext); return tIDENTIFIER; }
[0-9]+    { yylval.numval = atoi(yytext); return tNUMBER; }
[ \t\n]   /* ignore whitespace */
.         { return *yytext; }

%%
```

Here is the grammar specification, p2c.y, including actions to build the tree:

```
%{
#include <stdio.h>
#include "tree.h"
%}

%union {
    int    numval;
    char   *idval;
        tree    *tval;
}
%token tBEGIN
```

```
%token tEND
%token tIF
%token tTHEN
%token tELSE
%token tASSIGN
%token <idval> tIDENTIFIER
%token <numval> tNUMBER
%type  <tval> statement statements expression

%start pascal
%left '>'
%left '+'
%left '-'

%%

pascal:        statement { print_tree($1); }

statement:     tIDENTIFIER tASSIGN expression
                     { $$ = mknode(t_assign, 0, mkid($1), $3); }
             | tIF expression tTHEN statement
                     { $$ = mknode(t_if, 0, $2, mknode(t_else, 0, $4, NULL)); }
             | tIF expression tTHEN statement tELSE statement
                     { $$ = mknode(t_if, 0, $2, mknode(t_else, 0, $4, $6)); }
             | tBEGIN statements tEND
                     { $$ = mknode(t_block, 0, $2, NULL); }
;

statements: statement
                     { $$ = mknode(t_join, 0, $1, NULL); }
             | statement ';' statements
                     { $$ = mknode(t_join, 0, $1, $3); }
;

expression: tNUMBER { $$ = mknum($1); }
             | tIDENTIFIER { $$ = mkid($1); }
             | expression '+' expression { $$ = mknode(t_op, '+', $1, $3); }
             | expression '-' expression { $$ = mknode(t_op, '-', $1, $3); }
             | expression '>' expression { $$ = mknode(t_op, '>', $1, $3); }
;

%%

int main()
{
  yyparse();
}

int yyerror(char *s)
{
  fprintf(stderr, "%s\n", s);
  return 0;
}

#include "lex.yy.c"
```

Notice that we have added calls to `mknode` and helper functions to create the tree nodes from parts of the tree already built by the parser. We have also added a new non-terminal, `pascal`, to act as the start symbol alone. This gives a single point at which to call `print_tree`, rather than having to do so in each of the alternatives given for `statement`.

Finally, here is the definition of a function to traverse the tree and print it out. This should be inserted at the appropriate place in `tree.c`:

```
print_tree(tree *t)
{
  if(!t) return;
  switch(t -> type) {
  case t_block:
    printf("{\n");
    print_tree(t -> left);
    printf("}\n");
    break;
  case t_join:
    print_tree(t -> left);
    if(t -> right)
      print_tree(t -> right);
    break;
  case t_if:
    printf("if( ");
    print_tree(t -> left);
    printf(")\n");
    t = t -> right;
    print_tree(t -> left);
    if(t -> right) {
      printf("else\n");
      print_tree(t -> right);
    }
    break;
  case t_assign:
    print_tree(t -> left);
    printf(" = ");
    print_tree(t -> right);
    printf(";\n");
    break;
  case t_op:
    printf("(");
    print_tree(t -> left);
    printf(" %c ", t -> op);
    print_tree(t -> right);
    printf(")");
    break;
  case t_num:
    printf(" %d ", t -> value.numval);
    break;
  case t_id:
    printf(" %s ", t -> value.idval);
    break;
  }
}
```

Now we can build the application:

```
$ bison -y p2c.y
$ flex -l p2c.l
$ gcc -o p2c y.tab.c tree.c -lfl
```

When we run the program using our Pascal fragments as input, it prints them out again in a different form:

```
$ ./p2c
fred := 2
^D
 fred  =  2 ;
$ cat sample.pas
if fred-7 > 34
then x := x+1
else
      begin
            y := y-1;
            bill := 2-fred
         end
$ ./p2c <sample.pas
if( (( fred  -   7 ) >   34 ))
  x  = ( x  +   1 );
 else
 {
  y  = ( y  -   1 );
  bill  = ( 2  -   fred );
 }
$
```

It may not be pretty, but here we have the beginnings of a program that can read Pascal statements and produce the equivalent in C – the start of a Pascal to C translator perhaps? It should be clear that it's fairly straightforward to add grammar rules and tree building functions to increase the size of the subset of Pascal this application can handle. It could also be used within other applications to add some additional richness to command line functions or macro definitions.

Options to bison

There are a number of options that you can use with the bison program to control various aspects of the parser generation. Some of the ones you're most likely to use are:

-b --file-prefix	Specify a prefix to be used on all of the output files.
	The input file *name*.y would generate an output *prefix-name*.c.
-d --defines	Generate an include file containing macro definitions for the token names defined in the grammar.
	The include file will be called *name*.h if the parser output file is *name*.c.

`-o` `--output-file`	Specify the name of the parser output file.
`-v` `--verbose`	Write an extra output file (ending in `.output`) containing information about the generated parser states and conflicts, if any.
`-y` `--yacc`	yacc compatible mode. Output files will be named `y.tab.c`, `y.tab.h` and `y.output`.
`-h` `--help`	Print a summary of options.

Conflicts in Grammars

While developing the grammar for the example above we glossed over an apparent error. `bison` and `yacc` report conflicts. So, what is a conflict in this sense? The full answer is rather complex, but in general terms, conflicts arise from ambiguities in a language. These will occur whenever there's more than one way that some input might match grammar rules.

The `if-then-else` statement in common programming languages gives an archetypal example. If we have a part of the grammar rule for the statement as:

```
<statement> = "if" <expression> "then" <statement>                              /* Rule 1 */
            | "if" <expression> "then" <statement> "else" <statement>   /* Rule 2 */
            | "print" <expression>                                                         /* Rule 3 */
```

The input:

```
if a > b then if b > c then print d else print e
```

can match the rule for statement in two different ways. In the diagrams below, the notation s[n] indicates that the underlined input is matched as a statement by rule n in the grammar above:

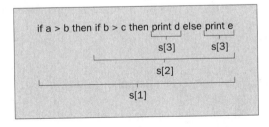

or alternatively,

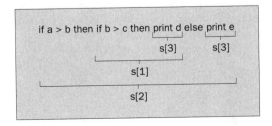

367

This is commonly known as the 'dangling else' problem. When analyzing the grammar rule for the statement, yacc and bison notice that they will have a choice whenever they encounter input like this. The problem comes when the else is encountered. Should the parser take the complete if-then it has already, and treat that as a whole statement (that is, **reduce** the statement) or continue with the else (**shift** it from the input) to build an if-then-else. This choice illustrates an ambiguity in the language defined by the grammar. The tools therefore report it as a conflict; in this case a shift/reduce conflict.

Conflicts in grammars need to be resolved, that is, a choice must be made as to whether to shift or reduce when encountering problems like this. yacc and bison have a default behavior, which is to shift. In this case it means that the parser will press on and build an if-then-else, which is exactly what we want to happen. The else part will become associated with the closest preceding if, which is the correct behavior for C, Pascal and all other common programming languages that have this ambiguity in their grammars.

Another kind of conflict is the reduce/reduce conflict, where input matches two rules at the same time. This can often occur when dealing with non-terminals that can match empty strings. Where possible in such cases, the grammar ought to be re-written to eliminate the conflict.

Possibly the greatest source of conflicts arises in the specification of arithmetic expressions, so much so that the tools we've been looking at contain features that have been implemented specifically to deal with them.

Arithmetic Expressions

As we've already seen, certain inputs can match simple grammar rules in several ways, and this inevitably leads to conflicts. In the case of arithmetic expressions, we would like to be able to write grammatical rules like this:

```
expression: expression '+' expression
          | expression '*' expression
          | expression '^' expression
        ;
```

However, when we do this we create a whole raft of conflicts, since we've not taken into account the relative precedence of the operators. The input

```
1 + 2 * 3
```

would be parsed as meaning (1+2)*3, since by default, the parser will continue to collect items that form an expression for as long as possible. What worked nicely for if statements fails horribly here. We could re-write the grammar, introducing types of expressions that only involve operators of the same precedence, but we don't actually have to.

The directives %left and %right are used to specify that an operator (or group of operators) are left- or right- associative. This information is used to help the parser generator create a parser that's sensitive to operator precedence and associativity. It also resolves potential conflicts. Here is a partial grammar that would deal correctly with common arithmetic operations:

```
%token tNUMBER
%token tIDENTIFIER
%token MINUS

%left '-' '+'
%left '*' '/'
%left MINUS
%right '^'

%%

expression: tNUMBER
          | tIDENTIFIER
          | expression '+' expression
          | expression '-' expression
          | expression '*' expression
          | expression '/' expression
          | expression '^' expression
          | '(' expression ')'
          | '-' expression %prec MINUS
          ;
```

The operators' associativity is listed in order of increasing precedence, so the grammar defines addition and subtraction as lower precedence than multiplication and division, and so on.

This grammar also deals with negative numbers by introducing a unary operator for negation. We use the special syntax %prec to indicate precedence for a rule that doesn't involve a binary operator, and a fake token MINUS to establish the correct precedence.

We can easily extend this grammar rule to include other operators by adding appropriate associativity directives and alternatives to the expression grammar.

Resources

For more information on scanners, parsers, compiler construction and related tools, you may want to check out some of these on-line resources:

❑ The Yacc Page – http://www.combo.org/lex_yacc_page

❑ ANTLR, another popular parser generator – http://www.antlr.org

❑ The ANTLR newsgroup – news:comp.compilers.tools.pccts

❑ The compilers newsgroup – news:comp.compilers

❑ Free tools catalog – http://www.idiom.com/free-compilers

❑ Compiler construction kits catalog – http://www.first.gmd.de/cogent/catalog/kits.html

❑ The 'Dragon book' – possibly the best known printed work on compilers: *Principles of Compiler Design*, by Aho and Ullman, Addison-Wesley (*ISBN 0-201000-22-9*).

❑ *Understanding and Writing Compilers*, by Bornat, Macmillan (*ISBN 0-333217-32-2*).

Summary

In this chapter we have tried to give an insight into the power and flexibility of some of the tools available for handling structured input. Lack of space has meant that we have barely even scratched the surface – bison in particular has many features and options we have not touched upon.

We hope to have encouraged you to think about using lex/flex and yacc/bison in your own applications. By now, you should be confident enough to start creating your own programs using them, and maybe even tackle their manual pages!

Online discussion at http://www.p2p.wrox.com

11

Testing Tools

As we've seen, debugging information in our program helps us to locate faults when they occur. This means we can do our best to ensure that the program won't crash when we leave it in the famously unpredictable hands of the end-user. So far, so good; but how do we know for sure that the program does what it is supposed to do? We started out with a carefully defined set of user requirements. Of course, we keep them in mind throughout the development process, but it's crucial that we formally qualify the program at some stage. Whether or not there's a contract involved, we've set out certain clearly defined goals; we need to know about any that we've not achieved, and if not, why not. This, of course, is the remit of testing.

Testing is all too often left until the end of development. Although testing and debugging usually proceed hand in hand, it is a good idea to plan your testing well in advance. As we have seen in earlier chapters, there are many things we can do during the development of our application that can help in the later stages. Examples include the introduction of a coding style that makes debugging easier and the early establishment of a test environment. Before we get anywhere near a public release, we should be extensively testing early versions of our application as development progresses.

Testing Requirements Types

To make sure that our application is ready for release we should test that all of our predefined requirements have been met. For each of them we should devise a test, or set of tests, that show the requirement being satisfied.

We must take care to cover all of the different requirements types. These include:

❑ Functional Requirements – the functions the software must perform

❑ Performance Requirements – how fast, how much data, what throughput

❑ Reliability Requirements – robustness against errors

❑ Maintenance Requirements – how easy is it to change and support

❑ Compatibility Requirements – does it run on different hardware, read all the data formats it is supposed to, conform to specified third-party standards

❑ Interface Requirements – does it talk to other systems correctly

❑ Usability Requirements – ease of use, complexity of interface

In this chapter we will try to cover some of the tools and techniques you can use to smooth the path of testing, ensuring that your application is released with as much confidence as possible that it will perform satisfactorily for your users. We will look in particular at testing the functional, reliability and performance requirements types.

Application Architecture

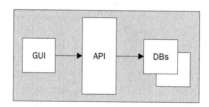

By dividing our application into three layers (or tiers) we can develop separate implementations of each layer to help with testing. Each layer is independent of the others and the interaction between them is based on a clearly defined interface.

For our DVD store, the first step was to define the APIs we were going to use to support the functionality of the system. Once done, this allowed us to implement the GUI independently of the database. In actual fact we developed more than one data implementation. The first, a reference implementation using simple flat files was used primarily to check that the API set was complete. It was also used to allow the GUI implementation to proceed, and create an initial version of the complete application. When the database was fully implemented it was able to 'slot in' behind the API. The API provides an abstraction to our database, independent of the technology used.

This layered approach can also be used when testing an application. We can write a simple, alternative front end to test out our database implementation. A command line program – responding to commands like "add member" and reporting the return result from the appropriate API – can be used before the GUI is done. In this way, testing can proceed in parallel with the development, reducing the chances that we find a nasty problem too late to fix it.

Steps

1. Define API

2. Create reference (flatfile) implementation

3. Create command line interface to API

4. Test reference implementation, and fix bugs found

5. Implement and test GUI using reference

6. Implement (final) database

7. Re-run tests (4) on final database

8. Test GUI with final database

9. Release version 1.0

10. Fix bugs and re-release

In this chapter we will look at tools for managing steps 3, 4, and 6.

General Testing

If our application architecture follows the pattern from the last section, we can implement a suite of test programs to test out parts of the API as they are developed. The DVD store reference application was tested with a few such simple programs. One of these, `testtitle`, we'll see in use throughout this chapter. It is a program that performs a few API calls and reports the results. Here's a small portion of the main test function `test_titles` that performs some searching:

```
int test_titles()
{
  dvd_title dvd;
  char **genres = NULL;
  char **classes = NULL;
  int ngenres = 0, nclasses = 0;
  int err =+ DVD_SUCCESS;
  int count = 0;
  int *results;
  int i = 1;

  show_result("get_genres", dvd_get_genre_list(&genres, &ngenres));
  show_result("get_classes", dvd_get_classification_list(&classes, &nclasses));
  ...

  /* Now let's search and print what we find */
  show_result("name search", dvd_title_search(NULL, "Jean", &results, &count));
  printf("Searched for name \"Jean\": \n");
  for(i = 0; i < count; i++) {
```

```
        dvd_title_get(results[i], &dvd);
        print_title(&dvd);
    }
    free(results);

    return DVD_SUCCESS;
}
```

This program is useful during the development of the application, when we have a few of the APIs written. It can also act as a check that we haven't seriously broken the code if we run it from time to time during development. When executed, the program prints a record of what it is doing (which we could save for later comparison after we change the program), and the results of the API calls.

```
$ ./testtitle
creating dvd title 1
creating dvd title 2
. . .
created dvd title 25
dvd_open_db: no error
get_genres: no error
get_classes: no error
name search: no error
Searched for name "Jean":
DVD Title #1: Grand Illusion
Directed by Jean Renoir (1938), Rated: U, Action
Starring: Jean Gabin
ASIN 0780020707, Price 29.99
DVD Title #5: The 400 Blows
Directed by Francois Truffaut (1959), Rated: 12, Education
Starring: Jean-Pierre Leaud
ASIN 1572525320, Price 23.98
. . .
test_titles: no error
```

The test data simply consists of 25 fake DVD titles, which we use exclusively for testing.

Regression Testing

Each time we make a change to our application, we run the risk of introducing problems, or breaking code that used to work. One way to check that everything is still OK is to rerun each of the tests that we have run before, making sure that the code still passes. This is what's known as **regression testing**. It can be very time-consuming and, frankly, quite dull, so what we need is a way to automate our testing. Automation will ensure that the same testing is performed each time.

> *Commercial tools are available for UNIX to help with regression testing; some can simulate quite sophisticated load conditions.*

One simple way to automate regression testing is to stick with some simple test programs like testtitle here, and use a makefile with make to automate the running and checking of the results.

The idea is to run a number of test programs and capture their output to a file. Later, when we have changed the implementation, rerun the test programs and check that the output is still the same. A very brief makefile (or a few lines added to an existing one) can make the process quite straightforward.

Here's an example:

```
TPROGS = testmember testtitle

all: $(TPROGS)

flatfile.o: dvd.h
testmember.o: dvd.h
testtitle.o: dvd.h

testmember: testmember.o flatfile.o

testtitle: testtitle.o flatfile.o

expected: $(TPROGS:=.expected)
%.expected : %
    $< > $@

check: $(TPROGS:=.out)
%.out : %
    $< > $@
    diff $@ $(@:.out=.expected)
```

The target `expected` runs each of the test programs defined in the variable `TPROGS` and captures their output in files with the extension `.expected`. This would be executed at the end of a test session when the results are known to be correct. To perform regression testing, the `check` target runs the test programs that have been updated and captures their output into files with extension `.out`. These are then compared using `diff`. The `make` will abort if there are any differences. Here's a sample session:

```
$ make expected
testmember > testmember.expected
testtitle > testtitle.expected
$
```

In our example, we have not captured the standard error, only the standard output. It only requires a small change to capture both into separate files and, if required, to compare them with results from future runs.

Now if we change the implementation, rebuild, and rerun the test programs, we need to check that the new output matches the old:

```
$ make check
testmember > testmember.out
diff testmember.out testmember.expected
testtitle > testtitle.out
diff testtitle.out testtitle.expected
$
```

If something has broken with the member functionality (so that the output does not match) we will see the differences reported and the make will stop:

```
$ make check
testmember > testmember.out
diff testmember.out testmember.expected
7c7
< No. 10002: Mr Ben Matthew
---
> No. 10022: Mr Ben Matthew
make: *** [testmember.out] Error 1
$
```

377

If you are going to use this kind of automated regression testing, you need to be careful that the output you capture and compare contains only information that will be unchanged from run to run. Things to look out for that can cause problems include timestamps, dates, and program-generated serial numbers that may legitimately change from run to run. You can replace the simple use of diff in the makefile with a more sophisticated comparison, or develop a more sophisticated approach yourself using scripts.

A Test Program

The test programs we've looked at so far have been simple affairs, and for some applications they might be sufficient. For a larger application it may well prove worthwhile to develop a more general test program that you can perform more complex testing with.

Here's a portion of a general-purpose test program for the DVD store APIs. It interacts with a user, rather than just calling a few API functions. The user (or a script created for testing) types a command, and the program calls the appropriate API and returns a result. In this way, we can use the program with a wide range of test data.

The test program commands are of the form:

```
command sub-command argument,argument,...
```

Examples include:

```
title get 6
title search Seven,Kurosawa
```

Now let's take a look at the code.

Headers and Declarations

First, we include library headers and declare functions that will be called later:

```
/*
    Test Program for the DVD store APIs
*/

#include <stdlib.h>
#include <stdio.h>
#include <readline/readline.h>
#include <readline/history.h>
#include <string.h>
#include "dvd.h"

int show_result(char *, int);
int execute_command(char *);
void initialize_readline(void);
```

main()

The main program opens the DVD database, and loops reading commands that are executed by a call to execute_command. We use the readline library to provide command line editing and a command history, just to make things a little more user-friendly.

```
int main()
{
  char *command;

  printf("DVD Store Application\n");

  dvd_open_db();

  /* Do not open the database, so we can test */
  /* printf("Warning, database is not open\n"); */

  /* Set up the command line interface */
  initialize_readline();

  /* Main loop, read commands and execute them */
  while(1) {
    command = readline("> ");
    if(command == NULL)
      break;
    if(*command != '\0') {
      add_history(command);
      show_result("!", execute_command(command));
    }
    free(command);
  }
  exit(EXIT_SUCCESS);
}

void initialize_readline()
{
  /* Turn off TAB file completion */
  rl_bind_key('\t', rl_insert);
}
```

show_result()

The results of all the calls to APIs are reported through the show_result function that decodes any error and prints a descriptive message:

```
int show_result(char *msg, int err)
{
  char *err_msg;

  (void) dvd_err_text(err, &err_msg);
  printf("%s: %s\n", msg, err_msg);
  return err == DVD_SUCCESS;
}
```

APIs

The APIs are divided into groups dealing with members, titles and disks, with one function responsible for all sub-commands within a group. A table, `functions`, connects typed commands to the correct handling function, and provides a help string for a `help` command. For brevity's sake this version of the program does not handle all of the APIs. A complete version can be downloaded from www.wrox.com.

```c
int help_function(int argc, char *argv[]);
int quit_function(int argc, char *argv[]);
int member_function(int argc, char *argv[]);
int title_function(int argc, char *argv[]);
int disk_function(int argc, char *argv[]);

typedef int Func(int, char **);

struct {
  char *name;
  Func *func;
  char *help;
} functions[] = {
  {"help", help_function, "summary of functions"},
  {"quit", quit_function, "quit the application"},
  {"title", title_function, "create, set, get, search titles"},
  {"member", member_function, "create, set, get, search members"},
  {"disk", disk_function, "create, set, get, search disks"},
  {NULL, NULL, NULL}
};

int help_function(int argc, char *argv[])
{
  int f;

  printf("These functions are available:\n");
  for(f = 0; functions[f].name; f++)
    printf("%s \t%s\n", functions[f].name, functions[f].help);
  printf("To get more help try <command> help\n");

  return DVD_SUCCESS;
}
```

quit_function()

The simplest function to implement is the one to quit the program:

```c
int quit_function(int argc, char *argv[])
{
  dvd_close_db();
  exit(EXIT_SUCCESS);
}
```

print_title(), title_function()

The following functions implement the commands for handling DVD titles. The first, `print_title` provides a neat output of the details of a DVD. The second, `title_function`, will handle all of the title commands. Here we only show retrieving DVD title details and searching the database for a title:

```
void print_title(dvd_title *dvd)
{
  printf("DVD Title #%d: %s\n", dvd -> title_id, dvd -> title_text);
  printf("Directed by %s (%s), Rated: %s, %s\n", dvd -> director,
    dvd -> release_date, dvd -> classification, dvd -> genre);
  printf("Starring: %s %s\n", dvd -> actor1, dvd -> actor2);
  printf("ASIN %s, Price %s\n", dvd -> asin, dvd -> rental_cost);
}

int title_function(int argc, char *argv[])
{
  if(argc < 2)
    return DVD_ERR_NOT_FOUND;

  if(argc == 3 && strcmp(argv[1], "get") == 0) {
    dvd_title dvd;
    if(show_result("title get", dvd_title_get(atoi(argv[2]), &dvd)))
      print_title(&dvd);
  }

  if(argc == 4 && strcmp(argv[1], "search") == 0) {
    int count;
    int *results;
    int i;

    show_result("title search",
      dvd_title_search(argv[2], argv[3], &results, &count));
    for(i = 0; i < count; i++)
      printf("[%d]",results[i]);
    printf("\n");
  }
  else {
    return DVD_ERR_NOT_FOUND;
  }
  return DVD_SUCCESS;
}
```

member_function(), disk_function()

The other command handling functions would be written in the same way; here they are just non-functional stubs:

```
int member_function(int argc, char *argv[])
{
  return DVD_SUCCESS;
}


int disk_function(int argc, char *argv[])
{
  return DVD_SUCCESS;
}
```

execute_command()

The commands are executed by the function `execute_command` that splits the command line into arguments and calls the appropriate command function:

```c
int execute_command(char *command)
{
    /* Break the command into comma separated tokens */
    char *string = command;
    char *token;
    char *items[20];
    int item = 0, i;
    char *cmd1, *cmd2;
    int f;

    /* Commands consist of either a single command word
        or two words followed by a comma separated list of args */

    cmd1 = strsep(&string, " ");
    items[item++] = cmd1;

    cmd2 = strsep(&string, " ");
    if(cmd2 == NULL)
      items[item] = NULL;
    else
      items[item++] = cmd2;

    if(cmd2) {
      /* Split up the arguments */
      while(1) {
        token = strsep(&string,",");
        if(token == NULL) {
    /* Last one */
    /* items[item++] = string; */
    break;
        }
        else
    items[item++] = token;
      };

      items[item] = NULL;
    }

    for(i = 0; i < item; i++)
      printf("[%s]", items[i]);
    printf("\n");

    /* Now call the right function for cmd1 */
    for(f = 0; functions[f].name != NULL; f++) {
      if(strcmp(cmd1, functions[f].name) == 0) {
        (*functions[f].func)(item, items);
        break;
      }
    }
    if(functions[f].name == NULL)
      return DVD_ERR_NOT_FOUND;

    return DVD_SUCCESS;
}
```

Testing the dvdstore Program

The program, dvdstore, implements only a few APIs, but does illustrate some key features of a usable test program. Firstly it contains help – even if it only ever gets used by you, it's a nice touch to include. It's all too easy to forget just what a 'disposable' test program is supposed to do. Secondly it uses the GNU readline library to provide command line editing with a history, so you can scroll back and issue the same (or similar) command again. Let's see it in action.

```
$ ./dvdstore
DVD Store Application
> title get 6
[title][get][6]
title get: no error
DVD Title #6: Beauty and The Beast
Directed by Jean Cocteau (1946), Rated: 18, Thriller
Starring: Jean Marais
ASIN 0780020715, Price 39.95
!: no error
> title search Seven,Kurosawa
[title][search][Seven][Kurosawa]
title search: no error
[2][11]
!: no error
> title get 2
[title][get][2]
title get: no error
DVD Title #2: Seven Samurai
Directed by Akira Kurosawa (1954), Rated: 12, Comedy
Starring: Takashi Shimura Toshiro Mifune
ASIN 0780020685, Price 27.99
!: no error
> quit
[quit]
$
```

It's not terribly pretty but it does the job. The tester is given a lot of feedback on return results, and is prompted for the next command with a simple prompt. This will prove useful when we automate its use. We when use the program we can react to the results, such as the titles returned here as a result of a search, and check that they make sense. Here we see that the classification and genre of the movies are clearly awry!

Scripting Tests

We can begin to script our test program by placing commands in a file and using shell input redirection. If the file script contains the lines:

```
title get 6
title search Seven,Kurosawa
title get 2
quit
```

we could run the test with the command:

```
$ ./dvdstore <script
```

This is all very well, but we lose the ability to react to the results as they are returned. To do that, we need a more powerful scripting mechanism.

expect

expect is a utility from the GNU project that allows you to automate a dialogue with an interactive program like the DVD store test program. It can run another program, send it commands, read the result and act upon what it receives. It is based on the general-purpose scripting language Tcl and therefore brings all of the power of that language to scripting tests. In fact, you can use expect directly from C and C++ too.

> *Check your Linux distribution for the documentation for* expect, *or get it from http://ex pect.nist.gov_or http://www.gnu.org.*

We'll take a very brief look at getting started with expect, using our test program as a subject. Let's write an expect script that will run the program, perform a search and print the details of all the DVD titles it finds:

```
#!/usr/bin/expect

# Script to search for a title given name and director

if $argc<2 {
    send_user "usage: search.exp title name\n"
    exit
}

# Set up search strings from arguments
set title [lindex $argv 0]
set name [lindex $argv 1]

# Loop through the returned title numbers printing them out
proc print_titles {l} {
  send_user "in print: $l"
  set list [split $l \[\]]
  foreach t $list {
    if [llength $t] {
      send "title get $t\n"
      expect ">"
    }
  }
}

# Start the program, wait for the first prompt
spawn ./dvdstore
expect DVD
expect ">"

# Perform the search
send "title search $title,$name\n"
expect -re \n
expect -re \n
expect -re \n
expect -re \n {
  set titles $expect_out(buffer);
  expect ">"
  print_titles $titles
}

# All done
send "quit\n"
expect eof
```

Here's an example run on the script:

```
$ ./search.exp Seven Kurosawa
spawn ./dvdstore
DVD Store Application
> title search Seven,Kurosawa
[title][search][Seven][Kurosawa]
title search: no error
[2][11]
!: no error
> in print: [2][11]
title get 2
[title][get][2]
title get: no error
DVD Title #2: Seven Samurai
Directed by Akira Kurosawa (1954), Rated: 12, Comedy
Starring: Takashi Shimura Toshiro Mifune
ASIN 0780020685, Price 27.99
!: no error
> title get 11
[title][get][11]
title get: no error
DVD Title #11: The Seventh Seal
Directed by Ingmar Bergman (1957), Rated: 12, Science Fiction
Starring: Gunnar Bjornstrand Max Von Sydow
ASIN 6305174083, Price 27.99
!: no error
> quit
[quit]
$
```

When we run this script, it starts the dvdstore application, performs a search for DVDs either with Seven in the title or directed by Kurosawa, and then loops through all of the DVD title numbers returned, printing out the details. It therefore reacts well to changes in the database that might result in the DVD title numbers changing. It is a simple matter to ignore parts of the output that are not relevant, such as time and date.

Using expect and a general purpose test program like this can replace the specific test programs (like test_titles) that we saw at the beginning of this chapter. Scripts for expect are easily incorporated into makefiles, and can provide for fairly comprehensive regression testing.

Memory Problems

A program generally performs operations on data. This data may be held in persistent storage, such as files on a hard disk, but it is almost always used in memory. Global variables, local variables, function arguments are all held in memory. It is no wonder that many errors in our programs are attributable to misuse of memory of one kind or another.

Any program you write has access to three different types of memory; memory used for different purposes is separated and managed in different ways. These are:

❑   static memory

❑   the stack

❑   dynamic memory (the heap)

Static Memory

When you declare a global variable in your program, a location is allocated to that variable when the program starts. Whenever you refer to the variable, the allocated location is used. All of your global variables will usually be allocated memory in neighboring locations that do not change as the program runs.

This is static memory. If our program writes beyond the end of a global array it will very probably corrupt another global variable stored alongside. These kinds of corruptions can be hard to locate.

The Stack

The second type of memory your program uses is stack memory. While a C program is running it makes extensive use of the CPU stack to store local variables and to keep track of where to return to when the current function has finished.

All local variables within functions, including `main`, share the same stack, so it is possible for errant code in one function to corrupt the values of local variables in another. This kind of error, known as **stack overwriting**, is most likely to occur when local arrays are misused.

> **The following program and the discussion that follows it is specific to Linux implementations on the Intel architecture. Other operating systems and processor architectures may behave slightly differently.**

We can see the layout of the C stack by examining memory from a debugger such as GDB. We can also explore memory layout if we write a program to deliberately wander outside of a function.

```
#include <stdlib.h>
#include <stdio.h>

/* A program to explore the stack frame */

void showstack()
{
  int local = 0xDD111111;
  int *ptr = &local;
  int i;
  for(i = 18; i >= 0; i--)
    printf("%02d: [%08x] %08x\n", i, ptr+i, ptr[i]);

  /* Now clobber main:local2 */
  ptr[12] = 0xDD222222;
}

int myfunction(int arg1, int arg2)
{
  int local1 = 0xFF111111;
  int local2 = 0xFF222222;
  int array[2] = {0xFFAA1111, 0xFFAA2222};
  showstack();
  return 0xFF333333;
}

int main(int argc, char *argv[], char **environ)
{
```

```
    int local1 = 0x11111111;
    int local2 = 0x22222222;
    int local3 = 0x33333333;

    /* Get our bearings */
    printf("main is at %08x, argc: %d, argv: %08x, env: %08x\n",
        &main, argc, argv, environ);
    printf("myfunction is at %08x\n", &myfunction);
    printf("showstack is at %08x\n", &showstack);

    /* Make a call with arguments */
    local3 = myfunction(0xAA111111, 0xAA222222);

    /* Do it again to see where return result went */
    local3 = myfunction(0xAA111111, 0xAA222222);
    exit(EXIT_SUCCESS);
}
```

When we run the program, the local variables, function arguments, and return addresses build up on the stack as we call main, myfunction and showstack. On most computer systems the stack builds downwards. That is, each new addition to the stack is made at a memory location smaller than the one before. The top of stack is initially set to a high location in memory and works its way down. So starting from a location on the stack and proceeding to high addresses, we ought to see data from earlier in the life of the program.

The function showstack takes the address of one of its own local variables to get an address on the stack:

```
    int local = 0xDD111111;
    int *ptr = &local;
```

It then uses this address as an array to access stack elements further up the stack, and prints them out. This first output will look something like this:

```
$ gcc -o stackframe stackframe.c
$ ./stackframe
main is at 080484d0, argc: 1, argv: bffff8a4, env: bffff8ac
myfunction is at 08048490
showstack is at 08048410
18: [bffff868] bffff8ac ^     [environ]
17: [bffff864] bffff8a4 |     [argv]
16: [bffff860] 00000001 |     [argc]
15: [bffff85c] 40038313 |     [return address, exit program]
14: [bffff858] bffff878 ++    [stack link]
13: [bffff854] 11111111 |     [main:local1]
12: [bffff850] 22222222 |     [main:local2]
11: [bffff84c] 33333333 |     [main:local3]
10: [bffff848] aa222222 |     [myfunction:arg2]
09: [bffff844] aa111111 |     [myfunction:arg1]
08: [bffff840] 0804853c |     [return address: main+0x6c]
07: [bffff83c] bffff858 -++   [stack link]
06: [bffff838] ff111111 |     [myfunction:local1]
05: [bffff834] ff222222 |     [myfunction:local2]
04: [bffff830] ffaa2222 |     [myfunction:array[1]]
03: [bffff82c] ffaa1111 |     [myfunction:array[0]]
02: [bffff828] 080484b7 |     [return address: myfunction+0x27]
01: [bffff824] bffff83c --+   [stack link]
00: [bffff820] dd111111      [showstack:local]
```

You can see that the mechanism for calling a function, for example the call to myfunction from main is as follows:

- ❏ remember current stack position
- ❏ add function arguments to the stack in reverse order
- ❏ add current program counter to stack as a return address
- ❏ add stack position to the stack

The combination of a return address, stack link, function arguments and local variables is called a **stack frame**.

The arguments to C functions are placed on the stack in reverse order so that they appear to the function in the correct order. That is, they are placed on the stack in order of increasing memory.

This argument ordering allows us to write functions that take a variable number of arguments, like printf. In cases like this we do something very similar to what showstack is doing here, take the address of the first argument and wander along the stack using what we find as arguments. In the case of printf the first argument is a format string that tells printf how many arguments to expect. If we pass too few, printf will print rubbish, the contents of the stack beyond the arguments we passed.

The compiler uses the stack links to restore the stack to its original state after a function call is completed.

We can see that the local variables of one function, the stack links, return addresses, arguments to a function we have called, and local variables of that function are all close to one another on the stack. It is therefore crucial that we do not stray across these boundaries. For example you can see that if we access array[2] in myfunction we will actually reference the same memory location as that used by myfunction:local2. Furthermore, setting array[3] will clobber myfunction:local1, and so on. Local arrays are therefore potentially very harmful if we accidentally write to them with an invalid index.

In the example program showstack deliberately overwrites one of the local variables in main, which we can see when showstack executes for the second time:

```
18: [bffff868] bffff8ac
17: [bffff864] bffff8a4
16: [bffff860] 00000001
15: [bffff85c] 40038313
14: [bffff858] bffff878
13: [bffff854] 11111111
12: [bffff850] dd222222   *** main:local2 corrupted by showstack
11: [bffff84c] ff333333   *** main:local3 has result from myfunction
10: [bffff848] aa222222
09: [bffff844] aa111111
08: [bffff840] 08048553
07: [bffff83c] bffff858
06: [bffff838] ff111111
05: [bffff834] ff222222
04: [bffff830] ffaa2222
03: [bffff82c] ffaa1111
02: [bffff828] 080484b7
01: [bffff824] bffff83c
00: [bffff820] dd111111
```

Overrunning local arrays can have far-reaching effects that can be very difficult to track down, so we must be especially careful in using them.

Debugging local variable corruption is further complicated by compiler optimization. If we compile the stackframe program again, this time asking the compiler to optimize, we get quite different results.

```
$ gcc -o stackframe -O6 stackframe.c
$ ./stackframe
main is at 080484b0, argc: 1, argv: bffff8a4, env: bffff8ac
myfunction is at 08048460
showstack is at 08048410
18: [bffff89c] 40014090
17: [bffff898] bffff89c
16: [bffff894] 4000ac70
15: [bffff890] 080485a8
14: [bffff88c] 080482bc
13: [bffff888] bffff8a4
12: [bffff884] 00000001
11: [bffff880] 080484b0
10: [bffff87c] 08048371
09: [bffff878] 00000000
08: [bffff874] 08048350
07: [bffff870] 00000001
06: [bffff86c] 40013a44
05: [bffff868] bffff8ac [environ]
04: [bffff864] bffff8a4 [argv]
03: [bffff860] 00000001 [argc]
02: [bffff85c] 40038313 [return address: exit program]
01: [bffff858] bffff878 [stack link]
00: [bffff854] dd111111 [showstack:local]
```

The compiler has been able to eliminate the storage used for the local variables in main and myfunction (either by using registers instead, or not at all if we did not use them). It also removed the need for a return address for myfunction because the call to showstack is effectively the last thing it does. The optimizer has vastly reduced our stack usage.

Now the corruption in showstack will affect a different area of the stack, with unknown consequences. What this means is that the symptoms of a memory bug like this may vary depending on compiler settings and code you add to track down the bug. Very nasty!

One trick it can be useful to try when you think you are suffering the effects of local variable corruption is to allocate a large local array as the first and last local variable in the function you suspect is causing problems. If the problem 'goes away' you will probably have localized the cause to that function.

There are a number of commercial tools that can help to debug static memory access problems like this. One is 'Purify' from Rational Software. It uses a proprietary technique called object-code insertion to create a version of your program that contains additional code to check that all memory accesses are valid at runtime. It has a performance penalty as you might expect, but it can be a lifesaver. At the time of writing, Rational had not released a version of Purify for Linux, but the company was showing an interest. Check out http://www.rational.com for the latest news.

Some versions of gcc can be used with a GNU utility called Checker. It aims to perform much the same job as Purify using a slightly different technique. It requires that you compile your program with a modified compiler rather than use object code insertion on an existing executable. To get the most from the tool you need to use special ("Checkered") versions of the C libraries and any other libraries required. At the time of writing Checker was available for gcc 2.8.1 and can be downloaded from the GNU website at http://www.gnu.org.

Another way to track down problems like this is to completely avoid the use of local arrays while developing and debugging the application. If we consider using dynamic memory allocation instead, we can bring to bear tools that were specifically written to help with dynamic memory errors. These are the subjects of the next section.

Dynamic Memory

Dynamic memory is memory allocated by Linux when your program is running, usually when you call one of the memory allocation functions, malloc, calloc and realloc. Dynamic memory may also be allocated on your behalf by other library functions you may call, so that they can return a variable amount of data to your program. An example here is the search functions of the DVD store APIs. You must call free to deallocate the memory allocated for search results when you are done with them. In C++ dynamic memory is used by the new and delete operators. In addition we can use code in destructors to ensure that memory is freed when objects go out of scope.

Dynamic memory allocated by malloc and its friends is often called the 'heap', separate from local and global variables declared in your program, the static memory and stack. The allocation functions manage memory taken from the heap, growing it if necessary by requesting more heap memory from the operating system. The memory managed by malloc is also known as the 'malloc arena'. Implementations of malloc vary, but typically malloc will keep track of blocks of memory of different sizes, splitting them up if necessary to allocate blocks for your program to use.

If your program continues to allocate memory, but does not free it, then a memory leak occurs. The amount of memory that your program occupies will grow and grow, eventually the physical memory of the machine will be exceeded and performance may suffer as the system is forced to supplement real memory with virtual memory swapped out to disk. (There are other subtleties concerning virtual memory management and operating systems, but this is the general idea.) In the end, Linux will forcibly terminate your program. Other programs running while this is going on will also suffer. Avoiding memory leaks is not only a good idea - it's also polite.

> *If you find you need to allocate dynamic memory that will only be used inside one function, you might consider using* alloca. *This function allocates a block of memory of the requested size (in bytes) on the stack and returns a* void * *pointer, and is therefore similar to* malloc. *However, the returned pointer value will be invalidated and the memory effectively freed as soon as the function that calls* alloca *returns. However,* alloca *is not supported on all systems, and its use is now deprecated.*

It is important to realize that the operating system also keeps tabs on how much dynamic memory your program consumes (through requests to extend the heap). When your program ends, all of the memory allocated to it by the operating system is automatically recovered. This is true at least for Linux and many other UNIX-like systems. Other operating systems may not be quite so thorough. It is tempting to think that for programs that allocate small amounts of memory and do not have long running time, it is acceptable to allow sloppy memory allocations. Do not fall into this trap. You never know what someone else might use your program for, it may one day find itself allocating (and leaking) large memory blocks, and be running 24 hours a day. Besides, care with dynamic memory is a good habit to get into.

It is worth noting that most implementations of free do not give back memory to the operating system, but keep it in a pool, ready for malloc to re-allocate. It can be useful to program an application to keep an eye on the total memory it has allocated by using functions such as getrusage or by using external utility programs like ps and top.

When we allocate memory with malloc, we are given a pointer into the heap. If we misuse this pointer we can wreak untold havoc. It is likely that the memory we are allocated was part of a chain of free blocks managed in the malloc arena. If we accidentally write beyond the bounds of the memory we have been allocated we might corrupt the next block along, or damage the structures that malloc uses to maintain the heap. If this happens we might only discover it when we come to allocate more memory or free another block at a point far removed from the point of the error.

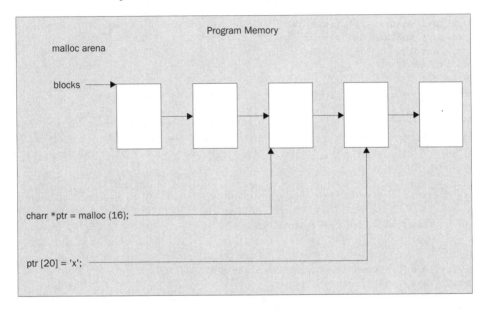

The most common errors that occur in using dynamic memory are:

1. Failing to allocate memory in the first place (unassigned pointers)

2. Failing to free up allocated memory (leaks)

3. Writing beyond the end (or before the beginning of an allocated block)

4. Using a block after it has been freed

All of these errors can be detected during testing by using appropriate tools, including malloc debuggers. These generally take the form of a replacement library that includes implementations of malloc and friends with special features. These features include logging of allocations, detection of leaks and help with finding corruption nearer the point of the error. We'll take a quick look at one such malloc replacement, mpatrol by Graeme Roy, which may be found at http://www.cbmamiga.demon.co.uk. Alternatives may be found listed at http://www.cs.colorado.edu/~zorn/MallocDebug.html.

The standard Linux `malloc` *library functions in GNU libc 2.x can be configured to be tolerant of some simple errors such as calling* `free` *twice with the same memory block, and overwriting by a single byte. It uses the environment variable* `MALLOC_CHECK_` *to enable these features. Set to 0 it silently ignores errors, set to 1 it prints diagnostics to the standard error, and set to 2 it will call* `abort` *to terminate the program if it detects heap corruption. Check the manual page for more details.*

Installing `mpatrol`

Once you have found and downloaded the source for `mpatrol`, installation is fairly easy, though at version 1.1.1 there was no automatic install script. We need to unpack the sources and build the library:

```
$ tar zxvf mpatrol_1.1.1.tar.gz
$ tar zxvf mpatrol_doc.tar.gz
$ cd mpatrol
$ cd build/unix
$ make all
$ cd ../..
```

This will have created a set of replacement `malloc` libraries. There is one static library and two shared libraries, one of which is suitable for use with multi-threaded programs. Full documentation is provided in many formats (including HTML) and covers the use of `mpatrol` in much more detail than we have space for here.

To install `mpatrol` we need to move the libraries and support files to an appropriated shared location. The `/usr/local` hierarchy is a good choice, but if you have local files stored elsewhere simply substitute for `/usr/local` where it appears here.

```
$ su
# mv build/unix/libmpatrol* /usr/local/lib
# mkdir /usr/local/include
# cp src/mpatrol.h /usr/local/include
# cp build/unix/mpatrol /usr/local/bin
# cp man/man1/mpatrol.1 /usr/local/man/man1
# cp man/man3/mpatrol.3 /usr/local/man/man3
# exit
```

Using mpatrol

To use `mpatrol` we do not need to alter the source code of our program, we simply have to link with the `mpatrol` library. Here's an example using the DVD store test programs:

```
$ gcc -o testtitle testtitle.o flatfile.o -lmpatrol -lbfd -liberty
$ ./testtitle
created dvd title 1
created dvd title 2
...
test_titles: no error
$
```

Note that we also need to link with the binary file library (-lbfd) and the Liberty library (-liberty) as mpatrol uses functions from those libraries to provide detail for its logs.

The test program appears to run normally, but we now find that a log file, mpatrol.log, has been created in the directory where the program was executed. This is the file that mpatrol uses to communicate its findings. The default level of detail simply provides a memory usage summary:

```
$ cat mpatrol.log
@(#) mpatrol 1.1.1 (00/03/09)
Copyright (C) 1997-2000 Graeme S. Roy

This is free software, and you are welcome to redistribute it under certain
conditions; see the GNU Library General Public License for details.

system page size:  4096 bytes
default alignment: 4 bytes
overflow size:     0 bytes
overflow byte:     0xAA
allocation byte:   0xFF
free byte:         0x55
allocation stop:   0
reallocation stop: 0
free stop:         0
unfreed abort:     0
lower check range: -
upper check range: -
failure frequency: 0
failure seed:      954833145
prologue function: <unset>
epilogue function: <unset>
handler function:  <unset>
log file:          mpatrol.log
program filename:  /proc/1970/exe
symbols read:      3723
allocation count:  57
allocation peak:   431320 bytes
allocation limit:  0 bytes
allocated blocks:  8 (1408 bytes)
freed blocks:      0 (0 bytes)
free blocks:       6 (477824 bytes)
internal blocks:   55 (225280 bytes)
total heap usage:  704512 bytes
total compared:    0 bytes
total located:     0 bytes
total copied:      63401 bytes
total set:         349772 bytes
total warnings:    0
total errors:      0
```

The level of detail can be set by using an environment variable, MPATROL_OPTIONS. The mpatrol functions act on flags set as part of the value of this variable. To get a complete log of memory transactions we can set it to LOGALL:

```
$ MPATROL_OPTIONS="LOGALL" ./testtitle
created dvd title 1
...
$
```

If we take a look at mptrol.log now we see that there is a record for every memory allocation and deallocation:

```
ALLOC: malloc (46, 176 bytes, 4 bytes) [-|-|-]
    0x400B385B __new_fopen
    0x08049A54 open_db_table
    0x08049B39 dvd_open_db
    0x08049930 create_db
    0x08049468 main
    0x40077313 __libc_start_main
    0x080493C1 _start

returns 0x0805F0B0
```

Here we can see the dynamic memory allocated for the file stream we use for accessing one of the database files. When a block of memory is deallocated, mpatrol also reports the place where that block was allocated.

```
FREE: free (0x0805F0B0) [-|-|-]
    0x400B343B __new_fclose
    0x08049C47 dvd_close_db
    0x08049A25 create_db
    0x08049468 main
    0x40077313 __libc_start_main
    0x080493C1 _start

  0x0805F0B0 (176 bytes) {malloc:46:0} [-|-|-]
    0x400B385B __new_fopen
    0x08049A54 open_db_table
    0x08049B39 dvd_open_db
    0x08049930 create_db
    0x08049468 main
    0x40077313 __libc_start_main
    0x080493C1 _start
```

As you might expect, the other allocation functions are included as well, here is a call to realloc:

```
REALLOC: realloc (0x0805F210, 32 bytes, 4 bytes) [-|-|-]
    0x0804A5D1 dvd_title_search
    0x08049839 test_titles
    0x08049495 main
    0x40077313 __libc_start_main
    0x080493C1 _start

  0x0805F210 (16 bytes) {realloc:57:0} [-|-|-]
    0x0804A5D1 dvd_title_search
    0x08049839 test_titles
    0x08049495 main
    0x40077313 __libc_start_main
    0x080493C1 _start

returns 0x0805F210
```

Other memory operations are recorded, such as memory copies via the memcpy function as these are often the source of errors that are difficult to track down.

mpatrol is able to detect a number of memory use errors as your program runs. It can allocate blocks that are larger than necessary, fill these 'buffer' areas with known values and detect when they change. The detection takes place when functions provided by mpatrol are called (malloc, free, memcpy etc), which might be some time after the error took place.

An alternative detection method is to use the CPUs hardware protection mechanism to detect overwrites. mpatrol can do this at the expense of increasing each allocated block to the processors pages size, 4K on Intel x86 and Pentium. A program that usually allocates many small blocks will then consume much more memory while being tested.

Here's a small example program to illustrate the use of mpatrol options:

```
#include <stdio.h>
#include <stdlib.h>

void bad(char *p)
{
  p[20] = 'x';
}

main()
{
  char *ptr = malloc(16);
  bad(ptr);
  printf("We've been naughty!\n");
}
```

We are deliberately writing just beyond the limit of a dynamically allocated buffer. This is one of the common errors we mentioned earlier. When we compile and run without mpatrol the program appears to work just fine:

```
$ gcc -o memory memory.c
$ ./memory
We've been naughty!
$
```

This is potentially catastrophic and demonstrates why using mpatrol to watch your memory allocation can be essential –otherwise your program may exhibit 'good' behaviour during testing only to corrupt data or crash inexplicably during production use.

If we try again using mpatrol we find that the program is abnormally terminated. This is an indication that mpatrol has detected a problem:

```
$ gcc -o memory memory.c -lmpatrol -lbfd -liberty
$ ./memory
We've been naughty!
Aborted
$
```

Now when we take a look in the log we see what has happened:

```
ERROR: free memory corruption at 0x0805A0C4
    0x0805A0C4  78555555 55555555 55555555 55555555   xUUUUUUUUUUUUUUU
    0x0805A0D4  55555555 55555555 55555555 55555555   UUUUUUUUUUUUUUUU
```

As you can see mpatrol has detected corruption of unallocated memory beyond our allocated block - it reports this as corruption in free memory and records the contents of the affected block. You can see the character x we have written. You will also notice that the program carried on after the fault occurred, in this case until the program ended.

We can use 'buffer' areas to detect the fault without corrupting neighboring blocks with the OFLOWSIZE option to mpatrol. We set it to the size of the additional memory we want to add to our blocks for detecting overwrites of underwrites. When the overwrite is detected mpatrol will know which block has been overrun:

```
$ MPATROL_OPTIONS="OFLOWSIZE=8" ./memory
We've been naughty!
Aborted
$ cat mpatrol.log

ERROR: allocation 0x0805A0C8 has a corrupted overflow buffer at 0x0805A0DC
    0x0805A0D8  AAAAAAAA 78AAAAAA                      ....x...

  0x0805A0C8 (16 bytes) {malloc:46:0} [-|-|-]
    0x0804925D main
    0x40077313 __libc_start_main
    0x080491A1 _start
```

Furthermore, we can protect this buffer with the memory management hardware support by using the PAGEALLOC option:

```
$ MPATROL_OPTIONS="OFLOWSIZE=8 PAGEALLOC=UPPER" ./memory
Aborted
$
```

In this case the program is terminated as soon as the offending write takes place, and the log file attempts to record the position in the program, although this can sometimes be out by a function call or so:

```
$ cat mpatrol.log

ERROR: illegal memory access

    call stack
    0x0804926E main
    0x40077313 __libc_start_main
    0x080491A1 _start
```

Once we have fixed our overwrites we can also discover if we have failed to free any of our allocated blocks by using the SHOWUNFREED option of mpatrol. The log file will then contain a summary of orphaned blocks:

```
$ MPATROL_OPTIONS=SHOWUNFREED ./memory-fixed
We've been naughty!
$ cat mpatrol.log

unfreed allocations: 2 (192 bytes)
  0x0805A000 (176 bytes) {malloc:1:0} [-|-|-]
    0x400B385B __new_fopen
    0x0804E5DE __mp_openlogfile
    0x0804978D __mp_init
    0x08049932 __mp_alloc
    0x080492A8 malloc
    0x0804925D main
    0x40077313 __libc_start_main
    0x080491A1 _start

  0x0805A0B0 (16 bytes) {malloc:46:0} [-|-|-]
    0x0804925D main
    0x40077313 __libc_start_main
    0x080491A1 _start
```

Using replacement `malloc` implementations usually incurs a performance penalty. For testing this is normally acceptable.

Testing Coverage

As we develop and execute tests, we hope to show that our program contains no errors. The only way we can ever be sure that our program is correct is if we can prove that for every possible value of the data we give it, it returns the correct answer. For all but the most trivial program this is almost impossible to do – there are some ways to approach proving programs are correct, but they are beyond the scope of this book. It would take forever to test a calculator program for every single value we could pass to its square root function – and where on earth would we get a list of correct answers?

We need to find a compromise that does not short change our testing. Typically we might develop a test set for each function that our program performs. We run the tests with a selected set of data, maybe some typical values plus some extremes and some invalid values. We try to partition the possible data values into sets. We select the sets such that every member of the set causes the same behavior in the program. We then proceed to test with just one member from each set. We hope that this selection will exercise our program sufficiently that we can be confident that it works. Can we be a little more precise than this? In fact we can, by considering test coverage.

The idea behind test coverage is to assess the fraction of our program that has been executed in the course of our testing. If we can determine that the whole of the program has been run at one point or another during our tests, then we can perhaps feel more confident than we otherwise might.

Statement Coverage

There are three main types of coverage that we can consider, and each is more stringent than the last. The first is statement coverage, which tries to assess whether every line of code in our program has been executed at least once during testing. This would at least tell us that we have ventured into every nook and cranny of the code.

Statement coverage has the disadvantage that it does not take into account any interaction between parts of our program. Take a simple example of a small function with a couple of `if` statements:

```
 1: int myfunction (int a, int b)
 2: {
 3:    int r = 1;
 4:    if(a > 0) {
 5:         r = 0;
 6:    }
 7:    if(b > 0) {
 8:         r = 3/r;
 9:       }
10:    return r;
11:}
```

The key executable lines are 4,5,7 and 8. If during our tests the function `myfunction` gets called at all we will execute lines 4 and 7. If we call `myfunction(1,0)`, that is with a positive first argument, we will execute line 5 (setting `r` to zero). If we call `myfunction(0,1)` we will enter the second conditional section and complete the execution of all the statements in the function. So, our tests will have achieved complete statement coverage.

We have not necessarily tested a case in which both sections are executed. A test that calls `myfunction(1,1)` would do this, and we will uncover a potential problem if we do so. This call will generate a fault by dividing by zero as we execute both of the conditional sections.

A fourth test, calling `myfunction(0,0)` fills in the remaining case, where neither conditional section is executed.

Branch and Data Coverage

The consideration of the path the program takes through the code is called branch coverage and is the second level of coverage. The number of paths through a section of code grows enormously quickly if there are conditionals and loops involved, the number of test cases to cover all of them would need to be equally large.

The third type consists of the unattainable case alluded to earlier, which we might call data coverage – the value of every item of data, in every combination has been executed in testing.

> *Good programmers write their programs with problems of test coverage in mind. Intelligent design and planning can help get the most from the tools covered in this chapter.*

There are some tools we can use to help discover how well our tests are covering our code, and we will look at one shortly. Most tools are only able to help with the first level of coverage, statement coverage. Because of this we must take care to write our program and choose our test data carefully

Test coverage tools generally work by instrumenting your program. They add their own extra code when the application is compiled. This code collects data about which statements are executed and how often. Because they work at the statement level it is a good idea to avoid C constructs that either explicitly or implicitly combine more than one statement on one line. Examples include writing if statements or loops on one line. Other less obvious ones perhaps include the use of pre-processor macros that contain code, and the ternary conditional expression. For example:

```
/* Bad style for statement coverage */

#define SOME_TEST(X) { if(X>0) X--; else X++ }
z = a > b? func(a): func(b);
for(i=0; i<a; i++) func(i);
```

In these cases the fact that the line gets executed may not tell us which branch of the conditional was taken, or in the case of the loop, whether the loop was executed at all.

The choice of test data should be determined by the boundary conditions in your application. If you have some data input, choose both simple and extreme cases. Suppose you have to deal with a password that can be up to 12 characters long. Test your program with passwords that are zero-length, several characters long, 12 long, 13 long, and contain non-printing characters and nulls. Try to make sure that your tests exercise all of the conditions in your functions.

Keeping your functions short and simple, with few branches and only one entry and exit will reduce the complexity of the paths the program can take. This will help to make statement coverage more useful.

OK, now it's time to take a look at a test coverage tool in action.

GCOV - a Statement Coverage Tool

The GNU coverage tool, gcov, has tended to go unnoticed in the Linux community. Its popularity is not helped by the fact that a typical Linux distribution may lack any documentation for it, although it might well be installed. You can find some information about it at http://gcc.gnu.org/onlinedocs/.

To use gcov we need to prepare a special version of our application, in much the same way as we prepare for debugging or profiling (as we will see shortly). In this case we have to use the GNU C compiler and use a number of special flags. These are:

```
-fprofile-arcs
-ftest-coverage
-fbranch-probabilities
```

The -ftest-coverage flag causes the compiler to create a couple of special files in addition to the normal object file. These files are related to the source filename, having the extension .bb and .bbg. These files record the branch structure of the functions in the source code, and will be used by gcov to create an execution map.

The -fprofile-arcs flag request the compiler to place additional code into our program to record which statements have been executed. This information will be written to a file, again derived from the source filename, but with extension .da, when the program exits normally (that is, via a call to exit or return from main). As this additional code will inevitably slow the program down the third option (-fbranch-probabilities) invokes optimizations based on the program flow. For example if a block of code has no conditionals in it the entire block can be marked as executed if the block is entered at all.

Let's take a look at an example.

In the reference implementation of the DVD store APIs, we created a set of functions in a single source file, flatfile.c. This was used to test out the API, making sure it was suitable for the application, before creating a PostgreSQL implementation in parallel with a graphical user interface.

To test the reference implementation several simple test programs were written, each intended to test out a subset of the API. So, a `testmember` program was used to test out functions relating to membership, a `testtitle` program to test out functions relating to adding DVD titles to the database, and so on.

What we'd like to find out is whether we have managed, by running these test programs, to exercise every part of the reference implementation.

First of all we create an instrumented version of our APIs:

```
$ gcc -ftest-coverage -fprofile-arcs -fbranch-probabilities -c flatfile.c
$ ls -lstr
...
  16 -rw-r--r--   1 matthewn matthewn   14924 Mar 31 21:08 flatfile.o
   8 -rw-r--r--   1 matthewn matthewn    7504 Mar 31 21:08 flatfile.bbg
   8 -rw-r--r--   1 matthewn matthewn    4244 Mar 31 21:08 flatfile.bb
$
```

Here we can see both the object file and the branch analysis files.

Then we re-compile and run the test programs:

```
$ gcc -o testmember  testmember.c flatfile.o
$ ./testmember
dvd_open_db: no error
dvd_today: no error
date is: 20000331
genres: no error
Action Education Comedy Thriller Foreign Romance Science Fiction
classes: no error
E U PG 12 15 18
member_create: no error
created member #1
member_create: no error
created member #2
member_get: no error
Member ID #2
No. 10002: Dr Ben Matthew
...
member_delete: no error
member_get: no match found
member_set: no error
member_get_id: no error
member 10002 has id 2
member_get_id: no match found
member_search: no error
1 2
```

The test program runs and produces the expected results. As it ran the additional code was busy collecting information that it then wrote a file in the directory where the program was running. For each source file that has been instrumented by the compiler a corresponding file with the extension `.da` is produced. This is a record of the executed parts of the original source.

```
$ ls -lstr
...
 16 -rw-r--r--   1 matthewn matthewn    14924 Mar 31 21:08 flatfile.o
  8 -rw-r--r--   1 matthewn matthewn     7504 Mar 31 21:08 flatfile.bbg
  8 -rw-r--r--   1 matthewn matthewn     4244 Mar 31 21:08 flatfile.bb
  4 -rw-r--r--   1 matthewn matthewn       60 Mar 31 21:19 reserve.dat
  4 -rw-r--r--   1 matthewn matthewn      876 Mar 31 21:19 member.dat
  4 -rw-r--r--   1 matthewn matthewn     1920 Mar 31 21:19 flatfile.da
$
```

The .dat files shown here are the flat file database files created by the test program.

Now we can use gcov to find out to what extent the code in flatfile.c has been exercised. The gcov program accepts a number of optional arguments as we shall see, but for now the default will be fine. We just run gcov specifying the source file of interest.

```
$ gcov flatfile.c
 31.07% of 412 source lines executed in file flatfile.c
Creating flatfile.c.gcov.
$
```

As you can see gcov reports that less than a third of our code has been executed during out test program run. This is not too surprising since the test program concentrates on only a portion of overall functionality. What gcov has done is analyze the .da file that was created during the test run and calculated some summary coverage statistics. It has also created a new file, flatfile.c.gcov which is an annotated version of the source file showing which lines have been executed and how many times. We will take a look at this file in a moment.

The data file written when we ran the test program is cumulative – as we run more and more tests, the file is extended and updated. This even extends to other programs that use the code we are trying to assess for coverage. So, if we compile and run another test program we increase the recorded coverage. For example, if we now compile and run the test program dealing with DVD titles we will see an improvement in coverage.

```
$ gcc -o testtitle testtitle.c flatfile.o
$ ./testtitle
created dvd title 1
created dvd title 2
created dvd title 3
...
created dvd title 24
created dvd title 25
dvd_open_db: no error
get_genres: no error
get_classes: no error
name search: no error
Searched for name "Jean":
DVD Title #1: Grand Illusion
Directed by Jean Renoir (1938), Rated: U, Action
Starring: Jean Gabin
ASIN 0780020707, Price 29.99
DVD Title #5: The 400 Blows
```

```
Directed by Francois Truffaut (1959), Rated: 12, Education
Starring: Jean-Pierre Leaud
ASIN 1572525320, Price 23.98
DVD Title #6: Beauty and The Beast
Directed by Jean Cocteau (1946), Rated: 18, Thriller
Starring: Jean Marais
ASIN 0780020715, Price 39.95
DVD Title #25: Alphaville
Directed by Jean-Luc Godard (1965), Rated: U, Science Fiction
Starring: Eddie Constantine
ASIN 0780021541, Price 20.99
title search: no error
...
test_titles: no error
$
```

The test program runs normally and the data file is updated. Running gcov again shows us that we have now exercised a larger proportion of our source:

```
$ gcov flatfile.c
 44.42% of 412 source lines executed in file flatfile.c
Creating flatfile.c.gcov.
$
```

You will need to reset the coverage files (*.da) if you change your application, to maintain consistency. This can be done by adding a rule in your makefile to delete them if the application changes.

Let's take a look at the gcov output to see if there are any things that we have missed in the testing. At this stage there are functions that are not tested at all (like renting and returning DVDs), but we still might find some surprises. The output shown below has been abbreviated to save space. The numbers to the left of the lines of code indicate the number of times each line has been executed:

```
$ more flatfile.c.gcov
...
        int dvd_member_get_id_from_number(char *member_no, int *member_id)
        {
          /* Search for a member by member number.
             Note that this is an case insensitive EXACT match
             in case we ever want to use alpha member "numbers"
          */
      6         dvd_store_member member;
      6         int id = 1;
        int err;

      6         while(err = dvd_member_get(id, &member),
     15         err == DVD_SUCCESS || err == DVD_ERR_NOT_FOUND) {
     12             if(err == DVD_SUCCESS &&
          strcasecmp(member_no, member.member_no) == 0) {
      3                 *member_id = id;
      3                 return DVD_SUCCESS;
      9             }
      9             id++;
      9         }
      3         return DVD_ERR_NOT_FOUND;
      6     }
```

Here we can see that the function `dvd_member_get_id_from_number` has been executed a number of times, in fact, every line has been executed at least once. From the execution counts we can deduce that we called the function six times and on three occasions failed to find the member. For functions that are incompletely exercised gcov highlights the uncovered lines so that they are easy to spot. Here's another extract from the output:

```
        int dvd_title_get(int title_id, dvd_title *title_record_to_complete)
        {
     88        int err = DVD_SUCCESS;

     88        if(title_record_to_complete == NULL)
######            return DVD_ERR_NULL_POINTER;

     88        err = file_get(title_file,
           sizeof(dvd_title) * title_id,
             sizeof(dvd_title),
             (void *) title_record_to_complete);

        /* If we cannot get the title there may be an error
           with the data, or the title may not exist */
     88        if(err != DVD_SUCCESS)
      3            return err;

        /* If the retrieved title id is not as expected there
           may be an error, or the title may be deleted */
     85        if(title_record_to_complete -> title_id == 0)
######            return DVD_ERR_NOT_FOUND;
     85        if(title_id != title_record_to_complete -> title_id)
######            return DVD_ERR_BAD_MEMBER_TABLE;
```

Here we can see that although we have tested the case where a DVD title does not exist (3 out of 88 calls) we have not tested the case where a null pointer is passed as an argument. This highlights a gap in our testing, we have not made sure that the function copes with a wide range of inputs. Worse, we have not tested the case where a title is sought after it has been deleted, which might cause problems if we use this test program with a different implementation.

We can ask gcov to provide some more detail in its summary by specifying the -f flag. This adds function by function coverage statistics so we can pin down the functions we need to look at more closely.

```
$ gcov -f flatfile.c
87.50% of 16 source lines executed in function open_db_table
 60.00% of 15 source lines executed in function dvd_open_db
100.00% of 9 source lines executed in function dvd_close_db
 66.67% of 6 source lines executed in function file_set
 83.33% of 6 source lines executed in function file_get
 75.00% of 4 source lines executed in function dvd_member_set
 83.33% of 12 source lines executed in function dvd_member_get
 87.50% of 16 source lines executed in function dvd_member_create
100.00% of 4 source lines executed in function dvd_member_delete
100.00% of 12 source lines executed in function dvd_member_get_id_from_number
 95.83% of 24 source lines executed in function dvd_member_search
 75.00% of 4 source lines executed in function dvd_title_set
 75.00% of 12 source lines executed in function dvd_title_get
 90.00% of 10 source lines executed in function dvd_title_create
 ...
$
```

Branch coverage can be attempted if we ask gcov to provide information about branches taken by specifying the -b flag.

```
$ gcov -b flatfile.c
 44.42% of 412 source lines executed in file flatfile.c
 43.60% of 250 branches executed in file flatfile.c
 32.80% of 250 branches taken at least once in file flatfile.c
 52.50% of 120 calls executed in file flatfile.c
Creating flatfile.c.gcov.
$
```

Now if we look at the gcov output we see that there is additional information pertaining to the branches taken at conditional statements. For each statement that has more than one possible outcome the percentage for each outcome is given. Statements that branch include if, case, for, while and so on, as well as function calls (since a function may or may not return). Some examples may make things clear.

```
           25        if(file_records == 0) {
branch 0 taken = 84%
                     /* We just created the file. As we use id zero as a
                        sentinel we need to reserve the first entry in the
                        file, so add a dummy record here */
            4            file_records = 1;
            4        }
```

Here we see a simple if statement. The underlying code will evaluate the test condition and then branch around the block of code. We see here that gcov records that the branch (skipping the if) was executed 84% of the time. A more complex test might generate additional branches that will get recorded separately. A function call in a test will count as a further branch as with this example:

```
           12        if(err == DVD_SUCCESS &&
branch 0 taken = 0%
call 1 returns = 100%
branch 2 taken = 75%
                     strcasecmp(member_no, member.member_no) == 0) {
            3            *member_id = id;
            3            return DVD_SUCCESS;
branch 0 taken = 100%
```

The branches are for the test against DVD_SUCCESS (failing) the call to strcasecmp returning, and the test of the return result (failing). The return statement also counts as a branch, and is always taken. Case statements will typically produce one branch per case, so you can see which ones have been exercised.

As you can see, interpreting branch information from gcov can be a little tricky, but with practice it is possible to untangle complex statements and get close to the benefits that a full branch coverage tool could provide.

```
The options with gcov are summarized below.

gcov [-b] [-v] [-n] [-l] [-f] [-o OBJDIR] file

-b output branch summary
-v print version
-n do not create .gcov file
-l use long file names
-o specify object file directories
```

The `-o` option allows you to direct `gcov` to the location of its data files, the `.bb` and `.bbg` files, if they are not in the current directory. The `-l` flag caters for the case where executable code is used in `include` files, and therefore effectively appears in more than one source file. The `-l` flags tells `gcov` to produce `.gcov` files for each use of the code separately, so if there is code in `inc.h` which is included in both `file1.c` and `file2.c` we will get coverage files `inc.h.file1.c.gcov` and `inc.h.file2.c.gcov`.

Performance Testing

An important aspect of testing is that of performance. Our application must not only perform the functions we need, but also be usable. Often usability is related to speed of response (latency) or rate of update (throughput). In cases like this it can be useful to find out where a program is spending its time. We can do this by profiling the application and run some tests designed to evaluate performance.

As with debugging and coverage testing, we can use the compiler and tools to help with analyzing the execution profile of our application. We build a special version of the program, run our tests and examine data collected as the program runs.

We will take a quick look at one profiler tool, `gprof` and show how that can help to track down inefficiencies. The aim is to guide optimization of a program that is working and debugged. There is little point in eking every last drop of performance out of a function that is hardly used, or is already fast enough if there are larger gains to be made elsewhere. Careful consideration of profiling information can help you decide where to expend your effort.

We prepare a profiled version of our application by using the `-pg` option to the compiler:

```
$ gcc -pg -o testtitle testtitle.c flatfile.c
```

For demonstration purposes the flat file implementation of the DVD store APIs has been doctored to introduce some delays in processing file reads and writes. This simulates the work that would need to be done accessing a real database.

When we run our program it executes normally, except that when it has finished it writes a new file, `gmon.out`, which is a record of the execution profile. What has happened is that the program has essentially been measuring the time taken for functions to execute and collecting data. When the program ends, this data is written out.

We use the `gprof` program to analyze the collected data and provide reports about our application's performance. There are a number of options to `gprof` – check the manual page for more details.

By default `gprof` produces a long report with descriptions of each of the reported statistics. We just need to run `gprof` in the directory where the `gmon.out` file was written (the directory where the application was started) and pass the name of the executable that produced the output file so that `gprof` can relate function names to the raw execution profile data:

```
$ ./testtitle
$ ls -ls gmon.out
   8 -rw-r--r--   1 neil      users         4809 Apr  4 09:39 gmon.out
$ gprof testtitle
Flat profile:
```

Each sample counts as 0.01 seconds.

% time	cumulative seconds	self seconds	calls	self ms/call	total ms/call	name
64.00	0.96	0.96	88	10.91	10.91	file_get
36.00	1.50	0.54	50	10.80	10.80	file_set
0.00	1.50	0.00	88	0.00	10.91	dvd_title_get
0.00	1.50	0.00	50	0.00	10.80	dvd_title_set
0.00	1.50	0.00	25	0.00	10.80	dvd_title_create
0.00	1.50	0.00	10	0.00	0.00	open_db_table
0.00	1.50	0.00	10	0.00	0.00	print_title
0.00	1.50	0.00	6	0.00	0.00	dvd_err_text
0.00	1.50	0.00	6	0.00	0.00	show_result
0.00	1.50	0.00	2	0.00	0.00	dvd_open_db
0.00	1.50	0.00	2	0.00	283.64	dvd_title_search
0.00	1.50	0.00	1	0.00	270.00	create_db
0.00	1.50	0.00	1	0.00	0.00	dvd_close_db
0.00	1.50	0.00	1	0.00	0.00	dvd_get_classification_list
0.00	1.50	0.00	1	0.00	0.00	dvd_get_genre_list
0.00	1.50	0.00	1	0.00	1230.00	test_titles

Here we can see that the bulk of the execution time was spent in the file access routines file_get and file_set. Notice that the time is accumulated by function. That is, the total time per call for the function create_db includes the time spent in the lower level functions that actually manipulated the data files. The bulk of remaining time was spent in functions called from dvd_title_search. Let's take a closer look at what is going on here.

The default gprof report continues with a call graph that shows which functions called which others and how long the calls took to execute. The output here is edited to save space, and shows the analysis for the functions dvd_title_get, file_get and dvd_title_search.

```
      ---------------------------------------------------
                  0.00    0.39    36/88      test_titles [2]
                  0.00    0.57    52/88      dvd_title_search [5]
      [3]  64.0   0.00    0.96    88       dvd_title_get [3]
                  0.96    0.00    88/88      file_get [4]
      ---------------------------------------------------
                  0.96    0.00    88/88      dvd_title_get [3]
      [4]  64.0   0.96    0.00    88       file_get [4]
      ---------------------------------------------------
                  0.00    0.57    2/2        test_titles [2]
      [5]  37.8   0.00    0.57    2        dvd_title_search [5]
                  0.00    0.57    52/88      dvd_title_get [3]
      ---------------------------------------------------
```

The function dvd_title_get (marked with [3] here) was called 88 times in total, 36 times from test_titles and 52 times from dvd_title_search. It accounts for all 88 calls to file_get. The search function dvd_title_search was called twice.

A careful analysis of an execution profile can lead to important information about your program. In this case, as the test program only calls dvd_title_search twice we can see that searching is very expensive in this implementation. In fact we are using a linear search through all of the title records which is very slow for large numbers of records. The profile has helped to finger the searching function as a target for optimization.

NOTE: This example is a little contrived since we would never consider such a poor search algorithm for a production application. The full DVD store program uses a database as we have seen in earlier chapters. Good algorithm selection and design is an essential part of programming practice, all too often overlooked.

The gprof program can also accumulate execution data across many runs of your test program. To do this we need to use the -s flag to gprof. Profile information will be accumulated in a gprof.sum file.

It is important to be aware that some of the information that gprof provides is statistical in nature. When the program is running its execution location is sampled at regular intervals, building up a picture of what it is doing. For some programs you might see a part of the execution time being reported in functions related to the profile data collection itself. In these cases the simplest thing to do is ignore data on functions you do not recognize.

Summary

In this chapter we have taken a look at some of the tools and techniques that you can use to make testing your application less of a chore and more rewarding in terms of information about the runtime behavior of the program.

We looked at test programs, flexible test harnesses, automating regression testing and scripting tests with expect. We covered the different types of memory available to your application and some of the problems that can arise. We looked at memory debugging tools, and ways to measure the performance of the application and the coverage of its testing.

With many of these tools available on the Linux platform, we have no excuses for making poor quality software!

Online discussion at http://www.p2p.wrox.com

12

Secure Programming

What is Secure Programming?

At its most basic level, security is the ability to have control over others' use of your resources: the ability to say no (or yes) to people and be able to back it up.

In the computer world, security encompasses many concepts. At one level, security is akin to reliability; a secure system is one that will be available despite the efforts of others to make it unavailable. At another level, security involves some form of access control; only certain people should be able to access the system, and then only in certain ways, all determined by the administrators of the system. Another security goal involves preventing information leakage, ensuring that when a legitimate user accesses information legitimately, no one else can gain a chance to access the same information.

Programming securely involves keeping all of these pitfalls in mind. The programmer must determine what security threats are important, and guard against them. A secure program may need to react positively to attacks as well as they are recognized by keeping good logs, alerts, and possibly even countermeasures to prevent the attack from continuing.

Secure programming is as much about knowing what *not* to do as knowing what to do. Thus, this chapter contains information about traps and mistakes to avoid as well as the usual new techniques and tips. It is not a comprehensive treatment; such a book could not be written, as attackers continue to invent new ways of compromising their targets. Rather, it is intended as a primer to secure programming practice, as well as a tutorial in the most common and useful security tips and pitfalls, so you can start writing more secure code right away.

Why Secure Programming is Hard

If there is one universal truth about secure programming, it is this: Writing secure code is hard work.

Evidence for this fact abounds in the various lists and online resources devoted to cataloging and exposing security weaknesses. If it were any easier, most programmers would choose to avoid the public embarrassment that goes along with an exploit.

Yet, despite this motivation and others, the field of secure programming seems to be littered with the failures of countless systems, some designed by the best minds in the industry. Why is it that implementing security in a program is so much more difficult than implementing other features?

Stealthy Bugs

Many security systems are well designed on paper. Unfortunately, they must be implemented before they can be used, and fallible programmers often introduce bugs while implementing the system. Security bugs are not unique in this regard; however, security bugs are unique in that they are much more difficult to detect than other bugs.

If you fail to allocate enough space in a form for a label, or you accidentally substitute one operator for another in a calculation, the error leaps out at you; the label is cut off, or the result of the calculation is wrong. Tracking down the source of the problem may be difficult, but the existence of the problem is never in doubt.

Security features, on the other hand, are often coded to be completely invisible to the user, and are often even difficult for the programmer to see. Many of the non-obvious security bugs found come in the form of a side-effect to an algorithm's normal execution that leaks important information; others have to do with neglected housekeeping duties which don't affect the program's execution, but which would prevent security violations. This means that a program may pass every test and be shown to be fully operational, and yet be totally insecure.

For example, a pass phrase may be hashed after the user enters it to generate an encryption session key, but the logic to erase the unhashed pass phrase from memory may have a bug causing it to not function. As the program no longer needs the pass phrase, the program will continue to work properly, using the hashed session key in all of its operations, and it may pass all tests with flying colors. However, an attacker, upon finding this oversight, can now completely circumvent the program's security; by causing the program to crash after the pass phrase is entered, the attacker may be able to create a crash dump file containing the program's data and isolate the pass phrase from the dump.

Not all security bugs need to be this subtle. Sometimes, a simple lack of bounds checking on a memory buffer can be the catalyst for a complete security breach. For example, many of the recent bugs in Microsoft's Internet Explorer browser are caused by the URL translator; a particular URL that can cause a breach may be blocked by one security update. However, since these checks work on the URL before decoding %escapes, attackers have been able to exploit the same bugs by encoding part of the attack URL (for example, encoding all A characters with %41). Viruses have used similar methods for years to attempt to evade virus scanners, with varying degrees of success.

The Virtue of Paranoia

Many programmers, upon seeing security breaches in programmers by respected programmers (some with years of experience in implementing secure systems), descend into despair; if the 'experts' cannot manage to write secure code, how can someone like me do it? Indeed, there is the feeling among many observers of the online community that security is an impossible goal; that no tower of code can long endure the studied consideration of a curious teen.

To an extent, this impression is true. Security has always been a matter of degrees rather than an absolute solution, so most physical security systems have aimed at making penetration too costly rather than making it impossible. The same is true of digital security. When designing a secure system, one must always keep in mind the specific threats the system is supposed to be able to resist, and implement countermeasures that reduce the risk of compromise to an acceptable level. Sometimes a breach may simply be the result of a determined attacker pushing a security system beyond its designed tolerance, much like an overloaded bridge may collapse in rush hour traffic if the weight of the cars on the bridge exceeds its designed weight tolerance.

At the same time, programmers used to writing secure code tend to develop a high degree of paranoia. The hallmark of secure programming is managing trust, whether trust in a particular cryptosystem, trust that a section of code is operating correctly, trust that a user will give you correct input, or trust of the system that a particular code section is authorized to perform a task. Thus, minimizing trust - as much as possible without sacrificing necessary functionality - is a surefire way for programmers to minimize security bugs.

Can You Trust Your Compiler?

In his acceptance speech for the Turing Award in 1984, Ken Thompson, one of the original creators of UNIX, described how he was able to create an undetectable security weakness in a utility, even with source available.

Thompson described how he was able to modify the C compiler on an early version of UNIX to detect when it was compiling the code for login(1)*, and insert code that would cause a certain password to always be accepted, allowing someone who knew the password to log in as any user. He then modified the source to the C compiler to detect when it was compiling itself (the C compiler was itself written in C, then as now) and insert this code (to detect login and insert the Trojan horse) into the C compiler. He then removed the changes he had made to the source.*

From then on, the UNIX C compiler would always include his trojan whenever compiling the login(1) *program. No amount of auditing of the source code for login, or for the C compiler, would have revealed any problems.*

Examples such as this help to illustrate how much the modern programmer trusts the modern computing environment. We trust many system components - the compiler, program loader, dynamic linker, and even the microcode decoder on the CPU - to do exactly what we ask; any of these - especially components used at run time, such as the program loader or dynamic linker - could itself be a source of a security weakness.

Minimizing trust can be done in a number of ways. Here are a few examples:

Choose components for your system that come with full source code (preferably open-source) including all vendor modules. If you can, audit (or pay a professional to audit) all of these modules, or look for public audit results on security sites on the Internet. This can be hard to do, and isn't always practical to implement fully; however, vendor libraries and OS components can be a fertile source of security problems. If the vendor refuses to provide you with source, consider switching to a vendor that does, or at least perform as much of an audit as you can by stressing it; for example, feeding invalid data to the library and seeing how it fails.

Run with as few privileges as possible. Isolate code that requires special privileges (such as code that opens a privileged network port) from the rest of the program. If possible, complete all of your privileged tasks at program startup, and drop all privilege for the majority of the program's run. If privilege is needed on an ongoing basis, consider splitting that section of the code into a separate process that communicates with the rest of the program via some IPC method (although see the next point; this method has risks of its own).

Don't trust data that originates outside the program - even from code you write. Write validation routines that ensure that data that comes from outside the program is correct. Remember that data outside the program includes data generated from the operating system or the system libraries; and they can be manipulated too.

Filesystem Security

Security on UNIX systems (and UNIX-like ones, such as Linux) hinge on two fundamental concepts: user privileges and file system permissions. By far, file system permission issues are more likely to be encountered in the day-to-day work of the average programmer.

The Standard Permissions

Most UNIX users and programmers are familiar with the standard security matrix, as described in the previous volume and illustrated by the ls -l command:

```
user group world
  \    |    /
  rwx rwx rwx
   |   |    |
  read write execute
```

These attributes are represented in a bit field that is stored in the directory entry; it can be accessed by the chmod(2) and stat(2) families of system calls. This bit field is most often referred to in octal (base 8) notation; this notation is particularly convenient here because each permissions set (for user, group, or world permissions) can be represented by a single octal digit. The permissions themselves can be calculated by adding the octal values for each permission type together.

Read	4
Write	2
Execute	1

The Sticky Bit

In addition to the standard permissions bits, most UNIX systems (including Linux) have a bit called the *sticky bit*. It can be changed by setting or clearing the bit at octal 1000 in the permissions bit field, or by using chmod with +/-t. The sticky bit is indicated under ls -l by a t in the user column, world permissions place.

Historically, the sticky bit was designed to flag program files that 'stuck' in memory or swap after completing, as a performance optimization on slower systems. On Linux, programs with the sticky bit set are kept in swap even after completing execution. This is mostly kept as a compatibility feature; few systems today are slow enough or sensitive enough to require such hacks.

When the sticky bit is applied to directories, it takes on a newer and more interesting role. If a directory has the sticky bit set, files in that directory cannot be deleted by anyone except root, the owner of the file, or the owner of the directory. In particular, in group-writable and world-writable directories with the sticky bit set, any user (or any user in the proper group) may create new files in such directories, but they may not delete the files of any other user unless they own the directory.

You can use this facility for any situation where you need users to interact with each other or with a common service. For example, your program may allow users to drop files off in a 'staging area' for later processing by a cron job or another daemon. To prevent users from deleting other users' jobs (either maliciously or accidentally), you can set the sticky bit on the staging directory.

The sticky bit is also popular for shared temporary directories, such as /tmp and /var/tmp, for obvious reasons. If your program creates any temporary directories that multiple users can access, you can use the sticky bit on those directories.

Setuid and Setgid Attributes

There are two other advanced file security attributes commonly used: the setuid (for 'set user ID') and setgid (for "set group ID") bits. A file can be set or unset setuid by setting or clearing the bit at octal 4000, or with the u+s or u-s symbolic arguments to chmod, and can be set or unset setgid with the bit at octal 2000, or with the g+s or g-s symbolic arguments. It is possible to set files setuid or setgid without setting them to be executable; in practice this is almost never done with files, and is only rarely seen on directories.

These bits have two meanings, depending on whether they are used on files or directories. On executable files, the attributes change the privileges of the process running them, and on directories, they change the default ownership on newly created files.

Setuid and Setgid Executable Files

When an executable file is executed that has the setuid and/or setgid attributes set, the effective user and/or group IDs are changed to match the owner and/or group of the file executed. This gives the current user the rights of that user and/or group within that single process; but other processes the user may be running do not gain any extra privilege. If the file is setuid, executable, and owned by root (a situation commonly referred to as being setuid root), the user executing the file will, for that process only, gain full superuser privilege.

There is one exception to this: the setuid and setgid attributes are ignored on many systems, including Linux, if the executable file is a script. This is because there is a security problem with allowing scripts to be setuid or setgid; see below, under Race Conditions, for an explanation.

This powerful ability can be used by programmers to allow users or processes to gain greater privilege than they normally have, while allowing the programmer to control how they are allowed to use those privileges. This is most often implemented in terms of file permissions, where a user temporarily is given the right to read or write a file or directory, but only through the particular program, and only in ways that the program allows.

For example, programs dealing with e-mail are often made setgid to the mail group (setgid mail), with each user's mail files set as group writeable and owned by the mail group. This ensures that each user is not normally allowed to read another user's mail, but allows a delivery agent run by the user to deliver mail to another user (by appending the message to the other user's mail file).

The unlimited power of the superuser can be managed closely through setuid root programs, allowing users and processes to access only certain superuser functions, and without having to give them the root password. The su(1) utility, for example, does its magic by being setuid root. As another example, only the superuser may access hardware directly on Linux systems, but the X Window System requires direct hardware access to fully utilize a video card's functions (as of XFree86 3.x and Linux 2.2). Thus, X servers on today's Linux distributions are most often setuid root, allowing the server to function properly. The X server is also designed to tightly restrict what the user is allowed to do, preventing the user from using the X server to (for example) read another user's files.

Setgid Directories

On directories, the setuid attribute does nothing. The setgid attribute causes the system to set the group owner on all new files in the directory to the group owner of the directory, instead of the default group of the user. This is often used as a convenience to allow for shared directories, where new files are automatically set to allow other group members access. It is mostly intended as a convenience for users and system administrators, rather than programmers; most programs that rely on proper group ownership of new files should set them manually to avoid the possibility of operator error when changing directory permissions.

It should be pointed out that this is true on most System V-based systems and their work-alikes, including Linux. Systems based on the BSD family ignore the setgid bit on directories, and treat them all as if they were setgid.

Using Setuid and Setgid Safely

Setuid and setgid permissions on executable files provide very powerful tools for the programmer to manage privilege; however, they are also very dangerous tools. Their power derives directly from their ability to act with higher privileges; if the user cannot presumably be trusted with these privileges outside of the program, then the system's integrity relies on the controls the program can place on the user's use of the privileges. This is particularly true of setuid root programs, since a security breach could potentially allow a user to gain full superuser privilege.

As an illustration, consider the mail example presented above. A setgid mail delivery agent may be written to only allow the program to append data to already-existing files. However, suppose that the programmer included debugging code in the agent that caused it to write log information to a file named in a certain mail header line. If that code were not removed in production, the user could point the log information at any file he or she had permission to access, and destroy that file's original contents.

Normally, this isn't a problem, as users already have the ability to destroy any of their own information. But in a setgid mail environment, the user gains the ability to write to any file that the mail group can write to; thus, a malicious user could direct the agent to use another user's mailbox file as the log file, effectively deleting all of the user's mail.

This is an extreme and somewhat contrived example; most real-world weaknesses are much less obvious. It is therefore especially important to follow the principles mentioned above for minimizing trust. For example, your mail delivery agent could be written as more than one program; a normal program with no privileges, could perform most of its required duties, and call a second, setgid mail enabled helper program when necessary – it's much easier to secure a small program designed for one task than a large, complex program performing many tasks.

Authenticating Users

As handy as file permissions are, they provide no benefit if users can easily assume each other's identities. Authentication – the process of proving that a user is who he or she claims to be – is therefore a very important facet in providing privilege.

The most common form of authentication in use today is the process of asking for a username and password from the user. The idea that you hold some secret that is shared with the computer, which proves who you are, has been around since the first multi-user systems. The standards for storing, comparing, and transporting passwords may change, but the basic idea remains the same.

Traditional Authentication on UNIX

Linux, in drawing heavily on its UNIX heritage, has adopted the traditional UNIX methods of authenticating users. These methods are often still used as the default user authentication method. We will quickly review this method, as it shows both how a good system was designed and why it eventually failed to provide adequate security.

Basic Techniques

Standard UNIX authentication information is kept in two files: /etc/passwd and /etc/group. Each file contains records, one per line, with fields separated by spaces. Entries for each are usually retrieved through the getpw* and getgr* functions. The first and second fields are used for authentication and contain the username and password.

Passwords are stored in hashed form, using the crypt(3) hash function, with the two-character salt prepended to the hash. Authentication is done by requesting the username and password from the user, looking up the username with getpwnam(3) and retrieving the hashed password, encrypting the password given by the user with crypt(3) and the salt from the stored password, and comparing the results; if the returned hash string from crypt(3) is identical to the stored hash, the passwords match, and the user is authenticated. (See below, under Encryption, for a better explanation of manual password authentication.)

Limitations

Traditional password authentication has one advantage – it is backwardly compatible with almost every UNIX variant. Apart from this one virtue, traditional authentication is unsatisfactory from just about any other viewpoint.

The crypt(3) algorithm was considered very good when it was first adopted in the early 1970s, but advances in technology (such as faster CPUs for cracking, large-capacity storage methods for storing precomputed password lists, and so on) have made it very weak to many attacks. Additionally, the need to authenticate across a network has introduced other weaknesses, most notably the ability to sniff plaintext passwords or password hashes off the net as they pass by. Most UNIX implementations limited passwords in this system to 8 or 14 characters, which is not very long. Finally, there is often a need to adapt to a non-UNIX system's methods of authentication; this is simply not possible with simple authentication methods.

PAM - Pluggable Authentication Modules

To address these limitations, Sun Microsystems wrote a new system for authenticating users on UNIX, and released the system as a standard. The standard – Pluggable Authentication Modules, or PAM – is implemented as a modular system, allowing the system administrator to switch authentication schemes as the need arises without having to rebuild an entire system. PAM is now supported as the standard authentication system on almost every Linux distribution, and its popularity on Linux and Solaris has caused it to catch on with most other UNIX vendors as well.

PAM in Theory

PAM is implemented as an API and a series of modules. Each module is expected to provide four types of services to the PAM system:

❑ **Authentication services.** These functions allow PAM to perform the task of authenticating the user. A username is passed, but not a password; if necessary, the module can invoke a callback to the program to ask for a password.

❑ **Account services.** These functions take care of any non-authentication functions for user validation. For example, a module could restrict certain classes of users from logging in outside business hours, or it could limit the number of concurrent sessions that are allowed. Another common task performed here is password expiration; if a password has expired, an account service could take responsibility for asking for a new password and setting it properly.

❑ **Session services.** These functions take care of the tasks necessary to set up the user's session. Typical tasks done here include logging successful access, dynamically creating the home directory if it doesn't exist, and setting up tokens for a distributed authentication system such as Kerberos.

❑ **Password services.** These functions implement the ability to change passwords. Utilities such as passwd(1) would use these facilities.

Steps in Authenticating With PAM

Applications that use PAM generally follow the same steps, with minor variations. This is not an exhaustive treatment of the entire PAM API; rather, it seeks to describe the standard procedures used by applications wanting to use PAM.

First, applications that use PAM should include the proper files in their C/C++ programs, and link to the proper libraries. The include file is security/pam_appl.h. A link line should look like one of the following:

```
... -lpam -ldl


... -lpam -lpam_misc -ldl
```

The former line is called for by the PAM standard, and will work on any platform that PAM supports. The latter includes some extra Linux-specific enhancements to PAM; these should only be used if portability to non-Linux systems is not an issue. (If these functions are needed, the program should also include security/pam_misc.h.)

The next step is to initialize PAM. This is done with a call to pam_start(3):

```
int pam_start(const char *service_name, const char *user_name, const struct
pam_conv *conversation, pam_handle_t **pamhandle);
```

The service_name is a simple text string that identifies the service to the PAM system. It is used to find and load the PAM configuration for the particular service. The program name makes a good service name; some service names you might find already used might include ssh, login, or su. You should never read this name from an external program source, such as the environment, argv[], or an external file.

The user_name is the name of the user we intend to authenticate. It is expected that the username has already been received from somewhere, whether from user input, a configuration file, current information about the current user, or somewhere else.

The conversation parameter will be dealt with more closely below. It registers a callback function with PAM that will be called when more user input is necessary.

The pamhandle parameter provides a place for PAM to return a session handle to the application.

Most PAM functions return an error code, defined in the PAM include file, which start with PAM_. Success is indicated with a return of PAM_SUCCESS; this should always be checked after each call to a PAM function. User-friendly descriptions of errors can be retrieved with a call to pam_strerror(3):

```
const char * pam_strerror(pam_handle_t *pamhandle, int error);
```

Next, the application calls pam_authenticate(3). This function requests authenticating information from the user (such as a password), and tests the response to ensure it matches what the module expects. The function is defined as follows:

```
int pam_authenticate(pam_handle_t *pamhandle, const int flags);
```

The flags field supports options that can use bitwise or together; it should be set to zero if no options are needed. Two flags are supported: PAM_SILENT, which suppresses user interaction through the callback function, and PAM_DISALLOW_NULL_AUTHTOK, which causes PAM to return a failure if the user's authorization token is NULL (for example, if a user has a blank password field) instead of simply returning success.

The return value, if it is not PAM_SUCCESS, could be one of the following:

PAM_AUTH_ERR	This indicates an authentication failure, such as an incorrect password.
PAM_CRED_INSUFFICIENT	This indicates that the application itself does not have sufficient access rights to check the user's authentication. In almost all cases, this is because of a fault in the configuration of the system by the system administrator.
PAM_AUTHINFO_UNAVAIL	This problem indicates that the authentication system is unavailable for some reason. For example, the system may use a networked authentication system, and the network could be down.

Table continued on following page

PAM_USER_UNKNOWN	This indicates that the username cannot be found.
PAM_MAXTRIES	This indicates that one of the authentication modules has indicated that the maximum number of retries has been reached. If the application receives this error, it should stop trying to authenticate.

> **A word of caution** – there are security implications in passing some of this information on when reporting an authentication failure to the user. For example, attackers have been known to feed likely usernames to an authentication service, watching the different responses to see if they scored a 'hit' or not. Therefore, best security practice is to treat PAM_AUTH_ERR and PAM_USER_UNKNOWN identically at least, unless there is a good reason otherwise. The other errors should likely also be treated the same way, at least to the user attempting to log in; of course, the information should likely be saved somewhere else so it can be accessed to diagnose problems.

If pam_authenticate(3) returns PAM_SUCCESS, then the user has been authenticated. However, there may be other factors besides the user's identity that govern access to the system. To check for these factors, the program should next call pam_acct_mgmt(3):

```
int pam_acct_mgmt(pam_handle_t *pamhandle, const int flags);
```

The flags here are the same as for pam_authenticate(3). The possible return values, besides PAM_SUCCESS, PAM_AUTH_ERR, and PAM_USER_UNKNOWN (which all have the same meaning as in pam_authenticate(3)), are:

PAM_ACCT_EXPIRED.	The user's account has expired. This indicates a more permanent condition, such as the account being disabled.
PAM_PERM_DENIED.	The user is not allowed to log in. As opposed to PAM_ACCT_EXPIRED, this indicates a temporary condition, such as a restriction that a user cannot log in except during certain hours.
PAM_AUTHTOKEN_REQD.	This is used to indicate that the user's authentication token is valid, but has expired. The application should not allow further access until it has been changed.

If necessary (the application received the PAM_AUTHTOKEN_REQD error, for example), the application can call pam_chauthtok(3) to change the authentication tokens for the user. This function is defined as follows:

```
int pam_chauthtok(pam_handle_t *pamhandle, const int flags);
```

Besides PAM_SILENT (a valid, if somewhat contradictory flag for this function), only one flag is supported: PAM_CHANGE_EXPIRED_AUTHTOK. This tells PAM to only attempt to change the tokens if they have expired; the default is to change them no matter what.

There are several errors that this function can return. Besides PAM_SUCCESS and PAM_USER_UNKNOWN, they are:

PAM_AUTHTOK_ERR	For some reason, the new authentication token couldn't be received. For example, the user may have attempted to cancel the process.
PAM_AUTHTOK_RECOVERY_ERR	The system couldn't receive the old authentication token. An authentication module might, for example, ask that the user enter his/her old password before asking for the new one, and it might have been mistyped.
PAM_AUTHTOK_LOCK_BUSY	The system was unable to update the authentication tokens because of a lock; for example, a record lock on a database.
PAM_AUTHTOK_DISABLE_AGING	One of the authentication modules does not support expiration on authorization tokens.
PAM_PERM_DENIED	The user does not have permission to change his/her authorization token.
PAM_TRY_AGAIN	One of the authentication modules in use reported an error, which aborted the whole process. The application should try again.

After all this, the user can be considered fully authorized by the system. However, there are still some housekeeping tasks that may need to be done before proceeding. Session management is the most important; this includes tasks such as providing access to home directories for users, setting up the environment, logging the user's access, registering the user in the utmp and wtmp databases, and so on.

Session handling is performed with the following two functions:

```
int pam_open_session(pam_handle_t *pamhandle, const int flags);
int pam_close_session(pam_handle_t *pamhandle, const int flags);
```

The first should be called to open the session, and the second should be called to close it (once the user has logged off). Both functions only accept the PAM_SILENT flag, and both functions return simple success (PAM_SUCCESS) or failure (PAM_SESSION_ERR).

Another option involves setting up credentials. These are special tokens an authentication system may keep track of to enable additional access. Two common examples of credentials are Kerberos tickets and group membership information.

Credentials are set up using the pam_setcred(3) function:

```
int pam_setcred(pam_handle_t *pamhandle, const int flags);
```

The flags (bitwise ored into the *flags* parameter) are used to determine what action is needed:

PAM_ESTABLISH_CRED	Establish credentials.
PAM_DELETE_CRED	Delete credential information.
PAM_REINITIALIZE_CRED.	Reinitialize credentials
PAM_REFRESH_CRED.	Refresh credentials to prevent them from expiring

The function can return one of several errors. Besides PAM_SUCCESS and PAM_USER_UNKNOWN, they are:

PAM_CRED_UNAVAIL.	For some reason, the user's credentials are unavailable.
PAM_CRED_EXPIRED.	The user's credentials have expired.
PAM_CRED_ERR.	One of the authentication modules had some other error in setting credentials.

The last step in working with PAM is to close the PAM session cleanly, which can be done after any sessions have been closed. This is done with pam_end(3):

```
int pam_end(pam_handle_t *pamhandle, const int pam_status);
```

The pam_status parameter should contain the last return value returned from a PAM function. It is probably prudent to report any return values other than PAM_SUCCESS back to the user with pam_strerror(3); otherwise, the return value can be ignored.

Registering Callbacks

The process of authentication needs, on occasion, information from the user logging in. To allow this to happen, the pam_start(3) function asks for a *conversation structure*; the primary purpose of this structure is to point PAM at a callback function provided by your application. This *conversation function* allows PAM to prompt for information from the user and receive the user's response.

Here is the definition of the conversation structure:

```
struct pam_conv {
    int (*conv)(int num_msg,
                const struct pam_message **msg,
                struct pam_response **resp,
                void *appdata_ptr);
    void *appdata_ptr;
};
```

The first field of the structure is a pointer to the conversation function, which must be declared with the given prototype. The second field can be NULL, or it can point to some arbitrary data; whatever its value, it is passed unchanged to the conversation function as the fourth parameter.

Each call to the conversation function contains a set of messages and expected responses. The messages are contained in the `msg` parameter, with the total number of messages stored in the `num_msg` parameter. Each message should be displayed to the user in an appropriate fashion for the application (to `stdout` or `stderr`, in a popup window under X, etc.). If the message type requires a response, the function should accept input from the user and store it in the array of `pam_response` structures (with `num_msg` entries) pointed to by `resp`; the entries in `resp` correspond to the entries in `msg`, so the response received for `message[n]` should be stored in `resp[n]`. Finally, the function should return `PAM_SUCCESS` under normal circumstances; if there is an error, the function should return `PAM_CONV_ERR` and not change any of the information in `resp`.

The `pam_message` and `pam_response` structs are defined as follows:

```
struct pam_message {
    int msg_style;
    const char *msg;
};

struct pam_response {
    char *resp;
    int resp_retcode;
};
```

The `msg` member of the `pam_message` structure is a pointer to the message string to display to the user. The `resp` field of the `pam_response` structure points to a buffer to fill with the user's response; the buffer is `PAM_MAX_MSG_SIZE` bytes long, so no more information than that should be copied by the function into the buffer. (The `msg` field should never be longer than `PAM_MAX_MSG_SIZE` bytes either; however, this behavior should not be expected by the application, as it is not enforced by PAM.) The `resp_retcode` field should be set to zero; it is not currently used.

This leaves the `msg_style` field of `pam_message`. The value of this field determines what kind of message it is, and whether a response is expected from the user. It may be set to the following values:

PAM_PROMPT_ECHO_OFF	This message should be displayed, and the user should enter a response. Echoing of the response while the user is typing it should be turned off; PAM has no requirements about what to display in its place, so the application is free to use whatever convention is appropriate (no response, echoing asterisks, etc.).
PAM_PROMPT_ECHO_ON	The message should be displayed, and the user should enter a response. Echo can be turned on.
PAM_ERROR_MSG	The message should be displayed in a manner appropriate for error messages. No input is expected.
PAM_TEXT_INFO	No input is expected. The message should be displayed. The message is not an error, so it can be displayed in whatever manner is appropriate.

Table continued on following page

PAM_BINARY_PROMPT	This message type is an extension supported by Linux. It contains a binary message intended for client-server authentication protocols, and expects a response. In most cases, the prompt and response are very dependent on particular authentication protocols, so determining whether the prompt should be displayed or how to receive the response is very dependent on the application and protocol
PAM_BINARY_MSG	This message type, like the last, is Linux-specific. It also contains a binary message, for which a response is not expected.

A large number of applications interact via text-based sessions without special needs for formatting input and output (such as ncurses). For these applications, the pam_misc library provides misc_conv; this function is a complete working conversation function that performs all its functions through simple reads and writes to the stdio file streams. This saves the effort needed to write custom conversation functions, all of which would likely implement almost exactly the same behavior.

An Example

Let's suppose that we have a need to store sensitive files, only accessible to valid users of the system (with other possible restrictions that could be defined in the future). Let's further assume that there is a concern about unattended terminals, and that we therefore want to require users to re-enter their password before being allowed access to these files.

The goal can be largely met by writing a file viewer that requires the user to be authenticated before viewing the file. We can then create a user, set the owner of our sensitive files to our new user, make them owner-readable only, and set our file viewer setuid to our user; this ensures that the only way to read the files is through our viewer.

To start off, we'll use PAM for authentication, and we'll use the misc_conv conversation function to save us some work. So, counting the non-PAM things we need to do, we'll need the following header files:

```
#include <stdio.h>
#include <stdlib.h>
#include <sys/types.h>
#include <pwd.h>
#include <syslog.h>
#include <security/pam_appl.h>
#include <security/pam_misc.h>
#include <security/_pam_types.h>
```

We don't need very sophisticated error checking; we can live with considering expired passwords and the like as errors. So, we only need to check for PAM_SUCCESS at every stage. We don't need anything like retries, either, since the app can just be run again if the first attempt fails. To avoid the tedium of doing the same check over and over, let's create an error testing function, displaying a generic message to the user and logging the real error to syslog(3):

```
void test_pam_error(pam_handle_t *ph, int pam_retval)
{
  if (pam_retval != PAM_SUCCESS)
    {
```

```
          fputs("authpam: auth error\n", stderr);
          syslog(LOG_ERR, pam_strerror(ph, pam_retval));
          exit(EXIT_FAILURE);
      }
  }
```

Next, we initialize `main`, declare our variables, and check that we've been called with the proper command line arguments:

```
int main(int argc, char *argv[])
{
  int retval;
  struct passwd *myinfo;
  struct pam_conv myconv;
  pam_handle_t *pamhandle = NULL;
  FILE *secure_file;
  char buf[256];

  openlog("authcat", LOG_PID, LOG_AUTHPRIV);
  if (argc != 2)
    {
      fputs("usage: authcat filename\n", stderr);
      exit(EXIT_FAILURE);
    }
```

At this point, we need a username before we can initialize PAM. Since we're re-authenticating the current user, we can get this by calling `getuid(2)` for the real UID (remember, we're running `setuid`, so the effective UID will always be for the user that owns these files), followed by a `getpwuid(3)` call to retrieve the username associated with this UID:

```
  myinfo = getpwuid(getuid());
  if (myinfo == NULL)
    {
      fputs("authcat: cannot determine the current user\n", stderr);
      exit(EXIT_FAILURE);
    }
```

Now, we've got the right username. Let's start PAM up:

```
  myconv.conv = misc_conv;
  myconv.appdata_ptr = NULL;
  retval = pam_start("authcat", myinfo->pw_name, &myconv, &pamhandle);
  test_pam_error(pamhandle, retval);
```

One important point: We could have used `argv[0]` here to pass in the service name, but we didn't. This is because `argv[0]` is not a secure source for the true application name. An attacker could weaken the security settings for the program in this case by creating a hard link or symlink for our program in the current directory, naming the link to be the same as some other PAM-based program with a more permissive configuration. Our application would then pass the link name to PAM from `argv[0]`, and PAM would load and use the more permissive settings.

Next, we can do the actual authentication. We don't care about credentials or session management, as this is a one-time authentication, so all we need are authentication and account services:

```
retval = pam_authenticate(pamhandle, 0);
test_pam_error(pamhandle, retval);

retval = pam_acct_mgmt(pamhandle, 0);
test_pam_error(pamhandle, retval);
```

If we make it this far without our error function killing us, then we're legitimate. So, we can now show the file:

```
secure_file = fopen(argv[1], "r");
if (secure_file == NULL)
  {
    fputs("authcat: cannot open file\n", stderr);
    exit(EXIT_FAILURE);
  }

while (!feof(secure_file))
  {
    if (fgets(buf, 256, secure_file))
      fputs(buf, stdout);
  }

fclose(secure_file);
```

Now we're done. We can shut PAM down now and return normally:

```
retval = pam_end(pamhandle, retval);
test_pam_error(pamhandle, retval);

return EXIT_SUCCESS;
}
```

Note that we didn't implement the part in our specification about 'other restrictions as needed'. The reason is simple: since we're using PAM, additional restrictions can be configured in the PAM configuration file. Thus, adding restrictions becomes the job of the system administrator, not the programmer.

For example, below is a relatively straightforward PAM configuration file that might be used for the above utility. In our case, the utility file is called authcat.c, so we must name our configuration file authcat, and save it in the directory /etc/pam.d/. You may find that you do not have the file pam_unix.so, in which case use pam_unix_auth.so, and pam_unix_acct.so respectively.

```
auth     required     pam_unix.so
account  required     pam_unix.so
```

A system administrator, however, may decide that the program should only be run from certain 'secure' terminals in a certain setting. This additional restriction is easy to add without programming:

```
auth      required     pam_listfile.so onerr=fail item=tty sense=allow \
                                       file=/etc/authcat-ttys
auth      required     pam_unix.so
account   required     pam_unix.so
```

In similar ways, other restrictions could be added to our program, or other authentication methods specified, without any change to our program.

The binary is compiled along the following lines:

```
$ gcc authcat authcat.c -lpam -ldl -lpam_misc
```

Now we can run the program on any file, and just enter the password when prompted, as shown below:

```
$ authcat temp.asc
Password:
```

At this point, the file will be written to stdout, and can be piped to less or some equivalent if necessary. If there's a problem, the user will see this:

```
$ authcat temp.asc
Password:
authpam: auth error
```

The administrator can find out what error occurred by looking in the system logs where authentication information is kept (typically /var/log/secure or /var/log/auth.log) for the actual error.

Managing Privileges

The Superuser's privilege is vast. The superuser needs to be able to do literally anything to the system: read and write any file, reformat the hard disk, abuse the hardware, shut down the system, or any number of other things. As a result, only trusted system administrators should have the ability to run as the superuser. Yet, superuser privilege is also required to perform many other system services: to bind to a privileged port, to access hardware directly, or to even log in.

To mitigate the potential for a security bug in program that must run as root, the system provides processes the ability to release root privilege when necessary. It is even possible to temporarily release root privilege and take it back. This way, a daemon could choose to center all root-privileged operations in a separate helper process from the main daemon, or could perform all of its privileged operations at startup and drop all special privileges immediately afterwards.

Dropping and Regaining Privileges

There are eight different IDs associated with each Linux process: two each (for user and group) of four different types. Six are portable to most modern UNIX systems, while two are not. They are:

❑ **Real ID.** The real ID is the so-called "authoritative" ID; this is the ID that indicates which user or group you "really" are.

❑ **Effective ID.** The effective ID controls what privilege you currently have. This is the ID that changes, for example, when you run a setuid/setgid program.

❑ **Saved ID.** Under certain circumstances, when a process changes one of its IDs, the old ID is stored in the saved ID. This can be used for a process to "gain back" privilege it once had.

❑ **Filesystem ID.** This is the ID that is consulted to determine if you have permission to access a filesystem object. This ID is Linux-specific, and is mostly implemented to assist in securing NFS; generally, it should not be used, as the filesystem ID gets set automatically to the effective ID as that changes.

When changing IDs, the basic rule that must be followed is this: if none of the real, effective, or saved UIDs is 0 (or root), then the real ID can only be changed to the current value of the effective ID, and the effective ID can only be changed to the current value of the real or saved IDs. The superuser can change any of the IDs to any valid value.

The system will change the saved ID periodically as the other IDs change. It is set to the effective ID whenever the real ID changes, and whenever the effective ID is changed to a different value than the real ID. Additionally, it can be manually changed with the setresuid(2) and setresgid(2) calls (described below).

get*id and set*id

There are many functions available for retrieving and setting IDs. They can generally be classified into several families, each with variants for getting and setting IDs and separate sets of functions for setting user or group IDs. Except where noted, all of these are provided for by POSIX, and should be present on any modern UNIX. The families are:

❑ **{g,s}et[e]{u,g}id.** These functions (getuid, setuid, getgid, setgid, geteuid, seteuid, getegid, and setegid) operate on the effective ID (the e versions) or the real ID alone, providing a simple method of manipulating IDs. The get* functions return the ID requested; the set* functions return 0 on success, or -1 on error (with errno set appropriately). As a special case, setuid and setgid will change the effective and saved IDs as well as the real ID if the old ID is 0. The general form of these functions is as follows (using getuid and setuid):

```
uid_t getuid(void);

int setuid(uid_t uid);
```

❑ **setre{u,g}id.** These functions (setreuid and setregid) operate on the effective and real ID at the same time. Either parameter can be set to -1, which tells the function to leave the ID as it is (a very important feature; see below for an example of why). The return value is the same as with setuid(2) and company. These functions are defined as follows (using setreuid):

```
int setreuid(uid_t realuid, uid_t effectiveuid);
```

❑ **{g,s}etres{u,g}id.** These functions (getresuid, setresuid, getresgid, and setresgid) manipulate the real, effective, and saved ID all at once. The get* versions take pointers to uid_t or gid_t variables, which are filled in with the appropriate values. They always return 0 on success or -1 on error, with errno set, just as setuid(2) and company do.

❏ The `setres*id` calls extend the ability of regular users to manipulate their IDs; any of the IDs can be set to the current value of any of the other IDs. Unlike the other families described so far, these are not standard; they are only available on Linux systems with version 2.2 kernels or above, and may not be available on other UNIX systems. They are defined as follows (using `getresuid` and `setresuid`):

```
int getresuid(uid_t *realuid, uid_t *effectiveuid, uid_t *saveduid);
int setresuid(uid_t realuid, uid_t effectiveuid, uid_t saveduid);
```

❏ `setfs{u,g}id`. These functions allow the application to set the filesystem ID, and are defined identically to the `setuid` family. They are normally not used, and are specific to Linux.

Strategies for Managing Privilege

The goal in managing user privileges is to prevent an attacker from increasing his/her privileges upon compromising a program in some way, while allowing the program to still take advantage of these same privileges.

For daemons started at boot, or programs that are `setuid` or `setgid` root, the most obvious way of doing this is to perform all privileged operations at startup, and reducing privilege immediately thereafter. This is the easiest situation to handle; the service can start as root, perform whatever tasks are needed, and perform the following steps immediately afterwards:

```
/* newuid is the uid of the user to run as,
   newgid is the gid of the group to run as */

if (setgid(newgid))
   handle_error();
if (setuid(newuid))
   handle_error();
```

Because of the special case behavior of `setuid` and `setgid` when called by root, this causes all IDs to be set to the new user. Note that group privileges are dropped first; this preserves the proper behavior of `setgid(2)` when run as root, ensuring that the saved GID is set as well.

Programs that are `setuid` or `setgid`, but not to root, are a little different. For portable code that works on most UNIX systems, it's impossible to set the saved ID directly; this can be a security breach if the program assumes that privileges have been completely dropped, as an attacker can regain `setuid/setgid` privilege by setting the effective ID directly. To clear the saved ID, it's better to swap the real and effective IDs, and then set the real ID to the effective ID; this has the effect of setting the effective ID to the real ID, with the added benefit of setting the saved ID as well:

```
if (setreuid(geteuid(), getuid()))
   handle_error();
if (setreuid(geteuid(), -1))
   handle_error();
```

Of course, if portability isn't an issue and you have `setresuid`/`setresgid` available, they provide a direct way to drop privileges completely:

```
int myuid = getuid();

if (setresuid(-1, myuid, myuid))
  handle_error();
```

If elevated privileges are needed long-term, there still are ways to reduce exposure. By using the saved ID, the program can run unprivileged until the specific times that higher privilege is needed. If an attacker can compromise the application to convince it to perform actions on his/her behalf, but cannot persuade it to run arbitrary code, this greatly restricts the damage that can be done.

Again, this can be tricky if the program doesn't have root privilege available and portability is needed. The important thing is to save the effective ID before changing it, as it's not possible to find out the saved ID in a portable fashion:

```
int oldeuid;

oldeuid = geteuid();
if (seteuid(getuid()))
  handle_error();

/* do dangerous things */

if (seteuid(oldeuid))
  handle_error();
```

Using Cryptography Securely

File and user security are very useful, but they are often not enough. For example, file permissions will not protect data from the superuser, and user-level security alone affords no protection over a network. For these situations, *cryptography* is often needed. Cryptography is the practice of *encrypting* data, or encoding it with an algorithm such that a key is required to unlock it; it also covers other practices of secure information transfer.

In the past, strong cryptography was the exclusive domain of the military and high finance. Today's digital public networks have made cryptographic techniques indispensable to data security. Like the rest of the security trade, however, cryptographic programming is exact; one mistake can completely defeat the security of a product.

A Short Introduction to Cryptography

For most of its history, cryptography was of the form now known as 'symmetric cryptography'. This involves scrambling the plaintext message with an algorithm by means of some key; unscrambling the resulting ciphertext requires that the same key be invoked (or a separate key that can easily be derived from the original).

Even with modern innovations, symmetric cryptography remains important. Almost all encryption today involves a symmetric algorithm at some level; this is due to the increased speed and efficiency of modern symmetric cryptography.

Some examples of symmetric ciphers are DES and its cousin Triple DES, IDEA (used in PGP), Blowfish, and RC4.

Public-Key Crypto

Public-key cryptography (or asymmetric cryptography) was first introduced in the 1970s. These systems involve multiple keys, usually two, that are related in this way: messages encrypted with one of the keys can only be decrypted using the other key. It is essential that the decryption key cannot be derived easily from the encryption key; otherwise, the system constitutes a special case of symmetric cryptography, since both keys must be kept secret.

Under an asymmetric system, the encryption key can be made public, such that anyone can encrypt a message (thus the name 'public-key'). This greatly simplifies problems with key distribution; it's possible to post public keys on the Internet, or send them in plain sight of your adversaries.

While key distribution is much less of a problem, key authentication is more so. Public-key cryptography is more vulnerable to attacks where an attacker intercepts the public key, sending his/her own in its place. Thus, it is important to validate public keys in some way to ensure that the key really belongs to whom it claims.

As a practical matter (due to security and other problems with pure asymmetric cryptosystems), most 'public-key' cryptosystems actually only use the asymmetric cipher to encrypt a key for a traditional symmetric cipher, used only for a particular transaction or set of transactions (this is often called a *session key*). This has essentially the same result, assuming that the symmetric cipher chosen is as secure or more secure than the asymmetric one.

Some examples of public-key ciphers include DSA, RSA, and ElGamal ciphers.

Secure Hash Algorithms

You may recall that a 'hash algorithm' takes an input and produces a result suitable for indexing in a lookup table; the idea is that it is unlikely (to some degree) for two inputs to result in the same hash, making lookups by hash value more efficient than lookups by the original values.

A secure hash algorithm has these additional properties:

> It is difficult to find a plaintext that produces a given hash.

> It is difficult to find two plaintexts that produce the same hash value.

Secure hash functions have many uses. For example, passwords can be stored in hashed form; this prevents cracking the password, while still allowing the password to be validated. Secure hashes can also be used as identification tags for data; if a given set of data produces the same hash, it is most likely the same data that was hashed before. In this way, secure hashes are similar to, although more robust than, checksums, and can be used for this purpose; traditional checksum algorithms, however, usually do not provide the guarantees above, and can usually be spoofed easily with some concerted effort.

Examples of secure hash functions include MD5 and SHA. The `crypt(3)` algorithm also attempts to fill the role of a secure hash function, although its security is much lower.

On Writing Custom/Proprietary Algorithms

Many programs implement their own proprietary cryptographic techniques, rather than use open, well-tested standards. This is almost always a grave mistake.

Almost all known secure cryptographic algorithms are widely published and studied. Contrary to popular belief, this provides better security, not worse. Secret algorithms rarely remain so for long; after all, computer implementations of the algorithm provide analysts (and attackers) with a working example they can reverse-engineer and disassemble.

Open, published systems have the advantage that legitimate security researchers can examine, criticize, and break the system if possible; the analysis can be used to improve the system or design better ones. And if an algorithm can withstand the penetrating analysis of the world's best minds for years, it's likely that it will be more than adequate for almost any use.

Additionally, home-grown algorithms written by inexperienced cryptographers often fall into the same traps over and over again. The shelves are full of systems with 'new unbreakable security features' that turn out to be rediscoveries of systems that have been broken for years. As an example, the encryption in several Microsoft Office products long ago was so easy to break, one cracking tool implemented delay loops so it would look like it was working hard, saving Microsoft some embarrassment.

Thus, when implementing a cryptographic solution, the best course is to use a well-known and well-tested system. If possible, keep as much of the encryption as possible in external libraries with established track records.

Some Common Techniques

Researchers have developed several applications for cryptography that go beyond the traditional 'keep a message safe from prying eyes' application. This is especially true with recent advancements in the field. A few of the most common cryptographic protocols are detailed below.

Digital Signatures

Digital signatures are implemented using public-key cryptography. Essentially, they work by standing public-key cryptography on its head; a message is 'encrypted' with a secret key, and 'decrypted' with a public key. If the public key can decrypt the message, it proves that it was encrypted by the private key.

Full-fledged encryption and decryption are not really necessary, since the message itself is not private. The only requirement is that a message 'encrypted' with the private key not be 'decryptable' with anything other than the public key. Additionally, the message itself is rarely used, for speed and security reasons. Instead, the message is hashed with a secure hash function, combined with identifying information (such as the current date and time), and 'encrypted' with the private key; the recipient can hash his or her own copy of the message, decrypt the signature with the public key (thus proving the source), compare the hashes and make sure they are identical (thus proving which message was signed), and note the other information.

Password Authentication

The problem of password authentication is actually two problems in one. The initial problem lies in password storage; how can passwords be stored securely? Once that problem is solved, a further difficulty presents itself: how can authentication information be transported over a possibly insecure network?

The standard solution to the first problem is to use a secure hash function. Passwords are stored as hashes, not as plaintext strings; since it is difficult to find a string that will generate the same hash, reading the hash from storage tells a potential attacker nothing. Validation routines can then accept a password from the user, hash it, and compare the hashes; if they are identical, then the user has supplied the proper password.

Most systems use an additional technique called *salting* the password. This involves calculating a number of random bits (the 'salt') and attaching them to the plaintext password before hashing it; the salt is then stored with the hash in the password store, and is attached in the same way to a user-supplied password during the authentication process. The salt does not add any real secrecy to the password itself, since it is stored in plain text, but it does ensure that the same password with a different salt will produce a different hash. This protects users who use the same password on multiple systems, and makes dictionary attacks more difficult; precomputed dictionaries would have to be calculated for each possible hash value, which can be prohibitively expensive given a large enough salt.

So far, we have been assuming that users can transport their passwords securely to the system. This is mostly true when logging on directly through the console, but is certainly not true when logging on over a network, which can be easily tapped. Password hashing helps the situation somewhat, as it keeps plaintext passwords off the network; however, simple systems that simply pass a hash in place of a password are still open to attack from modified client software that replays hashes sniffed off the network.

There are many solutions to this problem, with varying degrees of security. Challenge-response protocols, for example, typically treat the hashed password as a key in a symmetric algorithm; the two sides send plaintext and encrypted data between themselves, and if the unencrypted data matches the data decrypted with the hashed password, then the user is authenticated. These protocols work, but can be vulnerable to sophisticated attacks. Microsoft uses challenge-response protocols extensively to authenticate many of their protocols, including Windows NT domain authentication and PPTP.

Digital signatures can provide another solution. One way to do this is to have the host store public keys instead of password hashes for each user. When the user wants to log in, the host sends a random string, and the user signs that string and sends it back. The user is authenticated if the signature is validated with the proper public key. Just as with challenge-response protocols, a sophisticated attack is possible; additionally, there is the ever-present problem with public-key cryptography of man-in-the-middle attacks if public keys are not verified properly. This is the method used by SSL to authenticate servers (and users, where that is supported); ssh also uses a variant of this in RSA authentication mode.

Session Encryption

The problem of authenticating becomes much easier if the data channel between the host and the user can be secured; in this case, it is sufficient to simply send a plaintext password over the secure channel and hash it on the host end.

Session encryption typically involves some form of authentication, followed by a secure key exchange for a symmetric key algorithm. Two keys need to be exchanged, one for each direction, to prevent certain attacks. Then, every packet's contents are encrypted before being sent on the wire.

This method is used by several systems. Most SSL-enabled solutions use a variant of this; the plaintext password method is transported over an encrypted connection set up with SSL. When ssh is used in simple password mode, it acts this way as well. Finally, any encrypted VPN, such as the IPSec standards, make this possible without any session hassles; the packets are encrypted as a natural part of routing them across the Internet to their destination.

Random Number Generation on Linux

Random numbers are often required in cryptographic applications for such things as key generation, message padding (to hide the length of messages), and so on. 'Randomness', here, is a relative term; most computers outside of military applications only have access to better or worse approximations of randomness (and many people even wonder if the military has access to anything like true randomness).

Normal programs have no problem generating pseudo-random numbers from functions like rand(3); however, security applications should never use these. If an attacker can guess the sequence of numbers generated by a security system's random number generator, he or she can often use that sequence to extract passwords, private keys, and other information from that system. Unfortunately, GNU libc's rand(3) function was not designed for that kind of robustness; very few vendors provide implementations that do.

Linux provides an alternative source for random numbers where security is an important factor: the 'random' character device. This device acts as an interface to the kernel's internal randomness generator, which generates an 'entropy pool' from random background events in various device drivers and other sources not under the system's control.

There are two device files that hook into the random driver: /dev/random and /dev/urandom. The /dev/random device returns random bytes from the entropy pool only; if the pool is emptied, the device will block until more bytes are available. Conversely, /dev/urandom never blocks; if the entropy pool runs out or is empty, it will generate random bits from its own random number generator. The entropy pool is considered to be a better source of "true randomness", and is preferred for long-life applications such as user key generation; however, the random number generator is considered to be cryptographically secure, and can act as a 'second-best' source for 'temporary' uses, such as session keys.

Reading from these devices is just like reading from other devices; they return a stream of random bytes. Information can be written to them in 512-byte blocks; this information is treated as a random seed for the generator. Generally, Linux takes care of initializing the seed for you during system startup.

As an example, the following C code will return a number suitable for use as a session key for a 128-bit algorithm:

```c
/* Remember: this isn't a string! */
unsigned char key[16];
int randomfile;
ssize_t bytes;

randomfile = open("/dev/urandom", O_RDONLY);
bytes = read(randomfile, key, 16);
if (bytes != 16)
{
    /* We need 16 bytes; anything else is an error. */
    handle_error();
}
```

It should be noted that most applications should get random numbers from the more traditional sources; cryptographic security is not required, for example, to shuffle a deck of cards for a solitaire game. This preserves the entropy pool for applications that need it (such as key generators). Additionally, programs that use /dev/[u]random are generally not portable to other operating systems.

Key Management

Another major source of security problems is insecure key management. Any key information that is intended to be kept secret (symmetric keys or private keys) must be treated carefully in order to ensure that it is not inadvertently leaked.

Obviously, simple mistakes are a common source. Secret key files should be kept in files with proper file system permissions: specifically, all world permissions should be turned off (and preferably group permissions as well unless you need them). Very sensitive keys should be kept on removable media, only mounted when the key is needed; this is obviously not always practical, but should especially be considered in situations where a secret key is only needed intermittently.

Prudence suggests that issues such as backup security should also be considered whenever keys are stored, as insecure backups form a particularly easy target for compromise. It is better to not keep keys in shared memory or pass them over any other IPC method if possible, although network sockets are, obviously, especially dangerous in this regard.

Additionally, keys should never be embedded into code; they should always be generated by the end user, or at least supplied in a configuration file. If the key is impossible to change, and if ever gets compromised, programs that rely on this key cannot be secured without replacing the key. Vendor-supplied keys are also attractive targets for attacks, as the compromise of a single key can open up the program's entire userbase. As an exception, it is allowable (and even valuable) for a vendor to supply a public key for the purpose of secure communication with the vendor; even here, however, the key should be replaceable if needed.

It is often useful to store keys encrypted with a symmetric algorithm, using as the key a secure hash of a pass phrase entered by the user. This prevents stolen key files from being immediately usable; with a strong enough pass phrase and a strong algorithm, the key could be safe even if stolen. Using weak encryption techniques to secure the keys, or embedding a 'master key' somewhere unprotected, gives little more security than simply storing the key in plaintext, and can create a false sense of security.

Keys should be long enough to resist brute-force attacks. In general, symmetric algorithms with key lengths of 128 bits are considered secure for almost all purposes. All current asymmetric algorithms are vulnerable to easier attacks than brute-force, due to the way they work; the recommended key length is dependent on the algorithm. For RSA, ElGamal, and DSA (the three most popular asymmetric algorithms at this time), key lengths of 2048 bits should be sufficient.

Bear in mind, that at the time of writing, several countries restrict the use or export of encryption technologies with long key lengths; you should therefore check into the legalities of encryption use and export when designing your application.

Secure Network Programming

Traditional host-based systems are relatively easy to secure. If all of the processing and data management take place inside the host, it becomes difficult to 'tap' the host for passwords or snoop inside internal communications. A system administrator could do well by simply watching for suspicious damage to terminal lines and locking the computer room door.

Networking has drastically changed that ideal. Tapping no longer requires arcane alterations to physical cables; any computer on a shared-bandwidth network (such as unswitched Ethernet) can set a hardware flag and get a complete copy of all traffic, even traffic between two unrelated systems. Switched networks are little safer; with a bit of manipulation of the underlying protocols, man-in-the-middle attacks (where the attacker inserts him or herself in between the two sides of a communication channel, eavesdropping as the traffic goes by) are possible.

Writing Protocols

It's important, therefore, to design network protocols to be easy to secure. Even if security is not an immediate goal, designing a securable protocol makes sense in the long run; goals can change in mid-project, and protocols can find applications far beyond their original intent.

Use Standards Where Possible

The first step in designing a protocol is often choosing not to. Many standard protocols exist, and most established ones have well-known security implications. This is especially true of popular, extensible protocols. Consider whether one of the standard protocols could fit the task, or if one could work with some extensions.

HTTP is particularly attractive as a protocol. Its security implications are well-studied, it works well with all firewalls and all proxy servers, and is easily secured via SSL. Many high-quality servers – including Apache, easily the most popular server application on the Internet outside of DNS – can handle the low-level details of the protocol, and the APIs for programming these servers are well-established (CGI, PHP, mod_perl, and so on). It supports atomic two-way (query-response style) requests as well as more persistent transactions through cookie-based sessions and keep-alive.

Whether HTTP or some other protocol, there is likely to be a protocol out there that will do what you need it to. Besides the obvious benefits of not reinventing the wheel, standard protocols are time-tested to be good, secure protocols. If you can, therefore, use a standard protocol.

Firewall Friendliness

Protocols intended to be used across trust domains, or protocols used over the Internet, will inevitably come into contact with some firewall/proxy security system. Success in these arenas will depend largely on how well the protocol cooperates with these systems.

There are several kinds of security systems:

❑   **Packet-filtering firewalls.** These simple devices are often implemented as a feature on routers. They allow packets to move back and forth based on a set of rules that can block packets by port number and IP address; more advanced packet filters can filter on other considerations, and can dynamically add rules based on other conditions.

❑   **Masquerade/NAT firewalls.** Firewalls that implement IP masquerade or network address translation (NAT) perform the same functions as packet filters; however, in addition, they rewrite the source addresses of the packets to make them all appear to come from some shared address range, or the firewall itself, instead of the originating computer. Sessions are identified using several means; incoming packets are identified as belonging to a session and are forwarded to the proper hosts.

❑   **Proxy servers.** These systems act as explicit relays for various protocols. A system wishing to make a connection contacts the proxy server and requests a connection to a remote system; the proxy server performs the connection for the client ('by proxy', as it were), and returns the results. Proxy servers can perform security tasks, such as validation, filtering of unwanted data, and authenticated access. Proxying can be done for both transaction-response protocols (such as HTTP) and persistent connections (such as SMTP, POP3, or FTP).

❑   **Transparent proxies.** These servers combine elements of proxy servers and NAT firewalls. Like proxy servers, they perform connections for clients and return the results. Like NAT firewalls, this is done transparently; the client does not know that the request is being proxied. This differs from simple NAT firewalls in that the translation is done at a higher level; therefore, transparent proxies provide the benefits of a proxy server (authenticated access, data filtering, etc.) in addition to the benefits of NAT firewalls.

Ideally, protocol designs should take all of these considerations into account. If possible, the following guidelines should be followed:

❑ Where possible, use a single TCP connection. UDP is problematic on many networks, as it's not generally possible to track sessions or otherwise manage the ability to connect through UDP except for protocol-specific hacks. Similarly, systems that require multiple TCP connections can run into problems, especially with server 'dial-back' services (where the server tries to connect back to the client).

❑ Never assume that either the client's or the server's idea of the client's IP address or port number is correct. Don't embed the IP address or port number in the protocol stream, or require connections to come from a particular client port.

❑ Consider adding explicit proxy support, either through a custom proxy server or through a generic system such as SOCKS. Proxy servers don't have to be complex; one could simply act as a simple intermediary between the client and the server. If desired, the proxy could take advantage of its position to enhance the protocol in some way, perhaps by caching requests at the proxy.

Web Application Security Issues

Much Internet development today centers around the world wide web, easily the most popular service on the Internet. The Web has, in many cases, moved far beyond its original goals of hyperlinked information to encompass virtual storefronts and complex application environments.

As the Web has grown, so have the security issues associated with it. Browsers and servers have grown more capable, providing many hooks for attackers to use. Browser makers seem, in many cases, indifferent to the problems their new hooks cause. And with credit card numbers, private tracking information, and other identifying information traveling across the Web today, attackers have a lot of incentives to find those hooks.

In most cases, it's simply not possible for users to be able to manage their security; the issues are too complex, the environment is too flexible, and most browsers (for better or worse) do not allow users easy access to important security information. Most of the responsibility for security must therefore fall on the Web developer, who must code defensively to try and prevent security problems.

Session Management Issues

Often, sensitive data is controlled through session management on a Web server. After being authenticated (either using HTTP authentication or a forms-based system), a token of some kind is attached to the session and embedded somehow in each Web page; the Web server determines if certain actions or data are accessible by consulting the token. (Cookies and hidden form fields are two popular ways to achieve this.)

Authentication is a considerable problem on the Web. The simplest methods – simple HTML forms or HTTP Basic authentication – are also the least secure, as they transmit passwords in clear text over the Internet. HTTP supports Digest authentication, which uses MD5 to hash the password before sending it; this is little better, however, as an attacker can simply use modified client software to sniff the hash from the network and resend it.

For security on sessions transmitting sensitive information, using SSL session encryption is mandatory; (See below for information on using SSL). Under these circumstances, clear text authentication isn't a serious problem, since passwords can't be sniffed from the network. However, in situations where SSL cannot be provided or isn't justifiable (for whatever reason), there are steps that can be taken to improve authentication security.

For example, a login form could use a simple challenge-response protocol to prevent passwords from being transmitted. With a system like this, the form could have a random challenge byte stored in a hidden form field. The submit button would then not submit the form directly; instead, it might concatenate the challenge and the password, hash them with a secure hash, clear the password field in the request, and submit the form with the hashed password only. For password storage requirements on the server, the password might have to be hashed twice; once to generate the password hash as stored on the server, and a second time to include the challenge.

The Cross-Site Scripting Problem

The greater capabilities of modern browsers have led to a new and different problem with Web security. The name 'cross-site scripting' is a bit of a misnomer, as it covers more than just attacks through scripts; however, it is the common name for whole classes of attacks that attempt to exploit trust between a user and a site.

The problem arises when an otherwise trusted site incorporates dynamic data supplied by its users into itself without fully verifying the input. Malicious users can exploit this problem by supplying data to the site that has unexpected side effects when displayed. These effects usually involve sending data to the attacker via another, less-well-trusted site, although they can (in rare cases) use the site itself to transmit information.

An example is in order. Suppose that a news site takes comments from users on its stories and displays them as part of each story. One way to implement this would be (in Perl):

```perl
# WARNING: this is insecure!  Use with caution!

# The @comments array contains an array of hashes, with the comment
# attributes in each hash.

foreach $comment (@comments)
{
  print "<p>Comment by ", $$comment{"name"}, "</p>\n";
  print "<p>\n";
  print $$comment{"text"}, "\n";
  print "</p>\n";
}
```

This code looks entirely reasonable, and it isn't really insecure – by itself. But consider what would happen if a user submits a comment like this:

```
You know what I think of this article?  The author is a:
</p>
<img src="http://www.example.com/offensive.jpg">
<p>
```

If the site did nothing to validate comments, then the off-site picture would be displayed as part of the page; indeed, to an untrained eye, it might even appear to be a part of the story itself, and be endorsed by the site.

While humorous, this example does not do justice to the possibilities. The <IMG> tag could just as easily have been a <SCRIPT> tag; with some knowledge of the site, the script could have pulled other information from the site and submitted it to a server controlled by the attacker. Within a <FORM> tag, the attacker's input could alter the behavior of the form, even to the extent of causing the information to go to a different source. Or, the <IMG> could have been a 1x1 transparent GIF with a cookie attached instead of an offensive image; by sprinkling news sites with comments such as these, an attacker could build up impressive profiles of users, even possibly linking them to real identities, and use that information to violate their privacy or cheat them in some way.

There are steps that can be taken to help prevent these kinds of attacks:

Always validate input from outside sources. This includes documents pulled from other sites, such as RSS/RDF news summaries, any input from forms (even from hidden form fields – it's trivial to POST arbitrary values into any URL), cookies, or file uploads.

Strictly define allowed data types. By rejecting anything but valid input (instead of rejecting only known invalid input), you prevent attackers from coming up with novel ways to bypass your validator.

Always validate input after decoding it, not before. This prevents attackers from pushing URL-encoded variants of exploit code through.

Always specify the charset for every dynamic page (and, preferably, every page). Browsers use different default charsets depending on many varied factors. Exploits have been written that exploit charset ambiguity to push innocuous-looking text into a site that, when displayed on a certain charset, produces a cross-site activation effect.

Standard Network Cryptography Tools

Networked applications often must rely on cryptography to provide security. As a result, several standards have arisen to assist developers use cryptography over networks; these standards are usually easy to implement, interoperate well, and are mostly transparent to the application.

SSL/TLS

SSL was one of the first general-purpose encryption systems for the Internet, and remains the most popular today. It was originally developed to facilitate secure Web transactions, but it can be applied to any TCP-based protocol with little effort.

ssh

The ssh utility (and associated sshd service) provides a feature-complete secure replacement for rsh services. Many applications use rsh to implement networked services, as it works well with the UNIX tools philosophy, but rsh is very insecure; by replacing it with ssh, these applications instantly gain encrypted sessions, two-way host authentication, and optional public-key user authentication.

Additionally, ssh has the handy ability to perform *port forwarding* across any secure connection; this allows insecure protocols to be forwarded over a secure ssh channel, keeping their contents from being sent on the Internet in plaintext. Any simple TCP-based protocol can be forwarded over ssh in this way.

Using ssh to perform a networked service usually involves simply executing the ssh command and reading the standard output (and standard error for errors). For example, a remote directory listing can be obtained as follows:

```
/* Be careful about unvalidated input here! */
int retval;
char cmd[256];
FILE *result;

snprintf(cmd, 256, "ssh -l %s ls %d", remuser, dirpath);
result = popen(cmd, "r");
if (result == NULL)
  handle_error();

/* Read the result. */

pclose(result);
```

General Security Tips and Techniques

A *race condition* exists whenever two events assume some relationship between them, which is not guaranteed to be true. They are common bugs in multi-threaded and multi-tasking applications, where two threads may attempt to grab some resource at the same time (with a random thread 'winning the race') if they are not explicitly synchronized.

In security situations, race conditions almost always involve an attacker performing operations at the same time a secure program is running. The target is a small window of time between when a program tests a certain condition and when it acts on the results of that test; if the condition can be changed during that time, the program may act incorrectly, resulting in a security breach.

For example, the setuid and setgid bits are ignored on scripts on most UNIX systems (including Linux) because of a race condition. Scripts are executed as a two-part process: the kernel first checks the script and opens it to determine what interpreter to run, and then runs the interpreter, which opens the script a second time. The setuid/setgid check must be done in the first step, since the kernel must set the effective ID before running the interpreter.

An attacker can take advantage of this by executing a setuid/setgid script through a symlink, and changing the link to point to a different script immediately after the permissions are checked by the kernel. The interpreter, when it runs, then follows the changed symlink and executes a different script than the one expected - with the privileges granted by the kernel to the first script.

Race conditions are likely whenever a program tests for some condition before performing some action. Whenever possible, the resource being tested should be locked first, and the lock should not be released until it can be considered safe for the condition to change. For example, a program may need to open a file, but only if the permissions are correct; to prevent a race condition, the program could open the file with O_EXCL set before testing its permissions. If the permissions are wrong, the program could simply close the file and continue; if they are correct, the file is already open, preventing an attacker from substituting a different file after the permissions are checked. There are many other mechanisms possible for implementing locks, including System V semaphores, lock files, and the lockf(3), flock(2), and fcntl(2) system calls.

Problems With the Environment

Environment variables are handy ways for the system (or users) to pass information to child processes. Unfortunately, they must essentially be treated as untrusted input; since any calling process can manipulate the environment passed to the child, there is no way of authenticating the source of the variables.

Setuid and setgid programs (and their child processes) are particularly vulnerable to this, because they manage elevated privileges on behalf of a user. A utility may, for example, use the file pointed to by the TMPFILE environment variable as a temporary file, deleting any old one in the process; this is normally safe (from a security standpoint) because the utility runs with regular privilege. But if a setuid root program calls the utility to perform some task, and an attacker can execute the setuid program with TMPFILE set to /etc/passwd, then the attacker gains the ability to delete /etc/passwd, either as a destructive act or in preparation to replace the file with a less secure one.

As a result, it's common practice for security-sensitive programs to use execve(2) when executing a child program, supplying an environment that has been completely sanitized. Ideally, none of the values in the replacement environment come from the old one; all of them should be built from common system defaults or from otherwise trusted sources.

Special Environment Variables

In addition to the risk associated with trusting environment variables, certain variables contain higher risks than others, because of the unexpected side effects they make possible.

*LD_**

The dynamic linker on Linux (and several other operating systems) uses several environment variables to control its behavior. In particular, the LD_PRELOAD variable tells the dynamic linker to load the libraries listed in it before loading any other libraries needed, while LD_LIBRARY_PATH specifies an alternate path to use when searching for libraries to load.

Attackers can take advantage of these settings to take control of a dynamically linked program. By pointing LD_PRELOAD at a custom library, the attacker can provide his/her own versions of library calls that are used by the program, making them execute code of the attacker's choosing. Similarly, by using LD_LIBRARY_PATH, the attacker can place his own custom libraries ahead of the standard ones in the search path, with a similar effect.

Many UNIX systems (including Linux) mitigate the problem to a degree by ignoring LD_PRELOAD when executing setuid/setgid programs, and by only loading libraries from LD_LIBRARY_PATH under certain conditions. This only makes the problem less severe; if the setuid/setgid program calls another program with normal permissions, then the restrictions are not enforced. Thus, it is good practice to always clear these environment variables before executing any programs in a sensitive environment.

IFS

Many shells, including bash (the default shell on most Linux distributions), use the IFS environment variable to determine how to split command line arguments. It is expected to contain all of the possible characters that can be used to separate arguments. By default, whitespace characters are used. Since the shell is often invoked by system calls (for example, when calling system(2)), setting this can have interesting repercussions.

For example, a program may execute ls to get directory listings under certain circumstances. Even if it validates the directory string passed, it could be fooled with a line like this:

```
/tmp*&&*rm*-f*/etc/passwd
```

To the untrained eye, this looks like a really strange (but valid) path name. But if IFS is set to *, this gets interpreted like this:

```
/tmp && rm -f /etc/passwd
```

If the systems call looks something like this:

```
snprintf(buf, buflen, "ls %s", dir);
system(buf);
```

then the attacker has just caused the program to delete /etc/passwd.

For safety's sake, therefore, this variable should always be unset before executing external programs.

PATH

Remember that the PATH variable is also unsafe. If PATH is set to `.:/bin:/usr/bin` and the program tries to run `ls`, all an attacker needs is an executable in the current directory named `ls` to take over. PATH should always be set to a sane value before executing other programs, usually only including trusted directories and never including the current directory; additionally, the weakness here can be lessened by calling external programs with absolute paths where possible.

Temporary File Handling

The use of temporary files can be an unexpected source of security problems. This is especially true when privileged programs make use of a common temporary directory, such as `/tmp`.

The problem is that shared temporary directories are usually set to be world-writable; thus, attackers can set traps in these directories to catch unwary programs. For example, one common trick is to guess the name of a future temporary file some program will use and create a symlink to some other file; when the program attempts to create the temporary file, it will follow the symlink and overwrite the file it points to. If this happens to root, any file on the system can be removed in this way; the goal may be denial of service or destruction of some sensitive data, or the attacker may be able to substitute a file of his/her own choosing for the destroyed file, allowing greater access into the system.

When working with temporary files, therefore, these guidelines are useful:

Consider trying to get along without using temporary files, if you can. Most other IPC mechanisms are preferable for passing data between processes. Using temporary storage to minimize memory usage is sometimes necessary; at the same time, it might be worth profiling your application to gauge the memory savings (and the need for it) against the security costs.

Consider structuring your program to use a non-shared area for temporary files. If possible, create a directory in the user's home directory for housing temporary files.

If more than one user can access a temporary directory at the same time, the sticky bit should be set on that directory (see above, under 'File Permissions'). This prevents attackers from deleting or otherwise manipulating the temporary files of other users, as well as disabling some traps.

Never follow symlinks when creating temporary files in shared areas. This can be done with the O_NOFOLLOW flag when running on Linux 2.2 or later; if running on earlier versions (or on other UNIXes), you can use `stat` to test for symlinks before opening the file, but be warned that this method is vulnerable to a race condition.

Avoid overwriting files that already exist in shared temporary directories (unless you expect them to exist). This can be done by creating files with O_CREAT | O_EXCL, which will fail if the file already exists.

Create a subdirectory in the shared temporary area, and put all your temporary files in there. The directory should be created to not be group-accessible or world-accessible (mode 0700). The call to `mkdir(2)` will fail if the file exists; if this happens, use a different filename rather than attempting to remove the file.

When creating directories and files, use random names. Don't base the names entirely on the time of day, process ID, username, or any other easily guessable parameter; all names should include some hard-to-guess component, such as a call to `rand(3)`. Cryptographic randomness isn't required; the idea is to prevent guessing of filenames in order to set traps.

Honor the TMPDIR environment variable, if it exists. Many administrators and users will set TMPDIR to point to an alternate temporary area to implement tighter security. You shouldn't necessarily trust TMPDIR; all of the previous items should apply to TMPDIR just as much as to /tmp. In particular, before attempting to use TMPDIR, check that you have permission to use it, and that the sticky bit is set if it is world-writable.

Using "chroot"

UNIX provides a very handy security tool in the chroot(2) system call. This call changes the apparent location of the root directory within the file system for the current process and all child processes. It cannot be reversed, even by root (although root can sometimes reach outside the virtual root file system under certain circumstances). This can be used as a last resort barrier to attackers; if the worst happens and someone is able to obtain unauthorized access through a program or service, the attacker will be unable to touch anything outside the chroot jail.

It is important to realize that *all* outside files are inaccessible to processes in a chroot jail; thus, the virtual root directory must contain certain files in order for the system to function. The following files should be provided for a minimal environment:

/etc/passwd	This file should contain as little information as possible: only the user IDs that are used inside the jail, and possibly root as well. No encrypted passwords should be present in the file; the password fields can be left blank or marked with an 'X'.
/etc/group	The same rules as for /etc/passwd apply here.
/dev/null	This should be a null device file, with the same major and minor number as the real /dev/null.
/lib/libc.so.* and /lib/ld *	This is a copy of the standard C library and the dynamic linker. Other libraries may be needed as well. Alternatively, all programs running in the chroot jail could be statically linked; this is slightly more secure.

In addition, any files that your application needs will have to be copied into the virtual root somewhere. You can load information from files outside the virtual root before calling chroot(2), but you must not hold any files open outside the virtual root after the call, as they can be used to break out.

Programs sensitive enough to require chroot(2) should also use syslog(3) to log information; unfortunately, syslogd on Linux operates through a UNIX socket in /dev/log, which won't be available within a chroot jail. Recent versions of syslogd solve this problem by supporting the -a option; this tells syslogd to open additional UNIX sockets and receive log information from them. Point this at the /dev/log path within the virtual root; when the application calls syslog(3), the call will continue to use /dev/log, which will point to the new socket within the jail.

For added effect, you can drop privileges after entering the chroot, switching to a unique user ID set up especially for this program. Some methods of breaking out of the jail involve root access, so this will make the jail even more secure. Additionally, important files in the jail could be set read-only to the user, keeping an attacker from being able to do damage within the jail.

After all this, the actual code mechanics for going into chroot mode (and switching IDs) is simple:

```
int uid, gid;   /* User and group IDs of the user and group to switch to. */
char *path;     /* Path of the chroot jail. */
int retval;

if (chroot(path))
  handle_error();

if (setregid(gid, gid))
  handle_error();
if (setreuid(uid, uid))
  handle_error();
```

At this point, the program is running in a chroot jail as the specified user and group.

Language-Specific Issues

Without a doubt, the number one security problem associated with C and C++ is the problem of buffer overflows. In fact, many security experts consider buffer overflow issues to be the top security issue in any language, because of C's popularity as a systems language and as an implementation language for interpreters for other languages.

How Buffer Overflows Work

A buffer overflow situation is created when the program copies some information into a fixed-length buffer. If the information is larger than the buffer, the standard C memory and string routines won't notice, and will happily trash any information beyond the buffer. This can be used by an attacker to overwrite information about function call returns, tricking the program into executing the wrong code.

This can be exploited in many different ways; for an example, let's consider what can happen when a buffer overflow occurs on an Intel-based system. Normally, when this happens, the program will crash with a SIGSEGV on UNIX systems; Windows users see the same thing when programs fail with a GPF (General Protection Fault) dialog box or the infamous 'blue screen of death'.

Consider how memory is allocated for a function call in C on Intel systems. Normally, all variables with function scope, as well as function parameters, are stored on the *stack*, a temporary holding place in memory for very short-term storage. The stack is normally managed by the CPU itself, and is arranged as a LIFO (last-in-first-out) queue; it is usually set up so that the top of the memory block is used first, with the current location on the stack moving downwards as items are added.

When a function call is made, each of the parameters is pushed onto the stack first. Then the call is made; the CPU implements function calls by pushing the current location of the instruction pointer (IP) onto the stack as well. The first task of the function, once it gains control, is to allocate more portions of the stack for its local variables.

So, a function call that looks like this:

```
void foo(char *bar)
{
  char baz[16] = "quux";

  [...]
}
```

ends up looking like this on the stack:

```
baz ------------>return addr->bar---->
quux\0-----------[void *]-----[char *]
```

It should be fairly clear now where the problem lies. In our example above, if data longer than 16 bytes were copied into the `baz` buffer, then the overflow would overwrite the pointer back to the calling routine, which would be interpreted as the code address to return to when the function returns. This usually causes a SIGSEGV; usually, the pointer is overwritten with garbage that points to an invalid memory location.

Now consider what happens if the data being copied is supplied by an attacker. If the string being written into the buffer just happened to have a valid address stored in it, the program would jump to that location instead of crashing, and execute from there. Since the buffer is itself stored in a valid address in memory, the address in the buffer could point to, say, the beginning of the buffer.

If the buffer contained valid machine code, the program would execute code unintentionally, with all of the privileges the program itself holds. A common thing to do is to include code that calls `exec(2)` to run a shell; if the program were running as root, the resulting shell would have full root privilege.

These are the basic mechanics of a stack-based buffer overflow on Intel systems; almost the same mechanics can be pursued on many other hardware platforms. Similar attacks are also possible using heap buffers. For more information on the low-level aspects of call semantics, including stack traces and the like, see Chapters 6 and 11.

How to Avoid Buffer Overflow Problems

Buffer overflow exploits are caused by blind copying of untrusted data; that is, data that does not originate from a trusted source. Therefore, the obvious solution to the problem is to always check that untrusted data is not longer than the buffer it is being copied into.

The easiest way to do this is to avoid using library routines to receive data that do not accept a maximum length argument. For example, `strcpy(3)` should never be used in sensitive situations; instead, use `strncpy(3)`.

Unsafe	Safe
strcpy	strncpy
strcat	strncat
sprintf	snprintf
gets	fgets

Other library functions, while safe in and of themselves, can be used unsafely. For example, the `scanf` family of functions provides the `%s` format specifier, indicating a whitespace-delimited string to be found in the input. Since any string found is copied into a buffer, a maximum field length should always be provided when dealing with untrusted input; this ensures that an attacker cannot simply provide a long input without spaces and overflow the buffer.

Beyond this, you should always be careful when working with buffers directly. If the buffer is treated as a null-terminated string, always ensure that the null terminator is there; in particular, some of the above 'safe' functions will not add a null byte if the maximum buffer length is reached. Better yet, always explicitly zero out buffers with memset(3) or some other method. Whenever possible, it is best to work with buffer lengths instead of relying solely on the NULL terminator.

Error Checking and Exceptions

Previous chapters discussed error handling, but the lessons there bear repeating. Buffer overflow conditions are only one popular case where attackers take advantage of lax error checking. It's fairly common in C to simply ignore error return codes or to blindly assume that function calls succeed; repeated checking of errors with every call can be tedious. By designing a comprehensive error handling facility into your program that can deal with errors gracefully, you can reduce the tedium considerably.

C++ programmers have an advantage in this regard: exceptions. With exceptions, you no longer need to check for success at every function call, since the compiler will interrupt the normal program flow for you when something goes wrong, alleviating the need for most explicit checking of results. Better yet, the C++ standard libraries provide extensive exception support for most of their operations.

When writing your own C++ code, implementing exception support at an early stage is recommended. It's better to throw an exception if you can when something doesn't work properly, rather than pass a return code back that must be checked.

Perl

Perl has a special mode called *taint mode* for handling untrusted user input. It can be turned on using the -T option, either on the command line or in the #! line.

When in taint mode, data from untrusted sources like command-line arguments, environment variables, locale information, file input, and certain system calls – are marked as 'tainted'. Tainted data cannot be used to invoke a subshell command (except through system or exec), or to modify a directory, file, or process; attempting to do so results in a runtime error. Tainting is 'contagious'; data generated from tainted data is itself tainted.

Variables containing tainted data can be untainted by clearing out the tainted data and setting the variable to clean data. In particular, this works with environment variables, with some exceptions; for example, Perl will 're-taint' $ENV{"PATH"} if you set it to include any world-writable directories.

Perl does not pass taint through a regular expression substring match (using parentheses and positional parameters); this provides a mechanism for untainting data. This is intentional; the intent is that you would use a regular expression to pull 'safe' information out of tainted data. Thus, when untainting data, it's best to write a regular expression that tests to make sure the resulting untainted data is truly safe.

Taint mode also turns on other security checks that are helpful. For a more complete description, see the man page for perlsec(3).

Setuid/Setgid Perl Scripts

Perl supports setuid and setgid scripts on almost all UNIXes, including Linux. It does this by detecting the setuid/setgid permissions on scripts after it is loaded and using a wrapper program to securely execute the script with elevated privileges. This avoids the race condition present in the kernel's script execution method. To provide additional protection, Perl automatically turns on taint mode when a script is run setuid or setgid.

Python

Python provides a class called REXec, which provides similar functionality to eval, execfile, exec, and import. Code executed through REXec, however, is not allowed to import modules or call functions except for those deemed safe.

REXec provides two sets of functions: r_ functions, which disallow access to the standard file streams (sys.stdin, sys.stdout, and sys.stderr), and s_ functions, which provide restricted access to the standard file streams.

Within each group, the same functions are provided (except for r_open, which does not have a corresponding s_open. They are (using the r_ versions):

r_eval(code)	This evaluates the Python code expression, returning the expression's return value.
r_exec(code)	This evaluates the Python code expression, returning no return value.
r_execfile(file)	This evaluates the Python code stored in the named file.
r_import(module, globals, locals, fromlist)	This imports a Python module. Each of the argument except the first is optional, although they must appear in order.
r_open(file, mode, bufsize)	This opens a file, returning a file object. Files can be opened for reading, but not for writing. Each of the arguments except the first is optional, although they must appear in order.
r_reload(module)	This reloads a module.
r_unload(module)	This unloads a module.

PHP

Since PHP is a Web development platform, it is sensitive to all of the concerns with Web-based security, including secure session management and cross-site scripting issues. PHP provides several functions for security purposes, including functions for encryption (when compiled with libmcrypt), secure hashing, HTTP basic authentication, cookies, and so on.

Resources

'Applied Cryptography' by Bruce Schneier, John Wiley & Sons, 1996, (*ISBN 0-471-11709-9*)

'Firewalls and Internet Security' by William R. Cheswick and Steven M. Bellovin, Addison-Wesley Publishing Company, 1994, (*ISBN 0-201-63357-4*).

Internet Information

The fast-paced nature of Internet security has given rise to a number of Internet sites, mailing lists, and newsgroups that cover security issues. Here are a few of them.

The comp.security hierarchy of newsgroups contains general security information for a number of systems.

The comp.risks newsgroup discusses the risks of using information technology, including security risks. While it doesn't specifically discuss security, it is a good resource for acquiring a healthy paranoia about the security of one's own code.

SecurityFocus (www.securityfocus.com) is a comprehensive web site, with papers, documentation, vulnerability databases, and other important reference information for the security programmer. SecurityFocus is also the home of the bugtraq mailing list, which is the premier mailing list for notification and discussion of security problems as they are discovered in various products.

Counterpane Systems is the security consulting company headed by Bruce Schneier, author of *Applied Cryptography*. Schneier publishes a bimonthly Web newsletter called Crypto-Gram, available on Counterpane's web site at www.counterpane.com.

The CERT (Computer Emergency Response Team) web site, at www.cert.org, contains historical security alerts, up-to-date security announcements, and other security information. While CERT is sometimes a bit behind other sources in terms of announcing vulnerabilities, their security research and vendor information is outstanding.

Summary

In this chapter we have explored the difficulties encountered when attempting to program in a secure way. We have started out with basic file security, examined its weaknesses and looked at tools and methods that will allow us to refine the authentication process.

We then moved on to consider cryptographic tools and the principles of secure network programming, including ssh.

Before concluding with language-specific issues, we covered language-independent dangers inherent in race conditions and the use of the chroot jail.

Online discussion at http://www.p2p.wrox.com

13

GUI Programming with KDE/Qt

Introduction

The X Window System has numerous widget libraries for the programmer to choose between. For a long time, the commercial **Motif** was the dominant toolkit. Motif, however, was not free. New toolkits were made, particularly to take advantage of the increasingly prevalent object-oriented languages, and today there are numerous ones available, most of which are free. Qt is one of the most popular of them, and we will look at it in this chapter. After that, we will take a look at the K Desktop Environment, or KDE, which is built on top of Qt. KDE/Qt is an alternative to GNOME/GTK+, and vice versa.

The reader is expected to be proficient in C++.

About Qt

Qt is a highly portable C++ GUI framework, which is available not only for Linux, but a dozen other UNIX variants, as well as Microsoft Windows. There's been a lot of historical problems with Qt's licensing, and whether or not it is truly free, so to clarify: Qt for UNIX is free when used to write free, open source software, and the source code for the UNIX version is freely available under the terms of the Qt Public License (QPL). Trolltech, the company behind Qt, is very supportive of the free software community, and has made sure that in case of bankruptcy, Qt will be released to this community under a BSD-like license. With the huge KDE and Qt free software community, the future of Qt is as safe as it can be. Qt has been in the center of some controversy because of its licensing. However, this has calmed down since the release of Qt 2.x, which introduced the QPL license. If you are concerned about the freedom of your code, you should read the license to make sure you are happy with it.

From a technical viewpoint, Qt is even more attractive. We have already mentioned the portability of Qt. Moreover, the toolkit is truly object-oriented and developing reusable software components with Qt comes naturally. Qt provides all the standard user interface components you expect to find in a GUI framework, such as push buttons, lists, menus, and check boxes. However, the beauty of Qt lies very much in the ease of creating what Qt does *not* have. Special, or customized versions of the available user interface components, for example, are essential in most applications. This is easily and naturally accomplished in Qt.

Another Qt feature is its support for custom look and feel, or themes. But Qt has more than just GUI support. Internationalization, utility classes such as lists and dictionaries, file management classes, and regular expressions classes are some of the other functionality you will find in Qt.

As we know, technical excellence does not necessarily equal success. The success of Qt also lies much in its outstanding documentation. It seldom leaves anything unanswered, and if it does, you have the source code to look at, and a very friendly and supportive mailing list.

About KDE

KDE is a powerful, open source, and free desktop for UNIX. KDE is, like many open source programs, an Internet project with its developers spread throughout the world. The project was born because one developer, Matthias Ettrich, proposed a free desktop environment for Linux. This was not long after Trolltech released the first version of Qt. Ettrich looked at the library and suggested using it because of its quality and friendly, open license. This led to the creation of KDE in October, 1996. Its name stands for K Desktop Environment. The K doesn't stand for anything. Today, several hundreds of developers and more than a hundred translators are participating in the KDE project.

KDE is interesting for both developers and users – for users mostly, perhaps, because it enforces consistency across applications. The look of KDE applications is to a large degree centrally configurable by the user. For the developer, KDE offers many classes that make it easier to develop applications. With the release of KDE 2, interaction and reuse between applications will become easier, creating an even more powerful and integrated desktop.

In this chapter, we will look at:

- ❏ Installation of Qt and KDE.
- ❏ Using `tmake` to simplify `Makefile` creation and management.
- ❏ Creating a simple Qt application.
- ❏ The signal/slot concept.
- ❏ Creating widgets.
- ❏ Layout widgets.
- ❏ The Qt utility classes.
- ❏ Introducing KDE programming by writing a simple text editor.

Installing Qt

The source code for Qt can be downloaded from ftp://ftp.trolltech.com/qt/source/. For installable packages such as those in RPM format, look in ftp://ftp.trolltech.com/qt/dist/, or check the web site of the Linux distribution you are using. We will look at installing from the compressed source tarball archive here. In the archive there is an INSTALL file explaining in painstaking detail how to install Qt. However, the basic install procedure, which should work on most systems, is as follows.

The suggested folder to place Qt into is /usr/local, but you are free to place Qt anywhere you want. In SuSE distributions, for example, Qt will be found in /usr/lib/qt. We will assume /usr/local:

```
$ cd /usr/local
```

We need to unpack the archive using something like this:

```
$ tar -xvzf qt-x11-2.1.1.tar.gz
```

Since you may want to have multiple Qt versions installed, we make a link to the Qt folder:

```
$ ln -s /usr/local/qt-2.1.1 /usr/local/qt
```

Qt needs a couple of environment variables:

```
QTDIR=/usr/local/qt
PATH=$QTDIR/bin:$PATH
```

The path update is necessary to tell the shell how to locate Qt's meta-object compiler (which we will meet later). Place these variables in the configuration file of the shell you are using, e.g. .bash_profile in your home directory for the bash shell. The INSTALL file contains a full explanation for different shells. If you only place the QTDIR in the shell configuration file, you need to restart your shell (that is, log out and log in again), or you can do:

```
$ export QTDIR=/usr/local/qt
```

to set up the variable in the current shell environment. Now, Qt is ready to be compiled. To see the list of compilation options, type:

```
$ ./configure -help
```

You may want to include JPEG and GIF support, neither of which are included in a default compilation. To do that, type:

```
$ ./configure -system-jpeg -gif
```

If you are satisfied with the defaults (you can see them using the -help parameter), you just need to type:

```
$ ./configure
```

In some rare cases, you must specify the platform you are compiling for. You do that like this:

```
$ ./configure -platform linux-g++
```

This will create the makefiles for the library and all the examples. Simply type:

```
$ make
```

To compile it all. There is no make install. Now add the following line to /etc/ld.so.conf:

```
/usr/local/qt/lib
```

Log in as root and run:

```
# ldconfig
```

That's it. If you are experiencing trouble, consult the INSTALL file or the installation FAQ. See the resources section for links.

Installing KDE

We will use the latest version of KDE, namely KDE 2. KDE is very large so downloading it may not be practical for you. Instead, it is recommended that you install it as part of your Linux distribution, and since KDE comes with almost all distributions, this should not be a problem. If you need to download KDE, follow the up-to-date installation instructions on the KDE website http://www.kde.org/

Libraries

Qt has various extensions and KDE comes with many libraries. We are only going to concentrate on the four central libraries. Once familiar with these, extending your application to use additional libraries is easy.

Library	Description
libqt	Qt consists of one library, libqt. There are Qt extensions in separate libraries, but we are not going cover those here.
libkdecore	All KDE programs use this library. It provides basic functionality, such as a configuration system and internationalization.
libkdeui	This library contains most of the user interface components KDE provides.
libkfile	This library provides many classes for dealing with files, such as file open and save dialogs, and file preview (to show a small preview of a file, say a thumbnail image) in the file open dialog.

Programming Applications Using Qt

Although there are several tools for developers to build GUIs using KDE/Qt, such as Qt Architect, QtEZ, and KDE Studio (links are given in the resources section), we will write our first GUIs by hand. There are two reasons for this: Firstly, Qt GUIs are pretty easy to write manually. Secondly, the best way to learn how to program Qt is by actually using it directly, and not let a GUI builder do it for us. It is useful to know what is going on behind the GUI builders, so that we can extend the code ourselves when the tools fall short.

The reader is encouraged to consult the reference manual for Qt for a full overview of the capabilities of the classes we will use.

Getting Started: Hello World

To get started, we'll take a conceptual overview of Qt and create a graphical hello world program. We will then enhance it a little bit before we look at Qt in more detail. The program will consist of a single push button with a predictable caption. Let's dive straight in:

```cpp
#include <qapplication.h>
#include <qpushbutton.h>

int main(int argc, char **argv)
{
    QApplication app(argc, argv);
    QPushButton button("Hello World", 0);
    app.setMainWidget(&button);
    button.show();
    return app.exec();
}
```

That's it! It could hardly have been much shorter. We compile and run it like this:

```
$ g++ -c -I$QTDIR/include main.cpp
$ g++ -o helloworld main.o -L$QTDIR/lib -lqt
$ ./helloworld
```

The QApplication object recognizes a few options. Consult the reference documentation for the QApplication class for a full list – we will only look at one, the -style argument. Try running helloworld again, each time specifying one of the two other styles Qt supports (Motif is the default); Windows and Platinum:

```
$ ./helloworld -style=platinum
```

and

```
$ ./helloworld -style=windows
```

Platinum, by the way, is the name Apple use to describe the look and feel of MacOS. Below are screen shots of the three different looks. Since there is only one button, the difference is very subtle, but you can see it in the shape and style of the bevel around the button. The `style` argument can be given to any Qt program. If the application does not explicitly force a look, the argument will change the style of the whole application.

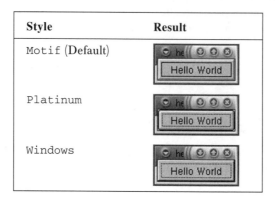

Style	Result
Motif (Default)	Hello World
Platinum	Hello World
Windows	Hello World

Let's take a closer look at the code:

```
#include <qapplication.h>
#include <qpushbutton.h>
```

We first include the necessary files. We are only going to use two classes, QApplication and QPushButton, so this is all we need:

```
QApplication app(argc, argv);
```

The command line arguments are passed to the QApplication constructor in order to allow it to recognize -style, for example. The QApplication class takes care of application initialization, finalization, control flow, and the main settings of the application. Qt provides many utility classes, and also a networking extension, so it is possible to develop non-GUI applications with Qt, in which case there is no need for a QApplication object. Although you will usually have a QApplication object, it is not a class that is much used other than at the very beginning of the application, as shown above. In many cases, the few lines above are all you need to know about QApplication.

```
QPushButton button("Hello World", 0);
```

This is the creation of the push button. The first argument is the caption of the button, and the second argument is the so-called parent of the push button. We will get back to the parent relationship in detail. For now, we will just say that all widgets in Qt have a parent, except top-level windows (which, by convention, have the root window as parent). Top-level windows are created by passing a null pointer as the parent.

```
app.setMainWidget(&button);
```

Here we specify to the application object the widget that is the main one in the application. The main widget has a special role; if it is closed, the application will quit.

```
button.show();
```

So far, the button has only been created, not shown. This line will show the push button. Since we passed a null pointer as the parent (we had no other option here as there were no other widgets), the button will appear in its own window.

```
return app.exec();
```

Here we leave the control to Qt, which will now take care of the program flow by listening for various events that happen and execute the appropriate code. In order for us to enhance the program a little, we need to introduce signal and slots. But before we do that, let us introduce a tool to simplify the compilation; tmake.

Simplifying Makefile Management With tmake

tmake is a small but useful tool to simplify creating and maintaining makefiles. The developers of Qt found it convenient to develop tmake because of all the different makefiles they needed for their extensive platform support. Moreover, Qt source code that uses the signal/slot system we will introduce shortly must be run through the meta object compiler that comes with Qt before the source code can be compiled with a C++ compiler. tmake takes care of this for us. Consequently, tmake is useful to more users than just the developers of Qt, and we will use it as well.

What tmake does is to take a project file as input, and generate a makefile from it. A project file (the naming convention is to let project files have a .pro extension) is basically just a list of all the source and header files in your project:

```
TARGET    = runme
SOURCES   = mainwindow.cpp main.cpp
HEADERS   = mainwindow.h
```

tmake, if it's not included in your distribution, can be downloaded from ftp://ftp.trolltech.com/freebies/tmake/.

We run the project file through tmake like this:

```
$ tmake test.pro -o Makefile
```

Simply typing make now should preprocess our source code with the meta object compiler and compile the code to create the executable runme.

With this tool, dealing with signals and slots will be easier, as we do not have to worry about the meta object compiler, moc.

Signals and Slots

Signals and slots are Qt's way of handling **event-driven programming**. The most common use of signals and slots is to connect events in the user interface triggered by the user, to code in the application that is responding to the event. For example, when the user selects a menu item, we want to take the appropriate action. Since user interfaces are generally filled with this kind of logic, it would be convenient if there was a way to simplify this code for us. This is where signals and slots come in. What Qt will do when the user selects a menu item is to emit a **signal**. We can listen to this signal, and this is done by connecting a **slot** to it. If this 'connection' sounds like a function callback to you, you are correct; Signals and slots are simply function callbacks, but they are type-safe, and easier to use as they hide many of the gory details.

The signal/slot system is very flexible: A Qt object can send any number of signals, and a Qt object can listen to any number of signals. A signal can have any number of slots connected to it and vice versa. It is even possible to connect signals to signals (first signal triggers the second), but in practice this is rarely done. Signals can take any number of arguments of any type, and they are typesafe.

There are a few limitations, but they are mostly academic. The two most important restrictions you are likely to encounter are that:

❑ signals cannot be used in templates, and

❑ when using multiple inheritance, the QObject class must be the first class in the list.

The first limitation should not give any problems as signals and slots are mostly used together with widgets, and a template widget class is not very likely. The second issue is not so much a limitation, as just something you will have to remember.

Signals and slots, then, are going to be an important tool for us in order to bring life to the interfaces we create. As mentioned, a signal needs to be connected to a slot. It is done like this:

```
connect(    signal_emitter, SIGNAL(a_signal()),
            slot_owner, SLOT(a_slot()));
```

The connect function is in the QObject class, so we assume the above line is called from a class derived from QObject. It follows that all classes that contain signals and/or slots must derive from QObject. This may sound like a bothersome restriction, but signals and slots are most commonly used in GUI code. Since QWidget, the base class for all widgets, derives from QObject, the requirement is rarely a problem in practice.

Here's a sample connect function. We'll see how to build the other things it needs in a moment:

```
connect(    button, SIGNAL(clicked())),
            this, SLOT(shutdown()));
```

The first argument is the sender of the signal, usually a widget. The second argument is which signal in the sender we are connecting to, in this case clicked. The third argument is the receiver of the signal, usually also a widget, and lastly we pass the slot, the shutdown function in this case. The slot is naturally located in the receiver object. We turn the functions in question into signals and slots using the SIGNAL and SLOT macros, which we'll come to later.

Although shutdown is a regular function and can be treated as such, we need to specify that it is a slot. This is done in the header file. Let's take a look at a header file, mywidget.h, that has all that is required to work with signal and slots:

```
class MyWidget : public QWidget
{
    Q_OBJECT
public:
    MyWidget();
    virtual ~MyWidget();

signals:
    void mysignal();
```

This non-standard label is probably a bit worrying. As we shall see, Qt classes that uses signal and slots will be run through a preprocessor which will ensure that the above is digestible for the C++ compiler. The preprocessor will also take care of this label:

```
private slots:
    void shutdown();

private:
    ...
}
```

We derive from `QWidget` and thus also `QObject` (see the class diagram below). Deriving from `QObject` is the first requirement in order to use signals and slots. The second requirement is that we must include the `Q_OBJECT` macro in the class declaration. These are the only two requirements, and the class is ready for signal and slot usage. If we want to define our own signals and/or slots, this must also be specified in the header file. Above we declared a signal, `mysignal`, and the mentioned slot, `shutdown`.

We have also specified a signal in the header file. To emit the signal, we simply write:

```
emit mysignal();
```

anywhere in the code for `MyWidget`. Notice that unlike slots, signals do not have any implementation (the implementation is effectively handled by the receiving slots). They are only function declarations. Slots are regular functions, and defined as such as well:

```
void MyWidget::shutdown()
{
    ...
}
```

Signals and slots can also have arguments. In the header file, they are specified as any other function declaration. Slots are implemented like any other function with arguments. Note that when using the `SIGNAL` and `SLOT` macros, you will have to specify the *types* and *not the variables*. For example, `QListView`, a class for creating trees and multi-column lists, defines a signal like this:

```
void clicked(QListViewItem *, const QPoint &, int);
```

In order to connect this signal to a slot in our own widget, we need to write something like this:

```
connect(    listview, SIGNAL(clicked(QListViewItem*, const QPoint&, int)),
            this, SLOT(our_slot(QListViewItem*, const QPoint&, int)));
```

Notice that the signatures of the signal and the slot must match. Signals must have `void` as the return type. This makes sense, since a signal could be received by any number of slots, or none at all, each with different results. To avoid this causing a problem, the signal sender doesn't receive any feedback about the result of the signal at all.

Now, obviously signals:, private slots:, and emit are keywords the C++ compiler would choke on. This is where the meta object compiler, or moc, comes in. moc is a preprocessor that scans through the class declaration looking for the Q_OBJECT macro. If it finds this, moc will create an additional C++ file which contains meta object code for this class. The created file can be included in the source file, but more commonly it is compiled separately and linked with the rest of the objects. This is how moc works, but as we've seen, tmake will take the code, run it through moc, compile and link for us. So, in practice, all you need to know is to derive from QObject (or a subclass) and include Q_OBJECT in the class declaration.

It is important to understand the concepts of signals and slots. They are absolutely essential when writing Qt applications.

> When the **SIGNAL/SLOT** system is used incorrectly, an error message like this is common:
>
> ```
> myobject.o(.text+0x390): undefined reference to 'MyObject virtual table'
> ```
>
> This is usually because the **Q_OBJECT** statement has not been included in the header file and/or moc has not been run on the files in question. We will be using **tmake** so we do not usually have to worry about this.

'Hello world' Revisited

Now we will change the code so that the application quits when the button is clicked. Only one line of code is needed:

```
#include <qapplication.h>
#include <qpushbutton.h>

int main(int argc, char **argv)
{
    QApplication app(argc, argv);
    QPushButton button("Hello World", 0);
    QObject::connect(&button, SIGNAL(clicked()), &app, SLOT(quit()));
    app.setMainWidget(&button);
    button.show();
    return app.exec();
}
```

The signal (clicked, defined in QButton, the base class of QPushButton) is connected to the slot (quit, defined in QApplication). The application is compiled and run the same way as before. Now, when we click on the button, the button widget emits a clicked signal, which causes the quit slot of the application to execute.

Deriving From Base Classes

When we develop real applications, we use widgets differently than we have done so far. The general way of creating a GUI is to derive from an appropriate base class and fill the constructor of the new class with code creating and placing widgets. For example, in order to create a dialog box, you would derive a class from, say, QDialog, and design the GUI in the new constructor.

Qt provides many such base classes for creating windows or dialog boxes. You could derive from the basic QWidget, or more commonly, perhaps, from QDialog. There is also a QTabDialog for creating dialogs with pages in them. We will introduce QMainWindow, a class you are likely to use in most, if not all applications. QMainWindow provides us with easy creation of a menu bar, tool bars, and a status bar.

To get a better overview of Qt's design, here's a very simplified and incomplete inheritance hierarchy:

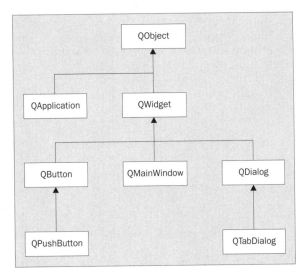

Let's look at how to use QMainWindow as a base class. We will start simple, first the header file mainwindow.h:

```
#include "qmainwindow.h"
class MainWindow : public QMainWindow
{
public:
    MainWindow(QWidget *parent = 0, const char *name = 0);
    virtual ~MainWindow();
};
```

This is all we need in order to create a main window. In fact, we could even have dropped the constructor arguments as we will not use either of them, but you should get used to always creating those two arguments in all new widgets you make. They are the standard arguments and are present in all widgets - we do not want to break this consistency. As you see, we give default values for both arguments so that we can ignore them when we actually use the class. First is the parent widget, and secondly is the name of this widget. If you look back at the 'Hello world' example, we passed the string caption of the button as the first argument, and the parent widget as the second argument. That, however, was *not* the name of the widget. The name is only used internally, and never visible to the user. We will look at both arguments in detail later.

The source code is just as simple:

```
#include "mainwindow.h"

MainWindow::MainWindow(
QWidget *parent,
const char *name)
: QMainWindow(parent, name)
{
}

MainWindow::~MainWindow()
{
}
```

Now we have a fully valid widget ready to be used. Admittedly, it cannot be used for anything useful, but it will be a skeleton to build upon. In order to show this window, the code will be almost identical to the 'Hello world' code. The reason is that both the push button and our main window are derived from QWidget, and we are using the QWidget interface in main:

```
#include <qapplication.h>
#include "mainwindow.h"

int main(int argc, char **argv)
{
    QApplication app(argc, argv);
    MainWindow m;
    app.setMainWidget(&m);
    m.show();
    return app.exec();
}
```

We create the main window, set it to be the main widget, and show it. The exec call enters the main event loop, and it will stay there until the main window is closed, exactly the same way as in 'Hello world'.

We create a project file, let's call it mainwindow.pro:

```
TARGET  = mainwindow
SOURCES = main.cpp mainwindow.cpp
HEADERS = mainwindow.h
```

The project file is sent to tmake which creates a makefile, so that we can compile and finally run our code:

```
$ tmake mainwindow.pro -o Makefile
$ make
$ ./mainwindow
```

We get this:

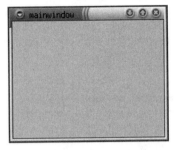

By deriving from QMainWindow as we have done here, what we are coding is specialization. This applies to any other Qt (or KDE) widget as well. If, for example, we did not like the default behavior of QPushButton, we could just derive from it and customize it to our needs.

We will leave the window as it is, and instead take a detailed look at the two biggest parts of Qt programming (apart from signals and slots). They are **widgets** and **layouts**.

Widgets

Every visible component in a Qt GUI, whether it is interactive or not, is a widget. QWidget is the base class for all widgets. All widgets are connected together in a parent-child relationship. This is done by passing the parent to the child's constructor when creating new widgets. We have already briefly touched upon this. For example, if we were to create a new push button in our main window above, the code may look something like this:

```
MainWindow::MainWindow(QWidget *parent, const char *name)
: QMainWindow(parent, name)
{
QPushButton *quit_button = new QPushButton("&Quit", this, "quitbutton");
...
}
```

The ampersand before the Q tells Qt to make Q the shortcut key for the button, and to underline that letter. The main thing we have done here, however, is to create a push button that is the child of the main window. Passing 'this' to constructors is something you will see a lot in Qt. Passing a null pointer as the parent will make the widget a new top-level window. That is, if we passed null to the push button constructor above, we would get a small window with a single push button separate from the dialog box. Null is the default value for widget constructors.

The other argument all widgets take is the name the widget shall have. In Qt, you can give all widgets a name, which is only used internally. Do not confuse it with text labels visible to the user. In the line above, 'Quit' is the caption of the button, and *not* its name. The name is quitbutton. We could have left it out, specifying the button instead like this:

```
QPushButton *quit_button = new QPushButton("&Quit", this);
```

We used this form in the first hello world program. The name is mostly useful for debugging purposes. For example, Qt may print out warnings, and if they belong to a widget, Qt will print the name so that you can easily track down the widget that is incorrectly used. Another debugging tool dumps all the QObjects that exist in a tree (the parent-child relationship). You can also use the names to look up the widget later, but you are unlikely to need this. For convenience, we will not name our widgets here, but it is a useful habit to get into.

> **All widgets in Qt with a parent (i.e. not top-level windows) *must* be created using 'new'. Qt automatically de-allocates these widgets for us.**

If you do not need to access the widgets you create, such as for reading values from it or for enabling or disabling, there is no need to store the pointers for de-allocation, and therefore, you will often find your destructors will be empty.

Below is a screen shot of the `widgets` example application that is included in the Qt distribution. The window does not show all the widgets Qt provides, but many of them, and it gives an impression of what you can you achieve with Qt. As you can see, the `Windows` look and feel is being used:

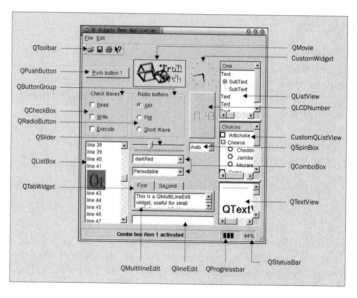

Layouts

Now that we know how to create widgets, we need some control over how they are placed. The best way to do that is to use the **layout** classes. A layout is not a widget, although Qt also provides a few widgets that can be used for placing other widgets. This is important to remember, because widgets can only have widgets as parents, and not layouts. In a few cases, this can mean it is necessary to use one of Qt's layout-widgets for placement. Either way, however, it may seem awkward to use them if you are used to placing widgets by fixed co-ordinates, but with layouts, we create neatly aligned, font-sensitive, and resizable GUIs automatically.

Qt provides a number of layout classes and you can even create your own if you have some special layout requirements, such as placing widgets in a circle, for example. Usually, though, the ones available are sufficient. We will mainly use `QVBoxLayout` and `QHBoxLayout` for vertical and horizontal placement respectively.

Layouts hold widgets and/or other layouts. For example, if we want a layout like this:

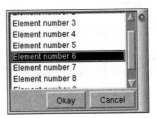

The list and button widgets are located like this (we don't worry about placing the scroll bar, since it is part of the list):

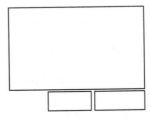

Before we start on the code, let's try to get a overview of what we need to do. If we mentally group the components of this dialog box, we have a list box above two horizontally ordered buttons. In other words, at the outer-most level, we need to place the two groups above each other. The most natural way to do that is using a vertical layout. Qt provides us with `QVBoxLayout` for such purposes. Let's build an object hierarchy of the layout. With a little practice, you will be able to build such hierarchies naturally. So, we have the vertical layout and two groups:

```
QVBoxLayout
    Group1
    Group2
```

Graphically:

The first group is simply the list box and is therefore not really a group of anything. The buttons, however, needs to be grouped horizontally. If we insert two buttons in the vertical layout, we will get the buttons above each other:

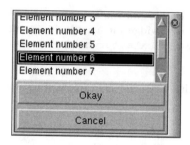

That is not what we want for this layout. So, we need a horizontal layout, or more specifically, QHBoxLayout. Inside this layout, we place the two buttons. The final hierarchy looks like this:

```
QVBoxLayout
    QListBox
    QHBoxLayout
        QPushButton
        QPushButton
```

If you look closely at the first screen shot, you see a blank area at the left of the two push buttons. Resizing the dialog will keep the push buttons the same size as the blank area gets larger. This is accomplished by inserting a so-called **stretch** at the left of the buttons.

With the logic and architecture of the dialog box sorted out, let's look at the code:

```
#include "dialog.h"
#include <qlayout.h>
#include <qlistbox.h>
#include <qpushbutton.h>

Dialog::Dialog(QWidget *parent, const char *name) : QDialog(parent, name)
{
```

Here we are deriving from `QDialog`, but we could just as well used `QWidget` as the base class. `QDialog` is derived from `QWidget`, and offers modality and default buttons, amongst other things.

```
QVBoxLayout *vertical   = new QVBoxLayout(this);
QHBoxLayout *horizontal = new QHBoxLayout;
```

Here we have the two layouts in the dialog box. Notice that only one of them has the dialog box as parent. You will get a run-time warning if you try to have more than one layout with a particular widget as parent. The horizontal layout will later become a child of the vertical layout.

```
QListBox *listbox = new QListBox(this);

for(int i = 1; i <= 10; i++)
{
    QString str = QString("Element number %1").arg(i);
```

QString is one of the non-GUI classes Qt provides. QString is powerful, and Qt uses it extensively. The string class use reference counting, and since it is used by Qt almost everywhere, it is therefore very efficient. Using another string class, such as the STL string class, together with Qt, would result in unnecessary copying. Moreover, it uses Unicode internally, opening up for support of any language. Here we build a string with a variable in it:

```
        listbox->insertItem(str);
    }
```

Creates the list box and its content:

```
    QPushButton *okay      = new QPushButton("Okay", this);
    QPushButton *cancel    = new QPushButton("Cancel", this);
```

Our two push buttons. Notice that both the list box and the push buttons have the dialog box as parent, and not the layouts they will be placed in. This is because widgets can only have widgets as parents, and layouts, as we know, are not widgets. With all the widgets created, we are ready to organize our widgets in our desired layout:

```
    horizontal->addStretch();
    horizontal->addWidget(okay);
    horizontal->addWidget(cancel);
```

Here we have created the horizontal layout. Widgets, spaces, and stretches are added in left-to-right order. By adding the stretch, we keep the horizontal size of the buttons fixed (their vertical size is already fixed by the implementation of QPushButton).

```
    vertical->addWidget(listbox);
    vertical->addLayout(horizontal);
```

Here we create the vertical layout with the list box on top and the horizontal layout at the bottom (top-to-bottom order). Notice that we use a different function for adding a layout.

```
    resize(200, 150);
    }
```

Lastly, we set the size for the dialog box. For completeness, here is the main function for opening the window:

```
    #include <qapplication.h>
    #include "dialog.h"

    int main(int argc, char **argv)
    {
        QApplication app(argc, argv);
        Dialog dlg;
        app.setMainWidget(&dlg);
        dlg.show();
        return app.exec();
    }
```

We create a `layout.pro` file:

```
TARGET  = layout
SOURCES = main.cpp dialog.cpp
HEADERS = dialog.h
```

Running the project file through `tmake`, compiling, and running it:

```
tmake layout.pro -o Makefile
make
./layout
```

As mentioned at the beginning of this section, we sometimes have to use what we sloppily referred to as 'layout-widgets'. Specifically, these are `QGrid`, `QHBox`, `QVBox`, and `QGroupBox` (and its derivatives). We are not going to cover all of these, but we will show you `QButtonGroup`, which is derived from `QGroupBox`, as an example.

`QGroupBox` provides a bevel around its contents, and a caption. This is useful when you want to group related widgets. `QButtonGroup` is similar to `QGroupBox`, but it is specialized to deal with `QButton` widgets, and has a set of useful features for dealing with such widgets. For example, a `QButtonGroup` can be set to be 'exclusive'. In this mode, the button group will ensure that only one button is toggled at a time. This is especially useful for radio buttons. Here is an example of a group box:

In general, the layout classes provide functionality for placing widgets, spaces, stretches, and sub layouts. The widgets mentioned above provide very limited positioning, but they do offer functionality for dealing with their contents, or providing beveled borders.

Although the vertical and horizontal layouts are simple building blocks, we can create pretty much any GUI we want by just combining them. In some cases, we may want to place widgets in a grid-like fashion, and although it can be done with horizontal and vertical layouts, it is more convenient to use `QGridLayout`.

That's it for Qt! It does, however, offer much more than we have covered here, and the reader is encouraged to look at features such as drag and drop, session management, and internationalization. With the foundation you have gained through this chapter, you can make use of the rest of Qt, and move on to KDE programming.

Programming Applications Using KDE

In general, developing KDE applications is done much the same as developing Qt applications. Naturally, KDE provides many of its own classes and classes extended from Qt, but the concepts of widgets, layouts, and the SIGNAL/SLOT system still applies. One of the most important aspects of developing KDE applications, is not of a technical nature, but rather one of good practice. Follow the style guide. The style guide is specified (it's not included in the packages) at http://developer.kde.org/documentation/standards/kde/style/basics/index.html.

This section is not about GUI design. We will focus on the technical side, and not let the style guide obscure the focus.

A Simple Text Editor

We will develop a simple text editor as an example KDE application. It will have:

❏   Menu bar with new, open, save, and quit capabilities.

❏   Tool bar with new, open, save, and quit capabilities.

❏   The editor itself.

Let's start with the main window right away – it will be the only window we will create ourselves. For the load and save dialogs, we will use an existing class. As with our Qt example, we want to use a 'main window' class. Now, the class is called KTMainWindow, though the general idea of deriving from it remains. KTMainWindow provides full session management (saves its position, geometry, and positions of toolbars), and is aware of the KDE settings, so fonts, colors, and themes will automatically be set to match the current KDE settings. The editorwindow.h file looks like this:

```
#include <ktmainwindow.h>
#include <keditcl.h>

class EditorWindow : public KTMainWindow
{
    Q_OBJECT
public:
    EditorWindow();
```

Unlike Qt, the KDE main window does not take a parent widget. It is also discouraged to specify the name because all the main windows in the application must have a unique name in order for the session management to work correctly. By not specifying a name, the class will ensure that the main window will get a unique name. Consequently, we will only have the default constructor:

```
    virtual ~EditorWindow();


private slots:
    void newFile();
    void openFile();
    void saveFile();

private:
    KEdit *m_pEditor;
};
```

As we can see, the header file is just as a Qt header file would have been, except that we are using KDE classes. Now, for the implementation of our editor (`editorwindow.cpp`):

```
#include "editorwindow.h"

#include <kaction.h>
#include <kapp.h>
#include <kfiledialog.h>
#include <kmenubar.h>
#include <kmessagebox.h>
#include <kstdaccel.h>
#include <qfile.h>
#include <qpopupmenu.h>
#include <qtextstream.h>

EditorWindow::EditorWindow()
{
```

KDE provides the class `KAction`, for conveniently creating related menu items and tool bar buttons. So, if we had this tool bar created:

`KAction` would create our menu items to be consistent with the tool bar, and so our menu would look something like this:

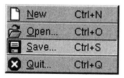

`KAction` centralizes state-setting, so you won't run the risk of enabling a menu item, but disabling its corresponding tool bar button. Another feature of `KAction` is that it will try to locate a tool bar icon according to the current theme:

```
KAction *new_action = new KAction(
    "&New",
    "filenew",
    KStdAccel::key(KStdAccel::New),
    this,
    SLOT(newFile()),
    this);
```

The string &New is the menu item string. The ampersand specifies which character to underline when indicating the short cut key Ctrl-N. The string `filenew` is the file name (from the KDE icon directories – no extension is specified) of the icon we want the tool bar button to have. A miniature version of the icon will also be put next to the menu item, as shown above. KDE will locate the best icon for us according to theme and size.

KStdAccel provides us with many standard keyboard shortcut keys. One standard item is the New menu item. We will follow the style guide and use it here. Next is the object and SLOT which we are going to connect to both the menu item and the tool bar button. Lastly is the parent of the action itself.

For common actions such as New, KDE provides us with KStdAction, which is even simpler to use:

```
KAction *new_action = KStdAction::openNew(this, SLOT(newFile()), this);
```

We create a similar action object for each menu item and tool bar button:

```
KAction *open_action = new KAction(
    "&Open...",
    "fileopen",
    KStdAccel::key(KStdAccel::Open),
    this,
    SLOT(openFile()),
    this);

KAction *save_action = new KAction(
    "&Save...",
    "filesave",
    KStdAccel::key(KStdAccel::Save),
    this,
    SLOT(saveFile()),
    this);

KAction *quit_action = new KAction(
    "&Quit...",
    "stop",
    KStdAccel::key(KStdAccel::Quit),
    KApplication::kApplication(),
    SLOT(quit()),
    this);
```

Now it is time to create our menu using Qt's QPopupMenu. We will place the popup menu under a 'File' label in the menu bar:

```
QPopupMenu *file_menu = new QPopupMenu;
menuBar()->insertItem("&File", file_menu);
```

We are now ready to design our menu, by using the action's plug function. This inserts the action into the given widget, (typically a menu or toolbar). That is, plugging the menu into the action will result in the menu getting a new item, with an icon and a short cut key. We will combine this with a direct call to the menu to insert separators in the menu:

```
new_action->plug(file_menu);
file_menu->insertSeparator();
open_action->plug(file_menu);
save_action->plug(file_menu);
file_menu->insertSeparator();
quit_action->plug(file_menu);
```

The tool bar is also created with the actions' `plug` function:

```
new_action->plug(toolBar());
open_action->plug(toolBar());
save_action->plug(toolBar());
quit_action->plug(toolBar());
```

Lastly, we create the editor widget, and set it to be the 'view' in the main window. This just means that the editor will occupy the main area of the main window:

```
m_pEditor = new KEdit(this);
setView(m_pEditor);
}
```

That was the GUI design. Now for the implementation of the actual functions. We will try to make the editor at least marginally user friendly, and quite apart from this, we should also make sure not to quit the application if there is unsaved data, unless it's OK by the user. We could put this data-saving code in the destructor, because the destructor is called when the user closes the main window. This may not be the best way to do things – for example, the user cannot just save the file and remain in the application, but we will keep things simple.

An alternative way to do this, would be to override the close event, so if the user wanted to leave the application running, s/he could reject the event. This, however, is beyond the scope of this introduction chapter. Notice that, just as with Qt, no KDE widgets are deleted in the destructor either. This is because the KDE widgets are derived from Qt:

```
EditorWindow::~EditorWindow()
{
```

The `KEdit` widget has a modified flag. We only ask the user if s/he wants to save the file if it has been modified:

```
if(m_pEditor->isModified())
{
```

KDE, as well as Qt, provides several kinds of dialog boxes for querying the user about the typical OK/Cancel situations. Here we use `KMessageBox`'s warning dialog box, with `Yes`/`No` buttons:

```
int rc = KMessageBox::warningYesNo(
    this,
    "There are unsaved changes. Do you want to save\n"
    "the changes?");

if(rc == KMessageBox::Yes)
    saveFile();
}
}
```

The 'New' action will blank the editor widget. Like the destructor, we must make sure to ask the user for permission in case the text is not saved:

```cpp
void EditorWindow::newFile()
{
    if(m_pEditor->isModified())
    {
        int rc = KMessageBox::warningYesNo(
            this,
            "There are unsaved changes. Are you sure you want to\n"
            "start a new file?");

        if(rc == KMessageBox::No)
            return;
    }
```

Now the editor can be cleared. We must also clear the edited-flag because we define no text as being unedited. If we didn't, the user would be asked to save an empty file when quitting the application.

```cpp
    m_pEditor->clear();
    m_pEditor->setModified(false);
}
```

For the open action, we are going to use KDE's file dialog and ask the user for a file name:

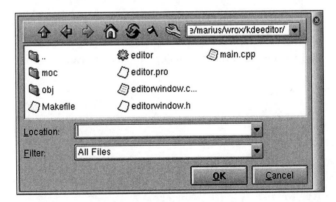

KFileDialog is the dialog we use in KDE for the selection of files and directories. It is similar to Qt's QFileDialog, but has greater functionality, and a different GUI. It provides several static functions for easy use, such as the two we will look at, as well as opening an URL and multiple file selection. More interesting, perhaps, is the ability to specify a preview widget. This could be used for something like showing thumbnails of images:

```cpp
void EditorWindow::openFile()
{
    QString file = KFileDialog::getOpenFileName();
```

If the user did not specify a file, an empty string will be returned. We check for that here:

```
if( ! file.isEmpty())
{
    QFile f(file);

    if(f.open(IO_ReadOnly))
    {
```

Now that the file is open, we can read from it. We will use a text stream class for that, namely QTextStream. This class is very similar to the STL iostream class, but we will use Qt's stream class for a particular reason.

If this had been a pure Qt application, we would have to read from the stream ourselves, and put the text into the editor. However, we are using KDE's KEdit editor, and it has the functionality to read and write directly from and to streams. That makes our code easy:

```
QTextStream s(&f);
m_pEditor->insertText(&s);
```

Again, we clear the modified flag because we have just loaded a file from disk:

```
m_pEditor->setModified(false);
        }
    }
}
```

The save action is similar to opening a file (the dialog box is identical):

```
void EditorWindow::saveFile()
{
    QString file = KFileDialog::getSaveFileName();

    if( ! file.isEmpty())
    {
        QFile f(file);

        if(f.open(IO_WriteOnly | IO_Truncate))
        {
            QTextStream s(&f);
```

Again, we let the editor widget write directly to the stream itself:

```
m_pEditor->saveText(&s);
            m_pEditor->setModified(false);
        }
    }
}
```

And that's the entire main window, with tool bar, menu bar, editor, and all its functions! We are not quite done yet, however, as we still need to open this window:

```
#include <kapp.h>
#include <kaboutdata.h>
#include <kcmdlineargs.h>

#include "editorwindow.h"

int main(int argc, char **argv)
{
```

Starting with KDE 2 (for which we are developing), applications must have a KAboutData object. This class is used to give information about the application, such as name, description, copyright, and homepage. If you are using an early version of KDE, you might get a warning that no data was specified, even though it was:

```
KAboutData aboutdata(
    "simplekeditor",
    "Simple KDE Editor",
    "1.0",
    "Wrox Demo Application; Text Editor",
    KAboutData::License_GPL,
    "(c) 2000, Wrox Press",
    "http://www.wrox.com",
    "The KDE example application conceived in\n"
    "'Professional Linux Programming'\n"
    "Wrox Press 2000",
    "none");
aboutdata.addAuthor("Marius Sundbakken");
```

KDE also requires us to pass the command line parameters to KCmdLineArgs. This way, our application will automatically support several generic arguments, such as '--help':

```
KCmdLineArgs::init(argc, argv, &aboutdata);
```

Since this is a KDE application, we will use KApplication, and not QApplication as the application object:

```
KApplication app;
```

The next lines are similar to what we have already seen:

```
EditorWindow w;
w.show();
return app.exec();
}
```

That's it! We have now written a simple, but nevertheless fully usable text editor with both load and save functionality. The application is aware of changes in the KDE configuration, such as theme and font. Before we can compile the source, though, we will write a project file, `editor.pro`:

```
TARGET              =       editor
MOC_DIR             =       moc
OBJECTS_DIR         =       obj
INCLUDEPATH         =       /opt/kde2/include
TMAKE_LIBDIR_X11   +=       -L$(KDEDIR)/lib
TMAKE_LIBS_X11     +=       -lkdeui -lkdecore -lkfile
SOURCES             =       main.cpp \
                            editorwindow.cpp
HEADERS             =       editorwindow.h
```

Run it through `tmake` as usual, compile, and run:

```
$ tmake editor.pro -o Makefile
$ make
$ ./editor
```

And this is what we get:

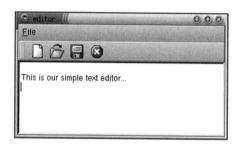

Resources

Qt can be found at: http://www.trolltech.com/

Qt mailing list: http://qt-interest.trolltech.com/

Qt Installation FAQ: http://www.trolltech.com/developer/faq/install.html

KDE can be found at: http://www.kde.org/

KDE mailing lists: http://lists.kde.org/

There are two KDE newsgroups: comp.os.windows.x.kde (English), de.alt.comp.kde (German)

Qt Architect: http://qtarch.sourceforge.net/

QtEZ: http://qtez.ibl.sk/

KDE Studio: http://www.thekompany.com/projects/kdestudio/

KDevelop: http://www.kdevelop.org/

Summary

In this chapter, we made a few basic Qt applications. We went through a relatively detailed explanation of both the SIGNAL/SLOT system, widgets, and layouts. We looked at how to use tmake, and although the material was brief, it is enough to get you up and running.

Lastly, we developed a simple KDE application, and showed a few aspects of KDE. Covering all of KDE would be at least a book in itself, but we have shown you how to get started. You may want to look at the following:

- ❏ Kconfig.
- ❏ KDE's configuration file parser.
- ❏ KbugReport.
- ❏ A dialog box for users to send bug reports.
- ❏ The extensive docking support (making it possible for the user to re-arrange the user interface by "drag and drop").
- ❏ The XMLGUI system where it is possible to build the GUI from an XML document.
- ❏ Command line parsing.
- ❏ Interprocess communication.
- ❏ And much more.

The reader is strongly urged to take a look at both the Qt and the KDE reference documentation.

Online discussion at http://www.p2p.wrox.com

14

Writing the DVD Store GUI Using KDE/Qt

In this chapter, we'll be looking again at how to implement the DVD Store user interface, this time using KDE and Qt. To keep things as simple as possible to start with, we'll only use Qt. We'll therefore see how similar it is to using Qt with KDE, but maximize portability (given that Qt is supported on more platforms than KDE). We'll then demonstrate how to add KDE-awareness to the application.

In this chapter, we will:

❑   Give an overview of some of the dialogs.

❑   Show how to use the database library in our GUI.

❑   Adapt the Qt-only version to make use of some of KDE.

Note that we will not be listing the complete code here – however, as with all code in this book, it's available for download from www.wrox.com.

Application Design

In order to help make it easier to compare the original GNOME/GTK+ version of the application with the version we will create in this chapter, differences in functionality will be as small as possible. The features we will include are:

- database login dialog
- a log showing every transaction
- adding, editing, and deleting members
- adding, editing, and deleting titles
- adding disks to titles
- member and title search
- checking the rental status of a disk (disk search)
- renting titles to members
- returning of particular disks displaying whether they are overdue or not
- reservation of titles
- configuration saving

With the database backend already written, our job is mainly to create a GUI. In order to execute all the functions in the list above, we'll have a main window with a menu bar and toolbar. Beyond that, we should support the following functionality:

- The user can add members, titles, and disks from the menu bar, opening the **member dialog**, the **title dialog**, or the **disk dialog** respectively; they can also add members from the tool bar.
- The three different searches are all collected into the **search dialog**.
- The same dialogs are used for editing **member** and **title** data, invoked in both cases from the search dialog.
- The user can right-click on an item to bring up a popup menu with **edit** and **delete** options.
- The user can invoke separate dialogs for **renting**, **returning**, and **reserving** titles from both the menu and the toolbar.
- The dialog for returning disks will open a second dialog to show whether any of the disks returned were overdue or not.
- Finally, there is a configuration dialog where the user can specify various options, such as the log file name.

These are the widgets we'll be using:

Widget name	Widget type	Description
ConnectDialog	QDialog	**Login dialog**. This will establish a connection to the database and make the application ready to use. Before a connection has been made, the only accessible function in the application is the preferences window.
DiskSearchPage	QWidget	**Search page for disks**. This dialog box will be where the user can check the rental status of a disk.
DVDSearchPage	QWidget	**Search page for DVDs**. Here the user can search for DVDs by title and/or actor and/or directory. The dialog box also acts as the starting point for editing and deleting titles.
GeneralPage	QWidget	**General preferences page**. This is where the user can specify the log file name and the maximum renting period before a rental is overdue. It is the first of the two pages in the preferences window.
MainWindow	QMainWindow	**Main window**. This is the starting window of the application. Most actions will be invoked from here, either by using the menu or the tool bar. The window also has the transaction log and the loan list.
MemberDialog	QDialog	**Dialog for adding members**. This dialog box can be invoked from the main window where it acts as the dialog for adding new members. Invoked from the search dialog, the user can edit an existing member here.
MemberSearchPage	QWidget	**Search page for members**. Here the user can search for members either by member number or last name. This is where editing and deleting members will be done.
PreferencesDialog	QTabDialog	**Preferences dialog**. This is the dialog that holds the two pages containing the various adjustable options.
RentDialog	QDialog	**Rental dialog**. From this dialog, the user specifies what disks a member is going to rent.
RentedDialog	QDialog	**Rental results dialog**. This is the dialog that pops up after the user is done in the rent dialog. It shows the address of the user and a list of the titles that the member wants to rent and which disks to rent out. If a title is not available (all disks are rented out), this will also be shown.

Table continued on following page

Widget name	Widget type	Description
ReserveDialog	QDialog	**Reserve dialog**. This where the user can make a reservation for a member.
ReturnDialog	QDialog	**Return dialog**. When a member returns rented disks, this is the dialog the user will report that in.
SearchDialog	QTabDialog	**Search dialog**. This is the dialog that holds the three search pages.
SearchWindowPage	QWidget	**Search preferences page**. This is the second of the two pages in the preferences window. Here the user can enable and disable various fields in the member and title search pages the user wants to see.
TitleDialog	QDialog	**Dialog for adding new DVDs**. When invoked from the main window, this is the dialog where new titles will be entered. Invoked from the title search page, this dialog acts as a dialog for editing the title.
No class	QInputDialog	**Dialog for adding disks to titles**. This uses an inbuilt Qt dialog.

The diagram below shows the relationship between the various dialog boxes, and their relationship (if any) to the database backend. The preferences dialog is simplified (its two pages are not shown in the diagram), however those in the search dialog are. Logging-related relationships to the main window are not shown.

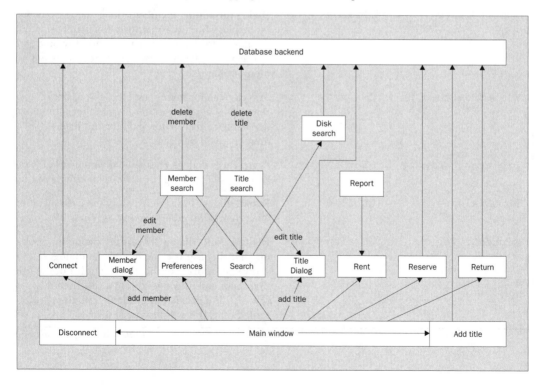

Not all the code you will see is directly related to KDE or Qt, and you may well come up with better ways to do certain things. Our primary focus will be the KDE and Qt code, and in other areas, such as logging, we've chosen simple solutions that won't obscure the central theme of the chapter. Consequently, some of the shortcuts taken may be out of place in a fully-fledged application.

We will now start on a description of the various parts of the GUI. It's by no means complete, but we've deliberately covered more or less the same dialogs as those discussed in the GNOME/GTK+ implementation chapter, so you can readily compare the two. These dialogs also cover most of the Qt functions we use, and is therefore a nice subset of the entire application to look at. Those we'll cover in the Qt section are:

- ❑ the main window
- ❑ the member dialog
- ❑ the rent dialog
- ❑ the rental report dialog
- ❑ the search window and its pages
- ❑ the settings manager

Main Window

Inside the main window, we need a menu bar for the various actions. It would be useful to include a toolbar with the most frequently used actions. The main area of the main window will contain the **log window** and a **loan list**. We want these to be separated, so we'll put them on separate pages by using a tab widget. Once we have the main window ready, we can start adding the various dialog boxes that we'll need for the other features.

Let's take a brief look at the header file:

```
class MainWindow :
    public QMainWindow
        {
        Q_OBJECT public:
            MainWindow();
            virtual ~MainWindow();
```

As we saw in the previous chapter, the Q_OBJECT macro is required in all classes that will use signals and/or slots.

One of the application requirements is the implementation of a transaction log, which will mainly be used to report the results of modifications to the database. Since the various dialogs each have their own code for dealing with the database, it's necessary that we should be able to add to the log from anywhere within the application.

There are many ways to achieve this; what we're going to do is place the log in the main window, and add a static function to the main window class:

```
static void addLog(const QString& msg);
```

Now, to the slots:

```
private slots:
    void connectDatabase();
    void disconnectDatabase();
    void addMember();
    void addTitle();
    void addDisk();
    void find();
    void rentDVD();
    void returnDVD();
    void reserve();
    void preferences();
    void about();
    void shutdown();
    ...
}
```

These slots are closely related to the list of features our application will have. We can go ahead and implement these slots in more or less an arbitrary order, but the database connection code must be made first. The preferences part is completely independent of the database; we'll touch just briefly on the preferences dialog box as it is fairly simple with purely GUI components and little additional code.

Let's look at the main window, which we open in the same way as we did in the previous chapter:

```
MainWindow::MainWindow() :
    QMainWindow(0, "dvdstore")
        {
        setCaption("DVDstore");
        m_pStoreMenu = new QPopupMenu(this);
```

Here we set the caption of the window and create a new menu for our menu bar. We use the QPopupMenu class for this, which can also be used to create context-sensitive popup menus; we'll see how to create menus like this when we discuss the search dialog box.

As usual, we specify the parent by passing the main window object to the QPopupMenu constructor. In order to connect to the database we want a menu item *and* a toolbar button.

Menu Items

First, we create the menu item:

```
m_ConnectItem = m_pStoreMenu->insertItem(
                                "&Connect...",
                                this,
                                SLOT(connectDatabase()));
```

The function returns an identifier for the inserted item. You can often ignore it, but we don't in this case, since we'll want to enable and disable this menu item; it makes little sense to offer the option of connecting to the database when we already are connected to it, so once we're connected we'll disable the item. We do so via the ID (as we shall see later) and we save it in m_ConnectItem.

insertItem

This function exists in many variants; the following code adds a menu item with a shortcut key:

```
m_AddMemberItem = m_pStoreMenu->insertItem(
                                   "Add Member...",
                                   this,
                                   SLOT(addMember()),
                                   CTRL + Key_M);
```

The rest of the menu is created in exactly the same way.

Once all the menus are created, we attach them to the menu bar. The QMainWindow class that we're using provides us with a menu bar, so we don't have to create it ourselves. The only thing we have to do is attach our menus to it:

```
menuBar()->insertItem("&DVDstore", m_pStoreMenu);
```

By default, a menu item is enabled. As mentioned, we use a menu item's identifier to enable and disable it. For example, to disable the database connect menu item:

```
m_pStoreMenu->setItemEnabled(m_ConnectItem, false);
```

Toolbar

We also want a toolbar, and QToolBar is the class for that:

```
m_pToolBar = new QToolBar("toolbar", this);
```

We can then use the QToolButton class to add buttons to our toolbar:

```
m_pConnectButton = new QToolButton(
            QPixmap(DVDSTORE_ICON_CONNECT),
            "Connect",
            "Connect to database",
            this,
            SLOT(connectDatabase()),
            m_pToolBar);
```

Note that any widget can be placed in the toolbar, but that the toolbar itself can *only* be placed in a QMainWindow object.

This tool button corresponds to the **Connect...** menu item. The first two arguments specify the pixmap to use for the tool button along with a text label to be shown below the icon: "Connect". The next string, "Connect to database", is the text to be shown on the status bar when the mouse is over the button. The two next lines are exactly like the ones in the insertItem call for menu items. Finally we specify the toolbar on which we want this button placed.

With the toolbar built up, we're ready to insert it into our main window. We also want the text labels to be shown, which we do like this:

```
addToolBar(m_pToolBar);
setUsesTextLabel(true);
```

Note that both of these functions are members of `QMainWindow`, our base class. Note also that we can disable tool buttons very simply, with a command like this:

```
m_pDisconnectButton->setEnabled(false);
```

and create toolbar separators with a line like:

```
m_pToolBar->addSeparator();
```

Central Widget

Now the menu bar and toolbar are done, we come to the central part of the window. Here we want two tabs, the first containing the log and the second the loan list. We create tabs with the `QTabWidget` class:

```
m_pCentralWidget = new QTabWidget(this);
```

For the log listing, we'll use the text editor widget that Qt provides, but in read-only mode.

> *Qt actually provides a read-only widget with `RichText` markup, called `QTextBrowser`, which is better suited for logs like this, but we choose the editor in order to stay as close to the GNOME/GTK+ version as possible:*

```
m_pLog = new QMultiLineEdit(m_pCentralWidget);
m_pLog->setReadOnly(true);
```

Notice the change in the parent field; the main window is no longer the parent. Since we want the log to be inside the tab widget, we're using the tab widget as parent instead.

For the loan list, we're going to use the `QListView` class. As with the editor, we want the list to be inside the tab widget, so we pass the tab widget to the list constructor. We then create a few columns in the list:

```
m_pList = new QListView(m_pCentralWidget);
m_pList->addColumn("Member No.");
m_pList->addColumn("DVD");
m_pList->addColumn("Title");
m_pList->addColumn("Due Back");
```

With the contents of the tab widget ready, we're ready to assign each of them a tab:

```
m_pCentralWidget->addTab(m_pLog, "DVDStore");
m_pCentralWidget->addTab(m_pList, "On Loan");
```

There are just two things left to do before our main window is complete. Firstly, we must let it know that our tab widget is to be the central widget. Secondly, we must give it a reasonable initial size (we can leave positioning to the window manager):

```
setCentralWidget(m_pCentralWidget);
resize(460, 300);
}
```

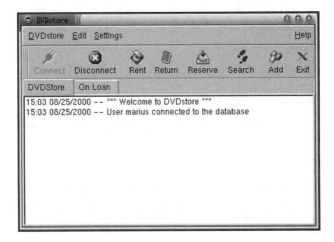

Transaction log

Every effort should be made to ensure that the transaction log is kept safe, and that as little information as possible is lost in the event of an application crash. The solution we choose here is by no means ideal, however, as discussed before, we will concentrate our focus on the Qt part, and we have therefore chosen the simplest solution. The log will only be saved when the application is closed properly (i.e. no crash).

We are going to place the log file saving in the destructor of the main window. We are going to use the QFile class, and let a text stream, QTextStream, work on the file. This is the common way to work on files. Qt also has a QDataStream class for binary data. We will use a simple ASCII text file for the log.

```
MainWindow::~MainWindow()
{
        QString logfile = SettingsManager::instance()->getString("logfile");
        if(logfile == "")
                logfile = "logfile.txt";

        QFile f(logfile);

        if(f.open(IO_WriteOnly | IO_Raw | IO_Append))
        {
                QTextStream s(&f);
                s << m_pLog->text();
                s << "\n";
                f.close();
        }
}
```

The destructor code looks to see if a log file name has been specified (using a default name if there is none), and passes it to the QFile constructor, which opens it in 'write and append' mode, without any buffering.

As you see, the streams work in much the same way as the standard I/O streams work. You may ask why you should choose the Qt classes. One reason is portability; apart from the database library we use, our application could compile on Windows with no changes at all to the code! Another reason is that if you stick to Qt you won't have to link against other libraries since you're likely to have all you need in Qt.

You may also find it easier to extend the Qt streams as Qt operates on a `QIODevice` class, which can be sub-classed, while the standard `iostream` doesn't work on such a class. Creating `cout`, `cin`, and `cerr` wrappers is simply a matter of:

```
QTextStream cout(stdout, IO_WriteOnly);
QTextStream cin(stdin, IO_ReadOnly);
QTextStream cerr(stderr, IO_WriteOnly);
```

You can also work on `QString` objects and byte arrays with the stream classes if you need to.

Member Dialog

This is where we add new members to our application, and to do so requires access to the database backend. We therefore use the C library that was implemented in Chapter 4. Since we are using C++, we will add a thin wrapper around the `dvd.h` header file. We call it `qdvd.h`:

```
#ifdef __cplusplus
extern "C"
{
#endif

#include "dvd.h"

#ifdef __cplusplus
}
#endif
```

The `memberdialog.h` looks like this:

```
#include <qdialog.h>
#include <qlineedit.h>

class MemberDialog : public QDialog
{
        Q_OBJECT
public:
        MemberDialog(const char *member_no, QWidget *parent = 0,
                                            const char *name = 0);
        virtual ~MemberDialog();

private slots:
        void okay();

private:
        QLineEdit *m_pTitle;
        QLineEdit *m_pFirstName;
        QLineEdit *m_pLastName;
        QLineEdit *m_pHouseNum;
        QLineEdit *m_pAddr1;
        QLineEdit *m_pAddr2;
        QLineEdit *m_pTown;
        QLineEdit *m_pState;
        QLineEdit *m_pZip;
        QLineEdit *m_pPhone;
        QString *m_MemberNo;

};
```

In the `okay` slot, we will copy all the text in the line edits and place it in a structure which we will pass to the database. The `memberdialog.cpp`:

```
MemberDialog::MemberDialog(
                const char *member_no,
                QWidget *parent,
                const char *name)
                : QDialog(parent, name, true)
{
```

We pass `true` as the final argument to the `QDialog` constructor meaning that the member dialog will be modal. This makes things easier for us, although the non-modal alternative would potentially give the user more flexibility.

We choose a vertical layout to place our widgets in, with a four-pixel border and four pixels between the contents:

```
QVBoxLayout *main = new QVBoxLayout(this, 4, 4);
```

Members are identified by a name and an address. For a user friendly GUI, we want to emphasize this natural grouping. We want a border around each group, and the way to do that is to use `QGroupBox` or one of its derivatives. We will use the horizontal kind, `QHGroupBox`:

```
QHGroupBox *namebox = new QHGroupBox("Name", this);
```

Inside this box, we want a left column with labels describing the single-line edit fields in the right column. We want them neatly aligned, so we've chosen to use a grid, or to be specific, a `QGrid`. We cannot use layouts within a group box:

```
QGrid *topgrid = new QGrid(2, namebox);
topgrid->setSpacing(4);
```

We've created a grid with two columns (and any number of rows) inside the box `namebox` by letting the box be the grid's parent. We set the spacing between components in the grid to four pixels.

We populate it by simply letting each widget in it have the grid as a parent:

```
(void) new QLabel("Title:", topgrid);
m_pTitle = new QLineEdit(topgrid);
m_pTitle->setMaxLength(PERSON_TITLE_LEN - 1);
    ...
}
```

These two widgets will now populate the first row of the grid. The grid will continue to fill out in this manner:

1	2
3	4
5	6
...	

Note that we don't need to store the label object, and therefore use (void) in front of new. All widgets with parents must be created on the heap; this is because when a parent is deleted, all its children will be as well. We therefore don't need to de-allocate the widget ourselves, and since we don't need access to the QLabel object, we don't store it. Using (void) in this form is something that comes in handy every now and then.

We have now laid out the controls; if the user clicks the **Okay** button, Qt will call our okay slot. The next step is to take values from the GUI and put them into the database. Since all the line edit fields have been given a maximum length (according to the size of the corresponding fields in the structure we are going to fill in), there's no need to check for the length of the text fields:

```
void MemberDialog::okay()
{
    dvd_store_member new_member;
    int member_id, rc;
    dvd_member_get_id_from_number(m_MemberNo, &member_id);
    dvd_member_get(member_id, &new_member);
    strcpy(new_member.title,          m_pTitle->text().local8Bit());
    strcpy(new_member.fname,          m_pFirstName->text().local8Bit());
    strcpy(new_member.lname,          m_pLastName->text().local8Bit());
    strcpy(new_member.house_flat_ref, m_pHouseNum->text().local8Bit());
    strcpy(new_member.address1,           m_pAddr1->text().local8Bit());
    strcpy(new_member.address2,           m_pAddr2->text().local8Bit());
    strcpy(new_member.town,           m_pTown->text().local8Bit());
    strcpy(new_member.state,          m_pState->text().local8Bit());
    strcpy(new_member.zipcode,            m_pZip->text().local8Bit());
    strcpy(new_member.phone,          m_pPhone->text().local8Bit());
```

Here, we fill in the dvd_store_member structure with the values from the GUI. Now that we have a new member structure, we must check whether it constitutes a change to an existing member or is a brand new member. The variable m_MemberNo contains the member number, if any, given in the constructor:

```
    if( ! m_MemberNo.isEmpty())
    {
        rc = dvd_member_set(&new_member);
    }
    else
    {
        rc = dvd_member_create(&new_member, &mem_id);
```

We pass the structure on to the database library, and it returns a member ID for the new member along with other data. If the function fails, we'll display an error message (code not shown):

```
if(rc == DVD_SUCCESS)
{
QString str = QString("%1 %2 %3 added as new member. Member no. %4")
                    .arg(m_pTitle->text()).arg(m_pFirstName->text())
                    .arg(m_pLastName->text().arg(mem_id);
```

We add the message to the log and also show the log message in a dialog box:

```
MainWindow::addLog(str);
QMessageBox::information(this, "DVDstore", str,
                    QMessageBox::Ok | QMessageBox::Default);
    }
    else
    {
    ...
    }
}
accept();
}
```

This should close the dialog box, returning a code to the caller to specify that everything went OK. Alternatively, you can call `reject` in case of errors or cancellation. This will also close the dialog, but with a different return code.

Rent Dialog

This dialog handles the renting out of DVD titles. The user can invoke this dialog from the menu, the toolbar, or the popup menu in the DVD search window. It contains a field in which user can specify a member ID, and a list to which the user can add the ID numbers of the titles the member wants to rent. For the sake of user friendliness we add a button to remove entries from the list, just in case the user makes a typo:

Rent List

We will begin by looking at the use of the list; we have an **Add** button connected to the add slot:

```
void RentDialog::add()
{
      dvd_title dvd;
      dvd_title_get(m_pTitleId->text().toInt(), &dvd);
      (void) new QListViewItem( m_pList,
m_pTitleId->text(),
dvd.title_text);
}
```

We fill in the `dvd_title` structure dvd with the title ID specified by the user. We then add an item to the list. When the user clicks the **Rent** button, we have to run through this list:

```
void RentDialog::rent()
{
      dvd_store_member mem;
      int member_id = m_pMember->text().toInt();
      int rc = dvd_member_get(member_id, &mem);

      if(rc != DVD_SUCCESS)
      {
            QMessageBox::warning(this, "DVDstore", "No such member");
      }
```

What this code does is to retrieve the appropriate member information from the database, as per the member ID specified by the user. We then make sure that the member actually exists; if not, we give an error. Notice that we don't actually close the dialog box, so that the user has another chance to enter the member number.

If the member does exist, we go through the list built in add. We want to show a rental report dialog box (this is also where we'll do the actual renting), so this will need to know about the rent list. There are many ways to do this – we've chosen to build a list of title IDs and pass it on to the rental report dialog box via the constructor.

We build the title ID list by going through the list view in the GUI:

```
QListViewItem *item = m_pList->firstChild();
```

This returns the very first element in the list. For the title IDs, we can use Qt's `QValueList` class:

```
QValueList<int> titlelist;

while(item != 0)
{
      titlelist.append(item->text(0).toInt());
      item = item->nextSibling();
}
```

Now we hide the rent dialog box and show the rental report dialog box:

```
hide();
RentedDialog dlg(m_pMember->text(), titlelist, this);
dlg.show();
```

When the user closes the `RentedDialog`, we go on to close this one:

```
accept();
```

Rental Report Dialog

As we've seen, the rent dialog box brings up the rental report dialog; this goes through the list of title IDs that was passed to it, and rents each one to the specified member:

```
...
int disk_id, title_id, rc;
QListViewItem *item;
QString log;

for(uint i = 0; i < titlelist.count(); i++)
{
        title_id = titlelist[i];
        rc = dvd_rent_title(member_id, title_id, &disk_id);
        item = new QListViewItem(list);
        item->setText(0, QString::number(title_id));
        item->setText(1, findTitle(title_id));
        if(rc == DVD_SUCCESS)
        {
                item->setText(2, "OK");
                log.sprintf("Rented disk %d to Member: %d",disk_id,member_id);
                MainWindow::addLog(log);
        }
        else
                item->setText(2, "N/A");
        item->setText(3, QString::number(disk_id));
}
```

This is what it the rental report dialog box looks like:

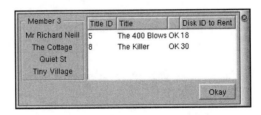

Search Window

As we've specified from the very start, the user must be able to search for DVD titles, actual disks, and members. These are clearly three different searches, and we want the GUI to reflect this. We therefore create one search dialog with three tabs in it; the search dialog is therefore a tab dialog.

Each page requires several widgets, and two of the pages also have a popup menu from which we can conveniently rent, reserve, return, or even delete DVD titles. It's therefore the most complicated dialog box in the application and requires some careful attention.

We touched briefly on the subject of tabs when discussing the main window; we used QtabWidget in that case, whereas we're now going to derive from QTabDialog, since it provides us with a **Close** button. We will start by having a look at the constructor, so that we can figure out how to go about using QTabDialog:

```
#include "searchdialog.h"
#include "dvdsearchpage.h"
#include "membersearchpage.h"
#include "disksearchpage.h"

SearchDialog::SearchDialog(
      QWidget *parent,
      const char *name)
      : QTabDialog(parent, name, true)
{

      setOkButton("Close");

      DVDSearchPage *page1    = new DVDSearchPage(this);
      MemberSearchPage *page2 = new MemberSearchPage(this);
      DiskSearchPage *page3   = new DiskSearchPage(this);

      addTab(page1, "DVD Title");
      addTab(page2, "Member");
      addTab(page3, "Disk");
}
```

We can see that each tab page is a widget. In our main window, we only needed a multi-line edit on one page and a list on the other; that meant that we could add the widgets directly. However, in our search window, we need more than one widget per page. In a case such as this, it's usually best to create a new widget (derived from QWidget) and build it up as we have the dialogs that we've seen so far.

Remember that a dialog is a widget as well, so setting up a widget with layouts and widgets is exactly as shown earlier.

We've created three widgets, one for each page in our search dialog.

DVD Search Page

This page will let the user search DVDs according to title and/or director/actor name. Once again we will skip the layout of the widgets, and go directly to the search routine. To get an impression of how the GUI works, here's a screen shot:

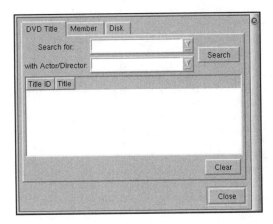

The Search button is connected to the search slot:

```
void DVDSearchPage::search()
{
        m_pList->clear();

        int *result;
        int count, colno;
        dvd_title dvd;

        dvd_title_search( m_pSearchFor->currentText(),
                        m_pActor->currentText(),
                        &result,
                        &count);
```

The dvd_title_search function fills out the result array with title IDs that match the specified criteria. We then iterate through the array and look up the detailed information for each title so as to populate the GUI with data:

```
        QListViewItem *item;
        for(int i = 0; i < count; i++)
        {
                dvd_title_get(result[i], &dvd);
                item = new QListViewItem(
                                m_pList,
                                QString::number(dvd.title_id),
                                dvd.title_text);
```

The first two columns (Title ID and Title) are always present; the user cannot turn them off. The others, however, can be turned off from the preferences window. We determine which columns to show or not via the settings manager. Since we identify the columns by number, we need to keep track of the column number so that we can place text in the correct column:

```
        colno = 2;
```

We are shortly going to start making extensive use of the settings manager's getBool method. Since Booleans are stored as "TRUE" and "FALSE" strings, this is fairly inefficient. A better solution would be to have a list of Booleans *and* a list of strings in the settings manager:

```
        if(sm->getBool("show_refnum"))
                item->setText(colno++, dvd.asin);
        if(sm->getBool("show_director"))
                item->setText(colno++, dvd.director);
        if(sm->getBool("show_genre"))
                item->setText(colno++, dvd.genre);
        if(sm->getBool("show_classif"))
                item->setText(colno++, dvd.classification);
        if(sm->getBool("show_actor1"))
                item->setText(colno++, dvd.actor1);
        if(sm->getBool("show_actor2"))
                item->setText(colno++, dvd.actor2);
        if(sm->getBool("show_reldate"))
                item->setText(colno++, dvd.release_date);
        if(sm->getBool("show_rentcost"))
                item->setText(colno++, dvd.rental_cost);
    }
```

Finally, free the memory allocated for the result array:

```
        free(result);
    }
```

The user must be able to edit and remove DVD titles. We will implement these functions in the search window, by adding a popup menu with **Edit** and **Delete** items. We will also add two convenience functions: **Rent** and **Reserve**. In order to show the popup menu, the user must right-click on an element in the list; we therefore need to set up a little menu in the constructor of the search page widget:

```
m_pPopup = new QPopupMenu(this);
m_pPopup->insertItem("Rent...", this, SLOT(rent()));
m_pPopup->insertItem("Reserve...", this, SLOT(reserve()));
m_pPopup->insertSeparator();
m_pPopup->insertItem("Edit...", this, SLOT(edit()));
m_pPopup->insertItem("Delete", this, SLOT(deleteDvd()));
```

This is the popup menu. We now need to listen up for the user right-clicking in the list view:

```
connect(
    m_pList,
    SIGNAL(rightButtonClicked(QListViewItem*, const QPoint&, int)),
    this,
    SLOT(showPopup(QListViewItem*, const QPoint&, int))
);
```

This signal has a more complicated signature than we've seen before. No variables are placed in the SIGNAL and SLOT parts, but the variables types are instead. The showPopup slot is straightforward:

```
void DVDSearchPage::showPopup(QListViewItem *item, const QPoint &p, int)
{
        if(item)
                m_pPopup->popup(p);
}
```

By checking the item for zero, we avoid showing the menu if the user clicked in a blank area. This will show the popup menu we created in the constructor. There we connected a slot to each item. If the user selects Rent... we enter the rent slot:

```
DVDSearchPage::rent()
{
        QListViewItem *item = m_pList->currentItem();
        int title_id = item->text(0).toInt();
        RentDialog dlg(title_id, this);
        dlg.show();
}
```

We built the rent dialog so that it accepts a title ID, which will then be placed in the rent dialog GUI.

This is the way to create popup menus. You may want to make the popup menus context-sensitive; this just involves checking in the showPopup slot for the kind of item the user clicked on.

Member Search Page

The second search requirement involves being able to search for members; the member page supports member searches by either last name or member number:

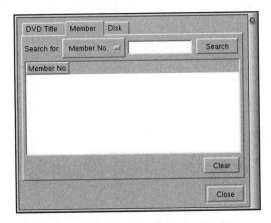

Again a search slot is connected to the Search button:

```
void MemberSearchPage::search()
{
        m_pList->clear();

        int *result;
        int count = 0;
```

The user can select to search on either member number or last name. Either way, we use an array of member IDs as a basis for building the list in the GUI.

```
if(m_pSearchFor->currentItem() == 0)
{
// Search for member no.
result      = (int*)malloc(1);
```

We use malloc here and not new because the we interface with a C library and memory will therefore be de-allocated by free:

```
int member_id;
int rc = dvd_member_get_id_from_number(m_pSearch->text(), &member_id);

if(rc == DVD_SUCCESS)
        {
                result[0]   = member_id;
                count       = 1;
        }
}
else
{
        // Search for last name.

        dvd_member_search(m_pSearch->text().local8Bit(),
                        &result,
                        &count);
}

dvd_store_member mem;
QListViewItem *item;
int colno, rc;
SettingsManager *sm = SettingsManager::instance();

for(int i = 0; i < count; i++)
{
        colno = 1;
        rc = dvd_member_get(result[i], &mem);

        if(rc == DVD_SUCCESS)
        {
                item = new QListViewItem(m_pList, mem.member_no);
                if(sm->getBool("show_title"))
                        item->setText(colno++, mem.title);
                ...
```

The user can choose which columns to show in the preferences dialog box. The population of the list and these columns is similar to that of the DVD search page.

Disk Search Page

Our third and final search requirement is the option to search for actual disks, so that we can see who, if anybody, they are on loan to:

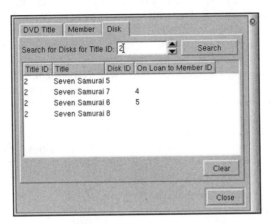

For the sake of completeness and comparison, we will list the disk search code. It is relatively simple, as the columns are not configurable:

```
void DiskSearchPage::search()
{
        m_pList->clear();

        int title_id = m_pSearchFor->value();
        int *result;
        int count;
        int rc = dvd_disk_search(title_id, &result, &count);

        if(rc == DVD_SUCCESS)
        {
                dvd_title dvd;
                dvd_title_get(title_id, &dvd);
                QListViewItem *item;
                char date_rented[9];
                int r, member_id;

                for(int i = 0; i < count; i++)
                {
                        item = new QListViewItem(    m_pList,
                                                QString::number(title_id),
                                                dvd.title_text,
                                                QString::number(result[i]));

                        r = dvd_rented_disk_info(result[i],
                                                &member_id,
                                                date_rented);

                        if(r == DVD_SUCCESS)
                                item->setText(3, QString::number(member_id));
                }
        }
}
```

The Settings Manager

Our application benefits greatly from the ability to persistently save its configuration; that is, the user can specify a log file name and which columns to enable in the search dialog box, and we want these settings to persist from one session to the next.

As in the main window destructor, we're going to use our own settings manager class; this acts like a simple keyword-based lookup table for settings that we want to be globally readable and writeable. In other words, the class is, in essence, just a dictionary with convenience functions for storing and retrieving simple data types. This is all we need in our application. There are no complex data structures we need to save that aren't already saved through the database interface.

The SettingsManager class is implemented as a singleton, in order to achieve a clean global access point; a singleton is a class with only one instance to which it provides a global point of access, achieved by using the static instance function and keeping the constructor private.

> *Mind you, the implementation here is not terribly efficient. All values are stored internally as strings, for example, even Booleans and integers.*

First, let's look at the interface to get an overview of the class:

```
#include <qmap.h>

class SettingsManager
{
public:
        virtual ~SettingsManager();

        static SettingsManager* instance();

        bool        isSet(const QString& key) const;
        void        set(const QString& key, bool value);
        void        set(const QString& key, const QString& value);
        bool        getBool(const QString& key) const;
        QString     getString(const QString& key) const;
        void        save();
        void        load();

private:
        SettingsManager();

        QMap<QString,QString> m_Settings;
        static SettingsManager *m_pInstance;
};
```

We could have used the standard map<> template classes instead of QMap, but this is a Qt tutorial and QDataStream provides us with a nice a function to save QMaps directly to disk as well. One of the set functions:

```
void SettingsManager::set(const QString& key, const QString& value)
{
        m_Settings.replace(key, new QString(value));
}
```

One place where the settings manager is used extensively is in the preferences dialog box. This reads and saves the state of each page to the settings manager. Here are some snippets of the state retrieval:

```
SettingsManager *sm = SettingsManager::instance();
m_pRefNum->setChecked(sm->getBool("show_refnum"));
m_pDirector->setChecked(sm->getBool("show_director"));
...
```

and state storage:

```
SettingsManager *sm = SettingsManager::instance();
sm->set("show_refnum", m_pRefNum->isChecked());
sm->set("show_director", m_pDirector->isChecked());
...
```

Now that we have all the settings in one place, it's easy to add persistent storage, at least in this case, where we don't have to deal with any complex data structures. We implement basic save and load functions:

```
void SettingsManager::save()
{
        QFile f("settings");

        if(f.open(IO_WriteOnly | IO_Raw | IO_Truncate))
        {
                QDataStream s(&f);
                s << m_Settings;
        }
}
```

QDataStream has an operator for saving QMaps, making the save code trivial. Reading is just as easy:

```
void SettingsManager::load()
{
        QFile f("settings");

        if(f.open(IO_ReadOnly))
        {
                QDataStream s(&f);
                s >> m_Settings;
        }
}
```

For simplicity, we only load the settings at the start of the application. The settings will be saved to disk once the settings dialog box is closed.

Adjusting the Code to KDE

If you don't need the portability and the small memory footprint offered by Qt, but feel a need for more ready-made widgets or utility classes, you may want to consider using KDE. KDE provides much that Qt does not, such as a central configuration manager from which you can modify the look of your application. It also provides a configuration parser, many more widgets (such as a fully-fledged HTML parser and widget), and helper classes (such as a spell checker).

Before we start though, a few words of caution:

❑ At the time of writing, KDE 2 is not yet released; the code in this chapter was written and tested under KDE beta 2. Hopefully, there will not be too many incompatibilities between this beta and the final version that impact on the code shown here.

❑ We want to continue to keep our application as similar as possible to the GNOME/GTK+ version. Because of this, we will not fully comply with the many conventions that have been established for 'true' KDE applications. These conventions can be seen in the style guide at: http://developer.kde.org/documentation/standards/kde/style/basics/index.html.

The style guide, however, is exactly that, a style guide for issues regarding GUI design. The technical aspects will still be the same, and that's what we're going to focus on here. In this section, we will look at how to make our Qt application more KDE-compliant. We'll look at:

❑ the KApplication object

❑ the main window

❑ the title dialog

❑ KConfig and SettingsManager

As mentioned in the previous chapter, the first step in making our application a KDE application is to replace Qt's QApplication with KDE's KApplication. KDE2 applications must also have a KAboutData object. This class is used to store information about the application, such as name, description, copyright, and homepage. It should be possible to pass a username and password from the command line. KDE provides a command line parser (KCmdLineArgs), although this is faulty in some beta versions of KDE2, and will be left out of our code (in beta versions of KDE2, you may get a warning saying that 'no about data was specified', even though it has been):

```
#include <kapp.h>
#include <kaboutdata.h>
#include <kcmdlineargs.h>
#include "mainwindow.h"
#include "settingsmanager.h"

int main(int argc, char **argv)
{
    KAboutData aboutdata(  "dvdstore",
                           "DVDstore",
                           "1.0",
                           "Wrox Press Demo Application",
                           KAboutData::License_GPL,
                           "(c) 2000, Wrox Press",
                           "http://www.wrox.com",
                           "A KDE GUI for the DVDstore conceived in\n"
                           "'Professional Linux Programming'\n"
                           "Wrox Press 2000",
                           "none");
```

```
aboutdata.addAuthor("Marius Sundbakken");

KCmdLineArgs::init(argc, argv, &aboutdata);
KApplication app;
...
```

By simply replacing the application object, we have quite drastically changed the look of our application; the toolbar, font, and most of the widgets have changed throughout:

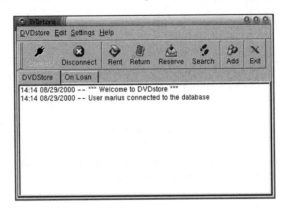

This look can now be configured centrally from the KDE control center.

The next step is to change our main window so that it derives itself from KTMainWindow rather than QMainWindow. By doing so, we get full session management. Toolbar positions will be saved along with window position and geometry.

Use of KTMainWindow requires a few other changes. We must use KMenuBar and KToolBar instead of their Qt equivalents; including kmenubar.h instead of qmenubar.h solves the first issue. For the toolbar, we need to update mainwindow.h to include ktoolbar.h, and replace QToolBar with KToolBar in both header and source files:

```
#include <ktmainwindow.h>
#include <ktoolbar.h>
...

class MainWindow : public KTMainWindow
{
...

private:
    KToolBar *m_pToolBar;
...
};
```

The KToolBar constructor is slightly different from QToolBar, but a larger change is that between the toolbar buttons. We're not going to use QToolButton any more; how we build our KDE toolbar will be more like how we previously built a menu. Consequently, we drop all of our tool button objects from the header file and replace them with simple integer IDs as we did for the menu. To create buttons, we are use insertButton in KToolBar.

For easy comparison, here's the code for both the initial Qt version and the new KDE version.

First, the Qt version:

```
m_pConnectButton = new QToolButton(
        QPixmap(DVDSTORE_ICON_CONNECT"),
        "Connect",
        "Connect to database",
        this,
        SLOT(connectDatabase()),
        m_pToolBar);
```

In the KDE version, we use the KDE icon loader to get us the QPixmap object. The icon loader is responsible for getting us icons that match the current theme selected by the user:

```
KIconLoader il;
QPixmap pixmap = il.loadIcon("socket", KIcon::Toolbar, 32);
```

Here, "socket" refers to the file name of the icon, but without any extension. We also specify in which icon group (toolbar) the icon loader is going to look in, and the size in pixels.

```
m_pToolBar->insertButton(
        pixmap,
        m_ConnectButton,
        SIGNAL(clicked()),
        this,
        SLOT(connectDatabase()),
        true,
        "Connect");
```

The pixmap is the same as before.

Next we pass the ID of the button, which will replace our QToolButton objects.

More interesting is the next parameter, specifying which signal we're going to listen to. We didn't specify this in the Qt version; Qt automatically used the clicked signal. In this case, we are going to use the clicked too (since it's the only one that makes sense).

The next two parameters specify the object and the slot. We then enable the button and give it a label.

> *This is the 'raw' way to create a toolbar button; KDE actually provides a KAction class, which simplifies this process for us, as well as ensuring consistency between corresponding menu items and toolbar buttons; however, we will not cover KAction here.*

A few function calls need to be changed:

❑   setCentralWidget is changed to setView,

❑   setUsesTextLabel to setIconText,

❑   and addSeparator to insertSeparator.

With these modifications to the toolbar, the look of our application has changed again. Finally, since we're not using QToolButton objects anymore (but integer IDs), we need to change the code that enables and disables the toolbar buttons:

```
m_pToolBar->setItemEnabled(m_DisconnectButton, false);
```

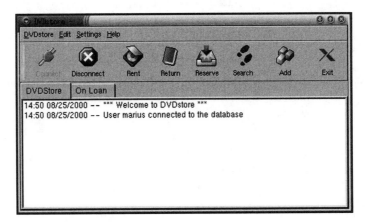

We will now convert one of our Qt dialogs to a KDE-compliant dialog. We choose the title dialog, so that we can replace its simple use of a line edit for the user to enter the date with KDE's date picker. The base class for KDE dialogs is KDialogBase. This class provides predefined layouts and standard buttons, such as OK and Cancel. First, the header file:

```
#include <kdatepik.h>
#include <kdialogbase.h>
...

class TitleDialog : QKDialogBase
{
...
```

We had an okay slot here, but since we are going to remove our own OK button and use the predefined one, we need to use the protected virtual slotOk in KDialogBase:

```
protected slots:
    void slotOk();

private:
    KDatePicker *m_pReleaseDate;
    ...
};
```

In titledialog.cpp:

```
TitleDialog::TitleDialog(int title_id, QWidget *parent, const char *name):

    KDialogBase(parent, name, true)
                    {
                    showButtonOK(true);
                    showButtonApply(false);
                    showButtonCancel(true);
```

With these three lines, we get the **OK** and **Cancel** button; we don't want an **Apply** button. `KDialogBase` comes with a number of predefined layouts; none of them fits our need though, so we create a widget placeholder for our own layout, and pass this widget to `KDialogBase`:

```
QWidget *thispage = new QWidget(this);
setMainWidget(thispage);
```

Also, we want to use the widget spacing that KDE suggests; the rest of the code referring to `this` must therefore be updated to `thispage` instead:

```
QVBoxLayout *main = new QVBoxLayout(thispage, 4, spacingHint());
...
```

The date picker:

```
...
m_pReleaseDate = new KDatePicker(topgrid);
...
}
```

Our new slot:

```
void TitleDialog::slotOk()
{
...
QDate d = m_pReleaseDate->getDate();
```

We must now build the date string to be passed to the database library. Usually, `QString::arg` is the function to use, but here we need it in YYYYMMDD format, so we use `QString::sprintf`:

```
QString str;
str.sprintf("%04d%02d%02d", d.year(), d.month(), d.day());
strcpy(new_title.release_date, str);
...
}
```

From the screenshot below, you see that a large date picker widget has replaced the small single-line edit field. However, the GUI is still perfectly aligned and tidy. This would not had been possible if we had placed the widgets at fixed co-ordinates; however, since we're using layouts, the actual placement is abstracted away from us, and we end up with the flexibility to add and remove widgets independent of their size. We also see the new **OK** and **Cancel** buttons:

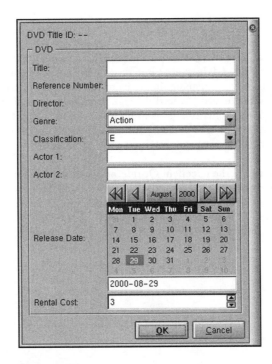

KConfig and SettingsManager

Since Qt doesn't have a configuration file parser, we wrote our own. KDE on the other hand, does provide us with such a class: KConfig. It's much more sophisticated than our settings manager class, but it works the same way as ours, by specifying keys and values. The KConfig object can be obtained from KApplication::sessionConfig, equivalent to our SettingsManager::instance function.

As we've seen, it's as simple to use the KDE classes as it is to use the Qt classes. Since KDE uses more or less the same naming conventions as Qt, mixing the two doesn't detract from the code's nice, clean, integrated feel. We could carry on like this, replacing every part in our application that had a KDE equivalent. Time and space limit us though, so we leave it to you to experiment with the full code, which you can download from the Wrox website at www.wrox.com.

Resources

Design Patterns: Elements of Reusable Object-Oriented Software, by Gamma et al, Addison Wesley (*ISBN 0-201-63361-2*).

Pattern Languages of Program Design 3, by Martin et al, Addison Wesley (*ISBN 0-201-31011-2*).

The Trolltech web site: http://www.trolltech.com/

The Qt-interest mailing list archive: http://qt-interest.trolltech.com/

Information about KDE, as well as its source code: http://www.kde.org/

KDE mailing lists archives: http://lists.kde.org/

Summary

In this chapter we looked at how to create a GUI using Qt, and then adjusted it to use some of KDE. We went through the creation of GUIs, and although we have not covered every GUI component in Qt, we have gone through the basics. Replacing the widgets and dialogs we have used with others should not offer too many problems. We also covered the signals and slots sufficiently for you to be able to use them efficiently. A GUI without functionality is of no use, so we also went through how to actually use the GUI components together with the C library for accessing the DVD Store database. Lastly, we looked at how to adjust a pure Qt application to make use of KDE.

The reader is encouraged to use the excellent Qt reference documentation extensively. If the documentation should fail to answer your questions, you can search in the Qt-interest mailing list archive at http://qt-interest.trolltech.com/. Either way, the mailing list is a highly recommended list to join, with it its relatively low volume, but excellent content. For KDE development, there are several mailing lists as well: http://www.kde.org/contact.html. For the archives, go to: http://lists.kde.org.

Online discussion at http://www.p2p.wrox.com

15

Python

Introduction

And now for something completely different...

—Monty Python's Flying Circus

Welcome to Python!

Python is a very high-level, object-oriented, dynamically typed, multiplatform, scalable, open-source programming language. Python is a language that maps well to the thought processes and abilities of the modern sophisticated programmer. Imagine scalable and readable Perl or Tcl, procedural and object-oriented Scheme, Ruby with minimalist syntax, and higher-level interpreted Java. Imagine ease of use and maintenance, and increased productivity. Put all of these together and you will have an approximation of what Python is.

Why learn another programming language? If you're like me, you collect programming languages, and so this question answers itself. But what if you're a hard-core C/C++ programmer, satisfied with your language of choice? Python is not a universal replacement for C or C++. Rather, it's another tool for a programmer's toolbox. Sometimes Python is a good alternative to C, and sometimes they are complementary. Python *is* often in direct competition with Perl, Tcl, JavaScript, and Visual Basic. If you are considering such a tool, or are dissatisfied with your current language, Python may be for you.

All programmers should have a range of tools at their disposal. So-called 'scripting' languages are traditionally used for small tasks, gluing other programs together, and automating processes. Python is unique in its scalability, from small scripts to very large systems. Your choice of programming languages is very personal, however: which one maps best to your thinking? If you already know several languages, I would not presume to try to convert you. Instead, I would like to present to you Python, a language that incorporates the best features of a variety of other languages, and introduces a few new ideas of its own, into a remarkably elegant, cohesive, and useful whole.

With Python, you can get the job done more quickly and simply. You can try out ideas of all sizes, with minimal coding overhead. You can prototype large or small systems, refining the design and proving the concept, before investing the time required to code it in C. You may find that the 'prototype' turns out to be all that's needed, and more. You can be more creative and have fun.

> *I never got beyond starting the data-structures in C++, I never got beyond seeing how it would work in Scheme. I finished it in one Python-filled afternoon, and discovered the idea sucked big time. I was glad I did it in Python, because it only cost me one afternoon to discover the idea sucks.*
>
> *—Moshe Zadka on comp.lang.python, 13 May 2000*

This chapter is a quick introduction to the language, with enough breadth to whet your appetite, and enough depth to get you started. It is an overview of what sets Python apart, what makes Python a valuable addition to any programmer's toolbox. It is not an introduction to programming, nor is it a complete reference.

Python was created by Guido van Rossum (Guido or GvR for short), and was first released in 1991. It takes its name from the British comedy troupe Monty Python. Python's roots are in ABC, a teaching language of limited practical success that Guido helped to create in the 1980s in Amsterdam. Guido took the best features of ABC and Modula-3, learned from the shortcomings of these and many other languages, and combined that with a vision of readability and usability, to produce this (in our humble opinion) wonderful language.

I will contrast Python with C, Perl (arguably Python's closest rival), and other common programming languages, point out Python's advantages and disadvantages, illustrate Python tricks, and identify Python traps.

So, how is Python different? Read on!

Features

Python's features are intentionally biased toward programmer efficiency and efficacy, sometimes at the expense of program efficiency. In other words, Python programs are faster to write, but sometimes slower to run, than the equivalent in C. Programmers' time is valuable, both in terms of money and in terms of creativity. Monetarily, Python is a boon for employers who recognize that programmers who get more done in less time will more than offset the cost of faster hardware. As for creativity, answer this: when was the last time you postponed or passed on a project because it was going to take too long to implement? Imagine taking up to 90% less time for that project; would you pass on it now?

Below are some of the features that are making Python into one of the hottest and most usable languages ever.

Very High Level Language (VHLL)

Often characterized as 'executable pseudo code,' Python programs are a high level representation of a programmer's ideas. Low-level 'housekeeping' details like memory allocation and reclamation are handled by Python itself; the programmer need not worry about them.

High-level means seeing the big picture and delegating the details. This is what Python does. Intelligent syntax reduces clutter. The interpreter understands program structure by examining the physical structure of the code; block delimiters are not required. Modules and classes provide exceedingly accessible abstraction, encapsulation, and modularity.

Interpreted

Python programs are interpreted, not compiled, at least not in the traditional sense of the C-source-to-machine-code compiler (more on this later). There is no 'edit, compile, link, then run' cycle; instead, it's 'edit, then run.' With dynamic loading and some planning, the cycle can even be 'run, edit, and reload the edited part into the running process without stopping'. The Python interpreter reads source files (called 'modules,' which usually have the extension .py), converts them to portable byte codes, and executes them by interpreting the byte codes (much like Java and Perl do, but at a higher level).

Python is sometimes referred to as a scripting language; this depends on your definition. Like shell scripts or Perl programs, Python source files and executables are (or can be) one and the same. But missing from Python are the limitations and cobbled-together feel of other scripting languages. Make no mistake; Python is a fully featured, general-purpose programming language.

Clean, Simple and Powerful Syntax

Python code is remarkably easy to write, read, and maintain. It remains easy to read weeks or even years after it was written. Unlike other programming languages, Python programs can be read and understood by non-Python programmers, and often even by non-programmers. Python also makes an excellent teaching or first language, being relatively devoid of the details that make other languages difficult for neophytes to learn. There is an initiative by Python's creator to develop a curriculum for non-computer science students to learn programming, dubbed CP4E, 'Computer Programming For Everybody.'

Python's syntax is minimalist. It lacks a lot of the 'noise' characters that other languages suffer from, like semicolons at the end of each statement, special dereferencing symbols, and braces or begin/end for nested code blocks. Compared to Perl, Python is refreshingly Spartan.

One feature of Python's syntax stands out more than any other: the significant use of whitespace for block structure. As opposed to some form of block start/end indicators ({ and } in Perl, C, and Java; begin/end in Pascal; if/fi, case/esac, and for/done in shell languages), the hierarchy of blocks of code in Python is indicated by that code block's indentation level. Experienced programmers are often turned off by this; some grow to love it, others never accept it. In the minds of many, Python is defined by this feature.

> What is hard is creating a language that makes as much sense to another human as it does to a machine. ... Python emphasizes much more than Perl the fact that when you write a program, you don't only write it for the compiler to read. You also it write it for your fellow programmers to read.
>
> −Guido van Rossum, creator of Python, in an interview with Sam Williams on BeOpen.com

Because of its simplicity, Python's syntax is also very powerful. An equivalent task will often require far less Python code than C code. Fewer lines of code also means fewer bugs, greater programmer productivity, and far less frustration.

'Small' languages tend to start out very nice and tidy, then as they become more popular they grown knobby bulges and unsightly additions, especially when they are extended in areas the original authors didn't foresee. The longer a language exists, the wartier it gets. Perl is a language that started out as an everything-*including*-the-kitchen-sink mixture of other languages, and has grown over time. Python began as a minimalist language; and change to the core language syntax has been planned and deliberately slow. Future versions of Python may even reduce the complexity of the language.

Object Oriented

Object orientation is not just tacked on to Python as an afterthought; the language is object oriented from the ground up. In Python, everything is an object. The implementation of classes and objects is much simpler in Python than in C++, and less pervasive than in Smalltalk. This simplicity makes OOP accessible, laying bare the essential nature of object orientation without complicated trappings that get in the way of the concept.

Dynamic Typing

In C, variables are statically typed. You must first declare the type of a variable, and that variable may only contain data of the type declared. In Python, variables are dynamically typed. Variables are created when they are assigned a value, and their type depends on the data they contain. An existing variable can be assigned a new value of a different type. With care and understanding, this feature leads to impressive programming power. Used carelessly, dynamic typing can be a major source of program bugs.

Large Standard Library

Python's core language is very minimalist, providing much less functionality than that of Perl. However, the standard Python distribution includes a large number and variety of modules, ready and easy to use in your own programs. Library modules include: string operations, regular expressions, file and operating system access, threads, sockets, database access, Internet protocols, and even access to Python's parser internals.

Multiplatform

Python has been ported to almost every hardware platform and operating system available, including Linux (of course), UNIX, MacOS, and Windows. General-purpose modules, if properly written, will run without modification on multiple platforms.

Multiple Implementations

In addition to the standard Python implementation, written in C (and commonly called CPython), there is also JPython and Stackless Python. JPython is a 100% Pure Java implementation, which runs on Java platforms, and provides seamless integration to Java classes. Stackless Python eliminates reliance on the C stack (thus the name), enabling Python to run in tight quarters (such as on handheld devices), and implements efficient continuations.

Scalable

Python scales very well. Simple 10-line scripts are easy to write and read. Large systems with thousands or millions of lines of code are feasible and maintainable. Compare that to Perl, Python's closest rival. Perl is great for one to ten line programs, but breaks down when you get into the hundreds or thousands of lines that a complex system will require. You can get a lot done with a one-line Perl program, but this comes at a price. With all the implicit behavior, line-noise-like syntax, and magic variables, Perl programs are indecipherable to all but Perl experts. And even for them, the larger a program grows, the less understandable and maintainable it becomes.

As a former Perl programmer, I speak from experience. I have written many thousands of lines of Perl code. Although I believe it was well written, I shudder to think of having to go back and maintain any of it. Although unreadable code can be written, I believe Python lends itself to legibility, more than any other language I've met. Although this is personal, any tool that helps other programmers' understanding of your code will extend the viable lifespan of your work.

Python implements encapsulation at multiple levels. Functions encapsulate reusable program code, classes combine data (attributes) with their associated functions (methods), modules contain related classes and functions, and packages encapsulate systems.

If native Python code is too slow or cannot access low-level functionality, extension modules can be written in C. If you have an application that needs to be scriptable, Python can be embedded (see Chapter 17)

Open-Source

Python is completely free for use, modification, redistribution, and commercial use, and even resale, with no strings attached (beyond the requirement to duplicate a copyright notice). Python's source code is freely downloadable.

Fun!

Given its roots in comedy, humour is almost a requirement in any discussion of Python, a 'seriously silly' language. In describing the features and functionality of other languages, often the names foo and bar are used in examples. In Python, the equivalents are spam and eggs, for reasons only a true Monty Python fan could tell you. Monty Python references are often used for application names, such as the Grail web browser, (obsolete) module ni, and the ArgumentClinic utility.

Although Python is *not* named after the snake, serpent references also abound, such as the Boa Constructor GUI builder, and the Vaults of Parnassus Python resource database. In addition, 'Py' is used as a prefix or suffix for modules and applications: PyUnit, NumPy.

As many Pythonistas (a name for Python aficionados) like to say,

Thank Guido for Python!

Python: The Right Tool for the Job

Python is a general purpose programming language, useful in many ways and fields. Examples include, but are not limited to: system administration, text and data processing (XML, HTML, etc.), Rapid Application Development (RAD) including Graphic User Interfaces (GUIs), numerical and scientific programming. Python is being adopted by the open-source community for its clarity, portability, and power.

...but not every job!

Being a very high-level language (VHLL), Python is not suitable for writing device drivers or operating system kernels. Being an interpreted language, Python can never be a match for compiled C in terms of speed; however, compiled C extension modules controlled by Python code may be the perfect balancing act of ultra-fast code and ultra-rapid development. Monolithic binary executables are not Python's forté, although (if you insist) there *are* ways to at least approximate this approach.

Installing Python

You may already have Python installed on your system. Several Linux distributions use Python for their installation scripts, and most come with Python pre-installed. To see if you have it, try running the interactive interpreter; if it is installed, you'll get something like this:

```
$ python
Python 1.5.1 (#1, Apr 30 1998, 11:51:50)   [GCC egcs-2.90.25 980302 (egc on linux2
Copyright 1991-1995 Stichting Mathematisch Centrum, Amsterdam
>>>
```

If you don't already have it, or if your version of Python is not up to date (as in the dated Python, above, that came with my Linux distribution), you can either download a precompiled binary or compile from the latest sources. Precompiled binary packages are available for Red Hat Linux, Debian GNU/Linux, and other Linux distributions from the usual archive sites. Installing such packages should be trivial.

If you can't find a compatible binary package, or the available binaries don't have the right mix of optional functionality that you require, you'll need to compile the source. Python is easy and straightforward to compile and install. Source code is available from the Python Language Website, http://www.python.org. As of writing this, the latest stable release version of Python is 1.5.2 (downloaded as py152.tgz), and version 2.0 (recently renumbered from 1.6) or later may be available by the time you read this. Let's install Python 1.5.2.

First, we unpack the source tarball:

```
$ tar -zxpf py152.tgz
$ cd Python-1.5.2
```

Be sure to read the README file in the top-level directory. It contains configuration instructions, specific platform installation instructions, and troubleshooting information.

```
$ ./configure
```

Configure will produce a lot of output as it checks your system for available features. It's quite forgiving and should complete the setup on any Linux system. Configure takes several options, the most commonly used being --with-thread to implement support for threads. Python is not threaded by default, because there is a performance hit involved, even if you don't actually use threads.

Before actually building the interpreter, you may want to edit the file Modules/Setup (copy it from Modules/Setup.in if necessary) to enable optional library modules and functionality in the Python interactive interpreter. You will probably want to enable the readline, termios, and curses modules as a minimum. If you have Tcl and Tk already installed, or if you don't mind getting and installing them first, you should enable the _tkinter module as well. The file Modules/Setup contains notes on each of the optional modules.

All code presented in this chapter will require only the modules installed by the default Modules/Setup.

Now we're ready to build the interpreter:

```
$ make
[voluminous output from make]
$ make test
[test output]
```

make test executes a set of test programs which put the interpreter through its paces. Some tests may be skipped or fail due to the lack of optional features, but that's normal.

To install Python into its default directory, /usr/local/bin/python (actually, the python executable is a hard link to python1.5), with libraries in /usr/local/lib/python1.5/:

```
$ su
Password: [your root password here]
# make install
[installation output]
# exit
```

If you reconfigure, before rebuilding you will need to clean up the files left behind by the first build process:

```
$ make clean
$ ./configure --with-thread     # for example
$ make
. . .
```

In certain cases, you will need to do a more thorough cleaning before rebuilding. First store a copy of your modified Modules/Setup file:

```
$ mv Modules/Setup Modules/Setup.old
```

Then bring the build directory back to its original pre-configuration state:

```
$ make distclean
```

After running configure again (perhaps with options), you should copy the stored file back to Modules/Setup:

```
$ ./configure --with-thread     # for example
$ cp Modules/Setup.old Modules/Setup
$ make
. . .
```

Running Python

There are several ways to execute Python code. Which way you chose will depend on how much you want to interact with Python itself.

The Interactive Interpreter

The simplest way to invoke the Python interpreter is to type:

```
$ python
```

at the shell prompt. This brings up the interactive Python interpreter, showing version, platform, and copyright information:

```
Python 1.5.2 (#4, Jun  3 2000, 14:20:48)  [GCC egcs-2.90.25 980302 (egcs-1.0.2 pr
on linux2
Copyright 1991-1995 Stichting Mathematisch Centrum, Amsterdam
>>>
```

>>> is Python's default first-level prompt, with . . . used as the prompt for nested code. I will use the interactive interpreter extensively to illustrate Python concepts.

From here you can type any Python statement or expression, such as the obligatory 'Hello world' program, Python-style:

```
>>> print "Spam!"
Spam!
>>>
```

In the interactive interpreter, when we enter a bare expression (i.e. not an assignment or print statement), the interpreter will echo its representation.

```
>>> "spam, egg, spam, spam, bacon and spam"
'spam, egg, spam, spam, bacon and spam'
>>>
```

This feature will be used a great deal in the remainder of this chapter.

Use ctrl-D or the following to exit the interpreter:

```
>>> import sys
>>> sys.exit()
$
```

Python also comes with IDLE, the Interactive DeveLopment Environment (named after Eric Idle). IDLE contains a GUI interface to the interpreter, a multi-window auto-indenting syntax-coloring text editor, and debugger. You can find it in the Tools/idle subdirectory of the source distribution, and possibly in a precompiled binary package. It is a multi-window GUI editor and debugger, written completely in Python (of course). IDLE requires Tkinter, Python's interface to Tcl/Tk.

Command Argument

Invoking Python with the `-c` option allows you to pass a command to the interpreter (normal shell quoting caveats apply):

```
$ python -c 'print "Lemon curry?"'
Lemon curry?
$
```

If you would like to invoke the interactive interpreter once the command is finished, use the `-i` option:

```
$ python -i -c 'print "What's all this then?"'
What's all this then?
>>>
```

Script Argument

By putting the code into an ordinary text file, we have created a script:

```
print "And now ... No. 1 ... The larch."
```

We execute the script as follows:

```
$ python hello1.py
And now ... No. 1 ... The larch.
$
```

The `.py` filename extension is not required in this case. Later, when we talk about reusing code through the import mechanism, we'll see that the `.py` extension *is* required, so it's good to get into the habit.

'Standalone' Executable

As with many scripting languages, we can add the shell's magic hash-bang first line:

```
#!/usr/bin/env python
print "Evening, squire!"
```

`#!/usr/local/bin/python` (or your system's equivalent) may also be used, but `#!/usr/bin/env python` is somewhat more portable.

By also enabling the source file's executable permissions, we can create the illusion of an apparently standalone executable:

```
$ chmod +x hello2.py
$ ./hello2.py
Evening, squire!
$
```

In this case, for generality and ease of typing, it may be advisable to drop the `.py` extension. The drawback is that without the `.py`, this file may not easily be imported (reused) by another Python program. Making a symbolic link solves that problem:

```
$ ln -s hello2.py hello2
$ hello2
Evening, squire!
$
```

The Details

Interpreter and Byte-Compilation

Although Python is an interpreted language, it *does* compile its programs in a way, just not as far as most C compilers do. When a module is imported (used by a Python program) for the first time, the Python interpreter will convert or compile the text source to byte code, and save the result as a `.pyc` (compiled Python) file. The next time that a module is imported, the interpreter will check for a `.pyc` file and use it, saving the compilation step. If the `.py` source file is newer than the `.pyc` file, however, Python will recompile the source and save the updated `.pyc` file for future use. Note that directly executed source files (named on the command line, and not imported), do not have `.pyc` files generated.

Byte-compiled `.pyc` files are completely portable, and can be executed on any platform (assuming, of course, that the Python interpreter and all required modules have been installed, and that the `.pyc` file's source code does not contain any platform-specific operations). Distributing only the `.pyc` files, without the source `.py` text files, is a way to protect source code from prying eyes, as is distributing binary executables without the C source.

However, Python byte code can be made human-readable by the disassembler (module `dis`) included in the standard Python distribution. Just as Python is much higher-level than C, so too is Python's byte code much higher-level than machine code, and disassembled Python byte code is much more readable than disassembled machine code. So distributing only the byte code `.pyc` files can only be described as weak source protection.

Comment Syntax

Python comments begin with the hash mark (sharp, or number sign) #, and extend to the end of the line. There are no multi-line comments in Python (although there are ways to simulate such comments with strings, as we shall see). Also, there is no Python preprocessor, so no equivalent to C's #ifdef compiler directives.

I will use comments in interactive code listings to illustrate concepts:

```
>>> print "it's..."   # This is a comment. It need not be typed in.
it's...
```

Case Sensitivity

Python names and keywords are case-sensitive. This is one of the features that are currently under discussion for possible future change. In future Python implementations, either the tools or the language itself may become case-insensitive.

Built-In Data Types and Operators

Python has many built-in data types. The commonly used data types can be grouped as follows:

- ❑ None: an object used to represent 'no value' or logical false.
- ❑ Numbers: integers, long integers, floating point numbers, and complex numbers.
- ❑ Sequences:
  - **a.** Mutable: lists
  - **b.** Immutable: strings and tuples
- ❑ Mappings: dictionaries
- ❑ Callable types: functions, methods, classes, and some class instances.
- ❑ Modules
- ❑ Classes
- ❑ Class Instances (objects)
- ❑ Files

Data types through mappings (dictionaries) are described below. Other data types are described later in this chapter.

None

There is only one None object, named None. It is used to signify 'no result,' 'absence of value,' or the logical false value.

Integers

Mathematical whole numbers, Python plain integers are at least 4-byte signed values between –2147483648 and 2147483647, inclusive. On some platforms integers may have a larger range. Integers may be created in decimal, octal, or hexadecimal:

```
>>> 10          # no prefix: base 10
10
>>> 010         # "0" prefix: base 8
8
>>> 0x10        # "0x" prefix: base 16
16
```

Many operations may be performed on integers, and most of these may also be performed on other types of numbers:

```
>>> - 1          # negation
-1
>>> + 1          # identity
1
>>> 1 + 1        # addition
2
>>> 2 - 3        # subtraction
-1
>>> 4 * 5        # multiplication
20
>>> 20 / 7       # division (note: integer division => integer result)
2
>>> 20 % 7       # modulo (remainder after integer division)
6
>>> divmod(20, 7)  # integer division: quotient & remainder
(2, 6)
>>> 6 ** 2       # power (6 squared)
36
>>> pow(6,2)     # power
36
>>> abs(-2)      # absolute value
2
>>> int(1.5)     # convert to plain integer
1
>>> long(4)      # convert to long integer
4L
>>> float(3)     # convert to floating point number
3.0
>>> complex(2,3)  # convert to complex number
(2+3j)
```

Integer division produces an integer result, rounded down (towards minus infinity); 1/2 gives 0, and –1/2 gives –1.

The only integer that evaluates to false is 0. All other integers evaluate to true. Here are the Python Boolean operators:

```
>>> not 0        # logical not. not false => true
1
>>> not 3        # not true => false
0
>>> 3 or 0       # logical or
3
>>> 3 and 0      # logical and
0
>>> 3 and 2
2
```

In the last example, the interpreter returned the actual value that evaluated to true, 2, not just the canonical 'true' value 1. If you require a return value of either 0 or 1 exclusively (as an index into a two-element list, for example), you will need to use the not operator, which is guaranteed to return 0 or 1 only:

```
>>> not not (3 and 2)   # double negation!
1
>>> (3 and 2) != 0      # another way
1
```

Python's and and or are short-circuit operators; their second arguments are only evaluated if necessary:

```
>>> 3 or 1        # 1 is never evaluated
3
>>> 0 and 1/0     # 1/0 is never evaluated
0
>>> 1/0           # if it were, it would result in an error:
Traceback (innermost last):
  File "<input>", line 1, in ?
ZeroDivisionError: integer division or modulo
```

Python's comparison operators work as you might expect:

```
>>> 3 > 2         # greater-than
1
>>> 3 < 2         # less-than
0
>>> 3 >= 3        # greater-than-or-equal-to
1
>>> 4 <= 3        # less-than-or-equal-to
0
>>> 3 == 3        # equal
1
>>> 3 != 3        # not equal. "<>" may also be used, but "!=" is preferred
0
```

Python's comparison operators may conveniently be chained, and work as expected from our long-forgotten math class:

```
>>> 5 > 3 > 2
1
>>> 5 > 1 > 2
0
>>> 5 > 6 > 2
0
```

Python's is operator compares object identities: are they the same object? In the current implementation of CPython, small numbers and certain strings constants may actually be shared objects:

```
>>> 3 is 3        # object identity: same object
1
>>> (1+2) is 3
1
>>> (1000+2000) is 3000  # larger number; not shared
0
```

Typically, we use the is operator on variables, which I describe later. In the meantime, please note that the shared object behaviour of small numbers (and other types as well) is an implementation detail and should not be relied upon.

The is not operator is the logical opposite of is.

```
>>> 1 is not 0
1
>>> not (1 is 0)
1
>>> 1 is (not 0)  # "a is not b" means "not(a is b)", not "a is (not b)"!
0
```

Bit-string operations can only be performed on integers and long integers:

```
>>> 5 | 6         # bitwise or
7
>>> 5 & 6         # bitwise and
4
>>> 5 ^ 6         # bitwise exclusive-or
3
>>> 1 << 3        # bitwise left-shift
8
>>> 16 >> 2       # bitwise right-shift
4
>>> ~ 5           # bitwise inversion/not (2's complement)
-6
```

Integers and all Python numbers are immutable. Once created, they cannot be changed; they can only be replaced. I will explain this concept further, when we discuss variables.

Long Integers

Long integers are just like plain integers, except they have platform-independent, arbitrarily large values. Of course, very large values may take up large amounts of memory space. Long integers are created by appending an L, (uppercase or lowercase, but uppercase is preferred for legibility), to the end of a whole number:

```
>>> 12345678901234567890L
12345678901234567890L
```

Mixed arithmetic operations will automatically convert as required: plain integers to long integers to floating-point numbers to complex numbers:

```
>>> 1 + 12345678901234567890L
12345678901234567891L
```

The zero value, 0L, is the only long integer that evaluates to false; all other values evaluate to true.

Floating-Point Numbers

Python floating-point numbers are implemented as C doubles, so the underlying C determines their precision. Floating-point numbers are created when a number literal includes a decimal point:

```
>>> 10.
10.0
>>> .1
0.1
```

When at least one of the operands of a division is a floating-point number, the other operand will be converted if necessary and the result will also be floating point:

```
>>> 10. / 3
3.33333333333
```

The zero value, 0.0, evaluates to false. All other floating-point values evaluate to true.

Complex Numbers

Complex numbers combine a real floating-point number with an imaginary floating-point number. The imaginary number part is displayed by appending a j (uppercase or lowercase; j represents the square root of −1) to a regular number:

```
>>> 2j            # imaginary number
2j
>>> 3+4j          # complex (real + imaginary) number
(3+4j)
>>> (3+4j) * (2+5j)   # complex numbers are, well, complex
(-14+23j)
```

Complex numbers can also be created with the complex function, and have a conjugate method which reverses the sign of the imaginary part:

```
>>> a = complex(3, 4)   # create a complex number variable "a"
>>> a
(3+4j)
>>> -a
(-3-4j)
>>> a.conjugate()
(3-4j)
```

Complex numbers cannot be converted to integers or floating-point numbers directly, since they are two-dimensional. You must convert the two-dimensional complex number to a one-dimensional value first, using the `real` or `imag` attributes, or the abs function:

```
>>> a.real        # real number part
3.0
>>> a.imag        # imaginary number part
4.0
>>> abs(a)        # "length" of complex number as a vector
5.0
```

The zero value, `(0j)`, evaluates to false; all other complex number values evaluate to true.

Lists

Lists are Python's mutable sequence type, one-dimensional arrays of object references. Mutable means the list's contents can be changed in-place. Lists are created with square brackets, with items separated by commas:

```
>>> b = [4, 3.14, 5+6j]   # a 3-item list
>>> b
[4, 3.14, (5+6j)]
```

A list may contain items of many different types. Integer indexing accesses sequence items:

```
>>> b[1]
3.14
>>> b[0] = 55     # change the first element in-place
>>> b
[55, 3.14, (5+6j)]
```

Python sequence indexes begin at 0 for the first element. The index of the last element of a sequence is the sequence's length less 1, but it can also be accessed with the index `-1`:

```
>>> b[2]
(5+6j)
>>> b[-1]         # indicates first item from the end
(5+6j)
>>> b[-2]         # indicates second item from the end
3.14
```

Sequences may be 'sliced,' obtaining a top-level (shallow) copy of the sub-sequence:

```
>>> b[0:2]        # elements 0 (inclusive) through 2-1
[55, 3.14]
>>> b[:2]         # omitting part of a slice implies the extremity
[55, 3.14]
>>> b[:]          # top-level (shallow) copy of b
[55, 3.14, (5+6j)]
```

b[:] creates a top-level, shallow copy of the list b. This means that if the list contains other lists, their contents are not copied but shared:

```
>>> list = [3.14, [1j, 2j], 1.01]
>>> list2 = list[:]
>>> list[2] = 'hi'
>>> list
[3.14, [1j, 2j], 'hi']
>>> list2
[3.14, [1j, 2j], 1.01]
>>> list[1][0] = 0
>>> list
[3.14, [0, 2j], 'hi']
>>> list2
[3.14, [0, 2j], 1.01]
>>>
```

Sequences (lists and strings) have several additional operators:

```
>>> b + [0]      # concatenation
[55, 3.14, (5+6j), 0]
>>> b * 3        # repetition
[55, 3.14, (5+6j), 55, 3.14, (5+6j), 55, 3.14, (5+6j)]
>>> 3.14 in b    # membership test
1
>>> 55 not in b  # inverse membership test
0
>>> len(b)       # length of b
3
>>> min(b)       # smallest value element of b
3.14
>>> max(b)       # largest value element of b
55
```

Lists have several methods:

```
>>> b.append(10)  # add an item to the end
>>> b
[55, 3.14, (5+6j), 10]
>>> b.count(55)   # how many 55's are in b?
1
>>> b.extend([1, 2])  # join a list to the end
>>> b
[55, 3.14, (5+6j), 10, 1, 2]
>>> b.index(10)   # what index is the item 10?
3
>>> b.insert(5, 3)   # add 3 before item #5
>>> b
[55, 3.14, (5+6j), 10, 1, 3, 2]
>>> b.pop()       # remove and return the last item
2
>>> b.remove(1)   # just remove the first 1
>>> b
```

```
[55, 3.14, (5+6j), 10, 3]
>>> b.reverse()   # reverse the list in-place; NO RETURN VALUE!
>>> b
[3, 10, (5+6j), 3.14, 55]
>>> b.sort()      # sort the list in-place; NO RETURN VALUE!
>>> b
[3, 3.14, (5+6j), 10, 55]
```

Items may be deleted from lists by index or slice:

```
>>> bb = b[:]    # make a shallow copy of b
>>> bb
[3, 3.14, (5+6j), 10, 55]
>>> del bb[3]    # delete item 3
>>> bb
[3, 3.14, (5+6j), 55]
```

The empty list, [], is the only list that evaluates to false. All other lists evaluate to true.

Strings

Strings are an immutable sequence type. This means they cannot be changed in-place. If you want to modify a string, you must replace it with a modified copy. Strings are created using single or double quotes; unlike Perl and the shells, there is no difference between quote types:

```
>>> c = '"Have you got any?" he asked, expecting the answer "no".'
>>> d = "I'll have a look, sir ... nnnnnnnnnno."
>>> print c, "\n", d      # "\n" is a newline
"Have you got any?" he asked, expecting the answer "no".
I'll have a look, sir ... nnnnnnnnnno.
```

Single quotes were used for c because the text contains double quotes. Double quotes were used for d because its text contains a single quote (apostrophe). To mix both single and double quotes in a single string, you can use backslash-escapes, or triple-quotes:

```
>>> e = "He said, \"My name is 'Gumby'.\""
>>> f = '''What's my name? "Gumby."'''
>>> print e, "\n", f
He said, "My name is 'Gumby'."
What's my name? "Gumby."
```

Triple-quoted strings (either triple-single-quotes or triple-double-quotes) may span multiple lines and may contain other quotes:

```
>>> g = """G'day Bruce.
... Oh, hello, Bruce.
... How are yer, Bruce?"""  # note the continuation prompts, "..."
>>> g                # Python automatically escapes control and unprintable characters:
"G'day Bruce.\012Oh, hello, Bruce.\012How are yer, Bruce?"
```

Line breaks are stored internally as newlines (\n), and converted to the platform's standard line separator character(s) on output.

Prefixing any type of string with an r creates a raw string: a string where backslash escapes are not interpreted:

```
>>> "\\"          # a single backslash, backslash-escaped
'\\'
>>> r"\\"         # two raw backslashes, displayed backslash-escaped
'\\\\'
```

In addition to the sequence operators shown with lists, above, strings also have a % formatting operator which implements C's sprints functionality:

```
>>> h = "%s of the Yard!"   # %s means string value
>>> h % "Flying Fox"        # % takes a single right argument
'Flying Fox of the Yard!'
>>> h % "Flying Thompson's Gazelle"
"Flying Thompson's Gazelle of the Yard!"
>>> "%s %s." % ("Start", "again")
'Start again.'
```

The % operator takes a single argument. If there are multiple % entries in the format string, the right-hand argument must be a tuple, as in the last example above.

Strings are sequences, so they can use all of the sequence operators shown for lists. In particular, strings can be concatenated with + and repeated with *:

```
>>> "spam, " + "eggs"
'spam, eggs'
>>> "spam, " * 3
'spam, spam, spam, '
>>> 3 * "spam, "
'spam, spam, spam, '
>>>
```

From version 2.0, Python strings will have several methods, currently implemented as functions in the string module. For example:

```
>>> f.split()  # splits on whitespace. Notice the intelligent quoting:
["What's", 'my', 'name?', '"Gumby."']
```

The empty string, "", evaluates to false. All other string values evaluate to true.

Tuples

Tuples are like immutable lists. Once created, their top-level items cannot be altered in-place. Tuples are created with the comma operator, usually (and preferably) enclosed with parentheses:

```
>>> i = 5, "hello", 0.2
>>> j = ()        # parentheses are required for an empty tuple
>>> k = (1,)      # a trailing comma is required for a single-item tuple
>>> print i, j, k
(5, 'hello', 0.2) () (1,)
```

Tuples are strictly immutable if they contain only immutable items. A tuple containing a list is not strictly immutable.

The empty tuple, (), evaluates to false. All other tuples evaluate to true.

Dictionaries

A dictionary is a mapping: a data structure that maps keys to values, like Awk and Perl's associative arrays or hashes. Dictionary keys must be strictly immutable data types (one reason for tuples and immutable strings!); values may be anything. Dictionaries are created by enclosing comma-separated 'key':'value' pairs with braces:

```
>>> m = {'name':'Arthur, King of the Britons',
...          'quest':'To seek the Holy Grail'}
```

Dictionary entries are indexed by key value:

```
>>> m ['name']
'Arthur, King of the Britons'
>>> m['favourite colour'] = 'green'   # creation of a new key
>>> m
{'quest': 'To seek the Holy Grail', 'name': 'Arthur, King of the Britons',
'favourite colour': 'green'}
```

Dictionaries sport their own set of methods:

```
>>> m.has_key('quest')   # test for existence of a key
1
>>>      # same as m['name'], but returns None if the key doesn't exist
>>> m.get('name')
'Arthur, King of the Britons'
>>> m.get('kids')   # returns None since key 'kids' doesn't exist
>>> m.get('kids', 0)   # default return value: 0
0
>>> m.items()       # returns list of (key, value) tuples
[('quest', 'To seek the Holy Grail'), ('name', 'Arthur, King of the Britons'),
('favourite colour', 'green')]
>>> m.keys()        # returns list of keys (in random order)
['quest', 'name', 'favourite colour']
>>> m.values()      # returns list of values (in random order)
['To seek the Holy Grail', 'Arthur, King of the Britons', 'green']
>>>                 # merges another dictionary
>>> m.update({'hometown':'Camelot', 'wife':'Guinevere'})
>>> m
{'favourite colour': 'green', 'hometown': 'Camelot', 'wife': 'Guinevere', 'name':
'Arthur, King of the Britons', 'quest': 'To seek the Holy Grail'}
>>> n = m.copy()    # makes a shallow copy
>>> n
{'name': 'Arthur, King of the Britons', 'favourite colour': 'green', 'quest': 'To
seek the Holy Grail'}
>>> del n['name']   # deletes one item
>>> n
{'quest': 'To seek the Holy Grail', 'favourite colour': 'green'}
>>> n.clear()       # clears the dictionary
>>> n
{}
```

Dictionary entries are arbitrarily ordered. However, if the keys, values, and items methods are called without any intervening modifications to the dictionary, the ordering of their results will match.

The empty dictionary, {}, evaluates to false. All other dictionary values evaluate to true.

Variables

Python variables are simply names that are bound to objects, much like C pointers, Java or C++ references. But in Python, all variables are names, so there is no need for explicit referencing or dereferencing. Assigning one variable to another simply binds both names to the same object. If the object is mutable, changing one variable in-place will also affect the other variable:

```
>>> a = ["one", "two", "three"]
>>> b = a           # now a and b refer to the same object
>>> b[1] = "deux"   # so changing b in-place...
>>> a               # ...also changes a:
['one', 'deux', 'three']
```

Block Structure Syntax

A distinguishing feature of Python's syntax is its use of indentation for code block nesting. This is a feature that at first strikes many programmers the wrong way, but it is very easy to learn, and quickly becomes second nature. Besides, it's natural; good programmers use indentation to aid program readability, so why shouldn't the language make use of this information? Here is the classic example of if-else ambiguity in C:

```
if (i > 0)
    if (a > b)
        x = a;
else
    x = b;
```

Although the (mistaken) indentation implies that the else goes with the outer (first) if, in fact, it goes with the inner (second) if. In the Python example, the else clause goes with the if with which it is aligned:

```
if i > 0:
    if a > b:
        x = a
else:
    x = b
```

Either tabs or spaces may be used for indentation. There is no rule as to how much indentation is required for each nesting level, as long as the indentation is consistent within a block. 4 spaces per indentation level is common. One tab is equivalent to 8 spaces, or more precisely, a tab aligns to the next 8-column tab stop. Although some programmers intermix tabs and spaces (4 spaces for the first indentation level, 1 tab for the second, 1 tab and 4 spaces for the third, and so on), it is better to be consistent and use either tabs or spaces, but not both. The emerging standard is to use 4 spaces for each indentation level, avoiding editor-related problems.

If you plan to distribute your code to the world, I recommend converting all tabs to spaces first. Different editors treat tabs differently, but spaces are universal. Some editors have a tab stop every 8 columns, some every 4; some, such as e-mail clients, convert each tab to a single space. The exclusive use of spaces will preserve the aesthetics of your code (including the alignment of comments).

Since there are no block start/end indicators (like { } in C or Perl) and since line breaks remove the requirement for statement separators (; in C and Perl), what happens when you want to break up a line that has grown too long? Logical lines may be broken into multiple physical lines using backslash escapes (\) at the very end of each physical line (except the last, of course), forcing a continuation. The indentation of the second and any subsequent lines is not significant; extra white space in the middle of a logical line is ignored. So the following two statements are equivalent:

```
# statement 1: all on one line
print "I'd like to have", "an argument,", "please."

# statement 2: broken up over multiple lines, with continuations
print "I'd like to have",\
      "an argument,",\
      "please."
```

In addition, if the statement you're breaking up contains an expression enclosed in parentheses (grouping, tuples, or function parameter lists), brackets [ ] (lists), or braces { } (dictionaries), the interpreter will infer line continuations automatically, until it finds the closing parenthesis/bracket/brace. So these two statements are also equivalent:

```
# statement 3: all on one line
spam = (eggs + ham - bacon)

# statement 4: broken up inside parentheses
spam = (eggs
         + ham
         - bacon)
```

Statement Syntax

Multiple statements can be written on one line, separated by semicolons (;). This is normally bad practice, however, and should be avoided.

Expression Statements

As we've seen many times already in the interactive interpreter, typing in an expression will compute and display the value:

```
>>> 1
1
>>> 6 * 7
42
```

Such statements in a program would have no meaning; they would compute a value and immediately discard it. In a program, an expression statement will only have meaning if it produces a side-effect. A call to a function that does something (a side-effect), but doesn't return a value (in other words, a call to a procedure in Pascal terms), is an example of a useful expression statement.

Assignment

Assignment statements are used to bind a name to an object.

This binds the name a to a new object whose value is 1:

```
a = 1
```

This binds both a and b to a new object (they share a single object), an integer whose value is 2:

```
a = b = 2
```

Assignment may have multiple targets (a comma-separated sequence) on the left-hand side. If so, the right-hand side must comprise a sequence containing the same number of objects. Thus:

```
a, b = 1, 2      # equivalent to: a = 1; b = 2
```

The right-hand side is evaluated first, so the traditional swap operation can be done in one line with Python:

```
a, b = b, a      # swap a, b
```

Any sequence can be used in this way, including strings:

```
a, b = "ni"      # equivalent to a = "n"; b = "i"
```

In Python, assignment does not return a value, and cannot be used within an expression

Simple Statements

pass

pass is a statement that does nothing. It is useful as a placeholder when required by the syntax of a compound statement, but no action is to take place (at least temporarily).

del

```
del variable [, variable] ...
del sequence[index]
```

Deletes a name from the current namespace (first form), or an item from a sequence (second form).

global

```
global variable [, variable] ...
```

Binds a name to the global module namespace. Assignment to the variable name made global will create a variable in the module's global namespace rather than in the function's, class's, or method's local namespace.

Import

There are two forms for the `import` statement.

```
import modulename [, modulename] ...
```

This finds a module (a file named `modulename.py` or `modulename.pyc` if available) in Python's import search path, initializes it if necessary (only the first time it's imported), and defines a name for the module in the local namespace. Modules are described in more detail later.

```
from modulename import object [, object2] ...
```

The second form works much like the first, except that instead of defining a name for the *module* in the local namespace, it defines names for each of the imported *objects*.

```
>>> import os
>>> os
<module 'os' from '/usr/local/lib/python1.5/os.pyc'>
>>> from sys import path
>>> sys            # this name is not bound
Traceback (innermost last):
  File "<input>", line 1, in ?
NameError: sys
>>> path
['', '/usr/local/lib/python/', '/usr/local/lib/python1.5/',
'/usr/local/lib/python1.5/plat-linux2', '/usr/local/lib/python1.5/lib-tk',
'/usr/local/lib/python1.5/lib-dynload']
>>>
```

A degenerate form of the `from ... import` statement is:

```
from modulename import *
```

This imports (copies) *all* names from the imported module into the local namespace. This last form should be used sparingly, and only for modules expressly designed to work this way. `from ... import *` can clobber variables in the local namespace without warning.

Once imported, all names defined in a module (variables, functions, and classes) are accessible by qualifying the name with the module name:

```
>>> import sys, getpass
>>> sys.path      # an attribute in the sys module
['', '/usr/local/lib/python/', '/usr/local/lib/python1.5/',
'/usr/local/lib/python1.5/plat-linux2', '/usr/local/lib/python1.5/lib-tk',
'/usr/local/lib/python1.5/lib-dynload']
>>> pw = getpass.getpass()  # a function in the getpass module
Password:
>>> print pw
mypassword
```

raise

```
raise
```

Used to re-raise the last exception, currently being handled by an exception handler.

```
raise exception [ , parameter ]
```

Raises a new exception, which will either be handled by an enclosing exception handler, or will cause program execution to cease. See `try` below.

assert

```
assert expression [ , parameter ]
```

If debugging mode is on (it can be turned off with the -O command-line option), and `expression` evaluates to false, an `AssertionError` exception will be raised, with an optional `parameter`. See `try` below.

print

```
print [ expression1 [ , expression] ... ]
```

Writes to the standard output, converting each expression to a string as necessary. Spaces are written out between expressions, unless the expression is at the beginning of a line. A new line will be printed at the end of the expressions, except when a trailing comma is present.

`print` is a convenience statement; the same functionality is available more directly through file objects, such as `sys.stdout`.

exec

```
exec "arbitrary Python code in a string"
```

Parses and executes Python code stored in a string. This can be a very powerful tool, but it must be used carefully. In addition to strings, exec can also be used with open file objects, and code objects. `eval` is the functional equivalent of `exec`.

Compound Statements

Python's compound statements are made up of *clauses*; each clause is a *header* followed by a *suite* of statements. Usually, the suite consists of multiple statements, which are indented below the header. If the suite consists of a single statement, the entire compound statement may be expressed in one line. (In the degenerate and highly un-Pythonic case, a suite of multiple statements that contains no further compound statements can be expressed on a single line, with statements separated by semicolons.)

if

The general form of Python's `if` statement is as follows:

```
if condition1:
    suite1          # executed if condition1 evaluates to true
elif condition2:    # evaluated if condition1 evaluates to false
    suite2          # executed if condition2 evaluates to true
else:
    suite3          # executed if no condition evaluates to true
```

Of course, both elif and else clauses are optional. Multiple elif parts may be present. elif is simply a convenience form of else: if which saves indentation, especially when there are multiple cases.

The single-line form of if...elif...else looks like this:

```
if condition1: statement1
elif condition2: statement2
else: statement3
```

Python has no equivalent to C's switch...case. These can be implemented as multiple if...elif statements.

while

The Python while statement executes its suite as long as its condition evaluates to true:

```
while condition:
    suite1
else:
    suite2
```

The else clause of the while statement is optional, and is executed once the condition evaluates to false.

The continue statement may be used within the first suite to skip the remainder of the suite and return to the top of the loop, testing the condition. The break statement causes immediate termination of the loop, *without* executing the else suite.

for

Python's for statement iterates over a sequence (list, tuple, string, or user-defined sequence-equivalent), assigning each element to a variable in turn:

```
for item in sequence:
    suite1
else:
    suite2
```

As with while, the else clause is optional; its suite is executed after the last item of the sequence has been used up. continue and break are also available, and operate as with while.

This example uses the repr function, which returns a string representation of its argument in Python syntax (in the form you would have to type):

```
>>> for char in "hello": print repr(char),
...
'h' 'e' 'l' 'l' 'o'
>>>
```

The `for` may not function correctly if the controlling sequence is modified within the loop. It is usually preferable to iterate over a copy of the sequence:

```
>>> a = range(10)
>>> for i in a:
...         if i % 2:
...                 a.remove(9 - i)
...
>>> a
[1, 2, 3, 5, 7, 9]
>>> a = range(10)
>>> for i in a[:]:   # iterating over a copy of a
...         if i % 2:
...                 a.remove(9 - i)
...
>>> a
[1, 3, 5, 7, 9]
>>>
```

try

The `try` statement implements exception handling within Python programs. It has two forms, `try...except` and `try...finally`.

try...except:

```
try:
    suite1
except [ expression [ , target ] ]:
    suite2
else:
    suite3
```

The `else` clause is optional. Multiple `except` clauses may be present. There may be one expressionless `except` clause, the last one.

If no exception occurs within the first suite, no exception handler is triggered, but the `else` suite (if present) is executed. If an exception occurs within the `try` suite, the except clauses are searched for a matching exception; if found, that clause's suite is executed. A final expressionless `except:` clause matches any exception. If no match is found, the exception is passed on to any surrounding `try` code, calling functions, and finally (if not caught) to the interpreter, where it is reported as a runtime error.

Here is a simple example of an exception handler in action:

```
>>> for n in range(-3, 4):
...         print "1 / %i =" % n,
...         try:
...                 print 1.0 / n
...         except ZeroDivisionError:
...                 print "infinity"   # or undefined, if you prefer
...
1 / -3 = -0.333333333333
1 / -2 = -0.5
1 / -1 = -1.0
1 / 0 = infinity
1 / 1 = 1.0
1 / 2 = 0.5
1 / 3 = 0.333333333333
```

try...finally:

```
try:
    suite1
finally:
    suite2
```

The second form of `try` creates a cleanup handler, to perform vital operations like closing files, for example. If an exception occurs within the `try` suite, the `finally` suite is first executed, and then the exception is re-raised for any surrounding `try` exception handlers to catch.

If the `try...finally` form is inside a loop, a `break` within the `try` suite will execute the `finally` suite on the way out, as will a `return` if it's inside a function or method.

The two forms of `try` may not be mixed, but they may be nested.

Functions

A function definition is a compound statement, which creates a user-defined function object and binds it to the function name in the current local namespace (say *that* ten times quickly!):

```
def function_name( [ parameter_list ] ):
    suite
```

A function definition's parameter list is required if the function is to accept arguments. The parameter list defines local names that are bound to the objects passed in the function call. Python function arguments are passed by assignment, so only mutable arguments (lists and dictionaries) can be changed by the function and have the changes visible once the function exits, and only if they are changed in-place.

Simple parameters are of the form name. In simple function calls, arguments are matched to parameters from their positions. However, arguments order may be altered if the function call includes keywords. The following function calls are equivalent:

```
>>> def f1(a, b):
...     print a, b
...
>>> f1(2,1)        # positional arguments
2 1
>>> f1(b=1,a=2)    # keyword arguments
2 1
```

Default parameters are of the form name=default. If a corresponding argument is omitted from a function call, the default value is used instead:

```
>>> def pet(name="Eric", kind="fish"):
...     return ""%(name)s the %(kind)s" " % locals()
...
>>> pet("Spot", "cat")
''Spot the cat'
>>> pet("Spot")                    # kind omitted since name is first
'Spot the fish'
>>> pet()                          # both name and kind omitted
'Eric the fish'
>>> pet(kind="half a bee")         # name omitted (using keyword)
'Eric the half a bee'
```

This example illustrates the use of the `return` statement, which allows a function to produce a value. It also shows another use of the string % operator: variable substitution. The `locals` function returns a dictionary (`{name:value}`) of all local variables. `vars` and `globals` may also be used with various effects.

A parameter of the form `*name` defines a name for excess positional parameters. If any excess positional parameters are present, they will be made into a tuple bound to `name`:

```
>>> def f2(*t):
...     print t
...
>>> f2(1, "two", ["III"])
(1, 'two', ['III'])
```

A parameter of the form `**name` defines a name for excess keyword parameters. Any excess keyword parameters will be made into a dictionary bound to `name`:

```
>>> def f3(**d):
...     print d
...
>>> f3(bird="swallow", kind="African", cargo="coconut")
{'kind': 'African', 'bird': 'swallow', 'cargo': 'coconut'}
```

The various different kinds of parameters may be used together in function definitions, with the condition that default parameters must come after all simple parameters, any excess positional parameter (`*name`) must come after that, and any excess keyword parameter (`**name`) must come last.

The function definition (the compound statement header beginning with `def`) is executed at load time, but the function body is not executed until the function is called. This has an important consequence for default values:

```
>>> def alist(mylist=[]):  # default value: an empty list
...     return mylist
...
>>> a = alist()
>>> b = alist()
>>> a.append("item")
>>> b
['item']
```

The default value in the example above, an empty list, is evaluated once when the function definition is executed. When both a and b are assigned from the function `alist`, both get bound to the same shared empty list object. This is a common source of bugs in Python programs.

```
>>> def alist(mylist=None):
...     if mylist is None: mylist = []
...     return mylist
...
>>> a = alist()
>>> b = alist()
>>> a.append("item")
>>> b
[]
```

Built-In Functions

Python defines many built-in functions. Here are some we haven't seen yet:

```
>>> chr(65)          # returns a string containing ASCII character 65
'A'
>>> ord('A')         # returns the ASCII value of 'A'
65
>>> cmp(1,2)         # compare: returns -1 (less), 0 (equal), 1 (greater)
-1
>>> coerce(1, 2.0)   # converts both arguments to a common numeric type
(1.0, 2.0)
>>> eval('2 * 3')    # evaluates the argument as Python code
6
>>> hex(31)          # hexadecimal (base 16) string
'0x1f'
>>> oct(63)          # octal (base 8) string
'077'
>>> a = 0
>>> id(a)            # unique object ID (implemented as object address)
17180908
>>> b = raw_input("Nudge, nudge: ")   # prompts for input from stdin
Nudge, nudge: Say no more!
>>> b
'Say no more!'
```

Namespaces

A namespace is a mapping from names to objects. Each module has a global (module-wide) namespace, and each function and class within that module has its own local namespace. When a name is accessed in a function, the local namespace is first searched, and then the global namespace; an entry in the local namespace 'shadows' a same-named entry in the global namespace. With assignment, by default the name is bound in the local namespace, unless the global statement is used with the name first.

Namespaces are a very powerful feature of Python. A full description is beyond the scope of this introduction. Please see the Python Reference Manual for more complete information

Modules and Packages

A Python source file ending in .py is a module. Modules encapsulate variables, functions, and classes in a namespace so that they won't interfere with objects with the same names in other modules. Importing a module creates a namespace for that module, and enables qualified access to the module's functions, variables, and classes from the importing module's local namespace via the module's name. For example, if there is a module called module1.py containing a function doIt, we can call the function like this:

```
>>> import module1
>>> module1.doIt()
```

Packages extend the concept of encapsulation to the computer's file system. A package is a directory on Python's import search path that contains an __init__.py file (required) and other Python modules and possibly subpackages (subdirectories). Access to those modules is qualified via the package name. For example, if we have a directory pkg containing a file module2.py, we can import the module like this:

```
>>> import pkg.module2
```

Package directories can be nested to arbitrary depth.

Some Modules From The Standard Distribution

Python's standard distribution contains a wealth of reusable modules. Here are just a few:

❑   sys – system-specific values and functions

❑   os – generic operating system services, multiplatform

❑   string – string manipulation

❑   parser – access to the parser internals

❑   dis – byte code disassembler

❑   pdb – interactive command-line debugger

❑   profile – code profiler

❑   urllib, httplib, htmllib, ftplib, telnetlib – Internet protocol services

❑   Tkinter – Python's interface to the Tk GUI toolkit

❑   copy – for making deep copies of a data structure

Classes and Objects

A class definition is a compound statement that creates a user-defined class object and binds it to the class name in the current local namespace:

```
class Class_name [ ( baseclass1 [ , baseclass2 ] ... ) ]:
    suite
```

A class has its own local namespace, as does each object instantiated from the class.

'Calling' a class (using the Class_name syntax) creates an object (a class instance). Variables defined in the top level of a class definition are called 'class attributes,' and are shared by all instances. Individual objects (class instances) can create their own 'instance attributes' and override class attributes with the same name. Functions defined in the top level of a class definition are called 'methods.' A class can inherit attributes and methods from one or more base classes (multiple inheritance).

In its simplest form, an empty class can be thought of as the equivalent of a C struct:

```
>>> class Struct:
...     pass
...
>>> parrot = Struct()
>>> parrot.kind = "Norwegian Blue"
>>> parrot.status = "dead"
```

But the real power of classes is realized when they combine data attributes with function attributes (methods)–information with behavior. This is the essence of object-oriented programming. Many good (and not so good) books have been written on the subject; I will not attempt to cover such important material in so short a space. What follows is simply the mechanics of how classes and objects are used in Python.

Methods

A method is a function bound to an object, a function defined within a class' namespace:

```
>>> class AClass:
...       def amethod(self):
...             return "Class.amethod here"
...       def another(self):
...             return "Class.another here"
...
>>> object = AClass()
>>> object.amethod()
'AClass.amethod here'
>>> object.another()
'AClass.another here'
>>>
```

When a method is called using the `object.method` syntax, Python automatically converts this into a `Class.method(object)` call.

self

Each method's parameter list begins with `self`; this is a name for the object itself when the object's bound method is called. The name `self` is merely a convention, albeit an almost-universal one. You could just as easily use `me, I, this` (for C++ die-hards), or any other name in place of `self`, as long as you are consistent within each method.

Inheritance

Classes may inherit class attributes and methods from other classes:

```
>>> class Subclass(AClass):
...       def another(self):
...             return "Subclass.another"
...
>>> s = Subclass()
>>> s.amethod()
'AClass.amethod here'
>>> s.another()
'Subclass.another'
```

Subclass above inherits the method `another` from `AClass`, and defines its own `another` method, which hides `Aclass'` another method.

Classes may inherit from multiple superclasses:

```
>>> class Other(AClass):
...     def amethod(self):
...         return "Other.method"
...     def another(self):
...         return "Other.another"
...     def athird(self):
...         return "Other.athird"
...
>>> class Multiclass(AClass, Subclass, Other):
...     pass
...
>>> m = Multiclass()
>>> m.method()
'AClass.amethod here'
>>> m.another()
'AClass.another here'
>>> m.athird()
'Other.athird'
>>>
```

The class `Multiclass` inherits `amethod` and `another` from `AClass`, and `athird` from `Other`. Multiple inheritance is a left-to-right, depth-first search. So any method defined in the first superclass (or any of its superclasses) will hide that same named method in one of the other superclasses. Multiple inheritance is useful for 'mixins', when there is some functionality that you want many classes to share, but the classes are not otherwise related.

Special Methods

Python has many special methods or hooks which classes can define to implement operator overloading and other behavior. All overloading methods' names begin and end with two underscores. The __init__ method is called upon object instantiation; it is used to initialize an object:

```
>>> class BClass:
...     def __init__(self, data):
...         self.data = data
...
>>> b = BClass('hello')
>>> b.data
'hello'
>>>
```

Python defines special methods for: string representation (`__repr__` and `__str__`), object length (`__len__`), index overloading (`__getitem__` and `__setitem__`), operator overloading (`__add__`, `__sub__`, `__mul__`, etc.) and many more.

Extending Python

Although the details are beyond the scope of this chapter, extension modules and extension types can easily be created for Python in C. A typical development scenario in Python might go like this:

- ❑   Write the program entirely in Python.

- ❑   Refine the concept and the code until it works properly.

- ❑   If the program runs too slowly, profile it to find the bottlenecks.

- ❑   Optimize the Python code.

- ❑   If the Python code is still too slow, recode the offending parts in C.

This approach gives us the best of both worlds: the raw speed of C when it's needed, and the high-level power of Python the rest of the time. If you give Python a chance, I'm sure you'll want to use its power as often and as much as you can.

An Example Program: Penny Pinching

In this section we will walk through a full example to get the sense of a living, breathing Python programme. The first line in the file is the magic hash-bang, as we've seen before. This is followed by the 'documentation string':

```
#! /usr/bin/env python

"""
Description
===========
This program was written by David Goodger to solve the Penny Pinching
puzzle: http://www.primroselodge.com/Playtime/weekly_puzzle_20.htm

Given:
- N players sit in a circle
- each player starts with one penny
- players alternately pass 1, then 2, then 1, then 2 (etc.)
  pennies to the next seated player
- a player leaves the circle when she has no pennies left

Players 1 & 2 will always leave the circle immediately. Sometimes, one
player will end up with all the pennies. The rest of the time, the
game will repeat in an infinite cycle.

Questions:
1. What is the smallest number of initial players in an
   infinitely cycling game?
2. With more than 10 players, what is the smallest number of players
   where the game finishes with one player holding all the pennies?
3. What is the pattern for the number of players that makes the
   game cycle infinitely?
```

```
    Usage
    =====
        pennies.py [-t] [-v] numplayers [to_numplayers]

    With one argument, an integer number of players, a single simulation
    for that number of players will be run. With two arguments, first and
    last: number of players, simulations are run for the entire range of
    numbers of players.

    Options
    -------
    -t : test mode: runs a test set of simulations.
    -v : verbose: show each step in the simulation; default
         is just to summarize the results.

    Examples
    --------
    1. "pennies.py -v 5" will run a verbose 5-player simulation.
    2. "pennies.py 1 100" will run & summarize simulations for
       1 to 100 players.
    """
```

If the first non-comment line in a module, function/method definition, or class definition is a lone string expression, it is known as the documentation string or docstring. The docstring serves both as a multiline comment and as extractable documentation. If this module were imported using `import pennies`, the docstring would be accessible as `pennies.__doc__`. Docstrings are usually delimited by triple-quotes, even if they don't span lines; this is just so that if at some later date the docstring were to grow, we wouldn't have to go back and add more quotes.

A lone string anywhere else in a module can act as a multiline comment, although it is not accessible as documentation. Using triple-quotes is one way to temporarily comment-out a section of code:

```python
class Player:
    """Represents a single player. Can pass and receive pennies."""

    def __init__(self, playerNo):
        self.pennies = 1
        self.number = playerNo

    def passes(self, toPass):
        """Pass pennies to my neighbor. Return pennies passed, and
           remaining pennies."""
        if toPass > self.pennies:    # check for enough pennies
            print ("Warning: Player %s has only %s penny, must pass %s"
                   % (self.number, self.pennies, toPass))
            print "(This shouldn't happen!)"
            toPass = self.pennies
        self.pennies = self.pennies - toPass
        return (toPass, self.pennies)

    def receives(self, toGet):
        """Receive pennies from my neighbor. Return total pennies."""
        self.pennies = self.pennies + toGet
        return self.pennies
```

A class definition. The Player class defines three methods and two instance attributes. The first method, Player.__init__, is a special-purpose method automatically called by Python when a Player object is instantiated.

The second method, Player.passes, returns a two-item tuple when it has finished its work. As we shall see, the calling code expects this:

```
class Simulation:
    """Penny Pinching puzzle simulator."""

    def __init__(self, nPlayers):
        self.nPlayers = nPlayers
        # create a list of Player objects:
        self.players = map(Player, range(1, nPlayers + 1))
        self.pennyList = [1] * nPlayers
        self.active = range(nPlayers)
        self.passer = ""              # player who is passing pennies
        self.toPass = ""              # number of pennies just passed
        width = len(str(nPlayers))
        self.playerFormat = ("%%-%ss  " % width) * nPlayers
        self.stateFormat = self.playerFormat + "P%s passes %s"
        self.header = (("P%%-%ss " % width) * nPlayers) % \
                        tuple(range(1, nPlayers + 1))
```

In Simulation.__init__, self.players is assigned from the map function. map is one of Python's functional programming constructs. It applies each item in turn from its second argument, a sequence, to its first argument, a function or callable object (in this case, a class), and returns a list of the results. map and its functional cohorts (apply, filter, reduce, and the lambda statement) make some programming tasks very simple; however, they are also easy to abuse and are often difficult to understand. They are not always faster, either.

self.playerFormat and self.stateFormat define format strings to be used with the % string format operator. Note that in self.playerFormat we take advantage of string formatting in order to build the repetitive format string itself. %% is used when a single % is desired in the formatted string.

Note the use of a backslash to split the last logical line onto two physical lines:

```
    def __str__(self):
        """String representation of the players."""
        return self.playerFormat % tuple(self.pennyList)
```

Simulation.__str__ is another special-purpose method, a hook into the str function, used to convert objects to strings. Other special methods are used for operator overloading, intercepting attribute access and assignment, and other more esoteric purposes.

The following method, Simulation.state, is an alternative way of implementing the same type of functionality. Note also that the return line is split over two physical lines, inside parentheses:

```
    def state(self):
        """String representation of the simulator's state."""
        return self.stateFormat % tuple(self.pennyList +
                                    [self.passer, self.toPass])
```

```
    def run(self, verbosely=1):
        """Run a single simulation. Returns two lists:
           active players and their penny totals."""
        if verbosely:
            print "Penny Pinching: %s Players\n" % self.nPlayers
            print self.header
        toPass = 1        # number of pennies to pass to next player
        toGet = 0         # number of pennies to get from last player
        states = {}       # record of all prior simulation states,
                          # to check for repeating cycles
        if verbosely: print str(self) + "initial"
        index = 0
        while 1:
            if len(self.active) == 1:    # only 1 player left?
                if verbosely: print str(self) + "final"
                break
            this = self.active[index]    # index of current player
                                         # index of next player:
            next = self.active[(index + 1) % len(self.active)]
            # assign 2-item return value to two targets:
            (toGet, self.pennyList[this]) = \
                                    self.players[this].passes(toPass)
            self.pennyList[next] = self.players[next].receives(toGet)
            toPass = 3 - toPass          # toggle between 1 & 2 pennies
            if not self.pennyList[this]:    # out of pennies?
                self.pennyList[this] = ""   # reduce screen clutter
                del self.active[index]      # make player inactive
                index = index % len(self.active)  # don't advance index
            else:                           # player still active.
                index = (index + 1) % len(self.active)  # advance index
            if verbosely:
                self.passer = this + 1  # +1 for 0-based lists
                self.toPass = toGet     # pennies actually passed
                print self.state()
            # create an immutable tuple, which can be used as a
            # dictionary key:
            state = tuple(self.pennyList + [self.passer, toPass])
            if states.has_key(state):    # check for repetition
                if verbosely: print str(self) + "repeats"
                break
            else:
                states[state] = 1        # store state for future checks
        if verbosely:
            print "\n"
        return (self.active, self.pennyList)
```

Several module-level functions are now defined, which control the simulations:

```
def runSimulations(minPlayers, maxPlayers, verbosely=1, summarize=0):
    """Run simulations for the given range of players.
       Returns list of (initial number of players, list of active
       players, list of penny totals)."""
                                    # initialize results array:
    results = [None] * (maxPlayers - minPlayers + 1)
```

```
        for n in range(minPlayers, maxPlayers + 1):     # acquire results
            results[n - minPlayers] = (n,) + Simulation(n).run(verbosely)
            if summarize:
                summarizeOne(results[n - minPlayers])
        return results

    def summarizeResults(results=[]):
        """Without an argument, just prints the summary header.
           Argument "results": same as output from runSimulations"""
        print "Initial    Final"
        print "Players    Players"
        for result in results:
            summarizeOne(result)

    def summarizeOne(result):
        print "%5s     %5s" % (result[0], len(result[1]))

    def test():
        """Runs simulations for 1 to 100 players."""
        results = runSimulations(1, 20, 1, 0)  # run verbosely for the first 20
        summarizeResults(results)
        runSimulations(21, 100, 0, 1)          # then just summarize

    def showUsageAndExit(message=None):
        import sys
        sys.stdout = sys.stderr                # print to stderr stream
        if message:
            print 'Error: %s' % message
        print __doc__                          # module's documentation string
        sys.exit(1)
```

What follows is a common Python idiom. When a module is executed rather than imported, a special variable __name__ in the module's namespace is set to the string "__main__" (when the module is imported, __name__ is set to the module's name). Testing for this allows us to determine how a module was executed and vary the actions taken as a result. This module is typical: if imported, it simply defines two classes and some functions, and allows the importing code to use it as a library. If executed directly, it will perform its default standalone behavior, which in this case is to process the command-line arguments and options:

```
    # do not execute this code if imported as a module:
    if __name__ == "__main__":
        import getopt, sys
        verbose = 0
        try:
            opts, args = getopt.getopt(sys.argv[1:], 'tv')
            # opts is a list of tuples containing two items each,
            # an option and its argument if any. The for loop below
            # assigns each tuple's option to o, and argument to a.
            for o, a in opts:
                if o == '-t':
                    test()
                    sys.exit()
                elif o == '-v':
                    verbose = 1
```

```
        else:
            raise getopt.error, 'Unknown option "%s"' % o
    if not 1 <= len(args) <= 2:
        raise getopt.error, 'One or two arguments needed.'
    firstnum = int(args[0])
    args.append(args[0])              # copy firstnum to lastnum
    lastnum = int(args[1])            # unless already specified
except:                               # catch all errors here
    type, value = sys.exc_info()[:2]  # extract exception info
    showUsageAndExit(value)
if not verbose:                       # will summarize as we go, so
    summarizeResults()                # just print the summary header
results = runSimulations(firstnum, lastnum, verbose, not verbose)
```

Note the use of chained comparisons (1 <= len(args) <= 2) above to test for a range of numbers of arguments.

You will recall that there are several ways to execute a Python program. We'll use the direct method here:

```
$ chmod +x pennies.py
$ pennies.py -v 5
Penny Pinching: 5 Players

P1 P2 P3 P4 P5
1  1  1  1  1  initial
   2  1  1  1  P1 passes 1
      3  1  1  P2 passes 2
      2  2  1  P3 passes 1
      2     3  P4 passes 2
      3     2  P5 passes 1
      1     4  P3 passes 2
      2     3  P5 passes 1
            5  P3 passes 2
            5  final
$ pennies.py 1 10
Initial  Final
Players  Players
   1        1
   2        1
   3        1
   4        1
   5        1
   6        1
   7        3
   8        3
   9        1
  10        1
$
```

So, what are the answers to the questions posed at the beginning? You now have the solution program, why not run it and see if you can answer them yourself?

Online Resources

The Python Language Website at http://www.python.org is the first place you should look for Python-related information. It contains the official Python reference documentation set, special interest groups, source code for the current distribution, multiple search engines, and many links to other sites.

The Python development team moved to BeOpen.com and formed PythonLabs in May 2000. Their website http://www.pythonlabs.com has late-breaking information.

The comp.lang.python newsgroup is very active, and very civilized. Its contributors post announcements of all kinds, programming questions, and implementation issues, patches and bug reports. Newbies can get answers to their questions here. Although controversial issues (including the ever-present Python vs. Perl 'religious debates') are discussed, there are rarely the kind of flame wars that are often seen on other newsgroups.

FAQTS is a knowledge base, with questions and answers extracted from the newsgroup and other sources: http://python.faqts.com.

The Vaults of Parnassus is a database of Python resources: http://www.vex.net/parnassus. Python does not yet have an equivalent of CPAN for Perl, unfortunately, but Parnassus maintains a database of pointers to where third-party modules and applications can be found.

Summary

> *Python is a language that gets its compromises exactly right.*
>
> *—attributed to Don Beaudry by Mark Hammond on comp.lang.python*

Python is built on a solid foundation of established ideas, borrowed from many sources. Although few features are original to Python, it's feature set was carefully chosen to make it a 'best of breed' product with great potential already being realized. Python has an indefinable feeling of *quality* about it, of *rightness.* It is Python's elegant and coherent design and inspired implementation that let it soar high.

Computers have become faster to the point where interpreted languages can painlessly be used for large systems. The tradeoffs of program efficiency versus programmer efficiency have become weighted on the programmer's side, and Python leads the way. Python allows the modern programmer to leverage its power and efficiency in a very enjoyable way.

Online discussion at http://www.p2p.wrox.com

16

Creating Web Interfaces with PHP

The advent of the world wide web has brought in its wake several technologies that facilitate the more serious business of deploying applications on the web as opposed to simply displaying pages or images. Not all of them have been products of commercial software companies – several of the more successful ones have been in the open source or free software realm. One such technology is PHP or Hypertext Preprocessor, which is a server side scripting language for generating dynamic pages.

It has become possible with the introduction of PHP to deploy professional web-based applications on Linux, with much less effort than before. PHP as a server-side scripting language complements the robustness and openness of Linux and together they form a serious and professional alternative to the commercial solutions for deploying web-based applications.

In this chapter we shall explore PHP, specifically as a tool for deploying web-based applications on Linux using the DVD database from previous chapters. Some of the topics we will be looking at are:

- ❑ PHP as a web-server scripting language.

- ❑ A syntactic introduction to PHP.

- ❑ Installing and Configuring PHP for Linux.

- ❑ Further investigation of technologies that are relevant to the deployment of our application.

- ❑ A fully-fledged interface to the DVD store database.

PHP and Server-Side Scripting

The world wide web as we know it has evolved from serving static web pages where web sites acted as little more than electronic billboards, through to the advent of pages with programmability using CGI (Common Gateway Interface). Today's web sites have more sophisticated user-interfaces in the form of dynamic web pages that are responsive to the user's actions. Scripts running on either the server and/or the browser allow access to applications and data in a way that hitherto had only been available using traditional non web-based user interfaces.

While client-side scripting (commonly JavaScript, but also occasionally VBScript) is limited to being interpreted by the browser, the server-side scripts, which are embedded in server pages or stand-alone script files, are interpreted by the web-server. This then generates the HTML that is passed on to the browser. The actual power of server-side scripting languages is not due to this capability alone, but due to the fact that several of these languages (PHP is a prime example) have a wide repertoire of connectivity and accessibility APIs that allow these scripts to interact with various databases, mail servers, and other application modules. Java applets, and Sun Microsystems' solution to achieving programmability within web-pages does not seem to have done as well on the client side as it was expected to.

Server-side scripting

The creation of dynamic content that is necessary for real-world applications to be accessed though web pages, has largely been achieved through server-side scripting languages such as PHP. How they do this usually depends on the scripting language, which brings us to the various server-side technologies and how they compare with PHP.

CGI scripts

Traditionally the creation of web pages was largely achieved through CGI or Common Gateway Interface. The actual script can be written in any scripting language (or any language as long as the compiler or interpreter is available on the server machine) provided the output generated is intelligible to the CGI interface. This approach slows performance, as the web-server has to spawn a separate process to handle the execution of a CGI script.

Active Server Pages

ASP or Active Server Pages, Microsoft's server-side scripting solution, allows the programmer to combine HTML, JScript (Microsoft's client-side scripting offering – similar to Netscape's JavaScript), and VBScript to generate dynamic HTML pages. With the COM or Component Object Model interface, it is possible to link to many other application modules. Its main shortcoming is that ASP is largely supported only on Microsoft platforms.

Java Server Pages and Servlets

JSP or Java Server Pages is an all Java solution and pretty similar to PHP, the difference being that the script is interpreted by a Java Virtual Machine (JVM). When a JSP script is requested, the Web server generates a Java Servlet, which runs in the JVM to produce the HTML. The other issue with JSP is the longer learning curve associated with familiarizing oneself with the technology, due to a very large number of features.

PHP scripting

PHP is currently supported on a number of platforms and in conjunction with a number of web servers. With the Apache web server, PHP can be installed as either a CGI interpreter or as an Apache module. The latter is the preferred means of installation when performance is the main criteria, since it does not involve spawning a separate process as would be the case with the CGI-style installation. If you are already keen on using PHP then you might want to go directly to the installation section later on in this chapter.

With Apache on Linux, PHP is a very able competitor to any of the technologies that we mentioned earlier. Apart from Linux, PHP is also supported on Microsoft Windows NT, and Windows 95/98 platforms. Some of the supported web servers include fhttpd (open-source), IIS3 up to 5, OmniHTTPd etc. On all these Web servers except Apache, PHP works only as a CGI interpreter and not as a built-in module. Finally, but most importantly, PHP is free and open-source.

As a generalization, most server-side scripting languages usually embed their scripting components within a HTML document. So, when the web server reads them from the file system to service a request from a browser, it interprets the script and generates the appropriate HTML to be returned to the browser. This contrasts with ordinary web pages where the server fetches an HTML-only static page directly from the file system and passes it on to the browser without any interpretation. The examples below illustrate this with slight variations on the inevitable Hello World theme. The first example shows a static HTML page, the second shows a dynamic HTML page.

```
<HTML>
<HEAD><TITLE>Hello Static World</TITLE></HEAD>
<BODY>
Hello World
</BODY>
</HTML>
```

```
<HTML>
<HEAD><TITLE>Hello Dynamic World</TITLE></HEAD>
<BODY>
<?php printf( "Hello World\n" ); ?>
</BODY>
</HTML>
```

Both examples generate roughly the same output, but the second one is the result of the web server interpreting the PHP script. More precisely, it might not actually be the web server that interprets the script – it would be the PHP interpreter (either as a web server module or CGI interpreter) that is doing the actual interpretation.

PHP capabilities

The actual power of PHP arises from the fact that it is possible to seamlessly access several other modules from PHP using the API support that PHP provides. At this point, it is worthwhile to take a quick look at the various modules that PHP supports:

❏ A large number of databases are supported for connectivity by PHP. As of PHP 4, these include Adabas, dBase, Empress, FilePro, Informix, InterBase, mSQL, MySQL, Oracle, PostgreSQL, Solid, Sybase, Velocis and dbm. ODBC (Open Database Connectivity) is also supported. We shall be looking at the database APIs closely as we shall be using some of them during the time we develop the DVD store application later in this chapter.

❏ LDAP (Light-weight Directory Access Protocol) is another supported protocol. PHP provides APIs for writing LDAP client programs. LDAP is a protocol used to store directory related information such as address books, white pages etc. The LDAP chapter has further details on this directory access technology.

❑ XML (eXtended Markup Language), touted as the future language of the Web, is also supported. XML (among others) aims at separating the content or information that a Web page holds from the presentation of the page. The XML chapter has more details. WDDX (Web Distributed Data eXchange) a technology derived form XML, is also supported.

❑ Mail protocols such as IMAP (Interactive Mail Access Protocol) and SMTP (Simple Mail Transport Protocol) are supported. IMAP is a protocol used for mail retrieval and SMTP is used for routing mail on the Internet.

❑ Image generation and manipulation functions are supported, and using PHP we can generate images dynamically. The PDF (Portable Document Format) for distributing documents on the web is also supported – PHP scripts can generate PDF documents on the fly using this interface.

❑ SNMP (Simple Network Management Protocol) is supported so that remote network management can be achieved.

Of course, the list above is by no means exhaustive and PHP support for more and more technologies is continuously evolving. At the time of writing, version 4 has been released and this comes with Zend, which is a much faster and tighter interpretation engine.

Installing and Configuring PHP

It is time for us to actually try to get PHP working on our Linux boxes, so that we can get on with our real task of exploring PHP hands-on.

For the application example in this chapter we require Apache, PHP and PostgreSQL to be installed on the machine. Several Linux distributions, including RedHat6.1 have Apache and the PHP module distributed with them by default (usually in `/usr/lib/apache/`), but the Apache configuration file `httpd.conf` seems to have the required settings turned off. We could enable these settings by uncommenting the following lines in this file:

❑ Under "Extra modules" uncomment or modify the following lines

```
AddModule mod_php
LoadModule php_module modules/libphp.so
```

❑ Under global configuration add the following:*(somewhere near the top of the file)*

```
AddType application/x-httpd-php .php
```

After we make these changes, we need to restart Apache for them to take effect. This can be done by:

```
# apachectl stop
# apachectl start
```

This is essentially the quickest way to get started with using PHP, provided Apache and PHP come pre-installed with the distribution.

In the event that Apache or PHP does not come pre-installed in a particular distribution, we might need to install them either by building them from the sources or installing from packages such as RedHat RPMs or Debian .debs. Having said that, in this chapter we shall try to install PHP and configure it so that it is best suited for the application at hand. A more exhaustive discussion on installing and configuring PHP can be found in Chapter 2 of *Professional PHP Programming* by Wrox Press. We could obtain the PHP distribution as an executable binary, as an RPM, or the source distribution. We shall go the Linux way and build the sources. The sources are available from the official PHP website http://www.php.net.

Building and Installing PHP as a CGI Interpreter

We assume that we have Apache and PostgreSQL already installed (as described in the PostgreSQL chapter). We need to know the directory in which Apache and PostgreSQL are installed. We also need a source distribution of PHP.

❏   Make sure we have Apache, which is PHP's web-server of choice. In particular, look for the apache executable, the location of which is dependant on your Linux distribution.

❏   We need to uncompress the distribution and extract the files first.

```
$ tar xvfz php-4.x.y.tar.gz
```

❏   We change directory into the distribution directory and run the configure script which will generate the necessary Make files. We can pass options to the configure script, to tell the script the composition of modules that we need for our installation and also certain configuration parameters. We shall look at each of these options soon.

```
$ ./configure --with-pgsql=DIR
```

This tells the configure script that we intend to build PHP with PostgreSQL support. We need PostgreSQL for the DVD application later on. The DIR argument to the --with-pgsql option is to indicate the distribution directory of PostgreSQL. The default location assumed if DIR is not specified is /usr/local/pgsql.

❏   If the earlier configure script ran successfully, the necessary files for compilation must have been generated. We need to compile the distribution at this point:

```
$ make
```

In the unlikely event that you see a link time failure, it is usually due to non-availability of libraries required for the specified modules or due to some of these libraries being installed in non-standard locations. If a particular library is in a non-standard location, check the environment variable LD_LIBRARY_PATH and if it is missing, add the path to this library in the variable. We could use the ldd command to see if the executable knows where to look for the shared libraries. For example, if the library libxyz.so is in a non-standard location /var/mylibdir, we would need to do the following on a Bash shell and re-run make again:

```
$ export LD_LIBRARY_PATH=$LD_LIBRARY_PATH:/var/mylibdir
```

❏ Once the source files have compiled successfully and have been linked, it is time to install the distribution. We might need to assume root privileges if we are installing in the standard location.

```
# make install
```

We now have a PHP binary that can be used as a CGI interpreter. If everything went fine, we have an interpreter that we could use to interpret PHP scripts. Finally, remember to take a look at the *Configuring PHP* section further below to see how we could configure PHP minimally to get started.

However, as mentioned earlier, PHP can also be installed as an Apache module. If you would rather install PHP this way, take a look at the next section

Building and Installing PHP with Apache as an Apache module

To build PHP as an Apache module we also need the source distribution for the Apache Web server. This is available for download from the Apache home page http://www.apache.org.

❏ We need to first uncompress and un-archive the PHP and Apache distributions:

```
$ tar xvfz apache_1.3.x.tar.gz
$ tar xvfz php-4.x.y.tar.gz
```

❏ Then change directory into the apache distribution directory and run the configure script

```
$ cd apache_1.3.x
$ ./configure --configuration-options-for-apache
```

The configure scripts can take build-time options for the Apache build. The option –prefix=/www results in the distribution targeted for the /www directory, rather than the default which is usually /usr/local/apache.

❏ We change directory back into the newly unpacked PHP distribution and run the configure script here

```
$ cd ../php-4.x.y
$ ./configure --with-apache=../apache_1.3.x --with-pgsql
```

The option --with-apache=../apache_1.3.x indicates that we wish to build this as an Apache module – it also specifies the directory where the Apache sources are.

❏ If the earlier configure script ran successfully, the necessary files for compilation must have been generated. We need to compile the distribution at this point:

```
$ make
```

❏ Once the source files have compiled successfully and have been linked, it is time to install the PHP distribution. We might need to assume root privileges if we are installing in the standard locations.

```
# make install
```

- Now to take care of the Apache distribution. We change directory back into the Apache distribution directory and run the `configure` script:

```
$ cd ../apache_1.3.x
$ ./configure --activate-module=src/modules/php4/libphp4.a –other-apache-
options
```

Note the library `src/modules/php4/libphp4.a` – this library has been created and copied into the Apache distribution directory during the PHP build process earlier. This library would be `src/modules/php3/libphp3.a` for PHP3.x.

- If the earlier `configure` script ran successfully, the necessary files for compilation must have been generated. We need to compile the distribution at this point:

```
$ make
```

- Once the source files have compiled successfully and have been linked, it is time to install the distribution. We might need to assume root privileges before doing this. If Apache was already running, we need to stop it and install the new Apache server (with the PHP module):

```
# /usr/local/apache/bin/apachectl stop
```

We need to do this only if we already have an Apache server already installed and running. If your linux distribution does not have the `apachectl` *command, you could kill a running instance of Apache by doing a* `'killall -9 apache'`.

```
# make install
```

- We are almost there. We now have an Apache server that has the PHP module built into it. We may need to do some tweaking of the Apache configuration files before we get Apache to recognize PHP scripts and use the PHP module for interpreting them. Take a look at the *Configuring PHP* section further below to see how to do this.

- Now to start the newly installed Apache server with the PHP module built into it:

```
# /usr/local/apache/bin/apachectl start
```

Installing PHP from an RPM

For die-hard RPM fans who want to shun the setup-configure-make routine and want to take the RPM way out (or as for that matter installing PHP from a package format specific to a distribution), there is a word of caution – pre-compiled binaries (distributed as RPMs) of PHP suffer from the drawback that they do not offer the flexibility of specifying the right mix and match of *add-on* modules that we want. Furthermore, RPM installation does not take care of some post-install stuff such as changing or adding entries in some configuration files like Apache's `httpd.conf` configuration file. Nevertheless if you choose to go the RPM way, remember to modify the Apache configuration file `httpd.conf` (usually `/etc/httpd/conf /httpd.conf`) and restart Apache. See the section below on configuring your PHP installation.

Configuring PHP

Now that we have succeeded in installing the PHP distribution, we need to configure it at least minimally so that we can start to use PHP. For a detailed description on configuring PHP, consult *Professional PHP Programming* published by Wrox.

We need to copy the sample configuration file for PHP, which comes with the distribution, into the installation directory. Assuming that this is `/usr/local/lib`, we would do the following:

```
# cp php.ini-dist /usr/local/lib/php.ini
```

We might also need to make some changes to the Apache configuration file to have PHP running with Apache.

On most Linux distributions the Apache configuration file is `/etc/httpd/conf/httpd.conf`. However under some distributions, this could be `/etc/apache/conf/httpd.conf`.

Here are some of the things that we need to add to or modify in the configuration file:

❑ Under "Extra modules" add, uncomment or modify the following lines

```
AddModule mod_php
LoadModule php4_module modules/libphp4.so
```

❑ Under global configuration add the following:(somewhere near the top of the file)

```
AddType application/x-httpd-php .php .php3
```

The `AddType` directive causes Apache to recognize files with the extension `.php` or `.php3` to be PHP scripts and use the PHP module to interpret them.

To test the success of the installation, create a small PHP script called `test.php` as below and leave it in the Apache directory which houses the rest of the HTML files, usually `/usr/local/apache/htdocs`. (i.e the document root of Apache).

```php
<?php
phpinfo( );
?>
```

If you installed PHP as a CGI interpreter, say in `/usr/local/bin/php`, then the script should look like this:

```php
#/usr/local/bin/php
<?php
phpinfo( );
?>
```

If Apache is running on **mymachine.mydomain.com**, we use a browser to access the URL http://mymachine.mydomain.com/test.php. If we see a set of variables maintained internally by PHP, rather than error messages, we know that the installation has been successful. You should essentially see something like below:

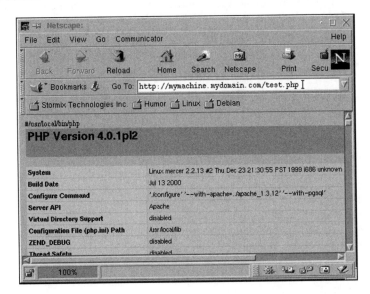

> The choice of installing **PHP** as an Apache module or as a CGI interpreter is often dictated by the primary considerations of the deploying site. Using **PHP** as a CGI interpreter may actually bog down performance as the interpreter runs as a separate process as opposed to as an Apache module that runs in the address space of the web server. Certain features such as persistent database connections are available only in the Apache module version and the module installation is safer from the security standpoint. However, the CGI version allows users to run PHP scripts under different user-ids. If it is required that non-privileged users who cannot install PHP as an Apache module install it, the CGI version is a better alternative.

Finally before we move on to the details of PHP syntax, let us take a look at an example that shows how PHP can be embedded with HTML in a web page:

```
<HTML>
<TITLE>PHP script embedded in HTML</TITLE>
<BODY>
What did Austin Powers say when he came out of the freezer ?
<BR>
<?php
$aargh = "It is good to be me!!";
echo( $aargh );
?>
<BR>
</BODY>
</HTML>
```

Introducing PHP syntax

In this section we shall take a look at the basic syntax of PHP. As this is one chapter in a wider book, we do not have space to dwell on the finer aspects of the syntax – we recommend *Professional PHP Programming* published by Wrox as a comprehensive guide instead. Nevertheless, we shall explore in detail those parts that are crucial to the application that we develop later on in the chapter.

Variables, Constants and Data types

Since PHP scripts can be embedded in HTML and especially since they almost always generate HTML, we shall take a look at how HTML and PHP co-exist. As we saw earlier, PHP scripts can be embedded in HTML pages between the tags `<?php` and `?>`. In fact we could also enclose PHP scripts between `<?` and `?>` tags or `<%` and `%>` tags. It is fine to embed PHP code in HTML files, but remember to name the name files with an extension `.php` or `.php3` so that the web-server interprets the embedded scripts. We could very well have a file with just a PHP script in it named with an extension `.php3` or `.php`.

Let us take a look at variables in PHP. We don't have to declare variables in PHP as we do with many other programming languages. Let us look at an example:

```php
<?php
$foo = "Hello World"; // Assigning a string to variable foo
echo ( $foo );
?>
```

The script above produces the ubiquitous programmer greeting. The script also shows one of several ways of marking out comment code in PHP. In fact, we could also enclose comments between `/*` and `*/` or add a comment after the `#` sign or after `//` until the end of the line.

Variables are always prefixed with a $. Fundamentally PHP has three data types – integer, double and string. Arrays and objects could be formed using these basic data types.
You assign a PHP variable with an = sign like this:

```php
$str = "This is a string variable "; // String
$a = 1.5; // Double
$b = 6; // Integer
```

Let us look at some functions that come in handy when using variables. `gettype` allows us to determine the type of a variable as shown below:

```php
<?php
$x = 2;
echo( gettype( $x ));
?>
```

The code snippet above prints `integer`, which is the data type of the variable $x. `gettype( )` returns double, string, array, object, class and unknown type for variables of these types.

`settype( )` is used to set the type for a variable as the code below illustrates. It returns false if it fails to do the conversion and true on success:

```
<?php
$wasADouble = 3.5;
settype( $wasADouble, "integer" ); // converts the variable to the integer type
echo( $wasADouble ); // outputs 3
?>
```

isset( ), empty( ), and unset( ) - isset( ) determines if a variable has been assigned. It returns true if it has been and false if not. empty( ) is the opposite of this in that it returns true if a variable has not been set and false if it has been. unset( ) is used to unset an assigned variable.

Constants can be declared using the define( ) function as shown below:

```
<?php
define( "helloString", "Hello World" );
echo( helloString);
?>
```

PHP has several built-in constants, e.g. PHP_OS is a constant that is defined as the name of the operating system that the PHP binary is running on. The version number of the PHP distribution that is used defines PHP_VERSION. The constants are accessed literally, i.e without prepending a $ to them. For example, to print the PHP version, we would use echo(PHP_VERSION);.

Operators in PHP

As you would expect PHP has a rich set of operators to construct simple to complex expressions and statements. Let us take a closer look at some of the important operator types in PHP:

Arithmetic Operators

The arithmetic operators are +, -, *, / and % for addition, subtraction, multiplication, division and modulus respectively.

Comparison Operators

These are used to test conditions. The comparison operators are listed below:

==	Left operand equals right operand.
<	Left operand is lesser than right operand.
>	Left operand is greater than right operand.
<=	Left operand is lesser than or equal to right operand.
>=	Left operand is greater than or equal to right operand.
!=	Left operand is not equal to right operand.
<>	Left operand is not equal to right operand.

Logical operators

Logical operators are used to evaluate truth-value of statements. They are used to combine expressions, as we shall illustrate. The logical operators supported are shown below:

&&	Evaluates to true if the left expression and the right expression are true.
||	Evaluates to true if the left expression or the right expression or both is true.
And	Evaluates to the true if left expression and the right expression are true.
Or	Evaluates to true if the left expression or the right expression or both is true.
Xor	Evaluates to true if only one of either the left or right expression is true.
!	Toggles the truth value of the operand.

Various other operators

The unary operator – negates the value of a number. The ternary operator ? evaluates a Boolean condition and return one of the two values based on its result. The . (dot) operator can be used to concatenate two strings. There are several other operators like the Bitwise operators, Object operators, and Error suspension operators, which are seldom used and hence we shall not discuss here. More information on these is available from several resources including the afore-mentioned *Professional PHP Programming* by Wrox Press. The following piece of code demonstrates the action of the unary, ternary, and dot operators:

```php
<?php
$a = 1;
$a = -$a;
$prepend = "This variable is ";
$str = $a < 0 ? "negative" : "positive";
echo( $prepend.$str ); // This should print the string negative
?>
```

Statements

Statements in PHP hold the various expressions together and determine the logical flow of the script. PHP statements can be broadly classified as conditional statements and loop statements. Those familiar with the C language, and other languages that have borrowed from C their statement syntax, will find PHP statements quite familiar.

The major conditional statements are the if and switch statements. The code below illustrates these statements:

```php
<?php
$a = 10;
if ( $a < 10 )
    echo( "Less than 10  " ); // This statement executes
else
    echo( "Greater than or equal to 10  " );
switch ( $a ) {
    case 8: echo( "Eight" ); break;
    case 9: echo( "Nine" ); break; // This statement executes
    case 10: echo( "Ten" ); break;
}
?>
```

Loop statements are used when we need to conditionally execute a code segment several times. The different loop statements are while, do .. while and for statements. The code below illustrates how we use these operators – they all produce the same output:

```php
<?php
$i = 1;
while ( $i <= 10 )
{
echo( $i );
++$i;
}

 $i = 1;
do {
echo( $i );
++$i;
}
while ( $i <= 10 );

for ( $i = 1; $i <= 10; ++$i )
    echo( $i );
?>
```

Functions

We use functions in PHP pretty much for the same reasons that we do in other programming languages. Functions help to modularise code that is often invoked in the program. We declare functions in PHP using the function keyword. As we saw earlier, variables in PHP do not have to be declared before use. By default, variables used in functions will result in the creation of a new local variable, accessible only inside that function. If we want to access a global variable from inside a function, we must declare it using the global keyword. The code below illustrates this:

```php
<?php
$a = 10;
$b = 20;

function SayHello( $first, $last ){
global $a; // Causes the function to use the global variable $a

$final = $first.$last; // This line concatenates the two strings
echo( $final );

$b = $b + 1; //Increments the local variable $b – change not visible outside this
function
$a = $a + 1; //Increments the global variable $a – change visible outside this
function
}
$hello = "Hello "; $world = "World";
SayHello( $hello, $world ); //You guessed right – prints Hello World
echo( $a ); // Prints 11
echo( $b ); // Prints 20
?>
```

The default way for functions is to have the arguments passed to it by values, i.e. modifications to the local copy of the passed argument are not reflected in the calling function. As an example, if the value of the variable $first was changed to ello from Hello, this would only be in effect in the function SayHello. The variable $hello in the calling function would remain unchanged with the value Hello.

However functions can be passed by reference too. What this means is that, if the variable passed by reference is modified in the called function, the change is reflected in the calling function. We prepend the & character to the argument in the function definition to indicate that it is a variable passed by reference. The example below illustrates this:

```php
<?php

function SayHello( &$first, $last ){
$first = "ello ";
$final = $first.$last; // This line concatenates the two strings
echo( $final );
}
$hello = "Hello "; $world = "World";
SayHello( $hello, $world ); //You guessed right - prints ello World
?>
```

Arrays

We use arrays in PHP to store several values of the same data type just like in other programming languages. The difference is that the arrays in PHP are much more versatile. PHP can index arrays using two methods – numerical indexing and associative or string indexing. In numerical indexing we use the location of the values of a variable to index into the array, whereas with associative indexing, we assign a string associated with a value to index into the array. This will become clearer as we take a look at the example that follows.

Arrays in PHP are also supplemented with several built-in functions that can be used to manipulate them. So, we could use the current( ) function to obtain the value of the current element that we have accessed in the array. Below are some examples of arrays in PHP:

```php
<?php
$color[0] = "violet ";
$color[1] = "indigo ";
$color[2] = "blue ";

$abbreviations["ps"] = "Post Script";
$abbreviations["etc"] = "Et Cetera";
$abbreviations["PHP"] = "Personal HomePage tools";

echo( $color[0] ); // Prints the string violet;
echo( $abbreviations["PHP"] ); // Prints Personal HomePage tools
?>
```

Using PHP with the DVD project

In the previous sections we took a few tentative steps into PHP-land and explored the installation and syntax of the language to some extent. For the rest of the chapter the focus is on using PHP and PostgreSQL in order to build the PHP application that will provide an interface for the DVD store project.

HTTP, HTML and PHP

As you would have wondered by now, we need some mechanism to accept user input from the HTML pages that are displayed. We normally use HTML forms to obtain user input, so we need a mechanism to obtain the value of a form element, say a textbox in an HTML form such that it is available to a PHP script. To facilitate this, a PHP variable with the same name as a form element contains the value of the form element. The script below illustrates this:

```
<HTML><BODY>
<FORM ACTION="getform.php" METHOD=GET>
Who goes there? :
<INPUT TYPE=TEXT NAME=yourname>
<BR><BR>
<INPUT TYPE=SUBMIT>
</FORM></BODY></HTML>
```

The script below is the `getform.php` file, which is used to process the form submitted using GET:

```
<HTML><BODY>
<?php
echo( "Hmm, So you are ". $yourname);
?>
</BODY></HTML>
```

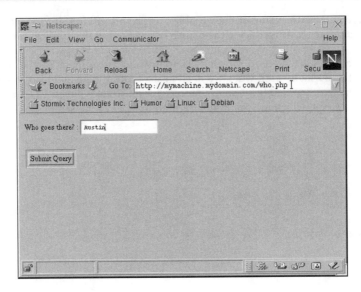

Our processed form will look like this:

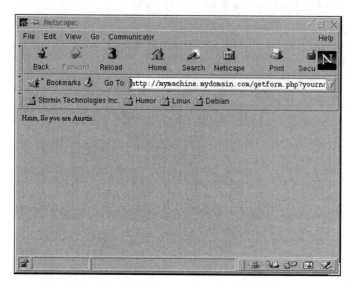

We see that the form variable `yourname` which was part of the HTML form is available to the PHP script as a PHP variable named `$yourname`.

Data can be returned to the server in one of two ways. Firstly, by encoding the data in a URL and sending it to the web server using the GET method. Let us assume that an HTML form takes as input the name of a user and needs to pass it to a PHP script so that the script can act upon it. GET will generate a URL that is sent to the web server (and thereby to the script) that will look something like:

http://www.example.net/php/egofind.php?user=incognito

The PHP script can access the value of the variable `$user` and will find it to be 'incognito'. We shall learn how to encode such a string during the course of developing the application.

We could also use the POST method, which does not involve encoding a URL to send data back to the PHP script. POST is normally used when we need to send lots of data and also when the data sent usually changes the existing data store on the server. For illustrative purposes let us put together an HTML form and a script, which use the POST method to achieve the same functionality of the earlier script using GET.

```
<HTML><BODY>
<FORM ACTION="getform.php" METHOD=POST>
Who goes there ?:
<INPUT TYPE=TEXT NAME=yourname>
<BR><BR>
<INPUT TYPE=SUBMIT>
</FORM></BODY></HTML>
```

We can use this PHP script shown below to process the form submitted using the POST method:

```
<?php
echo( "Hmm, so you are ". $yourname );
?>
```

GET is often used to send small amounts of data, often to query the data store at the server side. Again, with GET, the submitted data is visible in the URL and therefore less secure as the data can be seen on the URL on the browser (assuming someone is looking over your shoulder).

Variables can be passed between scripts by encoding them in URLs. We shall see further examples of this when we take a look at the application itself. A session for an application can be maintained by passing these variables between scripts. We shall see more of this soon.

Application

Now we can move on to building the full PHP application. As well as being able to query the database through a browser, the user can also reserve (or relinquish) reservations on DVDs through the website.

The code in the example application is both modular and uses functional abstraction to separate HTML and PHP coding. As far as possible the same semantics and syntax of the database access functions are preserved from earlier chapters.

Login

❑ Obtains name from the user and uses the last name for authentication. Basic authentication is achieved by matching the member's ID and last name pair against the database value for this pair.

❑ Obtain member-id and match with last name to log the user in.

❑ Member ID should be preserved for subsequent scripts which will require them.

❑ After logging in, offer options of checking reservation status and searching the database.

Reservation status

❑ Check if the member has reserved any titles. If yes, display complete details. Display a cancel link for the reserved link, clicking on this will allow the user to cancel his or her reservation for the title.

❑ If there are no reservations, indicate so.

Search for titles

❑ Present the search form – a query can be made on the title of the movie and also the director.

❑ Call search function to get matches.

❑ Each match should have a reserve link, clicking on this should allow the user to reserve that title.

Reserve Titles

❑ Check if there are any reservations already for this user – if yes, display an error message.

❑ Obtain a date for which the title is to be reserved. Enforce the rule that a title cannot be reserved more than 7 days before hand.

❑ Check availability again for the desired date; if not available, display an error message.

❑ If available, reserve this title for the member for the requested date.

Cancellation

❑ Call the database access function to cancel the reservation made by the user for that title.

The code itself is below. The script file below contains the database access functions. You will notice that a few of these functions are not ultimately used by the main application code. They are just here for illustrative purposes and also so that the reader might use them to extend the application later. Remember to have the code from Chapter 4 made and installed before trying to run this code. Instructions on how to do this can be found in the relevant README files.

dvdstorefunctions.php

Here we define and assign a bunch of variables which are used only for the database access. The db_name variable is the name of the database and this has to be the same as that of an existing database used by the other interfaces to the DVD store application. The database user is defined by the variable $db_user:

```php
<?php
//dvdstoredbfunctions.php
// Global Variables
$host="localhost";
$port="";
$db_name="dvd_store";
$options="";
$tty="";
$db_user="dvd_user";
$db_password="";
$err_mesg;
$db_conn;
```

dvd_open_db()

This function opens a persistent connection to the database. A persistent connection saves us the overhead of initiating a connection to the database every time we need to access the database. Persistent connections are connections that do not close when the execution of a particular script ends. When a database connection is requested and persistent connections are enabled, PHP checks whether there's already a pre-existing connection and if yes, it uses the connection, if no, it initializes a new one:

```php
function dvd_open_db() {
    global $db_conn, $err_mesg;
    global $host, $db_name, $db_user, $db_password;
```

```
        // Open a persistent database connection
        if (($db_conn = pg_pConnect("host=$host dbname=$db_name user=$db_user
password=$db_password ")) == false) {
                $err_mesg = "Could not connect to the database";
        }
        return $db_conn;
}
```

dvd_err_text()

This function populates the error message string:

```
function dvd_err_text() {
      global $err_mesg;

      return $err_mesg;
}
```

dvd_close_db()

This function is executed to close a database connection:

```
function dvd_close_db() {
      return;
}
```

dvd_member_get()

This function populates a member structure by querying the database, and we test to see if a persistent database connection is already available by testing the variable $db_conn. If it is not, we initiate one by calling the dvd_open_db function. We use the pg_exec function to execute the SQL queries to the database:

```
function dvd_member_get($member_id, &$member_object) {

      global $db_conn, $err_mesg;

      // Get the database connection
      if (!$db_conn) {
          if (!($db_conn = dvd_open_db())) {
              return null;
          }
      }
      // Execute the select query
      if (( $result_id = pg_exec($db_conn, "select * from member
                       where member_id=$member_id")) == false) {
          $err_mesg=pg_errormessage($db_conn);
          return false;
      } else {
          $member_object = pg_Fetch_Object($result_id, 0);
          return true;
      }
}
```

dvd_member_search()

This function searches for members given a last name, as well as doing the usual check for a persistent database connection. We execute a SELECT query to search for records with the lastname field that we are looking for, and then populate the ID structure with member IDs of matching members:

```
function dvd_member_search($lname, &$ids) {

global $db_conn, $err_mesg;

    // Get the database connection
    if (!$db_conn) {
        if (!($db_conn = dvd_open_db())) {
            return null;
        }
    }

    if (( $result_id = pg_exec($db_conn, "select * from member
            where lname= '$lname'")) == false) {
        $err_mesg=pg_errormessage($db_conn);
        return false;
    } else {
        $row=0;
        for($row=0; $row<pg_numrows($result_id); $row++) {
            $store_member_object = pg_Fetch_Object($result_id, 0);
                $ids[$row] = $store_member_object->member_id;
        }

        return true;
    }
}
```

dvd_title_get()

This function populates a DVD title object given a DVD title ID, and does a database SELECT based on various search criteria. It also fetches the actual title object based on the result of the SELECT:

```
function dvd_title_get($title_id, &$title_object) {
    global $db_conn, $err_mesg;

    if (!$db_conn) {
        if (!($db_conn = dvd_open_db())) {
            return null;
        }
    }

    if (( $result_id = pg_exec($db_conn, "select title_id, title_text, asin,
director,  classification, actor1, actor2, release_date, rental_cost, genre_name
from title, genre where title_id=$title_id and title.genre_id = genre.genre_id"))
== false) {

        $err_mesg=pg_errormessage($db_conn);
            return false;
        } else {
            $title_object = pg_Fetch_Object($result_id, $row);
            return true;
        }
    }
}
```

dvd_title_search()

This function searches for DVDs with a given title, and executes the SQL query to get the DVDs with the required title:

```
function dvd_title_search($title, $name, &$matches) {
    global $db_conn, $err_mesg;
    // Get the database connection
    if (!$db_conn) {
        if (!($db_conn = dvd_open_db())) {
            return null;
        }
    }

    $title = strtolower($title);
    $name = strtolower($name);


    // Generate the sql query
    if ((strlen(trim($title)) == 0) && (strlen(trim($name)) == 0)) {
        return false;
    } else if ((strlen(trim($title)) == 0) || (strlen(trim($name)) == 0)) {
        if (strlen(trim($title)) == 0) {
            $sql_query = "SELECT * FROM title WHERE lower(director) LIKE
'%$name%' or lower(actor1) LIKE '%$name%' or lower(actor2) LIKE '%$name%'";
        } else {
            $sql_query = "SELECT * FROM title WHERE lower(title_text) LIKE
'%$title%'";
        }
    } else {
            $sql_query = "SELECT * FROM title WHERE lower(title_text) LIKE
'%$title%' or lower(director) LIKE '%$name%' or lower(actor1) like '%$name%' or
lower(actor2) LIKE '%$name%'";

    }


    if (( $result_id = pg_exec($db_conn,$sql_query)) == false) {
        $err_mesg=pg_errormessage($db_conn);
        return false;
    } else {
        for($row=0; $row<pg_numrows($result_id); $row++) {
            $title_object = pg_Fetch_Object($result_id, $row);
            $matches[$row] = $title_object->title_id;
        }
        return true;
    }
}
```

dvd_title_available()

This function checks whether a given title is available for a particular date:

```
// Check if the title is available
function dvd_title_available($title_id, $date, &$disk) {
    global $db_conn, $err_mesg;
    if (!$db_conn) {
        if (!($db_conn = dvd_open_db())) {
            return null;
        }
    }
    // Get the list of all the disks from the table disk
    if (( $result_id = pg_exec($db_conn, "select * from disk
                    where title_id = $title_id ")) == false){
        $err_mesg=pg_errormessage($db_conn);
        return false;
    } else {
        $disk=0;
        for($row=0; $row<pg_numrows($result_id); $row++) {
            $disk_object = pg_Fetch_Object($result_id, $row);
            if ($disk_object->member_id == 0) {
                $disk = $disk_object->disk_id;
            }
        }
        return true;
    }
}
```

dvd_reserve_title()

This function reserves a DVD title for a particular date:

```
function dvd_reserve_title($date, $title_id, $disk_id, $member_id) {
    global $db_conn, $err_mesg;

    if (!$db_conn) {
        if (!($db_conn = dvd_open_db())) {
            return null;
        }
    }

    if (( $result_id = pg_exec($db_conn, "insert into member_booking(member_id,
title_id, date_required) values
                    ($member_id, $title_id, '$date')")) == false) {
        $err_mesg=pg_errormessage($db_conn);
        return false;
    } else if (( $result_id = pg_exec($db_conn, "update disk set
member_id=$member_id where disk_id=$disk_id "))== false) {
        $err_mesg=pg_errormessage($db_conn);
        return false;
    } else{
        return true;
    }
}
```

dvd_reserve_title_cancel()

This function cancels an already reserved title:

```php
function dvd_reserve_title_cancel($member_id) {
     global $db_conn, $err_mesg;

     if (!$db_conn) {
          if (!($db_conn = dvd_open_db())) {
               return null;
          }
     }
     // This function assumes that there will be only one
     // reservation for the member in the member_booking table
     if (( $result_id = pg_exec($db_conn, "delete   from member_booking
                    where member_id= $member_id ")) == false) {
          $err_mesg=pg_errormessage($db_conn);
          return false;
     } else if (( $result_id = pg_exec($db_conn, "update disk set member_id=0
                    where member_id= $member_id ")) == false) {
          $err_mesg=pg_errormessage($db_conn);
          return false;

     }else {
          return true;
     }

}
```

dvd_reserve_title_query_by_member()

This function queries to see the titles reserved by a particular member:

```php
function dvd_reserve_title_query_by_member($member_id, &$tmpTitle)
     global $db_conn, $err_mesg;

     // Get the database connection
     if (!$db_conn) {
          if (!($db_conn = dvd_open_db())) {
               return null;
          }
     }

     // This function assumes that there will be only one
     // reservation for the member in member_booking table
     if (( $result_id = pg_exec($db_conn, "select * from member_booking
                    where member_id= $member_id ")) == false) {
          $err_mesg=pg_errormessage($db_conn);
          return false;
     } else {
          if (pg_NumRows($result_id) > 0) {
               $member_booking_object = pg_Fetch_Object($result_id, 0);
               $tmpTitle = $member_booking_object->title_id;
          }
```

```
        else {
                $tmpTitle= 0;
        }
        return true;
    }
}
```

dvd_begin_transaction()

This function initiates a database transaction:

```php
function dvd_begin_transaction() {
    global $db_conn;

    // Get the database connection
    if (!$db_conn) {
        if (!($db_conn = dvd_open_db())) {
            return null;
        }
    }

    return pg_exec($db_conn, "begin");

}
```

dvd_commit_transaction()

This function commits a database transaction to the database:

```php
function dvd_commit_transaction() {
    global $db_conn;

    // Get the database connection
    if (!$db_conn) {
        if (!($db_conn = dvd_open_db())) {
            return null;
        }
    }
    return pg_exec($db_conn, "commit");

}
```

The script below has some common definitions and functions used by other scripts. Most of the functions below are implemented so as to achieve the objective of separating the HTML rendering from the business logic of the application.

dvdstorecommon.php

```php
<?php
// dvdstorecommon.php
// Functions and other definitions used by other scripts

require( 'dvdstoredbfunctions.php' );
```

These constants are used to disambiguate between calls to rendering functions from either "Status check" routines or "Search routines":

```
define( "FROM_STATUS", 0 );
define( "FROM_SEARCH", 1 );
```

GenerateLoginForm()

This `function` generates a login page using an HTML form, the action script for which will authenticate the login. Note that the `$memberID` and `$lastName` variables will be available to this action script when the form is submitted:

```
function GenerateLoginForm( )
{
printf( "<FORM METHOD=POST ACTION=dvdstorelogin.php>\n" );
printf("<TABLE>");
printf( "<TR><TD><B>Lastname:</B></TD><TD> <INPUT TYPE=text SIZE=30
NAME=lastName><TD></TR><BR>\n" );
printf( "<TR><TD><B>Member ID:</B> </TD><TD><INPUT TYPE=text SIZE=30
NAME=memberID></TD></TR><BR>\n" );
printf( "<TR><TD><INPUT TYPE=submit VALUE=\"Submit\"></TD></TR>\n" );
printf("</TABLE>");
printf( "</FORM>" );
}
```

GenerateHTMLHeader()

This simply displays a header message. The readers could use their imagination to make this more fanciful by adding HTML to include images, banners, etc:

```
function GenerateHTMLHeader( $message )
{
printf( "<H1>%s</H1>\n", $message );
}
```

DisplayErrorMessage()

This function displays error messages in HTML. The HTML code below is more designed to suit formatting on a page than to aid readability. Basically it displays an error message very conspicuously. It is called by other functions that need to report an error to the user:

```
function DisplayErrorMessage( $message )
{
printf( "<BLOCKQUOTE><BLOCKQUOTE><BLOCKQUOTE><H3><FONT
COLOR=\"#cc0000\">%s</FONT></H3></BLOCKQUOTE></BLOCKQUOTE></BLOCKQUOTE>\n",
$message );
}
```

DisplaySearchMenu()

This function displays a search menu, so that the store user can search the DVD database:

```
function DisplaySearchMenu($memberID)
{
printf("<FORM METHOD=POST ACTION=dvdstoresearch.php?memberID=%s>\n", $memberID);
printf("<TABLE>\n");
printf( "<TR><TD><B>Movie title:</B></TD> <TD><INPUT TYPE=text SIZE=40
NAME=title></TD></TR>\n" );
printf( "<TR><TD><B>Director/ Actors:</B></TD> <TD> <INPUT TYPE=text SIZE=30
NAME=director><BR></TD></TR>\n" );
printf( "<TR><TD><INPUT TYPE=submit VALUE=\"Search\"></TD></TR>\n" );
printf("</TABLE>\n");
printf( "</FORM>" );
}
```

DisplayUserMenu()

This function gives a choice of checking existing reservations or searching for a new title:

```
function DisplayUserMenu( $memberID )
{
printf( "<A HREF=\"dvdstorestatus.php?memberID=%s\"><H3>Check your reservation
status</H3></A>", $memberID );
printf( "<A HREF=\"dvdstoresearch.php?memberID=%s\"><H3>Search for
movies</H3></A>", $memberID );
}
```

DisplayDVDDetails()

This function displays a DVD either reserved by the user, or ones that were returned as a result of the search. Depending on which function called this function, it displays the appropriate heading. So, if the calling function is the search or the reservation status function, it displays a page with a Search or a Status header respectively. If this function is called to display search results, it also gives the user the option to reserve a matching title. If the function is called to display reservation status, it also gives the provision to the user to cancel a reserved title:

```
function DisplayDVDDetails( $titleID, $searchORstatus )
{
global $memberID;

if (dvd_title_get( $titleID, $title_object) == false) {
    DisplayErrorMessage( "dvd_title_get failed" );
} else {
    if ( $searchORstatus == SEARCH ) {
        printf( "<B>Search results:</B><BR>\n" );
    }
    if ( $searchORstatus == STATUS ) {
        printf( "<B>You have the following DVD reserved:</B><BR>\n" );
    }

    printf( "<BR><BR> <B>Title:</B> %s<BR>\n", $title_object->title_text);
    printf( "<B>Director:</B> %s<BR>\n", $title_object->director );
    printf( "<B>Genre:</B> %s<BR>\n", $title_object->genre_name );
```

```
        printf( "<B>Rated:</B> %s<BR>\n", $title_object->classification );
        printf( "<B>Cast:</B> %s", $title_object->actor1);
        if (strlen($title_object->actor2)>0) {
                printf(", %s<BR>\n", $title_object->actor2);
        } else {
                printf("\n");
        }
        printf( "<B>Year:</B> %s<BR>\n", $title_object->release_date );
        printf( "<B>Rental cost:</B> %s<BR>\n", $title_object->rental_cost );

        if ( $searchORstatus == SEARCH )
                printf( "<BR><BR>Click <A
HREF=\"dvdstorereserve.php?memberID=%s&titleID=%s&date=0\">here </A> to reserve
this title<BR><BR><BR>\n", $memberID, $titleID );

        if ( $searchORstatus == STATUS )
                printf( "<BR><BR>Click <A HREF=\"dvdstorecancel.php?memberID=%s\">here
</A> to unreserve this title<BR><BR><BR>\n", $memberID );
        }
        }
```

GetReserveDate()

This function gets a date from the user for reserving a DVD title:

```
function GetReserveDate( $memberID, $titleID )
{

GenerateHTMLHeader( "Reserve a DVD title" );
printf( "<FORM METHOD=POST
ACTION=\"dvdstorereserve.php?memberID=%s&title=%s\">\n", $memberID, $titleID );
printf( "<B>Enter a date to reserve this title (MM/DD/YYYY format):</B> <INPUT
TYPE=text SIZE=10  NAME=dateToReserve><BR>\n" );
printf( "<INPUT TYPE=submit VALUE=\"Submit\">\n" );
printf( "</FORM>" );
}
```

The script below handles the login authentication of the user by obtaining the last name of the user and the member id and matching the two.

dvdstorelogin.php

The require function makes the functions and variables defined in dvdstorecommon.php to be available to this script file:

```
<?php
// dvdstorelogin.php
// Process login with this script

require( './dvdstorecommon.php' );
```

This script may be invoked either the first time without any values to $lastName and $memberID or with values assigned to them. In the first case, the script needs to display a login form and in the latter case it needs to process the login information.

```php
if ( empty( $lastName ) && empty( $memberID ))
{
//First time this script is invoked
     GenerateHTMLHeader( "Login to DVD store online" );
     GenerateLoginForm( );
} else {
     if ( empty( $lastName ) || empty( $memberID ))
     {
          //User submitted an incomplete form
          GenerateHTMLHeader( "Login to DVD store online" );
          DisplayErrorMessage( "Lastname and MemberID needs to be entered" );
          GenerateLoginForm( );
     } else {
          //We search for matching last names
          if (dvd_member_search( $lastName, $matches) == false) {
               DisplayErrorMessage("Error in dvd_member_search");
          } else if ( !$matches ||( count($matches) == 0) ) {
               //No matches for last name
               GenerateHTMLHeader( "Login Error" );
               DisplayErrorMessage( "No such User in the database" );
          } else {
               //Found at least one match for lastname
               for ( $i = 0; $i < count($matches); $i++ )
               {
                    if ( $matches[$i] == $memberID )
                    {
                         //Login succeded
                         GenerateHTMLHeader( "Welcome to DVD store online" );
                         DisplayUserMenu( $memberID );
                         return;
                    }
               }
               // Login Error
               GenerateHTMLHeader( "Login Error" );
               DisplayErrorMessage( "Last Name and the Member ID don't
match!");
          }
     }
}
?>
```

The application would look like the screenshot below in the normal course of a user's interaction with it. The following screen is the Login screen presented to the user:

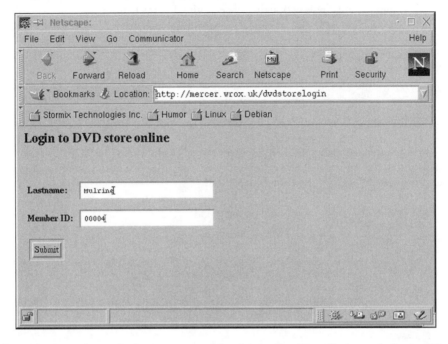

The following screen shows the login processed by the application, offering a choice to either check reservation status or to search for DVD titles:

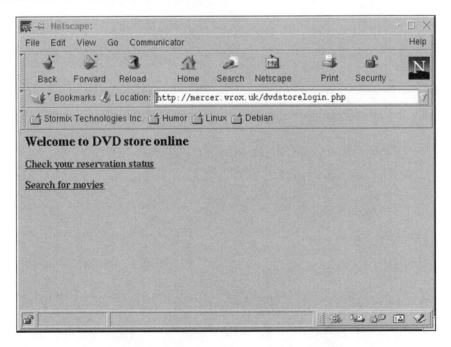

dvdstoresearch.php

The script below implements the functionality of searching for DVD titles:

```php
<?php
// dvdstoresearch.php
// Search for DVDs

require( './dvdstorecommon.php' );

GenerateHTMLHeader( "DVD titles search" );
```

This script may be invoked either the first time without any values to $title and $director or with values assigned to them. In the first case, the script needs to display a search menu and in the latter case it needs to process the search information passed to it:

```php
if ( empty( $title ) && empty( $director )){
    //First call to this script
    DisplaySearchMenu($memberID);
}else {
    //The case where search criteria is sent to the script through the form
    if (dvd_title_search( $title, $director, $matches)== false) {
        DisplayErrorMessage( "dvd_title_search() failed" );
    } else if ( count($matches)== 0) {
        //Zero matches
        DisplayErrorMessage( "No matches found" );
    } else {
        //Display all the matches found
        for ( $i = 0; $i < count($matches); ++$i ) {
            DisplayDVDDetails( $matches[$i], SEARCH );
        }
    }
}

?>
```

The following is the search screen of the application where the user can search for a DVD title:

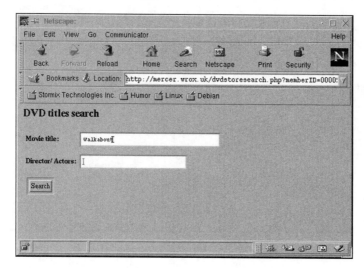

The search results are in the next screen shot, and the user could click on the link below to reserve this title:

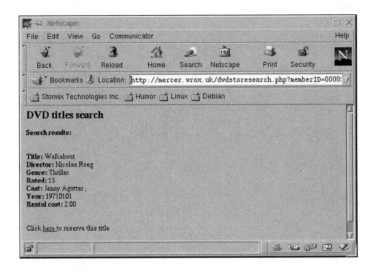

dvdstorestatus.php

The code below handles the checking of reservation status for a given user by querying for the titles currently reserved by the user and displaying the reservation if any:

```php
<?php
// dvdstorestatus.php
// Check a user's reservation status

require( './dvdstorecommon.php' );

GenerateHTMLHeader( "Reservation Status" );


if (dvd_reserve_title_query_by_member( $memberID, $titleID) == false) {
    DisplayErrorMessage("dvd_reserve_title_query_by_member failed");
} else if ($titleID > 0) {
    //Found the DVD reserved by this user

    DisplayDVDDetails( $titleID, STATUS );

} else {
    //No DVDs found
    printf( "<B>You have no DVDs reserved as of now.</B>\n" );
}

?>
```

The following screen shows the reservation status page of the user. The user could click the link at the bottom to cancel this reservation.

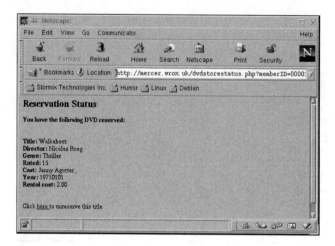

dvdstorecancel.php

The code below handles cancelling of the reservation of a title for a given user:

```php
<?php
// dvdstorecancel.php
// Cancel the title reserved by this member

require( './dvdstorecommon.php' );


if ( dvd_reserve_title_cancel( $memberID ) == false )
    DisplayErrorMessage( "dvd_reserve_title_cancel failed" );
else
    printf( "<B>Cancel succeeded</B>" );
?>
```

and hence:

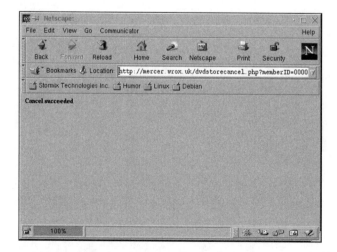

dvdstorereserve.php

The code below handles reserving a title for a given user:

```php
<?php
// dvdstorereserve.php
// Reserve a title for this member

require( './dvdstorecommon.php' );



if ( $dateToReserve == 0 )
{
    //User has not yet specified a date to reserve the title
    //Prompt the user to enter a date
    GetReserveDate( $memberID, $titleID );
} else {

    // Begin the transaction
    dvd_begin_transaction();
    //We have the reservation date, member ID and the title ID now
    if ( dvd_reserve_title_query_by_member( $memberID, $tmpTitle ) == false )
        DisplayErrorMessage( "dvd_display_title_query_by_member failed" );
    else {
        if ( $tmpTitle > 0 )
            //Member already has a title reserved
            DisplayErrorMessage( "Sorry you already have a title reserved"
);
        else {
            //Try reserving the title for this member
            $dateArray = split( '[/.-]', $dateToReserve );
```

We parse the date string to obtain the date for reserving this title:

```php
            $absReserveTime = mktime( 0, 0, 0, $dateArray[0], $dateArray[1],
$dateArray[2] );
            $absToday = time( );
            if (( $absReserveTime - $absToday ) > ( 24 * 60 * 60*7 ))
            {
                //Reservations can only be made 7 days in advance
                DisplayErrorMessage( "You can reserve a title only 7 days
in advance" );
                GetReserveDate( $memberID, $title );
            } else {
                //Check if the title is available for the day
                if ( dvd_title_available( $title, $date, $disk ) == false )
                    DisplayErrorMessage( "dvd_title_available failed" );
                else
                    if ( $disk == 0 )
                        DisplayErrorMessage( "The title is not available on
this date" );
                    else
                        if ( dvd_reserve_title( $dateArray[2] .
```

```
$dateArray[0] . $dateArray[1], $title, $disk, $memberID ) == false ) {
                                    DisplayErrorMessage( "dvd_reserve_title
failed" );

                        } else {
                        printf( "<B>Reservation succeeded</B>" );
                    }
            }
        }
        // End the transaction
        dvd_commit_transaction ();
    }
}
?>
```

Summary

In this chapter we explored PHP as a server-side scripting language and compared it with other similar solutions. We looked at the issue of installing PHP on a Linux box and configuring it to our needs. We went on to outline the syntax of the scripting language at an introductory level. During the course of this we explored variables, constants, operators, functions and arrays. Finally we attempted to apply our understanding of PHP by building an application that was an extension of the DVD store application that we developed in other chapters.

Resources

❑   Professional PHP programming, Jesus Castagnetto et. Al, Wrox Press

❑   PHP manual, Stig Baekken et al - http://www.php.net/manual/

❑   Beginning Linux Programming, Rick Stones and Neil Mathews, Wrox Press

17

Embedding and Extending Python with C/C++

Python includes many modules, through which a wide variety of features are provided. Many third-party modules are also available, including support for CORBA, XML and extensive web server functionality. Occasionally, Python and its modules may not meet all our needs, either because the necessary functionality doesn't exist, or because the performance of the Python scripts is inadequate.

These two problems can both be solved by creating C/C++ "extension" modules that we can call from Python scripts; by doing so, we're literally **extending** Python, granting Python programs access to functionality and object types that are not included in its base environment, and sometimes improved performance as well. What's more, these modules can be used to define new object types as well as new functions.

Python provides a rich set of APIs that ease extension module development. These APIs also allow C/C++ programs to call Python scripts by **embedding** the Python interpreter in an existing C/C++ program. Typically, programs that embed the Python interpreter will also extend Python, allowing scripts to access functions declared in the host program.

In this chapter, we'll extend Python by creating several C/C++ extension modules. We'll start by using **SWIG** (Simplified Wrapper Interface Generator) to develop a few simple modules. We'll then create more advanced extension modules, using the Python C API directly. Finally, we'll use the API to embed Python in a C/C++ host program. We'll allow Python to callback to the host program by making the host program an extension module itself.

Extending Python with a C/C++ extension module

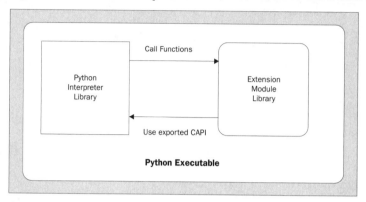

A typical extension scenario is shown above. The Python executable loads the Python interpreter library, which in turn executes a Python script. At some point the script **imports** an extension module. The Python interpreter dynamically loads the extension module library and initializes it. The functions and object types defined in the extension module then become available to the Python script.

It's important to bear in mind that Python scripts don't know that the imported module is an extension module and not a regular Python module; from the script's perspective, there's no difference.

Embedding Python in a Host Program

The Python interpreter library can also be loaded into C/C++ programs, giving them powerful Python scripting functionality.

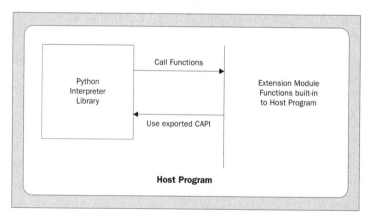

This diagram shows a typical Python embedding scenario. In this example, the host C/C++ program has loaded the Python interpreter library. The host program calls into the Python interpreter, using the Python C API to execute Python scripts. Those Python scripts can call back to the host program using an extension module.

In this case, the host program is also an extension module, even though it's not dynamically loaded. It is also possible to dynamically load other extension modules when the Python interpreter is embedded in a C/C++ host program.

Developing Extension Modules in C/C++

The following steps describe how to create a Python extension module in C/C++:

- ❑ Identify the functions, structures and objects you wish to make available to Python.
- ❑ Create interface functions (often wrapper functions) that can be called by the Python interpreter.
- ❑ Compile the interface functions (wrapper module).
- ❑ Link the wrapper module against the target function library and Python library.
- ❑ Test the module.

The interface functions, or **wrappers**, may be written by hand or created automatically by SWIG. We'll start off by using SWIG to create wrapper code for a few functions and structures. Later on, we'll create wrapper functions using the Python C API directly.

Required Software Tools

To extend or embed Python, you must have the base Python interpreter and Python development libraries installed. These are available in RPM form or .tar format from http://www.python.org. To develop extensions using SWIG, you'll need to download and install SWIG from http://www.swig.org.

Python Interpreter

The Python package includes the Python executable, Python interpreter, and Python library. Check your system for these files, typically (for version 1.5.2 at least) located in /usr/bin/python, /usr/lib/python1.5 and /usr/lib/python1.5/config respectively.

Python Development Libraries

The Python library is typically located in the /usr/lib/python1.5/config directory, where you'll find libpython1.5.a, Makefile.pre.in, and python.o. If you don't have these files, you'll need to install a Python development package or download and install the source from the Python website.

SWIG – Simplified Wrapper Interface Generator

SWIG can generate wrappers for TCL, Perl and Python, and runs on both UNIX and Windows; we're now going to use it to automatically generate our wrapper functions. There are several different versions of SWIG available; our examples were made using Version 1.1 Patch 5; you can download the latest version from http://www.swig.org.

```
$ swig -version

SWIG Version 1.1 (Patch 5)
Copyright (c) 1995-98
University of Utah and the Regents of the University of California

Compiled with c++
```

When this chapter was written, the 1.3 swig versions were unreliable, so users should stick with the latest stable release, version 1.1.

Extending Python Using SWIG

Python provides a comprehensive C API that is used to both extend and embed Python; however, it's large and not fully documented, making its use rather difficult. We often need to let a Python script access one or two simple functions or structures; apparently an easy task, but one that can take a lot of code to accomplish using the C API. SWIG was designed with such simple tasks in mind.

SWIG makes extending Python easy; we create a simple **interface file**, describing the functions we want to access from Python. SWIG then automatically generates the code required to interface Python with the specified functions. SWIG directives provide additional control over the wrapping process.

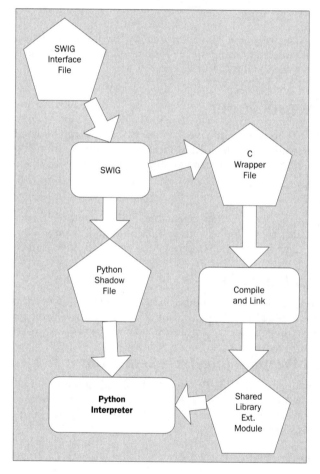

This diagram shows the process used to create an extension module from a SWIG interface file. SWIG reads the interface file and produces a Python **shadow file**. The shadow file contains helper class definitions, which ease the task of interfacing with C structures. SWIG also creates a C source file, containing code based on the contents of the interface file; this is called a **wrapper file**.

The process of making C functions available to Python is common referred to by Python developers as "wrapping".

The SWIG-generated wrapper file is compiled and linked against the Python interpreter library, producing a shared extension module. The wrapper file could also be linked directly into a custom version of the Python interpreter, or linked into a host program that will be embedding the Python interpreter.

Finally, Python loads the shadow file and the extension module to provide access to the functions and structures declared in the SWIG interface file.

Simple Functions

We'll make our first Python extension module by using SWIG to wrap the sysinfo function and structure. If you examine the man page for sysinfo, you'll see that it describes a structure called sysinfo, along with a function of the same name. The structure is defined in /usr/include/linux/kernel.h, but the function itself is not defined in any include files.

By convention, SWIG interface files use an extension of .i; let's then create our first SWIG interface file and call it sysinfo.i. You should create a new directory to contain the files that comprise the extension module – several files will be used for each. You *can* build more than one module in a single directory, but in this example we'll just create one in a fresh directory.

The sysinfo.i interface file contains the following text.

```
%module sysinfo
%{
#include <linux/kernel.h>
#include <linux/sys.h>
%}

%include "linux/kernel.h"

%name(getsysinfo) int sysinfo(struct sysinfo *info);
```

There are several things to note about this file:

❑ SWIG directives are denoted by a leading percent (%) symbol.

❑ Text enclosed between %{ and %} is placed in the generated C wrapper file without interpretation.

❑ The first line of the interface file, %module sysinfo, specifies the name of the Python module that is to be created.

In this example, the first two #include statements will be written to the generated C wrapper file. The man page for sysinfo specifies that both of these files should be included.

❑ The %include directive tells SWIG to process the specified file, creating wrapper code for structures and functions defined in the included file.

In this example, we only process linux/kernel.h, since it's the file that defines the sysinfo structure. Note that SWIG does not have a full C preprocessor, so it sometimes fails on complicated .h files.

When wrapping many functions described by existing .h files, it is sometimes necessary to rewrite the .h files, removing constructs that SWIG doesn't understand. In this case, SWIG has no problem with linux/kernel.h.

❏ Finally, when SWIG generates the shadow file it creates a class named sysinfo to represent the C sysinfo structure.

Since Python uses a single namespace for objects declared at the module level, the class name 'sysinfo' conflicts with the function name 'sysinfo'. To resolve this conflict, we use the %name directive to rename the sysinfo function as getsysinfo in the shadow file.

Having created the sysinfo.i interface file, we use SWIG to create the C wrapper file sysinfo_wrap.c thus:

```
$ swig -python -I/usr/include -shadow -make_default sysinfo.i
Generating wrappers for Python
/usr/include/linux/kernel.h : Line 85. Warning. Array member will be read-only.
/usr/include/linux/kernel.h : Line 93. Warning. Array member will be read-only.
```

SWIG reports two warnings while processing the interface file; later on, we'll discuss what these mean.

Several command line options can be used to control the generation of the C wrapper file:

Option	Specifies
-python	produce code for extending Python (rather than TCL or Perl)
-I/usr/include	where to look for include files
-shadow	create a shadow Python file
-make_default	create a default constructor for structures
sysinfo.i	the name of the interface file

Unlike a C/C++ compiler SWIG will, by default, look for include files in the current working directory and the swig_lib directory. As we're including linux/kernel.h in sysinfo.i, we used the -I/usr/include command line option to tell SWIG to also look in the /usr/include directory.

The -shadow command causes SWIG to produce a shadow Python file. Shadow files make it easier to access C structures and functions from Python by defining the structures as Python classes.

SWIG generates the C wrapper file sysinfo_wrap.c, and the Python shadow file sysinfo.py. A portion of the shadow file, sysinfo.py is shown below:

```
# This file was created automatically by SWIG.
import sysinfoc
class sysinfo:
    def __init__(self,*args):
        self.this = apply(sysinfoc.new_sysinfo,args)
        self.thisown = 1
```

```
    def __del__(self,sysinfoc=sysinfoc):
        if self.thisown == 1 :
            sysinfoc.delete_sysinfo(self)
    __setmethods__ = {
        "uptime" : sysinfoc.sysinfo_uptime_set,
        "totalram" : sysinfoc.sysinfo_totalram_set,
        "freeram" : sysinfoc.sysinfo_freeram_set,
        "sharedram" : sysinfoc.sysinfo_sharedram_set,
        "bufferram" : sysinfoc.sysinfo_bufferram_set,
        "totalswap" : sysinfoc.sysinfo_totalswap_set,
        "freeswap" : sysinfoc.sysinfo_freeswap_set,
        "procs" : sysinfoc.sysinfo_procs_set,
    }
    def __setattr__(self,name,value):
        if (name == "this") or (name == "thisown"):
            self.__dict__[name] = value; return
        method = sysinfo.__setmethods__.get(name,None)
        if method: return method(self,value)
        self.__dict__[name] = value
<snip>
```

There are two important items to note in the shadow file shown above:

The first is the line import sysinfoc. When the shadow file sysinfo.py is imported into Python, sysinfo.py expects to import the extension module as sysinfoc. When the sysinfo_wrap.c file is compiled, you must therefore be able to import it as sysinfoc, and not sysinfo.

The second is that the sysinfo structure is represented by a class of the same name, and includes both a constructor (__init__) and a destructor (__del__).

Compiling and Testing a SWIG-generated Wrapper File

The C wrapper file sysinfo_wrap.c must be compiled and linked before Python can use it. (We won't list the wrapper file here due to its length.) The Python distribution includes a Makefile template, which can ease the task of building extension modules. We need to copy the following files to our working directory (your exact paths may vary depending on your installation):

❏ /usr/lib/python1.5/config/Makefile.pre.in (the Makefile template)

❏ /usr/lib/python1.5/config/Setup (the template control file)

The Setup file defines the default modules that are built into the Python interpreter. This file includes instructions on how to create our own Setup file for use with the Makefile template. To make our lives a little easier, we rename Setup to Setup.doc in our working directory. We can then refer to the comments in the Setup.doc file for instructions on building Python extension modules using the template.

In our example, we'll create a Setup.in file containing these two lines:

```
*shared*
sysinfoc sysinfo_wrap.c
```

The first tells the template to create a shared module, while the second specifies that a module sysinfoc should be created from the source file sysinfo_wrap.c. In the previous section, we examined the shadow file sysinfo.py and found that SWIG expects compiled extension modules to be the module name we specified in the interface file sysinfo.i, but with the letter 'c' appended to the name. Consequently, we've specified sysinfoc as the name of the shared module to be created in the Setup.in file.

Now we have the Setup.in file, we create the Makefile according to the instructions specified in Makefile.pre.in:

```
make -f Makefile.pre.in boot
```

The 'boot' process copies Setup.in to Setup and creates the Makefile. After the initial build of Makefile, changes made to Setup.in will be ignored since Makefile will read the Setup file instead. Any future changes we'll need to make to the Setup file.

We can now compile the sysinfo C wrapper file using the make command:

```
$ make
gcc -fPIC  -g -O2 -I/usr/include/python1.5 -I/usr/include/python1.5 -
DHAVE_CONFIG_H -c ./sysinfo_wrap.c
gcc -shared  sysinfo_wrap.o  -o sysinfocmodule.so
$
```

Testing the Extension Module

The wrapper file sysinfo_wrap.c has now been compiled into a shareable module that can be loaded by Python. To test the extension module, simply start the Python interpreter in the same directory as the sysinfocmodule.so file. (If we don't run it in the same directory, it will not be able to load the sysinfoc module because the module is not on the Python path.)

```
$python
Python 1.5.2 (#1, Sep 17 1999, 20:15:36)  [GCC egcs-2.91.66 19990314/Linux]
Copyright 1991-1995 Stichting Mathematisch Centrum, Amsterdam
>>> import sysinfo
>>> si = sysinfo.sysinfo()
>>> sysinfo.getsysinfo(si)
0
>>> print si.totalram, si.freeram, si.sharedram
97861632 2396160 38313984
>>> print si.totalswap, si.freeswap, si.procs
139788288 133033984 73
>>>
```

The statement import sysinfo causes Python to load the shadow file sysinfo.py. This in turn loads the compiled extension module sysinfocmodule.so by executing the import sysinfoc statement we mentioned previously.

Next, we create a sysinfo object with the assignment si = sysinfo.sysinfo(). This statement causes si to refer to an instance of the sysinfo class defined by the shadow file sysinfo.py. This is equivalent to allocating memory for a sysinfo structure in C.

We call the `sysinfo` function (which we've renamed `getsysinfo`) with the statement `sysinfo.getsysinfo(si)`. The return code from this function is 0, which is what's printed by the Python interpreter. We've basically passed `getsysinfo` the last created `sysinfo` structure referenced by the `si` variable.

Finally, we have two `print` statements that print out some of the attributes of the `sysinfo` structure.

Accessing Arrays Using SWIG Pointers

SWIG eases the task of quickly adding C functions to Python programs. One area in which SWIG does not perform well is handling arrays. When we ran SWIG on the `sysinfo.i` file, it reported two warnings:

```
$ swig -python -I/usr/include -shadow -make_default sysinfo.i
Generating wrappers for Python
/usr/include/linux/kernel.h : Line 85. Warning. Array member will be read-only.
/usr/include/linux/kernel.h : Line 93. Warning. Array member will be read-only.
```

Examining `/usr/include/linux/kernel.h` we see that line 85 contains the following declaration:

```
unsigned long loads[3];        /* 1, 5, and 15 minute load averages */
```

When we try to print out the value of the loads attribute in Python, we get the following result:

```
>>> print si.loads
_80e958c_unsigned_long_p
```

Rather than returning the contents of the array, SWIG returns a pointer to an unsigned long. One of the reasons it does this is that there's no way to specify the index of the array element we wish to access. However, SWIG does allow Python programs to access a variety of simple array types using pointers; it includes an interface file named `pointer.i` that defines several pointer access functions. This file resides in the `swig_lib` library directory. We gain access to these functions by simply including the interface file in our base interface file, `sysinfo.i`:

```
%module sysinfo
%{
#include <linux/kernel.h>
#include <linux/sys.h>
%}

%include "pointer.i"
%include "linux/kernel.h"

%name(getsysinfo) int sysinfo(struct sysinfo *info);
```

We can now use these functions to access the `loads` array. Run SWIG, and rebuild the `sysinfocmodule.so` file by running make. Restart Python, import sysinfo, create a `sysinfo` structure and call `getsysinfo` with that structure; finally print the contents of `loads`:

```
$python
Python 1.5.2 (#1, Sep 17 1999, 20:15:36)  [GCC egcs-2.91.66 19990314/Linux]
Copyright 1991-1995 Stichting Mathematisch Centrum, Amsterdam
>>> import sysinfo
```

```
>>> si = sysinfo.sysinfo()
>>> sysinfo.getsysinfo(si)
0
>>> for i in range(0,3): print sysinfo.ptrvalue(si.loads,i,"long")
...
224
1664
0
```

The statement `print sysinfo.ptrvalue(si.loads,i,"long")` calls the pointer function `ptrvalue` defined in `pointer.i`. The `ptrvalue` function takes three arguments: the pointer, the index, and an optional pointer typecast.

> *Note that `ptrvalue` does not support unsigned longs; however, we can access the `unsigned long` values that `loads` refers to, by casting them to `longs` instead.*

Adding Virtual Methods to Structures

Using `ptrvalue` to access the `loads` array is actually rather crude though. The `ptrvalue` function doesn't know the size of the `loads` array, and will gladly try to access any index passed to it, even beyond the end of the array. SWIG allows you to add arbitrary methods to C/C++ structures.

> *This feature makes C structures look and act somewhat like C++ objects.*

Let's add a method to the `sysinfo` structure to return `loads` information. We'll use the `%addmethods` SWIG directive in `sysinfo.i`:

```
%module sysinfo
%{
#include <linux/kernel.h>
#include <linux/sys.h>
%}

%include "pointer.i"
%include "linux/kernel.h"
```

```
%addmethods sysinfo {
        unsigned long getload(int index) {
                if(index >= (sizeof(self->loads)/sizeof(unsigned long)) ||
                    index < 0) {
                        return 0;
                }
                return self->loads[index];
        }
}
```

```
%name(getsysinfo) int sysinfo(struct sysinfo *info);
```

This adds the method `getload` to the `sysinfo` structure. When the `getload` function is executed, SWIG will automatically pass a pointer to the underlying structure (`sysinfo`) as the variable `self`. Similar to the `this` pointer in C++, `self` refers to the instance of the object on which the method is operating.

The `getload` function checks to see whether index is within the bounds of the `loads` array. If index is out of bounds it returns 0. We can test the `getload` method by running SWIG and `make again`, and then loading Python as before:

```
$python
Python 1.5.2 (#1, Sep 17 1999, 20:15:36)   [GCC egcs-2.91.66 19990314/Linux]
Copyright 1991-1995 Stichting Mathematisch Centrum, Amsterdam
>>> import sysinfo
>>> si = sysinfo.sysinfo()
>>> sysinfo.getsysinfo(si)
0
>>> for index in range(-1,4): print si.getload(index)
...
0
63008
63104
55328
0
>>>
```

If index is out of bounds, the `getload` function will return 0. A better solution would be for `getload` to raise an `IndexError` exception when index is out of bounds.

Raising and Handling Exceptions Using Typemaps

One of the nice features of the Python language is its support of exceptions. The `try`, `except` and `raise` statements provide a powerful mechanism for handling infrequent conditions while supporting fast typical control flow. SWIG supports both the generation of exceptions, and the processing of exceptions that occur in wrapped functions.

The `sysinfo` function, for example, returns the value –1 when an invalid `sysinfo` structure address has been passed. System functions and libraries frequently use a specific return code value to indicate an error condition. For example, most system function calls return –1 to indicate an error. This consistent return code value can provide the basis for automatic exception generation by raising an exception whenever a failure return code, such as -1, is encountered.

We can improve our `sysinfo` extension module by raising an exception when `sysinfo` returns -1. SWIG has a **typemap** directive that allows us to control how SWIG converts Python data to its C representation, and vice-versa. SWIG also uses typemaps to specify how to handle an exception.

Creating SWIG typemaps is something of a black art; typemaps can ease the automatic conversion of large function libraries. However, improper typemaps can create unusable C code. Be sure to carefully study the typemap documentation and examples that come with SWIG before getting too ambitious.

SWIG is currently undergoing a large rewrite in preparation for the release of version 2; its author has said that typemaps may not be implemented in this new version. However, in the event that they're not, it's perfectly likely that some alternative mechanism will be provided.

SWIG also includes an exception.i interface file, which provides a convenient, language-neutral mechanism for raising exceptions. We'll use both of these features to add exception support to the sysinfo function. Our new sysinfo.i interface file looks like this:

```
%module sysinfo
%{
#include <linux/kernel.h>
#include <linux/sys.h>
#include <string.h>
#include <errno.h>
%}

%include "pointer.i"
%include "linux/kernel.h"
%include "exception.i"

%addmethods sysinfo {
        unsigned long getload(int index) {
                if(index >= (sizeof(self->loads)/sizeof(unsigned long)) ||
                   index < 0) {
                        return 0;
                }
                return self->loads[index];
        }
}

%typemap(python,except) int {
        $function
        if( $source < 0) {
                _SWIG_exception(SWIG_RuntimeError,strerror(errno));
                $cleanup
                return NULL;
        }
}

%name(getsysinfo) int sysinfo(struct sysinfo *info);
```

We're now including <string.h> and <errno.h> to support the strerror function. The statement %include "exception.i" imports the exception-handling code into sysinfo_wrap.c.

SWIG typemaps are defined by three parameters: the target language, the "typemap type" and the parameter type. In this example, we've added a typemap of type "except" for the Python language, for functions returning an int. Any such functions defined in the interface file after this declaration, will have this typemap applied to them.

SWIG inserts the exception handling code in the wrapper file where it would normally call the underlying library function that's being wrapped. The exception handler can modify the return value, raise an exception or do nothing. If the exception handler does nothing, SWIG will return the result code to Python without modification, just as if the exception handler had not been specified.

We've also made use of a number of macros:

- ❏ `$function` expands to the actual function call to sysinfo.

- ❏ `$source` expands to the variable name holding the result of the sysinfo call.

- ❏ `$cleanup` expands to any C code needed to free memory used in the wrapper function.

If `$source` is less than zero, the _SWIG_exception function is called to raise an exception condition of type SWIG_RuntimeError. The strerror function converts errno to a string. The `$cleanup` macro frees any allocated memory and the wrapper function returns NULL. Bear in mind that the wrapper function is being called from Python, which expects C functions to return NULL when an exception has occurred.

If `$source` is greater than or equal to zero, SWIG will return that result code to Python.

After re-running SWIG and rebuilding sysinfocmodule.so, we can test the exception handler by creating an invalid sysinfo object:

```
$ python
Python 1.5.2 (#1, Sep 17 1999, 20:15:36)  [GCC egcs-2.91.66 19990314/Linux]
Copyright 1991-1995 Stichting Mathematisch Centrum, Amsterdam
>>> import sysinfo
>>> badSI = sysinfo.sysinfoPtr(sysinfo.ptrcast(0,"sysinfo_p"))
>>> sysinfo.getsysinfo(badSI)
Traceback (innermost last):
  File "<stdin>", line 1, in ?
RuntimeError: Bad address
>>>
```

To create an invalid sysinfo object, we use the ptrcast function to create a NULL C pointer to an object of type sysinfo_p. Calling getsysinfo with this object raises an exception. The strerror function converted errno to the string "Bad Address".

Admittedly, this is rather a contrived example, but it shows how to use exception typemaps to properly handle invalid conditions. Using this technique we can go back and fix the getload function to raise an exception when the index value is out of range.

Let's modify the getload method in sysinfo.i as follows:

```
%include "exception.i"

%typemap(python,except) unsigned long {
        $function
        if(PyErr_Occurred()) {
                $cleanup
                return NULL;
        }
}
```

```
%addmethods sysinfo {
        unsigned long getload(int index) {
                if(index >= (sizeof(self->loads)/sizeof(unsigned long)) ||
                   index < 0) {
                        _SWIG_exception(SWIG_ValueError,"Index out of range");
                        return 0;
                }
                return self->loads[index];
        }
}
```

We've now added a new exception typemap for functions that return unsigned long values. The Python function PyErr_Occurred returns TRUE if an exception has been raised; in this case the exception typemap executes the $cleanup macro, and then returns NULL.

In the getload function, we've added a call to _SWIG_exception. In the example shown above, we return the dummy value 0 after raising the exception condition; this is ignored by the exception typemap, which detects the raised exception because PyErr_Occurred returns TRUE.

```
$python
Python 1.5.2 (#1, Sep 17 1999, 20:15:36)  [GCC egcs-2.91.66 19990314/Linux]
Copyright 1991-1995 Stichting Mathematisch Centrum, Amsterdam
>>> import sysinfo
>>> si = sysinfo.sysinfo()
>>> sysinfo.getsysinfo(si)
0
>>> si.getload(-1)
Traceback (innermost last):
  File "<stdin>", line 1, in ?
  File "sysinfo.py", line 9, in getload
    val = sysinfoc.sysinfo_getload(self.this,arg0)
ValueError: Index out of range
>>>
```

Calling getload with an invalid index now raises an exception of type ValueError.

Handling variables by reference using typemaps

We've now pretty much exhausted the examples we can demonstrate using the sysinfo structure and sysinfo function. Let's tackle a common problem of handling variables by reference, also known as in/out variables. We'll use the function getdomainname declared as follows:

```
int getdomainname(char *name, int len);
```

This function expects to receive a pointer to a character buffer, and the length of that buffer. It will fill in the passed buffer with the domain name and return a result code. However, Python does not allow you to pass variables by reference, which is how the name variable is being used.

There are a variety of ways to tackle this problem. The simplest is to create one typemap for the name buffer, and another for len; these can be applied to the getdomainname function. In this example, we'll use a fixed length buffer of 255 bytes. Here are the appropriate modifications to sysinfo.i:

```
%name(getsysinfo) int sysinfo(struct sysinfo *info);
```

```
%typemap(python,ignore)
    STRINGLEN {
        $target = 255;
    }
```

Like the except typemap shown earlier, ignore defines a mapping that controls how SWIG converts values between Python and C. In this case, the ignore typemap does two things:

❑   it causes the argument to be invisible when the function is called from Python.

❑   it defines a default value for the argument.

Python scripts cannot provide a value for an ignored argument because the default value specified in the interface file will always be used. The SWIG $target macro expands to the name of the variable that will be passed to the called function. We set that variable to the value 255:

```
%name(getsysinfo) int sysinfo(struct sysinfo *info);
```

```
%typemap(python,ignore)
    STRINGOUT (char _temp[255]) {
        _temp[0] = 0;
        $target = _temp;
    }
```

The ignore typemap defines a mapping called STRINGOUT; this creates a null-terminated character buffer named _temp, of length 255 bytes. Like the STRINGLEN typemap, STRINGOUT will pass the address of this temporary buffer to the called function:

```
%typemap(python,argout)
    STRINGOUT  {
    PyObject *o;

    o = Py_BuildValue("s",$source);
    if (!$target) {
      $target = o;
    } else {
      $target = t_output_helper($target, o);
    }
  }
```

This argout typemap tells SWIG how to convert the argument value into an output value. In other words, functions that have STRINGOUT arguments see the temporary string as input values, but SWIG must convert them to output values in order to return them to Python.

In this example, the $source macro expands to the name of the temporary character array allocated by the ignore typemap shown above. The Python function Py_BuildValue converts the character array into a Python string.

Finally, the Python string value is returned directly (if the $target value expands to NULL), or appended the current return value as an additional tuple member:

```
%apply STRINGOUT {char *name};
%apply STRINGLEN {int len};
int getdomainname(char *name, int len);
%clear STRINGOUT, char *name;
%clear STRINGLEN, int len;
```

We've defined the two typemaps as STRINGLEN and STRINGOUT, in place of int and char * respectively. Any functions defined after these typemaps' declaration would use the typemaps for any int and char * parameter. Since we've named them using an arbitrary (but unique) name, we can apply them to a function selectively using the %apply SWIG directive as shown above.

For example, the %apply STRINGOUT {char *name}; directive causes the STRINGOUT typemap to be applied to any subsequent function declaration with an argument of type char *name.

Finally, the %clear STRINGOUT, char *name; directive disables the typemap application, so that subsequent functions with arguments of char *name will not get the STRINGOUT typemap applied.

Rebuild sysinfo.i, make the sysinfocmodule.so file and test as follows:

```
$ python
Python 1.5.2 (#1, Sep 17 1999, 20:15:36)  [GCC egcs-2.91.66 19990314/Linux]
Copyright 1991-1995 Stichting Mathematisch Centrum, Amsterdam
>>> import sysinfo
>>> sysinfo.getdomainname()
(0, 'murkworks.com')
>>>
```

Note that the getdomainname function (as called from Python) does not take any arguments. This is because both arguments had an ignore typemap that caused SWIG to hide the arguments from Python, and set the default value to pass to the C getdomainname function.

The return value from the Python getdomainname function is a two-element tuple. The first element is the return code from the C getdomainname function. The second element is the name argument.

Creating New Object Types with SWIG

SWIG's %addmethods directive allows us to add arbitrary methods to any structure. We can also bind Python special method names to structures. Adding special methods such as __getitem__ to a structure allows the structure to support iteration using the Python for operator. Other special methods support object comparison, hashing and string representation.

In this section we'll create several 'object types' from structures by adding Python special methods to those structures. These will be used to support iteration, comparison and string representation. Our example is based on struct servent, returned from getservbyname, getservbyport and getservent.

Creating the basic SWIG interface file

First we create a minimal SWIG interface file called `servtyp.i`. The layout of this interface file is similar to the `sysinfo.i` file:

```
%module servtyp
%{
#include <string.h>
#include <errno.h>
#include <netdb.h>
%}
```

We begin the interface file by specifying the name of the module with the `%module servtyp` directive. We then 'inject' several include statements in the wrapper file using the `%{` and `%}` directives:

```
%include "exception.i"
%include "typemaps.i"
```

We include exception and typemap support with the `%include` directive:

```
%typemap(python,except) struct servent *, char *, PyObject *,int {
    $function
    if(PyErr_Occurred()) {
        $cleanup
        return NULL;
    }
}
```

In `servtyp.i`, we create one exception handler that supports four different function return types: `struct servent *`, `char *`, `PyObject *` and `int`. This single exception handler can support all four types of functions because it explicitly checks for a raised exception using the `PyErr_Occurred` function. The remainder of `servtyp.i` follows:

```
struct servent {
    %addmethods {
        servent(PyObject *name_or_port,char *proto="tcp") {
            struct servent *res = NULL;

            if(PyInt_Check(name_or_port))
                res = getservbyport(ntohs(PyInt_AsLong(name_or_port)),
                    proto);
            else if(PyString_Check(name_or_port))
                res = getservbyname(PyString_AsString(name_or_port),
                    proto);
            else {
                SWIG_exception(SWIG_ValueError,"Invalid name or port type");
            }
            if(NULL == res) {
                SWIG_exception(SWIG_RuntimeError,strerror(errno));
            }
            return res;
        } /* end servent constructor /
        ~servent() { } / do nothing in destructor */
```

```
            PyObject *__str__() {
                char info[128];

                sprintf(info,"servent %s port %d proto %s",
                    self->s_name,ntohs(self->s_port),self->s_proto);
                return PyString_FromString(info);
            }
        }   /* end addmethods */
    %readonly
        %name(name) char *s_name;
        %name(aliases) char **s_aliases;
        %name(port) int s_port;
        %name(proto) char *s_proto;
    %readwrite
    }
```

Finally, we define the `servent` structure and three additional methods:

❑   the constructor `servent`

❑   the destructor `~servent`

❑   the Python special method `__str__`

In this example we've placed the `%addmethods` directive before specifying the structure attributes (s_name, s__aliases, etc). We've done this to allow methods we define using `%addmethods` to override any methods that are automatically generated by SWIG when processing structure attributes. We'll encounter this condition later in the chapter.

Rather than having SWIG process `netdb.h` directly, we've manually specified the `servent` structure attributes by carefully replicating the real `servent` structure layout specified in `netdb.h`. We've done this for two reasons: firstly, we can more easily use the `%readonly` SWIG directive to flag the attributes as readonly; secondly we've used the `%name` directive to give the attributes prettier names – for example, `%name(port) int s_port` lets us to refer to the attribute as `port` from Python, without the leading 's_'.

Let's take a moment to examine the three methods we've added.

First, the constructor `servent` is used to create a `servent` instance object. The constructor takes two arguments:

❑   a `PyObject *`, which we've dubbed `name_or_port`,

❑   and a `char *` named `proto` that defaults to the string "tcp".

SWIG provides the support for argument defaults; it is not part of the Python C API.

In the `servent` constructor, we check to see if `name_or_port` is an integer using the Python C API function `PyInt_Check`. This function returns true if the `PyObject` passed to the function is an integer, or supports the `__int__` Python special method.

If `name_or_port` is an integer, we use `getservbyport` to get a `servent` structure for the specified port.

If `name_or_port` is a string, we use `getservbyname` to get a `servent` structure for the specified name.

If `name_or_port` is not an integer or a string we raise an exception of type `SWIG_ValueError`.

Finally, if a `servent` structure is not found then `NULL == res` will be true and we raise a `SWIG_RuntimeError`.

Note that in the constructor we're using `SWIG_exception`, a macro that calls the `_SWIG_exception` function and then returns `NULL`. Be careful to choose the macro or function as appropriate. The `SWIG_exception` macro does not include its own C braces `{}`, so it must be the last statement in a code block or enclosed in braces to effect a proper function return.

However, there's a problem with the `servent` constructor shown above. The functions `getservbyport` and `getservbyname` return a pointer to a static structure. If two `servent` objects are created, they'll both refer to the same data – even if the second one specifies a different port.

SWIG assumes that constructors will return new objects that must be freed when deleted; but we're returning a pointer to the *same* static object, which must not be freed. The second method we've added is therefore the destructor ~`servent`. It has an empty body, so it doesn't actually *do* anything, but by defining it explicitly, we override SWIG's default destructor that would have called `free` on the `servent` structure.

Unfortunately, we're still only able to have one `servent` object at a time; creating a second `servent` structure would alter the contents of the shared static structure, thus changing the values referenced by the previously created `servent` structure. This is a problem we'll work round later on.

The third method we've added to `struct servent` is the `__str__` Python special method. This returns the string (that is, human-readable) representation of a given object. In the `servent` example, we'll return a Python string that specifies the port, protocol and name of the `servent` object. Note the use of `ntohs` throughout to convert `s_port` from network order to host order for the sake of presentation.

Processing, compiling and testing the interface file

As with `sysinfo.i`, we process the interface file `servtyp.i` with the following command:

```
$ swig -python -make_default -shadow servtyp.i
Generating wrappers for Python
```

We then create a new `Makefile` using the 'boot' procedure described previously. The `Setup.in` file contains these two lines:

```
*shared*
servtypc servtyp_wrap.c
```

Executing the make command produces this output:

```
$ make
gcc -fPIC  -g -O2 -I/usr/include/python1.5 -I/usr/include/python1.5 -
DHAVE_CONFIG_H -c ./servtyp_wrap.c
gcc -shared  servtyp_wrap.o  -o servtypcmodule.so
$
```

Now we're ready to test the module:

```
$ python
Python 1.5.2 (#1, Sep 17 1999, 20:15:36)  [GCC egcs-2.91.66 19990314/Linux]
Copyright 1991-1995 Stichting Mathematisch Centrum, Amsterdam
>>> import servtyp
>>> i = servtyp.servent(25)
>>> str(i)
'servent smtp port 25 proto tcp'
```

Now that we've imported the servtyp extension module, we instantiate an instance of the servent object by calling the servent constructor with the single argument '25'; the protocol is not specified, defaulting to tcp because this is what we specified as the default value for the proto argument. We then call the __str__ special method by applying the str function to the servent instance.

We can test the exception handling functionality by specifying an unsupported port or protocol when calling the servent constructor, like this:

```
>>> b = servtyp.servent(999,'udp')
Traceback (innermost last):
  File "<stdin>", line 1, in ?
  File "servtyp.py", line 46, in __init__
    self.this = apply(servtypc.new_servent,(arg0,)+args)
RuntimeError: No such file or directory
>>>
```

Because port 999 does not correspond to any known service, the getservbyport function returns NULL. The strerror function converts errno to the string "No such file or directory" which is then returned by the SWIG_exception macro.

Because we used the %name SWIG directive to give the servent attributes prettier names, we can access the attributes as follows:

```
>>> print i.proto, i.port, i.name
tcp 6400 smtp
>>>
```

The proceeding print statement prints the protocol, port number and name of the service. The servent shadow class accesses the s_port attribute directly; since s_port is stored in network order though, it displays as 6400 and not 25 (on the Intel architecture machine this example was developed on).

Overriding attribute access functions

We can fix the port network order problem by overriding SWIG's default attribute accessor function. SWIG automatically creates functions to get and put values from and to structure attributes. We can use the %addmethod directive to define our own get function for the port attribute.

Add a new method to the servent structure in servtyp.i as follows:

```
} /* end servent constructor */
~servent() { } /* do nothing */
int port_get() {
        return ntohs(self->s_port);
}
PyObject *__str__() {
```

Processing the updated servtyp.i file with SWIG produces the following output:

```
swig -python -docstring -make_default -shadow servtyp.i
Generating wrappers for Python
servtyp.i : Line 54. Variable servent_port_get multiply defined (2nd definition
ignored).
```

Note that SWIG reports a warning at line 54 (%name(port) int s_port;) that servent_port_get is multiply defined; this function has already been defined by the method port_get. We define our own port_get function first, before SWIG's default function is generated. SWIG therefore reports that the function is already defined and ignores the second (default) definition.

The port attribute now returns the expected value:

```
$ python
Python 1.5.2 (#1, Sep 17 1999, 20:15:36)  [GCC egcs-2.91.66 19990314/Linux]
Copyright 1991-1995 Stichting Mathematisch Centrum, Amsterdam
>>> import servtyp
>>> i = servtyp.servent(25)
>>> print i.port
25
```

Creating an iterator object

One of the servent structure's attributes is s_aliases. This is a char ** that points to a NULL-terminated array of strings. When we access this attribute from Python we get a pointer object, rather than a list of aliases:

```
>>> print i.aliases
_80e7824_char_pp
```

We'd actually rather get a list of aliases, or an object that can be used with Python's for operator. In this section we'll create a new object type, an **iterator object** that will support the for operator. Iterator objects are easy to create; they are simply objects that support the Python special method __getitem__.

When used with the for operator, __getitem__ will receive an increasing index number beginning at zero. The iterator object needs only to return a value that corresponds to the index, and raise an IndexError exception when there are no more values to return.

To create an iterator object, we're going to define a new structure in `servtyp.i` called `servent_alias`. It shouldn't have any Python-accessible attributes apart from the special method `__getitem__`. In order to hide the other attributes, the `servent_alias` structure will be defined twice in the `servtyp.i` interface file:

❑ The first definition will be in the wrapper section – that is, the definition will be written to the `servtyp_wrap.c` file without interpretation by SWIG. It will contain the real attributes needed by the `servent_alias` structure.

❑ The second definition of `servent_alias` will be interpreted by SWIG. It will contain only the `__getitem__` special method, and no attribute definitions.

Although SWIG can't see any attribute definitions, the wrapper file `servtyp_wrap.c` will contain the first definition with the appropriate attribute definition. On the other hand, our `__getitem__` method *does* see these attributes, since it is also C code that is placed directly in the wrapper file.

We begin by adding the first `servent_alias` definition to the `servtyp.i` interface file:

```
%module servtyp
%{
#include <string.h>
#include <errno.h>
#include <netdb.h>

struct servent_alias {
        char **aliases;
};

%}
```

The `servent_alias` structure has only one attribute: `char **aliases`. We'll set this attribute to the `s_aliases` value in the `servent` structure, and since this structure definition is contained within `%{` and `%}` SWIG directives, it will be written directly to the wrapper file without interpretation.

We now add the second `servent_alias` structure definition to the `servtyp.i` interface file. This definition is processed by SWIG:

```
            if(PyErr_Occurred()) {
                    $cleanup
                    return NULL;
            }
    }
}

struct servent_alias {
        %addmethods {
                char *__getitem__(int index) {
                        char **i = self->aliases;
                        while(i && *i) {
                                if(0 == index)
                                        return *i;
                                index--;
                                i++;
```

```
                        }
                        SWIG_exception(SWIG_IndexError,"index out of bounds");
                }
        }           /* end addmethods */
}

struct servent {
        %addmethods {
```

The __getitem__ special method of the servent_alias structure accepts an integer as the index. It uses the index value and the aliases variable to determine which string alias to return. It raises an IndexError exception if index is out of range.

Finally, we need to modify the servent structure to return an instance of servent_alias. The logical way to do this is to create an aliases_get accessor function that overrides SWIG's default accessor, as follows:

```
int port_get() {
        return ntohs(self->s_port);
}
%new struct servent_alias *aliases_get() {
        struct servent_alias *i = malloc(sizeof(*i));
        i->aliases = self->s_aliases;
        return i;
}
PyObject *__str__() {
```

The aliases_get function is declared to return a struct servent_alias * value. Note the use of the %new SWIG directive. Although SWIG knows that constructors return allocated memory, it has no way of knowing that this function is returning a new object that must be freed when deleted. The %new directive tells SWIG that this function is returning a new object.

Finally, we alter the definition of the s_aliases attribute to define it as being a struct servent_alias * value:

```
%name(name) char *s_name;
%name(aliases) struct servent_alias *s_aliases;
%name(port) int s_port;
```

We're now ready to test the iterator object. We'll create a servent instance for the discard protocol:

```
>>> import servtyp
>>> i = servtyp.servent('discard')
```

Now we reference the aliases attribute of the servent instance to get an instance of a servent_alias structure:

```
>>> print i.aliases
'_80f67f8_struct_servent_alias_p'
```

Oops! This is not what we expected – we got an instance of a `servent_alias` structure, but it's not wrapped up in its respective Python shadow class. Therefore there's no way for Python's `for` operator to call the __getitem__ special method on the instance.

We can see why this problem has occurred by examining the `servtyp.py` shadow file:

```
class serventPtr :
    def aliases_get(self):
        """"""
        val = servtypc.servent_aliases_get(self.this)
        val = servent_aliasPtr(val)
        val.thisown = 1
        return val
    def __getattr__(self,name):
        if name == "aliases" :
            return servtypc.servent_aliases_get(self.this)
```

This modified example shows that when getting the value of `aliases` from a `servent` structure with the `getattr` method, the `servent_aliases_get` function defined in the wrapper file is called directly. Although the `aliases_get` function makes the same call to the wrapper file, it then encapsulates the returned value in a `servent_aliasPtr` instance before returning the value.

Compare the return value from `aliases_get` with the aliases value shown previously:

```
>>> print i.aliases_get()
<C servent_alias instance>
```

This shows up an important limitation in the version of SWIG that was used to create these examples. Although SWIG 'does the right thing' for the function `aliases_get`, and knows that `aliases_get` overrides the default wrapper function for the `aliases` attribute, it doesn't make the proper adjustments to the wrapper file to encapsulate the attribute value in a `servent_aliasPtr` instance.

Your version of SWIG may not have this limitation. For the moment, let's use the `aliases_get` function directly, rather than accessing the `aliases` attribute.

We can continue to test the `servent_alias` structure by calling the Python special method __getitem__ using an increasing index value:

```
>>> print i.aliases_get()[0]
'sink'
>>> print i.aliases_get()[1]
'null'
>>> print i.aliases_get()[2]
Traceback (innermost last):
  File "<stdin>", line 1, in ?
  File "servtyp.py", line 10, in __getitem__
    val = servtypc.servent_alias___getitem__(self.this,arg0)
IndexError: index out of bounds
>>>
```

The `servent_aliases___getitem_` special method raises an `IndexError` when the index value is out of range. We can use the `servent_aliases` instance with the Python `for` operator as follows:

```
>>> for alias in i.aliases_get():
...     print alias
...
sink
null
>>>
```

Correcting the single instance problem

As we've observed, the `servent` constructor returns the same copy of the `servent` structure because the C Library returns a pointer to a static object. To fix this, we need to persuade the `servent` constructor to return a *copy* of the structure, rather than a pointer to the single static instance that the C Library provides.

We can do this by providing a wrapper function, which we'll call `CopyServent`. Its function is to create a new dynamic copy of the `servent` structure, including aliases. This code isn't Python-specific, but is necessary to improve the quality of the following examples.

Note that this code does very little error checking and makes some gross assumptions about structure sizes. Error checking has been left out due to space limitations, and to simplify the example.

Change the `servtyp.i` file by inserting the following code:

```
        if(PyErr_Occurred()) {
                $cleanup
                return NULL;
        }
}
%wrapper %{
#define MAX_MY_ALIASES 10
struct my_servent {
        struct servent s;
        char    *aliases[MAX_MY_ALIASES];
        char    data[1024];
        char    name[255];
        char    proto[16];
};
struct servent *CopyServent(struct servent *res)
{
        struct my_servent *copy;
        char *cp,**icp;
        int     index;

        copy = (struct my_servent *) calloc(1,sizeof(struct my_servent));

        if(NULL == copy) {
                SWIG_exception(SWIG_MemoryError,"out of memory");
        }
        memcpy(copy,res,sizeof(*res));
        strcpy(copy->name,res->s_name);
        copy->s.s_name = copy->name;
```

```
        strcpy(copy->proto,res->s_proto);
        copy->s.s_proto = copy->proto;
        /* now fixup aliases */
        index = 0;
        copy->aliases[0] = NULL;
        cp = copy->data;
        copy->s.s_aliases = copy->aliases;
        icp = res->s_aliases;
        while(icp && *icp && index < MAX_MY_ALIASES &&
                (cp - copy->data) < sizeof(copy->data)-255) {
                copy->aliases[index++] = cp;
                strcpy(cp,*icp);
                cp = cp + strlen(cp)+1;
                icp++;
        }
        copy->aliases[index] = NULL;
        return (struct servent *) copy;
    }
%}
```

```
struct servent_alias {
        %addmethods {
```

Note the use of the `%wrapper` SWIG directive. This is in some respects similar to the `%{` and `%}` directives, in that any code contained within is written to the wrapper file without interpretation. The `%wrapper` directive, however, is principally used to inject large sections of C code into the wrapper file, whereas the `%{` and `%}` directives are typically reserved for including header files and declaring structures.

Finally, we need to alter the `servent` constructor and eliminate the dummy destructor `~servent`, since we're now returning new objects that must be freed when deleted.

```
        if(NULL == res) {
                SWIG_exception(SWIG_RuntimeError,strerror(errno));
        }
        return CopyServent(res);
    } /* end servent constructor */
    int port_get() {
            return ntohs(self->s_port);
    }
```

Supporting object comparison

Now that we're returning unique instances of servent objects, we can add support for the `__cmp__` Python special method. This method is used by comparison operations, such as <, ==, and >.

Add the following code to the `servtyp.i` interface file, and then re-run SWIG, make and Python to test:

```
%new struct servent_alias *aliases_get() {
        struct servent_alias *i = malloc(sizeof(*i));
        i->aliases = self->s_aliases;
        return i;
    }
```

```
    int __cmp__(PyObject *other_obj) {
        /* compare to other object */
        struct servent *other;
        PyObject *temp_obj;

        if(NULL != (temp_obj =
    PyObject_GetAttrString(other_obj,"this")))
            other_obj = temp_obj;
        else
            PyErr_Clear();
        if(!PyString_Check(other_obj) ||
        SWIG_GetPtr(PyString_AsString(other_obj),
        (void **) &other, "_struct_servent_p")) {
            _SWIG_exception(SWIG_TypeError,
                            "other object must be type servent");
            return 0;
        }
        if(self->s_port < other->s_port)
            return -1;
        else if(self->s_port == other->s_port)
            return strcasecmp(self->s_proto,other->s_proto);
        else
            return 1;

    }    /* end __cmp__ */

PyObject *__str__() {
```

Python starts by calling the __cmp__ special method to perform a comparison. This __cmp__ implementation supports comparison only with other servent instances.

The first step in the comparison operation is to get a pointer to the other servent structure. Our comparison function can be compared either to a shadow class instance of the servent structure, or to a low level C instance of the servent structure.

In the former case, other_obj will be a Python object that has an attribute named this. The this attribute will be a string that names the low level C instance of the other servent structure.

We use the Python C API function PyObject_GetAttrString to get the value of the this attribute of the other_obj. If there isn't one, PyObject_GetAttrString will raise an exception. We clear the exception by calling PyErr_Clear. If other_obj did contain an attribute named this, we update other_obj to point to that attribute value.

We then check to see if other_obj is a string. If it is, we call the SWIG_GetPtr function to convert the string to a pointer of type _struct_servent_p. Otherwise, we raise a TypeError exception, reporting "other object must be type servent".

How did we know that SWIG_GetPtr should be used this way, and how did we know that the servent structure is called "_struct_servent_p"? We knew by examining the C code in the servtyp_wrap.c file. SWIG includes comments that describe how to use SWIG_GetPtr, and we can see how SWIG implements method functions. Much of the __cmp__ code is taken directly from the servtyp_wrap.c file.

After obtaining a pointer to the other `servent` structure, we can compare them and return a suitable value for sorting purposes. In this example, we sort based on port number, then protocol.

We can test the __cmp__ special method as follows:

```
$ python
Python 1.5.2 (#1, Sep 17 1999, 20:15:36)  [GCC egcs-2.91.66 19990314/Linux]
Copyright 1991-1995 Stichting Mathematisch Centrum, Amsterdam
>>> import servtyp
>>> i = servtyp.servent('smtp')
>>> b = servtyp.servent(9)
>>> print i == b
0
>>> print i < b
0
>>> print i > b
1
>>> print str(i), " ? ", str(b)
servent smtp port 25 proto tcp  ?  servent discard port 9 proto tcp
```

Supporting object hashing

A Python object that supports the __hash__ special method may be used as a key in a dictionary. The servent structure isn't very practical as a key in a dictionary, but this section will show how to implement a __hash__ special method using SWIG.

Like the __cmp__ special method, we use the %addmethods directive to add __hash__ to the servent structure by modifying the servtyp.i interface file as follows:

```
                        return 1;
}           /* end __cmp__ */
int __hash__() {
        unsigned long v = self->s_port;
        if(!strcasecmp(self->s_proto,"udp"))
                v = v + 0x100000;
        return v;
} /* end __hash__ */
PyObject *__str__() {
```

The __hash__ special method must return the same numeric value for the 'same' object. In this example, we assume that the hash function is based solely on the servent s_port and s_proto value. The line 'v = v + 0x100000' is used to generate a unique value when the port is the same, but the protocol differs.

After rebuilding the extension module, we can test it in Python as follows:

```
$ python
Python 1.5.2 (#1, Sep 17 1999, 20:15:36)  [GCC egcs-2.91.66 19990314/Linux]
Copyright 1991-1995 Stichting Mathematisch Centrum, Amsterdam
>>> import servtyp
>>> i = servtyp.servent('smtp')
>>> b = servtyp.servent(22)
>>> testDict = {}
```

```
>>> testDict[i] = "email"
>>> testDict[b] = "ssh"
>>> for v in testDict.keys(): print str(v)," ==> ",testDict[v]
...
servent ssh port 22 proto tcp   ==>   ssh
servent smtp port 25 proto tcp  ==>   email
>>
>>> print testDict[i]
'email'
```

Using an object destructor to cleanup

Our final SWIG example shows how to use an object destructor to perform side-effect cleanups, such as closing an open file or C library iteration. In this example, we'll create another iterator object. This will encapsulate the `setservent`, `getservent` and `endservent` functions.

We'll create a new iterator object called `ServentIterator`. It will return `servent` objects from its __getitem__ special method. These are the final changes we'll make to the `servtyp.i` interface file:

```
struct servent_alias {
        char **aliases;
};

struct ServentIterator {
        int isopen;
};


%}
```

We first add a C definition for the `ServentIterator` structure in the wrapper section of the interface file. The `ServentIterator` structure has one attribute, `isopen`, which is non-zero if `setservent` has been called.

At the end of the `servtyp.i` interface file, we add the following definition for the `ServentIterator` structure:

```
struct ServentIterator {
    %addmethods {
        %new struct servent *__getitem__(int index) {
            struct servent *res;

            if(!self->isopen) {
              self->isopen++;
              setservent(1);
            }
            res = getservent();
            if(NULL == res) {
              endservent();
              self->isopen = 0;
              SWIG_exception(SWIG_IndexError,"no more entries");
            }
            return CopyServent(res);
        }   /* end __getitem__ */
```

```
            ~ServentIterator() {
                if(self->isopen)
                    endservent();
                free(self);
            }
        } /* end addmethods */
};
```

The __getitem__ special method returns the next servent structure returned by the getservent function. If no more servent entries are available, __getitem__ raises an IndexError exception. Note the use of the %new SWIG directive. It tells SWIG that this function returns a new object that must be freed when deleted.

We also use the CopyServent helper function defined previously to create a unique copy of the servent structure returned from the getservent function.

The first time __getitem__ is called, the ServentIterator attribute isopen will be 0 (false) because calloc is used to allocate memory for the ServentIterator structure. We set the attribute to 1 (true) and call setservent to start the iterator process.

The destructor ~ServentIterator checks the isopen attribute to determine if the endservent function should be called. It also frees the memory allocated for the ServentIterator structure.

We can now test the ServentIterator object by listing all the services in /etc/services using the Python for operator.

```
>>> for i in servtyp.ServentIterator():
...     print str(i)
...     for a in i.aliases_get(): print "   ",a
...
servent tcpmux port 1 proto tcp
servent echo port 7 proto tcp
servent echo port 7 proto udp
servent discard port 9 proto tcp
    sink
    null
servent discard port 9 proto udp
    sink
    null
<snip>
```

The C library assumes that only one task will be using the getservent library calls at any one time, so it's actually unsafe to have more than one ServentIterator active at any time. It's therefore not a terribly practical example, but still serves as a useful demonstration of extension techniques.

We've now completed our look at using SWIG to wrap C functions for use with Python; remember that SWIG also has limited support for using C++ functions with Python. It also includes a large amount of documentation that more completely explains how to use the features we've been looking at.

Also remember that there are several ways to accomplish each the things we've done. It's well worth experimenting with SWIG to find the ones that are best suited to your application.

Extending Python Using the C API

As we've seen, SWIG substantially eases the task of building C extension modules for Python – unfortunately though, it doesn't produce the most efficient C code. The new second version promises to produce better code, but it will still be the case that some applications will be better built by hand, writing the necessary wrapper functions manually rather than relying on SWIG to write them for us. What's more, the Python C API allows extension modules to provide object interfaces and functionality over and above that which can be provided through SWIG alone.

The Python C API provides all the functionality we need to develop extension modules in C or C++. After all, SWIG uses this same API when *it* generates wrapper files. We can often get a sense of how to use certain functions, or how to structure our extension module, by examining the code in a SWIG-produced wrapper file.

Python Object Types

The Python language supports a variety of object types, including strings, integers, floats, lists, tuples, dictionaries, modules, classes, and instances, and there's a corresponding C API for each of these types. The Python documentation provides a complete reference for these functions.

When working with simple data types such as strings, integers, longs and floats, there are three basic functions provided for each:

❑ testing a Python object for type compatibility

❑ extracting a C value from Python data

❑ creating a Python value from C data

For example, these basic object types have similar management functions:

Data Type	Check	From Python to C	From C to Python
string	PyString_Check	PyString_AsString	PyString_FromString
int	PyInt_Check	PyInt_AsInt	PyInt_FromInt
long	PyLong_Check	PyLong_AsLong	PyLong_FromLong
float	PyFloat_Check	PyFloat_AsDouble	PyFloat_FromDouble

The C API treats all Python objects literally as PyObject types. That is, we'll manipulate Python objects as pointers to PyObjects. For example, to create a Python string object from a C string, we would use the following code:

```
PyObject *pystring = PyString_FromString("sample string");
```

Similarly, to convert a Python object to a C string, the following code could be used:

```
if (PyString_Check(pystring)) {
    char *mystring = PyString_AsString(pystring);
}
```

The PyString_AsString function also calls PyString_Check. We can slightly improve performance by using PyString_AS_STRING instead of PyString_AsString, but we should only do this if we're certain that the passed object is a string (or string type), because PyString_AS_STRING bypasses the call to PyString_Check.

Similar functions exist for integers and floats.

Reference Counting and Ownership

Python manages memory by counting references to each allocated object. Rather than using garbage collection (like Java) or explicit alloc/free (like C) it keeps track of how many references are held for a given object. When the del operator is applied to a Python object, the object itself is not directly freed; rather the reference count is decremented. If the reference count falls to zero, then the object is freed.

The PyString_FromString function, for example, returns a Python object whose reference count is set to one. This object can be directly returned to Python from a C function. However, if the object is no longer needed we must explicitly decrement the object reference count using the Py_DECREF function.

There are three types of references: owned, borrowed or stolen.

❑ We **own** a reference to an object when it has been created for us by a C API function, such as the PyString_FromString function. If this is the case, we must either call Py_DECREF on the object when we're done using it (thereby giving up ownership of the reference) or pass on ownership to something else.

For example, we can give away object ownership by returning the object from a C function called from Python. Generally, any Python C API function that creates an object will return a reference that we own.

❑ A **borrowed** reference is a reference to an object that we do *not* own. Since we don't own the reference, we can't give it away. Calling C API functions may cause the object to be deleted, thereby invalidating the handle to the object.

Borrowed references must be managed carefully; for example, the C API function PyDict_GetItem returns a borrowed reference to an object. We can acquire ownership of a borrowed reference using the Py_INCREF function. However, we must remember to give up ownership using Py_DECREF when we have finished with the object.

❑ Finally, a **stolen** reference is one that is taken from us by a C API function. For example, the PyList_SetItem and PyTuple_SetItem functions assume ownership of references that we pass to them; they are the only two that do. They are commonly used to create lists and tuples of objects constructed using C API functions that return owned references.

You should check the Python documentation carefully to be sure what kind of object reference you receive from C API functions, and what kind of object references are expected by functions that you call.

It's very important to carefully manage reference ownership and reference counts. An object is never freed while an owned reference for it exists. If you have a lot of these 'owned but unused' objects, you'll waste a great deal of memory. In addition, objects whose reference count is decremented below zero can cause a protection fault and program failure.

Most C API functions return owned references, however, functions such as `PyTuple_GetItem`, `PyList_GetItem`, `PyDict_GetItem`, and `PyDict_GetItemString` all return borrowed references. Furthermore, `PyList_SetItem` and `PyTuple_SetItem` actually *steal* the owned reference to objects we pass them, so we must *own* any references we pass in; if we call these two functions with a borrowed reference, we'll have serious problems.

Remember that any C API call can invalidate borrowed references. This includes `Py_DECREF` itself, which often does cause an object to be deleted; that object may in turn delete another object to which we hold a borrowed reference.

Overview of Developing C Extension Modules

Creating a C extension module using the C API involves the same steps as we used with SWIG. We need to create a `Setup.in` file and follow the instructions outlined in `Makefile.pre.in` to bootstrap the creation of a `Makefile`.

After copying `Makefile.pre.in` to the current directory (we'll start this project in a new, empty directory), create a `Setup.in` file with the following contents:

```
*shared*
capi capi.c
```

Then execute the following boot procedure:

```
$ make -f Makefile.pre.in boot
```

This generates a `Makefile` that depends on the C source file `capi.c`.

Extension Module Structure

Unlike SWIG interface files, there's no particular format requirement for C extension module source files. There are only four things you *must* do:

- ❑ include `Python.h` to gain access to the C API
- ❑ construct an array of `PyMethodDef` structures describing each Python-callable function
- ❑ export a single function named `init<modulename>` (such as `initcapi`)
- ❑ call the `Py_InitModule` function from within the exported function to initialize our module

The *init* Function

Let's create a simple extension module that doesn't define any Python-callable functions. This will serve as a starting point for our examples. Create a file called `capi.c` with the following text:

```c
#include "Python.h"

static PyMethodDef capi_functions[] = {
        { NULL, NULL }
};
```

```
void
initcapi()
{
        Py_InitModule("capi",capi_functions);
}
```

The `capi.c` file imports `Python.h` (note the capital 'P'). Within this file we create an array of `PyMethodDef` structures; the array is terminated by a `NULL` definition. We declare all variables and functions as static, except for the `init` function.

> *The `PyMethodDef` typedef is defined by `methodobject.h`, which is automatically included by `Python.h`.*

The `init` function is named after the module name; in this case `initcapi`. Within this function, we call `Py_InitModule`, passing it the name of the module and the array of `PyMethodDef` structures.

We can compile and test the module as follows:

```
$ make
gcc -fPIC  -g -O2 -I/usr/include/python1.5 -I/usr/include/python1.5 -
DHAVE_CONFIG_H -c ./capi.c
gcc -shared  capi.o  -o capi.so
$ python
Python 1.5.2 (#1, Sep 17 1999, 20:15:36)  [GCC egcs-2.91.66 19990314/Linux]
Copyright 1991-1995 Stichting Mathematisch Centrum, Amsterdam
>>> import capi
>>> dir(capi)
['__doc__', '__file__', '__name__']
>>>
```

Note that the `capi` module automatically has a doc, file and name string assigned by Python. Otherwise there are no functions defined within the module. We are now ready to define our first function.

Simple Functions

We'll start by defining a simple C function by making the following changes to `capi.c`:

```
#include <stdio.h>
#include "Python.h"

static PyObject *
PrintString(PyObject *self, PyObject *args)
{
        const char *str;

        if(!PyArg_ParseTuple(args,"s:PrintString",&str))
                return NULL;

        printf("print: %s\n",str);
        Py_INCREF(Py_None);
        return Py_None;
}

static PyMethodDef capi_functions[] = {
        { "PrintString", PrintString, METH_VARARGS},
        { NULL, NULL }
```

We've defined a function called PrintString. Python passes two arguments to C functions:

❑ The first, self, is NULL unless the function is a method of an instance object (more about that later).

❑ The second, args, is a tuple containing all of the arguments passed from Python.

Python provides the handy function PyArg_ParseTuple for processing function arguments. This function takes the args tuple, a template string and zero or more output variables. In our example, PyArg_ParseTuple expects to receive a single string object. It will convert that string object to a char * and save it in the variable str.

> *Note that str is a constant because the char * address returned from PyArg_ParseTuple points to a string that should not be modified.*

The PyArg_ParseTuple function returns non-zero on success; it returns zero when it fails, having already raised an exception. C functions must return NULL when an exception has been raised. Most Python C API functions will also return NULL when they fail (having already raised an exception). If we receive NULL from a Python C API function, then we must release ownership of all references we own and return NULL from our function. This is how exceptions are passed up the calling chain.

If PyArg_ParseTuple succeeds, str will point to the string text. We call printf, passing in the str variable.

Finally, we return Py_None as a result code from the PrintString function. Py_None is defined in Python.h and is an **identity object** telling Python that "no value is being returned". Returning Py_None is like declaring a C function as type void.

Note that we increment the reference count of Py_None using Py_INCREF. This grants us ownership of a reference, which we then return to Python. C functions must either return NULL (after having raised an exception), or return an owned reference to a Python object.

We can test the new module by running make, loading Python and importing the capi module:

```
>>> import capi
>>> capi.PrintString("hi there")
print: hi there
>>> capi.PrintString(1)
Traceback (innermost last):
  File "<stdin>", line 1, in ?
TypeError: PrintString, argument 1: expected string, int found
>>> capi.PrintString("hi there","hello")
Traceback (innermost last):
  File "<stdin>", line 1, in ?
TypeError: PrintString requires exactly 1 argument; 2 given
>>> ^D
```

There are some interesting things to note about this example:

When we pass PrintString a single string, it dutifully prints the string. PyArg_ParseTuple fails if we pass PrintString a Python object that isn't a string or doesn't support the __str__ Python special method. It automatically raises an exception, which is automatically printed as part of the traceback from the Python interpreter. Note that the word "PrintString" in the TypeError statement comes from the ":PrintString" portion of the format string passed to PyArg_ParseTuple.

We can also see what happens when two arguments are passed to `PrintString`. The `PyArg_ParseTuple` function is very powerful.

Consult the Python documentation for a complete list of the format options you can use.

A Slightly More Complex Function

Let's modify `PrintString` to accept either an integer or a string, by making the following changes to `capi.c`:

```
PrintString(PyObject *self, PyObject *args)
{
        PyObject *o;

        if(!PyArg_ParseTuple(args,"O:PrintString",&o))
                return NULL;

        if(PyString_Check(o))
                printf("print string: %s\n",PyString_AS_STRING(o));
        else if(PyInt_Check(o))
                printf("print int: %d\n",PyInt_AS_LONG(o));
        else {
                PyErr_SetString(PyExc_TypeError,
                    "invalid type passed to PrintString");
                return NULL;
        }
        Py_INCREF(Py_None);
        return Py_None;
```

We've now changed the format string passed to `PyArg_ParseTuple` to accept *any* Python object; the variable o is set to point to that object, while `PyArg_ParseTuple` returns a borrowed reference to the object. This means that we don't need to decrement the object's reference count.

We use the `PyString_Check` function to see if the object passed is a string. If it is, we print out a string value. Otherwise, if the object is an integer, we print out an integer value. Finally, we raise a `TypeError` exception if the object passed is neither a string nor an integer, or an object that cannot be coerced to either of these types because it doesn't support the __str__ or __int__ Python special method.

We can test these changes by rebuilding `capi.c` and loading it in Python:

```
>>> import capi
>>> capi.PrintString("hi there")
print string: hi there
>>> capi.PrintString(1)
print int: 1
>>> capi.PrintString(None)
Traceback (innermost last):
  File "<stdin>", line 1, in ?
TypeError: invalid type passed to PrintString
>>> capi.PrintString(1,"string")
Traceback (innermost last):
  File "<stdin>", line 1, in ?
TypeError: PrintString requires exactly 1 argument; 2 given
>>>
```

The changes work as expected. Note though, that `PyArg_ParseTuple` still raises an exception in the event that two arguments are passed to `PrintString`.

The Global Interpreter Lock

Before we go much further with creating Python-callable functions, the issue of the Python Global Interpreter Lock must be discussed. Although Python is capable of multi-threading, internally only one thread at a time can be executing Python code. To allow multi-threaded Python programs to perform well, C functions must release the global interpreter lock before calling any C library function that may block the thread.

For example, if your function reads from a file or socket, that read may take several milliseconds to complete. You should release the global interpreter lock before the read function, and re-acquire the lock after the function returns.

Python provides two simple macros that ease this task:

```
int rc;
Py_BEGIN_ALLOW_THREADS
rc = read(..);
Py_END_ALLOW_THREADS
```

Note that these macros do nothing if Python was compiled without thread support. Also, you must not call any Python C API functions while the thread lock is released.

Creating New Python Object Types

We can use the Python C API to create new object types directly in C. Typically, it's easier to create new types in Python, and have those types call into a lower level C API, rather than creating an entirely new type in C. However, there are some situations that necessitate user simplicity (no .py file required) or slightly faster operation.

Python allocates all objects from the heap. Each object instance has a corresponding type, a reference count and a storage location for the allocated per-instance memory. To create a new object type, we first define a structure (or C++ class) that stores per-instance data for the object. We must also create an object type structure that defines the interfaces supported by the object.

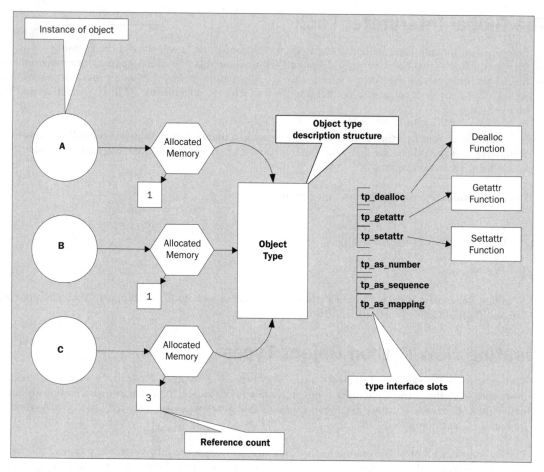

This diagram represents the relationship between:

❑   Python object instances (shown in circles),

❑   their corresponding allocated memory (in hexagons),

❑   reference count (small square)

❑   and their shared object type structure.

All instances of a given type share a single object type structure (rectangle). This contains information about the object type, such as the object type name, methods for de-allocating per-instance memory, and getting and setting attributes. Python provides the object type structure definition, so developers need only fill in the gaps with the appropriate information.

Python objects support multiple interfaces, that is, a single object may be used as a numeric type, a dictionary, a sequence, and so on. Each of these uses is generally defined by a single interface. Each object type interface is implemented by a function specific to that interface and that object type. Python accesses these interfaces through the associated 'slot' in the object type structure, such as tp_getattr, tp_setattr and so on.

Objects that don't support a given interface leave the associated slot set to NULL.

The Minimum Object Type

Let's modify `capi.c` to create a minimal object type. Python provides several structure definitions in `object.h` that define the required layout of the object type structure and related support structures. We need only include `Python.h` and use those structures to define our basic object:

```
#include "Python.h"
```

```
typedef struct {
        PyObject_HEAD    /* required header */
        int value;
} BasicObject;
```

First we define the per-instance memory structure for our new type. The typedef structure `BasicObject` includes `PyObject_HEAD` as its first element. This required header contains the reference count for the instance, along with a pointer to the object type structure. We've also added `int value` as a per-instance attribute:

```
static void
bobject_dealloc(BasicObject *self)
{
        if(self)
                free(self);
}
```

Next, we define the `bobject_dealloc` function for the `BasicObject`. This will be called when the reference count for the object has fallen to zero. The `dealloc` function should perform whatever per-instance cleanup is required, and then free the memory allocated for the object. Note that the `dealloc` function does not return a value. It receives a pointer to the per-instance memory, which is a `BasicObject` structure.

```
PyTypeObject BasicObject_Type = {
        PyObject_HEAD_INIT(&PyType_Type)  /* required header */
        0,                                /* variable object size */
        "basic_object",                   /* name of object type */
        sizeof(BasicObject),              /* size of per-instance memory */
        0,                                /* size of per-item element */
        (destructor) bobject_dealloc      /* tp_dealloc */
};
```

Here we create a minimal object type structure. `PyObject_HEAD_INIT` is required as the first element of the structure. `PyTypeObject` declares the layout of the object type structure. We fill in the slots as appropriate, with data specific to our new object type. In this case, we support only one interface slot, `tp_dealloc`.

Python allows us to create objects containing an array of items whose size is determined when the object is allocated. To accomplish this, the per-item element size and variable object size fields are used. We won't be creating variable length objects in our examples.

For more information about variable length array objects, see `object.h`.

Note that in our minimal object type example we've only filled in three slots in the object type structure:

❑   The name of the object type: `"basic_object"`

❑   The size of per-instance memory: `sizeof(BasicObject)`

❑   The dealloc function: `bobject_dealloc`

We now need to add a function that creates new BasicObjects. The following function will return a BasicObject:

```
PyObject *
NewBasicObject(PyObject *self, PyObject *args)
       /* return a new instance of basicobject */
{
       if(!PyArg_ParseTuple(args,":BasicObject"))
              return NULL;

       return (PyObject *) PyObject_NEW(BasicObject, &BasicObject_Type);
}
```

Since the `BasicObject` constructor doesn't accept any arguments, we call `PyArg_ParseTuple` with an empty string, so as to be certain that no arguments have been passed to the constructor. If arguments *are* passed to the constructor, `PyArg_ParseTuple` will raise an exception.

The macro `PyObject_NEW` allocates memory for the specified per-instance data (`BasicObject`), sets the object's type to `BasicObject_Type` and sets the reference count to one. New instances created with this macro are owned references and may be returned directly to Python.

Finally, we make the `NewBasicObject` function callable through the `capi` module by modifying the `capi_functions` `PyMethodDef` array:

```
static PyMethodDef capi_functions[] = {
        { "PrintString", PrintString, METH_VARARGS},
        { "BasicObject", NewBasicObject, METH_VARARGS},
        { NULL, NULL }
};
```

There is no special relationship between the function name `NewBasicObject` and the `BasicObject` it returns. Any Python-callable C function can create new objects of any type. Unlike C++, it's not the function's name that makes it a constructor; rather the code it executes makes it behave like a C++ constructor by returning new objects.

We're now ready to test our new BasicObject in Python:

```
>>> import capi
>>> obj = capi.BasicObject()
>>> print repr(obj)
<basic_object object at 80c4f58>
>>> obj.value
Traceback (innermost last):
  File "<stdin>", line 1, in ?
AttributeError: 'basic_object' object has no attribute 'value'
>>> del obj
>>> ^D
```

In our test, we import the capi module and create a new instance of BasicObject. The repr function returns the object type as basic_object, the value we specified in the object_type structure. We try to print the per-instance value of the object, but this raises an exception.

Finally we delete the object instance.

Supporting getattr

When accessing an instance's attributes, Python attempts to use the getattr type interface; but we didn't define that type interface in our BasicObject. Let's go back and add support for getattr. Note that we include structmember.h, in order to gain access to some utility functions:

```c
#include "Python.h"
#include "structmember.h"

typedef struct {

#define OFF(x)  offsetof(BasicObject, x)

static struct memberlist bobject_memberlist[] = {
        {"value", T_INT, OFF(value)},
        {NULL}
};

static PyObject *
bobject_getattr(BasicObject *self, char *attr)
{
        return PyMember_Get((char *) self, bobject_memberlist, attr);
}
```

Next, we define OFF, a handy macro to compute the offset of a specified structure element. This is used in the bobject_memberlist array, which defines a list of per-instance attributes and each one's Python data type. In our example, the value attribute is T_INT. The structmember.h file defines other Python data types that are supported using the memberlist structure.

The bobject_getattr function uses PyMember_Get (declared in structmember.h) to locate the specified attribute and return its value. PyMember_Get automatically raises an exception if the specified attribute is not found; otherwise it returns an owned PyObject with the correct value, which can be directly returned to Python.

Finally, we add bobject_getattr to the BasicObject_Type structure:

```c
        (destructor) bobject_dealloc,     /* tp_dealloc */
        0,                                /* tp_print, aka str */
        (getattrfunc) bobject_getattr,    /* tp_getattr */
}
```

Note that we skipped the tp_print slot by setting it to zero, meaning it's undefined and won't be used by Python. We can now test these changes:

```
>>> import capi
>>> obj = capi.BasicObject()
>>> print obj.value
65536
>>> obj.value = 1
Traceback (innermost last):
  File "<stdin>", line 1, in ?
TypeError: object has read-only attributes
>>> ^D
```

Here we create an instance of BasicObject and print its value attribute. Notice that value is not 0, as might be expected. This is because PyObject_NEW uses malloc, not calloc, to allocate memory for the per-instance data. We need to explicitly set the initial value of all per-instance attributes.

We also try to set the value attribute, but raise an exception because the setattr method is not defined.

Supporting setattr

Adding support for setattr is very similar to adding getattr support. We make a few simple changes to capi.c:

```
static int
bobject_setattr(BasicObject *self, char *attr, PyObject *value)
{
        if(value == NULL) {
                PyErr_SetString(PyExc_AttributeError,"can't delete attributes");
                return -1;
        }
        return PyMember_Set((char *) self, bobject_memberlist, attr, value);
}
```

We start by adding the bobject_setattr function. Note that the return value for this function is an integer, not a PyObject. Each type interface has its own requirements for return type and argument type; they will not all be the same. The function bobject_setattr checks to see if value is NULL. If it is, that means that Python is trying to delete the attribute entirely. This doesn't make sense for a C-based object, so we raise an exception.

The PyMember_Set function (declared in structmember.h) returns the appropriate result code, raising an exception if the specified attribute cannot be set, or the supplied value is of the wrong type:

```
        0,                              /* tp_print aka str */
        (getattrfunc) bobject_getattr,  /* tp_getattr */
        (setattrfunc) bobject_setattr,  /* tp_setattr */
```

Finally, we add `bobject_setattr` to the `BasicObject_Type` structure and we are ready to test:

```
>>> import capi
>>> obj = capi.BasicObject()
>>> obj.value = 1
>>> print obj.value
1
>>> del obj.value
Traceback (innermost last):
  File "<stdin>", line 1, in ?
AttributeError: can't delete attributes
>>> obj.missing = 1
Traceback (innermost last):
  File "<stdin>", line 1, in ?
AttributeError: missing
>>>
```

Note that attempting to delete `value` from the object raises an exception as expected. Attempting to set an attribute that's not a member of the instance will also raise an exception.

Supporting Method Calls

Object method calls are implemented in a similar fashion to module functions. An array of `PyMethodDef` structures defines the methods that can be called against a particular object type:

```
static PyObject *
bobject_stringvalue(BasicObject *self, PyObject *args)
{
        char text[128];

        if(!PyArg_ParseTuple(args,":stringvalue"))
                return NULL;

        sprintf(text,"value is: %d",self->value);
        return PyString_FromString(text);
}
```

We first define a method called `bobject_stringvalue`. This method takes no arguments and returns a Python string containing the per-instance `value`. Unlike module functions that receive a `NULL` value for `self`, method functions receive `self` set to the per-instance data. This is how object methods gain access to per-instance data.

To keep things simple, we don't check for a possible string buffer overflow in this example, but in practice it's important to always check for such potential errors.

```
static PyMethodDef bobject_methods[] = {
        {"stringvalue",(PyCFunction) bobject_stringvalue, METH_VARARGS},
        { NULL, NULL}
};
```

An array of `PyMethodDef` structures lists all the methods supported by our object. In this case only one method is supported: `stringvalue`.

```
static PyObject *
bobject_getattr(BasicObject *self, char *attr)
{
        PyObject *res;

        res = Py_FindMethod(bobject_methods, (PyObject *) self,attr);
        if(NULL != res)
                return res;
        else {
                PyErr_Clear();
                return PyMember_Get((char *) self, bobject_memberlist, attr);
        }
}
```

Finally, we modify `bobject_getattr` to search through `bobject_methods` for the specified method name using `Py_FindMethod`. If a method is found that matches the attribute name, we return that method to Python. Otherwise, we use `PyMember_Get` to see if an attribute with the specified name exists.

`Py_FindMethod` will raise an exception if the specified attribute is not in the `bobject_methods` array. We use `PyErr_Clear` to cancel the exception before calling `PyMember_Get`. When `bobject_getattr` returns a bound method object to Python (returned by `Py_FindMethod`), Python will call the method passing in the per-instance data as `self`.

```
>>> import capi
>>> obj = capi.BasicObject()
>>> obj.value = 1
>>> print obj.stringvalue()
value is: 1
>>> print obj.stringvalue("spam")
Traceback (innermost last):
  File "<stdin>", line 1, in ?
TypeError: stringvalue requires exactly 0 arguments; 1 given
>>> print obj.stringvalue
<built-in method stringvalue of basic_object object at 80c4f58>
>>>
```

Here we can see that the `stringvalue` function behaves as expected; it won't accept arguments, and raises an exception when arguments are passed to it. Finally, printing `obj.stringvalue` shows that it's a bound method object.

Object Initialization

Earlier we saw that the `value` attribute of `BasicObject` was not set to any particular value when an object is created. Similar to a class' `__init__` method, C objects can also initialize themselves and accept constructor arguments during initialization. To add support for constructor arguments, we need to change the `NewBasicObject` function to accept arguments, as follows:

```
PyObject *
NewBasicObject(PyObject *self, PyObject *args)
        /* return a new instance of basicobject */
{
        int defaultValue = 0;
        BasicObject *obj;

        if(!PyArg_ParseTuple(args,"|i:BasicObject", &defaultValue))
                return NULL;

        obj = PyObject_NEW(BasicObject, &BasicObject_Type);
        if(obj)
                obj->value = defaultValue;
        return (PyObject *) obj;
}
```

`PyArg_ParseTuple` has a new format string, which accepts an optional integer. Note that `defaultValue` is set to a default value before the call to `PyArg_ParseTuple`. If no arguments are specified, `PyArg_ParseTuple` will not alter `defaultValue`.

We call `PyObject_NEW` to create an instance of `BasicObject`. If the object was created successfully, we set its `value` attribute to `defaultValue`.

```
>>> import capi
>>> obj = capi.BasicObject(5)
>>> print obj.value
5
>>> xobj = capi.BasicObject()
>>> print xobj.value
0
>>>
```

Encapsulating C++ Objects Using the C-API

In the `BasicObject` example we used a C structure for the per-instance storage, and individual C functions as interface functions. Python also allows the use of C++ classes as Python objects. One downside to using C++ for creating Python objects is that all the Python type interface functions must be declared as static methods. This is because Python is explicitly using `self` argument to pass in the per-instance data.

Here is `BasicObject` re-written as a C++ module named `cplus.cpp`:

```
#include <stdio.h>
#include "Python.h"
#include "structmember.h"
```

```
class BasicObject: public PyObject
{
public:
    BasicObject(int defaultValue=0);
    ~BasicObject();

    /* python specific interfaces */
    static void dealloc(PyObject *obj);
    static PyObject *getattr(PyObject *obj, char *name);
    static int setattr(PyObject *obj, char *name, PyObject *value);

    static PyObject *stringvalue(PyObject *obj, PyObject *args);
    static struct memberlist memberlist[];
    static PyMethodDef methodlist[];

    int value;
};


BasicObject::~BasicObject()
{
    /* nothing to do here */
}

void
BasicObject::dealloc(PyObject *obj)
{
    delete (BasicObject *) obj;
}

#define    OFF(x)      offsetof(BasicObject, x)

struct memberlist BasicObject::memberlist[] = {
    {"value", T_INT, OFF(value)},
    {NULL}
};

PyObject *
BasicObject::stringvalue(PyObject *obj, PyObject *args)
{
    BasicObject *self = (BasicObject *) obj;
    char text[128];

    if(!PyArg_ParseTuple(args,":stringvalue"))
        return NULL;

    sprintf(text,"value is: %d",self->value);
    return PyString_FromString(text);
}

PyMethodDef BasicObject::methodlist[] = {
    {"stringvalue",(PyCFunction) BasicObject::stringvalue, METH_VARARGS},
    { NULL, NULL}
};
```

```
PyObject *
BasicObject::getattr(PyObject *obj, char *attr)
{
    PyObject *res;
    BasicObject *self = (BasicObject *) obj;

    res = Py_FindMethod(methodlist, (PyObject *) self,attr);
    if(NULL != res)
        return res;
    else {
        PyErr_Clear();
        return PyMember_Get((char *) self, memberlist, attr);
    }
}

int
BasicObject::setattr(PyObject *obj, char *attr, PyObject *value)
{
    BasicObject *self = (BasicObject *) obj;
    if(value == NULL) {
        PyErr_SetString(PyExc_AttributeError,"can't delete attributes");
        return -1;
    }
    return PyMember_Set((char *) self, memberlist, attr, value);
}

PyTypeObject BasicObject_Type = {
    PyObject_HEAD_INIT(&PyType_Type)  /* required header */
    0,                      /* variable object size */
    "basic_object",              /* name of object type */
    sizeof(BasicObject),        /* size of per-instance memory */
    0,                      /* size of per-item element */
    (destructor) BasicObject::dealloc,/* tp_dealloc */
    0,                      /* tp_print aka str */
    (getattrfunc) BasicObject::getattr,/* tp_getattr */
    (setattrfunc) BasicObject::setattr,/* tp_setattr */
};

BasicObject::BasicObject(int defaultValue=0)
{

    ob_type = &BasicObject_Type;
    _Py_NewReference(this);

    value = defaultValue;
}
```

The BasicObject constructor accepts defaultValue as the initial value:

```
PyObject *
NewBasicObject(PyObject *self, PyObject *args)
    /* return a new instance of basicobject */
{
    int defaultValue = 0;

    if(!PyArg_ParseTuple(args,"|i:BasicObject",&defaultValue))
            return NULL;

    return new BasicObject(defaultValue);
}
```

NewBasicObject is the actual function that Python calls to create an instance of BasicObject. It accepts an optional integer argument (default 0):

```
static PyMethodDef cplus_functions[] = {
    { "BasicObject", NewBasicObject, METH_VARARGS},
    { NULL, NULL }
};


extern "C"
void
initcplus()
{
    Py_InitModule("cplus",cplus_functions);
}
```

In all respects BasicObject in the cplus module functions identically to the BasicObject in the capi module. Note the use of the extern "C" modifier for the init function to avoid C++ name-mangling.

Embedding Python in C/C++ Programs

As we've observed, the Python interpreter can also be **embedded** in other programs, providing these **host programs** with Python scripting functionality. Simply embedding the Python interpreter in a host program isn't particularly useful by itself; the host program should extend Python in some way, by adding functions, callbacks, variables, or new object types.

For example, you could embed the Python interpreter in a word processor program. End users could then create Python scripts that edit text by calling functions within the word processor, such as 'move to', 'mark', 'copy', and so on.

Host programs can extend Python using the techniques we've already seen; using SWIG or writing wrapper functions manually. In the course of this section, we'll use both techniques to demonstrate some simple embedding examples.

The Embedding Development Environment

Our first step towards embedding the Python interpreter in a host program is to assemble the development environment. Our first embedding example will be based on a single C source file, ebdemo.c.

We'll start by creating a suitable Makefile for the example; the easiest way to create a Makefile that works with Python is to refer to one that's been generated by the Makefile.pre.in boot process that we discussed previously. Extract the necessary options from that Makefile to create one that's specific to our embedding example.

Here's the `Makefile` that we'll be using for the first example:

```
# Demo Makefile for ebdemo.c
VERSION= 1.5
CC=      gcc
OPT=     -g -O2
LIBS=    -ldl -lpthread -lieee
installdir= /usr
exec_installdir=/usr
DEFS=-DHAVE_CONFIG_H
INCLUDEDIR=     $(installdir)/include
INCLUDEPY=      $(INCLUDEDIR)/python$(VERSION)
EXECINCLUDEPY=  $(exec_installdir)/include/python$(VERSION)
LIBP=           $(exec_installdir)/lib/python$(VERSION)
LIBPL=          $(LIBP)/config
PYTHONLIBS=     $(LIBPL)/libpython$(VERSION).a

CFLAGS= $(OPT) -I$(INCLUDEPY) -I$(EXECINCLUDEPY) $(DEFS)

default: ebdemo

ebdemo: ebdemo.o
        $(CC)   -o ebdemo ebdemo.o $(PYTHONLIBS) $(LIBS)

ebdemo.o: ebdemo.c
        $(CC) $(CFLAGS) -c ebdemo.c
```

Yours may need adjustment to match the directory paths used on your system.

Embedding Python Using High-level Functions

You can find a simple embedding example in the Python documentation; we're going to start with a similar example that simply clones the functionality of the Python program, which simply passes all command line arguments and `stdin` to the Python interpreter for evaluation.

A typical host program interacts with the interpreter in the following sequence:

❑   initialize the Python interpreter

❑   initialize statically linked extension modules

❑   execute the body of the host program

❑   finalize the Python interpreter

The initial version of `ebdemo.c` is very simple:

```
/* ebdemo.c - embed python demo */

#include <stdio.h>
#include "Python.h"

int main(int argc, char **argv)
{
        int rc;

        Py_Initialize();
        rc = PyRun_AnyFile(stdin,"???");
        Py_Finalize();
        return rc;
}
```

The `main` function calls `Py_Initialize` to initialize the Python interpreter. We then call `PyRun_AnyFile`, passing in the file handle for `stdin` as the input file and setting the filename to the string `"???"`.

The Python interpreter recognizes that the input file is `stdin`, and operates in interactive mode – it will do this whenever *any* of these conditions is met:

❏ `isatty` returns true on the file handle passed

❏ the file name is `NULL`, `"<stdin>"` or `"???"`; yes, we've passed `"???"` as the file name to force the Python interpreter to run in interactive mode, even if `stdin` is a file and not a terminal.

After `PyRun_AnyFile` returns, we shut down the Python interpreter by calling `Py_Finalize`, and return the result code from `main`.

Now `make` and execute the file, and you should see the following:

```
$ make
gcc -g -O2 -I/usr/include/python1.5 -I/usr/include/python1.5 -DHAVE_CONFIG_H -c
ebdemo.c
gcc   -o ebdemo ebdemo.o /usr/lib/python1.5/config/libpython1.5.a -ldl -lpthread -
lieee
$ ./ebdemo
>>> import sys
>>> print sys.path
['/usr/lib/python1.5/', '/usr/lib/python1.5/plat-linux-i386',
'/usr/lib/python1.5/lib-tk', '/usr/lib/python1.5/lib-dynload',
'/usr/lib/python1.5/site-packages']
>>> print sys.argv
Traceback (innermost last):
  File "???", line 1, in ?
AttributeError: argv
>>> ^D
$
```

As expected, the Python interpreter runs in interactive mode.

There are three important points to note from the above interactive example:

❏ `^D` (*Ctrl-D*) at the interpreter prompt causes the Python interpreter to exit back to the `ebdemo` program.

❏ `sys.path` does not include the current working directory in the Python path. When we execute the Python program without any arguments, Python inserts the directory specification for the executing program (if any) into `sys.path`. In the `ebdemo` example we have not told Python what the program name is, therefore the path to the executable is not included in `sys.path`.

❏ `sys.argv` hasn't been set because the `ebdemo` example doesn't set it.

We can fix these problems by making the following changes to `ebdemo.c`:

```
Py_SetProgramName(argv[0]);
Py_Initialize();
PySys_SetArgv(argc, argv);
rc = PyRun_AnyFile(stdin,"???");
```

We've added a call to `Py_SetProgramName`, passing in `argv[0]` as the name of the program; this must come before `Py_Initialize` is called. We also added a call to `PySys_SetArgv`, passing in the current `argc` and `argv` variables. We can test our changes by rebuilding `ebdemo.c` and executing it:

```
$ ./ebdemo
>>> import sys
>>> print sys.path
['.', '/usr/lib/python1.5/', '/usr/lib/python1.5/plat-linux-i386',
'/usr/lib/python1.5/lib-tk', '/usr/lib/python1.5/lib-dynload',
'/usr/lib/python1.5/site-packages']
>>> print sys.argv
['./ebdemo']
>>> ^D
```

There are several high level functions available for executing, parsing and compiling strings, or executing files. Check the Python documentation reference for a complete list of functions.

Statically Linking a Host Program to an Extension Module

We noted earlier that a host program that doesn't provide any extension functionality to Python is not very useful. We'll now see how to statically link an extension module to a host program. In this particular example, we'll link to the `sysinfo_wrap.c` file that we produced earlier using SWIG.

The first step in the linking process is to modify the `Makefile` as follows:

```
ebdemo: ebdemo.o sysinfo.o
        $(CC)   -o ebdemo ebdemo.o sysinfo.o $(PYTHONLIBS) $(LIBS)

sysinfo.o: ../sysinfo/sysinfo_wrap.c
        $(CC) $(CFLAGS) -c ../sysinfo/sysinfo_wrap.c -o sysinfo.o

ebdemo.o: ebdemo.c
        $(CC) $(CFLAGS) -c ebdemo.c
```

In this particular example, we're building `ebdemo` in a sibling directory of `sysinfo`, where `sysinfo_wrap.c` resides. The `Makefile` reflects the relative paths used to reach the `sysinfo_wrap.c` file.

We need to make two simple changes to `ebdemo.c`:

Firstly, we declare the init function for the sysinfo module as external:

```
#include "Python.h"

extern void initsysinfoc();

int main(int argc, char **argv)
```

Then we add a call to the sysinfo module initialization routine:

```
PySys_SetArgv(argc, argv);
initsysinfoc();
rc = PyRun_AnyFile(stdin,"???");
```

Now we're almost ready to test our changes. However, there's one more step that must be completed before we can use the sysinfo module. Recall that the sysinfo module consists of both the sysinfo_wrap.c file *and* a Python shadow file named sysinfo.py. Both these files are produced by SWIG when it processes the sysinfo.i interface file.

When we import the sysinfo module, Python is actually importing sysinfo.py, which in turn imports sysinfoc (the extension module, itself contained in sysinfo_wrap.c). Since we've not put sysinfo.py in the Python path, we must find a way to make it available to the ebdemo program; the quickest is to copy sysinfo.py to the current working directory before starting the ebdemo program:

```
$ cp ../sysinfo/sysinfo.py .
```

Typically, we'd install sysinfo.py in the Python path, but to keep things straightforward, we'll use the simple file copy method:

```
$ ./ebdemo
>>> import sysinfo
>>> si = sysinfo.sysinfo()
>>> sysinfo.getsysinfo(si)
0
>>> print si.totalram
97861632
>>>
```

So, we run the ebdemo program, which imports the sysinfo module. This imports sysinfo.py, which in turn imports the sysinfoc module. As the sysinfoc module was already initialized (by the call to initsysinfoc in ebdemo.c), Python didn't look for a shared extension module sysinfocmodule.so as it did in the earlier sysinfo examples.

From Python's perspective, the shared extension module sysinfocmodule.so and the statically linked sysinfoc module function are exactly the same.

Embedding Python Using Lower-level Calls

The high level Python API makes embedding quick and easy; however most host applications require a greater level of control over how Python scripts execute. Host programs can be extension modules simply by creating their own module interface and defining an appropriate set of functions within that module. Using this functionality, host programs can allow Python scripts to call back to the host to obtain or supply information.

The Python C API also allows host programs to call individual functions in Python modules, to call methods of instances, and manipulate module dictionaries. This functionality provides a finer level of control over the execution environment than the high level functions alone.

We'll now demonstrate the use of some of the lower level C API functions.

Executing Strings

Let's modify ebdemo.c to add a little more functionality:

```
Py_SetProgramName(argv[0]);
Py_Initialize();
initsysinfoc();
if(argc < 2)  {
        PySys_SetArgv(argc, argv);
        rc = PyRun_AnyFile(stdin,"???");
} else {
        PySys_SetArgv(argc-1, argv+1);
        sprintf(cmd,"execfile('%s')",argv[1]);
        rc = PyRun_SimpleString(cmd);
}
printf("Result Code is %d\n",rc);
Py_Finalize();
return rc;
```

We've changed ebdemo.c to accept a command line argument. If one is specified, it is executed by Python as a script using the execfile function. In this case, we also modify the arguments passed to the Python script, eliminating argv[0] from the argument list. The PyRun_SimpleString function is used to execute the execfile statement. If ebdemo is executed without a command line argument, we operate in interactive mode, as in the previous version.

Finally, we've added a print statement to display the result code returned from Python.

Let's also create a simple script file to test ebdemo with; we'll call it ebdemo1.py:

```
# test ebdemo
print "hi, ebdemo running Python"
import sys
print sys.argv
```

Rebuild ebdemo and execute it with ebdemo1.py as a command line argument:

```
$ ./ebdemo ebdemo1.py arg1 arg2 arg3
hi, ebdemo running Python
['ebdemo1.py', 'arg1', 'arg2', 'arg3']
Result Code is 0
```

We can see that ebdemo1.py is the first argument, and it's followed by the other command line arguments we passed in. The result code from PyRun_SimpleString is displayed as 0.

Overriding Built-in Python Functions

Suppose we run ebdemo without any command line arguments, and execute Python's sys.exit function:

```
$ ./ebdemo
>>> import sys
>>> sys.exit(5)
$
```

Note that the result code from PyRun_AnyFile is not displayed. Python's sys.exit function directly calls the C runtime library exit function, thereby exiting the ebdemo program. This behavior is undesirable in an embedded program.

We can override the sys.exit function (or any other function for that matter) by declaring our own C-based function to be called in its place.

Add the following code to ebdemo.c:

```
extern void initsysinfoc();
PyObject *
NoExit(PyObject *a, PyObject *args)
        /* disallow all exiting */
{
        PyErr_SetString(PyExc_RuntimeError,"No exit allowed");
        return NULL;
}

static PyMethodDef hostModuleMethods[] = {
        { "NoExit", NoExit, METH_VARARGS },
        { NULL, NULL}
};

void
SetupHostModule(void)
{
        PyObject *hostmod, *sysmod;

        hostmod = Py_InitModule("hostModule",hostModuleMethods);
        sysmod = PyImport_ImportModule("sys");
        if(NULL != sysmod) {
```

```
                    PyObject *sysDict, *noExitObj, *hostDict;
                    sysDict = PyModule_GetDict(sysmod);
                    hostDict = PyModule_GetDict(hostmod);
                    if(NULL != sysDict && NULL != hostDict) {
                            noExitObj = PyDict_GetItemString(hostDict,"NoExit");
                            if(NULL != noExitObj)
                                    PyDict_SetItemString(sysDict,"exit",noExitObj);
                    }
                    Py_DECREF(sysmod);
            }
    }
```

What we've added are two functions and a module initialization structure. The function NoExit is a standard Python-callable C function, which simply raises a RuntimeError exception.

The function SetupHostModule initializes the hostModule module. It then acquires a reference to the sys module, locates the exit function in the module's dictionary, and replaces it with the NoExit function defined in the hostModule module.

Finally, during initialization, we call the SetupHostModule function:

```
    Py_Initialize();
    initsysinfoc();
    SetupHostModule();
    if(argc < 2)   {
```

We can test these changes as follows:

```
$ ./ebdemo
>>> import sys
>>> sys.exit(5)
Traceback (innermost last):
  File "???", line 1, in ?
RuntimeError: No exit allowed
>>> ^D
Result Code is 0
$
```

You can use this technique to override any other function definitions. However this is probably not the best way to handle sys.exit, since most Python scripts expect to exit rather than encounter an exception using this function.

Note that the complicated process of replacing sys.exit with hostmodule.NoExit can be simplified by performing the assignment in Python rather than C.

Calling Python Functions

Any function defined in a Python script at the module or class level can be called from a host program. As a simple example, let's modify the NoExit C function to callback into Python. This function will look in the __main__ module (the primary module executed by the Python interpreter) for the function named ExitFunction; if it exists, NoExit will call it, passing in a string argument:

```
PyObject *
NoExit(PyObject *a, PyObject *args)
        /* disallow all exiting */
{
        PyObject *mainModule, *mainDict;

        mainModule = PyImport_ImportModule("__main__");
        if(NULL != mainModule) {
                PyObject *mainDict;

                mainDict = PyModule_GetDict(mainModule);
                if(NULL != mainDict) {
                        PyObject *func  =
                                PyDict_GetItemString(mainDict,"ExitFunction");
                        if(NULL != func) {
                                PyObject *res = PyObject_CallFunction(func,
                                        "s","NoExit was called");
                                Py_DECREF(mainModule);
                                return res;
                        }
                }
                Py_DECREF(mainModule);
        }

        PyErr_SetString(PyExc_RuntimeError,"No exit allowed");
        return NULL;
}
```

Note that `PyImport_ImportModule` returns an owned reference to the selected module. This reference must be released with the `Py_DECREF` macro. The `NoExit` function uses the reference to obtain the module dictionary, and then calls `PyDict_GetItemString` to retrieve the `ExitFunction`. The `PyDict_GetItemString` function returns a borrowed reference that should not be released.

Finally, we use `PyObject_CallFunction` to call the `ExitFunction` (if it's defined). `PyObject_CallFunction` takes a format string similar to the `Py_BuildValue` function. In our example, we pass a single string to the function object.

We can test our changes by running `ebdemo` without command line arguments and using the Python interpreter in interactive mode:

```
$ ./ebdemo
>>> import hostModule
>>> hostModule.NoExit()
Traceback (innermost last):
  File "???", line 1, in ?
RuntimeError: No exit allowed
>>> def ExitFunction(s):
...     print "ExitFunction called with '", s, "'"
...     return "I got " + s
...
>>> print hostModule.NoExit()
ExitFunction called with  ' NoExit was called '
'I got NoExit was called'
>>>
```

First, we call hostModule.NoExit to demonstrate its original behavior (it raises an exception). We define a function named ExitFunction, which prints a statement and returns another string. Now, when we call hostModule.NoExit, we see that ExitFunction is executed and the return value passed through NoExit is printed.

Instantiating a Python Instance and Calling an Instance Method

This rather contrived example will demonstrate how to instantiate Python class objects (creating an instance), and calling methods of an instance object. Like the previous two examples, we need to acquire a reference to the target module, obtain a reference to the module's dictionary, and then extract the desired item from that dictionary.

We add the following function to ebdemo.c:

```c
void
CallMethodInInstance(char *klassname, char *method)
{
        PyObject *mainModule, *mainDict, *klassobj, *args, *instance;

        mainModule = PyImport_ImportModule("__main__");
        if(NULL == mainModule)
                return;

        mainDict = PyModule_GetDict(mainModule);
        Py_DECREF(mainModule);
        if(NULL == mainDict)
                return;

        klassobj = PyDict_GetItemString(mainDict,klassname);
        if(NULL == klassobj) {
                printf("Could not find class named %s in __main__\n",klassname);
                return;
        }
        args = Py_BuildValue("()");      /* create empty tuple for args */
        if(NULL == args)
                return;

        instance = PyInstance_New(klassobj,args,NULL);
        if(NULL == instance) {
                printf("Could not create instance of %s\n",klassname);
                return;
        }

        PyObject_CallMethod(instance, method, "s", "Call From CMII");
        Py_DECREF(instance);
}
```

The CallMethodInInstance function accepts two arguments: the name of the class to instantiate and the name of the method to call in the created instance of that class. After getting the module's dictionary reference, we extract the class object from that dictionary based on the klassname variable.

When a class instance is created, the Python special method __init__ is called. In our example, this will accept only one argument: self. Arguments are passed to __init__ as a tuple; we create an empty tuple with the Py_BuildValue function.

We then call `PyInstance_New`, passing the reference to the class object, the empty tuple, and `NULL` as the keywords dictionary.

If `PyInstance_New` creates an instance of the desired class, we then use `PyObject_CallMethod` to call the method specified in the method string. We pass the specified method a single string argument "Call from CMII".

We need to make one more modification to `ebdemo.c`, placing a call to `CallMethodInInstance` after the `PyRun_SimpleString` statement. By executing the specified Python script first, the script can define the target class to call. We can then test the `CallMethodInInstance` function in the event that we received both the class name and the method name on the `ebdemo` command line:

```
rc = PyRun_SimpleString(cmd);
if(argc > 3)    /* argv[2] == class, argv[3] == method */
        CallMethodInInstance(argv[2],argv[3]);
}
```

We now create a simple test Python script called `ebdemo2.py` with the following code:

```
#demo class instantiation and callback
class    ebdemo:
        def __init__(self):
                print "ebdemo object created"

        def Test(self,s):
                print "In function Test, got arg '"+s+"'"
```

Finally, we test these changes as follows:

```
$ ./ebdemo ebdemo2.py ebdemo Test
ebdemo object created
In function Test, got arg 'Call From CMII'
Result Code is 0
$
```

Multi-threading

Thread support is available in Python as long as your interpreter was compiled with the `--with-threads` configuration option. If you installed Python from an RPM or distribution package (or it was pre-installed on your system) you'll most likely have thread support enabled.

Using multiple threads within a C or C++ host program takes a bit more code than the simple programs we've seen thus far. Remember that Python has a Global Interpreter Lock, which it uses to ensure that only one thread executes Python code at any one time. Python also uses a `PyThreadState` structure to keep per-thread information, such as `errno` and pending exception. Every thread in a Python program has a single `PyThreadState` structure associated with it.

Python can also support multiple interpreters per program. An interpreter state (or `PyInterpreterState` structure) contains all the runtime information for a given interpreter, such as imported modules, module search path, `sys.stdout`, and so on.

Each `PyThreadState` structure refers to a `PyInterpreterState` structure. However, more than one `PyThreadState` can refer to a single `PyInterpreterState` structure, as shown in the following diagram:

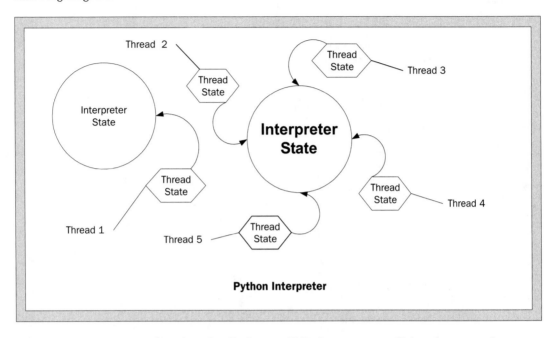

Whenever we spawn new threads within Python itself, Python manages all these structures for us. However, to create a multi-threaded host program that embeds the Python interpreter, we must manage the thread states, Global Interpreter Lock and `PyInterpreterState` structures manually.

tdemo.c

Let's create a multi-threaded host program named `tdemo.c`. This will use a single `PyInterpreterState` with multiple `PyThreadState` structures and will spawn new threads whenever commanded to by a Python script. These threads will sleep for a specified number of seconds, print a message, and then sleep some more. Having printed the message a few times, the threads will exit and die.

We start off with the usual includes, and we've added `pthread.h` so as to give us access to threading functions:

```
/* tdemo.c - threaded embed python demo */

#include <stdio.h>
#include <pthread.h>
#include "Python.h"

PyThreadState *mainThreadState;
```

InterpretPythonString

This function accepts a string containing Python instructions, which it executes in the context of the main module:

```
int
InterpretPythonString(char *s)
        /* return 1 if exiting */
{
        PyObject *m, *d, *v;
        int gotnl = (NULL != strchr(s,'\n'));

        m = PyImport_AddModule("__main__");
        if (NULL == m)
                return;
        d = PyModule_GetDict(m);
        v = PyRun_String(s, gotnl ? Py_file_input : Py_single_input, d, d);
        if (NULL == v)  {
                if(PyExc_SystemExit == PyErr_Occurred()) {
                        PyErr_Clear();
                        return 1;
                }
                return 0;
        }
        Py_DECREF(v);
        return 0;
}
```

We assume the Global Interpreter Lock is held by the current thread when this function is called; it uses the `PyRun_String` function to execute the supplied command string. If this string contains newlines, we tell `PyRun_String` that the input is of type `Py_file_input` rather than `Py_single_input`.

If `PyRun_String` returns `NULL`, an exception has been raised. We check to see if that exception is `PyExc_SystemExit`. If it is, we return 1 from `InterpretPythonString`, otherwise we decrement the reference count on the returned value and return 0.

StartThread

`StartThread` is the function that will be executed by the created thread.

```
void    *
StartThread(void *arg)
{
        char cmd[256];
        PyThreadState *tstate;
        int loopcount = 0;

        int i = (int) arg;
        sprintf(cmd,"print 'Thread %d says hi!'\n",pthread_self());

        PyEval_AcquireLock();   /* acquire global lock */
        tstate = PyThreadState_New(mainThreadState->interp);
        PyThreadState_Swap(tstate);     /* use this new threadstate */
        while(1) {
```

```
                    Py_BEGIN_ALLOW_THREADS
                    sleep(i);
                    Py_END_ALLOW_THREADS
                    if(0 != InterpretPythonString(cmd))
                            break;
                    if(2 < loopcount++)
                            strcpy(cmd,"import sys\nsys.exit(1)\n");
            }
            printf("Thread %d exiting\n",pthread_self());
            PyThreadState_Swap(NULL);        /* reset Python thread state */
            PyThreadState_Clear(tstate);     /* clear thread state */
            PyThreadState_Delete(tstate);    /* delete thread state */
            PyEval_ReleaseLock();
            return NULL;
    }
```

It acquires the Global Interpreter Lock using the `PyEval_AcquireLock` function. The `PyThreadState_New` function creates a new thread state structure, which we save in the variable `tstate`. This function requires a pointer to the `PyInterpreterState` structure that this thread will be using. We pass in the `PyInterpreterState` structure used by the 'main thread'.

`PyThreadState_Swap` sets the current thread state to the newly created state held in `tstate`. We drop into the `while` loop and use the `Py_BEGIN_ALLOW_THREADS` macro to release the Global Interpreter Lock before calling the system `sleep` function.

After sleep returns, the `Py_END_ALLOW_THREADS` macro reacquires the Global Interpreter Lock, and restores the current `PyThreadState`. At this point it's safe for the current thread to execute Python C API functions. The `StartThread` function calls `InterpretPythonString` to execute the cmd string. If `InterpretPythonString` returns a non-zero value (because `sys.exit` was called in Python), we break out of the `while` loop.

If we've looped several times, `loopcount` will cause cmd to be replaced with:

```
import sys
sys.exit(1)
```

The next time through the `while` loop, `InterpretPythonString` will execute the new cmd value, causing the `InterpretPythonString` function to return a non-zero value.

Finally we print out a message indicating that the thread is exiting, reset the current thread state to NULL, clear the current thread's `PyThreadState` structure and free it. `PyEval_ReleaseLock` is the last function executed, releasing the Global Interpreter Lock.

LaunchThread

The `LaunchThread` function is called from Python to spawn a new thread:

```
PyObject *
LaunchThread(PyObject *a, PyObject *args)
        /* disallow all exiting */
{
        int i = 5;
```

```
        pthread_t tid;
        int rc;

        if(!PyArg_ParseTuple(args,"|i:LaunchThread",&i))
                return NULL;

        if(pthread_create(&tid,NULL,StartThread,(void *) i) < 0)
                return PyErr_SetFromErrno(PyExc_RuntimeError);

        if(pthread_detach(tid) < 0)
                return PyErr_SetFromErrno(PyExc_RuntimeError);

        return PyInt_FromLong(tid);
};
```

It accepts just one optional argument: the time delay. LaunchThread creates a new thread using pthread_create, and passes it StartThread, the function to execute. The pthread_detach function allows the newly spawned thread to execute, and we return the thread id of the new thread to Python.

host_functions

This is the array of functions exported by the host module:

```
PyMethodDef host_functions[] = {
        { "LaunchThread", LaunchThread, METH_VARARGS},
        { NULL, NULL }
};
```

SetupHostModule

This function uses the host_functions array to initialize the host module:

```
void
SetupHostModule(void)
{
        PyObject *hostmod, *sysmod;

        hostmod = Py_InitModule("hostModule",host_functions);
}
```

InitializePython

The InitializePython function initializes the Python interpreter and sets up the initial thread environment:

```
void
InitializePython(int argc, char **argv)
{
        Py_SetProgramName(argv[0]);

        PyEval_InitThreads();   /* initialize threading, acquire global lock */
```

```
        Py_Initialize();
        PySys_SetArgv(argc, argv);
        SetupHostModule();

        mainThreadState = PyEval_SaveThread(); /* release global lock */
}
```

It calls `Py_SetProgramName` to set the program name, `PyEval_InitThreads` to switch Python to threaded mode, `Py_Initialize` to initialize the Python interpreter, `PySys_SetArgv` to set the value of `sys.argv`, and `SetupHostModule` to initialize the hostModule. Finally we call `PyEval_SaveThread` to retrieve a pointer to the current `PyThreadState` and release the Global Interpreter Lock.

The global variable `mainThreadState` is used in `StartThread` to return a pointer to the main `PyInterpreterState` structure.

main

In main, we call `InitializePython` to set up the initial threading environment, initialize Python and set up the `hostModule`:

```
int
main(int argc, char **argv)
{
        int rc;
        char cmd[1024];

        InitializePython(argc, argv);

        PyEval_AcquireLock();    /* acquire global interpreter lock */
        PyThreadState_Swap(mainThreadState);
        rc = PyRun_AnyFile(stdin,"???");
        Py_Finalize();
        /* just die without releasing lock so other threads don't call Python */
        return rc;
}
```

`PyEval_AcquireLock` acquires the Global Interpreter Lock (which was released by the `InitializePython` function). We then use `PyThreadState_Swap` to set the current PyThreadState to `mainThreadState` and call `PyRun_AnyFile` to execute the Python interpreter in interactive mode.

When `PyRun_AnyFile` returns we call `Py_Finalize` to clean up the Python interpreter and return from main – without releasing the Global Interpreter Lock. It's probably more appropriate to wait for the threads spawned by `StartThread` to exit before calling `Py_Finalize` than to 'pull out the rug' as we do here. However, as we're trying to keep the example quite simple, we just exit as soon as the interactive session completes.

We're now ready to test the `tdemo` program by typing in commands to spawn new threads in interactive mode:

```
$ ./tdemo
>>> import hostModule
>>> hostModule.LaunchThread(10)
1026
>>> dir()
```

We execute the `dir` function just to demonstrate that the interactive interpreter is still working after we've launched thread 1026 (using the `LaunchThread` function). Note that thread numbers on Linux are really process numbers, and are unlikely to be the same from one run to the next:

```
['__builtins__', '__doc__', '__name__', 'hostModule']
>>> hostModule.LaunchThread(5)
2051
```

We launch another thread:

```
>>> Thread 1026 says hi!
Thread 2051 says hi!

>>> Thread 2051 says hi!
Thread 1026 says hi!
Thread 2051 says hi!

>>> Thread 2051 says hi!
Thread 1026 says hi!
Thread 2051 exiting
```

Both threads print their message, and thread 2051 exits:

```
>>> dir()
['__builtins__', '__doc__', '__name__', 'hostModule', 'sys']
```

This command demonstrates that the Python interpreter is still working, even after thread 2051 has died:

```
>>> Thread 1026 says hi!
Thread 1026 exiting

>>> hostModule.LaunchThread(1)
3074
>>> Thread 3074 says hi!
Thread 3074 says hi!
Thread 3074 says hi!
Thread 3074 exiting

>>> ^D
```

We launch one more thread after the first two have died, then finally quit the program with *Ctrl-D*.

General Suggestions

When developing new programs it's often easier to prototype them in Python rather than writing them in C. If you find that the prototype doesn't perform as desired, you can typically recode the "slow code" in C as an extension module. This hybrid approach to software development gives you quicker results than writing in C alone.

Existing C/C++ programs can gain comprehensive functionality by embedding the Python interpreter. Static programs quickly become more configurable and more powerful by allowing the end user to control the program via Python. Again, a hybrid approach often provides impressive reduction in development time.

The Python interpreter can be used to automate module and system testing of C/C++ programs. By wiring up a test harness in your C program as you develop it, you can test program modules as they are developed using Python scripts. Later revisions to the program can be quickly tested and compared to baseline results to detect unexpected side effects.

Resources

For more information on Python: http://www.python.org.

To find out more about SWIG: http://www.swig.org.

Summary

This chapter demonstrates how to extend Python with both SWIG- and hand-written C/C++ code. You can give Python scripts access to just about any function, library or C++ object using the techniques shown here.

We've seen that SWIG can be used to quickly create interface functions based on existing header files, although its limitations may mean some tweaking is necessary.

Nevertheless, SWIG's shadow class file provides a powerful mechanism for easing access to structures, while the %addmethods directive provides useful encapsulation features that often outweigh SWIG's limitations. Examining the SWIG-generated C wrapper file can provide clues on how to use the Python C API and how to structure a hand-written C/C++ module.

Online discussion at http://www.p2p.wrox.com

18

Remote Procedure Calls

Overview

Up until now, both the application-user interaction and the business logic behind the DVD Store database manipulation all took place in the one application process, and only on the local machine. We already have a defined interface to the database for the application – described in the dvd.h source file. Now let us assume our DVD storeowner has decided to connect two or more branches together using a single centralized database. This will facilitate the administration of the database, and allow backups and security functions to be maintained.

We now have a new requirement to separate our application into distinct tiers, or components. Let's have a think about this:

- ❑ User Interface: the user interface stands out as a candidate for a class (object instance) of its own. We have now provided a GTK+/GNOME (Chapter 9) based implementation, KDE/Qt implementation (Chapter 14) and web front end (Chapter 16). We might also decide eventually to port it to another operating system (BeOS for instance? Did I hear someone suggesting Windows?). How the interface is displayed is, for the most part, independent of the 'business logic' of the application.

- ❑ Business Logic: making decisions based on the results of database searches and queries. This is a good candidate for a tier.

- ❑ Finally the Database itself: the function of storing and retrieving the information for our DVD Store is sufficiently self-contained and significant to warrant its own tier.

What we have done here is to stumble across the concept of multi-tiered application development. By separating the application into different components, and specifying interfaces between them, we can distribute the components across the network. In addition, we can easily support many-to-many relationships between users of the information, and the information database at the back-end. At a first level, this allows multiple users to access the interface. More powerfully, however, it allows differing 'views' or filtering of this information, depending on the user; for example, the storeowner or manager might get more information than an assistant working in the store.

In this chapter, we will consider separating these from the database access functions, and introduce the concept of remote procedure calls.

We will start by examining a first potential candidate for adding network functionality to our database – using the socket API, which was invented for use in BSD but is now part of the POSIX definition. We will examine both client and server software using sockets, and look at some of the difficulties in programming to this interface.

We will introduce Remote Procedure Calls (RPCs) as our chosen solution, showing how they save the developer time, in both the program development cycle, and also during the debugging, by simplifying the API. We will incrementally develop the code necessary for an RPC implementation of the DVD store data access functions, based on the reliable, connection-oriented, TCP protocol.

Finally, we will introduce some more sophisticated mechanisms to enable network communication using component-based software, and object-oriented development techniques.

A Simple Networked DVD Store Database

In our initial attempt at making the DVD store application network-enabled, we will use BSD sockets to perform all the network communication for us. This will put into perspective the ease of use afforded by the use of RPCs.

First of all, we will quickly review the concepts of the BSD Socket API.

BSD Sockets

Applications can communicate either locally, or across the network through the use of sockets. A server application creates a socket, and names it by binding a particular address to it. It then listens for incoming connection requests on the socket.

There are many different types of sockets, each with its own address type. To connect to processes running on different machines, the most common type of sockets are TCP/IP sockets. In TCP/IP terms, the address of the socket consists of the protocol used (usually TCP or UDP), the hostname and the port number to connect to.

The client application somehow obtains the address of the socket. Common applications may have standardized port numbers that are called 'well-known' port numbers, such as TCP port 25 for SMTP (the Simple Mail Transport Protocol) and TCP port 80 for HTTP (the HyperText Transfer protocol). Once the client application has the server address, it connects to the socket.

The server is listening for these connection requests, and accepts them according to some arbitrary connection strategy defined by the programmer.

At this point, both client and server are free to use the socket as a file descriptor to UNIX I/O in order to transfer data. Let's have a look at this in code, starting first with the server. (the code for this chapter, including a makefile, is available for download from http://www.wrox.com.)

Simple Socket Server

This simple socket-based server writes `Hello, World!` to the client and closes the connection:

```c
/* svc_socket.c */

#include <stdio.h>
#include <stdlib.h>
#include <string.h>
#include <sys/utsname.h>
#include <sys/types.h>
#include <sys/socket.h>

#include <netinet/in.h>
#include <arpa/inet.h>
#include <netdb.h>
#include <unistd.h>
#include <errno.h>
#include <limits.h>

static int Get_Host_Name(char *buffer, int len);
static int Write(int sock_descr, const void *msg_ptr, int bytes_to_send);

static const char _message[] = "Hello, World!\n";

int main(int argc, char *argv[])
{
    int svc_socket = 0,
        on = 0,
        port = 0;
    struct hostent *host_ptr = 0;
    char hostname[80] = "";
    struct sockaddr_in server_name = { 0 };
    struct linger linger = { 0 };

    /* first, get the port number that the server will run on */
    if (2 != argc) {
        fprintf(stderr, "Usage: %s <port_num>\n", argv[0]);
        exit(EXIT_FAILURE);
    }

    port = strtol(argv[1], 0, 10);
    if ((LONG_MAX == port) || (LONG_MIN == port))
    {
        perror("strtol");
        exit(EXIT_FAILURE);
    }
```

We have now parsed the command line arguments, and know the port number to bind to. We now need to create a socket, construct an address and bind the address to the socket:

```
/* create the server socket */
svc_socket = socket(PF_INET, SOCK_STREAM, IPPROTO_TCP);
if (-1 == svc_socket) {
    perror("socket");
    exit(EXIT_FAILURE);
}


/*
 * set socket options to reuse the address quickly if the server dies,
 * and to linger on sending data once the connection closes
 */
setsockopt(svc_socket, SOL_SOCKET, SO_REUSEADDR,
    (const char *)&on, sizeof(on));
linger.l_onoff = 1;
linger.l_linger = 30;
setsockopt(svc_socket, SOL_SOCKET, SO_LINGER,
    (const char *)&linger, sizeof(linger));

/* get my hostname */
if (-1 == Get_Host_Name(hostname, sizeof(hostname))) {
    perror("Get_Host_Name");
    exit(EXIT_FAILURE);
}

host_ptr = gethostbyname(hostname);
if (0 == host_ptr) {
    perror("gethostbyname");
    exit(EXIT_FAILURE);
}

/* create and bind to IP Address:Port */
memset(&server_name, 0, sizeof(server_name));
memcpy(&server_name.sin_addr, host_ptr->h_addr, host_ptr->h_length);

server_name.sin_addr.s_addr = htonl(INADDR_ANY);
server_name.sin_family = AF_INET;
server_name.sin_port = htons(port);
if (-1 == bind(svc_socket, (struct sockaddr *)&server_name,
    sizeof(server_name))) {
    perror("bind");
    exit(EXIT_FAILURE);
}
```

Now, it is just a question of listening for incoming connections, accepting them and writing a message back to the client:

```
/* listen for incoming connection requests */
if (-1 == listen(svc_socket, 5)) {
    perror("listen");
    exit(EXIT_FAILURE);
}
```

```
        /* for each incoming connection... */
    for (;;) {
        struct sockaddr_in clnt_name = { 0 };
        int clnt_socket = 0,
            clnt_len = sizeof(clnt_name);

        /* accept the connection */
        memset(&clnt_name, 0, sizeof(clnt_name));
        clnt_socket = accept(svc_socket, (struct sockaddr *)&clnt_name,
            &clnt_len);
        if (-1 == clnt_socket) {
            perror("accept");
            exit(EXIT_FAILURE);
        }

        /* find out who the client peer is */
        if (-1 == getpeername(clnt_socket, (struct sockaddr *)&clnt_name,
                &clnt_len))
            perror("getpeername");
        else
            printf("Connection request from %s\n",
                inet_ntoa(clnt_name.sin_addr));

        /* write the message to the client, handling short writes */
        Write(clnt_socket, _message, strlen(_message));
        close(clnt_socket);
    }
}

static int Get_Host_Name(char *buffer, int len)
{
    struct utsname sys_name = { { 0 } };
    int status = uname(&sys_name);

    if (-1 != status)
        strncpy(buffer, sys_name.nodename, len);

    return (status);
}
```

Since it is possible that the kernel will interrupt a process during a socket write, we will need to ensure that short writes are also handled. This is done as follows:

```
static int Write(int sock_descr, const void *msg_ptr, int bytes_to_send)
{
    int bytes_written, num_sent = 0;

    for (bytes_written = 0; bytes_written < bytes_to_send; bytes_written +=
num_sent) {
        num_sent = write(sock_descr, (void *)((char *)msg_ptr + bytes_written),
                    (bytes_to_send - bytes_written));

        if (num_sent < 0) {
            perror("write");
```

```
                    if (errno != EINTR) {
                            exit(1);
                    }
            }
      }

      return 0;
}
```

Simple Socket Client

And now, the corresponding client:

```
/*
 * clnt_socket.c
 */

#include <stdio.h>
#include <stdlib.h>
#include <sys/types.h>
#include <sys/socket.h>
#include <unistd.h>
#include <netinet/in.h>
#include <arpa/inet.h>
#include <netdb.h>

int main(int argc, char **argv)
{
  int clnt_socket = 0,
    remote_port = 0,
    status = 0;
  struct hostent *host_ptr = 0;
  struct sockaddr_in svc_name = { 0 };
  char buffer[256] = "";
  char *remote_host = 0;

  if (3 != argc) {
    fprintf(stderr, "Usage: %s <remote_host> <remote_port>\n", argv[0]);
    exit(EXIT_FAILURE);
  }
  remote_host = argv[1];
  remote_port = atoi(argv[2]);
```

Again, we have parsed the command line arguments and have learnt the remote host and port number. Since the user can pass the remote host as either a hostname or as an IP address, we must handle both in the code. Now, we create a socket, and determine the remote address to connect to:

```
  /* create a socket */
  clnt_socket = socket(PF_INET, SOCK_STREAM, IPPROTO_TCP);
  if (-1 == clnt_socket) {
    perror("socket");
    exit(EXIT_FAILURE);
  }
```

```
    /*
     * find the host address - first see if the user passed a hostname on
     * the command line. If not, try an IP address. If this fails also,
     * then report it as an error and terminate execution
     */
    host_ptr = gethostbyname(remote_host);
    if (0 == host_ptr) {
      host_ptr = gethostbyaddr(remote_host, strlen(remote_host), AF_INET);
      if (0 == host_ptr) {
        perror("Error resolving server address");
        exit(EXIT_FAILURE);
      }
    }


    /*
     * build the address of the remote structure, and attempt to connect to
     * it
     */
    svc_name.sin_family = AF_INET;
    svc_name.sin_port = htons(remote_port);
    memcpy(&svc_name.sin_addr, host_ptr->h_addr, host_ptr->h_length);

    status = connect(clnt_socket, (struct sockaddr*) &svc_name,
            sizeof(svc_name));
    if (-1 == status) {
      perror("connect");
      exit(EXIT_FAILURE);
    }
```

Now we have a connection to the server, we will continue reading from the socket until the server has nothing further to transmit:

```
    /*
     * until the server is finished transmitting and has closed
     * the connection, keep reading from the socket
     */
    while (0 < (status = read(clnt_socket, buffer, sizeof(buffer) -1))) {
      buffer[status] = '\0'; /* null terminate string */
      printf("CLNT_SOCKET: Received %d bytes - \"%s\"\n", status, buffer);
    }

    if (-1 == status) {
      perror("read");
    }

    /* all done */
    close(clnt_socket);
    return 0;
  }
```

For more information on the programming techniques and APIs used in either the socket server or client, please refer to Chapter 14 of *Beginning Linux Programming*, Second Edition, published by Wrox Press (*ISBN 1861002971*).

Coding Issues Using the BSD Socket Interface

You can see from these two code examples how time-consuming just creating the client and server sockets is, never mind actually transferring any data across them! Using sockets is also prone to coding error. The interface is complex, and requires large amounts of code.

Having said this, socket code is quite often re-useable; it's a formula. Once you have a working framework for client and server side code, you can just re-use it forever.

For applications that do not involve flow of control, but are more data stream oriented (such as FTP or HTTP), using sockets directly makes the most sense – they are more efficient. The programmer must be pragmatic and use the appropriate solution for the problem in hand.

It is important to realize that the socket API, much like the UNIX concept of a file, does not handle any of the issues associated with representation of data being transmitted across the network. By this, we mean issues such as:

❑ The endianness of the machine (in other words the order in which it stores the bytes of its native types, such as integers and longs).

❑ The natural word size of the architecture – for example, the remote machine may be a 64-bit machine (Compaq Alpha running Linux or Compaq Tru64), whereas the local machine might be based on the 32-bit Intel 80x86.

❑ The form of more complicated data structures – such as C structs, zero-terminated strings etc. The machines at either end of the network connection may be of differing architectures, or use different compilers. This may lead to differences in the padding and alignment of the members of a structure.

❑ Any dispatching of control messages over the link – for example, application level requests to perform certain tasks have to be explicitly decoded and dispatched to the appropriate routine by the programmer.

The practice of packaging data into a form suitable for transmission across a network is called Marshaling. The reverse procedure, extracting this information back into a form usable in a program, is called De-Marshaling. As can be imagined, this is not a trivial task. The BSD socket API provides a number of macro functions for transporting simple data types across the network in a portable fashion – htons for host to network short, htonl for host to network long, etc. However, when structures, pointers and more complex types like arrays of structures are involved, this requires quite an amount of coding on the part of the developer. Surely there must be a better way?

ONC RPC Architecture and Concepts.

Enter the Open Network Computing Remote Procedure Calls, or ONC-RPC for short. ONC-RPC is based on a remote procedure call standard developed by Sun Microsystems, and promoted as an IETF (Internet Engineering Task Force, the entity responsible for standardizing the various protocols used on the Internet) standard since the early 1980s [RFC 1831]. It has become the de facto RPC standard amongst the UNIX developer community.

The attractiveness of using remote procedure calls to handle distributed network programming stems from the fact that it extends a familiar metaphor – that of the procedure call. By making network programming as close to writing a procedure call as possible, RPC aims to take the drudgery and potential for error out of the task. In fact, it is quite easy to view client-server interactions as procedure calls – the client makes a request of the server and the server responds with the result; the caller calls the procedure, passing in various arguments, and the procedure call may return a result when finished.

In ONC-RPC, the remote procedure interface is specified using a special language called remote procedure description language. These files are usually given the suffix .x. A protocol compiler converts these description language files into source modules that the programmer links with. Together with support from the C runtime library, these modules perform all the networking functionality.

Remote procedures run within the context of execution of a remote server. To be able to execute a remote procedure, the client must first find this remote server. RPC handles this by use of a well-known server that acts as a directory of services running on the machine. To locate any particular server, the client contacts this directory server (called the portmap) first, and then it is able to communicate with the server it requires.

Datagram (Connectionless) or Stream (Connection-oriented)

ONC-RPC supports both datagram-based remote procedure calls, and also stream-based procedure calls. The datagram-based calls use the UDP protocol from the TCP/IP suite. UDP does not guarantee reliable transfer of data, so datagram-based RPCs will retransmit the RPC request, if necessary. After a fixed number of unsuccessful attempts, the RPC will time out and report an error to the client. With UDP, the maximum size of the RPC message is limited by the size of the UDP packet. This in turn is limited by the maximum transmission unit size (MTU) of the link.

Stream-based RPCs will report an error message if the server is not running, and they can also be configured to timeout after a certain period of time. The use of timeouts is explained later on in this chapter.

eXtended Data Representation (XDR).

In a local procedure call, one function calls another, passing it various arguments, and possibly receives a return value. On Intel 80x86 CPUs, this is generally done through the use of a stack frame. If the function has a small parameter list and return type, this may be done through the use of registers in the CPU as a compiler run-time optimization. The programmer can pass variables by value, or by reference using pointers in C. All the code is running in the same virtual address space, so it is perfectly valid to use the pointer in the called function.

Things become a little trickier when dealing with functions that are potentially remote – either in a different process, or on a different machine entirely. Now, it is no longer valid to pass a pointer to an object to a separate process, or even a separate machine. Instead the value pointed to by the pointer must be bundled up into a portable package and sent to the other side. In ONC-RPC, this is handled automatically for you by the eXtended Data Representation (XDR) package. The RPC protocol compiler automatically generates XDR routines that will perform all this marshaling and de-marshaling of information transparently. XDR is defined in [RFC 1832].

The main components of ONC RPC on Linux are:

❑ the RPC protocol Compiler

❑ the Program Service to Server Mapper

❑ the XDR standard for encoding data portably between different systems.

❑   the glibc library, which contains the runtime implementation of the RPC and XDR routines.

Why Use RPC in the DVD Store Application?

The interaction of a DVD Store client with a DVD Store server is control-based. The client interrogates the server, and then receives responses. The system is protocol-centric, rather than data throughput-centric. If we were to write this application using the Socket API, we would spend considerable time writing the routines to perform the marshaling and de-marshaling.

Additionally, we would need to parse commands coming from the data stream over the socket, and dispatch them to a suitable handler routine to execute the command and generate the response.

We can solve both of these issues by taking advantage of the features provided by RPCs. The RPC protocol compiler will generate the routines to handle all marshaling activity, and since RPC is based on the function call metaphor, it implicitly handles all the required command dispatching.

The PostgreSQL database used to store the data in the DVD store application already presents a network interface, and it would be possible to use this interface instead to provide distributed access to the database. However, there are a number of advantages to using an RPC-like mechanism instead of the native network capabilities of PostgreSQL:

❏ The client-side application is better abstracted from the server/database implementation. This allows the project to be potentially scaled up to a larger database, or even a database from a different supplier, if customer demands necessitate it.

❏ The developer is able to use RPC-based authentication of the client-side request.

❏ Multiple databases could be connected on the server-side, whilst presenting only a single interface to the client.

RPC was born out of necessity. In fact, the origins of ONC-RPC were for NFS. When Sun Microsystems wanted to allow remote machines share file systems, the most obvious method for doing this was to extend the existing UNIX file API across the network. The remote procedure call was the perfect tool for this application! Both NFS and NIS still use RPC.

RPC Tools and Utilities

To begin developing RPC-based applications in Linux, you need the following tools and utilities:

❏ gcc, the GNU Compiler (we tested this chapter with egcs v1.1.2).

❏ glibc, the GNU C library (we tested with glibc v2.1.3). This contains RPC support in the library, and the required include files.

❏ portmap.

❏ A Linux kernel with SunRPC support compiled in, or available as a module.

The code examples in this chapter were developed and tested using Red Hat 6.2. However, any suitably configured distribution should suffice, with a little tinkering.

Let's now discuss some of the support tools commonly used in developing and using remote procedure call applications.

rpcgen – the RPC Protocol Compiler

The rpcgen tool parses the RPC protocol from an RPC language file and converts it into C. As used in this chapter, it takes one input file and generates three C code output files, and one C header file. The file dvd_store.x contains the RPC protocol description for the DVD Store application, a full code listing for which can be found in Appendix B.

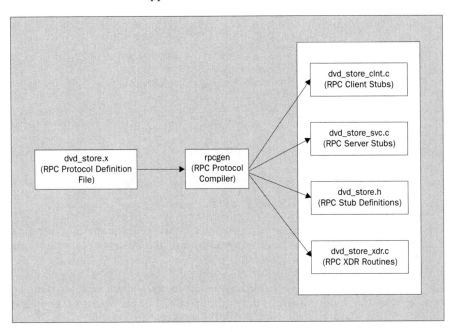

The use of rpcgen, as illustrated in the diagram, will be described in more detail throughout the chapter.

Structure of the RPC Protocol Definition File

It is a good idea to structure the RPC protocol definition file into three main sections, as this allows us to quickly find a particular item of interest. Here is the structure we are going to use to add RPC capabilities to the DVD store:

```
/*
 * dvd_store.x - RPC Protocol Definition File
 */

/* constant values go first */

/* type definitions go next */

/* finally, the program protocol definition */
```

The RPC protocol definition language is a C-like language, but is a special subset that has its own limited set of variable types, its own data abstraction.

portmap – Port Address to RPC Program Number Mapper

portmap converts RPC program numbers into local socket port numbers. The portmap must be running in order to map RPC calls. When a client RPC program wishes to execute a remote procedure, it first contacts the portmap processes running on the remote side, and interrogates it to find the port number that the server process is listening on. The portmap itself is a server running on a well-known (i.e. dedicated) port – port 111.

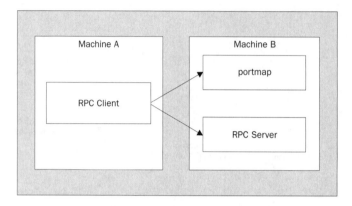

RPC servers register themselves with portmap when they start up. It is important therefore to ensure that if the portmap process is restarted for some reason, that all RPC services are also restarted. The above diagram shows the portmap in operation.

Note that because the communication is based on the function call, all information returned to the client is passed via the standard 'return' mechanism. For this reason, the arrows in the digram are not bi-directional, as they indicate flow of control through the function calls.

rpcinfo – Query for RPC Information

rpcinfo makes a remote procedure call to a specified RPC server, and reports back what it learns. The most common case is to connect to the portmap processes on a machine and report back what it learns. Note that the information about RPC services is transmitted over the network in plain text. This is an ideal way for a hacker to learn important information about your system. RPC is NOT secure and may be inappropriate in all networks that you do not own and control the 'wire'.

```
$ rpcinfo -p localhost
  program vers proto  port
  100000  2   tcp   111 portmapper
  100000  2   udp   111 portmapper
  100021  1   udp   1900 nlockmgr
  100021  3   udp   1900 nlockmgr
  100021  1   tcp   2893 nlockmgr
  100021  3   tcp   2893 nlockmgr
  100024  1   udp   950 status
  100024  1   tcp   952 status
  100005  1   udp   977 mountd
  100005  1   tcp   979 mountd
  100005  2   udp   983 mountd
  100005  2   tcp   985 mountd
  100009  1   udp   686 yppasswdd
 536871065  1   tcp   2896 dvd_store
```

rpcinfo can also verify that a particular server is running correctly by making an RPC call to procedure 0 of the service. Procedure 0 is a special 'ping' type procedure used to indicate that the server is alive. There are two versions of this command – one to check datagram servers (-u for UDP) and the other to check stream servers (-t for TCP):

```
$ rpcinfo -u localhost mountd 1
program 100005 version 1 ready and waiting
$ rpcinfo -t localhost 100005 2
program 100005 version 2 ready and waiting
```

As you can see, rpcinfo can interrogate based on either the service name (from /etc/rpc), or the service program number.

Broadcasts to all hosts on a particular program number and protocol are also possible:

```
$ rpcinfo -b mountd 1
192.168.1.2.239   gold
192.168.13.21.52  bronze
192.168.2.4.42    silver
```

Finally, rpcinfo allows the user to delete a particular program registration from a portmap server. However, you must run as the superuser to do this (note you don't need to be superuser to run the RPC server process itself):

```
$ rpcinfo -d 536871065 1
Sorry. You are not root
$ su
Password:
# /usr/sbin/rpcinfo -d 536871065 1
#
```

The server process will automatically reregister itself when it is restarted.

Applying RPCs to the DVD Store

The steps in building an RPC application are:

- ❏ generation of interface description file
- ❏ using the protocol compiler
- ❏ implementing client and server stubs, and using rpcgen to generate XDR routines
- ❏ integration with the reference implementation stubs described in Chapter 1

First, we will show how to convert two simple DVD Store functions (that have no parameters and return values) into remote procedure calls. We will generate the interface descriptions, create the client and server stubs, and finally compile both sides and execute both programs.

Functions Without Arguments or Return Types

We'll start by adding the simplest of functions to our RPC interface:

```
void dvd_open_db(void);
void dvd_close_db(void);
```

These functions are relatively simple to implement as remote procedure calls. We define these function interfaces in the program definition section of dvd_store.x file as follows:

```
/*
 * dvd_store.x RPC interface definition
 */

/* constant value declarations */

/* type definition section (return types, argument types) */

/* dvd_store protocol definition */
program DVD_STORE_PROG {
    version DVD_STORE_VER {
        int DVD_OPEN_DB = 1;
        int DVD_CLOSE_DB = 3;
    } = 1; /* protocol version */
} = 0x20000099; /* protocol identifier */
```

At this stage, we don't need to define any constants, return types or argument types, so these sections of the dvd_store.x file are blank for now.

The protocol for a particular program is defined inside a 'program block'. Each program protocol is assigned a unique number – in our case, the number 0x20000099 in hexadecimal is from the public address range specified in [RFC 1831]:

```
0x00000000 - 0x1fffffff defined by Sun Microsystems
0x20000000 - 0x3fffffff defined by the user
0x40000000 - 0x5fffffff transient
0x60000000 - 0xffffffff reserved for future use.
```

A single .x file can contain multiple program definitions. Within each program, there may be multiple versions of the protocol. For example, the NFS application, the original application for ONC-RPC from Sun, is now on NFS version 3. From the example above, you can see that we are using version 1 of the DVD Store RPC protocol.

Inside this version block, each procedure, or function, is numbered uniquely. Procedure numbers start at 0 – but procedure number 0 is reserved as a NULL or 'ping' procedure. It is automatically generated by the rpcgen compiler, doesn't require any arguments, and returns nothing. However, it is useful to ensure that the remote server is running.

The procedure number for DVD_OPEN_DB is 1, it takes no arguments and returns an int (the status). Similarly for DVD_CLOSE_DB, the procedure number is 3, it also takes no arguments and returns the status.

Don't worry about the fact that the procedure numbers are not contiguous. We have implemented the functions in the dvd_store.x based on the order that they appear in dvd.h. The completed dvd_store.x has all the missing functions in it.

Running rpcgen on dvd_store.x [see the diagram] generates the following files:

❏ dvd_store_clnt.c – the client side-stubs

❏ dvd_store_svc.c – the server-side stubs

❏ dvd_store_xdr.c – the XDR routines

❏ dvd_store.h – the common RPC header file for this protocol

The routines in the stub files handle the entire network programming for you. The XDR routines handle the data marshaling into a network-transportable format, and de-marshaling into the native type of the opposite end. We now need to connect our implementations of the dvd.h API and also the user of the API to these RPC stubs. This is done through the use of client and server-side 'wrappers'.

The server wrappers map directly to the DVD API, as described in dvd.h. Here is the server side wrapper source code for the two functions defined above:

```
/*
 * dvd_server_wrapper.c
 */

#include <stdio.h>
#include <rpc/rpc.h>
#include "dvd.h"
#include "dvd_store.h"      /* automatically generated by rpcgen */

int * dvd_open_db_1_svc(void *dummy_ptr, struct svc_req * svc_req_prt)
{
    static int result = DVD_NO_ERROR;  /* must be static */
#ifdef RPC_DEBUG
    fputs("RPC_SERVER: dvd_open_db_1_svc called\n", stderr);
#endif

    result = dvd_open_db;

    return (&result);
}

int * dvd_close_db_1_svc(void *dummy_ptr, struct svc_req * svc_req_prt)
{
    static int result = DVD_NO_ERROR;  /* must be static */
#ifdef RPC_DEBUG
    fputs("RPC_SERVER: dvd_close_db_1_svc called\n", stderr);
#endif

    result = dvd_close_db;

    return (&result);
}
```

As you can see, each function name is the name of the function from the `dvd_store.x` file, in lower case, with an underscore, the protocol revision number, and the string `_svc` appended to it. The RPC definition used in this chapter will always take exactly one argument, and return exactly one result. This is the default (initial) functionality supported by the `rpcgen` compiler – more complex arguments and return types are handled using structures.

Newer functionality allows the use of more C-like arguments – but beware: the compiler does not always generate correct C from this, especially when you use structures as one of the arguments. It is best to stick with the original method, as it is more portable, and more reliable.

The `rpcgen` compiler is quite dumb – in the case of a `void` argument, and changes this to `void *`. This can be seen from the previous source listing. Since the parameter is not used anywhere, it has been labeled `dummy_ptr` to note this. The functions also take a pointer to structure `svc_req` as the second argument – more on this later.

We are using a preprocessor directive `RPC_DEBUG` to compile in some code to print out the name of a server procedure being invoked on the console that ran the server application.

It is important that the scope of the return variable be greater than that of the server procedure, since it is returned to the underlying RPC mechanism for marshaling and transmission through to the other side. For this reason, the `result` variables have been declared static in the above example.

Here is the corresponding client side code for this implementation:

```
/*
 * dvd_client_wrapper.c
 */

#include <stdio.h>        /* fprintf */
#include <stdlib.h>       /* exit */
#include <rpc/rpc.h>      /* always required for RPC */
#include "dvd.h"
#include "dvd_store.h"    /* generated automatically by the rpcgen compiler */

static char *server_host_name = "localhost";
static  CLIENT *client = 0;

static void dvd_rpc_client_init(void);
static void dvd_rpc_client_shutdown(void);

int dvd_open_db(void)
{
    int *result;
    int status = DVD_ERR_BAD_DATABASE;

    if (0 == client) {
        /*
         * if a client handle does not exist, try to create one
         */
        dvd_rpc_client_init;
    }

    result = dvd_open_db_1((void *)0, client);
```

```
        if (NULL != result) {
            status = *result;
        } else {
            clnt_pcreateerror(server_host_name);
        }

        return (status);
}

int dvd_close_db(void)
{
    int *result;
    int status = DVD_ERR_BAD_DATABASE;

    if (0 != client) {
        result = dvd_close_db_1((void *)0, client);
        dvd_rpc_client_shutdown;
    }
    else {
        /*
         * looks like something beat us to it in tearing down the
         * RPC connection... has dvd_close_db been called before
         * dvd_open_db or dvd_open_db_login?
         */
#ifdef RPC_DEBUG
        fprintf(stderr,
            "RPC_CLIENT - dvd_close_db: handle is null at %s:%d\n",
            __FILE__, __LINE__);
#endif

        status = DVD_ERR_BAD_DATABASE;
    }

    if (NULL != result) {
        status = *result;
    } else {
        clnt_pcreateerror(server_host_name);
    }
    return (status);
}
```

We want the fact that we are using RPCs, to allow the DVD Store components to be distributed, to be as transparent as possible. The RPC code automatically initializes itself on the client-side when dvd_open_db or dvd_open_db_login are called – hiding the fact that RPC itself needs initialization from the programmer:

```
/*
 * ensure that when dvd_open_db or dvd_open_db_login is called
 * the RPC connection is created to the server process
 */
static void dvd_rpc_client_init(void) {
    client = clnt_create(server_host_name, DVD_STORE_PROG,
                         DVD_STORE_VERS, "tcp");
    if (NULL == client) {
        /*
```

```
         * unable to establish a connection with the server
         * so print an error message and stop
         */
        clnt_pcreateerror(server_host_name);
        exit(1);
    }
}

/*
 * tear down the RPC connection when dvd_close_db is called
 */
static void dvd_rpc_client_shutdown(void) {
    if (0 != client) {
        clnt_destroy(_client);
        client = 0;
    }
}
```

As you may have guessed, there is quite a bit more to the client implementation than the server implementation!

We'll start with the rather odd two functions at the end – dvd_rpc_client_init and dvd_rpc_client_shutdown. Both of these do not appear in dvd.h – in fact, there are local helper functions for the RPC client implementation:

❑   dvd_rpc_client_init is responsible for creating a connection to the RPC server. Usually it does this when a database session is started i.e. when dvd_open_db is invoked. It creates the connection to the server by calling:

```
CLIENT *clnt_create(const char *host, const u_long prognum, const u_long
versnum, const char *nettype);
```

and passing it the server host name, the program number (remember this from the program definition in dvd_store.x?), the program protocol version and the network protocol to use – in this case 'TCP', the Transmission Control Protocol from the TCP/IP suite.

clnt_create returns a pointer to an RPC structure called CLIENT – this is the client's handle to the RPC server. The client uses this handle in communicating with the server.

If the return value is a NULL pointer, then the call to clnt_create failed for some reason. In this case, we use:

```
void clnt_pcreateerror(const char *s);
```

to print the corresponding error message to standard error, and we terminate execution of the client.

You may notice that the server hostname is hard-coded to localhost. You can leave it like this if you plan to run both the server and client on the same machine – alternatively you can change this to the name of a distinct server machine. Ideally, a resource like this should be input from a configuration file, or use some other mechanism, such as broadcasting.

❑   dvd_rpc_client_shutdown is called to release the handle to the RPC server – this is indirectly invoked when dvd_close_db is called to end a database session. It releases the connection using:

```
void clnt_destroy(CLIENT *clnt);
```

passing it the client's handle to the RPC server as the only argument.

It should now become apparent why we showed both dvd_open_db and dvd_close_db being added to the RPC interface simultaneously, even though they are both simple functions. dvd_open_db creates the connection to the RPC server, and dvd_close_db releases it.

We now need to link these files with the files generated by rpcgen, and our application implementation, to enable us to test at least these two functions (dvd_open_db and dvd_close_db) over RPC. Before we do this, we need a short test file on the client side – we can use flatfile.c on the server side:

```
/*
 * dvd_test_client.c
 */

#include <stdio.h>
#include "dvd.h" /* note that this test file doesn't know anything about RPC
                  * - only the standard DVD API */

int main(int argc, char *argv[])
{
    int status;

    /******************************************************************
     * TEST 1 - Testing dvd_close_db without RPC connection setup
     *
     * this will print an error to the client console because
     * dvd_open_db/dvd_open_db_login has not happened first to setup
     * the RPC connection to the server
     ******************************************************************/
    {
        printf("\nTEST 1 - Testing dvd_close_db without"
               " RPC connection setup\n");
        status = dvd_close_db;

        if (DVD_SUCCESS != status)
            printf(" - passed\n");
        else
            printf(" - FAILED!\n");
    }


    /******************************************************************
     * TEST 2 - Testing dvd_today without pre-existing RPC connection
     ******************************************************************/
    {
        char *date;
```

```
        printf("\nTEST 2 - Testing dvd_today without pre-existing"
                " RPC connection\n");
        status = dvd_today(&date);

        if (DVD_SUCCESS == status) {
            printf(" - Todays date is %s [YYYYMMDD]\n", date);
            printf(" - passed\n");
        } else {
            printf(" - FAILED!\n");
        }

    }

    /*****************************************************************
     * TEST 3 - Testing dvd_open_db
     *****************************************************************/
    {
        printf("\nTEST 3 - Testing dvd_open_db\n");
        status = dvd_open_db;

        if (DVD_SUCCESS == status)
            printf(" - passed\n");
        else
            printf(" - FAILED!\n");
    }
```

At this stage, we are in a position to compile these simple routines into binaries ready to test. First, we generate the stub files:

$ **rpcgen dvd_store.x**

Now we link the files required for the server – the wrapper file we created, the server stub generated by the rpcgen compiler, the XDR stub, and the actual backend implementation – for simplicity here, we will use the flat file version:

$ **gcc –DRPC_DEBUG –o dvd_rpc_server dvd_server_wrapper.c dvd_store_svc.c dvd_store_xdr.c flatfile.c**

Similarly, the client is built from the client wrapper, client stub, XDR stub, and the client application:

$ **gcc –DRPC_DEBUG –o dvd_rpc_client dvd_client_wrapper.c dvd_store_clnt.c dvd_store_xdr.c dvd_test_client.c**

So far, so good! This build process can be used to build all of the examples, as functionality is added and developed through this chapter. To give you an impression of the final product, the output from the client should look something like:

```
RPC_CLIENT - dvd_close_db: handle is null at dvd_client_wrapper.c:110
RPC_CLIENT - dvd_today: handle is null at dvd_client_wrapper.c:765
RPC_CLIENT - dvd_today: making temporary RPC connection
localhost: RPC: Success
```

```
TEST 1 - Testing dvd_close_db without RPC connection setup
 - passed

TEST 2 - Testing dvd_today without pre-existing RPC connection
 - Todays date is 20000717 [YYYYMMDD]
 - passed

TEST 3 - Testing dvd_open_db
 - passed

TEST 4 - Testing dvd_today
 - Todays date is 20000717 [YYYYMMDD]
 - passed

TEST 5 - Testing dvd_err_text
 - 001 : unknown error type: 1 - passed
 - 000 : no error - passed
 - -01 : cannot open file - passed
        etc. (more error codes…)


TEST 6 - Testing dvd_get_genre_list
 - Number of genres - 007
 - 000 : Action
 - 001 : Education
 -       etc… (more genres…)
 - passed

TEST 7 - Testing dvd_get_classification_list
 - Number of classes - 006
 - 000 : E
 - 001 : U
 - 002 : PG
 - 003 : 12
 - 004 : 15
 - 005 : 18
 - passed

TEST 8 - Testing dvd_member_create
 - assigned member id is #5
 - passed

TEST X - Testing dvd_member_search
 - count is 001
 - result[000] is 005
 - passed

    etc… (other API tests…)

TEST X - Testing dvd_close
 - passed
```

and the server test output (edited for brevity) should be:

```
RPC_SERVER: dvd_today_1_svc called
RPC_SERVER: dvd_open_db_1_svc called
RPC_SERVER: dvd_today_1_svc called
RPC_SERVER: dvd_err_text_1_svc called
RPC_SERVER: dvd_err_text_1_svc called
        .
        .
        .
RPC_SERVER: dvd_get_genre_list_1_svc called
RPC_SERVER: dvd_get_classification_list_1_svc called
RPC_SERVER: dvd_member_create_1_svc called
RPC_SERVER: dvd_member_search_1_svc called
RPC_SERVER: dvd_member_get_id_from_number_1_svc called
RPC_SERVER: dvd_title_create_1_svc called
RPC_SERVER: dvd_disk_create_1_svc called
RPC_SERVER: dvd_disk_delete_1_svc called
RPC_SERVER: dvd_title_delete_1_svc called
RPC_SERVER: dvd_member_delete_1_svc called
RPC_SERVER: dvd_close_db_1_svc called
```

The following diagram shows the flow of control when the client application invokes one of these DVD functions:

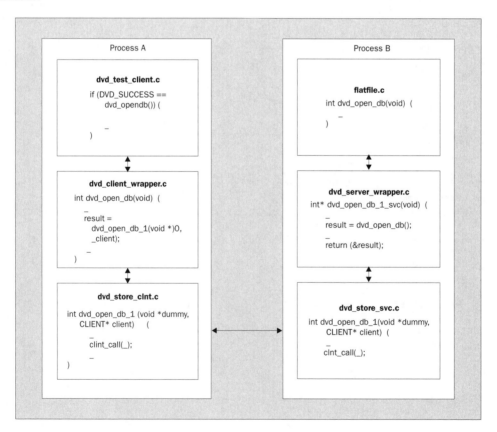

The client wrapper presents the client application with the standard DVD API, but in effect it constructs the message for the RPC stub. This is marshaled and transported from the client process to the server process. Here, it is received by the server stubs and de-marshaled. Then the procedure decoded and dispatched to the server wrapper, which reconstructs the standard DVD API call. It then takes the response from the database, and returns the value; again back across the RPC interface to the client process.

It makes no difference to the client code whether the server application is located on the same machine, or in an entirely different machine. In fact, it doesn't even matter if the remote machine is a different CPU, running a different operating system, with a different endianness and word-size, as long as both support the ONC-RPC protocol.

Functions with Simple Arguments and Simple Return Types

OK, let's consider the case where the function takes an argument:

```
int dvd_member_delete(const int member_id);
```

There is not much more involved here than the previous example. Here is the additional code required to add a procedure definition to the dvd_store.x file:

```
int DVD_MEMBER_DELETE(int) = 7;
```

Here is the code for the server wrapper of this procedure:

```
/* server wrapper function for dvd_member_delete */
int * dvd_member_delete_1_svc(int *member_id_ptr, struct svc_req * svc_req_ptr)
{
  static int result;

#ifdef RPC_DEBUG
  fputs("RPC_SERVER: dvd_member_delete_1_svc called\n", stderr);
#endif

  result = dvd_member_delete(*member_id_ptr);

  return (&result);
}
```

Nothing much to remark about here, except perhaps that the first argument to the function is now a pointer to the member_id value. Here is the corresponding client wrapper function for this procedure:

```
/* client wrapper function for dvd_member_delete */
int dvd_member_delete(const int member_id)
{
  int *result;
  int status = DVD_ERR_BAD_DATABASE;

  if (0 == _client) {
    /*
     * if the client handle is zero, i.e. this function has been called
     * before either dvd_open_db or dvd_open_db_login, then flag this
     * as an error and die
```

```
        */
#ifdef RPC_DEBUG
    fprintf(stderr,
        "RPC_CLIENT - dvd_member_delete: handle is null at %s:%d\n",
        __FILE__, __LINE__);
#endif
    return (status);
  }

  result = dvd_member_delete_1(&member_id, _client);

  if (NULL != result) {
    status = *result;
  } else {
    clnt_pcreateerror(server_host_name);
  }

  return (status);
}
```

You can see here that we check if the client handle to the RPC server is 0 before invoking the client stub to issue the RPC request. If so, we print the function name, filename and line number to standard error, and terminate execution.

We now need to check the result of the RPC stub call to ensure it is not NULL. It could be NULL if the stub function failed completely. If so, we call clnt_pcreateerror to print the error message to standard error.

Otherwise, we copy the result status into our status variable, and return this. Actually, this step isn't needed for this particular example, since the return type is the status int. For more complicated return types, as will be presented in the next section, we will need to copy out of a status field in the return from the RPC stub.

Note that there is no need to explicitly call free to release the memory returned by the RPC client stub. If you have a look at the code for dvd_store_clnt.c, you will see that the return variable is actually statically defined inside the scope of the stub function, and that a reference to it is returned. As a result, it would be a mistake to call free – in fact, it would most likely generate a segmentation violation.

More Complex Examples

Now, for something more challenging. This function takes a structure pointer as the parameter, and returns an int. However, all may not be as it seems at first glance:

```
int dvd_member_create(dvd_store_member *member_record_to_add,
         int *member_id);
```

Notice the fact that the member_record_to_add and the member_id variables are passed by reference to the function. In the DVD store application, any parameter to a function that is not changed by the function is explicitly typed as const. These parameters are modified inside the function, and as a result are passed in by address rather than by value. We know from our knowledge of the DVD application that this function is passed a partially filled in dvd_store_member structure, and that it returns the completed structure, a member_id number, and also a status value.

This function shows that it is important to understand the semantics of the API, and not just the syntax of the language it is implemented in. In essence, the dvd_member_create function takes one argument – the partially completed dvd_store_member structure. It returns three values – the completed dvd_store_member, the member identifier, and also the status value.

Here are the additional lines to define this return structure in the type definition section of the dvd_store.x file:

```
/*
 * RPC protocol interface for dvd_member_create
 * The % character means do not the interpret line, but pass it directly
 * through to C code
 */

%#ifndef _DVD_H
%#define _DVD_H

/* const size definitions */
const MEMBER_KNOWN_ID_LEN = 6;
const PERSON_TITLE_LEN = 4;
const NAME_LEN = 26;
const ADDRESS_LEN = 51;
const STATE_LEN = 3;
const PHONE_NO_LEN = 31;
const ZIP_CODE_LEN = 11;
const DVD_TITLE_LEN = 61;
const ASIN_LEN = 11;
const GENRE_LEN = 21;
const CLASS_LEN = 11;
const DAY_DATE_LEN = 9;
const COST_LEN = 7;

/* type definitions */
struct dvd_store_member {
  int member_id;
  char member_no[MEMBER_KNOWN_ID_LEN];
  char title[PERSON_TITLE_LEN];
  char fname[NAME_LEN];
  char lname[NAME_LEN];
  char house_flat_ref[NAME_LEN];
  char address1[ADDRESS_LEN];
  char address2[ADDRESS_LEN];
  char town[ADDRESS_LEN];
  char state[STATE_LEN];
  char phone[PHONE_NO_LEN];
  char zipcode[ZIP_CODE_LEN];
};

%#endif

struct dvd_member_create_res {
  int status;
  dvd_store_member updated_member_record;
  int member_id;
};
```

The dvd_store_member structure needs to be defined in the dvd_store.x file, to enable the rpcgen compiler to generate the correct XDR stubs to transport this structure across the network. However, this can cause us problems – especially since this structure is defined in dvd.h, and our client and server stubs will be inheriting this file also (for error codes, for example). The solution is to guard dvd.h by using the standard C pre-processor mechanism to prevent multiple inclusions. In this case, we are using a #define based on the file name – i.e. _DVD_H. We can then check for this in the dvd_store.x file. The % character instructs rpcgen not to interpret the line, but to pass it through directly to the generated C code.

The lengths of the string fields in dvd_store_member are fixed. This allows us to use a fixed char array in our protocol definition, rather than the generic string foo definition.

And we define the function interface in the dvd_store.x file like this:

```
dvd_member_create_res DVD_MEMBER_CREATE(dvd_store_member) = 6;
```

The server wrapper for this function deserves some discussion, as it is the first time we will use a structure for the return type:

```
/* server wrapper function for dvd_member_create_res */

dvd_member_create_res * dvd_member_create_1_svc(dvd_store_member *member_ptr,
struct svc_req * svc_req_ptr)
{
  static dvd_member_create_res result;
  result.updated_member_record = *member_ptr;

#ifdef RPC_DEBUG
  fputs("RPC_SERVER: dvd_member_create_1_svc called\n", stderr);
#endif

  result.status = dvd_member_create(&(result.updated_member_record),
&(result.member_id));

  return(&result);
}
```

result is now a static instance of the return structure. The updated_member_record field is initialized from the partially filled-in structure passed (via a pointer) as an argument into the function.

Then, the real dvd_member_create function is called, with a reference to this structure and the member id field.

On return, dvd_member_create has initialized the member_id field, and filled in the missing values in the dvd_member_structure. Now, the work of the server wrapper is done, and we can return this to the RPC mechanism underneath.

As usual, the client side code required is more verbose:

```
int dvd_member_create(dvd_store_member *member_record_to_add, int *member_id)
{
  dvd_member_create_res *result;
  int status = DVD_ERR_BAD_DATABASE;

  if (0 == _client) {
    /*
     * if the client handle is zero, i.e. this function has been called
     * before either dvd_open_db or dvd_open_db_login, then flag this
     * as an error and die
     */
#ifdef RPC_DEBUG
    fprintf(stderr,
      "RPC_CLIENT - dvd_member_create: handle is null at %s:%d\n",
      __FILE__, __LINE__);
#endif
    return (status);
  }

  result = dvd_member_create_1(member_record_to_add, _client);

  if (NULL != result) {
    if (DVD_SUCCESS == result->status) {
      /* structure copy */
      *member_record_to_add = result->updated_member_record;
      *member_id = result->member_id;
    }

    status = result->status;
  } else {
    clnt_pcreateerror(server_host_name);
  }

  return (status);
}
```

First, we perform the usual check to ensure we have a valid handle to the RPC server. Then we call the stub function to perform the RPC call, and then invoke the functionality on the server side.

Again, we check the result of the RPC stub call to ensure it is not NULL. If not, we check the status of the returned value to ensure that the function completed successfully according to the DVD Store API. If so, we copy the updated_member_record into the structure passed by reference to the local dvd_member_create call in the client, we update the member_id. We don't do this if the status reports unsuccessful – does not equal to DVD_SUCCESS.

Either way, we return the status value.

Returning Arrays

Some of the functions in the `dvd.h` API return lists of items:

```
int dvd_get_genre_list(char **genre_list[], int *count);
int dvd_disk_search(const int title_id, int *result_ids[], int *count);
```

To illustrate how to return a list (or array), we'll show the RPC Language definition for these functions, and also the C implementation of the server and client-side wrappers for both:

```
/* new additions to dvd_store.x */
typedef int int_array<>;
typedef string string_array<>;
```

`<>` means create an array of unspecified size. The `rpcgen` compiler will realize this using a structure containing a pointer to the type of the array, and a size value:

```
struct dvd_get_genre_list_res {
  int status;
  string_array genre_list<>;
  int count;
};

struct dvd_disk_search_res {
  int status;
  int_array result_ids;
  int count;
};

    dvd_disk_search_res DVD_DISK_SEARCH(int) = 19;
    dvd_get_genre_list_res DVD_GET_GENRE_LIST(void) = 21;
```

We first create a type called `string_array`, which holds a variable number of strings. Then we create the return structure for `dvd_get_genre_list` – with a status value, a count of the number of strings returned, and a variable array of strings of variable length.

For `dvd_disk_search`, we do something similar – we create the return structure, with a status value, a count of the number of disk identifiers being returned, and the array itself.

Here is the server implementation of these functions:

```
dvd_disk_search_res * dvd_disk_search_1_svc(int *disk_id_ptr,
            struct svc_req * svc_req_ptr)
{
  static dvd_disk_search_res result;

#ifdef RPC_DEBUG
  fputs("RPC_SERVER: dvd_disk_search_1_svc called\n", stderr);
#endif

  result.status = dvd_disk_search(*disk_id_ptr,
     &(result.result_ids.int_array_val),
     &(result.count));
```

```
      result.result_ids.int_array_len = result.count;

      return (&result);
   }


   dvd_get_genre_list_res * dvd_get_genre_list_1_svc(void *dummy_ptr,
                   struct svc_req * svc_req_ptr)
   {
     static dvd_get_genre_list_res result;

#ifdef RPC_DEBUG
     fputs("RPC_SERVER: dvd_get_genre_list_1_svc called\n", stderr);
#endif
     result.status = dvd_get_genre_list(&(result.genre_list.genre_list_val),
&(result.count));
     result.genre_list.genre_list_len = result.count;

     return (&result);
   }
```

The important point to note about the server implementation is how the arrays are initialized for the return. For dvd_disk_search, the results_id array becomes a structure with two fields – int_array_val, which is an actual int pointer, and int_array_len, which must be set to the number of elements in the array. Note that the rpcgen compiler has named the fields in the results_id structure after their type – int_array.

For dvd_get_genre_list, the rpcgen compiler again creates two fields – genre_list_val, which is the pointer to the list of NULL-terminated strings, and genre_list_count, which is the number of strings being returned. Note that in this case, rpcgen has named the fields in the genre_list after the name of the structure.

The corresponding client wrapper implementation for these functions looks like this:

```
   int dvd_disk_search(const int title_id, int *result_ids[], int *count)
   {
     dvd_disk_search_res *result;
     int status = DVD_ERR_BAD_DATABASE;

     if (0 == _client) {
       /*
        * if the client handle is zero, i.e. this function has been called
        * before either dvd_open_db or dvd_open_db_login, then flag this
        * as an error and die
        */
#ifdef RPC_DEBUG
       fprintf(stderr,
          "RPC_CLIENT - dvd_disk_search: handle is null" at %s:%d\n",
          __FILE__, __LINE__);
#endif
       return (status);
     }
```

```
    result = dvd_disk_search_1((int *)&title_id, _client);

    if (NULL != result) {
      if (DVD_SUCCESS == result->status) {
        *result_ids = (result->result_ids).int_array_val;
        *count = result->count;
      }

      status = result->status;
    } else {
      clnt_pcreateerror(server_host_name);
    }

    return (status);
}

int dvd_get_genre_list(char **genre_list[], int *count)
{
  dvd_get_genre_list_res *result;
  int status = DVD_ERR_BAD_DATABASE;

  if (0 == _client) {
    /*
     * if the client handle is zero, i.e. this function has been called
     * before either dvd_open_db or dvd_open_db_login, then flag this
     * as an error and die
     */
#ifdef RPC_DEBUG
    fprintf(stderr, "RPC_CLIENT - dvd_get_genre_list: handle is null at %s:%d\n",
      __FILE__, __LINE__);
#endif
    return (status);
  }

  result = dvd_get_genre_list_1((void *)0, _client);

  if (NULL != result) {
    if (DVD_SUCCESS == result->status) {
      *genre_list = (result->genre_list).genre_list_val;
      *count = (result->count);
    }

    status = result->status;
  } else {
    clnt_pcreateerror(server_host_name);
  }

  return (status);
}
```

At this stage, the implementation of both of the above functions should be relatively easy to understand. We know that both functions are returning their results in a structure, which contains the array, a count of the array size and also the status. The wrapper function just needs to extract this information and return it back to the caller in the correct format.

However, the arrays have been declared in the RPC Protocol Definition file, `dvd_store.x`, as of variable length. In this case, the client stubs will dynamically allocate memory to hold this array on the stack. It is the responsibility of the programmer to ensure that this memory is freed at a later stage.

For the arrays used in the DVD Store Application, it is possible just to use `free` to release the memory. However, if there were arrays of more complicated structures (especially structures containing structures, etc.), you should use XDR to release XDR allocated memory. The procedure for doing this is to copy the array into locally allocated space in the client wrapper function, and to use XDR to free the previous memory allocated in the stub. The following example illustrates this for `dvd_get_genre_list`:

```
if (NULL != result) {
  if (DVD_SUCCESS == result->status) {
    /*
     * original code:
     *
     * *genre_list = (result->genre_list).genre_list_val;
     * *count = (result->count);
     */

    int i;
    XDR xdr;

    *count = (result->count);
    *genre_list = malloc(sizeof(char **) * (result->count));

    for (i = 0; i < ((result->genre_list).genre_list_len); i++)
    {
      int string_len =
        strlen((result->genre_list).genre_list_val[i]) + 1;

      (*genre_list)[i] = malloc(sizeof(char) * string_len);
      strcpy((*genre_list)[i],
        ((result->genre_list).genre_list_val)[i]);
    }

    xdr.x_op = XDR_FREE;
    xdr_bytes(&xdr,
      (char **) &((result->genre_list).genre_list_val),
      &((result->genre_list).genre_list_len), 0);
  }

  status = result->status;
} else {
  clnt_pcreateerror(server_host_name);
}
```

Client Timeouts

In some situations, it may be that the server processes get overloaded with requests. In particular, this might be the case if there were a large number of DVD Stores all using the same centralized server. In circumstances like this, it is often useful to have the client application *timeout* its requests to the server after a particular period of time – perhaps then prompting the user, and allowing them to retry to procedure if appropriate.

It is possible to explicitly add a timeout value to client requests, rather than accept the default. Initializing a `struct timeval` parameter, and using `clnt_control` to set this on the client's server handle achieves this. In our RPC example, the place to do this is in file `dvd_client_wrapper.c`, function `dvd_rpc_client_init`:

```
/* function from dvd_client_wrapper.c */
static void dvd_rpc_client_init(void) {
    client = clnt_create(server_host_name, DVD_STORE_PROG,
                         DVD_STORE_VERS, "tcp");
    if (NULL == client) {
        /*
         * unable to establish a connection with the server
         * so print an error message and stop
         */
        clnt_pcreateerror(server_host_name);
        exit(1);
    }

    /* this following code sets up a 60 second timeout on client requests */
    {
        struct timeval tv;

        tv.tv_sec = 60;
        tv.tv_usec = 0;
        clnt_control(client, CLSET_TIMEOUT, (char *)&tv);
    }
}
```

Authentication

So far in our DVD Store RPC application, the server did not require the client to identify itself. In fact, the client never even attempted to. Authentication is the name given to the process whereby the client provides this information to the server, and the server uses it to determine whether to service the request from the client, or to reject it.

Authentication can be done either using the authentication mechanisms supported by RPC itself, or entirely at an application level (for example, using functions like `dvd_open_db_login`). The author of an application may choose to use an authentication scheme apart from the RPC application. For example, we could demand a Kerberos ticket before processing an RPC request. Better still, we could use Pluggable Authentication Modules (PAM), which we investigated in Chapter 12, and pick a simple scheme while testing and then plugging in a better scheme for production. Obviously, one thing to be aware of when using non-encrypted passwords is that transmission of plaintext over a physical network is open to the possibility of eavesdropping.

There are a number of authentication mechanisms supported by RPC:

- ❑ AUTH_NONE – this is for no authentication, and is the default value

- ❑ AUTH_UNIX – this is authentication using UNIX system credentials – UIDs and GIDs

- ❑ AUTH_DES – this is the use of the DES algorithm

- ❑ AUTH_KERBEROS – this is RPC authentication based on Kerberos tickets

We are going to show a simple example of using AUTH_UNIX in our DVD Store RPC wrappers

AUTH_NONE

As mentioned, AUTH_NONE is used to specify no authentication is being used over the link. No data structures are allocated for authentication on the client side, and no clean-up needs to be done afterwards. If the programmer does not explicitly select an authentication style, this is the default.

AUTH_UNIX

Here, we will add the simplest of the RPC supported authentication mechanisms to our client and server wrapper files – authentication using UNIX system credentials (hostname, uid, and gids). Bear in mind that this would be transmitted in plain text over the wire, and could be considered even worse than no authentication. It reveals to the world all kinds of interesting information about your network.

Client-Side Authentication Support

As with the client timeout, all modifications to authentication are performed inside the dvd_rpc_client_init function in dvd_client_wrapper.c:

```
/* functions from dvd_client_wrapper.c */
static void dvd_rpc_client_init(void) {
    client = clnt_create(server_host_name, DVD_STORE_PROG,
                         DVD_STORE_VERS, "tcp");
    if (NULL == client) {
        /*
         * unable to establish a connection with the server
         * so print an error message and stop
         */
        clnt_pcreateerror(server_host_name);
        exit(1);
    }

    /* add default UNIX-based authentication here */
    client->cl_auth = (AUTH *)authunix_create_default;
}

/*
 * tear down the RPC connection when dvd_close_db is called
 */
static void dvd_rpc_client_shutdown(void) {
    if (0 != client) {
        /*
```

```
         * if we have added an authentication mechanism, then we
         * need to clean-up here
         */
        auth_destroy(client->cl_auth);

        clnt_destroy(client);
        client = 0;
    }
}
```

The `client` structure used to store the server's handle contains a field specifying the authentication style being used – `cl_auth`. Here we are initializing this field with UNIX credential authentication – we do this by calling:

```
AUTH * authunix_create_default(void);
```

When we use a form of authentication other than the default `AUTH_NONE`, we must ensure that we delete any allocated memory when the RPC connection is being closed. We do this using `auth_destroy`, and passing it the `cl_auth` field of the `CLIENT` structure:

```
void auth_destroy(AUTH *auth);
```

Server-Side Authentication Support

Earlier in the chapter, we introduced `svc_req`, and mentioned that it is used by the server routines. We are now going to make use of this structure, as it passes in authentication information to the server wrapper routines.

The format of the `struct svc_req` structure is:

```
struct svc_req {
    u_long rq_prog;              /* service program number */
    u_long rq_vers;              /* service protocol version */
    u_long rq_proc;              /* procedure number */
    struct opaque_auth rq_cred;  /* raw credentials (from network) */
    caddr_t rq_clntcred;         /* credentials (Read Only) */
    SVCXPRT *rq_xprt;            /* pointer containing information on
                                  * associated transport */
}
```

The server application is then presented the authentication information in the credentials pointer of the `svc_req_prt`. However, these credentials are presented in a 'raw' format – basically the format they were transmitted over the wire. In order to be of any use to us, we need to convert this 'raw' format to the structure we are using for our authentication style. The format of the `AUTH_UNIX` credentials structure is:

```
/* AUTH_UNIX credentials */
struct authunix_parms {
    u_long aup_time;        /* creation time for the credentials */
    char *aup_machname;     /*client host name */
    uid_t aup_uid;          /* users' uid */
    gid_t aup_gid;          /* users' primary gid */
    u_int aup_len;          /* number of extra gids in aup_gids array */
    gid_t *aup_gids;        /* array of gids */
};
```

Here is how we modify a function wrapper from `dvd_server_wrapper.c` to handle authentication:

```
/* function from dvd_server_wrapper.c */
int * dvd_open_db_1_svc(void *dummy_ptr, struct svc_req * svc_req_prt)
{
    static int result = 0;  /* must be static */
#ifdef RPC_DEBUG
    fputs("RPC_SERVER: dvd_open_db_1_svc called\n", stderr);
#endif

    /*
     * authentication for this function - if this is to be used across all
     * functions, then it should be moved out into a function call of its
     * own
     */
    {
        struct authunix_parms* unix_cred;

        switch ((svc_req_ptr->rq_cred).oa_flavor) {
        case AUTH_UNIX:
            unix_cred = (struct authunix_parms *)svc_req_ptr->rq_clntcred;
            fprintf(stderr, "RPC_SERVER: AUTH-UNIX - UID of client is %d\n",
                unix_cred->aup_uid);
            fprintf(stderr,
                "RPC_SERVER: AUTH-UNIX - machine name of client is %s\n",
                unix_cred->aup_machname);
            break;

        case AUTH_NONE:     /* fallthrough is deliberate */
        case AUTH_DEFAULT:
            svcerr_weakauth(svc_req_ptr->rq_xprt);
            result = DVD_ERR_BAD_DATABASE; /* in real life we would
                                            * define a new error code */
            return (&result);
    }

    result = dvd_open_db;

    return (&result);
}
```

We check the 'flavor' of authentication by performing a switch on the `oa_flavor` field of the `rq_cred`. In our example, we are using `AUTH_UNIX`. We copy the 'raw' credentials from the format transported into a `struct authunix parms`, as described above. This then gives us access to the UID, and the hostname, as shown, and also to the GIDs. At this stage, it is up to the application to somehow determine whether these credentials are suitable for access to the service.

Obviously Unix authentication may not be so useful when the UIDs and GIDs do not correspond from client host to server host – the use of a distributed namespace service like NIS may help here.

NIS provides unified login between a number of systems. It also provides for a limited form of unified configuration name space (sharing information typically found in files such as /etc/passwd, /etc/hosts, /etc/services, /etc/group etc.)

687

If another form of authentication is being used other than the form we expect, we can call `svcerr_weakauth`, passing in the pointer to the transport information from `struct svc_req`.

If we were basing our authentication on a particular UID, or a particular hostname, we could call `svcerr_systemerr` instead to indicate that the error was due to an application issue, and not an RPC issue. `svcerr_systemerr` also takes the pointer to the transport information from `struct svc_req`.

Using RPC Servers with /etc/inetd.conf

By passing a command line argument to `rpcgen`, it is possible to get the stub compiler to generate server stubs that can be spawned automatically by `inetd`, the Internet super-server when an RPC request arrives:

```
$ rpcgen -I dvd_store.x
```

The main difference in the code generated here is that `inetd` handles most of the socket-related networking and instead presents the RPC application with a network endpoint bound to standard in and standard output. Thus, the RPC stub server must, in its internals, use file descriptors 0 and 1 to receive and transmit data. This is what the `-I` command line argument enables.

The following line shows how the `dvd_rpc_server`, linked with the server stubs created using `rpcgen` as above, would be configured to run using `/etc/inetd.conf`, the configuration file for `inetd`:

```
# name/vers endpoint rpc/proto wait|nowait user.group svc_prog svc_prog_args
dvd_store/1 stream rpc/tcp nowait dvd.dvd /home/dvd/dvd_rpc_server
```

The fields are:

- ❏ `dvd_store/1` – the service name and version number. A version range is also allowed (that is `nfsd/2-3`).

- ❏ `stream` – the endpoint for a stream socket (that is TCP, since it is used in the DVD_Store application). `dgram` would be used for a datagram socket (for example UDP).

- ❏ `rpc/tcp` – specifies the service uses the RPC protocol and TCP-based communication.

- ❏ `nowait` – do not wait to release the socket.

- ❏ `dvd.dvd` – the username to run the server as is `dvd`, the group is `dvd`.

- ❏ `/home/dvd/dvd_rpc_server` – the pathname to run the program.

- ❏ any command line argument would go next (including argument 0 – the program name).

Since the service is identified by name in `/etc/inetd.conf`, the `portmapper` has to be able to map a service number to this name. This is done by adding the following line to `/etc/rpc`, the RPC program number database:

```
# name_of_svc prog_number aliases
dvd_store    536871065   dvd_rpc_server
```

It is quite common that such servers would typically respond to a request, and then stay running for a period of time to determine if further requests are likely. If no request arrives in this period, then the server shuts down again.

This timeout value is specifiable in seconds by using the -K command line argument:

```
$ rpcgen -I -K 15 dvd_store.x
```

This will generate an inetd compatible server that, after receiving a request, will wait for 15 seconds before shutting down.

This would probably not make much sense using the DVD Store application from inetd.conf – we are not really worried about load on machine, and besides, the server side should keep running, since it probably has an open connection to the PostgreSQL database.

Other Methods to Simplify Network Programming

RPC was invented quite a while ago now. Since then, new technologies such as C++, Java and the concepts of software components have arrived. Many developers are now working using the object-oriented paradigm, and considered this a suitable model for network communications. As a result, there are many mechanisms to provide remote communication between objects – however most developers are segregated into one of two camps:

❑ Microsoft has developed its own technology, by extending its Component Object Model (COM) in Windows and calling it the Distributed Component Object Model (DCOM). DCOM invokes object methods layered upon the Microsoft implementation of DCE-RPC to support remote objects. DCE-RPC is a slightly different variant of remote procedure calls, developed by the Open Software Foundation (now the Open Group), the developers of Motif. Unfortunately, DCE-RPC is incompatible with ONC-RPC. Microsoft's DCE-RPC implementation may even be incompatible with standard DCE-RPC. DCE-RPC is available for Linux, and ONC-RPC is also available for Windows.

❑ Almost everyone else has rallied around an open standard called the Common Object Request Broker Architecture (CORBA). We will read about CORBA in Chapters 20 and 21.

Resources

In Linux, RPC generally comes as part of the `glibc` package. Unfortunately, many Linux distributions at the time of writing do not come with help manual pages describing the RPC functions such as `clnt_create`, `clnt_control`, etc.

Quite a share of information can be found on-line on the Internet in relation to ONC-RPCs. Many of the documents below provide useful background information on the topics presented in this chapter. In particular, the Compaq Tru64 documentation (and to a slightly lesser extent the UnixWare 7 documentation) is, for the most part, generally applicable to the implementation of ONC-RPC for Linux.

❑ Programming with RPCs, UnixWare 7 Documentation, Santa Cruz Operation Inc., http://uw7doc.sco.com/SDK_netapi/CTOC-rpcpN.intro.html.

❑ Programming with ONC-RPCs, Tru64 v4.0G Documentation, Compaq Computer Corporation Inc. http://www.unix.digital.com/faqs/publications/base_doc /DOCUMENTATION/V40G_HTML/AQ0R5BTE/TITLE.HTM.

❑ RPC: Remote Procedure Call Protocol Specification Version 2, R. Srinivasan, Sun Microsystems, August 1995, RFC 1831.

❑ XDR: External Data Representation Standard, R. Srinivasan, Sun Microsystems, August 1995, RFC 1832.

❑ Authentication Mechanisms for ONC RPC, A. Chiu, Sun Microsystems, September 1999, RFC 2695.

❑ NFS Version 3 Protocol Specification, B. Callaghan et al, Sun Microsystems, June 1995, RFC 1813.

❑ CORBA – http://www.omg.org/.

❑ DCOM for Linux – http://www.softwareag.com/entirex/services/faq.htm.

Summary

In this chapter, we have discussed some of the reasons for moving from a local procedure-based application to the use of remote procedure calls. The benefits of moving from a single-process, single-machine implementation of the application to a distributed system were explained.

As a first attempt at network-enabling the DVD Store application, we used the BSD socket API. This allows tremendous flexibility in coding the client/server programs, but at the expense of tediousness and verbosity of code. As such, it is often quite prone to error.

Remote Procedure Calls were then introduced as a programming technique to simplify the life of the developer. It reduces development time, and helps ensure that the resulting application is less prone to network-related coding errors.

We have just scratched the surface of remote procedure calls. There is an additional wealth of features available to the programmer, depending on how low-level you wish to start your coding. There is also the category of datagram-based RPCs, which we have not mentioned in this chapter.

Nevertheless, we have shown how a typical medium to large application, such as the DVD Store, can make use of RPCs in moving from a monolithic system to a more distributed architecture. In future chapters, we will introduce a more advanced network programming technique to enable this: the Common Object Request Broker Architecture (CORBA).

19

Multimedia and Linux

We're now going to take a break from our main DVD Store theme and focus on an area in which DVDs themselves play no small part. Multimedia can be defined as the integrated presentation of text, graphics, video, animation, and sound on a computer.

First, we'll take a look at the current support for multimedia in Linux.

We're going to look at various audio devices, formats and their corresponding players, and take a brief look at how we can play sound ourselves. Likewise, we'll look at some of the animation and video formats that are available, and again, some players that can be used to play them. Finally, we will look briefly at some recent efforts to create software or software-assisted DVD players, and provide some pointers to where you can find more information.

The Current State of Affairs

Linux is not currently well known as a multimedia platform; this is principally due to the lack of device driver support that exists. There are several reasons for this:

❑ Most people creating hardware drivers are interested only in writing them for specific (usually business-related) tasks. That's why, if you take a look in the kernel, you'll see a plethora of drivers for network cards and networking in general, ISDN cards, SCSI drivers and very little fun-related (although the joystick section had quite a few entries in version 2.2.15).

❑ Companies manufacturing multimedia devices are rather tight-lipped when it comes to the inner workings of their products. This may be because of contractual obligations – their hardware uses technologies licensed from other companies, or proprietary algorithms embedded in their firmware.

A notorious example of this is that of the cheap DVD (MPEG-2) decoder cards that you can find in stores nowadays for about $75 or less. Until recently, the manufacturers of these cards were not willing to give up their specifications for fear of being sued by the MPAA, the Motion Picture Association of America.

❑ Economics. Linux isn't currently the platform generating the most revenue for multimedia hardware manufacturers, so they are unwilling to devote a lot of time and resources to writing Linux drivers (even though it might actually be easier to do so for Linux than it is for Windows).

With Linux gaining in popularity, some of these manufacturers are starting to say that they will support Linux in the future; so far though, none have fulfilled that promise. However, there are beta drivers available for many popular cards that may work for you; you can find out more about these at http://www.linuxvideo.org .

❑ Some companies believe that writing a device driver for Linux is too much work. In some cases this is true, since they're often unwilling to publish the drivers' source code. Drivers therefore have to be released in binary form, with a different version for every possible kernel configuration. It's a familiar problem – This type of company usually thinks that releasing the specifications on what they produce would give their competitors an unfair advantage.

This doesn't necessarily have to be the case in future, particularly considering the speed of current developments in the world of multimedia. Linux multimedia is by no means impossible; if we thought it was, then this would be a very short chapter! However, it does require a careful choice of hardware.

If you're already the owner of a piece of hardware that doesn't work with Linux, you can do a lot worse than complaining (and complaining loudly) to its manufacturer.

Software companies can be just as bad – at time of writing there are several fully functional software DVD players for Windows, but none for Linux. There are currently two projects attempting to remedy that situation (one of which we'll look at towards the end of the chapter), and one of the companies behind a Windows player has promised that there will be one for Linux 'soon'.

Of course, as Linux gains in popularity, it should just be a matter of time before companies recognize it as a serious factor – there are already companies producing capture cards designed especially for Linux. Furthermore, there are various websites (http://www.linuxtv.org for example) that try to unify thoughts about a DVD programming interface; have a look – you may be able to contribute!

Program Integration

If you are writing a program that will use multimedia elements, then you may well consider using an existing program. For example, if you simply wanted to add a soundtrack to your program's existing output, you'd just add a call or two to an external player and save yourself the trouble of reinventing the wheel.

This is the approach taken by most e-mail programs and web-browsers such as Netscape Navigator. To find an external viewer appropriate to the extension or MIME type used, they read system-specific files (usually /etc/mailcap and /etc/mime.types) find the associated viewer, and start it up.

This is called loose integration, and is the opposite of tight integration (where program and viewer usually run in the same memory space and talk to each other by means of a predefined API). Web browsers usually support both, supporting the latter form by means of **plugins**. The advantage of tight integration over loose integration is most apparent in the case of graphical content: tightly integrated graphical data usually looks like an integral part of a page, while an external viewer has no context and opens up a separate window. In most cases this will distract from the rest of the information being presented. Tight integration is not limited to web-browsers; the GIMP also relies on several plugins, which adhere to the GIMP API.

Sound

A large number of sound cards are now supported under Linux. Unfortunately though, not all the necessary drivers are included with the standard Linux kernel. In most cases though, you can find the ones you need on the Web – either on the card vendor's site, on 4Front Technologies' site, or at Alsa Linux. For those of you unfamiliar with these names, here's a little bit of history.

In the early days of Linux, when soundcard vendors weren't eager to hand out specifications for free, they were sometimes willing to make them available under non-disclosure agreements and only to companies, not individuals.

The people writing Linux soundcard drivers at the time decided that it would be better to have distributable binary drivers than no drivers at all, so they started their own company '4Front Technologies' and created binary distributions, under a unified low-level API, known as OSS (OpenSoundSystem). They still contributed some of their work to the kernel as OSS/Lite. The complete version is OSS/Full and can be found at http://www.opensound.com.

Others did not agree with this philosophy. Unsatisfied with the state of affairs, they started their own project, one that would be API-compatible with OSS. However, it would only support cards whose driver specifications were given out freely, along with cards that could easily be reverse-engineered. This is called the Advanced Linux Sound Architecture (ALSA) project. More information can be found at the project website: http://www.alsa-project.org/.

Due to this variety of soundcard support, along with changing availability, we're not going to try and cover the installation process here. However, you can find a great deal of relevant information in the Sound-HOWTO at http://www.linux.org/help/ldp/howto/Sound-HOWTO.html.

Devices

Soundcards are usually rather complex devices; they can handle a number of input and output sources such as microphones and speakers and auxiliary devices such as the CD-ROM. They are usually able to handle intricate effects, ranging from digital sound processing to 3D effects. To allow for all these different I/O sources and modes of operation, there are a number of standard devices, which can be found in /dev.

These are the most standard device file names; some Linux distributions may use slightly different names.

Devicename	Description
/dev/audio	A legacy device, originally found on Sun systems. The Linux device mimics the Sun device's behavior. By default, this device accepts 8 kHz audio A-law compressed files.
/dev/dsp	The Digital Sound Processor is the interface to your soundcard's normal sound functions of. This device accepts 44.1 kHz, 16 bit, little-endian audio files by default.
/dev/mixer	The mixer determines what devices can be used for playback and recording and determines their relative volume level. If the soundcard supports it, the mixer can also be used to control a master volume.
/dev/sequencer	A special form of a MIDI device.
/dev/midi	MIDI port (either external or internal).
/dev/sndstat	Displays sound driver status when read.

Make sure that you have at least these devices on your system. Normally these are created during installation but maybe you did not have your soundcard installed at the time. If they are not created, then you can run a script called /dev/MAKEDEV as root, which will create the necessary device files for you, like this:

```
# cd /dev
# ./MAKEDEV sound
# ls -l /dev/sndstat
   crw-rw-rw-   1 root     audio     14,   6 Nov  4 1999 /dev/sndstat
#
```

Now, if your soundcard is correctly installed and configured, you can use the /dev/sndstat file to get more information about your current configuration. On this particular system, a soundcard with the Aureal Vortex (or Aureal 8830) chip is installed:

```
# cat /dev/sndstat
OSS/Free: 0x30802
Load type: Driver loaded as a module
Kernel: Linux motif 2.2.15 #4 SMP Mon Jun 19 19:19:15 CEST 2000 i686
Config options: 0

Installed drivers:
Type 0: Aureal Vortex

Card config:
(Au8830 at 0xca800000 irq 9)

Audio devices:
0: Au88xx (DUPLEX)

Synth devices:
Not supported by current driver
```

```
Midi devices:
0: Au88xx

Timers:
0: System Clock

Mixers:
0: Au88xx
#
```

The final test of whether everything works correctly is to play something over your speakers. Any file will do, but as an example we will use our current kernel /vmlinuz as this is a file that is guaranteed to produce random noise. Make sure your volume is not turned all the way up though!

```
# cat /vmlinuz >/dev/dsp
```

Later on, we will show you how to produce sound that's rather more easy on the ears.

Handling Standard Audio Formats

Before we delve into the nitty-gritty details of programming the audio device, we will first look at a number of commonly used audio formats, along with some of the players available for those formats. While it's impossible to give an exhaustive list, this should at least give you a starting point. Source code is available for all the players mentioned, as well as binary packages for various Linux distributions. Descriptions and specifications for the various formats can be found on the Internet; http://www.wotsit.org is a good starting point, should you want to write some code for one of these formats yourself.

Uncompressed Audio – Raw

The raw format uses a simple stream of bytes, without any header information; the sort of audio you would extract from an audio CD, for example. This kind of file stores either 8 or 16 bits values corresponding directly to sampled wave amplitudes. Common sample rates include 11025, 22100, 44100 and 48000 Hz, where 44100Hz is the standard for a CD music track.

> *Sampling is really nothing more than taking a snapshot of the strength of an audio signal, assigning it a number, and mapping that number to a specified scale. The range of values in that scale is called the* **resolution***. In the case of a CD, the resolution is 16 bits for each channel, left and right channels sampled independently of one another. Each sampled value can therefore correspond to an integer between 1 and 2^{16}, allowing each one to represent any of 65536 distinct levels.*

For one second of CD audio you therefore need 44100 x 4 (16 bits x 2 channels) = 176400 bytes of audio data. These bytes are stored in 2352 byte groups called sectors, which means there are 75 sectors of audio played in a second. The length of an average CD-R is around 74 minutes, so a quick calculation tells us that 176400 x 74 x 60 = 783216000 bytes, which is approximately 746 MB, a commonly listed value for the capacity of a CD-R.

This is only true for audio, though. For other data storage, only 2048 bytes of each sector are used. The others are used for error checking and correction purposes. Another quick calculation gives us 2048 x 75 x 74 x 60 = 681984000 bytes, which is 650 MB, perhaps a more familiar value.

You can play this kind of audio file by simple redirection to an appropriate audio device. For example, if you extracted music from a CD, you would use the dd command or the cat command to send the file to the specified device, in this case /dev/dsp as you can see in the example in the previous section.

Compressed Audio

Audio compression uses complex algorithms to strip off redundant information and reduce the amount of data needed to faithfully reproduce a recorded sound. Because of fundamental differences between the way we tend to record sound (sampling the amplitude of a oscillating signal, or wave) and the way our brains register sound (detecting the intensity of certain frequencies in the wave), there's a great deal of this useless information. Consequently, compressed audio files often occupy a lot less space than their uncompressed counterparts.

Not all compression is necessarily 'lossy', that is, throwing away information – a second of uncompressed silence can occupy just as much disk space as a CD-quality recording of the author saying "What a waste of space!" Replace the 44100 consecutive zeroes with a single zero and a rule to repeat the last value 44100 times, and you've got yourself a nice, small file. However, the sort of space savings you can practically achieve with such methods are tiny compared to those of the lossy formats, some of which we'll now take a look at.

Nowadays, most audio compression methods are 'lossy', simply throwing away information that won't be registered by a human listener. As we've noted, there's an awful lot of this information, which means that they can achieve a *very* high level of compression.

Probably the most well known example is the MP3 format. MP3 is shorthand for MPEG-1 Layer 3, as the compression used was originally defined in the MPEG-1 standard. Its popularity is principally due to the fact that it produces a relatively high quality of reproduction despite high compression ratios (typically around 10:1); it's therefore very well suited as a medium for music downloads on the Web, as the recording industry and their lawyers have recently come to realize (see Political and Legal Issues).

In its entirety, MPEG-1 is a standard for moving pictures *and* sound – 'layer 3' refers to the audio component. MP3 files can be played under Linux by a variety of programs, including mpg123 and xmms.

MP3 is not the only compressed audio format available for Linux, although it's arguably the most popular. Work is underway to create a fully open, non-proprietary, patent-and-royalty-free MP3-like format; more information can be found at http://www.xiph.org/ogg/vorbis/index.html, which is also the place to look for players and the like. Another compressed audio format is RealAudio, for which a Linux player is available from Real Corporation at http://www.real.com.

WAV

You'll probably be familiar with the WAV format if you have worked with Microsoft Windows. It's structured according to Microsoft's **RIFF** (Resource Interchange File Format) specification, which in turn is little more than a little endian version of Electronic Arts' **IFF** (Interchange File Format) specification.

It consists of 'chunks', each one having a type that tells the RIFF processor what kind of data it holds. The simplest WAV is a header chunk holding various file characteristics, such as whether it's in stereo or mono, the sampling rate used, and what type of data chunk follows on from it. A second chunk holds the data, which can either be uncompressed (as we discussed above), or in some cases compressed.

A variety of programs can be used to play WAV files in Linux. One of the simplest is bplay, which is very small but does the job admirably. Its companion brecord can record a WAV file from one of your soundcard's input sources.

AIFF

The AIFF format, like WAV, is capable of holding multiple sources of audio data both compressed and uncompressed. It is one incarnation of the IFF originally put forward by Electronic Arts and very popular on the Commodore Amiga, which used IFF files to store both audio and video; AIFF is the audio variant. Like WAV, it contains a header chunk followed by a data chunk.

Converting Between Audio Formats – sox

sox is billed as "the Swiss Army Knife of sound processing programs". It's been around for a number of years, and is a command-line program that can be used to convert between audio file formats. The Linux version also serves as a player for these formats, which include AIFF. The sox homepage, which can be found at http://home.sprynet.com/~cbagwell/sox.html, will tell you virtually everything you'll ever need to know about audio file format conversion and the application of digital sound processing effects. Some systems support a **play** command, which automatically uses sox to play several types of audio file.

Do-It-Yourself

We will now look at programming the various sound devices, starting with a simple program and then moving on to a program that actually produces some output on your speakers. Note that this section will talk about the OSS API only, as it is the lowest common denominator and (virtually) guaranteed to be supported by your soundcard driver, either directly or by a small emulation layer. If all goes well, the final program will play two seconds of sound.

/sys/soundcard.h

This is the file in which all constants and structures are defined for playing sounds. It is included with the Linux kernel header files. Usually the /dev/sys directory will contain a reference to this file, while the actual file will be in your kernel header files directory /usr/include/linux.

To communicate directly with the audio system, we use the ioctl system call, which is prototyped in the file /sys/ioctl.h. Since we are dealing with files at a very low level, we also need definitions for opening low level files and some constants, which are defined in the files unistd.h, stdlib.h and fcntl.h. Any errors we may encounter are defined in errno.h, and everything we want to report we should report through the high level I/O functions of the stdio.h library. We must therefore include files as follows:

```
#include <stdio.h>
#include <errno.h>
#include <string.h>
#include <stdlib.h>
#include <unistd.h>

#include <sys/ioctl.h>
#include <fcntl.h>
#include <sys/soundcard.h>
```

ioctl

This is a system call that we will use extensively to communicate with the soundcard, so it is worth a close look. Its prototype is:

```
int ioctl(int devicedescriptor,int command,... parameters)
```

It is a generic call to allow user-space programs to talk to kernel-space device drivers so as to pass driver-specific settings back and forth. The parameters passed are dependent on the command, both in number and type. The advantage of using this call is that it saves you using a lot of system calls to the kernel itself, instead providing you with a hook into the driver internals. The drawback is that you don't get any form of type checking; so your program may silently crash if, say, you passed a number as a function argument, when the function expected a *pointer* to a number.

If the `ioctl` command is not valid for the given device, or if the parameters given are not valid for the given command, -1 is returned and `errno` will hold the reason for the failed call. `errno` will usually take a value of `EINVAL` if the command is not supported.

In order to play something, we must take the following steps:

❑ Open an audio device.

❑ Set play parameters – audio format, number of channels, sample frequency.

❑ Setup an audio buffer.

❑ Write the buffer to the device.

❑ Close the device when finished.

This framework can be extended to include additional checking at various points to see whether the device actually supports what we would like it to do.

soundtest.c

Let's start our test program with a simple `main` function that takes an optional parameter on the command line. This parameter will specify the audio device to open. If no audio device is passed on the command line, we will use `/dev/dsp` as the default.

Usage

For purposes of clarity, we define a function `Usage`, which we will call if too many parameters are given to the program, or if the user requests help:

```
void Usage(FILE *output, const char *progname)
{
  fprintf(output,
          "Usage:\n\n%s [sounddevice]\n\n",
          progname);

  fprintf(output,
          "If sounddevice is not specified,\n"
          "then /dev/dsp is used by default.\n"
          );
}
```

main

Here is the skeleton code for our `main` function; note that we are opening the device for writing. If we wanted to make this as foolproof as possible, we would use a `stat` or `fstat` call to check whether the filename passed was actually a device. If it's not, we'll have to be careful, as the referenced file will be created empty. Therefore, in the following code, we'll first open the device as read-only, then try to ensure that it's an audio device; only once we're sure will we reopen the device.

```
int main(int argc, const char *argv[])
{
  const char *device    = "/dev/dsp"; /* the standard name of the sound device. */

  int         device_fd = -1;         /* we have not opened anything yet */

  switch (argc)
        {
          case 2: device = argv[1];   /* device name was specified. */
                  if (strcmp(argv[1],"-?") == 0)
                      {
                          Usage(stdout,argv[0]); /* provide help */
                          exit(EXIT_SUCCESS);
                      }
                  break;
          case 1: break;              /* no arguments, use standard device. */

          default: /* too many arguments, show help: */
                  Usage(stderr,argv[0]);
                  exit(EXIT_FAILURE);
        }
```

We know that to play something, we only need to write to the device; likewise if we just want to record, we can specify O_RDONLY. However, writing to the wrong place could be rather dangerous, so the `open_device` call must check that the filename passed actually points to a device:

```
    device_fd = open_device(stderr, device, O_WRONLY);

    if (device_fd == -1) /* if this is true,the open call failed and an
                          * error will have been given.
                          */
    {
      exit(1);
    }

  /* playing code will go here */

    close(device_fd);

    return 0;
}
```

open_device

The `open_device` call simply opens the device and writes an error message to the specified log file – in this case we use the `stderr` stream – and returns the handle (or file descriptor) to the opened device, or –1 if the device was not opened successfully. For safety reasons, we also include a call to `stat` to see whether the filename passed actually points to a device. `stat` and associated constants are defined in the file `stat.h`:

```
int open_device(FILE *errorlog, const char *device_name, int open_flags)
{
  struct stat device_info;
  int audio_fd;

  if (stat(device_name,&device_info) == -1) /* file does not exist */
    {
      fprintf(errorlog,
              "ERROR: device <%s> could not be opened: it does not exist.\n",
              device_name);
      return -1;
    }

  if ((device_info.st_mode & S_IFCHR) != S_IFCHR) /* is this a device ? */
    {
      fprintf(errorlog,
              "ERROR: filename <%s> is not a devicefile.\n",
              device_name);

      return -1;
    }

  audio_fd = open(device_name, open_flags, 0);

  if (audio_fd == -1) // opening the device failed
    {
      int reason_for_failure = errno;
      fprintf(errorlog,
              "ERROR: device <%s> could not be opened with flags %d.\n",
              device_name, open_flags);

      fprintf(errorlog,
              "        The reason given was:   <%s>.\n",
              strerror(reason_for_failure));
    }

  return audio_fd;
}
```

Determining the Capabilities of the Soundcard Device

The capabilities of different soundcards are many and varied. In some, particularly the older ones, there are fundamental limitations at the level of the hardware; newer cards may also be limited by immature drivers. The sound API provides three `ioctl` calls to help you determine your soundcard's capabilities, each taking a pointer to an integer as a parameter. On returning, `ioctl` will assign a value to this integer; either a bitmask with bits set according to capabilities or formats supported, or a series of bytes grouped together in an integer, or even a combination of the two.

The following call will return the version of the OSS API used by the device, or (in the case of ALSA) the version of OSS that the compatibility layer is trying to emulate. Note that the OSS API doesn't support this call prior to version 3.6.1.

```
ioctl(device_fd, OSS_GETVERSION, &version)
```

The following sections of code, which should be inserted just after the open_device function, demonstrate the use of this call:

decode_version

```c
int decode_version(FILE *output, int version)
{
  int major_version = (version >> 16) & 0xff;
  int minor_version = (version >>  8) & 0xff;
  int revision      = (version      ) & 0xff;

  fprintf(output,
          "The OSS Version of this device-driver is %d.%d.%d\n",
          major_version,minor_version,revision);

  return (major_version << 16) |
         (minor_version <<  8) |
         revision;
}
```

report_version

```c
int report_version(FILE *output, const char *device_name, int device_fd)
{
  int version = 0;

  if (ioctl(device_fd, OSS_GETVERSION, &version) == -1)
    {
      /* the device does not support this call */

      int reason_why_GET_VERSION_failed = errno;

      fprintf(output,
              "The device <%s> reported the error %d (%s),\n"
              "while asking for its OSS driver version.\n",
              device_name,
              reason_why_GET_VERSION_failed,
              strerror(reason_why_GET_VERSION_failed));

      if (reason_why_GET_VERSION_failed == EINVAL) /* may be an old driver*/
        return 0x0300000; /* make up a version number, reasonably recent */

      return 0;
    }
  else /* we should now be able to decode the version supported: */
    {
      return decode_version(output, version);
    }
}
```

As you can see, the version number consists of a major release byte, a minor release byte and a revision byte, all packed together in the integer that is returned.

Capabilities of the Device

```
ioctl(device_fd, SNDCTL_DSP_GETCAPS, &capability_mask);
```

This call returns the capabilities of the device. Currently the following capabilities are defined:

Bitmask	Meaning
DSP_CAP_REVISION	The revision number of the driver/card – this part of capability_mask is actually a number, rather than a bitmask.
DSP_CAP_DUPLEX	The driver/card is full duplex – it can record and play at the same time.
DSP_CAP_REALTIME	The driver/card is capable of real-time processing.
DSP_CAP_BATCH	The driver/card is capable of batching – it has a number of internal buffers.
DSP_CAP_COPROC	The driver/card has a co-processor.
DSP_CAP_TRIGGER	The driver/card can supply triggers to your application.
DSP_CAP_MMAP	The driver can use the mmap call to map part of the memory space to its internal buffers, speeding up operation.

The following code shows how to report the capabilities on a standard device. Note that we separate the reporting code from the error-checking code for the sake of clarity. Also note that we cheat a little with the revision part, pretending that it's a bitmask and only printing it if it has some value.

sound_capability

```
typedef struct
{
    int         scBitmask; /* the bitmask that corresponds to this capability */
    const char *scName;   /* a human readable representation for this capability */
} sound_capability;
```

list_capabilities

```
void list_capabilities(FILE *output, int capability_mask)
{
  static const sound_capability capability_list[] =
        {
            { DSP_CAP_REVISION, "revision" },
            { DSP_CAP_DUPLEX,   "full duplex" },
            { DSP_CAP_REALTIME, "real-time processing" },
            { DSP_CAP_BATCH, "batching" },
            { DSP_CAP_COPROC, "co-processing" },
            { DSP_CAP_TRIGGER, "trigger" },
            { DSP_CAP_MMAP, "mmap()" },
            { 0, 0 }
        };
```

```
    int i;

    for (i = 0 ; capability_list[i].scBitmask != 0; ++i)
      {
        if (capability_mask & capability_list[i].scBitmask)
          {
            fprintf(output,
                    "The device has the %s capability (%x -> %x).\n",
                    capability_list[i].scName,
                    capability_list[i].scBitmask,
                    capability_mask & capability_list[i].scBitmask
                  );
          }
      }
}
```

report_capabilities

```
int report_capabilities(FILE *output, const char *device_name, int device_fd)
{
  int capability_mask = 0;

  if (ioctl(device_fd, SNDCTL_DSP_GETCAPS, &capability_mask) == -1)
    {
      /* the device does not support this call */

      int reason_why_DSP_GETCAPS_failed = errno;

      fprintf(output,
              "The device <%s> reported the error %d (%s),\n"
              "while asking for its supported capabilities.\n",
              device_name,
              reason_why_DSP_GETCAPS_failed,
              strerror(reason_why_DSP_GETCAPS_failed));

      return 0;
    }
  else /* we should now be able to list the capabilities supported: */
    {
      fprintf(output,
          "The device <%s> supports the following capabilities: (%d %x)\n",
              device_name, capability_mask, capability_mask);

      list_capabilities(output, capability_mask);
    }

  return capability_mask;
}
```

Supported Formats

Finally, we can use the following call to get the formats supported:

```
ioctl(device_fd, SNDCTL_DSP_GETFMTS, &format_mask)
```

The corresponding bitmasks are as follows:

Bitmask	Format
AFMT_MU_LAW	mu-law
AFMT_A_LAW	a-law
AFMT_IMA_ADPCM	IMA ADPCM
AFMT_U8	8 bit unsigned
AFMT_S16_LE	signed 16 bit, little-endian
AFMT_S16_BE	signed 16 bit, big-endian
AFMT_S8	8 bit signed
AFMT_U16_LE	unsigned 16 bit, little-endian
AFMT_U16_BE	unsigned 16 bit, big-endian
AFMT_MPEG	MPEG audio

It is quite possible for a driver to support more formats than it returns with this call. Only natively supported formats will show up here; others may be supported by way of some internal conversion process. Nevertheless, it will be far more efficient to use a format that is natively supported.

The following code will report what formats are supported, in a similar fashion to the capability functions above:

sound_format

```
typedef struct
{
   int         sfBitmask; /* the bitmask that corresponds with this format */
   const char *sfName;   /* a human readable representation for this format */
} sound_format;
```

list_formats

```
void list_formats(FILE *output, int format_mask)
{
   static sound_format format_list[] =
        {
            { AFMT_MU_LAW, "mu-law" },
            { AFMT_A_LAW,  "a-law" },
            { AFMT_IMA_ADPCM, "IMA ADPCM" },
            { AFMT_U8, "8 bit unsigned" },
            { AFMT_S16_LE, "signed 16 bit, little endian" },
            { AFMT_S16_BE, "signed 16 bit, big endian" },
            { AFMT_S8, "8 bit signed" },
            { AFMT_U16_LE, "unsigned 16 bit, little endian" },
            { AFMT_U16_BE, "unsigned 16 bit, big endian" },
            { AFMT_MPEG, "MPEG audio" },
            { 0, 0 }
        };
```

```
    int i;

    for (i = 0 ; format_list[i].sfBitmask != 0; ++i)
        {
          if (format_mask & format_list[i].sfBitmask)
            {
              fprintf(output,
                      "The device supports %s audio.\n",
                      format_list[i].sfName);
            }
        }
}
```

report_formats

```
int report_formats(FILE *output, const char *device_name, int device_fd)
{
  int format_mask = 0;

  if (ioctl(device_fd, SNDCTL_DSP_GETFMTS, &format_mask) == -1)
      {
        /* the device does not support this call */

        int reason_why_DSP_GETFMTS_failed = errno;

        fprintf(output,
                "The device <%s> reported the error %d (%s),\n"
                "while asking for its supported formats.\n",
                device_name,
                reason_why_DSP_GETFMTS_failed,
                strerror(reason_why_DSP_GETFMTS_failed));

        return 0;
      }
  else /* we should now be able to list the formats supported: */
      {
        fprintf(output,
                "The device <%s> supports the following formats: (%d %x)\n",
                device_name, format_mask, format_mask);

        list_formats(output, format_mask);
      }

  return format_mask;
}
```

Soundtest – Putting It All Together

We will now see how to use the functions we've described by adding appropriate calls to our main function. First we need some extra variables, which we will use to store the results from each call:

```
int main(int argc, const char *argv[])
{
  const char *device    = "/dev/dsp"; /* standard name of sound device. */

  int         device_fd = -1;         /* we have not opened anything yet */
  int         version         = 0;    /* the version of the OSS driver   */
  int         capability_mask = 0;    /* what the device is capable of.  */
  int         format_mask     = 0;    /* what formats the device can play.*/
```

```
switch (argc)
    {
```

Next, we add calls to the various reporting functions defined above:

```
device_fd = open_device(stderr, device, O_WRONLY);

if (device_fd == -1)
    /* if true the open call failed and an error will have been given.*/

{
  exit(1);
}
```

```
/* we have succesfully opened our device. now report what it can do: */

version        = report_version(stdout, device, device_fd);
capability_mask = report_capabilities(stdout,device,device_fd);
format_mask     = report_formats(stdout,device,device_fd);

if ((version == 0) ||
    (capability_mask == 0) ||
    (format_mask == 0))
  {
    /* remember that we were going to -write- to the device.
     * If this device happened to be a harddisk which got passed to
     * this program by mistake (or maybe the devicefile itself got
     * messed up by accident) we would be destroying the filesystem
     * and lose important data. We therefore try to dwell on the side
     * of caution and exit the program.
     */

    fprintf(stderr,
  "This device did not respond to one of the required audio functions.\n"
  "It may not be an audio output-device. Exiting, just in case.\n"
            );
    exit(1);
   }

/* playing code will go here */
```

As you can see, we are being very conservative in dealing the device we're about to open – the `open_device` call made sure we were dealing with a device, while the `report_` calls assured us that we were actually dealing with a sound device. If we're in *any* doubt, we exit the program immediately.

If you now recompile the program, you'll see that the output now includes information about the version of OSS used, as well as the capabilities and formats supported by our sound device.

```
$ ./soundtest /dev/dsp
The OSS Version of this device-driver is 3.8.2
The device </dev/dsp> supports the following capabilities: (13056 3300)
The device has the full duplex capability (100 -> 100).
The device has the real-time processing capability (200 -> 200).
The device has the trigger capability (1000 -> 1000).
```

```
The device has the mmap() capability (2000 -> 2000).
The device </dev/dsp> supports the following formats: (27 1b)
The device supports mu-law audio.
The device supports a-law audio.
The device supports 8 bit unsigned audio.
The device supports signed 16 bit, little endian audio.
$
```

Setting Up The Device

Now that we know what the device is capable of, we can pick a supported format and sample frequency. We must also specify the number of channels to use. Older versions of the OSS API only support one or two channels (mono or stereo). Later versions provide us with a call to set an arbitrary number of channels. This allows us to support soundcards that can drive more than two speakers – a fairly common feature on newer soundcards.

Care must be taken to specify settings in the following order:

- ❑ the format to be played
- ❑ the number of channels to be used
- ❑ the sample frequency

Each of these is set by a separate call. Some soundcards do not support all sample frequencies in all modes for all formats. By applying the settings in this order, the soundcard can accurately tell you which of the remaining settings it supports for each stage. Note that most drivers will actually use an approximation of what you've specified – you should check carefully what the sound driver returns, to see if it's still within an acceptable range for the format you want to play. Our program will only accept an exact match.

Also note that the device needs to be set up before *anything* is written to it; it's not possible to modify any of these settings during playback. To do this, you'll need to close and open (or reset) the device.

In code, these rules translate to:

```
int set_play_params(int device_fd,
                    int play_format,
                    int channels,
                    int sample_frequency)
{
  /* make sure we get back what we ask for: */

  return (set_play_format(device_fd, play_format) == play_format) &&
         (set_channels(device_fd, channels) == channels) &&
    (set_sample_frequency(device_fd, sample_frequency) == sample_frequency);
}
```

Note that this function returns a non-zero number if it succeeds, and zero if it does not.

The ioctl calls we need to set format, channels and sample frequency are:

```
ioctl(device_fd, SNDCTL_DSP_SETFMT, &new_play_format)
```

709

```
ioctl(device_fd, SNDCTL_DSP_CHANNELS, &new_channels)

ioctl(device_fd, SNDCTL_DSP_SPEED, &new_sample_frequency)
```

For the channel call with older drivers, you may need to use:

```
ioctl(device_fd, SNDCTL_DSP_STEREO, &stereo)
```

Note that this uses 0 (mono) and 1 (stereo), while the above uses the number of channels.)

As you can see, these calls don't take an integer as argument, rather a pointer to an integer. This is done so that we can return actual format of the audio data, the number of channels and speed (sample frequency) that have been set. As we've already said, you should check these return values carefully. The actual implementation of the functions is now rather simple:

set_play_format

```
int set_play_format(int device_fd, int play_format)
{
  int new_play_format = play_format;

  if (ioctl(device_fd, SNDCTL_DSP_SETFMT, &new_play_format) == -1)
    {
      return -1; /* format (or ioctl()) not supported by device */
    }

  return new_play_format; /* could be different from the one asked for! */
}
```

set_channels

```
int set_channels(int device_fd, int channels)
{
  int new_channels = channels;

  if (ioctl(device_fd, SNDCTL_DSP_CHANNELS, &new_channels) == -1)
    {
      if (channels <= 2)
              /* maybe the previous call failed because of an old driver */
        {
          /* we are now going to use the old call, and
           * need to adjust our parameter accordingly.
           */

          new_channels = channels - 1;

          if (ioctl(device_fd, SNDCTL_DSP_STEREO, &new_channels) == -1)
            return -1;

          return new_channels + 1;
          /* return type will be 0 or 1,  should
           * be consistent with the 'new' driver case
           */
```

```
        }
      else
        return -1;
        /* this number of channels (>2) is not supported by an old driver */

    }
  return_new_channels
    return new_channels; /* this will be the number of channels actually available.
  */
  }
```

set_sample_frequency

```
    int set_sample_frequency(int device_fd, int sample_frequency)
    {
      int new_sample_frequency = sample_frequency;

      if (ioctl(device_fd, SNDCTL_DSP_SPEED, &new_sample_frequency) == -1)
        {
          return -1; /* format (or ioctl()) not supported by device */
        }

      return new_sample_frequency;
          /* could be different from the one asked for! */
    }
```

Note the fallback to the older SNDCTL_DSP_STEREO call if the SNDCTL_DSP_CHANNELS call is not supported and the specified number of channels is less than or equal to two.

We're now ready to use these functions in our main program. First, we must check whether the driver actually supports the format we've chosen; then we configure the driver with play format, number of channels and sample frequency. We exit the program if we don't get what we expected.

Let's define some variables to store the number of channels, format to use and sample frequency:

```
    int         version        = 0;    /* the version of the OSS driver */
    int         capability_mask = 0;    /* what the device is capable of. */
    int         format_mask     = 0;   /* what formats the device can play.*/

    int         channels       = 1;
    int         play_format    = AFMT_U8;
    int         sample_frequency = 48000;
                /* change this to 44100 or 22050 if this high
                 * a frequency is not supported by your soundcard.
                 */
```

With these in place, we can now add the rest of the code:

```
      fprintf(stderr,
    "This device did not respond to one of the required audio functions.\n"
    "It may not be an audio output-device. Exiting, just in case.\n"
              );
      exit(1);
    }
```

```
/* playing code will go here */

    /* ok, we are ready to play something now */

  if (!(format_mask & play_format))
    {
      fprintf(stderr,
              "This device is not capable of playing the desired format.\n");

      exit(1);
    }

  if (!set_play_params(device_fd, play_format, channels, sample_frequency))
    {
      fprintf(stderr,
              "This device is not capable of playing the combination of:\n"
              "Format   : %d\n"
              "Channels : %d\n"
              "Frequency: %d\n",
              play_format, channels, sample_frequency);

      /* usually when this happens, the sample frequency is not supported;
       * try changing it to a lower value.
       */

      exit(1);
    }

  fprintf(stdout,
          "This device is now set up to play the combination of:\n"
          "Format   : %d\n"
          "Channels : %d\n"
          "Frequency: %d\n",
          play_format, channels, sample_frequency);
```

Playing Actual Sound Data

Now, the only thing left to do is to play some data. This is actually very simple compared to all that we've done so far: just call the `write` function with a buffer of data. For purposes of demonstration we've written a simple function to create a buffer and fill it with two seconds' worth of data:

bytes_needed

```
int bytes_needed(int play_format,
                 int channels,
                 int sample_frequency,
                 int seconds)
{
  int bytes_per_channel = 0;

  switch (play_format)
        {
          case AFMT_MU_LAW:
```

```
                case AFMT_A_LAW:
                case AFMT_IMA_ADPCM:
                case AFMT_S16_LE:
                case AFMT_S16_BE:
                case AFMT_U16_LE:
                case AFMT_U16_BE:
                case AFMT_MPEG:
                    return 0; /* format not supported by this program */

                case AFMT_U8:
                case AFMT_S8:
                    bytes_per_channel = 1;
                    break;
        }
    return seconds * sample_frequency * bytes_per_channel * channels;
}
```

setup_buffer

```
int setup_buffer(unsigned char **buffer, size_t *buffersize,
                 int play_format,
                 int channels,
                 int sample_frequency)
{
  unsigned char *walker = 0 ; /* used to walk through the buffer
                               * we will allocate
                               */
  int seconds         = 2;

  int needed = bytes_needed(play_format,
                            channels,
                            sample_frequency,
                            seconds);
  int i;

  if ((needed == 0) || (!buffer) || (!buffersize))
    return 0;

  walker = malloc(needed);

  if (!walker)
    {
      *buffersize = 0;
      return 0;
    }

  *buffer     = walker; /* save the beginning of the buffer */
  *buffersize = needed;

  needed /= channels;

  for (i = 0 ; i < needed ; ++i)
    {
      int j;
```

```
        for (j = 0 ; j < channels; ++j)
            /* the following formula generates a sawtooth waveform */
            *walker++ = -1 * (j+1) * i & 0xff;
    }

    return 1;
}
```

We've done our best to keep this function as general as possible, so that you can experiment with different numbers of channels and different formats. We can now use it in our main program; we need a buffer to hold the data, so we add it to our variable section:

```
int         channels        = 1;
int         play_format      = AFMT_U8;
int         sample_frequency = 48000;
            /* change this to 44100 or 22050 if this high
             * a frequency is not supported by your soundcard.
             */
```

```
unsigned char *buffer       = 0;
size_t         buffersize    = 0;
```

and once we've set the various parameters, we create the buffer:

```
fprintf(stdout,
        "This device is now set up to play the combination of:\n"
            "Format    : %d\n"
            "Channels : %d\n"
            "Frequency: %d\n",
            play_format, channels, sample_frequency);
```

```
    /* initialize a buffer with the desired playing format */

    if (setup_buffer(&buffer, &buffersize,
                    play_format, channels, sample_frequency))
    { /* code to play buffer goes here */
    }
```

```
close(device_fd);
```

Finally, here's the actual code to play the buffer and clean it up once we're done with it:

```
    /* code to play buffer goes here */
```

```
    size_t bytes_written =  0;

    fprintf(stdout,
            "Now writing %d bytes to the device.\n",
            buffersize);

    bytes_written =  write(device_fd, buffer, buffersize);
```

```
            fprintf(stdout,
                    "Managed to write %d bytes to the device.\n",
                    bytes_written);

            reset_device(device_fd);

            free(buffer);
        }

    close(device_fd);
```

Cleaning up

There are a number of ways to return the device to a known state, as may be necessary in order to terminate the playback of a lengthy sound file. One way is to **close** the device (by calling the `close` function); another is to wait until all of the device's internal buffers are flushed:

wait_till_finished

```
int wait_till_finished(int device_fd)
{
  if (ioctl(device_fd, SNDCTL_DSP_SYNC, 0) == -1)
    {
       return -1; /* format (or ioctl()) not supported by device */
    }

  return 1; /* all sound has been played */
}
```

Another possibility is to **reset** the device; this stops whatever is playing and readies the device to play more, as opposed to the `close` function which first lets the device finish what it's doing. After a reset, you can set different parameters for the device.

We used the following function in the code above, to make sure that the music stopped before we exited the program – we used an early driver for our soundcard, which would sometimes hang if we did not:

reset_device

```
int reset_device(int device_fd)
{
  if (ioctl(device_fd, SNDCTL_DSP_RESET, 0) == -1)
    {
       return -1; /* format (or ioctl()) not supported by device */
    }

  return 1; /* sounddevice has been reset */
}
```

Moving Pictures

Linux support for video and animation can be roughly divided into three categories:

❑   software players

❑   hardware players (a hardware driver assisted by a thin software layer)

❑   hybrids (hardware players assisted by software modules)

We will look briefly at each of these categories in turn.

Software Players

xanim

The software player that has been around the longest is undoubtedly `xanim`, and while it currently appears to be unmaintained, it nevertheless supports quite a large number of formats, including:

FLIC

These are animated files, which can (and occasionally do) include sound. The two official types are FLI (a resolution-limited older format) and FLC (featuring configurable resolution and better compression). These used to be quite popular as an output format for 3D rendering because of their support in Autodesk, but with the advent of other animated formats its use seems to have declined. The main reason for its decline is the limited sound capabilities the format has. For more information, see: http://www.compuphase.com/flic.htm

AVI

AVI stands for "Audio/Video Interleaved"; this format is commonly used in MS Windows. It falls into the 'umbrella format' category, meaning that it can hold many different forms of compressed video and audio, such as Indeo (a compression format devised by Intel), Cinepak and numerous others. Some of these video formats are compressed according to proprietary standards. `xanim` therefore features a plugin architecture, using binary **codec** (compress-decompress) modules to interpret the formats. Note that many Linux distributions including `xanim` do not include these modules.

QT/MOV

These are originally native to the Apple world. QT stands for QuickTime, another umbrella format. Unlike AVI formats, not all QT-compressed video is supported.

In particular, QT video compressed with Sorenson codecs is growing in popularity on the internet. It delivers high quality video in relatively small files, but has not yet been ported to Linux, apparently because Sorenson has not received permission from Apple to do so.

MPEG-1

Last, but not least, `xanim` supports MPEG-1 movies, both audio and video. However, there are players that do a better job for MPEG-1; check out `SMPEG` and `MpegTV`, both available from a Linux archive near you.

RealPlayer

This supports both **RealVideo** and **RealAudio** formats. The former is one of the few streaming video formats available for Linux. It can be downloaded from Real's website at: www.real.com.

Other Formats

Two more major formats have so far gone unmentioned:

MPEG-2

The second version of the MPEG standard, aimed at high-bandwidth video streaming. This is the video (and audio) standard used for DVDs, also used in digital (TV) broadcasts. MPEG-2 files can be decoded with `nist` and `mpeg2dec`. See the 'Hybrids' section for more details.

ASF – Advanced Streaming Format

This is the Microsoft standard format for streaming multimedia. Originally designed by several different companies, it is now used almost exclusively on Microsoft platforms, although there is a beta player available for the Mac. Like AVI, ASF is an umbrella format, which means that the streamed video data can be compressed with a number of different algorithms. In practice however, MPEG-4 is used most of the time. At time of writing, no Linux programs are available to decode ASF or MPEG-4 compressed files.

Hardware Players

Hardware-only Linux multimedia almost invariably comes back to soundcards, television tuners and video capture cards that have been based on the Brooktree 848 and 878 chipset. You can find more information about this chipset and the Video4Linux specification these cards use at Alan Cox's website: roadrunner.swansea.uk.linux.org/v4l.shtml. The Video4Linux API is currently no longer actively updated, although a second version, Video4Linux II, is in the works.

However, a different player is appearing on the hardware front: the latest release of the Linux X11 Window System implementation 'XFree86 4.0' incorporates the Xv video extension, a hardware abstraction layer for video overlays and direct access to the underlying hardware. You can find more information on the Xfree86 website, at http://www.xfree86.org.

Hybrids

Since this book has an underlying DVD theme, it would seem almost inappropriate not to mention the only software DVD player that currently works for Linux.

OMS – the Open Media System

OMS is a spin-off from the development of a Linux driver for the hardware DVD extension of a series of video cards based on the Matrox G200 chipset. Running parallel to this was the development of various software audio decoders, along with the DVD decoding logic. This hybrid evolved into the Open Media System.

OMS features a plugin architecture, allowing the use of multiple decoders, one of them being the DVD extension mentioned above. However, it's also possible to use pipes (FIFOs) to pass the various streams from the DVD to external decoders. If you want to do everything in software though, you should be prepared to have high demands put on your hardware: a Pentium III (or equivalent) running at no less than 500 MHz is required to get a satisfactory movie viewing experience.

At present, no special hardware is required to run OMS.

How to get it

Because of the continual development of OMS, the best way to retrieve it is through CVS, which means that you'll need a cvs package installed:

```
$ mkdir ~/livid
$ cd ~/livid
$ export CVSROOT=:pserver:anonymous@cvs.linuxvideo.org:/cvs/livid
$ cvs login
  (Logging in to anonymous@cvs.linuxvideo.org)
  CVS password:
```

There is no password set right now, so just press *Enter*. You can now proceed to download the software:

```
$ cvs -z3 co -P ac3dec oms mpeg2dec mgadvd
```

Note that you don't need to specify mgadvd *unless you have a Matrox G200/G400-based card with hardware DVD decoder.*

The tools will now download to their respective directories.

> **Bear in mind that this is a work in progress, so it's possible that the build you grabbed from the website will not compile properly.**

OMS has a few prerequisites, such as the existence of various developer tools including:

❑ GNU autoconf and automake

❑ GTK+ and imlib

The configure scripts will tell you which versions they need.

Now enter the various directories, and use configure to configure, build and install the packages. It's usually easiest to do this as root, because of the necessary permissions required for installation.

```
# cd ac3dec; ./configure; make; make install
# cd ../mpeg2dec; ./configure; make; make install
```

You'll need to 'make install' before configuring oms, or it won't be able to find the library routines from the two programs above. Finally, configure oms itself:

```
# cd ../oms; ./configure; make; make install
```

It's quite possible that the build of oms will fail because a header file cannot be found. If that happens, go down to the directory libvo, do a **make** and **make install**, and then try again in the top-level directory. Don't forget to do a final **make install** in the oms directory, or the program will not be able to find the various plugins it needs.

Now, the only thing that is left to do is run oms:

```
$ oms
```

If all went OK, you will be rewarded with an interface that looks approximately like this:

Now insert a DVD in your DVD player, click on PlayList and retrieve the play list for your DVD. Then hit the play button and click on the Play icon (highlighted in the picture above). Then sit back and enjoy!

Political and Legal Issues

The world of multimedia is surrounded by legal battles; every day we hear about another lawsuit filed against projects involved in web-related distribution and multimedia tools (Napster, Scour, DeCSS to name but a few).

The last of these in particular, recently put Linux in the spotlight – depending on who you ask, it was either an innocent means to viewing DVDs on Linux, or a concerted effort to crack the built-in physical copyright protection and open the way to widespread DVD piracy.

Entire books have been (and will continue to be) written on the subject of multimedia distribution, legal or otherwise. Copyright law has always been a minefield of precedents and subtle technicalities, and we're not even going to try and represent the plethora of opinions that have been expressed on this very wide-reaching issue. However, if you want an interesting perspective on the DeCSS case, you may want to take a look at http://www.opendvd.org.

References

Linux Video, OMS and other DVD related links:
http://www.linuxvideo.org

Video4Linux API:
http://roadrunner.swansea.uk.linux.org/v4l.shtml

The OSS/Full versions for various soundcards and the OSS API:
http://www.opensound.com

Its non-commercial alternative ALSA:
http://www.alsa-project.org

Installing a soundcard under Linux:
http://www.linux.org/help/ldp/Sound-HOWTO.html

Playing various sound formats under Linux:
http://www.linux.org/LDP/Sound-Playing-HOWTO.html

Making MP3s:
http://www.linux.org/help/ldp/howto/MP3-HOWTO.html

Drivers for Creative Labs Dxr2 and Dxr3 cards:
http://opensource.creative.com

A tutorial to get these drivers working, written by Jonathan Blank:
http://caspian.twu.net/tech/writing/tutorials/dvdlinux.html

References to programs, tools, tutorials and other things sound and Linux related:
http://www.clug.in-chemnitz.de/vortraege/multimedia/SOFTWARE/linux_soundapps.html

References to video and animation-related programs and tools:
http://www.linuxstart.com/applications/multimedia/video.html

Summary

In this chapter we addressed a number of issues regarding multimedia in Linux. First, we looked at audio file formats and how to play audio using external players. We moved on to describe the OSS API in more detail, developing a program to play audio files with it.

In the second part of the chapter we looked at the state of affairs in the world of graphics. We looked at animation and video formats, and looked briefly at the installation of a prototype software DVD player.

Online discussion at http://www.p2p.wrox.com

20

CORBA

CORBA stands for the Common Object Request Broker Architecture. It is a standardized scheme for constructing distributed object-based applications, allowing components to 'talk to one another' regardless of platform or implementation language.

One view of the architecture of a CORBA system may be seen in the following diagram where the Client and Application Server represent programs that you might write:

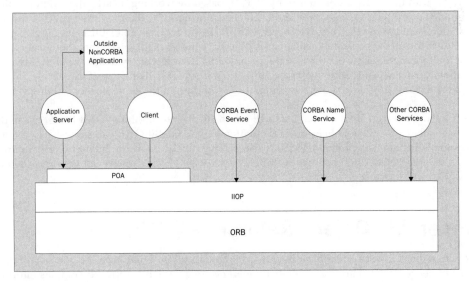

CORBA consists of a number of components and layers.

Interface Definition Language (IDL)

This is the language that is used to declare interfaces to objects. It strongly resembles C++ class declarations.

IDL is used to declare the data structures and methods available for use via CORBA in the application. IDL is usually compiled into 'stubs' (static interfaces), and 'skeletons' (dynamic interfaces) for any given combination of ORB (see below) and language. You would then include the stubs with a client, or skeletons with servers, and the code that is generated by the IDL compiler is used to manage communications between the code you use in the client or server and the ORB. IDL information tells the ORB about the type system that is in use, indicating what kinds of data may be communicated, as well as what kinds of requests may be performed with the data.

Object Request Broker (ORB)

This is the base layer on top of which everything else is built.

The ORB represents a remote invocation facility, at its most basic level providing a proxy to allow clients to request operations, and to pass parameters back and forth between client and server. It might forward a request through another ORB, if that ORB is managing the service.

The critical component that makes this useful is the ability for ORBs to communicate with one another regardless of their implementation. CORBA defines a general framework for this, known as the General Inter-ORB Protocol, or GIOP. GIOP provides a Common Data Representation (CDR), common message formats, and common assumptions to be made concerning any network transport layer that might be used to transfer GIOP messages. (And that only scratches the surface; there are more acronyms available to those that are interested!)

These days, with the relative dominance of TCP/IP-based networking, nearly all communications between ORBs and the processes they serve take place using TCP/IP, and thus a specific transport specification is added to GIOP, providing us with IIOP, the Internet Inter-ORB Protocol. These protocols are themselves specified using CORBA IDL, which has the result that there truly is a high level of interoperability between ORB implementations. If an ORBit, which is the GNOME ORB, application can access an ORBit object via IIOP, then it is highly likely that it can access an object implemented using a different ORB, say omniORB, whether on the same host or another.

There is a standardized ORB-to-ORB protocol called IIOP (Internet Inter-ORB Protocol), so that you may reasonably expect that a client program written for the ORBit ORB can successfully request services implemented using omniORB. This requires no special effort on the part of the programmer; so long as a suitable object reference (see IOR below) is available, the request can get forwarded to the remote ORB and processed.

Interoperable Object Reference (IOR)

In order to request invoking an object method, the request to the ORB must include an Interoperable Object Reference (IOR). This is a 'stringified' reference to a CORBA object. It contains information that includes the IDL type, the host where the object resides, and the endianness of that host, and, on TCP/IP systems, the socket that can be used to submit the request to the ORB on that host.

It may be worthwhile, when debugging things, to try to decode parts of the IOR, but it should generally be treated as opaque, something that only your ORB should try to interpret.

Getting a CORBA system initialized typically involves transferring some IORs around so that clients know how to get at their servers, and this process is, overall, one of the more irritating parts of getting a CORBA application working.

Object Adapter

In between the ORB and the implementation of the object comes the Object Adaptor. An Object Adaptor provides functions to support the creation, identification, activation, and, ultimately, disposal of an object.

Originally, CORBA defined a Basic Object Adaptor (BOA); it was unfortunately under-specified. Different ORBs implemented the calls quite differently, which severely limited interoperability of applications. Since then, a Portable Object Adaptor (POA) was defined that allows many 'life-cycle' activities to be specified in a much more portable manner.

This means that if one ORB proves unacceptable, you can take that code, and, so long as a language mapping is available, you should be able to port the code to use a different ORB without needing to do too much rewriting of code.

Servers

Servers provide implementations of objects, allowing clients to request that methods be invoked on those objects. CORBA Services have been defined using standardized IDL definitions to provide ways of doing common things. The Name Service allows building a registry of objects that are available for use so that CORBA applications may look up the services that they need. The Event Service supplies 'event queues' so that applications that use event-based programming with CORBA requests do not need to hack together a service from scratch.

Clients do not need to directly know the identity of the server that they are trying to access. Server components may reside on different hosts all over the place, and there is no need for clients to be aware of the specific location. They merely request the desired object operations, and the ORB will forward requests to the server on the right host. There are several CORBA Services designed to allow programs to register services that they offer, which means that a CORBA application can explore, at runtime, the services available for use,

Note that CORBA is not purely a 'client/server' system, but often has peers communicating with peers. Many of the CORBA Services require that servers reverse the role to become clients, requesting services of other servers.

For instance, in the DVD application, the application server process that supports queries can be regarded as a server, but it takes the role of client when it requests data from a database server, or asks a security server for authentication.

Naming and Trading services

By using CORBA Naming and Trading Services, many CORBA applications may simultaneously use the same 'registry', and this might even allow us to use generic system management utilities that would track status information for all registered objects. Without a standardized scheme like the Naming Service, there would be no way of creating a generic utility for this purpose. It also allows binding into directory services such as LDAP.

None of this has mentioned anything about the use of UDP versus TCP, host names, or what language is used to implement clients or servers. With RPC or sockets, there is a need for applications to be aware of the states of the hosts and how to connect to servers. With CORBA, these all represent environmental details that are left up to the implementation, and, being managed by the ORB, generally don't need to intrude into your application. Sockets provide a raw format bound to some standard protocols. They require that the application be aware of the protocol, as well as the format of the data to be transferred. CORBA IDL specifies the format, and protocol is left for the ORB to manage, thus eliminating the need for you to parse the raw data. The use of IDL to specify strongly typed data helps to ensure that well-structured data is being transmitted from system to system, regardless of what operating system, network protocol, language, or ORB is in use.

Evaluating CORBA

Whilst there is an initial development cost to using CORBA rather than just plumbing components directly into each other, the payoff comes from long-term development gains. For the purposes of the DVD rental application, using CORBA to split it into client and server portions will not provide dramatic improvements over using sockets or RPC. What it does provide is a sound infrastructure that would make the *next* set of changes easier to manage, whether that would be:

❑ to interface the rental application to a financial accounting application

❑ to hook up a bar code reader so that movie returns are processed at the moment that the customer slides the DVD case in the return slot and past a sensor

❑ to move data into a PostgreSQL database without the client front end having any reason to notice the change

❑ to port the server software to Java

❑ to divide up the application so that the member database is managed on one host, the DVD titles are managed on another host, and access to other portions of the application may reside on different hosts

All of these environmental changes may take place without there being any need to modify the client 'front end' of the application. In cases where new interfaces are introduced, all that need be done is for the added software to connect to the existing DVD servers, which will not disturb the existing clients in the slightest.

If changes reshape the server functionality, clients' CORBA connections are likely to need re-initializing in order to get references to the new locations of object services. Assuming the interfaces didn't change, getting the DVD client to access the new server may be as simple as logging out and then logging back in.

Further services can be added seamlessly. An implementation of the CORBA Security Service might include having verification of authentication take place with specific support from the ORB. That would diminish the need to trust both clients and servers; the alternative would be for them to individually include authentication code. This is also true for several of the CORBA Services; their behavior might be improved by implementing some portions of their functionality within the ORB.

Separating IDL definitions from the languages used to implement clients and servers becomes increasingly valuable as development teams get more widely distributed. It is crucial to have interfaces precisely and concisely documented, particularly if the system is intended to represent some form of open standard where some implementers may be in different organizations, and perhaps in different countries.

While the interface may be quite strictly defined, how you implement the service is your choice, and an important point is that both environment and implementation may be changed without the necessity of changing interfaces.

Unlike many of its alternatives, CORBA supports the connecting together of all sorts of operating system platforms and all sorts of languages. The Object Management Group (OMG), the consortium that maintains CORBA standards, has agreed on standard ways of mapping IDL constructs onto several computer languages, including Ada, C, C++, COBOL, Common Lisp, Java, and Smalltalk. Other organizations have established less formalized mappings for other languages like Perl, Python, and TCL.

Some languages, such as C, do not support direct 'object' abstractions, meaning that objects must be simulated. This unfortunately can result in rather awkward looking code, but rewards our efforts with flexible objects that would be difficult to produce in any other way.

CORBA and RPC

CORBA most strongly resembles RPC (see Chapter 18), allowing clients to request remote function calls. The critical difference is that locations of servers are not indicated via host/socket information managed by the client, but rather via an "object reference," used to properly forward requests by the ORB. In effect, the ORB directs traffic between clients and servers rather than clients managing this themselves.

The basic problem with alternatives such as RPC and sockets is not that they provide awful abstractions, but rather that as the complexity of applications using these mechanisms grows, they become more and more difficult to manage, as applications need additional services, registries, and proxies. CORBA, on the other hand, includes a framework for adding additional services, and the OMG has agreed on a number of useful CORBA Services to support additional object abstractions, as well as application-oriented CORBA Facilities to support some specific application areas. Both will be discussed in greater detail later.

CORBA addresses several significant limitations of RPC:

❏   RPC requires that APIs be statically declared at compile time.

   While RPC and CORBA both provide interface definition languages, defining the permitted operations, or "protocol," CORBA also offers a Dynamic Invocation Interface, whereby programs may explore at runtime what methods are available to be invoked by querying an Interface Repository. RPC provides no equivalent to this.

❏ RPC provides only synchronous messaging.

With CORBA, client-to-ORB communications are traditionally synchronous, as are ORB-to-server communications, but it is straightforward to attach "proxies" to provide additional messaging models. Thus, while the connection to the ORB may remain synchronous, a CORBA server that accepts and stores the request may provide an adequate simulation of asynchronous messaging when "talking to" the server that actually services the request.

There is a new Asynchronous Method Invocation (AMI) scheme that provides true asynchronous messaging, and is being implemented in a number of ORBs.

❏ RPC only addresses procedures, whereas, these days, systems tend to reference and use objects.

❏ RPC is pretty strongly tied to TCP/IP.

In contrast, CORBA assumes some communications characteristics similar to those provided by TCP/IP, but the architecture consciously contemplates the use of alternative communications transport systems such as IPX, ATM, Xerox XNS, IBM SNA, DECNet, as well as, for monstrous speed, local shared memory.

In particular, the use of shared memory can allow immense performance improvements, and is fairly much obligatory if you wish to use CORBA for fairly low-level graphical abstractions such as controlling windowing systems, as is the case for Berlin (http://www.berlin-consortium.org/), a windowing system that uses CORBA as the communications layer between its API and the graphics controller.

The critical point here is that these mechanisms have, between them, substantially different semantics, CORBA consciously tries to stay out of being tied to one or another. While "everyone" uses TCP/IP these days, that outcome was by no means a foregone conclusion ten years ago, and it is not impossible that, in 2010, we'll all be using ATM to get personal Gigabit-per-second bandwidth. CORBA can cope with that outcome transparently. With few working to extend RPC capabilities, it is unlikely that modifications will be made to cope with such changes.

❏ CORBA is still undergoing design and development efforts, whereas the ONC and DCE RPC efforts are now effectively defunct as their sponsors have moved on to CORBA. If you enhance ONC RPC, you may be the lone user of your enhancements. There was a project to produce a "free" DCE implementation; it seems to have fallen out of fashion.

CORBA and Sockets

In a similar fashion, we can compare CORBA to sockets:

❏ The use of IDL to specify strongly typed data helps to ensure that well-structured data is being transmitted from system to system, regardless of what operating system, network protocol, language, or ORB is in use.

Sockets provide a "raw" format bound to some standard protocols. They require that the application be aware of the protocol, as well as the format of the data to be transferred. CORBA IDL specifies the format, and protocol is left for the ORB to manage, thus eliminating the need for you to parse the raw data.

❏ Sockets do not provide any generally accepted scheme for providing asynchronous or proxied connections.

HTTP proxies are certainly quite common, but they are specialized to a very specific socket-based protocol, and do not support socket-based protocols as a whole.

Systems Similar To CORBA

In addition to RPC, which we have already explored in Chapter 18, there are a number of other systems that resemble CORBA, providing tools for the construction of distributed applications.

DCOM or COM+

This system, available from Microsoft, is the distributed computing system most like CORBA. Originally, DCOM was the distributed version of COM; more recently, the combination of COM and DCOM has been named COM+. A port of DCOM to Linux, also called EntireX, is available, and its installation and configuration is described in the Wrox Press book, *Professional Linux Deployment* (*ISBN 1861002874*).

Like CORBA, DCOM provides a relatively language-independent IDL to describe interfaces. Unlike CORBA IDL, however, Microsoft IDL commonly includes quite detailed system configuration information, indicating data that would normally be managed using the Windows Registry.

Microsoft has also added a plethora of services, including:

❑ MTS for transaction processing

❑ MSMQ for asynchronous messaging

❑ DAO and ADO for data access

These parallel several of the CORBA Services.

As the product of a single-vendor system, COM and DCOM are provided with the benefit of Win32 facilities like the Windows Registry and the uniform availability of identical implementations of dispatchers and services. In contrast, CORBA cannot even assume the availability of file systems, as components are intended to even be able to run on embedded computers that have little more hardware than is needed to support communications and a sensor.

The fact that you cannot assume the availability of registries, database systems, and such, increases the complexity of booting up a CORBA application.

On the other hand, enterprises that need to use diverse platforms must essentially rule out COM/DCOM, whether due to the practical necessity of having platforms on which DCOM will not function, or due to a reluctance to rewrite components.

If you need to combine CORBA and DCOM objects within a system, there are 'bridge' products to allow communications back and forth, and the OMG is actively working on standards for such interoperability.

Java Remote Method Invocation (RMI)

This is a distributed object system for Sun's Java environment; it does not involve the sophistication and complexity of CORBA Services. Since it only needs to cope with interoperating with Java, it is simpler to use than CORBA. CORBA and RMI share the property of being relatively platform-independent, but, unfortunately, RMI only works with Java programs.

Recent efforts have involved implementing RMI using the same network protocol, IIOP, as is typically used with CORBA for ORB-to-ORB communications. This represents something of a convergence of two technologies. While the increased use of IIOP may provide some synergies, it does not necessarily lead to improved interoperability.

Enterprise JavaBeans

Enterprise JavaBeans (EJB) provide a somewhat similar scheme to CORBA and DCOM, providing a standardized and fairly sophisticated way of invoking distributed components that includes a framework for robustly handling persistent data.

As with Java RMI, JavaBeans are restricted to the Java language, and suffer from all performance problems to which Java-based systems have proven susceptible. As Java compilers improve, performance should become less of an issue.

A CORBA component framework to interoperate with Enterprise JavaBeans is under construction; as with Java RMI, the technologies are converging to some extent. There are a number of EJB implementations out there, including the open source Enhydra, which makes it promising that EJB may prove to provide some truly useful results. This should be contrasted with past CORBA plans to provide "compound document" functionality using OpenDOC, which, whether for good or ill, fell by the wayside when Apple and IBM lost their commitment.

IBM MQSeries

This asynchronous messaging system, with various followers including Microsoft's MSMQ, Falcon MQ, amongst others, provides a model which reverses the CORBA design assumption of synchronous connections.

CORBA, at its base, involves synchronous messaging, where clients set up synchronous 'message channels' to servers, using proxy servers on those occasions when asynchronous operations are required. Message Queuing provides exactly the opposite result; processing is asynchronous by default, whilst establishing synchronous connections requires special programming effort.

Both approaches are useful, and CORBA Messaging Service seeks to integrate CORBA with such systems. The well-regarded QNX and BeOS operating systems make extensive use of message queues to manage interprocess (and sometimes inter-thread) communications. This is a very useful abstraction for event-based systems.

SOAP

Microsoft is promoting the Simple Object Access Protocol (SOAP). In this scheme, remote procedure calls are requested using the HTTP protocol, with data passed in XML form.

It seems not unlikely that this will ultimately be merged with MSMQ, providing a more reliable transport, where messages are represented in XML.

If you find XML a rather wordy format then you may discover IIOP's use of CDR is more efficient, both from the perspective of quantity of data transmitted and from that of the parsing effort that is required to interpret the contents of messages. The popularity of XML as a buzzword almost certainly helps promote SOAP, despite these deficiencies.

Since we have yet to see completion of large-scale SOAP-based projects, it is still early days to draw conclusions as to the ultimate viability of SOAP. Data compression and other sorts of 'protocol tuning' may improve SOAP's efficiency.

SOAP notably differs from CORBA in that the messages that are transmitted are either represented as text, or in a form that is trivially transformed into text. This means that the data being passed around may be easily examined and transformed while in transit, which may be helpful in debugging the system.

Summing up, there are quite a number of systems that provide frameworks for building distributed applications. You can accomplish similar things with them, and as they all offer useful abstractions, there are ongoing efforts to allow them to interoperate with CORBA.

The various schemes support different programming abstractions, and it is well worth looking at the underlying ideas, regardless of which framework you choose in the end. Even if you don't use the specific systems, you may look at their implementations for techniques that you may use with one of the other systems.

For software written on Linux to interoperate with GNOME, the only realistic choice is CORBA. We will use the GNOME ORB, ORBit, to illustrate this.

IDL: Defining Interfaces

CORBA provides the Interface Definition Language to express object interfaces. IDL resembles C++ or Java class declarations, and although it is not a programming language, as such; it is used to form these declarations. You cannot write code that 'does stuff' in IDL.

Modules

Modules are the top-level structure in IDL; they are used to group together related interfaces within a single namespace, which can lead to conflicts. For instance, let's consider an IDL sample containing two modules, ECHOING and NOTECHOING. In the following line the ECHOING module provides a namespace for its interface called Echo:

```
module ECHOING {
```

Here IDL supports type definitions that are used much like those in C and C++. Type input is local to the ECHOING module:

```
    typedef string input;
```

The Echo interface, and the operations inside it, are localized to the ECHOING namespace:

```
    interface Echo {
      void echo (in input str);
    };
  };
```

Then the NOTECHOING module provides a separate namespace for its interface with the same name Echo:

```
module NOTECHOING {
   interface Echo {
      void noecho (in ECHOING::input str);
   };
};
```

Note that when we use the input type, local to the ECHOING module, we need to indicate that it is being imported from that namespace by using the prefix ECHOING::. This is similar to the way C++ manages references into foreign namespaces.

In this example there were two interfaces called Echo, as well as an operator called echo. The interfaces are only established as distinct by being carefully applied in separate modules.

Pitfalls

Beware of both careless use of capitalization. CORBA assumes that it is being used with languages that are not case sensitive, and thus treats identifiers in a case-insensitive manner. If you create two declarations that differ only in case, an IDL compiler should indicate that this is an error.

When writing your code, bear in mind the language that you will be using to create clients for your CORBA service. If it interprets characters like underscores in a particular way, then it is best not to use them. In C, where there is no native 'object system', the language mapping constructs names for objects by appending together pieces using underscores. For instance, the noecho operator might be named, in C, NOTECHOING_Echo_noecho.

Interfaces

Interfaces are used to group together related data structures and operations.

For the DVD application, a reasonable set of interfaces, within the DVD module, looks to be:

```
module DVD {
  interface MEMBERSHIP { // Methods to manipulate DVD Store MEMBERS
  };
  interface TITLING { // Methods to manipulate DVD Store TITLES
  };
  interface DISKS { // Methods to manipulate DVD DISKS
  };
  interface RENTAL { // Methods for processing disk RENTALs and returns
  };
  interface RESERVATIONS { // Methods for managing reserving TITLES
  };
  interface UTILITIES { // Other methods that don't fit well elsewhere
  };
  interface FACTORY { // Base interface that provides access to the others
  };
};
```

Each interface provides an object reference. We will provide some control over how these are established and passed to clients in the DVD application by having a base FACTORY interface that will contain operations that return references to the other interfaces. The FACTORY could be used as a security tool, only returning references in response to client requests if it was satisfied that requestors are properly authenticated. It is not valid to nest one interface inside another, nor can one module nest inside another.

Basic Data Types

CORBA defines a set of basic data types that are the basic components of data shipped around from ORB to ORB in the Common Data Representation (CDR) format. The following table shows the CORBA data types:

IDL Type	Description
short	16 bit integer
long	32 bit integer
long long	64 bit integer
unsigned short	unsigned 16 bit integer
unsigned long	unsigned 32 bit integer
unsigned long long	unsigned 64 bit integer
float	32 bit IEEE floating-point number
double	64 bit IEEE floating-point number
char	8 bit character
wchar	16 bit character
boolean	boolean type taking TRUE or FALSE
octet	opaque character type untouched by communications
any	can represent any basic or constructed type

Most of the types are very similar to those provided in C and C++. It is worth elaborating on more unique octet type, which is an 8 bit character type which may be used to transmit binary data that is supposed to remain untouched. If you are transmitting text data using the char type between an ASCII-based UNIX system and an IBM AS/400 system that uses EBCDIC, it would be a fine idea for the ORB to automatically translate that data from the native form at the source into the native form at the destination, thus eliminating the need for client and/or server to do translations. On the other hand, if you want the data to be left completely alone, then use octet.

Template Types

These are types that are of variable size.

sequences

Sequences are variable length vectors. They may contain any element type. They may either be unbounded in size, thus allowing you to pass an unlimited number of string values:

```
sequence<string> message;
```

or alternatively, be bounded to some maximum number of elements:

```
sequence<char, 80> line;
```

strings and wstrings

strings are just like C strings: a vector of characters (type char) of variable length that is NULL terminated. wstrings extend this by using a vector of wchar wide characters, which are designed for use with languages with multi-byte characters.

They are equivalent to the sequence sequence<char> , but are established as a distinct type since some language environments provide functions specifically made to manipulate strings efficiently.

fixed

The fixed type is new in CORBA 2.3, and not yet universally implemented. It provides a data type for storing decimal values of up to 31 significant digits with a fixed decimal point. This parallels the PIC data type used in COBOL, and may be used to support the MONEY data type sometimes available in SQL.

This type is particularly useful in financial applications, where applications need to provide consistent policies for rounding, overflow, and treatment of precision.

```
fixed<10,2> totalamt;
```

COBOL and Ada both provide fixed decimal types; in other languages, it is necessary for the IDL language mapping to provide a representation in the local 'tongue'.

In C, the representation is not quite as natural; the ORBit IDL compiler generates the following:

```
typedef struct
{
    CORBA_unsigned_short _digits;
    CORBA_short _scale;
    CORBA_char _value[6];
} CORBA_fixed_10_2;
```

which represents a packed 2-digits-per-byte format, which requires having functions to manipulate fixed values rather than using the ordinary C arithmetic operations.

Constructed Data Types

Constructed types are constructed out of more basic types. They can contain elements that are themselves constructed types.

typedef

typedefs work much like the C typedef keyword.

```
typedef long dvdidt;
typedef fixed<10,2> money;
```

This declares a constructed type called dvdidt, which stores 32 bit integer values, and a money data type, with ten digits, of which two are decimal places.

Structures

Structures resemble C structures, albeit with a slightly different syntax.

```
struct dvddisks {
  dvdidt diskid;
  TITLING::titlet titleid;
};
```

In this example, the name of the structure is dvddisks, with the structure component diskid is declared using the dvdidt type that was declared earlier, and is thus a 32 bit signed integer.

Structure component titleid is declared using type titlet , which is declared in namespace TITLING. This illustrates the use of namespaces to reference a 'foreign' type declared in a separate interface.

Enumerations

These are rather like C/C++ enumerated types:

```
enum movieratings { G, PG13, NC17, R, NR, XXX };
```

Note that there is no way to specify a starting value, as you might do in C or C++; that means that there is no portable way of exchanging enumerated ordinal values between clients and servers; you must use the enumerators themselves. This restriction is intentional, as some languages support enumerations without there being any numbers involved. For instance, in the Common Lisp mapping, the enumerators are directly represented as symbols, thus:

```
(setf ratings-list (:G :PG13 :NC17 :R :NR :XXX))
```

In the sample application, we won't use this enumeration, as that would permanently lock the application into a fixed set of movie ratings. Instead, the values are stored in a table, so that they might be modified at a later time without needing to change the interfaces.

Arrays

Arrays provide vectors with fixed numbers of elements. You may declare single dimensioned arrays:

```
typedef char line[80];
```

as well as multidimensional arrays:

```
typedef double bezier[3][3];
```

Unions

IDL unions differ from C/C++ counterparts in that they are required to be discriminated, allow multiple case: labels for a single member, and support a default case:

```
union PCode switch(Country) {   /* International Postal Codes */
        case USA:      /* Like 75063-2921 */
            long main;
            short sub;
        case Canada:  /* Like K0A 2N0 */
            char p1;
            short p2;
            char p3;
            short p4;
            char p5;
            short p6;
        default:
            string pcode;
};
```

This example provides a representation for international postal codes, allowing the format to vary from country to country based on the value of the Country field. It is aware of special formats for Canada and the United States, and leaves the field as a generic string for other countries.

Operations

These represent object methods; they look rather like C or C++ function calls. They consist of:

An optional operation attribute indicating communications semantics; the one attribute supported is *oneway*, which indicates asynchronous processing, where the call returns immediately without returning any value. This attribute is deprecated in favor of the CORBA Messaging Service, which provides better defined properties for quality of service.

A type specification, indicating what type of value the method returns. This may be any of the IDL-declared types, or void.

An identifier, indicating the name of the operation.

A parameter list, indicating data to be passed to the server, or returned back. These consist of a parameter attribute that indicates the direction in which the parameter is to be passed. Valid attributes are:

`in`	indicating the parameter is passed from client to server
`out`	indicating the parameter is passed from server to client
`inout`	indicating the parameter is passed in both directions

This attribute may be implemented by deleting the `in` values, and allocating fresh `out` values, so it is certainly not safe to assume that the data will stay in the same place.

A parameter type specification, indicating the type of the parameter, and

A parameter name, indicating what this parameter is to be called.

Here are some examples. This is the simplest operation:

```
void simplemethod ();
```

A method to set a value:

```
void set(in storemembers recordtoupdate);
```

A method to search for a value and `memberid`, returning the value in `recordtocomplete`:

```
void get(in memberidt memberid,
        out storemembers recordtocomplete)
    raises (NOSUCHMEMBER);
```

If the operation fails, the server can return an exception, NOSUCHMEMBER, to indicate the failure.

A method that changes its input:

```
long modifyrecord(inout memrecordtype member)
    raises (TOTALLYMESSEDUP, TOTALLYRADICALDUDE);
```

An optional `raises` expression is used here, indicating application-declared exceptions that the operation may raise. Several of the operators above illustrate the declaration of exception expressions that we will deal with next. An optional context expression indicates context information. This strongly resembles the way UNIX environment variables are passed to processes. Unfortunately, context values are not type safe, which makes it problematic to look them up, and thus their use is not encouraged.

Exceptions

It would be a nice thing if interfaces worked in a straightforward manner, with no need to interpret the results. Unfortunately, things happen outside intended sequences. They might, for instance ask the Naming Service for information on a **Logging Service** that has not been registered. Or request information about a customer that doesn't exist. Or request information they are not permitted to look at. As a result, CORBA provides a set of system-defined exceptions to allow communication of ORB-related error conditions that may arise. These include:

UNKNOWN	PERSIST_STORE
BAD_PARAM	BAD_INV_ORDER
NO_MEMORY	TRANSIENT
IMP_LIMIT	FREE_MEM
COMM_FAILURE	INV_IDENT
INV_OBJREF	INV_FLAG
NO_PERMISSION	INTF_REPOS
INTERNAL	BAD_CONTEXT
MARSHAL	OBJ_ADAPTER
INITIALIZE	DATA_CONVERSION
NO_IMPLEMENT	OBJECT_NOT_EXIST
BAD_TYPECODE	TRANSACTION_REQUIRED
BAD_OPERATION	TRANSACTION_ROLLEDBACK
NO_RESOURCES	INVALID_TRANSACTION
NO_RESPONSE	

IDL also offers the ability to declare exceptions that either represent boolean indicators of there being some error condition, as with:

```
exception NOSUCHMEMBER {};
```

or that can provide further feedback concerning the nature of the exception so that the client may more intelligently react to the problem, as with:

```
exception FIELDOVERFLOW {long maxsize, long offendingsize,
string shorttext, string longtext};
```

The standard CORBA exceptions may be raised anywhere, and are most likely to be raised by your ORB or in function stubs/skeletons when there are failures at the ORB level when you try to invoke operations. In contrast, you must explicitly declare where exceptions declared in your own IDL may be used, as with:

```
void updatesurname (in memberidt memberid, in string surname)
    raises (FIELDOVERFLOW);
```

Attributes

Attributes allow you to, with one implicit operation, declare a state variable associated with an interface, allowing you to both set and get the value. The following two IDL interfaces are equivalent:

```
interface SomeDumbInterface{
   attribute int count;
};
```

```
interface SomeDumbInterface{
   int _get_count();
   void _set_count(in int c);
};
```

You can also have a `readonly` `attribute`, which will result in the omission of the `_set_count` function.

The fact that you can readily declare such methods by hand makes this of somewhat limited usefulness.

Example DVD Application

Here is a sample IDL file that describes an API for the DVD application:

```
module DVD {
  typedef string datec;
// The IDL is split into several interfaces:
//     MEMBERSHIP    - to work with the set of DVD store members
//     TITLING       - to work with the titles of DVDs that _may_ be available
//     DISKS         - to work with the set of actual physical DVDs that are
//                       available to be rented
//     RENTAL        - the transactions for renting out DVDs
//     RESERVATIONS  - allowing members to reserve titles on future dates
//     UTILITIES     - some operators that don't fit in elsewhere
//     FACTORY       - the "interface factory" that is used to provide
//                       clients with references to the other interfaces

// Methods to manipulate DVD Store MEMBERS
  interface MEMBERSHIP {
     exception NOSUCHMEMBER {};
     // The internal representation is a long integer
     typedef long memberidt;

     // memberidList is used to allow operators to return a list of
     // members
     typedef sequence<memberidt> memberidList;

     // The information tracked for each member:
     struct storemembers  {
       memberidt memberid;                 /* internal id [1..] */
       string memberno;   /* the number the member knows */
       string title;       /* Mr Mrs Ms Dr Sir */
       string fname;             /* first name */
       string lname;             /* last name */
       string houseflatref;      /* i.e. 5, or 'The birches' etc. */
       string address1;        /* Address line 1 */
       string address2;        /* Address line 2 */
       string town;            /* Town/City */
       string state;             /* needed in US only */
       string phone;           /* +44(0)123 456789 */
       string zipcode;         /* LE1 1AA or whatever */
     };
```

Next the operators allow creating, deleting, getting, and setting values for a member:

```
void set(in storemembers recordtoupdate);
void get(in memberidt memberid,
         out storemembers recordtocomplete)
   raises (NOSUCHMEMBER);
void create (in storemembers recordtoadd,
             out memberidt memberid);
void delete (in memberidt memberid)
   raises (NOSUCHMEMBER);
```

If you search for a surname, you get back a list of matching members:

```
void search (in string lname,
             out memberidList resultids);
// idfromnumber translates from the "public" member ID to the
// private values used internally.
void idfromnumber (in string memberno,
                   out memberidt memberid)
   raises (NOSUCHMEMBER);
};
```

Methods to manipulate DVD Store titles:

```
interface TITLING {
  exception NOSUCHTITLE {};
  exception NOSUCHGENRE {};
  typedef string classif;
  typedef sequence<classif> classList;
  typedef string genres ;
  typedef sequence<genres> genreList;
  typedef long titlet;
  typedef sequence<titlet> titleList;
  struct dvdtitles {
    titlet titleid;              /* internal ID [1..] */
    string titletext;   /* 'The silence of the lambs' */
    string asin;        /* 10 digit reference number */
    string director;    /* restricted to a single name */
    genres genre;               /* 'Horror', 'comedy', etc. API for
                                   standard list later */
    classif classification;
    string actor1;       /*  'Jeremy Irons' */
    string actor2;       /* 'Ingmar Bergman' */
    datec releasedate;          /* YYYYMMDD plus the null */
    string rentalcost;   /* cost of a day rental for this title
                            $$$.cc */
  };
```

Note that set, get, create, delete, and search are reused in the TITLING namespace. They will be used again in later interfaces as well:

```
      void set (in dvdtitles recordtoupdate);
      void get (in titlet titleid,
                out dvdtitles recordtocomplete)
        raises (NOSUCHTITLE);
      void create (in dvdtitles recordtoadd,
                   out titlet titleid);
      void delete (in titlet titleid)
        raises (NOSUCHTITLE);
      void search (in string title, in string name,
                   out titleList resultids);
   };
   // Methods to manipulate DVD DISKS
   //
```

A 'disk' is an actual physical DVD that the store has in stock that could be rented out to a member, such as one of seven copies of 'Seven Samurai':

```
   interface DISKS {
     exception NOSUCHDISK {};
     typedef long dvdidt;
     typedef sequence<dvdidt> dvdList;
     struct dvddisks {
       dvdidt diskid;    /* internal ID [1..] (not related to title_id) */
       TITLING::titlet titleid;
     } ;
     // Note the continuing reuse of the same operator names,
     // set/get/create/delete
     void    set (in dvddisks recordtoupdate);
     void    get (in dvdidt diskid,
                  out dvddisks recordtocomplete)
       raises (NOSUCHDISK);
     void    create (in dvddisks recordtoadd,
                     out dvdidt diskid);
     void    delete (in dvdidt diskid)
       raises (NOSUCHDISK);
     void    search (in TITLING::titlet titleid,
                     out dvdList resultids);
   };
```

The RENTAL and RESERVATIONS interfaces provide rather more complex operators that are descriptive of what is done with a title:

```
   interface RENTAL { // Methods for processing disk RENTALs and returns
     exception FORBIDDENRATING {}; // Kids are not permitted to rent porn
     void renttitle (in MEMBERSHIP::memberidt memberid,
                     in TITLING::titlet titleid,
                     out DISKS::dvdidt diskid)
       raises (DISKS::NOSUCHDISK, MEMBERSHIP::NOSUCHMEMBER,
               TITLING::NOSUCHTITLE, FORBIDDENRATING);
     void rentdiskinfo (in DISKS::dvdidt diskid,
```

```
                              out MEMBERSHIP::memberidt memberid,
                              out datec daterented)
            raises (DISKS::NOSUCHDISK);
        void diskreturn (in DISKS::dvdidt diskid,
                         in datec returndate,
                         out MEMBERSHIP::memberidt memberid)
            raises (DISKS::NOSUCHDISK);
        long titleavailable (in TITLING::titlet titleid, in datec date)
            raises (TITLING::NOSUCHTITLE);
        void overduedisks (in datec fromdate, in datec todate,
                           out DISKS::dvdList latedisks);
    };
    interface RESERVATIONS { // Methods for managing reserving TITLES
        void reservetitle (in datec needed, in TITLING::titlet titleid,
                           in MEMBERSHIP::memberidt memberid)
            raises (TITLING::NOSUCHTITLE, MEMBERSHIP::NOSUCHMEMBER,
                    RENTAL::FORBIDDENRATING);
        void cancelreservation (in MEMBERSHIP::memberidt memberid)
            raises (MEMBERSHIP::NOSUCHMEMBER);
        void queryreservationbymember (in MEMBERSHIP::memberidt memberid,
                                       out TITLING::titlet titleid)
            raises (MEMBERSHIP::NOSUCHMEMBER);
        void queryreservationbytitle (in TITLING::titlet titleid,
                                      in datec date,
                                      out MEMBERSHIP::memberidList memberids)
            raises (TITLING::NOSUCHTITLE);
    };
    // Other methods that don't fit well elsewhere
    interface UTILITIES {
        void getgenres(out TITLING::genreList genrelist);
        void getclassifications (out TITLING::classList classlist);
        void errtext(in long errnumber, out string messagetoshow);
        void today(out datec date);
        // Time _could_ be managed via the Time Service, but our needs
        // here are pretty simple
    };
```

The FACTORY is the base interface which provides operators that return references to all the other interfaces. It represents the bootstrap for the system. We could change the way the system is distributed by changing the way these interfaces are returned:

```
    interface FACTORY {
        MEMBERSHIP MEMBERSHIPFactory ();
        TITLING TITLINGFactory ();
        DISKS DISKSFactory ();
        RENTAL RENTALFactory ();
        RESERVATIONS RESERVATIONSFactory ();
        UTILITIES UTILITIESFactory ();
    };
};
```

Language Mappings

Since CORBA is intended to interoperate with a variety of languages, there needs to be a way of establishing how the functions and data structures described in IDL are to be represented in the languages that client and server processes are to be written in. For any language that is to be used, there needs to be a mapping. Historically, the first mappings were to C and Smalltalk, and the most widely used and maintained mappings these days appear to be for C++ and Java.

There is not necessarily universal support for complete functionality for all languages; the Emacs Lisp implementation, for instance, is really only capable of being used as a client. It may prove easier to use dynamic or scripting languages like Python or Lisp to support Dynamic Invocation Interface (DII) objects as they do not resolve value types until runtime, quite congruent with DII. One Python mapping, PyORBit, effectively appears to only use DII.

The mappings formally specified by the OMG include:

- Ada
- C
- C++
- COBOL
- Java
- Smalltalk
- Common Lisp

It would be a good idea to obtain a copy of the OMG documentation on whichever of these mappings you intend to use from (http://www.omg.org/technology/documents/formal /corba_language_mapping_specifica.htm). The OMG makes these documents available in Adobe PDF and Postscript form.

Mappings also exist for other languages that have not been officially adopted by the OMG, but which have been prepared with a bit less formality by interested third parties. These include the following:

- An Eiffel Language Mapping for CORBA IDL.
- An IDL Mapping for Python (http://www.python.org/sigs/do-sig/corbamap.html).
- An IDL Mapping for Erlang (http://www.erlang.org/doc/doc/lib/orber-2.0.2/doc/html /ch_erl_map.html).
- CORBA support for Haskell. (http://www.cse.unsw.edu.au/~chak/haskell/gnome /gnome-small/node11.html).
- CORBA Mapping for Perl. (http://people.redhat.com/otaylor/corba/mapping.html#CORBA_mapping_for_Perl).
- corba.el (http://www.lysator.liu.se/~lenst/corba/corba.el) - an Emacs client-side implementation of CORBA.

Language Mapping Components

A language mapping provides the means of expressing the following information in the language in question:

❑ all basic data types from IDL

❑ all constructed data types from IDL

❑ references to constants declared in IDL

❑ references to objects declared in IDL

❑ invocation of operations, including the transmission of parameters and receipt of results

❑ exceptions, including what occurs when an exception is raised, and the transmission of exception parameters

❑ access to attributes

❑ signatures for ORB-defined operations such as in the DII, object adaptors, and so forth

A good mapping will permit programmers to access all ORB functionality, expressing it in ways that are reasonably convenient for the given programming language. If the language does not provide native support for IDL functionality, as is the case for exceptions in C, the language mapping for this may wind up being somewhat clumsy.

The point of standardizing the mapping is so that the same code may be used with any ORB. After all, it would be more than a little irritating to write C++ code for the omniORB ORB, and find that the application needs to be substantially rewritten in order to use it with the TAO ORB.

C Mappings

This section will walk through various IDL mappings to C, many based on the IDL used in the DVD application. This really only touches on a fraction of all that is expressible using the standard C mapping, but should be useful in providing the flavor of how it works.

Basic IDL Data Type Mappings

The basic CORBA data type mappings for C are as follows:

IDL Type	C type mapping
short	CORBA_short
unsigned short	CORBA_unsigned_short
long	CORBA_long
unsigned long	CORBA_unsigned_long
long long	CORBA_long_long
unsigned long long	CORBA_unsigned_long_long

IDL Type	C type mapping
float	CORBA_float
double	CORBA_double
long double	CORBA_long_double
boolean	CORBA_boolean
char	CORBA_char
wchar	CORBA_wchar

Rather than using `long some_long_variable`, programs must use `CORBA_long some_long_variable`. That has the result that the specific type required by CORBA is used, rather than leaving the choice as one for the individual C implementation to apply. This issue may not be terribly important on the average IA-32 system, where the basic C types pretty much conform to the CORBA types, but is certainly going to be an issue as we progress to use 64 bit architectures, where "native" types tend to be 64 bits wide.

Thus, for `typedef long memberidt;` in interface MEMBERSHIP we get:

```
typedef CORBA_long DVD_MEMBERSHIP_memberidt;
```

and for `typedef long titlet;` in interface TITLING we get:

```
typedef CORBA_long DVD_TITLING_titlet;
```

Constructed and Template Data Types

The mappings include:

Strings

Consider the date string type:

```
typedef string datec;
```

The C mapping for this definition is:

```
typedef CORBA_char *DVD_datec;
```

This reflects that C strings are just arrays of characters.

Structures

The mapping here is not overly surprising. For instance the IDL for `storemembers` in interface MEMBERSHIP in module DVD is:

```
struct storemembers {
    memberidt memberid;              /* internal id [1..] */
    string memberno;    /* the number the member knows */
```

```
    string title;          /* Mr Mrs Ms Dr Sir */
    string fname;              /* first name */
    string lname;              /* last name */
    string houseflatref;       /* i.e. 5, or 'The birches' etc. */
    string address1;       /* Address line 1 */
    string address2;       /* Address line 2 */
    string town;           /* Town/City */
    string state;              /* needed in US only */
    string phone;          /* +44(0)123 456789 */
    string zipcode;        /* LE1 1AA or whatever */
};
```

This maps to the following C structure:

```
typedef struct
{
    DVD_MEMBERSHIP_memberidt memberid;
    CORBA_char *memberno;
    CORBA_char *title;
    CORBA_char *fname;
    CORBA_char *lname;
    CORBA_char *houseflatref;
    CORBA_char *address1;
    CORBA_char *address2;
    CORBA_char *town;
    CORBA_char *state;
    CORBA_char *phone;
    CORBA_char *zipcode;
} DVD_MEMBERSHIP_storemembers;
```

The module, interface, and structure name are appended together to get the C name,
`DVD_MEMBERSHIP_storemembers`

Sequences

Sequences result in the generation of a structure to collect the components together as an array.
For instance, interface `MEMBERSHIP` declares a sequence `memberidList`:

```
typedef sequence<memberidt> memberidList;
```

This leads to generating the following structure:

```
typedef struct
{
    CORBA_unsigned_long _maximum,
```

`_maximum` is permitted to contain the maximum number of elements permissible in the sequence:

```
    _length;
```

_length is a mandatory element, representing the number of entries being passed in the sequence:

```
DVD_MEMBERSHIP_memberidt *_buffer;
```

_buffer is an array of pointers to the variety of values being passed, in this case, IDL type memberidt, and C type DVD_MEMBERSHIP_memberidt:

```
CORBA_boolean _release;
```

_release is a variable that indicates whether or not the sequence info should be released by the ORB once data transmission is complete:

```
} CORBA_sequence_DVD_MEMBERSHIP_memberidt;
```

To use this, you might code something like:

```
/* Set up sequence variable */
CORBA_sequence_DVD_MEMBERSHIP_memberidt membs;
/* Allocate entries in the sequence */
membs._buffer = CORBA_alloc_DVD_MEMBERSHIP_memberidt(6);
membs._length = 6; /* Guess how many entries we have? */
membs._buffer[0] = member1;
membs._buffer[1] = member2;
membs._buffer[2] = member3;
membs._buffer[3] = member4;
membs._buffer[4] = member5;
membs._buffer[5] = member6;
```

This provides membs, ready to be passed to a server as an argument, or back to a client, as a result.

Enumerations

This isn't a sample from the DVD application, but could have been:

```
enum emovieratings {G, PG13, NC17, R, NR, XXX};
```

This could map to:

```
typedef enum { DVD_G, DVD_PG13, DVD_NC17, DVD_R, DVD_NR, DVD_XXX }
    DVD_emovieratings;
```

Arrays

Looking at:

```
typedef double memid[8][12];
```

We get the definitions:

```
typedef CORBA_double DVD_memid[8][12];
typedef CORBA_double DVD_memid_slice[12];
```

The slices represent the 'secondary pieces' of the array, that could be allocated separately if you so wished.

Constant References

You may declare constants of the various basic types, and they will be rendered as C #define definitions. They may involve computations using basic mathematical and boolean operators such as addition, multiplication, exclusive OR, and shift operators.

This is perhaps best outlined by outlining some examples in IDL, and showing their rendition in C. Here are some constant declarations in IDL of various types, some of them using calculations:

```
module CONSAMPLES {
  enum Colour { Red, Green, Blue, Brown, Fuschia, Lime };
  const Colour FAVORITECOLOUR = Fuschia;
  const long LV = 3;
  const long long sdiff = (2500000 << 4) - (254 >> 2) * LV;
  const double Pi = 3.14159265358979323846;
  const double Piover2 = Pi / 2.0;
};
```

The IDL transforms into the following set of C declarations:

```
typedef enum {
      CONSAMPLES_Red, CONSAMPLES_Green, CONSAMPLES_Blue,
      CONSAMPLES_Brown, CONSAMPLES_Fuschia, CONSAMPLES_Lime
} CONSAMPLES_Colour;
#define CONSAMPLES_FAVORITECOLOUR CONSAMPLES_Fuschia
#define CONSAMPLES_LV 3
#define CONSAMPLES_sdiff 39999811
#define CONSAMPLES_Pi 3.141593
#define CONSAMPLES_Piover2 1.570796
```

Invoking Operations

This represents the 'meat' of what one does with CORBA . Here are some operations declared in IDL:

```
module opsamples {
  interface ops {
    void op1 ();  /* Which passes no values */
    void op2 (in long in1); /* Passing in a long */
    void op3 (in long in1, out long out1); /* Receives and outputs a long */
    long op4 (inout long io1);  /* Changes a long value, and produces a long */
  };
};
```

These map to the following C declarations:

```
/** prototypes **/
void opsamples_ops_op1(opsamples_ops _obj, CORBA_Environment * ev);
void opsamples_ops_op2(opsamples_ops _obj, const CORBA_long in1,
                    CORBA_Environment * ev);
void opsamples_ops_op3(opsamples_ops _obj, const CORBA_long in1,
                    CORBA_long * out1, CORBA_Environment * ev);
CORBA_long opsamples_ops_op4(opsamples_ops _obj, CORBA_long * io1,
                    CORBA_Environment * ev);
```

Server code will implement these functions; client code will use them to request work to be done.

Exception Handling

This is one area where the mapping to C is particularly clumsy. IDL defines a structured exception system that is fairly similar to the C++ exception system. C is lacking in this area of functionality. As a result, the C mapping involves adding an additional return value to each method, which returns an 'exception environment' which the program must then interpret. You may find you want to build helper functions so that you only use the native mapping once or twice.

Suppose we declare a set of exceptions thus:

```
module main {
  exception foo {};  // Exception without argument
  interface secondary {
    exception bar {  // Exception WITH argument
      string msg;
    };
  };
};
```

The C mapping produces the following declarations:

```
 #define ex_main_foo "IDL:main/foo:1.0"
#define _main_foo_defined 1
typedef struct {
  int dummy;
} main_foo;
#define ex_main_secondary_bar "IDL:main/secondary/bar:1.0"
#define _main_secondary_bar_defined 1
typedef struct {
  CORBA_char *msg;
} main_secondary_bar;
```

After returning from a CORBA operation invocation, an exception structure of the following form is generated:

```
typedef struct CORBA_environment {
  CORBA_exception_type _major;
  ... other ORB-dependent stuff
} CORBA_environment;
```

The _major value may contain either CORBA_NO_EXCEPTION, indicating there was no exception, CORBA_USER_EXCEPTION, indicating that one of the exceptions declared in the IDL was raised, and CORBA_SYSTEM_EXCEPTION, if one of the standard CORBA exceptions was raised. You can determine the exception name by calling CORBA_exception_id, and its value by calling CORBA_exception_value.

Attributes

This mapping is most readily illustrated via an example. Suppose we declare a set of exceptions thus:

```
module attsamp {
  interface circle {
    attribute float radius;
  };
};
```

The C mapping produces the following declarations:

```
/** prototypes **/
CORBA_float attsamp_circle__get_radius(attsamp_circle _obj,
                                    CORBA_Environment * ev);
void attsamp_circle__set_radius(attsamp_circle _obj,
                             const CORBA_float value,
                             CORBA_Environment * ev);
```

These methods will be used just like ordinary operators, which means that the only diminishment of effort occurs when writing up the IDL file, which is generally the easy part.

An Introductory Example: A Simple Messaging System

We'll start by presenting the complete code for a fairly simple system. The program will be passed two arguments – the name of a sender, and that of a recipient, and then reads a message from stdin and submits it to a CORBA message server. The full code listing for this example is available for download from the Wrox website http://www.wrox.com.

This example will illustrate several things:

❑ a small, but complete, IDL interface

❑ how to use ORBit-IDL to generate stub files

❑ the basic wrapper code required to use CORBA in an application

❑ care and feeding of an IOR

❑ illustrate interlanguage interoperability, as the server will be written in Python

Simple Messaging

The application here is to provide a simple way of submitting messages to a server. A message consists of:

❑ an identity of the 'sender'

❑ an identity of the 'recipient' to which the message is directed

❑ and a sequence of lines that make up the message

This isn't directly very useful, but if you tweak the meaning of sender and recipient, and perhaps add some additional fields, there are a lot of applications that require submitting messages from one place to another.

IDL for this is:

```
module MESSAGING {
    typedef sequence#&60;string#&62; msgLines;
    struct msg {
```

```
      string fr;
      string to;
      msgLines body;
   };
   interface mail {
     void submit (in msg message);
   };
};
```

Using ORBit With The IDL

The primary ORB used with the GNOME Project is ORBit, so our examples will be based on its use. If you have the GNOME development tools installed, this should include ORBit.

Take the MESSAGING IDL from the previous section and put it in a file as msg.idl. The command orbit-idl msg.idl will generate four files, which are unfortunately too verbose to include in detail:

Msg.h	This contains the 'public' data types and function definitions that will be used by any program that uses the interfaces declared in msg.idl.
msg-common.c	This file contains common functions and data types that will be used both by client and servers for the interfaces. This notably includes functions to allocate and free the data structures defined in the interfaces.
msg-skels.c	This file contains 'skeleton' functions and other definitions to receive requests from ORBit. Its purpose is to provide functions that receive requests directly from ORBit, unmarshall and pass them on to the C functions written to implement the operations, as well as to provide functions that take values to be passed out to clients, marshall and pass them back to the ORB. Thus, this would be compiled into an ORBit -based message server.
msg-stubs.c	This represents a converse to the 'skeletons' of msg-skels.c, providing stubs to communicate between the requests, in your program, and the ORB. The stubs manage the 'marshalling' of requests, submission, and then receipt and 'unmarshalling' of the results.

The Message Client

We'll write the client in C, which allows us to show off the C mapping:

```
/* A Simple Client */
#include "stdio.h"
#include "orb/orbit.h"   /* ORBit header */
#include "msg.h"         /* IDL header file */
int readlines (void);
```

```
#define MAXMSGLEN 2500    /* Maximum lines in msg */
char *contents[MAXMSGLEN+1];

int main (int argc, char *argv[])
{
  /* Variables used for IOR-reading */
  FILE *ifp; char *ior, filebuffer[1024];
  /* Critical variables for the POA */
  CORBA_Environment ev;
  CORBA_ORB orb;
  CORBA_Object msg_client;  /* Link to the Message object */

  /* Variables used to store object data for a message to be
     sent. */
  MESSAGING_msg *ourmessage;
  MESSAGING_msgLines *mbody;
  /* Miscellanea */
  int lines, i;

  /* Standard initialization of the orb. Notice that ORB_init 'eats'
     input from the command line */
  CORBA_exception_init(#&46;ev);
  orb = CORBA_ORB_init(#&46;argc, argv, "orbit-local-orb", #&46;ev);
```

The next section gets the IOR (object reference). It should be written out by msg-server in the form of a string into the file msg.ior. If you are running the server in the same place as the client, this should be fine. Otherwise, we have the 'IOR distribution problem':

```
ifp = fopen("msg-server.ior","r");
if( ifp == NULL ) {
  g_error("No msg-server.ior file!");
  exit(-1);
}
fgets(filebuffer,1024,ifp);
ior = g_strdup(filebuffer);
fclose(ifp);
```

Now, let's get a link to the actual message interface object:

```
msg_client = CORBA_ORB_string_to_object(orb, ior, #&46;ev);
if (!msg_client) {
  printf("Cannot bind to %s\n", ior);
  exit(-2);
}
```

Then, let's set up a simple message – first, allocate a message structure:

```
ourmessage=MESSAGING_msg__alloc();
```

And attach basic fields to it:

```
if (argc < 3) {
  printf("Need two arguments: from to\n");
  exit(-3);
}
ourmessage->fr=argv[1];
ourmessage->to=argv[2];
mbody = MESSAGING_msgLines__alloc();  /* Allocate the structure... */
lines = readlines();           /* Read the body in */

mbody->_length = lines;
mbody->_buffer = CORBA_sequence_CORBA_string_allocbuf(lines);
for (i = 0; i < lines; i++) {
  mbody->_buffer[i] = contents[i];
}
ourmessage->body = *mbody; /* And now link that sequence into the
                              message */
/* Now, to submit the message... */
MESSAGING_mail_submit(msg_client, ourmessage, #&46;ev);
```

Catch any exceptions (eg, network is down):

```
if(ev._major != CORBA_NO_EXCEPTION) {
  printf("we got exception %d from submit!\n", ev._major);
  return 1;
}
/* Clean up, somewhat... */
CORBA_Object_release(msg_client, #&46;ev);
CORBA_Object_release((CORBA_Object)orb, #&46;ev);
return 0;
}
```

And finally a function that reads in a bunch of lines and puts them in the buffer:

```
int readlines (void) {
  char linebuff[4096];  /* Temporary buffer for lines... */
  int nlines, llen;
  for (nlines = 0; fgets(linebuff, 4096, stdin); !feof(stdin)) {
    llen = strlen(linebuff);
    contents[nlines] = (char*) malloc(llen+1);
    linebuff[llen-1]=0;   /* Nuke the line terminator */
    strcpy (contents[nlines], linebuff);
    nlines++;
    if (nlines >= MAXMSGLEN) {
      return nlines;
    }
  }
  return nlines;
}
```

The Message Server

The message server illustrates language independence by being presented in Python. It also illustrates the way that Python provides a more elegant mapping than C, in that it has language features that conveniently support such things as objects, classes, and (not used here) exceptions.

In addition, the fact that Python provides garbage collection means that we don't have the messiness of having to pepper your code with `malloc` and `free` calls so that the process doesn't chew up memory. Memory still needs to be allocated and de-allocated, but this does not need to intrude on the code. This is file `msg-server.py`:

```python
#!/usr/bin/env python
import CORBA
class mail:
        msgs = 0    # Message counter
        def submit(self, msg):
                print "Message Received from:", msg.fr
                print "Message for:", msg.to
                for line in msg.body:
                        print line
                self.msgs = self.msgs + 1
                print "Messages Served: ", self.msgs
CORBA.load_idl("msg.idl")
CORBA.load_idl("/usr/share/idl/name-service.idl")
orb = CORBA.ORB_init((), CORBA.ORB_ID)
poa = orb.resolve_initial_references("RootPOA")

servant = POA.MESSAGING.mail(mail())
poa.activate_object(servant)
ref = poa.servant_to_reference(servant)
open("./msg-server.ior", "w").write(orb.object_to_string(ref))
print "Wrote out IOR: ", orb.object_to_string(ref)
poa.the_POAManager.activate()
orb.run()   # Server now is in an ORBit event loop, awaiting requests
```

Compiling the ORBit Application

Here is a makefile for this application:

```make
### Makefile for message application
# ORBit configuration:
ORBIT_IDL = /usr/bin/orbit-idl
ORBIT_CFLAGS = -I/usr/lib/glib/include -I/usr/include
ORBIT_LIBS = -L/usr/lib -lORBit -lIIOP -lORBitutil -lglib -lm
CFLAGS = $(ORBIT_CFLAGS) -g
LFLAGS = $(ORBIT_LIBS)

all: msg-client msg.hh msgSK.cc

### Some ORBit IDL transformations
%.h : %.idl
        orbit-idl $<
%-common.c : %.idl
```

```
        orbit-idl $<
%-skels.c : %.idl
        orbit-idl $<
%-stubs.c : %.idl
        orbit-idl $<
### omniORB Dependencies...
%SK.cc: %.idl
        omniidl2 $<
%.hh : %.idl
        omniidl2 $<

### Our favorite bits of dependencies:
msg.h: msg.idl
msg-common.c: msg.idl
msg-stubs.c: msg.idl
msg-skels.c: msg.idl

### omniORB2 bindings are set up here to provide a secondary verification
### that the IDL is well-formed from the perspective of another
### language, ORB, and parser.  If you don't have it installed, this
### bit will fail, which is a benign error.
msg.hh: msg.idl
msgSK.cc: msg.idl

### Compiling the Message Client
msg-client: msg-client.o msg-common.o msg-stubs.o
        $(CC) -o msg-client msg-client.o msg-stubs.o msg-common.o \
                $(LFLAGS)

msg-client.o: msg-client.c
```

These may not be the best transformations for getting Make to automatically generate stubs from IDL, but they do work. Note that this makefile produces bindings files for C++, using omniORB. We don't actually use this, but using it has proven useful in finding errors in IDL files, as omniORB looks for problems with C++-related issues.

Running The Message Application

You first need to make sure that ORBit, Python and ORBit-Python are all installed on your system. The first two might have already been installed on system by your Linux distribution. ORBit-Python, which provides Python bindings for ORBit, can be downloaded from http://projects.sault.org/orbit-python.

Now, let's suppose that all of the files listed thus far are in the directory /usr/local/src/ORBitsamples. Head to that directory, and type:

```
$ make
```

This will generate IDL stubs, msg-client, and perhaps even generate msg.hh and msgSK.cc, if you have omniORB installed.

Next, we need to run `msg-server`, to effectively 'boot up' this distributed application:

```
$ ./msg-server
```

This takes over the present console/terminal, so you will want to set it up as a background process if you want to reuse the same console to run the client.

This will start up the server, and write out an IOR, in string form, to `/usr/local/src/ORBitsamples/msg-server.ior`. You might want to look at that file to see what the IOR looks like. Now, for the moment of truth: head to an available terminal/console/window, and type:

```
$ ./msg-client me you < msg-server.ior
```

The console on which `msg-server` is running should now display a message number, the information about the message, and the contents of the IOR file. Presto! You have your first CORBA application running. If you have another computer around which is connected via TCP/IP, you can try a remote connection. You will need several things: you need to have `msg-client` on that host and you need to have the `msg-server.ior` file available. One way of accomplishing this is by having `/usr/local` mounted on both hosts; another would be to use FTP or a floppy disk to copy `msg-client` and `msg-server.ior` over. On a Compaq Alpha box, it was necessary to recompile `msg-client`, after which it worked fine.

In any case, this shows that you can submit a message from the client to the server. The Python server was 'pounded' in testing with messages, where two servers threw messages at it, and it handled 15,000 messages over a period of ten minutes without complaint.

Resources

These are useful web sites:

- ❏ Object Management Group (http://www.omg.org)
- ❏ ORBit (http://www.labs.redhat.com/orbit)
- ❏ Enhydra (http://www.enhydra.org)
- ❏ Dr. Douglas Schmidt's CORBA Links (http://www.cs.wustl.edu/~schmidt/corba.html)
- ❏ Tom Valesky's Free CORBA ORB Listing (http://patriot.net/~tvalesky/freecorba.html)
- ❏ Enhydra (http://www.enhydra.org) Open Source Java and XML Application Server
- ❏ Simple Object Access Protocol (SOAP) (http://www.ietf.org/internet-drafts /draft-box-http-soap-00.txt)

Summary

This chapter has introduced CORBA as a way of building distributed object-based applications, and its major components, including Object Request Brokers (ORB), and the Interface Definition Language, IDL.

CORBA has been compared to some systems used to accomplish similar purposes. Functionality is tending to converge, particularly as CORBA supporters either implement services that resemble those of other systems, or implement bridges to communicate with other systems.

We looked in some detail at the structures of IDL, and how they are used to define interfaces to objects. We looked at how CORBA applications join together the language-independent IDL and specific languages, looking particularly at the C language mapping.

Source code was presented to implement a simple messaging system with components in C and Python, using the ORBit ORB.

Online discussion at http://www.p2p.wrox.com

21

Implementing CORBA with ORBit

Some time ago, the GNOME Project was looking to use an ORB. They examined a number of options. Whilst there were a number of C++-based ORBs at the time, there were only a few that used C.

ILU, the Inter Language Unification package, developed at Xerox, provided CORBA services and supported quite a number of languages, including C. However, in 1998 it was not clear that its licensing would be acceptable, and Xerox didn't provide the sorts of clarifications that would have allowed the adoption of ILU.

ILU has another problem in that it is not precisely a CORBA implementation, but rather uses its own IDL-like language, ISL, as well as some of its own protocols, which would induce additional translations when using it to support CORBA applications. It is an interesting platform for experimenting with CORBA-like techniques, but it is not exactly CORBA.

Primarily as a result of the licensing issues, Dick Porter and Elliot Lee constructed an IDL parser, marking the beginning of the ORBit CORBA implementation. They continue to enhance the system to this day.

Licensing issues have since been clarified with ILU, but in the meantime ORBit has become fairly well established. ORBit still has the merit of being small in size and designed solely as a CORBA implementation, which makes it more focused on one type of service than ILU.

Using CORBA for the DVD Store Application

The goal in this chapter is to demonstrate how one may construct a CORBA-based application with minimal change to the original DVD store GUI application. Improvements over the 'monolithic' approach include:

❑   The application allows multiple users to concurrently connect to a single data store without using a relational database manager; in effect, the DVD server is the database manager.

❑   It eliminates the need for clients to worry about synchronizing data accesses themselves.

File-based client/server systems have traditionally needed to go to great pains to provide locking schemes to ensure that users would not trample on one another's work. The most modern version of the Berkeley Database, Sleepycat DB, includes a `lock server` process devoted to this purpose. One of the longstanding criticisms of NFS is its less than satisfactory file locking semantics.

In contrast, CORBA DVD store application does not need to provide a distributed locking scheme since access to data only occurs in one place – within the server process supporting the DVD interfaces. While PostgreSQL also provides this data management function, in larger scale systems, it may prove necessary to explore which approach will prove most beneficial. A mixed approach, combining both a DBMS as well as some form of transaction system is fairly likely to scale best. This is evidenced by the fact that when vendors try to construct transaction processing benchmarks, they often use both a relational database, like Oracle, along with a separate transaction processing monitor such as BEA Tuxedo.

Our application is split into three pieces.

The DVD Client

This is the GNOME-based application that has already been seen in various forms. The changes to this program are largely restricted to changing the data access API in `flatfile.c`, renamed to `corbaclient.c`, so that it references CORBA methods instead of accessing files locally.

There are some other changes: `dvdc.h`, `dvdc-common.c`, and `dvdc-stubs.c`, generated by `orbit-idl`, are added in to support the CORBA operators, and `main.c` has code added to request access to the CORBA services.

The DVD Server

This program, written in Python, acts primarily as a CORBA server, providing functions that perform the various operations declared by the interfaces.

It stores data in Berkeley DB style database files; one for each of the MEMBERSHIP, TITLING, DISKS, RESERVATIONS, and RENTALS interfaces. The data gets 'stringified' for storage, not entirely unlike the way that information about CORBA object references may be serialized as an IOR. In the role of a CORBA client, it also makes use of the separate logging server, tracking requests that come in.

A Logging Server

This component monitors actions taken by the DVD server. For the purposes of this system, the logging server is mostly useful as a debugging tool, and it does not provide a way to 'fail back' to some form of local message logging if the network is down.

In a more sophisticated system, the logging server would be a critical security tool, providing the means to establish the non-repudiation of transactions, as well as to provide a data repository, which is useful if a breach occurs and you need to find out who did what when.

A further improvement in reliability may be obtained using the log server. A technique used in database management systems to improve system reliability is called 'transaction logging'. Every change made to the database is written to the transaction log in chronological order. If the database becomes corrupted, typically due to a hardware failure, you may recover the system by going back and reading an old copy of the database, reading transactions from the transaction log, and replaying them to recover the system up to the time of the failure.

In a more sophisticated version, it would be logical to introduce some further sets of interfaces, including a login process that requires authentication. It would be straightforward to introduce a simple interface, which would admit or deny access to the other interfaces based on the information the user passes it at login time. There is a Co-Security interface defined for the Security Service that could provide a fairly sophisticated authentication scheme; unfortunately, this service is not yet generally available with any free CORBA implementations.

Validation Server

One of the major merits of using a relational database like PostgreSQL is that it provides ways to express relationships between pieces of data, as well as to enforce the integrity of those relationships. For instance, a foreign key relationship might be used to ensure that DVDs can only be rented to members that are in good standing. As with the 'locking' issue, small-scale applications may be able to be implemented either by enforcing relationships in a relational database, or by having application server objects validate and maintain the relationships.

With larger applications that have busy databases, performance will be improved if at least some validation takes place within a CORBA service, before attempting to update the database. If all the validation is done by the RDBMS, then an unsuccessful attempt to do an update results in considerable effort as the database works to start the update, detect and report the error condition, and then roll back the changes. In contrast, if the error is caught before any attempt is made to touch the database, the database needs to do fewer rollbacks.

Client Code

The first source code change occurs in `main.c`:

```
  int main (int argc, char *argv[])
{
  GnomeClient *client;

#ifdef ENABLE_NLS
  bindtextdomain (PACKAGE, PACKAGE_LOCALE_DIR);
  textdomain (PACKAGE);
```

```
#endif
  user = NULL;
  passwd = NULL;
  /* New bit of code for CORBA Application! */
  ConnectORB(argc, argv);  /* Connect to DVD Server */

  gnome_init_with_popt_table("dvdstore", VERSION, argc, argv,
                             options, 0, NULL);
  /* ... and so on ... */
}
```

Log Server

The log server provides a structured set of log information, based on the following IDL:

```
module LOG {
  struct loginfo {
    string hostname;
    string userid;
    string application;
    string messagetype;
    string shortmessage;
  };
  interface LOG {
    void addlog (in loginfo info);
  };
};
```

This is an intentionally simple interface, because we want to give it the rather important property of having little opportunity to go wrong:

```
#!/usr/bin/env python
# $ID$
import CORBA, sys, regex, string, random, time
from string import split, strip, joinfields
from time import localtime, strftime, time
# Here are the functions to support the LOG interface
class LOG:   # interface
    def addlog (self, info):
        logfile = open("./logs.log", "a")
        logfile.write(joinfields([info.hostname,
                                  strftime("%Y/%m/%d %H:%M:%S %Z",
                                           localtime(time())),
                                  info.userid, info.application,
                                  info.messagetype, info.shortmessage], "|"))
        logfile.write("\n")
        logfile.close()

CORBA.load_idl("logger.idl")
orb = CORBA.ORB_init((), CORBA.ORB_ID)
poa = orb.resolve_initial_references("RootPOA")
```

```
servant = POA.LOG.LOG(LOG())
poa.activate_object(servant)
ref = poa.servant_to_reference(servant)
open("./logger.ior", "w").write(orb.object_to_string(ref))

print "Done initialization: Proceed!"
poa.the_POAManager.activate()
orb.run()
```

This provides only a single interface, with a single function defined in it. That's about all you need for pushing messages into the log.

The log file is opened and closed for each entry, which may cost a bit in terms of performance, but it guarantees that all updates are immediately flushed to disk, which, if you are watching programs crash on you, is just what you need. This also means that if a log manager process renames the log file, so that older logs eventually get purged, this can occur without the log server needing to worry about this.

DVD Server

The DVD server is implemented in Python, using the ORBit-Python (http://projects.sault.org/orbit-python/) mapping of CORBA onto Python.

We start by defining a set of utility functions to be used internally by the server. This includes defining the data repositories, where data is stored using bsddb.btopen in B-Trees on disk. Functions that use these databases need to force updates to disk via calls like SHMEMBERS.sync:

```
.#!/usr/bin/env python

import CORBA, sys, string, random, time, bsddb, os
from string import split, strip, joinfields
from random import randint
from time import localtime, strftime, time

### Connect Associative arrays to Files
SHDISKS=bsddb.btopen("disks.db", "c")
SHMEMBERS=bsddb.btopen("members.db", "c")
SHRENTALS=bsddb.btopen("rentals.db", "c")
SHRESERVATIONS=bsddb.btopen("reservations.db", "c")
SHTITLES=bsddb.btopen("titles.db", "c")
```

The functions in the class SETUPCOUNTERS provide the ability to create new entries in the disk, member, and title tables. This illustrates that the implementation does not need to limit itself to the set of operations enumerated in the IDL. The IDL represents the public interfaces; the server includes a number of private interfaces that it uses internally:

```
### Now, utilities...
class SetUpCounters:
    def maxforall(self):
        self.maxfordisks()
        self.maxformembers()
        self.maxfortitles()
    def maxfordisks(self):
```

```
        if DBMAX.has_key("disks"):
            max = DBMAX["disks"]
        else:
            max = 1
        try:
            i=SHDISKS.first()
            while i != None:
                iint = string.atoi(i)
                if iint > max:
                    max=iint+1
                i=SHDISKS.next(i)
        except:
            DBMAX["disks"] = max
    def maxformembers(self):
        if DBMAX.has_key("members"):
            max = DBMAX["members"]
        else:
            max = 1
        try:
            i=SHMEMBERS.first()
            while i != None:
                iint = string.atoi(i)
                if iint > max:
                    max=iint+1
                i=SHMEMBERS.next(i)
        except:
            DBMAX["members"] = max
    def maxfortitles(self):
        if DBMAX.has_key("titles"):
            max = DBMAX["titles"]
        else:
            max = 1
        try:
            i=SHTITLES.first()
            while i != None:
                iint = string.atoi(i)
                if iint > max:
                    max=iint+1
                i=SHTITLES.next(i)
        except:
            DBMAX["titles"] = max
```

Function `logit` is used as a wrapper for the operation that is being used from the Logging Server, simplifying its use:

```
  uname = os.uname()
hostname = uname[1]
def logit(type, info):
    try:
        LOGORB.addlog(LOG.loginfo(hostname=hostname,
                                  userid="%d" % os.getuid(),
                                  application="dvd-server",
                                  messagetype=type,
                                  shortmessage=info))
    except:
        print "logging server broken!"
```

There are a number of functions to 'stringify' and 'destringify' values. The problem here is to transform the CORBA data structures back and forth into strings that can be put into the `bsddb` databases:

```
### Functions to pack/unpack the DBM file information
def idtostring (id):
    return "%d" % id

def destringizereservationinfo(sres):
    rout=DVD.RESERVATIONS.reservation
    (mbr, ttl, dd)=string.split(sres, "\\")
    rout.memberid=string.atoi(mbr)
    rout.titleid=string.atoi(ttl)
    rout.dwanted=dd
    return rout
def stringizereservation(res):
    return string.join(("%d"%res.memberid, "%d"%res.titleid, res.dwanted), "\\")
def destringizerentinfo(srental):
    rout=DVD.RENTAL.rentinfo
    (dsk, mbr, dd) = string.split(srental, "\\")
    rout.diskid=string.atoi(dsk)
    rout.memberid=string.atoi(mbr)
    rout.drented=dd
    return rout
def stringizerentinfo(rrec):
    return string.join(("%d"%rrec.diskid, "%d"%rrec.memberid, rrec.drented), "\\")
def destringizedisk(sdisk):
    disk=DVD.DISKS.dvddisks()
    (sd, st) = string.split(sdisk, "\\")
    disk.diskid = string.atoi(sd)
    disk.titleid = string.atoi(st)
    return disk
def stringizedisk(disk):
    return string.join(("%d"%disk.diskid, "%d"%disk.titleid), "\\")
def stringizetitle(title):
    return string.join(("%d" % title.titleid, title.titletext, title.asin,
title.director, title.genre, title.classification, title.actor1, ti-tle.actor2,
title.releasedate, title.rentalcost, title.image), "\\")
def destringizetitle(stitle):
    title=DVD.TITLING.dvdtitles()
    (mttl, title.titletext, title.asin, title.director, title.genre, ti-
tle.classification, title.actor1, title.actor2, title.releasedate, ti-
tle.rentalcost, title.image) = string.split(stitle, "\\")
    title.titleid=string.atoi(mttl)
    return title

def stringizemember(member):
    return string.join(("%d" % member.memberid, member.memberno,
                        member.title, member.fname, member.lname,
                        member.houseflatref, member.address1,
                        member.address2, member.town, member.state,
                        member.phone, member.zipcode), "\\")
def destringizemember(smember):
    member=DVD.MEMBERSHIP.storemembers()
    (mid, member.memberno, member.title, member.fname, member.lname,
     member.houseflatref, member.address1, member.address2,
     member.town, member.state, member.phone, member.zipcode) =
string.split(smember, "\\")
    member.memberid=string.atoi(mid)
    return member
```

Future enhancements to the system could include making use of the Python `shelve` or `pickle` classes, which provide more sophisticated ways of serializing data structures, or ultimately, having the DVD server communicate with a PostgreSQL server.

Let's complete the setup of the non-CORBA components by establishing associative arrays for the error message tables and running the function `maxforall` to establish the record creation counters:

```
    ### Initialization of non-ORB stuff...
FACTORYOBJECT = {}
DBMAX = {}
ERRNDICT = {
      0 : "DVD_SUCCESS"              ,
     -1 : "DVD_ERR_NO_FILE"          ,
     -2 : "DVD_ERR_BAD_TABLE"        ,
     -3 : "DVD_ERR_NO_MEMBER_TABLE"  ,
     -4 : "DVD_ERR_BAD_MEMBER_TABLE",
     -5 : "DVD_ERR_BAD_TITLE_TABLE"  ,
     -6 : "DVD_ERR_BAD_DISK_TABLE"   ,
     -7 : "DVD_ERR_BAD_SEEK"         ,
     -8 : "DVD_ERR_NULL_POINTER"     ,
     -9 : "DVD_ERR_BAD_WRITE"        ,
    -10 : "DVD_ERR_BAD_READ"         ,
    -11 : "DVD_ERR_NOT_FOUND"        ,
    -12 : "DVD_ERR_NO_MEMORY"        ,
    -13 : "DVD_ERR_BAD_RENTAL_TABLE" ,
    -14 : "DVD_ERR_BAD_RESERVE_TABLE" }

ERRMSGDICT = {
    "DVD_SUCCESS" : "no error",
    "DVD_ERR_NO_FILE" : "cannot open file",
    "DVD_ERR_BAD_TABLE" : "corrupt table file",
    "DVD_ERR_NO_MEMBER_TABLE" : "no member table",
    "DVD_ERR_BAD_MEMBER_TABLE" : "corrupt member table",
    "DVD_ERR_BAD_TITLE_TABLE" : "corrupt title table",
    "DVD_ERR_BAD_DISK_TABLE" : "corrupt disk table",
    "DVD_ERR_BAD_RENTAL_TABLE" : "corrupt rental table",
    "DVD_ERR_BAD_RESERVE_TABLE" : "corrupt reserve table",
    "DVD_ERR_BAD_SEEK" : "cannot seek in file",
    "DVD_ERR_NULL_POINTER" : "null data pointer",
    "DVD_ERR_BAD_WRITE" : "cannot write to file",
    "DVD_ERR_BAD_READ" : "cannot read file",
    "DVD_ERR_NOT_FOUND" : "no match found",
    "DVD_ERR_NO_MEMORY" : "out of memory"}

SETUP=SetUpCounters()
SETUP.maxforall()
```

The Python class `Factory` provides the functions that initialize and provide clients with object references to the DVD interfaces:

```
class Factory:
    def generateFactory(self, name, instance):
        new_instance = instance
        poa.activate_object(new_instance)
```

```
        FACTORYOBJECT[name] = poa.servant_to_reference(new_instance)
        return FACTORYOBJECT[name]
    def DISKSFactory(self):
        if FACTORYOBJECT.has_key("disks"):
            return FACTORYOBJECT["disks"]
        else:
            logit("Factory", "Create DISKS Interface")
            return self.generateFactory("disks", POA.DVD.DISKS(Disks()))
    def UTILITIESFactory(self):
        if FACTORYOBJECT.has_key("utilities"):
            return FACTORYOBJECT["utilities"]
        else:
            logit("Factory", "Create utilities interface")
            return self.generateFactory("utilities",
                                    POA.DVD.UTILITIES(Utilities()))
    def MEMBERSHIPFactory(self):
        if FACTORYOBJECT.has_key("membership"):
            return FACTORYOBJECT["membership"]
        else:
            logit("Factory", "Create membership interface")
            return self.generateFactory("membership",
                                    POA.DVD.MEMBERSHIP(Membership()))
    def TITLINGFactory(self):
        if FACTORYOBJECT.has_key("titling"):
            return FACTORYOBJECT["titling"]
        else:
            logit("Factory", "Create titling interface")
            return self.generateFactory("titling",
                                    POA.DVD.TITLING(Titling()))
    def DISKSFactory(self):
        if FACTORYOBJECT.has_key("disks"):
            return FACTORYOBJECT["disks"]
        else:
            logit("Factory", "Create disks interface")
            return self.generateFactory("disks",
                                    POA.DVD.DISKS(Disks()))
    def RENTALFactory(self):
        if FACTORYOBJECT.has_key("rental"):
            return FACTORYOBJECT["rental"]
        else:
            logit("Factory", "Create rental interface")
            return self.generateFactory("rental",
                                    POA.DVD.RENTAL(Rental()))
    def RESERVATIONSFactory(self):
        if FACTORYOBJECT.has_key("reservations"):
            return FACTORYOBJECT["reservations"]
        else:
            logit("Factory", "Create reservations interface")
            return self.generateFactory("reservations",
                                        POA.DVD.RESERVATIONS(Reservations()))
```

Class MEMBERSHIP implements the server side of the membership interface:

```python
class Membership:
    def set (self, recordtoupdate):
        logit("Membership", "Set contents for %d" %
                recordtoupdate.memberid)
        SHMEMBERS[idtostring(recordtoupdate.memberid)]=
                    stringizemember(recordtoupdate)
        SHMEMBERS.sync()
    def get (self, memberid):
        try:
            record=SHMEMBERS[idtostring(memberid)]
        except:
            logit("Membership", "Failure of get() contents for member %d"
                    % memberid)
            print "Couldn't get member", memberid
            raise DVD.MEMBERSHIP.NOSUCHMEMBER
        logit("Membership", "Success of get() contents for member %d"
                % memberid)
        return destringizemember(record)
    def delete (self, memberid):
        try:
            del SHMEMBERS[idtostring(memberid)]
            logit("Membership", "delete contents for %d" % memberid)
            SHMEMBERS.sync()
        except:
            raise DVD.MEMBERSHIP.NOSUCHMEMBER
    def create (self, recordtoadd):
        lastid = DBMAX["members"]
        lastid = lastid + 1
        logit("Membership", "Create new member record - %d" % lastid)
        DBMAX["members"] = lastid
        recordtoadd.memberid = lastid
        recordtoadd.memberno = "%d" % lastid
        SHMEMBERS[idtostring(lastid)]=stringizemember(recordtoadd)
        SHMEMBERS.sync()
        logit("Membership", "Create new member  for %d" % lastid)
        return lastid
    def search (self, lname):
        rseq = []
        try:
            (key,value)=SHMEMBERS.first()
            while 1 == 1:
                lst=string.split(value, "\\")
                surname=lst[4]
                if string.upper(surname) == string.upper(lname):
                    rseq.append (string.atoi(key))
                (key,value)=SHMEMBERS.next()
        except:
            done = ""
        logit("Membership", "Search for %s" % lname)
        rseq.sort()
        return rseq
    def idfromnumber (self, memberno):
```

```
        logit("Membership", "id-to-number for %s" % memberno)
        try:
            (key,value)=SHMEMBERS.first()
            while 1 == 1:
                lst = string.split(value, "\\")
                no = lst[1]
                if no == memberno:
                    return string.atoi(key)
                (key,value) = SHMEMBERS.next()
        except:
            raise DVD.MEMBERSHIP.NOSUCHMEMBER
```

Classes TITLING and DISKS implement the server side of their respective interfaces. As the code strongly resembles that for MEMBERSHIP, they are not shown.

Class RENTALS implements the server side of the rental operations. Not all of the GUI has been implemented yet, so a few operations are left to be completed.

Notice that while the IDL does not define set or get functions (so clients cannot access those functions), they are implemented and used privately within other functions in this interface:

```
def set(self, disk, rentinfo):
    SHRENTALS[idtostring(disk)] = stringizerentinfo(rentinfo)
    # This should raise exceptions, but doesn't, at this point.
    # It's only being used internally in the server by the other
    # functions, and error checking is done in them
def get(self, disk):
    try:
        record=SHRENTALS[idtostring(disk)]
    except:
        logit("DISKS", "Failure of get() contents for disk %d"
            % disk)
        raise DVD.DISKS.NOSUCHDISK
    logit("DISKS", "Success of get() contents for disk %d" % disk)
    return destringizerentinfo(record)
def renttitle (self, memberid, titleid):
    MEM= FACTORYOBJECT["membership"]
    TTL= FACTORYOBJECT["titling"]
    DSK= FACTORYOBJECT["disks"]
    RNT= FACTORYOBJECT["rentals"]
    RES= FACTORYOBJECT["reservations"]
    try:
        mbr=MEM.get(memberid)
    except:
        raise DVD.MEMBERSHIP.NOSUCHMEMBER
    try:
        ttl=TTL.get(titleid)
    except:
        raise DVD.TITLING.NOSUCHTITLE
    ### If we stored info on what classifications were permissible
    ### for each member, we'd process handling of
    ### DVD.RENTAL.FORBIDDENRATING here...
    dlist = DSK.search(titleid)  # Get disk list...
```

```
        # Next, check the items on the list to see if they are available
        availabledisk = 0
        for d in dlist:
            # Look for rental
            #    If rented, continue
            try:
                r=RNT.get(d)
                if r.datec != "":
                    skip="Y"
            except:
                skip="N"
            # Look for reservation
            # If reserved, by matching memberid, then we've got a result
            if skip == "N":
                try:
                    r=RES.get(d)
                    if (r.memberid == memberid) and
                        (r.titleid == titleid):
                        founddisk = d
                except: pass
            # If all is OK, set availabledisk, then break
            if skip != "Y":
                founddisk = d
                break
        # Now, rent the disk...
        try:
            logit("Rental", "rentdiskinfo - disk %d - failed" % diskid)
            rrec=DVD.RENTAL.rentinfo(diskid=founddisk,
                memberid=memberid, drented="20000801")
            SRENTAL[idtostring(founddisk)]= stringizerentinfo(rrec)
            logit("Rental", "rentdisk - disk %d member %d"
                    % (founddisk, memberid))
            # If the member had reserved this title, then cancel that
            # now...
        except:
            logit("Rental", "rentdiskinfo - failed for %d" % titleid)
            raise DVD.DISKS.NOSUCHDISK
        try:
            rtitle = RES.queryreservationbymember(memberid)
            if rtitle == titleid:
                RES.cancelreservation(memberid)
        except:
            raise DVD.MEMBERSHIP.NOSUCHMEMBER
        return founddisk
        #returns diskid, if it exists...
    def rentdiskinfo (self, diskid):
        print "Finish RENTAL::rentdiskinfo()"
        try:
            rtl=destringizerentinfo(SRENTAL[idtostring(diskid)])
            mbr=rtl.memberid
            dt=rtl.drented
            logit("Rental", "rentdiskinfo - disk %d - Found member %d date %s"
                    % (diskid, mbr, returndate))
        except:
```

```
            logit("Rental", "rentdiskinfo - disk %d - failed" % diskid)
            raise DVD.DISKS.NOSUCHDISK
        return mbr, dt
    def diskreturn (self, diskid, returndate):
        try:
            dsk= destringizerentinfo(SRENTAL[idtostring(diskid)])
            del SRENTAL[idtostring(diskid)]
            logit("Rental", "Return disk %d %s" % (diskid, returndate))
            return dsk.memberid
        except:
            raise DVD.DISKS.NOSUCHDISK
    def titleavailable (self, titleid, date):
        print "titleavailable not yet used, so no need..."
        return [2, 3, 4]
    def overduedisks (self, fromdate, todate):
        print "overduedisks not yet used, so no need..."
        return []
```

The RESERVATIONS interface, much like RENTALS, publishes a set of action-oriented operations for public use, as well as implementing some private functions for internal use.

Class UTILITIES implements the server side of the utility operations:

```
class Utilities:
    def getclassifications(self):
        logit("Utilities", "Query Classifications ")
        return ["E", "U", "PG", "12", "15", "18", "XXX"]
    def getgenres(self):
        logit("Utilities", "Query Genres")
        return ["Action", "Education", "Comedy", "Thriller",
        "Foreign", "Romance", "Science Fiction"]
    def errortext(self, errnumber):
        logit("Utilities", "Get Errnum for %d" % errnumber)
        # This uses dictionaries defined below...
        try:
            errname=ERRNDICT[errnumber]
            errmsg=ERRMSGDICT[errname]
        except:
            errmsg="Unknown error type: %d " % errnumber
        return errmsg
    def today(self):
        return strftime("%Y%m%d", localtime(time()))
```

Finally comes the part of the code that loads the IDL, sets up connections to ORBit using the Portable Object Adaptor (POA), and then starts an event loop via `orb.run` that waits for requests from DVD clients:

```
 # First, parse the IDL.  This provides a correspondence
# between the operators defined in the IDL and Python
# classes and methods.
CORBA.load_idl("dvdc.idl")
CORBA.load_idl("logger.idl")
# Initialize ORBit, and attach to the Portable Object Adaptor
```

```
orb = CORBA.ORB_init((), CORBA.ORB_ID)
poa = orb.resolve_initial_references("RootPOA")
# Now, attempt to get an object reference, stored in LOGORB,
# that connects to a Logging Service server
try:
    logior = open("./logger.ior").readline()
    LOGORB = orb.string_to_object(logior)
    print LOGORB.__repo_id
    LOGORB.addlog(LOG.loginfo(hostname="knuth", userid="cbbrowne",
                              application="dvd-server",
                              messagetype="info",
                              shortmessage="Start up DVD Server"))
except:
    print "Could not open Logger!"
# Set up a Servant, which will start up the services of the DVD server
servant = POA.DVD.FACTORY(Factory())
poa.activate_object(servant)
# Next, we need an object reference to this servant, to pass that
# on to other processes that would like to use its services.
# The IOR is written to a file to publish how to access the
# server
ref = poa.servant_to_reference(servant)
open("./dvd-server.ior", "w").write(orb.object_to_string(ref))

# Now that the reference is published, we activate the POA, and then
# let ORBit "take over," running the event loop
poa.the_POAManager.activate()
orb.run()
```

Mapping the C API to the CORBA Operators

This section runs through the C code that attaches in between the CORBA methods and the existing C code in the DVD application.

First, we start with critical setup:

```
/*
  DVD Store Application Reference API Implementation

  This file contains definitions of functions conforming
  to the DVD Store application database APIs.
 */
#include <stdlib.h>
#include <stdio.h>
#include <string.h>
#include <time.h>
#include "dvd.h"
#include "dvdc.h"

static void open_factory_error (CORBA_Object interface,
                                char *interfacename);
/* CORBA structures */
static CORBA_Environment ev;
static CORBA_ORB orb;
static CORBA_Object dvd_client;
```

```
/* This function does the setup to establish the connection to
   ORBit. */

#define IORLOCATION "../server/dvd-server.ior"

void ConnectORB (int argc, char *argv[]) {
  FILE *ifp;
  char *ior;
  char filebuffer[1024];
  /* Start up the exception handler */
  CORBA_exception_init(&ev);
  /* Request a connection to ORBit */
  orb = CORBA_ORB_init(&argc, argv, "orbit-local-orb", &ev);
  ifp = fopen(IORLOCATION,"r");
  if( ifp == NULL ) {
    printf("No dvd-server.ior file!");
    exit(-1);
  }
  fgets(filebuffer,1024,ifp);
  printf("%s\n", filebuffer);
  ior = g_strdup(filebuffer);
  fclose(ifp);
  dvd_client = CORBA_ORB_string_to_object(orb, ior, &ev);
  if (!dvd_client) {
    printf("Cannot bind to IOR: %s\n", ior);
    exit(-1);
  }
}
```

At present, the particular file location `../server/dvd-server.ior` that `dvdstore` uses to look for the IOR, is coded explicitly. It would be good to add an option that lets the user select where to look for the IOR.

This illustrates the wider issue that booting up a CORBA application is not trivial. In order to get connections working, some object reference needs to be available through some non-CORBA mechanism.

A multi-host system needs to distribute the base IOR to all client machines, whether via a shared file system using NFS, transmitted via FTP, pushed to client machines using the configuration manager CFengine, or perhaps published on a web server in an established location. The CORBA Naming Service may be useful for managing lists of object references, but you still need an object reference in order to find the Naming Service.

The function `Build_Factories` sets up connections to the interfaces. This represents a second level of booting up:

```
static DVD_MEMBERSHIP membership;
static DVD_TITLING titling;
static DVD_DISKS disks;
static DVD_RENTAL rental;
static DVD_RESERVATIONS reservations;
static DVD_UTILITIES utilities;
```

```
static void open_factory_error (CORBA_Object interface, char *interfacename) {
  if (!interface) {
    g_error ("Could not bind factory for interface %s", interfacename);
  }
}

int Build_Factories (int argc, char *argv[]) {
  FILE *ifp;
  char *ior;
  char filebuffer[1024];
  CORBA_exception_init(&ev);
  orb = CORBA_ORB_init(&argc, argv, "orbit-local-orb", &ev);
  ifp = fopen("../server/dvd-server.ior","r");
  if( ifp == NULL ) {
    g_error("No dvd-server.ior file!");
    exit(-1);
  }
  fgets(filebuffer,1024,ifp);
  ior = g_strdup(filebuffer);
  fclose(ifp);
  dvd_client = CORBA_ORB_string_to_object(orb, ior, &ev);
  if (!dvd_client) {
    g_error("Cannot bind to %s\n", ior);
    return 1;
  }

  /* A logical extension at this point would be to insert some
     security validation, so that only those interfaces that the user
     is permitted to access are in fact set by this process.

     We'd add an "authentication token" as an argument to each of
     these factory functions; the instantiations of interfaces would
     then fail as "needed" in that the server would refuse to return
     the interface reference. */

  membership = DVD_FACTORY_MEMBERSHIPFactory( dvd_client, &ev);
  open_factory_error(membership, "membership");
  titling = DVD_FACTORY_TITLINGFactory( dvd_client, &ev);
  open_factory_error(titling, "titling");
  disks = DVD_FACTORY_DISKSFactory( dvd_client, &ev);
  open_factory_error(disks, "disks");
  rental = DVD_FACTORY_RENTALFactory( dvd_client, &ev);
  open_factory_error(rental, "rental");
  reservations = DVD_FACTORY_RESERVATIONSFactory( dvd_client, &ev);
  open_factory_error(reservations, "reservations");
  utilities = DVD_FACTORY_UTILITIESFactory( dvd_client, &ev);
  open_factory_error(utilities, "utilities");
  return 1;
}
```

A logical extension to this would be for the various FACTORY functions to do some security validation, so that only those interfaces that the user is permitted to access are actually made available. The security scheme would involve transmitting some sort of 'authentication token' to the server, where, if the user's privileges were not sufficient, no object reference would be passed back.

We will only look at one interface, MEMBERSHIP, in any detail. The layout of code in the other interfaces is comparable.

dvd_member_set uses operation set from interface MEMBERSHIP:

```
    int dvd_member_set(dvd_store_member *member)
{
  DVD_MEMBERSHIP_storemembers *memout;
  printf("Set: dvd_store_member\n");
  memout= DVD_MEMBERSHIP_storemembers__alloc();
  if(member == NULL) {
    return DVD_ERR_NULL_POINTER;
  } else {
    memout->memberid = member->member_id;
    memout->memberno = member->member_no;
    memout->title = member->title;
    memout->fname = member->fname;
    memout->lname = member->lname;
    memout->houseflatref = member->house_flat_ref;
    memout->address1 = member->address1;
    memout->address2 = member->address2;
    memout->town = member->town;
    memout->state = member->state;
    memout->phone = member->phone;
    memout->zipcode = member->zipcode;
    DVD_MEMBERSHIP_set (membership, memout, &ev);
    if (ev._major != CORBA_NO_EXCEPTION) {
      g_error("Got CORBA exception %d/%s", ev._major,
              CORBA_exception_id(&ev));
      return DVD_SUCCESS;
    }
  }
  return DVD_SUCCESS;
}
```

Input comes from member, and the function populates the structure that DVD_MEMBERSHIP_set uses. In this case, we need only make reference to the values that are to be passed on to the server. The code in dvdc-stubs.c contains functions responsible for marshalling the data, making copies to be used by the server. You may examine the function DVD_MEMBERSHIP_set in the stubs file to see how this works:

```
      dvd_member_get() provides the opposite operation, querying the server for
information about a member.
  int dvd_member_get(int member_id, dvd_store_member *member)
{
  DVD_MEMBERSHIP_storemembers *cmember;
  int rc;
  if(member == NULL) {
    return DVD_ERR_NULL_POINTER;
  } else {
    DVD_MEMBERSHIP_get (membership, member_id, &cmember, &ev);
  }
  /* If we cannot get the member there may be an error
     with the data, or the member may not exist */
```

```
/* EXCEPTION SAMPLE */
switch (ev._major) {
case CORBA_NO_EXCEPTION:
  rc = 0;
  break;
case CORBA_SYSTEM_EXCEPTION:
  g_error("Got CORBA exception %d/%d from DVD_MEMBERSHIP_get", ev._major,
          CORBA_exception_value(&ev));
    return (int) DVD_ERR_NOT_FOUND;

case CORBA_USER_EXCEPTION:
  printf("Error: %s\n", CORBA_exception_id(&ev));
  return (int) DVD_ERR_NOT_FOUND;
}
if (rc != 0)    /* If we had an exception above... */
  return rc;
/* If the retrieved member id is not as expected there
   may be an error, or the member may be deleted */
if(member -> member_id == 0)
  return (int) DVD_ERR_NOT_FOUND;
if(member_id != cmember->memberid)
  return (int) DVD_ERR_BAD_MEMBER_TABLE;

member->member_id = cmember->memberid;
strncpy(member->member_no, cmember->memberno, 6);
strncpy(member->title, cmember->title, 4);
strncpy(member->fname, cmember->fname, 26);
strncpy(member->lname, cmember->lname, 26);
strncpy(member->house_flat_ref, cmember->houseflatref, 26);
strncpy(member->address1, cmember->address1, 51);
strncpy(member->address2, cmember->address2, 51);
strncpy(member->town, cmember->town, 51);
strncpy(member->state, cmember->state, 3);
strncpy(member->phone, cmember->phone, 31);
strncpy(member->zipcode, cmember->zipcode, 11);
printf("Member: %d %s %s %s %s", member->member_id,
       member->member_no, member->fname, member->lname,
       member->zipcode);
return DVD_SUCCESS;
}
```

This function nicely demonstrates the problem that an attempt to provide reasonably complete error checking involves writing far more code than the operations themselves directly involve.

Functions dvd_title_create and dvd_title_delete provide no more insight, only additional code, and so are not shown here.

Function dvd_title_search is quite interesting, in that it demonstrates how a request can receive a sequence data structure, and transform it into the form used by the GNOME application:

```
int dvd_member_search(char *lname, int *result_ids[], int *count)
{
  DVD_MEMBERSHIP_memberidList *CList;
  int *results = NULL, i;
```

```
      DVD_MEMBERSHIP_search(membership, lname, &CList, &ev);
      printf("Found... %d\n", CList->_length);
      if (ev._major != CORBA_NO_EXCEPTION) {
        g_error("Got CORBA exception %d/%s\n", ev._major,
                CORBA_exception_id(&ev));
        return DVD_ERR_NOT_FOUND;
      }
      printf("No exception... Got some results...  Count: %d\n", CList->_length);
      /* Alternatively, there _were_ good results in CList->.. */
      results=calloc(CList->_length, sizeof(int));
      printf("Allocated memory...\n");
      if (results == NULL) {
        return DVD_ERR_NO_MEMORY;
      }
      printf("Search results: ");
      for (i = 0; i < CList->_length; i++) {
        printf(" %d %d ", i, CList->_buffer[i]);
        results[i] = CList->_buffer[i];
      }
      CList->_release = TRUE;
      *result_ids = results;
      *count = CList->_length;
      CORBA_free(CList);
      return DVD_SUCCESS;
    }
```

Unlike the previous C version, where the code would do repetitive `realloc` calls, we get the whole thing passed over in one fell swoop. As a result, we need only one `calloc` call in order to allocate space for the entire set of results.

This function is one where it is particularly important to use `CORBA_free(CList)` to clean up after establishing the results to be passed back. The CORBA operator `DVD_MEMBERSHIP_search` will, if searches that are requested find a lot of members, allocate quite a lot of memory in the client program.

Putting It All Together

In order to run the DVD store application, we will need to perform a number of steps. We first need to install ORBit-Python, which can be found at http://projects.sault.org/orbit-python/. Let's extract it in a suitable location, perhaps /usr/local:

```
$ tar zxfv orbitpython-0.1.3.tgz
$ cd orbit-python-0.1.3
$ ./configure
$ make all
$ su -
Password:
# make install
```

Now we need to install our DVD store application. The source file dvdcorba.tar.gz can be downloaded from the Wrox web site. Extract it to a suitable location, perhaps /usr/local, and compile the GUI front end:

```
$ cd dvdcorba
$ ./configure
$ make
```

This will result in the file src/dvdstore being compiled; this is the GUI front end.

If you wish to reconfigure the location of the IOR file, look for IORLOCATION in src/corbaclient.c.

Now, with all the components compiled, we can fire up the application. This involves invoking three programs, in order.

First, run the log server, in directory /usr/local/dvdcorba/server:

```
$ python log-server.py
Done initialization: Proceed!
```

This server will block immediately, waiting for CORBA requests, so you'll probably want to invoke it in the background.

Second, run the dvd server, also in directory /usr/local/dvdcorba/server:

```
$ python dvd-server.py
IDL:LOG/LOG:1.0
Starting up DVD Server
```

Again, this server blocks, waiting for CORBA requests, and so should probably be run as a background process.

We might try running the script dvd-tester.py, a Python script in the same directory, that tries to invoke some of the DVD CORBA operations.

Lastly, we start up the GUI front end:

```
$ cd ../src
$ ./dvdstore
```

Using libgnorba

GNOME provides an additional library, libgnorba, which simplifies the creation of GNOME applications that are to be CORBA servers. The services provided by this library include the following:

❑ The function gnome_CORBA_init can be used to replace CORBA_ORB_init. This integrates the ORBit and GTK event loops together, so that you do not need to manage their events separately, switching manually from event loop to event loop. If you leave your CORBA servers with no GUI, as is done with the DVD application, then this provides little value. On the other hand, making a GNOME application like Gnumeric scriptable via CORBA does require having a GUI, so this may prove quite useful in the long run.

It can also query X Properties to determine what Name Server to use, and can use X cookies to validate security access at a very basic level. Unfortunately, if an ORBit-based server is configured to do this, all ORBit clients and servers must validate access in this manner, which makes it difficult for such servers to interoperate with clients that use other ORBs.

On the other hand, it may be regarded as a pretty good idea to diminish the vulnerability of users who aren't very security conscious, and are using ORBit-based desktop applications on a single machine. What balance is struck depends very much on the environment that the program is used in.

❑   gnorba_CORBA_init is equivalent to gnome_CORBA_init, except that it does not provide GTK event loop integration. This would be useful for a GUI-less daemon.

❑   goad_server_register and goad_server_unregister are used to register a server with the GOAD (Gnome Object Activation Directory) at runtime, indicating that a service has been made available for other applications.

❑   goad_server_list_get is used to query GOAD to get a list of servers that are available.

❑   goad_server_activate, goad_server_activate_list_get, and goad_server_activate_with_id allow activating a GOAD server. If the server is already running, this may merely send it a message; if the server is not running, GOAD will spawn a new process.

Configuring ORBit for Multi-Host Use

ORBit has a security feature intended to protect not-terribly-security-conscious home users, which may cause inconvenience if you wish to distribute an application across multiple hosts.

There is a configuration file, likely to be found as /etc/orbitrc, which controls what kinds of connections ORBit will accept. You will likely find it contains the following:

```
ORBIIOPUSock=1
ORBIIOPIPv4=0
ORBIIOPIPv6=0
```

These three lines indicate different kinds of input sources – 0 indicates that the source will be rejected, and 1 indicates that the source will be accepted.

The entry ORBIIOPUSock=1 indicates that ORBit will accept Unix Socket Files as input, which in turn means the ORB will only accept requests from local processes. It's fast, and comparatively secure, but may prove irritating if you want to allow processes on other hosts to access the services.

In order to allow ORBit to support multiple hosts, the second line must be amended to ORBIIOPIPv4=1.

GOAD - GNOME Object Activation Directory

GOAD is a registry that is used to associate servers with services, so that ORBit can start CORBA servers on demand rather than needing to run them all on the off-chance that someone might need the service. It is, loosely speaking, an Implementation Repository, that "contains information that allows the ORB to locate and activate implementations of objects". It does not conform to any particular standard – the OMG declined to define a standard for this, because the mechanisms that are available will vary significantly from platform to platform.

The GOAD process is started up during GNOME's session initialization, and it reads configuration from a series of .gnorba files in either /etc/CORBA or /usr/etc/CORBA. There is also a CORBA interface that allows applications to introduce GOAD at a later time.

So, to add servers to the GOAD, you will need to maintain the contents of the .gnorba files. Each file in this configuration directory may contain one or more server definitions. For instance, the GNOME Panel configuration uses the following sequence of settings:

`[gnome_panel]`	*Name*, used by the Name Server.
`type=exe`	*Application type*, used by GOAD to determine how to invoke the server. Other options include **shlib**, for shared libraries, and **factory**, that appears to refer to Bonobo factory objects.
`location_info=panel`	*Server Location*, used in conjunction with the *Application type*, to determine where the application may be found.
`repo_id=IDL:GNOME/Panel:1.0`	*Repository ID*, used to determine which IDL to use from the Interface Repository.
`description=GNOME Panel`	*Description* of the service.

Note that the GOAD is intended to start up local processes on the local host. It does not provide a mechanism for starting up servants on remote hosts.

The Use of CORBA in GNOME

With all that has been said about CORBA being intended to cope with the burgeoning complexity of distributed applications, it may come as something of a surprise that most of the interfaces declared in GNOME thus far are in fact not very complex.

The problem with providing highly expressive and thus complex IDL interfaces is that both clients and servers are forced to be correspondingly complex, and this intimacy can also damage the resilience of the system.

Consider the following moderately sophisticated IDL for invoking a text editor:

```
module EDITOR {
  interface editing {
    struct position {
      long line;
      short position;
    };
```

```
    struct screen {
        short width;
        short height;
    };
    struct font {
        string family;
        short pointsize;
        enum { bold, italics, bolditalics, normal };
    };
    typedef sequence<string> pathcomponents;
    void edit_file ( in string host, in pathcomponents,
                     in position pos, in screen scrn, in font fontinfo );
  };
};
```

This provides considerable flexibility by having the text editor head to a particular position in the file, and displays the file in a particular way.

Unfortunately, it puts a considerable burden on anyone who plans to provide an interface to a particular text editor, because it requires rather a lot of code to be written in order to control all these attributes.

It usually makes a lot more sense to keep it simple, and have the IDL keep to the basics:

```
interface editing {
  void editfile (in string fullfilename);
};
```

Many of the interfaces declared for GNOME applications are of such simple components that they can be easily used. Simple interfaces will tend to be utilized more than complex ones. Furthermore, simple interfaces may be incrementally extended without necessarily breaking old code.

The Bonobo Compound Document Architecture will use somewhat more sophisticated interfaces. Applications that plan to use this include Evolution (an integrated communications tool, combining mail, calendar, and contact management), Nautilus (file manager), and Gnumeric (spreadsheet). Gnumeric is one of the first applications offering scriptability via the CORBA interface. Although it is currently not well documented, the developing source code is worth a look.

Advanced CORBA Functionality

It is practically impossible to give more than an outline of CORBA in just two chapters, and so in the interests of showing at least one working example we have overlooked some of CORBA's most powerful features. We would be selling you short if we did not show you the facilities that allow CORBA to be the keystone of any medium to large-scale project.

Dynamic Interface Invocation

Dynamic Interface Invocation represents a way to dynamically accept or generate requests at run time, based on interface information they receive from an Implementation Repository.

In this sort of configuration, the client doesn't know the signature of the object, so it queries the Implementation Repository to determine what set of parameters it should submit and accept in return. In effect, this amounts to providing an interpreter engine alongside the client that can translate between the data types it knows, and the data types the IR indicates it should be using.

The mapping of this for C is fairly clumsy. It is far easier to use the DII facility with languages that provide more sophisticated dynamic allocation of data as well as more object-oriented abstractions.

CORBAServices

Quite a number of services, that tend to be oriented towards object abstraction, have been defined over the last few years. That is, they provide extensions to allow you to do additional things with objects. These services are intended to be widely usable across many different kinds of applications. Contrast this with CORBAFacilities, discussed later in the chapter, which provide interfaces intended for very specific kinds of applications.

OMG Standards may be found under CORBA Services Specifications (http://cgi.omg.org/library/csindx.html. Be aware that not all services are widely implemented. ORBit so far only includes the Naming and Event Services. That said, an ORBit-based application may be able to use services implemented by another ORB, but the need to manage access to multiple ORBs will make running the application more complex. See the essay *CORBA, GNOME, CMUCL, and other macabre tales* at http://ww.telent.net/corba/gnome-lisp.html for an example that uses services from about three ORBs at once.

Naming Service

The naming service is similar in function to the Internet Domain Naming Service (DNS). It provides a registry where object references may be associated with symbolic names. It is probably the most commonly used service – servers may commonly register themselves using the Naming Service. Once this is done clients need only query the Naming Service in order to discover where the services they need may be found. This diminishes the need to pass around files containing IORs. ORBit does include a Naming Service server.

Trading Service

The Trading Service represents a sophisticated extension of the Naming Service. A server would, as with the Naming Service, register itself with the Trading Service, but rather than merely supplying a name, it provides a set of properties representing service types and service offerings.

For instance, a print server might register the resolutions it supports (speed in pages-per-minute, color or lack thereof, physical location, and other such properties) with the Trading Service. A process looking for a printer would then set up a query requesting the desired properties, and select a printer based on the options the Trading Service returns.

This service is primarily needed with systems involving large numbers of objects that manage dynamic redirection of requests. It is unlikely that it will be needed for the deployment of personal applications atop GNOME, but is used to enable scalability to large complex applications. ORBit does not include this service.

Event Service

The Event Service is supported by ORBit. It permits the establishment of event queues to provide a proxy that relaxes CORBA's usual use of synchronous messaging. A process that wishes to accept/supply event requests on an asynchronous basis will submit requests of `connect_pull_consumer`, `connect_push_consumer`, `connect_pull_supplier`, `connect_push_supplier` to indicate its readiness to accept/supply events, and on what basis it will do so.

Notification Service

The Notification Service extends the Event Service by providing more sophisticated ways for hosts to register themselves, and to receive notification of events that are of interest. This parallels the way the Naming Service is extended to provide the Trading Service.

The Notification Service is of interest in systems where a diverse set of objects need to monitor a complex set of events. Other systems describe this as a design pattern called Publish and Subscribe.

ORBit does not include this service, nor does it support any of the later services (yet).

Concurrency Control Service

This service provides an interface for managing concurrency using a number of different types of distributed locks:

❑   Read locks

❑   Write locks

❑   Upgrade locks: Upgrades from a read lock to a write lock without deadlock.

❑   Intention locks: Allows variable granularity for what is to be locked.

Messaging Service

The Messaging Service is intended to provide the equivalent of the asynchronous messaging commonly associated with message queuing middleware such as IBM MQSeries, Microsoft MSMQ, Tibco TIB. It should be possible to use such services to support the Service.

It is also intended to overcome the semantic problem with the *oneway* IDL declaration, where there are no guarantees of quality of service, and where it would be correct according to the standards (albeit evidence of a pathologically bad implementation) for an ORB to simply drop all *oneway* requests.

This service would be extremely valuable for implementing financial applications and other applications involving batch processing. It is not yet widely implemented, even on commercial ORBs.

Time Service

The Time Service is intended to allow the CORBA user to obtain current time along with an error estimate. Uses for this include:

❑   Determining the order in which events occur.

❑   Generating time-based events like timers and alarms.

❑   Computing intervals between events.

It is not likely to be of vast importance on Linux systems, where it is quite straightforward to install NTP client or server software, which provides considerably more sophisticated time synchronization capabilities than the CORBA Time Service offers.

The service is, however, relatively simple to implement, and there is a free implementation for the MICO ORB.

Life Cycle Service

This provides conventions for creating, deleting, and moving objects to different locations.

Relationship Service

This service establishes two new kinds of objects, relationships and roles, to permit explicit representation and navigation of relationships between CORBA objects.

Persistence Service

The idea of this is to provide a way for objects to have values that persist even when computers are shut off.

This service has had a rather rocky history – the initial Persistent Object Service (POS) was made obsolete before being commonly implemented. It suffered from having a complex interface, a lack of current or planned implementations, and failed to satisfy needs. The new Persistent State Service (PSS) intends to provide the ability for objects to maintain their own state. However, with the diversity of data stores, including files, relational databases, and object databases, implementation is rather complex. There are not yet any open source implementations of this service.

Transaction Service

This service provides the ability to support 'transactional guarantees' that changes are being robustly dealt with. A transactional CORBA message provides, with two phase commit semantics, the transaction processing system ACID characteristics:

Atomicity

All transactions are either performed completely, committed, or not done at all. This means a partial transaction that is aborted must be rolled back.

Consistency

The effects of a transaction must preserve required system properties, often described as database integrity. For instance, if funds are transferred between accounts, a deposit and a withdrawal must appear to be committed to the database as a single action, so that the accounting system does not appear to fall out of balance (even though the multiple updates may truly leave things out of balance temporarily).

Isolation

Intermediate stages must not be made visible to other transactions. So, in the case of a transfer of funds between accounts, both sides of the double-entry bookkeeping system must change together. This means that transactions appear to execute serially (e.g. in order) even if the work is done concurrently.

Durability

Once a transaction is committed, the change must persist, even in the face of a catastrophic failure. Further, if a commit is in progress, and a less than catastrophic failure occurs, the commit must be concluded when operations resume.

This service is considered particularly valuable for managing financial information. At one point, there was a project to implement this service for ORBit, but this has not gone very far.

Security Service

The Security Service provides a framework for building trustworthy applications. It uses cryptographic components to protect data from examination and to implement authentication protocols. This includes:

- ❑ identification and authorization of users
- ❑ authorization and access control
- ❑ activity auditing
- ❑ communications security
- ❑ establishing non-repudiation of activities
- ❑ security administration

Unfortunately, security is not simply a feature that can be patched onto an application as an afterthought, but rather represents an emergent property that must be pervasive throughout the design. Ideally, the ORB should authenticate requests against the requestor's identity, and the permissions assigned to the requestor. Unfortunately, while omniORB has many of the hooks in place to support it, no free ORB supports this service yet.

Work is ongoing to encrypt IIOP transmissions for ORBit using SSL (Secure Socket Layer). This will help to support communications security, but does little about the other aspects of the security model.

Externalization Service

The Externalization Service allows an object's state to be transformed into a data stream, and moved to another location. This is required, if you want to support moving an object from one host to another via the Life Cycle Service.

Object Properties Service

This service allows attaching properties to objects that can then be queried using the Query Service.

Object Query Service

This service allows constructing SQL-like queries on the properties of CORBA objects.

Licensing Service

The Licensing Service enables the construction of policies to control access to services. Of course, since part of the point of using free software like GNOME and ORBit is to avoid the need to worry about usage constraints, this is about the last CORBAService likely to be implemented for ORBit.

CORBAFacilities

These are application-oriented services, also known as OMG Domain Technologies, (http://cgi.omg.org/library/cdomain.html) which include the following:

- ❑ CORBA Finance Specifications (http://cgi.omg.org/library/cfinindx.html) – including a general ledger specification, currency, party management.

- ❑ CORBA Manufacturing Specifications (http://cgi.omg.org/library/cmfgindx.html).

- ❑ CORBAMed Specifications (http://cgi.omg.org/library/cmedindx.html) – consisting of specifications that relate to the OMG-compliant interfaces for healthcare systems.

- ❑ CORBA Telecoms Specifications, (http://cgi.omg.org/library/ctelindx.html) – consisting of specifications that relate to telecom technologies, which at present include Audio/Video Streams.

- ❑ CORBA Business – including task/session management, and workflow.

- ❑ CORBA E-Commerce – including a negotiating facility.

- ❑ CORBA Life Science – including genomic maps, biomolecular sequence analysis.

- ❑ CORBA Transportation – including an Air Traffic Control Facility.

The CORBAFacilities have met with varying degrees of success, and many represent works in progress. As a result, while they may represent sources of ideas and examples of reasonably sophisticated CORBA systems, they do not necessarily represent sources of usable code.

If you plan to build applications that relate to these application areas, the specifications that others have published can help guide you past the problems that others have already seen and written about. And even if you have no plans to create a CORBA-based Air Traffic Control system, the documentation allows you to see realistic examples of non-trivial CORBA-based applications.

Designing and Running Scalable CORBA Services

The CORBA Services and Facilities outlined in the final sections show that there is a considerable body of additional material on constructing more sophisticated applications using CORBA.

There seem to be two trends manifested in the way CORBA is developed:

- ❑ The creation of relatively simple services, like help servers, logging servers, authentication servers, and directory servers. These can provide useful tools to help manage systems, and, if designed to provide somewhat generic functionality intended for reuse, these will be useful to extend the functionality of the GNOME desktop and applications.

- ❑ The creation of more sophisticated interfaces and services targeted at specific applications, like the DVD store application, or the GNOME Pilot interfaces designed specifically to use pilot-link to communicate with PalmOS handheld computers. These sorts of interfaces allow construction of sophisticated distributed applications, but aren't directly reusable.

The GNOME Bonobo system is intended to provide a third option, of sophisticated compound document services intended to embed GNOME applications/documents inside one another. It remains to be seen how successfully Bonobo will turn out. As a general principal, CORBA is such a multileveled architecture that jumping into sophisticated uses all at once is likely to give you an arcane system design, that even you, the designer, may not properly understand.

The more complex the system is, the more complex the sets of error conditions and deadlocks will become. This may be briefly illustrated in the DVD application function `dvd_member_delete(int member_id)`. In this function there is several times more exception-handling code than there is code for useful work. It would be wiser to start out less ambitious, with relatively simple facilities, perhaps extending the functionality of the message server, and turning that into a 'system activity logger'.

There are some major issues that we have not yet touched on, which become important if we wish to scale up the use of CORBA. Let's explore these now.

Managing Concurrency

If we look carefully at the operations that have been defined in these examples, we find that all are intended to represent relatively brief transactions. None are expected to take any significant length of time for a response.

We have done things like:

❑ Querying a table for a value, or a few values.

❑ Updating an entry in a database.

❑ Submitting a brief message.

None of these require substantial processing effort, and as a result, it is reasonable for requests to run serially. So, if a request comes in while another is being processed, it is not unreasonable to wait a few milliseconds until the request underway has completed.

If, however, there are operations that will require more substantial computational effort, managing concurrency becomes an important part of the program's design. Some of the approaches to improving responsiveness of applications should be addressed by the CORBA 3.0 specifications.

Threading

If a server needs to be responsive to multiple operations at the same time, then it may need to spawn multiple threads.

Multiple Dispatch

You may want to have an 'object factory' instantiate multiple instances of a particular sort of object that may run on separate hosts, and have some form of gatekeeper or dispatcher that can direct requests to whichever of the objects is most appropriate or perhaps least busy.

This illustrates where the Trading Service comes in handy; servants may register themselves with the Trading Service, perhaps even updating this registry occasionally with information on how busy they are, and clients can then query the Trading Service to get a list of possible servants. If some group of objects is expected to experience intensive use, you might want to have an explicit dispatcher that balances the load across server processes.

Asynchronous Processing and Callbacks

If a particular operation is always going to take quite a long time to process, it may be a good idea to turn it into an asynchronous process.

Thus, the client marshals together the arguments and submits them, perhaps to a proxy, or perhaps a more sophisticated version of the simple message server presented earlier.

The work processes can then head to the message queue, and do the work as and when they have the opportunity. It may be necessary to return the results, for instance, if the client requested that a report be generated, perhaps because there was a desire to display the contents of that report.

It must be acknowledged that this whole sequence of marshalling of values does come at some cost – queuing does not come for free. If it improves reliability, that is likely a very worthwhile trade off. If it substantially diminishes the number of objects that need to be active, that can also be worthwhile.

Once the results have been calculated, the server needs to, in some fashion, call back, and return the results. There are several options.

The client could have registered a CORBA callback, passing an object reference so that we see a role-reversal, with what we thought was a server now behaving as a client. It submits a `here_are_the_results` operation to what we thought was a client, now behaving as a CORBA server.

A disadvantage to this approach is that it makes the server process somewhat dependent on the status of the 'client', which will somewhat diminish the reliability of the system. The client may register callback with the CORBA Event Service. In this case, the server reports to the Event Service that it has results; the client might either pull them across via the Event Service, or submit an `I_Hear_You_Have_My_Results_Ready` call the server again to the operation to get the results.

Since the Event Service server now takes responsibility for managing the connections, rather than our application server managing this by itself, the reliability of the system is hopefully improved.

As an alternative, we could use a form of message queue, using abstractions similar to those provided by IBM MQSeries to transfer the results back in an asynchronous manner. The server marshals the results as a message, addresses it to the client, and throws it into a message queue. The client may poll the queue for results, may await the queue submitting a message to indicate that results are ready, or use a polling scheme with a `back-off signal`, not unlike the way Ethernet avoids deadlocks (the client stops attempting to request a service and waits for a period of time before trying again).

All of these options are possible. The reliability and responsiveness of the resulting system services will vary, so there is no unambiguous best way.

Managing Robustness

Distributed systems provide all sorts of new opportunities for system failures as a result of there being additional components like network interfaces, ORBs, and multiple separate processes and services. For instance:

- ❑ The IOR file may be inaccessible, whether due to permission problems, or someone deleting it.
- ❑ An IOR may refer to a servant that is no longer working.
- ❑ Network connections may break.
- ❑ A firewall may not let you through.
- ❑ A servant may get too busy, and start ignoring requests.
- ❑ A servant may see its work queue fill up, and drop queued requests.

Resilient software copes with such problems with some grace, or at least offers you some tools to diagnose in greater detail. You should consider Tools and techniques for System Management Interfaces.

System Management Interfaces

In an application involving a horde of objects, it is vitally important to build in some interfaces and operators, in order to monitor what objects are out there, what they are up to, and to provide some degree of central control over the system. The message server example shows a simple way to provide centralized logging of error information. It's so simple that if anything of a CORBA nature on the system is working, it should work too.

If your system reports what's going on, whether in clients or in servers, that makes it vastly easier to figure out what was happening just before the DBMS server went down.

Complex, intimate interfaces, where everything has to be running in order for anything to work are not your friends; it may be better to have several simple, restartable interfaces.

Efficiency may encourage keeping servers running as long as possible, but it is very useful if pieces of the system can be 'hot' restarted while it's running without clients needing to be too worried about it.

It is instructive to look at the way a typical Linux system gets going:

❑ The Linux kernel starts up.

❑ The Linux kernel loads a process called init. If you run the command ps aex | head, you will most likely find that process ID 1 is init.

❑ init is crucial in the system, when it shuts down, the entire system is taken down.

❑ Under the control of the data in /etc/inittab, init then initializes the network configuration, and starts up services that might include NFS, Sendmail, atd, cron, Apache, lpd, ntp, CFengine, and any other things that should run automatically.

Nearly all of these processes may be restarted while the system is running, for instance:

```
# cd /etc/init.d
# ./nfs-server restart
# cd /etc/init.d
# ./pcmcia lpd start
```

The fact that so many of the system services may be restarted without rebooting is a big part of what makes UNIX so resilient. We can learn from this in our own work. Our applications will have some critical components, much like the Linux kernel or init, without which the remainder of the system cannot function. With some careful design, it may be possible to eliminate the need to treat any particular object as being critical to the running of the system.

There will be some objects that are fairly critical to the system, much like the services referenced in /etc/rc.d or /etc/ini7.d. They might be automatically restarted after a reboot – if they shut down for other reasons, it is likely that they require human intervention to resolve a system problem.

For instance, if PostgreSQL runs out of disk space, restarting it before doing some maintenance is not a good idea. If there are a set of objects in a CORBA system that manage data in a PostgreSQL database, they will have no better ability to cope with that problem than PostgreSQL itself.

Finally then, there will be objects that parallel UNIX's `getty`, objects that support such things as users logging in to do work. These objects can, and should, be supported by 'object factories' that can establish them on demand.

Resources

Open Source ORBs available for Linux include:

- ❑ ORBit (http://www.labs.redhat.com/orbit/)
- ❑ ORBit-Python (http://projects.sault.org/orbit-python/)
- ❑ MICO - a GNU ORB (http://www.mico.org/)
- ❑ Real-time CORBA with TAO (The ACE ORB) (http://www.cs.wustl.edu/~schmidt/TAO.html)
- ❑ omniORB (http://www.uk.research.att.com/omniORB/)
- ❑ ILU (Inter-Language Unification) at PARC (ftp://ftp.parc.xerox.com/pub/ilu/ilu.html)
- ❑ JacORB - GPLed Java ORB (http://www.inf.fu-berlin.de/~brose/jacorb/)
- ❑ Sun's IDL Compiler in Java (http://developer.java.sun.com/developer/earlyAccess /idlc/index.html)

These are resources for some other services that were discussed in the chapter:

- ❑ CORBAservices Specifications (http://www.omg.org/)
- ❑ NTP - Network Time Protocol, a sophisticated standard for synchronizing computer systems (http://www.ntp.org/)

Summary

In this chapter, we have seen how GNOME came to have ORBit as its preferred ORB. Then we walked through the implementation of the DVD application as a multi-tiered client/server system using CORBA. Then we outlined the installation of the components needed to use ORBit. We concluded with an overview of the more advanced aspects of CORBA and considered the design aspects of planning a scalable CORBA application.

Online discussion at http://www.p2p.wrox.com

22

Diskless Systems

You've been working with, playing with, and generally messing with computers for years. You are currently using two or three PCs at once, running Windows 2000, Windows 98, Windows ME, and several Linux flavors. You have even networked them together in your den and around the house. You have a garage rapidly filling up with left over bits from the last upgrade frenzy. Sound familiar?

Maybe you use PCs at the office and have a mixture of new and not-so-new machines, with some discarded low-spec computers that nobody can bear to throw out. Pehaps they still have a paper value in the accounts department, or appear to be beyond economic repair with broken disk drives.

If you've got a Linux machine accessible on a network, you can bring some of this older equipment back to life. In fact you can do it with just about any server that can provide BOOTP and TFTP protocols, but here we're going to be using Linux.

In this chapter we are going to take a quick look at diskless Linux systems. The idea is a simple one: take a bare-bones PC with some memory, a cheap display card and a network card (and not much else!) and turn it into a workstation or computing engine, or a system for surfing the Internet in the lounge.

It might be a little difficult to truly justify the time and effort, but this is a "take-a-break" chapter, so let's have a little fun!

A Little History

Way back in the 1980s, memory and hard disk space were very expensive, so ways were found to make desktop workstations affordable. More and more application interfaces were becoming graphical, requiring sophisticated color displays rather than the older character-based VDU (Visual Display Unit) terminals.

In universities and large corporations, shared departmental computers could run the X Window system, and a new breed of displays – X terminals – were born. These had no local storage of their own, and very little memory. Their sole purpose was to provide an X display for use by applications running on the server. Typically they'd run a simple operating system of their own, just enough to support the X server program.

As personal workstations became popular and processing power increased, the next logical step was taken: run the application on the workstation itself. However, storage was still expensive. One way around this was to continue using a server to provide all the storage that the workstations would need, which could include supplying the operating system for the workstations.

X terminals and diskless workstations found favor in many organizations. They were an affordable way to get modern computing to the desktop. A central server controlled all the software, so they were relatively easy to maintain (particularly when compared to today's PCs) as there was only ever one place that changes needed to be made – on the server. If a workstation or X terminal failed, it could be swapped with another in moments – a one-line change (or possibly no change at all!) at the server, and the user would be up and running again.

The network clearly played a large part in the success of this way of working, but is perhaps also the cause of the workstations' downfall. As workstation power increased, the capacity of the networks could not keep up. The demands of reading large applications and data files from the server became too heavy. Eventually workstations acquired local hard disks, applications were installed locally and the workstation became a personal computer. Diskless systems became a thing of the past, and in the process, many of the administrative benefits of centralized computing were lost.

In the 1990s diskless systems saw something of a revival, as networks started to become consumer items. They are simple to construct, and support a larger bandwidth. Examples of the application of diskless (or near-diskless) systems abound:

- ❑   the network computer
- ❑   home movie set-top boxes
- ❑   internet kiosks

In our DVD store for example, we could use a diskless system to provide multiple user access or the public kiosk.

All these devices rely on obtaining their operating system – or prime functionality – via a network connection, so they have little or no local storage. Their software is instantly updated by a change of files on the network, so they have low maintenance overheads – ideal in a mass consumer marketplace.

One of the authors took the diskless concept to a novel extreme, noting that a diskless machine is quieter than a regular PC as it has no noisy hard disk. The near-empty case also runs at a lower temperature. He decided to create a totally silent PC. Removing the fan from the power supply and replacing the CPU fan with a large heat sink he created a PC that was eerily silent. As we said, great for surfing the Internet in the lounge!

But folks, don't mess with the power supply hardware like this unless you know what you're doing. Fans tend to be there for a reason.

Linux has supported diskless operation almost since the beginning. Key features in the kernel allow a Linux system to download its operating system from the network and obtain all its files from a server. It's entirely possible to build a Linux-based X terminal or a diskless workstation.

In this chapter we're going to see how it's done, step by step, by considering the following questions:

❑ What is a diskless system?

❑ Why would you want to build one?

❑ How do diskless systems work?

❑ How are diskless systems configured?

❑ What diskless systems applications are there?

What, No Disk?

A truly diskless system has **no** local storage – in fact it has a long list of "no"s:

❑ no hard disk

❑ no CD-ROM

❑ no floppy disk

❑ no monitor (maybe)

Every single file that the system needs for its operation is obtained from a server, across a network connection. Typically the network connection will be an Ethernet – either 10 or 100 Mbits/s. Other possibilities include ATM and xDSL (as used by some video-on-demand set-top boxes). If you can transfer files over it, you can run diskless over it. We'll concentrate here on the use of a TCP/IP network using Ethernet, but the principles apply equally well to other network types.

Why Go Diskless?

Diskless systems have many advantages to offer:

❑ With no disk or CD a diskless system can be very low cost.

It's possible to build a diskless PC for a lot fewer hard-earned dollars than a regular PC. If the diskless system is going to be a simple X terminal, you don't need the leading edge in CPU technology either. You can build a perfectly serviceable diskless system from a 486-based machine, the sort of equipment that's now widely considered obsolete – particularly for running Microsoft Windows. A Pentium-100 with 32Mb RAM is quite a challenge for Windows NT4 (never mind Windows 2000!), but just fine for running Linux diskless.

❑ With no local storage, a diskless system can be made very secure.

They are ideal machines for students to use while experimenting with Linux. There's no local file system to corrupt if the machine crashes – files on the server can be easily controlled or replaced.

❑ Administration of a group of diskless systems is simpler for being server-based.

As mentioned earlier, new systems can be added very quickly, all of them can be backed up at the same time, and disaster recovery is quick and easy. This kind of central administration is especially beneficial if the diskless systems are spread over a campus, or several offices in a company.

Naturally though, there are also disadvantages:

❑ Diskless systems require a server to provide files and other resources.

Nevertheless a reasonably modern, well-specified PC can act as a server to a surprisingly large number of diskless systems; the limiting factor is likely to be the network itself. Because all files are transferred as required across the network, the network can get very busy, and act as a bottleneck.

❑ The speed of a 10 Mbits/s LAN cannot rival that of a local hard disk.

Having said that, if the applications being run on the diskless systems are well chosen it can be a workable solution – we will discuss suitable applications later. Using a segmented network and Ethernet switches can help to lessen the impact to other users of diskless systems' network traffic.

❑ A totally server-based solution provides a single point of failure.

This is a key issue, and one that has played a significant role in the proliferation of desktop PCs and distributed computing. However, this isn't actually much worse than the central dependency that many distributed systems have upon a file or mail server; in both circumstances, what's crucial is that the server is properly managed.

How Does It Work?

Once it's up and running, a diskless system simply uses a network file system to access its files. In this case we'll be using the Network File System, NFS. In fact we will have two or more file systems provided by a file server. Each diskless system has read and write access to an area on the file server that is reserved for its sole use. This will be the diskless system's root file system '/'. In addition, the diskless systems will share a single /usr partition. To prevent write conflicts in the /usr file system, we arrange that the /usr partition is mounted read-only.

It's actually quite possible to run multiple diskless systems from a single read-only root filesystem, thus providing extra security – it's rather hard to hack a read-only system.

It's often overlooked, but in the standard UNIX file system, files in /usr are intended to be read-only – it's therefore possible for systems to share a single copy. Files that have traditionally resided in /usr and have to be writeable (such as message logs that used to live in /usr/adm) have moved to a /var (for variable) area which remains writeable. Check out the Linux Filesystem Hierarchy Standard at http://www.pathname.com/fhs/ for details of the read-only nature of /usr under Linux.

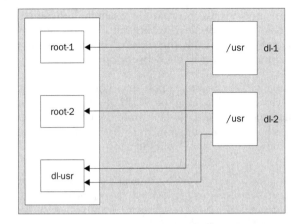

In the diagram above, two diskless workstations (dl-1 and dl-2) use separate areas on the server for their root partitions and a shared /usr. In effect they're running as if they had executed the following NFS mount commands:

On dl-1:

```
mount -t nfs server:/root-1 /
mount -t nfs -o ro server:/dl-usr /usr
```

On dl-2:

```
mount -t nfs server:/root-2 /
mount -t nfs -o ro server:/dl-usr /usr
```

In fact, some Linux distributions have missed this subtle read-only feature of /usr and persist with some writeable files in the /usr area. We'll take a look at this problem a little later on.

We can actually take the sharing of the /usr area slightly further. If the server is the same type of computer as the diskless systems, we can use the server's own /usr files as the shared /usr. The only extra space we need to accommodate the diskless systems will be for a root file system for each of them.

Starting a Diskless System

So how do we get to this happy state of file access from a server if we don't have an operating system installed in the first place?

There are three steps in starting a diskless system:

- ❏   Initial Boot – obtain an IP address
- ❏   Secondary Boot – download an operating system image and start it
- ❏   Multi-user Boot – normal Linux startup

In the initial boot stage the diskless system makes contact with its network environment. This is commonly done by running a small program (less than 32K in size) on the diskless system. It contains just enough network protocol to contact a server on the network. The program is small enough to be burned into an EPROM and located on the diskless system's network card.

For trying out diskless configurations it's also possible to run the program from a bootable floppy disk or CD-ROM. OK, that's not strictly a diskless system, but it's a good way to get started. If you can't arrange to boot from the network card at all, this may be your best option. Otherwise, once everything's ready and working, you can move across to the network card version!

PCs generally try to boot an operating system that's stored on a floppy disk, hard disk or CD-ROM. The order in which these devices are tried is set in the PC BIOS. A common setting is 'CD-ROM, A:, C:'. This indicates that the machine will first try to boot from the CD (if there's a disc in the drive), then try the floppy (again, if there's one present), and finally the hard disk. For a diskless system to boot properly, its BIOS must know to try to boot from the network device.

> *If the network card has a socket for an EPROM, it's usually possible to configure the card to install its EPROM code as a BIOS extension, adding network-booting capability to the computer. This often means that the system will first try to boot from the network, so you'll need to keep the network card configuration program handy while trying things out.*

There are many Ethernet cards that can be used to boot a diskless system using the method we'll be looking at here. They include:

- 3Com 3c503,507,509,590,595,905
- Novell NE1000/2000/2100 and compatibles
- Digital DE100 and DE200
- Intel EtherExpress Pro/100
- SMC 83c170 EPIC/100

as well as numerous cards that are based on the same chips as these. Details can be found in the documentation for the `etherboot` package, which we'll meet a little later.

Network Identification for Diskless Systems

On a TCP/IP network, each computer is assigned an IP (Internet Protocol) address that's used for all communications between computers. This address will often be configured into the operating system when the system is first installed. It can also be assigned automatically when the operating system starts up, using the Dynamic Host Configuration Protocol (DHCP).

When a diskless system starts up, it has no idea of its IP address or even what type of operating system it's supposed to run. It needs to get this information from a server on the network, but initially it doesn't even know where that is! The initial boot therefore starts with a cry for help.

All network cards have a unique address assigned to them when they're manufactured. This is known as the Media Access Control (**MAC**) address. A diskless system starts its life by broadcasting its MAC address across the whole network as part of a request for information about itself.

The server can then determine the IP address that corresponds to this MAC address using one of several protocols, such as **RARP** (Reverse Address Resolution Protocol), **BOOTP** (Boot Protocol), and **DHCP**. Here we will use BOOTP.

A server running the BOOTP service will receive the request for an IP address and (if it has been configured to respond) will return the IP address that the client system is to use. Since the BOOTP request is *broadcast* – that is, addressed to all computers on the network – the client doesn't need to know the address of the server.

> *Some care needs to be taken if you configure more than one BOOTP server on the same network, but it is certainly possible to so.*

Once the diskless system has determined its IP address, it still has no idea what it has to do; this is exactly what BOOTP was designed for. The diskless system puts out another request, this time for an operating system. It asks whether any server on the network has an operating system image for it to run, specifying its IP address. The BOOTP server responds accordingly, giving the location on the server of an operating system to load.

Running an Operating System

In our diskless Linux systems we will use a RAM disk approach to booting the operating system. What we prepare is effectively the image of an imaginary floppy disk that will be downloaded to the diskless client and started. The diskless system will load the image into RAM and run it, booting the system just as if it were on stored on the floppy. To get started, we will provide a special Linux kernel as the operating system image. Once running, the system will have access to a full Linux system via the server.

At this point we could choose not to run Linux, but some other operating system. Any system that can be started in a fairly small space (a floppy disk is ideal, but RAM disks can be larger) can be run. One example would be MS-DOS 6.22, which is quite happy to run with no disks, with its local storage being entirely contained within the RAM disk. If you add the Microsoft Network Client for DOS, you can access Microsoft servers to gain access to more storage and applications. It's also possible to install Microsoft Windows 3.11 on a server connected this way, and run an entirely diskless Windows. Windows 95 is trickier but still possible, whereas Windows 98 is practically impossible. Linux, however, is very easy.

The RAM disk image is transferred from the server to the diskless client using yet another protocol, this time a very simple file transfer protocol: **TFTP** (Trivial File Transfer Protocol).

Now we're getting close to completing the diskless boot sequence. Once the Linux kernel has started to run, it can access the server. There are a few special things we have to do to create this Linux kernel, as it has to cope without any local storage. We configure the kernel to determine its IP address via BOOTP (just as the initial boot did), and to use NFS to mount its root file system from the server.

Once the root file system is mounted, Linux functions as usual, running scripts and starting services as configured by the startup files in the root file system. At some point in the boot sequence it will mount /usr read-only from the server, as we saw in the diagram above. That's all there is to it!

Just to recap, we take a look at an imaginary conversation on the network:

Event	Client	Protocol	Server
Power UP	"I'm alive!"		
Initial Boot			
	"I have MAC address m"		
	"Who am I?"	BOOTP(m)	"Aha, a client!"
		BOOTP(I)	"You have IP address I"
	"I have IP address I"		
	"Anyone got an image?"	BOOTP(I)	"One of my clients"
		BOOTP(F)	"Your image file is here: F"
	"Give me the image F"	TFTP(F)	"Here you are"
Secondary Boot			
	"Booting RAM disk"		
	"Linux starting"		
	"What is my IP address"	BOOTP(m)	
		BOOTP(I)	"You have IP address I"
	"Mount / for address I"	NFS(I)	"OK"
Multi-user Boot			
	"Mount /usr"	NFS(I)	"OK"

Note that the client has to ask for its IP address twice – once when it's running the boot loader, and once more when running the kernel. This is simply because the boot code has no way to communicate with the kernel, so it can't pass the information on.

Server Configuration

Now that we understand how the diskless system is going to get started, let's take a look at how we need to configure the server in order for it to support all this business about addresses and images. We will return to the client configuration a little later on.

We'll try to keep the configuration as simple as possible, so that if you want to try this yourself, you should have no trouble recreating what we discuss here.

We're going to use a single server for all of the network services, mapping the MAC addresses to IP address, storing the RAM disk boot images, and providing the root and /usr file systems for the client diskless systems.

To start with, we need to create an area on the server where all our diskless operations are going to be carried out. This area will contain boot images and the clients' root file systems. In this example we have chosen to create an area called /tftpboot (a name that stretches back into antiquity and Sun workstations). You could choose another area if required. This area needs to be readable and searchable by all, so that the non-privileged services can supply boot images from it.

Next, we need to configure support for BOOTP and TFTP. We do this by editing the /etc/inetd.conf file, either uncommenting existing lines or adding new ones, as shown here:

```
tftp    dgram   udp   wait   nobody /usr/sbin/tcpd  in.tftpd /tftpboot
bootps  dgram   udp   wait   root   /usr/sbin/bootpd bootpd -c /tftpboot
```

You should check that these services are present in /etc/services. There must be lines like this:

```
bootps      67/tcp
bootps      67/udp
tftp        69/tcp
tftp        69/udp
```

To activate the changes, we need to restart the Internet Daemon, inetd. We do this by sending it a Hangup signal, most readily done as superuser with the killall command:

```
# killall -v -HUP inetd
```

Now when a BOOTP or TFTP request is received the server will be able to respond to it. We must now configure the BOOTP service so that it responds to requests appropriately.

The default configuration file for BOOTP is /etc/bootptab. It is a fairly simple file with a format that has much in common with other Linux configuration files, notably /etc/termcap and /etc/printcap. If it doesn't already exist, we need to create it and populate it with one entry for each diskless client we want to support. Here is a complete example file:

```
.def:ht=ethernet:

barney:ha=00608CF11872:ip=192.168.0.77:bf=/tftpboot/linux.diskless:
```

Each entry consists of a host name followed by tags separated by colons. Each tag consists of a boolean flag (that takes no value) or a variable assigned a value. The special host name .def is used to supply defaults. Documentation on the fields and flags that can be specified are to be found in the bootptab(5) manual page. The most commonly used ones are:

bf	boot file
dn	domain name
ds	domain name server address list
ha	host hardware address (MAC address of the client)
ip	host IP address (IP address of the client)
hn	send client's host name to client
ht	hardware type
sa	TFTP server address
rp	root path to mount as root
tc	table continuation

Not all of these tags can be used for booting diskless Linux systems. The critical ones for mapping MAC addresses to IP addresses are ha and ip, along with bf for booting an operating system image.

If you want to create a large number of similar diskless configurations, you can use the defaults under the .def entry, or use the continuation tag tc to specify that the entry should carry on as the start of the entry named as part of the tag. Here we use a default to specify that all of our diskless systems are using an Ethernet network. Other values for the ht tag include token-ring and ax.25 for Token Ring and AX.25 amateur radio. A full list can be found in the manual page.

Since our Linux kernel will establish its own IP address, we can reuse the same RAM disk boot image for all of our clients, and either add it as a default tag or introduce a continuation (using the tc tag) to be used for all clients of the same type. A continuation effectively joins one entry to another, allowing you to collect groups of tags together like this:

```
barney:ha=...:ip=...:tc=linux:
obiwan:ha=...:ip=...:tc=linux:
athena:ha=...:ip=...:tc=dos:

linux:bf=/tftpboot/linux.diskless:
dos:bf=/tftpboot/dos.diskless:
```

You will need to make sure that any IP addresses you allocate with BOOTP are part of your network and unused elsewhere. Here we are using one of the private IP address ranges, 192.168.0.XXX. All machines on this network are allocated addresses in this range. If there is a DHCP server on your network, you will need to allocate addresses that are not managed by the DHCP server.

Let's move on now, and create a bootable image for our clients.

Boot Image Creation

There are two main steps in creating a boot image for a diskless system. The first is to create an initial boot loader. This is the small program that will run from the network card (or floppy) in the diskless machine and start off communication with the server. The second step is the creation of the downloaded operating system image that the secondary boot will start from.

We can use the freely available `etherboot` and `netboot` packages to perform both of these. The `etherboot` package contains a large number of programs for controlling many different types of network card and performing the initial boot. It's also supplied with a version of `netboot`, which helps make bootable RAM disk images for operating systems such as DOS and Linux. Both packages can be downloaded from http://etherboot.sourceforge.net.

To build the `etherboot` package simply unpack the source code tarball and `make`:

```
$ tar zxvf etherboot-4.6.2.tar.gz
$ cd etherboot-4.6.2/src
$ make
```

Many ROM images for different cards will be produced in the directories `bin16` and `bin32`. In this example we are using an old ISA Ethernet card, a 3Com 3c509. The file that we need to burn into an EPROM and install on the card is called `bin32/3c509.rom`. If you have a different card, look for a suitable `.rom` file to use.

If you are not yet ready to use (or cannot use) an EPROM file, and have a near-diskless system that retains a floppy disk drive you can make a floppy disk with the equivalent of the EPROM image on it by executing:

```
$ make bin32/3c509.fd0
```

with a floppy disk in the first drive (`/dev/fd0`).

If we want to try out our initial boot we can use this floppy and try booting the diskless system. We should see that the initial boot program starts up and identifies the Ethernet card in the machine, like this:

```
Loading ROM image......
ROM segment 0x1000 length 0x4000 reloc 0x9800
Boot from (N)etwork or from (L)ocal? N
Etherboot/32 version 4.6.2(GPL) for [3x5x9]
Probing...[3c5x9]3c5x9 board on ISA at 0x300 - 10baseT
Ethernet address: 00:60:8X:F1:18:72
Searching for server ...
```

If we have correctly configured our server we may also see an IP address being returned by our BOOTP service:

```
Me: 192.168.0.77, Server 192.168.0.66
Loading /tftpboot/linux.diskless...
```

At this point the client is trying to access the boot image that we specified in /etc/bootptab, but we haven't created it yet, so this will fail.

The netboot package will be used to create the missing linux.diskless operating system image. This image consists of a loader (the netboot loader) and a Linux kernel specially built for diskless systems.

We build the netboot package that is included with etherboot by changing into its subdirectory (mknbi-1.0) and building in the usual way:

```
$ cd etherboot-4.6.2/mknbi-1.0
$ make
$ su
# make install
```

The install procedure requires superuser permissions as it will place the resulting programs in /usr/local/bin and also create some manual pages.

The main programs provided by netboot are mknbi-linux and mknbi-dos. The name mknbi means MaKe Net Boot Image. We will be using mknbi-linux a little later to create our diskless Linux image.

If we want to try it out, we can use a bootable DOS floppy and mknbi-dos to create a diskless DOS machine, just for fun! To do this, place the bootable floppy in the drive and type:

```
$ dd if=/dev/fd0 of=floppy.image
$ mknbi-dos floppy.image > dos.diskless
```

If you copy the output file dos.diskless to /tftpboot and edit /etc/bootptab you can try to boot your diskless system into DOS. A Windows 98 startup disk works well for this.

But we want Linux on our system, so let's move on to creating a Linux kernel for our diskless wonders.

Diskless Linux Kernel

These days Linux kernels are very modular, with many drivers loaded as needed after Linux has started. For a diskless system we need to make sure that all of the drivers we need for booting are included in the kernel itself, not loaded as modules.

The key driver here is the Ethernet card driver, typically loaded from /lib/modules during the Linux startup – however, we need to be able to access the network to get to /lib in the first place! This is one of the reasons we need to build our own kernel. You will need to make sure that you have the kernel sources installed, and change to the kernel source directory, /usr/src/linux.

We will create a kernel with the following options set:

❑ Ethercard driver built into the kernel, not a module

❑ NFS file system support enabled and in the kernel

❑ IP autoconfiguration

❑ Root on NFS

As a general rule we should strive to make our diskless kernel as small as possible by enabling only those features and drivers we absolutely need. This has two advantages. The first is that the kernel size will be less so that it will occupy less RAM in the diskless system. The second is that the diskless system will be *slightly* more secure if it does not have a floppy disk driver in its kernel. An enterprising hacker adding a floppy drive to the diskless system should not be able to use our kernel in ways we don't want them to.

Remember that we don't need drivers for hard disks, SCSI devices, CD-ROMS, or support for their file systems. Be drastic, just keep what we absolutely need. If, later on you find that something doesn't work, you can always rebuild the kernel, adding what you need. The key options are:

- ❏ CONFIG_EXPERIMENTAL (Code Maturity Level Options)

  Enable *Prompt for development and/or incomplete code/drivers* – this enables the selection of *Root on NFS* in later menus if you're using a kernel version earlier than about 2.2.14. Otherwise, the option should be available anyway.

- ❏ CONFIG_NET (General Setup)

  Enable *Networking support* – this turns on general networking.

- ❏ CONFIG_IP_PNP and CONFIG_IP_PNP_BOOTP (Networking Options)

  Enable *IP: kernel level autoconfiguration* and *enable BOOTP support* – this configures the kernel to use BOOTP to determine its network settings, principally its IP address.

- ❏ CONFIG_EL3 (Network device support | Ethernet)

  Enable *Network device support* and *3Com 3c509/3c579* support (or an appropriate driver for whichever network card you're using). Make sure to select YES (y) and not MODULE (m). You can include as many different drivers as you wish if you need to make a kernel that will run on a number of diskless systems using different network cards.

- ❏ CONFIG_NFS_FS and CONFIG_ROOT_NFS (Filesystems | Network File Systems)

  Enable *NFS filesystem support* – this enables root file system on NFS

These options configure general support for the network file system into the kernel, and specifically cause the kernel to try to mount its root file system across the network. It will attempt to mount a file system at the location /tftpboot/<ip-address> on the boot server discovered in the initial boot.

So, for our sample system 'barney' configured as IP address 192.168.0.77, we need to provide a root file system on our server at /tftpboot/192.268.0.77. We'll do this shortly.

You can set these options by running one of the menu interfaces for kernel configuration. This diskless configuration was tested using xconfig (under the X Window System) which you can run as superuser by invoking:

```
# make xconfig
```

If you're not using X you can use a character based configuration program, menuconfig:

```
# make menuconfig
```

Having configured the kernel we now need to build it – if you're unfamiliar with building kernels we suggest you start by reading the README file. Before we start though, it's sensible to backup the server's own kernel configuration. If it exists, put a copy of the file .config somewhere safe. We will be overwriting this file with a configuration for the diskless kernel.

Now you can build the kernel with:

```
# make dep
# make zImage
```

If all goes well you will be left with a kernel in arch/i386/boot/zImage. Let's move it to a more appropriate place:

```
# mv arch/i386/boot/zImage /tftpboot/kernel.diskless
# cd /tftpboot
```

We are almost ready to make our image. First though, we need to make sure that the kernel is set to boot from the network, rather than a hard disk. This should have been taken care of in the kernel configuration, but we can make sure by using the rdev command to explicitly set the boot device to the pseudo-device /dev/nfs:

```
# rdev kernel.diskless /dev/nfs
```

If you don't have a /dev/nfs device you can make one with:

```
# mknod   /dev/nfs c 0 255
```

Now all that remains is to create the boot image using the netboot tool mknbi-linux that we mentioned earlier on. This is very simple:

```
# mknbi-linux kernel.diskless > linux.diskless
```

Now we have a boot image that will run our custom kernel. If we install this image in /tftpboot, we can try booting our diskless client again and see the Linux kernel startup. After the same initial boot messages we saw before we now see the kernel loading and a netboot copyright message:

```
Loading /tftpboot/linux.diskless...

Linux Net Boot Image Loader Version 0.8.1 (mknbi-linux)
Copyright (C) 1996,1997 G. Kuhlmann and M. Gutschke
GPLed by G. Kuhlman
```

As the kernel starts it configures the network card and gets its IP address and then fails to mount its root file system:

```
eth0: 3c509 at 0x300 tag 1, 10baseT port, address  00 60 8c f1 18 72, IRQ 10
Sending BOOTP and RARP requests..... OK
IP-Config: Got BOOTP answer from 192.168.0.66, my address is 192.168.0.77
Looking up port of RPC 100003/2 on 192.168.0.66
Looking up port of RPC 100005/1 on 192.168.0.66
Root-NFS: Server returned error -13 while mounting /tftpboot/192.168.0.77
```

The next step is to create a root file system for our client.

Before we do that we can take care of the server NFS. We need to make sure that the server will allow access to the client root file system once it is made, and provide read-only access to any other file systems we may need. To do this we first of all have to enable the NFS service. This can be done from one of the system utilities available with Linux such as YaST on SuSE or linuxconf on RedHat. Then we need to add the file systems we need to make available to the NFS exports file, /etc/exports, creating it if it does not exist. Here is a complete example:

```
# See exports(5) for a description.
# This file contains a list of all directories exported to other computers.
# It is used by rpc.nfsd and rpc.mountd.

/tftpboot/192.168.0.77         barney(rw,no_root_squash)
/usr              (ro)
/opt              (ro)
```

We make available the client specific root file system, /usr and /opt (for access to some optional applications stored there). The options used in the exports file are ro (for read-only) in the case of /usr and /opt, while for the client we reserve root file system access to the host named barney, allowing it read-write access even as root.

The no_root_squash option disables NFS's default action which disallows superuser access as a security precaution. As Linux boots up, it effectively runs as superuser, so this option is necessary in order for the client to get started.

To complete the job of making the file systems available we need to export them using the exportfs command:

```
# exportfs -a
```

The -a (all) option instructs exportfs to make avalable all of the file systems described in /etc/exports.

Root File Systems

We need to create several root file systems on our server, one for each diskless client machine. Each needs to include all the files that the client will require to boot. Unless we want to create further file systems for the clients to mount, it must also contain all the files that the client will need to write to. It will therefore need to contain all the files in:

> /etc – configuration files
>
> /var – log files
>
> /lib – libraries used at boot time
>
> /dev – device files

A full root file system for a well-specified Linux system runs to about 135Mb. We can use the server's own root file system as a starting point for the client, removing files that we don't need. It's easy to reduce the required space to below 40Mb or so.

For the second and subsequent clients, it is possible to share some of the files through hard links. Those files that are never likely to be written to (such as the C library) can be stored in one place, and links made from there into the client's root file system areas.

However, disk space is cheap these days, and the simpler method is good enough to get started with. Here is a shell script (makeroot) derived from one provided in the netboot package that will copy the server root file system into a client area, ready for configuring:

```
#!/bin/sh
if [ $# != 1 ]
then
        echo Usage: $0 client-IP-addr-or-name
        exit 1
fi

cd /

umask 022

mkdir -p /tftpboot/$1

# just make these ones
for d in home mnt proc tmp usr opt
do
        mkdir /tftpboot/$1/$d
done

chmod 1777 /tftpboot/$1/tmp

touch /tftpboot/$1/fastboot
chattr +i /tftpboot/$1/fastboot
# copy these ones
cp -a bin lib sbin dev etc root var /tftpboot/$1

cat <<EOF
Now, in /tftpboot/$1/etc, edit

        [RedHat] sysconfig/network
        [RedHat] sysconfig/network-scripts/ifcfg-eth0
        [SuSE]   rc.config
    fstab
        conf.modules
    hosts

and configure

        rc.d/rc*.d
EOF
```

To make a start on a root file system for our client, we call the script with the IP address of the diskless machine being created:

```
# makeroot 192.168.0.77
```

The script creates the directory in /tftpboot and copies in the files that we need. It also takes care of making some directories that need to be present but can be empty (like /home and /proc) and sets the permissions of the temporary directory /tmp.

> **Note that this script copies the superuser's home directory /root. You may want to make sure that the files it contains are appropriate to the diskless client's superuser before installing.**

When a typical Linux system boots, it routinely checks to see whether it was shutdown properly – if not, it performs a file system check on its root file system. In this case that won't be possible, since the file system isn't on a hard disk but across the network.

To prevent this file system check from happening, we can make use of the fact that Linux looks for a file called /fastboot. If this is present, it assumes that the disks are in good order and skips the check. Normally, this file is created as the system shuts down and deleted when the check is run.

In a diskless environment we will not be able to write this file, as it is done after the network file systems are unmounted. We therefore create a /fastboot file and make it undeleteable using the chattr command. Our diskless client will now always think that its file system is in good order, and never try running an unnecessary file system check.

Finally, the script prints a message reminding us that we need to tailor the root file system for this client's requirements. The network configuration will require some work, and the startup scripts will require some drastic editing (as the client is highly unlikely to need to start all of the services we might need on a server).

The precise files that need changing differ slightly from distribution to distribution; the ones presented here are correct for SuSE 6.3.

In the client root file system, we must set up the NFS mounts so that the diskless system will access the correct files. Here is a client /etc/fstab file:

```
192.168.0.66:/tftpboot/192.168.0.77    /       nfs     rw      0 0
192.168.0.66:/usr              /usr    nfs     ro      0 0
192.168.0.66:/opt              /opt    nfs     ro      0 0
proc /proc proc  defaults 0 0
devpts      /dev/pts    devpts  defaults 0 0
```

The network configuration needs tailoring to make sure that the correct IP address is used. It is possible to use a DHCP server, as long as the IP address provided by the server can be guaranteed to be the same as the one returned by BOOTP on our server.

On SuSE the IP address is set in /etc/rc.config:

```
IP_ADDR_0="192.168.0.77"
...
IFCONFIG0="192.168.0.77 broadcast 192.168.0.255 netmask 192.168.0.255 up"
```

On RedHat and Mandrake Linux similar changes need to be made to /etc/sysconfig/network and the network start script /etc/sysconfig/network-scripts/ifcfg-eth0. On Slackware Linux, the file is /etc/rc.d/rc.inet1.

It is advisable to edit the /etc/hosts file on the client's root file system to include the client's own address and that of the server being used. This can speed up name resolution for some services such as ftp. Ideally you would add all of the clients to the server's hosts file before making a copy for the client root file system, that way all of the clients would have addresses for all the others.

The bulk of the remaining work concentrates on trimming down the services that are started and stopped when Linux is booted and powered down. All unnecessary services should be removed from the startup scripts. This has to be done by hand, but on SuSE it is simply a matter of editing the /etc/rc.config script and setting the service variables appropriately. On RedHat we need to remove unwanted scripts from the /etc/rc.d directories.

Once you've created a tailored set of startup scripts, you should be able to boot your client diskless system all the way into a multi-user configuration and be rewarded with a login prompt!

Problems

Depending on your distribution you may run into certain difficulties starting up and shutting down your diskless clients.

A key thing to watch out for is the use of files living in /usr before the NFS mounts have been executed. Until that time there is no /usr for your client to use! Offenders in the past have been RedHat with its use of linuxconf in the startup sequence, and SuSE with its use of loadkeys when booting single user. Both of these programs use files stored in /usr. Another potential problem program is rpc.klockd, which is used at just about the point the NFS mounts are performed.

A simple way to correct this problems is to create a /usr directory in the client root file system and copy in any file you find is needed before the NFS mounts are done. The NFS mount will still happen, hiding the files you have copied, but making visible the 'real' copies on the server.

Shutting down a diskless Linux box can be a problem too – again it is the order of things that is at fault. Linux will try to unmount all of its networked file systems before it has finished with its root file system. To avoid this the easiest thing is to delete the stop script for NFS in the /etc/rc.d directories. Typically rc6.d and rc0.d are the ones to target as they house the scripts that are executed as Linux is halted or rebooted.

You'll find some useful links at the etherboot home page http://etherboot.sourceforge.net. There's also a HOWTO document for diskless systems available, which will be found in /usr/doc (assuming the documents have been installed).

The Linux Terminal Server Project at http://www.ltsp.org has a lot of useful information on configuring diskless clients and the servers they boot from.

Finally, http://www.disklessworkstations.com can supply suitable Ethernet cards and EPROMS if you need them.

Client Applications

Once you have a basic diskless Linux system booting you can move on to configuring other applications. Perhaps the most useful is the X Window System.

If your distribution already uses X configuration files in /etc (or anywhere outside /usr) you should be able to run the X configuration utilities as per a normal installation. However, you will have to make sure that the server has installed the X server that your client needs.

For example, if the server has an ATI Mach 64-based graphics card it's likely that it has just the XF86_MACH64 X server available. If your diskless client has a Matrox graphics card you'll need the XF86_SVGA X server. This will need to be installed on the server and made available in the /usr/X11R6/bin directory so that the X configuration programs can find it.

We have not enabled any swap space on the client. This is because, at present, the use of NFS for swap is experimental. For now, we need to make sure that the client systems have enough RAM for the applications we wish to run. If we run out of memory, Linux will start to close our applications.

Say we want to run X and browse the Internet with Netscape; this is just about possible in 32Mb of RAM. You can trim the X installation memory usage by choosing simpler applications to run. For example:

- Use rxvt instead of xterm
- Use icewm instead of KDE or GNOME and Enlightenment
- Use a smaller X installation, like tinyX

Another way of avoiding RAM usage on the client is to run the applications on the server, using the client as a display only – in other words, as an X terminal. To do this, you must first enable incoming connections to your X session, then login to the server and start applications using the DISPLAY environment variable:

```
$ xhost +
$ telnet server
$ export DISPLAY=client:0
$ netscape &
```

With a suitable server configuration, it's possible to invoke Netscape remotely in a single line:

```
$ rsh server /usr/local/bin/netscape -display client:0
```

Now Netscape runs on the server, using the server's RAM and Internet connection, while the client just displays the results.

A diskless Linux system can be used for many applications – new uses appear almost every day. These include:

- network firewalls
- routers or bridges
- workstations
- X terminals
- Java stations
- set-top boxes

Hopefully we've encouraged you to explore the possibilities that diskless operation can provide. A diskless application might soon breathe life into an old PC near you!

Summary

A diskless system is a computer that contains virtually no storage media, accessing its data from a separate server via a network. In this chapter, we've looked at the history and reasons for diskless systems, and seen how they work and how to implement them using Linux.

Diskless systems make use of centrally stored data, and therefore offer many advantages over other models, such as low cost, high security and ease of administration. Disadvantages include increased dependence on a single machine and the limitations of network speed and capacity.

Starting Linux on a diskless system involves three steps:

❑ Initial Boot – a small program on the diskless system broadcasts the network card's MAC address across the network; the configured server responds with the diskless system's IP address.

❑ Secondary Boot – the diskless system broadcasts a request for a kernel image; the configured server sends it the appropriate data.

❑ Multi-user Boot – the diskless system boots the kernel from RAM; once it's up and running, it uses a network file system to access its files.

Each diskless system has exclusive read-write access to its own 'root' file system (stored in a predetermined area on the file server), as well as sharing a single /usr partition with other diskless systems running from the same server.

In the course of this chapter, we saw how to configure a server, create a boot image, and compile a Linux kernel suitable for use in a diskless system. Finally, we saw how to use a diskless Linux system as an X terminal, one of many possible applications including firewalls, routers, Java stations, and *quiet* Web browsers.

Online discussion at http://www.p2p.wrox.com

23

XML and libxml

XML, or to give it its full title, **eXtensible Markup Language,** is currently a very hot topic. Everywhere you look in the computer press, XML is mentioned, often alongside a raft of other related abbreviations such as SAX, XSLT, DOM, DTDs, and many others. Look through book catalogues and you also see a host of books on XML, SGML, and related titles.

When we were talking to Wrox about the nature and content of this book, and the sample application we were going to use as a vehicle to demonstrate some of the techniques in each chapter, we needed some sample data for our DVD store catalogue. Wrox immediately sent us some sample data (thanks DanM!) in XML format. Just to give you a flavor, here is the start of dvdcatalog.xml (the prices are fake by the way!):

```
<?xml version="1.0" encoding="UTF-8" standalone="yes" ?>
<!DOCTYPE catalog [

<!ELEMENT catalog (dvd+) >
<!ELEMENT dvd (title, price, director, actors, year_made)>
<!ATTLIST dvd
          asin CDATA #REQUIRED >
<!ELEMENT title (#PCDATA)>
<!ELEMENT price (#PCDATA)>
<!ELEMENT director (#PCDATA)>
<!ELEMENT actors (actor+)>
<!ELEMENT actor (#PCDATA)>
<!ELEMENT year_made (#PCDATA)>

]>
```

```
<catalog>
    <dvd asin="0780020707">
        <title>Grand Illusion</title>
        <price>29.99</price>
        <director>Jean Renoir</director>
        <actors>
            <actor>Jean Gabin</actor>
        </actors>
        <year_made>1938</year_made>
    </dvd>

    <dvd asin="0780020685">
        <title>Seven Samurai</title>
        <price>27.99</price>
        <director>Akira Kurosawa</director>
        <actors>
            <actor>Takashi Shimura</actor>
            <actor>Toshiro Mifune</actor>
        </actors>
        <year_made>1954</year_made>
    </dvd>

    . . .

</catalog>
```

This was great sample data, and there was no real surprise about the format chosen, but how were we going to transform the sample data into something we could easily load into our database? Originally we had assumed we would start with a comma separated variable (CSV) file or other file format that could be trivially imported into the database.

We could of course have written a C (or Python, or Perl...) program from scratch to change the format. We thought about using flex and bison to help with the syntax. We wondered about writing an **eXtensible Stylesheet Language** (XSL) transform, attacking it with awk, or maybe Perl's pattern matching would be a good tool...

We came to the conclusion that the 'right' answer was to parse the XML using an XML parser – after all, why build your own parser where there are several excellent free ones available – and that's what we'll be showing you how to do in this chapter.

In this chapter we will:

❑   Give a very brief overview of XML documents and how they are defined

❑   Look at how you can use some of the tools available on Linux to help process XML documents

❑   Walk through SAX callback routines to extract data from an XML document

XML Document Structure

Before we move on to the problem of our dvdcatalog.xml, it's important to look at exactly what XML is, and how XML documents are formed.

XML Syntax

At first sight an XML document looks much like HTML, with tags, tag attributes, and data between the tags. This is because both HTML and XML follow on from work done on the **Standard Generalized Markup Language** (SGML). Indeed XML is a subset of SGML. XML is superficially very similar to HTML, but there are some very important differences:

❑ HTML is primarily used for display purposes.

Although the original versions of HTML concentrated on describing elements of a document (such as 'this is a heading'), later versions acquired many markup tags to provide information about how to display the data, but never expanded on the tags to tell you what different parts of the document actually mean. Tags in XML, on the other hand, say nothing about how the data should be displayed – rather they tell us about the meaning of the data. Of course, we can then use that meaning to decide how to display the data, but that's a very important distinction. Look at the first DVD in the list. In an HTML page describing a film we may well seen the text "Jean Renoir" and "Jean Gabin" appearing, clearly being peoples names. However without some context information we would have had no way of telling who was an actor in the film, and who was the director. In XML we would tag these fields as being actors or directors, so as to provide an indication of what they were.

❑ HTML documents are not legal XML.

This applies even to those documents that are conformant to the HTML version 4 definition. A new version of HTML, XHTML, which is a slight variant on HTML, is also defined, which provides a standard for HTML, such that documents can be simultaneously legal XHTML and legal XML.

❑ XML is case sensitive.

In HTML the tag <H1> has exactly the same meaning as <h1>, but in XML the two are distinct and different tags. Although in English there is little confusion when characters are converted between upper and lower case, this is not true of languages in general, and making XML case sensitive allows it to be used in many different languages avoiding the pitfalls of automatic case folding. XML data is not limited to ASCII; it can use a full set of UNICODE characters if this is required. However you may not use tag names that start with the three letters xml or xsl, irrespective of case. All names starting with those three characters are reserved for the World Wide Web Consortium (W3C), the committee that developed the XML standard.

Well-formed XML

Rather like the more recent versions of the HTML standard, XML document standards are tightly defined by syntax rules laid down by the **World Wide Web Consortium**, (often referred to as the W3C). For further information, see the resources section at the end of this chapter. All XML documents must conform to these rules in order to be considered 'well-formed'. If it doesn't conform, then it's not XML.

In this section we will look briefly at the syntax rules of XML, which must be followed in all XML documents.

Sections

Each XML document can have three sections, rather than the two (head and body) that an HTML document has. These three sections are **prolog**, **body**, and **epilog** (although the standard does not actually use the term epilog). Only the body section is mandatory; either or both of the others may be omitted.

Prolog

The prolog section of an XML document, in the words of the standard 'may, and should, begin with an XML Declaration'. So although we said a moment ago that the prolog was optional, the standard strongly suggests that at a minimum a prolog containing an XML declaration be included in all XML documents. An XML declaration looks like this:

```
<?xml version="1.0"?>
```

As you can guess, it not only tells us that the document is in XML format, it also tells us the version of the specification, 1.0, which the document conforms to. We may also optionally include in the XML declaration a language specification, and information telling the reader, human or computer, if any external documents are required to interpret the XML in the document. In our example:

```
<?xml version="1.0" encoding="UTF-8" standalone="yes" ?>
```

tells us that the eight-bit encoding defined by Unicode UTF-8 (ISO-LATIN1) is being used, and that no external documents are required. Also in the prolog you can put a document type definition, starting `<!DOCTYPE` as we have in our example XML, but since we have not met those yet, we will come back to the topic of document type definitions shortly. The prolog can also contain comments, which we will also meet shortly.

Body

The body of the XML document is where all the useful data is contained. It contains a single element, the document root, in much the same way as HTML documents are encased in a single `<HTML>...</HTML>` tag pair. However, in XML each element can have elements nested to any level. In our example the single element is the catalog element, nested inside which are many other elements, which themselves contain elements, and so on. We will postpone the rather more difficult definition of 'element' until the next section.

You can also add comments to the body section.

Epilog

The epilog is often omitted. It may contain processing instructions, an advanced topic that we do not need to consider further here.

Elements

When we defined the body of an XML document, we conveniently avoided defining what at element was. However, the element is the main data container of an XML document, so it's an important concept. This is why we've brought it out into a section by itself.

Elements are containers that contain data, attributes, other elements, or a combination of the above. Tags, using angle brackets like HTML tags, delimit each element. However, unlike HTML it's never permissible to *omit* the end tag, as is frequently done with HTML tags such as `<P>`. As we mentioned earlier, another difference from HTML is that the case of the tag name is case sensitive.

A start tag consists of an angle bracket, a name, an optional attribute set, then a closing angle bracket; the end tag is identical except a solidus (or forward slash), is inserted before the tag name. Hence a well-formed XML tag looks like:

```
<my_tag_name>The data content goes here</my_tag_name>
```

It's perfectly valid to have no content between tags. In this case, rather than writing:

```
<my_tag_name> </my_tag_name>
```

a short form is allowed, which is:

```
<my_tag_name/>
```

Having an empty tag might seem a little strange, but that's because we've not yet met tag attributes. These allow us to qualify information inside the tag, in much the same way as in HTML, where we can qualify the meaning of a tag. For example, we might want to specify a table with border and padding:

```
<TABLE BORDER="2" CELLPADDING="10">
...
</TABLE>
```

We can add attributes with values to XML tags in a similar way. For example:

```
<my_tag_name text_type="example">The data content goes here</my_tag_name>
```

gives the tag an attribute of `text_type`, and that attribute has the value `example`.

The rules for XML attributes are much stricter than those for HTML:

❑ In XML, all attribute values must be enclosed in either double or single quotes. Therefore the HTML fragment `<TABLE BORDER=2>`, which would be considered legal HTML, is not legal in XML.

❑ In HTML it's possible, though probably a mistake, to have the same attribute name appearing more than once in a tag. In XML this repetition is not allowed.

❑ Two special characters may not appear in the attribute value, `<` and `&`. The special escape sequences `&lt;` and `&amp;` familiar from HTML must be used instead.

❑ If you need the same type of quotes to appear inside your attribute values as the quotes you have used to delimit the value, then the two escape sequences `&apos;` and `&quot;` may be used to insert `'` and `"` respectively.

Clearly there is a choice to be made between putting information in the attribute section of a tag, and as data between the tag delimiters. In general if the information does not change the meaning, merely qualifies it, then use an attribute. If the information is independent, then make it the data. For example, if you had some XML describing a car, then color might appear as an attribute, since it does not essentially change the car, just a detail of its appearance. The engine size would probably be useful as data, since it significantly changes the car. If you are not sure which is appropriate, then putting the information as data rather than as an attribute is probably a safer choice.

Element nesting

An XML document would not be of much value if we could only put a single tag in it. A lot of the usefulness of XML comes from its ability to nest tags. In our example at the start of the chapter, we have a catalog tag, and inside the catalog tag we have a dvd tag, and inside the dvd tag we have several tags, including title and actors. Usefully, we can have the same tag appearing more than once – the dvd 'Seven Samurai' lists two actors. What the XML is describing for us is a tree-type structure. If we draw the structure, we see that catalog contains multiple dvd entries, dvd contains title, price, director, actors and year made, and actors contains one or more actor elements.

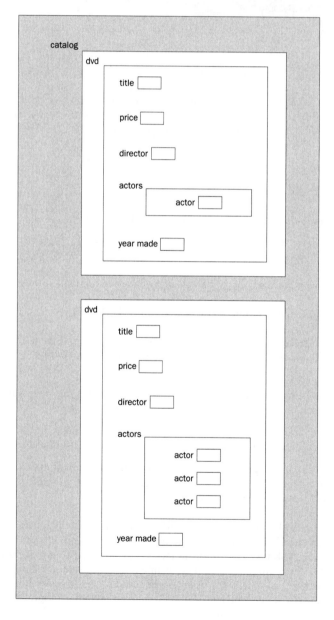

One thing that XML is very unforgiving about is the nesting sequence of tags. All tags must be strictly ordered. Although illegal in HTML, tag sequences such as:

```
<B>Hello<I>Word</B></I>
```

with incorrectly nested tags, will usually be interpreted by browsers in a 'reasonable' way. In XML such a sequence would be considered a major error, and invalidate the whole XML document.

Comments

In XML comments are very similar to their HTML counterpart. A comment starts with `<!--` and ends with `-->`.

Inside a comment you may not put two dashes, nor may the comment end in a dash.

Unlike HTML, XML parsers are under no obligation to pass through comment data, so the common HTML 'trick' of hiding scripts inside comments is not a valid technique in XML. Hopefully such tricks will not be needed because XML defines a way of providing processing instructions.

Valid XML

In the last section we saw an overview of the syntax rules of XML, which must always be followed for a document to be considered as XML. These rules say nothing about the contents, or sequence of tags in XML, providing they follow the XML syntax. However, this is normally not sufficient to define a format that can be processed. Suppose our DVD catalog had some data in it like this:

```
<dvd asin="0780020707">
    <title>Grand Illusion</title>
    <price>29.99</price>
    <actors>
        <actor>Jean Gabin</actor>
    </actors>
    <year_made>1938</year_made>
</dvd>
<director>Jean Renoir</director>
<wibble>Black Adder</wibble>
<year_made>1954</year_made>
<dvd asin="0780020685">
    <title>Seven Samurai</title>
    <price>27.99</price>
    <director>Akira Kurosawa</director>
    <actors>
        <actor>Takashi Shimura</actor>
        <actor>Toshiro Mifune</actor>
    </actors>
</dvd>
```

What do these elements mean?

```
<director>Jean Renoir</director>
<wibble>Black Adder</wibble>
<year_made>1954</year_made>
```

Since they are outside any particular dvd tag we have no way of knowing which dvd entry they are referring to. In addition, we are unable to deduce any meaning for the tag named wibble. Although the above XML fragment is well-formed and is syntactically correct, it is of little use because it is not semantically meaningful. What is needed is a way of defining XML document structure that goes beyond the syntax, to define exactly the tags and sequences of tags that may appear in any particular XML document. One way this can be done in XML is to define a **Document Type Definition**, or DTD.

DTDs

A DTD is an exact specification of what may appear in a given XML document, and constrains the document structure to a particular set and sequence of tags. XML documents that have a DTD to which they conform are classed as 'valid'. This is an additional requirement above and beyond 'well-formed', so an XML document cannot be 'valid' unless it is also 'well-formed'.

It's easy to see why we need to specify a structure for XML documents since we generally wish to use them for transferring information. Unlike HTML, there are no implicit meanings or predefined tags in XML. Without a 'phrase book' to interpret an XML document, we cannot know what its particular meaning is. Before two or more parties can reliably exchange documents using XML, they must agree a structure. This can be done with a DTD.

Defining a DTD

DTDs are the backbone of XML, so let us look at the essentials of defining one. We don't have anything like the space in this chapter to look at all aspects of DTDs; what we will do is present the basics. Readers who need more information are directed to the resources listed at the end of the chapter. The foundation of a DTD is the ELEMENT declaration, which looks like this:

```
<!ELEMENT mytagname … >
```

This declaration defines that 'mytagname' is a tag in the XML document structure. After the tag name that we are defining we can specify what sub-elements the tag can contain. Rules are used for specifying the sub-elements, to allow us to define lists of sub-elements, choices of sub-elements, and the numbers of sub-elements that can appear. The rules are quite simple:

Operator	Meaning
,	Allows us to list sub-elements, which must appear in the order listed
|	Allows a choice between sub-elements
?	Allows a sub-element to be optional
*	Allows a sub-element to appear zero or more times
+	Allows a sub-element to appear one or more times
(…)	Allows grouping of sub-elements

The operators * ? + follow the element to which they apply.

Suppose we wanted to define a `sandwich` element, consisting of a pair of `bread` elements, containing between them another element of either `honey` or `jelly`. We could write this:

```
<!ELEMENT sandwich (bread, (honey | jelly), bread) >
```

Some XML that conforms to this mini-specification would be:

```
<sandwich><bread/><honey/><bread/></sandwich>
```

Suppose we wanted to make the filling optional. We add an optional specifier like this:

```
<!ELEMENT sandwich (bread, (honey | jelly)?, bread) >
```

Now the filling is optional. We can use brackets as required to nest as many levels of complexity as we need.

Let's return to our DVD catalogue example. We need to specify that the catalog element consists of a number of DVDs, but there must always be at least one `dvd` present. Hence we write:

```
<!ELEMENT catalog (dvd+) >
```

Now we need to say that the `dvd` also consists of sub-elements, in this case `title`, `price`, `director`, `actors`, and `year_made`, all of which must be present. The element declaration for `dvd` is:

```
<!ELEMENT dvd (title, price, director, actors, year_made)>
```

Our last level of nesting is to say that the `actors` element must consist of one of more `actor` elements, like this:

```
<!ELEMENT actors (actor+)>
```

We have now defined the structure of our tags, but have not yet said anything about possible attributes of those tags. We need to say that our `dvd` element must contain an `asin` number. We do this by adding an `attlist` element to our DTD. To specify our requirement for an `asin` number, we add an element like this:

```
<!ATTLIST dvd
          asin CDATA #REQUIRED >
```

This tells us that the element `dvd` has an `asin` attribute, it consists of character data (a string) and it is a required attribute. In general the `ATTLIST` tag has the format:

```
<!ATTLIST name-of-tag name-of-attribute attribute-data-type qualifier>
```

The `name-of-tag name-of-attribute attribute-data-type` qualifier section may be repeated as many times as required, providing you do not repeat any attributes. There is a range of data types allowed, summarized below:

Data type	Meaning
CDATA	A string
ID	A name unique in the XML document
IDREF	A reference to another element with the given ID
IDREFS	A reference to a list of other elements with the given IDs
ENTITY	The name of an external entity
ENTITIES	A list of external entity names
NMTOKEN	A name
NMTOKENS	A list of names
NOTATION	An externally defined notation name, such as TEX or PNG
Explicit value	A series of explicitly defined values

A discussion of all of these is beyond the scope of this chapter.

The qualifier part of the `ATTLIST` has the following allowed values:

Value	Meaning
#REQUIRED	The attribute must appear
#IMPLIED	The attribute is optional
#FIXED <value>	The attribute must have the given value
<default value>	If the attribute is not specified, then it automatically gets this default value

Since our `dvd` element has one possible attribute, we only need a single `ATTLIST` declaration in our DTD element specification.

Last, but not least, we must specify the type of data that each of the elements can contain between the start and end tags of that element. Generally the lowest level of all data is the known as Parseable Character Data, which is written in XML as `(#PCDATA)`. We complete our DTD by saying that all lowest level elements can contain character data, like this:

```
<!ELEMENT title (#PCDATA)>
<!ELEMENT price (#PCDATA)>
<!ELEMENT director (#PCDATA)>
<!ELEMENT actor (#PCDATA)>
<!ELEMENT year_made (#PCDATA)>
```

Let's summarize by looking at the whole DTD again:

```
<!ELEMENT catalog (dvd+) >
<!ELEMENT dvd (title, price, director, actors, year_made)>
<!ATTLIST dvd
          asin CDATA #REQUIRED >
<!ELEMENT title (#PCDATA)>
<!ELEMENT price (#PCDATA)>
<!ELEMENT director (#PCDATA)>
<!ELEMENT actors (actor+)>
<!ELEMENT actor (#PCDATA)>
<!ELEMENT year_made (#PCDATA)>
```

This DTD tells us that a catalog consists of one or more dvd elements. A dvd element must have an attribute, asin, which has some data associated with it. dvd elements contain title, price, directory, actors, and year_made elements. The actors element itself contains one or more actor elements. Finally, each of the lowest level elements must enclose character data!

We think you will agree the specification is actually easier to understand than the explanation, once you understand the basics of DTDs.

Schemas

Although DTDs can provide exact definitions of document structure, they are rather inflexible. For this reason the W3C is working on a more rigorous but flexible method, called schemas. These will be much more suitable for defining the way XML files should be processed, to better enable applications to exchange data in XML format.

At the time of writing several proposals have been submitted for consideration, and this is currently a very hot topic in the XML world, with competing proposals, and attempts by various companies and consortia to force a *de facto* standard by providing tools and web sites to support particular proprietary proposals. Hopefully this will soon be resolved with an agreed and supported standard emerging. However, at the time of writing no final schema for defining XML has been defined, so for the rest of this chapter we will concentrate on DTDs, even though they will probably be superceded by schemas for more complex documents in the future.

Relating a DTD to an XML Document

Once we have defined our DTD, we need to associate it with the XML document, or documents, whose structure it defines. For our purposes it is sufficient for our DVD catalogue to simply carry with it its own DTD. Note that this is not a very good solution in general; if two companies are trying to exchange information using XML, there is little point in each message carrying its own specification with it. What is needed is an agreed external standard to which all XML documents messages will conform. XML schemas will provide this in due course.

In our XML document the DTD is embedded using the <!DOCTYPE tag, which defines a catalog document type:

```
<!DOCTYPE catalog [

<!ELEMENT catalog (dvd+) >
<!ELEMENT dvd (title, price, director, actors, year_made)>
<!ATTLIST dvd
```

```
              asin CDATA #REQUIRED >
<!ELEMENT title (#PCDATA)>
<!ELEMENT price (#PCDATA)>
<!ELEMENT director (#PCDATA)>
<!ELEMENT actors (actor+)>
<!ELEMENT actor (#PCDATA)>
<!ELEMENT year_made (#PCDATA)>

]>
```

XML Parsing

Now that we understand our XML catalogue data, we need to parse it in order to be able to process the data it contains. At which point we have a difficult choice to make – which parser to choose. There are two distinct models for parsing XML, the **Document Object Model** (DOM) approach, and the **Simple API for XML** (SAX) approach. We will look briefly at each before making our choice, and writing some code.

DOM

The W3C has produced a standard specification for a Document Object Model for XML, which allows developers to access the internals of documents in a standardized and language independent fashion. To access a document through the DOM, the document is first loaded and parsed; at which point it is available to your program and can be accessed and altered. Once you have finished manipulating the object model you can then write it out again as a new XML document.

However, there is a downside to DOM – the entire document has to be held in memory before it can be processed, and this can be a serious problem with very large XML files. For this reason a less official standard, SAX, is also in common use.

SAX

SAX is the Simple API for XML, and was originally implemented in Java. The latest version of the specification is maintained by David Megginson; for more information refer to his web site – the URL is in the Resources section at the end of this chapter.

The specification is very straightforward, and has been implemented almost universally by Java XML parsers, although C and C++ implementations are also available; again, see the Resources section.

Rather than load the document into memory, SAX reads the document in stages, and issues 'callbacks' to user-written code as different conditions occur, such as a tag starting, a comment being found, or the document ending. This forces the developer to do slightly more work, since they must accept the XML document in the order it is parsed, rather that being able to access it randomly.

In some ways it's similar to the callbacks that GNOME uses to handle events. SAX is also a read-only interface, providing no assistance in generating XML documents. However, for many practical purposes a SAX interface is perfectly sufficient, and its removal of the 'all in memory at the same time' constraint of DOM means that it may be the only practical approach for very large XML documents.

libXML a.k.a. gnome-xml

For our DVD store application we decided to use a SAX interface, and in particular the library now known as libxml (it was formerly called gnome-xml) because:

- ❑ We knew it was already used for Glade, the GUI builder for GNOME applications, and so was a reliable implementation.

- ❑ It has a C interface, and that is the main programming language we are using in this book.

- ❑ We only needed to read XML documents, not create them.

- ❑ It is being actively developed.

If you have GNOME installed on your Linux machine then you almost certainly will have libxml already installed. If you use a different GUI you may be missing libxml, but it's available in RPM format.

The libxml page has links to download locations – see Resources. Note that you will need both the standard and -devel versions for compiling XML programs, unless you install it from source code.

At first sight, code that uses libxml looks a little unusual. This is partly because it is a C implementation of what was essentially a Java-specific specification. It's also partly because it relies on callback routines, which may not be an entirely familiar approach to all C programmers.

The basic structure for using SAX with an XML document is very simple:

- ❑ Create an instance of the parser.

- ❑ Write a set of routines to be called when the parser detects certain constructs.

- ❑ Tell the parser about your routines.

- ❑ Tell the parser to parse the file.

- ❑ The parser then calls your routines as it processes the XML file, to notify you of the data it has processed.

In practice there are a few more hurdles to overcome, but the basic idea should not vary too much from this format.

Graphically we could represent the sequence like this:

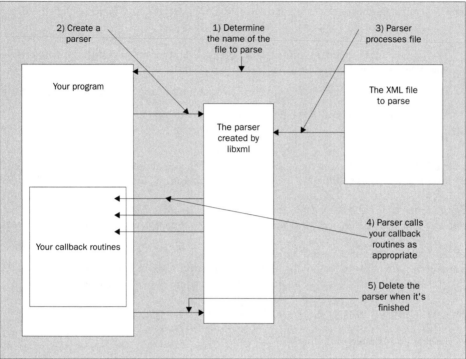

Creating and Calling the Parser

Well enough of the theory – let's have a look at a program that uses the parser in libxml. This is sax1.c, a minimal program that uses libxml:

```
#include <stdlib.h>
#include <stdio.h>

#include <parser.h>
#include <parserInternals.h>


int main() {

  xmlParserCtxtPtr ctxt_ptr;

  ctxt_ptr = xmlCreateFileParserCtxt("dvdcatalog.xml");
  if (!ctxt_ptr) {
    fprintf(stderr, "Failed to create file parser\n");
    exit(EXIT_FAILURE);
  }

  xmlParseDocument(ctxt_ptr);
```

```
    if (!ctxt_ptr->wellFormed) {
      fprintf(stderr, "Document not well formed\n");
    }

    xmlFreeParserCtxt(ctxt_ptr);

    printf("Parsing complete\n");
    exit(EXIT_SUCCESS);
  }
```

The program is rather short, as we've not yet added any callback routines. Don't worry, they are coming soon.

To compile this program you will need to specify in the include search path the directory where the parser.h and perserInternals.h files reside on your system. On machines with installations prior to version 2 of libxml this will probably be in /usr/include/gnome-xml, but from version 2 onwards it will be /usr/include/xml. You will also need to link with the xml and zlib libraries (the latter because libxml can read compressed XML files, and thus requires the zlib routines to be available). Your compile command will therefore be a variant on:

```
$ gcc -I/usr/include/gnome-xml sax1.c -lxml -lz -o sax1
```

or

```
$ gcc -I/usr/include/xml sax1.c -lxml -lz -o sax1
```

Let's now have a look at the code in more detail:

```
xmlParserCtxtPtr ctxt_ptr;

ctxt_ptr = xmlCreateFileParserCtxt("dvdcatalog.xml");
if (!ctxt_ptr) {
  fprintf(stderr, "Failed to create file parser\n");
  exit(EXIT_FAILURE);
}
```

This section creates a parser for us, which is pointed to by the ctxt_ptr. This:

```
xmlParseDocument(ctxt_ptr);
```

tells the parser to parse the file, and this:

```
if (!ctxt_ptr->wellFormed) {
  fprintf(stderr, "Document not well formed\n");
}
```

is called once parsing is finished, to warn us if the file was not considered well-formed. Finally:

```
xmlFreeParserCtxt(ctxt_ptr);
```

releases the parser once we have finished with it.

When we run it, all we see is:

```
$./sax1
Parsing complete
$
```

This is a start, but isn't terribly useful; all we know is that the parser apparently considers our XML file to be well-formed. Let's try corrupting our XML file and check how the parser reacts.

Let's deliberately insert a stray <B> tag in one of the dvd entries, like this:

```
<dvd asin="0780020707">
      <title>Grand Illusion</title>
      <price>29.99</price>
      <director>Jean<B>Renoir</director>
      <actors>
          <actor>Jean Gabin</actor>
      </actors>
      <year_made>1938</year_made>
   </dvd>
```

When we run the parser again we get:

```
$./sax1
dvdcatalog.xml:7: error: Opening and ending tag mismatch: B and director
      <director>Jean<B>Renoir</director>
                                        ^
dvdcatalog.xml:12: error: Opening and ending tag mismatch: director and dvd
   </dvd>
       ^
dvdcatalog.xml:25: error: Opening and ending tag mismatch: dvd and catalog
</catalog>
         ^
dvdcatalog.xml:26: error: detected an error in element content

 ^
dvdcatalog.xml:26: error: Premature end of data in tag <catalog>
   <dvd asin="07800

 ^
Document not well formed
Parsing complete
```

So we do know that the parser is at least processing our document, and provides helpful error messages when it finds problems.

Before going any further, restore the XML file to its original clean state. We will return to error handling a bit later, when we discover that it is possible to provide your own callback routines for error handling, if the default behavior is not suitable.

Document Information

In the first example, we saw the expression:

```
ctxt_ptr->wellFormed
```

which enabled us to check that the document was well-formed. The libxml structure has some other useful elements in this context structure. If we look in the header file parser.h, we will find a typedef structure _xmlParserCtxt, which has several other structure elements, notably version and encoding character information. We could use these to get the parser to tell us more about the XML file. This is an extract of sax2.c, which is otherwise identical to sax1.c:

```
if (!ctxt_ptr->wellFormed) {
    fprintf(stderr, "Document not well formed\n");
}
printf("XML version %s, encoding %s\n", ctxt_ptr->version, ctxt_ptr->encoding);


ctxt_ptr->sax = NULL;
```

When we run this we get:

```
$./sax2
XML version 1.0, encoding UTF-8
Parsing complete
$
```

Using Callbacks

Now we know that the parser is processing our file, checking its validity, and extracting basic information successfully, it's time to write some callback routines, so we can get at the data in our XML file.

There is a structure defined (as an xmlSAXHandler) in parser.h that lists the callback points that are available to us. We will see this structure shortly.

Also defined are the prototypes for the functions that you, the user, must provide if you wish to write a callback routine:

```
typedef xmlParserInputPtr (*resolveEntitySAXFunc) (void *ctx,
                                          const CHAR *publicId,
                                          const CHAR *systemId);

typedef void (*internalSubsetSAXFunc) (void *ctx, const CHAR *name,
                                          const CHAR *ExternalID,
                                          const CHAR *SystemID);

typedef xmlEntityPtr (*getEntitySAXFunc) (void *ctx, const CHAR *name);

typedef void (*entityDeclSAXFunc) (void *ctx, const CHAR *name, int type,
                                          const CHAR *publicId,
                                          const CHAR *systemId,
                                          CHAR *content);
```

```
typedef void (*notationDeclSAXFunc)(void *ctx, const CHAR *name,
                                    const CHAR *publicId,
                                    const CHAR *systemId);

typedef void (*attributeDeclSAXFunc)(void *ctx, const CHAR *elem,
                                     const CHAR *name,
                                     int type, int def,
                                     const CHAR *defaultValue,
                                     xmlEnumerationPtr tree);

typedef void (*elementDeclSAXFunc)(void *ctx, const CHAR *name,
                                   int type, xmlElementContentPtr content);

typedef void (*unparsedEntityDeclSAXFunc)(void *ctx,
                                          const CHAR *name,
                                          const CHAR *publicId,
                                          const CHAR *systemId,
                                          const CHAR *notationName);

typedef void (*setDocumentLocatorSAXFunc) (void *ctx,
                                           xmlSAXLocatorPtr loc);

typedef void (*startDocumentSAXFunc) (void *ctx);

typedef void (*endDocumentSAXFunc) (void *ctx);

typedef void (*startElementSAXFunc) (void *ctx, const CHAR *name,
                                     const CHAR **atts);

typedef void (*endElementSAXFunc) (void *ctx, const CHAR *name);

typedef void (*attributeSAXFunc) (void *ctx, const CHAR *name,
                                  const CHAR *value);

typedef void (*referenceSAXFunc) (void *ctx, const CHAR *name);

typedef void (*charactersSAXFunc) (void *ctx, const CHAR *ch, int len);

typedef void (*ignorableWhitespaceSAXFunc) (void *ctx,
                                            const CHAR *ch, int len);

typedef void (*processingInstructionSAXFunc) (void *ctx,
                                              const CHAR *target,
                                              const CHAR *data);

typedef void (*commentSAXFunc) (void *ctx, const CHAR *value);

typedef void (*warningSAXFunc) (void *ctx, const char *msg, ...);

typedef void (*errorSAXFunc) (void *ctx, const char *msg, ...);

typedef void (*fatalErrorSAXFunc) (void *ctx, const char *msg, ...);

typedef int (*isStandaloneSAXFunc) (void *ctx);

typedef int (*hasInternalSubsetSAXFunc) (void *ctx);

typedef int (*hasExternalSubsetSAXFunc) (void *ctx);
```

> Notice the use of **CHAR** rather than **char** – this is a new type declared in the headers, not a typing mistake.

Fortunately, only a few of these callbacks are required to parse an XML file and extract useful information. Before working through the main callback functions that we will need, let's add two very simple callback routines to our code, so we can see how the callback mechanism works in practice.

What we will do is provide callback routines for the start and end of the document, which we will ask to be called when the parser detects the document start and the document end. From the list above these are `startDocumentSAXFunc` and `endDocumentSAXFunc`. These routines are often used to enable us to perform initialization and cleanup operations.

To use a callback we must do three things:

❑   Write the callback function

❑   Setup `libxml`'s callback structure to call them

❑   Tell the parser about the callback structure

Let's do the easy bit first, and write two callback functions. We can ignore the parameters for now:

```
static void start_document(void *ctx) {
  printf("Document start\n");
}

static void end_document(void *ctx) {
  printf("Document end\n");
}
```

Now for the tricky bit, which is to set up the callback structure. To do this we must declare ourselves a structure of type `xmlSAXHandler`, and assign pointers to our routines in the appropriate places.

The structure `xmlSAXHandler`, which declares the callbacks available, is declared in `parse.h`:

```
typedef struct xmlSAXHandler {
    internalSubsetSAXFunc internalSubset;
    isStandaloneSAXFunc isStandalone;
    hasInternalSubsetSAXFunc hasInternalSubset;
    hasExternalSubsetSAXFunc hasExternalSubset;
    resolveEntitySAXFunc resolveEntity;
    getEntitySAXFunc getEntity;
    entityDeclSAXFunc entityDecl;
    notationDeclSAXFunc notationDecl;
    attributeDeclSAXFunc attributeDecl;
    elementDeclSAXFunc elementDecl;
    unparsedEntityDeclSAXFunc unparsedEntityDecl;
    setDocumentLocatorSAXFunc setDocumentLocator;
    startDocumentSAXFunc startDocument;
    endDocumentSAXFunc endDocument;
    startElementSAXFunc startElement;
    endElementSAXFunc endElement;
    referenceSAXFunc reference;
    charactersSAXFunc characters;
    ignorableWhitespaceSAXFunc ignorableWhitespace;
    processingInstructionSAXFunc processingInstruction;
    commentSAXFunc comment;
    warningSAXFunc warning;
    errorSAXFunc error;
    fatalErrorSAXFunc fatalError;
} xmlSAXHandler;
```

As you can see, the callback function pointers are well named, so it's easy to spot the ones you want.

All the callback routine locations that we do not wish to handle get a NULL, so libxml knows we have not written routines for these. To safeguard against this structure changing, we use memset to clear the whole structure to NULL, and then explicitly overwrite the callback function pointers we need. Anyone who has worked with structures of callbacks will know the chaos that can result from putting a function pointer in the wrong place in a long list of callback routines...

```
static xmlSAXHandler mySAXParseCallbacks;

    memset(&mySAXParseCallbacks, sizeof(mySAXParseCallbacks), 0);
    mySAXParseCallbacks.startDocument = start_document;
    mySAXParseCallbacks.endDocument = end_document;
```

Finally, we must tell the parser about our callback structure:

```
if (!ctxt_ptr) {
    fprintf(stderr, "Failed to create file parser\n");
    exit(EXIT_FAILURE);
}

    ctxt_ptr->sax = &mySAXParseCallbacks;

    xmlParseDocument(ctxt_ptr);


    ctxt_ptr->sax = NULL;
```

Notice we set the pointer in the context back to NULL once parsing has finished.

If we put these all together we get sax3.c, which calls our routines automatically as the document is being parsed:

```
$./sax3
Document start
Document end
Parsing complete
$
```

For this example, we took out the version and encoding code, since it's now just clutter in the file.

As you can see, setting up the callbacks is actually quite easy. Now it's time to look down all that list of possible callbacks, and see what they can be used for. In practice we can solve 95% of all our parsing needs with just five callback routines (plus three more for error handling if the default error behavior is not suitable), so these are the ones we will describe here. All of these routines take a void *ctx pointer as the first parameter. We will discover a use for this in the next section, when we look at maintaining information between different callback routines.

Error routines

All the error routines have the same format, but different callbacks are invoked depending on the seriousness of the error. The three routines are:

```
typedef void (*warningSAXFunc) (void *ctx, const char *msg, ...);
typedef void (*errorSAXFunc) (void *ctx, const char *msg, ...);
typedef void (*fatalErrorSAXFunc) (void *ctx, const char *msg, ...);
```

The `warningSAXFunc` is for warnings, `errorSAXFunc` is for errors, and `fatalErrorSAXFunc` is for errors where the parser cannot continue. Notice that these are unlike most of the earlier callbacks and do use a conventional `char`, not a `CHAR`.

All of these routines take a variable number of arguments. They should be accessed by using the `stdarg` functions. The error message can be displayed (after including `<stdarg.h>`) thus:

```
va_list args;
va_start(args, msg);

vprintf(msg, args);
va_end(args);
```

For use on the command line, which is how we are using `libxml` in this chapter, the default error behavior is generally fine. If you were writing a GUI, then the default behavior would not be so acceptable, and we would need to write a more appropriate routine and configure it as a callback.

For example, here is a brief extract from `saxp.c`, which implements a callback for error handling. The `saxp.c` file is part of the Glade test suite:

```
static void gladeError(GladeParseState *state, const char*msg, ...) {
va_list args;

va_start(args, msg);
g_logv("XML", G_LOG_LEVEL_CRITICAL, msg, args);
va_end(args);
}
```

Start Document

This routine is called once when the document parsing starts, and will always be called before any other callback routines. Its prototype is:

```
typedef void (*startDocumentSAXFunc) (void *ctx);
```

End Document

This routine is called once when parsing of a document finishes, either because the document has ended, or because an unrecoverable error has occurred. Its prototype is:

```
typedef void (*endDocumentSAXFunc) (void *ctx);
```

Start element

This routine is called each time a new element is detected:

```
typedef void (*startElementSAXFunc) (void *ctx, const CHAR *name,
                                      const CHAR **atts);
```

The `name` parameter gives the name of the element, and the `atts` parameter is either `NULL`, or a `NULL` terminated list of pointers to attribute names and values, for example in our DVD catalog the `dvd` element has an attribute of `asin` with a value of a string the `atts` array would have two pointers, the first to a string `"asin"`, the second to the actual string (which just happens to consist of digits). We will see some example code accessing element attributes in the next version of our SAX example file.

End element

This routine is called each time an element ends, even if the element was an empty element, such as <fud/>. Thus every call to the start element callback will have a matching end element call, providing no fatal error occurs:

```
typedef void (*endElementSAXFunc) (void *ctx, const CHAR *name);
```

Characters

This routine is called every time a character sequence is found that is not something more specific, such as an element, or comment for example:

```
typedef void (*charactersSAXFunc) (void *ctx, const CHAR *ch, int len);
```

It's possible for long strings of characters to be split into multiple calls to this routine, so the application may need to take steps to handle this possibility.

A Callback Example

Now we know what callback routines look like, we can write some code that does more than tell us about events – we can actually get at the data and attributes in the elements. Here is sax4.c, which demonstrates our first realistic parsing attempt on the document:

```c
#include <stdlib.h>
#include <stdio.h>

#include <string.h>

#include <parser.h>
#include <parserInternals.h>

static void start_document(void *ctx);
static void end_document(void *ctx);
static void start_element(void *ctx, const CHAR *name, const CHAR **attrs);
static void end_element(void *ctx, const CHAR *name);
static void chars_found(void *ctx, const CHAR *chars, int len);

static xmlSAXHandler mySAXParseCallbacks;

int main() {

  xmlParserCtxtPtr ctxt_ptr;

  memset(&mySAXParseCallbacks, sizeof(mySAXParseCallbacks), 0);
  mySAXParseCallbacks.startDocument = start_document;
  mySAXParseCallbacks.endDocument = end_document;
  mySAXParseCallbacks.startElement = start_element;
  mySAXParseCallbacks.endElement = end_element;
  mySAXParseCallbacks.characters = chars_found;

  ctxt_ptr = xmlCreateFileParserCtxt("dvdcatalog.xml");
  if (!ctxt_ptr) {
    fprintf(stderr, "Failed to create file parser\n");
    exit(EXIT_FAILURE);
  }
```

```
    ctxt_ptr->sax = &mySAXParseCallbacks;


    xmlParseDocument(ctxt_ptr);
    if (!ctxt_ptr->wellFormed) {
      fprintf(stderr, "Document not well formed\n");
    }

    ctxt_ptr->sax = NULL;

    xmlFreeParserCtxt(ctxt_ptr);

    printf("Parsing complete\n");
    exit(EXIT_SUCCESS);
} /* main */


static void start_document(void *ctx) {
  printf("Document start\n");
} /* start_document */

static void end_document(void *ctx) {
  printf("Document end\n");
} /* end_document */

static void start_element(void *ctx, const CHAR *name, const CHAR **attrs) {
  const char *attr_ptr;
  int curr_attr = 0;
  printf("Element %s started\n", name);
  if (attrs) {
    attr_ptr = *attrs;
    while(attr_ptr) {
      printf("\tAttribute %s\n", attr_ptr);
      curr_attr++;
      attr_ptr = *(attrs + curr_attr);
    }
  }
} /* start_element */

static void end_element(void *ctx, const CHAR *name) {
  printf("Element %s ended\n", name);
} /* end_element */

#define CHAR_BUFFER 1024

static void chars_found(void *ctx, const CHAR *chars, int len) {
  char buff[CHAR_BUFFER + 1];
  if (len > CHAR_BUFFER) len = CHAR_BUFFER;

  strncpy(buff, chars, len);
  buff[len] = '\0';
  printf("Found %d characters: %s\n", len, buff);

} /* chars_found */
```

It's a little long, but it's quite straightforward, apart from two parts that warrant special attention:

❑ start_element shows how we must detect the presence of attribute strings, and how we can access their names and values.

❑ chars_found prints out the data found. Notice that (at least in the current implementation) the string passed is not NULL terminated, so we must take special measures to print out only the number of characters we were told to.

When we run sax4, what we see (abbreviated for clarity) is:

```
$ ./sax4
Document start
Element catalog started
Found 5 characters:

Element dvd started
        Attribute asin
        Attribute 0780020707
Found 8 characters:

Element title started
Found 14 characters: Grand Illusion
Element title ended
Found 8 characters:

Element price started
Found 5 characters: 29.99
Element price ended
Found 8 characters:

Element director started
Found 11 characters: Jean Renoir
Element director ended
Found 8 characters:

Element actors started
Found 11 characters:

Element actor started
Found 10 characters: Jean Gabin
Element actor ended
Found 8 characters:

Element actors ended
...
```

The astute among you will promptly spot a difficulty. When the start_element routine is called, we don't yet know the contents of the element, and when the chars_found routine is called, we no longer know which element we were processing. Furthermore, chars_found is called in places where we're not interested in processing the characters. This is the drawback of using a SAX-type parser. What we need to do is save some state information.

Maintaining State

The need to maintain some state information while sequentially parsing structured data is almost a given, and `libxml` has some built-in features to help you.

In the context structure, as well as a pointer for the callback structure, there is a `void *` pointer for `userData`, which can be used to store our state information. No pre-defined structure is provided for this information, which is handy, because often we wish to store slightly more than pure state information. Each time a callback function is invoked, a pointer to our structure is passed as the first argument, the `void *ctx` pointer to callback routines, which we have not so far used.

To maintain our state information, we first need to declare a structure to hold the information. For our XML file we need one extra piece of information over and above the state information – we need to track the number of actors we have listed for each title. We made a decision in previous chapters, as part of our simplification of the problem, that we would hold exactly two actors' names per DVD, using NULLs when names were missing.

In the XML file, the DTD tells us that there is always at least one actor (see the DTD: the actors element must be present, and it consists of one or more actor elements), but there may be entries where three or more actors are listed. We need to catch the case of only having a single actor, so we can insert a NULL actor for the second entry.

First we enumerate some states that our parser might be in:

```
typedef enum {
    parse_start_s = 0,      /* starting                               */
    parse_finish_s,         /* ending                                 */
    parse_dvd_s,            /* processing a dvd element               */
    parse_price_s,          /* processing a price element             */
    parse_actor_s,          /* processing an actor element            */
    parse_year_made_s,      /* processing the year made element       */
    parse_valid_string_s,   /* processing a some other valid element  */
    parse_skip_string_s,    /* processing an element we want to ignore */
    parse_unknown_s         /* processing something not understood    */
} parse_state;
```

Then we declare a structure to hold the state and actor count:

```
typedef struct {
    parse_state current_state;
    int actors_this_movie;
} catalog_parse_state;
```

In the main routine we can declare an instance of this structure, and assign a pointer to it to the parser context structure:

```
xmlParserCtxtPtr ctxt_ptr;
catalog_parse_state parsing_state;

ctxt_ptr = xmlCreateFileParserCtxt("dvdcatalog.xml");
if (!ctxt_ptr) {
    fprintf(stderr, "Failed to create file parser\n");
```

```
        exit(EXIT_FAILURE);
    }

    ctxt_ptr->sax = &mySAXParseCallbacks;
    ctxt_ptr->userData = &parsing_state;

    xmlParseDocument(ctxt_ptr);
```

In each of our callback routines, we can access this state structure, through the `ctx` pointer:

```
static void start_element(void *ctx, const char *name, const char **attrs) {
    const char *attr_ptr;
    int curr_attr = 0;
    catalog_parse_state *state_ptr;

    parse_state curr_state;
    parse_event curr_event;

    state_ptr = (catalog_parse_state *)ctx;
    curr_state = state_ptr->current_state;
```

The Complete Parser

The final version of the program used to parse our XML file puts together many of the features we have met earlier in the chapter, and additionally includes a state/event machine to decide how each event requires processing. We consider the machine to be in a particular state, and the function callbacks from the parser are converted into events. The combination of current state and received event is passed to the state machine to determine how the combination should be processed.

We have not provided our own error handling, as the routines built into `libxml` that are called by default are ideal for our purpose.

Rather than show a file that outputs the CSV ready for loading in the database, here is `sax5.c`, which is still human-readable, so you can see the processing output.

We start with some standard includes and forward declarations:

```
#include <stdlib.h>
#include <stdio.h>

#include <string.h>

#include <parser.h>
#include <parserInternals.h>
```

Now some `typedef` enumerations in order to provide an easy way to process event and state definitions:

```
/* Event map */
typedef enum {
    parse_start_e = 0,
    parse_finish_e,
```

```
    parse_catalog_e,
    parse_dvd_e,
    parse_title_e,
    parse_price_e,
    parse_director_e,
    parse_actors_e,
    parse_actor_e,
    parse_year_made_e,
    parse_end_element_e,
    parse_other_e
} parse_event;


/* State map */
typedef enum {
    parse_start_s = 0,
    parse_finish_s,
    parse_dvd_s,
    parse_price_s,
    parse_actor_s,
    parse_year_made_s,
    parse_valid_string_s,
    parse_skip_string_s,
    parse_unknown_s
} parse_state;
```

We declare a structure to hold the information we need passing between callback routines. This consists of the state that we are in, plus the count of the number of actors:

```
/* Structure to store state and actor count between callbacks */
typedef struct {
    parse_state current_state;
    int actors_this_movie;
} catalog_parse_state;
```

We declare prototypes:

```
/* Callback prototypes */
static void start_document(void *ctx);
static void end_document(void *ctx);
static void start_element(void *ctx, const char *name, const char **attrs);
static void end_element(void *ctx, const char *name);
static void chars_found(void *ctx, const char *chars, int len);

/* Utility functions */
static parse_event get_event_from_name(const char *name);
static parse_state state_event_machine(parse_state curr_state, parse_event
curr_event);
```

and the callback structure:

```
static xmlSAXHandler mySAXParseCallbacks;
```

main()

Now, we're ready for the main routine. All this does is:

- ❑ create a parser
- ❑ set up the callbacks
- ❑ set up a pointer to the data holding state in between callbacks
- ❑ request that the document is parsed
- ❑ remove the callbacks
- ❑ delete the parser

It takes hardly any more lines of code to write the actual C program than it does to describe it:

```c
int main() {

  xmlParserCtxtPtr ctxt_ptr;
  catalog_parse_state parsing_state;

  memset(&mySAXParseCallbacks, sizeof(mySAXParseCallbacks), 0);
  mySAXParseCallbacks.startDocument = start_document;
  mySAXParseCallbacks.endDocument = end_document;
  mySAXParseCallbacks.startElement = start_element;
  mySAXParseCallbacks.endElement = end_element;
  mySAXParseCallbacks.characters = chars_found;


  ctxt_ptr = xmlCreateFileParserCtxt("dvdcatalog.xml");
  if (!ctxt_ptr) {
    fprintf(stderr, "Failed to create file parser\n");
    exit(EXIT_FAILURE);
  }

  ctxt_ptr->sax = &mySAXParseCallbacks; /* Set callback map */
  ctxt_ptr->userData = &parsing_state;

  xmlParseDocument(ctxt_ptr);
  if (!ctxt_ptr->wellFormed) {
    fprintf(stderr, "Document not well formed\n");
  }

  ctxt_ptr->sax = NULL;

  xmlFreeParserCtxt(ctxt_ptr);

  printf("Parsing complete\n");
  exit(EXIT_SUCCESS);
} /* main */
```

start_document()

This callback is invoked when document parsing starts, and resets the state machine information:

```
static void start_document(void *ctx) {
   catalog_parse_state *state_ptr;
   state_ptr = (catalog_parse_state *)ctx;

   state_ptr->current_state = parse_start_s;
   state_ptr->actors_this_movie = 0;

} /* start_document */
```

end_document()

The following callback is called when document parsing ends, and sets the state machine information so any further callbacks will be detected as invalid:

```
static void end_document(void *ctx) {
   catalog_parse_state *state_ptr;
   state_ptr = (catalog_parse_state *)ctx;

   state_ptr->current_state = parse_finish_s;

} /* end_document */
```

start_element()

The `start_element` callback is called each time a new element in the XML document is detected. Its main action is to call the state machine to determine our new state. In addition, it counts actors and handles the attributes that the `dvd` element contains:

```
static void start_element(void *ctx, const char *name, const char **attrs) {
   const char *attr_ptr;
   int curr_attr = 0;
   catalog_parse_state *state_ptr;

   parse_state curr_state;
   parse_event curr_event;

   state_ptr = (catalog_parse_state *)ctx;
   curr_state = state_ptr->current_state;
   curr_event = get_event_from_name(name);

   state_ptr->current_state = state_event_machine(curr_state, curr_event);

   if (curr_event == parse_actor_e) {
     state_ptr->actors_this_movie++;
   }
   if (curr_event == parse_actors_e) {
     state_ptr->actors_this_movie = 0;
   }
```

```
      if (state_ptr->current_state == parse_dvd_s) {
        /* The DVD element should have attributes */
        printf("Element %s started\n", name);
        if (attrs) {
          attr_ptr = *attrs;
          while(attr_ptr) {
          printf("\tAttribute %s\n", attr_ptr);
          curr_attr++;
          attr_ptr = *(attrs + curr_attr);
          }
        }
      }

    } /* start_element */
```

end_element()

The `end_element` callback is invoked each time an element ends, and simply invokes the state machine to handle the event:

```
static void end_element(void *ctx, const char *name) {
  catalog_parse_state *state_ptr;
  parse_state curr_state;
  parse_event curr_event;

  state_ptr = (catalog_parse_state *)ctx;
  curr_state = state_ptr->current_state;
  curr_event = parse_end_element_e;

  state_ptr->current_state = state_event_machine(curr_state, curr_event);
} /* end_element */
```

chars_found()

The `chars_found` routine is called each time a string is detected that is not an element, comment, or attribute. We use the current state of the state machine to determine how the characters should be handled. We handle `price` and `year_made` slightly differently, to demonstrate how the state engine can detect a mix of specific and more general elements, using the `parse_valid_string_s` state for generic type elements:

```
/* In the interest of simplicity we assume a limited event name
length, and all characters returned in a single callback */

#define CHAR_BUFFER 1024

static void chars_found(void *ctx, const char *chars, int len) {
  char buff[CHAR_BUFFER + 1];
  catalog_parse_state *state_ptr;
  state_ptr = (catalog_parse_state *)ctx;

  if (len > CHAR_BUFFER) len = CHAR_BUFFER;
  strncpy(buff, chars, len);
  buff[len] = '\0';
```

```
      /* Depending on the state handle the string in different ways */
      switch(state_ptr->current_state) {
      case parse_start_s:
      case parse_finish_s:
      case parse_dvd_s:
        break;
      case parse_price_s:
        printf("Price %s\n", buff);
        break;
      case parse_actor_s:
        printf("Actor %s (%d)\n", buff, state_ptr->actors_this_movie);
        break;
      case parse_year_made_s:
        printf("Year %s\n", buff);
        break;
      case parse_valid_string_s:
        printf("Other valid %s\n", buff);
        break;
      case parse_skip_string_s:
        break;
      case parse_unknown_s:
        break;
      default:
        printf("DEBUG default case in chars_found %d\n", state_ptr->current_state);
        break;
      } /* switch */

    } /* chars_found */
```

get_event_from_name()

We have a utility to convert element names into event enumerations:

```
    /* Map element names to event enumerations */

    const struct {
      const char *name;
      parse_event event;
    } events[] = {
      {"catalog", parse_catalog_e},
      {"dvd", parse_dvd_e},
      {"title", parse_title_e},
      {"price", parse_price_e},
      {"director", parse_director_e},
      {"actor", parse_actor_e},
      {"actors", parse_actors_e},
      {"year_made", parse_year_made_e}
    };

    static parse_event get_event_from_name(const char *name) {
      int i;

      for (i = 0; i < sizeof(events)/sizeof(*events); i++) {
        if (!strcmp(name, events[i].name)) return events[i].event;
      }
      return parse_other_e;

    } /* get_event_from_name */
```

state_event_machine()

Last, but not least, we have the state machine that determines the new state, given the current state and an event:

```
/* State machine lookup */
const struct {
  const parse_event pe;
  parse_state ns;
} event_state[] = {
  {parse_start_e, parse_start_s},
  {parse_finish_e, parse_finish_s},
  {parse_dvd_e, parse_dvd_s},
  {parse_price_e, parse_price_s},
  {parse_actor_e, parse_actor_s},
  {parse_year_made_e, parse_year_made_s},
  {parse_title_e, parse_valid_string_s},
  {parse_director_e, parse_valid_string_s},
  {parse_year_made_e, parse_year_made_s},
  {parse_title_e, parse_valid_string_s},
  {parse_director_e, parse_valid_string_s},
  {parse_catalog_e, parse_skip_string_s},
  {parse_actors_e, parse_skip_string_s},
  {parse_other_e, parse_unknown_s},
  {parse_end_element_e, parse_skip_string_s}
};

static parse_state state_event_machine(parse_state curr_state, parse_event
curr_event) {
  int i;

  for (i = 0; i < sizeof(event_state)/sizeof(*event_state); i++) {
    if (curr_event == event_state[i].pe) return event_state[i].ns;
  }

  return parse_unknown_s;
} /* state_event_machine */
```

When we run this (on a subset of data for brevity) we get a nice clean output. Notice each actor is tagged with their 'number' in that DVD record, and we simply use the 'Other valid' message for both directors and film titles. This is more to demonstrate how we can simplify the parser where there are a number of elements that can be handled in a generic fashion, than from any lack of desire to separate the two meanings!

```
Element dvd started
    Attribute asin
    Attribute 0780020707
Other valid Grand Illusion
Price 29.99
Other valid Jean Renoir
Actor Jean Gabin (1)
Year 1938
Element dvd started
    Attribute asin
    Attribute 0780020685
```

```
Other valid Seven Samurai
Price 27.99
Other valid Akira Kurosawa
Actor Takashi Shimura (1)
Actor Toshiro Mifune (2)
Year 1954
Parsing complete
```

Resources

The main starting point for anything to do with XML is the W3C standards site at: http://www.w3.org/xml.

It's also well worth looking out the annotated version of the XML standard, which can be found from http://www.xml.com/pub/axml/axmlintro.html.

The Home page for the libxml library, previously known as gnome-xml, can be found at http://xmlsoft.org, and, as well as providing some documentation and download links, is also a good source of other XML links you may wish to investigate. An alternative source of libxml documentation can be found at http://www.daa.com.au/~james/gnome/xml-sax/xml-sax.html.

A great resource for Open Source XML work can be found at http://xml.apache.org/, in particular the Xerces XML parser, which is available in both Java and C++ flavors, runs under Linux, and implements a DOM parsing model that is closely tracking the W3C standard for XML schemas.

IBM is doing a lot of XML (and Linux) work, its alphaWorks site at http://www.alphaworks.ibm.com/ is often a good place to look for new and emerging technologies.

James Clark's Home Page, at http://www.jclark.com/ is also a good XML resource.

Another DOM interface, Gdome, built on top of libxml, can be found at http://levien.com/gnome/gdome.html.

The SAX interface standard for parsing XML can be found at http://www.megginson.com/SAX.

The XML FAQ can be found at http://www.ucc.ie/xml.

An Open Source XML editor (written in Java) can be found at http://www.merlotxml.org/.

There are so many XML books out there, it's a little difficult to know where to start. One weighty tome that's well worth considering is *Professional XML*, Wrox Press (*ISBN 1-861003-11-0*).

Summary

In this chapter we have provided an overview of XML document structures, and the DTDs that define them. We discussed the difference between a 'well-formed' XML document that is syntactically correct, and a 'valid' XML document that has a defined Document Type Definition (DTD) to which it conforms.

We then looked briefly at the two main parser types for XML documents, the Document Object Model (DOM), and the Simple API for XML (SAX) Model.

We then looked in detail at libxml, a library originally part of the Gnome GUI, but now a tool in its own right, that provides a SAX-based parser with a C programming interface.

Finally we built a parser using libxml to process our dvdcatalog.xml file.

24

Beowulf Clusters

During the past decade, there has been a tremendous increase in performance and a rapid decline in the price of personal computers and networking hardware. Computer users have also seen the availability of free, high quality system software for these computers. The source code of these software packages is also made available to the public to allow enhancements and modifications. In 1994, NASA GSFC started a project to build a parallel computer for their computing needs using commodity hardware and freely available software packages. This computer called the **Beowulf** was built using 16 Intel x86 processors with 10 MBit/s Ethernet and ran the Linux operating system and other freely available software distributed under the GPL. In recent years, these computer clusters have become very popular due to their low cost, good performance, and high reliability.

In this chapter, you will learn about the architecture, the software configuration, and the programming of Beowulf clusters. The primary emphasis will be on the programming aspect where we provide several sample programs to experiment with on these computer clusters. These programs will run on a single computer as well as a computer cluster.

Hardware Setup

A Beowulf cluster consists of a set of computers interconnected by a network to form a **tightly coupled** or **shared memory** computing system. The diagram below shows the typical configuration of a Beowulf cluster. In this figure, the boxes labeled n0 to n7 represent computers and the box labeled S represents a network switch or hub.

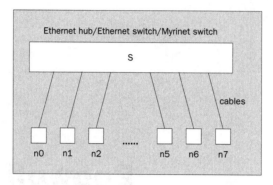

Due to their low cost and relatively high performance, a popular choice for the computers is the Intel Pentium based system. The choice of networking hardware could range from a 10 Mbit/sec Ethernet based hub for a low-end system to a Myrinet (a low cost, high performance communication and packet switching device developed by Myricom inc.) or Gigabit Ethernet based switch for a high-end system. A 10 Mbit/sec Ethernet hub based system is suitable for a typical home user who wishes to experiment or learn about Beowulf clusters. These clusters are suitable for parallel programs with a small amount of inter-processor communication relative to computations. A good choice for a small company or a research institution operating on a moderate budget is a 100 Mbit/s switched Ethernet based system. There are 64-port switches currently available that allow up to 64 computers to be connected to the same switch. Larger systems could be built by cascading two or more switches. You can also get switches with more than 64 ports and this number will increase over time. The high-end networks that employ Myrinet or Gigabit Ethernet are mainly used by government agencies that use Beowulf clusters as an alternative to traditional supercomputers. One example is the **Hive** computer at NASA Goddard Space Flight Center with a 200 processor system connected by fast Ethernet and Myrinet. The Myrinet based systems are typically 10 times faster than the 100 Mbits/s Ethernet systems.

Software Configuration

As mentioned before, a Beowulf cluster is configured using freely available software packages distributed under the GNU General Public License. The commonly used operating system is Linux. A Beowulf cluster can be easily configured to run under the Linux operating system. In this chapter, it is assumed that you are already familiar with installing a Linux operating system on a personal computer. If a Beowulf cluster has only few nodes, the nodes can be configured one by one using the same CD. However, there are some important points to remember when configuring a Beowulf cluster:

❑ One of the nodes of the cluster is set up as a master and the other nodes as slaves.

❑ The master and the slaves are interconnected by a network as explained before. In addition, the master node will usually have access to the outside world using the Ethernet network or a modem. Therefore, it is necessary to select the appropriate network support and driver modules to support the network functionality when configuring the nodes.

- ❏ It is convenient to set up each user to have a common home directory for all nodes. This directory usually resides on the master and is exported to the other nodes of the cluster. If you are unfamiliar with how to NFS export and mount drives, the procedure was described in Chapter 22 and is repeated below:

  Firstly, the master node needs to have some entries in the `/etc/exports` file. In this file, you enter what shares you want available to share. You could enter `/home rw` to make that available as a write-enabled drive. The format of this file is similar to that of `/etc/fstab`. Then each node needs to make available each drive in the `/etc/fstab` file as `master:/home /home` line, for instance.

- ❏ As the nodes form a tightly coupled cluster, each is configured to allow `rsh`, `rcp`, and `rlogin` access to all users (including the root user) from other nodes without a password. This essentially creates a system that looks like one machine, with a single point of access through the master node. Only the master node needs to be made fully secure, as it is the only node that communicates with the outside world. You need to ensure that either `/etc/hosts.equiv` or `$HOME/.rhosts` contains all of the hosts in the cluster, including the local hostname and the master. You might want to make this file available on a shared drive.

Programming a Beowulf Cluster

Beowulf clusters are implemented using a message-passing programming model. In this model, a parallel program consists of a set of processes each working on a subset of the data. The processes communicate with each other using messages to access and modify data that belongs to other processes. The most popular message-passing library is the Message Passing Interface (MPI) that was developed by the MPI forum – a consortium of universities, government agencies, industry, and other research institutions. Several software packages implement the MPI standard. Another message passing library is the Parallel Virtual Machine (PVM) package developed at the Oakridge National Laboratory, which will be covered later.

Programming Using MPI

In this chapter, we use the MPICH software package that is freely available from the Argonne National Laboratory. The web address for the MPICH home page is http://www-unix.mcs.anl.gov/mpi/mpich/index.html. The first step before programming a Beowulf cluster is to connect to this web site and download the software package by appropriately following the links. MPICH also comes with an installation manual and user guide that can be downloaded from the same web site. These manuals explain the installation process and the various MPI library calls in detail. Once you download the tarball, `mpich.tar.gz`, to your host (say n0), the software can be easily installed using the following few steps:

1. Login as root.

2. Unzip and untar the distribution.

3. Change to the `mpich` directory.

4. Run `./configure` to select the default architecture.

If you have an SMP cluster with multiple CPUs per node, you can configure MPICH to include SMP support as follows:

```
# ./configure -opt=-O-comm shared
```

In this case, MPICH can use shared memory for intra-node communication and TCP/IP for inter-node communication between processors.

5. Compile the software:

```
# make > make.log 2>&1
```

6. Examine the make.log to check for errors.

7. If the compilation was successful, install the software:

```
# make PREFIX=/usr/local/mpi install
```

8. Create or edit the file /usr/local/mpi/util/machines/machines.LINUX to add the machine names. For our sample system, this file is as follows:

```
n1
n2
n3
n4
n5
n6
n7
```

The format of this file is similar to the standard .rhosts file with one entry per node. The root node (say n0) from which a MPI program is executed is not listed in the machines.LINUX file because MPI always starts the first task on the master node by default. Therefore, for our eight-node system, there will be seven entries in the file. However, this file, for some reason, has to have at least five entries. If you are using less than five nodes, you can just repeat some of the entries so that there are five lines in there.

If you have an SMP cluster with two processors per node, the machines.LINUX file for our eight node system will be as follows:

```
n0
n1
n1
n2
n2
n3
n3
...
...
n7
n7
```

Note that n0 is listed only once and all other nodes are listed twice for a total of 15 entries in the file for our 8 node system. Again, the root node is listed only once because MPI starts the first task on this node by default. With this file, MPICH will spawn two processes per node starting with node n0.

9. Duplicate the `/usr/local/mpi` directory on the remaining nodes, n1-n7 if `/usr` is not shared among nodes. It should be, however.

The Basic Functionality of an MPI Program

All MPI programs must include a call to the `MPI_Init` routine to initialize the programming environment. This routine must be called before any other MPI library routine. It has two arguments: a pointer to the number of arguments and a pointer to the argument vector as shown below:

```
int MPI_Init(int *argc, char **argv)
```

Every MPI program must also make a call to `MPI_Finalize` to clean up the execution environment. You are not allowed to make any other MPI library calls after calling `MPI_Finalize`. It has the form:

```
int MPI_Finalize(void)
```

When an MPI program is started, each process is assigned a unique integer called the rank. If there are N processes, the rank will vary from 0 to N-1. The send/receive routines use the rank of a process to identify the destination/source of a message.

MPI programs use the `MPI_Comm_size` and `MPI_Comm_rank` routines in order to obtain the number of processes and the rank of the calling process. These library routines have the following form:

```
int MPI_Comm_size(MPI_Comm comm, int *size)
int MPI_Comm_rank(MPI_Comm comm, int *rank)
```

The first argument to both these routines is an MPI communicator that identifies the group of processes participating in a communication operation. Most of the MPI library routines need an MPI communicator as an argument. The most commonly used communicator is `MPI_COMM_WORLD` which is an MPI defined communicator to denote all the processes executing an MPI program. For example, if there are N processes executing a parallel program, the set denoted by `MPI_COMM_WORLD` will have a size N. For most practical purposes, the group defined by `MPI_COMM_WORLD` is the only communicator needed to write parallel programs. However, MPI also gives the programmer the option of defining additional communicators for subsets of the processes. This gives the programmer the option to assign subsets of the processes for performing specialized tasks within a parallel program.

Below is the MPI implementation of a parallel version of the standard *Hello World* program:

1. Make the necessary include files and declare the variables:

```
#include <stdio.h>
#include "mpi.h"

int main(int argc, char *argv[])
{
```

```
    int nproc;
    int iproc;
    char proc_name[MPI_MAX_PROCESSOR_NAME];
    int nameLength;
```

2. Initialize the MPI programming environment:

```
MPI_Init(&argc, &argv);
```

3. Obtain the number of processes and process rank:

```
MPI_Comm_size(MPI_COMM_WORLD, &nproc);
MPI_Comm_rank(MPI_COMM_WORLD, &iproc);
```

4. Obtain the host name:

```
MPI_Get_processor_name(proc_name, &nameLength);
```

5. Each process executes a printf statement to print the information obtained in steps 3 and 4:

```
printf("Hello world, I am host %s with rank %d of %d\n",
    proc_name, iproc, nproc);
```

6. End the MPI program:

```
MPI_Finalize();

return 0;
}
```

Compiling and Executing a Simple MPI Program

In this section, we describe how to compile and execute an MPI program on a Beowulf cluster using the standard *Hello World* program as an example. We have installed the MPI library in the directory /usr/local/mpi/. Before we compile and execute an MPI program, it is necessary to modify our search path for executables to include the directory /usr/local/mpi/bin. The hello.c program is compiled using the mpicc command as follows:

```
$ mpicc -o hello hello.c
```

The mpicc command uses the C compiler to compile an MPI program. You can pass the usual C compiler options to the mpicc command. This command also provides the options for MPI include files and libraries needed to compile an MPI program. You can execute the mpicc command with the -show option to find out what mpicc does without actually compiling the program:

```
$ mpicc -show -o hello hello.c
```

The output will be:

```
cc -DUSE_STDARG -DHAVE_STDLIB_H=1 -DHAVE_STRING_H=1
   -DHAVE_UNISTD_H=1 -DHAVE_STDARG_H=1 -DUSE_STDARG=1
   -DMALLOC_RET_VOID=1  -I/usr/local/mpi/include
    /usr/local/mpi/build/LINUX/ch_p4/include -c -O hello.c

cc -DUSE_STDARG -DHAVE_STDLIB_H=1 -DHAVE_STRING_H=1
   -DHAVE_UNISTD_H=1  -DHAVE_STDARG_H=1 -DUSE_STDARG=1
   -DMALLOC_RET_VOID=1  -L/usr/local/mpi/build/LINUX/ch_p4/lib
    hello.o -O -o hello -lpmpich -lmpich
```

MPI programs must be executed using the mpirun command. We assume that a user has a common home directory for all nodes. This home directory will reside on one of the nodes (say n0) and be NFS mounted by other nodes of the cluster. If the user has separate home directories for each node instead, the executable must be copied from the master to each client using the rcp command. The *Hello World* program is executed on eight nodes of our cluster as follows:

```
$ mpirun -np 8 hello
```

The output of this program should be:

```
Hello world, I am host n4 with rank 4 of 8
Hello world, I am host n2 with rank 2 of 8
Hello world, I am host n3 with rank 3 of 8
Hello world, I am host n5 with rank 5 of 8
Hello world, I am host n6 with rank 6 of 8
Hello world, I am host n7 with rank 7 of 8
Hello world, I am host n1 with rank 1 of 8
Hello world, I am host n0 with rank 0 of 8
```

If you execute this program another time the output could be in a different order.

A Distributed MP3 Encoder

The second example we consider is a distributed MP3 encoder. We develop a parallel program that can convert multiple WAV-files to MP3 files on a Beowulf cluster. The parallel program uses Blade's MP3 encoder distributed under the GNU Lesser General Public License. Following are the steps involved in implementing the distributed version of this program:

1. Download the stable source tarball from the web site, http://bladeenc.mp3.no/.

2. Uncompress and untar the source distribution:

```
$ tar xvzf bladeenc-n-src-stable.tar.gz
```

This will create the directory bladeenc-n-src-stable, where n is the version number.

3. Change to the bladeenc-n-src-stable directory:

```
$ cd bladeenc-082-src-stable
```

857

4. Make the following changes to the source code:

    a. Rename `main.c` to `bladeenc.c`:

    b. Edit `bladeenc.c` and replace "main" with "bladeenc"

5. Modify Makefile as follows:

    c. Add `bladeenc.o` to the `OBJS` to be made

    d. Replace `gcc` with `mpicc`

6. Replace main.c with the program described below:

Include the necessary header files, declare the variables, and call the MPI initialization routine:

```c
#include <stdio.h>
#include <mpi.h>

static int nproc;
static int iproc;
extern void bladeenc(int argc, char **argv);

int main(int argc, char **argv)
{
    MPI_Init(&argc, &argv);
    MPI_Comm_size(MPI_COMM_WORLD, &nproc);
    MPI_Comm_rank(MPI_COMM_WORLD, &iproc);
```

Each process determines the number of files to process. If there are M files and N processes, the first (M%N) processes will process (M/N+1) files and the rest will process M/N files. For example, if you have eight files and three processors, two of the processors will convert three files and the other processor will convert the remaining two.

```c
    {
        int first;
        int n;
        int remainder;
        int nt;

        nt = argc - 1;
        remainder = nt % nproc;
        n = nt / nproc;

        if (remainder > 0)
        {
            if (iproc < remainder )
            {
                n++;
                first = iproc * n ;
            }
            else
            {
                first = (n+1) * remainder + (iproc - remainder) * n;
            }
        }
        else
        {
            first = iproc * n;
        }
```

Each process calls the `bladeenc` routine to process its files:

```
        bladeenc(n+1, argv+first);
    }
```

Finally, `MPI_Finalize` is called to end the MPI program:

```
    MPI_Finalize();

    return 0;
}
```

7. We can compile and execute this program on a Beowulf cluster as follows:

```
$ make
$ mpirun -np 3 bladeenc x1.wav x2.wav x3.wav x4.wav
```

This will convert the four wav files to mp3 files using three processors of a Beowulf cluster. This demonstrates why it is important to used shared drives, as not only do you need all of the WAV files located on each node, the mp3 files are only saved to the node that performed the processing and so if the location isn't shared, then every file has to be copied to the final destination.

This program uses a static approach to distribute the files to processors because each processor will convert a set of files determined at the beginning. This approach is suitable if the files to be encoded are approximately the same size. However, if the files vary widely in size, this approach will result in poor load balance between processors. In this case, a client-server programming model should be used where a server sends the name of the file to be processed in response to a request from the client.

Communication Performance of a Beowulf Cluster

In this section, we provide a simple program to measure the round trip time of messages of various lengths between two nodes of a Beowulf cluster. The program uses the `MPI_Send` and `MPI_Recv` library routines for sending and receiving messages. The syntax of these two function calls is as follows:

```
int MPI_Send(void *buf,  int count, MPI_Datatype datatype,
    int dest, int tag, MPI_Comm comm)

int MPI_Recv(void *buf, int count, MPI_Datatype datatype,
    int source, int tag, MPI_Comm comm, MPI_Status *status)
```

The `MPI_Send` routine sends `count` number of data elements of type `datatype` stored in `buf` to the node with rank `dest` in the communication domain `comm`. Similarly, the `MPI_Recv` routine receives `count` number of data elements of type `datatype` into `buf` from the node with rank `source` in the communication domain `comm`. The two routines also use an integer identifier called the `tag` that helps a receiver to differentiate between messages from the same sender. The various data types are defined in the header file `mpi.h`. These are listed overleaf:

C data type	MPI data type
char	MPI_CHAR
short int	MPI_SHORT
int	MPI_INT
long int	MPI_LONG
unsigned char	MPI_UNSIGNED_CHAR
unsigned short int	MPI_UNSIGNED_SHORT
unsigned int	MPI_UNSIGNED
unsigned long int	MPI_UNSIGNED_LONG

The program, `roundtrip.c`, is as follows:

1. Insert the header files:

```
#include <stdio.h>
#include <stdlib.h>
#include "mpi.h"
#include <sys/time.h>
```

2. Define some macro calls for measuring the time:

```
static struct timeval time_value1;
static struct timeval time_value2;
#define START_TIMER gettimeofday(&time_value1, (struct timezone*)0)
#define STOP_TIMER  gettimeofday(&time_value2, (struct timezone*)0)
#define ELAPSED_TIME((double) ((time_value2.tv_usec - \
        time_value1.tv_usec)*0.001 \
        + ((time_value2.tv_sec-time_value1.tv_sec)*1000.0)))
```

3. Global variable declaration:

```
static char *buffer ;
static int iproc ;
static int nproc ;
```

4. Following is the function to measure the round trip time. It has two arguments: The first is the number of times a message is sent and received. The second is the size of the message in bytes:

```
double roundtrip ( int count, int size )
{
    MPI_Status status;

    int i;
```

5. Start the timer:

```
START_TIMER;
```

6. The processes send and receive messages. A message length is size bytes; a message type is MPI_BYTE; the tag number is 0:

```
if ( iproc == 0 )
{
    for (i = 0 ; i < count ; i++)
    {
        MPI_Send(buffer, size, MPI_BYTE, 1, 0, MPI_COMM_WORLD);
        MPI_Recv(buffer, size, MPI_BYTE, 1, 0, MPI_COMM_WORLD,
            &status);
    }

}
else
{
    for (i = 0 ; i < count ; i++)
    {

        MPI_Recv (buffer, size, MPI_BYTE, 0, 0, MPI_COMM_WORLD,
            &status);

        MPI_Send (buffer, size, MPI_BYTE, 0, 0, MPI_COMM_WORLD);

    }

}
```

7. Stop the timer and return the elapsed time:

```
STOP_TIMER;

return (ELAPSED_TIME / ((double) count));
}
```

8. The main program begins here. The program begins with calls to the MPI routines to initialize and obtain the values of nproc and iproc. The program accepts one command line argument, count - the number of messages to send and receive. This program runs only on two processes:

```
int main(int argc, char *argv[])
{
    int count ;

    MPI_Init(&argc, &argv);
    MPI_Comm_size(MPI_COMM_WORLD, &nproc);
    MPI_Comm_rank(MPI_COMM_WORLD, &iproc);
    if (argc != 2)
        perror("Usage: roundTrip <Number of iterations>");

    count = atoi (argv[1]);

    if (nproc != 2)
        perror("Fatal run time error: number of processors must be two");
```

9. Allocate a buffer and fill it with arbitrary values:

```
/* allocate a buffer of size 1 MByte */
{
    double *p;
    int i ;
    double elapsed_time;
    p = (double *) malloc(1024 * 128 * sizeof(double));

    if (!p)
        perror ("Malloc failed");

    /* fill buffer with some arbitrary values */
    buffer = (char *) p;

    for (i = 0 ; i < 1024 * 1024 ; i++) buffer[i] = 1;
```

10. Measure and print the round trip times:

```
    /* measure times */
    if ( iproc == 0 ) printf("Bytes\t\tElapsed Time (mS)\n");
    for ( i = 2 ; i < 1024 * 1024 ; i *= 2 )
    {
        elapsed_time = roundtrip(count, i);
        if (iproc == 0)
        {
            printf ("%d\t\t%.4f\n", i, elapsed_time);
            fflush ( stdout );
        }
    }
```

11. Free buffers and call `MPI_Finalize` to end the program:

```
    free ( p ) ;
    }
    MPI_Finalize () ;

    return 0;
}
```

Let us compile and execute this program as follows:

```
$ mpicc -O -o roundTrip roundTrip.c
$ mpirun -np 2 roundTrip
```

The output of this command on a cluster with 100 MBits/s Ethernet was as follows:

```
Bytes              Elapsed Time (ms)
2                  0.5674
4                  0.5546
8                  0.5604
16                 0.5632
32                 0.5556
64                 0.5667
128                0.5993
256                0.6253
512                0.6781
1024               0.8384
2048               1.1323
4096               1.7464
8192               2.3025
16384              3.8878
32768              7.0513
65536              13.2913
131072             28.5340
262144             56.4394
524288             110.4963
```

The latency and bandwidth are two important parameters that characterize a network. The latency measures the overhead associated with sending or receiving a message and is often measured as half the round trip time for a small message. Therefore, we observe from the results that the latency of a 100 MBits/s network is about 0.28 ms. The bandwidth measures the rate of data transmission. Using the round trip time for the largest message, the actual bandwidth of the network using MPI for large messages is 75 Mbits/s, which is about 75% of the peak.

The send and receive library calls used in the example are called **blocking** routines. In a blocking send, the function call does not return until the send buffer is available for use again. However, this does not mean that the data has been received or that it has actually even been sent. In a blocking receive, the function does not return until the requested data is available in the receive buffer. MPI has another **non-blocking** version of the send/receive functions, which is explained, in the next section.

A Review of Advanced Features of MPI

The MPI initialization routines and the blocking send and receive routines are sufficient to implement most MPI programs. However, MPI also comes with numerous other features to help programmers implement efficient parallel programs. These include non-blocking send/receive routines for point-to-point communication, user defined data types, and group communication primitives.

Point-to-point Communication Primitives

In addition to the `MPI_Send` and `MPI_Recv` communication primitives described in a previous section, MPI offers several other routines to implement message passing between pairs of nodes. One useful routine is the `MPI_Sendrecv` routine that is useful for implementing an exchange operation. In this case, the two processes involved in the communication send and receive data from each other.

```
int MPI_Sendrecv(void *sendbuf, int sendcount, MPI_Datatype sendtype,
    int dest, int sendtag,void *recvbuf, int recvcount,
    MPI_Datatype recvtype, int source,
    MPI_Datatype recvtag, MPI_Comm comm, MPI_Status *status)
```

Following is an example using two processes:

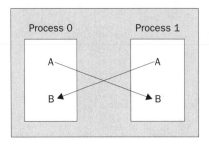

The piece of code that implements the exchange operation follows:

```
{
    int A;
    int B;
    int src;
    int dest;
    MPI_Status status;

    int iproc;   /* rank of processes (0 or 1 for two process case) */

    . . . . . . . . . .
    . . . . . . . . . .

    src = ( iproc == 0  ? 1 :  0  );
    dest = src;

    MPI_Sendrecv (&A, 1, MPI_INT, dest, 0, &B, 1, MPI_INT, src,
        0, MPI_COMM_WORLD, &status);
    . . .
}
```

Another variant of the point-to-point communication primitives that MPI offers is the non-blocking send and receive calls that allow overlapped computations with communications. Using non-blocking versions of send and receive calls will result in better performance of parallel programs on networking hardware equipped with direct memory access (DMA) channels. This includes any PC or workstation produced in the past 10 years; the programmer can assume DMA hardware support unless using a very old legacy system.

In a non-blocking send, the sender posts a send request and returns immediately to perform other work. Before reusing the message buffer, the process must either use a **wait** or **test** operation to determine its availability. MPI provides special library calls to implement these operations. A **wait** is a blocking operation and a **test** is a non-blocking operation that returns immediately with a 0 (not available) or 1 (available). Therefore, a test operation permits the process to perform more work if the buffer is not available.

Similarly, in a non-blocking receive, the receiver posts a receive request and returns immediately to perform other work. When the receiver needs the data, it has to use a wait or test operation to check for the completion of the receive operation.

The non-blocking send and receive routines have the form:

```
int MPI_Isend(void *buf, int send_count, MPI_Datatype data_type,
    int destination, int tag, MPI_Comm communicator,
    MPI_Request *request)

int MPI_Irecv(void *buf, int send_count, MPI_Datatype data_type,
    int destination, int tag, MPI_Comm communicator,
    MPI_Request *request)
```

The last argument to these routines is used by MPI_Wait and MPI_Test to check for the completion of the send or receive operation.

```
MPI_Wait(MPI_Request *request, MPI_Status *status)
MPI_Test(MPI_Request *request, int *isDone, MPI_Status *status)
```

In MPI_Test, the isDone flag is set to 1 if the request has completed and to 0 otherwise. These routines also have another variant that allows a programmer to check for the completion of multiple communication requests in a single library call.

User Defined Data Types

All MPI communication routines accept a data type as an argument. In addition to the library-defined data types listed in the above table, MPI gives the option of user-defined data types. These add a lot of power and flexibility when creating MPI based parallel programs. In this section, we will review some of the important library routines for defining data types.

MPI_Type_contiguous is the simplest of the data type constructors. It allows the creation of a contiguous data type.

```
int MPI_Type_contiguous(int count, MPI_Datatype old_type,
    MPI_Datatype *new_type)
```

The following diagram shows a 4x4 matrix. Each row of this matrix is a contiguous array of size 4.

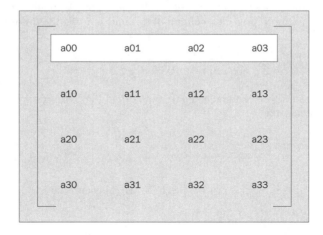

Assuming the data type is integer, we can create a new data type, row, to represent a row of this matrix using the following piece of code:

```
MPI_Datatype row;
MPI_Type_contiguous(4, MPI_INT, &row);
```

The MPI_Type_vector and MPI_Type_hvector library routines are used to create a strided vector data type. In the first form of this function, the stride is in number of elements and in the second the stride is in bytes.

```
MPI_Type_vector(int count, int block_length, int stride,
    MPI_Datatype old_type, MPI_Datatype *new_type)

MPI_Type_hvector(int count, int block_length, int stride,
    MPI_Datatype old_type, MPI_Datatype *new_type)
```

For example, the following figure shows the same 4x4 matrix as in the previous example but with a column highlighted.

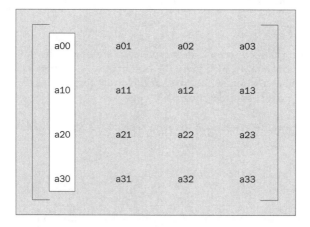

Each column of this matrix is a strided vector of size (count) 4, block length 1 and stride 4. We can create a data type, column to represent a column of this matrix using the following piece of code:

```
MPI_Datatype column;
MPI_Type_vector(4, 1, 4, MPI_INT, &column);
```

Using the data type column, we can create a data type called the transposed_matrix that is a transposed form of the matrix:

```
MPI_Datatype transposed_matrix;
MPI_Type_hvector(4, 1, sizeof(int), column, &transposed_matrix);
```

In this case, the MPI_Type_hvector routine has to be used because the stride is measured in bytes.

A derived data type must be committed using `MPI_Type_commit` before it can be used in a communication operation:

```
int MPI_Type_commit(MPI_Datatype *datatype)
```

A derived data type can be de-allocated using `MPI_Type_free`:

```
int MPI_Type_free(MPI_Datatype *datatype)
```

We provide an example of using these library routines later in the chapter in a sample program to transpose a square matrix.

Collective Operations

Group communication functions are very useful in implementing parallel programs on Beowulf clusters. The most important group communication functions are reduce, broadcast, scatter, gather, all-to-all and barrier. These group communication functions can operate on the MPI predefined data types listed on page 860 or on user-defined data types. They also can support a variety of predefined operations listed in the following table as well as user-defined operations.

Operation	MPI Operation Type
Maximum	MPI_MAX
Minimum	MPI_MIN
Sum	MPI_SUM
Product	MPI_PROD
Logical OR	MPI_LOR
Bit-wise OR	MPI_BOR
Logical XOR	MPI_LXOR
Bit-wise XOR	MPI_BXOR
Logical AND	MPI_LAND
Bit-wise AND	MPI_BAND

Broadcast

In a broadcast operation, a root process sends data to all processes of a communicator group.

```
int MPI_Bcast (void *buffer, int count, MPI_Datatype data_type,
    int root, MPI_Comm comm)
```

The broadcast operation is illustrated in the following diagram:

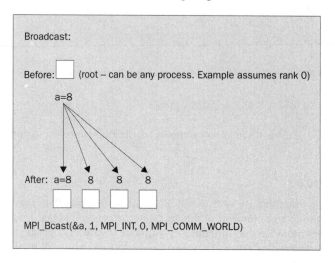

Scatter

In a scatter operation, a root process distributes a data array to other processes. If N is the total number of processes and M elements are sent to each process, the size of the array at the root will be MxN.

```
int MPI_Scatter (void * send_buf, int send_cnt, MPI_Datatype send_type,
    void *recv_buf, int recv_cnt, MPI_Datatype recv_type,
    int root, MPI_Comm comm )
```

The scatter operation is illustrated in the following diagram. In addition to the one shown here, there are several other variants of the scatter operation.

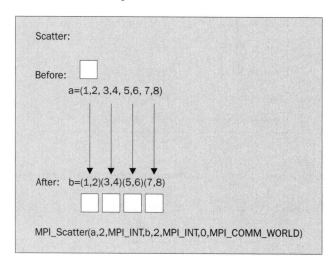

Gather

In a gather operation, a root process accumulates data from other processes. If there are M processes and each process has an array of size N, the accumulated array at the root has a size MxN.

```
int MPI_Gather (void *send_buf, int send_cnt, MPI_Datatype send_type,
    void *recv_buf, int recv_cnt, MPI_Datatype  recv_type,
    int root, MPI_Comm comm )
```

The gather operation is illustrated in the following figure. MPI also supports several variants of the gather operation.

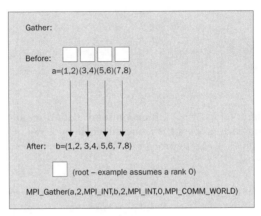

Reduce

A reduce function performs a global reduction operation such as sum, max, or min on data distributed across all the processes of a communicator group. The two important reduce operations are MPI_Reduce and MPI_Allreduce. In the first case, the final result is returned only to a root process. In the second case, the final result is returned to all members of the communicator group.

```
int MPI_Reduce (void *send_buf, void *recv_buf, int count,
    MPI_Datatype data_type, MPI_Op op, int root,
    MPI_Comm comm )

int MPI_Allreduce(void *send_buf, void *recv_buf, int count,
    MPI_Datatype data_type, MPI_Op op, MPI_Comm comm )
```

The two reduce routines are illustrated in the following two diagrams:

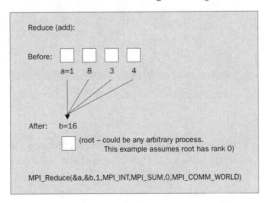

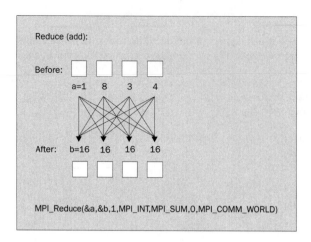

MPI_Reduce(&a,&b,1,MPI_INT,MPI_SUM,0,MPI_COMM_WORLD)

All-to-all

As implied by its name, the `MPI_Alltoall` function sends data from all to all processors.
If there are `N` processes and each process has a one dimensional array of size `M*N`, process `i` sends `M` elements starting at location `M*(j-1)` to process `j`. Process `j` stores the data received from process `i` starting at location `M*(i-1)`.

```
int MPI_Alltoall( void *send_buf, int send_count, MPI_Datatype send_type,
    void *recv_buf, int recv_cnt, MPI_Datatype recv_type,
    MPI_Comm comm )
```

The `MPI_Alltoall` function is illustrated in next diagram. This routine also has several other variants.

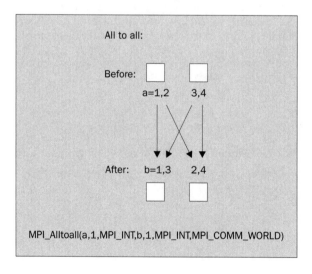

MPI_Alltoall(a,1,MPI_INT,b,1,MPI_INT,MPI_COMM_WORLD)

Barrier

A barrier is used to synchronize the processes belonging to a communicator group.
No process can move past a barrier until all the members of the communicator group have reached it.

```
int MPI_Barrier(MPI_Comm comm)
```

Some MPI Programming Examples:

In this section, we consider programs to demonstrate the use of several MPI library routines. The examples include group communication, non-blocking send and receives, and creating user defined data types.

A Program to Compute Pi

The first example is a program that computes the value of pi using a numerical scheme. This program makes use of the `MPI_Reduce` group communication function.

The numerical scheme used for computing is illustrated in the following figure:

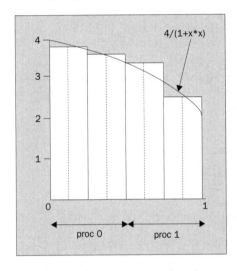

According to this figure, the value of pi can be approximated as the sum of the area of N rectangles, where N=4 in the above diagram. The figure also shows how the workload is distributed across the processors (for the two processor case). In the parallel implementation, each process computes the sum of the area of the rectangles in its domain followed by a call to the `MPI_Reduce` function to compute the global sum that approximates the value of pi. This value finishes on the root process that prints the value.

The parallel program to compute is as follows:

1. The include files are listed first:

```
#include <math.h>
#include <stdlib.h>
#include "mpi.h"
```

2. Some macro definitions are listed next. The value of pi is computed as the area under the function `f(x)` defined here:

```
#define f(x) (4.0/(1.0+(x)*(x)))
#define PI 3.141592653589793238462643
```

3. The main routine begins here. We also declare variables and call some MPI routines:

```
int main (int argc, char *argv[])
{
    int nproc;
    int iproc;
    int nameLength;
    int intervals;
    double interval_length;
    double pi;
    double local_area = 0.0;

    MPI_Init(&argc, &argv);
    MPI_Comm_size(MPI_COMM_WORLD, &nproc);
    MPI_Comm_rank(MPI_COMM_WORLD, &iproc);
```

4. The number of intervals used for computing pi is entered as a command line argument. As the x value varies from 0 to 1, the length of the interval is simply the reciprocal of the number of intervals:

```
if (argc != 2)
    perror("Usage: pi <number of intervals>");

intervals = atoi(argv[1]);

if (intervals % nproc)
    perror("Fatal runtime error: intervals not divisible by nproc\n");

interval_length = 1.0 / ((double) intervals);
```

5. Each process computes the sum of the area of rectangles in its domain:

```
    {
        int i;
        int intervals_local;
        double current_x;

        intervals_local = intervals / nproc;
        current_x = (((double) (iproc * intervals_local))
            + 0.5 ) * interval_length;
        for (i = 0; i < intervals_local; i++)
        {
            local_area += interval_length * f(current_x);
            current_x += interval_length;
        }
    }
}
```

6. The `MPI_Reduce` function is used to compute the global sum of the area. This value ends up on the root process:

```
MPI_Reduce(&local_area, &pi, 1, MPI_DOUBLE, MPI_SUM, 0,
    MPI_COMM_WORLD);
```

7. The root process prints the value of pi. The processes then call `MPI_Finalize` to end the program:

```
if( iproc == 0 )
{
    printf("computed pi is %.16f, error is %.16f\n",
        pi, fabs(pi - PI));
}

MPI_Finalize () ;

return 0;
}
```

You can compile and execute this program on a Beowulf cluster as follows:

❑   To compile:

`$ mpicc -O -o pi pi.c`

❑   To run the program using 8 processors and 2000 rectangles:

`$ mpirun -np 8 pi 2000`

The output should be computed as 3.1415926744231264, the error as 0.0000000208333333

Computation of the Mandelbrot Set

The second example is a program that computes the Mandelbrot set. This program makes use of the gather function.

The Mandelbrot set M is the set of values of c that leads to a stable solution of the complex iterative equation $z = z^2 + c$ starting from $z = 0$. It can be shown that if the modulus of z ever becomes greater than 2 when iterating, then z will ultimately increase without bounds leading to an unstable solution. This rule is used to calculate an approximate solution to the Mandelbrot set by iterating the equation a specific number of times for each c. Each value of c for which the modulus of z remains less than two will belong to the Mandelbrot set. A colorful image is usually generated by assigning black to the points that belong to the Mandelbrot set and by assigning a color proportional to the number of iterations it takes for modulus of z to increase beyond 2 to the rest of the points.

The Mandelbrot set is computed for the set of points inside a square region of length 4 centered at the origin of the complex plane. The parallel program uses a mapping scheme in which the computational grid is divided into rectangular regions parallel to the y-axis and assigned to processors. The only inter-processor communication in this program is when gathering the image array distributed across the processors to the root node for writing to a file. The MPI_Gather function is used for gathering this data.

Following is an MPI based parallel program, `mand.c`, to compute the Mandelbrot set:

1. The Mandelbrot set program needs two command line arguments. The first is the number of iterations and the second is the variable `nt` where `nt * nt` is the size of the grid. The variable `nt` should be divisible by the number of processors.

873

```
#include <stdio.h>
#include <stdlib.h>
#include "mpi.h"

int main(int argc, char **argv)
{
    int n;
    int nt;
    int ite;
    float *image;
    float *image_g;
    double s;
    int x;
    int y;
    int i;
    int j;
    double zr;
    double zi;
    double  cr;
    double  ci;
    double tr;
    double ti;
    int flag;
    double sq_mod;
    int nproc;
    int iproc;
    int y_first;
    int y_last;

    MPI_Init(&argc,&argv);
    MPI_Comm_size(MPI_COMM_WORLD,&nproc);
    MPI_Comm_rank(MPI_COMM_WORLD,&iproc);

    if (argc != 3)
        perror("usage: mand <number of iterations> <number of grid points>");

    ite = atoi(argv[1]);
    nt = atoi(argv[2]);

    if(nt%nproc)
        perror ("number of grid points should be divisible by number of
            processors");
```

2. Each processor works on an n * nt grid. The processors also allocate memory for the arrays:

```
    n = nt / nproc;
    image = (float *) malloc (nt * n * sizeof(float));
    if (!image)
        perror ("malloc image");

    image_g = (float *) malloc (nt * nt * sizeof(float));
    if (!image_g)
        perror ("malloc image_g");
```

3. The variable s is the length of the interval when the 4 * 4 square region is divided in to an nt x nt grid:

```
    s = 4.0/((double) (nt-1));
```

4. Each processor loops over the set of grid points in its domain:

```
i = 0;
y_first = n * iproc;
y_last = y_first + n;
for ( y = y_first; y < y_last; y++)
{
    ci = -2.0 + ((double) y)*s;
    for( x = 0; x < nt; x++)
    {
        zr = 0.0;
        zi = 0.0;
        cr = -2.0 + ((double) x)*s;
        flag = 0;
```

5. Each grid point is iterated for ite iterations or until $z^2(r^2+i^2) > 2.0$:

```
for( j = 0; j < ite;  j++)
{
    tr = (zr*zr - zi*zi) + cr;
    ti = 2.0*zr*zi + ci;
    zr = tr;
    zi = ti;
    sq_mod = zr*zr + zi*zi;
    if( sq_mod > 2.0)
    {
        flag = 1;
        break;
    }
}
```

6. The image is generated:

```
if (flag)
{
    image[i] = ((float) j);
}
else image[i] = 0.0;
{
    i ++;
}
}
```

7. The processors execute a gather routine. The final image ends up on the root processor:

```
MPI_Gather(image, nt*n, MPI_FLOAT, image_g, nt*n, MPI_FLOAT, 0,
    MPI_COMM_WORLD);
```

8. The root processor writes the image to a file:

```
if (iproc == 0)
{
   FILE *fp;
   int c;
   fp = fopen ("mand.out", "w");
   if (!fp)
      perror("Error opening file mand.out");

      c = fwrite(image_g, sizeof(float), nt * nt, fp);

      if (c != (nt * nt))
         perror ("Error writing to file mand.out");
}
```

9. Clean up and exit:

```
   free(image);
   free(image_g);

   MPI_Finalize();

   return 0;
}
```

Let's compile and execute the Mandelbrot set program on our Beowulf cluster:

```
$ mpicc -O -o mand mand.c
$ mpirun -np 8 mand 100 512
```

This will compute the Mandelbrot set using 100 iterations and a 512x512 grid.

The output will be written to a file mand.out. The image shown below was generated using the saoimage utility for displaying images in an X-Window environment. This package, developed at the Smithsonian Astrophysical Observatory, can be downloaded from: http://tdc-www.harvard.edu/software/saoimage.html.

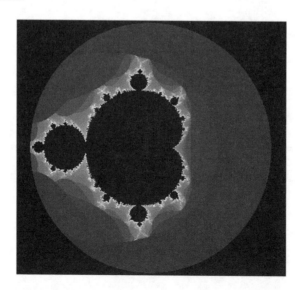

The mapping scheme used in the Mandelbrot set computation is called a block-oriented scheme because a group of adjacent columns is assigned to each processor. When examining the image, we observe that a block-oriented mapping scheme does not result in a good, load balanced program because some nodes process more points that belong to the Mandelbrot set than others. It takes more time to process a point that belongs to the set because in this case the equation has to be iterated for the maximum number of iterations. A better mapping strategy is to assign the columns to the processors in a round robin manner starting from column identifier 0.

Matrix Transpose

The next example we consider is a program to compute the transpose of a square matrix. In this program, we will make use of MPI library routines for creating user-defined data types, performing non-blocking communication, and performing scatter operations.

The matrix transpose is an important operation in many scientific algorithms. The method of partitioning a matrix to processors is usually determined by the communication behavior of the overall program. In our program, we use a 1-D, block-oriented partitioning of the matrix to the processors as shown in the diagram. This type of partitioning method is suitable for algorithms that involve fast Fourier transform computations.

0	1	2	3
4	5	6	7
8	9	10	11
12	13	14	15

1-D partitioning of 4 x 4
matrix on to two processors

The next figure illustrates the algorithm used for transforming a matrix. If the matrix has dimensions $N * N$ and if there are M processors with N exactly divisible by M, the matrix is divided into M^2 sub-matrices of dimensions $(N/M) * (N/M)$. The figure illustrates this for a 4x4 matrix and two processors. Each processor has M sub-matrices. Aij denotes the jth sub-matrix of processor i. When transposing the matrix, processor i exchanges its (transposed) sub-matrix j with (transposed) sub-matrix i of processor j. In our program, each processor posts M MPI_Isend calls followed by M MPI_Irecv requests to transpose the matrix. After posting the send and receive requests, the processors simply wait until the tasks complete. We also notice that use of the derived data types greatly simplifies the program by avoiding the need for explicitly transposing the sub-matrices.

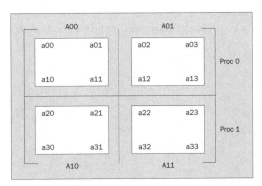

1. The include files and global declarations are listed here:

```
#include <stdio.h>
#include "mpi.h"
static int nproc ;
static int iproc ;
```

2. A function to print an N * N matrix is listed below:

```
void print_matrix (char *mesg, int N, int *a)
{
   int *p;
   register int i;
   register int j;
   printf("%s\n", mesg);
   p = a;
   for (i = 0 ; i < N ; i++)
   {
      for(j = 0 ; j < N ; j++)
      {
         printf("%4d ", *p ++);
      }
      printf("\n");
   }
}
```

3. Following is the matrix transpose routine:

```
void transpose(int n, int *a, int *b)
{
   int i;
   int nl;
   MPI_Datatype svec;
   MPI_Datatype s_matrix;
   MPI_Datatype rvec;
   MPI_Datatype r_matrix;
   MPI_Request *send_request;
   MPI_Request *recv_request;
   MPI_Status *send_status;
   MPI_Status *recv_status;
   nl = n / nproc;
```

4. We first create data types for sending and receiving sub-matrices:

```
MPI_Type_vector(nl, 1, n, MPI_INT, &svec);
MPI_Type_hvector(nl, 1, sizeof(int), svec, &s_matrix);
MPI_Type_commit(&s_matrix);
MPI_Type_contiguous(nl, MPI_INT, &rvec);
MPI_Type_hvector(nl, 1, sizeof(int)*n, rvec, &r_matrix);
```

5. Some arrays are allocated here:

```
send_request = (MPI_Request *) malloc(nproc * sizeof(MPI_Request));
recv_request = (MPI_Request *) malloc(nproc * sizeof(MPI_Request));
send_status = (MPI_Status *) malloc(nproc * sizeof(MPI_Status));
recv_status = (MPI_Status *) malloc(nproc * sizeof(MPI_Status));
```

6. Each processor issues `nproc` non-blocking sends:

```
for ( i = 0 ; i < nproc ; i++ )
{
    MPI_Isend(a + i * nl, 1, s_matrix, i, 0, MPI_COMM_WORLD,
        send_request +i);
}
```

7. Each process issues `nproc` non-blocking receives:

```
for (i = 0 ; i < nproc ; i++)
{
    MPI_Irecv(b + i * nl, 1, r_matrix, i, 0, MPI_COMM_WORLD,
        recv_request + i);
}
```

8. The processors wait for their send requests to complete:

```
for (i = 0 ; i < nproc ; i++)
{
    MPI_Wait (send_request + i, send_status + i);
}
```

9. The processors wait for their receive requests to complete:

```
for (i = 0 ; i < nproc ; i++)
{
    MPI_Wait (recv_request + i, recv_status + i);
}
```

10. Free the memory for the allocated arrays:

```
    free(send_request);
    free(recv_request);
    free(send_status);
    free(recv_status);
}
```

11. The main program begins here:

```
int main(int argc, char *argv[])
{
    int N;
    int NL;
    int *a;
    int *a_local;
    int *b;
    int *b_local;
    int i;
```

12. These are the MPI initialization functions:

```
MPI_Init(&argc, &argv);
MPI_Comm_size(MPI_COMM_WORLD, &nproc);
MPI_Comm_rank(MPI_COMM_WORLD, &iproc);
```

13. The program works on an N * N matrix. The value of N is entered as a command line argument. It should be exactly divisible by nproc:

```
N = atoi(argv[1]);
if (argc != 2)
    perror("Usage: transpose <N, for a N x N matrix>");
if (N % nproc)
    perror("N must be divisible by nproc");
NL = N / nproc;
```

14. The processors allocate the data array. The root processor initializes the input matrix:

```
a = (int *) malloc(N * N * sizeof(int));
if (!a)
    perror("malloc a");
a_local = (int *) malloc(N * NL * sizeof(int));
if (!a_local)
    perror("malloc a_local");
b = (int *) malloc(N * N * sizeof(int));
if (!b)
    perror ("malloc b");
b_local = (int *) malloc(N * NL * sizeof(int));
if (!b_local)
    perror("malloc b_local");
if (iproc == 0)
{
    for (i = 0 ; i < N * N ; i++)
    {
        a[i] = i;
    }
}
```

15. MPI_Scatter is used to send portions of the input matrix to each processor:

```
MPI_Scatter(a, N*NL, MPI_INT, a_local, N*NL, MPI_INT, 0, MPI_COMM_WORLD);
```

16. The processors perform the matrix transpose:

```
transpose(N, a_local, b_local);
```

17. The matrix is gathered by the root processor:

```
MPI_Gather (b_local, N*NL, MPI_INT, b, N*NL,, MPI_INT, 0, MPI_COMM_WORLD);
```

18. The root processor calls the `print_matrix` routine for printing the input and output matrices:

```
if (iproc == 0)
{
    print_matrix(("Input",  N,  a);
    print_matrix("Output", N, b);
}

free(a);
free(a_local);
free(b);
free(b_local);
```

19. The `MPI_Finalize` function is called to end the program:

```
MPI_Finalize();

exit(0) ;
}
```

Programming with PVM

The Parallel Virtual Machine (PVM) software package is another message passing library that can be used to program Beowulf computer systems. The PVM project started at Oakridge National Laboratory in 1989. However, the PVM software package is still widely used in developing message passing parallel programs.

Comparison with MPI

With the introduction of the MPI standard for developing message passing programs and the availability of high quality software packages based on this standard, more and more people are moving towards using MPI for implementing parallel programs. The primary reason for the wide popularity of MPI over PVM is that MPI supports a wide range of functionality that is not available with PVM. This includes non-blocking send/receive communication primitives, user-defined data types, communicators for increasing the power of point-to-point and collective operations, and the ability to define virtual process topologies to assign processes to physical processors.

The MPI standard supports heterogeneity, allowing parallel programs using MPI to run on computers with incompatible data representations. However, the MPI standard does not mandate that an MPI implementation should support communication between heterogeneous computers. If you are building a Beowulf cluster consisting of heterogeneous nodes, the easiest way to get a parallel application running is to use PVM. PVM supports heterogeneity at the user application level. If the computers in a virtual machine have incompatible data representations, a parallel program could specify a special encoding scheme when sending data. This means that PVM will convert the data to a standard format when packing it into the buffers for transmission. When the data is unpacked at the receiver, it will be converted from the standard format to the receiver's internal data format.

Obtaining and Installing PVM

The PVM source code is freely available from http://www.netlib.org/pvm3/index.html. The gzipped tar version could be downloaded from this site. PVM also comes with a user guide that explains the installation process along with a tutorial for networked parallel computing. For the rest of this discussion, we assume that you have downloaded and installed PVM in to a directory /usr/local/pvm3. This directory should be duplicated on all nodes of the cluster. If the cluster consists of heterogeneous computers, PVM must be built on each node architecture of the cluster.

In order to use PVM, we have to do the following:

- ❑ Set the environment variable PVM_ROOT to /usr/local/pvm3.
- ❑ Set the environment variable PVM_DPATH to $PVM_ROOT/lib/pvmd.
- ❑ Add the location of the PVM binaries to the search path for executables. These are located in $PVM_ROOT/bin.
- ❑ Add the location of the PVM manual to the search path for manual entries.

Also, when spawning processes, the PVM daemon looks for user executables in the directory pvm3/bin/LINUX under the user's home. This directory should be added to the search path for executables.

A Review of PVM Library Routines

A PVM program is a program augmented with calls to the PVM library routines to spawn processes and handle message passing. The pvm_mytid function must be the first call in any PVM program. It returns a positive integer called the task identifier or a negative value on error. This routine has the form:

```
int pvm_mytid(void)
```

The pvm_parent library routine returns the PVM task identifier of the parent of the calling process or a negative value on error. This routine has the form:

```
int pvm_parent(void)
```

New PVM processes are started with calls to pvm_spawn. Processes that are not started with pvm_spawn have a parent ID of -1. The library routine has the form:

```
int pvm_spawn(char *progName, char **argv, int spawnOption,
    char *where, int ntasks, int *tids)
```

The first argument is the name of the program to be executed. The second is the set of run-time arguments to the program. The third argument specifies how the processes are to be spawned. This variable can have the following values:

Option	Meaning
`PvmTaskDefault`	The machine is chosen by PVM
`PvmTaskHost`	User specified machine using the `where` option
`PvmTaskArch`	User specified architecture using the `where` option
`PvmTaskDebug`	Start the process under the debugger
`PvmTaskTrace`	Generate trace data for the process

The `pvm_spawn` routine returns the number of tasks spawned. A negative value or a value less than the number requested denotes an error.

PVM processes can join a group using the `pvm_joingroup` library routine. This routine has the form:

```
int pvm_joingroup(char *group)
```

This routine returns an integer instance number for the calling process or a negative value on an error. The primary use of joining a group is for synchronization with other group members. In PVM, processes synchronize using calls to the `pvm_barrier` routine. It has the form:

```
int pvm_barrier(char *group, int n)
```

A process belonging to the `group` arriving at a barrier cannot leave until a total of n processes have arrived at the barrier. This library routine returns a status code that denotes a success or an error.

In PVM, processes communicate by sending and receiving messages. Sending a message is a three step sequence. First, the `pvm_initsend` routine is called to clear the message buffers and prepare a message for sending. This routine has the form:

```
int pvm_initsend(int encoding)
```

The library routine has one argument – the encoding scheme for sending the message. Its values are:

Encoding Scheme	Meaning
PvmDataDefault	XDR encoding for heterogeneous systems
PvmDataRaw	No encoding
PvmDataInPlace	Data left in place

The second step is to pack the message to be sent. PVM has packing routines for each of the supported data types. These are:

```
int pvm_pkbyte (char *data, int nitems, int stride)
int pvm_pkcplx(float *data, int nitems, int stride)
int pvm_pkdcplx (double *data, int nitems, int stride)
int pvm_pkdouble (double *data, int nitems, int stride)
int pvm_pkfloat(float *data, int nitems, int stride)
int pvm_pkint(int *data, int nitems, int stride)
int pvm_pklong(long *data, int nitems, int stride)
int pvm_pkshort(short *data, int nitems, int stride)
int pvm_pkstr(char *data)
```

The packed message is sent to the destination using the pvm_send routine. This routine has the form:

```
int pvm_send(int task_id, int message_tag)
```

The message_tag is a positive integer and is used by the receiver to differentiate between messages from the same source.

Receiving a message in PVM is a two-step process. First, the message has to be received using the pvm_recv library routine. This has the form:

```
int pvm_recv(int task_id, int message_tag).
```

Then, the received message has to be unpacked using the corresponding routine for the particular data type. These routines are similar to the data packing routines and are:

```
int pvm_upkbyte (char *data, int nitems, int stride)
int pvm_upkcplx(float *data, int nitems, int stride)
int pvm_upkdcplx (double *data, int nitems, int stride)
int pvm_upkdouble (double *data, int nitems, int stride)
int pvm_upkfloat(float *data, int nitems, int stride)
int pvm_upkint(int *data, int nitems, int stride)
int pvm_upklong(long *data, int nitems, int stride)
int pvm_upkshort(short *data, int nitems, int stride)
int pvm_upkstr(char *data)
```

A Sample PVM Program

1. Following are the list of include files, definitions, and variable declarations. The program will run on four processes. You have to change the definition for nproc to run on a different number of processors.

```
#include "pvm3.h"
#include <stdio.h>
#include <unistd.h>
#include <stdlib.h>
#define nproc 4

int main(int argc, char **argv)
{
    int tid;
    int parent_id;
    int *tids;
    int tid_recv;
    int c;
    int i;
    char hname[128];
```

2. Each process obtains its task ID and parent ID:

```
tid = pvm_mytid();
parent_id = pvm_parent();
```

3. The root process spawns `nproc` client processes:

```
if ( parent_id < 0 )
{
   tids = (int *) malloc(nproc * sizeof(int));

   c = pvm_spawn(argv[0], (char **) NULL, PvmTaskDefault,
      NULL, nproc, tids);
   if (c != nproc)
   {
      fprintf(stderr, "Failed to spawn %d processes\n", nproc);
      pvm_exit();
      exit(1);
   }
#ifdef DEBUG
   for(i=0; i<nproc; i++)
   {
      printf("task id %00x\n", tids[i]);
   }
#endif
   free (tids);
}
```

4. All the processes join a group:

```
pvm_joingroup ("nodes");
```

5. The root process receives a message from each client and prints to the screen:

```
if (parent_id < 0)
{
   for ( i = 0 ; i < nproc; i++ )
   {
      pvm_recv(-1, -1);
      pvm_upkint(&tid_recv, 1, 1);
      pvm_upkstr(hname);
      printf("Hello world from tid %00x running on %s\n", tid_recv, hname);
   }
}
else
{
```

6. Each client process sends a message to the parent. The message sent includes the task identifier and the host name on which the process is running.

```
   gethostname(hname, 128);

   pvm_initsend(PvmDataDefault);
   pvm_pkint(&tid, 1, 1);
   pvm_pkstr(hname);
   pvm_send(parent_id, 0);
}
```

7. All the processes synchronize using pvm_barrier:

```
pvm_barrier("nodes",  nproc + 1);
pvm_exit();
return 0;
}
```

Compiling and Executing a PVM Program on a Beowulf Cluster

Let's compile and execute the hello_pvm.c program on our Beowulf cluster.

The program is compiled as follows:

```
$ cc -O -o hello_pvm -L/usr/local/pvm3/lib/LINUX \
   -I/usr/local/pvm3/include hello_pvm.c -lpvm3 -lgpvm3
$ cp hello_pvm ~/pvm3/bin/LINUX/
```

Before executing the program on a Beowulf cluster, we have to start the PVM daemon. There are several methods for starting the PVM daemon. For a system with few nodes the daemon can be started by typing pvm at the prompt:

```
$ pvm
```

The output will be the prompt of the pvm console:

```
pvm>
```

The pvm console accepts commands from the standard input. To add machine n0:

```
pvm> add n0
```

Repeat this process to add the remaining machines to the pvm virtual machine.

```
pvm> help
```

...will give the set of commands available from the pvm console. You can now enter the quit command as the pvm daemon will continue to run.

Assuming the pvm daemon is running, the program can be executed as follows:

```
$ hello_pvm
```

The output of this program running on 4 processes is as follows:

```
Message from tid 40011 running on n0
Message from tid 80007 running on n1
Message from tid c0008 running on n2
Message from tid 40012 running on n0
```

Resources

BEOWULF: A Parallel Workstation for Scientific Computation, by Donald J. Becker, Thomas Sterling, Daniel Savarese, John E. Dorband, Udaya A. Ranawake and Charles V. Packer, Proceedings of ICPP'95.

MPI: A Message-Passing Interface Standard, Message Passing Interface Forum (www-unix.mcs.anl.gov/mpi/mpich/index.html).

Installation Guide to mpich, a Portable Implementation of MPI Version 1.2.0, William Gropp and Ewing Lus (http://www-unix.mcs.anl.gov/mpi/mpich/index.html).

The Fractal Geometry of Nature, by B. Mandelbrot, Freeman & Co. (ISBN 0-716711-86-9).

PVM 3.0 User Guide and Reference Manual, Al Geist, Adam Beguelin , Jack Dongarra, Weicheng Jiang, Robert Manchek, and Vaidy Sunderam, February, 1993.

Summary

In this chapter, we have discussed the setting up of a Beowulf cluster. We also gave some sample programs to demonstrate how to program a Beowulf cluster using the C programming language and the MPI and PVM communication libraries.

Some Useful Beowulf Links

http://www.beowulf.org	This is the official Beowulf site and gives a description of the project history and shows some links to currently available Beowulf systems.
http://newton.gsfc.nasa.gov/thehive	This is a Beowulf system available at NASA GSFC, USA and provides benchmark results and freely downloadable software for monitoring these clusters.
http://www.beowulf-underground.org	This site has some useful information on building and using Beowulf systems.

Online discussion at http://www.p2p.wrox.com

25

Documentation

Documentation is one of the most needed, yet most often overlooked aspects of development. Requirements for writing documentation differ from organization to organization. In some organizations, writing documentation is a required part of the whole process of producing software, in others, documentation is only often added as an afterthought (especially in situations that deal with deadlines and real-world pressures). In practice, there tends to be only time to get the job done, and almost no time for a proper description of how the goal was accomplished, or what the thoughts of the programmer were when writing the code. If you are a programmer who has ever had to look at code written by others, you will probably be nodding in agreement.

Unless required by law or contract, documentation is usually only done in a sparse manner, if at all. Often comments within code will be inconsistent with the code itself; this is because code is often corrected or changed, but the comments are left the same.

If we shift our focus from the programming professional to those who will use the programs we write, we encounter a similar phenomenon. If the documentation we have written for our users remains unchanged while we add or change certain features to suit their needs, inconsistencies creep in leading to minor irritations or major disasters.

This is not easily remedied. Writing documentation is like writing code – it takes discipline to get it right. Learning how to write good documentation takes practice and the ability to take a lot of criticism. On the positive side, it is one of the most visible parts of the project and, if done well, can help garner repeat business or add to your reputation as a good programmer.

This chapter gives an overview of where to find useful information about programs and tools that we can use when writing our own programs. It will also provide us with the information necessary to start writing documentation for our own software. The main focus will be external documentation such as manual pages and other printable documents, with less emphasis on commenting code.

Defining the Audience

The first step in writing documentation is to properly define your audience. People that only use your software are unlikely to be interested in the same things as the people who have to keep your software running. Roughly, it is possible to divide the people who will look for documentation into four categories and, while these definitions are strict about the roles assumed by the user, over time the same user may come to need all aspects of our documentation.

❑ **End Users:** End Users use documentation for primary learning purposes (What does this button do? How do I make a reservation?). We can usually assume they will never have to use the command line aspects of a package.

❑ **Power Users or System Administrators:** A Power User or System Administrator is someone who is interested in making things work and then keeping them running. When someone like that is interested in knowing more, it usually means that something is not working properly, or that a certain task needs to be tweaked.

❑ **Integrators:** An Integrator is someone who wants to build upon existing functionality by using a software package or program as part of a bigger project.

❑ **Developers:** This is someone who wants to enhance existing functionality by adding features to our software.

End User Documentation: GUIs

An End User will, in most cases, use a Graphical User Interface in some form or other. Throughout this book we have used the example of a DVD store, so we will use this application as our example. Straight away we can distinguish between two different End Users – those operating the store and those who are on the Web and connecting to the store's web site. We'll start with the local users.

Documenting GUIs Running on the Local Machine

GUIs are best documented by providing online help, with lots of pictures. Context-sensitive help (the help users get depending on what they are currently doing or looking at), is also something that is good to have. Context-sensitivity takes many forms, ranging from tool tips, and little popup windows that display a short explanation, through to dedicated help windows that appear when the user presses a certain combination of keys (usually CTRL-F1). Care must be taken that every element of the GUI and its relationships are documented.

Unfortunately, it is rather hard to provide consistent help – in most toolkits it is not available, and most people roll their own implementations anyway. As a result, we will be looking at a form of lowest common denominator of GUI help later on.

Context Sensitive Help

The best way of providing help is by making it available as close as possible to the problem it tries to address. Under Microsoft Windows this usually means pointing at something with your cursor and then pressing the CTRL and F1-key. At that point help will come up, or, when using one of the Office products, the Office Assistant will offer 'helpful' suggestions.

Right-clicking with the mouse will bring up a context menu, showing you the actions that can be taken with the object you are pointing to – sometimes a help option is offered in that menu as well. The obvious advantage of being context-sensitive is that it provides immediate feedback. Unfortunately, it is very hard to implement if the GUI toolkit in use does not support it directly. In that case, you usually have to do it yourself, which is by no means an easy task because it involves catching keystrokes and mouse events.

Another option is a global help function, which is obviously not context-sensitive. Usually this kind of online help is presented as a hierarchical list of topics that cover more or less (but usually less) what the application is capable of. An elegant compromise is to have a single help function that can jump directly to a specific topic with a little intuitive prompting.

Poor Man's Context Sensitivity

A neat trick to get structured help is to employ the services of a web browser and write HTML pages. With some knowledge of HTML, we will present a very basic recipe for providing support, to which we can add more flavor using JavaScript event handlers, framesets, style sheets, and whatever else we have. For now, we will stick to the minimum in order to illustrate the concept better.

Under the Help button of the GUI front end to the DVD store application that we developed in Chapter 9, we had only the option of reading more about the author of the application. What we are going to do now is add our help functionality. Adding this functionality is little more than adding a button (which we learned in the same chapter), and adding the handler for the code, which is an invocation of an HTML browser and our help URL.

- ❑ **Screenshots**: For every menu, dialog (either popup or tabbed), and general window within your GUI-program, create a screenshot. The largest of all screenshot makers is xwd, but you can find more sophisticated ones in the ImageMagick package or the standalone program xgrabsc. In order for it to be usable, the xwd format has to be changed into a picture format that a browser can display – PNG is one such example. You can use the xwdtopnm and pnmtopng programs from the PBMPLUS toolkit or ImageMagick to do this. The GIMP, a full-fledged image editor for Linux, also has screen capture capabilities, as well as the possibility to save your file in PNG or a host of other formats.

- ❑ **HTML pages**: Create an empty HTML page for every screenshot you just made.

- ❑ **Add the Image to the HTML page**: Add an image to this HTML page. If we do not use a WYSIWYG HTML editor, then we can do this with the ISMAP and USEMAP attributes, like this:

```
<IMG SRC="dvdstore.png"
    ALT="This picture shows the DVDStore"
    ISMAP="ismap"
    USEMAP="#dvdstore-map">
```

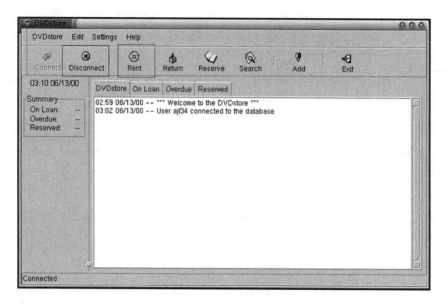

❑ **Add an image-map to an HTML page:** Next, we have to create and add an image-map to our HTML page. This is a list of areas in our picture that correspond to user elements in our screenshot. For our example page, this will look like this:

```
<MAP NAME="dvdstore-map">
  <AREA SHAPE="rect"
       COORDS="102,39,186,83"
       ALT="Disconnect Button"
       HREF="#ExplanationOfDisconnectButton">
  <AREA SHAPE="rect"
       COORDS="200,39,299,83"
       ALT="Rent Button"
       HREF="#ExplanationOfRentButton">
  <!-- ETC. -->
</MAP>
```

The described regions are shown in the picture above as dotted rectangles. This can be an arduous process so don't hesitate to use a design tool like Netscape Composer.

❑ **Add explanations to your HTML page**: Now the only thing left to do is explain what every button does. So we would write something like the code that follows. This allows a user to click on different parts of the picture as if they were buttons from our application, this then instructs the browser to jump to the appropriate spot in our documentation. Remember, we should start our explanations with the anchor points mentioned by the HREF above, and then we are done.

```
<CENTER>
<A NAME="ExplanationOfDisconnectButton">
<H1>The Disconnect Button</H1>
</A>
</CENTER>
The explanation of what the Disconnect Button does goes here.
<P>
```

```
<CENTER>
<A NAME="ExplanationOfRentButton">
<H1>The Rent Button</H1>
</A>
</CENTER>
The explanation of what the Rent Button does goes here.
<P>
```

Of course, we can add animations to our HTML page. We could even use a frameset approach where our dialog is on top of the page and have a frame for each element that pops up whenever we click on the element in the picture. In other words, we can be as creative as we wish with an approach like this.

The advantage of this approach is that we can use a printed version of the online documentation we have produced as a user's manual. Another benefit is that if you decide to revamp your GUI, or rewrite it for another toolkit or environment, this approach retains its validity, because little apart from the screenshots in your documentation need changing.

Documenting Web GUIs

When designing for web interfaces to our system, we have a number of advantages. Firstly we are only implementing a limited subset of functions, so the user can usually experiment safely without damaging our data. We also have the space to provide verbose instructions that would be cumbersome for a GUI user who has to use our application intensively.

It is important to clearly indicate what fields are used for what purpose and to ensure that all fields have a clear meaning; for example, 'Title' is used (and interpreted) in addresses to mean one of 'Mr.', 'Mrs.' and 'Ms.' as well as 'Job Title'.

It is a good idea to include the ALT attribute for every tag that supports it – so that when the user hovers the cursor over the entryfield or button, the browser can show a tooltip with the corresponding text. Another option for entryfields with a corresponding label is to turn the label into a link to where more help can be found. So:

```
<TABLE>
<TR>
<TD>Your name:
<TD><INPUT TYPE="text" NAME="name" LENGTH=250>
</TABLE>
```

would become:

```
<TABLE>
<TR>
<TD><A HREF="#ExplanationOfNameField">Your name:</A>
<TD><INPUT TYPE="text" NAME="name" ALT="Short description of namefield goes here"
LENGTH=250>
</TABLE>
```

For a specific action, it is vital that you describe the steps that are to be taken. In our example, the procedure for booking a DVD might consist of adding items to a shopping cart, and then submitting the bookings. These steps should be clearly and graphically marked.

Remember that not all browsers are created equal; some people may be viewing your web page on an organizer or other type of PDA, on their mobile phone, or on other devices with similar limitations on available screen estate. Keep this in mind when writing your online documentation.

Power User/System Administrator Documentation

As a Power User or System Administrator we will, in most cases, be more knowledgeable about how our system, or subsystem, works. In most cases we will work with maintaining programs that may or may not be GUI based. GUIs were covered in the previous section, and GUI documentation generation for this kind of audience differs only in the level and knowledge of the target audience. So, we will now move to the world where daemons rule and tools are full of purpose.

Command-line Options: Providing - -help

When working with command-line tools, even the ones we use frequently, we sometimes want to use a slightly obscure option or just get a list of available options. For the GNU family of tools, life is easy – every GNU program has a --help option, which produces a list of options (or a synopsis, for those programs that have a lot of options, such as gcc). For example, this the output for the cat command.

```
$ cat --help
Usage: cat [OPTION] [FILE]...
Concatenate FILE(s), or standard input, to standard output.

  -A, --show-all           equivalent to -vET
  -b, --number-nonblank    number nonblank output lines
  -e                       equivalent to -vE
  -E, --show-ends          display $ at end of each line
  -n, --number             number all output lines
  -s, --squeeze-blank      never more than one single blank line
  -t                       equivalent to -vT
  -T, --show-tabs          display TAB characters as ^I
  -u                       (ignored)
  -v, --show-nonprinting   use ^ and M- notation, except for LFD and TAB
      --help               display this help and exit
      --version            output version information and exit

With no FILE, or when FILE is -, read standard input.

Report bugs to <bug-textutils@gnu.org>.
```

Following this example, we can see that command-line help should include at the very least the following items:

❑ **Name:** The name of the program. People may want to redirect the output of your usage information to a file, and having the name of the program serves as a reference point.

❑ **Usage:** The usage information should include the order of the options and the arguments that should be provided. We must make sure that we indicate which arguments are optional and which arguments are mandatory and the order of the arguments if important.

❑ **Detailed Usage:** Depending on the number of arguments our program accepts, we may want to give a line-by-line description of all the options and arguments. Care must be taken not to include the entire manual in our usage information. One or two pages should usually be the maximum; people will usually use your usage-information as a quick-reference. Remember that more than a page means that people will have to use a pager such as more, less or most, which might be annoying.

Manual Pages

People who are going to use our programs now have a quick-reference. For a more detailed look at software, they will usually turn to a somewhat more comprehensive source of information – the manual pages, or manpage.

Manpages are one of the earliest forms of online documentation and can be found on the earliest forms of UNIX.

A manpage can be displayed by the man command. To know how the man command works, we use man man. We will see how to roll our own manpage shortly, but let's take a look at some background information first.

The man command has a sibling apropos that can help you locate information by keyword, rather than by command name. apropos is usually an alias for man -k, and we can give as arguments any keyword we like and get a list of appropriate programs or manual pages in return. Here is an example:

```
$ apropos noweb
nodefs (1)           - find definitions in noweb file
noindex (1)          - build external index for noweb document
noroots (1)          - print roots of a noweb file
notangle (1)         - noweb, a literate-programming tool
nountangle (1)       - noweb, a literate-programming tool
noweave (1)          - noweb, a literate-programming tool
noweb (1)            - a simple literate-programming tool
nowebfilters (7)     - filters and parsers for use with noweb
nowebstyle (7)       - LaTeX package for noweb
nuweb2noweb (1)      - convert nuweb files to noweb form
```

Manpage Sections

Manpages exist for quite a variety of material, from command-line utilities, to programming routines from the Standard C Library, to file formats used by various programs. However, if we threw all of these together, things would get unwieldy rather fast. Manpages would be rather large and people would not know where to start looking for information. That is why the concept of sections was introduced. Every section holds the manpages for a specific kind of information.

There are 9 principal categories:

1. Executable programs or shell commands that are accessible by all users

2. System calls (functions provided by the kernel)

3. Library calls (functions within system libraries)

4. Special files (usually found in /dev)

5. File formats and conventions, for example /etc/passwd

6. Games

7. Macro packages and conventions

8. System administration commands (usually only for root)

9. Kernel routines (Non standard)

People refer to a `manpage` in a specific section by putting the number of the section in brackets behind the command in question. The man command for example would be referred to as man(1), because it is an executable program (or shell command).

It is possible that a program and a library call have the same name, for example `printf` is both an executable program and a library call. To read the `manpage` for the former, we can just type:

```
$ man printf
```

Although, we could also type:

```
$ man 1 printf
```

to explicitly request the `manpage` for the program in section 1. For the latter (the library call), we can type:

```
$ man 3 printf.
```

On some systems there can be additional categories, a popular one being `local`.

Keeping Things Manageable

Since the birth of UNIX, a lot of libraries have been written, and some of them are really quite large. On my system, the documentation for the X library contains 935 `manpages` documenting structures and functions that can be used when writing programs for the X11 Window System. `Manpages` in subsections are referred to by their major section number, and a series of letters. For example, these 935 `manpages` can be found in subsection 3x, and the Tk-library has its functions documented in section 3tk.

Sections commonly found in manpages

A `manpage` has a certain structure; it has mandatory and optional sections that are usually found in a certain order. The more common sections are:

- ❑ **NAME**: The NAME section is the only mandatory section. It contains the name of the program and a one-line description for quick reference.

- ❑ **SYNOPSIS**: This section briefly describes the program or function's interface. This is the section intended for the people who just need a quick refresh of how the program should be used. No explanation is given, just common usage or function prototype.

- ❑ **DESCRIPTION**: The DESCRIPTION section describes what the command or function actually does. It tells us how the command uses its arguments, what it consumes and what it produces. Note that this section usually does not go into depth with respect to internals or options – that level of detail is more appropriate for the USAGE or OPTIONS section.

- ❑ **RETURN VALUES**: The RETURN VALUES section describes the possible values that a function may return to its caller, and the circumstances that may lead to certain values being returned.

- ❑ **EXIT STATUS**: A program may also have a return value, but usually in the case of a program we talk about its exit status. As a result, the `manpage` may have this section instead of RETURN VALUES.

❑ **OPTIONS**: The OPTIONS section describes the options that are accepted by a program, or the arguments accepted by a function call, and how they change its behavior.

❑ **USAGE**: The USAGE section gives examples of common usage of the program or function.

❑ **FILES**: The FILES section describes the files a program or function may use. This includes configuration files, startup files, and the files that the program directly operates on. It is customary to refer to those files by their full pathname.

❑ **ENVIRONMENT**: The ENVIRONMENT section lists all the environment variables that influence the working of a program or function, and describes the specific effect they have.

❑ **DIAGNOSTICS**: Most programs have quite a number of error messages or warnings. This section should list the more common warning or error messages and the circumstances that could cause them to occur.

❑ **SECURITY**: The SECURITY section lists the possible dangers that a program may pose to your system. For example, this could range from having the setuid bit set, to being susceptible to race conditions in the /tmp directory.

❑ **CONFORMING TO**: This section describes any standards or conventions a program or function implements, such as POSIX.1 or ANSI.

❑ **NOTES**: Any notes not appropriate in any other section.

❑ **BUGS**: People who write code are not perfect. Their code usually works very well, but there may be circumstances where this is not the case. These circumstances, with workarounds if available, and an indication of when (if ever) the situation will be fixed, should be described in the BUGS section.

❑ **AUTHOR**: The people who contributed to the program should be listed in the AUTHOR section. Usually contact information is included as well.

SEE ALSO: The SEE ALSO section lists related manpages, usually in alphabetical order, as well as other related documents. By convention, this should be the last section.

Sometimes, you just want to know a short description of what a command does, rather than an in-depth explanation. This is where the man sibling whatis comes in. The whatis command (usually an alias for man -1) will look in the manpage for the argument given, and extract the contents of the NAME section for you.

The man Behind the Curtain: troff

The man program does not do its magic all by itself. Under the hood is a powerful engine that does all the formatting required. man itself, adhering to the powerful UNIX philosophy of keeping things simple and modular, merely administers the manpages and displays them using a program from the roff(1) (for run off) family of programs, These include troff(1) (typesetter roff) and nroff(1) (new roff). The public domain groff(1) (GNU roff) will perform all the functions of both and more.

troff was originally written as a typesetting program for a specific printer, the Graphic Systems phototypesetter. This typesetter had four fonts in various styles (roman, italic, and bold), a Greek alphabet and quite a number of special characters and mathematical symbols. Characters could be placed anywhere on the output page. Due to this tie-in to a specific typesetter, the low-level troff commands resemble machine language.

897

Fortunately, people have written quite a few front-end applications (macro packages) that make writing `troff` documents quite a bit easier. These are usually installed on Linux systems as the `troff` emulator, which in turn enables us to read `manpages`. `Groff` is quite a bit more sophisticated than its 1974 predecessor and boasts quite a number of back-ends to produce PostScript and other kinds of output. This has the side effect that we can not only produce `manpages` on screen, but also in quite good printing quality on PostScript printers.

Rolling Your Own manpage

Of course, the easiest way to start with a manual page would be to copy an existing one and change it. It is still useful though to know a little bit more about the `troff` syntax, or, more accurately, about the `troff` MAN macros that are used. An example will be given later, but let's delve first into the theory. Should you want to review these online, then you can always look in the `manpage` on how to write `manpages` using the command:

```
$ man 7 man
```

Now, we can get by with just a few rules of thumb:

- ❑ Commands (or macros) in `troff` consist of a period (.) followed by two letters. These letters are case sensitive, so `.pp` is different from `.PP`.

- ❑ Commands are usually found on a line by themselves, possibly followed by their arguments. This improves readability.

- ❑ There are a few inline commands (those start with a \ followed by a letter), and we will encounter some of the more common ones later on in the chapter.

- ❑ Special characters and predefined strings start with either * and a letter or *(and two letters.

- ❑ You can use comments in a `manpage`; just start your command with \" and everything else on that line will be ignored.

If your manual page uses some kind of a `troff` pre-processor (for example, it interprets `tbl` for tables, or `eqn` for mathematical equations) then your file should start with a comment line like this:

```
\" t
```

This means that your `manpage` should be pre-processed by the `tbl` command. You should, however, be careful with this. On quite a few systems, manual pages are no longer processed with a genuine `troff` implementation, but by programs that implement a subset of the `troff` macro command set. You should therefore use as little `troff` trickery as possible. A `manpage` should start with the `.TH` command, which stands for 'Table Header'. This command has the following syntax:

```
.TH title section date source manual
```

where:

- ❏ title: This is the title of the manpage.

- ❏ section: The section this manpage should go into (1 through 9, as described above).

- ❏ date: This is the last time the manpage was updated. Remember to change it every time you change the manpage!

- ❏ source: This is the place the program came from. In today's Linux distribution world, this could be the distributionname, the distributionsection or the package from the distribution this program came in.

- ❏ manual: is the manual that this program belongs to.

Date, source, and manual are optional, and if any of these arguments contain spaces, then they should be enclosed in double quotes " ".

Manpages have various parts or sections as outlined above, but only one is mandatory – the NAME section. Every section is formatted with the .SH macro, followed by the name of the section. The NAME section is special, because it's contents are (or can be) used by other programs that make use of this special format:

```
.SH NAME
hello \- THE greeting printing program.
```

Note the \ in front of the – sign.

Throughout the years, a number of conventions have made their way into manpage writing. The rules of thumb in the Linux world are:

- ❏ For functions, the arguments are always specified using italics, even in the SYNOPSIS section, where the rest of the function is specified in bold:

int myfunction(*int argc, char **argv*);

- ❏ Filenames are always in italics (*/usr/include/stdio.h*), except in the SYNOPSIS section, where included files are in bold:

- ❏ **#include <stdio.h>**

- ❏ Special macros, which are usually in upper case, are in bold:

- ❏ **MAXINT**

- ❏ When enumerating a list of error codes, the codes are in bold (this list usually uses the .TP macro).

- ❏ Any reference to another man page (or to the subject of the current man page) is in bold. If the manual section number is given, it is given in Roman (normal) font, without any spaces, like this:

man(7)

Fonts

You can use the following commands (taken from the `groff_man(7) manpage`):

- ❑ **.R** text

  Causes text to appear in roman font. If no text is present on the line where the macro is called, then the text of the next line appears in roman. This is the default font to which text is returned at the end of processing of the other macros.

- ❑ **.B** text

  Causes text to appear in bold face. If no text is present on the line where the macro is called, then the text of the next line appears in bold face.

- ❑ **.I** text

  Causes text to appear in italic. If no text is present on the line where the macro is called, then the text of the next line appears in italic.

- ❑ **.SB** text

  Causes the text on the same line if any or the text on the next line to appear in small boldface font.

- ❑ **.BI** text

  Causes text on the same line to appear alternately in bold face and italic font. The text must be on the same line as the macro call. Thus '. BI this word and that' would cause 'this' and 'and' to appear in bold face, while 'word' and 'that' appear in italics.

- ❑ **.IB** text

  Causes text to appear alternately in italic and bold face. The text must be on the same line as the macro call.

- ❑ **.BR** text

  Causes text on the same line to appear alternately in bold face and roman. The text must be on the same line as the macro call.

- ❑ **.RB** text

  Causes text on the same line to appear alternately in roman and bold face. The text must be on the same line as the macro call.

Paragraphs

You can start a new paragraph within the section with a **.PP** command.

Tables

You can use the macros from the `tbl` program to create tables, but it usually better (and easier) to use the **.TP** macro for this. The **.TP** macro creates an indented paragraph with a label, which is equivalent to a poor man's table. To start a table, put the **.TP** macro on a line by itself, followed by the amount of indentation. A **.TP** by itself ends the indented paragraph.

Installing Your manpage

Typically, manpages are kept in a directory with the name man, which will hold several subdirectories named man1, man2, and so on, with one subdirectory per section. The common place to have the hierarchy would be in /usr/man, or /usr/local/man for those programs specific to your set up and system.

The man program looks for those top-level directories by checking an environment variable called MANPATH. Like the PATH variable, this variable should contain a colon-delimited list of top-level man hierarchies.

Example Manual Page

Here is the example we promised – we present a small manual page for the command-line options that the DVD store GUI program has.

```
.TH DVDSTORE 1
.\" Note that the name should be in CAPS, followed by the section.
.SH NAME
dvdstore \- The GUI frontend to the DVD-store database management program.
.SH SYNOPSIS
.B dvdstore
.I [\-u USER] [\-p PASSWORD] [\-\-help] [ GNOME options ]
.SH DESCRIPTION
This manual page documents briefly the
.BR dvdstore
GUI program.
This manual page was written for Professional Linux Programming.
.PP
The
.B dvdstore
program is the graphical frontend for the DVD-store program. It allows one
to manage the DVD-store's inventory as well as general maintenance of
everything that goes on in the store.
.SH OPTIONS
.TP
.B \-?, \-\-help
Show summary of options.
.TP
.B \-u, \-username
Connect as the specified user.
.TP
.B \-p, \-password
Use the specified password for the user.
.TP
.I GNOME options
The standard GNOME options apply to this program. For full details, read
the chapter on GNOME in the Professional Linux Programming Book.
.SH AUTHOR
This manual page was written by Ronald van Loon.
```

The following two screenshots give an indication of what this manpage looks like in a terminal, and what it looks like converted to HTML. To display the terminal version save the file as dvdstore.1 in the man1 directory (some distributions store man pages in gzipped form so you may have to do this as well), then issue the command:

```
$ man dvdstore
```

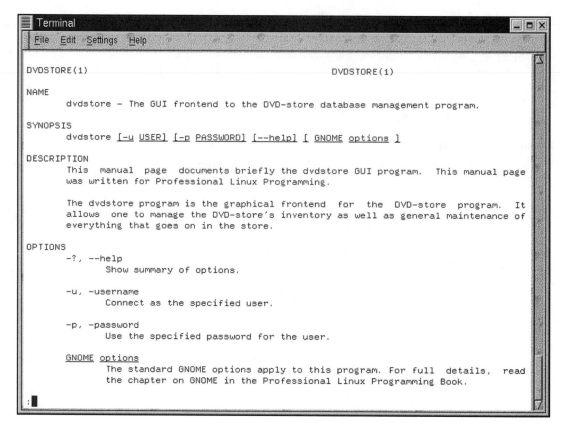

```
DVDSTORE(1)                                           DVDSTORE(1)

NAME
       dvdstore - The GUI frontend to the DVD-store database management program.

SYNOPSIS
       dvdstore [-u USER] [-p PASSWORD] [--help] [ GNOME options ]

DESCRIPTION
       This  manual  page  documents briefly the dvdstore GUI program.  This manual page
       was written for Professional Linux Programming.

       The dvdstore program is the graphical frontend  for  the  DVD-store  program.  It
       allows  one to manage the DVD-store's inventory as well as general maintenance of
       everything that goes on in the store.

OPTIONS
       -?, --help
              Show summary of options.

       -u, -username
              Connect as the specified user.

       -p, -password
              Use the specified password for the user.

       GNOME options
              The standard GNOME options apply to this program. For full  details,  read
              the chapter on GNOME in the Professional Linux Programming Book.

:
```

With the following method, you can create an HTML page from the `dvdstore.1` file, and have it displayed in a browser. You must ensure that you have a newer version of `groff` that will support HTML – the `groff` manpage will tell you whether it does or not. Once you have this, you can enter the commands shown below:

```
$ groff -T html -man dvdstore.1 >dvdstore.html
$ netscape dvdstore.html
```

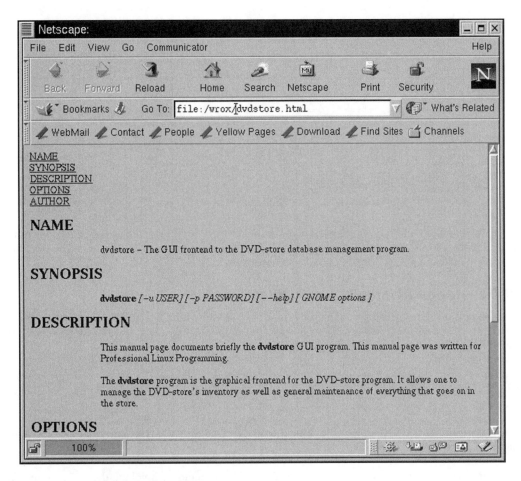

Writing Manual Pages for APIs

You may have written an application with a user-interface part and a library part where the latter contains functions that can be reused by other applications. Our database API is an example. People who want to use the API might forget the specific syntax of a function and would like to look it up online, rather than go and look for this book. This is where manual pages can also be useful. Most system functions have manual pages, here, for example, is the manual page (copyrights deleted for brevity) for memcpy:

```
.\" References consulted:
.\"     Linux libc source code
.\"     Lewine's _POSIX Programmer's Guide_ (O'Reilly & Associates, 1991)
.\"     386BSD man pages
.\" Modified Sun Jul 25 10:41:09 1993 by Rik Faith (faith@cs.unc.edu)
.TH MEMCPY 3  "April 10, 1993" "GNU" "Linux Programmer's Manual"
.SH NAME
memcpy \- copy memory area
.SH SYNOPSIS
.nf
```

```
.B #include <string.h>
.sp
.BI "void *memcpy(void *" dest ", const void *" src ", size_t " n );
.fi
.SH DESCRIPTION
The \fBmemcpy()\fP function copies \fIn\fP bytes from memory area
\fIsrc\fP to memory area \fIdest\fP.  The memory areas may not
overlap.  Use \fBmemmove\fP(3) if the memory areas do overlap.
.SH "RETURN VALUE"
The \fBmemcpy()\fP function returns a pointer to \fIdest\fP.
.SH "CONFORMING TO"
SVID 3, BSD 4.3, ISO 9899
.SH "SEE ALSO"
.BR bcopy "(3), " memccpy "(3), " memmove "(3), " strcpy "(3), " strncpy(3)
```

If you have written a library, it might be a good idea to write separate manual pages for your functions as well. Later in this chapter we will try to show that it can also work differently – writing code and documentation can go hand in hand, and stay consistent to boot.

Next Generation Manpages – info Files

The GNU Project has developed quite a number of UNIX tool look-alikes that come with many Linux distributions. These programs usually have a manpage, but a lot of additional information is usually found in a different place – the info page.

info pages are generated from a special kind of file called a texinfo file. It is a structured format from which a number of other formats can be generated. This concept is also used in a number of other documentation programs, which are discussed in the next section.

The online format is called an info-file. This file is organized in nodes, and you can navigate to the info pages with the help of hyperlinks.

You can start browsing information for a specific GNU command by invoking the info command. When invoked without arguments, info will present you with a menu of choices, and:

```
$ info progname
```

should take you directly to the information about progname.

In order to be able to use this information, you should have the info command installed at your system. If you are an Emacs user, you can also use the special mode that allows you to browse it from within Emacs.

If you want the info pages in a more graphic manner, then you can also use the xinfo command, but unfortunately it is rather old and not commonly found in distributions. You should be able to find it at ftp.x.org. If you are a GNOME user, then you can use the GNOME help browser. Typing:

```
$ info command
```

will call up the manual page for the specified command, or the indicated file. Here is the info file fileutils.info, which you see if you issue the command:

```
$ info ls
```

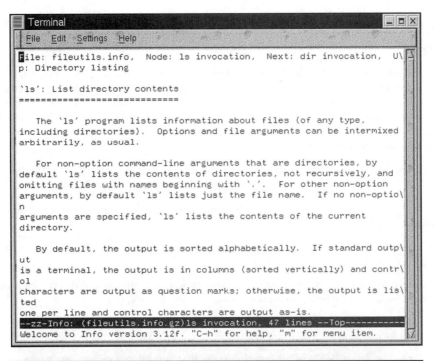

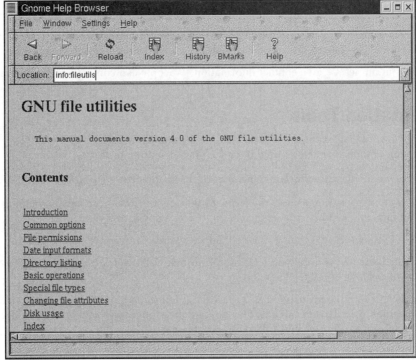

It's All About Structure: From Single Program to Distributed Systems

In the previous section we described some methods to document single modules, such as a stand-alone program, function, or file format. Usually though, a program is but a small part of the greater whole. The DVD-store example that is used throughout this book is a good example of this. There is not one application but several – some are used as the storefront, others are used for the back office. Each of these parts has specific tasks, and even their interoperability deserves some attention. We have seen each part described in a different chapter.

The description of manpages has showed you some signs of internal structure. In the following sections, I will try to show you how you can use other tools to describe the whole that is greater than the parts.

Writing concise, clear, and above all useful documentation is a skill – almost an art. There are a few rules, though:

❑ Try to put all programs that are used in a broader perspective – which program depends on the output of some other program, etc.

❑ Make a list of all the applications your application depends on and the versions you tested them with. This includes obvious ones such as shells, awk, perl.

❑ Give an estimate of the minimum diskspace and CPU requirements necessary to install and run your program.

❑ Make an exhaustive list of all security issues that you know exist or may occur (even though there is only a slight chance of them occurring), such as race conditions, use of /tmp etc.

❑ Make a step-by-step description of how to compile (for applications distributed in source form) and install (for binary distributions or after compilation) your application's files.

❑ Last but not least – give contact information so people can contact you for bug reports or code contributions.

Documentation Tools

We could go on and give examples, but there is not a general one-size-fits-all-recipe, so I will move on to a description of tools that can be used to create documentation instead.

The tools that will be described in the remainder of the chapter have a number of things in common:

❑ They are markup languages, which means they concentrate primarily on helping you structure your material, and intersperse the commands in a non-intrusive manner.

❑ They are text-based, suitable to be edited with almost any editor on any OS.

❑ All the basic text is usually in a US-ASCII format (7-bit characters) and they have a special way of defining 'foreign' characters.

❑ At their core is the principle that typesetting is not something that a writer should be overtly concerned with. In other words, they are definitely not based on a What-You-See-Comes-Close-To-What-You-Would-Like-To-Get principle.

This has a distinct advantage over programs such as Microsoft Word, in that you do not have to spend hours editing the table you created in the beginning of your document and removing a paragraph halfway through, only to find that your document is suddenly in Norwegian – well, according to the spellchecker anyway.

Old, But Still Going Strong: TeX, LaTeX

The first program (or maybe 'typesetting system' would be more apt) to tackle is TeX, created by Donald E. Knuth. The first version of TeX was in use in 1978 and had a major revision in 1984. TeX is not actively being developed – it doesn't need to be. Its latest version is 3.14159, and if any more (minor) versions are to be released, they will add further decimal places of pi. There is also an accompanying program, called METAFONT, which allows you to define fonts. LaTeX and TeX are usually bundled with your Linux distribution. For our purposes we discuss them together.

TeX is almost a programming language in itself. As a matter of fact, people have written 'code' that solves the Towers of Hanoi puzzle in TeX! It allows for a very tight control of everything on the page, if you delve deep into its bowels. Yet it was made not to have to do so.

Writing raw TeX is rarely a pleasure – like `troff`, it becomes easier to use when you use macro packages for it. One macro package that became rather popular is LaTeX, conceived by Leslie Lamport in 1985. In the table at the end of this section, there is a list of mostly LaTeX macros, rather than their TeX counterparts. TeX is very useful in environments that are heavy on formulae:

$$\sqrt[n]{\frac{x^n - y^n}{1 + u^{2n}}} + \int_a^b f_i(x) g_i(x)\, dx$$

It is very easy to write, even within the current body of the text, as shown above. As a matter of fact, the first draft of this chapter was written with the help of LaTeX, and then converted to Microsoft Word with some of the tools we encounter later.

How TeX and LaTeX Work

Like all good programming languages, LaTeX utilizes symbols that are not commonly in use in everyday text. For example, the \ introduces either a command (with or without arguments) or a special character, and the percentage sign % introduces comments. Introducing accents on characters, for example, áèïô is simply a matter of prefixing them with a \ and the appropriate ASCII representation of the accent character:

```
\'a\'e\"\i\^o\~n
```

was used to create the accents in the previous example.

LaTeX uses {} for grouping and for arguments to internal macros, commands given within an opening brace are only valid till the next closing brace.

LaTeX minimizes the number of braces and manages sections by means of so-called environments. These start with a `\begin{sectionname}` and end with a `\end{sectionname}`, in between, processing appropriate to the section occurs. So, if we wanted an enumerated list, we would start with an `enumerate` environment, and an unnumbered list would start with an `itemize` environment.

A LaTeX document starts with a preamble, which sets things like title and author, and then starts with the `document` environment. Before you can do so, however, you need to tell LaTeX the kind of document environment it will be processing.

For example, this paragraph is part of a book, so we would it tell LaTeX that its `documentclass` is `book`; this is done by means of the `\documentclass{book}` macro call. Macros can take optional arguments, which are specified before the required arguments within square brackets []. The `\documentclass` has an optional `papersize` argument, `a4paper`, which sets various `paperdimensions` and margins internally to those appropriate for A4 paper.

Usually you do not need to specify the papersize, because the 'native' papersize will be setup on the destination system automatically – this takes care of most formatting issues for different papersizes. You only need to use it if you want to cater for specific papersizes, which you might need to do when generating PDF files, which we will deal with later.

Let's start with an example.

```
% This is a comment line which will not appear in the actual output
% text.

% Some information about this book for the titlepage

\title{Professional Linux Programming}
\author{Neil \and Rick \and Ronald \and Others}
\date{\today}

% This document is for a book

\documentclass[a4paper]{book} % LaTeX 2e style.

% \documentstyle[a4]{book} % LaTeX 2.09 style - deprecated now

% The actual document starts here:

\begin{document}

\maketitle % make a titlepage

\tableofcontents % generate the table of contents right after the
                 % titlepage

\chapter*{Introduction} % The first chapter.

Introduction goes here...

Let us introduce you to an enumeration:

An introduction should start with:

\begin{enumerate}
\item Shaking hands
\item Mentioning of your name
\item Swapping of business cards
\end{enumerate}

\chapter{Requirements} % Another chapter

\section{Important Requirements} % A section within the chapter

\section{Etc.} % Another section

\chapter{Final words}

\end{document}
```

In this example we saw a few things we haven't mentioned yet, such as chapters and sections. Those will be rendered according to LaTeXs internal rules. The nice thing, though, is that I am not concerned about what a chapter should look like; I can leave that to the publisher, who can add his or her appropriate style file to this document, so it will be typeset in accordance with the specified house rules. The document itself, however, remains exactly the same, which means you can truly concentrate on writing the actual text, instead of worrying whether you have turned on italics in the correct spot and so on. Compare this to `troff` where you had to do everything yourself!

Producing Output

Processing this is simple:

```
$ latex filename
```

It is traditional, but not mandatory, to give your files a `.tex` suffix.

LaTeX processes your file one line at a time and puts the text it encounters in boxes (horizontally oriented boxes or `hbox`, and vertically oriented boxes or `vbox`), which are sequentially arranged in an aesthetic fashion on the page. The designers of GNOME copied this idea in their layout managers. It will also number your chapters automatically for you, as well as your sections, unless you especially tell it not to. This is done by adding a `*` to the Introduction chapter.

The whole process will produces four files, all beginning with the prefix of the given file:

- ❑ `.dvi` – This file holds the actual output of your document.
- ❑ `.log` – This file logs what LaTeX has done with your document.
- ❑ `.aux` – This file contains commands for a future run of LaTeX.
- ❑ `.toc` – This is a file generated during this run of LaTeX, it holds all information relevant to the table-of-contents.

We are not quite done yet. Let's view what we have produced so far.

Viewing Output

The `.dvi` file that was produced by running LaTeX is a device independent file. It contains information on how the document should be rendered. This is akin to the way Java works. Instead of the Java Virtual Machine you are using a TeX Virtual Machine. Various implementations exist – the more common ones are `dvips`, which create PostScript-files from DVI files, and `xdvi`, which displays the document on your graphical desktop. For those who do not run X on their machines there is also `dvisvga`, which will display it on the SVGA mode of your console (if your console supports it).

If this is your first document, and you run one of the aforementioned programs, you will notice that a number of fonts have been produced. This is normal behavior – TeX is resolution-independent, which means that the fonts it uses are (or should be) resolution-independent also. Because it would be unwieldy to have fonts present for every imaginable printer or display device, fonts are usually generated for the desired resolution as needed by a program called Metafont. After being generated, these fonts usually reside in a font cache, so the next run of your DVI viewer will be a lot faster. This may seem like a cumbersome process, but it has the advantage that your output will be better as soon as it is generated for a better printer, so guaranteeing the best possible output at every resolution.

Producing Better Output

If you view your document now, you will see that a number of things will be missing. The document starts with a title page, but there is an empty table of contents page (it only says 'Contents'). This is normal, LaTeX is not clairvoyant, and so does not know where everything will end up. A table of contents typically will have page numbers, but those will not be known until LaTeX has finished processing the document! In order to be able to do this, LaTeX will write everything that should go in the table of contents to a file with the .toc extension. The \tableofcontents macro will look for the .toc file, and will include it if it is found. LaTeX will then continue with the remainder of the document as before.

As a consequence, you will have to run LaTeX three times. The first time to produce an initial table of contents file, the second time to include the table of contents file generated the first time and the third time to compensate for the additional pages that the table of contents has generated.

The same goes for references from one part of a document to another. References are also not known until after LaTeX has run at least once.

There are tips and tricks that will help to run LaTeX faster, and more efficiently, but those methods are better left for a different book, such as 'A Guide to LaTeX' by Helmut Kopka and Patrick W. Daly, published by Addison-Wesley (*ISBN 0-201398-25-7*).

Info Files Revisited

You will remember the mentioning of the 'info' file. An info file is actually produced from something called a 'TeXinfo' file. This is a specific file-format that became popular with the GNU family of tools invented by Richard Stallman of Emacs and FSF fame. A TeXinfo file is a combination of typesetting commands from printing (the TeX part), and hyperlinks and references for online documentation (the info part). Depending on the program used, you can produce a .dvi file if you want to, suitable for printing, or .info files for browsing with the info command.

A New Breed: HTML, XML, and DocBook

LaTeX and TeX are not the only kids on the block that can make it easy for you to create structured documents without caring much about layout issues. SGML (a meta-markup language) was created especially for this purpose. It does not define a markup language itself, but allows you to describe the elements your documents are made up of by means of Document Type Definitions. Then there is a second candidate that could be used for structuring documents: XML. XML is just another SGML Document Type Definition or DTD for short but it has tighter requirements on the presence of tags. For example, every tag should have a corresponding close tag, and no tags are optional.

Both SGML and XML are basically meta-languages, in the sense that it does not mean anything if you are using SGML or XML, unless you provide a detailed description of the tags you use and their attributes.

The underlying principal behind SGML and XML is again one of structure, rather than one of presentation. Interpretation of tags is left to external programs, although the forms of SGML and XML are defined and can be syntactically checked by programs such as sgmls, provided a DTD for your tags is available.

HTML

A concrete example of an SGML DTD that is in rather common use today is HTML. Judging from the variety of colorful and flashy web pages that are on the Web, you would be likely to forget that HTML originally started out as a simple way to structure documents and add hyperlinks to documents. The original HTML specification is rather lacking in the document presentation department. Instead, displaying, and formatting in documents, such as headings and fonts, were left to the browser.

Now, years after the original HTML specification was released, people are starting to go back to the original concept of structured documents and separating the presentation from the actual text by means of Cascading Style Sheets and their XML equivalents.

Literally hundreds of books have been written on HTML, which has overshadowed other important document technologies such as DocBook.

DocBook at a glance

The aim of DocBook is to provide structure without imposing formatting rules to those people who need to write structured text, with a slight bias towards technical reference material.

DocBook, like HTML, is also an SGML based standard, but its origins are different. DocBook was started in 1991 as a joint project of HaL Computer Systems and the publisher O'Reilly. It currently is maintained by the Organization for the Advancement of Structured Information Standards (OASIS). Its latest incarnation, version 3.1, saw the light of day in February 1999 and the first one released under OASIS. A complete description and reference of this document description method can be found in 'DocBook: The Definitive Guide', published by O'Reilly (*ISBN: 1-565925-80-7*). As it weighs in at 600 pages, we will just give some of the rationale behind DocBook, rather than a complete reference. An online reference can be found at http://docbook.org. The Debian distribution has a Docbook package, which contains the necessary files for working with DocBook.

DocBook is all about structured documentation. It shares a great many similarities with the reasoning behind LaTeX in that respect. You, as the author, have the responsibility for the content, while the publisher will deal with all the formatting and typesetting issues. Some authors do not want to give up the control over their formatting – this is OK, but not if a publisher wants to present a consistent look to the readers, especially if the book is part of a series.

DocBook adheres to this philosophy by providing only elements of structure, and no elements for presentation; these will be provided by a style sheet writer. Designing those style sheets is an art in itself, but once done it ensures that not only every document using DocBook in your organization, but also those you receive from the outside world, will have a consistent look.

The advantage of using DocBook is that a number of tools exist to convert a DocBook file and a style sheet to a variety of other formats, including HTML, `TexInfo` files, and `manpages`. This saves you the trouble of learning about formatting and layout, as well as the added benefit of being able to make your documents available in a variety of other well-known formats.

The table overleaf summarizes some structure elements in the various documentation tools mentioned earlier. The implicit assumption here is that you will be writing a manual with chapters, like a book. For articles, the elements will be similar. This list is not meant to be comprehensive, but you can have a look and see what kind of tool you like best.

The table should at least whet your appetite for one particular flavor. You may find that LaTeX is more for the mathematically inclined; HTML is for everyone, but it does not offer much to the documentation writer, who needs all kinds of tools (references, tables, table of contents). DocBook might be the beginner's choice, as it is XML/SGML based and can be learned fairly quickly and comes with a number of tools that make life easier.

Description	HTML	DocBook	LaTeX
Comment Character	<-- everything in the -- tag will be ignored>	<-- everything in the -- tag will be ignored>	% everything behind a % is ignored.
Document Preamble	<HTML><HEAD>	<!DOCTYPE book PUBLIC "-//OASIS//DTD DocBook V3.1//EN><book>	\documentclass[a4paper]{book}
Book Information		<bookinfo>	
Author Information	<AUTHOR>Authorname One, Authorname Two</AUTHOR>	<authorgroup> <-- for multiple authors> <author> <firstname>First</firstname> <surname>Name</surname> </author> <author> <firstname>Second</firstname> <surname>Name</surname> </author> </authorgroup>	\author{Authorname One \and Authorname Two}
End of Book Information		</bookinfo>	
Title	<TITLE>Title goes here</TITLE>	<title>Title goes here</title>	\title{Title goes here}
Start of Document	</HEAD>		\begin{document}
Titlepage	<BODY>	implicitly generated from the bookinfo above	\maketitle

Description	HTML	DocBook	LaTeX

Table of Contents	*not available, unless you make one yourself*	`<toc>` <!-- usually generated automatically -->
		 `<tocpart>`
		 `<tocchap>`
		 `<tocentry pagenum="1">Chapter one</tocentry>`
		 `<toclevel1>`
		 `<tocentry pagenum="1">Section one</tocentry>`
		 `</toclevel1>`
		 `</tocchap>`
		 `</tocpart>`
		 `</toc>`
			`\tableofcontents`

Start of Chapter	*not available, unless you make one yourself (or have it generated)* `<H1>Chapter Title</H1>`	`<chapter>` `<title>Chapter Title</title>`	`\chapter{Chapter Title}`
Start of Section	`<H2>Section Title</H2>`	`<sect1><title>Section Title</title>`	`\section{Section Title}`
Start of Subsection	`<H3>Subsection Title</H3>`	`<sect2><title>Subsection Title</title>`	`\subsection{Subsection Title}`
Start of Subsubsection	`<H4>Subsubsection Title</H4>`	`<sect3><title>Subsubsection Title</title>`	`\subsubsection{Subsubsection Title}`
Start Numbered List	`<OL>`	`<orderedlist>`	`\begin{enumerate}`
Numbered Item	`<LI>Item goes here.`	`<listitem>Item goes here.</listitem>`	`\item Item goes here.`
End Numbered List	`</OL>`	`</orderedlist>`	`\end{enumerate}`
Start Unnumbered List	`<UL>`	`<itemizedlist>`	`\begin{itemize}`
Item	`<LI>Item goes here.`	`<listitem>Item goes here.</listitem>`	`\item Item goes here.`
End Unnumbered List	`</UL>`	`</itemizedlist>`	`\end{itemize}`
End of Document		`</book>`	`\end{document}`

Painting the Big Picture: HOWTO and FAQ Files

The previous sections dealt with tools and how to use them for writing documentation before the release of your application. That however, is not the end of the documentation cycle.

As time goes by, you will receive a number of questions over and over again. These questions are usually on some minor topic like something not clear in the documentation, or concerning usage scenarios, where your application is a building block towards achieving some sort of greater goal, perhaps one you did not think of when writing the application in the first place.

At first you will probably be inclined to answer all the questions personally, but answering the same question five times, gets old rather quickly. At that point, it might be a good idea to bundle your answers to these frequently asked questions in, you guessed it, a Frequently Asked Questions file, or FAQ.

It's also a good idea to write a HOWTO file, where you answer configuration questions about how your application can be configured to fit a particular scenario. It should give quick guidelines that users of your application can follow to get your application up and running, and in less time than it would take if they actually were to study your documentation.

It is also a good idea to include a README file, where you mention the things to keep in mind, contact information, and installation caveats. Other things that have proved invaluable are TODO files, Changelogs detailing the changes made (even small ones!), with major changes and features added recounted in a NEWS file.

Developer Documentation

At this point, you will have written online documentation for those who are using your programs and a manual that puts things in a broader perspective; maybe even a FAQ and a HOWTO file for your application. Your mailboxes, both electronic and physical, are overflowing with thank-you notes and copies of birth certificates showing that several people have named their firstborn after you as a token of their eternal gratitude for putting your application out there in the open.

Praise is not the only thing likely to pour into your mailboxes, though. Bug reports, feature requests, requests for clarification of code – all those are just as likely to appear on the scene.

You probably will not have time to deal with all those requests. Fortunately, (and this is part of the point of open source development), you do not have to. Depending on the usefulness and popularity of your application, people will volunteer to help you fix bugs, and to improve your application and rewrite your code. Your application will evolve from a single person or small group effort towards a large scale operation. The perils that this brings are documented in Eric Raymond's 'The Cathedral and the Bazaar'. A URL to the online version can be found in Chapter 1.

Logistics of undertaking open source projects aside, it is helpful that your code will be well documented. The usage documentation I mentioned a few paragraphs ago will have given people the idea of what your program does on a functional level. Developers, on the other hand, care more for how things are done on a technical and implementation level. This begs for well-documented code.

Some might say that well-documented code is an oxymoron, and in practice it is true that source material contains very few comments. In a number of cases the comments that are there are incorrect, because original code was superseded by new code, with different logic from the original. The comments of the old code usually remain, but are no longer valid. Exceptions to this rule are found in areas where it is mandatory to have correct code, like the military, or with critical embedded systems such as those used in aviation.

One of the main reasons that documenting software and algorithms is even less popular than the writing of usage documentation is that it cannot be easily validated or checked. Another reason is that documentation and code are often separated, especially when the documentation goes beyond a few lines of text.

If you are writing code to implement a standard, then references to the relevant section of that standard can be useful; standards could include RFCs and RFPs, for example. Where a design document such as an RFC is missing, you may have to create one yourself with the methods shown earlier.

Let's start with an example.

Perl's 'POD' Method

If you are familiar with Perl you will be acquainted with comment delineation using the # character. What you may not know, is that in Perl you can intersperse complete pieces of prose without having to resort to long sections of lines starting with #. More importantly, you can generate manpages for your perl-script from these pieces of prose, by using only a few rules of thumb. This mechanism is called 'POD', which stands for 'Plain Old Documentation'.

The full documentation of POD can be found in the perlpod(1) manpage. Here is a quick summary:

- ❑ You can start a POD section at any point in your perl code where you can begin a new statement.

- ❑ A POD-extractor/translator will look for an empty line preceding a pod section. That line should really be empty, and not just look empty. Watch out for stray spaces.

- ❑ A POD section starts with an equals sign, followed by a POD-command.

- ❑ A POD section ends with a line that starts with =cut. Everything else on that line is ignored.

Within a POD section there are three kinds of paragraphs:

- ❑ **Verbatim Paragraph**: A verbatim paragraph is an indented block (starts with a space or tab) of text that should be copied verbatim by a POD processor.

- ❑ **Command Paragraph**: A command paragraph is a paragraph that starts with an equals sign, followed by a command, followed by the arguments for that command.

- ❑ **Literal text**: A block of text. The text can be anything. Within the text some additional inline sequences can be used (see below).

The PODs can have the following commands:

- ❑ pod starts an ordinary pod section.

- ❑ cut ends a pod section.

- ❑ head1, head2, Level 1, and Level 2 are level headings.

- ❑ Lists are created with the over n, item text, back commands. The n after over is the amount of indentation; the text is an indication for the sort of list. numbers is used for numbered lists, * for bulleted list, arbitrary text for a heading. The actual text of the item should be on the next line.

- ❑ for format text; if the format format is used, insert the text into the output stream.

- ❑ begin format, end format; same as for but for larger blocks of text.

Last but not least, you can add some smarkup to your text by using the X<text> construct, where X is one of:

Letter	Meaning
I	Italicize text, used for emphasis or variables
B	Embolden text, used for switches and programs
S	text contains non-breaking spaces
C	Literal code
L	A link (cross reference) to text
F	text is a filename
X	text is an index entry
Z	A zero-width character (text should be empty)
E	text is an escape character

Examples of POD can be found in any Perl distribution.

There are several programs available to get from POD (or Perl script) to a number of other formats:

- ❑ pod2html: Formats the POD part of a perl script in HTML format.
- ❑ pod2man: Formats the POD part of a perl script in troff (man) format.
- ❑ pod2latex: Formats the POD part of a perl script in LaTeX format.
- ❑ pod2text: Formats the POD part of a perl script in plain text format.

Literary Programming

The previous section showed examples of constructs within the language itself. Unfortunately this does not help those whose language does not have these kind of facilities built in.

Fortunately, there is a solution for almost any kind of programming language in use today, but it takes a bit of a change of attitude to start using it.

The major mental adaptation you need to make is that the documentation is the important thing, not the actual coding. In other words, it's the idea that counts, not the implementation. If you have ever worked as a software architect, someone who designs systems or applications, but who does not necessarily have to do all the coding, then this adaptation will be quite natural.

Unless you are superhuman, and are able to produce perfect code first time round, you will usually first brainstorm with yourself, or with colleagues, about the best way to tackle a problem. When you have a rough idea, you sit down and code. Unfortunately, the moment you start coding, how you arrived at that particular implementation, and your original ideas, are lost to others unless you write your thoughts down first. In practice, however, alternatives you considered, and then discarded because of impracticality or dead ends in reasoning, are usually not documented. This can be a major disadvantage to anyone who needs to develop your project further.

You can remedy this situation, though, by employing a technique known as 'literary programming'. This technique was, if not conceived, then at least demonstrated by Donald Knuth. For his TeX program, which was originally written in Pascal, he created two tools, called `tangle` and `weave` that were used to extract code (`tangle`) and documentation (`weave`) from a single document. This document is called a `web`.

How it Works

In this section we will use a literary programming tool called `noweb`, available for at least the Debian distribution of Linux; there will probably be other packages for other distributions as well. The `'no'` in `noweb` is the first two letters of its author's first name: Norman Ramsey. There are more tools that allow you more control over typesetting and formatting, but `noweb` is one of our favorites because it is so easy to understand and use, while still packing enough power so that you are not limited in the basic idea behind literary programming. If you need more powerful features, you can use `fweb`, `funnelweb`, or revert to the proven worth of `cweb`.

In `noweb` there are two types of section, called 'chunks' they are either documentation chunks, in which a certain concept is explained, or code chunks.

A documentation chunk starts with a single @, followed by a new line or space. A code chunk starts with a double angular left bracket << in the first column, followed by the chunk name (which can contain spaces), followed by >> and an equal sign =.

Within the documentation chunk, you can use your favorite documentation typesetter, such as LaTeX or HTML. If you need to provide code snippets within the documentation chunk, you can enclose it within double square brackets like so: [[code]].

The code chunk can contain anything you like, in terms of code, as well as references to other chunks. Simply putting its name in angular brackets makes a reference to another chunk << and >>. There are no restrictions on the language used, and you can mix languages within your document.

Let's take a look at an example of a small C program that will implement a recursive factorial calculation function:

```
@ This noweb file demonstrates the use of noweb and its tools. We will
implement a function that will use recursion to calculate a factorial. Let's
start with the outline of our program. What we will do is call our program
file [[factorial.c]] and implement a simple [[main()]] that will call our
function for us and write the result to [[stdout]], then exit gracefully.

<<factorial.c>>=
<<Include necessary headerfiles>>

<<Implementation of factorial function>>

int main(void)
{
    int result = <<Call to factorial function with 5 as the argument>> ;

    printf ("The factorial function returned %d as the answer.\n",result);

    return 0;
}
```

Here you see the top-down approach of literary programming. First there is an explanation of what follows, and then the source file called `factorial.c` is created, using other chunks, that have not been defined yet. In a few simple lines of code we have explained what is going to happen, and have presented the basic outlines, and by concentrating on one thing at a time, we haven't overburdened the casual reader with too much information.

Here is the rest of the file:

```
@ In order for this [[main()]] function to work, we need to include the
[[stdio.h]] headerfile, for the definition of [[printf()]].

<<Include necessary headerfiles>>=
#include <stdio.h>

@ What is the definition of factorial? Simply put, [[n! = n * (n-1)!]]. This
suggests that our factorial function will have one argument, and that its
implementation will use recursion. Let's call our function [[factorial()]]
and assume that an [[int]] will be sufficient for both argument and result.

<<Implementation of factorial function>>=
int factorial(int n)
{
  <<Check if n is in range>>

  return <<result of calling [[n * factorial(n-1)]]>>;
}
@ When is our parameter [[n]] not in range? The correct answer is: when it
is less or equal to zero. In this case, the factorial function has no clear
answer. It seems a bit severe to halt the program when this happens, so
let's just return 1 as the answer if we are called with such a parameter:

<<Check if n is in range>>=
  if (n <= 0)
    return 1;

@ The added advantage of this approach is, that we now have a termination
point for our function, which is a requirement for recursive functions, or
they will not terminate.

Implementing the remainder of our function is a breeze: just call ourselves
again, but with a decremented parameter:

<<result of calling [[n * factorial(n-1)]]>>=
  n * factorial(n-1)

@ Now our function is fully defined, we can call it from our main program
and we are done:

<<Call to factorial function with 5 as the argument>>=
factorial(5)
```

That's it! Now, to create the file `factorial.c` all I have to do is use the `notangle` program:

```
$ notangle -Rfactorial.c factorial.nw >factorial.c
```

This will result in the `factorial.c` file being created. If you look at the generated output you will see:

```c
#include <stdio.h>

int factorial(int n)
{
    if (n <= 0)
      return 1;

  return   n * factorial(n-1) ;
}

int main(void)
{
  int result = factorial(5) ;

  printf ("The factorial function returned %d as the answer.\n",result);

  return 0;
}
```

This code can now be compiled by a C compiler and will produce the expected output (120). If you wanted to include the original comment/documentation chunks, then you could use the `nountangle` command instead. In practice you should not really need it, as you should make your changes in the noweb source, not in the generated code, but it sometimes helps to see where all the comments end up.

But that's not all! The documentation has not been generated yet. You can do this by calling the `noweave` command. Noweave can generate automatic indexes for all the functions we define; just call it like this:

```
$ noweave -autodefs c -index factorial.nw >factorial.tex
```

You now have a LaTeX file that you can run through LaTeX three times as explained earlier. When viewed with xdvi you should see something like:

```
July 19, 2000                                    faculty.nw    1


      This noweb file demonstrates the use of noweb and its tools. We willimplement
      a function that will use recursion to calculate a faculty. Let's start with the
      outline of our program. What we will do is call our program file faculty.c
      and implement a simple main() that will call our function for us and write the
      result to stdout, then exit gracefully.

1a    ⟨faculty.c 1a⟩≡
      ⟨Include necessary headerfiles 1b⟩

      ⟨Implementation of faculty function 1c⟩

      int main(void)
      {
          int result = ⟨Call to faculty function with 5 as the argument 2c⟩ ;

          printf ("The faculty function returned %d as the answer.\n",result);

          return 0;
      }

      Defines:
        main, never used.
      Uses faculty 1c.

      In order for this main() function to work, we need to include the stdio.h
      headerfile, for the definition of printf().

1b    ⟨Include necessary headerfiles 1b⟩≡                          (1a)
          #include <stdio.h>

      What is the definition of faculty ? Simply put, n! = n * (n-1)!. This suggests
      that our faculty function will have one argument, and that its implementation
      will use recursion. Let's call our function faculty() and assume that an int
      will be sufficient for both argument and result.

1c    ⟨Implementation of faculty function 1c⟩≡                     (1a)
          int faculty(int n)
          {
              ⟨Check if n is in range 2a⟩

              return ⟨result of calling n * faculty(n-1) 2b⟩;
          }

      Defines:
        faculty, used in chunks 1 and 2.
```

Navigation buttons (right side):
Quit, Abort, Again, Help, Reread, 100%, 33%, 25%, 17%, First, Page-10, Page-5, Prev, Next, Page+5, Page+10, Last, View PS, Back, File

That's all there is to it, really. A simple, but powerful method for writing well documented code, or maybe we should say well-coded documents?

Lightweight Literary Programming

Maybe you are a bit overwhelmed by the idea of writing books about your coding. Or maybe you are not as much at home in explaining as you are in coding. In most cases, a more lightweight approach to literary programming might be the right thing for you.

What we will describe now only works for C. The tool is called c2man. It uses a very simple concept – you place comments after every symbol, enum element, structure element, and function parameter, like this (example taken from the c2man manpage):

```
enum Place
{
    HOME,        /* Home, Sweet Home */
    WORK,        /* where I spend lots of time */
    MOVIES,      /* Saturday nights mainly */
    CITY,        /* New York, New York */
    COUNTRY      /* Bob's Country Bunker */
}
;

/*
 * do some useful work for a change.
 * This function will actually get some productive
 * work done, if you are really lucky.
 * returns the number of milliseconds in a second.
 */
int dowork(int count,       /* how much work to do */
           enum Place where, /* where to do the work */
           long fiveoclock  /* when to knock off */);
```

When you run the c2man program on a header file, it will produce a manual page with NAME, SYNOPSIS, PARAMETERS, DESCRIPTION, and RETURNS sections where the comments above are inserted, with correct capitalization. For enums, the valid values are listed as well.

As said, this might be sufficient for documenting library functions, but does not have the advantages of literary programming as outlined earlier.

Document Interchange

If you have written documentation, but it cannot be read by its intended audience, your efforts will be a total waste of time. This occurs when a Microsoft Windows user gives you, a Linux user, a Microsoft Word file. Unless you have one of the Linux Office suites installed, or the program mswordview that converts Word to HTML, you will not be able to do much with it. Even so, with these programs, the conversion is usually close, but will not always achieve the desired level of accuracy.

Of course, the same applies if you have a document written in troff and give it to the aforementioned Windows user. Even though troff is probably available, it is not the ideal format for document exchange.

Clearly, a common denominator is needed. There are a few possibilities:

Plain Text: Plain text always works, at least for English language and possibly other ISO8859-documents. The Chinese, Japanese, and Russians are out of luck here. You lose formatting and graphical capabilities, though. This can be an advantage, but often isn't.

HTML: HTML is a format that has the advantage of being plain text based, and also has some structure elements which can be displayed on a lot of systems.

PDF: The Portable Document Format or PDF is a format invented by Adobe; it is based on the PostScript language, but is a bit more restrictive which makes it easier to parse. A large number of platforms have the Acrobat Reader ported to them, including Linux. Others can make do with ghostscript, the GNU version of PostScript, which also supports PDF. Ghostscript can also help you to extract the text of a PDF file. An alternative viewer for PDF files on Linux is xpdf, also available from a Linux archive near you.

PDF Files

Writing PDF files by hand is better left to the experts who live and breathe PostScript. For mere mortals, it is not a or language/format that is easy to write manually.

At the time of writing, Adobe did not have a Linux version of its Acrobat program. Fortunately, there is an alternative – if you write LaTeX documents, then you can use the pdflatex program. This is not the usual backend used for producing dvi files, and it produces PDF files instead, which are suitable for use on any platform. You only have to substitute pdflatex for latex on the command line for this to work.

Summary

In this chapter, we have said a lot about different forms of documentation. The difference in target audiences (end-user, power-user/system administrator, and developer) was explained. Various forms of online documentation were discussed, such as context-sensitive help for GUIs, the manpage, and info files.

If your application is not a simple one, but consists of a number of modules, it is useful to use a specific documentation system to put things in perspective. LaTeX and DocBook were discussed as possible options.

We then tried to show you some options to turn your programming into a more literary experience by introducing the concept of literary programming, thus killing two birds with one stone.

Online discussion at http://www.p2p.wrox.com

26

Device Drivers

In this chapter we're going to take a look at kernel programming. This is a topic which could quite easily fill a whole book on its own, so it's not going to be a complete tutorial. Instead, we're only going to look at writing a device driver. Most people will not need to get their hands this dirty, but if you have a piece of hardware that the Linux kernel is not yet capable of supporting, you may want to attempt to write a driver for it.

What we're going to do is concentrate on the basics – how to make sure your initialization code is called at the right time, how to detect and configure PCI devices, how to merge your driver into the build system, and some of the more esoteric aspects of kernel programming, which many people either get wrong, or have difficulty understanding. In particular we'll look at the various locking primitives which are used to protect data structures and code from concurrent access and the situations in which each is used, and we'll point out some of the more common race conditions (bugs caused by an unusual timing of events leading to irregular behavior) and how to avoid them. We'll also look at the rules for accessing data that resides in the memory pages of a normal Linux process (user-space), rather than safely in kernel pages (kernel-space) that cannot be paged to disk.

The driver that we're going to use for our examples will be a character device driver for an intelligent fieldbus (factory network) controller – an update for the code which is in the 2.3 development series. We don't need to know much about it, except that the card has a memory buffer shared on the PCI bus through which it exchanges packets of data with the user-space libraries. For the curious, the cards handled by this driver are produced by Applicom International S.A. (http://www.applicom-int.com/) and are intelligent devices capable of communicating over most common factory networks and fieldbusses.

Execution Context

Every process has a virtual memory map that maps each page in its own virtual address space to physical pages either in RAM or in swap. Each process also has the kernel's pages mapped, but the permissions are such that they cannot be accessed while the CPU is in non-privileged mode.

Most kernel code runs in the context of a user process – when a process makes a system call, the CPU switches into privileged mode and continues to run with the same virtual memory map as the calling process. This means that unless the code plays memory management tricks, the CPU can access only kernel-space pages, or the user-space pages of the process it's running in the context of.

Any kernel code that is running in this context may access the process's memory via the `copy_to_user` and `copy_from_user` functions which we'll describe later. It may also call functions which can sleep (give up the CPU temporarily to allow other processes to run, while waiting for an event or timeout).

Some code, however, should complete quickly without attempting to sleep. This includes code that may interrupt (or preempt) any process at any time, including interrupt handlers, which are called immediately when a hardware IRQ occurs, and functions set up as timers by asking the kernel to invoke them when a certain time is reached. Such code will run in the context of the process that happens to be running on the same CPU when the event happens, and should not cause that process to sleep.

It is possible for any code to hold a lock that an interrupt handler may require to complete its task. Any code that holds such a lock should also ensure that the lock is released as quickly as possible without sleeping.

The normal method of memory allocation within the Linux kernel is the `kmalloc` function, which takes the size parameter, measured in bytes, plus one extra argument. This extra argument is most often set to `GFP_KERNEL`, which indicates that the caller is willing to sleep if necessary while waiting for space to become available.

It is best to call `kmalloc` from a context where sleeping is permitted. For example, a network card driver may attempt to keep empty buffers queued ready to receive packets, so that the interrupt handler does not have to allocate a new buffer when the card generates an IRQ to say that it has received a new packet.

If it is necessary to allocate memory from a context where sleeping is not permitted, the `GFP_ATOMIC` flag is used. This indicates that the `kmalloc` routine should return failure unless it can satisfy the allocation request without waiting.

Module and Initialization Code

Almost every driver will have to have an initialization routine, to probe for the hardware that the driver can handle, and to register its functionality in order for it to be accessed. We need to make sure that our initialization routine is called at the right time – which, if our driver is linked into the kernel, is when the kernel boots, or otherwise when the module containing the driver is loaded into the kernel.

In the 2.2 series and previous versions of the Linux kernel, there was a large list of calls (in the `init/main.c` file) to initialization functions for various subsystems and drivers. If you compiled your driver into the kernel, then you had to add a call to its initialization function to that list, either directly or indirectly (by adding it to another function that is called from the main list).

If you compiled your driver as a loadable module, then you had to call your initialization routine 'init_module', because the functions in the kernel that handle the loading of modules will use that special name to identify the routine to call when the module is first loaded.

In the 2.4 series, all this has been simplified, and you can use the same code whether your driver is compiled into the kernel or not. All you need to do is use a simple pre-processor macro to identify the routine to be called at initialization, and another to identify a routine needed before unloading (if your driver is a loadable module).

To identify the initialization routine, use the module_init macro, and to identify the cleanup routine, use the module_exit macro. Each takes a single argument – the name of the routine to be used. An example is given a few paragraphs below.

Neither the initialization nor the exit routine is passed any arguments. The initialization routine returns an int indicating success or failure – a non-zero return code means that the probe or initialization was unsuccessful. If the driver was compiled as a module, and its init_module routine returns non-zero, then the system will automatically unload the module without calling the exit function. In the 2.4 kernels, the return code from init_module will be returned as an error code to the process attempting to load the module (usually insmod or modprobe).

The exit function is called just before the module is unloaded, but only if the driver is a loadable module. By the time the exit function is called, it is too late to prevent the module from being unloaded – you must just make the best of it and clean up as well as possible. There are, however, ways to prevent your module from being unloaded while it's in use – we'll look at them a little later.

Linker Sections

When a driver is linked into the kernel, its initialization routine will only get called once during the boot procedure, and the exit routine will not be called – the kernel must remain complete even when all of user-space has shut down – until modules need to be unloaded. To leave all the code and data required for the initialization and exit routines in memory would be wasteful – the Linux kernel cannot be paged to disc, so this unused code would be taking up valuable physical RAM.

To fix this, the kernel build system gives the programmer a way to mark certain data and functions so that they can be discarded when they will no longer be used.

The most commonly used of these is the __init macro, which is used to mark initialization functions. There is also __exit, for module unload functions, and __initdata and __exitdata, are used for data that may be discarded. They work by placing the entities with which they are associated into a different ELF section from most of the normal code and data. We've shown how to use each macro in the example module below.

If you look closely at the output of the kernel while it boots, or use the dmesg command to review the kernel's console output buffer, you'll see that immediately after mounting the root filesystem it emits a line which looks like this:

```
Freeing unused kernel memory: 108k freed
```

This means that it's released 108 KB of kernel memory containing code and data that it knows it will not require again. The parts discarded at runtime are none other than the contents of the __init and __initdata sections. As it is known even at compile time that the parts marked __exit and __exitdata will never be used except for modules, they are simply omitted from the final linkage of the bootable kernel image.

Example Module Code

Here's an example of a skeleton driver, which prints an appropriate message upon initialization and exits. It also uses the __init, __exit, __initdata and __exitdata macros appropriately, and is written to work with a kernel from the 2.4 series. Assuming the kernel source is in the normal place (/usr/src/linux), and that the code below is placed into a file name 'example.c', it can be compiled with the command:

```
$ gcc -DMODULE -D__KERNEL__ -I/usr/src/linux/include -c example.c
```

All kernel code is compiled with __KERNEL__ defined, so that the include files that are shared between the kernel and the C library (libc) can include parts that are private to the kernel. Loadable modules also have MODULE defined. More details on adding drivers to the kernel's Makefiles and configuration system are included nearer the end of this chapter.

```
#include <linux/kernel.h>
#include <linux/module.h>
#include <linux/init.h>
static char __initdata hellomessage[] = KERN_NOTICE "Hello, world!\n";
static char __exitdata byemessage[] = KERN_NOTICE "Goodbye, cruel world.\n";

static int __init start_hello_world(void)
{
    printk(hellomessage);
    return 0;
}

static void __exit go_away(void)
{
    printk(byemessage);
}

module_init(start_hello_world);
module_exit(go_away);
```

The compilation command above should produce a file called example.o, which can be loaded into the kernel with the insmod command, and subsequently removed with the rmmod command:

```
$ /sbin/insmod example.o
$ /sbin/rmmod example
```

If you are at a virtual console when you load the module, you should immediately see the messages it prints in each of its initialization and exit functions. If you are logged in remotely, or are running in X-Windows, then you will need to use the dmesg command to view the kernel's output.

PCI Devices and Drivers

Now we've seen how to get our code into the kernel, it's time to look at the way that the Linux kernel handles PCI devices.

struct pci_dev

The struct `pci_dev` is the basic structure that Linux uses to hold information about a physical PCI device. The structure is defined in full in the file `/include/linux/pci.h` (depending on your set up), which contains far more in it than we're going to mention here. However, there are a few fields that are immediately relevant to us. Firstly, there are the fields that help us to identify a given device.

These numeric fields are all basic parts of the PCI specification, and a table giving mappings from the ID numbers to actual names of vendors and devices may be found in the file `linux/drivers/pci/pci.ids` in the source of a 2.4 series kernel, or as part of the `pciutils` package:

```
unsigned short vendor              PCI vendor ID
unsigned short device              PCI device ID
unsigned short subsystem_vendor    PCI subsystem vendor ID
unsigned short subsystem_device    PCI subsystem device ID
unsigned int class                 Combination of Base Class,
                                   Subclass and Program Interface
```

Then there are the fields that allow us to find the memory, I/O, and interrupt resources used by the PCI device. These resources are generally set up on a PC by the BIOS, but may be remapped by the kernel, or in some cases completely set up by the kernel from scratch. When Linux reassigns resources, it may not write the changed values to the configuration space of the PCI device, so it is important that you do not read these values from the device itself, but instead use the values stored in the struct `pci_dev` associated with the device:

```
unsigned int irq              Interrupt line (IRQ)
struct resource resource[]    I/O and memory regions
```

The I/O and memory resources are described by a structure which is defined in the file `include/linux/ioport.h`. The parts of the structure that may be relevant to you at this stage are:

```
unsigned long start, end
unsigned long flags
```

The `start` and `end` fields give the address range that the device occupies, and the `flags` field contains flags also defined in `include/linux/ioport.h`. In this case each resource should have either the `IORESOURCE_IO` (for I/O ports) or `IORESOURCE_MEM` (for MMIO region) bits set, depending on the type of access the card provides. For compatibility across potential structure changes, it's best to use the `pci_resource_start`, `pci_resource_end`, and `pci_resource_flags` macros to access this information. These take two arguments each – the PCI device structure and the number of the resource as an offset into the resource array listed above. They are currently defined in `include/linux/pci.h` as follows:

```
#define pci_resource_start(dev,bar)    ((dev)->resource[(bar)].start)
#define pci_resource_end(dev,bar)      ((dev)->resource[(bar)].end)
#define pci_resource_flags(dev,bar)    ((dev)->resource[(bar)].flags)
```

There is also a `pci_resource_len` macro, which performs the necessary arithmetic to obtain the length of a region from its start and end addresses.

Finally, for now that is, there is a field that identifies the PCI driver currently controlling the device (if there is one), and a space for storage (by the driver) of any private data that may be required to keep track of the current state of the device:

```
struct pci_driver *driver      PCI driver structure (of which more later)
void *driver_data              Private data for PCI driver
```

Finding PCI Devices

There are actually two ways for your driver to find the PCI devices in the system that it is capable of driving. The driver can manually scan the available busses at initialization time, and immediately start using the devices that it recognizes. Equally, it can register itself with the kernel's PCI subsystem, giving a structure containing callback routines and listing a set of criteria for the devices in which it is interested, and then do nothing until the callback routines are invoked (which will happen whenever a matching device is added to, or removed from the system).

The former method, manual scanning, is used in the 2.2 series and previous versions of the Linux kernel, but doesn't support hot-swappable PCI (CompactPCI, CardBus, etc.). Although it is still possible to do this in the 2.4 kernel, the method is deprecated in favor of the new PCI driver callback system.

Manual Scanning

Although we said that the manual scanning method is deprecated in the 2.4 series, it's still worth explaining it briefly, because it's still necessary in code intended to be used in the 2.2 series kernels.

The simplest form of search uses the pci_find_device function, which takes three arguments – a Vendor ID, a Device ID, and a struct pci_dev * that indicates the position in the kernel's global list of present PCI devices from which to start the search. This is so that you can find the second and subsequent devices that match your criteria, rather than only the first.

To start the search at the beginning of the global list, use NULL as the third argument. To continue the search from the last matching device, use its address. It is permitted to use the constant PCI_ANY_ID as a wildcard. So, if you wish to match any device from a given vendor whose assigned vendor ID in include/linux/pci_ids.h is PCI_VENDOR_ID_MYVENDOR, you might use code such as:

```
struct pci_dev *dev = NULL;

while ((dev=pci_find_device(PCI_VENDOR_ID_MYVENDOR,
        PCI_ANY_ID, dev)))
    setup_device(dev);
```

There are also other functions that allow drivers to search for PCI devices matching other critieria – such as pci_find_class, pci_find_subsys, and pci_find_slot. All these are defined in the header file include/linux/pci.h:

```
struct pci_dev *pci_find_device (unsigned int vendor, unsigned int device,
                                 const struct pci_dev *from);
struct pci_dev *pci_find_subsys (unsigned int vendor, unsigned int device,
                                 unsigned int ss_vendor, unsigned int ss_device,
                                 const struct pci_dev *from);
struct pci_dev *pci_find_class  (unsigned int class, const struct pci_dev *from);
struct pci_dev *pci_find_slot   (unsigned int bus, unsigned int devfn);
```

PCI Drivers

Although the method given above will still work in the 2.4 series, the recommended way to write a PCI device driver for a 2.4 kernel is to register the presence of your driver's probe routine, along with some data about the relevant devices, with the PCI subsystem. This PCI subsystem is specific to the 2.4 series, and is not present in 2.2 kernels. All the relevant information about the driver is stored in a `struct pci_driver`, which your initialization routine should populate and then register with the function `register_pci_driver`. The structure and the routines are defined in `include/linux/pci.h`:

```
int pci_register_driver(struct pci_driver *);
void pci_unregister_driver(struct pci_driver *);
```

The fields of the struct `pci_driver` that need to be populated are as follows:

`char *name`	The name of the device driver.
`const struct pci_device_id *id_table`	A list of device IDs that are supported (of which more in a moment).
`int (*probe) (struct pci_dev *dev, const struct pci_device_id *id)`	Probe routine, called by the kernel's PCI subsystem when a device matching one of the `id_table` entries is found.
`void (*remove) (struct pci_dev *dev)`	Called by the kernel's PCI subsystem when a device is removed or upon unregistering the `pci_driver`.
`void (*suspend) (struct pci_dev *dev)`	Called by power management code to notify the driver that the device has been suspended.
`void (*resume) (struct pci_dev *dev)`	Called by power management code to notify the driver that the device has been woken up, and may need re-initialization.

The struct `pci_device_id`, also defined in `include/linux/pci.h`, contains information similar to that which was passed to the `pci_find_` routines. That is:

`unsigned int vendor, device`	Required vendor/device ID numbers or `PCI_ANY_ID` to indicate "Don't care."
`unsigned int subvendor, subdevice`	Required subsystem ID numbers or `PCI_ANY_ID`.
`unsigned int class, class_mask`	Combination of one byte for each of (class, subclass, program-interface), and a bitmask that has bits set to '1' for each bit which is to be matched. Bits in the class field for which the corresponding bit in the `class_mask` field is not set do not need to be matched.
`unsigned long driver_data`	Private data for use by the driver.

As the precise `pci_device_id` that was matched is passed to the driver's `probe` routine, the `driver_data` field can be used for board-specific information that differs in the various devices supported by a driver. For example, a driver that supports various revisions of a board or chipset may place a set of `flags` in the `driver_data` field, to indicate the capabilities of the board(s) matched by each `pci_device_id` structure, so that the driver's `probe` routine doesn't need to re-check the exact device numbers.

The `id_table` field of the `pci_driver` structure should point to an array of these `pci_device_id` structures, terminated with an all-zero entry.

When the driver is first registered, its `probe` function is called for every PCI device in the system that matches an entry in the `pci_device_id` list, and isn't already assigned to another driver. If matching hot-pluggable devices are later added, the kernel's PCI subsystem will call the `probe` function for each registered driver that matches the new device, until one of them returns zero to indicate that it has accepted the device.

You are guaranteed that your driver's `probe` function will be called in a process context (see the section on 'Execution Context' near the beginning of the chapter), and this means that the function is permitted to sleep if necessary. The function should return zero if it has accepted the device and will drive it; otherwise, it should return a non-zero error code to allow the PCI subsystem to offer it to other drivers whose ID list it matches. Error codes are defined in the files `include/linux/errno.h` and `include/asm/errno.h` and as with all functions in the Linux kernel, it is normal to return a negative value to signal the error. For example:

```
return -EIO;    /* I/O error encountered */
```

The driver's `remove` function will be called only for devices that the `probe` function has accepted. It will be called automatically by the kernel's PCI subsystem when hot-pluggable devices are removed from the system, or when the driver is unregistered by calling `pci_unregister_driver`. At this point, the `remove` function will be called for each device that has been allocated to the driver.

Some kernels may not have the power management code enabled, and in those cases the `suspend` and `resume` functions may never be called. The fields in the structure are still present in all cases, however, the driver being able to indicate that such functionality is not supported by setting them to NULL.

PCI Access Functions

To start with, before your driver attempts to access the I/O ports or shared memory of a device, it should ensure that the device is enabled by calling the `pci_enable_device` routine. This will attempt to allocate I/O and memory regions as necessary, and ensure that the device is fully powered up. You should be prepared to handle the possibility that `pci_enable_device` will fail, and deal with that appropriately, probably by printing a warning message and returning a non-zero result from the initialization procedure. The routine returns a non-zero value to indicate failure, or zero to indicate success:

```
int pci_enable_device(struct pci_dev *dev);
```

Also, if you are intending to use bus mastering functionality, you should enable that separately by using the `pci_set_master` function. This function may not fail:

```
void pci_set_master(struct pci_dev *dev);
```

Once the device is enabled, you can access the PCI configuration space using `pci_read_config_byte` and its associated routines for all combinations of read/write and byte/word/dword accesses. Note that the `pci_read_config_*` routines don't return the value that was obtained; instead they take a pointer to a place to store the value and return an error code (or zero to indicate success):

```
int pci_read_config_byte(struct pci_dev *dev, int where, u8 *val);
int pci_read_config_word(struct pci_dev *dev, int where, u16 *val);
int pci_read_config_dword(struct pci_dev *dev, int where, u32 *val);
int pci_write_config_byte(struct pci_dev *dev, int where, u8 val);
int pci_write_config_word(struct pci_dev *dev, int where, u16 val);
int pci_write_config_dword(struct pci_dev *dev, int where, u32 val);
```

Resource Allocation

Before accessing either I/O ports or memory regions, they must be properly allocated, and in the case of memory, the physical regions need to be mapped into the CPU's virtual address space – just as any other physical pages need to be mapped to virtual addresses.

To allocate either I/O or memory space, the functions `request_region` and `request_mem_region` are used respectively. Each take as arguments the start address and length of the required region, and a name, which will be used in the displaying of the allocation map via the `/proc/ioports` or `/proc/iomem` files – assuming that the special 'proc' filesystem is mounted in its normal place.

The return value of these functions will be either NULL in the case of a failure to allocate the requested region, or a pointer to the newly-allocated `struct` resource, if the allocation was successful. Actually, in the 2.4 series of kernels, these are macros that use a single generic `__request_region` function to allocate regions from a different base 'resource', but this fact should be transparent to the code that uses the macros, and they may be used as if they were defined as follows:

```
struct resource *request_region(unsigned long start,
                         unsigned long n, const char * name);
struct resource *request_mem_region(unsigned long start,
                           unsigned long n, const char * name);
```

It is not necessary to store the returned address of the new resource, because the region can be deallocated with the `release_region` or `release_mem_region` functions later. These two functions take the same arguments as the corresponding allocation functions. All these functions are defined in `include/ioport.h`. Again, these are actually macros based on a more generic 'resource' handling function, but they can be used as if they were functions defined as follows:

```
void release_region(unsigned long start, unsigned long n);
void release_mem_region(unsigned long start, unsigned long n);
```

Once the resource has been allocated, you may start using I/O ports immediately, but memory areas must still be mapped into the kernel's virtual address space before they can be accessed. For this, you use the `ioremap` function call, passing it the physical address that was found in the resource structure for your device, and the length in bytes of your desired mapping. Usually, these will be the exact values of `start` and `length` that were provided by the `pci_resource_start` and `pci_resource_len` macros that were documented earlier.

The mapping set up by `ioremap` should be destroyed at a later date, by passing the address that it returned to the converse `iounmap` function.

```
void *ioremap(unsigned long offset, unsigned long size);
void iounmap(void * addr);
```

The `ioremap` function will return a address in the CPU's 'virtual' address space, which you must not use directly as a pointer, but through the access macros `readb`, `readw`, `readl`, `writeb`, `writew` and `writel`. Although directly accessing the mapped area happens to work at the moment on 32-bit Intel machines, it is not portable and is definitely not correct. Alpha 21064 processors, for example, do not have the capability to address individual bytes, and actually have to use different virtual addresses for different widths of access to the bus, letting the PCI chipset fix up the access. In this case, it is absolutely essential that the access macros are correctly used.

Interrupt Handlers

Aside from I/O and memory regions, you will probably also need to set up an interrupt handler – a piece of code that is executed each time the hardware asserts an IRQ line on the PCI bus.

Interrupt handlers were mentioned briefly in the section on "Execution Context" near the beginning of the chapter – interrupts may happen at any time, and handlers should operate very quickly without sleeping or accessing user-space memory areas.

An interrupt handler has the following prototype:

```
void my_irqhandler(int irq, void *dev_id, struct pt_regs *regs);
```

The first argument, `irq`, is the numeric value of the IRQ line that has been triggered. The interrupt handler may use this value if it is registered as a handler for more than one interrupt level – for example if a board has more than one interrupt line, or if the same interrupt handler is registered multiple times for different boards. The second argument, `*dev_id`, is an opaque pointer, never dereferenced by the kernel, which will have been passed by the driver at the time the interrupt handler was registered. Finally, `*regs` contains a pointer to the place in memory where the registers were stored when the CPU was interrupted. Normally, you will not need to access the registers, but for example the floating point exceptions on Intel 386 processors are signaled by an interrupt, and the interrupt handler for that interrupt has to be able to access and modify the registers before returning.

To register an interrupt handler for a certain IRQ, the `request_irq` routine, defined in `include/linux/sched.h`, is used:

```
int request_irq(unsigned int irq,
                void (*handler)(int, void *, struct pt_regs *),
                unsigned long irqflags, const char *devname,
                void *dev_id);
```

Working our way through the arguments, the first gives the number of the IRQ line that is to be requested, and the second gives a pointer to the actual interrupt handler that is to be invoked on any subsequent assertion of the IRQ line by the hardware. Meanwhile, `devname` is used for printing the interrupt assignments in the special `/proc/interrupts` file, and `dev_id` is the opaque pointer that was already mentioned, and is passed to the interrupt handler each time it is invoked. The `irqflags` argument may contain any of the flags defined in `include/asm/signal.h`. Many of the possible flags are obsoleted or unsupported, and the main ones it's necessary to know about are:

SA_SHIRQ	Accept shared interrupts. Unless this flag is set on all handlers, only one interrupt handler may register on each IRQ level. For sanely-designed PCI devices, it should never be necessary to register an interrupt handler without SA_SHIRQ.
SA_INTERRUPT	When invoking the interrupt handler, disable interrupts on the CPU which is running. This flag should not be set by normal device drivers.
SA_SAMPLE_RANDOM	Use the timing of this interrupt to contribute to the 'entropy pool' which is used to generate data for the /dev/random device.

Finally, an interrupt handler is deregistered with the free_irq function, which should be passed the same irq and dev_id arguments that were passed to the request_irq function.

```
void free_irq(unsigned int irq, void *dev_id);
```

Note that although the kernel never dereferences the dev_id pointer, it does use it to determine which IRQ handler should be freed when more than one handler is registered for the same interrupt. Because of this, your driver shouldn't just set it to NULL if it doesn't need to use it – set it to something specific to your driver instead.

Applicom Module PCI Driver Code

Now a chapter that's all theory and no practice makes Jack the programmer a dull boy, so in this section, we're going to work through some code. In this case, it's a pci_driver registration, with simple probe code for the Applicom fieldbus card I mentioned at the beginning of the chapter.

We begin with the function declaration:

```
static int apdrv_probe(struct pci_dev *dev, const struct pci_device_id *devid)
{
```

We also need to declare two local variables. The first will store the virtual address at which the board's MMIO region is mapped, and the other will maintain the 'board number' with which the jumpers on the board are configured:

```
void *VirtIO;
int boardno;
```

Initialization over, we first try to enable the device. If the pci_enable_device routine returns a non-zero result indicating that it failed to assign resources to the device, then we cannot continue, so we return immediately with an appropriate error code:

```
if (pci_enable_device(dev))
    return -EIO;
```

Assuming we can enable the device, we attempt to map the device's memory space into the kernel's virtual memory map. Again, we check for failure and return an appropriate error code if necessary. Note that in neither this case nor the case above do we print an error message – these failure modes could be triggered simply by running low on resources, and if every driver were to print error messages when that happened, then resources would be wasted even more.

```
VirtIO = ioremap(pci_resource_start(dev, 0), pci_resource_len(dev, 0));
if (!VirtIO)
    return -EIO;
```

Now we call a function that probes the board to see if it's behaving as we think an Applicom board should. There will usually be some kind of test specific to the hardware for which your driver is written, which can be used to check if it is in working order. In this case, because it's not particularly important that you know exactly how to check the particular board we're using for the example, we've moved this test into a separate function: ac_probe_board.

If the board doesn't seem to be behaving normally, we don't want to take responsibility for it, and again we return an error code having first used iounmap to undo the mapping performed by ioremap above.

As this is an unexpected (although not unanticipated) failure mode, we also print an error message in this case. The printk routine, is very similar to printf and the KERN_INFO macro, producing just an extra piece of text added at the beginning of the output to signify the importance of the line on which it occurs. It is defined in include/linux/kernel.h.

```
if ((boardno = ac_probe_board(dev->resource[0].start,
                (unsigned long)VirtIO)) == -1) {
    printk(KERN_INFO "ac.o: PCI Applicom device doesn't have"
        " correct signature.\n");
    iounmap(VirtIO);
    return -EIO;
}
```

If all still seems OK, we must go on to register an interrupt handler for the interrupt number that is found in the pci_dev structure for this device. We use the SA_SHIRQ flag to signify that we support shared IRQs. Again, we will complain, iounmap, and quit if it doesn't happen as expected:

```
if (request_irq(dev->irq, &ac_interrupt, SA_SHIRQ,
        "Applicom PCI", dev)) {
    printk(KERN_INFO "Could not allocate IRQ %d for "
        "PCI Applicom device.\n", dev->irq);
    iounmap(VirtIO);
    return -EIO;
}
```

If we've made it this far without already returning an error code, then all has gone well, so we return a successful return code to indicate that we are going to control this device and that it shouldn't be offered to any other drivers that happen to match it:

```
    return 0;
}
```

Access to User Space Memory

So now we've found the device and we know how to talk to it – we need to be able to copy data packets to and from the user-space programs that want to communicate with the device.

As we mentioned before, user-space data needs special treatment when you access it from within the kernel. There are three main problems that may occur when using a buffer provided by the user:

❏   Firstly, the user may have passed an invalid pointer – it may try to trick your code into overwriting an area of kernel or user memory to which it does not have permission to write. Or it may try to get your code to read from an area that contains sensitive data, which it is not permitted to read directly.

❏   Secondly, while kernel data structures are never paged out to disc, the buffer that a user has provided may not actually be present in physical RAM, so any access to it may incur a page fault and your code will have to wait for the page to be brought back in from swap space.

❏   Thirdly, you must be aware that different processes do not share the same address space. User-space pointers must obviously only be used in the same process context as the process that passed the buffer pointer.

The fact that accessing user-space pointers may cause a page fault means that you may not access user-space addresses in any situation when you may not sleep – when the CPU on which your code is running has interrupts disabled, or when your code is holding a spinlock, for example. (We'll look at spinlocks and other types of lock later.)

Also, you may not access user-space from within an interrupt handler - not only because it may cause your interrupt handler to sleep while it waits for a page to be brought in, but because you have no idea in which process's context, if any, your handler will be executed.

To help overcome these pitfalls, the Linux system provides the `copy_to_user` and `copy_from_user` macros for accessing user-space data. These macros handle the necessary permission checks and behave correctly if a page fault occurs for whatever reason.

There are two main types of reason why a page fault may occur. It is expected that the most common will be the case where the page exists, but is not currently mapped into physical memory. This may happen either if a data page is moved to swap space to make room in physical RAM, or if pages reside in an executable on the file system and need to be demand-loaded (Linux does not load programs into memory immediately when they're executed, it waits for each page to be accessed before 'demand-loading' it.)

In these cases, the page fault handler will sleep and wait for the requested page to be brought into memory, before continuing with the copy as if nothing had happened.

The other class of page faults occur when the requested access is invalid – perhaps because an invalid pointer was dereferenced, or because an attempt was made to write to areas marked as read-only. If this class of page fault occurs, then the macro 'returns' a non-zero result to indicate this fact.

As mentioned before, because of the possibility that the page fault handler may sleep, and because interrupts may occur in the context of any process (not just the process that set up the buffer), you may not touch user-space from within an interrupt handler.

```
copy_to_user(to, from, n)
copy_from_user(to, from, n)
```

Each of these routines copies data in one direction between a user-space buffer and the kernel, waiting for paging to occur if necessary. The third argument gives the number of bytes to be copied. Upon success they return zero, or on failure they return the number of bytes that were remaining to be copied when the error occurred. So it's common to see them used as follows:

```
if (copy_to_user(buf, result, sizeof(result)))
    return -EFAULT;   /* Bad address */
```

These routines are used throughout the Linux kernel, and it is probably not necessary to go into more detail regarding their use – but you should be aware of the above restrictions on their use, and make sure that you don't use them when you shouldn't.

The kiobuf Architecture

Under the 2.2 kernel, it was not possible for interrupt handlers or DMA-capable hardware to access buffers in user-space directly. It was necessary to copy data via a buffer in kernel space, which in some cases could cause a severe performance hit, especially to drivers that rely on copying large amounts of data between the hardware and the user-space process, such as framegrabber and sound cards.

During the development of the 2.3 kernel series, a method was devised to allow drivers to lock down pages of user-space memory, so that they could be used for direct access without all the restrictions above – the kiobuf facility.

This works first by ensuring that the desired pages are present in physical memory, bringing them in from swap space if necessary, and then locking them down so that they cannot be paged back out or moved. Once this is done, it is safe to access them from any code until the pages are later unlocked.

To use the kiobuf facility, you must first allocate an array of kiobuf structures in which the system will keep data about the mapping. For this you use the `alloc_kiovec` routine:

```
int alloc_kiovec(int nr, struct kiobuf **bufp);
void free_kiovec(int nr, struct kiobuf **bufp);
```

These routines simply allocate and free an array of kiobuf structures, for use with the 'real' kiobuf operations, which are described below. The reason for dealing with kiobufs in arrays rather than individually is to allow us to support the scatter/gather operation of devices easily. Each kiobuf can only represent a single contiguous address range, so to be capable of dealing with data from different areas of memory in a single transfer, we need to group the kiobufs together into kiovecs.

A scatter/gather operation is a form of DMA where the device is passed an ordered list of pages into which the data should be copied, rather than just a single physical address and length, which is all that primitive DMA-capable devices could manage. It means that the kernel no longer needs to be able to allocate large chunks of contiguous physical memory, and does not have to work so hard to keep memory allocations defragmented.

Having allocated space for an array of kiobufs, each must then be configured correctly with the virtual address and size of the memory range that it should represent, allowing the memory management code to verify the existence of each page and ensure that each is correctly accessible for either reading or full access, depending on the parameters passed to the map_user_kiobuf routine:

```
int map_user_kiobuf(int rw, struct kiobuf *iobuf,
                    unsigned long va, size_t len);
```

The rw argument indicates whether the kiobuf is to be used for read-only or full access – zero means read-only, and one is used to request write access. Attempting to enable write access to pages for which the currently active process does not have sufficient permissions will cause the mapping to fail. Other less obvious restrictions on the behavior of the map_user_kiobuf routine are that the va argument (short for 'virtual address') must be page-aligned (must be an exact multiple of the page size on the system, defined as PAGE_SIZE in include/asm/page.h), and the length of the addressed range must not be larger then 64 KB. For larger ranges, you can use multiple kiobufs.

Once each kiobuf is correctly set up to point at the required area of memory, the final stage necessary before the pages can be safely accessed is to lock the whole range of pages into physical memory. This is achieved by using the lock_kiovec routine:

```
int lock_kiovec(int nr, struct kiobuf *iovec[], int wait);
int unlock_kiovec(int nr, struct kiobuf *iovec[]);
```

The wait argument to lock_kiovec controls its behavior when one of the pages is found to be absent, and requires paging in from swap space. If wait is zero, the routine may return an error of -EAGAIN to indicate that one or more pages were not present. Otherwise, the routine will wait until all pages are available and locked.

Once the pages are mapped, the address of each page within a kiobuf is accessible through the maplist field, which points to an array of struct page structures, one for each page mapped in the kiobuf. A further complication is that on recent Intel processors with the Physical Address Extension (PAE), these physical pages may be in high memory (above 4 GB), which isn't directly accessible by the kernel, so although you may have already locked them into physical memory, you may also need to ensure that they are mapped into the current virtual memory map. To do this, you use the kmap routine, which returns a real virtual address that you can finally use to access the locked page. After you have finished accessing the page, use the kunmap function to remove the virtual mapping. These two routines are defined in include/linux/highmem.h, which may also include include/asm/highmem.h:

```
unsigned long kmap(struct page *page);
void kunmap(struct page *page);
```

Because it plays clever games with virtual memory regions to avoid expensive cache flushes (it re-uses a pre-allocated range of virtual memory addresses), the kmap routine may have to sleep to wait for a virtual address to become free. It doesn't matter if you don't understand the reasoning – just be aware that it can sleep.

Applicom kiobuf Code

Getting back to the Applicom board driver, we can see that in order to prevent the interrupt handler from attempting to access the board while we are transferring a packet into or out of it, we should disable interrupts while we perform the transfer. This means that we cannot touch the user's buffer directly during the transfer – we cannot just copy the packet directly from the user to the Applicom card.

Either we need to copy the whole packet into a kernel-space 'bounce buffer' first (so called because the data 'bounces' in and out of it), then disable interrupts while we transfer it to the card, or we should use the kiobuf code to lock down the user's buffer before doing the transfer. Bounce buffers are a waste of time and resources, so this code taken from the `ac_write` routine uses the latter option.

First, we allocate a single kiobuf entry – we only have one region to lock down:

```
struct kiobuf *iobuf;

ret = alloc_kiovec(1, &iobuf);
    if (ret)
        return ret;
```

If the allocation fails, we return the error code. If all is well, we set up the mapping of our single kiobuf. This is tricky because kiobuf mappings always have to be page-aligned. So the area we actually map in the kiobuf runs from the beginning of the first page in the user's buffer to the end of the last page. (The struct `mailbox` used here is just the structure that is passed to and from the Applicom board. Hence `sizeof(struct mailbox)` is the length of the buffer to be copied when the user wants to send or receive a packet.)

```
bufadr=((unsigned long)buf) & PAGE_MASK;
bufofs=((unsigned long)buf) & ~PAGE_MASK;

ret = map_user_kiobuf(READ, iobuf, bufadr,
                    sizeof(struct mailbox) + bufofs);
```

Again, if it fails we need to free the previously allocated kiovec and return an appropriate error code to the caller:

```
if (ret) {
    free_kiovec(1, &iobuf);
    return ret;
}
```

If that succeeded, we lock down the buffer immediately. The early version of the kiovec patches developed for the 2.2 kernels didn't require this step – the mapping also locked the buffers in place. But in the final version of the kiobuf code in the 2.4 kernels, the locking is a separate step.

```
ret = lock_kiovec(1, &iobuf, 1);
if (ret) {
    unmap_kiobuf(iobuf);
    free_kiovec(1, &iobuf);
    return ret;
}
```

Next we need to extract the actual addresses to which the pages are mapped, now that they've been locked into memory. Luckily, we know we'll only need access to two pages at most – our packet is less than a page long, so the worst case is that it'll go over the end of the first page and onto a second. The nr_pages field of iobuf tells us how many pages were mapped.

As mentioned earlier, we have to use kmap to ensure that each page is mapped into the kernel's virtual memory before we disable interrupts, because of the possibility that it may need to sleep:

```
pageadr[0] = kmap(iobuf->maplist[0]);
if (iobuf->nr_pages > 1)
    pageadr[1] = kmap(iobuf->maplist[1]);
```

Now all the buffers are locked down, we can disable interrupts and copy the packet to the card. The spin_lock_irq function disables interrupts, and is explained later. Actually, to be pedantic, we should check here whether the card is ready to receive a packet, and wait until it's ready if necessary – the code to do so is omitted here for simplicity but is included later as an example of wait queue handling.

```
spin_lock_irq(&apbs[IndexCard].mutex);
```

The source address is the address at which the first page is mapped, plus the offset in the page at which the packet was found. We calculated this offset earlier, just before the map_user_kiobuf function call.

```
from = (char *)pageadr[0] + bufofs;
```

The destination address is a constant offset into the address where we mapped the PCI card's memory region. This was set up and recorded by the apdrv_probe routine, which we saw earlier.

```
to = (unsigned long) apbs[IndexCard].VirtIO + RAM_FROM_PC;
```

Now the addresses are set up, we can perform the copy:

```
for (i = 0; i < sizeof(struct mailbox); i++) {
    writeb(*(from++), to++);
```

The second page isn't guaranteed to be located immediately after the end of the first, so, after we have dealt with the final byte on the first page, we need to change the source address to point to the first byte of the second page.

```
    if (!(((unsigned long)from) & PAGE_MASK))
        from = (char *)pageadr[1];
}
```

Now we're done, we can release the lock and re-enable interrupts...

```
spin_unlock_irq(&apbs[IndexCard].mutex);
```

... and finally unmap each page, and unlock, unmap, and free the kiobuf we've been using:

```
kunmap(iobuf->maplist[0]);
if (iobuf->nr_pages > 1)
    kunmap(iobuf->maplist[1]);
unlock_kiovec(1, &iobuf);
unmap_kiobuf(iobuf);
free_kiovec(1, &iobuf);
```

Locking Primitives

There are several basic lock operations available within the Linux kernel, each of which is designed for use in different situations appropriate to its behavior and the restrictions on its use.

Semaphores

The simplest of these is a traditional semaphore, which is often used as a mutual exclusion lock to allow different sections of code to mutually exclude each other. That is, to prevent concurrent access to data structures or procedures.

A traditional semaphore contains a counter, which is increased by the up operation, and decreased by the down operation. However, the value of the counter may never be negative, so when the value of the counter is zero, any call to down will cause the calling process to sleep until another process makes a call to up. If the up operation doesn't happen, the process attempting the down operation will sleep for ever.

The Linux implementation of a semaphore conveniently provides functions for the up and down operations, which are called up and down, respectively. These are defined in include/asm/semaphore.h, along with the data structure that holds the counter and other internally-used state information – the struct semaphore.

```
void down(struct semaphore *sem);
void up(struct semaphore *sem);
```

Before it can be used, the struct semaphore must be initialized. The normal way to do this is to use the init_MUTEX or init_MUTEX_LOCKED functions, which set up the internally-used data and reset the counter to one and zero, respectively:

```
struct semaphore MySem, MySem2;
init_MUTEX(&MySem);
init_MUTEX_LOCKED(&MySem2);
```

Alternatively, for a semaphore where the storage space is statically allocated (where the struct semaphore is a global variable rather than a local variable within a function), the DECLARE_MUTEX and DECLARE_MUTEX_LOCKED macros may be used in place of the declaration of the struct semaphore. Therefore, the above example would become:

```
DECLARE_MUTEX (MySem);
DECLARE_MUTEX_LOCKED(MySem2);
```

Once the semaphore is correctly initialized, the down and up functions may be used to manipulate the lock. It is important to remember that while the down operation is waiting for a lock, it places the calling process in a sleeping state, and calls the kernel's schedule function (which is examined in more detail later in this chapter) to allow other processes to utilize the CPU. Because it is not permitted to schedule within an interrupt handler, this means that an interrupt handler may not use the down function. It is, however, permitted to use the up function, because that can never sleep.

There is another function that operates on semaphores, and which may also be used in a context where the caller may not sleep. It is the down_trylock function, which will attempt to decrease the value of the semaphore's counter but which will return an error (a non-zero value) rather than sleeping if it is not possible to do so immediately (because the counter is already zero).

```
int down_trylock(struct semaphore *sem);
```

Spinlocks

Spinlocks are also used in the kernel for mutual exclusion purposes, but have a significant difference from semaphores. While waiting to obtain a spinlock, a process will not relinquish the CPU, but will 'spin' as the name implies, hogging the CPU and repeatedly checking the state of the lock until it is possible to 'obtain' the lock. This means that spinlocks may be used in interrupt handlers, and also means that they should be locked only for extremely short periods of time. Also, it means that a process should never relinquish the CPU while holding a spinlock; if another section of code were to attempt to obtain the lock then a deadlock could occur – the new section of code would never be able to obtain the lock, and would never relinquish the CPU to allow the original code to release the lock, thereby locking up the system permanently.

Spinlocks are declared to be of type `spinlock_t` and must be initialized with the `spin_lock_init` function before use. The `spin_lock` and `spin_unlock` routines lock and unlock the spinlock respectively. These definitions can be found in `include/linux/spinlock.h`, which includes in turn `include/asm/spinlock.h`.

```
void spin_lock(spinlock_t *lock);
void spin_unlock(spinlock_t *lock);
```

Because spinlocks may be used within an interrupt handler, a further complication is necessary. A deadlock could occur if an interrupt occurred while the spinlock was locked, and the interrupt handler attempted to re-obtain the same lock. Therefore, when obtaining a spinlock that may also be obtained from an interrupt handler, we should make sure that interrupts are disabled on the local CPU (the CPU on which the original `spin_lock` function is called; it doesn't matter if a different CPU attempts to obtain the lock at the same time). Two further spinlock functions provide the required functionality for us – they are `spin_lock_irq` and `spin_unlock_irq`, which disable and enable interrupts on the local CPU respectively, as well as performing the requested action upon the spinlock.

```
void spin_lock_irq(spinlock_t *lock);
void spin_unlock_irq(spinlock_t *lock);
```

The Big Kernel Lock

When Linux was first made to run on multiprocessor machines during the 1.3 development series, the locking was extremely simple and inefficient. There was a single lock, known as the 'big kernel lock' (BKL), which prevented two CPUs from being in kernel mode at the same time. If a process running on one CPU made a system call while another CPU was already in the kernel, then it had to wait for the other to finish. This lock still lives on, but by now large amounts of code have been taken out from under its protection, allowing the kernel to make far better use of multiple CPUs. In the 2.4 kernel, initialization code and file system code still hold the BKL most of the time, and it's also obtained during many system calls. Most device drivers, however, don't hold the BKL outside their initialization routine. While this makes the 2.4 kernel far more efficient on multiprocessor machines, it does mean that driver code must be SMP-aware and take care to avoid race conditions.

The kernel lock is special, because it's automatically released when a process relinquishes the CPU, and re-obtained when that process is rescheduled. Another common mistake made by programmers is to call a function that may sleep, such as `copy_from_user` or `kmalloc`, while holding the BKL, and assume that the lock was never released. This is a false assumption – as we've just explained.

For a more detailed discussion of the locking available within the Linux kernel, you could do far worse than to study Paul Russell's "Unreliable Guide To Locking", at http://www.samba.org/netfilter /unreliable-guides/kernel-locking/lklockingguide.html.

Scheduling and Wait Queues

There are times when your driver will have to wait for something to happen. Generally, busy-waiting is a bad thing to do because it wastes CPU time that could be used by other processes. So you should put your process to sleep, and arrange to have it woken up at an appropriate time.

schedule()

The schedule function, the prototype for which is in include/linux/sched.h, is called when a process wants to give up the CPU. Within Linux, kernel code is not preempted – the only way that kernel code may be taken off the CPU is if it explicitly takes itself off the scheduler's run queue, with the exception of temporary interruptions such as hardware interrupts. When you call schedule, it stores the CPU registers and then other processes are given the opportunity to run on the CPU. When your process is returned to the CPU, usually because it has been 'woken' by one of the functions we're about to look at, the schedule function call restores the registers and returns control to the function from which it was called. Aside from the time difference, it is as if nothing had ever happened.

```
void schedule(void);
```

set_current_state()

After calling schedule your code may be rescheduled after a short period of time, after other processes have been given a 'fair' amount of time on the CPU. Sometimes this is a useful thing to do in itself; for example, if you are in the middle of a CPU-intensive piece of code and wish to avoid hogging the CPU.

More often however, your code is waiting for an external event and doesn't wish to be rescheduled until that event occurs. In that case, you can mark the process as being in a non-runnable state, which will prevent the scheduler from putting it back on the CPU. The set_current_state macro performs this function. There are three states that are of interest initially – for a complete list, see include/linux/sched.h:

TASK_RUNNING	This is the normal state for runnable processes.
TASK_UNINTERRUPTIBLE	Not runnable. Must be explicitly woken up.
TASK_INTERRUPTIBLE	Not runnable, but will be automatically switched back to TASK_RUNNING if a signal arrives.

schedule_timeout()

A common requirement by drivers is to wait for an event, but to timeout after a set period of time. This functionality is provided by the schedule_timeout routine, which takes a single argument signifying the length of time, in 'jiffies' or clock ticks, to allow before rescheduling the process. The length of a 'jiffy' is dependent upon the type of system – but there is a macro HZ, defined in include/asm/param.h, which is defined as the number of jiffies per second. For 32-bit Intel machines, this is normally 100, making 1 jiffy equal to 10ms. In Alpha-based computers, the value of HZ is 1024, giving approximately 1ms per jiffy.

Upon return, schedule_timeout returns either a zero value if the timeout expired, or the number of jiffies that were remaining when the process was woken up by some other means (which we're just about to explain).

```
signed long schedule_timeout(signed long timeout);
```

wake_up()

We've seen how to put a process to sleep – the obvious next step is to learn how to wake it up again. To do this, Linux uses a construct known as a 'wait queue'. Before giving up the CPU, the sleeping process must put itself on a queue of processes that want to be woken up when a certain event happens. Then, when the event happens, whichever code is responsible for receiving the event notification – generally an interrupt handler – uses the wake_up function to switch the state of all the waiting processes back to TASK_RUNNING and place them back on the scheduler's queue of runnable processes.

The 'head' of a wait queue is declared to be of type wait_queue_head_t and must be initialized with the init_waitqueue_head function before it's used. As with semaphores and spinlocks, there's a shortcut for static declarations, which declares the structure and initializes it all at once. In this case, the shortcut is:

```
DECLARE_WAIT_QUEUE_HEAD(name);
```

which replaces:

```
wait_queue_head_t name;
init_waitqueue_head(&name);
```

The above are defined in include/linux/wait.h.

The wake_up function itself is actually a macro that calls a __wake_up function with an extra argument. If you're curious you can look up the definition in include/linux/sched.h, but otherwise you can just treat if as if it were defined as:

```
void wake_up(wait_queue_head_t *q);
```

add_wait_queue()

Before a process can be woken up, of course, you have to have placed it on the wait queue. To do this, you declare a structure of type wait_queue_t, initialize it with the task structure of the current process, and add it to the wait queue head. This goes as follows:

```
wait_queue_t wait;
init_waitqueue_entry(&wait, current);
add_wait_queue(&name, &wait);
```

Again, there's a shortcut for the declaration and initialization of the wait_queue_t:

```
DECLARE_WAITQUEUE(wait, current);
```

The macro current is best thought of as a global variable that always points to the task data structure for the currently-running process. Aside from knowing that its type, struct task_struct *, by a happy coincidence (or not) matches the prototype of the init_waitqueue_entry function, and is defined in include/linux/sched.h, you don't need to know much more about it at this stage.

```
void init_waitqueue_entry(wait_queue_t *q, struct task_struct *p);
void add_wait_queue(wait_queue_head_t *q, wait_queue_t * wait);
```

remove_wait_queue()

Once your progress has been woken up, you need to remove the wait queue entry from the queue to prevent the same process from being woken up again later by another occurrence of the same event. This is done by using the remove_wait_queue function, which takes exactly the same arguments as the add_wait_queue function:

```
void remove_wait_queue(wait_queue_head_t *q, wait_queue_t * wait);
```

sleep_on() and Race Conditions

There's a simple function that groups together a number of these functions to allow a process to set up a wait queue and sleep with a single function call. It's called sleep_on and it takes a single argument – the address of the wait queue head. There are also variants for TASK_INTERRUPTIBLE sleep and for using schedule_timeout instead of schedule.

I'm going to explain how it works because it's a prime example of how not to use wait queues if you want safe code – there's a simple heuristic for determining whether you should use sleep_on and friends: "If you have to ask, it's not safe to use it". In fact, Linus Torvalds has agreed to remove it entirely in the early stages of the 2.5 series of development kernels.

This (with a little rearrangement) is the code of sleep_on (found in the file kernel/sched.c):

```
void sleep_on(wait_queue_head_t *q)
{
    unsigned long flags;
    wait_queue_t wait;
    init_waitqueue_entry(&wait, current);

    set_current_state(TASK_UNINTERRUPTIBLE);
    add_wait_queue(q, &wait);
    schedule();
    remove_wait_queue(q, &wait);
}
```

This is all very well – but often it has been used in the following way:

```
while (!event_has_happened)
    sleep_on(event_wait_queue);
```

Now consider what happens if the event and the wake_up call happen on another CPU between the check and the call to sleep_on. The naïve code above will just go to sleep, even though the event has already happened, and stay asleep for ever unless the event is repeated. On a single-CPU machine, this is less of an issue, but if the wake_up is performed from an interrupt handler, it could still occur during the vulnerable period between the check and the sleep_on.

What we should do is put ourself on the wait queue, then check the status of the event, and call schedule if necessary. Then, if the wake_up happens after we've checked the status, it will still switch the process back into TASK_RUNNING state, and the schedule call will only give up the CPU for a short period of time before returning.

Note that you should obviously set the process state to TASK_INTERRUPTIBLE before adding yourself to the wait queue – otherwise the event could happen before you do so, and you still may sleep forever.

Having warned you off sleep_on and the associated routines interruptible_sleep_on, sleep_on_timeout and interruptible_sleep_on_timeout, we should probably admit that there are a few situations in which it is actually safe to use them.

In particular, when both the sleeping code and the waking code are protected by the Big Kernel Lock, it's safe to use them because the lock won't be dropped until sleep_on calls into schedule, and the wake_up therefore can't happen in the middle of going to sleep. This covers a lot of file system code in the 2.4 kernels, although that fact may well change during 2.5 development. Even this exception, though, has a caveat – you must not do anything between the status check and the sleep_on that may cause the process to sleep and hence temporarily drop the kernel lock. This includes accessing user-space memory, and certain calls to kmalloc, as described above in the section on the BKL.

Back to the Applicom Card

The Applicom driver is not one of the few cases where it's safe to use sleep_on, so we have to handle the wait queues properly for ourselves. This is some of the extra code that we omitted from our earlier kiobuf example taken from ac_write.

Once we've locked down and mapped the user's buffer to be copied to the card, rather than going ahead immediately as we did in the earlier code, we need to wait until the card is ready to receive a packet from us – if we blindly copy data to the card's buffer while it's not ready to receive anything, then we'll accomplish nothing except to discard our data and waste CPU cycles.

First, having obtained the spinlock and disabled interrupts, we put the current task onto the wait queue that is used for tasks wishing to write to the board:

```
set_current_state(TASK_INTERRUPTIBLE);
add_wait_queue(&apbs[IndexCard].FlagSleepSend, &wait);
```

Now we enter a loop that will continue until the card indicates that it is ready to receive data – which it does by returning zero in response to a read from the DATA_FROM_PC_READY register. Until it returns zero, we have to wait, because it isn't ready. Note that, in this case, the exact use of this particular register on this particular card isn't important – most peripheral cards will have a similar register that needs to be checked for readiness before copying data to or from the shared memory region:

```
while (readb(apbs[IndexCard].VirtIO + DATA_FROM_PC_READY) != 0) {
```

If the card is ready immediately, then the inside of the loop is skipped entirely and the execution continues. However, if the card isn't yet ready, we need to sleep and wait for it to generate an interrupt. We release the spinlock, re-enable interrupts, and call the schedule function to wait until we're woken:

```
spin_unlock_irq(&apbs[IndexCard].mutex);
schedule();
```

At this point, the process sleeps until it's woken. This will happen either when the interrupt happens and the interrupt handler code calls wake_up on the FlagSleepSend wait queue to which we added ourselves, or, as we set our state to TASK_INTERRUPTIBLE, it could happen if a signal arrives while we're waiting. First, we check for the latter condition:

```
        if (signal_pending(current)) {
```

If the condition is true, then we were woken by a signal, so we remove ourselves from the wait queue, free up all the kiobuf stuff and return with an appropriate error code:

```
        remove_wait_queue(&apbs[IndexCard].FlagSleepSend, &wait);
        kunmap(iobuf->maplist[0]);
        if (iobuf->nr_pages > 1)
            kunmap(iobuf->maplist[1]);
        unlock_kiovec(1, &iobuf);
        unmap_kiobuf(iobuf);
        free_kiovec(1, &iobuf);
        return -EINTR;
    }
```

Having eliminated the possibility of a signal, we know that the card was ready to talk to someone. However, we can't just go ahead and send data to the card, because there might be more than one process waiting to write to it, and they still might have got to this place in the code before us. So we re-obtain the spinlock, and loop back to the beginning of the while loop. If another process has beaten us to it, it will take some time to re-obtain the spinlock, and by the time we do manage, the card will be busy again so we'll just have to release the spinlock and wait again.

```
    spin_lock_irq(&apbs[IndexCard].mutex);
}
```

This is the end of the while loop. By the time we get here, we know that we are holding the spinlock that protects access to the card, and that it's ready to accept a packet from us.

We now remove ourselves from the wait queue and set the task state back to TASK_RUNNING, in case the card was ready the first time we checked it, and hence we didn't have to wait for an interrupt, which will have performed those two tasks for us:

```
    set_current_state(TASK_RUNNING);
    remove_wait_queue(&apbs[IndexCard].FlagSleepSend, &wait);
```

Now we perform the actual copy of the packet to the card, as in the example earlier, and when that's done, we release the spinlock for the last time.

Module Use Counts

Another common mistake made by kernel programmers regards the handling of module use counts. The principle behind module use counts is very simple. Each module keeps a count of the number of times it is in use, and when that reaches zero, it is safe for the module to be removed. The two macros that are used to manipulate the module's use count are MOD_INC_USE_COUNT and MOD_DEC_USE_COUNT. A driver implemented as a module should ensure that its use count is non-zero at all times when code or data structures that it contains could be referenced by the kernel.

In the 2.2 series kernels, it was normal practice for the open routine of a device driver to increase the usage count, and for the release routine to decrease it again. Before calling either of these routines, the kernel would obtain the Big Kernel Lock, which prevented the module from being unloaded while the routine was actually running, because the function that is called to unload a module also required the Big Kernel Lock. Of course, let's not forget that a module cannot be unloaded unless it does something that might sleep during its execution.

This kind of code used to be common:

```
int my_driver_open(struct inode *inode, struct file *filp)
{
    struct my_driver_private priv;

    priv = kmalloc(sizeof(*priv), GFP_KERNEL);
    if (!priv)
        return -ENOMEM;

    filp->private_data = priv;
    MOD_INC_USE_COUNT;
    return 0;
}
```

Now consider what happens if the kmalloc call has to sleep to allocate the requested memory, and if while it's sleeping another process attempts to remove the module. By the time the kmalloc returns, the function to which it's attempting to return has been removed and BOOM!

The correct approach in the 2.2 kernels is to increase the use count speculatively, then reduce it again if anything goes wrong. Not only that, but you need to be aware that module removal is a two-stage process, and if your module_exit routine can sleep, then the module might already have been marked for deletion before the open routine was called. In the 2.2 kernels, there's not a lot you can do about this except say "Don't sleep in your module's cleanup function".

To accommodate this situation, a new function, try_inc_mod_count, has been made available in the 2.4 series, which returns a success code of 1 if the increment was successful, or zero if the module has already been marked for deletion. Unlike the MOD_INC_USE_COUNT macro, try_inc_mod_count needs to be passed a pointer to the module information structure of the module it's supposed to be dealing with. In modular code, this is always a static variable with the name __this_module.

Thus the safe version of the above code becomes:

```
int my_driver_open(struct inode *inode, struct file *filp)
{
    struct my_driver_private priv;

    if (!try_inc_mod_count(&__this_module);
        return -EAGAIN;

    priv = kmalloc(sizeof(*priv), GFP_KERNEL);
    if (!priv) {
        MOD_DEC_USE_COUNT;
        return -ENOMEM;
    }

    filp->private_data = priv;
    return 0;
}
```

The use count handling in the 2.2 version of the Applicom driver was very simple, because the open and release routines don't actually do anything else. Every time the device is opened, the use count is increased, and every time it is closed again, the use count is decreased:

```
static int ac_open(struct inode *inode, struct file *filp)
{
    if (!try_inc_mod_count(&__this_module))
        return -EAGAIN;
    return 0;
}

static int ac_release(struct inode *inode, struct file *filp)
{
    MOD_DEC_USE_COUNT;
    return 0;
}
```

In the 2.4 version, this can become even easier – there is no need for the open and release routines to exist at all. This is because as of the 2.4.0-test4 release, the Linux kernel will automatically increase the use count of the module before calling the open routine, and decrease it again after calling the release routine. This was changed in order to allow us to eliminate yet another place where the old "Big Kernel Lock" was used, as part of the ongoing effort to allow Linux to scale more efficiently to larger numbers of CPUs.

To clarify that – in the 2.4 kernels, a simple driver need not manipulate its own module's use count when its open and release functions are called, and those functions may no longer assume that the Big Kernel Lock is held when they are called.

Making It Build

Once you've written the code of your driver, to complete your task you will need to merge your new driver into the kernel's configuration and build system. This will involve adding it to the configuration options, and instructing the kernel Makefiles on what to do when the configuration option for the new driver is enabled.

Adding Configuration Options

To start with, you need to select a name for your new configuration option. You can see these names when you run make config in the kernel build tree. Obviously you should choose a name that bears some relation to the driver that it enables, and one that is unlikely to match any existing or future name. For the Applicom boards, I chose CONFIG_APPLICOM – unimaginative is good. To add your option to the list made available, you need to edit the file called Config.in, which you will find in the drivers subdirectory for the driver you have written. In the case of the Applicom driver, it is a character device, so it is added to drivers/char/Config.in. The format of these files is fairly simple, and allows you to make the options dependent on the previous selections made by the user.

The simplest way to declare a new configuration option is the bool declaration. For example:

```
bool 'Direct Rendering Manager (XFree86 DRI support)' CONFIG_DRM
```

This allows the user to select either 'Yes' or 'No'. It is used for code that has not been made to work as a loadable module (APM for example), and is also sometimes used in other situations. For example, the CONFIG_NET_ETHERNET option does not directly affect the code, but if the user responds 'No' then they will not be asked individually whether they want to include drivers for each of the numerous types of Ethernet cards that Linux supports.

A more commonly used declaration is `tristate`, which allows the user to choose from 'Yes', 'No' or 'Module' – a common set of options for kernel drivers. (The 'Yes' option means to compile the driver statically into the kernel image, while the 'No and 'Module' options ought to be self-explanatory.)

Often, however, the user's choice will be restricted by choices they have made previously. For example, you can't use the Applicom device driver if you don't have PCI support, so saying 'Y' to the former but 'N' to the latter would be meaningless. If it were possible to compile PCI support as a loadable module and that option was selected, then valid options for `CONFIG_APPLICOM` would be 'M' or 'N' but not 'Y' – because the Applicom driver depends on the PCI code and cannot function without it.

To handle these dependencies, it is possible to use a `dep_tristate` declaration to make this simpler. This is what we'll use for the Applicom board:

```
dep_tristate 'Applicom intelligent fieldbus card support' CONFIG_APPLICOM
             $CONFIG_PCI
```

This directive causes the build system only to allow the user to select options for `CONFIG_APPLICOM` that are compatible with the previously chosen value for `CONFIG_PCI`. This would enforce the sensible restriction that you can't compile the Applicom driver into the kernel while leaving out PCI. We should probably admit at this point that the PCI code is currently only a 'Yes/No' choice, because nobody has bothered to expend the effort required to make it modular – so this example is perhaps a little contrived.

Makefiles

Having defined a new configuration option, you need to alter the Makefiles so that they compile the your code appropriately when it is selected by the user.

The Makefiles in the Linux kernel are currently undergoing an almost complete rewrite with the intention of making them non-recursive. That is, so there is a single tree of dependencies rather than multiple separate trees in different directories. There is an essay on the Web about the reasoning for this, and it's not worth going into it in detail here. See http://www.tip.net.au/~millerp/rmch/recu-make-cons-harm.html for more information if you really care about such things.

As it is, the 2.4 kernel is still using a recursive make setup, and you need to alter the Makefile in the directory in which you added your driver to make it compile.

Generally, the way to do this is to add the name of the object file (such as `applicom.o`) to the relevant list of object files that are created during the build. Here's where it starts to get a little complex.

If your driver is to be a module, then the name of your driver needs to be added to the variable `M_OBJS`. If it's to be linked into the kernel, then you need to look at whether the directory creates an archive or a single object file from all the object files therein. If it defines a variable `L_TARGET` then it creates an archive, and you should add your driver's name to the variable `L_OBJS`. On the other hand, if the Makefile defines a variable `O_TARGET` then it creates a single object file, and you should add your driver's name to the variable `O_OBJS`.

If your driver is exporting symbols that are to be used by other modules, which you probably won't want to do at this stage, then that all changes – the lists to which you should add your driver become `MX_OBJS`, `LX_OBJS` and `OX_OBJS` respectively.

All the configuration options are imported as variables into the make process, so the addition to the Makefile would look something like this:

```
ifeq ($(CONFIG_APPLICOM),y)
   L_OBJS += applicom.o
else
    ifeq ($(CONFIG_APPLICOM),m)
       M_OBJS += applicom.o
    endif
endif
```

However, in an attempt to make all this simpler, some Makefiles, including the Makefile in the `drivers/char` directory to which we want to add our example driver, have been changed around. The new-style Makefiles still have the same final targets as before, but the process of creating the object lists is made simpler. If your object file needs to export symbols, then you add it to the variable called `export-list` – whether it's a module or not. You also add it to either the variable called `obj-m` or `obj-y`. This allows the addition for the Applicom driver into 2.4 to be a single line:

```
obj-$(CONFIG_APPLICOM) += applicom.o
```

Some Makefiles have already been converted, and some haven't, and all of them are expected to be thrown away during the 2.5 development cycle and replaced with an entirely more sensible system. In the meantime, you will need to know a little bit about Makefiles and make a decision about how to add your driver in the place where you think it should live. Don't panic, though – when you actually look at the existing Makefiles and configuration rules, it's not that difficult to see where to add the necessary lines to match your own driver, and if you have put in the effort required to produce a driver, the members of the Linux-kernel mailing list (see below) are quite likely to take pity on you and help you merge it properly if you ask for help.

What to Do with Your New Driver

Once you have completed your driver, you will probably be wondering what to do with it next. There are two common options:

❑　You can place your code under a licence compatible with the licence of the Linux kernel (essentially GPL), or

❑　You can distribute your driver in binary form only.

To a large extent, this will depend on the Intellectual Property that you have drawn from in writing your driver. If you have obtained any information that was required for your driver (such as hardware specifications) under a Non-Disclosure Agreement, then your choices may be restricted by that agreement.

Before making a decision, you should be familiar with the terms of the GNU Public Licence, under which the Linux kernel is distributed. It grants users the right to obtain and modify the source code of any software which is linked into their Linux kernel. If you do not release the source code to your driver, then you may only distribute it in the form of a loadable module – you may not distribute kernels with the driver built-in. That loadable module will not only be likely to work only on the same CPU architecture and version of the kernel, but in some cases may fail if different configuration options are selected by the user, or if a different version of the compiler is used. By deciding not to distribute the source code, you are tying yourself in to building multiple different versions of your driver to match each of your user's needs.

Furthermore, those users will no longer be able to expect any support from the core Linux development team or many commercial enterprises. Upon receiving a bug report from a user who admits to using binary-only loadable modules, the first response is almost always to tell the reporter to attempt to reproduce it without the module loaded. If the problem can't be reproduced with only known code running on the system, then most people will not look any further.

Linus Torvalds himself has made this position very clear, in an e-mail sent to the kernel developers' mailing list in February of 1999:

> *Basically, I want people to know that when they use binary-only modules, it's THEIR problem. I want people to know that in their bones, and I want it shouted out from the rooftops. I want people to wake up in a cold sweat every once in a while if they use binary-only modules.*

For this reason, it is strongly recommended that any new drivers are licensed under the GPL, and submitted to Linus for inclusion in the official kernel. Not only will your users be able to expect support for their system, but you may also find that subtle bugs are fixed and your driver updated as the Linux kernel evolves and internal APIs change.

Submitting a New Driver

To submit a new driver to Linus, you should first verify that it builds and operates correctly on the latest development version of the kernel. If it can be both compiled into the kernel and as a loadable module, then check that it works in both configurations.

A common mistake made by programmers new to Linux is to assume that "all the world's a PC". Linux runs on many platforms, including 64-bit and big-endian processors. You should make sure your driver will behave correctly on those architectures, if it's at all possible that it will be used on them. If your driver is for a PCI board, then it can be used on more than one CPU architecture, so test it on as many different platforms as possible – especially trying to vary the endianness and word size. Platforms other than IA32 (x86) that take PCI cards include Alpha, PowerPC, IA64, SPARC, UltraSPARC, and others. If you don't have access to such machines, ask on the Linux-kernel mailing list for testers. People are usually happy to help, especially if your driver is commercially supported, and you are able to send them the hardware to be tested in their computer.

Once you're convinced that your driver will work on all platforms, in all configurations, make a patch that adds it to a clean copy of the latest development kernel. A simple way to do that is to extract the clean kernel into one directory, copy it to another and merge your new driver in to one of the copies. Then run a diff command similar to:

```
diff -uNr linux-clean linux-patched
```

to produce the patch. The most important part of the above command is the -u (or --unified) option, which selects an output format which is preferred by Linus and other kernel developers because it is easier to apply on top of other patches, and because it is easier to understand what it's doing just by looking at it.

Once you've created your patch, apply it to a clean copy of the kernel, rebuild it and test it again. You'll often find that you've missed out an important file, which you forget was present in your build tree, or that you've accidentally included a useless temporary file or two. Repeat as necessary.

Now you're sure that your patch is fine, you need to get it tested by other people, and also looked over for correctness. If it's quite small, you can post it directly to the kernel developers' mailing list at linux-kernel@vger.rutgers.edu with a request for testing and/or opinions. If it's large, put it on an FTP site somewhere and post a similar request with a URL for where to download it. To make your visit a more pleasant experience for all concerned, please make sure you carefully read the FAQ (Frequently Asked Questions) at http://www.tux.org/lkml/ before posting anything to the list.

Once you have positive feedback, and have resolved any bug reports or criticism that followed from your posting to the mailing list, then you can consider sending the patch to Linus. When you do so, make sure the patch is in the main body of the mail, not attached by MIME, and include a short explanation of the functionality that the patch provides. If you're going to attempt sending HTML mail, then you might as well not bother.

Now be patient. Linus is extremely busy, and getting him to accept patches is a fine art that nobody has yet perfected. Only if you're extremely lucky will he either apply or reject it on the first attempt. If not, be prepared to resubmit it at reasonable intervals until he either applies it or tells you why he doesn't like it. It may help to carbon-copy the developers' mailing list each time you submit the patch to Linus.

Summary

We've covered a number of topics here that anyone who is interested in kernel development should be aware of, but there's still a lot more to do. In fact, there's far more to investigate than we have space left for in this book. What we have shown here, however, should get you well on the way past the initial issues you'll encounter while building a driver for your PCI card/device.

Until Wrox releases Professional Linux Kernel Programming, however (and no, it's not even penned in at this stage – Ed) it remains up to you to search out the documentation you require. There's quite a bit to be found in the Documentation subdirectory of the Linux kernel source tree, and of course, Alessandro Rubini's book *Linux Device Drivers* (*ISBN 1-56592-292-1*) is readily available, although it doesn't cover the 2.4 kernel.

Online discussion at http://www.p2p.wrox.com

27

Distributing the Application

In this chapter we will take a look at preparing our application for distribution, making source and binary packages to distribute, and dealing with bugs that are reported by our users. In this chapter we will:

- ❑ explore the RPM package installer
- ❑ use `autoconf` and `configure` to create installation specific makefiles
- ❑ outline the process of creating an RPM
- ❑ look at the creation and distribution of patches
- ❑ consider post release bug tracking

When developing for Microsoft DOS, it's fairly easy – a program that runs on one machine will most likely work on all others. Windows is slightly trickier in that you may need to deal with variations between CE (Pocket PC), NT, 9x, 2000. Nevertheless, you can compile for each of these platforms and ship a binary executable.

Open Source software presents some new challenges when it comes to distributing the finished applications. We generally have to try to cater for a much wider variation of hardware platform and processor architecture. Furthermore, if you intend to distribute an Open Source product, you will by definition be making the source code available.

If you develop on Linux you may still find that your users will try compiling your code on other UNIX-like systems including FreeBSD, Solaris, HP-UX, and many more. Each of these systems differs in some way, often significantly enough to stop your application from compiling. Even the various distributions of Linux can introduce differences sufficient to trip up the unwary. Having said that though, Linux does attempt to comply with the marketplace; to thrive, it must be adopted, used and extended by others. We therefore need to make the installation and upgrade of our application as painless as possible.

One way to achieve this is to provide a binary package that can be installed simply. If we also provide a source package, interested parties can take a look and make improvements to our code. Many Linux users will already be familiar with the idea of packages. We will take a look at the most popular type, the RedHat RPM package, from the points of view of both the user and the developer creating a package.

It's possible that our application is built on top of some other software, which may be beyond our control. For example, a graphical interface to the debugger GDB, would only be useful if our user already had installed GDB. Not only that; we may be dependent on a *particular version* of GDB.

Rather than bundle a copy of GDB with our application, we need to make such dependencies explicit within our binary package. That way, when the user installs our application, they will be warned if GDB is missing or out of date on their system. Later on, we will see how RPM packages handle dependencies.

Installation of our application may be as simple as storing program executables in a directory such as /usr/local/bin or somewhere in /opt. On the other hand, we may need to run a configuration program, initialize a database, or perform housekeeping functions on package installation, or come to that, on package removal. The RPM package format can arrange for all of these things to happen automatically.

> *It is even possible to create your own Linux distribution, designed explicitly to deploy and run just your applications. This can be useful for specialist applications such as communications servers.*

Since we expect Open Source software to be improved by the user community, we must consider how to integrate those changes into vendor-neutral international standards such as POSIX. To help with the complexity of target platform requirements, there are many tools available that can be used to ensure that your program will work on as many different machines as possible – we'll see configure and autoconf in action a little later on. Of course, sticking to the standards can also help a great deal.

There is an enormous wealth of free software for Linux, and our application will be competing for attention. We saw back in Chapter 2 how a source code control system such as CVS can be used across a network to give access to source code and therefore provide a way to publishing code. In this chapter, we'll take a look at the patch utility, which can be used to distribute source code changes, both small and large.

A popular program may generate a large level of interest, including general comments, suggestions for improvement, and problem reports. To help handle these communications we will make a mention of the GNU bug tracking system, GNATS.

RPM Packages

Since its first introduction in Red Hat Linux, the RPM (RedHat Package Manager) format has become widely adopted as a way to distribute installable Linux applications. RPMs are supported on many distributions such as Red Hat (of course!), Mandrake (which is based on Red Hat), and SuSE (which isn't). Since the RPM format is widely known and there are Open Source applications that support it, there are few reasons why RPM should not be supported on many other Linux and UNIX platforms some day.

Other packing formats do exist, notably the GNU/Debian DEB package used in Debian-based distributions. Many of the principles discussed here are equally applicable to DEB packages. If you are running a Debian-based system, check out the documentation for dpkg and dselect. You can run RPM tools on Debian if you wish.

The RPM User

A Linux user will typically first come across RPM files during installation. Both Red Hat and SuSE Linux almost completely fill their CDs and DVDs with RPM package files. The installation program typically presents a menu of available packages (or collections thereof) and installs the ones chosen. The RPM installer (the program called rpm) is used behind the scenes.

Later on, after installation is complete, many distributions provide a graphical package installer. Here we will cover the basic RPM manager, rpm, since it can be used before the X Window system is up and running.

The rpm program will be used when changes are necessary to the Linux installation. These will be:

❑   removing a package that is no longer needed

❑   adding a package from the distribution that was not initially installed

❑   upgrading an installed package to a later version

❑   adding a new package from another source

These tasks are usually all very straightforward, but require superuser permissions as they require access to system areas of the file system; we'll take a look at each of these shortly. There are also operations that ordinary users can perform with rpm, and we will start with these.

The rpm program can appear to be incredibly intimidating at first glance. If you type:

```
$ rpm --help
```

you will be confronted with a two-page long listing of all the options that can be used with rpm, both as a user installing and manipulating binary packages, and also as a developer creating source or binary RPM packages. Here we will cover some of the easier options, those that help us to perform the tasks we will need to perform most often.

The rpm program can run in a number of modes, depending on what we have asked it to do. These include:

❑   query mode

❑   install and upgrade mode

❑   build mode

We'll now use the first of these to pick a package for use, as an example of installation and removal of a package. Query mode is invoked by using the -q option to rpm.

What Do I Have Installed?

To get a listing of all of the packages that have been installed by rpm, use the query mode and use the -a option to specify all packages:

```
$ rpm -q -a
aaa_base-99.11.11-2
aaa_dir-99.11.12-0
base-99.11.2-1
bash-2.03-26
bdflush-1.5-101
cpio-2.4.2-99
...
gnuchess-4.0.pl80-5
...
xboard-4.0.0-68
...
dia-0.81-1
pg_datab-6.5-21
pg_ifa-6.5.1-18
pg_iface-6.5.1-15
postgres-6.5.1-18
$
```

On this well-endowed SuSE system, we get a listing of over 1000 packages in the order they were installed. The final few show that the PostgreSQL database was the most recent package.

The package names take a standard form:

```
<package-name>-<package-version>-<release>
```

The package name is usually the name of the main application or library. The package version is the version number of the application contained within the RPM package. The release number is a number that's incremented each time the RPM package is built for distribution. For example, the PostgreSQL package postgres-6.5.1-18 is the eighteenth RPM package to be built containing PostgreSQL version 6.5.1.

Packages are rebuilt for many reasons; usually to adjust the install location, or scripts that are executed automatically when the package is installed. A new package containing a new version of an application will start again at release 1, as with dia-0.81-1 in our listing above.

The RPM Database

To keep track of all the packages it has installed on a Linux system, the rpm program maintains a database of the packages, the files within those packages and the dependencies. This database is typically located in /var/lib/rpm. The files in this directory are mostly database files (using the UNIX dbm database) that we cannot look at directly. The rpm program provides us with many different ways of querying it, though.

For now it is enough to realize that whenever we use rpm to install, upgrade or remove RPM packages this database is being updated.

What's in a Package?

We can ask rpm to tell us what files have been installed by a particular package. In the listing above there were two packages that we will use for our examples: gnuchess and xboard. These are the GNU chess program and a graphical user interface for it.

```
$ rpm -q xboard gnuchess
xboard-4.0.0-68
gnuchess-4.0.pl80-5
$
```

We can get a complete listing of all the files installed by a package by using the query mode option -l (list files):

```
$ rpm -q -l gnuchess
/usr/bin/game
/usr/bin/gnuan
/usr/bin/gnuchess
/usr/bin/gnuchessc
/usr/bin/gnuchessn
/usr/bin/gnuchessr
/usr/bin/gnuchessx
/usr/bin/postprint
/usr/lib/eco.pgn
/usr/lib/gnuchess.data
/usr/lib/gnuchess.eco
/usr/lib/gnuchess.lang
/usr/man/man6/game.6.gz
/usr/man/man6/gnuan.6.gz
/usr/man/man6/gnuchess.6.gz
/usr/man/man6/postprint.6.gz
$
```

Conversely if we want to find out which package a particular file belongs to we can use the query mode option -f:

```
$ rpm -q -f /usr/X11R6/bin/xboard
xboard-4.0.0-68
$
```

We can specify multiple files if we wish; rpm will report the source package for each file we ask about. Check out the manual page for details of further query mode options.

Removing a Package

To make changes to a Linux installation, superuser permission is required. Always take care when using rpm as root; it's all too easy to destroy a working system by accidentally removing a crucial package. Let's remove something harmless, like the GNU chess program interface, xboard.

We can try to remove a package by specifying the -e (erase) option to the rpm program and giving the package name. RPM package names can often be abbreviated, and we can do this here; we need only give the package name without the version or release parts. This is possible because it is usually only possible for one version of a package to be installed at any given time. You may have noticed that we have already been abbreviating the package names in the earlier query examples.

```
$ su -
Password:
# rpm -e xboard
#
```

Now when we try to query the package, it's reported as not installed:

```
# rpm -q xboard
package xboard is not installed
#
```

Now let's try to remove the GNU chess program itself:

```
# rpm -e gnuchess
error: removing these packages would break dependencies:
        gnuchess is needed by glchess-0.10d-67
#
```

Here we can see that there is another package, glchess, already installed, that relies on the presence of the GNU chess program. Let's find out what it is.

Package Status

We can ask rpm to give us more information about an installed packed with the query mode -i (information) option:

```
$ rpm -q -i glchess
Name        : glchess                Relocations: (not relocateable)
Version     : 0.10d                  Vendor: SuSE GmbH, Nuernberg, Germany
Release     : 67                     Build Date: Sat 13 Nov 1999 16:13:38 GMT
Install date: Sun 02 Jan 2000 17:50:14 GMT     Build Host: stott.suse.de
Group       : unsorted               Source RPM: glchess-0.10d-67.src.rpm
Size        : 171581                 License: GPL
Packager    : feedback@suse.de
Summary     : 3D frontend for gnuchess
Description :
glchess is a fine 3D mesa frontend for gnuchess

Authors:
--------
    Tomi.Sarvela@iki.fi
$
```

Here we see that the glchess package is another graphical interface for gnuchess, this time in 3D. It will cease to work if we press ahead with our removal of gnuchess. If we are intent on stripping this machine of chess-playing abilities we will need to remove glchess too:

```
# rpm -e glchess gnuchess
#
```

This time there is no problem. Notice that we remove two packages at the same time by specifying both packages as arguments. rpm is happy to remove them together as the combined operation will not break the dependency glchess has on gnuchess.

We will return to the subject of dependencies a little later.

Installing Packages

If we have a file containing an RPM package that we want to install, we can simply use the `rpm` program's `-i` (install) option. For packages provided with a Linux installation, we probably need to track down the file we need on the original CD. Unfortunately the `rpm` database doesn't keep track of where previously installed packages were installed from.

Let's reinstate the chess-playing facilities.

First we need to find the RPM package files. Their location will vary between different systems and installation media. For example, if you have downloaded a package from the internet, you simply need to give the filename to `rpm` to install it. In this example we will re-install from the SuSE DVD:

```
# mount /cdrom
# cd /cdrom/suse/fun1
# ls
3d_chess.rpm    figlet.rpm      oonsoo.rpm      xbl.rpm         xpilot.rpm
3dpong.rpm      fishtank.rpm    pacman.rpm      xblast.rpm      xpinguin.rpm
INDEX           flying.rpm      pingus.rpm      xboard.rpm      xpuzzles.rpm
INDEX.english   fortune.rpm     pipeman.rpm     xboing.rpm      xracer.rpm
INDEX.german    freeciv.rpm     playone.rpm     xbomb.rpm       xroach.rpm
MD5SUMS         frisk.rpm       puzzle.rpm      xbombs.rpm      xrobots.rpm
TRANS.TBL       frotz.rpm       pysol.rpm       xdemine.rpm     xshogi.rpm
abuse.rpm       glchess.rpm     rockdiam.rpm    xearth.rpm      xskat.rpm
aleclone.rpm    gnuchess.rpm    sastroid.rpm    xengine.rpm     xsnow.rpm
anachron.rpm    gnugo.rpm       space.rpm       xfract.rpm      xsok.rpm
antipoli.rpm    gshogi.rpm      spellc.rpm      xgammon.rpm     xsol.rpm
asclock.rpm     hextris.rpm     tf.rpm          xgas.rpm        xspringi.rpm
astrolog.rpm    imaze.rpm       tfhelp.rpm      xjewel.rpm      xtacy.rpm
batalion.rpm    lincity.rpm     thrust.rpm      xlife.rpm       xtartan.rpm
battball.rpm    maelstr.rpm     tux_aqfh.rpm    xlyap.rpm       xteddy.rpm
bsdgames.rpm    manix.rpm       tuxeyes.rpm     xmahjong.rpm    xtetris.rpm
bzflag.rpm      meltflip.rpm    vgacard.rpm     xmemory.rpm     xthing.rpm
craft.rpm       mirrma.rpm      x3d.rpm         xmine.rpm       xtron.rpm
crafty.rpm      moontool.rpm    xabacus.rpm     xmines.rpm      xvier.rpm
crosfire.rpm    net3d.rpm       xancur.rpm      xmountns.rpm    yahtzee.rpm
daliclck.rpm    nethack.rpm     xaos.rpm        xmris.rpm
emiclock.rpm    netmaze.rpm     xball.rpm       xpat2.rpm
empire.rpm      oneko.rpm       xbill.rpm       xphoon.rpm
#
```

Here we can see a whole host of RPM packages, including `gnuchess` and `xboard`. If we try to install `xboard` on its own we will get a dependency warning, as expected:

```
# rpm -i xboard.rpm
error: failed dependencies:
        gnuchess is needed by xboard-4.0.0-68
#
```

We can install more than one package at a time (as we would have to if they had a mutual dependency) by specifying more files on the command line:

```
# rpm -i xboard.rpm gnuchess.rpm
#
```

Upgrading a Package

If an earlier version of a package is already installed, we can tell rpm to upgrade by specifying the -U (upgrade) option instead of -i. This works just like an installation except that files are overwritten with new ones, whereas the -i option will fail if rpm detects that a version of a package you're trying to install is already present.

Graphical Installers

As installing RPM packages is quite a common task, there are now a number of utilities available to help make it even more painless. In the GNOME environment, the program gnorpm provides a way of graphically selecting packages and installing (or uninstalling) them. The KDE desktop features a similar utility called kpackage (shown below). Old Red Hat distributions use another called glint. Outside the X Window System, there are character-based interfaces including YaST in SuSE distributions.

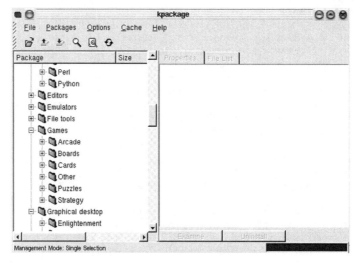

These tools can be very helpful for everyday package maintenance, although to date none of them allows access to *all* features of the base rpm program.

Checking Dependencies

We can ask rpm about the dependencies of an installed package by using the query mode -R (or -- requires) option:

```
$ rpm -q -R xboard
gnuchess
/bin/sh
/usr/bin/perl
ld-linux.so.2
libICE.so.6
libSM.so.6
libX11.so.6
libXaw.so.6
libXext.so.6
libXmu.so.6
libXt.so.6
libc.so.6
libc.so.6(GLIBC_2.0)
$
```

Here we can see that the xboard package requires gnuchess and some other things such as X Window libraries, perl, and a shell.

Each of the items listed is termed a capability. Each RPM package provides one or more capabilities and requires zero or more other capabilities to be present on the system when installed. The RPM file itself records the capabilities. A package's dependencies simply reflect its reliance on other programs to provide capabilities it doesn't have itself. We can explore the capabilities provided by a particular package with the query mode --provides option.

Let's now use this to investigate the XML library a little. This library, which we investigated in Chapter 23, allows programs to read and write XML files and is fast becoming an important data interchange tool.

Let's check the version we have:

```
$ rpm -q libxml
libxml-1.7.3-5
$
```

Now let's see what it provides:

```
$ rpm -q --provides libxml
libxml
libxml.so.1
libxml.so.1(GCC.INTERNAL)
$
```

Here we can see that the package lists a number of capabilities; both general and specific capabilities are listed. The package provides an XML library (libxml) and this particular installation provides a specific version of the shared library (libxml.so.1).

> **We need to be careful when querying packages for dependencies; some may require a specific version of a capability, not simply the general capability.**

We can find out which package provides a particular capability by using the query mode --whatprovides option.

```
$ rpm -q --whatprovides libxml
libxml-1.7.3-5
$
```

Conversely, we can ask which installed packages require a capability with the query mode --whatrequires option.

```
$ rpm -q --whatrequires libxml
libglad-0.7-5
libxmld-1.7.3-5
$
```

Here we see that a couple of other library packages require `libxml` to be present; but what about applications? They will typically require a specific version of a shared library, so let's check for that:

```
$ rpm -q --whatrequires libxml.so.1
gnorpm-0.9-3
gnprint-0.10-5
gnumeric-0.41-5
libglad-0.7-5
$
```

Here we can see that the GNOME RPM package installer `gnorpm` and some others require the `libxml` shared library at version 1 explicitly.

Overriding Dependencies

Sometimes packages may specify a dependency on a package that you don't have installed, or perhaps one you have installed in a different manner. To get around such eventualities, you can override the `rpm` program dependency checking by using the install mode `--nodeps` option:

```
# rpm -i xboard.rpm
error: failed dependencies:
        gnuchess is needed by xboard-4.0.0-68
# rpm -i --nodeps xboard.rpm
#
```

If you try to install a package that's already installed, the `rpm` program will refuse. You can override this behavior with the install mode `--force` option. This can be handy for installing a previous version of a package over a later one.

Other Options

There are several other useful options for the user of RPM packages. If you want to see the scripts that a package will run when you install or uninstall it, you can use the query mode `--scripts` option:

```
$ rpm -q --scripts postgres
postinstall script (through /bin/sh):
if [ -x bin/fillup ] ; then
  bin/fillup -q -d = etc/rc.config var/adm/fillup-templates/rc.config.postgres
else
  echo "ERROR: fillup not found. This should not happen. Please compare"
  echo "etc/rc.config and var/adm/fillup-templates/rc.config.postgres and"
  echo "update by hand."
fi
touch var/log/postgresql.log
if [ "$UID" = "0" ] ; then
  chown postgres.daemon var/log/postgresql.log
fi
preuninstall script (through /bin/sh):
if [ -x sbin/init.d/postgres ] ; then
    sbin/init.d/postgres stop
    sleep 2
fi
$
```

For example, here we can see that before uninstalling the PostgreSQL package, the pre-uninstall script will stop the `postgres` service.

If we want to prevent these scripts from running when installing (-i) or erasing (-e) packages, we can specify the option `--noscripts`.

We can test that an installation will be OK by specifying the `--test` option. This will check dependencies but not actually go through with installing the package files.

The -v option to `rpm` will enable some more verbose output for some queries.

When upgrading or installing many packages at once it is helpful to see an indication of progress. You can get a progress bar constructed from hash marks by using the -h option:

```
# rpm -i -v -h xboard.rpm gnuchess.rpm
xboard                  ####################################################
gnuchess                #####################
#
```

> *Single character options may be combined into a single argument, so that* -ivh *has the same effect as* -i -v -h *in the example above.*

The `rpm` program is also able to install packages directly from the internet via FTP or HTTP. To do this, you simply use an FTP or HTTP URL as the package name when installing. See the `rpm` manual page for options concerning non-standard port numbers and the use of proxy servers.

Finally, the RPM database allows you to verify that packages are installed correctly. If you accidentally delete some files and want to check what has been damaged, use the -V (verify) option.

```
# rm /usr/bin/gnuchess
# rpm -V gnuchess
missing     /usr/bin/gnuchess
```

Here we can see that the gnuchess installation is damaged, missing the main program file.

You can combine -V with -a (all) to verify all of the installed packages at the same time. (This can take a little while for large installations.) Each file that has been installed as part of a package undergoes a number of tests. Those files that fail one or more of them are listed, with the results of the tests:

```
# rpm -V -a
S.5....T c /etc/modules.conf
S.5....T c /etc/hosts
.....U..   /var/spool/fax
Unsatisfied dependencies for shlibs5-99.11.10-1: libgif.so
missing     /var/catman
$
```

Each output line consists of an eight character test result, an indication that the file is a configuration file (marked as c) or not, and the file name. Unsatisfied dependencies and missing files are also listed. The test results show a comparison of the actual file attributes with those stored for that file in the RPM database. Attributes that differ are noted by a character as follows:

.	(period) test passed
S	file size
M	modes (permissions)
U	user
G	group
5	MD5 checksum
T	modification time
L	symbolic link
D	device

Some care needs to be taken when reading the output of a verify operation. Not all test failures are problems. Many files will change legitimately as the system is used. In the example above, the file /etc/hosts will have been updated with local network host addresses.

Uninstalled Packages

Most of the query operations we have seen have been operating on installed packages. Sometimes we need to find out which of the uninstalled packages we need to install to provide a capability or a file. To do this we need to enlist the help of the -p (package file) option.

If we need to find the RPM package that provides a particular file, say /usr/bin/gnuchess, and we don't have that file installed, the query we saw earlier will not work. Similarly, the query on the capability gnuchess will not work either:

```
$ rpm -q -f /usr/bin/gnuchess
file /usr/bin/gnuchess: No such file or directory
$ rpm -q --whatprovides gnuchess
no package provides gnuchess
$
```

We need to resort to querying the RPM package files themselves. We can ask about the version, the capabilities provided, the files contained in the package, see the scripts (if any), and check dependencies:

```
$ cd <wherever-the-rpms-are>
$ rpm -q -p gnuchess.rpm
gnuchess-4.0.p180-5
$ rpm -q --provides -p gnuchess.rpm
gchess
gnuchess
$ rpm -q -l -p gnuchess.rpm
/usr/bin/game
/usr/bin/gnuan
/usr/bin/gnuchess
...
```

Unfortunately we cannot use the --whatprovides or --whatrequires options on a group of uninstalled RPM package files, so we have to resort to querying each package separately:

```
$ for p in *.rpm
> do
> rpm -q -R -p $p | grep -s gnuchess
> if [ "$?" = "0" ]
> then
>   echo $p
> fi
> done
glchess.rpm
xboard.rpm
$
```

Here we discover that of the packages in this directory only glchess and xboard require gnuchess. Now we have located gnuchess, we can fix up the damaged installation that we found with rpm -V by reinstalling the gnuchess RPM.

Anatomy of an RPM Package

Let's take a look at a typical RPM package file. Here is postgres.rpm taken from the SuSE distribution:

```
$ ls -ls postgres.rpm
2844 -rw-r--r--   1 neil     users       2905041 Apr 16 13:09 postgres.rpm
$ file postgres.rpm
postgres.rpm: RPM v3 bin i386 postgres-6.5.1-18
$
```

The file type is recognized by the file command because the file structure has been added to the /etc/magic database. The file is recognized because it starts with a defined header that describes the file as an RPM package. This header includes a magic number, denoting whether the package is a binary one or contains source code. For binary packages, the hardware type for which it has been compiled is also noted. Finally, there is a string that names the package, including version and release numbers. These header attributes are printed by the file command.

Essentially an RPM package file is an archive (like tar and cpio) containing the files that need to be installed. RPM files also support compression and contain checks to ensure that the package is complete.

To get a better look inside an RPM package file we can convert it to a cpio archive using rpm2cpio, which given an RPM package file as argument (or on the standard input) writes a cpio archive to the standard output:

```
$ rpm2cpio postgres.rpm > postgres.cpio
$
```

We can get a listing of the files included in the archive, using `cpio` to obtain a directory listing:

```
$ cpio -t <postgres.cpio
etc/profile.d/postgres.csh
etc/profile.d/postgres.sh
sbin/init.d/postgres
sbin/init.d/rc2.d/K15postgres
sbin/init.d/rc2.d/S25postgres
sbin/init.d/rc3.d/K15postgres
sbin/init.d/rc3.d/S25postgres
usr/doc/packages/postgres
usr/doc/packages/postgres/COPYRIGHT
usr/doc/packages/postgres/CVS
...
```

Should we ever need to, we can use this technique of converting to a `cpio` archive to extract individual files from an RPM without having to install the package.

Source Packages

Although very many applications are distributed as binary packages in formats such as RPM, there are times when building from source code is the only option. The very latest version of an application may not yet be available as an RPM, or perhaps the application needs tailoring to the local installation environment for it to function; either way, a compilation is necessary.

It is entirely possible to create an RPM package that contains source code. These are often known as source RPMs, SRPMs, or spm files. Typically, source code is distributed as a `tar` archive. These are known as 'tarballs', and are usually compressed, containing the application source, often accompanied by a specification that can be used to build a binary RPM package. Source RPMs usually contain just such a compressed source tarball.

For users of source tarballs, the installation process is often very similar and runs like this:

```
$ tar zxvf application.tar.gz
$ cd application
$ ./configure
$ make
$ su -
# make install
```

Sometimes there will be a `make check` step if the application has been provided with test programs or scripts.

Anyone who has ever installed software from the Free Software Foundation will recognize this sequence of events. This is the standard method developed by the GNU project for their software, and has been adopted very widely. It is aimed at making compilation of applications as painless as possible on as wide a variation of hardware platforms as possible. Let's take a closer look at the steps.

❑ The first simply unpacks the tar archive into the current directory. Most often, this will result in a new subdirectory being created, including the application code.

❏   The second step (after we step into the new directory if there is one) is to run the `configure` script. The principal job of this script is to create a **makefile** that is tailored to the machine on which the application is being compiled. It is also able to create an **include file** (usually called `config.h`) that the application can `include` to define options for compilation. For example it might define macros that are set depending on the availability of libraries, or on aspects of the machine hardware, like integer size.

❏   The third step compiles the application using the tailored makefile and include files.

❏   As long as all goes well, the last step is to install the application. Normally superuser privilege is needed for this.

If we take a look at the application directory, we normally find a number of helpful files. These are part of the build standard and include:

COPYING	license details, conditions on copying
ChangeLog	descriptions of recent changes
FAQ	Frequently Asked (Answered) Questions
INSTALL	how to install the application
NEWS	new features and hints
README	application description and purpose
TODO	items planned for the future

Using files of this sort in your applications will help the user find answers to questions they may have, without resorting to sending you a bug report!

configure, autoconf and automake

There are several tools that can be used to help create a standard source code directory ready for distribution – these are `configure`, `autoconf`, and `automake`. The full use of these tools is a little outside the scope of this chapter; indeed many experts state that the best way of using them is to copy someone else's working setup. Here we will take a brief look at some of the files that are used to create a source code directory and configuration that will enable an application to be made portable. For further information take a look at the `info` pages for `autoconf` and `automake`.

As we saw a little earlier, the `configure` shell script is an important part of the standard source code distribution. It is a neat script that is able to check versions of applications, test for the presence (or absence) of libraries, and set options to be used in creating a makefile.

Probably the most common option used to run a configure script is `--prefix`. This sets a top-level directory for the installation of the application being configured. It allows the user to decide whether to accept or override a default. Usually a configure script will set things up so that the resulting application will live somewhere in `/usr/local`, with the executable located in `/usr/local/bin`, the manual pages in `/usr/local/man` and so on. The `--prefix` option allows the top level (`/usr/local`) to be changed (perhaps to `/opt`, or a version-specific directory such as `/usr/local/app-1.0`). Other applications may define their own configure script options, for example to build all or just part of a suite of applications.

The `configure` script itself is not generally written by hand as it contains much that is reusable. Rather it is generated by the `autoconf` program. The script that `autoconf` produces does not require `autoconf` to run; it is a simple (if long!) shell script. The `autoconf` program builds the script from a template that contains an indication of the features or other packages that our application needs.

Let's take a look at a simple application of `autoconf`. Our test program for the DVD store application uses `readline`, the GNU input library. If we try to compile the test application on a system that does not have `readline` available, we will fail. This is a shame because although the test program uses `readline` it is not reliant on it. It is used only to provide command line editing, a feature that, if missing, does not render the program useless. It is a simple matter to write the code so that the calls to `readline` functions are made conditional on a `#define` say.

The first step is to create an input file for `autoconf` to use. This is `configure.in`. If you need to write your own tests for features (such as the availability of some tool or other) you may need to create shell scripts to execute those tests. These are usually held in a file called `aclocal.m4`. A site-wide version might be found in `acsite.m4`. The `autoconf` program makes heavy use of the m4 macro processor, so if you do need to delve more deeply it would be worthwhile checking out the `info` pages for m4 as well. If you need to create a C include file to control your application's use of features you will need to create at least a `config.h.in` file.

There are very many macros supplied with `autoconf` to perform tests; it is very likely that these will suffice for most needs. Full details can be found in the `autoconf` documentation.

There are two things that we would like to achieve with `configure` in our application. The first is to generate a configuration header file that we will use to switch on our `readline`-dependent code. The second is to create a makefile that will link the correct libraries.

To create the header file we create a template, `config.h.in`, that looks like this:

```
/*

    config.h

    Set compile time options
*/

/* Set this if you have the readline library
#define HAVE_READLINE   0
```

The variable `HAVE_READLINE` will be redefined by `configure` when it runs. We will create a configure script that will set the value of `HAVE_READLINE` to 1 or 0 depending on whether the `readline` include file is present on the system.

Here is a very simple `configure.in` file:

```
dnl Process this file with autoconf to produce a configure script.
AC_INIT(dvdstore.c)
AC_CONFIG_HEADER(config.h)

dnl Checks for programs.
AC_PROG_CC
```

```
dnl Checks for libraries.

dnl Checks for header files.
AC_HEADER_STDC
AC_CHECK_HEADERS(readline/readline.h, AC_DEFINE(HAVE_READLINE))

dnl Checks for typedefs, structures, and compiler characteristics.

dnl Checks for library functions.

AC_OUTPUT()
```

The lines starting with `dnl` are comments that the `m4` macro processor just deletes to the end of the line (`dnl` stands for delete to new line). The file consists of a number of macro calls that can be made in more or less any order. The call to `AC_INIT` and `AC_CONFIG_HEADER` must come first, and the call to `AC_OUTPUT` must come last. The other sections shown here are mostly empty, but illustrate a recommended ordering of tests; the ones that cause the greatest problems if they fail coming earlier.

The `AC_INIT` macro is used by `configure` for initialization. It is passed the name of a file that must exist in the source directory. The `configure` script checks that this file exists and that therefore it is running in the right place.

The `AC_CONFIG_HEADER` macro declares a name for a configuration header file; here we choose `config.h`.

The first test this `configure` script will run is `AC_PROG_CC`, which makes sure that a C compiler is present. In the header test section you can see a test for the presence of the standard C library headers. Then we come to the primary purpose of this script: to determine if the `readline` header file is present. If it is, then variable `HAVE_READLINE` will be defined.

Finally the `AC_OUTPUT` macro call causes `configure` to update its output files (in this case `config.h`) with any changes that need to be made as a result of the tests.

Let's try it out. First run `autoconf` to create the configuration script:

```
$ autoconf
$
```

Now run the script to create the header file:

```
$ ./configure
creating cache ./config.cache
checking how to run the C preprocessor... cc -E
checking for ANSI C header files... yes
checking for readline/readline.h... yes
updating cache ./config.cache
creating ./config.status
creating config.h
$
```

If we take a look at the header file, we can see that the `#define` has been changed to reflect the fact that we do indeed have `readline` installed on this system:

```
/* config.h.  Generated automatically by configure.  */
/*
      config.h

      Set compile time options
*/

/* Set this if you have the readline library */
#define HAVE_READLINE 1
```

Other predefined `configure`-script macros allow us to test for the existence of the physical code library (rather than just the header file), and also to check that the functions we want to call are included in that library. We will assume that if the header file is there, all is well with `readline`!

We will also need to make sure that our `makefile` can cope with `readline` being absent. To do this we can create a variable within our configure script that will cause a makefile to be edited in the same way as we have seen `config.h` get changed.

We need to create a makefile template that the configure script can edit. In this case we use variable names bracketed by @-signs in a file called `Makefile.in`:

```
RLIB = @RLIB@

dvdstore: dvdstore.o
    $(CC) -o dvdstore dvdstore.o dvd_pg.a $(RLIB)
```

This is just a simple makefile for illustrative purposes. We want `configure` to set the variable `RLIB` to a sensible value for linking with the `readline` library, or leave it blank if the library is absent.

Next we have to make some small additions to our `configure.in` file to accommodate this change:

```
...
dnl Checks for library functions.
AC_CHECK_LIB(readline, rl_bind_key,
                RLIB="-lreadline -lncurses",
                [],
                -lncurses)
AC_SUBST(RLIB)

AC_OUTPUT(Makefile)
```

The `AC_CHECK_LIB` macro checks to see if we can link a test program that calls the `rl_bind_key` function (one of the calls we use in the test program). The parameters to `AC_CHECK_LIB` are:

```
<library>, <function>, <action-if-found>, <action-if-not-found>, <other-libraries>
```

If compiling a test program with `-lreadline` works, the macro sets the shell variable `RLIB`. In this case we need to link with the curses library too, so that makes an appearance as the *<other-libraries>* argument. We use empty square brackets to indicate that no action is taken if the library is missing.

When debugging configure *scripts it is a good idea to clear the configure cache. This is a file,* config.cache, *that* configure *uses to remember the results of tests between runs. You can remove it quite safely, and force* configure *to redo all of its tests. This is a good habit to get into when you change the* configure.in *file and rerun* autoconf.

```
$ rm config.cache
$ autoconf
$ ./configure
creating cache ./config.cache
checking how to run the C preprocessor... cc -E
checking for ANSI C header files... yes
checking for readline/readline.h... yes
checking for rl_bind_key in -lreadline... yes
updating cache ./config.cache
creating ./config.status
creating Makefile
creating config.h
config.h is unchanged
```

Now we can see that a makefile called Makefile has been created from our Makefile.in by the call to AC_OUTPUT(Makefile) and contains an appropriate library definition:

```
# Generated automatically from Makefile.in by configure.

RLIB = -lreadline -lncurses

dvdstore: dvdstore.o
    $(CC) -o dvdstore dvdstore.o dvd_pg.a $(RLIB)
```

Along similar lines to autoconf, the automake program generates standard Makefile.in files from templates called Makefile.am files. The idea is to standardize the use of macros and rules within makefiles. If you are interested in taking this further, checkout the automake info files.

By using autoconf and configure we are able to create portable source code that we can distribute to our users with the hope that they will be able to use the application on a wide range of systems with different sets of installed tools and libraries.

Source RPM Packages

As we mentioned earlier, a source RPM is a special kind of RPM that includes the source code for an application, along with any patches that the RPM creator needed to apply to make the RPM, and a specification for building the application into a binary RPM.

When installed, a source RPM will typically place its source code (generally as a tarball) in /usr/src/packages/SOURCES and the specification file in /usr/src/packages/SPECS. The precise location may vary from distribution to distribution; another common location is /var/lib/rpm and subdirectories therein.

Let's take a look at an example source RPM, in this case the XBoard application in its SuSE 6.3 incarnation, xboard.spm.

If we list the contents with the rpm program we can see the source, patch, and specification:

```
$ rpm -q -l -p xboard.spm
xboard-4.0.0.dif
xboard-4.0.0.tar.gz
xboard.spec
$
```

We can extract the files (to /usr/src/packages/SOURCES or wherever rpm is configured to place them) by installing the RPM:

```
$ rpm -i xboard.spm
```

Building an RPM Package

The RPM package is an ideal way for us to distribute our own applications. It is easy for the user to work with, supporting simple installation, uninstallation, querying, and dependency resolution. So how do we go about making one of our very own?

The simplest way to create our own RPM is to cheat. There are many options available to the creator of an RPM, many of which are rarely used. In the spirit of Open Source we can 'borrow' the specification and techniques used in the creation of another RPM to make our own.

As RPM creation can be very complex (it possibly even warrants a book in its own right) we will stick to a simple example in this chapter, one that should be enough to distribute a reasonable application as source or binary. We will leave the more esoteric options and support for packages derived via patches to the interested reader. Check out the manual page for the rpm program, or the RPM HOWTO (usually found in /usr/doc) for more information.

Let's now make an RPM for our DVD store application, dvdstore.

The heart of the RPM creation process is the spec file, which we will name dvdstore.spec. The specification file contains a number of sections that describe how the application is built, how it is installed and what its dependencies are.

When we create an RPM the rpm program will go through a number of steps, each of which we will be able to exercise some control over. We will use sections of the specification file to state what we wish to happen.

In general, the rpm program will use the /usr/src/packages (or /var/lib/rpm) tree for its operations. Source code tarballs are stored in SOURCES, spec files in SPECS, source RPM packages will be created in SRPMS, binary RPM packages in RPM. Applications are built in subdirectories of BUILD.

Given a specification file, the rpm program will look in SOURCES for the source tarball, unpack it into a subdirectory of BUILD, enter that directory, build the application, install it, and create RPM packages.

We'll give an outline of the process as controlled by the specification file.

The first part of the specification contains items that describe the application – what capabilities it provides and what others it requires:

```
#
# spec file for package dvdstore (Version 1.1)
#

Vendor:             Wrox Press
Distribution:       Any
Name:               dvdstore
Release:            1
Packager:           neil@tilde.co.uk
Copyright:          2000 by Wrox Press
Group:              Applications/Media
Provides:           dvdstore
Requires:           postgres-6.5
Autoreqprov:        on
Version:            1.1
Summary:            DVD Rental Store Application
Source:             dvdstore-1.1.tar.gz
```

Most of the items here are self-explanatory. The RPM packages will have names that are of the form:

```
Name-Version-Release.architecture.rpm
```

where `architecture` will be either `src` for a source RPM, or `noarch` for an RPM that is not platform-specific, or `i386` for a binary RPM prepared for an Intel CPU-based machine. Linux systems running on other architectures use different names for the architecture, for example, `sparc` for the Sun SPARC. Some packages containing applications that were compiled specifically for a particular member of a processor family may use an indicative architecture. An example would be a kernel compiled for Intel Pentium processors using `i586` as the architecture.

The `Group` item is used to guide graphical package installers. It specifies an application grouping that this package should be filed under.

The `Autoreqprov` setting allows the `rpm` program to add its own dependencies if needed. We will see an example of this later.

The next part is a free form (but mandatory) section for a description of the application, often used to provide author details and contacts:

```
%description
DVD Rental Store Application

An application to manage a DVD rental store, including membership, rental and
return of titles and reservations.

This version requires PostgreSQL 6.5.

Authors: Neil Matthew and Richard Stones
```

The next sections contain commands that are used by the RPM `build` process to prepare the source code for building, doing the build, and then installing the application:

```
%prep
%b

%build
make

%install
make install
```

The `%prep` section is used to **prepare** the source code for building, applying any patches if necessary. There is a macro (`%setup`) that can be used for unpacking a source tarball. For our application this is sufficient.

The `%build` section contains instructions on *how* to build the application. For us, a simple `make` is enough; for more complex applications an invocation of the `configure` script with parameters relating to this particular build might be used, for example, if this is going to be used to make a binary RPM of a package with special options set.

The `%install` section contains instructions for installing the application locally.

Each of the `%prep`, `%build`, and `%install` sections is effectively a shell script and can therefore use any command that can be called from the shell, including conditionals.

When requested to build an RPM package, the `rpm` program will execute these sections in turn. Options that control the building of RPMs all begin with `-b`:

`-bp`	execute `%prep` section
`-bc`	execute `%build` section
`-bi`	execute `%install` section
`-bs`	build a source package (after `%prep`, `%build` and `%install`)
`-bb`	build a binary package (after `%prep`, `%build` and `%install`)
`-ba`	build both source and binary packages

To create a binary RPM package, the `rpm` program needs to know which files are installed during the install process. We need to list the files in a `%files` section of the specification file:

```
%files
/usr/local/lib/dvd_pg.a
/usr/local/include/dvd.h
/usr/local/man/man3/dvd.3
```

To check that the listed files exist we can use the -bl (list check) option to the rpm program:

```
$ rpm -bl dvdstore.spec
Processing files: dvdstore
File not found: /usr/local/man/man3/dvd.3
Provides: dvdstore
Requires: postgres-6.5
$
```

Once we have ensured that our application builds and installs from source, and that our file list is correct, we can go ahead and build the RPM packages. Remember that we may need superuser permissions for the install part of the process to work. Again, the output shown here has been abbreviated to save space:

```
$ rpm -ba dvdstore.spec
Executing: %prep
+ umask 022
+ cd /usr/src/packages/BUILD
+ cd /usr/src/packages/BUILD
+ rm -rf dvdstore-1.1
+ /bin/gzip -dc /usr/src/packages/SOURCES/dvdstore-1.1.tar.gz
+ tar -xvvf -
drwxr-xr-x neil/users          0 2000-04-25 10:54 dvdstore-1.1/
-rw-r--r-- neil/users       1093 2000-04-25 10:54 dvdstore-1.1/Makefile
-rw-r--r-- neil/users       5391 2000-04-08 20:23 dvdstore-1.1/pg_disk.pgc
-rw-r--r-- neil/users       6889 2000-04-08 20:23 dvdstore-1.1/pg_title.pgc
...
+ STATUS=0
+ '[' 0 -ne 0 ']'
+ cd dvdstore-1.1
++ /usr/bin/id -u
+ '[' 500 = 0 ']'
++ /usr/bin/id -u
+ '[' 500 = 0 ']'
+ /bin/chmod -Rf a+rX,g-w,o-w .
+ exit 0
Executing: %build
+ umask 022
+ cd /usr/src/packages/BUILD
+ cd dvdstore-1.1
+ make
gcc -Wall -g -I/usr/lib/pgsql/include   -c dvd_gen.c -o dvd_gen.o
ecpg -t -I/usr/lib/pgsql/include pg_util.pgc
gcc -Wall -g -I/usr/lib/pgsql/include   -c pg_util.c -o pg_util.o
ecpg -t -I/usr/lib/pgsql/include pg_functional.pgc
gcc -Wall -g -I/usr/lib/pgsql/include   -c pg_functional.c -o pg_functional.o
ar -r dvd_pg.a dvd_gen.o pg_util.o pg_functional.o pg_member.o pg_lookup.o
pg_title.o pg_disk.o
+ exit 0
Executing: %install
+ umask 022
+ cd /usr/src/packages/BUILD
+ cd dvdstore-1.1
+ make install
```

```
cp dvd.h /usr/local/include
cp dvd_pg.a /usr/local/lib
+ exit 0
Processing files: dvdstore
Finding provides...
Finding requires...
Provides: dvdstore
Requires: postgres-6.5
Wrote: /usr/src/packages/SRPMS/dvdstore-1.1-1.src.rpm
Wrote: /usr/src/packages/RPMS/i386/dvdstore-1.1-1.i386.rpm
$
```

We can now distribute the source and binary RPM packages to our users!

If we need to execute any scripts on installation or uninstallation we can add those to the specification file. For more details, check out the RPM HOWTO. As a quick example let's add a script to e-mail the superuser when the package is installed. We add a script to a %post (for post-install) section in the specification file:

```
%post
mail root -s "DVD installed - please register" </dev/null
```

Now when we build the RPM package we see that the rpm program adds a dependency of its own, that of /bin/sh, as this will be needed to execute the post-install script we have just added:

```
$ rpm -bb dvdstore.spec
...
Finding requires...
Provides: dvdstore
Prereqs: /bin/sh
Requires: postgres-6.5
Wrote: /usr/src/packages/RPMS/i386/dvdstore-1.1-1.i386.rpm
$
```

If we query the resulting RPM we can see the script that will be executed on installation:

```
$ rpm -q --scripts -p /usr/src/packages/RPMS/i386/dvdstore-1.1-1.i386.rpm
postinstall script (through /bin/sh):
mail root -s "DVD installed - please register" </dev/null
$
```

Other scripts that run at other times are created in a similar way.

Patches

If we have chosen to distribute a source tarball (or source RPM) of our application we can make use of patches to distribute small source code changes to our programs. A patch is a just a difference between two versions of a file, or set of files. If we were careful enough in our use of a source code control system (such as CVS) we will have made sure that our releases were all tagged. That way we would know exactly and precisely which versions of our source (and other) files constituted each and every release of the code that we made.

To save our users having to download a complete set of source code each time we release a new version, we can also publish patches with which users can update their copy to the latest revision level.

The patch program (developed by Larry Wall and now part of the POSIX standard) allows patch files to be applied to source code automatically. The Linux kernel source code distribution relies heavily on this mechanism, as the complete source is well over ten megabytes in size. A typical minor revision to the kernel comprises a few tens of kilobytes of new source code. Patching is a very efficient way of distributing updates, and sharing fixes and changes between developers.

Making a Patch

A patch file is generally just the output of the diff program, made with a couple of specific options to allow errors to be detected more readily.

First of all we need to create subdirectories that contain the last released version (the old version) and the latest code (the new version). Then we run the diff program to compare the directories, creating a list of differences.

> It is essential that our starting point (the old version) is the same as the version the users will apply the patch to, and that we immediately save the new version as a release so that we can reliably created patches against that version in the future.

The patch manual page recommends a procedure for creating patches that ensures the greatest possibility of success. The diff command that should be used to create the patch is given as:

```
$ LC_ALL=C TZ=GMT0 diff -Naur old new
```

The environment variable LC_ALL sets the locale for the diff command, in this case ensuring that all local translations of formats such as time, date, messages and so on are inhibited as they will not necessarily be relevant on the user's machine.

The variable TZ set to GMT0 ensures that the time and dates used in the output from diff are in Universal Time so that (if needed) the times and dates can be set correctly on the patched files.

The options to use with diff are:

-N	Treat files found only in one of the directories as present, but empty in the other. This will cause patch to create new files as required as the difference will be given as the entire content of the file that is present.
-a	Treat all files as text, and compare line by line.
-u	Use the unified format output, which includes some context around the differences to help patch find the right place to apply the changes. *This option may not be available in all versions of diff on non-Linux systems. If it is not in yours try -c for a context diff, or install GNU diff!*
-r	When comparing directories, use a recursive search into sub-directories.

Let's see this in action by creating a patch from version 1.0 of our DVD store application to version 1.1. First we create directories containing just the source files for each version of the application.

> *It is often useful to have a target `distclean` in your makefile to clean up all of the intermediate files created in the build process for your application. This target typically would delete object files, libraries, editor backup files, and the application binaries, leaving just the text files and the source code, ready for a source distribution or a patch.*

```
$ ls -F
dvd_app_1.0/       dvd_app_1.1/
```

Now let's create the patch that describes the differences between these two versions of the application. The output shown here is abbreviated to save space:

```
$ LC_ALL=C TZ=GMT0 diff -Naur dvd_app_1.0 dvd_app_1.1
diff -Naur dvd_app_1.0/Makefile dvd_app_1.1/Makefile
--- dvd_app_1.0/Makefile    Sat Apr  8 14:09:21 2000
+++ dvd_app_1.1/Makefile    Tue Apr 25 07:42:49 2000
@@ -39,3 +44,7 @@
        rm -f *~
        rm -f core

+distclean:
+    rm -f *.o *~ core test_pg dvd_pg.a dvd_app final_file
+    rm -f pg_member.c pg_util.c pg_functional.c
+    rm -f pg_lookup.c pg_title.c pg_disk.c
diff -Naur dvd_app_1.0/pg_lookup.pgc dvd_app_1.1/pg_lookup.pgc
--- dvd_app_1.0/pg_lookup.pgc Sat Apr  8 19:23:56 2000
+++ dvd_app_1.1/pg_lookup.pgc Tue Apr 25 07:43:14 2000
@@ -135,7 +135,7 @@
        sprintf(db_text, "Unknown Error: %d", err_number);
        pg_print_debug(__FILE__, __LINE__, sqlca, "Bad err code");
    }
-    strcpy(*message_to_show, db_text);
+    *message_to_show = db_text;

    exec sql COMMIT WORK;
  } /* pg_get_err_text */
...
$
```

Here you can see that the file `Makefile` has changed (the `distclean` target has been added) and a bug has been fixed in `pg_lookup.pgc` at around line 135.

To publish this patch we should capture the output, compress it, and make it available to our users:

```
$ LC_ALL=C TZ=GMT0 diff -Naur dvd_app_1.0 dvd_app_1.1 | gzip > patch-1.0-1.1.gz
```

The compressed patch file is just over 1000 bytes in size, compared with over 100K for the complete source.

Applying a Patch

When users receive our patch they will be able to update their copy of the source code to match our latest. To do this they simply need to use the patch command, but there are a couple of things to watch out for.

Each of the differences in our patch refers to files in subdirectories called dvd_app_1.0 and dvd_app_1.1. The user may not have placed his or her copy of the source in a directory with the same name as our original.

The patch program allows us to ignore one of more parts of the filenames used for applying the patch. The foremost use for this is to overcome the problem of directory names at the top level. You should tell your users to change into the directory where they have placed the application source code and run the command:

```
$ patch -Np1
```

using the uncompressed patch file as the input. This can be achieved in one command like this:

```
$ ls -F
dvd_app/        patch-1.0-1.1.gz
$ cd dvd_app
$ gzip -dc ../patch-1.0-1.1.gz | patch -Np1
patching file Makefile
patching file dvd_gen.c
patching file pg_lookup.pgc
patching file pg_util.pgc
$
```

The options used to patch are:

-p<number>	Strip off the first part of the filename recorded in the patch file. In our case dvd_app_1.0/Makefile becomes Makefile, which is correct as we are running the patch command in the top-level directory.
-N	Assume a normal (rather than reverse) patch. The patch program is able to undo patches (reverse patch) if it detects a patch has already been applied. The -N option ensures that patch will not offer to do this should the patch be accidentally applied a second time.

GNATS

Once released into the wild, your application will no doubt come across a wide range of different users, uses, and problems. Some of your users will report problems back to you, for you to fix. If your application is popular you may receive many requests for fixes, updates, new features.

The GNATS application is a database for tracking bugs and is well worth a closer look. For an installable package for GNATS and more information look at the Cygnus web site, at http://sourceware.cygnus.com/projects.html.

The GNATS system uses a database to record the status of bugs that are being tracked. A server process listens for incoming problem reports that can arrive in a number of ways. The system accepts reports as:

❑ e-mail

❑ web site posting

❑ direct from applications

A simple UNIX application `send-pr` is distributed with your application. This arranges for problem reports to be sent to the GNATS system on your machine. If problems are reported by e-mail you need to setup a process to intercept messages addressed to GNATS and process them. Bugs can be assigned to developers, and reports of outstanding faults can be generated.

A web interface (WebGNATS) has been developed and is distributed along with the GNATS source code.

Summary

In this chapter we have taken quite an extensive look at the RPM package manager. We have seen how it can be used to control the packages installed on a Linux system through installing, uninstalling, and querying packages. We have also seen how easy it is to create our own source and binary RPM packages for distributing our own applications.

We have seen how providing patches instead of complete source code can be an effective way to keep to a minimum the amount of data the user has to manage to keep up to date.

We also looked briefly at GNATS, the bug tracking tool that can help keep problem reports under control.

28

Internationalization

One of the most important aspects of working as a professional programmer is being prepared to accept responsibility for developing applications with *all* the functionality demanded by a set of user requirements. In today's global economy, complete functionality often means that you'll need to offer support for input and output in multiple languages, along with appropriate, culturally specific data formatting.

For example, although Americans and Europeans both recognize '1/2/99' as a date, Americans would interpret it as January 2nd, 1999, while Europeans would read it as 1st February 1999. This problem can be dealt with on output simply by using an unambiguous format; spelling out the month and using a four-digit year is one possibility.

However, requirements may demand an alternative, potentially ambiguous format (perhaps in support of "backward compatibility"). We may allow the user to enter dates freehand, or they may prefer a shorter, all numeric format. User-friendliness can be further enhanced by requesting confirmation of ambiguous formats, giving the best guess according to local custom.

Say you're implementing flexible date-handling in an application that was ordered by a multinational corporation; you'll probably face a requirement that the application handle date conventions for *all* the countries that client can foresee operating in, preferably without any need to recompile.

Internally, businesses are likely to use 'international format' (YYYY-MM-DD) since it's widely familiar, Y2K-safe, and sorts properly; however, one of the most important areas for **internationalization** is in business-to-consumer e-business. While employees can quickly be trained to work to corporate convention, customers are likely to be much less tractable. This is especially true outside of North America and northern Europe (even in countries like Japan), where customers are still used to having human assistants translate their input into something acceptable to the organization's formatting conventions.

Evidently, given the large number of date formats in common use, handling them all perfectly is impossible, even in principle. Writing a robust, convenient application will therefore be expensive, both in terms of programmer labor and calendar time. Furthermore, since a professional programmer will also commit to delivering a product by a deadline *and* within budget, there's apparently a conflict in the requirements.

Fortunately, the problem needn't be as tough as it looks, at least not for the application programmer. A set of standards is available, which codifies common needs for multicultural customers, including:

- ❑ technical features such as character sets and encodings
- ❑ user interface parameters like date and currency formats
- ❑ input of characters not directly available on keyboards
- ❑ the language for message display

Furthermore, these standards are implemented in libraries available in Linux systems. Internationalization for Linux is one of the areas where the GNU Project has been an essential leader, helping Linux to catch up to established standards and proprietary implementations. GNU libc will provide all of the advanced internationalization features specified in standards such as POSIX and UNIX98, going far beyond what was normal practice in the Linux development community. In fact, this commitment to support by Linux's default libc implementation has encouraged the Linux development community to turn to standards-based internationalization, and inspired projects like the **GNU Translation Project**.

Li18nux, the **Linux Internationalization Initiative** (http://www.li18nux.net), is supported by some of the big names in computing like IBM and Sun Microsystems besides the usual faces of Red Hat, SuSe and so on, and holds out the promise that Linux internationalization facilities will be competitive with those of commercial platforms such as Solaris, Windows, and the Macintosh. The Li18nux 2000 draft standard (http://www.linux.net/root/LI18NUX2000/li18nux2k_draft.html) contains references to all of the relevant standards, and many examples of their implementation. The text is very dry, so don't read it. Think of it as a kind of annotated bookmarks file: it contains URLs for everything mentioned below.

Most of the standard facilities described later are available in version 2.1 of GNU libc, and more are planned for version 2.2. Others are provided by Xlib or by toolkits like Motif and GTK+. Special-purpose libraries and functionality incorporated in application-specific libraries round out the programmer's internationalization toolbox. The purpose of this chapter is to provide the professional GNU/Linux programmer with a framework for identifying these common requirements and the basic knowledge of the libraries and their functionality.

The main difficulty in creating programs flexible enough to be readily used in many cultural environments is that the standard facilities are a very recent development. The implementations are still unstable (as can be seen from the continuing work on GNU libc, and the state of GTK+ and other toolkits), and there are few examples of "best practice" that Linux programmers can refer to, although most GNU utilities at least support native language message catalogs. New standards for more advanced facilities (for example GUI layout widgets capable of automatically handling the bidirectional layout problems of languages like Hebrew and Arabic) are proposed or revised weekly. It is hoped that this chapter will encourage you readers to pioneer in this area and communicate "best practices" to fellow developers, and provide some basic hints to guide your efforts.

I18N Terminology

The basic process of adapting a software program to a given culture is **localization**. Localization can be accomplished by changing the source of a program in a manner reminiscent of porting software to a new platform: redefining functions, reordering parameters, translating strings, and so on. This suggests that the efficiency of the process can be enhanced by proper attention to "cultural portability" in the development of the first version of the program.

And so it can: this practice is called **internationalization**. Internationalizing a program means using a standard set of variables and callbacks in the program. These variables and callbacks reduce the process of localizing the program to a different culture to proper initialization of the variables, linking in the callbacks from a standard library, and translating messages. That is, although localization could involve massive changes to the source code, in a properly internationalized application all of the cultural differences will be handled by loading appropriate data files. Not only will this reduce programmer effort, but it is more likely to produce correct output. For example, translation can be handled by translators who specialize in the natural language, rather than programmers.

It is worth noting that in almost all applications, the program need handle only one culture at a time. Input, output, and error messages will all be given in the same language. A few classes of application, however, demand that multiple languages be handled by the same program at the same time. (An editor used for translation is an obvious example, but any messaging application, such as a mail user agent or a newsreader, should be able to handle messages in various languages, and even multilingual messages.) The process of adapting a program to simultaneous use of several cultural conventions is called **multilingualization**. It is interesting to note that because of the client-server architecture, as a system our DVD store application can be multilingual, allowing different users simultaneous interaction with the application in their native languages, even though neither the server nor the client is multilingual.

There is a set of common abbreviations for these jawbreaking terms: L10N for localization, I18N for internationalization, and M17N for multilingualization. The abbreviations are derived by replacing all the letters but the first and last with the count of the letters omitted. For example, "localization" has 12 letters, and thus there are 10 letters between the "L" and the "N", giving "L10N."

The rest of the chapter will be divided into a description of models of internationalization available to the application programmer, a description of the APIs available to the professional GNU/Linux programmer, and a selection of applications of these techniques to the DVD store sample application.

Isn't Unicode the Answer?

Yes, Unicode is the answer to a lot of questions about I18N, by virtue of its goal of assigning a unique code point to each character used in text by all of the world's languages; but it's not the answer to all of them, not even a majority.

Unicode

What It Is...

Unicode is a universal character set created by the unification of the work of the Unicode Consortium and the International Standards Organization's (ISO JTC1/SC2) "Universal Multiple-Octet Coded Character Set" (UCS), standardized as ISO-10646. It is intended to be able to represent all text in all of the world's languages. It is also a standard specifying an encoding of these characters as a map from the character set to the integers. The current version of the standard includes several ways to represent the range of the map in memory. These representations are called **Unicode Transformation Formats**, abbreviated UTF. Finally, the standard specifies certain properties of characters such as the numerical values of digits, and standard algorithms for manipulations like sorting.

A character set is an ordered set of characters. Characters have various properties, including the glyph used to display them and syntactic classifications like whitespace and punctuation. An encoding is a one-to-one mapping from the characters in a character set to a set of objects that a computer can handle, typically the set of bitstrings or byte strings. (Note that Unicode departs from this practice by specifying the integers.)

Normally the length of the bitstring-encoding of a character is a multiple of 8. In modern computers, this is the same size as a byte. Since at one time bytes could have different sizes on different architectures, the term octet was invented to unambiguously mean a bitstring of length 8. If the bitstrings for all characters encoded by the encoding have the same number of bits, the encoding is called a wide-character encoding. ASCII is a (degenerate) wide-character encoding, using 7 (or 8) bits per character. Unicode (as originally conceived) is a 16-bit (or two-octet) wide-character encoding. Otherwise, the encoding is a multibyte encoding. UTF-8 is a multibyte encoding. "Fixed width" encoding and "variable width" encoding would be more accurate terms, but the terms "wide character" and "multibyte" are now in universal use.

The Unicode Consortium was organized to develop a commercially practical unified character code (thus, "Unicode"). These considerations led to its original 16-bit format, limiting the code space to 65536 characters. In practice, somewhat less, as characters are generally assigned in blocks aligned on "rows" of 256 code points. Each block corresponds to an alphabet, such as "Greek", or a set of related alphabets, like "Latin", or other groupings less familiar to Western programmers, such as the Cherokee (native American) syllabary or the block of Han (Chinese) ideographs.

On the other hand, the UCS was intended to provide a comprehensive framework for all standardized characters, so that any text could be translated into a single universal encoding without loss. Since the Japanese and Chinese comprehensive character dictionaries for Chinese characters each contain about 50,000 characters, and there are nearly 12,000 Hangul syllables for Korean, not to mention the hieroglyphics, there is no room left for the paltry 26 letters of the Roman alphabet, let alone Greek, Cyrillic, and mathematical symbols, in the 16-bit code space. So the designers of the UCS realized that they would need more than 16 bits to encode all the characters of interest (even given Han unification, which identified many Japanese characters with the Chinese characters from which they were originally derived). Considering modern computer architecture, it was decided that the code space would be representable in 31 bits (reserving the last bit to identify a 32-bit word as assigned to a non-UCS-character usage, and to avoid problems of signed vs. unsigned representations).

However, the ISO working group recognized the need for a compact subset representable in 16 bits. This subset, called the **Basic Multilingual Plane** (BMP), was from the outset very similar to the Unicode character set, since it was designed on similar principles. Even the committee memberships overlapped substantially, so it was quickly decided to unify those efforts, bringing the BMP into line with the Unicode standard.

Similarly, the Han unification controversy (see later for more details) and the fact that even with Han unification there wouldn't be enough space to include all the character sets satisfying the Unicode Consortium standards for inclusion led the Consortium to design an augmented character space via the "UTF-16" format, which set aside certain pairs of 16-bit "surrogate" characters to encode an addition 1024x1024 space of code points.

The inconsistency of the 16-bit surrogates (which means that the count of characters in an array is not the same as the count of Unicode characters in the string it represents) led to the definition of the flat "UTF-32" format. UTF-32 uses 32-bit characters but can represent exactly the same characters as "UTF-16", by restricting usage to the first 1,114,112 code points of the 4,294,967,296 available in the space of 32-bit unsigned integers. The rest are considered illegal in a Unicode text.

The unification of the Unicode and ISO 10646 standards was completed when the ISO agreed not to assign characters to any code point above 1,114,111.

Thus we have arrived at a stage where there is a single, undisputed universal character set, a single encoding from characters to integers, and a small number of well-defined Unicode transformation formats (UTF) for representing those integers. Besides the formats mentioned above, there is the famous UTF-8 variable width format, which has the property that all ASCII characters represent themselves in a single byte, and that all other characters are encoded in more than one byte, all of which are in the range 0x80-0xFF. This means that 8-bit clean mechanisms based on ASCII, such as the Unix file system and many shells and programming languages, will not accidentally treat UTF-8 strings as containing keywords or syntactic constructs. There are other Unicode transformation formats, but their use is severely deprecated today.

Format	Definition	Typical Use
Unicode, UCS	An invertible mapping from standardized characters to non-negative integers.	Abstract (the integer representation is not defined) and ambiguous (depending on context, "Unicode" may mean the whole character set, the two-byte UCS-2 representation without surrogates, or the UTF-16 representation with surrogates).
UCS-4	Unicode code points are represented as 31-bit unsigned integers.	A superset of UTF-32, not strictly standard conformant; glibc's internal wide character format.
UTF-32	Unicode code points are represented as 31-bit unsigned integers, but restricted to the range 0x0 to 0x1FFFF.	The standard-conforming wide character representation capable of representing all Unicode code points.
UTF-16	Unicode characters in the BMP, 0x0 to 0xFFFF, are represented as 16-bit unsigned integers; characters with code points above 65535 are represented as pairs of surrogates, the first from the range 0xD800 to 0xDBFF, and the second from the range 0xDC00 to 0xDFFF.	For applications where "string is character array" semantics are desirable but not absolutely required, but ability to transmit the full range of Unicode characters is required, and a more compact representation than UTF-32 is desired.

Table continued on following page

Format	Definition	Typical Use
UCS-2, BMP	Restricted to Unicode characters in the BMP, 0x0 to 0xFFFF.	For applications where "string is character array" semantics are absolutely required, but ability to transmit the full range of Unicode characters is not, and a more compact representation than UTF-32 is desired.
UTF-8	A variable width format, with ASCII characters represented as 8-bit unsigned integers, and others represented by a varying number of bytes with the high bit set.	Normally used as an external format, especially for input to byte-oriented programs (such as shells and the file system) that treat certain ASCII bytes as syntactically significant, but are 8-bit clean (treat all high-bit-set bytes as non-syntactic characters and pass them untransformed); also provides a fairly efficient encoding for applications where text data is expected to contain a high proportion of ASCII, such as computer programs or SGML data.

Another aspect of Unicode that must be mentioned is that it's a standard for text processing and not merely for character encoding. In this it goes beyond the ISO-10646 standard. In fact, in the future the Unicode Consortium has committed to accepting the ISO's designations of newly standardized characters, while its developers concentrate on algorithmic aspects of text processing. While the Unicode Standard admits that it is not likely to be comprehensive or universally applicable for some time, it defines many facilities and baseline algorithms. These include the following:

❑ Alternative representations of composed characters: many extended Latin letters can be decomposed into a base letter plus a diacritical accent – both representations are possible in Unicode.

❑ Algorithms for comparing composed characters (since the same text may represent the same character in different ways at different places).

❑ Assigning properties such as numeric values for digits and textual unit boundaries for words and sentences.

❑ Algorithms for sorting and searching.

❑ Algorithms for rendering nested bi-directional text.

There remain a few unstandardized areas. Some are basically omissions (for example, because the Ukraine was a part of the Soviet Union at the time, the Cyrillic character set incorporated into Unicode versions 1 and 2 was Russian-specific, and a few Cyrillic characters specific to Ukrainian were omitted). These may be expected to be resolved in future versions of the standard.

Another is a difference of principle, such as the "Han Unification" problem, for example. The point of contention is that Japanese, Korean, and (traditional) Vietnamese writing systems all use derivatives of the Chinese ideographic characters, and all agree on the lineage of each character; characters that are "the same" in each system can therefore be commonly agreed. On this basis, these sets of characters, including one at most from each national character set, are identified as a single "unified Han" character.

However, a vocal minority of critics (mostly Japanese) insists that each national variant is in fact a different character, and should be assigned a separate code point in the Unicode standard. There are three points to their argument:

❑ It is convenient in multilingual texts to be able to determine the language from the characters used.

❑ Many Japanese feel there is something special about their language, and some feel that by sharing character codes with other languages they will somehow diminishes this "Japanese spirit".

❑ Finally, it becomes more difficult to change national standards, as that could break the way in which the unified Han characters are 'attached' to their national variants. This is important, at least in Japan, because some officially registered personal and place names use characters that are not present in the JIS X 0208 and JIS X 0212 standards used to help define the Basic Multilingual Plane.

Clearly, this cannot be resolved to the satisfaction of all disputants. Unification will stay, but various means (both inside the Unicode standard – the so-called "Plane 14 tags" – and outside it – such as the language attributes in XML tags) will be provided to distinguish different Han variants where necessary.

A final, more serious, problem is "characters" that cannot be included in Unicode for one reason or another. Some, like music or electronic circuit notation, are arguably characters in the sense that they can be implemented as fonts of stylized glyphs to be positioned appropriately on output. However, the Unicode standard explicitly excludes them on the ground that Unicode is for text that is representable as linear streams, rather than two-dimensional notations. (This didn't stop the Consortium from including box-drawing characters in the BMP at block 0x2500. This was justified by the common inclusion of such characters in hardware terminal fonts and the IBM PC character set, but is clearly inconsistent.)

Others, such as the Ukrainian characters mentioned above or some rare personal and place name characters in Japanese cannot be included because they are not standardized by the appropriate national body. Some characters have not been invented yet; the currency symbol for the European currency unit, the Euro, is just one recent addition; surely there will be many others. Finally, since Unicode proper is limited to officially standardized characters, special purpose characters (such as corporate logos) and character sets (e-mail 'smilies') will not be incorporated.

To some extent, all of these problems can be solved by using the standard facilities of Unicode. The addition of small numbers of characters can be done privately by using the private space provided in the Unicode standard, codes 0xE000 to 0xF8FF (6400 points in the BMP), and 0xF0000 to 0x10FFFF (131,072 points at the top of the Unicode code space). Microsoft and Apple have already helped themselves (in conflicting ways) to portions of the private space in the BMP. "Han disambiguation" can be handled while conforming to the Unicode standard by use of language tags, either those defined by Unicode itself, or at a higher level in a markup language such as SGML or XML.

If you know that your application will only be used in its own context, then you can hard-code your private character set into the private space in the BMP. For example, Klingon is available in the Linux kernel in this way. However, if you expect (as the Japanese would) that users would be likely to want to add characters for personal or corporate reasons, or wish your application to be portable to environments where vendors like Microsoft have already grabbed large parts of the private space, you will need to provide for dynamic allocation of private space, and relocation of your private characters from one instance of the application to the next.

...What It Can Do...

Because each character is assigned a unique code point in Unicode, it is the obvious choice for internal representation. As long as text is simply translated to Unicode from an external representation on input, then translated in reverse on output, no data corruption will occur. This property is designed into the fundamental criteria for assembling the Unicode character set.

Also, in principle this makes it simple to check what characters are handled by fonts and other facilities. Since the encoding is standard, a font only needs to give a list of the characters it provides.

Unicode makes it possible to define standard libraries for handling properties of characters like type (letter, digit, etc.) and directionality (Hebrew characters are read right-to-left) since each character has a unique identifying code. Even where Unicode's baseline algorithms may not be optimal, they do provide a fallback and are likely to be widely implemented in libraries and toolkits. Java's streams and IBM's Unicode Classes for C++ are two examples.

Thus, Unicode basically allows the extension of the standard C string facilities to all the world's scripts, as well as extending the kinds of string and character manipulations that can be delegated to standard libraries. In many ways, this is a huge improvement over the status quo.

...and What It Can't Do

First of all, as Hideki Hiura (a principal designer of the XIM and IIIMF protocols for I18N user input) likes to emphasize, Unicode only solves problems related to scripts (collections of characters); but these are the easiest of language-related problems to deal with. There are many others.

A few representative examples are:

- ❑ **Translation**
  Just because you have a system capable of printing error messages in Japanese for your application doesn't mean that you have Japanese error messages to print! The original error messages will need to be translated.

- ❑ **Text Formatting**
  Unicode cannot guarantee that formatting will be correct. Although Americans and Britons can both write dates entirely in ASCII, the preferred formats are different, and the interpretation of some common abbreviated formats will be different. In fact, in some sense Unicode makes it more difficult, since applications cannot use the character set as a hint about formatting preferences.

- ❑ **Font Choice**
  Chinese, Japanese, and Korean scripts share thousands of characters, but not only are the preferred styles different, the actual shapes can vary quite substantially for a given character. That is, historically it is possible to trace how character shapes have evolved in each culture, through independent waves of standardization and simplification. But all of these ideographic characters originated with the Chinese many hundreds of years ago. Thus there are objective criteria to say the glyphs represent the same character, despite the rather different shapes. Since the character is the same, the Unicode code is the same.

- ❑ **GUI Layout**
  While most Japanese GUIs present their text left-to-right, the historical vertical orientation of Japanese writing has left its imprint on Japanese sensibilities with respect to layout, and many Japanese GUI designers will place buttons and other GUI components in rather different places than American designers would. No purely textual device, such as a character set, can help with this kind of issue.

The Character Encoding Problem

Despite the introduction of Unicode, one of the problems facing the application programmer wishing to internationalize their software is the large number of character encodings in use. Not only does each language have its own encodings, but most have several possible encodings. Japanese Linux users must deal with data in three different encodings. EUC-JP is the standard encoding for Unix platforms because it is compact and file system safe. Shift JIS is used on Microsoft and Apple platforms. ISO-2022-JP is more verbose, but it is mandated for use in Internet mail and news. Soon Unicode will be added to the traditional three. It won't replace them: they will remain in legacy databases and will be produced by legacy software. It is true that the user can often easily distinguish these cases by the source of the data, but programs will generally not be able to do so.

Another problem is that the different encodings all use the same set of bit strings as codes. EBCDIC and ASCII both use codes in the range 0x00 to 0x7F to encode English, but they are not the same. Encodings for different languages, ISO Greek and ISO Cyrillic, also overlap. Both use the octets in the range 0x00 to 0x7F to encode the ASCII character set but ISO Greek uses the octets 0xA0 to 0xFF to encode the Greek alphabet while ISO Cyrillic uses the same octets to encode the Cyrillic alphabet. Automatically determining the encoding used in a data stream will be risky, and the best guess will depend on user characteristics and the process that generates the stream. Whether such heuristics can be used safely will depend on the application.

ISO 2022: Extension Techniques for Coded Character Sets

The obvious solution is Unicode, that is, some universal character set. However, in the 1960s and 1970s when these problems were first dealt with, compact representation was very important, while multilingual data communication channels were quite rare. And of course it was politically difficult: clearly the basic Latin alphabet of 52 letters and 10 digits, a reasonable number of punctuation marks, several dozen accented Latin letters, and the Greek, Cyrillic, Hebrew, and Arabic alphabets cannot all coexist in 256 characters. Who would be willing to accept a multibyte representation for their alphabet?

So the solution to overlapping codespaces adopted then was to include signals that the encoding has changed in the data stream. This solution was standardized as ISO 2022, which uses escape sequences to designate character sets for later use, and to shift them into the current "register". ISO 2022 thus defines modal systems: the communicating processes need to keep track of the current mode (character encoding) to correctly interpret the stream of character codes. Unicode is nonmodal: a Unicode character code always represents the same character.

ISO 2022 remains important for two reasons. First, it is the basis for many existing applications. For example, Mule, the Multilingual Extension to GNU Emacs, uses an internal character encoding based on ISO 2022. Second, the need to be consistent with ISO 2022 has had great influence on the design of character set standards. For example, although an 8-bit byte can represent 256 characters, ISO-2022-conformant encodings can use at most 192 of them for printing characters.

The ISO 2022 system suffers from many defects:

❑   the need to keep an external registry of known character encodings and the escape sequences used to invoke them

❑   the non-robustness of communication to corruption of escape sequences

❑   the potential catastrophic failure of communication if an unrecognized escape sequence is used

For example, the VM mail agent (based on GNU Emacs) will refuse to display messages in the Windows-1252 encoding in its default configuration. The argument for this behavior is that unknown encodings may contain arbitrary characters, which the terminal may treat as control sequences. I have locked up Windows DOS boxes and even xterms many times by cating Japanese. However, in fact most mail encoded in Windows-1252 contains only US-ASCII character codes, and is perfectly safe. On the other hand, in a Unicode based environment, the rare codes not present in ASCII would simply fail in looking up glyphs in the font. So most of the time near-perfect display could be achieved.

> *Note that VM **is** a robust application, which both allows the user to display the "raw" character codes and to create aliases for encodings. VM's author simply wants it made clear that proprietary standards created solely for the purpose of making Microsoft-compatibility harder to achieve are not his problem – the user must take explicit action to view text using that encoding.*

Although ISO 2022 still has its fans, especially among Unicode's detractors, most experts deprecate it. However, it has had an enormous influence on I18N efforts for the last 30 years. The first consequence of this is that the X11 standard for interclient communication specifies X Compound Text, a version of ISO 2022, as the encoding for internationalized applications. The Motif toolkit uses a related technique, compound strings, based on the same principles. If you must communicate with legacy Xlib or Motif clients, you may need to learn about Compound Text and ISO 2022.

Second, because ISO 2022 ratified the ambiguity of code points and the proliferation of encodings, and helped greatly to standardize the national encodings, fonts available for X11 are generally indexed by those same character sets. This has the advantage of compacting the representation of a font (that is, a table mapping code points to bitmaps). However, users may often want to display some characters from one font, and others from a different one. For example, there are many very high quality fonts available in the "Times Roman" style for the ISO-8859-1 (ASCII plus Latin-1) character set, but very few for ISO-8859-2 (ASCII plus Latin-2). Yet all of the ASCII characters and quite of few of the accented characters are common to both encodings. So a user might wish to use ISO-8859-1 wherever possible, and fall back to the lower quality font only when necessary.

Evidently, this multi-stage mapping process would be easier if there was some standard intermediate code. And in fact, there is: Unicode. Today, the standard strategy for high quality font rendering is to create fonts with compact tables of glyphs (outlines or bitmaps that can actually be displayed on the screen or page), and associate them with a table mapping from Unicode to the limited range of indices actually needed for the font. Such fonts are called "CID-keyed" (CID means "character ID"); applications need know nothing about that actual internal font encoding. By creating Cmaps ("character maps"), or tables going from any other encoding to Unicode, such fonts can be used for any character encoding whose characters have glyphs in the fonts. However, this system is far from universal. In fact, at present it is only available for X11 in recently developed TrueType-compatible servers and font servers, or with the Display Postscript extension.

Programming with Unicode

The most basic function is encoding conversion.

You may be able to control the file formats used by your application, and thus specify Unicode for them. If any legacy data you have is in the form of text files, then the iconv(1) utility can be used to migrate them to Unicode or UTF-8. With GNU iconv, the --list option can be used to get a list of currently implemented encodings. Because GNU iconv will automatically use a "transitive conversion" from source encoding to UCS-4, and from UCS-4 to the target encoding, it is unnecessary to list source-target pairs. If any conversions are available for a given encoding, all conversions will be available. (Some conversions are "available" subject to the proviso that the iconv(3) function will give an error return if a character to be converted has no equivalent in the target encoding, terminating the conversion at that point.)

Unfortunately, it is likely for some time to come that user input and output will require character conversion. Furthermore, most legacy databases will not be in a format such that iconv(1) can be directly applied to them. This means that the programmer will be required to make conversions to Unicode internally. Fortunately, this is straightforward using the iconv(3) function from GNU libc. Its use is normally very routine:

1. Allocate a conversion descriptor with iconv_open(3).

2. Test for success. (This is important, since attempting to use the failure return value in a conversion results in a segmentation violation on at least some systems.)

3. Use the descriptor in a call to iconv(3) to convert the text in the input buffer and store it in the output buffer. (The descriptor allows the buffer to be filled and converted asynchronously; it remembers the state of the conversion.)

4. Test the status of the conversion.

5. Deallocate the conversion descriptor with iconv_close(3).

Here is the classic example program, "hello, world", rewritten with the message defined in Unicode, but printed to an ASCII stream. Note that iconv is not thread-safe, in the sense that a conversion descriptor returned by iconv_open(3) may only be safely used in one thread, because it contains context-dependent state. For example, a character may have only been partially read from an external stream. An application may have multiple conversion descriptors open. This allows one thread to read input and convert to the internal encoding using one conversion descriptor, while another converts the processed internal stream to the external encoding and writes the output using another. By the nature of the stream paradigm, this should be sufficient for almost all applications.

First some head matter. Data types and function prototypes for iconv(3) functions are defined in <iconv.h>. Prototypes for auxiliary functions are given here.

```
/*
 hello_iconv.c
 demonstrates use of the UNIX98 iconv function
*/
```

```
#include <iconv.h>
#include <stdio.h>
#include <errno.h>
#include <stdlib.h>

/* prototypes for functions defined */
void u2a (char *a_string, const unsigned short *u_string);
char *dotted (char *s, int n);
void usage ();
```

The input buffer is initialized here. The data should look familiar, if strangely formatted.

The Unicode Standard states that big-endian format is preferred, but that little-endian is also acceptable. The Unicode encoding is really a map from characters to integers, so endianness is only an issue for external data streams. The Standard also defines Unicode Transformation Formats (UTF), which are actually just various ways to encode integers in the range 0 to $17*2^{16}$-1.

We do not use wchar_t here because we do not know that it is 16 bits; in fact on GNU systems it is 32 bits. It could even be 8 bits! (The assumption that a short is 16 bits is traditional; it would be more exact to use the uint16_t type defined by ISO C 9X.)

Initialization of the output buffer is unnecessary, but used to emphasize that the last array element is actually a sentinel to ensure that the standard C string functions work.

```
unsigned short unicode_string[15] =
{
'h','e','l','l','o',',',' ','w','o','r','l','d','\n',0,
0 /* end of buffer sentinel since this will be cast to char[] and dotted()
  */
};

/* buffer for output */
char c_string[15] =
{
0,0,0,0,0,0,0,0,0,0,0,0,0,0,
0 /* end of buffer sentinal for a dotted() output string */
};
```

u2a is the function that does the interesting work; checking status is always a good idea, but in I18N not only do you have to deal with the most unreliable sources – human users and network streams – but you cannot even make assumptions about the format of the input beyond a raw stream of bytes. Unicode text as a byte stream will contain ASCII NUL, LF, ESC, and DEL characters.

Note that since **iconv(3)** handles wide characters of 1, 2, and 4 bytes, as well as multibyte (variable width) characters, buffers must be handled as byte arrays.

```
void u2a (char *to_c, const unsigned short *from_unicode)
{
  int status = 0;
```

```
/* shame C doesn't have references, isn't it? */
int u_count = 14*sizeof(unsigned short);
int c_count = 14*sizeof(char);

/*
   this cast _must_ be made; it is the way the iconv function is
   defined
*/
const char *unicode_buffer = (const char *) from_unicode;
```

Declare and open the conversion descriptor. Note the specification of UNICODELITTLE; Unicode is by default big-endian, but little-endian versions are allowed – the programmer must check. This is hardcoded for an Intel box; on big-endian platforms this must be changed to UNICODEBIG.

Alternatively, many Unicode streams are prefixed by the byte-order mark (BOM) 0xFEFF (ZERO-WIDTH NO-BREAK SPACE). 0xFFFE is not a Unicode character, so this allows autodetection of endianness for such streams. (Code 0xFFFE is not a character precisely so that 0xFEFF can be used as the BOM.) This must be handled by the programmer, because iconv(3) will not discard this character, if recognized. A naïve attempt to use it in a program like this results in EILSEQ, since there is no such ASCII character.

```
iconv_t cd = iconv_open ("ASCII","UNICODELITTLE");

/*
   not necessary for ASCII, but suppose the target was input by a user?
   -- on my machine, attempting to use an invalid conversion descriptor
   ends in tears with a SIGSEGV
*/
if (cd == (iconv_t) (-1))
{
   printf ("Conversion to ASCII not available.\n");
   exit (EXIT_FAILURE);
}
```

Do the conversion, checking status, and reporting errors:

```
switch (status = iconv (cd, &unicode_buffer, &u_count, &to_c, &c_count))
{
case 0:
   /*
      depending on allocation and string representation,
      you may need to terminate the string
   */

   *to_c = '\0';
   break;

case -1:
   printf ("Error in conversion:  ");

   switch (errno) {
   case E2BIG:
      printf ("output buffer too small");
      break;
```

```
        case EILSEQ:
            printf ("invalid multibyte sequence");
            break;

        case EINVAL:
            printf ("incomplete multibyte sequence");
            break;

        default:
            printf ("iconv error not listed in man page (%d)", errno);
        }

        printf ("\n");

        /*
           depending on allocation and string representation,
           you may need to terminate the string
           E2BIG and EINVAL are normally not fatal; the state of CD will
           allow restarting after the last successfully converted character
           it's not obvious how to recover here, fake it
        */

        *to_c = '\0';
        break;

    default:
        /*
           depending on allocation and string representation,
           you may need to terminate the string
           this is probably the best we can do here
        */

        *to_c = '\0';
        printf ("%d characters irreversibly converted\n", status);
    }

    /*
       ... and a gold star for cleaning up:  the cd data structure can
       contain quite large tables, so this could plug a substantial
       memory leak
    */
    iconv_close (cd);
}
```

A simple driver program, a utility to make NULL bytes visible as periods, and the usage function:

```
/*
driver program which does several variants on printing the Unicode
string to the terminal; see usage() for usage
*/

int main (int argc, char *argv[])
{
  if (argc != 2 || argv[1][1] != '\0')
```

```
{
   usage (argv[0]);
   exit (EXIT_FAILURE);
}

switch (argv[1][0]) {
case '1':
   u2a (c_string, unicode_string);
   printf (c_string);
   break;

case '2':
   printf (dotted ((char *) unicode_string, 13*sizeof(unsigned short)));
   break;

case '3':
   printf ((char *) unicode_string);
   break;

case '4':
   u2a (c_string, unicode_string);
   printf (dotted (c_string, 14));
   break;

default:
   usage (argv[0]);
   exit (EXIT_FAILURE);
}
exit(EXIT_SUCCESS);
}

/*
a little utility to replace all null bytes in a string with dots
*/

char *dotted (char *s, int n)
{
 while (n > 0)
    if (s[--n] == '\0')
       s[n] = '.';
 return s;
}

/*
purely compulsive...
*/
void usage (char *s)
{
 printf ("usage: %s {1|2|3|4}\n", s);
 printf ("1 - printf converted C string\n");
 printf ("2 - printf Unicode string with dots replacing null bytes\n");
 printf ("3 - printf raw Unicode string\n");
 printf ("4 - printf converted C string with dots replacing null
         bytes\n");
}

/* end hello_iconv.c */
```

Here is a short session with the program in an xterm:

```
$ gcc -Wall -g -o test hello_iconv.c
$ ./test
usage: ./test {1|2|3|4}
1 - printf converted C string
2 - printf Unicode string with dots replacing null bytes
3 - printf raw Unicode string
4 - printf converted C string with dots replacing null bytes
$ ./test 1
hello, world
$ ./test 2
h.e.l.l.o.,. .w.o.r.l.d.
.$ ./test 3
h$ ./test 4
hello, world
.$
```

Comparing the results of ./test 2 and ./test 3, it is clear that ordinary string functions cannot be used with wide characters. Since the ASCII characters have the same integer values in Unicode, but are represented as shorts, on my little-endian machine only the 'h' is output, and printf then sees the NUL high byte and returns. On a big-endian machine the NUL comes first and nothing would be output by ./test 3.

> *If an additional function printing the Unicode string with wprintf were added, it would output the whole string as a series of 16-bit entities. This function is not included in the sample code, however, since the result would depend on the implementation of the terminal emulator, and could cause the terminal to lock up or crash.*

Although this program only produces output, getting input and converting to Unicode internally is equally simple. Another thing to notice about the iconv_open(3) interface is that the encodings are named by ASCII strings. There are two reasons for this. First, it is possible to define a module to implement a new conversion and load it dynamically. Use of macros (or an enum) to define C identifiers for encodings would make practical use of such modules difficult. Second, it means that an encoding name can be passed directly from the user to iconv_open. It might be an amusing exercise for the reader to modify hello_iconv.c to take the target encoding as a command-line argument. Because they are designed for ASCII-compatibility, conversion to the EUC-* encodings and UTF-8 is safe but boring. EBCDIC-US doesn't cause great harm in an xterm on my machine, but beware that it could change the terminal's mode or even crash it.

A final note: this program doesn't use any locale functions. This isn't really an omission. Even for the modified program suggested as an exercise (taking the target encoding as an argument), use of the locale functions would be unreliable and complicated because there is no standard way to determine things like the character set from the locale string, which is typically an alias. (Some help is available from the alias files provided by GNU libc and X11R6, typically in /usr/share/locale/locale.alias and /usr/X11R6/lib/locale/locale.alias respectively. But those files are not standardized, and there are no standard functions for parsing them.) Unfortunately, applications must provide their own heuristics (perhaps based on the locale.alias files), and if there seems to be risk of confusion about encodings, document the need for fully specified locale strings to the users. In the not-so-distant future, the most difficult problem (determining encoding of user input and output) should be eliminated by the universal use of UTF-8 for text streams. The remaining uses for conversion functions will be converting among Unicode transformation formats depending on the needs of the application, and converting data from legacy databases. But at least the latter should be a slow-moving target!

I18N Models and the System Environment

I18N models basically correspond to standards set up to define libraries useful for writing internationalized programs, and the functionality of each module in such a library. It is important for the application developer to be familiar with the various models and their domains of application. This determines the kinds of internationalization that are relatively straightforward to accomplish. Application designers should be aware of these models as well; they help to indicate not only the programmer resources that will be required for various kinds of functionality, but also other resources such as translators and associated software like "input method servers."

The POSIX Locale Model

The technical description of what we vaguely term "culture" is called a "locale". A locale is a set of values for such parameters as language, region, character set, encoding, date format, currency format, and so on. It is debatable exactly what is needed to compactly characterize a locale, but the POSIX standard provides a basic definition, called the **POSIX locale model**. The POSIX locale model makes the following assumptions:

1. The most important characteristics of text are determined by the user's native language, with allowance made for regional variation (such as the spelling differences between American English, "en_US", and British English, "en_GB"). For historical reasons, the encoding of the character set (for example, ASCII vs. Unicode) is added to language and region. (Note that language is not sufficient to determine encoding. Most European languages are supported by at least three encodings: a 7-bit variant of ASCII, an 8-bit ISO-8859 variant, and Unicode.) Finally, an implementation-dependent "modifier" is allowed, but not described at all in the standard.

2. Users will have applications in which the standard locales are in part inappropriate, requiring the ability to redefine some categories of the locale.

3. Redefinitions can be accomplished by mixing the practices of several locales.

Thus, the full specification of a POSIX locale looks like en_US.iso646-irv@unused.

- ❏ "en" stands for the English language. The language component is a two-letter code from the list defined by the ISO 639 standard.

- ❏ "US" stands for the United States. Normally the region code is a two-letter code from the list defined by ISO 3166.

- ❏ "iso646-irv" is the ISO version of the ASCII standard, and is identical to US ASCII except for name. Many national variants of ASCII were defined when many systems used 7-bit bytes; ISO 646 attempted to regularize them. "irv" stands for "international reference version".

- ❏ "unused" is a placeholder; actually it should be omitted. Its function is wholly implementation dependent, and it is not used at all in glibc or Linux.

The only required part of the locale is the language. The other three parts may be omitted along with their prefix. The system should choose a sensible default. Thus, in the US "en" should default to "en_US.iso646-irv", while in a system configured for use in England it would be interpreted as "en_GB.iso8859-15". Furthermore, most POSIX systems provide for aliases for locales. On Linux systems, the list of aliases is in the file /usr/share/locale/locale.alias. This is very system-dependent.

The first assumption – that the user's native language determines most properties of the locale – actually causes problems, especially for multilingual programs, because it led the POSIX working group to define the locale as a global property of a process. This means that dealing with multiple languages requires changing the locale, a fairly expensive operation. In particular, a multilingual application is likely to have to deal with multiple encodings at the same time. It will not be thread-safe. This assumption will be relaxed in future versions of glibc by providing a non-standard context parameter for an extended set of locale functions, but it is not certain that glibc's approach (though logical) will be adopted as an international standard. Programmers worried about the portability of their code to non-glibc platforms need to take this into account.

The third assumption amounts to a notational convention, since it is quite easy to define new locales and to derive them from old ones.

One approach to the I18N problem that is often available is to side-step it partially by using a client-server architecture. The idea is that the server will handle texts stored in its database as binary objects, assuming that the client is capable of formatting them. Thus internationalization of the server only affects its interaction with the operator. The interactions with database and clients will be "internationalized" by switching the data returned for a query based on the locale of the client. This often must be done anyway; if two branches are located in San Diego and Tijuana, prices in one will be quoted in US dollars, the other in Mexican pesos. So we are merely extending this notion to the texts.

The problem with this approach occurs when the order of text entries returned is important; since collation depends on the locale, the database server would need to be able to switch to the appropriate locale. There are two obvious approaches to side-step this most of the time: running a database backend for each locale, and sorting the data at the client. The first may be too expensive in terms of server resources, and the second in terms of bandwidth; it eliminates the possibility of using facilities like database cursors. So I18N can even impact your choice of system architecture.

The POSIX locale, as mentioned, is an internal variable, which is global to the process. In glibc it is implemented by dynamically changing internal functions called by the standard sorting and classification functions as well as by the stream input/output functions. Thus, changing the locale is a fairly expensive operation.

The categories of behavior affected by the locale are specified as "atoms". Each atom is implemented as a variable in the environment, and as a macro (or possibly enumerated constant) in C programs (see <locale.h>). The atom specifying date and time formatting is LC_TIME. Thus, a user who wants to use American English conventions for date formatting would set LC_TIME=en_US in his environment. A programmer wanting to hardcode those conventions in her program would invoke setlocale(LC_TIME,"en_US").

There are two environment variables defined by the POSIX standard that do not define a specific behavior, LANG and LC_ALL. The value of LANG is taken as the default for each category if neither the category-specific variable nor LC_ALL is set in the environment. It is typically set in shell configuration scripts such as ~/.bash_login. LC_ALL overrides all settings of the specific categories, and is typically used to force the locale to a known value.

The POSIX standard defines the following categories, but does not prohibit implementations from defining additional categories. (Thus the function of LC_ALL cannot be accomplished by setting individual category variables, unless the system where the code will be executed is known in advance.)

Collation

The collation category determines the order of characters in the encoding. It may also compose characters, such as the Ch and Ll ligatures in traditional Spanish. (Although modern standard Spanish has abolished the special treatment for these character pairs, languages like Thai and Hindi require character composition.) Other languages may split a single character into several, as for the German "sharp S" which is collated as "SS". Finally, languages differ in their treatment of accents. Some languages consider accented letters to be equivalent to the base character, unless the accent is the only way to break a tie. Others consider accented letters to be individual characters rather than variants of the base. This affects sorting outcomes and search algorithms, and it also determines the interpretation of range expressions and equivalence classes for the regular expression library. Represented by the atom `LC_COLLATE`.

Character Type

The character type category determines definitions of classes like upper and lower case, decimal and hex digits, punctuation, and so on. This affects the character classes in the regular expression library, the standard classification functions and macros, case conversion, and wide-character usage. Represented by the atom `LC_CTYPE`.

Messages

The message category determines the language used for localizable natural-language messages. In the POSIX standard, the definition of "localizable" is not made precise, except that equivalents for "yes" and "no" must be defined (there exist languages where "y" is the initial of a common negative and "n" the initial of an affirmative word). Messages are actually a rather difficult problem. In cases where a message is parameterized, the order of the arguments to a printf-like function may differ depending on the language. Represented by the atom `LC_MESSAGES`.

Monetary

The monetary category affects the output formatting of monetary values. This includes use of appropriate currency symbols, and possibly variant numeric formatting. Represented by the atom `LC_MONETARY`.

Numeric

The numeric category affects the output formatting of numeric values, including the character used for the decimal separator (typically period or comma), and the character used for grouping, if any. Represented by the atom `LC_NUMERIC`.

Time

The time category affects the output formatting of dates and times. Represented by the atom `LC_TIME`.

Note that the POSIX model does not help with the issues of input. All of the POSIX locale categories are concerned with output or internal processing, except for the `LC_MESSAGES` category. Even there, only an input of yes/no answers is defined.

The POSIX model is useful to developers because a compliant implementation provides:

- ❑   initialization functions that set up the library to provide behavior conforming to the specification of the user's desired locale, and a standard way of getting information about user preferences

- ❑   entry points embodying the specified functionality (sorting, classification, output formatting)

- ❑   a library of predefined locale definitions

- ❑   a means for defining new locales without rebuilding the function library

So for those functions defined in the POSIX model (collation, character typing, formatting of numeric, monetary, and temporal strings, and the formatting of yes/no dialog strings), the programmer need do nothing beyond using the appropriate functions from the library. In some cases the standard C function is internationalized transparently to the application programmer; in others, a special internationalized function must be used. For most locales, definitions will already be available in the library. Where pre-existing definitions are not available, or are incorrect, the ability to define new locales without rebuilding the library means that the locale definition activity can be delegated to a linguistic specialist with a little bit of training in the definition language. Locale definition need not be done by programmers who may not even speak the language very well (as would be expected in an internationalized application targeted for several cultures).

Furthermore, when the "global locale" model is useful, more advanced services like input methods and layout managers (described below) often use the POSIX locale settings to determine the user's preferences.

The X/Open Portability Guide (XPG)

The X/Open Group produced standards for portability among UNIX systems in many areas. Internationalization was no exception. The three important extensions to the POSIX locale model are the functions for handling multibyte characters (variable-width characters such as UTF-8) and wide characters (fixed-width characters such as Unicode), a general system for creating message translations based on the library function `catgets(3)`, and the `iconv(3)` subsystem for translating character encodings.

The multi- and wide-character functions are an advanced topic, mostly important for specialized uses (in particular, in truly multilingual applications). These are well covered (although tersely) in the Info manual for GNU libc. You can get summary lists with:

$ **man -k multibyte**

and

$ **man -k 'wide character'**

as in the table presented below. This shows that multibyte functions are mainly used to convert external multibyte streams to internal wide character format for processing, and wide character functions not only perform the inverse function, but also have analogues to most of the standard file I/O and string library functions.

Mbstowcs(3)	Convert a multibyte string to a wide character string
mbtowc (3)	Convert a multibyte character to a wide character
utf-8 (7)	An ASCII compatible multibyte Unicode encoding
Wcstombs(3)	Convert a wide character string to a multibyte character string
wctomb (3)	Convert a wide character to a multibyte character
Mbstowcs(3)	Convert a multibyte string to a wide character string
mbtowc (3)	Convert a multibyte character to a wide character
wcstombs(3)	Convert a wide character string to a multibyte character string
wctomb (3)	Convert a wide character to a multibyte character

The catgets(3) module is available in GNU libc, but was basically superceded for Linux development by the gettext(3) module, described below. catgets(3) might be useful if you are porting a program from an alternative environment, or, if you are cooperating with a project where the possibility of contamination from the GPL is unacceptable.

The gettext module itself is probably available from the GNU libc sources, and thus should be covered by the GNU Library General Public License. However, the auxiliary binaries, and the standalone library libintl produced by the gettext source distribution are covered by the GNU General Public License. According to the FSF, this means that all software that is intended to be linked with libintl, must be distributed under the GNU GPL. catgets(3) usage is quite similar to that of gettext(3), except that the API is somewhat less clear. It is well documented in the info manual for GNU libc.

The iconv(3) subsystem is a set of functions used for converting between different encodings of the same character set. It is a modern definition, demanding reentrancy and good exception handling. This means that character sets that are only partially compatible with each other (such as ASCII and EBCDIC) can be translated. It also provides support for applications like transliteration (for example, of Cyrillic letters into combinations of Roman letters). The use of these functions will ensure robust and efficient conversions, including conversions to and from Unicode, and between Unicode and UTF-8. These functions are primarily relevant for backwards compatibility with archived files and for converting user input. It is strongly recommended that storage of current data files and user output be done with Unicode or UTF-8. (If space is an issue, a little reflection shows that except for a small amount of overhead in the coding dictionaries, a file encoded in Unicode and then compressed with a general algorithm like gzip will have the same size as one encoded in ASCII and compressed by the same algorithm.) The iconv module makes it easy, efficient, and reliable for the programmer to use Unicode or UTF-8 as the external representation of text, regardless of the locale.

GNU libc Extensions to the POSIX and X/Open Models

The GNU implementation of libc, version 2 and above, implements the POSIX and X/Open models completely. (As of version 2.1, there are some problems with wide-character functions for Asian languages; these issues should be resolved in version 2.2.) The most important additional facility is the alternative API for message catalogs called "GNU gettext," written by Ulrich Drepper. The problem with the catgets(3) interface is that it essentially involves keeping an ordered mapping of all messages along with an index number. Then a call to the catgets(3) function uses the index number to access the catalog. This makes catalog maintenance very difficult; if a new message is inserted between 1 and 2, it must be numbered 3. Thus the programmer must keep track of the message number. This is going to result in many collisions in a distributed development environment like CVS. Two programmers looking at the same catalog would see the same "next index"; some sort of allocation scheme would be necessary. Furthermore, in the case that some locale's catalog does not get updated, or perhaps no catalogs are available, there must be a hardcoded fallback string, which may or may not be the same as the string in the relevant catalog in the program's "native language" (usually English).

GNU gettext (based on the method defined by the Uniforum group led by Sun Microsystems) collapses the fallback string and the index number into a single object by the ingenious device of using a hash table indexed by the fallback string. GNU gettext also optimizes the common case where there is a single message catalog for each language for an application by allowing the message catalog to be bound globally. This means that where a call to catgets(3) has four arguments (a catalog, a set number within the catalog, a message number, and a default message), gettext(3) normally has only one, the default message.

An important advantage of this is that it makes "gettext-izing" a program rather simple; quite a good job can be done by a sed(1) script that simply looks for quoted strings and wraps them in calls to the function gettext(3). Furthermore, one common usage is to define a macro with one argument named _ (yes, simply an underscore). This means that a reference to a string like:

```
"Please gettext-ize me!"
```

becomes a macro call:

```
_("Please gettext-ize me!")
```

This rapidly becomes no more obtrusive than the C comment convention, unlike catgets(3), where a similar "lightweight macro" approach would be defeated by the presence of the extraneous index argument. (In fact, the catgets(3) API requires two other arguments, the catalog and the set number, but for simple applications a wrapper function or macro that glosses over these arguments could be defined. The index number and the fallback message, however, would be required.)

Furthermore, GNU gettext (and libc with the gettext facility) defines two more locale-related environment variables. LANGUAGE, a generalization of LANG, allows a "search path" of languages. This affects only the LC_MESSAGES locale categories, but it allows the user to specify that message catalogs for several languages be tried before resorting to the default language hard-coded in the program. LINGUAS is a GNU gettext-specific variable, which determines which message categories from those available will be installed on the system. (LINGUAS really is quite different from the other locale categories described. It is used by distribution packagers and system administrators, though not normally by application developers, and is mentioned here only for completeness since it could plausibly be assumed to be related.)

The Separate Library and Documentation for GNU gettext

GNU gettext is distributed in two forms, as an auxiliary library libintl.a and as part of GNU libc. They share a common interface, libintl.h. These have different licensing terms; the former is licensed under the GNU GPL, while the latter is licensed under the GNU LGPL. Also, the auxiliary programs gettextize(1), msgfmt(1), msgmerge(1), and xgettext(1) for program development are distributed only with the separate library, since they are not needed merely to run internationalized programs. This means that where "gettext documentation" is referred to, check both the documents distributed with gettext itself (the only source for auxiliary programs like xgettext(1) and msgfmt(1)) and the libc documentation on the gettext library entry points (which is more detailed and accurate).

Output Formatting and Input Processing

The fundamental requirement of I18N is that the user be able to view output and create input in his or her preferred language. The X Windows System (X11) makes this capability hardware-independent by performing output to a bitmapped graphics display, and providing for highly configurable keyboard mapping. Application programmers normally should never alter the keyboard mapping. The flexibility is hidden in the vendor's configuration, so that the application programmer should never need to read the keyboard directly for any kind of text input.

The X Window System

X11 provides crucial support for Linux I18N: the bitmapped graphic display and flexible input handling frees internationalized applications from concerns about hardware capabilities. It doesn't matter whether the hardware lacks the odd character such as the Spanish enye (n tilde), the whole Cyrillic alphabet, or even the thousands of characters used by Asian languages. X11 supplies its own fonts with an open standard so that new ones can be created and installed. Neither you nor the X server itself will know the difference. This guarantees that all written languages can be supported by X11.

Since X11 provides a set of standard font formats, output in any language can be enabled simply by creating an appropriate font and registering it with the X server, using `mkfontdir(1x)` and `xset(1x)`. Once this is done, neither the X server nor the user can tell whether the font was provided by the X11 distribution, or as an add-on.

X11 provides two functions supporting internationalized input. First, the flexible keyboard mappings mean that the X server can be told to interpret the hardware's signals as arbitrary characters or control functions, such as composition of a base character with an accent. Second, it provides hooks to input methods that allow arbitrary processing of input. For example, most Asian languages require lookup in external dictionaries and interactive choice of the appropriate candidate because the thousands of characters cannot all be given separate keys, or even unique key combinations – a limitation of the human users. These hooks are standardized as X Input Methods (XIM).

Formatted Output

Of course, some fonts look better than others, and some font description languages are more conducive to attractive rendering than others. It's a shame that X has taken so long to support TrueType, for example. And nobody supports Arabic very well. The language requires less than one hundred basic characters to write. However, each character is shaped differently depending on whether it occurs first, last, or internally in a word. Furthermore, Arabic is a cursive script, and attractive joining of two characters depends on both of them. High-quality Arabic fonts contain thousands of glyphs to ensure that these context dependencies are handled correctly. But that's not a general problem for programmers; we usually just want to `printf` some text with some control over size and position, and the X11 model allows us to do that. Another issue is layout: users of languages that default to right-to-left text (such as Hebrew and Arabic) typically expect their GUI components on the opposite sides of the labels from the standard placement in English (for example, radio or toggle buttons on the right, not the left).

Fortunately, with the agreement between TrueType proponents and (Adobe) Type 1 proponents to create a new OpenType format to supercede both TrueType and Type 1, both of these issues look likely to be solved satisfactorily in the next year or so. OpenType will provide means for high-quality text rendering, and although problems of right-to-left scripts (which actually implies bidirectional rendering, since Arabic numerals and embedded Western languages are written left-to-right in Hebrew and Arabic text) are not solved by OpenType, X11R6 introduced the X Output Method (XOM). As of X11R6, the X Output Method standard is part of the X11 definition; it provides the necessary hooks for specialists to create output methods to handle things like right-to-left output and context-dependent glyphs. Under normal circumstances, this will be transparent to the application programmer, as long as you initialize the XOM subsystem. This is considered the responsibility of toolkits like Motif and GTK+.

User Input

As anybody who has wrestled with the standard scanf(3) functions knows, output is by comparison a piece of cake. It takes a real programmer to handle input with flair. Input I18N is no exception. Strictly speaking, it's not the input that is the problem, but discerning the meaning of the stream. Reading the input into the buffer is done once, but the program may need to make any number of passes across segments of the input stream to parse it. This is why most hardcore C programmers do not bother with the limits of fscanf(3), but use either fgets(3) or fread(3). This allows the program to try several different conversions for the user's input, rather than assuming an integer via the %d conversion. At least the English-speaking programmer trying to read a number can be pretty sure the code is ASCII. But in many languages there are several ways to encode the numeral "one" (Japanese has at least three).

In the simplest situation, internationalized input is trivial, because it is handled by the hardware. There are special keyboards for typing French or Hebrew. You stroke the appropriate keys, and the keyboard sends character codes already encoded in ISO-8859-1 (for French) or ISO-8859-8 (for Hebrew) to the CPU. At almost as low a level, keyboards may be remapped via the X server, and even certain combinations of characters can be remapped to automatically produce "composed characters" (for example, commonly in "French mode" typing a followed by ' will produce á).

On the application side, as well, handling this kind of input is trivial. At worst, the program must convert from strings in the user's locale to Unicode. But this is easily done using the iconv(3) facility provided by GNU libc.

However, for the great majority of the world's population (if not yet a majority of computer users), it is simply not feasible to have a keyboard that allows direct input of any character the user might use. An educated Chinese has a repertoire of about five to ten thousand Han characters, and Koreans can algorithmically construct 11,172 Hangul. There are several schemes that can be used to input text using such large character sets, but the most popular approach is to input a phonetic rendering (often using the Roman alphabet) of the text. Then the phonetic rendering is compared to a dictionary (and often further pruned or reordered by use of common phrases and knowledge of the language's grammar, and possibly the user's own past input habits). This produces a list of candidates for final insertion into the text. The user's manipulation of the phonetic representation and the candidate list is called preedit, to distinguish it from the overall editing process of inserting, deleting, and moving characters and blocks of characters.

Obviously this method involves substantial feedback. Yet such an expensive process involving databases and AI will often be run in a separate process. This means that the text processing application and the input server must communicate about both the content and the presentation of the feedback to the user.

The X Input Method is a standard introduced in X11R5 that was revised and made mandatory in X11R6. It provides for several alternative presentation techniques. In the simplest, the input manager itself will pop up a separate preedit window, whose placement is under the control of the window manager (and ultimately the user). This method is evidently clumsy and distracting, especially if the use of the input manager is intermittent (as it would be in writing a C program with Japanese comments). Other methods are more flexible but more complex, culminating in the "on-the-spot" method where the application passes callbacks to the input manager, allowing the input manager to delegate preedit and status feedback to the application. This allows the application to (for example) present the preedit text in the same font but different color. This gives a much smoother appearance, and does not force the user to move their eyes back and forth between the application receiving the input, and the preedit window managing the details.

The following figures show how Japanese input occurs with the common combination of `kterm(1x)`, `kinput2(1x)`, and `cannaserver(1)`. `kterm(1x)` is a derivative of `xterm(1x)` that can handle output of Japanese characters. `kinput2(1x)` is a Japanese input manager that supports the XIM protocol.

Most Linux distributions provide Canna, KInput2, and KTerm in package form, so it should be quite easy to install them and try out the example. Canna packages will normally start the server automatically, and install a boot script as well; Kinput2 and KTerm must be run by hand.

However, distributions vary greatly in how well they configure the packages to cooperate. The Debian `kinput2-canna` and `kinput2-canna-wnn` packages work 'out of the box', but other distributions' packaged versions may require some manual configuration before you persuade Canna to talk to Kinput2, and Kinput2 to talk to KTerm.

The `ae(1)` text editor is used to contain the text since `bash(1)` gets confused by Japanese, and echoes garbage to the kterm. `ae(1)` doesn't understand Japanese, and in fact it is possible to delete half of a character (the editing buffer is treated as an array of bytes). With care though, Japanese can be inserted and modified.

> *We decided to use ae(1) because it's the default editor for the Debian distribution, on which these examples were produced. However, nvi, a version of vi(1) is also known to work, as well as most other versions of vi(1) and emacs(1) as well. 'Internationalized' versions like Emacs/Mule should be avoided as they don't usually use XIM, but often accept Japanese via other mechanisms, therefore confusing the example.*

The procedure depicted in the accompanying screen shots is as follows:

❑ As superuser, run `/usr/sbin/cannaserver` to start the "Canna" Japanese character dictionary server.

❑ Next as a normal user, start the XIM server with `kinput2 &`.

❑ Open `kterm` with **XMODIFIERS="@xim=kinput2" kterm -xim &**, and start a text editor from within it:

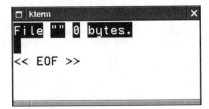

Press *Shift-Space* to activate XIM:

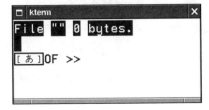

Now type "korehanihongodesu". This is the phonetic rendering of the Japanese for "This is Japanese". in the Latin alphabet. The input server automatically converts the Latin to phonetic kana as displayed in the next screenshot. If the input makes no sense as kana, it is displayed as Latin letters. Scientific and technical Japanese tend to use this input format. They learn to touch-type the Latin alphabet, since many of their papers and programs are written in the Latin alphabet. Non-technical secretaries prefer keymaps that produce kana with one keystroke.

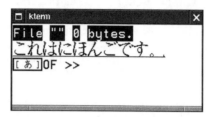

Type *Space* to produce the mixed phonetic and ideographic output shown below. Believe it or not, this is actually the correct result:

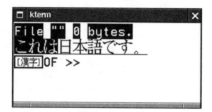

Type *Space* again, popping up the Candidate Selection list in a separate window, as shown below. Keyboard focus is set to the popup window, and the list can be traversed with the arrow keys:

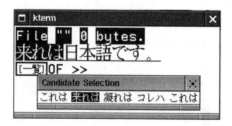

Use left arrow to return to the phonetic version of the first phrase, and type Enter to accept the candidate for the first phrase. The screen returns to the state as seen in the previous figure. Press *Enter* again to accept the whole sentence. Note how the status window follows the cursor:

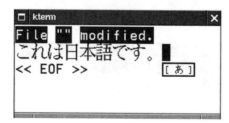

Typing *Shift-Space* deactivates XIM (see below). You can now type ASCII, or *Shift-Space* to re-enter Japanese input mode.

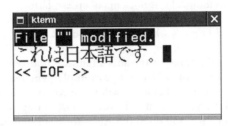

A relative newcomer to the field of input managers is the Intranet-Internet Input Method Format (IIIMF) standard, originally for Java. It eliminates some of the rarely used complexities of XIM, while codifying and making more usable some of the ambiguities in the XIM specification. This is a technology to watch, especially since it is mandated by the Li18nux 2000 standard (see References) for internationalized Linux systems drafted by the Linux Internationalization Initiative.

Although toolkits and GUIs are beginning to encapsulate these capabilities, they are generally restricted currently. IIIMF is not implemented outside Java, and toolkits generally implement only the simpler of the preedit styles. In any case, managing the complex styles is difficult. However, experience shows it is well worth it in terms of user satisfaction for languages like Japanese. Programmers targeting Asian markets should carefully consider the costs and benefits of learning these techniques.

Practical Considerations of I18N Programming

How does all this complexity affect the professional Linux programmer? Fortunately not very much for most tasks, in principle at least. Although high-quality output and efficient input are far more complex than simply writing strings to windows with an appropriate graphics context and reading strings from simple input functions, the complexity can be made routine and left up to specialists. In fact, input managers conforming to XIM have been available for ten years or so, and layout managers conforming to XOM are under active development by proprietary X vendors.

One of the truly exciting developments of the commercialization of Linux is that vendors like IBM, at the forefront of these important technologies, seem likely to donate excellent implementations of various standards to the open source movement. Linux will be the first beneficiary since it is the most commercially successful, but ports to other open source platforms will surely follow.

Thus, programmers can look forward to the day in the near future when even at the low level of Xlib programming, they can expect to use very stylized code sequences to initialize XIM and XOM managers, get the user's preferences, and all the rest will be handled by the standard components. Furthermore, the I18N standards for I/O are explicitly designed for incorporation into toolkits. So applications suited to use of high-level toolkits will typically not need to be concerned with basic functionality at all.

However, in the near future there are two obstacles to such simplicity. First, the technologies are as yet experimental, or only partially implemented. This is especially true of the layout components for XOM. So for the near term, programmers will have to deal with much of the initialization and low-level operations themselves. They also may find themselves frustrated by inadequate support in toolkits, which nonetheless interfere with lower level functionality.

Second, XIM and XOM are both X11-specific, and the first complete standards of their kinds. While this is not a problem for Linux for the next decade, since GUIs are clearly necessary and Linux GUIs are and will continue to be based on X11, it does make cross-platform portability difficult. For this reason, it seems likely that XIM will be augmented and perhaps replaced (as the usual API) by the Internet-Intranet Input Method Framework (IIIMF) developed by Sun for Java.

The reference implementation, the Internet-Intranet Input Method Protocol (IIIMP), explicitly relies on XIM to provide IIIMF functionality on X11-based Java implementations. This means that XIM-based applications will continue to work, and that users will not have to learn one input method for GTK+ applications and another for Java applications. However, it does impose a burden on programmers, who will need to learn the characteristics, and often the APIs, for both standards.

The XOM standard deals with output, which is a better understood problem than input. It also has the benefit of more experience (including that of early XIM and Java implementations) than the designers of XIM had. But the XOM API may also be augmented or even superceded in the medium term. Furthermore, unlike the case of XIM, where the Java IIIMF standard explicitly relies on XIM for input services on X, the Java GUI toolkits (Swing and the older AWT) do not integrate XOM, at least not yet.

Thus, modularization, always a good idea, is imperative for internationalized input and output. This is greatly complicated by the advantages to declaring and initializing messages near the point of usage. Fortunately, for simple cases, GNU gettext makes this straightforward, with just enough syntactic sugar to make it obvious at a glance whether a given body of code has been gettext-ized yet or not.

I18N and Internal Text Processing

How I18N is going to affect code for your application's internal functionality is going to be very application-specific. If your program does text analysis beyond regular expression searches and simple collation, you will be forced to deal directly with various character sets and to learn about each language you wish to handle properly. For example, in languages like Japanese and Chinese, words are not delimited by spaces. Furthermore, although there are some standards for defining words, they will often not meet your needs even in simple applications like regular expression searches.

It is beyond the scope of this book to discuss in detail the techniques that will be used in applications like full-fledged text editors. However, beyond careful modularization of code affected by I18N, a number of considerations can be listed. Most important is that all strings to be manipulated internally should be stored in Unicode, preferably in the UCS-4 format. This may seem to be a waste of space (UCS-4 requires 4 bytes per character). Consider the analogy to saving megabytes by removing your GUI. Even though the GUI code itself is in a shared library, and thus doesn't cost much to any one application, applications do have customized pixmaps, "skins," and audio clips, maybe movies. Still, most information is transferred in text form. If you care whether or not your program can be easily extended to other cultures, surely the investment in space is generally small for the benefits in simplicity and maintainability gained. Most informational messages can be stored in UTF-8 since they will just be sent to the screen. That is very inexpensive if you use gettext and your base language is English; your default messages will be encoded in one byte per character.

The main theoretical reason for using UCS-4 is that it is the only truly universal character set, guaranteed to be able to encode all characters for the foreseeable future. The primary practical reason is that glibc uses UCS-4 internally as its wide-character format. If you always translate strings to UCS-4 before operating on them, you will never find yourself with mismatched encodings. You can be fairly sure that efficient code for making the translation will be available through the iconv suite of standard functions, and furthermore you can expect that standard string optimizations like regular expression search will also be optimized for the UCS-4 case.

There is one caveat here, however; that communities developing different libraries and APIs have made differing decisions about the character encodings they will use internally. For example, in PostgreSQL 6.5.3 the only universal character set available for databases is the internal encoding of MULE, the multi-lingual extension to GNU Emacs. Apparently the attractions of the MULE encoding were, first, that the contributor was familiar with it. Second, the MULE encoding supports algorithmic translations to most national standard encodings, while Unicode requires large tables.

But the MULE encoding is implementation-defined; there is no standards document defining conformance. Now PostgreSQL 7.0 provides UTF-8 support for databases. Similarly, the Samba team is migrating Samba's internal encoding to UCS-2 (or perhaps UTF-16). According to Jeremy Allison, a core Samba developer, the choice of a wide character format rather than UTF-8 was to ensure that any code that's not "Unicode clean" would break in a purely English environment (due to the null bytes) just as quickly as in an international environment.

It is important to note that although GNU libc, Postgres, and Samba have all standardized on Unicode, in fact the internal encodings are incompatible and require transformation. Unicode compatibility is not enough to guarantee the transparent exchange of data! However, there are no problems of ambiguity here that require AI to automatically distinguish them (for example, the use of the same codes – 0xA0 to 0xFF – in ISO-8859-5 and ISO-8859-8 to represent the Cyrillic and Hebrew alphabets, respectively). Furthermore, GNU libc provides standardized, convenient, and efficient implementations of the algorithms for translating among Unicode transformation formats in the iconv(3) group of functions. Since the different Unicode formats require only simple invertible translations, and the different formats are easily and extremely reliably distinguishable, no AI is needed. Check the documentation for packages that "support Unicode" carefully, to see exactly which variant is meant.

Programming with Locales

Despite the caveat about encodings, and the hope that most non-Unicode encodings will gradually fade away and be relegated to issues of backward compatibility with fixed systems, locales themselves are going to continue to be relevant. Encodings are transparent to the end-user; as long as they can input their text and reliably receive appropriate output, they don't care what integer values correspond to each character. But they will ferociously resist changing their date formats and currency symbols, and will strongly prefer systems that speak to them "in their own language", including sorting lists "in the right order".

Using locales well is more difficult than using the iconv functions correctly. Since encoding conversion is by far most commonly applied to input and output streams, it can generally be localized to a very few functions dealing with such streams. On the other hand, locales affect all kinds of formatting that typically is done piece by piece and spread throughout the user interface code. It requires more attention to modularization and greater discipline to make sure that all strings are gettext-ized, all dates and currency items are formatted in portable ways, and so on. Character classification, including case conversion, is generally transparent in the sense that the implementation of functions like toupper(3) and isdigit(3) have been changed to account for locale differences. However, the collation functions like strcmp(3) have not; to get locale-respecting comparison, you must use strcoll(3) (for one-shot comparisons) or strxfrm(3) (which transforms strings so that they compare correctly but efficiently). (Functions like strcasecmp(3) are partially locale-respecting: they use the locale to determine the case-folding properties, but not the collation order. Be careful!)

Although preprocessing with strxfrm(3) is supposed to be more efficient, one must take care that in some implementations it can use as much as six to eight times as much space as the original string. For moderately large files, this could easily make the difference between an in-memory sort using strcoll, and an external sort using direct byte-by-byte comparisons; typically the latter will be slower. The glibc implementation does not seem to suffer this problem. The documentation strongly suggests that the processed string is approximately the same size as the raw string, and testing with a few English, Japanese, and Unicode strings bears this out. It is an issue to be aware of for efficient porting to systems like Solaris and HP/UX.

A list of GNU libc functions related to I18N is presented in the following table. Some functions are simply generalizations of standard string handling to multibyte and wide characters. However, many are implicitly affected by locale. The Locale Dependence column describes these effects. That is, it shows when a function's behavior will change for the same input depending on the locale. For example, MB_CUR_MAX is the maximum number of bytes used by a character in the current locale. In the default POSIX locale, whose encoding is ASCII, this is 1. In a locale using UTF-8, it could be as high as 6.

Category – Dimensions

Functions	Description	Locale Dependence
MB_CUR_MAX, MB_LEN_MAX	Maximum sizes of multibyte characters	MB_CUR_MAX
mblen, mbrlen	Number of bytes in multibyte character	None
wcslen, strlen	Number of characters in (wide character) string	None
wcswidth, wcwidth	Columns needed to display a wide character string	None

Category – Conversions

Functions	Description	Locale Dependence
mbrtowc, mbsnrtowcs, mbsrtowcs, mbstowcs, mbtowc, wcrtomb, wcsnrtombs, wcsrtombs, wcstombs, wctomb, wcrtomb, btowc, wctob	Convert among bytes (b), multibyte characters (mb), and wide characters (wc) or strings (mbs and wcs respectively)	None
iconv, iconv_open, iconv_close	Translate among character encodings	None

Category – I/O

Functions	Description	Locale Dependence
fgetwc, fgetws, getwc, getwchar, ungetwc	Read wide characters or strings from FILE streams	None
fgetc, fgets, getc, getchar, ungetc	Read unibyte characters or strings from FILE streams	None
fputwc, fputws, putwc, putwchar	Wide character output, including formatted conversion	None
fputc, fputs, putc, putchar	Character output, including formatted conversion	None

Category – String formatting

Functions	Description	Locale Dependence
wprintf, fwprintf, swprintf, vfwprintf, vswprintf, vwprintf, wcsftime, wcsfmon	Wide character string formatting and output	Positional parameter extension; locale-specific format
printf, fprintf, sprintf, vfprintf, vsprintf, vprintf, strftime, strfmon	String formatting and output	Positional parameter extension; locale-specific format

Category – Character classification

Functions	Description	Locale Dependence
iswalnum, iswalpha, iswblank, iswcntrl, iswctype, iswdigit, iswgraph, iswlower, iswprint, iswpunct, iswspace, iswupper, iswxdigit, wctype	Classify wide characters	All; wctype allows implementation-dependent extension of classes for a locale
isalnum, isalpha, isblank, iscntrl, isctype, isdigit, isgraph, islower, isprint, ispunct, isspace, isupper, isxdigit	Classify wide characters	All

Category – Conversions

Functions	Description	Locale Dependence
towlower, towupper, towctrans, wctrans	Convert a wide character to a given class	All
tolower, toupper	Convert a character to lower or upper case	All

Category – String copying and filling

Functions	Description	Locale Dependence
wcpcpy, wcpncpy, wcscpy, wcsncpy, wcsspn, wmemset	Copy a wide character string	None
cpcpy, cpncpy, cscpy, csncpy, csspn, memset	Copy a wide character string	None

Category – String searching

Functions	Description	Locale Dependence
wcschr, wcscspn, wcspbrk, wcsrchr, wmemchr	Search for wide characters in a wide-character string	None
strspn, strcspn, index, memchr, rindex, strchr, strpbrk, strsep, strstr, strtok	Search for characters in a string	None

Category – Collation

Functions	Description	Locale Dependence
strcoll, strxfrm, wcscoll, wcsxfrm	Compare (wide character) strings or "compile" them for repeated comparison	Collation order

Category – Regular expressions

Functions	Description	Locale Dependence
regcomp, regexec, regerror, regfree	Regular expression search	May add additional character classes; comparison may be locale specific

Category – Locale manipulation

Functions	Description	Locale Dependence
`setlocale, localeconv,` `nl_langinfo`	Set and get locale information	

Category – Message catalogs

Functions	Description	Locale Dependence

`gettext, dgettext, dcgettext,`
`textdomain, bindtextdomain,`
`catgets, catopen, catclose`
	Manipulate locale-specific messages	

The basic procedure for adapting your program to use the current locale is very simple:

1. Call the function `setlocale`, once for each locale category that needs to be set (you can imagine that a French report on the US economy would use French conventions for language and date, but tables of US financial data would be output according to US currency format).

2. Use `gettext` to localize messages.

3. Use locale-respecting functions to format output.

But it does require discipline to be thorough about this process. Here's a not very plausible program that uses several of the techniques described. In the default configuration, this program expects the message catalogs to be named `PLiP_hello.mo` and installed below the current directory, in:

```
./{$LOCALE1,$LOCALE2,...}/LC_MESSAGES/PLiP_hello.mo)
```

where LOCALEn is a locale name such as `ja_JP.eucJP` (the usual Japanese locale). To find the catalogs in the usual place for your system, leave `GETTEXT_DATA_ROOT` undefined. On an FHS-compliant Linux system that is equivalent to:

```
#define GETTEXT_DATA_ROOT "/usr/share/locale"
```

implying the catalogs are installed in:

```
/usr/share/locale/{$LOCALE1,$LOCALE2,...}/LC_MESSAGES/PLiP_hello.mo)
```

The other configuration `#define` is `USE_YESNO_STR`, which if defined (the default) gets the POSIX-defined yes/no strings for the locale. Few of the locales supplied with GNU libc define these strings, so this should be avoided (it's the default here for "educational purposes").

These defines are followed by standard includes:

```
/*
locale.c
demonstrates use of locale support and gettext
*/

#define GETTEXT_DATA_ROOT getcwd(NULL,0)
#define USE_YESNO_STR

/* get facilities needed ... */
#include <locale.h>        /* for setlocale(3) and friends */
#include <langinfo.h>      /* for nl_langinfo(3) and friends */
#include <stdio.h>
#include <stdlib.h>
#include <string.h>
#include <time.h>
#include <regex.h>
#include <unistd.h>
/* ... whew! */
```

Now set up the gettext facilities. The underscore macros are conventionally in gettext applications to reduce the visual impact (and avoid contributing too much length to a line), but are not defined in the header file. The N_ form is used to mark static data initializers. (See the definition of the function usage below for an example.)

```
#include <libintl.h>
#define _(String)  gettext (String)
#define N_(String) String

/* prototypes for functions defined */
void usage (char *);
void do_date ();
void do_hello ();

/* globals are evil, but I'm lazy */
char *default_locale;
```

Here is the driver program which sets locales:

```
int main (int argc, char *argv[]) {

#ifdef GETTEXT_DATA_ROOT
   const char *gettext_data_root = GETTEXT_DATA_ROOT;
#endif
```

Initialize the locale based on the environment. See setlocale(3) for the semantics. This is a fairly expensive operation, as it involves setting up tables and callbacks for the functions whose behavior changes with the locale.

See the gettext docs for dangers of LC_ALL in some contexts. The problem is that the program may not need to control all the locale functionality, and this overrules the user's environment settings of such don't-care categories. It can be particularly confusing in multilingual applications such as text editors, where users often want LC_COLLATE and LC_CTYPE set appropriately for sorting and searching in "second-language" buffers, but want timestamps and numerical data to appear in their native format.

Set up the locale first, before parsing the command line, to provide message translation for usage. Note that if the locale setup fails, gettext cannot translate the message. So until the locale setup is known to be successful, we don't bother to mark the strings for gettext.

```
default_locale = setlocale (LC_ALL, "");

if (!default_locale)
{
    fprintf (stderr,
        /* libc also prints an error message here */
        "%s: Arggh!  can't set default locale, get a new system!\n",
        argv[0]);
    /* normally I would limp along, but this is fatal in this example */
    exit(EXIT_FAILURE);
}
```

Now we initialize gettext by binding the default catalog. This initialization also should be done before parsing the command line. The catalog is normally $GETTEXT_DATA_ROOT/$LOCALE/LC_CATEGORY /$TEXT_DOMAIN.mo, where $GETTEXT_DATA_ROOT is /usr/share/locale on Linux, $LOCALE is computed from default_locale initialized above, $LC_CATEGORY = LC_MESSAGES (see gettext docs for exceptions), and $TEXT_DOMAIN is set to PLiP_hello by calling textdomain below.

Note that a general use library can't very well use a call to textdomain(3) to set a default domain – it will likely conflict with the user program. Libraries will normally use the dgettext(3) function, whose first argument is the message domain, instead of gettext(3), which leaves it implicit. Of course, in the library code a macro or inline function can be used for convenience.

The gettext library isn't initialized yet, so we can't translate the failure messages here, either:

```
if (!textdomain ("PLiP_hello"))
{
    fprintf (stderr,
        /* nb:  absolutely useless to gettextize this */
        "%s: Arggh!  can't set gettext domain, get more memory!\n",
        argv[0]);

    /* this is fatal because textdomain() does no sanity check:
       must be due to (eg) ENOMEM */
    exit(EXIT_FAILURE);
}

#ifdef GETTEXT_DATA_ROOT
    if (!bindtextdomain ("PLiP_hello", gettext_data_root))
    {
        fprintf (stderr,
            /* nb:  absolutely useless to gettextize this */
            "%s: Arggh!  can't bind gettext domain, get more memory!\n",
            argv[0]);

        /* this is fatal, must be due to (eg) ENOMEM */
        exit(EXIT_FAILURE);
    }
#endif
```

Here is one possible sanity check, asking the user. It would be nice if there were an automatic way to do this. The problem is that for the program's native domain (typically English), there won't be a message catalog. So failing to find a message catalog is not really an error.

Especially with user-supplied locales there are problems in implicit checking. POSIX insists on standard ISO 639 language codes and ISO 3166 country codes. Those can be checked. GNU libc also normalizes encoding names (by changing them to lowercase and stripping punctuation like hyphens and underscores), but that's not really good enough. One approach to handling the encoding is to insist on message catalogs in UTF-8, and then convert on-the-fly if the terminal can't hack UTF-8. But this fails if the user will be specifying data sources and destinations (files and sockets) whose encoding the program cannot control. Finally, since the @modifier component of the standard locale string format is implementation dependent, the program cannot possibly guess what might be valid.

System administrators can help by setting up a `locale.alias` file with mnemonic aliases for locales commonly used on their system.

```
/*
    note to translators:  this message should be translated to
    "If you were not expecting this language, check your LANGUAGE, LANG,
    LC_MESSAGES, and LC_ALL variables.  If they are set correctly, then
    the message catalog for your language has been misplaced."
*/

puts (_("I hope you're happy with the default `POSIX' locale, because
        \nthat's what you've got!  No message catalog found for you."));
puts (_("Successfully initialized I18N."));
```

Now check arguments, and call the requested function:

```
if (argc != 2 || argv[1][1] != '\0')
{
    usage (argv[0]);
    exit (EXIT_FAILURE);
}

switch (argv[1][0]) {
case '1':
    do_date ();
    break;

case '2':
    do_hello ();
    break;

default:
    usage (argv[0]);
    exit (EXIT_FAILURE);
}

putchar('\n');
exit(EXIT_SUCCESS);
}
```

The localized print-date-and-time function. The `%c` and `%Z` conversion specifiers simply request the conversion of time and date, respectively, according to the locale's conventions:

```c
#define SIZE 256

void do_date ()
{
 char date[SIZE];
 time_t now;
 struct tm *tmnow;

 time (&now);
 tmnow = localtime(&now);

 /* strftime(3) seems broken in GNU libc 2.1.3; time is correctly
    localized for the default localtime correction, but setting TZ or LANG
    gives GMT the manual indicates strftime should handle correction
    automatically
 */

 if (strftime (date, SIZE, "%c %Z", tmnow))
    printf (_("The time now is %s.\n"), date);
 else

    /*
        `do_date' is a program identifier, and should not be translated.
       Of course the format specifier mustn't be "translated"!
    */
    printf ("do_date:  %s\n",
            _("one of the dates formatted had zero length."));
}
```

The print "hello" function:

```c
void do_hello ()
{
 char buffer[SIZE];
 regex_t yre, nre;

 /* prep the regexps */
 if (regcomp (&yre, nl_langinfo(YESEXPR), REG_NOSUB)
    || regcomp (&nre, nl_langinfo(NOEXPR), REG_NOSUB))
 {
    fprintf (stderr, "do_hello: %s\n", _("regex compilation failed\n"));
    exit (EXIT_FAILURE);
 }

 while (1)
 {
    /*
       prompt and read user input
       pretty unnecessary, actually, since yesstr and nostr are
       deprecated and few locales provide them
```

```
        ar_SA, cs_CZ, sk_SK, th_TH, and tr_TR do, as does POSIX (but not in
        the source!) in GNU libc 2.1.3
     */

     #ifdef USE_YESNO_STR
        printf (_("Would you like to see \"hello\" in some language
                   [%s/%s]?  "), nl_langinfo(YESSTR), nl_langinfo(NOSTR));
     #else
        printf (_("Would you like to see \"hello\" in some language
                   [yes/no]?  "));
     #endif
     scanf ("%255s", buffer);

     /* parse answer */
     if (!regexec (&nre, buffer, 0, 0, 0))
     {
        /* negative answer matched */
        printf (_("Later, bye!\n"));
        exit (EXIT_SUCCESS);
     }
     else if (regexec (&yre, buffer, 0, 0, 0))
     {
        /* positive answer didn't match */
        printf (_("Answer the question!\n"));
        continue;          /* redundant */
     }
     else
     {
        /* positive answer matched */
        break;
     }
}
```

do_hello continues with a silly example that demonstrates that the locale can be changed. Changing the locale doesn't have anything to do with gettext(3), though. In fact, in this example it does nothing.

```
/* prompt and read user input */
printf (_("Enter a POSIX-style locale:  "));
scanf ("%255s", buffer);

/* set locale */
if (setlocale (LC_ALL, buffer))
{
    printf (_("\"Hello\" in English is %s.\n"), "\"hello\"");
```

Here is how to change gettext's message catalog on the fly. The manipulation of _nl_msg_cat_cntr is a gross hack due to an optimization in the implementation of gettext(3) and dgettext(3). Note that only an environment variable is changed here; obviously if gettext(3) checked the environment on every call it would get expensive. So this check is optimized out, unless the catalog counter is changed. dcgettext(3) checks every time. It is used in the implementation of gettext and dgettext. It checks the environment variables LANGUAGE, LC_ALL, LC_MESSAGES, and LANG in that order, using the first one found.

This facility is rarely useful:

```
    /* Change language.  */
    setenv ("LANGUAGE", buffer, 1);

    /* Make change known.  */
    {
      extern int  _nl_msg_cat_cntr;
      ++_nl_msg_cat_cntr;
    }
  }
  else
    printf (_("%s is not a real locale!  Not one I know, anyway.\n"),
            buffer);

  /* clean up - obviously redundant here ...
     ... but it's the principle of the thing */
  setlocale (LC_ALL, default_locale);
}
```

This definition and the following function demonstrate how to translate statically allocated data. Note the call gettext (menu[i-1].tag) in the last printf.

```
/*
 purely compulsive...
*/
/* OPTIONS must be <= 9 */

#define OPTIONS 2

struct menu_item {
 char *tag;
 void (*function) ();
} menu[OPTIONS] = {
/*
  these static strings cannot have calls to gettext()
  wrapped around them, so use noop variant
*/
{ N_("see the date in your locale"), do_date },
{ N_("see \"hello\" in various locales"), do_hello }
};

void usage (char *s)
{
 int i;

 printf (_("usage: %s {"), s);
 for (i = 1; i <= OPTIONS; ++i)
    printf ("%d%s", i, i == OPTIONS ? "}\n" : "|");

 for (i = 1; i <= OPTIONS; ++i)
```

```
      /*
        I prefer the full identifier `gettext' here to emphasize that
        it is being applied to a computed value
      */
      printf ("%d - %s\n", i, gettext (menu[i-1].tag));
  }
/* end locale.c */
```

Running this program requires the .mo files. One was constructed for English, and another for Japanese. The following screenshot shows a couple of runs in a kterm (Japanese xterm):

```
bash-2.04$ gcc -Wall -o locale locale.c
locale.c: In function 'do_date':
locale.c:198: warning: '%c' yields only last 2 digits of year in some locales
bash-2.04$ ./locale 1
I hope you're happy with the default 'POSIX' locale, because
that's what you've got!  No message catalog found for you.
Successfully initialized I18N.
The time now is Fri Jul 28 23:32:25 2000 JST.

bash-2.04$ LANG=ja_JP ./locale 1
おめでとうございます。日本語のメッセージカタログが見付かりました。
I 1 8 Nは初期化されました。
只今の時刻はFri 28 Jul 2000 11:32:32 PM JST JSTです。

bash-2.04$ LANG=en_US ./locale 2
Congratulations!  Found an English message catalog.
Successfully initialized I18N.
Would you like to see "hello" in some language [/]?  y
Enter a POSIX-style locale:  ja_JP
英語の挨拶は "hello" です。

bash-2.04$ ▮
```

The compilation is interesting because GCC warns about faulty locale definitions. The invocation in the ja_JP locale seems to have tickled a bug in glibc 2.1.3 (the timezone JST is repeated). Interestingly enough, the en_US locale is one of the many which does not provide yes/no strings. Fortunately, this doesn't cause the program to crash. Note that the message catalog has changed from English to Japanese in the final line.

I18N and Xlib Programming

Although modern developers generally will not be programming user interfaces in raw Xlib, it serves to demonstrate some of the issues involved in internationalizing GUIs – it is normally necessary to convert Unicode text back to the "native encoding" of the font you wish to use.

The following program displays this capability and demonstrates how to handle multilingual text in Xt. The low-level functions would be hidden by a modern GUI toolkit, but the basic principles of dealing with the text (determining language and encoding) will be the same, except that sometimes these details are also hidden by the toolkits. In which case, if they get it wrong, you can't do anything about it. The higher level structure will not be affected by the GUI.

Even with Unicode, this is unlikely to change much. Like translation, font design is inherently culture-specific. You wouldn't hire a Japanese writer to translate to or from Hindi, and it doesn't make much sense to ask a Russian to design fonts for Thai. So even with CID and Cmaps, few fonts, especially locally attractive ones, will cover the entire range of Unicode. There are none, now, and as more and more characters are added, it's unlikely that fonts will keep up.

Also, there remains a certain ambiguity, especially with the Han characters. Although the users agree on which characters are equivalent across traditional Chinese, simplified Chinese, Japanese, and Korean, as is evident from the screen shot, styles vary greatly for the same characters.

The basic requirement for the program is that it must be able to display a window, whose main content is a table of (English) language names, their native names (where available), and their translations of the English word "hello".

The high-level design is simple. The basic data structure is an array of structs. Each struct has six string members: language name, translated name, hello translation, iconv-recognized coding name, font registry, and preferred font. All strings are encoded in UTF-8. The window layout will be done as an array of Xt Label widgets. The X stuff is pretty ugly; I never was much of an X programmer. Purely geometric sections are boring, and will be omitted here.

First, the header material. The program itself is really not internationalized (gettext is not used). So the only I18N-related header is iconv.h.

```
/*
m17n.c
demonstrates some aspects of multilingual output
I18N-related
*/
#include <iconv.h>

/* Generally necessary */
#include <stdio.h>
#include <string.h>
#include <stdlib.h>

/* Necessary Xstuff */
#include <X11/Intrinsic.h>      /* Intrinsics Definitions */
#include <X11/StringDefs.h>     /* Standard Name-String definitions */

#include <X11/Xaw/Label.h>    /* Athena Label Widget */
#include <X11/Xaw/Form.h>     /* Athena Form Widget */
```

Next, define the I18N-related application data types:

```
/*
Language record
Text data
Holds information about each language
*/

typedef struct _LangRec {

 /* these strings are expected to be UTF-8 */
 char *english;       /* language name in English */
 char *native;          /* native name of language */
 char *hello;         /* translation of hello */

 /*
    in a real application, these should be computed from the
    characters used via a database of languages/locales; there should
    also be an optional parameter to specify the language where it is
    ambiguous ("Deutsche" contains only characters in the ASCII set,
    but German words may not be limited to ASCII)

    lists should be allowed

    these strings are components of XLFDs so must be X Portable
    Character Set (basically ASCII)
 */
 char *iconv_charset;       /* yes, we need both of these ... */
 char *x_registry;       /* ... the strings don't always match */
 char *font;
} LangRec;

/*
LangRec method declarations
*/

int langRecValidP (LangRec*);    /* true if encoding restrictions OK */
char* englishName (LangRec*);    /* "convert" UTF-8 name to ASCII */

/* these function allocate memory; caller must free */
char* nativeName (LangRec*);    /* convert UTF-8 name to native encoding */
char* nativeHello (LangRec*);    /* convert UTF-8 hello to native encoding */
```

Next, the table of language information. The first three strings in each record are actually encoded in UTF-8. Notice how the ASCII characters are encoded as themselves, the extended Latin characters used by Spanish (the lowercase N tilde and the inverted exclamation mark) are two bytes, encoded as hexadecimal escapes for safety, and the Japanese, Chinese, and Korean characters are each three bytes:

```
#define NUMLANGS 6
LangRec languages[NUMLANGS] = {

 /* Table header */
 { "Language", "Native name", "Greeting", "ISO-8859-1", "iso8859-1",
   "Helvetica" },
```

```
    /* Languages */
    { "English", "English", "Hello", "ISO-8859-1", "iso8859-1",
      "Helvetica" },
    { "Spanish", "Espa\xC3\xB1ol", "\xC2\xA1Hola!", "ISO-8859-1",
      "iso8859-1", "Helvetica" },

  /* the Japanese font here is distributed with X11 */
    { "Japanese", "\xE6\x97\xA5\xE6\x9C\xAC\xE8\xAA\x9E",
      "\xE3\x81\x93\xE3\x82\x93\xE3\x81\xAB\xE3\x81\xA1\xE3\x81\xAF",
      "EUC-JP", "jisx0208.1983-0", "fixed" },

  /* Korean and Chinese fonts are rarer */
    { "Korean", "\xED\x95\x9C\xEA\xB8\x80",
      "\xEC\x95\x88\xEB\x85\x95\xED\x95\x98\xEC\x84\xB8\xEC\x9A\x94",
      /* if you have any Korean font at all, this should pick it up:
         "EUC-KR", "ks*", "*" }, */
      "EUC-KR", "ksc5601.1987-0", "mincho" },

    { "Chinese", "\xE6\xB1\x89\xE8\xAF\xAD", "\xE4\xBD\xA0\xE5\xA5\xBD",
      /* if you have any Chinese font at all, this should pick it up:
         "GB2312", "gb*", "*" } */
      "GB2312", "gb2312.1980-0", "song ti" }
  };
```

The next section of the program contains the declarations of data structures and functions implementing the table layout. These are uninteresting from the point of view of I18N, and are omitted here.

The English font is used in several subroutines. For convenience of the programmer it is hardcoded and declared as a global. A utility program constructing an XLFD from character encoding registry and font family is declared here, too:

```
/*
BORING GLOBAL STUFF
Global variables are evil, but I'm lazy.
*/

char *englishXLFD = "-*-Helvetica-medium-r-*-*-24-*-100-100-*-*-iso8859-1";
XFontStruct *englishFont = NULL;

/*
Utility function declarationss
*/

char *makeXLFD (char*, char*);
```

Next are the implementations of the I18N-related functions. utfToNative uses iconv(3) as we've seen before. But there is a twist, due to the fact that iconv(3) is designed to handle external streams:

```
/* LangRec method implementations */

/*
utfToNative()
more basic iconv manipulations
*/
```

```
#define UTNBUFSZ 256
char* utfToNative (const char *source, const char *iconv_charset)
{
  char *buffer = malloc (UTNBUFSZ);
  char *const retbuf = buffer;

  size_t ssz = strlen (source);
  size_t bsz = UTNBUFSZ;

  iconv_t cd = iconv_open (iconv_charset, "UTF-8");

  if (cd != (iconv_t) (-1)
      && iconv (cd, &source, &ssz, &buffer, &bsz) != (size_t) (-1))
  {
      *buffer = 0;
      iconv_close (cd);
```

Here's where things get twisted. The Japanese Industrial Standard JIS X 0208 defines a basic set of about 6000 characters for Japanese, and a two-byte encoding compatible with the ISO 2022 standard. This allows languages like Japanese to use multibyte encodings in a truly essential way: different number of bytes means different character sets. Two-byte characters are Japanese, and one-byte characters are ASCII (or JIS X 0201, the Japanese version of ISO 646, differing from ASCII in three characters). ISO 2022 provides two ways to distinguish a byte that is a full ASCII character from a byte that is half of a Japanese character: either use the high bit to signal character set (high-bit-set is Japanese), or use escape sequences. The high bit method is implemented by the EUC-JP encoding, and the escape sequence method by ISO-2022-JP. iconv(3) can produce both.

Unfortunately, the X11 text rendering functions can't handle either. They will ignore the initial ESC character in an escape sequence, but then print the printable ones. So ISO-2022-JP cannot be passed directly to those functions. On the other hand, EUC-JP is unacceptable because the encoding used by the Japanese fonts supplied for X11 expects each byte in the range 0x21 to 0x7E, while EUC-JP Japanese characters use bytes in the range 0xA1 to 0xFE.

So this program asks iconv(3) to output EUC codes for Asian languages, and masks the high bit to fit the code points into the format expected by the font.

This is typical of the kinds of obstacles I18N programmers currently face. Matters are improving, but it is still the case that even with a well-internationalized application, localization to some cultures may require surgery on the code. Of course, once you've handled that culture, you'll have the code in your toolbox for the next project. The point is that implementations of I18N routines often must be exposed to the application programmer, breaking encapsulation and losing some of the advantages of object-oriented programming.

```
    if (!strcmp (iconv_charset, "EUC-JP"))
      for (buffer = retbuf; *buffer; ++buffer)
         *buffer &= 127;
    return retbuf;
  }

  fprintf (stderr, "iconv failed for %s\n", iconv_charset);
  iconv_close (cd);
  return (char *) NULL;
}
```

Here is the code that handles fonts. It is possible to delegate the mapping of languages to fonts to Xlib by using X Font Sets. However, these basically use the ISO 2022 technology and are not recommended for maintainable applications. They will not work very well in a Unicode environment due to lack of complete fonts. They are also not very user-friendly; although both X11 itself and other toolkits (such as GTK+) provide helper applications or dialogs for choosing fonts, none of them is very helpful with X Font Sets.

Nor can you just use Unicode and hope for a good font choice, since several languages use the same character, but often have quite different ideas of what looks good. In the case of characters shared by Chinese, Japanese, and Koreans, the glyphs are typically differently shaped; a person unfamiliar with the conventions used by the Chinese and Japanese to simplify the traditional glyphs would not recognize them as the same character. For typical internationalized applications this isn't really a problem. Chinese would not have fonts that appeal to Japanese installed, or if they did they would be low priority. But in a multilingual application like this one, the problem is quite real.

```c
/*  LabelRow method implementations  */

/*
init()
Returns 1 on success, 0 on failure (to find nativeFont).
Aborts on failure to find englishFont.
*/

int init (LabelRow *labelRow, LangRec *lr, Widget parent)
{
  static int rownum = 0;
  char widgetname[128];
  XFontStruct *nativeFont;

  if (!englishFont)
  {
    if (!(englishFont = XLoadQueryFont (XtDisplay(parent), englishXLFD)))
    {
      /* No English (or locale, if you I18N-ize this) font is fatal */
      fprintf (stderr, "Bailing out, couldn't load English font:\n%s\n",
               englishXLFD);
      exit (EXIT_FAILURE);
    }
  }

  if (!(nativeFont = XLoadQueryFont (XtDisplay(parent),
                      makeXLFD (lr->font, lr->x_registry))))
  {
    /* This is not fatal; many systems won't have Japanese fonts, eg. */
    fprintf (stderr, "Couldn't find font %s for language %s (%s)\n",
             lr->font, lr->english, lr->x_registry);
    return 0;
  }

  snprintf (widgetname, 128, "english%d", rownum);
  labelRow->english =
    XtVaCreateManagedWidget (widgetname, labelWidgetClass, parent,
      XtNlabel,          englishName (lr),
      XtNborderWidth,    0,
      /* I18N stuff */
```

```
        XtNfont,            englishFont,
        XtNinternational, FALSE,
        XtNencoding,        englishFont->min_byte1 == englishFont->max_byte1
                            ? XawTextEncoding8bit
                            : XawTextEncodingChar2b,
        NULL);

snprintf (widgetname, 128, "native%d", rownum);
labelRow->native =
    XtVaCreateManagedWidget (widgetname, labelWidgetClass, parent,
        XtNlabel,           nativeName (lr),
        XtNborderWidth,     0,
        /* I18N stuff */
        XtNfont,            nativeFont,
        XtNinternational, FALSE,
        XtNencoding,        nativeFont->min_byte1 == nativeFont->max_byte1
                            ? XawTextEncoding8bit
                            : XawTextEncodingChar2b,
        NULL);

snprintf (widgetname, 128, "hello%d", rownum);
labelRow->hello =
    XtVaCreateManagedWidget (widgetname, labelWidgetClass, parent,
        XtNlabel,           nativeHello (lr),
        XtNborderWidth,     0,
        /* I18N stuff */
        XtNfont,            nativeFont,
        XtNinternational, FALSE,
        XtNencoding,        nativeFont->min_byte1 == nativeFont->max_byte1
                            ? XawTextEncoding8bit
                            : XawTextEncodingChar2b,
        NULL);

++rownum;
return 1;
}
```

The `main` program just sets up the Xt application loop and calls it. Boring, omittable, omitted.

The font and LangRec manipulations are straightforward. The exception is the `langRecValidP` function. It was planned to check that each LangRec is composed of three UTF-8 strings and two ASCII strings. For ASCII, just check that all character codes are in the range 0x20 to 0x7E. UTF-8 is more complex, because it is context dependent, but the signature is quite distinctive. If the first byte of a character is an ASCII character (high bit clear), it is a one byte character (actually an ASCII character). Otherwise, the number of leading 1 bits corresponds to the number of bytes in the character, and all following bytes in the character have the form 10xxxxxx. The code was not written due to time pressure.

```
/*  XLFD and XFont manipulations  */
char *makeXLFD (char *font, char *registry)
{
  char *xlfd = malloc (36 + strlen(font) + strlen(registry));
  sprintf (xlfd, "-*-%s-medium-r-*-*-24-*-*-*-*-*-%s", font, registry);
  return xlfd;
```

```
}

/* LangRec method implementations  */
int langRecValidP (LangRec *lr)
{
/* am I lazy or what? */
return 1;
}

char *englishName (LangRec *lr)
{
return lr->english;
}

char *nativeName (LangRec *lr)
{
return utfToNative (lr->native, lr->iconv_charset);
}

char *nativeHello (LangRec *lr)
{
return utfToNative (lr->hello, lr->iconv_charset);
}

/* end m17n.c */
```

More boring geometric implementation details were here, but have been omitted. That concludes the description of the program, and to remind you what exactly you'll get after compiling the complete code from the download at http://www.wrox.com, here's a repeat of the end result we saw earlier:

Language	Native name	Greeting
English	English	Hello
Spanish	Español	¡Hola!
Japanese	日本語	こんにちは
Korean	한글	안녕하세요
Chinese	汉语	你好

Fortunately, although the ins and outs of parsing input are much more difficult than generating output, the major GUIs like Qt and GTK+ already provide text widgets incorporating XIM input managers. So the application programmer often simply needs to be aware of the encoding used (some toolkits automatically translate to Unicode, others do not). Since it is recommended that the internal encoding be a Unicode variant, in the latter case a translation of the input from the native encoding to Unicode, the inverse of that used in the program above, will be required.

I18N and Linux GUIs

I18N at the level of the basic system library (libc) has certainly advanced in the last few years, both in standardization of facilities, APIs, and semantics, and in implementation, especially in GNU libc. Text handling is certainly easier than GUI presentation, since the former is basically linear (albeit "folded") while the latter is two- (or more) dimensional. Thus, at higher levels, in particular the GUI toolkits, neither standardization nor implementation is far advanced. The effort on I18N standardization for Linux is spearheaded by the Linux Internationalization Initiative. The Li18nux draft proposal (available at http://www.li18nux.net/, and which is scheduled for approval and publication as this book goes to press) specifically mentions GUIs as an area needing standardization, but not yet ready for any "final words".

The professional Linux programmer should have an appreciation for the difficulties, so he or she can assess whether it is worth working with cutting edge techniques, often as yet uncodified as libraries, to gain the extra functionality and portability.

For example, in plain text it is common to write a bulleted list like this:

```
o item 1
o item 2
```

Now, if presented in Hebrew, lines will be naturally started from the right side, and the bullets will "automatically" be lined up at the right margin. But in a GUI, it is likely that the underlying GUI places bullet pixmaps relative to a culture-independent origin such as "window top left", and then formats the item strings into label widgets. So the label widget may "know" to format Hebrew right-to-left, but the bullets will appear incorrectly on the left side of the labels.

Clearly, things which just "do the right thing" in linear ("folded") text will often need substantially more careful attention in multidimensional GUIs. It will likely become harder still as audio and animation follow images into GUI presentation. Although the image, audio, and animation dimensions may seem more universal than written languages, yet there are surely many traps yet to be sprung on standardizers and implementers in these areas.

Still, both standardization and implementation are proceeding. Although the GTK+ documentation remains very sketchy, Owen Taylor of Red Hat has published a "white paper" (available from www.gtk.org and www.gnome.org) on the internationalization of GTK+. The developers are currently in the process of converting the internal representation of GTK+ strings to a Unicode variant, although they are (unfortunately) creating yet another library of functions to convert to and from the GTK+ internal encoding (rather than using GNU libc or another existing library). The Li18nux 2000 standard also provides some guidance on GUIs, although the May 2000 draft mostly points to the very few examples of good practice, in particular, Mozilla.

Unsurprisingly, given its commercial nature, both documentation and implementation for Qt are farther advanced than for GTK+. Qt already is entirely Unicode-based internally, and supports most external encodings (the omissions are the bidirectional languages, Arabic and Hebrew, and the complex composing languages like Hindi and Thai). Qt has integrated message catalogs, using the `gettext` PO format for translations, but compiling into a proprietary format (due to Qt's inability to use GNU `gettext` on many of its platforms, where GNU libc is not the system library).

Like GTK+/GNOME, Qt/KDE conspicuously fails to supply documentation for the internationalization of layout management and interclient communications. But this is not a defect compared to the state of the art; merely something that belongs on the wish list. Overall, the biggest defect for Qt is that it is not free software. If that matters to your project (due to some philosophical bent or a simple commitment to existing GPLed code), of course you can't use it. But otherwise, Qt should be a strong contender for your time, especially in view of its cross-platform support for I18N. (The I18N documentation is available online at http://doc.trolltech.com/i18n.html.) On the other hand, if your strategic vision is long term, the turbulence in I18N standards and implementation surely increase the risks associated with "lock-in" to the Qt platform. It had better not turn out to be broken, because you can't fix it.

One gap in the current vision for I18N is in the very recently developed "network objects" area, exemplified by Microsoft's DCOM, the much more open CORBA standard, and the GNOME implementation of a network-friendly desktop for free Unix clones, especially Linux. Of course the CORBA set of data types is sufficiently expressive to implement the POSIX locale. What is worrisome is that CORBA data types are more than expressive enough to allow multiple incompatible implementations of I18N concepts. We advocate that programmers should try to be aware of, and compatible with, emerging standards in this area. A little bit of effort in compliance, starting early in the development cycle, will pay enormous dividends in the future as the standardization process really gets going.

Status of I18N for Linux Software Development

Up to this point in the chapter, we've looked only at the internationalization of the main system libraries (libc, Xlib, and the GUI libraries). I18N efforts on other libraries are proceeding, but they are uneven as no general rule is being applied to them all. Take, for example, the PostgreSQL database used in the DVD store application, which supported several encodings for data as of 6.5.3, and added crucial support for Unicode (UTF-8) in 7.0.x, but whose overall locale support is somewhat weak and considered very slow, even by the authors. The screen library, ncurses, is sufficiently low-level that it is not directly affected by locales, but on the other hand the multibyte and wide-character functions specified in the XSI standard for curses are not yet implemented, even for capable terminal emulators (the Linux virtual console does not yet support wide or multibyte characters at all).

As with the libraries, the GNU utilities are generally the best internationalized of the utilities. Many of the file utilities, text utilities, and shell utilities have complete message catalogs for many locales. Other programs, like the basic network utilities telnet and ftp, simply try to provide "8-bit clean" communication channels; nobody has considered gettext-izing them yet. Most such programs do have localized versions for Japan, but that is of little use in porting them to Chinese or French.

One important issue is scripting languages. Of the major shells, only tcsh currently has been internationalized; it has message catalogs for German, the Romance languages, Greek, and Japanese. Fortunately, as of version 5.6 the most important scripting language, Perl, has been converted to use Unicode internally, and it has a full suite of internationalization functions analogous to those provided by GNU libc. Python is somewhat behind Perl, but the next release of Python should also be Unicode-capable internally, and modules supporting Python I18N are starting to become available.

I18N in Real Software Development Projects

At this point, experienced programmers who have not worked in the I18N field are likely to be a little bewildered by the large area covered rather lightly. They also may be wondering if all the effort is worth it.

This chapter is intended as a brief introduction to the terminology, techniques, and technology of I18N. If it has convinced you that robust I18N is a painstaking effort, but that a lot of progress has been made in supporting this effort, that part of the task is done.

It also is intended to persuade you that I18N is a worthwhile undertaking. On the benefit side, think about the possibility of taking your product to a market of one billion Chinese, and another of one billion Indians, at the relatively low cost of localization. (In Tokyo, translators cost one-third or less what programmers do, and the size of the job is easy to estimate.) Also, remember that improving the basic user interface is subject to diminishing returns, because the users who value your application the most were probably willing to accept a relatively crude user interface. But I18N and subsequent localization to a new culture will bring out a whole new group of high value users, who could not have used your program no matter how slick the user interface was.

That logic doesn't apply to every application, of course. But it's worth thinking about!

Second, in practice, the I18N foundation is likely to be less costly than first glance might suggest. After all, every user interface can be improved, yet in many cases a simple approach is good enough for the task. It is likely that a rough-and-ready approach to I18N will also suffice. Also, object-oriented methods and tools for automatically adding I18N features to programs offer relief from the tedious tasks of managing low-level functions and marking messages.

Object Oriented Programming and I18N

One reviewer of this chapter was at great pains to point out that most I18N techniques are repetitive. It is an obvious application for object-oriented programming methods. He is right, of course. But it must be pointed out that at the current state of the art, the leverage from OOP is not as great as one might hope.

First, consider the advantages. The interfaces, such as `iconv(3)`, are very general, but they make use of hard to read constructs like double indirection, and use several objects in combination in a very stylized way. With `iconv(3)` you have two indirect buffers, two indirect indices, and the conversion context that must be referenced in every call. It is very natural to bundle these all up together, and add methods to fill, convert, and flush the buffers.

The main reason that you lose leverage is that most I18N features are poorly designed for encapsulation. POSIX locales are the worst; they are a global variable in the process. This means that you can't simply create an object to encapsulate a locale and then use it to change locale in a safe way.

> *Of course you can implement the locale set up as initialization of a locale object; but this is hardly using OOP, it's just structured programming, which could be done with a function or macro.*

The point is that to change the locale locally, you must prevent other threads from running, and you must explicitly change it back when you exit the routine. Automatic destruction of the locally allocated object does help with the discipline for restoring the locale. However, changing locale is an expensive operation that should not be too easy to do implicitly.

Similarly, the conversion descriptor used by `iconv(3)` cannot be shared by different threads. Again, OOP techniques can be used to help ensure that forbidden operations cannot be done via the public interface, for example, by creating an `IconvThread` class that allocates a new private descriptor for each stream. This is likely to be inefficient, and makes designing an orthogonal class that can be used in any context far more difficult.

The second reason for the weakened efficacy of OOP techniques is the complexity of the task. First, user interfaces are potentially highly complex in any case. There are many ways for the user to introduce errors in the input, and the developer wants to robustly handle as many as possible. This is itself a highly exacting task. Now consider that in I18N, you are developing for natural languages you have never heard of. You don't know even the forms of the errors you will have to handle! Errors that can't occur or can be ignored in ASCII input may be common and dangerous in Japanese, and vice versa. I18N is to ordinary interface design as Kreigspiel is to chess.

> *Kreigspiel is the variant of chess where each player uses a separate board, and the only information you have about your opponent's activities is the fact of a capture (but not the identity of the piece involved), and the referee's prohibition of your moves made impossible by blockading pieces of the opponent.*

Thus, OOP will deliver readability and discipline through encapsulation. Based on these benefits OOP techniques are highly recommended. But each application is likely to have rather different requirements of the I18N components, so that at present an extensive library of reusable components is just a dream.

Application Builders and I18N

Application builders will surely provide great support for I18N. One of the most interesting things about the DVD store applications user interface code is that much of the I18N work was already done when I first saw it. It is true that there was some discussion of the implications of I18N among the authors, but I had no idea that the application's developers would go ahead and just do it. But they did. Or, to be accurate, Glade did.

Let's take a look at what Glade did (and didn't) do for I18N, and how it did it. First, note that the application hasn't been localized at all. It won't do anything special in any other locale than the default POSIX locale; there are no translations yet. What has been done is the following:

- ❏ Initialization of the locale functionality of GNU libc (implicitly, by GTK+)
- ❏ Initialization of the message catalog (explicitly by calls to `textdomain` and `bindtextdomain`, added by Glade in `./src/main.c`)
- ❏ Initialization of the input methods (implicitly, by GTK+)
- ❏ Declaration of `gettext` facilities (explicitly, added by Glade in `./src/support.h`)
- ❏ Wrapping strings in calls to `gettext` (explicitly, added by Glade using the conventional "_" macro)
- ❏ Generation of a message catalog template in `./po/dvdstore.pot`

From the developer's point of view, this is quite automatic. As of Glade 0.5.7, all of the above is done by default except generation of the message catalog template. This is enabled by selecting Options | LibGlade Options and enabling "Save Translatable Strings" with filename po/dvdstore.pot. The message catalog is not complete, because it is generated at the time the sources are generated. So all messages in callbacks and the main program that are added later must be merged in by hand. This can probably be done by Glade by rebuilding the project, but Glade doesn't seem to invoke the gettext utilities; it does it itself. So you may prefer to use msgmerge(1), xgettext(1), or Emacs's po-mode (provided as po-mode.el with the gettext package).

There's really only a little left to do for the basic I18N functionality. First, the template for textdomain should be completed with dvdstore substituted for PACKAGE. This substitution also needs to be made in src/support.h. It is expected that later versions of Glade will do this automatically, but the current one does not.

The call to bindtextdomain is unnecessary for this application, and can be removed. (It is primarily useful when for some reason there is a name conflict among packages.)

That is sufficient to make the basic localized message functionality available; all that's necessary is to find translators to create the dvdstore.po files for each target locale, and compile them using msgfmt(1) to .mo files for installation.

There are three issues left. The major issue is that no provision has been made for handling different currencies. This is going to be difficult, however, because it will surely involve design changes in the database backend at the same time: the price schedule will need to differ for different locales. But locale may not be enough; for example, one might want to have different prices for big city and rural stores due to the cost of land. It's probably not a good idea to use the @modifier component of locale to proxy for store address, as it is insufficiently flexible. This should be handled by the database, not the locale mechanism. However, in preparation for such a move, it might be worthwhile to change the following code (in ./src/title_dialog.c):

```
strncpy((new_title.rental_cost), g_strdup_printf("%f", cost), COST_LEN);
```

to something like:

```
char *buffer = g_malloc (COST_LEN);
/* Note that cost is a float in strfmon, too */
strfmon (buffer, COST_LEN, "%n", cost);
strncpy((new_title.rental_cost), buffer, COST_LEN);
```

The second issue is that a similar change might be made for dates, to use the strftime function to format user-visible dates. The main reason to advocate this change is that a later maintainer might decide to "humanize" dates, at least for output, and the use of the strftime function to format dates in the similar ISO 8601 style (YYYY-MM-DD) would clearly distinguish between user-visible dates and those intended for internal use by the database itself in the user interface code.

The third issue is the use of positional parameters in the translated strings, where more than one format specification is present. For example, in ./src/disk_dialog.c, we have the following code:

```
msg = g_strdup_printf(_("Created Disk ID %d for Title ID %d"),
        new_disk.disk_id,
        new_disk.title_id);
```

Seems innocent enough, but some languages, like German and Japanese, seem "reverse Polish" to an English speaker. That is, the natural way (practically forced by Japanese grammar, in fact) for a Japanese to express that message is the equivalent of "For Title ID %d, Disk ID %d was created". Not impossible, although stilted, in English. But the problem is that there is no way for programmers to know such a thing. It's not their job; translators are experts for that. Not to mention that other target languages require the reverse of the Japanese order.

So what needs to be done is to use positional parameters. These are now a standard feature in the C library, and are certainly implemented in GNU libc. In the source code, we would have:

```
/* note the "%" INTEGER "$d" format strings */
msg = g_strdup_printf(_("Created Disk ID %1$d for Title ID %2$d"),
        new_disk.disk_id,
        new_disk.title_id);
```

and in the Japanese .po file, ./po/ja/dvdstore.po:

```
#: src/disk_dialog.c:30
msgid "Created Disk ID %1$d for Title ID %2$d"
msgstr "For Title ID %2$d, Disk ID %1$d was created"
```

Note how the positional parameters indicate the correct association of "Disk ID" with new_disk.disk_id and "Title ID" with new_disk.title_id. This shouldn't be too burdensome; surely inserting the positional parameter can automated with a Python or Perl script. And in fact only 5% (7 of 140) of the localized strings in the user interface have more than one format converter. That doesn't seem to be unusually low; such strings are relatively few.

All-in-all, the work involved in internationalizing this application seems not too great, considering that the original developers are not I18N specialists, and yet managed to get the job 95% done.

Where Next for Linux I18N?

The Linux Internationalization Initiative (http://www.li18nux.net/) is advancing the standardization of I18N facilities for Linux, and free UNIX systems in general. It's up to you to incorporate I18N in your own programs, and so advance the state of the art!

Annotated References

Internationalization is a large, very technical field. We've name checked quite a few of the most important references already in this chapter, but to make it simpler, here they are again. Starting from them you should be able to find information about most issues you will run into in I18N.

Li18nux – The Linux Internationalization Initiative

The consortium of Linux distributions, companies, and anyone else interested charged with drawing up standards and best practice guidelines for Linux internationalization. You can find the Li18nux 2000 draft standard (May, 2000) at http://www.linux.net/root/LI18NUX2000/ li18nux2k_draft.html).

ISO Standards, Especially Unicode

Many are cited in Li18nux 2000. Unfortunately, the printed versions are extremely expensive. Mostly there are cheaper alternatives, often better as well. Every developer serious about I18N should have access to ISO 10646 (the Universal Character Set definition), but it costs about $500! But the Unicode Standard, version 3.0, is only $50 or so, and not only contains the definition of the character set, but a wealth of additional information about text processing. Many tables, examples, and tools are available online at http://www.unicode.org/.

Internet RFCs, Especially MIME

The Internet Engineering Task Force Request for Comments (RFC) series is primarily of interest to specialists implementing particular protocols and standardizers themselves. It is not primarily concerned with I18N, of course. However, many RFCs bear on I18N, and the group of RFCs dealing with MIME (2045 to 2049) is extremely important, because the MIME standard defines how e-mail and Usenet can handle languages other than English. Furthermore, many MIME conventions are directly adopted by other protocols, such as HTTP. It's useful to browse `rfc-index.txt`. Most large archives mirror the RFCs.

CJKV Information Processing: Chinese, Japanese, Korean, and Vietnamese Computing

By Ken Lunde. Sebastopol: O'Reilly and Associates, 1999. The bible of Asian language processing, and the place to start for advanced study. Many examples and tools are available online: ftp://ftp.uu.net/vendor/oreilly/nutshell/cjkv/.

Implementations

Of course, this is Linux. Many tools and applications are already internationalized. Some not so well – but you can do better. Right? "Use the Source, Luke."

❏ System libraries: Linux kernel, GNU libc, X11R6

❏ GUIs/desktops: GTK+, GNOME, Qt, KDE

❏ System commands: GNU file|shell|text utilities

❏ Editors: GNU Emacs/Mule, XEmacs/Mule, yudit

❏ Browsers: Lynx, Mozilla

❏ Languages: C/C++, Perl, Python

❏ Application libraries: databases, etc.

There is no automatic sanity checker for I18N yet, and probably won't be for a long time. I18N is going to remain a job for human programmers for the foreseeable future. But with the rapidly proceeding globalization of the WWW and the market for software and software development in general, we can expect great rewards to developers responsible for good designs and implementations in this field.

Online discussion at http://www.p2p.wrox.com

GTK+ & GNOME Object Reference

This the API of the GTK+/GNOME widgets and functions used in the DVD store application in Chapter 9.

This reference is licensed under the GNU Free Documentation License (GFDL), and you can obtain the original copy from http://developer.gnome.org/. You can also download this appendix free of charge from our website, where it can be found in the code tarball, as an HTML file called `Appendix_A.html`.

GTK+ Widgets and Functions

GtkButton

A widget that creates a signal when clicked on.

Function	Parameters	Description
`gtk_button_new`	`(void)`	Creates a new GtkButton widget.
`gtk_button_new_with_label`	`(const gchar *label)`	Creates a GtkButton widget with a GtkLabel child containing the text contained in `label`.
`gtk_button_pressed`	`(GtkButton *button)`	Emits a `GtkButton::pressed` signal to the given GtkButton.

Table continued on following page

Function	Parameters	Description
gtk_button_released	(GtkButton *button)	Emits a GtkButton::released signal to the given GtkButton.
gtk_button_clicked	(GtkButton *button)	Emits a GtkButton::clicked signal to the given GtkButton.
gtk_button_enter	(GtkButton *button)	Emits a GtkButton::enter signal to the given GtkButton.
gtk_button_leave	(GtkButton *button)	Emits a GtkButton::leave signal to the given GtkButton.
gtk_button_ set_relief	(GtkButton *button GtkReliefStyle newstyle)	Sets the relief style of the edges of the given GtkButton widget. Three styles exist, GTK_RELIEF_NORMAL, GTK_RELIEF_HALF, GTK_RELIEF_NONE. The default style is GTK_RELIEF_NORMAL.
gtk_button_ get_relief	(GtkButton *button)	Returns the current relief style of the given GtkButton.

GtkCheckButton

Create widgets with a discrete toggle button.

Function	Parameters	Description
gtk_check_button_new	(void)	Creates a new GtkCheckButton.
gtk_check_button_ new_with_label	(const gchar *label)	Creates a new GtkCheckButton with a GtkLabel to the right of it.

GtkCList

A multi-columned scrolling list widget.

Function	Parameters	Description
gtk_clist_construct	(GtkCList *clist, gint columns, gchar *titles[ ])	Initializes a previously allocated GtkCList widget for use. This should not normally be used to create a GtkCList widget. Use gtk_clist_new instead.
gtk_clist_new	(gint columns)	Creates a new GtkCList widget.
gtk_clist_new_ with_titles	(gint columns, gchar *titles)	Creates a new GtkCList widget with column titles.

Function	Parameters	Description
gtk_clist_set_shadow_type	(GtkClist *clist, GtkShadowType type)	Sets the shadow type for the specified CList. Changing this value will cause the GtkCList to update its visuals.
gtk_clist_set_selection_mode	GtkCList *clist, GtkSelectionMode mode)	Sets the selection mode for the specified CList. This allows you to set whether only one or more than one item can be selected at a time in the widget. Note that setting the widget's selection mode to one of GTK_SELECTION_BROWSE or GTK_SELECTION_SINGLE will cause all the items in the GtkCList to become deselected.
gtk_clist_freeze	(GtkCList *clist)	Causes the GtkCList to stop updating its visuals until a matching call to gtk_clist_thaw is made. This function is useful if a lot of changes will be made to the widget that may cause a lot of visual updating to occur. Note that calls to gtk_clist_freeze can be nested.
gtk_clist_thaw	(GtkCList *clist)	Causes the specified GtkCList to allow visual updates.
gtk_clist_column_titles_show	(GtkCList *clist)	This function causes the GtkCList to show its column titles, if they are not already showing.
gtk_clist_column_titles_hide	(GtkCList *clist)	Causes the GtkCList to hide its column titles, if they are currently showing.
gtk_clist_column_title_active	(GtkCList *clist, gint column)	Sets the specified column in the GtkCList to become selectable. You can then respond to events from the user clicking on a title button, and take appropriate action.
gtk_clist_column_title_passive	(GtkCList *clist, gint column)	Causes the specified column title button to become passive, so it doesn't respond to events, such as the user clicking on it.
gtk_clist_column_titles_active	(GtkCList *clist)	Causes all column title buttons to become active. This is the same as calling gtk_clist_column_title_active for each column.

Table continued on following page

Function	Parameters	Description
gtk_clist_column_titles_passive	(GtkCList *clist)	Causes all column title buttons to become passive. This is the same as calling gtk_clist_column_title_passive for each column.
gtk_clist_set_column_title	(GtkCList *clist, gint column, const gchar *title)	Sets the title for the specified column.
gtk_clist_set_column_widget	(GtkCList *clist, gint column, const gchar *title)	Sets a widget to be used as the specified column's title. This can be used to place a pixmap or something else as the column title, instead of the standard text.
gtk_clist_set_column_justification	(GtkCList *clist, gint column, GtkJustification justification)	Sets the justification to be used for all text in the specified column.
gtk_clist_set_column_visibility	(GtkCList *clist, gint column, gboolean visible)	Allows you to set whether a specified column in the GtkCList should be hidden or shown. Note that at least one column must always be showing; so attempting to hide the last visible column will be ignored.
gtk_clist_set_column_resizeable	(GtkCList *clist, gint column, gboolean resizeable)	Lets you specify whether a specified column should be resizeable by the user. Note that turning on resizeability for the column will automatically shut off auto-resizing, but turning off resizeability will NOT turn on auto-resizing. This must be done manually via a call to gtk_clist_set_column_auto_resize.
gtk_clist_set_column_auto_resize	(GtkCList *clist, gint column, gboolean auto_resize)	Lets you specify whether a column should be automatically resized by the widget when data is added or removed. Enabling auto-resize on a column explicitly disallows user resizing of the column.
gtk_clist_optimal_column_width	(GtkCList *clist, gint column)	Gets the required width in pixels that is needed to show everything in the specified column.

Function	Parameters	Description
gtk_clist_set_ column_width	(GtkCList *clist, gint column, gint width)	Causes the column specified for the GtkCList to be set to a specified width.
gtk_clist_set_ column_min_width	(GtkCList *clist, gint column, gint min_width)	Causes the column specified to have a minimum width, preventing the user from resizing it smaller than specified.
gtk_clist_set_ column_max_width	(GtkCList *clist, gint column, gint max_width)	Causes the column specified to have a maximum width, preventing the user from resizing it larger than specified.
gtk_clist_set_ row_height	(GtkCList *clist, guint height)	Causes the GtkCList to have a specified height for its rows. Setting the row height to 0 allows the GtkCList to adjust automatically to data in the row.
gtk_clist_moveto	(GtkCList *clist, gint row, gint column, gfloat row_align, gfloat col_align)	Tells the CList widget to visually move to the specified row and column.
gtk_clist_row_ is_visible	(GtkCList *clist, gint row)	Checks how the specified row is visible.
gtk_clist_get_ cell_type	(GtkCList *clist, gint row, gint column)	Checks the type of cell at the location specified.
gtk_clist_set_text	(GtkCList *clist, gint row, gint column, const gchar *text)	Sets the displayed text in the specified cell.
gtk_clist_get_text	(GtkCList *clist, gint row, gint column, const gchar *text)	Gets the text for the specified cell.
gtk_clist_set_pixmap	(GtkClist *clist, gint row, gint column, GdkPixmap, *pixmap, GdkBitmap *mask)	Sets a pixmap for the specified cell.

Table continued on following page

Function	Parameters	Description
gtk_clist_ get_pixmap	(GtkClist *clist, gint row, gint column, GdkPixmap, *pixmap, GdkBitmap *mask)	Gets the pixmap and bitmap mask of the specified cell. The returned mask value can be NULL.
gtk_clist_set_ pixtext	(GtkClist *clist, gint row, gint column, const gchar *text, guint8 spacing, GdkPixmap *pixmap, GdkBitmap *mask)	Sets text and a pixmap/bitmap on the specified cell.
gtk_clist_get_ pixtext	(GtkClist *clist, gint row, gint column, const gchar *text, guint8 spacing, GdkPixmap *pixmap, GdkBitmap *mask)	Gets the text, pixmap and bitmap mask for the specified cell.
gtk_clist_set_ foreground	GtkClist *clist, gint row, GdkColor *color)	Sets the foreground color for the specified row.
gtk_clist_set_ background	GtkClist *clist, gint row, GdkColor *color)	Sets the background color for the specified row.
gtk_clist_set_ cell_style	GtkClist *clist, gint row, gint column, GtkStyle *style)	Sets the style for the specified cell.
gtk_clist_get_ cell_style	GtkClist *clist, gint row, gint column, GtkStyle *style)	Gets the current style of the specified cell.
gtk_clist_set_ row_style	GtkClist *clist, gint row, GtkStyle *style)	Sets the style for all cells in the specified row.
gtk_clist_get_ row_style	(GtkCList *clist, gint row)	Gets the style set for the specified row.
gtk_clist_set_ shift	(GtkCList *clist, gint row, gint column, gint vertical, gint horizontal)	Sets the vertical and horizontal shift of the specified cell.
gtk_clist_set_ selectable	(GtkCList *clist, gint row, gboolean selectable)	Sets whether the specified row is selectable or not.
gtk_clist_get_ selectable	(GtkCList *clist, gint row)	Gets whether the specified row is selectable or not.
gtk_clist_ prepend	(GtkCList *clist, gchar *text)	Adds a row to the CList at the top.
gtk_clist_ append	(GtkCList *clist, gchar *text)	Adds a row to the CList at the bottom.

Function	Parameters	Description
gtk_clist_insert	(GtkCList *clist, gint row, gchar *text)	Adds a row of text to the CList at the specified position.
gtk_clist_remove	(GtkCList *clist, gint row)	Removes the specified row from the CList.
gtk_clist_set_row_data	(GtkCList *clist, gint row, gpointer data)	Sets data for the specified row. This is the same as calling gtk_clist_set_row_data_full (clist, row, data, NULL).
gtk_clist_set_row_data_full	(GtkCList *clist, gint row, gpointer data, GtkDestroyNotify destroy)	Sets the data for the specified row, with a callback when the row is destroyed.
gtk_clist_get_row_data	(GtkCList *clist, gint row)	Gets the currently set data for the specified row.
gtk_clist_find_row_from_data	(GtkCList *clist, gpointer data)	Searches the CList for the row with the specified data.
gtk_clist_select_row	(GtkCList *clist, gint row, gint column)	Selects the specified row. Causes the "select-row" signal to be emitted for the specified row and column.
gtk_clist_unselect_row	(GtkCList *clist, gint row, gint column)	Unselects the specified row. Causes the "unselect-row" signal to be emitted for the specified row and column.
gtk_clist_undo_selection	(GtkCList *clist)	Undoes the last selection for an "extended selection mode" CList.
gtk_clist_clear	(GtkCList *clist)	Removes all of the CList's rows.
gtk_clist_get_selection_info	(GtkCList *clist, gint x, gint y, gint *row, gint *column))	Gets the row and column at the specified pixel position in the CList.
gtk_clist_select_all	(GtkCList *clist)	Selects all rows in the CList. This function has no affect for a CList in "single" or "browse" selection mode.
gtk_clist_unselect_all	(GtkCList *clist)	Unselects all rows in the CList.

Table continued on following page

Function	Parameters	Description
gtk_clist_ swap_rows	(GtkCList *clist, gint row1, gint row2)	Swaps the two specified rows with each other.
gtk_clist_set_ compare_func	(GtkCList *clist, GtkCListCompareFunc cmp_func)	Sets the compare function of the GtkClist to cmp_func. If cmp_func is NULL, then the default compare function is used. The default compare function sorts ascending or with the type set by gtk_clist_set_sort_type by the column set by gtk_clist_set_sort_column.
gtk_clist_set_ sort_column	(GtkCList *clist, gint column)	Sets the sort column of the CList. The sort column is used by the default compare function to determine which column to sort by.
gtk_clist_set_ sort_type	(GtkCList *clist, GtkSortType sort_type)	Sets the sort type of the GtkClist. This is either GTK_SORT_ASCENDING for an ascending sort order or GTK_SORT_DESCENDING for a descending sort.
gtk_clist_sort	(GtkCList *clist)	Sorts the GtkCList according to the current compare function, which can be set with the gtk_clist_set_compare_func function.
gtk_clist_set_ auto_sort	(GtkCList *clist, gboolean auto_sort)	Turns on or off auto sort of the GtkCList. If auto sort is on, then the CList will be resorted when a row is inserted into the CList.
gtk_clist_ columns_autosize	(GtkCList *clist)	Auto-sizes all columns in the CList and returns the total width of the CList.
gtk_clist_get_ column_title	(GtkCList *clist, gint column)	Gets the current title of the specified column.
gtk_clist_get_ column_widget	(GtkCList *clist, gint column)	Gets the widget in the column header for the specified column.
gtk_clist_get_ hadjustment	(GtkCList *clist)	Gets the GtkAdjustment currently being used for the horizontal aspect.
gtk_clist_get_ vadjustment	(GtkCList *clist)	Gets the GtkAdjustment currently being used for the vertical aspect.

Function	Parameters	Description
gtk_clist_ row_move	(GtkCList *clist, gint source_row, gint dest_row)	Allows you to move a row from one position to another in the list.
gtk_clist_set_ button_actions	(GtkCList *clist, guint button, guint button_actions)	Sets the action(s) that the specified mouse button will have on the CList.
gtk_clist_set_ hadjustment	(GtkCList *clist, GtkAdjustment *adjustment)	Allows you to set the GtkAdjustment to be used for the horizontal aspect of the GtkCList widget.
gtk_clist_set_ reorderable	(GtkCList *clist, gboolean reorderbale)	Sets whether the CList's rows are re-orderable using drag-and-drop.
gtk_clist_set_ use_drag_icons	(GtkCList *clist, gboolean use_icons)	Determines whether the GtkClist should use icons when doing drag-and-drop operations.
gtk_clist_set_ vadjustment	(GtkCList *clist, GtkAdjustment *adjustment)	Allows you to set the GtkAdjustment to be used for the vertical aspect of the GtkCList widget.

GtkCombo

A text entry field with a dropdown list.

Function	Parameters	Description
gtk_combo_new	(void)	Creates a new GtkCombo.
gtk_combo_set_ popdown_strings	(GtkCombo *combo, GList *strings)	Convenience function to set all of the items in the popup list.
gtk_combo_set_ value_in_list	(GtkCombo *combo, gint val, gint ok_if_empty)	Specifies whether the value entered in the text entry field must match one of the values in the list. If this is set then the user will not be able to perform any other action until a valid value has been entered. If an empty field is acceptable, the ok_if_empty parameter should be TRUE.
gtk_combo_set_ use_arrows	(GtkCombo *combo, gint val)	Specifies if the arrow (cursor) keys can be used to step through the items in the list. This is on by default.

Table continued on following page

Function	Parameters	Description
gtk_combo_set_ use_arrows_ always	(GtkCombo *combo, gint val)	Specifies if the arrow keys will still work even if the current contents of the GtkEntry field do not match any of the list items.
gtk_combo_set_ case_sensitive	(GtkCombo *combo, gint val)	Specifies whether the text entered into the GtkEntry field and the text in the list items is case sensitive.
		This may be useful, for example, when you have called gtk_combo_set_value_ in_list to limit the values entered, but you are not worried about differences in case.
gtk_combo_set_ item_string	(GtkCombo *combo, GtkItem *item, const gchar *item_value)	Sets the string to place in the GtkEntry field when a particular list item is selected. This is needed if the list item is not a simple label.
gtk_combo_ disable_activate	(GtkCombo *combo)	Stops the GtkCombo widget from showing the popup list when the GtkEntry emits the "activate" signal, which it does when the *Return* key is pressed. This may be useful if, for example, you want the *Return* key to close a dialog instead.

GtkEntry

The GtkEntry widget is a single line text entry widget. A fairly large set of key bindings are supported by default. If the entered text is longer than the allocation of the widget, the widget will scroll so that the cursor position is visible.

Function	Parameters	Description
gtk_entry_new	(void)	Creates a new GtkEntry widget.
gtk_entry_new_ with_max_length	(guint16 max)	Creates a new GtkEntry widget with the given maximum length.
		Note: the existence of this function is inconsistent with the rest of the GTK+ API. The normal setup would be to just require the user to make an extra call to gtk_entry_set_max_length instead. It is not expected that this function will be removed, but it would be better practice not to use it.

Function	Parameters	Description
gtk_entry_ set_text	(GtkEntry *entry, const gchar *text)	Sets the text in the widget to the given value, replacing the current contents.
gtk_entry_ append_text	(GtkEntry *entry, const gchar *text)	Appends the given text to the contents of the widget.
gtk_entry_ prepend_text	(GtkEntry *entry, const gchar *text)	Prepends the given text to the contents of the widget.
gtk_entry_ set_position	(GtkEntry *entry, gint position)	Sets the cursor position in an entry to the given value. This function is obsolete. You should use gtk_editable_set_position instead.
gtk_entry_ get_text	(GtkEntry *entry)	Retrieve the contents of the entry widget. The returned pointer points to internally allocated storage in the widget and must not be freed, modified, or stored. For this reason, this function is deprecated. Use gtk_editable_get_chars instead.
gtk_entry_ select_region	(GtkEntry *entry, gint start, gint end)	Selects a region of text. The characters that are selected are those characters at positions from start_pos up to, but not including end_pos. If end_pos is negative, then the characters selected will be those characters from start_pos to the end of the text. This function is obsolete. You should use gtk_editable_select_ region instead.
gtk_entry_ set_visibility	(GtkEntry *entry, gboolean visible)	Sets whether the contents of the entry are visible or not. When visibility is set to FALSE, characters are displayed as asterisks, and will also appear that way when the text in the entry widget is copied elsewhere.
gtk_entry_ set_editable	(GtkEntry *entry, gboolean editable)	Determines if the user can edit the text in the editable widget or not. This function is obsolete. You should use gtk_editable_ set_editable instead.
gtk_entry_ set_max_length	(GtkEntry *entry, guint16 max)	Sets the maximum allowed length of the contents of the widget. If the current contents are longer than the given length, then they will be truncated to fit.

GtkFrame

The frame widget is a Bin that surrounds its child with a decorative frame and an optional label. If present, the label is drawn in a gap in the top side of the frame. The position of the label can be controlled with gtk_frame_set_label_align.

Function	Parameters	Description
gtk_frame_new	(const gchar *label)	Creates a new Frame, with optional label, label. If label is NULL, the label is omitted.
gtk_frame_set_label	(GtkFrame *frame, const gchar *label)	Sets the text of the label. If label is NULL, the current label, if any, is removed.
gtk_frame_set_label_align	(GtkFrame *frame, gfloat xalign, gfloat yalign)	Sets the alignment of the Frame widget's label. The default value for a newly created Frame is 0.0.
gtk_frame_set_shadow_type	(GtkFrame *frame, GtkShadowType type)	Sets the shadow type for the Frame widget.

GtkHBox

A horizontal container box.

Function	Parameters	Description
gtk_hbox_new	(gboolean homogenous, gint spacing)	Creates a new GtkHBox.

GtkHButtonBox

A container for arranging buttons horizontally.

Function	Parameters	Description
gtk_hbutton_box_new	(void)	Creates a new horizontal button box.
gtk_hbutton_box_get_spacing_default	(void)	Retrieves the current default spacing for horizontal button boxes. This is the number of pixels to be placed between the buttons when they are arranged.
gtk_hbutton_box_get_layout_default	(void)	Retrieves the current layout used to arrange buttons in button box widgets.

Function	Parameters	Description
gtk_hbutton_box_ set_spacing_ default	(gint spacing)	Changes the default spacing that is placed between widgets in a horizontal button box.
gtk_hbutton_ box_set_layout_ default	(GtkButtonBoxStyle layout)	Sets a new layout mode that will be used by all button boxes.

GtkHSeparator

A horizontal separator.

Function	Parameters	Description
gtk_hseparator_ new	(void)	Creates a new GtkHSeparator.

GtkLabel

A widget that displays a small to medium amount of text.

Function	Parameters	Description
gtk_label_new	(const gchar *str)	Creates a new label with the given string of text inside it. You can pass NULL to get an empty label widget.
gtk_label_ set_pattern	(GtkLabel *label, const gchar *pattern)	Sets the pattern of underlines you want under the existing text within the GtkLabel widget. For example if the current text of the label says "FooBarBaz" passing a pattern of "___ ___" will underline "Foo" and "Baz" but not "Bar".
gtk_label_ set_justify	(GtkLabel *label, GtkJustification jtype)	Sets where the text within the GtkLabel will align. This can be one of four values: GTK_JUSTIFY_LEFT, GTK_JUSTIFY_RIGHT, GTK_JUSTIFY_CENTER, and GTK_JUSTIFY_FILL. GTK_JUSTIFY_CENTER is the default value when the widget is first created with gtk_label_new.
gtk_label_get	(GtkLabel *label, gchar *str)	Gets the current string of text within the GtkLabel and writes it to the given str argument. It does not make a copy of this string so you must not write to it.

Table continued on following page

Function	Parameters	Description
gtk_label_parse_uline	(GtkLabel *label, const gchar *string)	Parses the given string for underscores and converts the next character to an underlined character. The last character that was underlined will have its lower-cased accelerator keyval returned (thus "_File" would return the keyval for "*f*". This is only used within the Gtk+ library itself for menu items and such.
gtk_label_set_line_wrap	(GtkLabel *label, gboolean wrap)	Toggles line wrapping within the GtkLabel widget. TRUE makes it break lines if text exceeds the widget's size. FALSE lets the text get cut off by the edge of the widget if it exceeds the widget size.
gtk_label_set_text	(GtkLabel *label, const gchar *str)	Sets the text within the GtkLabel widget. It overwrites any text that was there before. Note that underlines that were there before do not get overwritten. If you want to erase underlines just send NULL to gtk_label_set_pattern.

GtkMenu

A drop down menu widget.

Function	Parameters	Description
gtk_menu_new	(void)	Creates a new GtkMenu.
gtk_menu_append	(GtkMenu *menu, GtkWidget *child)	Adds a new GtkMenuItem to the end of the menu's item list.
gtk_menu_prepend	(GtkMenu *menu, GtkWidget *child)	Adds a new GtkMenuItem to the beginning of the menu's item list.
gtk_menu_insert	(GtkMenu *menu, GtkWidget *child, gint position)	Adds a new GtkMenuItem to the menu's item list at the position indicated by position.
gtk_menu_reorder_child	(GtkMenu *menu, GtkWidget *child, gint position)	Moves a GtkMenuItem to a new position within the GtkMenu.
gtk_menu_popup	(GtkMenu *menu, GtkWidget *parent_meni_shell, GtkWidget *parent_menu_item, GtkMenuPositionFunc func, gpointer data, guint button, guint32 activate_time)	Displays a menu and makes it available for selection. Applications can use this function to display context-sensitive menus, and will typically supply NULL for the parent_menu_shell, parent_menu_item, func, and data parameters. The default menu positioning function will position the menu at the current pointer position.

Function	Parameters	Description
gtk_menu_set_accel_group	(GtkMenu *menu, GtkAccelGroup *accel_group)	Sets the GtkAccelGroup that holds global accelerators for the menu.
gtk_menu_set_title	(GtkMenu *menu, const gchar *title)	Sets the title string for the menu. The title is displayed when the menu is shown as a tear-off menu.
gtk_menu_popdown	(GtkMenu *menu)	Removes the menu from the screen.
gtk_menu_reposition	(GtkMenu *menu)	Repositions the menu according to its position function.
gtk_menu_get_active	(GtkMenu *menu)	Returns the selected menu item from the menu. The GtkOptionMenu uses this.
gtk_menu_set_active	(GtkMenu *menu, guint index)	Selects the specified menu item within the menu. The GtkOptionMenu uses this.
gtk_menu_set_tearoff_state	(GtkMenu *menu, gboolean torn_off)	Changes the tear-off state of the menu. A menu is normally displayed as drop down menu, which persists as long as the menu is active. It can also be displayed as a tear-off menu which persists until it is closed or reattached.
gtk_menu_attach_to_widget	(GtkMenu *menu, GtkWidget *attach_widget, GtkMenuDetachFunc detacher)	Attaches the menu to the widget and provides a callback function that will be invoked when the menu calls gtk_menu_detach during its destruction.
gtk_menu_detach	(GtkMenu *menu)	Detaches the menu from the widget to which it had been attached. This function will call the callback function, detacher, provided when the gtk_menu_attach_to_widget function was called.
gtk_menu_get_attach_widget	(GtkMenu *menu)	Returns the GtkWidget that the menu is attached to.

GtkMenuBar

A subclass widget for GtkMenuShell, which holds GtkMenuItem widgets.

Function	Parameters	Description
gtk_menu_bar_new	(void)	Creates a new GtkMenuBar.

Table continued on following page

Function	Parameters	Description
gtk_menu_bar_ append	(GtkMenuBar *menu_bar, GtkWidget *child)	Adds a new GtkMenuItem to the end of the GtkMenuBar.
gtk_menu_bar_ prepend	(GtkMenuBar *menu_bar, GtkWidgct *child)	Adds a new GtkMenuItem to the beginning of the GtkMenuBar.
gtk_menu_bar_ insert	(GtkMenuBar *menu_bar, GtkWidget *child, gint position)	Adds a new GtkMenuItem to the GtkMenuBar at the position defined by position.
gtk_menu_bar_ set_shadow_type	(GtkMenuBar *menu_bar, GtkShadowType type)	Sets the shadow type to use on the GtkMenuBar. The shadow types to use are: GTK_SHADOW_NONE, GTK_SHADOW_IN, GTK_SHADOW_OUT, GTK_SHADOW_ETCHED_IN, and GTK_SHADOW_ETCHED_OUT.

GtkMenuItem

The widget used for items in menus.

Function	Parameters	Description
gtk_menu_ item_new	(void)	Creates a new GtkMenuItem.
gtk_menu_item_ new_with_label	(const gchar *label)	Creates a new GtkMenuItem whose child is a simple GtkLabel.
gtk_menu_item_ set_submenu	(GtkMenuItem *menu_item, GtkWidget *submenu)	Sets the widget submenu, or changes it.
gtk_menu_item_ remove_submenu	(GtkMenuItem *menu_item)	Removes the widget's submenu.
gtk_menu_item_ set_placement	(GtkMenuItem *menu_item, GtkSubmenuPlacement placement)	Specifies the placement of the submenu around the menu item. The placement is usually GTK_LEFT_RIGHT for menu items in a popup menu and GTK_TOP_BOTTOM in menu bars. This function is useless in usual applications.
gtk_menu_item_ configure	(GtkMenuItem *menu_item, gint show_toggle_ indicator, gint show_submenu_ indicator)	Sets whether the menu item should show a submenu indicator, which is a right arrow.

Function	Parameters	Description
gtk_menu_item_ select	(GtkMenuItem *menu_item)	Emits the "select" signal on the given item. Behaves exactly like gtk_item_select.
gtk_menu_item_ deselect	(GtkMenuItem *menu_item)	Emits the "deselect" signal on the given item. Behaves exactly like gtk_item_ deselect.
gtk_menu_item_ activate	(GtkMenuItem *menu_item)	Emits the "activate" signal on the given item.
gtk_menu_item_ right_justify	(GtkMenuItem *menu_item)	Sets the menu item to be right justified. Only useful for menu bars.

GtkNotebook

Set of pages with bookmarks.

Function	Parameters	Description
gtk_notebook_ new	(void)	Creates a new GtkNotebook widget.
gtk_notebook_ append_page	(GtkNotebook *notebook, GtkWidget *child, GtkWidget *tab_label)	Appends to notebook a page whose content is child, and whose bookmark is tab_label.
gtk_notebook_ append_page_ menu	(GtkNotebook *notebook, GtkWidget *child, GtkWidget *tab_labe, GtkWidget *menu_label)	Appends to notebook a page whose content is child, whose bookmark is tab_label, and whose menu label is menu_label.
gtk_notebook_ prepend_page	(GtkNotebook *notebook, GtkWidget *child, GtkWidget *tab_label)	Prepends to notebook a page whose content is child, and whose bookmark is tab_label.
gtk_notebook_ prepend_page_ menu	(GtkNotebook *notebook, GtkWidget *child, GtkWidget *tab_labe, GtkWidget *menu_label)	Preappends to notebook a page whose content is child, whose bookmark is tab_label, and whose menu label is menu_label.

Table continued on following page

Function	Parameters	Description
gtk_notebook_ insert_page	(GtkNotebook *notebook, GtkWidget *child, GtkWidget *tab_label, gint position)	Inserts in notebook a new page whose content is child, and whose bookmark is tab_label. The page is inserted just before the page number position, starting with 0. If position is out of bounds, it is assumed to be the current number of pages.
gtk_notebook_ insert_page_menu	(GtkNotebook *notebook, GtkWidget *child, GtkWidget *tab_label, GtkWidget *menu_label, gint position)	Inserts in notebook a new page whose content is child, whose bookmark is tab_label, and whose menu label is menu_label. The page is inserted just before the page number position, starting with 0. If position is out of bounds, it is assumed to be the current number of pages.
gtk_notebook_ remove_page	(GtkNotebook *notebook, gint page_num)	Removes the page page_num from notebook. Pages are numbered starting at zero. Negative values stand for the last page; too large values are ignored.
gtk_notebook_ page_num	(GtkNotebook *notebook, GtkWidget *child)	Returns the page number of child in notebook.
gtk_notebook_ set_page	(GtkNotebook *notebook, gint page_num)	Switches to the page number page_num. Negative values stand for the last page; too large values are ignored.
gtk_notebook_ next_page	(GtkNotebook *notebook)	Switches to the next page. Nothing happens if the current page is the last page.
gtk_notebook_ prev_page	(GtkNotebook *notebook)	Switches to the previous page. Nothing happens if the current page is the first page.
gtk_notebook_ reorder_child	(GtkNotebook *notebook, GtkWidget *child, gint position)	Moves the page child, so that it appears in position, position. Out of bounds position will be clamped.
gtk_notebook_ set_tab_pos	(GtkNotebook *notebook, GtkPositionType pos)	Sets the position of the bookmarks.
gtk_notebook_ set_show_tabs	(GtkNotebook *notebook, gboolean show_tabs)	Sets whether to show the bookmarks or not.
gtk_notebook_ set_show_border	(GtkNotebook *notebook, gboolean show_border)	Sets whether to show the border of the notebook or not. Bookmarks are in the border.

Function	Parameters	Description
gtk_notebook_ set_scrollable	(GtkNotebook *notebook, gboolean scrollable)	Sets whether the bookmarks area may be scrollable or not if there are too many bookmarks to fit in the allocated area.
gtk_notebook_ set_tab_border	(GtkNotebook *notebook, guint border_width)	Sets whether there should be a border around the bookmarks or not.
gtk_notebook_ popup_enable	(GtkNotebook *notebook)	Enables the popup menu: if the user clicks with the right mouse button on the bookmarks, a menu with all the pages will be popped up.
gtk_notebook_ popup_disable	(GtkNotebook *notebook)	Disables the popup menu.
gtk_notebook_ get_current_page	(GtkNotebook *notebook)	Returns the page number of the current page.
gtk_notebook_ get_menu_label	(GtkNotebook *notebook, GtkWidget *child)	Returns the menu label of the page child. NULL is returned if child is not in notebook or NULL if it has the default menu label.
gtk_notebook_ get_nth_page	(GtkNotebook *notebook, gint page_num)	Returns the content of the page number page_num, or NULL if page_num is out of bounds.
gtk_notebook_ get_tab_label	(GtkNotebook *notebook, GtkWidget *child)	Returns the menu tab of the page child. NULL is returned if child is not in notebook or if it has the default tab label.
gtk_notebook_ query_tab_ label_packing	(GtkNotebook *notebook, GtkWidget *child, gboolean *expand, gboolean *fill, GtkPackType *pack_type)	Looks for the packing attributes of the bookmarks of child.
gtk_notebook_ set_homogeneous_ tabs	(GtkNotebook *notebook, gboolean homogenous)	Sets whether the tabs must have all the same size or not.
gtk_notebook_ set_menu_label	(GtkNotebook *notebook, GtkWidget *child, GtkWidget *menu_label)	Changes the menu label of child. Nothing happens if child is not in notebook.

Table continued on following page

Function	Parameters	Description
gtk_notebook_ set_menu_label_ text	(GtkNotebook *notebook, GtkWidget *child, const gchar *menu_text)	Creates a new label and sets it as the menu label of child.
gtk_notebook_ set_tab_hborder	(GtkNotebook *notebook, gboolean tab_hborder)	Sets whether the tabs should have a horizontal border.
gtk_notebook_ set_tab_label	(GtkNotebook *notebook, GtkWidget *child, GtkWidget *tab_label)	Changes the bookmark label of child. Nothing happens if child is not in notebook.
gtk_notebook_ set_tab_label_ packing	(GtkNotebook *notebook, GtkWidget *child, gboolean *expand, gboolean *fill, GtkPackType *pack_type)	Sets the packing parameters for the bookmark of child. See GtkBoxPackStart for the exact meanings.
gtk_notebook_ set_tab_label_ text	(GtkNotebook *notebook, GtkWidget *child, const gchar *tab_text)	Creates a new label and sets it as the bookmark label of child.
gtk_notebook_ set_tab_vborder	(GtkNotebook *notebook, gboolean tab_vborder)	Sets whether the tabs should have a vertical border.

GtkOptionMenu

A widget used to choose from a list of valid choices.

Function	Parameters	Description
gtk_option_ menu_new	(void)	Creates a new GtkOptionMenu.
gtk_option_ menu_get_menu	(GtkOptionMenu *option_menu)	Returns the GtkMenu associated with the GtkOptionMenu.

Function	Parameters	Description
gtk_option_ menu_set_menu	(GtkOptionMenu *option_menu, GtkWidget *menu)	Provides the GtkMenu that is popped up to allow the user to choose a new value. You should provide a simple menu avoiding the use of tear-off menu items, submenus, and accelerators.
gtk_option_ menu_remove_menu	(GtkOptionMenu *option_menu)	Removes the menu from the option menu.
gtk_option_ menu_set_history	(GtkOptionMenu *option_menu, guint index)	Selects the menu item specified by index, making it the newly selected value for the option menu.

GtkPixmapMenuItem

A special widget for GNOME menus.

Function	Parameters	Description
gtk_pixmap_menu_ item_new	(void)	Creates a new pixmap menu item. Use gtk_pixmap_menu_item_set_pixmap to set the pixmap, which is displayed on the left side.
gtk_pixmap_menu_ item_set_pixmap	(GtkPixmapMenuItem *menu_item, GtkWidget *pixmap)	Sets the pixmap of the menu item.

GtkScrolledWindow

Adds scrollbars to its child widget.

Function	Parameters	Description
gtk_scrolled_ window_new	(GtkAdjustment *hadjustment, GtkAdjustment *vadjustment)	Creates a new scrolled window. The two arguments are the scrolled window's adjustments; these will be shared with the scrollbars and the child widget to keep the bars in sync with the child. Usually you want to pass NULL for the adjustments, which will cause the scrolled window to create them for you.
gtk_scrolled_ window_get_ hadjustment	(GtkScrolledWindow *scrolled_window)	Returns the horizontal scrollbar's adjustment, used to connect the horizontal scrollbar to the child widget's horizontal scroll functionality.

Table continued on following page

Function	Parameters	Description
`gtk_scrolled_ window_get_ vadjustment`	`(GtkScrolledWindow *scrolled_window)`	Returns the vertical scrollbar's adjustment, used to connect the vertical scrollbar to the child widget's vertical scroll functionality.
`gtk_scrolled_ window_set_ policy`	`(GtkScrolledWindow *scrolled_window, GtkPolicyType hscrollbar_policy, GtkPolicyType vscrollbar_policy)`	Sets the scrollbar policy for the horizontal and vertical scrollbars. The policy determines when the scrollbar should appear; it is a value from the GtkPolicyType enumeration. If `GTK_POLICY_ALWAYS`, the scrollbar is always present; if `GTK_POLICY_NEVER`, the scrollbar is never present; if `GTK_POLICY_AUTOMATIC`, the scrollbar is present only if needed (that is, if the slider part of the bar would be smaller than the trough – the display is larger than the page size).
`gtk_scrolled_ window_add_ with_viewport`	`(GtkScrolledWindow *scrolled_window, GtkWidget *child)`	Used to add children without native scrolling capabilities. This is simply a convenience function; it is equivalent to adding the unscrollable child to a viewport, then adding the viewport to the scrolled window. If a child has native scrolling, use `gtk_ container_add` instead of this function. The viewport scrolls the child by moving its GdkWindow, and takes the size of the child to be the size of its toplevel GdkWindow. This will be very wrong for most widgets that support native scrolling; for example, if you add a GtkCList with a viewport, the whole widget will scroll, including the column headings. Thus GtkCList supports scrolling already, and should not be used with the GtkViewport proxy. A widget supports scrolling natively if the `set_scroll_adjustments_signal` field in GtkWidgetClass is non-zero, and so has been filled in with a valid signal identifier.
`gtk_scrolled_ window_set_ hadjustment`	`(GtkScrolledWindow *scrolled_window, GtkAdjustment *hadjustment)`	Sets the GtkAdjustment for the horizontal scrollbar.

Function	Parameters	Description
gtk_scrolled_ window_set_ placement	(GtkScrolledWindow *scrolled_window, GtkCornerType window_placement)	Determines the location of the child widget with respect to the scrollbars. The default is GTK_CORNER_TOP_LEFT, meaning the child is in the top left, with the scrollbars underneath and to the right. Other values in GtkCornerType are GTK_CORNER_ TOP_RIGHT, GTK_CORNER_BOTTOM_LEFT, and GTK_CORNER_BOTTOM_RIGHT.
gtk_scrolled_ window_set_ vadjustment	(GtkScrolledWindow *scrolled_window, GtkAdjustment *vadjustment)	Sets the GtkAdjustment for the vertical scrollbar.

GtkSpinButton

This as a widget that allows the system to retrieve an integer or floating-point number from the user using arrows.

Function	Parameters	Description
gtk_spin_button_ configure	(GtkSpinButton *spin_button, GtkAdjustment *adjustment, gfloat climb_rate, guint digits)	Changes the properties of an existing spin button. The adjustment, climb rate, and number of decimal places are all changed accordingly, after this function call.
gtk_spin_button_ new	(GtkAdjustment *adjustment, gfloat climb_rate, guint digits)	Creates a new GtkSpinButton.
gtk_spin_button_ set_adjustment	(GtkSpinButton *spin_button, GtkAdjustment *adjustment)	Changes which GtkAdjustment is associated with a spin button.
gtk_spin_button_ get_adjustment	(GtkSpinButton *spin_button)	Retrieves the GtkAdjustment used by a given spin button.
gtk_spin_button_ set_digits	(GtkSpinButton *spin_button, guint digits)	Alters the number of decimal places that are displayed in a spin button.
gtk_spin_button_ get_value_as_ float	(GtkSpinButton *spin_button)	Retrieves the current value of a GtkSpinButton. If the number has no decimal places, it is converted to a float before the function returns.

Table continued on following page

Function	Parameters	Description
gtk_spin_button_ get_value_as_int	(GtkSpinButton *spin_button)	Retrieves the current integer value of a GtkSpinButton.
gtk_spin_button_ set_value	(GtkSpinButton *spin_button, gfloat value)	Sets the value of a spin button.
gtk_spin_button_ set_update_policy	(GtkSpinButton *spin_button, GtkSpinButton UpdatePolicy policy)	Changes the way a spin button refreshes and updates itself. See GtkSpinButtonUpdatePolicy for more information.
gtk_spin_button_ set_numeric	(GtkSpinButton *spin_button, gboolean numeric)	Sets how the spin button's GtkEntry reacts to alphabetic characters. A value of TRUE to numeric means that all non-numeric characters (except '-' and a decimal point) are ignored.
gtk_spin_button_ spin	(GtkSpinButton *spin_button, GtkSpinType direction, gfloat increment)	Performs an explicit 'spin' on a spin button.
gtk_spin_button_ set_wrap	(GtkSpinButton *spin_button, gboolean wrap)	Sets a spin button's value to the lower limit when its upper limit is reached, and vice versa.
gtk_spin_button_ set_shadow_type	(GtkSpinButton *spin_button, GtkShadowType shadow_type)	Creates a border around the arrows of a GtkSpinButton. The type of border is determined by shadow_type.
gtk_spin_button_ set_snap_to_ticks	(GtkSpinButton *spin_button, gboolean snap_to_ticks)	Sets whether a number typed into a spin button should be snapped to the nearest step increment.
gtk_spin_button_ update	(GtkSpinButton *spin_button)	Refreshes a spin button. The behavior of the update is determined by gtk_spin_button_set_update_policy.

GtkTable

The GtkTable functions allow the programmer to arrange widgets in rows and columns, making it easy to align many widgets next to each other, horizontally and vertically.

Function	Parameters	Description
gtk_table_new	(guint rows, guint columns, gboolean homogenous)	Used to create a new table widget. An initial size must be given by specifying how many rows and columns the table should have, although this can be changed later with gtk_table_resize.
gtk_table_resize	(GtkTable *table, guint rows, guint columns)	If you need to change a table's size after it has been created, this function allows you to do so.
gtk_table_attach	(GtkTable *table, GtkWidget *child, guint left_attach, guint right_attach, guint top_attach, guint bottom_attach, GtkAttachOptions xoptions, GtkAttachOptions yoptions, guint xpadding, guint ypadding)	Adds a widget to a table. The number of cells that a widget will occupy is specified by left_attach, right_attach, top_attach, and bottom_attach. These represent the leftmost, rightmost, uppermost and lowest column and row numbers of the table. (Columns and rows are indexed from zero.)
gtk_table_ attach_defaults	(GtkTable *table, GtkWidget *widget, guint left_attach, guint right_attach, guint top_attach, guint bottom_attach)	As there are many options associated with gtk_table_attach, this convenience function provides the programmer with a means to add children to a table with identical padding and expansion options.
gtk_table_set_ row_spacing	(GtkTable *table, guint row, guint spacing)	Changes the space between a given table row and its surrounding rows.
gtk_table_set_ col_spacing	(GtkTable *table, guint column, guint spacing)	Alters the amount of space between a given table column and the adjacent columns.
gtk_table_set_ row_spacings	(GtkTable *table, guint spacing)	Sets the space between every row in table equal to spacing.
gtk_table_set_ col_spacings	(GtkTable *table, guint spacing)	Sets the space between every column in table equal to spacing.
gtk_table_set_ homogeneous	(GtkTable *table, gboolean homogenous)	Changes the homogenous property of table cells – whether all cells are an equal size or not.

GtkText

A GtkText widget allows one to display any given text and manipulate it by deleting from one point to another, selecting a region, and various other functions. It is inherited from GtkEditable.

Function	Parameters	Description
gtk_text_new	(GtkAdjustment *hadj, GtkAdjustment *vadj)	Creates a new GtkText widget, initialized with the given pointers to GtkAdjustments. These pointers can be used to track the viewing position of the GtkText widget. Passing NULL to either or both of them will make the GtkText create it's own. You can set these later with the function gtk_text_set_adjustment.
gtk_text_set_editable	(GtkText *text, gboolean editable)	Sets whether the GtkText widget can be edited by the user or not. This still allows you the programmer to make changes with the various GtkText functions.
gtk_text_set_word_wrap	(GtkText *text, gint word_wrap)	Sets whether the GtkText widget wraps words down to the next line if they can't be completed on the current line.
gtk_text_set_line_wrap	(GtkText *text, gint line_wrap)	Controls how GtkText handles long lines of continuous text. If line wrap is on, the line is broken when it reaches the extent of the GtkText widget viewing area and the rest is displayed on the next line. If it is not set, the line continues regardless of the size of the current viewing area. Similar to word wrap but it disregards word boundaries.
gtk_text_set_adjustments	(GtkText *text, GtkAdjustment *hadj, GtkAdjustment *vadj)	Allows you to set GtkAdjustment pointers, which in turn allows you to keep track of the viewing position of the GtkText widget.
gtk_text_set_point	(GtkText *text, guint index)	Sets the cursor at the given point. In this case a point constitutes the number of characters from the extreme upper left corner of the GtkText widget.
gtk_text_get_point	(GtkText *text)	Gets the current position of the cursor as the number of characters from the upper left corner of the GtkText widget.
gtk_text_get_length	(GtkText *text)	Returns the length of the all the text contained within the GtkText widget; disregards current point position.

Function	Parameters	Description
gtk_text_ freeze	(GtkText *text)	Freezes the GtkText widget, which disallows redrawing of the widget until it is thawed. This is useful if a large number of changes are going to be made to the text within the widget, reducing the amount of flicker seen by the user.
gtk_text_thaw	(GtkText *text)	Allows the GtkText widget to be redrawn again by GTK+.
gtk_text_ insert	(GtkText *text, GdkFont *font, GdkColor *fore, GdkColor *back, const char *chars, gint length)	Inserts given text into the GtkText widget with the given properties.
gtk_text_ backward_delete	(GtkText *text, guint nchars)	Deletes from the current point position backward the given number of characters.
gtk_text_ forward_delete	(GtkText *text, guint nchars)	Deletes from the current point position forward the given number of characters.

GtkVBox

GtkVBox is a container that organizes child widgets into a single column.

Function	Parameters	Description
gtk_vbox_new	(gboolean homogenous, gint spacing)	Creates a new GtkVBox.

GtkWindow

New windows on the screen emerge from this widget.

Function	Parameters	Description
gtk_window_new	(GtkWindowType type)	Creates a new GtkWindow.
gtk_window_set_ title	(GtkWindow *window, const gchar *title)	Sets the title of the specified window.
gtk_window_set_ wmclass	(GtkWindow *window, const gchar *wmclass_name, const gchar *wmclass_class)	Used for setting a unique name and a class for your window so that your window manager knows how to choose titles and icons when dealing with your window.

Table continued on following page

Function	Parameters	Description
gtk_window_ set_policy	(GtkWindow *window, gint allw_shrink, gint allow_grow, gint auto_shrink)	Changes how a top-level window deals with size and resize requests. There are really only two ways of calling this function, (GTK_WINDOW (window, FALSE, TRUE, FALSE) allows the window to be resized by users, and (GTK_WINDOW(window), FALSE, FALSE, TRUE) means the window is programmatically controlled and will be the optimal size to contain its children.
gtk_window_ activate_focus	(GtkWindow *window)	Activates the currently focussed widget.
gtk_window_ set_modal	(GtkWindow *window, gboolean modal)	Specifies whether a window should be modal or not. If a window is modal, it means that it always has focus and normally means that you have to confirm or deny something until control is returned to another window. (For example, a save request when a window has been closed.)

GNOME Widgets & Functions

GnomeAbout

Simple way to provide an About box.

Function	Parameters	Description
gnome_ about_new	(const gchar *title, const gchar *version, const gchar *copyright, const gchar **authors, const gchar *comments, const gchar *logo)	Creates a new GNOME About dialog.

GnomeApp

This is a top-level GNOME container.

Function	Parameters	Description
gnome_app_new	(const gchar *appname, const gchar *title)	Creates a new (empty) application window.
gnome_app_ set_menus	(GnomeApp *app, GtkMenuBar *menubar)	Sets the menu bar of app's application window.

Function	Parameters	Description
gnome_app_ set_toolbar	(GnomeApp *app, GtkToolbar *toolbar)	Sets the main tool bar of app's application window.
gnome_app_ set_statusbar	(GnomeApp *app, GtkWidget *statusbar)	Sets the status bar of app's application window.
gnome_app_ set_contents	(GnomeApp *app, GtkWidget *contents)	Sets the content area of the GNOME application's main window.
gnome_app_ add_toolbar	(GnomeApp *app, GtkToolbar *toolbar, const gchar *name, GnomeDockItemBehavior behavior, GnomeDockPlacement placement, gint band_num, gint band_position, gint offset)	Creates a new GnomeDockItem widget containing toolbar, and adds it to app's dock container (which is a flexible widget container) with the specified layout information. Notice that, if automatic layout configuration is enabled, the layout is overridden by the saved configuration, if any.
gnome_app_ add_docked	void gnome_app_add_docked (GnomeApp *app, GtkWidget *widget, const gchar *name, GnomeDockItemBehavior behavior, GnomeDockPlacement placement, gint band_num, gint band_position, gint offset)	Adds widget as a dock item according to the specified layout information. Notice that, if automatic layout configuration is enabled, the layout is overridden by the saved configuration.
gnome_app_ add_dock_item	void gnome_app_add_dock_item (GnomeApp *app, GnomeDockItem *item, GnomeDockPlacement placement, gint band_num, gint band_position, gint offset)	Adds item according to the specified layout information. Notice that, if automatic layout configuration is enabled, the layout is overridden by the saved configuration.
gnome_app_ enable_layout_ config	void gnome_app_add_ enable_layout (GnomeApp *app, gboolean enable)	Specifies whether app should automatically save the dock's layout configuration via gnome-config whenever it changes.
gnome_app_ get_dock	GnomeDock* gnome_app_get_dock (GnomeApp *app)	Retrieves the GnomeDock widget contained in the GnomeApp.
gnome_app_get_ dock_item_ by_name	GnomeDockItem* gnome_app_get_dock_item _by_name (GnomeApp *app, const gchar *name)	Retrieve the dock item whose name matches name.

GnomeAppBar

A bar that GNOME applications put on the bottom of the windows to display status, progress, hints for menu items, or a mini-buffer for getting some sort of response.

Function	Parameters	Description
gnome_appbar_new	(gboolean has_progress, gboolean has_status, GnomePreferencesType interactivity)	Creates a new GNOME application status bar.
gnome_appbar_set_default	(GnomeAppBar *appbar, const gchar *default_status)	This sets what to show when there is nothing else. It defaults to nothing. In other words, this states what is shown on the appbar when no information has been passed to the widget as to what should be displayed.
gnome_appbar_push	(GnomeAppBar *appbar, const gchar *status)	Pushes a new status message onto the status bar stack, and display it.
gnome_appbar_pop	(GnomeAppBar *appbar)	Removes current status message, and displays previous status message, if any. It is OK to call this with an empty stack.
gnome_appbar_clear_stack	(GnomeAppBar *appbar)	Removes all status messages from appbar, and displays default status message (if present).
gnome_appbar_get_progress	(GnomeAppBar *appbar)	Returns a GtkProgress widget pointer, so that the progress bar may be manipulated further.
gnome_appbar_refresh	(GnomeAppBar *appbar)	Refreshes the current state of the stack to the default. This is useful if you need to force a set_status to disappear.
gnome_appbar_set_prompt	(GnomeAppBar *appbar, const gchar *prompt, gboolean modal)	Puts a prompt in the appbar and waits for a response. When the user responds or cancels, a user_response signal is emitted.
gnome_appbar_clear_prompt	(GnomeAppBar *appbar)	Removes any prompt.
gnome_appbar_get_response	(GnomeAppBar *appbar)	Gets the response to the prompt, if any. Result must be g_free'd.

GnomeDateEdit

The GnomeDateEdit widget provides a way to enter dates and times with a helper calendar to let the user select the date.

Function	Parameters	Description
gnome_date_ edit_new	(time_t the_time, gint show_time, gint use_24_format)	Creates a new GnomeDateEdit widget, which can be used to provide an easy to use way for entering dates and times.
gnome_date_ edit_set_time	(GnomeDateEdit *gde, time_t the_time)	Changes the displayed date and time in the GnomeDateEdit widget to be the one represented by the_time.
gnome_date_ edit_set_ popup_range	(GnomeDateEdit *gde, gint low_hour, gint up_hour)	Sets the range of times that will be provided by the time popup selectors.
gnome_date_ edit_get_date	(GnomeDateEdit *gde)	Returns the date and time.

GnomeDialog

GnomeDialog gives dialogs a consistent look and feel, while making them more convenient to program. GnomeDialog makes it easy to use stock buttons, makes it easier to handle delete_event, and adds some cosmetic touches (such as a separator above the buttons, and a bevel around the edge of the window).

Function	Parameters	Description
gnome_dialog_new	(const gchar *title, ..., NULL)	Creates a new GnomeDialog, with the given title, and any button names in the argument list. Buttons passed to this function are numbered from left to right, starting with 0. These numbers are used throughout the GnomeDialog API.
gnome_dialog_ set_parent	(GnomeDialog *dialog, GtkWindow *parent)	This function will let the window manager know about the parent-child relationship of a dialog (which app owns the dialog).
gnome_dialog_ button_connect	(GnomeDialog *dialog, gint button, GtkSignalFunc callback, gpointer data)	Simply, this performs a gtk_signal_connect to the clicked signal of the specified button.

Table continued on following page

Function	Parameters	Description
gnome_dialog_ button_connect_ object	(GnomeDialog *dialog, gint button, GtkSignalFunc callback, GtkObject *obj)	gtk_signal_connect_object to the clicked signal of the given button.
gnome_dialog_run	(GnomeDialog *dialog)	Blocks until the user clicks a button, or closes the dialog with the window manager's close decoration (or by pressing *Escape*).
gnome_dialog_ run_and_close	(GnomeDialog *dialog)	See gnome_dialog_run. The only difference is that this function calls gnome_dialog_close before returning; if the dialog was not already closed.
gnome_dialog_ set_default	(GnomeDialog *dialog, gint button)	The default button will be activated if the user just presses *Return*.
gnome_dialog_ set_sensitive	(GnomeDialog *dialog, gint button, gboolean setting)	Calls gtk_widget_set_sensitive on the specified button number.
gnome_dialog_ set_accelerator	(GnomeDialog *dialog, gint button, const guchar accelerator_key, guint8 accelerator_mods)	Sets the accelerator key for a button.
gnome_dialog_ close	(GnomeDialog *dialog)	See gnome_dialog_close_hide. This function emits the close signal, which either hides or destroys the dialog (destroys by default). If you connect to the close signal, and your callback returns TRUE, the hide or destroy will be blocked.
gnome_dialog_ close_hide	(GnomeDialog *dialog, gboolean just_hide)	Some dialogs are expensive to create, so you want to keep them around and just gtk_widget_show them when they are opened, and gtk_widget_hide them when they're closed.
gnome_dialog_ set_close	(GnomeDialog *dialog, gboolean click_crosses)	By default, GnomeDialog has this parameter set to FALSE and it will not close. (This was a design error.) However, almost all the GnomeDialog subclasses, such as GnomeMessageBox and GnomePropertyBox, have this parameter set to TRUE by default.

Function	Parameters	Description
gnome_dialog_ editable_enters	(GnomeDialog *dialog, GtkEditable *editable)	In most cases, the user expects to type something in and then press *Enter* to close the dialog. This function enables that behavior.
gnome_dialog_ append_button_ with_pixmap	(GnomeDialog *dialog, const gchar *name, const gchar *pixmap)	The gnome_dialog_new function does not permit custom buttons with pixmaps, so use this function to add them later.
gnome_dialog_ append_buttons_ with_pixmaps	(GnomeDialog *dialog, const gchar **names, const gchar **pixmaps)	Simply, calls gnome_dialog_ append_button_with_pixmap repeatedly.

GnomeDock

GnomeDock is a container widget designed to let users move around widgets such as toolbars, menubars and so on.

Function	Parameters	Description
gnome_dock_new	(void)	Creates a new GnomeDock widget.
gnome_dock_allow_ floating_items	(GnomeDock *dock, gboolean enable)	Enables or disables floating items on dock, according to enable.
gnome_dock_add_ item	(GnomeDock *dock, GnomeDockItem *item, GnomeDockPlacement placement, guint band_num, gint position, guint offset, gboolean in_new_band)	Adds item to dock. The placement parameter can be GNOME_DOCK_TOP, GNOME_DOCK_RIGHT, GNOME_DOCK_BOTTOM, or GNOME_DOCK_LEFT and specifies what area of the dock should contain the item. If in_new_band is TRUE, a new dock band is created at the position specified by band_num; otherwise, the item is added to the band_num'th band.
gnome_dock_add_ floating_item	(GnomeDock *dock, GnomeDockItem *widget, gint x, gint y, GtkOrientation orientation)	Adds widget to dock and make it floating at the specified (x, y) coordinates (relative to the root window of the screen).
gnome_dock_set_ client_area	(GnomeDock *dock, GtkWidget *widget)	Specifies a widget for the dock's client area.
gnome_dock_get_ client_area	(GnomeDock *dock)	Retrieves the widget being used as the client area in dock.

Table continued on following page

Function	Parameters	Description
gnome_dock_get_item_by_name	(GnomeDock *dock, const gchar *name, GnomeDockPlacement *placement_return, guint *num_band_return, guint *band_position_return, guint *offset_return)	Retrieves the dock item name; information about its position in the dock is returned via placement_return, num_band_return, band_position_return, and offset_return. If the placement is GNOME_DOCK_FLOATING, *num_band_return, *band_position_return, and *offset_return are not set.
gnome_dock_get_layout	(GnomeDock *dock)	Retrieves the layout of dock.
gnome_dock_add_from_layout	(GnomeDock *dock, GnomeDockLayout *layout);	Adds all the items in layout to the specified dock.

GnomeDockItem

GnomeDockItem is a container widget that can be used to make widgets dockable. Making a widget dockable means that the widget gets a handle through which users can drag it around the dock widget or detach it so that it gets displayed in its own window thus becoming a floating item.

Function	Parameters	Description
gnome_dock_item_new	(const gchar *name, GnomeDockItemBehavior behavior)	Creates a new GnomeDockItem called name, with the specified behavior.
gnome_dock_item_get_child	(GnomeDockItem *dock_item)	Retrieves the child of dock_item.
gnome_dock_item_get_name	(GnomeDockItem *dock_item)	Retrieves the name of dock_item.
gnome_dock_item_set_shadow_type	(GnomeDockItem *dock_item, GtkShadowType type)	Sets the shadow type for dock_item.
gnome_dock_item_get_shadow_type	(GnomeDockItem *dock_item)	Retrieves the shadow type of dock_item.
gnome_dock_item_set_orientation	(GnomeDockItem *dock_item, GtkOrientation orientation)	Sets the orientation for dock_item.
gnome_dock_item_get_orientation	(GnomeDockItem *dock_item)	Retrieves the orientation of dock_item.
gnome_dock_item_get_behavior	(GnomeDockItem *dock_item)	Retrieves the behavior of dock_item.

GnomeEntry

This widget is a wrapper around the GtkEntry widget, but it provides a history mechanism for all the input entered into the widget. The way this works is that a special identifier is provided when creating the GnomeEntry widget, and this identifier is used to load and save the history of the text.

Function	Parameters	Description
gnome_entry_new	(const gchar *history_id);	Creates a new GnomeEntry widget. If history_id is not NULL, then the history list will be saved and restored between uses under the given history_id.
gnome_entry_ gtk_entry	(GnomeEntry *gentry)	Obtains pointer to GnomeEntry's internal text entry.
gnome_entry_ set_history_id	(GnomeEntry *gentry, const gchar *history_id)	Sets or clears the history_id of the GnomeEntry widget. If history_id is NULL, the widget's history_id is cleared. Otherwise, the given ID replaces the previous widget history_id.
gnome_entry_ prepend_history	(GnomeEntry *gentry, gint save, const gchar *text)	Adds a history item of the given text to the head of the history list inside gentry. If save is TRUE, the history item will be saved in the config file (assuming that gentry's history_id is not NULL).
gnome_entry_ append_history	(GnomeEntry *gentry, gint save, const gchar *text)	Adds a history item of the given text to the tail of the history list inside gentry.
gnome_entry_ load_history	(GnomeEntry *gentry)	Loads a stored history list from the GNOME configuration file, if one is available. If the history_id of gentry is NULL, nothing occurs.
gnome_entry_ save_history	(GnomeEntry *gentry)	Forces the history items of the widget to be stored in a configuration file. If the history_id of gentry is NULL, nothing occurs.

GnomePropertyBox

The GnomePropertyBox widget simplifies coding a consistent dialog box for configuring properties of any kind. The GnomePropertyBox is a top-level widget (it will create its own window), and inside it contains a GtkNotebook, which is used to hold the various property pages.

Function	Parameter	Description
gnome_property_ box_new	(void)	Creates a new GnomePropertyBox widget. The PropertyBox widget is useful for making consistent configuration dialog boxes.
gnome_property_ box_changed	(GnomePropertyBox *property_box)	When a setting has changed, the code needs to invoke this routine to make the OK/Apply buttons sensitive.
gnome_property_ box_set_state	(GnomePropertyBox *property_box, gboolean state)	Sets the state of the GnomePropertyBox.
gnome_property_ box_append_page	(GnomePropertyBox *property_box, GtkWidget *child, GtkWidget *tab_label)	Appends a new page to property_box.

References

The following URLs are included if you want more information than can be found in this Appendix.

The GNOME API:
http://developer.gnome.org/doc/API/libgnomeui/gnome-objects.html

GTK+ Reference Manual:
http://developer.gnome.org/doc/API/gtk/index.html

GDK Reference Manual:
http://developer.gnome.org/doc/API/gdk/index.html

GLib Reference Manual:
http://developer.gnome.org/doc/API/glib/index.html

Online discussion at http://www.p2p.wrox.com

The DVD Store RPC Protocol Definition

Here is the code listing of the protocol definition for the RPC interface from Chapter 18 in full:

```
/*****************************************************************
 *
 * dvd_store.x -  DVD Store RPC Interface Definition
 *
 * Demonstration code from 'Professional Linux Programming'
 *
 * Written by Neil Matthew, Rick Stones et. al.
 *
 * Copyright (C) 2000 Wrox Press.
 *
 * http://www.wrox.com
 *
 * This program is free software; you can redistribute it and/or
 * modify it under the terms of the GNU General Public License
 * as published by the Free Software Foundation; either version 2
 * of the License, or (at your option) any later version.
 *
 * This program is distributed in the hope that it will be useful,
 * but WITHOUT ANY WARRANTY; without even the implied warranty of
 * MERCHANTABILITY or FITNESS FOR A PARTICULAR PURPOSE.  See the
 * GNU General Public License for more details.
 *
 * You should have received a copy of the GNU General Public License
 * along with this program; if not, write to the Free Software
 * Foundation, Inc., 59 Temple Place - Suite 330, Boston, MA  02111-1307, USA.
 *
 *****************************************************************/
```

```
/*
 * there is a slight issue in that some of the definitions in dvd.h
 * need also to be defined here in dvd_store.x to allow the rpcgen
 * compiler generate the RPC stubs correctly.
 *
 * the problem occurs when dvd.h and dvd_store.h are both included
 * in the same C file -- the compiler complains about multiple definitions
 *
 * the solution is to use the % syntax in the .x file, which allows
 * code to be passed through to 'C' unmodified.  By protecting dvd.h
 * with a define (DVD_H) and ensuring that it is not defined here, we
 * safely include both in the same C source file.
 *
 * so, the workaround steps are:
 * 1.   added DVD_H to dvd.h to prevent multiple-inclusion, and also to give
 *      a suitable guard clause for the definitions in dvd_store.x
 * 2.   protected definitions in dvd_store.x with same guard cause (DVD_H)
 * 3.   ensure that dvd_store.h is included in a C file AFTER dvd.h
 */

%#ifndef DVD_H
/* Error definitions */
const DVD_SUCCESS = 0;
const DVD_ERR_NO_FILE = -1;
const DVD_ERR_BAD_TABLE = -2;
const DVD_ERR_NO_MEMBER_TABLE = -3;
const DVD_ERR_BAD_MEMBER_TABLE = -4;
const DVD_ERR_BAD_TITLE_TABLE = -5;
const DVD_ERR_BAD_DISK_TABLE = -6;
const DVD_ERR_BAD_SEEK = -7;
const DVD_ERR_NULL_POINTER = -8;
const DVD_ERR_BAD_WRITE = -9;
const DVD_ERR_BAD_READ = -10;
const DVD_ERR_NOT_FOUND = -11;
const DVD_ERR_NO_MEMORY = -12;
const DVD_ERR_BAD_RENTAL_TABLE = -13;
const DVD_ERR_BAD_RESERVE_TABLE = -14;
const DVD_ERR_BAD_DATABASE = -15;
const DVD_ERR_BAD_GENRE = -16;

/* size definitions */
const MEMBER_KNOWN_ID_LEN = 6;
const PERSON_TITLE_LEN = 4;
const NAME_LEN = 26;
const ADDRESS_LEN = 51;
const STATE_LEN = 3;
const PHONE_NO_LEN = 31;
const ZIP_CODE_LEN = 11;
const DVD_TITLE_LEN = 61;
const ASIN_LEN = 11;
const GENRE_LEN = 21;
const CLASS_LEN = 11;
const DAY_DATE_LEN = 9;
const COST_LEN = 7;
```

```
/* structures */
struct dvd_store_member {
    int member_id;
    char member_no[MEMBER_KNOWN_ID_LEN];
    char title[PERSON_TITLE_LEN];
    char fname[NAME_LEN];
    char lname[NAME_LEN];
    char house_flat_ref[NAME_LEN];
    char address1[ADDRESS_LEN];
    char address2[ADDRESS_LEN];
    char town[ADDRESS_LEN];
    char state[STATE_LEN];
    char phone[PHONE_NO_LEN];
    char zipcode[ZIP_CODE_LEN];
};

struct dvd_title {
    int title_id;
    char title_text[DVD_TITLE_LEN];
    char asin[ASIN_LEN];
    char director[NAME_LEN];
    char genre[GENRE_LEN];
    char classification[CLASS_LEN];
    char actor1[NAME_LEN];
    char actor2[NAME_LEN];
    char release_date[DAY_DATE_LEN];
    char rental_cost[COST_LEN];
};

struct dvd_disk {
    int disk_id;
    int title_id;
};

%#endif

struct dvd_open_db_login_arg {
    string user<>;
    string password<>;
};

struct dvd_member_get_res {
    int status;
    dvd_store_member completed_member_record;
};

struct dvd_member_create_res {
    int status;
    dvd_store_member updated_member_record;
    int member_id;
};

struct dvd_member_get_id_from_number_res {
    int status;
    int member_id;
};
```

```
typedef int int_array<>;

struct dvd_member_search_res {
    int status;
    int_array result_ids;
    int count;
};

struct dvd_title_get_res {
    int status;
    dvd_title completed_title_record;
};

struct dvd_title_create_res {
    int status;
    dvd_title updated_title_record;
    int title_id;
};

struct dvd_title_search_arg {
    string title<>;
    string name<>;
};

struct dvd_title_search_res {
    int status;
    int_array result_ids;
    int count;
};

struct dvd_disk_get_res {
    int status;
    dvd_disk completed_disk_record;
};

struct dvd_disk_create_res {
    int status;
    dvd_disk updated_disk_record;
    int disk_id;
};

struct dvd_disk_search_res {
    int status;
    int_array result_ids;
    int count;
};

typedef string string_array<>;

struct dvd_get_classification_list_res {
    int status;
    string_array class_list<>;
    int count;
};
```

```
struct dvd_get_genre_list_res {
    int status;
    string_array genre_list<>;
    int count;
};

struct dvd_err_text_res {
    int status;
    string message_to_show<>;
};

struct dvd_today_res {
    int status;
    string date<>;
};

struct dvd_rent_title_arg {
    int member_id;
    int title_id;
};

struct dvd_rent_title_res {
    int status;
    int disk_id;
};

struct dvd_rented_disk_info_res {
    int status;
    int member_id;
    string date_rented<>;
};

struct dvd_disk_return_res {
    int status;
    int member_id;
    string date<>;
};

struct dvd_overdue_disks_arg {
    string date1<>;
    string date2<>;
};

struct dvd_overdue_disks_res {
    int status;
    int_array disk_ids;
    int count;
};

struct dvd_reserve_title_query_by_member_res {
    int status;
    int title_id;
};
```

```
struct dvd_title_available_arg {
    int title_id;
    string date<>;
};

struct dvd_title_available_res {
    int status;
    int count;
};

struct dvd_reserve_title_arg {
    string date<>;
    int title_id;
    int member_id;
};

struct dvd_reserve_title_query_by_titledate_arg {
    int title_id;
    string date<>;
};

struct dvd_reserve_title_query_by_titledate_res {
    int status;
    int_array member_ids;
    int count;
};

program DVD_STORE_PROG {
    version DVD_STORE_VERS {
        int DVD_OPEN_DB() = 1;
        int DVD_OPEN_DB_LOGIN(dvd_open_db_login_arg) = 2;
        int DVD_CLOSE_DB() = 3;

        int DVD_MEMBER_SET(dvd_store_member) = 4;
        dvd_member_get_res DVD_MEMBER_GET(int) = 5;
        dvd_member_create_res DVD_MEMBER_CREATE(dvd_store_member) = 6;
        int DVD_MEMBER_DELETE(int) = 7;
        dvd_member_search_res DVD_MEMBER_SEARCH(string lname) = 8;
        dvd_member_get_id_from_number_res
            DVD_MEMBER_GET_ID_FROM_NUMBER(string member_no) = 9;

        int DVD_TITLE_SET(dvd_title) = 10;
        dvd_title_get_res DVD_TITLE_GET(int) = 11;
        dvd_title_create_res DVD_TITLE_CREATE(dvd_title) = 12;
        int DVD_TITLE_DELETE(int title_id) = 13;
        dvd_title_search_res DVD_TITLE_SEARCH(dvd_title_search_arg) = 14;

        int DVD_DISK_SET(dvd_disk) = 15;
        dvd_disk_get_res DVD_DISK_GET(int) = 16;
        dvd_disk_create_res DVD_DISK_CREATE(dvd_disk) = 17;
        int DVD_DISK_DELETE(int disk_id) = 18;
        dvd_disk_search_res DVD_DISK_SEARCH(int) = 19;

        dvd_get_classification_list_res
            DVD_GET_CLASSIFICATION_LIST(void) = 20;
        dvd_get_genre_list_res DVD_GET_GENRE_LIST(void) = 21;
        dvd_err_text_res DVD_ERR_TEXT(int) = 22;
        dvd_today_res DVD_TODAY(void) = 23;
```

```
          dvd_rent_title_res DVD_RENT_TITLE(dvd_rent_title_arg) = 24;

          dvd_rented_disk_info_res DVD_RENTED_DISK_INFO(int) = 25;

          dvd_disk_return_res DVD_DISK_RETURN(int) = 26;

          dvd_overdue_disks_res DVD_OVERDUE_DISKS(dvd_overdue_disks_arg) = 27;

          dvd_title_available_res
              DVD_TITLE_AVAILABLE(dvd_title_available_arg) = 28;

          int DVD_RESERVE_TITLE(dvd_reserve_title_arg) = 29;
          int DVD_RESERVE_TITLE_CANCEL(int) = 30;
          dvd_reserve_title_query_by_member_res
              DVD_RESERVE_TITLE_QUERY_BY_MEMBER(int member_id) = 31;
          dvd_reserve_title_query_by_titledate_res
              DVD_RESERVE_TITLE_QUERY_BY_TITLEDATE(
                  dvd_reserve_title_query_by_titledate_arg) = 32;

     } = 1;
} = 0x20000099;
```

Online discussion at http://www.p2p.wrox.com

Open Source Licenses

The GNU General Public License

This is the Free Software Foundation general license known as the GPL.

GNU GENERAL PUBLIC LICENSE

Version 2, June 1991

Copyright (C) 1989, 1991 Free Software Foundation, Inc.
59 Temple Place – Suite 330, Boston, MA 02111-1307, USA

Everyone is permitted to copy and distribute verbatim copies
of this license document, but changing it is not allowed.

Preamble

The licenses for most software are designed to take away your freedom to share and change it. By contrast, the GNU General Public License is intended to guarantee your freedom to share and change free software – to make sure the software is free for all its users. This General Public License applies to most of the Free Software Foundation's software and to any other program whose authors commit to using it. (Some other Free Software Foundation software is covered by the GNU Library General Public License instead.) You can apply it to your programs, too.

When we speak of free software, we are referring to freedom, not price. Our General Public Licenses are designed to make sure that you have the freedom to distribute copies of free software (and charge for this service if you wish), that you receive source code or can get it if you want it, that you can change the software or use pieces of it in new free programs; and that you know you can do these things.

To protect your rights, we need to make restrictions that forbid anyone to deny you these rights or to ask you to surrender the rights. These restrictions translate to certain responsibilities for you if you distribute copies of the software, or if you modify it.

For example, if you distribute copies of such a program, whether gratis or for a fee, you must give the recipients all the rights that you have. You must make sure that they, too, receive or can get the source code. And you must show them these terms so they know their rights.

We protect your rights with two steps: (1) copyright the software, and (2) offer you this license which gives you legal permission to copy, distribute and/or modify the software.

Also, for each author's protection and ours, we want to make certain that everyone understands that there is no warranty for this free software. If the software is modified by someone else and passed on, we want its recipients to know that what they have is not the original, so that any problems introduced by others will not reflect on the original authors' reputations.

Finally, any free program is threatened constantly by software patents. We wish to avoid the danger that redistributors of a free program will individually obtain patent licenses, in effect making the program proprietary. To prevent this, we have made it clear that any patent must be licensed for everyone's free use or not licensed at all.

The precise terms and conditions for copying, distribution and modification follow.

TERMS AND CONDITIONS FOR COPYING, DISTRIBUTION AND MODIFICATION

This License applies to any program or other work which contains a notice placed by the copyright holder saying it may be distributed under the terms of this General Public License. The "Program", below, refers to any such program or work, and a "work based on the Program" means either the Program or any derivative work under copyright law: that is to say, a work containing the Program or a portion of it, either verbatim or with modifications and/or translated into another language. (Hereinafter, translation is included without limitation in the term "modification".) Each licensee is addressed as "you".

Activities other than copying, distribution and modification are not covered by this License; they are outside its scope. The act of running the Program is not restricted, and the output from the Program is covered only if its contents constitute a work based on the Program (independent of having been made by running the Program). Whether that is true depends on what the Program does.

1. You may copy and distribute verbatim copies of the Program's source code as you receive it, in any medium, provided that you conspicuously and appropriately publish on each copy an appropriate copyright notice and disclaimer of warranty; keep intact all the notices that refer to this License and to the absence of any warranty; and give any other recipients of the Program a copy of this License along with the Program.

You may charge a fee for the physical act of transferring a copy, and you may at your option offer warranty protection in exchange for a fee.

2. You may modify your copy or copies of the Program or any portion of it, thus forming a work based on the Program, and copy and distribute such modifications or work under the terms of Section 1 above, provided that you also meet all of these conditions:

a) You must cause the modified files to carry prominent notices stating that you changed the files and the date of any change.

b) You must cause any work that you distribute or publish, that in whole or in part contains or is derived from the Program or any part thereof, to be licensed as a whole at no charge to all third parties under the terms of this License.

c) If the modified program normally reads commands interactively when run, you must cause it, when started running for such interactive use in the most ordinary way, to print or display an announcement including an appropriate copyright notice and a notice that there is no warranty (or else, saying that you provide a warranty) and that users may redistribute the program under these conditions, and telling the user how to view a copy of this License. (Exception: if the Program itself is interactive but does not normally print such an announcement, your work based on the Program is not required to print an announcement.)

These requirements apply to the modified work as a whole. If identifiable sections of that work are not derived from the Program, and can be reasonably considered independent and separate works in themselves, then this License, and its terms, do not apply to those sections when you distribute them as separate works. But when you distribute the same sections as part of a whole which is a work based on the Program, the distribution of the whole must be on the terms of this License, whose permissions for other licensees extend to the entire whole, and thus to each and every part regardless of who wrote it.

Thus, it is not the intent of this section to claim rights or contest your rights to work written entirely by you; rather, the intent is to exercise the right to control the distribution of derivative or collective works based on the Program.

In addition, mere aggregation of another work not based on the Program with the Program (or with a work based on the Program) on a volume of a storage or distribution medium does not bring the other work under the scope of this License.

3. You may copy and distribute the Program (or a work based on it, under Section 2) in object code or executable form under the terms of Sections 1 and 2 above provided that you also do one of the following:

a) Accompany it with the complete corresponding machine-readable source code, which must be distributed under the terms of Sections 1 and 2 above on a medium customarily used for software interchange; or,

b) Accompany it with a written offer, valid for at least three years, to give any third party, for a charge no more than your cost of physically performing source distribution, a complete machine-readable copy of the corresponding source code, to be distributed under the terms of Sections 1 and 2 above on a medium customarily used for software interchange; or,

c) Accompany it with the information you received as to the offer to distribute corresponding source code. (This alternative is allowed only for noncommercial distribution and only if you received the program in object code or executable form with such an offer, in accord with Subsection b above.)

1091

The source code for a work means the preferred form of the work for making modifications to it. For an executable work, complete source code means all the source code for all modules it contains, plus any associated interface definition files, plus the scripts used to control compilation and installation of the executable. However, as a special exception, the source code distributed need not include anything that is normally distributed (in either source or binary form) with the major components (compiler, kernel, and so on) of the operating system on which the executable runs, unless that component itself accompanies the executable.

If distribution of executable or object code is made by offering access to copy from a designated place, then offering equivalent access to copy the source code from the same place counts as distribution of the source code, even though third parties are not compelled to copy the source along with the object code.

4. You may not copy, modify, sublicense, or distribute the Program except as expressly provided under this License. Any attempt otherwise to copy, modify, sublicense or distribute the Program is void, and will automatically terminate your rights under this License. However, parties who have received copies, or rights, from you under this License will not have their licenses terminated so long as such parties remain in full compliance.

5. You are not required to accept this License, since you have not signed it. However, nothing else grants you permission to modify or distribute the Program or its derivative works. These actions are prohibited by law if you do not accept this License. Therefore, by modifying or distributing the Program (or any work based on the Program), you indicate your acceptance of this License to do so, and all its terms and conditions for copying, distributing or modifying the Program or works based on it.

6. Each time you redistribute the Program (or any work based on the Program), the recipient automatically receives a license from the original licensor to copy, distribute or modify the Program subject to these terms and conditions. You may not impose any further restrictions on the recipients' exercise of the rights granted herein. You are not responsible for enforcing compliance by third parties to this License.

7. If, as a consequence of a court judgment or allegation of patent infringement or for any other reason (not limited to patent issues), conditions are imposed on you (whether by court order, agreement or otherwise) that contradict the conditions of this License, they do not excuse you from the conditions of this License. If you cannot distribute so as to satisfy simultaneously your obligations under this License and any other pertinent obligations, then as a consequence you may not distribute the Program at all. For example, if a patent license would not permit royalty-free redistribution of the Program by all those who receive copies directly or indirectly through you, then the only way you could satisfy both it and this License would be to refrain entirely from distribution of the Program.

If any portion of this section is held invalid or unenforceable under any particular circumstance, the balance of the section is intended to apply and the section as a whole is intended to apply in other circumstances.

It is not the purpose of this section to induce you to infringe any patents or other property right claims or to contest validity of any such claims; this section has the sole purpose of protecting the integrity of the free software distribution system, which is implemented by public license practices. Many people have made generous contributions to the wide range of software distributed through that system in reliance on consistent application of that system; it is up to the author/donor to decide if he or she is willing to distribute software through any other system and a licensee cannot impose that choice.

This section is intended to make thoroughly clear what is believed to be a consequence of the rest of this License.

8. If the distribution and/or use of the Program is restricted in certain countries either by patents or by copyrighted interfaces, the original copyright holder who places the Program under this License may add an explicit geographical distribution limitation excluding those countries, so that distribution is permitted only in or among countries not thus excluded. In such case, this License incorporates the limitation as if written in the body of this License.

9. The Free Software Foundation may publish revised and/or new versions of the General Public License from time to time. Such new versions will be similar in spirit to the present version, but may differ in detail to address new problems or concerns.

Each version is given a distinguishing version number. If the Program specifies a version number of this License which applies to it and "any later version", you have the option of following the terms and conditions either of that version or of any later version published by the Free Software Foundation. If the Program does not specify a version number of this License, you may choose any version ever published by the Free Software Foundation.

10. If you wish to incorporate parts of the Program into other free programs whose distribution conditions are different, write to the author to ask for permission. For software which is copyrighted by the Free Software Foundation, write to the Free Software Foundation; we sometimes make exceptions for this. Our decision will be guided by the two goals of preserving the free status of all derivatives of our free software and of promoting the sharing and reuse of software generally.

NO WARRANTY
11. BECAUSE THE PROGRAM IS LICENSED FREE OF CHARGE, THERE IS NO WARRANTY FOR THE PROGRAM, TO THE EXTENT PERMITTED BY APPLICABLE LAW. EXCEPT WHEN OTHERWISE STATED IN WRITING THE COPYRIGHT HOLDERS AND/OR OTHER PARTIES PROVIDE THE PROGRAM "AS IS" WITHOUT WARRANTY OF ANY KIND, EITHER EXPRESSED OR IMPLIED, INCLUDING, BUT NOT LIMITED TO, THE IMPLIED WARRANTIES OF MERCHANTABILITY AND FITNESS FOR A PARTICULAR PURPOSE. THE ENTIRE RISK AS TO THE QUALITY AND PERFORMANCE OF THE PROGRAM IS WITH YOU. SHOULD THE PROGRAM PROVE DEFECTIVE, YOU ASSUME THE COST OF ALL NECESSARY SERVICING, REPAIR OR CORRECTION.

12. IN NO EVENT UNLESS REQUIRED BY APPLICABLE LAW OR AGREED TO IN WRITING WILL ANY COPYRIGHT HOLDER, OR ANY OTHER PARTY WHO MAY MODIFY AND/OR REDISTRIBUTE THE PROGRAM AS PERMITTED ABOVE, BE LIABLE TO YOU FOR DAMAGES, INCLUDING ANY GENERAL, SPECIAL, INCIDENTAL OR CONSEQUENTIAL DAMAGES ARISING OUT OF THE USE OR INABILITY TO USE THE PROGRAM (INCLUDING BUT NOT LIMITED TO LOSS OF DATA OR DATA BEING RENDERED INACCURATE OR LOSSES SUSTAINED BY YOU OR THIRD PARTIES OR A FAILURE OF THE PROGRAM TO OPERATE WITH ANY OTHER PROGRAMS), EVEN IF SUCH HOLDER OR OTHER PARTY HAS BEEN ADVISED OF THE POSSIBILITY OF SUCH DAMAGES.

END OF TERMS AND CONDITIONS

How to Apply These Terms to Your New Programs

If you develop a new program, and you want it to be of the greatest possible use to the public, the best way to achieve this is to make it free software which everyone can redistribute and change under these terms.

To do so, attach the following notices to the program. It is safest to attach them to the start of each source file to most effectively convey the exclusion of warranty; and each file should have at least the "copyright" line and a pointer to where the full notice is found.

one line to give the program's name and an idea of what it does.
Copyright (C) *yyyy name of author*

This program is free software; you can redistribute it and/or
modify it under the terms of the GNU General Public License
as published by the Free Software Foundation; either version 2
of the License, or (at your option) any later version.

This program is distributed in the hope that it will be useful,
but WITHOUT ANY WARRANTY; without even the implied warranty of
MERCHANTABILITY or FITNESS FOR A PARTICULAR PURPOSE. See the
GNU General Public License for more details.

You should have received a copy of the GNU General Public License
along with this program; if not, write to the Free Software
Foundation, Inc., 59 Temple Place – Suite 330, Boston, MA 02111-1307, USA.

Also add information on how to contact you by electronic and paper mail.

If the program is interactive, make it output a short notice like this when it starts in an interactive mode:

Gnomovision version 69, Copyright (C) *year name of author*
Gnomovision comes with ABSOLUTELY NO WARRANTY; for details
type 'show w'. This is free software, and you are welcome
to redistribute it under certain conditions; type 'show c'
for details.

The hypothetical commands 'show w' and 'show c' should show the appropriate parts of the General Public License. Of course, the commands you use may be called something other than 'show w' and 'show c'; they could even be mouse-clicks or menu items – whatever suits your program.

You should also get your employer (if you work as a programmer) or your school, if any, to sign a "copyright disclaimer" for the program, if necessary. Here is a sample; alter the names:

Yoyodyne, Inc., hereby disclaims all copyright
interest in the program 'Gnomovision'
(which makes passes at compilers) written
by James Hacker.

signature of Ty Coon, 1 April 1989
Ty Coon, President of Vice

This General Public License does not permit incorporating your program into proprietary programs. If your program is a subroutine library, you may consider it more useful to permit linking proprietary applications with the library. If this is what you want to do, use the GNU Library General Public License instead of this License.

The Lesser GNU Public License

This is the Free Software Foundation license known as the LGPL.

Version 2, June 1991

Copyright (C) 1991 Free Software Foundation, Inc.
59 Temple Place – Suite 330, Boston, MA 02111-1307, USA
Everyone is permitted to copy and distribute verbatim copies
of this license document, but changing it is not allowed.

[This is the first released version of the library GPL. It is
  numbered 2 because it goes with version 2 of the ordinary GPL.]

Preamble

The licenses for most software are designed to take away your freedom to share and change it. By contrast, the GNU General Public Licenses are intended to guarantee your freedom to share and change free software – to make sure the software is free for all its users.

This license, the Library General Public License, applies to some specially designated Free Software Foundation software, and to any other libraries whose authors decide to use it. You can use it for your libraries, too.

When we speak of free software, we are referring to freedom, not price. Our General Public Licenses are designed to make sure that you have the freedom to distribute copies of free software (and charge for this service if you wish), that you receive source code or can get it if you want it, that you can change the software or use pieces of it in new free programs; and that you know you can do these things.

To protect your rights, we need to make restrictions that forbid anyone to deny you these rights or to ask you to surrender the rights. These restrictions translate to certain responsibilities for you if you distribute copies of the library, or if you modify it.

For example, if you distribute copies of the library, whether gratis or for a fee, you must give the recipients all the rights that we gave you. You must make sure that they, too, receive or can get the source code. If you link a program with the library, you must provide complete object files to the recipients so that they can relink them with the library, after making changes to the library and recompiling it. And you must show them these terms so they know their rights.

Our method of protecting your rights has two steps: (1) copyright the library, and (2) offer you this license which gives you legal permission to copy, distribute and/or modify the library.

Also, for each distributor's protection, we want to make certain that everyone understands that there is no warranty for this free library. If the library is modified by someone else and passed on, we want its recipients to know that what they have is not the original version, so that any problems introduced by others will not reflect on the original authors' reputations.

Finally, any free program is threatened constantly by software patents. We wish to avoid the danger that companies distributing free software will individually obtain patent licenses, thus in effect transforming the program into proprietary software. To prevent this, we have made it clear that any patent must be licensed for everyone's free use or not licensed at all.

Most GNU software, including some libraries, is covered by the ordinary GNU General Public License, which was designed for utility programs. This license, the GNU Library General Public License, applies to certain designated libraries. This license is quite different from the ordinary one; be sure to read it in full, and don't assume that anything in it is the same as in the ordinary license.

The reason we have a separate public license for some libraries is that they blur the distinction we usually make between modifying or adding to a program and simply using it. Linking a program with a library, without changing the library, is in some sense simply using the library, and is analogous to running a utility program or application program. However, in a textual and legal sense, the linked executable is a combined work, a derivative of the original library, and the ordinary General Public License treats it as such.

Because of this blurred distinction, using the ordinary General Public License for libraries did not effectively promote software sharing, because most developers did not use the libraries. We concluded that weaker conditions might promote sharing better.

However, unrestricted linking of non-free programs would deprive the users of those programs of all benefit from the free status of the libraries themselves. This Library General Public License is intended to permit developers of non-free programs to use free libraries, while preserving your freedom as a user of such programs to change the free libraries that are incorporated in them. (We have not seen how to achieve this as regards changes in header files, but we have achieved it as regards changes in the actual functions of the Library.) The hope is that this will lead to faster development of free libraries.

The precise terms and conditions for copying, distribution and modification follow. Pay close attention to the difference between a "work based on the library" and a "work that uses the library". The former contains code derived from the library, while the latter only works together with the library.

Note that it is possible for a library to be covered by the ordinary General Public License rather than by this special one.

TERMS AND CONDITIONS FOR COPYING, DISTRIBUTION AND MODIFICATION

0. This License Agreement applies to any software library or other program which contains a notice placed by the copyright holder or other authorized party saying it may be distributed under the terms of this Lesser General Public License (also called "this License"). Each licensee is addressed as "you".

A "library" means a collection of software functions and/or data prepared so as to be conveniently linked with application programs (which use some of those functions and data) to form executables.

The "Library", below, refers to any such software library or work which has been distributed under these terms. A "work based on the Library" means either the Library or any derivative work under copyright law: that is to say, a work containing the Library or a portion of it, either verbatim or with modifications and/or translated straightforwardly into another language. (Hereinafter, translation is included without limitation in the term "modification".)

"Source code" for a work means the preferred form of the work for making modifications to it. For a library, complete source code means all the source code for all modules it contains, plus any associated interface definition files, plus the scripts used to control compilation and installation of the library.

Activities other than copying, distribution and modification are not covered by this License; they are outside its scope. The act of running a program using the Library is not restricted, and output from such a program is covered only if its contents constitute a work based on the Library (independent of the use of the Library in a tool for writing it). Whether that is true depends on what the Library does and what the program that uses the Library does.

1. You may copy and distribute verbatim copies of the Library's complete source code as you receive it, in any medium, provided that you conspicuously and appropriately publish on each copy an appropriate copyright notice and disclaimer of warranty; keep intact all the notices that refer to this License and to the absence of any warranty; and distribute a copy of this License along with the Library.

You may charge a fee for the physical act of transferring a copy, and you may at your option offer warranty protection in exchange for a fee.

2. You may modify your copy or copies of the Library or any portion of it, thus forming a work based on the Library, and copy and distribute such modifications or work under the terms of Section 1 above, provided that you also meet all of these conditions:

a) The modified work must itself be a software library.

b) You must cause the files modified to carry prominent notices stating that you changed the files and the date of any change.

c) You must cause the whole of the work to be licensed at no charge to all third parties under the terms of this License.

d) If a facility in the modified Library refers to a function or a table of data to be supplied by an application program that uses the facility, other than as an argument passed when the facility is invoked, then you must make a good faith effort to ensure that, in the event an application does not supply such function or table, the facility still operates, and performs whatever part of its purpose remains meaningful.

(For example, a function in a library to compute square roots has a purpose that is entirely well-defined independent of the application. Therefore, Subsection 2d requires that any application-supplied function or table used by this function must be optional: if the application does not supply it, the square root function must still compute square roots.)

These requirements apply to the modified work as a whole. If identifiable sections of that work are not derived from the Library, and can be reasonably considered independent and separate works in themselves, then this License, and its terms, do not apply to those sections when you distribute them as separate works. But when you distribute the same sections as part of a whole which is a work based on the Library, the distribution of the whole must be on the terms of this License, whose permissions for other licensees extend to the entire whole, and thus to each and every part regardless of who wrote it.

Thus, it is not the intent of this section to claim rights or contest your rights to work written entirely by you; rather, the intent is to exercise the right to control the distribution of derivative or collective works based on the Library.

In addition, mere aggregation of another work not based on the Library with the Library (or with a work based on the Library) on a volume of a storage or distribution medium does not bring the other work under the scope of this License.

3. You may opt to apply the terms of the ordinary GNU General Public License instead of this License to a given copy of the Library. To do this, you must alter all the notices that refer to this License, so that they refer to the ordinary GNU General Public License, version 2, instead of to this License. (If a newer version than version 2 of the ordinary GNU General Public License has appeared, then you can specify that version instead if you wish.) Do not make any other change in these notices.

Once this change is made in a given copy, it is irreversible for that copy, so the ordinary GNU General Public License applies to all subsequent copies and derivative works made from that copy.

This option is useful when you wish to copy part of the code of the Library into a program that is not a library.

4. You may copy and distribute the Library (or a portion or derivative of it, under Section 2) in object code or executable form under the terms of Sections 1 and 2 above provided that you accompany it with the complete corresponding machine-readable source code, which must be distributed under the terms of Sections 1 and 2 above on a medium customarily used for software interchange.

If distribution of object code is made by offering access to copy from a designated place, then offering equivalent access to copy the source code from the same place satisfies the requirement to distribute the source code, even though third parties are not compelled to copy the source along with the object code.

5. A program that contains no derivative of any portion of the Library, but is designed to work with the Library by being compiled or linked with it, is called a "work that uses the Library". Such a work, in isolation, is not a derivative work of the Library, and therefore falls outside the scope of this License.

However, linking a "work that uses the Library" with the Library creates an executable that is a derivative of the Library (because it contains portions of the Library), rather than a "work that uses the library". The executable is therefore covered by this License. Section 6 states terms for distribution of such executables.

When a "work that uses the Library" uses material from a header file that is part of the Library, the object code for the work may be a derivative work of the Library even though the source code is not. Whether this is true is especially significant if the work can be linked without the Library, or if the work is itself a library. The threshold for this to be true is not precisely defined by law.

If such an object file uses only numerical parameters, data structure layouts and accessors, and small macros and small inline functions (ten lines or less in length), then the use of the object file is unrestricted, regardless of whether it is legally a derivative work. (Executables containing this object code plus portions of the Library will still fall under Section 6.)

Otherwise, if the work is a derivative of the Library, you may distribute the object code for the work under the terms of Section 6. Any executables containing that work also fall under Section 6, whether or not they are linked directly with the Library itself.

6. As an exception to the Sections above, you may also combine or link a "work that uses the Library" with the Library to produce a work containing portions of the Library, and distribute that work under terms of your choice, provided that the terms permit modification of the work for the customer's own use and reverse engineering for debugging such modifications.

You must give prominent notice with each copy of the work that the Library is used in it and that the Library and its use are covered by this License. You must supply a copy of this License. If the work during execution displays copyright notices, you must include the copyright notice for the Library among them, as well as a reference directing the user to the copy of this License. Also, you must do one of these things:

a) Accompany the work with the complete corresponding machine-readable source code for the Library including whatever changes were used in the work (which must be distributed under Sections 1 and 2 above); and, if the work is an executable linked with the Library, with the complete machine-readable "work that uses the Library", as object code and/or source code, so that the user can modify the Library and then relink to produce a modified executable containing the modified Library. (It is understood that the user who changes the contents of definitions files in the Library will not necessarily be able to recompile the application to use the modified definitions.)

b) Use a suitable shared library mechanism for linking with the Library. A suitable mechanism is one that (1) uses at run time a copy of the library already present on the user's computer system, rather than copying library functions into the executable, and (2) will operate properly with a modified version of the library, if the user installs one, as long as the modified version is interface-compatible with the version that the work was made with.

c) Accompany the work with a written offer, valid for at least three years, to give the same user the materials specified in Subsection 6a, above, for a charge no more than the cost of performing this distribution.

d) If distribution of the work is made by offering access to copy from a designated place, offer equivalent access to copy the above specified materials from the same place.

e) Verify that the user has already received a copy of these materials or that you have already sent this user a copy.

For an executable, the required form of the "work that uses the Library" must include any data and utility programs needed for reproducing the executable from it. However, as a special exception, the materials to be distributed need not include anything that is normally distributed (in either source or binary form) with the major components (compiler, kernel, and so on) of the operating system on which the executable runs, unless that component itself accompanies the executable.

It may happen that this requirement contradicts the license restrictions of other proprietary libraries that do not normally accompany the operating system. Such a contradiction means you cannot use both them and the Library together in an executable that you distribute.

7. You may place library facilities that are a work based on the Library side-by-side in a single library together with other library facilities not covered by this License, and distribute such a combined library, provided that the separate distribution of the work based on the Library and of the other library facilities is otherwise permitted, and provided that you do these two things:

a) Accompany the combined library with a copy of the same work based on the Library, uncombined with any other library facilities. This must be distributed under the terms of the Sections above.

b) Give prominent notice with the combined library of the fact that part of it is a work based on the Library, and explaining where to find the accompanying uncombined form of the same work.

8. You may not copy, modify, sublicense, link with, or distribute the Library except as expressly provided under this License. Any attempt otherwise to copy, modify, sublicense, link with, or distribute the Library is void, and will automatically terminate your rights under this License. However, parties who have received copies, or rights, from you under this License will not have their licenses terminated so long as such parties remain in full compliance.

9. You are not required to accept this License, since you have not signed it. However, nothing else grants you permission to modify or distribute the Library or its derivative works. These actions are prohibited by law if you do not accept this License. Therefore, by modifying or distributing the Library (or any work based on the Library), you indicate your acceptance of this License to do so, and all its terms and conditions for copying, distributing or modifying the Library or works based on it.

10. Each time you redistribute the Library (or any work based on the Library), the recipient automatically receives a license from the original licensor to copy, distribute, link with or modify the Library subject to these terms and conditions. You may not impose any further restrictions on the recipients' exercise of the rights granted herein. You are not responsible for enforcing compliance by third parties with this License.

11. If, as a consequence of a court judgment or allegation of patent infringement or for any other reason (not limited to patent issues), conditions are imposed on you (whether by court order, agreement or otherwise) that contradict the conditions of this License, they do not excuse you from the conditions of this License. If you cannot distribute so as to satisfy simultaneously your obligations under this License and any other pertinent obligations, then as a consequence you may not distribute the Library at all. For example, if a patent license would not permit royalty-free redistribution of the Library by all those who receive copies directly or indirectly through you, then the only way you could satisfy both it and this License would be to refrain entirely from distribution of the Library.

If any portion of this section is held invalid or unenforceable under any particular circumstance, the balance of the section is intended to apply, and the section as a whole is intended to apply in other circumstances.

It is not the purpose of this section to induce you to infringe any patents or other property right claims or to contest validity of any such claims; this section has the sole purpose of protecting the integrity of the free software distribution system which is implemented by public license practices. Many people have made generous contributions to the wide range of software distributed through that system in reliance on consistent application of that system; it is up to the author/donor to decide if he or she is willing to distribute software through any other system and a licensee cannot impose that choice.

This section is intended to make thoroughly clear what is believed to be a consequence of the rest of this License.

12. If the distribution and/or use of the Library is restricted in certain countries either by patents or by copyrighted interfaces, the original copyright holder who places the Library under this License may add an explicit geographical distribution limitation excluding those countries, so that distribution is permitted only in or among countries not thus excluded. In such case, this License incorporates the limitation as if written in the body of this License.

13. The Free Software Foundation may publish revised and/or new versions of the Lesser General Public License from time to time. Such new versions will be similar in spirit to the present version, but may differ in detail to address new problems or concerns.

Each version is given a distinguishing version number. If the Library specifies a version number of this License which applies to it and "any later version", you have the option of following the terms and conditions either of that version or of any later version published by the Free Software Foundation. If the Library does not specify a license version number, you may choose any version ever published by the Free Software Foundation.

14. If you wish to incorporate parts of the Library into other free programs whose distribution conditions are incompatible with these, write to the author to ask for permission. For software which is copyrighted by the Free Software Foundation, write to the Free Software Foundation; we sometimes make exceptions for this. Our decision will be guided by the two goals of preserving the free status of all derivatives of our free software and of promoting the sharing and reuse of software generally.

NO WARRANTY

15. BECAUSE THE LIBRARY IS LICENSED FREE OF CHARGE, THERE IS NO WARRANTY FOR THE LIBRARY, TO THE EXTENT PERMITTED BY APPLICABLE LAW. EXCEPT WHEN OTHERWISE STATED IN WRITING THE COPYRIGHT HOLDERS AND/OR OTHER PARTIES PROVIDE THE LIBRARY "AS IS" WITHOUT WARRANTY OF ANY KIND, EITHER EXPRESSED OR IMPLIED, INCLUDING, BUT NOT LIMITED TO, THE IMPLIED WARRANTIES OF MERCHANTABILITY AND FITNESS FOR A PARTICULAR PURPOSE. THE ENTIRE RISK AS TO THE QUALITY AND PERFORMANCE OF THE LIBRARY IS WITH YOU. SHOULD THE LIBRARY PROVE DEFECTIVE, YOU ASSUME THE COST OF ALL NECESSARY SERVICING, REPAIR OR CORRECTION.

16. IN NO EVENT UNLESS REQUIRED BY APPLICABLE LAW OR AGREED TO IN WRITING WILL ANY COPYRIGHT HOLDER, OR ANY OTHER PARTY WHO MAY MODIFY AND/OR REDISTRIBUTE THE LIBRARY AS PERMITTED ABOVE, BE LIABLE TO YOU FOR DAMAGES, INCLUDING ANY GENERAL, SPECIAL, INCIDENTAL OR CONSEQUENTIAL DAMAGES ARISING OUT OF THE USE OR INABILITY TO USE THE LIBRARY (INCLUDING BUT NOT LIMITED TO LOSS OF DATA OR DATA BEING RENDERED INACCURATE OR LOSSES SUSTAINED BY YOU OR THIRD PARTIES OR A FAILURE OF THE LIBRARY TO OPERATE WITH ANY OTHER SOFTWARE), EVEN IF SUCH HOLDER OR OTHER PARTY HAS BEEN ADVISED OF THE POSSIBILITY OF SUCH DAMAGES.

END OF TERMS AND CONDITIONS

How to Apply These Terms to Your New Libraries

If you develop a new library, and you want it to be of the greatest possible use to the public, we recommend making it free software that everyone can redistribute and change. You can do so by permitting redistribution under these terms (or, alternatively, under the terms of the ordinary General Public License).

To apply these terms, attach the following notices to the library. It is safest to attach them to the start of each source file to most effectively convey the exclusion of warranty; and each file should have at least the "copyright" line and a pointer to where the full notice is found.

one line to give the library's name and an idea of what it does.
Copyright (C) *year name of author*

This library is free software; you can redistribute it and/or
modify it under the terms of the GNU Lesser General Public
License as published by the Free Software Foundation; either
version 2.1 of the License, or (at your option) any later version.

This library is distributed in the hope that it will be useful,
but WITHOUT ANY WARRANTY; without even the implied warranty of
MERCHANTABILITY or FITNESS FOR A PARTICULAR PURPOSE. See the GNU
Lesser General Public License for more details.

You should have received a copy of the GNU Lesser General Public
License along with this library; if not, write to the Free Software
Foundation, Inc., 59 Temple Place, Suite 330, Boston, MA 02111-1307 USA

Also add information on how to contact you by electronic and paper mail.

You should also get your employer (if you work as a programmer) or your school, if any, to sign a
"copyright disclaimer" for the library, if necessary. Here is a sample; alter the names:

Yoyodyne, Inc., hereby disclaims all copyright interest in
the library 'Frob' (a library for tweaking knobs) written
by James Random Hacker.

signature of Ty Coon, 1 April 1990
Ty Coon, President of Vice

That's all there is to it!

The GNU Free Documentation License

This is the latest Free Software Foundation License known as the **GNU Free Documentation License**.

Version 1.1, March 2000

Copyright (C) 2000 Free Software Foundation, Inc.
59 Temple Place, Suite 330, Boston, MA 02111-1307 USA
Everyone is permitted to copy and distribute verbatim copies
of this license document, but changing it is not allowed.

0. PREAMBLE

The purpose of this License is to make a manual, textbook, or other written document "free" in the
sense of freedom: to assure everyone the effective freedom to copy and redistribute it, with or without
modifying it, either commercially or noncommercially. Secondarily, this License preserves for the
author and publisher a way to get credit for their work, while not being considered responsible for
modifications made by others.

1102

This License is a kind of "copyleft", which means that derivative works of the document must themselves be free in the same sense. It complements the GNU General Public License, which is a copyleft license designed for free software.

We have designed this License in order to use it for manuals for free software, because free software needs free documentation: a free program should come with manuals providing the same freedoms that the software does. But this License is not limited to software manuals; it can be used for any textual work, regardless of subject matter or whether it is published as a printed book. We recommend this License principally for works whose purpose is instruction or reference.

1. APPLICABILITY AND DEFINITIONS

This License applies to any manual or other work that contains a notice placed by the copyright holder saying it can be distributed under the terms of this License. The "Document", below, refers to any such manual or work. Any member of the public is a licensee, and is addressed as "you".

A "Modified Version" of the Document means any work containing the Document or a portion of it, either copied verbatim, or with modifications and/or translated into another language.

A "Secondary Section" is a named appendix or a front-matter section of the Document that deals exclusively with the relationship of the publishers or authors of the Document to the Document's overall subject (or to related matters) and contains nothing that could fall directly within that overall subject. (For example, if the Document is in part a textbook of mathematics, a Secondary Section may not explain any mathematics.) The relationship could be a matter of historical connection with the subject or with related matters, or of legal, commercial, philosophical, ethical or political position regarding them.

The "Invariant Sections" are certain Secondary Sections whose titles are designated, as being those of Invariant Sections, in the notice that says that the Document is released under this License.

The "Cover Texts" are certain short passages of text that are listed, as Front-Cover Texts or Back-Cover Texts, in the notice that says that the Document is released under this License.

A "Transparent" copy of the Document means a machine-readable copy, represented in a format whose specification is available to the general public, whose contents can be viewed and edited directly and straightforwardly with generic text editors or (for images composed of pixels) generic paint programs or (for drawings) some widely available drawing editor, and that is suitable for input to text formatters or for automatic translation to a variety of formats suitable for input to text formatters. A copy made in an otherwise Transparent file format whose markup has been designed to thwart or discourage subsequent modification by readers is not Transparent. A copy that is not "Transparent" is called "Opaque".

Examples of suitable formats for Transparent copies include plain ASCII without markup, Texinfo input format, LaTeX input format, SGML or XML using a publicly available DTD, and standard-conforming simple HTML designed for human modification. Opaque formats include PostScript, PDF, proprietary formats that can be read and edited only by proprietary word processors, SGML or XML for which the DTD and/or processing tools are not generally available, and the machine-generated HTML produced by some word processors for output purposes only.

The "Title Page" means, for a printed book, the title page itself, plus such following pages as are needed to hold, legibly, the material this License requires to appear in the title page. For works in formats which do not have any title page as such, "Title Page" means the text near the most prominent appearance of the work's title, preceding the beginning of the body of the text.

2. *VERBATIM COPYING*

You may copy and distribute the Document in any medium, either commercially or noncommercially, provided that this License, the copyright notices, and the license notice saying this License applies to the Document are reproduced in all copies, and that you add no other conditions whatsoever to those of this License. You may not use technical measures to obstruct or control the reading or further copying of the copies you make or distribute. However, you may accept compensation in exchange for copies. If you distribute a large enough number of copies you must also follow the conditions in section 3.

You may also lend copies, under the same conditions stated above, and you may publicly display copies.

3. *COPYING IN QUANTITY*

If you publish printed copies of the Document numbering more than 100, and the Document's license notice requires Cover Texts, you must enclose the copies in covers that carry, clearly and legibly, all these Cover Texts: Front-Cover Texts on the front cover, and Back-Cover Texts on the back cover. Both covers must also clearly and legibly identify you as the publisher of these copies. The front cover must present the full title with all words of the title equally prominent and visible. You may add other material on the covers in addition. Copying with changes limited to the covers, as long as they preserve the title of the Document and satisfy these conditions, can be treated as verbatim copying in other respects.

If the required texts for either cover are too voluminous to fit legibly, you should put the first ones listed (as many as fit reasonably) on the actual cover, and continue the rest onto adjacent pages.

If you publish or distribute Opaque copies of the Document numbering more than 100, you must either include a machine-readable Transparent copy along with each Opaque copy, or state in or with each Opaque copy a publicly-accessible computer-network location containing a complete Transparent copy of the Document, free of added material, which the general network-using public has access to download anonymously at no charge using public-standard network protocols. If you use the latter option, you must take reasonably prudent steps, when you begin distribution of Opaque copies in quantity, to ensure that this Transparent copy will remain thus accessible at the stated location until at least one year after the last time you distribute an Opaque copy (directly or through your agents or retailers) of that edition to the public.

It is requested, but not required, that you contact the authors of the Document well before redistributing any large number of copies, to give them a chance to provide you with an updated version of the Document.

4. *MODIFICATIONS*

You may copy and distribute a Modified Version of the Document under the conditions of sections 2 and 3 above, provided that you release the Modified Version under precisely this License, with the Modified Version filling the role of the Document, thus licensing distribution and modification of the Modified Version to whoever possesses a copy of it. In addition, you must do these things in the Modified Version:

A. Use in the Title Page (and on the covers, if any) a title distinct from that of the Document, and from those of previous versions (which should, if there were any, be listed in the History section of the Document). You may use the same title as a previous version if the original publisher of that version gives permission.

B. List on the Title Page, as authors, one or more persons or entities responsible for authorship of the modifications in the Modified Version, together with at least five of the principal authors of the Document (all of its principal authors, if it has less than five).

C. State on the Title page the name of the publisher of the Modified Version, as the publisher.

D. Preserve all the copyright notices of the Document.

E. Add an appropriate copyright notice for your modifications adjacent to the other copyright notices.

F. Include, immediately after the copyright notices, a license notice giving the public permission to use the Modified Version under the terms of this License, in the form shown in the Addendum below.

G. Preserve in that license notice the full lists of Invariant Sections and required Cover Texts given in the Document's license notice.

H. Include an unaltered copy of this License.

I. Preserve the section entitled "History", and its title, and add to it an item stating at least the title, year, new authors, and publisher of the Modified Version as given on the Title Page. If there is no section entitled "History" in the Document, create one stating the title, year, authors, and publisher of the Document as given on its Title Page, then add an item describing the Modified Version as stated in the previous sentence.

J. Preserve the network location, if any, given in the Document for public access to a Transparent copy of the Document, and likewise the network locations given in the Document for previous versions it was based on. These may be placed in the "History" section. You may omit a network location for a work that was published at least four years before the Document itself, or if the original publisher of the version it refers to gives permission.

K. In any section entitled "Acknowledgements" or "Dedications", preserve the section's title, and preserve in the section all the substance and tone of each of the contributor acknowledgements and/or dedications given therein.

L. Preserve all the Invariant Sections of the Document, unaltered in their text and in their titles. Section numbers or the equivalent are not considered part of the section titles.

M. Delete any section entitled "Endorsements". Such a section may not be included in the Modified Version.

N. Do not retitle any existing section as "Endorsements" or to conflict in title with any Invariant Section.

If the Modified Version includes new front-matter sections or appendices that qualify as Secondary Sections and contain no material copied from the Document, you may at your option designate some or all of these sections as invariant. To do this, add their titles to the list of Invariant Sections in the Modified Version's license notice. These titles must be distinct from any other section titles.

You may add a section entitled "Endorsements", provided it contains nothing but endorsements of your Modified Version by various parties – for example, statements of peer review or that the text has been approved by an organization as the authoritative definition of a standard.

You may add a passage of up to five words as a Front-Cover Text, and a passage of up to 25 words as a Back-Cover Text, to the end of the list of Cover Texts in the Modified Version. Only one passage of Front-Cover Text and one of Back-Cover Text may be added by (or through arrangements made by) any one entity. If the Document already includes a cover text for the same cover, previously added by you or by arrangement made by the same entity you are acting on behalf of, you may not add another; but you may replace the old one, on explicit permission from the previous publisher that added the old one.

The author(s) and publisher(s) of the Document do not by this License give permission to use their names for publicity for or to assert or imply endorsement of any Modified Version.

5. COMBINING DOCUMENTS

You may combine the Document with other documents released under this License, under the terms defined in section 4 above for modified versions, provided that you include in the combination all of the Invariant Sections of all of the original documents, unmodified, and list them all as Invariant Sections of your combined work in its license notice.

The combined work need only contain one copy of this License, and multiple identical Invariant Sections may be replaced with a single copy. If there are multiple Invariant Sections with the same name but different contents, make the title of each such section unique by adding at the end of it, in parentheses, the name of the original author or publisher of that section if known, or else a unique number. Make the same adjustment to the section titles in the list of Invariant Sections in the license notice of the combined work.

In the combination, you must combine any sections entitled "History" in the various original documents, forming one section entitled "History"; likewise combine any sections entitled "Acknowledgements", and any sections entitled "Dedications". You must delete all sections entitled "Endorsements".

6. COLLECTIONS OF DOCUMENTS

You may make a collection consisting of the Document and other documents released under this License, and replace the individual copies of this License in the various documents with a single copy that is included in the collection, provided that you follow the rules of this License for verbatim copying of each of the documents in all other respects.

You may extract a single document from such a collection, and distribute it individually under this License, provided you insert a copy of this License into the extracted document, and follow this License in all other respects regarding verbatim copying of that document.

7. AGGREGATION WITH INDEPENDENT WORKS

A compilation of the Document or its derivatives with other separate and independent documents or works, in or on a volume of a storage or distribution medium, does not as a whole count as a Modified Version of the Document, provided no compilation copyright is claimed for the compilation. Such a compilation is called an "aggregate", and this License does not apply to the other self-contained works thus compiled with the Document, on account of their being thus compiled, if they are not themselves derivative works of the Document.

If the Cover Text requirement of section 3 is applicable to these copies of the Document, then if the Document is less than one quarter of the entire aggregate, the Document's Cover Texts may be placed on covers that surround only the Document within the aggregate. Otherwise they must appear on covers around the whole aggregate.

8. TRANSLATION

Translation is considered a kind of modification, so you may distribute translations of the Document under the terms of section 4. Replacing Invariant Sections with translations requires special permission from their copyright holders, but you may include translations of some or all Invariant Sections in addition to the original versions of these Invariant Sections. You may include a translation of this License provided that you also include the original English version of this License. In case of a disagreement between the translation and the original English version of this License, the original English version will prevail.

9. TERMINATION

You may not copy, modify, sublicense, or distribute the Document except as expressly provided for under this License. Any other attempt to copy, modify, sublicense or distribute the Document is void, and will automatically terminate your rights under this License. However, parties who have received copies, or rights, from you under this License will not have their licenses terminated so long as such parties remain in full compliance.

10. FUTURE REVISIONS OF THIS LICENSE

The Free Software Foundation may publish new, revised versions of the GNU Free Documentation License from time to time. Such new versions will be similar in spirit to the present version, but may differ in detail to address new problems or concerns. See http://www.gnu.org/copyleft/.

Each version of the License is given a distinguishing version number. If the Document specifies that a particular numbered version of this License "or any later version" applies to it, you have the option of following the terms and conditions either of that specified version or of any later version that has been published (not as a draft) by the Free Software Foundation. If the Document does not specify a version number of this License, you may choose any version ever published (not as a draft) by the Free Software Foundation.

How to use this License for your documents

To use this License in a document you have written, include a copy of the License in the document and put the following copyright and license notices just after the title page:

> Copyright (c) YEAR YOUR NAME.
> Permission is granted to copy, distribute and/or modify this document under the terms of the GNU Free Documentation License, Version 1.1 or any later version published by the Free Software Foundation; with the Invariant Sections being LIST THEIR TITLES, with the Front-Cover Texts being LIST, and with the Back-Cover Texts being LIST. A copy of the license is included in the section entitled "GNU Free Documentation License".

If you have no Invariant Sections, write "with no Invariant Sections" instead of saying which ones are invariant. If you have no Front-Cover Texts, write "no Front-Cover Texts" instead of "Front-Cover Texts being LIST"; likewise for Back-Cover Texts.

If your document contains nontrivial examples of program code, we recommend releasing these examples in parallel under your choice of free software license, such as the GNU General Public License, to permit their use in free software.

The Q Public License

This is the Trolltech Q Public License.

THE Q PUBLIC LICENSE version 1.0

Copyright (C) 1999 Trolltech AS, Norway.
Everyone is permitted to copy and
distribute this license document.

The intent of this license is to establish freedom to share and change the software regulated by this license under the open source model.

This license applies to any software containing a notice placed by the copyright holder saying that it may be distributed under the terms of the Q Public License version 1.0. Such software is herein referred to as the Software. This license covers modification and distribution of the Software, use of third-party application programs based on the Software, and development of free software which uses the Software.

Granted Rights

1. You are granted the non-exclusive rights set forth in this license provided you agree to and comply with any and all conditions in this license. Whole or partial distribution of the Software, or software items that link with the Software, in any form signifies acceptance of this license.

2. You may copy and distribute the Software in unmodified form provided that the entire package, including – but not restricted to – copyright, trademark notices and disclaimers, as released by the initial developer of the Software, is distributed.

3. You may make modifications to the Software and distribute your modifications, in a form that is separate from the Software, such as patches. The following restrictions apply to modifications:

a. Modifications must not alter or remove any copyright notices in the Software.

b. When modifications to the Software are released under this license, a non-exclusive royalty-free right is granted to the initial developer of the Software to distribute your modification in future versions of the Software provided such versions remain available under these terms in addition to any other license(s) of the initial developer.

4. You may distribute machine-executable forms of the Software or machine-executable forms of modified versions of the Software, provided that you meet these restrictions:

a. You must include this license document in the distribution.

b. You must ensure that all recipients of the machine-executable forms are also able to receive the complete machine-readable source code to the distributed Software, including all modifications, without any charge beyond the costs of data transfer, and place prominent notices in the distribution explaining this.

c. You must ensure that all modifications included in the machine-executable forms are available under the terms of this license.

5. You may use the original or modified versions of the Software to compile, link and run application programs legally developed by you or by others.

6. You may develop application programs, reusable components and other software items that link with the original or modified versions of the Software. These items, when distributed, are subject to the following requirements:

a. You must ensure that all recipients of machine-executable forms of these items are also able to receive and use the complete machine-readable source code to the items without any charge beyond the costs of data transfer.

b. You must explicitly license all recipients of your items to use and re-distribute original and modified versions of the items in both machine-executable and source code forms. The recipients must be able to do so without any charges whatsoever, and they must be able to re-distribute to anyone they choose.

c. If the items are not available to the general public, and the initial developer of the Software requests a copy of the items, then you must supply one.

Limitations of Liability

In no event shall the initial developers or copyright holders be liable for any damages whatsoever, including – but not restricted to – lost revenue or profits or other direct, indirect, special, incidental or consequential damages, even if they have been advised of the possibility of such damages, except to the extent invariable law, if any, provides otherwise.

No Warranty

The Software and this license document are provided AS IS with NO WARRANTY OF ANY KIND, INCLUDING THE WARRANTY OF DESIGN, MERCHANTABILITY AND FITNESS FOR A PARTICULAR PURPOSE.

Choice of Law

This license is governed by the Laws of Norway. Disputes shall be settled by Oslo City Court.

Online discussion at http://www.p2p.wrox.com

D

Support, Errata, and P2P.Wrox.Com

One of the most irritating things about any programming book is when you find that bit of code you've just spent an hour typing simply doesn't work. You check it a hundred times to see if you've set it up correctly and then you notice the spelling mistake in the variable name on the book page. Of course, you can blame the authors for not taking enough care and testing the code, the editors for not doing their job properly, or the proofreaders for not being eagle-eyed enough, but this doesn't get around the fact that mistakes do happen.

We try hard to ensure no mistakes sneak out into the real world, but we can't promise that this book is 100% error free. What we can do is offer the next best thing by providing you with immediate support and feedback from experts who have worked on the book and try to ensure that future editions eliminate these gremlins. We also now commit to supporting you not just while you read the book, but once you start developing applications as well through our online forums where you can put your questions to the authors, reviewers, and fellow industry professionals.

In this appendix we'll look at how to:

- ❏ Enroll in the peer to peer forums at p2p.wrox.com
- ❏ Post and check for errata on our main site, www.wrox.com
- ❏ e-Mail technical support a query or feedback on our books in general

Between all three support procedures, you should get an answer to your problem in no time flat.

The Online Forums at P2P.Wrox.Com

Join the Professional Linux Programming mailing list for author and peer support. Our system provides **programmer to programmer™ support** on mailing lists, forums and newsgroups all in addition to our one-to-one e-mail system, which we'll look at in a minute. Be confident that your query is not just being examined by a support professional, but by the many Wrox authors and other industry experts present on our mailing lists.

How to Enroll for Support

Just follow this six-step system:

1. Go to p2p.wrox.com in your favorite browser.
    Here you'll find any current announcements concerning P2P – new lists created, any removed and so on.

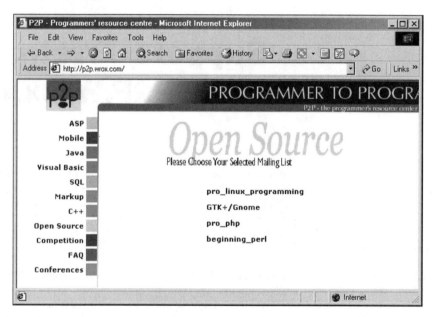

2. Click on the Open Source button in the left hand column.

3. Choose to access the pro_linux_programming list.

4. If you are not a member of the list, you can choose to either view the list without joining it or create an account in the list, by hitting the respective buttons.

5. If you wish to join, you'll be presented with a form in which you'll need to fill in your e-mail address, name and a password (of at least 4 alphanumeric characters). Choose how you would like to receive the messages from the list and then hit Save.

6. Congratulations. You're now a member of the Professional Linux Programming mailing list.

Why This System Offers the Best Support

You can choose to join the mailing lists or you can receive them as a weekly digest. If you don't have the time or facility to receive the mailing list, then you can search our online archives. You'll find the ability to search on specific subject areas or keywords. As these lists are moderated, you can be confident of finding good, accurate information quickly. Mails can be edited or moved by the moderator into the correct place, making this a most efficient resource. Junk and spam mail are deleted, and your own e-mail address is protected by the unique Lyris system from web-bots that can automatically hoover up newsgroup mailing list addresses. Any queries about joining, leaving lists or any query about the list should be sent to: `listsupport@wrox.com`.

Checking the Errata Online at www.wrox.com

The following section will take you step by step through the process of posting errata to our web site to get that help. The sections that follow, therefore, are:

- ❏ Wrox Developers Membership
- ❏ Finding a list of existing errata on the web site
- ❏ Adding your own errata to the existing list
- ❏ What happens to your erratum once you've posted it (why doesn't it appear immediately)?

There is also a section covering how to e-mail a question for technical support. This comprises:

- ❏ What your e-mail should include
- ❏ What happens to your e-mail once it has been received by us

So that you only need view information relevant to yourself, we ask that you register as a Wrox Developer Member. This is a quick and easy process, that will save you time in the long-run. If you are already a member, just update membership to include this book.

Wrox Developer's Membership

To get your FREE Wrox Developer's Membership click on Membership in the top navigation bar of our home site – http://www.wrox.com. This is shown in the following screenshot:

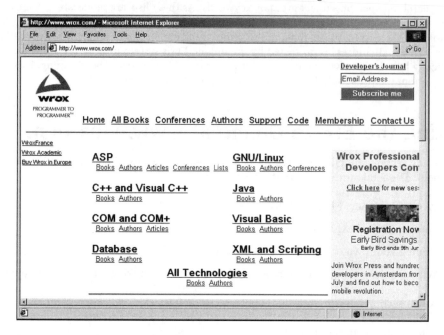

Then, on the next screen (not shown), click on New User. This will display a form. Fill in the details on the form and submit the details using the Register button at the bottom. Before you can say 'The best read books come in Wrox Red' you will get the following screen:

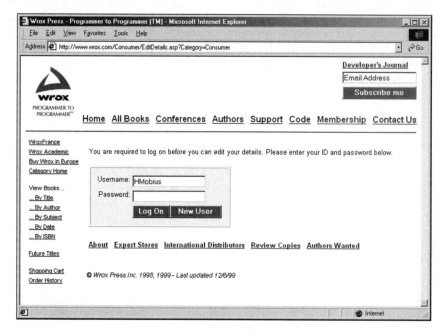

Type in your password once again and click Log On. The following page allows you to change your details if you need to, but now you're logged on, you have access to all the source code downloads and errata for the entire Wrox range of books.

Finding an Errata on the Web Site

Before you send in a query, you might be able to save time by finding the answer to your problem on our web site – http:\\www.wrox.com.

Each book we publish has its own page and its own errata sheet. You can get to any book's page by clicking on Support from the top navigation bar.

Halfway down the main support page is a drop down box called Title Support. Simply scroll down the list until you see Professional Linux Programming. Select it and then hit Errata.

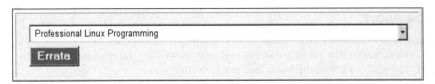

This will take you to the errata page for the book. Select the criteria by which you want to view the errata, and click the Apply criteria button. This will provide you with links to specific errata. For an initial search, you are advised to view the errata by page numbers. If you have looked for an error previously, then you may wish to limit your search using dates. We update these pages daily to ensure that you have the latest information on bugs and errors.

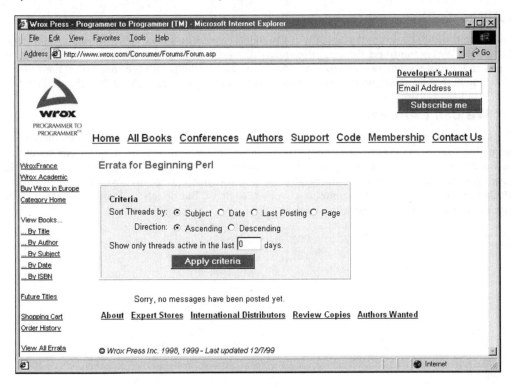

Add an Erratum: e-Mail Support

If you wish to point out an erratum to put up on the web site or directly query a problem in the book page with an expert who knows the book in detail then e-mail `support@wrox.com`, with the title of the book and the last four numbers of the ISBN in the subject field of the e-mail. A typical e-mail should include the following things:

The **name**, **last four digits of the ISBN**, and **page number** of the problem in the Subject field

Your **name**, **contact info**, and the **problem** in the body of the message

We won't send you junk mail. We need the details to save your time and ours. If we need to replace a disk or CD we'll be able to get it to you straight away. When you send an e-mail it will go through the following chain of support:

Customer Support

Your message is delivered to one of our customer support staff who are the first people to read it. They have files on most frequently asked questions and will answer anything general immediately. They answer general questions about the book and the web site.

Editorial

Deeper queries are forwarded to the technical editor responsible for that book. They have experience with the programming language or particular product and are able to answer detailed technical questions on the subject. Once an issue has been resolved, the editor can post the errata to the web site.

The Authors

Finally, in the unlikely event that the editor can't answer your problem, they will forward the request to the author. We try to protect the author from any distractions from writing. However, we are quite happy to forward specific requests to them. All Wrox authors help with the support on their books. They'll mail the customer and the editor with their response, and again all readers should benefit.

What We Can't Answer

Obviously with an ever-growing range of books and an ever-changing technology base, there is an increasing volume of data requiring support. While we endeavor to answer all questions about the book, we can't answer bugs in your own programs that you've adapted from our code. So, while you might have loved the chapters on file handling, don't expect too much sympathy if you cripple your company with a routine which deletes the contents of your hard drive. But do tell us if you're especially pleased with the routine you developed with our help.

How to Tell Us Exactly What You Think

We understand that errors can destroy the enjoyment of a book and can cause many wasted and frustrated hours, so we seek to minimize the distress that they can cause.

You might just wish to tell us how much you liked or loathed the book in question. Or you might have ideas about how this whole process could be improved. In which case you should e-mail feedback@wrox.com. You'll always find a sympathetic ear, no matter what the problem is. Above all you should remember that we do care about what you have to say and we will do our utmost to act upon it.

Online discussion at http://www.p2p.wrox.com

Index

A Guide to the Index

The index is arranged hierarchically, in alphabetical order, with symbols preceding the letter A. Most second-level entries and many third-level entries also occur as first-level entries. This is to ensure that users will find the information they require however they choose to search for it.

D

H

I

Online discussion at http://www.p2p.wrox.com

Wrox Conferences provide timely, practical and code-heavy information for the programming community - true to the core values of Wrox Press. Focused on the latest technologies, our conferences all feature speakers who are authors, solution providers and industry professionals. They have one thing in common: they are all programmers. As such, they are able to share their knowledge with fellow programmers, teach their code, and offer practical solutions to today's developing needs.

What makes a Wrox Conference different?

● Wrox Conferences deliver Wrox-edited, code-heavy programming solutions, independent of commercial bias.

● Peer-to-Peer, the central ethic of Wrox, means that expert programmers share their knowledge and experience to enable delegates to build their skills and get ahead in programming.

Session details and registration information for Wrox Conferences can be found on:

http://www.wroxconferences.com

LAMP Tree

The LAMP catagory represents more than just Linux - Wrox books in this area guide you through the whole open source community: Linux, Apache, MySQL and PHP. Whether you want to exploit the potential of Perl or get to the heart of the key features of Zope, we provide the information you need, bringing the Wrox Press Programmer to Programmer philosophy to the open source platform.

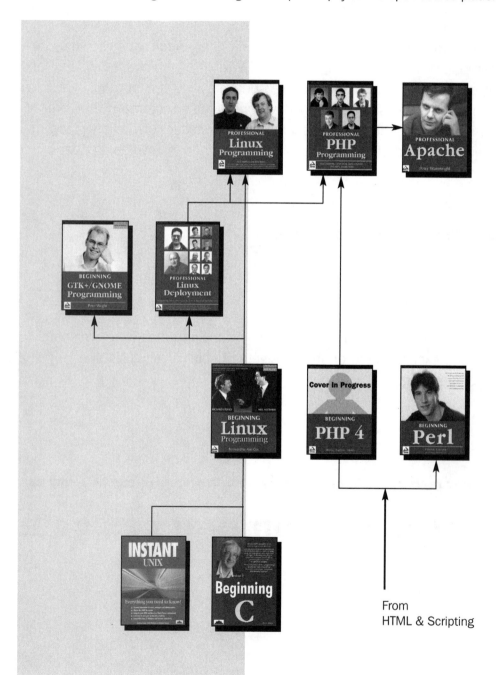

From
HTML & Scripting

Beginning Linux Programming is an easy-to-use guide to developing programs for the Linux and other UNIX-style operating systems. The focus is on C programming, looking at the GNU tools, and the UNIX C libraries with step-by-step instructions on how to write, build and debug serious application code.

This is the second edition of this title; published to coincide with the explosion of interest in Linux, the wealth of new features in the latest version of popular Linux distributions and the Kernel itself. This second edition covers all the same ground as the original, but adds coverage of the GNOME desktop, device drivers, and the latest Linux Kernal features. To get the most out of Beginning Linux you should be a competent C programmer with a good working knowlege of how to use and configure the Linux system.

- Latest Linux Kernel, current tools and C libraries
- Programming for GNOME
- Extensive examples illustrate theory and programming techniques

Neil Matthew
Richard Stones

1-861002-97-1

September 1999

US$ 39.99
C$ 59.95
£ 28.99

Summary of contents

LAMP BOOKS

Beginning Perl

Perl is an immensely popular scripting language that combines the best features of C, key UNIX utilities and a powerful usc of regular expressions. It has a wide range of uses beyond simple text processing and is commonly used for web programming - creating and parsing CGI forms, validating HTML syntax and hyperlinks - as well as e-mail and Usenet news filtering. The book promotes the use of Perl as a programming language, encouraging the creation of legible and sensible programs, dispelling the image of Perl as confusing and obscure. Whatever your current experience level in the world of Perl, this book has something for you.

- Complete tutorial in Perl on Windows and UNIX
- Making use of online Perl resources like CPAN
- Using Perl as an object-oriented language

Simon Cozens

1-861003-14-5

June 2000

US$ 39.99
C$ 59.95
£ 28.99

Summary of Contents

If you're a corporate NT server administrator, this book will show you how to move all of your company services over to the Linux platform. Containing detailed technical knowledge and case studies from the real world, this book covers the technical issues faced by a company making the move to Linux. Code examples and comprehensive talk-throughs are provided throughout. The full spectrum of real and potential enterprise deployments is covered.

- Setting up essential Internet and intranet services
- Creating web and FTP servers
- Using the free databases MySQL and PostgreSQL

Mike Banahan
Michael Boerner
Ian Dickson
Jonathon Kelly
Nikhilesh Kumar Mandalay
Richard Ollerenshaw
Jonathan Pinnock
Ganesh Prasad
Joel Rowbottom
Geoff Sherlock
Mark Wilcox

1-861002-87-4

January 2000

US$ 49.99
C$ 74.95
£ 35.99

Summary of Contents

Peter Wainwright

1-861003-02-1

November 1999

US$ 49.99
C$ 74.95
£ 35.99

Professional Apache is the book for anybody who needs to get the most out of the server that powers 60% of the web. If you're thinking of setting up Apache for the first time, or of moving an existing web site to a dedicated server, then this book will help you. It's full of information on how to add new capabilities to existing servers, like e-commerce, PHP, or server-side Java support. The key theme is 'Apache the way you want it' - through extensive examples, this book gives you the information you need to build, configure and extend Apache to suit your requirements.

- The Apache 1.3.x server, including new features in Apache 1.3.9
- Setting Apache up to deliver dynamic content efficiently and securely
- Adding SSL encryption support to your Apache Server

Summary of Contents

Beginning GTK+ /GNOME - Linux GUI Programming

Linux continues to go from strength to strength, not only taking 20% of the server market but becoming an increasingly popular choice as a standalone desktop platform. If you would like to contribute to this next big leap for Linux then this is the book for you. GTK+ and GNOME provide a powerful, easy-to-learn, object-oriented set of libraries to help you develop professional graphical interfaces. GTK+ and GNOME are exciting development technologies that allow you to create and manipulate windows, buttons, dialogs, menus, tool tips, status bars, tool bars, horizontal and vertical scroll bars. They also have facilities for handling colours and fonts. If you have installed Linux and know simple C programming you have all you need to begin reading this book and developing very sophisticated and attractive graphical interfaces.

- The GIMP Toolkit (GTK+) and Drawing Kit (GDK)
- The GNU Network Object Model Environment (GNOME)
- The GNOME Integrated Development Environment (gIDE)

Summary of Contents

Peter Wright

1-861003-81-1

April 2000

US$ 39.99
C$ 59.95
£ 28.99

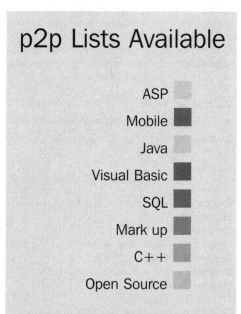